Golden Horrors

Golden Horrors

An Illustrated Critical Filmography of Terror Cinema, 1931–1939

BRYAN SENN

McFarland & Company, Inc., Publishers
Jefferson, North Carolina, and London

Frontispiece: The author (right), having driven nearly 200 miles to see a revival of *Frankenstein* and *Dracula* at Portland's Roseway Theater in 1992, worships at the cinematic altar (photo: Lynn Naron).

The present work is a reprint of the library bound edition of Golden Horrors: An Illustrated Critical Filmography of Terror Cinema, 1931–1939, *first published in 1996 by McFarland.*

LIBRARY OF CONGRESS CATALOGUING-IN-PUBLICATION DATA

Senn, Bryan, 1962–
  Golden horrors : an illustrated critical filmography of terror cinema, 1931–1939 / by Bryan Senn.
    p. cm.
  Includes bibliographical references and index.

  ISBN 0-7864-2724-8 (softcover : 50# alk. paper) ∞

  1. Horror films — History and criticism.   I. Title.
PN1995.9.H6S44   1996
791.43'616 — dc20   96-10936

British Library cataloguing data are available

©1996 Bryan Senn. All rights reserved

No part of this book may be reproduced or transmitted in any form or by any means, electronic or mechanical, including photocopying or recording, or by any information storage and retrieval system, without permission in writing from the publisher.

On the cover: One-sheet poster from the 1935 film *The Raven* (Universal Pictures/Photofest)

Manufactured in the United States of America

McFarland & Company, Inc., Publishers
  Box 611, Jefferson, North Carolina 28640
    www.mcfarlandpub.com

This book is dedicated to four people whose touch has affected my life for the better:

Gina Beretta, whose sense of perspective made sure the task remained an enjoyable one; **Terry and Sharon Senn**, whose interest and support was never less than encouraging; and **J. C. Olmsted** ("Uncle Buddy") — now you'll have to *read* it.

Table of Contents

Acknowledgments	*ix*
Introduction	*1*

THE FILMS

Dracula (1931)	9
Frankenstein (1931)	19
Dr. Jekyll and Mr. Hyde (1931)	30
Murders in the Rue Morgue (1932)	43
Freaks (1932)	52
Vampyr (1932)	68
White Zombie (1932)	81
Doctor X (1932)	91
The Lodger (1932)	102
The Most Dangerous Game (1932)	109
The Old Dark House (1932)	119
The Mask of Fu Manchu (1932)	129
The Mummy (1932)	137
Island of Lost Souls (1933)	144
The Vampire Bat (1933)	153
Mystery of the Wax Museum (1933)	159
King Kong (1933)	169
Murders in the Zoo (1933)	184
Supernatural (1933)	195
The Ghoul (1933)	205
The Invisible Man (1933)	212

TABLE OF CONTENTS

The Son of Kong (1933)	*221*
The Black Cat (1934)	*234*
Drums o' Voodoo (1934)	*241*
The Secret of the Loch (1934)	*247*
Maniac (1934)	*256*
Mark of the Vampire (1935)	*264*
Bride of Frankenstein (1935)	*276*
Werewolf of London (1935)	*288*
The Raven (1935)	*296*
Mad Love (1935)	*308*
The Black Room (1935)	*314*
Condemned to Live (1935)	*322*
The Crime of Doctor Crespi (1935)	*328*
The Invisible Ray (1936)	*337*
The Walking Dead (1936)	*345*
Dracula's Daughter (1936)	*352*
Revolt of the Zombies (1936)	*361*
The Devil-Doll (1936)	*368*
The Man Who Changed His Mind (1936)	*377*
Son of Frankenstein (1939)	*386*
The Man They Could Not Hang (1939)	*395*
Torture Ship (1939)	*402*
Tower of London (1939)	*409*
The Dark Eyes of London (1939)	*416*
The Return of Dr. X (1939)	*424*
Appendix A: Borderline Horrors, "Lost" Films, and Foreign Exclusions	*431*
Appendix B: The Ten Best Films from The Golden Age of Horror	*489*
Bibliography	*495*
Index	*501*

Acknowledgments

A book like this is shaped by many hands, and I extend mine in heartfelt thanks to the following:

Paul Jensen for his insightful editorial input. Without his guidance this would be a poorer work indeed.

Gina Beretta for her patience, support, and considerable editorial skills.

Lynn Naron for lending both his invaluable research skills and photographic expertise (not to mention his wonderful personal library and vast store of esoteric knowledge).

John Johnson for his general formatting ideas as well as his specific input on the *Island of Lost Souls* and *The Walking Dead* chapters (and a special thanks for his unswerving confidence and encouragement).

Brad Senn (once again) for his frequent computer assistance.

Ted Okuda for selflessly furnishing many of the finest stills included here (as well as providing his evaluation of *Night Life of the Gods*—a film very few have been privileged to see).

Tom Weaver for generously opening his voluminous files to me, and for providing several of the films themselves.

Ronald V. Borst for providing copies of pressbooks, articles, and films.

Freda Novello for her charitable assistance in researching (and procuring photos for) *The Lodger*.

Jean-Claude Michel (the ultimate Tod Slaughter authority) for his information on some of the lesser-known British films.

John Kisch (author of *A Separate Cinema*) and D. Lindsay Pettus (of the Lancaster County Society for Historical Preservation) for their expertise and assistance regarding the all-black films.

Forrest J Ackerman, Carroll Borland, Dwight Frye, Jr., Richard Gordon, Dan Sonney, and Gloria Stuart for sharing their time and personal reminiscences.

B. Alan Atkinson, Pat Battle, Eric Hoffman, Ken Landgraf, Stark Maynard, Dennis Payne, Bob Selvig, and Chuck Wilson for locating some of the more hard-to-find films in my hour(s) of need.

And to Edmund G. Bansak, Robert Bloch, Ted A. Bohus, Ray Bradbury, John Brunas, Michael Brunas, Keith J. Crocker, Joe Dante, William K. Everson, Bruce G. Hallenbeck, Ray Harryhausen, Tom Johnson, Dick Klemensen, John Landis, Gregory William Mank, Mark A. Miller, Tim Murphy, John E. Parnum, Fred Olen Ray, Don G. Smith, Gary J. Svehla, and Richard Valley for their participation and input.

Finally, I must thank the myriad researchers and writers who have come before and upon whose sturdy foundation this particular house of words is built. Their names and works can be found in the bibliography.

Introduction

THE BIRTH OF HORROR'S GOLDEN AGE

The "Golden Age of Horror" began on February 12, 1931, when Universal exposed *Dracula* to the rays of the (halogen) sun. As "the first all-out sound horror film"[1] of the era, *Dracula* virtually began the horror film cycle. Though one could argue that other talking pictures previous to *Dracula* could be loosely classified as "horror" (the 1930 entries *The Bat Whispers* and *The Cat Creeps*, for instance), these fledgling fright films are dressed-up murder mysteries which qualify only as tentative, borderline horror at best. *Dracula* was the first sound picture that did not make light of, or explain away, its supernatural element. At the time, however, Universal was none-too-sure of their new property and opted to promote their vampire picture along a romantic rather than horrific line, billing it as "The story of the strangest passion the world has ever known!"

Dracula's huge success at the box office quickly convinced the studio that "horror" was simply another word for "dollars" and Universal went all out in their promotion of shock and terror with their next offering of the macabre — *Frankenstein*. The studio even went so far as to shoot a brief pre-credit prologue to the picture in which cast member Edward Van Sloan advises the audience that "I think it will thrill you; it may shock you; it might even *horrify* you. So if any of you feel that you do not care to subject your nerves to such a strain, now's your chance to — Well, we've warned you!"

Curiously, the wholly unexpected success of *Dracula* made little immediate impact among the other studios. "U Has Horror Cycle All to Self," reported *Variety* on April 8, 1931. "With *Dracula* making money at the box office for Universal, other studios are looking for horror tales — but very squeamishly. Producers are not certain whether nightmare pictures have a box-office pull, or whether *Dracula* is just a freak. To date, no other studio has tried to follow in U's steps, one of the few occasions when a hit wasn't followed by a cycle of similar pictures." The monumental success of Universal's follow-up venture, *Frankenstein*, however, proved that *Dracula* was no "freak" after all, and horror was here to stay. While only two other studios, Paramount and MGM, had a horror project in production at the time *Frankenstein* hit the screens in late November 1931 (*Dr. Jekyll and Mr. Hyde* and *Freaks*, respectively), by fall of 1932 five of the eight major studios had climbed aboard the horror bandwagon. With Universal as the flagship, the genre sailed into its Golden Age.

Of the nascent terror field, *Variety* predicted in late 1931 (after the release of *Frankenstein*): "Sufficient to insure financial success if these pictures are well made," adding, "It took nerve for U[niversal] to do ['Frankenstein'] and 'Dracula.'" Once Pandora's cinematic box had been opened, there was no going back, though many critics of the day would have liked nothing better than to slam down the lid and sit on it. The burgeoning genre was generally met with great resistance by reviewers who were reluctant to acknowledge the many artistic merits of these early efforts, and instead tended to dismiss them out of hand for their frequently weird and sometimes unsettling subject matter. *Variety's* "Abel" typified this predominant attitude in his critical smashing of *The Old Dark House* (1932), voicing not only his contempt for the subject but for the audience as well: "With the horror school ... the audience seemingly doesn't expect coherence, and so everything goes by the boards." Fortunately, while the highbrow critics held their noses and pushed them away, the moviegoing public opened their arms (and pocketbooks) wide to embrace the early horror pictures. By 1935, this same reviewer had apparently come to grips with the genre as a legitimate branch of motion pictures, going so far as to call *The Raven* "a good horror flicker." Yes, the horror film was here to stay — only things would not always be so (blood-red) rosy.

THE HORROR "BAN"

In a rare personal article entitled "I Like Playing Dracula" published in *Film Weekly* (July 1935), Bela Lugosi concluded: "Every year a number of films with fantastic or supernatural characters are made, and will, it seems, continue to be made, whatever may happen to the horror 'cycle' of pictures. I have deliberately specialized in such characters — and I firmly believe there will be suitable roles for me for a long time to come!" Ironically, a scant one month later, an Associated Press headline (August 23, 1935) proclaimed, "HORROR FILMS TABOO IN BRITAIN — '*THE RAVEN*' LAST." Great Britain (which comprised over 40 percent of the all-important foreign distribution income) had become the site of a moral rebellion against the horror movie. Local parent groups, newspapers, and town councils across the British Isles took up a cry of outrage against a Hollywood product that promoted "moral decay" in its youth. "To take a child to see one of those Karloff and Bela Lugosi horrors is to outrage its nervous system and perhaps warp it for life," wrote a film critic reviewing *The Raven* for the *Alhambra Post-Advocate*, and these sentiments quickly became the voice of the British censors. This indignation was largely triggered by *The Raven* itself with its themes of torture, madness, and sexual aberration. The London City Council succumbed to the monumental pressure of the anti-horror sentiment and quickly drew up the recommendation that "...in addition to their two existing categories of film (U: Universal exhibition, and A: Adults only), there should be a third category, 'H,' passed as 'horrific,' i.e., for public presentation when no children under 16 years of age are present." In the wake of this proclamation, the British Board of Film Censors called for a complete halt to the importation of horror films for an indefinite period until all those terror pictures made since 1929 could be reviewed and reclassified. This boycott of horror films (along with support from like-minded and vociferous anti-horror PTAs and civic groups throughout the United States) sounded the death knell for American production. Since so much of the lucrative foreign market was now effectively closed to them, producers found it too much of a financial risk to invest in horror pictures.

This sad situation only worsened when Universal's president, Carl Laemmle, and vice president in charge of production, Carl Laemmle, Jr. (the father and son team that made Universal the "Home of Horror"), saw their cinematic empire wrested from their grasp by Charles Rogers and Standard Capitol Corporation. The year 1935 had been disastrous financially for Universal (with a loss of $677,185), and "Uncle Carl" sought a loan of $750,000 from Rogers and company to weather the storm. The loan came with a proviso that Standard Capitol receive an option to buy the studio at a fixed cost of $5.5 million, an amount Laemmle, Sr., felt certain Rogers would be unable to raise. Laemmle was wrong, and on March 14, 1936, father and son packed up and left Universal City forever. Charles Rogers took over Junior's post of vice president in charge of production and instituted an anti-horror policy in favor of musicals, comedies, and "B" actioners (even nixing Universal's scheduled Karloff/Lugosi vehicle, *The Electric Man*[2]). With "The New Universal" under horror-hostile management, the genre found itself among the homeless.

Thus, after a few last-minute releases in 1936, the genre slipped into a cataleptic trance which lasted for nearly two years. (As an indicator of the regard the industry held for horror during this down-time, *Variety*'s June 30, 1937, obituary for Colin Clive opined that the actor "reached his greatest fame in the stage and screen versions of 'Journey's End' " — failing to even *mention* the megahits *Frankenstein* or the more recent *Bride of Frankenstein*.) The dearth of horror product was so complete that Bela Lugosi (whose name had become synonymous with horror and who mistakenly thought that "there will be suitable roles for me for a long time to come!") could not find film work for over *fifteen months* in 1937–1938.

Then, in August of 1938, a Hollywood theater owner named Emil Ulmann attempted to stave off impending bankruptcy by purchasing three forgotten films for the incredibly cheap price of $99 per week. And so the first triple bill of horror was born, with *Dracula*, *Frankenstein* and *The Son of Kong* filling the screen along with this challenge: "We dare you to see them together."

Ulmann's desperation ploy succeeded beyond his wildest dreams. On the first night, eager patrons ignored the horror boycott and lined up around the block. And the lines continued, dictating that the pictures be shown almost continuously for 21 hours a day.

Universal quickly jumped on the refurbished horror bandwagon by reissuing *Dracula* and *Frankenstein* nationwide. This double bill was such a huge success across the country that it even exceeded the pictures' original release grosses in some cities. A near-rabid excitement gripped many moviegoers on the brink of horror's rediscovery (even in the unlikeliest of places) as evidenced by this *New York Times* report: "At the Victory Theater in Salt Lake City the house was sold out by ten o'clock in the morning. Four thousand frenzied Mormons milled around outside, finally broke through police lines, smashed the plate glass box office, bent in the front doors and tore off one of the door checks in their eagerness to get in and be frightened. The manager rented an empty theater across the street, bicycled the reels to it and in twenty minutes had it packed to the gunwales, with the street still full of frustrated phobiaphiles clamoring for admission." Horror was not dead after all and, much like Caligari's Caesar in the genre's premier picture, it awakened to walk once more when Universal hastily drew up plans to continue their dynasty with *Son of Frankenstein*. In 1939, the second age of the horror film dawned across the celluloid skies.

1939: HORROR RESURRECTED

" 'Nightmares for everybody' is the Hollywood slogan for a more horrible 1939," announced the February 28th issue of *Look* magazine. The end of the decade marked the beginning of horror's second wave, one which didn't crest until 1948 when the tide went out once again on terror topics, only to resurge and deposit the myriad alien invaders of the 1950s on cinematic shorelines.

Though strictly speaking, the "Golden Age of Horror" ended in 1936 with the British moratorium on terror pictures and the changing of the guard at Universal, for a variety of reasons the latter third of the decade (basically 1939) is included in this volume as well. First of all, much of the horror produced in that transitional year harkened back to the mood of the early thirties. As David J. Skal noted in *The Monster Show*, "Universal's *Son of Frankenstein* (1939) is sometimes considered part of a new cycle, but its production style, mood, and theme look back and not forward." Secondly, 1939 was the final year for some time of big-budget horror — in which prestige pictures like *Son of Frankenstein*, *Tower of London*, and *The Hunchback of Notre Dame* were allotted generous budgets and, if not quite "A" production schedules, then at least A-minus. With a few exceptions (such as Universal's opulent 1943 remake of *The Phantom of the Opera* and MGM's excellent *The Picture of Dorian Gray* in 1945), the forties saw the horror picture shoved compactly and irretrievably into the

"B" movie slot, there to remain. With World War II came problems for the film industry, including shortages of film stock, set-building materials, and leading men. Still, theaters remained busier than before, since the real-life crisis brought about a strong desire for escapist entertainment. Production difficulties, coupled with the voracious appetites of seemingly indiscriminate moviegoers, induced the studios to churn out low-level product simply to fill booking dates. Low-budget became the norm as volume increased. Consequently, the horror genre of the 1940s became an almost exclusively low-budget, slapdash realm.

Horror was no longer fresh, and while 1939 saw it rise phoenix-like from the ashes, that year was also the last gasp of the genre's Golden Age. No longer in the hands of innovative filmmakers with creative, forceful personalities like James Whale, Carl Freund, or Michael Curtiz, the industry fell into the efficient-but-workmanlike grasp of men like Arthur Lubin (*Black Friday*, 1940; *Phantom of the Opera*, 1943; *The Spider Woman Strikes Back*, 1946), Nick Grinde (*The Man They Could Not Hang*, 1939; *The Man with Nine Lives*, 1940; *Before I Hang*, 1940), and Jean Yarbrough (*The Devil Bat*, 1941; *King of the Zombies*, 1941; *House of Horrors*, 1946), whose forte was more one of rapid execution than creativity. After 1939, horror languished in the barn of the "B" movie as Universal milked their stable of monsters for all they were worth and the poverty row houses churned out quickie mad scientist movies in imitation of Columbia's (already cheap) Mad Doctor series. Val Lewton's RKO horror unit (which spawned the considerable talents of directors Jacques Tourneur, Robert Wise, and Mark Robson) represents the best of horror's "Silver Age" by providing the genre with the majority of its few classic films of the forties — movies like *Cat People* (1942), *I Walked with a Zombie* (1943), and *The Body Snatcher* (1945). Boris Karloff, who starred in three of the producer's films, referred to Lewton as "the man who rescued me from the living dead and restored my soul."

WHY THE "GOLDEN" AGE?

What (besides a respect for our sexagenarian elders) makes the 1930s the "Golden" Age of horror cinema? To answer this we must first ask why horror became so popular so quickly. Boris Karloff, the Grand Old Man of Horror himself, provided his personal theory in *Films and Filming*: "This genre of film entertainment obviously fulfills a desire in people to experience something which is beyond the range of everyday human emotion.... [For] millions of filmgoers they relieve the humdrum life of the average individual better than any other kind of story, and that after all is what entertainment should always do." While Karloff saw the horror film as an escape from the dull and ordinary, Margaret Mead considered terror pictures an escape from real-life horrors: "Today people are exposed to more actual crime and horror than ever before in history because of the tremendous advances in modern communication — on-the-spot radio and television, wirephotos, and so on. The monsters and mummies of the screen, which are always destroyed in the end just as the heroine is saved, are a relief from everyday horror."[3] Both these opinions were espoused in the 1950s, but their viewpoints are just as applicable to the 1930s. It is no coincidence that the Cinema of the Fantastic blossomed and flourished during the Great Depression. With millions out of work, poverty, loss of dignity, and starvation were the pervasive horrors of the day. So why not use that precious dime to seek "relief from everyday horror" and "experience something which is beyond the range of everyday human emotion"?

In the 1930s the genre was fresh and undefined (and thus unconfined). Particularly in the pre–Code days, it was no holds barred in the idea department. Being a new genre, there was huge room for originality and no pre-set parameters. Each of the horror films of the 1930s warrants an in-depth look because of its originality and relative rarity.[4] In contrast to today's market of sequelitis and copy-cat formulae, the horror of the 1930s seems all that much more creative and fascinating, encompassing a timelessness which bridges the decades to fire the imagination. Taken as a whole, the genre today produces not so much "horror" films as "special effects" pictures. All too often, the effects themselves have become the be-all and end-all in the modern horror movie. Rather than frighten with mood and atmosphere, today's product shocks with gruesome, eye-popping technical achievements. Such amazing visuals were simply beyond the technical scope of the 1930s and so the Golden Age terror picture had to wring its chills from story, character, and, above all else, mood.

Even more, these pictures have survived as examples of some of the most stylistic in the horror genre. The 1930s carried with it an expressionistic style overtly Teutonic in origin. As Andrew Tudor observed in his impressive 1989 cultural analysis of the horror film, *Monsters and Mad Scientists*, "the thirties horror-movie was the major beneficiary from the twenties influx of German technicians and from German stylistic influences in general." The Germanic style, with its emphasis on shadows, darkness, and odd perspectives, lent itself brilliantly to the macabre themes of the burgeoning horror genre. Tudor goes on to note that "this 'German Style' proved highly effective in suggesting a world in which dimly seen and dimly understood forces constrained, controlled and attacked its unsuspecting inhabitants" (and unsuspecting audience).

More than any other decade, horror films of the 1930s were aimed squarely at adult audiences. (This irrevocably changed in the 1950s when genre filmmakers realized their greatest potential patrons were teenagers escaping their Uncle Miltie-watching parents to frequent the local "passion pits.") As such, the best of the thirties terror pictures took a more sophisticated and intelligent approach to their dark themes of monsters, madness, and death. At the same time, the advent of sound created a more holistic moviegoing experience. The filmmakers responded by producing adult-oriented pictures like *The Most Dangerous Game* (1932), *The Old Dark House* (1932), and *The Black Cat* (1934), which all featured characters and themes directed toward a sophisticated audience. Some pictures even overshot their mark, as evidenced by the public outrage leveled at *Freaks* (1932) and *Island of Lost Souls* (1933). While this orientation did not necessarily ensure a mature attitude on the part of the filmmakers, it did make such an approach to the subject matter a more viable (i.e., profitable) option.

Many of the Golden Age horror films (a majority, in fact) were produced before the revamped Production Code became an all powerful censorial entity in 1934 under William H. Hays. Consequently, pre–Code pictures could deal with themes and topics effectively outlawed after 1934. While a rare genius like James Whale could circumvent the repressive censorship and express his "subversive" elements by couching them in black humor and symbolism, many issues (like sex and religion) could no longer be dealt with openly. Thus, the movies (and horror in particular) lost much of the freedom of ideas after 1934. Nine of the decade's top ten horror films (chosen by a panel of "experts"—see Appendix B) were produced before the Code's stringent enforcement.

Apart from the creation of Will Hays' idea-devouring dragon, the decade also saw the birth of most of Horrordom's classic cinematic monsters: Dracula, the Frankenstein Monster, the Mummy, the Invisible Man, and even the Werewolf (though Henry Hull's stodgy lycanthrope was soon—and rightly—eclipsed by Lon Chaney, Jr.'s more active version of *The Wolf Man* in 1941). Admittedly, these celluloid legends no longer hold the power to frighten as they once did. Over the decades, familiarity has bred, if not contempt, then at least ennui. What Golden Age horror films have to offer today's viewer (above their nostalgia value) is a strong sense of atmosphere. Rather than shocks, these pictures create an almost palpable mood, weaving their macabre threads into a rich tapestry often startling in its bizarre beauty.

THAT ILLUSIVE DEFINITION OF "HORROR" (OR WHY ISN'T *THAT* FILM INCLUDED?)

What exactly is a "horror" film? Many writers more erudite than myself have tried to define the genre of horror and none has been wholly successful. Perhaps that is because horror is such a personal concept, and so offers little agreement on defining boundaries.

First, I have excluded those strictly science fiction pictures like *FP1 Doesn't Answer* (1932) and *Things to Come* (1936; though I do discuss the latter picture in Appendix A). I have always felt that the best science fiction films incorporate significant horror elements. They explore the darkness of terror as much as the brilliance of science. For example, where would *Alien* (1979) be without its dim, organic interiors and dungeonesque atmosphere (not to mention its terrifying monster) or *The Thing* (1951) without its claustrophobic setting filled with dark corridors and forbidding passageways? (Of course, there are exceptions — the antiseptic sci-fi of *2001: A Space Odyssey* being a prime example — but they are few and far between.) *Things to Come* (1936) is a rare instance of a pure science fiction film from Hollywood's Golden Age. Despite spectacular special effects, it failed both economically and critically, for its moralizing and prophetic focus on science and technology proved too impersonal for most viewers. What I term "horror," however, is an intensely individual experience (if portrayed effectively), and can readily draw the viewer into a science fiction setting — something *Things to Come* failed to do.

Tradition is also a big part of the definition of "horror." Some films have "traditionally been thought of" as horror pictures, to quote a time-honored (or is that time-*worn*?) phrase. *Tower of London*, though more historical melodrama than terror tale, is one such film. *The Dark Eyes of London*, a horrific crime drama, is another. A "genre" provides such a loose and nebulous boundary that it becomes inevitable that one fall back on "tradition." After all, of what use is the term "genre" if there is no common history, no shared basis upon which to build and communicate?

"Horror" sports no hard and fast rules. Must it be limited to the realm of supernatural monsters like vampires and werewolves, or can horror be found in the monstrousness of a deranged mind? Simply because a film *lacks* a supernatural element doesn't automatically exclude it from the horror fraternity. In fact, over three-quarters of the recognized horror pictures from the 1930s contain no supernatural devices whatsoever. Conversely, just because a film features a supernatural element (a ghost for instance) does not make it a horror picture. (Not many people think of *Topper* as a terror film despite the fact that the two lead characters are *dead*.)

In talking with various authors, editors, and filmmakers, I found little agreement as to which pictures should be included. Many are obvious. No one quibbled about the inclusion of *Dracula* or *Dr. Jekyll and Mr. Hyde* (despite the latter's science fiction leanings). But even some ostensibly "obvious" choices had their dissenters. Respected genre historian William K. Everson, for example, did not feel that *King Kong* belonged, and frequent genre author (and screenwriter) Robert Bloch refused to categorize either *Freaks* or *Bride of Frankenstein* as horror films. And these were the "obvious" choices! Then there are the more shadowy areas in which reside such films as *M*, *The Lodger* and *Murder by the Clock*. Some say yes, some say no. Paul Jensen (author of *Boris Karloff and His Films* and *The Cinema of Fritz Lang*), for example, feels *M* does not belong to the horror genre and I agree (though I feel it is truly the most *horrifying* film of the decade in terms of subject matter), while *Cinemacabre* editor John Parnum lists it at number five in his top ten Golden Age horror films.

Through all this, I've concluded that "horror" is a very idiosyncratic notion — one viewer's meat is another viewer's poison. In the end, I have given a full chapter to all those pictures which *I* feel qualify as horror, and allotted those borderline cases (which may or may not have been generally thought of as falling within the hazy boundaries) that didn't make the cut a page or two in Appendix A. Because of space limitations, I have been forced to make some difficult choices. Doubtless, no two readers will agree on the wisdom of my selections, but try not to judge too harshly — I've done the best I can with this particular "poison."

INTRODUCTION

ABOUT THE BOOK

A number of Golden Age horror films have been previously detailed and analyzed thoroughly in books and periodicals (some nearly unto *death*). A few, such as *Dracula* and *King Kong*, even have entire volumes devoted to them. Yet, apart from the Universals and a few other notables, many (if not most) of their contemporaries have received short shrift in the research and analysis departments. Some have secured little more than a passing word here or there which barely acknowledges their existence (*Drums o' Voodoo*, *The Secret of the Loch*, *The Crime of Dr. Crespi*, to name but three). I've tried to focus more on these neglected pictures, giving in-depth preferential treatment to those features historically ignored or relegated to second-tier status. (This, hopefully, answers such burning questions as "Why does Dwain Esper's grindhouse curiosity, *Maniac*, warrant more space than Universal's lycanthropic groundbreaker, *Werewolf of London*?" or "Why does he allot Victor Halperin's tepid misfire, *Supernatural*, half again as many pages as Karl Freund's poetic masterpiece, *The Mummy*?") With the acknowledged classics, I've tried to focus on aspects which haven't yet become critical clichés (or at least provide a slightly different slant on same).

No other branch of cinema remains quite as fascinating to me as the horror genre. And like no other decade, thirties horror films engulf the receptive viewer in a sea of forbidden thought and dark emotion, swirling the audience about in id-infested eddies of light and dark, good and evil. With the most effective of the horror tales, a residual pool remains to moisten our too-often cut-and-dried intellect with rivulets of imagination and emotion long after the celluloid images evaporate under the heat of the harsh house lights. The Golden Age of Horror provides us with a living legacy worthy of the oft-misused term "cinematic heritage," one we can continue to enjoy and be proud of.

BRYAN SENN
Kent, Washington

NOTES

1. William K. Everson in *More Classics of the Horror Film*.
2. Universal eventually dusted off this property in 1941 (long after Rogers' departure in 1938) and cast Lon Chaney, Jr., and Lionel Atwill in the parts intended for Karloff and Lugosi. It was released as *Man Made Monster*.
3. Quoted in *Hollywood Anecdotes*, by Paul F. Boller, Jr., and Ronald L. Davis.
4. During the 1930s, horror pictures accounted for only about one percent of the total film distribution. In each succeeding decade, the terror film grabbed more and more of the proportional output, culminating with about a ten percent total in the 1980s.

The Films

DRACULA
(1931; Universal)

Release Date: February 12, 1931
Running Time: 84 minutes
Director: Tod Browning
Producer: Carl Laemmle, Jr.
Associate Producer: E. M. Asher
Screenplay: Garrett Fort (based on the novel by Bram Stoker and the play by Hamilton Deane and John L. Balderston)
Continuity: Dudley Murphy
Photography: Karl Freund
Art Director: Charles D. Hall
Editor: Milton Carruth
Supervising Editor: Maurice Pivar
Recording Supervisor: C. Roy Hunter
Cast: Bela Lugosi (Count Dracula), Helen Chandler (Mina), David Manners (John Harker), Dwight Frye (Renfield), Edward Van Sloan (Van Helsing), Herbert Bunston (Doctor Seward), Frances Dade (Lucy), Joan Standing (Maid), Charles Gerrard (Martin).

"To die, to be *really* dead — that must be *glorious*." — Dracula.

SYNOPSIS

A coach bearing Mr. Renfield, a young London solicitor, arrives at a rustic inn nestled in the Carpathian mountains of Transylvania. Renfield's destination is the Borgo Pass, where another coach is to meet him at midnight and take him to Castle Dracula. The natives fearfully cross themselves when Renfield mentions the aristocratic name. "We people of the mountains believe that at the castle there are *vampires*!" explains the innkeeper. "Dracula and his wives — they take the form of *wolves* and *bats*. They leave their coffins at night and they feed on the blood of the living." Despite the warning, Renfield insists on going to conclude his business with the Count; Dracula has purchased the ruined Carfax Abbey on the outskirts of London and intends to take up residence there.

The natives' "superstitions" (as Renfield labels them) turn out to be all-too-real and Renfield falls victim to the suave, uncanny Count Dracula at the vampire's ruined castle. Now a raving lunatic under Dracula's control, Renfield watches over his master's coffin as the unholy pair charter a ship for England. After violent storms, the ship runs aground on the English coast. "Crew of Corpses Found on Derelict Vessel," reads a newspaper headline, while the text tells us: "Sole survivor a raving maniac. His craving to devour ants, flies and other small living things to obtain their blood puzzles scientists. At present he is under observation in Doctor Seward's Sanitarium near London."

Dracula walks the fog-shrouded streets of London, where he victimizes a young flower girl on his way to the symphony. At the Opera

Bela Lugosi as *Dracula* (1931) recoils from a cross held in the unknowing hand of Renfield (Dwight Frye), soon to become the vampire's pitiful slave.

House, he introduces himself to Dr. Seward (whose sanitarium adjoins Dracula's new home); Seward's daughter, Mina; her fiancé, Jonathan; and her friend, Lucy. Later that night, Lucy falls prey to Dracula and becomes the mysterious "Woman in White," an ethereal creature who attacks small children near the cemetery.

Professor Van Helsing (a respected doctor and expert on the occult) concludes after analyzing Renfield's blood that "We are dealing with the undead" and sets out to secure proof. From hints dropped by the raving Renfield and the fact Count Dracula casts no reflection, the Professor concludes that "Dracula is our vampire."

In the meantime, Dracula has been systematically draining Mina of blood. Jonathan wants to take her away, but Van Helsing warns that "If you take her from under our protection, you will kill her." Despite Van Helsing's precautions (wolfbane, attendant nurse), Dracula continues his nocturnal attacks on Mina and makes her a living slave by forcing her to drink his own blood. "Our only chance of saving Miss Mina's life," counsels Van Helsing, "is to find the hiding place of Dracula's living corpse and to drive a stake through its heart." The following night, Dracula comes yet again to Mina and, hypnotizing the nurse, takes his intended bride back to Carfax Abbey.

Meanwhile, Renfield has escaped his cell. Van Helsing and Harker, out searching for Dracula's box of earth, follow the madman to the Abbey. When the two vampire-hunters arrive on the heels of Renfield, Dracula kills his inept servant and takes Mina down to the crypt. Van Helsing and Harker break in after him only to find *two* boxes. Inside one is Dracula (the sun having just risen), but the other is empty. (The dawn had prevented Dracula from consummating Mina's vampiric transformation.) As Van Helsing drives a stake into Dracula's undead heart, Mina comes out of her trance. Harker rushes to her side and the lovers are reunited.

MEMORABLE MOMENTS

Renfield's arrival at Castle Dracula heralds what is undoubtedly the most atmospheric and supernaturally-charged quarter-hour from the Golden Age of Horror Cinema. It begins with Dracula's speeding coach pulling into the castle courtyard. As the horses come to a halt, Renfield voices his indignation. "I say driver, what do you mean by going at this—" His protestation trails off when he finds only an empty seat atop the coach. As he looks about him in astonishment, the castle's massive wooden and iron door slowly creaks open of its own accord. Renfield, unsure, passes uneasily through the forbidding portal. Inside the cavernous interior, all huge windows, massive pillars, and shadowy archways, the sparse furnishings and centuries-old cobwebs are barely visible in the massive moonlit space. Renfield, small and insignificant as an insect (or "unwary fly"), steps cautiously into the gigantic chamber. As Renfield hesitates at the bottom of the wide stone staircase, a lone black-shrouded figure carrying a single inadequate candle descends the stairs. Renfield turns and looks about him in nervous alarm, while Dracula glides inexorably down the stairs towards him. Renfield stares at the approaching figure in trepidation until the figure gives a slight smirking smile and Bela Lugosi's sepulchral Hungarian tones issue forth with "I am—Dracula."

Throughout this entire sequence, an ominous silence lies heavily over the scene, the absence of sound seeming to build to an almost unbearable anti-crescendo, so that the ghostly coming of Dracula and his first innocuous utterance take on an almost shattering supernatural significance. For the next dozen minutes the macabre ambiance and unforgettable dialogue build exponentially, creating uncanny vignettes such as Dracula passing undisturbed through the giant spider web stretched across the staircase, the Count's congenial host transforming into a blood-maddened fiend when the unknowing Renfield pricks his finger, and Dracula's three spectral wives closing in on their prostrate prey. For two reels, anyway, *Dracula* has yet to be matched.

ASSETS

The Golden Age of Sound Horror glided into Hollywood on gossamer (bat)wings—sported by the King of the Undead himself, Dracula. Though not the first literary appearance of the dread nosferatu (*Varney the Vampire*, by Thomas Preskett Prest and *Carmilla*, by Sheridan Le Fanu preceded it by 50 and 25 years, respectively), Bram Stoker's *Dracula* is the father of all screen bloodsuckers. Vampires and Dracula arrived on the silver screen together with an unauthorized adaptation of Stoker's novel—*Nosferatu* (1922). Since then, Dracula has appeared onscreen in nearly 100 films, but none having more impact than the 1931 Universal adaptation[1] which skyrocketed an unknown Hungarian stage actor named Bela Lugosi to screen stardom (and typecasting purgatory). Every horror film made since then owes an enormous debt to *Dracula* (1931), for it was this immensely popular picture (assisted by Universal's follow-up feature, *Frankenstein*, released later the same year) which gave birth to the sound horror genre in America. It is very easy to find fault with *Dracula* today. Its flaws are legion and obvious. One should not overlook, however, its many assets as well, qualities that have kept it firmly ensconced in the "classic" pantheon over the years.

Actor David Manners (in David J. Skal's *Hollywood Gothic*) credited *Dracula*'s merits to cinematographer Karl Freund rather than director Tod Browning. "Tod Browning," recalled the actor, "was always off to the side somewhere. I remember being directed by Karl Freund. I believe that he is the one who is mainly responsible for *Dracula* being watchable today." Freund's gliding camera and exquisite lighting do much to generate the picture's effectively eerie atmosphere. In the shadowy recesses of his castle cellar, for example, Dracula stands unmoving as we first glimpse the undead fiend. His cape wrapped tightly around him, the dim, diffuse light transforms the garment into an enveloping, impenetrable shroud of blackness. With pinpoint precision, Freund illumines the vampire's face so that it appears to glow, shining forth from the twilight gloom with an unearthly (unholy?) inner light. In Dracula's first encounter with Mina at the Opera House, Freund utilizes lighting to underscore a moment's mood. "There are far worse things—" Dracula intones and pauses dramatically, while at that very moment the light dims (as the theater house lights go down) before he continues "— awaiting man — than death." At this last sepulchral utterance, the light raises at a reduced intensity as the stage footlights come up, which adds a glowing illumination to the supernatural speaker. Freund's perfectly timed changes in lighting amplify the dread impact of the ominous dialogue.

Critics often single out the static staginess of *Dracula*'s second half as the picture's greatest liability. While it's true that the latter portion fails to live up to the eerie promise made in the first twenty minutes (and it IS stagy — due to leisurely pacing and haphazard direction), *Dracula*'s nether-region (so to speak) is anything *but* static, containing moments of downright inventive cinematography — most likely courtesy of Karl Freund. The introduction to Dr. Seward's sanitarium is a good case in point. The scene opens with a high crane shot overlooking the sanitarium gate. The camera lowers and moves forward as if passing through the portal itself as the scene dissolves to the grounds inside. Still in an elevated position, the camera continues its smooth advance, gliding forward and turning from side to side as if looking about at the various attendants and patients moving around the grounds. A sudden piercing cry comes from the left, at which the camera swiftly swings *right* to focus on two patients sitting on a bench. "He probably wants his *flies* again!" screeches the nearest inmate, while an off-screen voice pleads, "No Martin, please!" The camera now swings left to trace the source of this tortured sound. Moving sideways and upwards (across a hedge and toward the building), the camera takes us to a second-story window and peers through the bars to discover two men huddled within. Throughout the fluid movement, we hear the tormented voice repeatedly entreating, "No Martin, please ... please, Martin!" backed by the first inmate's horrible, screeching laughter. Through his smooth and elaborate camera movements, Freund takes the viewer inside the sanitarium emotionally as well as physically. The initial motion *away* from the strained, plaintive voice (and toward the giggling inmate) inspires first surprise, then curiosity about the sound's source, and finally pity as we wonder at the unseen sufferer's torments (not yet knowing he simply wants his "fat, juicy spider" back). Finally, the abrupt, rapid motion toward the voice creates a palpable urgency as the pleadings continue and we finally approach the cell to peer within.

The fluid tracking shots continue throughout the film. Focusing on Lucy asleep in her bed, Freund pans right to reveal the sinister form of Count Dracula standing at the opposite end of the room. The camera follows him as he slowly approaches her prone form and then zooms in for emphasis as the vampire's face dips downward to her neck.

Van Helsing's introduction begins with a tight shot of the white-coated professor sitting at his desk measuring out liquid from a test tube. The camera then smoothly dollies backward to reveal a cluster of dark forms gathered about the desk, awaiting Van Helsing's bizarre pronouncement: "Gentlemen, we are dealing with the undead." The smooth motion adds visual impact to the dramatic statement by heralding a significant change in the complexion of the scene — and the man's character — from solitary scientist to revered authority.

For the pivotal moment when Van Helsing

realizes Dracula casts no reflection, the camera focuses on the images in the mirrored cigarette case and, with measured subtlety, creeps in closer — so gradually that we hardly notice until the scene cuts to Van Helsing bending close over the case for a better look — just as *we* have done via the camera.[2]

When Renfield, terrified he's said too much, spots a bat at the window, he exclaims, "No, no Master, I wasn't going to say anything. I've told them nothing. I'm loyal to you Master!" As the terrified "fly-eater" steps back in trepidation, the camera glides forward towards Renfield, closing in on him to heighten visually his mounting terror.

Inevitably, when one discusses *Dracula*, one discusses Bela Lugosi, for, as so many of *Dracula*'s critics/historians have concluded over the years, Lugosi IS Dracula. Other actors have followed (and made their own individual marks) but none has grasped the role as strongly as Lugosi. Like some tenacious undead duckling, Lugosi's Dracula has imprinted on our cinematic collective consciousness. Though the "Hungarian Romeo's" brand of continental suavity may not be so sexually appealing to today's audiences, he still exudes a powerful presence difficult to dismiss (and impossible to ignore). The actor's sometimes overpowering pantomimic skills (developed during years on the European stage) create an old world charm and intensity on the one hand, and capture the very essence of evil on the other. When Dracula approaches the sleeping Lucy, for instance, Lugosi's body curves in a graceful arc as he stalks slowly forward with his hand outstretched, his long bony fingers like talons, his entire malevolent being intensely focused on the supine form like some huge bird of prey. Once seen, Lugosi and Dracula become synonymous for most viewers.

Edward Van Sloan gives a veritable crash-course on how to play Old World Authority. His birdlike stance (hands held suspended in front, neck craned forward), owlish glances, and slow, studied movements both complement and contrast with Lugosi's unholy nighthawk. Ironically, Van Sloan was positively aghast at his own performance. "When I first saw myself on film I wanted to scream and run away, I thought I was so awful," remembered the venerable stage actor. "I said to myself, 'Is that all you've learnt about acting after appearing in 150 or so plays?' I just couldn't believe that Dracula would be a success in the cinema and I felt I should have stayed on the stage!"[3] Contrary to Van Sloan's self-critical perception, his and Lugosi's unhurried playing perfectly suits the slow, stately progression of events. The measured movements of the actors — and of the film itself — augment the picture's morbid atmosphere. (The "slowness" of *Dracula* so often attacked by the film's critics is a deliberate pace which, to some extent, proves successfully eerie.) The stately playing also creates a striking antithesis to Dwight Frye's jittery Renfield, who seems animated by an explosive, unthinking energy (with his lunatic laugh and mad pleadings like, "I'll be loyal master ... you'll see that I get lives? Not human lives, but small ones, with blood in them"). Frye makes of his "fly-eater" a veritable dynamo of insane lust and tormented guilt. (Dwight Frye's portrayal was so effective that Hollywood typecast him in similar roles for the remainder of his career, despite his coming from a successful stage career on Broadway and possessing a genuine affinity for comedy.)

While critics have often criticized Helen Chandler's performance (with words like "bloodless" cavalierly bandied about), she actually plays a number of scenes to good effect. When she meets Dracula at the Seward home, after her nocturnal "dream," the sight of her unholy paramour causes her breathing to visibly accelerate and she leans forward almost imperceptibly, a subtle look of excited expectancy on her face. One can almost *see* the blood quicken in her veins (yearning, no doubt, to flow out of them and onto the lips of Count Dracula). Later, after becoming the vampire's slave, Ms. Chandler reveals a frighteningly perverse transformation as the blood lust overpowers her. Suddenly, the lines of her mouth become fixed, while her eyes stare with a strange, malevolent intensity. An animal-like hunger crosses her face as she moves in to do

God-knows-what to her unsuspecting fiancé. All in all, Ms. Chandler does quite well given the frequently less-than-perfect performances of most of the other players (David Manners as the lusterless Harker, Herbert Bunston in the tepid non-presence of Seward, Charles Gerrard as the buffoonish Martin) — and obvious lack of direction from Browning. (Director Joseph Newman, who had worked under Browning in the 1930s, claimed in *Filmfax* #33 that "Tod Browning had the knack of making an actor probe for the unusual in characterization without the actor really being aware of being directed." For *Dracula*, did Browning do his job too well — or just barely at all? According to David Manners — and most of the supporting performances — one would have to take the latter, less charitable view.)

LIABILITIES

"Words, words, words," sneers Renfield contemptuously at one of Van Helsing's many pronouncements. It could almost be an epithet for the film's talky second half itself. Once Dracula arrives in London, the narrative bogs down in Van Helsing's endless expositions and Jonathan's continual obstructive protestations. Sadly, little is seen of Dracula after the mirror incident; through much of the film he remains as invisible as his image in the reflective cigarette case.

Tod Browning — was he an overblown, alcoholic hack riding on the coattails of his lucky partnership with the brilliant Lon Chaney or was he a true genius of light and shadow worthy of the (studio-awarded) appellation "The Edgar Allan Poe of the Screen"? As with most extremist viewpoints, reality undoubtedly lies somewhere in the middle. Of the four Golden Age horror pictures Browning directed (*Dracula*, *Freaks*, *Mark of the Vampire*, and *The Devil-Doll*), there's no denying the considerable (though varied) power found in each. At the very least, Browning provided some of the most atmospheric moments of the decade, while shedding light on some of the darkest themes of the period. Yet, he was rarely able to sustain a mood throughout an entire picture, either through lack of skill or simple lack of interest.

In *Dracula*, Tod Browning's haphazard direction is full of instances of just plain carelessness. In no fewer than four shots in Mina's bedroom, a tattered square of cardboard (utilized to shield a lamp while the set was being lit) is thoughtlessly left in full view. In one shot, this incongruous object appears prominently in the *foreground*! Cameraman Karl Freund *must* have realized the gaff, *must* have seen it through his viewfinder. One can conjecture that, annoyed with the apparently apathetic Browning, Freund spitefully remained silent and left the unobservant director to wipe the egg off his face later on. In any case, such obvious negligence leads one to suspect that the erratic director suffered more from lapses of impetus than dearth of talent.

Browning makes little use of Charles D. Hall's magnificent Castle Dracula and Carfax Abbey sets.[4] With such vast space and exquisitely macabre detail, Browning chose to keep the camera relatively still rather than giving Freund a free hand to prowl about and explore these wondrous gothic settings. Browning allowed a freer mobility later on, so why he held back on the most visually enthralling sets is difficult to fathom.[5] Even worse, he populated his cobwebbed cathedral with such bizarrely out-of-place fauna as cuddly possums and American armadillos.

At times, Browning seems simply to have chosen the path of least resistance. The director cheats the audience by first showing Lugosi's coffin lid rise, then panning the camera away to a window while the noise of the lid slamming down is heard, and finally tracking back to reveal Lugosi standing upright next to his coffin. Browning does this not once but *twice*, the two scenes shot in an almost identical fashion! Granted, one wants to avoid showing the sinister Count struggling to free his cape from beneath him as he swings a leg out of the box, but Browning makes no effort to imbue this cheap avoidance trick with any sense of justification. At the very least, Browning could have shown the light fading behind the window to give some excuse for the camera (and

Dracula's three wives glide across Charles D. Hall's atmospheric Castle Dracula set to close on the fallen Renfield.

audience) to look in that direction (as Lambert Hillyer later did in *Dracula's Daughter*). But no such reason is provided. This directorial laziness becomes almost unforgivable when compared to director George Melford's effective and atmospheric handling of this same scene in the Spanish language version: The coffin lid opens of its own accord while an eerie cloud of white smoke issues forth, rising upwards to dissolve and reveal the imposing figure of Count Dracula.

When Dracula first encounters Dr. Seward and family at the symphony, Browning allows Dracula to stand on a lower step as he meets Seward. This results in Dracula appearing a full head *shorter* than Seward and places the Count in the subservient position of having to look up at his soon-to-be-enemy. Why Browning would shoot the all-powerful Dracula in such a subordinate position is a question with no logical answer — except that the scene was carelessly staged. (Melford avoids this mistake by having Dracula meet Seward just after the latter steps out of his opera box so that the two stand on level ground, allowing the half-a-head-taller Dracula to look down upon his shorter nemesis.)

Browning often undermines the visuals by holding on a shot too long, creating a static staged impression, such as when Jonathan jumps about waving his arms at the bat hovering over Mina for what seems an interminable period of time. (Again Melford's handling proves superior; by shooting close-ups, Melford provides inserts that break the monotony.)

The film's slow pace and theatrical acting fit well with the gothic aura of the Castle Dracula sets (which only grow more fascinating as we linger among them), but in the more mundane drawing room sets of the picture's second half, the pace becomes a noticeable detraction. Browning extends the inertia by relying on dialogue rather than action. Dracula's sudden departure after the mirror incident, for instance, has Jonathan striding to the terrace after him, only to look out the window and state: "What's that — running across the lawn? Looks like a huge dog." We, however, never see the demonic hellhound in a bit of optic avoidance straight off the stage (as is Manners' stilted delivery). In the visual medium of cinema, it's a shame to lose such a rich opportunity by employing such a limiting theatrical technique (which only serves to make the picture seem more stagebound than it truly is). It is primarily the lethargic pacing and tendency to *talk* about horrific events instead of *showing* them which has earned *Dracula* the unwanted appellations "stagebound" and "flawed classic."[6]

Loose ends waft lazily on the Transylvanian breeze of Garrett Fort and Tod Browning's[7] screenplay. Whatever happened to Dracula's three wives? Are they still terrorizing the Carpathian countryside? And what about his numerous London victims (including the flower girl)? Vampirism must be running rampant through the English capital by now. What of the vampirized Lucy? Though much is made of her nocturnal attacks on children, there is no mention of the "Woman in White's" ultimate fate.[8] What does the poor unfortunate Renfield actually *do* for Dracula besides reveal information to the vampire's enemies? And Professor Van Helsing's rather cavalier protection of Mina (particularly by leaving her alone with the same nurse who'd allowed her to wander out into Dracula's clutches on the previous night) seems surprisingly incautious from such "a wise man."

The only truly funny comedy found in *Dracula* is purely unintentional. (The intended Comedy Relief—in the broad accent and clownish walk of Charles Gerrard's dim-witted Cockney attendant — falls flat.) When Renfield's coach pulls into the stage stop, his exchange with the Innkeeper is a howlingly funny see-saw of echoing questions and answers:

> Renfield: "There's a carriage meeting me at Borgo Pass at midnight."
> Innkeeper: "Borgo Pass?"
> Renfield: "Yes."
> Innkeeper: "Whose carriage?"
> Renfield: "Count Dracula."
> Innkeeper: "Count Dracula's? Castle Dracula?"
> Renfield: "Yes, that's where I'm going."
> Innkeeper: "To de castle?"
> Renfield: "Yes."
> Innkeeper: "Noooo."

Complete with arching eyebrows and pantomimic hand movements, Michael Visaroff's concerned Innkeeper becomes a heavily accented, mustachioed parrot.[9]

While *Dracula* has dated rather badly over the years, one cannot deny its powerful mystique. With all its flaws, *Dracula* still inspires an almost primal, hypnotic fascination which (much like Mina held by Dracula's burning gaze) a true lover of horror's Golden Age finds impossible to resist.

REVIEWS

Mordaunt Hall, reviewer for *The New York Times* (February 13, 1931) credited both Browning and Lugosi for the film's success: "What with Mr. Browning's imaginative direction and Mr. Lugosi's make-up and weird gestures, this picture succeeds to some extent in its grand guignol intentions." Incredibly, Mr. Hall claimed that "David Manners contributes good work," while stating that Dwight Frye does only "fairly well."

Even for this first of all sound horror films, Mr. Hall seemed to be offering an apology for the budding genre when he concluded that "this picture can at least boast of being the best of the many mystery films."

Variety (February 18, 1931) felt the key to the picture's success lay in "a remarkably effective background of creepy atmosphere" and "the mute perfection of the settings [which] carry the conviction that the characters lack." In essence, "the atmosphere makes anything seem possible." About Lugosi: "It is difficult to think of anybody who could quite match the performance in the vampire part of Bela Lugosi, even to the faint flavor of foreign speech [*faint* flavor?!] that fits so neatly."

PRODUCTION NOTES

Much publicity surrounded the premier of *Dracula*. The film was set to open on

Bela Lugosi strikes a contemplative pose on the Universal lot during the filming of *Dracula* (1931). (Courtesy of Ted Okuda.)

February 13, 1931, at the Roxy Theater in New York. However, the thirteenth was a Friday and an advertisement reprinting this supposed telegram appeared in *Variety* on February 7:

DEAR ROXY DON'T BLAME ME BUT I WAS BORN SUPERSTITIOUS STOP JUST HEARD YOU ARE OPENING DRACULA FRIDAY STOP THAT BAD ENOUGH BUT FRIDAY THE THIRTEENTH IS TERRIBLE STOP I HAVE PUT EVERYTHING I HAVE INTO THIS PICTURE AND AS A FAVOR TO ME CAN'T YOU OPEN YOUR PRESENTATION THURSDAY STOP BEST REGARDS — TOD BROWNING

"Roxy" good-naturedly went along with the publicity ploy and the picture opened on Thursday, February 12th (NOT on the 14th — Valentine's Day — as has been frequently — and erroneously — reported).

Costing a hefty $442,000, *Dracula* ran over budget to the tune of $87,000. The studio executives had little to complain about, however, for the picture earned Universal nearly $700,000 upon its initial release. By 1936, the figure was well over $1,000,000.

Universal trimmed nine minutes from the film before it ever hit the Roxy in an attempt to speed up the picture's glacial pace. The cutting seemed panicky, for a few of the injudicious deletions prove downright disastrous. In one scene, Renfield approaches a frightened maid, who faints and slumps to the ground. The sequence ends abruptly with Renfield leering over her, one hand reaching for her throat (or blouse top?). In actuality, the poor creature is simply after a fly which has alighted upon the girl's prostrate form. By excising the scene's final denouement, Renfield appears bent upon murder — or worse. Also deleted were all further references to the vampiric Lucy, so her fate remains undecided in the finished film.

Universal's first choice as Dracula was *not* Bela Lugosi, but Conrad Veidt, with Paul Leni (*The Wax Works*, *The Cat and the Canary*) to direct. On September 11, 1929, however, Leni suddenly died of blood poisoning and Veidt, who had relied heavily on the brilliant director during *The Man Who Laughs* (1928), bowed out and returned to Germany. (Ironically, Veidt withdrew from English language pictures altogether because of his poor grasp of English — a handicap shared by Lugosi; Veidt later overcame this while Lugosi never did.) Universal next chose Lon Chaney, Sr., for the role, the "Man of a Thousand Faces" and the first true horror star. The studio offered this "top male box office draw" (according to the annual Quigley Poll of exhibitors in both 1928 and 1929) a three-picture contract consisting of *Outside the Law* (a remake of Chaney's earlier vehicle), *The Return of the Phantom* (a sequel to *The Phantom of the Opera*), and *Dracula*. Sadly, Chaney died of throat cancer soon after.

Among the actors subsequently considered for the pivotal role of the King of the Vampires were William Courtenay, Ian Keith, perennial screen gangster Paul Muni, and, claimed the actor himself, the then-unknown John Carradine. (Carradine later *did* play the Count a total of four times — twice as many as Lugosi — in *House of Frankenstein* [1944], *House of Dracula* [1945], *Billy the Kid vs. Dracula* [1966] and *Nocturna, Granddaughter of Dracula* [1979]). Universal associate producer E. M. Asher even offered Chester Morris (star of *The Bat Whispers*) the part a mere *two weeks* before the production was to begin. Fortunately, Morris turned it down.

At the last minute, Universal finally chose Bela Lugosi. Lugosi had starred in the hit Broadway stageplay[10] and had been energetically lobbying for the part all along. Film historians often maintain that the studio's choice was predominantly a financial rather than creative decision, for they knew they could get Lugosi quite cheaply, and wound up paying him a pitiful $500 a week (while tepid leading man David Manners earned four times that sum at $2,000 weekly!).

For Lugosi, *Dracula* was both a blessing and a curse. Hurd Hatfield remembered (in *Forties Film Talk* by Doug McClelland) how his career was forever "haunted" by *The Picture of Dorian Gray*. Putting things in perspective, he reported, "One friend told me it's a good thing I didn't make *Dracula* and have my entire professional life dominated by that!"

Dracula's Jonathan Harker was Canadian-born David Manners' first role in a horror film, and he played similar parts in two later classics, *The Mummy* (1932), and *The Black Cat* (1934). In an interview with author David J. Skal (for *The Monster Show*), Manners admitted that he'd *never* seen *Dracula*! "I knew it was a stinker all the while we were making it," dismissed the actor contemptuously, "so I just never bothered to go."

A Spanish version of *Dracula* was filmed simultaneously with the English version, using the same sets but a different cast and crew. The

English version was shot during the day, with the Spanish crew working at night. Many critics feel that, while it sorely misses Lugosi's iconographic presence, *cinematically* the Spanish version is superior to the English one.

In early 1958 (two years after Lugosi's death), the first remake of *Dracula* was planned (*before* Hammer's version got underway) and, in a bit of Hollywood irony, was set to star ... Boris Karloff! According to Richard Gordon (Karloff's producer on *Corridors of Blood* and *The Haunted Strangler*), it was discovered that Universal still owned the film rights to Stoker's story, so the project was ultimately abandoned.

NOTES

1. Though based on the book *Dracula*, by Bram Stoker, Universal's film more closely follows the stage play adaptation by Hamilton Deane and John L. Balderston. The characters are Stoker's, but their actions are the playwrights'.

2. Edward Van Sloan noted that, "In fact, there weren't a great many differences between the stage version and the film, though I do recall one. On the stage, in the famous scene where Van Helsing confronts Dracula with a betraying mirror, we used a full-length wall mirror, and as soon as he saw it he tossed a vase at it and shattered it. In the film this became a small mirror box and I don't believe the scene was anywhere near as dramatic." (Quoted in *The Dracula Scrapbook*, by Peter Haining.)

3. Quoted in *The Dracula Scrapbook*, by Peter Haining.

4. British-born Charles D. "Danny" Hall was one of the great unsung heroes of Hollywood's Golden Age. His expansive and imaginative designs graced such films as *The Hunchback of Notre Dame* (1923), *The Phantom of the Opera* (1925), *The Cat and the Canary* (1927), *The Man Who Laughs* (1928), *All Quiet on the Western Front* (1930), *Frankenstein* (1931), *The Old Dark House* (1932), *The Invisible Man* (1933), *The Black Cat* (1934), and *Bride of Frankenstein* (1935). In later years, he was forced to make a living designing cheap sets for low-budget independents like *The Flying Saucer* (1950), *Red Planet Mars* (1952), and *The Unearthly* (1957; his next to last film).

5. Lupita Tovar, who starred in Universal's simultaneously-shot Spanish language version, remembered just how effective these sets were. "I was always an hour early because I wanted to be ready. And many a time I walk in there and I was all alone and it was really scary to see the sets and everything. If anybody will touch me, I think I would *scream*."

6. Some historians have conjectured that Browning, feeling pressure from Universal's front office, hurried through the latter portion of the screenplay (which was shot in roughly chronological order) in an attempt to finish on time, and so chose to stage and shoot some scenes as quickly and easily as possible. If so, he failed anyway, for he still took the production a full six days over its 36-day schedule.

7. Though Garrett Fort received sole screenplay credit on the finished film, the picture's fourth and final draft of the script credited "Adaptation and Dialogue by Tod Browning and Garrett Fort," revealing that Browning had a hand in the writing as well (as the director did on many a "Tod Browning Production").

8. The shooting script *does* include a nocturnal sequence in which Van Helsing (who carries "an oblong, paper-wrapped parcel") and Jonathan secretly watch as the vampiric Lucy returns to her crypt. If this scene was shot as written, it failed to make the final cut. Melford's Spanish version deftly handles the issue by including a brief (and rather atmospheric) scene in which Van Helsing and Juan (Jonathan) walk somberly out through the cemetery gate and the weary Van Helsing says, "It was a good deed — to drive a stake through the heart of that poor girl. Now, her soul will rest in peace."

9. In the Spanish language version, Melford wisely shortened this dialogue to avoid the ridiculous mimicry.

10. Lugosi was not the only veteran from the Broadway play to appear in the film version; Edward Van Sloan, Dwight Frye, and Herbert Bunston all reprised their stage roles for the movie.

FRANKENSTEIN
(1931; Universal)

Release Date: November 21, 1931
Running Time: 71 minutes
Director: James Whale

Producer: Carl Laemmle, Jr.
Associate Producer: E. M. Asher
Screenplay: Garrett Fort, Francis Edwards

Faragoh, *John Russell, *Robert Florey (based on the composition by John L. Balderston; from the novel by Mrs. Percy B. Shelley; adapted from the play by Peggy Webling)
**Scenario Editor: Richard Schayer
*Continuity: Thomas Reed
Photography: Arthur Edeson
Editor: Clarence Kolster
Supervising Editor: Maurice Pivar
Art Director: Charles D. Hall
*Set Designer: Herman Rosse
Recording Supervisor: C. Roy Hunter
*Makeup: Jack P. Pierce
*Assistant Director: Joseph A. McDonough
*Special Electrical Effects: Kenneth Strickfaden, Frank Graves, Raymond Lindsay
*Technical Advisor: Dr. Cecil Reynolds
*Music: David Broekman
Cast: Colin Clive (Henry Frankenstein), Mae Clarke (Elizabeth), John Boles (Victor Moritz), Boris Karloff (The Monster), Edward Van Sloan (Doctor Waldman), Frederick Kerr (Baron Frankenstein), Dwight Frye (Fritz), Lionel Belmore (The Burgomaster), Marilyn Harris (Little Maria), *Michael Mark (Ludwig), *Arletta Duncan (Bridesmaid), *Pauline Moore (Bridesmaid), *Francis Ford (Extra at Lecture/Wounded Villager on Hill).

*Uncredited on film print.
**As head of Universal's story department, Richard Schayer received a standard "Scenario Editor" credit, but (though he made suggestions and arbitrated disputes as necessary) he was not a collaborator per se.

"In the name of God, now I know what it feels like to *be* God!"[1]— Henry Frankenstein.
"Success is simply a matter of being on the right corner at the right time." — Boris Karloff.[2]

SYNOPSIS

Near the Bavarian mountain village of Goldstadt, the young scientist Henry Frankenstein, with the aid of his hunchbacked assistant Fritz, steals dead bodies to carry out his experiments on the secrets of life. His worried fiancée, Elizabeth, leads family friend Victor, along with Henry's former professor Dr. Waldman, to the isolated abandoned watchtower which Frankenstein uses as a laboratory. That very night, Henry performs his final experiment and, before the startled eyes of the three onlookers, brings to life a thing he made "with my own hands from the bodies I took from graves, from the gallows, *anywhere!*"

The creature fails to respond as Henry would have wished (no doubt due to the fact that the creature's skull houses a *criminal* brain which Fritz had stolen from the nearby medical college), and Henry must keep the brute chained. When the monster kills Fritz (who "always tormented him"), Dr. Waldman convinces Henry that the creature must be destroyed. After subduing his now-violent creation, Henry collapses from exhaustion as Elizabeth arrives with Baron Frankenstein (Henry's father) to take him away.

While Henry recuperates under the care of the adoring Elizabeth, Dr. Waldman prepares to dissect the drugged creature. The monster wakes, however, and kills Waldman. Escaping into the outside world, he comes upon a little girl playing by a lake. Unafraid of the hideous intruder, Maria invites him to join her game of tossing flowers into the pond. This idyllic scene is shattered when the enthusiastic monster runs out of petals and playfully tosses Maria into the water — where she promptly sinks.

Unaware of the monster's escape, the villagers celebrate on the day of Henry and Elizabeth's wedding. Before the nuptials can commence, however, the monster pays a visit to the bride, leaving Elizabeth in a swoon but otherwise unhurt. When Ludwig carries the body of little Maria through the streets, the revelers stop and follow him to the Burgomaster's. With Frankenstein's aid, the villagers form a search party to seek out "the fiend." As the torch-bearing mob combs the countryside, Henry becomes separated from his men in the mountains, where he comes face to face with his angry creation. The creature overpowers Henry and, with the villagers hot on his heels, drags his creator to an old windmill.

When Henry recovers his senses and attempts to escape the fiend's clutches, the enraged monster hurls him from the top of the windmill, where he falls at the feet of the villagers. The mob takes up Henry's limp body and sets fire to the building. As the monster screams in rage and pain, the burning structure collapses around him.

Back at the Frankenstein home, Elizabeth tends a recovering Henry while the Baron, standing outside his son's sickroom, toasts, "Here's to a son to the House of Frankenstein."

MEMORABLE MOMENT

Due to James Whale's unique staging, the monster's first appearance remains a startling moment, even after 60-odd years of overexposure. As Henry and Waldman talk earnestly at a table, the heavy thud of shuffling footsteps intrudes. Turning toward the noise, Henry whispers, "Here he comes. Let's turn out the light." As they look expectantly on, the recessed cell door swings slowly open to reveal a hulking figure in silhouette. When the form awkwardly moves forward, the camera cuts closer so that we see a broad back and oddly-shaped head. Only then do we realize that the creature is *backing* through the doorway. As it slowly turns we see a shadowy visage in profile before the movement brings the cadaverous countenance fully into the light. Before we can catch our breath (or suppress our building scream), two rapid jump cuts take us tight, then tighter still, into the hideous face so that for a moment the screen — indeed, our whole world — is filled with the nightmarish image.[3] The only sound throughout this sequence is the slow, shuffling noise of the creature's feet, the uncanny silence serving to magnify the shock.

ASSETS

In the six decades since Boris Karloff first turned his Jack Pierce makeup toward the camera, the Frankenstein monster has been transformed from an object of cinematic terror into such banal incarnations as a Saturday morning cartoon character and a breakfast cereal huckster. With familiarity frequently comes contempt, and it is far too easy for today's viewer (even the devout horror fan) to take for granted this old horror classic. Yet, far from being a dated chestnut like *Dracula* or *The Ghoul*, *Frankenstein* possesses enough raw power and primal fascination to enthrall even after decades of merchandising and overexposure.

A large part of the picture's staying power arises from the fact that *Frankenstein* is one of the *tightest* horror films of the Golden Age. Director James Whale takes the viewer from point A to point B in the most direct route possible, moving from unease to wonder to shock to horror to excitement and to sympathy at a smooth, rapid pace.

Beyond *Frankenstein*'s tight, linear construction, the film's overall success stems primarily from the efforts of three men — director James Whale, makeup maestro Jack P. Pierce, and a little-known bit player named Boris Karloff.

Through Karloff's sensitive portrayal and Whale's insightful direction, the monster becomes a sympathetic as well as frightening figure. This element of pathos is what gives *Frankenstein* its enduring fascination even after literally dozens of sequels, remakes, and knock-offs. Karloff's child-like yearning and open-handed pleading for the sunlight, his frantic straining against the chains that bind him, his all-too-temporary smiles of genuine joy at playing with Maria, and his subsequent panicked concern when the little girl sinks in the lake all combine to make this hideous outcast pitiable (though no less dangerous for that). Even at the very end, after venting his violent rage on the picture's ostensible hero, Karloff's high-pitched scream of terror at the consuming fire inspires pity along with fear, and his frantic, ineffectual struggle to free himself from a burning beam tempers the flaming excitement of the moment with an element of sadness (a trait which made *King Kong*'s climactic battle with the biplanes so heartrendingly memorable two years later). In Karloff's own words, "I think the popularity [of the character] was due to the compassion people felt for him, this poor tragic figure. His master, the only person he knew, had turned on him; he was helpless, alone, confused and terrified — how could one not feel sympathy for such a creature?"[4]

Whale's discerning direction augments this compassion. Through a clever use of point-of-view photography when Fritz torments the monster, for example, Whale places the audience firmly in the hapless creature's asphalt-spreader boots so that we, alongside the monster, feel the terror of a flaming torch thrust into our faces.

Whale's guiding hand and attention to detail can be found in every scene. With the picture's first sequence, for example, Whale provides subtle insight into the character of Henry Frankenstein, a man who cares little for normal convention and nothing at all for such sacred concepts as the laws of Man and Nature. When he eagerly approaches the fresh grave, Henry strips off his jacket and carelessly throws it into the dirt behind him, much as he strips off constraining societal and moral conventions with his resurrectionist activities. Then, in his excitement, Henry hastily shovels the dirt off the grave this way and that, one shovelful of earth flying square in the face of a nearby statue of the grim reaper! With this subtle, blackly humorous action, Whale suggests how little reverence Frankenstein holds for the subject of death, and how willing he is to fly in the face of dissolution much as the dirt flies in the face of the marble figure.

In *Frankenstein*, James Whale exhibits the technical skill, intelligence, sensitivity, and dark taste for irreverence which made him the greatest filmmaker of horror's Golden Age—and made each of his four genre efforts (*Frankenstein*, *The Old Dark House*, *The Invisible Man*, and *Bride of Frankenstein*) timeless classics. (One can only marvel at the possible result had Universal chosen Whale rather than Tod Browning to direct their initial horror effort, *Dracula*.) After the monster's first appearance, for example, Henry leads the creature out of the cell, retreating slowly backwards before the hulking figure. As the monster advances, his sinister shadow moves before him so that it leans and towers over Henry, foreshadowing (so to speak) the menacing conflict to come. (While one should not underestimate the contribution made by cinematographer Arthur Edeson, there is little doubt that Whale was in full command at all times. Gloria Stuart, who acted for Whale in *The Old Dark House* and *The Invisible Man*, told this author that Whale was "authoritative, always in complete control" and that he conferred with his cameraman on each and every shot.)

Not since the unveiling of the skeletal countenance of Lon Chaney's Phantom of the Opera had movie audiences been assailed by a face as shocking as that dreamed up by a fastidious 42-year-old former jockey and semi-pro shortstop named Jack Pierce. Born Janus Piccoulas, the diminutive Greek immigrant came to California from Chicago in 1910 and worked at a number of different jobs within the film industry (including projectionist, theater manager, cameraman, assistant director, and even actor) before joining Universal in 1926 as a makeup artist. Through hundreds of hours of painstaking research and weeks of trial-and-error testing with Karloff, Pierce fashioned a visage of cadaverous, horrible humanity. "I spent months of study on the anatomical possibilities of the monster alone," wrote Pierce in the May, 1932 issue of *American Cinematographer*. "I studied every operation that would be necessary to create such a body from 'spare parts,' as was related in the story. I studied the physical effect of each, and strove to reproduce them in Mr. Karloff's final character. Every line, every scar, every peculiarity of contour had to be just so for medical reasons; the eyes, for instance, were exact duplicates of the dead eyes of a 2800-year-old Egyptian corpse!"

Boris Karloff never failed to give full credit to the genius of Jack Pierce. "James Whale saw me and wanted me to test for the part of the monster," remembered the actor in a 1967 interview (*Famous Monsters* #47). "I had no idea of the importance of the role, but Jack Pierce knew. He stalled the test two weeks while working on the makeup, and the makeup sold the part."

While on the surface *Frankenstein* remains a gripping horror film, one should not overlook the many textures and subtle themes which lurk beneath its horrific exterior. Allusions to such diverse subjects as parental responsibilities, sexual conflict, the doppelganger motif, and political unrest have been recognized and explored by many an insightful scholar. While these thematic threads may be (and frequently *have* been) taken to the extreme, there's no denying that *Frankenstein* is spun from multilayered cloth. To take one of these strands as example, one can interpret the conflict caused by Frankenstein's creation of a man as the conflict arising from homosexual love and its subsequent rejection. In light of director James Whale's open homosexuality, this particular theme becomes irresistibly intriguing. The discord arises when Henry rejects his creature out of hand, feeling it ugly and brutal. Is this what happens when one disavows one's own sexual instincts? "There can be no wedding," announces Henry, "while this horrible creation of mine is still alive." Frankenstein cannot consummate "normal" love while his homosexuality lives to assert itself. While some may feel that these sorts of "speculative readings" don't belong in most horror picture analyses (Freud himself admitted that "sometimes a cigar is *just* a cigar"), the sheer volume of so many diverse interpretations put forth over the years provides evidence for the thematic richness and depth of *Frankenstein*.

Though *Frankenstein* lacks the quirky, macabre humor so pervasive in Whale's later productions (culminating in the baroque brilliance of *Bride of Frankenstein*), the director still managed to inject small moments of well-hidden humor, keeping subtle the dark comedy he was to let reign in *Bride*. When the harried and determined Fritz slams the door in the face of Henry's unwanted visitors, he waves his comically undersized stick at the door and rails, "Go on, knock!" at their futile pounding. Hurrying to hobble back up the stone stairs, Fritz pauses long enough to pull up a stubborn sock before continuing on his way. Later, during the Great Experiment, Henry and Fritz excitedly roll back the blanket covering the lifeless corpse — only to reveal a tidy white sheet underneath (as if the monstrous cadaver were simply asleep in its bed), which (in a bit of near-comical perversity) they in turn roll back in the *opposite* direction.

Whale takes care of his more obvious comedic needs through the character of the crotchety old Baron Frankenstein, though coloring him with darker hues than those shading the typical Comic Relief character. When Elizabeth tells the Baron that Henry is busy with his experiments, the Baron blusters, "I understand perfectly well. There's another woman — and you're afraid to tell me. Pretty sort of *experiments* these must be!" Later, when a maid announces the arrival of the Burgomaster, the Baron orders, "Well, tell him to go away." "But he says it's important," persists the maid, to which the Baron snorts, "Nothing the Burgomaster can say can be of the *slightest* importance." Overall, I personally find this subtler (and less noisome) comedy character superior to Whale's later (over)use of Una O'Connor's screeching harpy in *The Invisible Man* and *Bride of Frankenstein*.

Beyond the Baron's comedic value, Whale utilizes this character to make light not only of male-female relations (the "pretty sort of experiments") but of the social structure as well. Beyond denigrating the obvious authority figure of the Burgomaster, Whale also subtly pokes fun at the aristocratic class represented by the blustery, cantankerous Baron. When the Burgomaster praises Henry as "such a fine young man, the very image of his father," the Baron interjects a derisive "Heaven forbid!" showing the kind of haughty self-contempt that marks the jaded gentry. (The class-conscious, homosexual Whale delighted time and again in having a go at the "sacred" institutions he disdained.)

In Charles Hall and Herman Rosse's gothic watchtower/laboratory sets, oversized beams and stone walls angle inward to generate a sense of oppressive imbalance — an image perfectly suited to the occupants. The obvious (and often discussed) brilliance of these sets, however, tends to overshadow the impressive secondary settings, such as Frankenstein Manor. When Victor visits Elizabeth there, they meet in the Victorian-style splendor of the parlor, sumptuously and comfortably furnished with dark wood paneling, classical portraits, and plush overstuffed sofas. When the pair finally decide to seek out Henry, they exit the safe, warm living area into a foyer whose vaulted ceiling, huge overhead crossbeams, stone floor, and bare walls speak of the cold, forbidding nature of their quest. The sets become an analogy for abandoning the comfort of the known to seek out the cold knowledge of the *unknown*.

Dr. Waldman's office at the University is no typical professor's cubicle, either. On his desk sit rows of antiquated test-tubes, while a grinning skull stares sightlessly up at his visitors. On the wall behind him, a bookcase filled with oversized volumes is topped by an entire row of human skulls, lined up as if death itself presided over the knowledge contained in the tomes beneath.

Kenneth Strickfaden's bizarre array of machines mixes immense, primitive-looking globes and rings of steel with intricate banks of gauges and levers in a melding of gothic/futura to enhance the oppressive yet dangerously exciting aura of the laboratory set. When the sparks fly (literally), the weird equipment seems as if it truly could conduct the "spark of life." Strickfaden had no pretensions about his fantastic designs. "I made these things because I didn't know anything and I had fun doing it," he admitted to interviewer George E. Turner fifty years later. "It was just a matter of experimentation. I'd put something together and then sit back and marvel at it. The styling all depended on what kind of junk I had on hand." An electrical engineer, Strickfaden felt the scene's premise was not that far from reality. "Electricity is life," he theorized. "We're just a bunch of sparks with various quantities of air."

The remaining technical elements, including Arthur Edeson's fluid, mobile photography (often tracking through the very walls of the castle),[5] the shadowy lighting casting ominous pools of blackness across the imposing gothic sets, and even the sound effects (the violent claps of thunder punctuating Fritz and Frankenstein's frenzied movements) all coalesce under Whale's visionary hand to produce a shuddery masterpiece of gothic terror — and the primary progenitor (if not by right of nascence, then by weight of influence) of the sound horror genre.[6]

LIABILITIES

The supporting cast of *Frankenstein* acquit themselves brilliantly, from the learned voice of reason in the form of Edward Van Sloan and the half-mad archetypal hunchbacked assistant created by Dwight Frye to the concerned fiancée of Mae Clarke and the worldly contempt of the blustering Frederick Kerr, with one exception — John Boles as Victor. In his stilted playing of the concerned family friend, Boles comes off as a glowering, stodgy David Manners (though lacking Manners' puppyish charm). Boles' stolid performance ultimately makes an unwelcome (and decidedly unimportant) intruder of this extraneous character.

Aside from this admittedly minor flaw, the only other liabilities to be found in *Frankenstein* are two technical blemishes. The studio backdrop of the forbidding sky, while adding a brooding atmosphere to the mountain chase scenes, calls attention to itself since the creases of the painted screen give away the effect and ultimately serve to remind the viewer of the set's artificiality.

The second sore spot comes from employing a mannequin (*other* than John Boles). When the monster throws Henry from atop the windmill, Frankenstein's body bends and twists at angles which reveal its counterfeit nature. After landing on a turning windmill blade (a circumstance which would have at least broken the back of a real man), the body slips off and drops earthward with the rubbery legs bowing and curving like a deboned fish. Given the intensity and fortitude exhibited by Henry Frankenstein throughout the previous seventy minutes, it's a shame to see him end up as a spineless dummy.

REVIEWS

Variety (December 8, 1931): "Looks like a 'Dracula' plus, touching a new peak in horror plays and handled in production with supreme craftsmanship.... Maximum of stimulating shock is there, but the thing is handled with

The Monster (**Boris Karloff**) makes his shocking appearance in James Whale's classic landmark horror film, *Frankenstein* (1931).

subtle change of pace and shift of tempo that keeps attention absorbed to a high voltage climax, tricked out with spectacle and dramatic crescendo, after holding the smash shivver [*sic*] on a hair trigger for more than an hour."

The reviewer (*Rush*) noted the film's fine pacing and sense of timing: "The feeling of horror is not once let go past the point at which it inspires disbelief, where out of excess it would create a feeling of make believe. This is the trick that actually makes the picture deliver its high voltage kick. The technique is shrewd manipulation. After each episode dealing with the weird elements of the story there is a swift twist to the normal people of the drama engaged in the commonplace activities, a contrast emphasizing the next eerie detail."

Of the monster: "It has a face and head of exactly the right distortions to convey a sense of the diabolical, but not enough to destroy the essential touch of monstrous human evil.... Boris Karloff enacts the monster and makes a memorable figure of the bizarre figure with its indescribably terrifying face of demoniacal calm, a fascinating acting bit of mesmerism."

Film Weekly (January 23, 1932) was suitably impressed but not a little horrified: "It is no idle exaggeration to say that *Frankenstein* is the most revoltingly gripping melodrama of the macabre since John Barrymore gave his hair-raising impersonation of Mr. Hyde. You may laugh at it, but somehow I don't think you will. The producer, director, and players have done their work too well. They have put a particularly unpleasant nightmare on the screen with a devastating illusion of reality. In some ways they have gone a little too far.... If you want the best horrors, *Frankenstein* certainly has them."

Bioscope's reviewer (January 27, 1932) did not agree with *Variety* that the film was a work of "supreme craftsmanship", labeling it instead as "anything but a classic in filmcraft." With obviously shocked sensibilities, the reviewer added: "As a crudely constructed blood-curdler it will certainly thrill those who find their pleasures in things morbid and horrible."

Perhaps the most telling review is the reaction of the audiences themselves. Cal York reported in his "Monthly Broadcast from Hollywood" column in the January 1932 issue of *Photoplay* that when *Frankenstein* was previewed in a Santa Barbara theater, women screamed, men trembled, and children began crying. One man threatened to file suit against the theater because his nerves (and those of his wife and child) were shattered. Another man called the theater manager that night every five minutes to say, "I can't sleep because of that picture and you aren't going to either."

PRODUCTION NOTES

The classic chronicle, *Frankenstein (or, the Modern Prometheus)*, was conceived in 1816 by a 19-year-old woman named Mary Wollstonecraft, a "free thinker" and mistress of famed British poet Percy Bysshe Shelley. Mary Shelley's creation was first brought to the screen nearly a century later, in 1910, by Thomas Edison's pioneering film company as a 16-minute short. Two other silent shorts followed—1915's *Life Without Soul* (in which the monster is a normal-looking but murderous fellow) and the 1920 Italian entry, *Il Mostro di Frakestein* [sic]—before Universal produced their definitive adaptation. Of the three silent renditions, only the Edison version seems to have survived.

"This is going to be a big year in motion pictures," announced Carl Laemmle, Jr., to the *New York Times* in June 1931. "As a result of the reception given *Dracula*, we're pushing plans for *Frankenstein* and *Murders in the Rue Morgue*. The stories are well under way."

Indeed they were. In April, Universal had purchased the rights to a modern stage adaptation of *Frankenstein* by John L. Balderston and Peggy Webling and assigned French writer/director Robert Florey to write a treatment in which their new horror star, Bela Lugosi, could follow up his recent success as *Dracula*. Before agreeing to undertake this task, Florey shrewdly insisted that he be given a contract stipulating that he would direct as well as write the picture. This done, the director shot a 20-minute test reel with Lugosi as the monster, Edward Van Sloan playing Dr. Waldman, and Dwight Frye as Fritz. Though this historic test reel has seemingly been lost, a description of Lugosi's Golem-like version of the monster was provided by Edward Van Sloan in an interview conducted by Forrest J Ackerman in *Famous Monsters of Filmland*. According to Van Sloan, Lugosi's "head was about four times normal size, with a broad wig on it. He had a polished, claylike skin." Meanwhile, production head Carl Laemmle, Jr., had given Universal's new "Ace" director, James Whale, a long list of studio properties for potential projects. On the list was *Frankenstein* and Whale became interested. Laemmle then took the production away form Florey (whose test reel reportedly had yielded little enthusiasm, anyway) and handed it over to Whale. Florey, shouting breach of contract, discovered to his dismay that the agreement he'd signed stipulated that he would write and direct *a* film, not specified by name. As consolation, Universal awarded *Murders in the Rue Morgue* to the disheartened writer/director.

Florey's contributions which remain in the finished film include Frankenstein mistakenly placing a criminal brain into the body of the monster, transforming Mary Shelley's eloquent creature into an inarticulate hulk, and setting the fiery climax in an abandoned windmill.[7] In a shameful example of Hollywood ingratitude, Florey received *no* screen credit (though he *did* receive his just due on foreign release posters).

While much has been made of Bela Lugosi's rejection of the monstrous role (thus paving the way for his subsequent rival, Boris Karloff), Florey initially approached the Hungarian actor by offering him the part of *Doctor* Frankenstein rather than the monster. In an interview with Al Taylor in *Fangoria*, Florey recalled how Universal nixed his casting idea. "[Story Department head Richard] Schayer agreed with my conception of the film and told me to go ahead with an extended and detailed adaptation, adding that the front office would insist on Lugosi playing the part of the monster."

After the departure of Florey and Lugosi, Universal initially preferred Leslie Howard for the role of Henry Frankenstein. Whale, however, had other ideas — and the clout to enforce them — and instead chose Colin Clive from the director's earlier picture, *Journey's End* (1930).

With his principal cast now in place, Whale needed to fill one more role. Though Lugosi dismissed the part of the monster with a contemptuous "You don't need an actor for that part! Anybody can moan and grunt!," Whale saw the character as pivotal to his film.

While many versions of how Boris Karloff came to become the Frankenstein monster have surfaced over the years (at one time Lugosi even claimed to have suggested him), the most likely one (and the one espoused by Karloff himself) goes as follows. "James Whale, the director," related Karloff, "who had just come over from England triumphant from the success of his direction of R. C. Sherriff's *Journey's End*, was lunching at a nearby table [at Universal Studio's commissary where Karloff was playing a murderer in *Graft*]. Suddenly he caught my eye and beckoned me over. I leapt — he was the most important director on the lot. He asked me to sit down. I did, holding my breath, and then he said: 'Your face has startling possibilities…' I cast my eyes down modestly, and then he said, 'I'd like you to test for the monster in *Frankenstein*.' It was shattering — for the first time in my life I had been gainfully employed long enough to buy myself some new clothes and spruce up a bit — actually, I rather fancied myself! Now, to hide all this new-found beauty under monster makeup? I said I'd be delighted. Half a dozen actors,[8] including Bela Lugosi, who refused it, had been tested for the part, but I ended up the lucky one — I say lucky because any one of them could have played it just as well as I did, and would have reaped the benefits that came to me."[9] Most consider this last statement rather doubtful, for it was Karloff's sensitive portrayal which gave the brutish figure character and sympathy and created of this "monster" a cultural icon. Few could have done as much, as was later demonstrated when Lugosi finally *did* portray the monster in *Frankenstein Meets the Wolfman* (1943). (Though Lugosi was sixty at the time, and various storyline changes were made to his detriment, it was still painfully obvious that Lugosi did not have the wherewithal to infuse real life in the part as Karloff had done.)

Although it launched Boris Karloff into stardom, *Frankenstein* was by no means the beginning of his film career. Karloff had already made *16* films in 1931 alone before *Frankenstein*, bringing his total screen output up to that time to about eighty pictures (though the majority were in extra or bit parts).

Karloff always spoke of his monster with

Subsequent reissue posters for *Frankenstein* relied heavily upon the popularity of Boris Karloff's name, though for the film's initial 1931 release, the fourth-billed Karloff was deemed too unimportant by Universal even to invite to the picture's premiere.

affection. "Boris was a great professional," remembered occasional co-star Vincent Price (in *Filmfax* #42). "I was very fond of him. He was a man who loved his work and knew exactly what he was doing. Off the set, he was a very funny man. An extraordinary thing about Boris was his gratitude for *Frankenstein*. He had great pride in it, even though it was something that plagued him his whole life."

Not surprisingly, Karloff called *Frankenstein* his favorite of his own films, "because it was such a lucky film for me — and I think rather a good one" (interview in February, 1965 issue of *Famous Monsters*).

Though *Frankenstein* plucked the 43-year-old actor from obscurity and thrust him into instant stardom, it was by no means a painless transition. The part of the monster was a grueling one whose physical trials were only exacerbated by director James Whale. Although by most accounts and testimonials Whale behaved like the consummate professional that he was, Cynthia Lindsay (a close personal friend of the Karloffs) claimed that the director was not above petty jealousy towards the star he created in the form of the Frankenstein monster — and more specifically, Boris Karloff. In *Dear Boris*, Lindsay wrote, "Boris never understood why Whale insisted on his carrying Colin Clive up the hill to the mill in the famous scene where the monster dies. Whale shot the scene dozens of times, using primarily long shots in which a dummy could have been used, or an extra could have played the monster, but Whale insisted on using Boris and Clive over and over and over.

"Boris's own body was encased in a seven-foot, six-inch structure of heavy padding and putty weighing 65 pounds; his hands were coated with plaster; his feet dragged thirty-pound weighted boots. With the added weight of the high artificial skull, the gummy layers of greasepaint, the strips of cotton soaked in collodion on his face, his eyes stretched open with rubber lids, staggering up and downhill carrying Clive was torture. The experience undoubtedly contributed to worsening the already bad back that soon sent him to the hospital for spinal fusion.

"Whale had the reputation of being an egomaniac, and Boris always felt, though he never said so publicly, that the monster had caused such wild interest not only from the studio people, but from the press, that Whale was actually jealous of him and decided to punish the monster, and inadvertently the man who created him. Not Frankenstein, but Boris."[10]

With a budget of $262,007 and a 30-day shooting schedule, Whale began filming on August 24, on the graveyard set. Principal photography wrapped on October 3, five days over schedule and $29,122 over budget. After a preview screening in early November, Carl Laemmle, Sr., Universal studios president (and Junior's father), demanded a few changes. "No little girl is going to drown in one of my pictures!" thundered the studio head to his secretary, J. U. Miller, and the famous scene in which the monster tosses the little girl into the pond sank beneath the ripples right alongside little Maria. (Fortunately, this long lost footage has been restored to current release prints.)

In *Famous Monsters of Filmland* #100, Mae Clarke discussed the controversial censored scene. "They purposely wanted to keep it very simple so that the little girl wouldn't get upset or distracted. They had to work with her you know, letting her know Boris first, watch the makeup being put on, so she had absolutely no trouble being friendly with him.... Through NOT showing how it happened pictorially and what his reactions were, you missed the whole pathos — that this was unintentional." Clarke also described her director: "James Whale was a very sensitive man. He was a true artist through and through who understood the necessity and effect of the finest kind of music or color or smell or when to have tea. He was a joy and a pleasure to know."

Besides this "offensive" sequence, the ending simply would not do either. As originally shot, Henry Frankenstein died after the monster throws him from the windmill. The studio apparently felt troubled by this rough treatment of their picture's hero and insisted on Whale shooting the happy ending now seen on all prints. As *Variety* reported, "Finish is a change from the first one tried, when the scientist also was destroyed." The reviewer (*Rush*) did not altogether agree with the new ending, observing that "the climax with the surviving Frankenstein ... relieves the tension somewhat at the finale, but that may not be the effect most to be desired." Nor was Colin Clive, Frankenstein himself, pleased with the change, having told the *New York Times* in October how delighted he was with the "rather unusual ending for a talking picture," in which "I ... am killed by the monster I have created."

The new denouement was clipped from many existing prints by Universal for a later re-release which paired *Frankenstein* with *Bride of Frankenstein*. Because *Bride* begins with the assumed-dead Henry brought to the castle where they discover life still remains in his battered body, this alteration to the original was necessary to maintain continuity in the series. In 1957, when *Frankenstein* hit the television airwaves as part of the "Shock" package, the original happy ending was restored. (Incidentally, it is *not* Colin Clive in the bed [nor Mae Clarke by his side for that matter] behind the old Baron as he proposes his toast. Because we see the couple only through the door and out of focus in the background, Universal did not need to rack up the expense of bringing these two costly stars back for a retake and simply replaced them with two extras.)

Old Uncle Carl received his own happy ending to go along with Henry's, when his studio's initial investment netted Universal over $12 million upon *Frankenstein*'s initial release!

For years, die-hard *Frankenstein* fans have nearly foamed at the mouth whenever someone refers to the monster as "Frankenstein." Even as far back as December, 1931, *Variety* pointed out that "Frankenstein is the creator of the monster, not the monster itself." Despite this early attempt to circumvent the inevitable misappellation, the fight for monster autonomy goes on...

NOTES

1. This long-thought-lost line was not deemed too blasphemous for its original release audience, who heard it delivered in all its grandiose glory. Only when the picture went before the MPPDA for reissue clearance in 1938 did the all-powerful censors demand its removal to protect the sensitive ears of movie patrons.

2. Quoted in *Dear Boris*, by Cynthia Lindsay.

3. Alfred Hitchcock utilized this very same "jump-cut advance" over three decades later to highlight the shocking discovery of a gruesome corpse in *The Birds* (1963).

4. Quoted in *Dear Boris*, by Cynthia Lindsay.

5. Over his 35-year career, cinematographer Arthur Edeson photographed over 100 films, including the classic genre entries *The Lost World* (1925), *The Old Dark House* (1932), and *The Invisible Man* (1933) as well as the Bogart classics *The Maltese Falcon* (1941) and *Casablanca* (1942). He received two Academy Award nominations—*All Quiet on the Western Front* (1930) and *Casablanca* (1942)—though he never won.

6. Even at this early date, *Frankenstein* was already overshadowing its predecessor, with Mordaunt Hall of *The New York Times* (December 5, 1931) noting that "Beside it 'Dracula' is tame."

7. Florey's original story situated Frankenstein's laboratory in this windmill rather than the old Roman watchtower seen in the finished film. A remnant of Florey's original concept escaped the revisionists' hands when Henry's father asks, "Why does he go messing around in an old ruined windmill when he has a decent house, a bath, good food and drink, and a darned pretty girl to come back to?"

8. Another actor who supposedly was considered for the part of the monster was the then-unknown John Carradine. According to Carradine himself, he "never played a monster... I was offered one and turned it down. I turned down Frankenstein." His reason: "I wasn't going to play the monster. I was from the the-a-tuh!" (from the 1974 ABC TV special, "The Horror Hall of Fame").

9. Quoted in *Dear Boris*, by Cynthia Lindsay.

10. Quoted in *Dear Boris*, by Cynthia Lindsay.

DR. JEKYLL AND MR. HYDE
(1931; Paramount)

Release Date: December 31, 1931
Running Time: 98 minutes (90 minutes for the re-release version)
Director/Producer: Rouben Mamoulian
Screenplay: Samuel Hoffenstein and Percy Heath (based on the novel by Robert Louis Stevenson)
Photography: Karl Struss
*Art Director: Hans Drier
*Editor: William Shea

*Makeup: Wally Westmore
Cast: Fredric March (Dr. Henry Jekyll/Mr. Hyde), Miriam Hopkins (Ivy Pierson), Rose Hobart (Muriel Carew), Holmes Herbert (Dr. Lanyon), Halliwell Hobbes (Brigadier-General Carew), Edgar Norton (Poole), Tempe Pigott (Mrs. Hawkins), *Arnold Lucy (Utterson), *Colonel McDonnell (Hobson), *Eric Wilton (Briggs), *Douglas Walton (Student), *John Rogers (Waiter), *Murdock MacQuarrie (Doctor), *Major Sam Harris (Dance Extra).

*Uncredited on film print.

"It's the things that one *can't* do that always tempt me."—Dr. Jekyll.

SYNOPSIS

"Gentlemen, London is so full of fog that it has penetrated our minds, set boundaries for our vision." This is how Dr. Henry Jekyll, respected surgeon and researcher, begins his address to an assembly of his colleagues and students. He goes on to relate his theory on the nature of man: "My analysis of this soul, the human psyche, leads me to believe man is not truly one, but truly two.... One of him strives for the nobility—this we call his 'good' self. The other self seeks an expression of impulses that binds him to some dim animal relation with the earth—this we may call the 'bad.' These two carry on an eternal struggle in the nature of man.... Now if these two selves could be separated from each other, how much freer the good in us would be. What heights it might scale; and the so-called evil, once liberated, would fulfill itself and trouble us no more. I believe the day is not far off when this separation will be possible."

This is our introduction to Henry Jekyll, whose noble ideals and philosophies go tragically awry and ultimately take him "further than man should go."

After the lecture, Dr. Jekyll attends a dinner party at the house of his fiancée, Muriel Carew. Arriving late (the conscientious physician was attending to his charity patients in the Free Ward), Jekyll presses Muriel's father, Brigadier-General Carew, to move up the wedding which is still eight months away. But despite both his and Muriel's pleadings, the General remains unmoved. "There is such a thing as decent observance, you know," is his stuffy reply.

On the walk home with his friend Dr. Lanyon, a frustrated Jekyll observes a young woman being assaulted. Coming to the girl's aid, Jekyll takes her up to her room and attends to her injuries (merely a few bruises). The girl's name is Ivy Pierson and she takes a shine to the dashing Dr. Jekyll, flirting with him shamelessly. Jekyll laughs it all off (including one particularly passionate kiss) as good-natured frivolity.

After leaving the girl, Jekyll tells Lanyon of his plan. "I want to be clean, not only in my conduct but in my innermost thoughts and desires. There is only one way to do it. Separate the two natures in us." Locking himself in his lab for three days, Jekyll intends to do just that.

Working furiously, the young doctor finally completes his elixir. Quaffing the bubbling draught, the handsome Jekyll is transformed into a hideous simianlike creature, whom he dubs "Mr. Hyde" (thus his evil self is released). Jekyll's butler, Poole, overhears the commotion and becomes concerned. Alarmed by Poole's banging on the door, Hyde quickly downs an antidote and becomes Jekyll once more.

The young doctor has been shaken and, frightened by the experiment and what it has unleashed within him, he tries once again to speed up his impending marriage to Muriel. The couple's pleadings fall on deaf ears, however, and matters are made worse when the General takes Muriel to Bath with him for an extended trip.

The separation and waiting prove too much for the impatient Jekyll, and when he receives a letter informing him that Muriel will be away for yet another month, he makes a decision. Jekyll chooses release—in the form of the pleasure-seeking Mr. Hyde.

Fredric March, Miriam Hopkins, and director Rouben Mamoulian go over the script for *Dr. Jekyll and Mr. Hyde* (1931). (Courtesy of Ted Okuda.)

Hyde goes looking for Ivy and finds her at the local saloon/dance hall. There he demonstrates his brutality and frightens Ivy into submission ("You see, I hurt you because I love you. I *want* you. And what I want, I get!"). Forcing her to become his mistress, Hyde sets her up in an apartment, where she awaits in horror each succeeding visit by the brute.

Upon learning of Muriel's return to London, Jekyll makes a vow never to utilize the horrid release in the form of Mr. Hyde again. "From now on I'll use only the *front* door," he tells Poole, throwing away the key to the laboratory's rear entrance. In a fit of remorse, Jekyll also sends 50 pounds to the brutalized Ivy.

Meanwhile, Muriel chastises Jekyll for not communicating with her over the long absence and making her "suffer so." Jekyll offers no explanation (other than "I was ill in soul"), just a heartfelt apology and the promise that "no man ever needed another, or loved another, as I need and love you." Once again, the couple ask Muriel's father to consent to their early marriage. This time Muriel's entreaties win out, and the General gives permission for them to marry the following month.

Jekyll's excitement and happiness are cut short, however, when Poole announces that he has a visitor—"a Miss Pierson." Ivy returns Jekyll's money and pleads for help of another sort. "It's Hyde ... he ain't human, sir, he's a beast!" Hysterical in her fear and misery, she begs, "If you don't help me, you as has the kindest heart in the world, sir, then give me poison so I can kill myself!" Jekyll, tormented by guilt at what he's done to this girl, makes a solemn promise that she will never see Hyde again. Relieved, she accepts the noble Dr. Jekyll at his word and leaves.

The following day, on the way to the

"Come back soon," coos Ivy (Miriam Hopkins) in one of the most erotically charged scenes from horror's Golden Age.

Carews' for dinner (and the announcement of their upcoming wedding), Jekyll stops in the park. Spying a little singing nightingale on a branch, the contented doctor sits to ponder the serene sight. His blissful reverie is disturbed, however, when a black cat appears on the tree limb to silence the bird. The sudden animal violence prompts Jekyll to change — without the drugs — and Hyde is free once more.

As Muriel awaits the arrival of her love (who never appears), Ivy is celebrating her liberation from the beast Hyde. But as she toasts to his demise, the door opens and in walks that very beast, who strangles her. Racing away from the scene of the crime, Hyde finds he cannot obtain access to the haven of Jekyll's laboratory, having earlier thrown away the key to the back door (and Poole won't let the monster in the front).

Desperate, Hyde sends a message to Lanyon (signing it Henry Jekyll), imploring his friend to go and fetch certain chemicals from his lab, return to his house, and hand over the package to a man arriving there at midnight. At the appointed hour, Hyde appears, but a suspicious Lanyon insists on proof of Jekyll's safety. Having no choice, Hyde mixes the drugs then and there and transforms back into Jekyll before Lanyon's astonished eyes. The tortured doctor throws himself upon his friend's mercy and begs for his help. Jekyll vows never to take the drugs again, and to fight his evil other self with all his might. He also vows to give up Muriel ("This is my penance!").

Jekyll goes to see Muriel for one last agonizing time, to "set her free." Upon leaving the sobbing girl, he begins to transform as the evil Hyde once again reigns supreme. Sneaking back into the house, Hyde attacks Muriel and kills General Carew before making his escape. Racing back to the safety of Jekyll's house, with the police hot on his tail, he locks himself in the laboratory. When the police break down the door, they find only Dr. Jekyll, who tells them the man has run out the back.

But Lanyon (the doctor called in on the case) had found Jekyll's broken cane next to the General's body, and has realized the truth. Rushing to Jekyll's house, he arrives and points to Jekyll, "There, there he is, there's your man!" The police are incredulous, but Jekyll begins to change, and there before them stands the bestial murderer himself. Attacking the police, the vicious Hyde climbs a bookcase and grabs a knife hanging on the wall. A policeman's bullet brings him down, and the hideous face of Hyde transforms one last time back into the now-peaceful visage of the young Dr. Jekyll.

MEMORABLE MOMENT

The film's centerpiece and most unforgettable moment is the first transformation of Jekyll into Hyde. This sequence is brilliant on both the technical and emotional sides — a symphony of images, movement, and sound which is both frightening and exhilarating, offering a vicarious release not only for Dr. Jekyll, but for the audience as well.

The scene begins as Jekyll holds up the vial of bubbling liquid in front of a mirror. (In essence, the audience is now also looking into the mirror — out of Jekyll's eyes — and so is about to make the great experiment with him.) He stares intently for a moment, then quickly downs the draught. Jekyll immediately grimaces in pain and makes horrible choking noises as his hands fly up to his throat. As he struggles and gasps, his hands and face darken (before our very eyes). The camera pulls back and Jekyll desperately reaches out (as if to draw it back and keep it close) and begins to collapse. The camera collapses with him and falls to the floor. As Jekyll pants and gasps, and his rapid heartbeat becomes louder and louder, the camera begins to spin, whirling faster and faster, until the surroundings become a blur. ("We had a problem with the sequence in which Jekyll takes a drink and is physically transformed," related director Rouben Mamoulian to Charles Higham and Joel Greenberg in *The Celluloid Muse*, "how do you make the audience believe it? I decided to make them feel what Jekyll is feeling. Showing subjectively his demented whirlings round his laboratory. I had the camera revolve around upon its axis, and all four walls of the set were lit completely; this had never been done on the screen. The cameraman had to be tied to the top of the camera: he had to lean down and control the focus from up there. He was as small as a jockey, luckily.") Images flash by — Jekyll and Muriel ("Marry me now, I can't wait any longer!"), the General ("Positively indecent!"), the enticing Ivy ("Come back sooooon"), and Lanyon ("Your conduct was disgusting"). Finally, the camera slows. As the focus becomes clearer, we once again see the familiar surroundings of Jekyll's lab. Moving again to the mirror, the camera steps in front and we see (we *are*) the bestial Hyde.

The thrilling camera movements, coupled

with the jarring soundtrack and the dizzying whirling, places the audience in Jekyll's shoes, and so provides us with some of the same fearful excitement. Mamoulian, Struss, and March have combined to create the most exciting and involving transformation scene in the Golden Age of Horror.

If the transformation sequence represents the film's technical triumph and most intense case of audience involvement, then the following scene embodies the picture's horrific content and height of emotional power. In it, Hyde is at his most loathsome — a sadistic tormentor who subtly plays on his victim's (Ivy's) mounting fears to build her emotional agony into a crescendo of terror. It begins as Hyde tells Ivy that he is going away. The sneering brute quickly dashes her ill-concealed hope, however, by asking, "You wouldn't have me go tonight, would you? Of course not, quite unworthy of our great love, hmm?" Clutching her, he forcefully presses his lips to her bosom. Reveling in the loathing and fear this inspires in her, he continues to torture her verbally: "That's right, my little bird. The last evening is always the sweetest, you know." Trapped in his arms, struggling to control her dread of the horrors to come, Ivy nearly collapses in panic. Enjoying her torment, he continues his mocking taunts: "And what a farewell this one will be. What a farewell! I don't know whether I shall be able to tear myself away from you at all. In fact, I shall only go as far as the door and the sight of your tears will bring me back. Does that please you, my dear?" March (utterly convincing in his role of tormentor) and Miriam Hopkins (the embodiment of barely-suppressed horror) create one of the most chillingly cruel scenes ever filmed.

ASSETS

Given seven weeks and around $500,000 (only slightly more money than *Dracula* and less than half that provided for MGM's inferior 1941 Spencer Tracy remake), director Rouben Mamoulian took Robert Louis Stevenson's classic work of literature and created a brilliant cinematic study of the duality of man and man's struggle to control his primitive instincts. In Mamoulian's own words: "Mr. Hyde is the exact replica of the Neanderthal man, so he's our ancestor. We *were* that once. The struggle or dilemma is not between evil and good, it's between the sophisticated, spiritual self in man and his animal, primeval instincts" (*Cinefantastique* no. 3). Even beyond this, Mamoulian has chosen to extend the metaphor and explore the conflict of society vs. the individual (Dr. Jekyll as the representative of the repressed Victorian proper society and Mr. Hyde as the personification of the gratification of the individual). While Hyde does not live by society's rules (his actions are governed only by the cravings and whims of his own Id), Jekyll is restrained (and frustrated) by the dictates of societal mores. Mamoulian daringly explores this theme of repressed desires and pent-up sexuality, intimating that it is these unfulfilled desires which lead Jekyll to destruction, causing him to seek relief in the "evil" form of Mr. Hyde. And this release IS evil, as Stevenson's story and Hoffenstein and Heath's screenplay take great pains to point out. In the best tradition of the morality play (and of the horror film), one of the major messages of *Dr. Jekyll and Mr. Hyde* is that just as repression can lead to dangerous risks, so can unbridled self-gratification lead to complete self-destruction.

Mamoulian is a master of his craft, and he has utilized a plethora of techniques and themes to create one of the most cinematically *alive* films ever shot (in any genre). Even a technique as simple as a dissolve is transformed into a fluid purveyor of thought and emotion. For instance, during a scene change in which Jekyll has just left Muriel, the fading image of Muriel is superimposed for a few seconds onto the next scene of Jekyll walking with his friend Lanyon, demonstrating that her image is embedded deep within Jekyll's mind and thoughts of her fill his head. Later, after Jekyll's first rather steamy encounter with Ivy, Mamoulian superimposes a shot of Ivy's swinging naked leg as the scene dissolves to Jekyll walking down the stairs — the lingering sexual image revealing that the seed of lust has been planted. For

Fredric March and director Rouben Mamoulian on the laboratory set of *Dr. Jekyll and Mr. Hyde* (1931). (Courtesy of Ted Okuda.)

a full 25 seconds this arousing image of beautiful flesh is transposed over (or, more accurately, *under*) the scene in which Lanyon chides Jekyll about "controlling instincts." This second image serves a dual purpose. Not only does it expose what is lingering beneath the surface of Jekyll's mind, it also distracts the viewer just as Jekyll himself is distracted and so allies our thoughts and feelings with Jekyll's own. This serves to further cement the bond between the character and the viewer which Mamoulian had taken such pains to forge with his initial point-of-view shots at the film's opening.

Mamoulian even employs the split screen technique as a process of changing scenes and emphasizing conflict, allowing the audience to see one scene as it finishes while at the same time viewing the next as it begins. In one transition we see both Ivy and Muriel at the same time — before Ivy is finally wiped away as Jekyll meets with Muriel. This split image underscores Jekyll's inner conflict between the "good woman" (society's daughter and as such unattainable) and the "fallen woman" of the streets who is willing and able and very tempting. Thus we see simultaneously the two women in Jekyll's life — and the two very different sides of his "romantic interest." The duality of man (and his needs) is again emphasized.

The director also cleverly underlines the primary theme of man's dualistic nature by his use of mirrors throughout the picture. The mirror is presented as a metaphor for Jekyll's (and man's) binary nature. At the film's opening, Jekyll is introduced to us in a mirror — as the Victorian gentleman dandying himself up. Though the import of first seeing a reflection rather than the man himself is not readily apparent at the time, it can later be seen not only as an introduction to Jekyll the character but also as an introduction to, and portent of, the release to come (in the form of Mr. Hyde). When Jekyll finally does transform, this fateful event is once more witnessed in a mirror. The scene begins with a disheveled Jekyll, determined to succeed in his experiment, holding up the vial containing the elixir. The camera suddenly changes focus to reveal the mirror behind the vial and Jekyll himself. As he approaches the mirror, we see it is not Jekyll but rather his mirror image — his other self — about to take this first ill-fated plunge. It is no accident that this first transformation is seen in a mirror.

Significantly, the second transformation is done straight on, *without* a mirror. The evil, bestial side of Jekyll is that much closer to the surface now and no longer the hidden side, no longer needing to stay within the confines of the mirror. The first transformation was an experiment — an exploration — of the duality of man. This second, however, is merely a weakness, a succumbing on Jekyll's part as he voluntarily gives in to his animal desires and the bestial freedom found in his other self.

Fredric March gives an Oscar-winning performance as Jekyll and Hyde. As March plays him, Hyde is a beast, a brute in the form of a man (though Hyde's "form" is not altogether human). March excels in the physical aspect of the role, his quick movements showing his impatience to wring every possible pleasure from his newfound freedom. As Hyde stretches with an almost animal delight after his first release, or lifts his face to the rain in an exuberant display, March shows him to be the Id incarnate, determined to revel in every sensation. Later, when Hyde becomes a bit more "sophisticated" (i.e., sexual) in his pleasure-seeking, March adds to his brutal physical performance a dimension of subtle cruelty — namely, his openly sadistic dialogue delivery. In the scenes in which Hyde verbally taunts Ivy, March's sarcastic and double-edged delivery (coupled with his sudden physical movements and quick shifts in demeanor) creates a terrifying picture of unpredictability. While he at first confines himself to the *verbal* torture of Ivy, it is a certainty that uncontrollable violence lurks just beneath the surface. March's brilliant mannerisms and mocking tones reveal the depths of mental as well as physical cruelty which this evil being is wont to inflict.

Fredric March is well supported by a cadre of fine actors. Miriam Hopkins matches March's Mr. Hyde with a flawless performance as the street-wise Ivy Pierson. At ease singing bawdy songs in a tavern or coquettishly lifting up her skirt to reveal her shapely legs, her unpolished charm and good humor make of her a very likable and sympathetic figure. Ivy's brazen sexuality is not a "dirty" thing, not a secret to be hidden away behind locked doors, but a breath of fresh air amongst the stuffy attitudes portrayed in the film. While Rose

Hobart (*Tower of London* [1939], *The Mad Ghoul* [1943], *Soul of a Monster* [1944]) is given the rather thankless role of Muriel, her earnest and intelligent performance manages to make her character real. Likewise, character actor Halliwell Hobbes ably supports the leads in his role of the blustery and pompous Brigadier-General Carew ("This is positively indecent!"), the pillar (and representative) of the repressive Victorian society.

LIABILITIES

The opening in which the camera follows Jekyll's perspective is an effective tool used by Mamoulian to draw us in, literally to place the audience in Jekyll's shoes and forge a bond of identification with the character. At the beginning we see only what Jekyll sees and the camera moves as if it were Jekyll's eyes. Mamoulian explained his technique when the director appeared at a 1971 American Film Institute revival of *Dr. Jekyll* (as reported by Bill Thomas in *Cinefantastique*, Summer 1971): "The camera begins by being Jekyll and Hyde. In other words, *you* are Jekyll, the audience is Jekyll, being the camera... Now I did that because I wanted to use that device in the transformation of Jekyll into Mr. Hyde. In other words, I wanted to put the audience into Jekyll's shoes and make them feel a little sharper this vertigo that Jekyll goes through." In the truncated re-release version (the 90-minute pared-down cut which was issued when the film resurfaced in 1967), this works quite well as it begins with Jekyll (and the audience) arriving by carriage at the lecture hall. However, in Mamoulian's original cut of the film (the original release version and the one now readily available on videocassette), there is a long, drawn-out sequence at Jekyll's home in which the camera swoops about at eye-level as Jekyll plays the organ, walks from room to room, talks to his servant, and dons his hat and coat.

This overlong prelude in Jekyll's home adds nothing to the Doctor's character development and is much too unimportant to do anything but attract attention to this curious technique of character perspective (and thus ultimately spoil its effectiveness). The introduction in the truncated version is short and sweet and just the right length to accomplish its purpose without overwhelming the audience with precious technique. This is one of the few instances in which tampering with the director's cut actually improved a film.

It must be noted, however, that this particular cut is *the only one* of the many seemingly arbitrary changes made which actually benefited the picture. The remaining edits were definitely detrimental, and even devastating at times. For instance, for the scene in which Jekyll first transforms without the use of the drugs, Mamoulian had preceded it with one particular key sequence. Strolling through a park, Jekyll sits on a bench to observe a singing nightingale. Suddenly a cat creeps up the branch and springs upon the bird. A startled and disturbed Jekyll then transforms into Hyde. It was this sudden animal violence witnessed by Jekyll which triggers his transformation into the bestial Hyde. In the truncated version, however, the cat does not appear. All that is shown is Jekyll sitting on the bench watching the singing bird when he suddenly begins to transform. Without this key sequence, the audience has no inkling as to *why* Hyde is suddenly let loose without the drugs, and so must conclude that it is simply a matter of course. A powerful insight has been lost.

The acting of Fredric March, while also seen as an asset, can paradoxically be seen as a liability (ironically reflecting the dual nature of his role). While March is indisputably brilliant in his animalistic portrayal of Mr. Hyde, his Dr. Henry Jekyll is overflowing with melodramatic gestures and speech. March gesticulates and finger waves to no end as Jekyll (particularly at the film's beginning) and while fiery and enthusiastic, this performance dates rather badly for today's more naturalistic-minded audiences. One can almost see it as a performance from the silent era, as if March is playing a verbal form of silent melodrama. However (in yet another paradox of this remarkable film), while March's melodramatic performance is a very noticeable liability at the picture's beginning, his enthusiasm and sincerity

Hyde callously tramples a small child in a scene excised from *Dr. Jekyll and Mr. Hyde* (1931) before release.

draw us in as the film progresses. Jekyll is a man struggling against the repressive mores of his day, and as such his outbursts and seemingly overly dramatic mannerisms are a retaliation against a society which tolerates none of the passion and curiosity he feels. As we watch, March's dramatics are transformed — normalized — and we realize that his rebellious character is well drawn against the backdrop of his stiff and formal Victorian world.

While Hoffenstein and Heath's screenplay is filled with brilliant lines, they seem to have reached backwards to the silents (much as March appears to have done) for the love scenes between Jekyll and Muriel. The love-talk comes across as silly, dated, and repetitious. Heartfelt demonstrations such as "I love you darling, I love you," and "My love, my love" strike the viewer as shallow and frivolous. However, when this silly by-play takes a darker, more serious turn, it becomes doubly effective: "Oh, I do love you seriously," Jekyll confides. "So seriously that it—it frightens me. You opened a gate for me into another world. Before that my work was everything. I was drawn to the mysteries of science, to the unknown. But now the unknown wears *your* face, looks back at me with *your* eyes." Once again, what initially appears as a liability becomes something of an asset.

Mamoulian occasionally falls into the trap of being too obvious and heavy-handed in his symbolism. In the scene in which Jekyll receives a letter from Muriel stating she'll be away from him for yet another month, the frustrated Jekyll debates whether to use his elixir once again. Mamoulian intercuts shots of Jekyll brooding and tapping his foot impatiently (the idea forming) with shots of a cast iron kettle on the fire (his passions bubbling). Back and forth it goes, from Jekyll to the kettle and back again, until finally Jekyll moves into action—and the pot boils over. While elsewhere Mamoulian has made good use of subtle symbolism (the mirror, for instance), this is rather too obvious a metaphor for Jekyll's pent-up passions and seems an unnecessary and even childish overstatement.

Rose Hobart (who played Muriel), in an interview with Tom Weaver and Michael Brunas for *Filmfax* magazine (#29), noted that Mamoulian sometimes went overboard with his use of symbolism: "He really was a fine, fine director. There was only one thing that really bothered me about the way he directed. I figured he always must have dotted his "i's" and crossed his "t's," because when he finished a scene, he would always have to have something symbolic to finish it up with. That was really overdoing it!"

REVIEWS

Variety (January 5, 1932), despite lavishly praising the artistic merits of this "over-elaborated" version and considering it "assured of good returns," expressed some misgivings as to its palatability to the public: "The picture is infinitely better art than the old stage play—indeed, in many passages it is an astonishingly fine bit of interpreting a classic, but as popular fare it loses in vital reaction.... As a literary transcription, the picture is the last word in artistic interpretation, done by understanding adaptors and an extremely skillful director...."

Mordaunt Hall, of *The New York Times* (January 2, 1932) called this version "a far more tense and shuddering affair than it was as John Barrymore's silent picture." Like many critics of the day, however, he was not above complaining about (or at least apologizing for) the heightened horror element: "True, the producers are not a little too zealous in their desire to spread terror among audiences, but while there are pardonable roamings from the original, there is in most instances a good excuse for making the scenes as they are in this current study."

Of Fredric March, the reviewer was impressed: "Mr. March's portrayal is something to arouse admiration.... As Dr. Jekyll he is a charming man, and as the fiend he is alert and sensual."

PRODUCTION NOTES

Beginning as early as 1908, over 15 cinematic versions of Robert Louis Stevenson's classic tale, *The Strange Case of Dr. Jekyll and Mr. Hyde*, were produced prior to this one, as well as numerous stage and even vaudeville adaptations. Over 20 more variations have followed it, though none have achieved the quality and power of this definitive 1931 classic (including the 1941 Spencer Tracy remake, which is a handsomely mounted but ultimately lackluster carbon copy of the March version).

Critically acclaimed at the time (*Dr. Jekyll* made both the *New York Times* and *Film Daily*

"Ten Best" lists of 1932), this version of Stevenson's story was lauded even by members of the novelist's own family. Mamoulian told *Fangoria* magazine (#2): "You know, the nicest fan letter I received after the film appeared was this one from Stevenson's niece: 'Dear Sir: As a member of Mr. Stevenson's family I went to see your picture of Jekyll and Hyde with some apprehension, for I knew that it needed real genius to do that great work full justice. That you have shown, Mr. Mamoulian, for it is a magnificent production, and my only regret on seeing it was that Mr. Stevenson had not lived to see it. Please accept my sincere congratulations. Most gratefully yours, Mrs. Salisbury Fields.'"

Another descendent, R. L. Stevenson (a nephew of Robert Louis Stevenson) appeared in the film in a small (uncredited) role, according to a 1932 article in the *New York Times*.

Until late in 1967, this definitive 1932 version of *Dr. Jekyll and Mr. Hyde* went virtually unseen. MGM had purchased the film from Paramount and suppressed it in order to protect their 1941 remake from potentially unfavorable comparisons.

The unknown actor Fred Bickel got his start in show business in 1920 as understudy to matinée idol and soon-to-be horror star Lionel Atwill in the Broadway play "Deburau." Fred Bickel soon changed his name to Fredric March. March went home with the 1932 Academy Award for Best Actor for his fierce, dualistic performance in *Dr. Jekyll and Mr. Hyde*, the first time a Best Actor Oscar has been awarded to a performer in a horror film.[1] The film was also nominated for Academy Awards in Writing Adaption (Samuel Hoffenstein, Percy Heath) and in Cinematography (Karl Struss).

Early on, Paramount had offered John Barrymore an unheard-of $25,000 a week to reprise the role(s) he made famous in the 1920 silent version. However, when MGM's Irving Thalberg offered the actor $110,000 and a one-year $3,500-a-week non-exclusive contract — plus the opportunity to act with his brother Lionel for the first time in their careers — "The Great Profile" abandoned his two famous portrayals and made *Arsene Lupin* for MGM.

Irving Pichel (*Dracula's Daughter*, 1936) was the studio's next choice for their Dr. Jekyll and Mr. Hyde, and the front office pushed hard for Pichel (fortunately, Mamoulian pushed even harder for March). "They said he would make such a wonderful Hyde," remembered Mamoulian. "'I'm not worried about Hyde,' I said. 'I'm worried about Jekyll. I want Jekyll to be young and handsome, and Mr. Pichel can't play that.' I wanted to use Freddy March, who was at that time a light comedian. He had just done a film called *Laughter*. They said, 'You're crazy. How can March play this part?' I told them that if I couldn't use Freddy March, I wouldn't do the film. I'd never even met March, I'd just seen him on the screen. Finally, the studio gave in." [As a point of interest, before Pichel was chosen, David O. Selznick personally championed Emil Jannings for the part (Jannings was a Swiss-born actor who rose to prominence in silent films but retreated to Germany at the advent of sound. He later worked enthusiastically on Nazi propaganda films). In a memo (which was never sent) to in-house producer B. P. Schulberg dated April 15, 1931, Selznick stated: "Any script of *Dr. Jekyll and Mr. Hyde* would almost certainly be a pretty free adaptation — and certainly the character could be molded to fit the versatile Jannings... Granted that on most pictures, the name of Jannings is today no draw, the combination of his name with that of the celebrated story seems like a "natural." ... So, in my opinion, we are passing up an opportunity to have the most important horror attraction that could be conceived: Emil Jannings in *Dr. Jekyll and Mr. Hyde*."]

Actress Miriam Hopkins developed a reputation for being difficult to work with (in fact Bette Davis once opined that "I don't think there was ever a more difficult female in the world"), and her co-star on *Dr. Jekyll*, Rose Hobart, confirmed this in a *Filmfax* (#29) interview with Tom Weaver and Michael Brunas: "I had no scenes with her, but I used to go on the set and hear about her endlessly from Freddie March. For example, when they were doing the scene of their meeting at the pub, Mamoulian put the camera on the dance floor. She was sitting in the box. They started the scene, but by the time they were shooting it, Hopkins was right by the camera. So Freddie practically had to look over his back. When the scene was over, the 'Cut!' came from behind the curtain. She wheeled around and said, 'Is that where the camera was?' And Mamoulian said, 'That's where the camera was. Print!' She was always upstaging everyone all of the time. I don't even think she thought about it anymore because she was so used to doing it. She was an excellent actress though." Rouben Mamoulian, however, voiced no complaints about Ms. Hopkins. "All of the stories I hear about Miriam Hopkins," the director told David Del Valle (in an interview published in *Video Watchdog* #18), "her temper tantrums, and her demonic ego were not in play at the time we were filming *Dr. Jekyll and Mr. Hyde*.... Directing her performance is one of my fondest memories of the picture. And if anything, she was Bette Davis' equal!"

Ms. Hobart admitted that playing the "good" half of Jekyll's romantic interest (in the form of the straitlaced Muriel Carew) was not entirely satisfying. "I would have given anything to play the Miriam Hopkins part. That's why Ingrid Bergman chose it in the [1941] remake." Ironically, Miriam Hopkins initially wanted Rose Hobart's role, and it took a persuasive Mamoulian to convince her otherwise. Ms. Hopkins later realized the allure of playing the "bad girl," admitting, "I enjoyed playing that sort of woman. They have the courage of the damned. They know what they want and go right ahead."[2]

In a minor continuity gaff, Paramount's prop department misspelled Ivy Pierson's name in the newspaper item which Jekyll reads detailing her brutal murder. In the credits, the name is spelled as P*i*erson, but in the newspaper column it is now P*e*arson. Of course, considering how notoriously inaccurate newspapers can be, this mistake might be more true-to-life than not.

Director Rouben Mamoulian ran up and down stairs recording his own heartbeat to be used on the soundtrack during the film's incredible first transformation sequence. "So when I say my heart is in *Dr. Jekyll and Mr. Hyde*," joked the director, "I mean it literally." The scene itself has long been the subject of much conjecture about how it was achieved. Mamoulian finally revealed that the masterful transformation was accomplished through a series of colored filters being removed from the camera lens, allowing the special makeup on March's face to appear seemingly out of nowhere without the usual overlapping photography. Cinematographer Karl Struss elaborated in *Famous Monsters of Filmland* magazine (#115): "[Makeup artist] Wally Westmore used a lot of red makeup in the first transformation of Fredric March and by photographing through red gelatin filters about two inches square held close to the camera lens, it [the transformation] was undetectable." Struss had utilized a similar technique in the 1923 version of *The Ten Commandments* while filming the healed lepers.

Wally Westmore's wonderfully simian makeup for Mr. Hyde was often a test of endurance for Fredric March. The actor later remarked about the makeup: "For six weeks I had to arrive at the studio each morning at 6 A.M., so that Wally Westmore could spend four hours building pieces on my nose and cheeks, sticking fangs in my mouth, and pushing cotton wool up my nostrils." To make things even more challenging, Mamoulian's wish for fluid, continual transformation scenes required Westmore to be quite inventive and just plain quick in his makeup applications. For some of the transformations, March sat in a chair while the camera moved about to reveal the changes on various parts of his body. Cinematographer Karl Struss related (in Susan and John Harvith's *Karl Struss: Man with a Camera*) : "I can see the makeup man now. He squatted in back of Fredric wherever he was seated, and while we were photographing one part of the body, he reached around, put the false teeth in and then disappeared. Or when we did another part of the body, he'd put the hair on the arms. The camera would swing back quickly to Fredric's face while he inserted fingernails. Then back to the hands again while a wig went on his head, and so on. Four different wigs were used, and a number of sets of different length fingernails." Despite the various hardships, March felt the makeup "made" the part. "I must thank Wally Westmore," lauded the actor at the Fifth Academy Awards banquet on November 18, 1932, "who made my task an easy one. Wally, who I consider a great artist, is responsible for the greater measure of my success."

Struss would have preferred a more subtle version of Mr. Hyde (more along the lines of the later Spencer Tracy version). "I thought they made a very bad mistake," he admitted in *Hollywood Cameramen*, "the change from Jekyll should have been largely a psychological one, with subtle changes only in the makeup. But they foolishly changed the hair and put false teeth in, and made him look like a monkey. That was terrible. Jekyll's shouldn't be a physical change, after all, it should be a mental one." Comparing March's vibrant, "monkey" Hyde to Tracy's "psychological" interpretation, we can be thankful that Struss, then as now, was in the minority.

NOTES

1. The horror genre had to wait nearly 60 years before capturing a second Best Actor Oscar, when Anthony Hopkins won for his performance in *The Silence of the Lambs* (1991).

2. Quoted in *Bad Girls of the Silver Screen*, by Lottie Da and Jan Alexander.

MURDERS IN THE RUE MORGUE
(1932; Universal)

Release Date: February 10, 1932
Running Time: 62 minutes
Director: Robert Florey
Producer: Carl Laemmle, Jr.
Associate Producer: E. M. Asher
Screenplay: Tom Reed, Dale van Every
Adaptation: Robert Florey
Added Dialogue: John Huston
Scenario Editor: Richard Schayer (based on the immortal classic by Edgar Allan Poe)
Photography: Karl Freund
Art Director: Charles D. Hall
Editor: Milton Carruth
Supervising Editor: Maurice Pivar
Special Effects: John Fulton
Recording Supervisor: C. Roy Hunter
Cast: Sidney Fox (Mlle. Camille L'Espanaye), Bela Lugosi (Doctor Mirakle), Leon Waycoff (Pierre Dupin), Bert Roach (Paul), Betsy Ross Clarke (Mme. L'Espanaye), Brandon Hurst (Prefect of Police), D'Arcy Corrigan (Morgue Keeper), Noble Johnson (Janos, The Black One), Arlene Francis (Woman of the Streets).

"If you only last one more minute, then we shall see — we shall know if you are to be the *bride of science!*" — Dr. Mirakle.

SYNOPSIS

In 1845, at a Parisian carnival, Pierre Dupin and his fiancée Camille enter the sideshow tent of "Erik the Ape." Inside, the ape's owner, Dr. Mirakle, gives a brief lecture on evolution. (This a full 14 years before Darwin published his *Origin of Species*. If Mirakle had been a little saner, perhaps we'd be studying *Mirakle's* theory of evolution in school rather than Darwin's!) As Mirakle concludes his oration, he draws the curtain of Erik's cage and announces dramatically, "Behold — the first man." Mirakle answers shouts of "Heresy" from the audience with animated talk of his "great experiment." "I shall prove your kinship with the ape," he claims above his listeners' protests. "Erik's blood shall be mixed with the blood of Man!" After the show, Pierre and Camille approach Erik's cage to get a closer look. Suddenly, Erik snatches the bonnet from Camille's head and then nearly throttles Pierre when the young man tries to retrieve it. The ape is taken with her—as is Dr. Mirakle, who watches with an unhealthy curiosity.

Later that night, Mirakle and Erik follow Camille to her residence. They move on, however, and Mirakle soon spies a streetwalker in near-hysterics after witnessing two men kill each other over her in a deadly street fight. Mirakle first cajoles, then forces, the girl to enter his carriage, upon which she screams and they drive off. At a secret laboratory, Mirakle injects her with a sample of Erik's blood. When she dies, Mirakle blames his failure on her own contaminated blood. "Your blood is rotten, black as your sins," he rails at the corpse.

The girl's body is fished out of the river (the third such victim) and brought to the morgue. Pierre Dupin, a medical student, arrives at the morgue to procure "supplies." When he examines the fresh body, he notices "the same marks" on the corpse's arm as on those of the previous two victims. Pierre bribes the attendant for a blood sample, in which he finds "the same foreign substance in the blood of each victim ... something introduced into the bloodstream to cause their death."

Camille receives a new bonnet from Dr. Mirakle, who asks her to visit him that night. Upon learning of this, Pierre goes in her stead and receives a curt dismissal from the disappointed doctor. His suspicions aroused, Pierre follows Mirakle and watches him enter an abandoned house.

That night, Mirakle goes to Camille's apartment, but the frightened girl shuts the door in his leering face. Not to be denied, Mirakle sends Erik into the house after her. Meanwhile, Pierre discovers that the "foreign substance" in the women's blood is the blood of a gorilla. Suddenly concerned for Camille, he races off towards her apartment.

Erik climbs up the side of the building and enters Camille's room, upon which the girl screams and faints. Her cry awakens her mother, who rushes into the room only to confront the enraged Erik. Pierre arrives as the mother's screams and Erik's howls arouse the building's other residents. With help, Pierre breaks down the door. Inside they find Camille gone and the body of her mother stuffed up the chimney. Dupin tells the Prefect of Police about Mirakle and his ape, but the police think him insane. Gorilla hair clutched in the corpse's hand finally convinces them otherwise, and Pierre leads the gendarmes to Mirakle's house.

As the police try to break in, Mirakle lets Erik out of his cage. When Mirakle approaches the unconscious Camille, however, Erik "goes ape" and strangles his master (presumably because the simian has fallen in love with her—though this is only hinted at and never made clear). The gendarmes shoot Mirakle's servant, Janos, and break in, but Erik has carried Camille to the roof. Pierre follows as the gorilla races across the rooftops of Paris. Finally, Pierre corners Erik and shoots him with a gendarme's borrowed pistol. As Erik rolls off the roof into the rushing river below, Pierre and Camille embrace. At the morgue, the dour attendant receives the body of Dr. Mirakle.

MEMORABLE MOMENT

The picture's strongest sequence, both visually and emotionally, is also its most brutal. After Mirakle escorts the prostitute into his carriage, the screen fades to black. A scream of terror emanates from the darkness and the screen lightens to reveal the shadow of a woman tied to a giant X-shaped rack. A man's shadow enters the frame. As the woman shrieks and struggles, the man speaks: "Be patient. Are you in pain mademoiselle? It will only last a little longer." After uttering these chilling words, the shadow raises a hand and moves menacingly toward the writhing figure on the cross, merging with it into one indistinct pool of darkness. The camera then pans left to reveal the figures casting these shadows. As the streetwalker struggles against her bonds, the grim Mirakle raises a knife to her arm. "You're stubborn! Hush!" he shouts at her, angered when her writhing makes his work more difficult. "If you only last one more minute, then we shall see," he continues, more to himself than to her. "We shall know if you are to be—" his voice rises to a demonic crescendo,

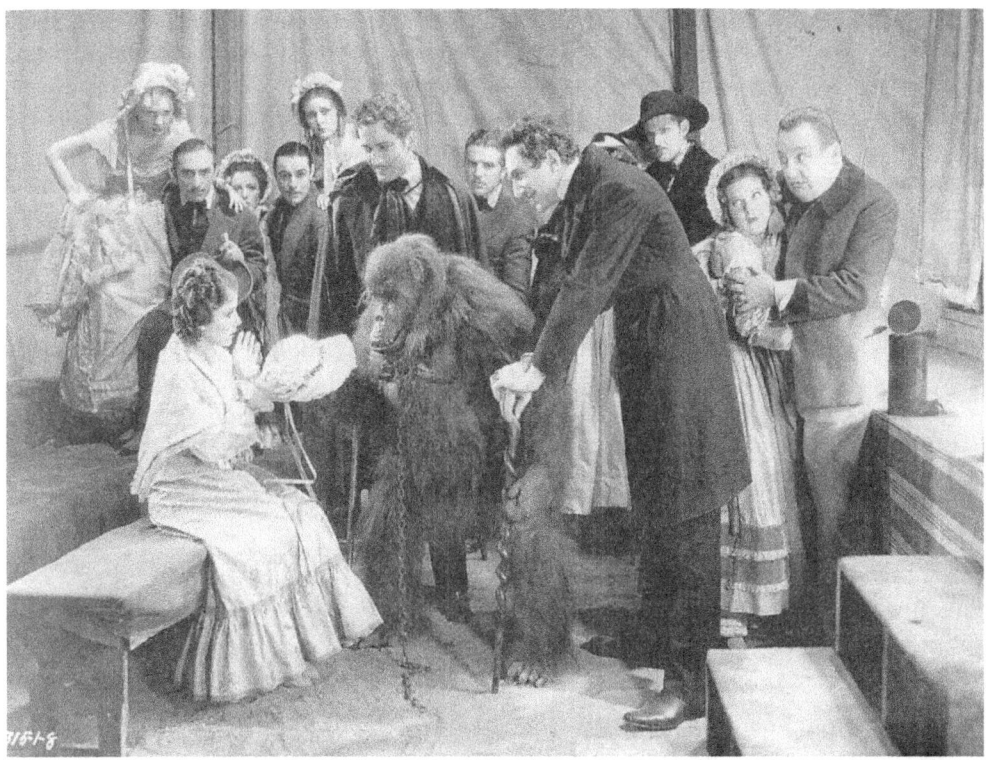

A group publicity shot from *Murders in the Rue Morgue*: Sidney Fox (seated), Charles Gemora (in ape suit), Leon Ames (behind Gemora), Bela Lugosi (leaning on cane), and Bert Roach (clutching girl). (Courtesy of Ted Okuda.)

"— the *bride of science*!" At this she utters an hysterical scream of pain.

The camera now tracks back and left to reveal a table covered with glass vials and bubbling beakers. While the girl hangs on the rack and sobs frantically in the background, Mirakle takes his fresh blood sample (brutally extracted from her arm) to the table and prepares a slide. Looking through the microscope, he utters a moan of despair. Suddenly, he knocks the instrument aside. "Rotten blood!" he shouts furiously, smashing equipment with another violent sweep of his arm. "You—" he accuses, turning to the now-unconscious girl. Approaching her, he holds up his fist and stares into her slack face. "Your blood is *rotten*! *Black* as your *sins*! You cheated me. Your beauty was a *lie*!" The girl moves once and then goes limp. Mirakle feels her pulse. "Dead," he says softly, all the fury drained from him. "You are— you're dead." He swallows hard and a look of sorrow plays across his face. A quick cut shows a low-angle close-up of the girl's head hanging down in the pose of a crucified martyr. The camera switches back to Mirakle who falls to his knees and clasps his hands together, raising them in a gesture of supplication, even prayer. In a moment his head drops and he sinks down in sorrow at the feet of his victim. A medium long shot now takes in the whole scene as we see him rise wearily to his feet. Motioning to his servant, he tells Janos to "get rid of it, get it away," the coldness in his voice indicating that his grieving has ended. In close up, Janos uses a hatchet to cut each of the ropes holding up the corpse, finishing with the bottom bonds so that we see only the corpse's legs. Then Mirakle's legs step into the frame and a quick movement of his foot releases the trap door over which the girl stood. Her body falls through it, passing quickly before our limited line of sight. "Will my search never end?" asks Mirakle, despairingly.

This sequence's brutal intensity stems from Arlene Francis' terrified whimpers and screams and from Lugosi's manic performance, while Florey's choice of shots and use of close-ups perfectly complements his actors. At the beginning, Lugosi's words and tones ring with a mad malevolence. Next he becomes impatient with her whimpering, then flies into a rage when he feels she has "cheated" him. Finally, he expresses genuine remorse (no doubt tinged with more than a little disappointment) when the girl succumbs to his "experiment." At the end, the cold, callous "disposal" of the body and his telling "Will my search never end?" brings Lugosi full circle back to his zealous insanity. (Incidentally, many State censor boards, including New York's, removed this scene from film prints shown in their regions, thus eliminating the picture's most powerful sequence.)

ASSETS

For their third horror production, Universal chose to follow the now-established (and lucrative) pattern of adapting the classic works of nineteenth century horror authors. Bram Stoker's *Dracula*, Mary Shelley's *Frankenstein*, and now Edgar Allan Poe's *Murders in the Rue Morgue* were brought to the screen to "thrill ... shock ... and even horrify" (in the words of Edward Van Sloan).[1] Horror was here to stay, and, tossing aside the promotional caution they showed on *Dracula* the previous year, Universal was ready to shout it to the theater rafters. "Only Poe dared imagine it! Only people who can stand excitement and shock should dare to see it!" warned the film's titillating trailer. In point of fact, it was Florey who "dared imagine it." The writer/director, with help from a variety of scenario writers, took Poe's admittedly gruesome detective story (arguably the first in that particular genre, by the way) and turned it into a horrific, full-blooded gothic study of a mad scientist's perversity.

While Florey did an admirable job on *Murders in the Rue Morgue*, the director has taken a critical pounding over the years. Critics point at the camera-mounted-on-a-swing sequence and shout phrases like "look-at-me precociousness" (*Universal Horrors*, Brunas, Brunas, and Weaver). Aside from this one (admittedly regrettable) excess, Florey made excellent visual decisions.[2] (The one valid criticism against Florey — and this is a great one — is that he did not properly direct his actors.) For instance, Florey deftly handles the pivotal unveiling of Erik the ape: Mirakle's servant reaches for the curtain covering the cage. As he draws it back, the viewpoint shifts and we see the curtain open not from outside looking in, but from *inside looking out*. All we glimpse of the dreaded creature is an indistinct shoulder and one side of the hirsute head as we look through the bars and watch audience members jump and shriek. We are placed in Erik's position and feel what it's like to be stared at and feared while simultaneously we experience that very fear ourselves as we strain to see the object of horror with which we share the cage. Unfortunately, this disorienting jolt and moment of suspense is quickly dispelled when the next shot reveals in close-up the face of an ordinary orangutan.

Of Lugosi, Robert Florey said: "It was at times difficult to control his tendency to chew the scenery." That is exactly what Lugosi DOES and what makes this performance so enjoyable to watch. While capable of subtlety, he generally heads in the opposite direction. In so doing, he often transforms overacting into an art form. While he chews, Lugosi puts his entire being into his jaw muscles and swallows with the deepest conviction. This sincerity makes his pregnant pauses, unwieldy accent, and fascinatingly improbable facial expressions real. Obviously, Lugosi believes it and, as a result, so do we. In *Murders in the Rue Morgue*, he gives a florid but forceful performance as the mad medico driven by his horrendous, perverse dream. His wicked smiles and exaggerated eyebrow movements lack subtlety but not efficacy. No one can smile more evilly than Lugosi, and he acts at full power here. When Mirakle encounters the hysterical prostitute, Lugosi's eyes are wide and gleaming and his lips curl upwards in a grotesque half-smile. "A lady — in distress?" he asks, his pregnant pause and grotesque gleam promising a distress far greater than her present predicament.

Lugosi's intensity reveals itself at the very beginning when he delivers his evolution pitch at the carnival tent. "Do they still burn men for heresy?" he asks when his audience balks at his radical ideas. "Then burn me, Monsieur. Light the fire." While on the surface Lugosi's tone is friendly and his smile inviting, something unhealthy and dangerous lurks beneath. "Do you think your little candle —" he begins good-naturedly when suddenly his brows descend angrily and his voice hardens as he finishes "— will outshine the flame of truth?!" That which only simmered now boils: "My life is consecrated to great *experiment*." In close-up his eyes gleam, and as he forces the words from his lips we can see in his face the disdain of a giant for mere mortals who dare doubt the speaker's greatness. Lugosi, having established his power and presence, now lets his character's madness shine through. "I tell you I will proooove — your kinship — with the ape." His drawing out of the word "prove" and insertion of pregnant pauses emphasize his conviction. At the same time, his voice takes on an almost desperate intensity as he raises the volume a notch, exposing the twisted roots of madness.

In addition to Robert Florey and Bela Lugosi, the third great star of *Murders in the Rue Morgue* is cinematographer Karl Freund. Due to Florey's direction and Freund's camerawork and lighting, the film possesses a visual richness far above its lurid story, inane dialogue, and melodramatic acting. Of his cameraman, Florey said, "It was a pleasure to collaborate with [Freund] as he understood exactly what I wanted. ... He responded to my specific efforts and helped me greatly with his suggestions. He was an expert in unnatural lighting effects." Freund makes good use of low-key lighting to create mood. In the important introduction to Dr. Mirakle, the lighting casts a giant shadow behind Mirakle as he moves and gestures dramatically on the stage, emphasizing the man's presence and power.

Under Florey's direction, Freund carefully constructs his images with an eye towards depth and balance. In the opening sequence in Mirakle's tent, Freund places two tent posts in the foreground to add visual depth. He carefully avoids arranging people and objects across a horizontal line, and instead staggers their positions to place some in the foreground, thereby creating a three-dimensional feel. The visuals are carefully composed, and Freund imbues these compositions with meaning. Erik's cage in the upper left-hand corner of the frame is balanced by an oil lamp placed in the lower right, creating a diagonal sight line. Through the middle of the frame runs the horizontal flight of four stairs up to the raised stage where Mirakle stands, balanced in the center of the horizontal line. When he moves to the side, the balance shifts and the now-unbalanced composition suddenly becomes a metaphor for Mirakle's unbalanced mind.

Camera movement plays a critical role in *Murders in the Rue Morgue*, creating mood and intensity. When Mirakle speaks of his "great experiment," for example, the camera tracks in so that Lugosi's face fills nearly the entire screen, inexorably drawing the viewer toward this visage until it becomes the whole world. Then, lighting from the side turns half his face into a mass of moving shadows as he speaks, while we are drawn to Lugosi's one visible eye, which shines with an insane gleam. The gradual, commanding camera movement, the pinpoint lighting, and Lugosi's malevolent presence all combine to create a moment of intensity.

Charles D. Hall's gothic sets and expressionistic backgrounds (the bizarre angles and painted shadows are reminiscent of 1919's *The Cabinet of Dr. Caligari*) evoke a dark, malevolent, almost surrealistic atmosphere. Mirakle's secret laboratory is a combination fifteenth century alchemy chamber and inquisition dungeon. Blank stone walls enclose a room filled with oversized tables and heavy wooden benches. Glass tubes, odd instruments, and jars of archaic origin litter their surfaces. In the center rises a wooden platform enclosed by a rough-hewn railing. A huge, upright,

Dr. Mirakle (Bela Lugosi) plots with his servant Janos (black actor Noble Johnson — in *whiteface*) to commit *Murders in the Rue Morgue* (1932).

wooden cross in the shape of an X dominates the dais — a device to which the madman straps his victims in a crucifixion pose and subjects them to his diabolical "great experiment." The macabre settings perfectly match the unwholesome characters and dire events.

Even the more mundane sets are treated with careful consideration and detailed art direction. Pierre's flat, for instance, with its exposed pipes, oversized rooftop window, and crude furniture, is cluttered with books and drawings while the walls sport student sketches and even charcoal caricatures drawn right on the plaster. These minor touches add visual interest, but, more importantly, they enhance the believability of the settings and so aid the viewer in suspending his disbelief over events that often prove highly *un*believable.

LIABILITIES

Apart from Lugosi, the remaining principals act as if they are in a stage-bound melodrama (or, in the case of Bert Roach, in a burlesque comedy). As Pierre, Leon Waycoff (later Leon Ames) gives an overblown, unconvincing performance. When his character becomes excited or angry, his exaggerated voice and gestures ring with insincerity (as if by overplaying he can make up for his lack of real conviction). Even in his calmer sequences, Waycoff displays no sense of subtlety. When Pierre pays his nighttime visit to Dr. Mirakle, the doctor tells him there will be "no show tonight, young man." Pierre replies, "I've already seen your performance — doctor." During the overlong, "dramatic" pause before "doctor," Waycoff reaches up to touch his throat and swivel his neck about, as his character supposedly remembers Erik grabbing him by the throat during the carnival. This gross theatrical trick is more suited to provincial theater than sinister cinema. Lugosi is able to pull something like this off, but Waycoff lacks the presence and conviction to make it work. (Florey's direction of actors didn't seem to improve with time. For instance, the director's final horror film, *The Beast with Five Fingers,* 1946, is nearly sunk by the toneless, insipid acting of its "world-weary" hero, Robert Alda.)

Sidney Fox has little appeal in the role of Camille. Why Pierre or Mirakle (or even Erik, for that matter) would be so captivated by this silly, colorless creature is a mystery. Of course, Mirakle primarily wanted her for her blood (though the Good Doctor seemed to develop a more natural secondary desire as well), but as for the other two, one can only conclude that they loved her because it was in the script. Said script gives her little to do (fawning over a new hat, singing a little ditty, or occasionally uttering a scream before fainting), and this may be just as well. Still, other actresses such as Fay Wray, Gloria Stuart, and Frances Drake were able to take similar wallflower characters and infuse them with life. Not so Sidney, whose alternately silly and near-invisible presence inspires no confidence in the unlikely proceedings. One suspects that her rumored romantic relationship with producer Carl Laemmle, Jr., may have had something to do with her winning the part (*and* receiving top billing).

As with many horror pictures of the Golden Age, the overblown romance becomes a stone around the film's neck. The love scenes between Pierre and Camille are ridiculous in their corny, antiquated dialogue. "You're like a flower," declares Pierre, gazing into Camille's moon-eyes, "soft and fragrant, pure and beautiful. You're like a star too — a white morning star. And your hair, it's full of stardust." Wait, he's not through yet: "You're like a song the girls of Provence sing on Mayday, and like the dancing in Normandy on Mayday, and like the wine in Burgundy on Mayday. Oh, Camille, I love you." *Enough* already! Equally excessive and ridiculous, the introduction to the lovers' "playful" scene in the park treats us to no fewer than seven pairs of young lovers engaged in romantic by-play before we finally find our hero and heroine (on the dreaded swing).

If the picture's love-interest comes off as a stone weight, then the "comedy" becomes a veritable *albatross* draped about the film's neck. As the whiny, cowardly Paul, Pierre's roommate and sidekick, Bert Roach's mincing portrayal of this silly, frivolous sissy is about as unfunny a comedy bit as one can find. Whenever Roach is onscreen, the picture comes to a screeching halt. The second wave of comedy relief comes in the form of the three "witnesses" who claim to have heard the assailant in Camille's flat speaking in a foreign language. First, the German bystander swears it was Italian. The second witness, an Italian, says no, it was Danish. Finally, the third bystander, a Dane, steps forward and claims, "it was German." This sets them all off. "Italian!" shouts the German; "Danish!" yells the Italian; "German!" roars the Dane. Then all three bellow at each other in their respective tongues. This noisy, nonsensical "comedy" lasts a full twenty seconds until a gendarme has the sense to shout "silence!" Before we can breathe a sigh of relief, however, the three get in a few more licks. This sequence goes on and on and ON, beyond silliness, almost (but not quite) to the point of slapstick.

The picture's credibility strains to the breaking point when shots of the gorilla-suited actor playing Erik are intercut with close-ups of a real chimp. These horribly mismatched shots are made even more ludicrous by the photography (a rare error in judgment on the part of Florey and Freund). The live monkey close-ups invariably feature a soft focus which contrasts markedly with the more natural hard focus of the medium and long shots of the gorilla suit. These jarring differences in cinematic texture within the same sequence only draw attention to the unconvincing cheat. In 1932, however, audience (and critical) expectations were apparently much lower than they are today, as *Variety* noted that "several switches from the real gorilla to a costume double are neatly veiled."

Further gorilla problems arise when Dr.

Mirakle "talks" with the ape. "I have learned his language," boasts Mirakle to his audience. Smiling benevolently, he approaches Erik's cage and begins speaking softly in some unknown language.[3] Between Mirakle's phrases, the monkey makes high-pitched whining and cooing noises, sounding nothing like the "language" Mirakle professes to know. This silly monkey baby-talk puts Mirakle in a ridiculous light. (Apparently, Erik understands English as well, for Mirakle eschews the gorilla tongue and speaks to the ape in English for the rest of the film.) The simian's "dialogue" doesn't help matters either. "I will translate what he says," announces Mirakle. "My home is in the African jungle, where I live with my father and my mother — and my brothers and sisters. But I was captured by a band of hairless white apes and carried away to a strange land. I'm in the prime of my strength — and I'm lonely." To his credit, Lugosi invests just as much heartfelt sincerity in this silly soliloquy as he does in his "great experiment" speech, but here the dialogue only makes Mirakle look ridiculous.

Despite these liabilities, *Murders in the Rue Morgue* deserves better than the critical knocks it has received in recent reassessments (*Universal Horrors* labeling it a "hokey, outdated stiff," for instance). Negative appraisals like these may either be a backlash against Robert Taves' recent Florey biography in which Taves more or less deifies the director, or reflect the expectation that since *Rue Morgue* is a Universal product, it should be better. While not on the same level as *The Mummy* or *The Black Cat*, *Murders in the Rue Morgue* still merits the respect it isn't getting. Florey's effective direction, Freund's fluid visuals, Hall's Caligaresque sets, and Lugosi's archetypal performance (setting the standard for his many subsequent Mad Doctor roles — and those of his imitators) make *Murders in the Rue Morgue* an unusual, artistic, and entertaining entry in the Golden Age of Horror.

REVIEW

"'Dracula' and 'Frankenstein' having softened 'em up," predicted *Variety*'s Bige (February 16, 1932), "this third of U's [Universal's] baby-scaring cycle won't have the benefit of shocking them stiff and then making them talk about it. Had it come first there's no doubt it would have created a stronger impression.

Of Lugosi, Bige states, "Dr. Mirakle [is] played in Bela Lugosi's customary fantastic manner," then complains that "Sidney Fox overdraws the sweet ingenue to the point of nearly distracting an audience from any fear it might have for her."

PRODUCTION NOTES

Murders in the Rue Morgue (1932) was director Robert Florey's "consolation prize" after *Frankenstein* was stolen away from him by James Whale. While Florey worked on *Frankenstein* (preparing the script and shooting test reels), Universal considered newcomer Bette Davis for the part of Elizabeth. When the studio bumped Florey from the project, Ms. Davis went with the director to his new production assignment of *Murders in the Rue Morgue*. Producer Carl Laemmle, Jr., however, was unimpressed by her screen test and Sidney Fox eventually received the female lead.

Despite a huge success with *Dracula*, the summer of 1931 was a disastrous time financially for Universal, who drew a gigantic deficit for the quarter. In September, E. M. Asher, a supervisor at Universal, ordered that the upcoming *Murders in the Rue Morgue* production be changed from its period setting of 1845 to modern-day 1931 in order to economize on costumes and sets. Fortunately, calmer heads prevailed and the film remained a period piece. Even so, the budget was cut from a proposed $130,000 to a mere $90,000, which caused director Robert Florey to walk out on the project. He soon returned, however, and the film ultimately sported a more respectable budget of $164,220 (which was still over $125,000 short of *Frankenstein*'s final cost). After principal photography was completed, seven days of retakes and additional shooting bumped *Murders in the Rue Morgue*'s final price tag up to $190,099.45.

Florey recalled the production in *The Films of Bela Lugosi*, by Richard Bojarski: "I wrote the *Rue Morgue* adaptation in a week and directed the film in four. That was during the fall of 1931. ... In *Rue Morgue* I used the same device I employed in my *Frankenstein* adaptation. Bela Lugosi became Dr. Mirakle — a mad scientist desirous of creating a human being — not with body parts stolen from a graveyard and a brain from a lab, but by the mating of an ape with a woman." (Note: This "mating" was toned down to become a mere mixing of blood in the film's final screenplay, which underwent six full rewrites before finally going before the cameras.) Florey remembered that Lugosi "was habitually silent and not given to conversation. Between scenes he retired in his dressing room."

The project was originally to have been directed by George Melford, who had previously helmed the cinematically superior Spanish language version of *Dracula* for Universal. But just as Whale bumped Florey from *Frankenstein*, so Florey bumped Melford from *Murders in the Rue Morgue*.

John Huston, at the time under contract to Universal as a writer, provided "additional dialogue." In his autobiography, *An Open Book*, Huston recalled, "I tried to bring Poe's prose style into the dialogue, but the director thought it sounded stilted, so he and his assistant rewrote scenes on the set. As a result, the picture was an odd mixture of nineteenth-century grammarian's prose and modern colloquialisms."

The picture suffered from some last-minute tampering in the editing room. Originally, it was to open with the scene of the street fight and Mirakle taking the prostitute to his laboratory. This sequence (the strongest in the film) was deemed too downbeat an opening and so was shuffled with the more breezy carnival scenes. Unfortunately, this rearrangement weakens the dramatic structure of the story. In the original structure, Mirakle's (and Erik's) unhealthy attraction to Camille at the carnival takes on a much darker, more sinister meaning and we can clearly see the contrast in Mirakle's mind between the "tainted" streetwalker and the "pure" Camille. This juxtaposition is lost in the current ordering. The scene switching also creates some continuity problems. Mirakle rides with Erik to Camille's residence, whereupon he gets out and the coach (with Erik inside) drives on. The next we see of Mirakle, he is back in the coach and Erik is nowhere to be seen. Besides that, a perfectly calm and clear night has inexplicably become a foggy and windy one.

Two other, minor gaffes have nothing to do with scene switching, however. The first comes when the streetwalker's body arrives at the morgue. When the attendant asks for identification, the orderly responds with, "None, she was naked." When Mirakle dropped her body through his trap door into the river, however, she was clothed in a smock. The other discrepancy is one of historical accuracy. In one street scene, a man rides an old-time bicycle, the style of which was not seen until several decades later.

Lugosi's onscreen victim is Arlene Francis, making her screen debut. Hero Leon Ames also made his film debut here using his real name of Leon Waycoff. The actor didn't acquire his stage moniker until 1935. Ames held a low opinion of his first picture, later calling it (in *Famous Monsters of Filmland*) "a perfectly awful film which still pops up on TV to haunt me!"

Statuesque black actor Noble Johnson (*The Most Dangerous Game*; *The Mummy*; *King Kong*) plays Mirakle's sadistic servant, Janos, in whiteface — despite being referred to as "The Black One" in the film's credits.

Poe's grotesque detective story was first adapted for film in 1908 as a Sherlock Holmes vehicle: *Sherlock Holmes in the Great Murder Mystery* (Denmark). *The Raven* (1912) also utilized elements of "Murders in the Rue Morgue" (among numerous others of Poe's stories). The original title finally reached the screen in 1914 as a Sol Rosenberg production. After the 1932 film, Warner Bros. tackled the tale in 1954 as *Phantom of the Rue Morgue*, though their adaptation starring Karl Malden as a mad zoologist was no closer to Poe's story than Universal's. *Phantom* is notable for two reasons. First, it is the only 3-D adaptation of a Poe story to date. Second, the ape suit in

Phantom was worn by Charles Gemora, who, 22 years earlier, had played Erik in Universal's picture. (Charles Gemora was not the only monkey-man in *Murders in the Rue Morgue*. Stuntman Joe Bonomo donned the hirsute disguise for the film's more vigorous sequences. Bonomo went on to portray not one but *two* of the manimal creatures stalking the *Island of Lost Souls* the following year.) In 1971, AIP's *Murders in the Rue Morgue* strayed even further from Poe than any of the previous adaptations by presenting a plot revolving around a killer who stalks a Grand Guignol theater presenting Poe's "Murders in the Rue Morgue" on stage. Finally, in 1986, Poe's tale made it to the screen in a faithful adaptation. Unfortunately, it was only the *small* screen, for *The Murders in the Rue Morgue* was a made-for-television movie (though with the advantage of having George C. Scott in the role of Poe's deductive detective, C. Auguste Dupin).

NOTES

1. In the onscreen preface to *Frankenstein* (1931).
2. This camera mounted on a swing gimmick was possibly suggested by cinematographer Karl Freund, who had used a similar technique in the 1925 German silent film *Variety*.
3. This language is not Lugosi's native Hungarian, but (according to two Hungarian acquaintances of mine) it does sound something like Romanian, a language the actor may have had some knowledge of.

FREAKS
(1932; MGM)

Alternate Titles: *Forbidden Love; The Monster Show; Nature's Mistakes*
Release Date: February 10, 1932
Running Time: 64 minutes
Director: Tod Browning
Screenplay: Willis Goldbeck, Leon Gordon; additional dialogue by Edgar Allen Woolf, Al Boasberg; (suggested by Tod Robbins' story "Spurs")
Photography: Merritt B. Gerstad
Editor: Basil Wrangell
Cast: Wallace Ford (Phroso), Leila Hyams (Venus), Roscoe Ates (Roscoe), Henry Victor (Hercules), Harry Earles (Hans), Daisy Earles (Frieda), Rose Dione (Madame Tetrallini), Daisy Hilton/Violet Hilton (Siamese Twins), Schlitze (Herself), Josephine Joseph (Half Woman-Half Man), Johnny Eck (Half Boy), Frances O'Connor (Armless Girl), Peter Robinson (Human Skeleton), Olga Roderick (Bearded Lady), Koo Koo (Herself), Randion (The Living Torso), Martha Morris (Armless Girl), Zip & Pip (Pinheads), Elizabeth Green (Bird Girl), Angelo Rossitto (Angeleno), Edward Brophy/Mat McHugh (Rollo Brothers).

"How many times have I told you not to be frightened. Have I not told you God looks after all his children."—Madame Tetrallini.

"Dirty!—slimy!—*freaks*!"—Cleopatra.

SYNOPSIS

"We didn't lie to you folks. We told you we had living, breathing monstrosities," promises a carnival barker to an eager crowd. "Their code is a law unto themselves. Offend one—and you offend them all." Directing his audience to a waist-high pen, the carny continues: "You are about to witness *the* most amazing, *the* most astounding living monstrosity of all time." As the onlookers gather around the pen (into which *we* cannot see), they gasp in horror. The barker then begins his story: "Friends, she was once a beautiful woman.... She was known as 'The Peacock of the Air.'" The scene dissolves to a bigtop interior where the beautiful aerialist Cleopatra is performing. Hans the midget watches intently from backstage. "She is the most beautiful big woman I have ever seen," he thoughtlessly tells his concerned fiancée Frieda, another midget.

Cleo notices Hans' interest and begins playing on his infatuation to extract gifts and loans from her diminutive admirer. Meanwhile, we meet the rest of the circus denizens and their daily lives. We are present after the birth of the bearded lady's baby; we witness the domestic squabbles of Daisy and Violet, the Siamese Twins, one of whom is married to Roscoe. ("You gotta cut out gettin' drunk every night," Roscoe orders his sister-in-law, Violet. "I'm not gonna have *my* wife layin' in bed half the day with *your* hangover!") We also meet Venus and Phroso, two "normals" who look on the "human oddities" as friends rather than freaks.

Cleopatra soon takes up with Hercules, the strong man, while still soliciting the attentions of Hans. Frieda goes to see her fiancé to warn him of Cleo's contempt. "To me you're a man," she tells Hans, "but to her you're only something to laugh at." Hans will have none of it, however. In a last-ditch effort to save the pride of the man she loves, Frieda goes to Cleo to try and convince her to stop this humiliating game. Frieda lets slip about the fortune Hans has inherited. With this knowledge, Cleo and Hercules form a plan.

Cleo marries Hans. At the wedding feast held by the freaks, Cleo slips something into her bridegroom's wine. The more she drinks, the more careless she becomes and her true feelings are revealed. "Our *wedding night*," she says contemptuously, and then laughs uproariously. Oblivious to Cleo's hateful behavior, the freaks prepare a loving cup. "We accept her, we accept her, one of us, one of us," they chant as the large cup is passed down the table from mouth to mouth. In a fit of rage and revulsion, Cleo hurls the cup's contents in their faces and orders them out. As a crowning humiliation, Hercules hoists Hans up onto Cleo's shoulders and she parades around the room in a perverse "horsy-back ride."

Later that night, Cleo and Hercules apologize to Hans (claiming they were drunk and it was all a joke). The matter is left unresolved, however, when Hans collapses from the poison. Venus is suspicious and confronts Hercules, threatening to go to the police if Hans worsens. The close-knit freaks set up a constant vigil; as Cleo nurses Hans, eyes peer at her from everywhere—through windows, from under stairs, from between the spokes of a wagon wheel. Cleo continues to administer the poison in Hans' medicine, but her husband now knows the truth. Spitting out the liquid when Cleo is not looking, Hans whispers "Tonight!" to his friends.

A terrible storm blows as the caravan moves out that night. Hercules goes to Venus' wagon to silence her, for she "knows too much." Phroso gets wind of this and follows, catching the strongman just as he bursts through Venus' door. Rolling outside into the mud, Hercules gets the better of Phroso, but a stiletto thrown by a dwarf stops the big man. The freaks advance upon the wounded strongman with knives drawn.

Meanwhile, Hans and his companions confront Cleo in his wagon. Just then, the wagon hits a rut and turns on its side. Shrieking, Cleo flees into the night with the freaks in fast pursuit. Lightning flashes, she utters one final scream, and the terrible scene dissolves back to the carnival barker at the edge of the pen. "How she got that way will never be known," he tells his audience. "Some say a jealous lover; others, the Code of the freaks; others, the storm. Believe it or not, there she is," and we see the fate of Cleopatra—she has been turned into a legless human chicken, forever suffering the sad plight of the freaks she once ridiculed.

In an epilogue, several years later Hans lives in seclusion. Phroso and Venus bring Frieda to see him. "Please go away, I can see no one," says Hans and turns away in shame. "But Hans," answers Frieda, "you tried to stop them... It wasn't your fault." As Phroso and Venus tactfully depart, Hans falls weeping into Frieda's loving arms.

MEMORABLE MOMENTS

Freaks abounds in memorable moments. Once having seen them, who is likely to forget the sight of Prince Randian, the "Living Torso," striking a match and lighting a cigarette using only his mouth, or the armless girl eating a meal and drinking a glass of beer with her feet, or the bizarre wedding feast in which "human oddities" dance wildly on the table and chant "we accept her, we accept her, one of us, gooble-gobble, one of us"? Still, all these unusual scenes pale next to the climactic sequence, in which the simmering tension and terror finally boils to the surface.

Actually, two climaxes occur concurrently, following the two separate, though parallel, fates of Cleopatra and Hercules. The dual cinematic threads are intertwined beautifully, combining to weave a tapestry of sheer terror. The sequence begins in Hans' wagon, where the midget, along with three of his friends (two dwarves and Johnny "the half-boy") confronts Cleopatra. A violent storm rages outside; the sounds of thunder and rain pounding on the carriage roof form an unnerving cacophony. While the first dwarf plays a weird, melancholy melody on a panflute, Hans demands the bottle of poison from Cleo. For emphasis, the second dwarf takes out a knife and begins polishing the blade while Johnny pulls a Luger from inside his jacket and begins to polish *it*. With one stage set, the scene changes to Venus' wagon. Hercules breaks through the door but Phroso follows the strongman inside and grapples with him. Suddenly, we are out in the storm and a wagon careens through the darkness only to hit a deep rut and tip over sideways. A beam of light streams into the darkness through the wagon's open door. We hear a scream and Cleo emerges to flee shrieking into the night with the freaks in close pursuit. Back in Venus' wagon, Hercules overpowers Phroso. Rolling out the door into the mud, the strongman begins to strangle Phroso. A dwarf, standing in the rain, throws a knife into Hercules' side. Phroso hits the big man and makes his escape. Struggling in the mud, Hercules looks up and sees the dwarf advancing with a (second) knife in his hand. From a different direction Slitzie the pinhead, no longer the childlike innocent, crawls through the mud under the wagon, her hand grasping a gleaming blade. Hercules, clutching his wounded side, crawls backwards, his eyes wide with fear. The camera follows him, pacing his retreat, and then cuts to view his pursuers' slow advance. Other freaks have come — a dwarf slides forward through the mud; a hairy beast-girl crawls on all fours in the mire; the "Living Torso" slithers forward with a knife clenched between his teeth. The slow, silent, determined advance is horrifying to behold as the freaks crawl, slink and slither through the mud towards their victim. Now we see them all together, descending as one nightmarish group upon the strongman. The picture changes to the nearby woods — dark and shadowy and indistinct. Suddenly, a burst of lightning illuminates the scene with an almost painful brilliance and we see a panic-stricken figure racing towards us. Lighting flashes again as she approaches and the figure shrieks. It is Cleopatra. She stops and turns to look behind her. With another brief blast of brilliant light, we see various freaks, led by the half-boy, come shambling across a fallen log and running towards us. Cleo screams once more in mortal terror and the scene dissolves to the carnival barker relating the story to his patrons. The terrible, horrible nightmare is over.

The fact that Hercules and Cleopatra are pursued separately compounds the terror of the climax by adding a feeling of helpless isolation. Each is alone, which makes the scenes more frightening than had they faced the freaks together. The two sequences are of different but complementary tones. The scenes of Cleo are high-speed terror as she flees wildly into the night with the more mobile freaks in fast and deadly pursuit. The glimpses of the freaks are quick and terrifying. The wounded Hercules, on the other hand, can only crawl slowly backwards in the mud, with the freaks advancing slowly and inexorably towards him (and the viewer). These scenes lack the frenetic terror of Cleo's flight, but they possess in full measure the frightful horror of the freaks themselves, who have become grotesque crawling *things* as they steadily advance on their terrified victim. While undeniably effective, the inclusion of these horrific shots is unfortunate because they transform these likable innocents, these "special people," into inhuman monsters and objects of terror. This is the

This reissue lobby card shows Phroso (Wallace Ford) demonstrating a gag to Madame Tetrallini (Rose Dione) and the three "pinheads," Schlitze, Zip, and Pip, in a scene cut from *Freaks* (1932).

very reaction the callous and exploitive sideshows historically strove for and *Freaks* (up until this climax) fought *against*. All our feelings of loathing, disgust, and fear are brought to the surface in these last moments, while the previous hour had worked hard to counteract these unworthy prejudices. In this instance, director Tod Browning has sacrificed message for shock. Still, in the process he also created the most horrific and terrifying climax of the Golden Age of Horror.

ASSETS

"To me *Freaks* is so loathsome that I am nauseated thinking about it." Thus spake the film reviewer for *Harrison's Reports* in 1932, and his virulent sentiments were frequently echoed by critics and audiences alike. What is it about the film that elicits such a violent reaction? True, it is a horror picture and the horror genre as a whole has garnered more than its fair share of bad press. Still, *Freaks* was something of an Olympian when it came to critics voicing vitriolic vehemence.

Publisher Martin Quigley, co-author of the Motion Picture Code in 1930, wrote a book called *Decency in Motion Pictures* in 1937. In this slim treatise, he singles out certain films as good examples of bad examples. Nearly five years after its disastrous release, *Freaks* was still high on Quigley's list: "It is a story concerned with the life and loves of circus freaks, and, because of the human abnormalities involved, its unwholesome shockery creates morbid audience reactions." In Quigley's eyes, these "morbid reactions" are decidedly unhealthy, for he complains that the film possesses "a [general] character which in consideration of the susceptibilities of mass audiences should be avoided."

Perhaps the reason for these knee-jerk reactions stems from the notion held by many that *Freaks* was exploitation, pure and simple — Tod Browning showing off his sideshow.

While in a superficial sense this is true, the numerous scenes focusing on the exceptional talents of these extraordinary individuals (the armless girl eating with a fork held in her toes; the "Living Torso" lighting a cigarette using only his mouth) actually do much to impress the viewer with the immense fortitude of these people in overcoming their handicaps and adapting to as normal a life as possible. Browning counterbalances these "exhibitionist" moments with scenes of the "normals" interacting socially with the "freaks." Venus and Frieda talk about man-problems over a load of washing, speaking as friends and equals. Phroso shows genuine wonder and joy at the birth of the bearded lady's baby. Later he jokes — without condescension — with Elvira and Slitzie (two childlike pinheads) about buying a hat. Film historian Robert F. Moss, calling *Freaks* "one of the most remarkable horror films ever made," observed that "the film is noteworthy both for its moments of fright and for its compassion towards the deformed circus people."[1] While the scenes most readily recalled are those in which Browning does indeed "show off his sideshow" or even exploit the horrific aspects of his unique cast (as in the terrifying climax), there are feelings aroused in — and explored by — the viewer which run far deeper than these superficial peepshow remembrances.

A more meaningful explanation of negative audience reaction is that *Freaks* simply makes its viewers uncomfortable. As a result, it inspires animosity, with some viewers transferring their uneasiness to indignation. This discomfort stems from the very nature of the picture for, like Fritz Lang's *M* (1931), *Freaks* is based on reality and not fantasy. One cannot enjoy the vicarious thrills and pathos of the picture and then go whistling happily away after the curtain falls, secure in the knowledge that it was all just fantasy. Unlike the horror offerings of 1931, *Freaks* offers no Eastern European Counts cringing from crosses, no man-made monsters powered by the bolts of heaven. *Freaks*' "monsters" are real human beings. After finishing their scenes, they did not saunter over to the makeup department to be restored to normalcy in an hour or two. No, they went back to their previous existence which, in most cases, was very much like that portrayed onscreen. The comfortable blanket of fantasy is missing from *Freaks* and the viewer must shiver in the cold reality of the situation. This is both what makes *Freaks* so hard to take and what gives the film its power. Though the story is contrived and the characters simplified, *Freaks* is *real*.

Director and guiding hand Tod Browning wastes no time in drawing us into the closed world of the "abnormal and the unwanted" (as the written prologue describes them). A few seconds after the title "*Freaks*" fills the screen, a hand suddenly rips through the background and violently peels it away, revealing it to be a mere sheet of poster paper — like a circus advertisement. The scene then dissolves to a bowler-hatted carnival barker wadding up a large sheet of paper as if it were *his* hand that we had just seen. This neat little trick pulls us in immediately, making us a part of the barker's on-screen audience. By ripping away the paper, the barker (and Browning) rips away the obstruction before our very eyes so that we may see the "living breathing monstrosities" close up. Or, metaphorically speaking, perhaps that title card was the safety of our own ignorant prejudice which he so callously tore away, leaving us without any protection against the onslaught of self-examination to come.

Browning then shows us the difficulties these unfortunates encounter and the resilience with which they overcome their handicaps, both physical and social (e.g., the marriage of the Siamese twins Daisy and Violet to two different men). But Browning doesn't let us get to know them well. Their world remains alien. The wedding feast is particularly disturbing, as they carry on in a bizarre, paganistic manner. Perhaps that was Browning's intention — to show that we can never fully understand these special people, and to make us realize that the revulsion we feel — even be it involuntary — stems from this very lack of understanding. Feelings are mixed, and we are shamed by our detestation. Browning holds our deepest feelings of abhorrence and fear up to the light and shows us how misguided they are — not a pleasant illumination, but a self-revealing one.

It is not unreasonable to attribute this intent to Browning. *Freaks* is definitely Browning's show. The opening credits even label it "Tod Browning's *Freaks*" and all other participants (except Tod Robbins) must wait until the closing credits to receive their due. Browning was intimately familiar with the circus milieu, having run away from home as a teenager to spend his formative years amid the sawdust and spectacle of a traveling carnival. His affinity for the circus world is evident in several of his previous pictures, including *The Mystic* (1925), *The Unholy Three* (1925), and *The Unknown* (1927). Without a doubt, *Freaks* is Browning's signature film. Whatever his general shortcomings, on *Freaks*, at least, Browning directed with a firm conviction (if not always a steady hand).

Cinematically speaking, *Freaks* is one of Browning's best efforts. He eschews the stagebound, static technique of his earlier *Dracula* (1931) and allows the camera to move about freely. This movement takes us into the special world of these people, allowing us to approach them readily and see things from their viewpoint. He also effectively uses the camera for emphasis (a technique generally lacking in *Dracula*). When Cleo and Hercules hatch their plot, for instance, the camera becomes something of an exclamation point. "I could marry him!" Cleo tells the laughing Hercules. "Yes, he would marry me!" she continues, her countenance animated by greed. Suddenly, as her face hardens and her eyes focus into a hard stare, the camera slowly glides towards her and stops suddenly just as she ominously intones, "Midgets are not strong. He could get sick." The smooth camera movement and the abrupt stop add dramatic impact to the scene by underlining the forming of the evil notion in Cleo's ruthless mind.

Browning makes good use of camera viewpoint. For example, when Cleo first seduces Hercules, she calls, "Ah, come on in," beckoning in a seductive, come-hither manner. The camera is placed directly in front of her so that this enticing invitation is directed squarely at the viewer. The subjective viewpoint readily involves us in the moment.

The sets add much to *Freaks*, creating an evocative tapestry upon which the drama is woven. The cramped wagons, drawn tightly together, evoke the closeness of the circus milieu, visually reminding the viewer of the close-knit nature of the group ("offend one and you offend them all"). When the midgets are in their scaled-down wagons, filled with fixtures and furniture proportionate to their small size, the surroundings establish an air of normalcy. Only when this Lilliputian world is invaded by a giant "normal" is this illusion shattered. Then it is the big people who seem monstrous and out-of-place, rather than the so-called freaks.

The realism of *Freaks* extends beyond both the setting and the nature of the freaks themselves to include the behavior and motives of the "normals." *Freaks* is definitely an adult film and as such does not shy away from mature themes. *Freaks* possesses a racy element which adds to its richness and fascination. In the Cleopatra/Hercules seduction sequence, Cleo offers to cook the burly brute some eggs (obviously working under the old axiom that "the way to a man's heart is through his stomach"). After breaking an egg in a pan, Cleo turns to Hercules and leans backwards, thrusting out her chest to ask, "How do you like them?" From her brazen stance and Hercules' appraising "Not bad" just before grabbing her in his arms, it is obvious that the query refers to something other than eggs.

In another scene, Venus goes to Phroso's caravan only to find him sitting naked in a bathtub outside his wagon. As they talk, we wonder at the almost shocking nonchalance of the two. Then the camera pulls back and Phroso ducks underneath the tub to reveal that it's just a gag for his act that he's working on — it's a fake tub and he's not naked after all, just bare-chested. While the scene is ultimately revealed to be an innocent one, we're left with the idea of nudity and closeness being an accepted part of their lives.

The character of Venus is definitely not your standard chaste heroine. (Even her name — denoting the goddess of love — conjures up visions of bacchanalian pleasures.) We are introduced to her just as she leaves Hercules, obviously after having lived with him for some time. It's good to see that a "fallen woman" (or "tramp" as Hercules unfairly calls her) can be a likable protagonist and find happiness (even getting the guy) at the end. Of course, this simply would not have been possible a mere two years later, after the strict enforcement of the Production Code began. One must be thankful that *Freaks* was filmed without the yoke of the Code, which undoubtedly would have demanded that her character be whitewashed and pure or alternatively would have required a messy end for her. *Freaks* is refreshing in its uncritical realism and lack of moralizing. It portrays people who are not necessarily "morally correct" according to the dictates of society and shows them to be warm and humane. This enlightened tolerance is a breath of fresh air and an unexpected bonus in this sometimes harsh and relentless film.

LIABILITIES

Freaks possesses a dichotomous nature — part exploitation, part exploration (which perhaps, is the best one can hope for in the business of moviemaking). As such, the film contains several long stretches of the various freaks exhibiting their special abilities. While these somewhat gratuitous scenes do, in fact, display the great adaptability of these people, they also slow the picture's pace considerably and fail to advance the story.

The picture's pacing problem begins even before the opening credits. Browning's original version opened with the freaks frolicking near the lake and closed with an emasculated Hercules singing falsetto in "Tetrallini's Freaks and Music Hall." After *Freaks*' initial preview screenings were met with an almost violent reaction, however, MGM ordered Browning to remove the picture's most "offensive" elements, starting with both the beginning and ending of his morbid production. The director hastily wrote the framing device of the carnival barker introducing the freaks and shot four days of retakes. In the film's official 1932 release, this tacked-on introduction was much longer than that seen by audiences today.[2] When Dwain Esper bought the picture from MGM and took it on the roadshow circuit, he drastically cut this sequence and added his own written prologue as a sort of moralistic disclaimer. (Since no prints of the MGM original release version seem to have survived, we are left only with Esper's altered version.) "Before proceeding with the showing of the following HIGHLY UNUSUAL ATTRACTION," begins Esper's written message, "a few words should be said about the amazing subject matter." These "few words" go on and on (and on) for a full two-and-one-half minutes! The ill-conceived diatribe talks of "misshapen misfits who have altered the world's course," citing the likes of *Goliath, Calaban, Frankenstein,*[3] *Gloucester, Tom Thumb* and *Kaiser Wilhelm,* some of whom are *fictional* characters! Between these ridiculous passages and other pointless lessons about how "malformed children were placed out in the elements to die" are sprinkled a few worthy sentiments such as "the majority of freaks themselves are endowed with normal thoughts and emotions" and "their lot is truly a heartbreaking one." These truisms are lost amid the remaining tripe, however, and this preachy attempt by Esper to justify his new acquisition falls flat. In the end, they are just words and the misshapen images of horror seen at the film's end linger in the minds of viewers long after these desperate pleadings have faded.

Just as unnecessary, and even more detrimental, is the final epilogue tacked on (by MGM this time) in order to soften the film's impact. This "happy ending" has Frieda come to Hans who has locked himself away to wallow in guilt over the deed (which, it is explained, wasn't his fault because he "tried to stop them"). By dragging out the picture long past the startling sight of Cleopatra transformed into some hideous human bird-creature,[4] MGM got what they wanted — a lessening of the shock. They also got a weaker picture, and the lame addition did nothing to improve the film's box-office showing.

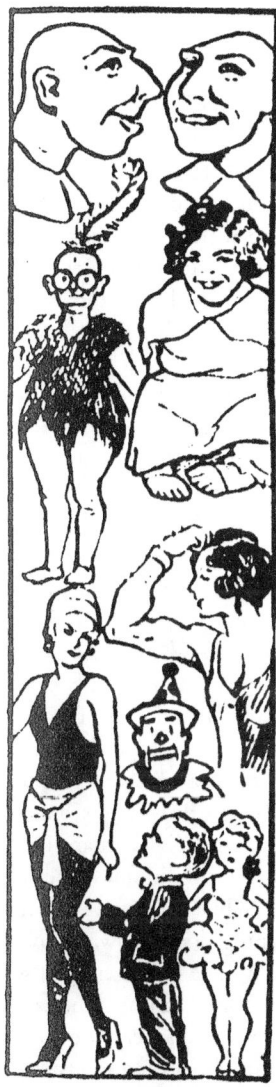

DAILY they are exhibited for the mockery and derision of the crowd!

Who cares for their lacerated feelings as pointing fingers and careless tongues flick and torture?

Who knows—and cares—if they are happy or sad; if they are deficient in body and normal in mind — craving all the things that make life worth living!

"Freaks" is not merely a picture of the tinsel and glitter of the side-show. IT'S LIFE! —lived by another race.

Don't Miss This Thrilling and Astounding Love Drama Which Will Cause Talk for Months to Come!

MGM played up their picture's poignancy rather than its horror content in their advertisements for *Freaks* (1932). (Courtesy of Ron Borst/Hollywood Movie Posters.)

The acting in *Freaks* leaves much to be desired. Three of the four "normal" stars tend to grossly overplay. Henry Victor (Hercules) constantly thrusts out his chest and booms out his lines. Olga Baclanova (Cleopatra) also frequently shouts and brays, playing her character as an evil witch in a storybook. Even Wallace Ford (as the sympathetic Phroso) brings little subtlety to his portrayal of an Everyday Joe-type (or as close as one gets to it in the circus) and seems always to speak without thinking first (though to be fair, he does usually appear sincere). Only Lelia Hyams, as Venus, seems like a truly rounded human being. The rather coarse acting is not entirely the fault of the cast, for their characters are all drawn too simply. However, with the exception of Ms. Hyams, who brings a genuine warmth to her role, the players do nothing to flesh out these simplistic characters.

One school of thought suggests that this crude playing of the "normals" is not necessarily a complete liability after all, since the freaks (most of whom are not really actors) are similarly sketchy in character and none of them does much in the way of subtle acting either. (One exception is Daisy Earles, who brings a tragic sadness to her role of the diminutive Frieda. She is quite touching when she comes to Hans, timidly and tearfully, to warn him about Cleopatra.) So, in the end, the "normal" people do not seem (or act) so normal after all—or at least no more normal than the freaks themselves.

Browning cast his friend and former compatriot, Harry Earles, in the pivotal role of Hans. Unfortunately, he isn't up to the demands of the part. As Earles plays him, Hans is not very likable or sympathetic in and of himself. He so frequently scowls that his forehead seems permanently creased. His nasal, high-pitched voice (often difficult to understand) carries little inflection, so he must nearly shout in order to betray any emotion. His expressions appear limited to fury and petulance, with a blank, downward stare standing in for shame. Thus, sympathy comes only from his small stature and his predicament—it is built in. We sympathize with the midget, not the man, and that is a pity. It distances us, but worst of all, it lets us rely on our own preconceived stereotypical notions—something the film seems at pains to prevent.

Browning does nothing to help Earles, either. With such a small face and small eyes, the actor at the very least needed a few extreme close-ups if he was to register anything other than gross changes in his diminutive countenance. Browning does not oblige, and Earles loses whatever chance at subtlety he might have had.

In regard to Browning's handling of actors, future-director Joseph Newman (*This Island Earth*, 1955), who had worked under Browning in the 1930s, told Robert Skotak in *Filmfax* #33 that "Tod Browning had the knack of making an actor probe for the unusual in characterization without the actor really being aware of being directed." Judging by the performances in *Freaks*, it is not at all difficult to imagine the actors "not really being aware of being directed" in this picture.

Freaks did not entirely escape the seemingly haphazard directorial decisions which plague *Dracula*. Although Browning seems to have taken more care with *Freaks* than many of his other projects, he still did not evince an entirely steady hand. While the camera is often quite mobile, Browning doesn't always know just what to do with it. The film's very first sequence illustrates this shortcoming. The camera moves in on the carnival barker as he makes his pitch about "living, breathing monstrosities." It starts to circle around him, but an awkward cut to a longer shot breaks the flow of movement, drawing attention to itself and *away* from the speaker. The camera again moves in closer as he talks, emphasizing a point. Then, a quick cut once more sends the camera (and the audience) into a long shot—distancing the viewer from the man just as he says "offend one and you offend them all," lessening the impact of this key statement. This sequence is filled with motion, but it is ill-used and, in the end, ineffectual. Cinematographer James Wong Howe (who worked for Browning on *Mark of the Vampire* three years later) claimed that Browning was "one of the old school who didn't know much about the camera" (*Hollywood Cameramen,* by Charles Higham). The director's unevenness — even on this, his best film — adds credibility to Howe's assessment.

Freaks is not a pleasant film. It is not one of the "oldies but goodies" which you can sit and watch again and again. Nor is it a film you feel comfortable with, like a favorite sweater or soft pair of slippers. It IS a film that generates emotion, be it revulsion, be it pity, or be it self-revelation. Despite its flaws, *Freaks* possesses a unique, raw power which sets it apart from (and lifts it above) most of its Golden Age contemporaries.

REVIEWS

The New York Times (July 9, 1932) had no doubt that "Metro-Goldwyn-Mayer definitely has on its hands a picture that is out of the ordinary. The difficulty is in telling whether it should be shown at the Rialto — where it opened yesterday — or in, say, the Medical Centre. *Freaks* is no normal program film, but whether it deserves the title of abnormal is a matter of personal opinion."

The reviewer seemed both fascinated and repelled by the picture, calling it "excellent at times and horrible, in the strict meaning of the word, at others." Cinematically, he was unimpressed: "Through long periods the story drags itself along, and there is one of the most profound anti-climaxes of them all to form the ending. Yet, despite this, *Freaks* is not a picture to be easily forgotten. The reason, of course, is the underlying sense of horror, the love of the macabre that fills the circus sideshows in the first place. Tod Browning, the director, has brought all of it out as fully as possible, trying to prove that the 'strange people' are children, that they do not like to be set apart."

Still unsure of the picture, the reviewer concluded that "The only thing that can be said definitely for *Freaks* is that it is not for children. Bad dreams lie that way."

Variety (July 12, 1932) realized the dichotomous nature of the picture when they observed, "As a horror story, in the 'Dracula' cycle, it is either too horrible or not horrible enough, according to the viewpoint." Alternately pleased and disappointed, the reviewer went on to say, "It has been sumptuously produced, admirably directed, and no cost was spared, but Metro heads failed to realize that even with a different sort of offering the story still is important.... It is gruesome and uncanny rather than tense, which is where the yarn went off the track.

About the freaks themselves (which he labeled "the finest selection of human curios ever assembled"), the reviewer seemed to have missed the point: "Most of the dependence is placed on the freaks, and these form background, but not story." Summing it up, the reviewer (incredibly) claims that "the real trouble with *Freaks* is that it fails to get under the skin." But that is *exactly* what it does — all too well.

PRODUCTION NOTES

As with many Hollywood productions, the genesis of *Freaks* is a convoluted and disputed one. One version has it that Harry Earles, the midget star of both versions of *The Unholy Three*, brought a short story by Tod Robbins called "Spurs" to the attention of his friend, Tod Browning. Fresh from his success with *Dracula*, the director pitched the idea to Universal, but the studio felt the story a bit too gruesome and declined. Browning then took it to Irving Thalberg at MGM, who gave the picture the go-ahead. According to Thalberg himself, however, it was *he* who instigated the project by assigning screenwriter Willis Goldbeck the job of coming up with something even more horrifying than *Frankenstein*. Goldbeck obliged by adapting the Robbins story (purchased for $8,000) into a screenplay and Thalberg then chose Browning to direct the production.

In any case, once *Freaks* was approved, Thalberg had to fight for the project tooth and nail. His associates at MGM, led by Supervisor of Production Harry Rapf, pleaded with him to drop the picture. Thalberg remained unmoved, retorting, "If it's a mistake, I'll take the blame."[5] It was, at least in the eyes of the outraged Louis B. Mayer.

Freaks originally ran 90 minutes, but MGM recut it immediately after the disastrous preview screenings (and tacked on the final "happy ending" as a denouement in an attempt to dissipate the horror of the picture's original climax). When finally officially shown in New York in July of 1932 (five months after its ill-fated preview), *Freaks* had been shorn of a full 26 minutes! After its New York screening, *Variety* related that, "planned by Metro to be one of the sensation pictures of the season, *Freaks* failed to qualify in the sure-fire category and has been shown in most parts of the country with astonishingly variable results. In spots it has been a clean-up. In others it was merely misery."

Even worse than the "misery" spots was Great Britain — the film was banned outright in England (with the ban remaining in effect for 31 years).

The many cuts included more explicit details of the mysterious climactic fates of the two antagonists. As originally filmed, when the fleeing Cleopatra pauses beneath a tree, lightning strikes and the falling trunk lands on her legs, pinning her to the ground. The pursuing freaks then swarm over her prostrate form. As for Hercules, in the final release print we are left to assume that the freaks, after disabling Hercules with a knife in the side, murder him. The original epilogue, however, showed us "Tetrallini's Freaks and Music Hall," in which the former strong man now sings in a high voice (a not-so-subtle hint that the freaks had emasculated him). The following is Browning's complete original ending:

> Ext. medium long shot — a foggy London street: Camera pans to second floor where an electric sign says: "TETRALLINI'S FREAKS AND MUSIC HALL" Dissolve to:
> Int. Long shot. Museum.
> Along the walls there are freaks on platforms, and in the center, two or three pits into which people are gazing. Through an arch near the entrance we can see theatre seats and people in them and we can hear music being played. Dissolve to:
> A large photograph. It is held in a woman's hand and it shows Hans and Frieda, the midgets. Frieda holds a tiny baby in her arms, while Hans stands beside her with a cane, faultlessly groomed and smiling. The photograph is signed: To Phroso and Venus, with love, from Hans and Frieda.
> M. Tetrallini's voice: Well, well — So, they're married, and have a baby. (cut to a medium shot of M. Tetrallini, Phroso and Venus. They are near the arch which leads into the theatre. Phroso and Venus are well dressed. They are clearly very prosperous.)
> Venus: Yes, we were at their wedding three years ago in Austria.
> M. Tetrallini: Three years! It seems only yesterday that they were working for me.
> Phroso: (looking around) Say — you've got a nice joint. Swell layout. How are you doing?
> M. Tetrallini: (shrugs) Paying expenses — It lets them work. Better than putting up for the winter.
> Venus: (who has been looking off at the freaks around the wall in the background) I see you've got the old bunch with you.
> M. Tetrallini: Yes — and Cleo is with me too.
> Phroso: Cleo? — Oh, yes, in a music hall.
> M. Tetrallini: No, in the first pit over there. (she points off)
> Venus: Cleo in a pit?
> M. Tetrallini: Yes, she's working as a freak now. (Venus and Phroso move over to the pit where two or three people are looking in. A curious sound comes from the pit, like the quack of a duck. They look down and see Cleo, horribly mutilated and dressed as a duck woman. Her legs are gone, one eye is gone, her nose is broken, scars are on her face. At intervals she utters the imbecilic cry that we have heard.)
> Cleo: Quack, quack. (In horror, Venus looks at Phroso, then pity comes to her and she leans forward toward Cleo.)
> Venus: Cleo! (At the sound of her name Cleo looks up. For a moment, there seems to be a glimmer of intelligence, of recognition in her eye, but this passes over at once.)
> Cleo: Quack, quack. (Venus, overcome, gets out her handkerchief and dabs at her eyes as they walk back to M. Tetrallini.)
> Venus: Oh, — it's too horrible, too wicked. That beautiful creature!
> M. Tetrallini: (philosophically) Yes, I guess it's best she can't remember.
> Phroso: (thoughtfully glancing back towards Cleo) Yeh, tough break. And that sweetie of hers, Hercules, what became of him?
> M. Tetrallini: Hercules? He, too, has changed a lot. He's working in the music hall now. (She looks off towards the theatre) Yes, his act's on next. (Venus and Phroso look off to a

small stage, Hercules walks onto the stage; he is a little fat now and is dressed in a tuxedo. The orchestra starts playing and Hercules begins to sing in a beautiful tenor voice. From the pit offscreen comes the sound of Cleo's voice:)
Cleo: Quack, quack.
THE END

Costing a hefty $316,000, *Freaks* was a financial failure, losing Mayer's studio $164,000. Mayer's loss, however, eventually proved Dwain Esper's gain. On August 7, 1932, a scant month after its release, MGM pulled *Freaks* from distribution. Enter exploitation filmmaker/distributor Dwain Esper, who, in 1947, offered to buy the rights to exhibit their cinematic monster-child for the next 25 years. MGM promptly removed their Leo the Lion logo, turned the dusty negative over to Esper, and breathed a belated sigh of relief.

Esper (maker of the bizarre grind-house horror oddity *Maniac* [1934] as well as *Marihuana, Weed with Roots in Hell* [1936], and *How to Undress in Front of Your Husband* [1937]) retitled *Freaks* variously as *Nature's Mistakes*, *The Monster Show* and *Forbidden Love*, and came up with horribly exploitative ad lines like "Can a Full Grown Woman Truly Love a Midget?" and "Do Siamese Twins Make Love?," profitably touring the picture on the adults-only roadshow circuit for a number of years. (For some of the more respectable venues, he retained the film's original title and employed an ad campaign centered around a positive 1932 review from columnist Louella Parsons.) Esper also edited out select footage and added the written prologue now found on all surviving prints. It has been reported that Esper even tacked on a reel composed of bizarre footage of other real-life freaks. (If so, it has not survived.) According to independent producer/distributor David F. Friedman, Esper went beyond simply adding another reel. "Ever the evil genius showman," wrote Friedman in his book *A Youth in Babylon*, "Esper framed a combination movie-live presentation, contracting a troupe of human oddities, headed by circus side-show veteran Sam 'The Man with No Face' Alexander, to travel with the picture. Esper sold and ran it like a tent show, hanging canvas banners on theater fronts. The performers worked from high stands in the lobbies, the floors of which Esper had covered with sawdust. He kept that unit on the road for five years."

Despite (or because of?) Esper's roadshowing efforts (with the rights ultimately changing hands several times) it wasn't until 1962 that *Freaks* received any serious attention, when it was shown at the Venice Film Festival. Since that time, it has played at revival houses and college campuses throughout the United States and even (for the first time after a 31-year ban) in Great Britain.

Henry Victor, who played Hercules, was born in London but raised in Germany. Beginning in the silents (he appeared in the 1916 versions of *She* and *The Picture of Dorian Gray*), Victor continued acting until his death in 1945 at the age of 52. Frequently cast in the Nazi-villain mold, he appeared in such films as *Confessions of a Nazi Spy* (1939), *King of the Zombies* (1941), and *Sherlock Holmes and the Secret Weapon* (1942).

MGM originally announced that Jean Harlow would play the sympathetic female lead, Venus. The part ultimately went to Leila Hyams, however, whom Browning had previously worked with on *The Thirteenth Chair* (1929). Leila Hyams was born into show business, the daughter of the vaudeville team "Hyams and McIntyre." After a stint at modeling (she was Listerine Mouthwash's first model), she began acting in pictures in 1924. Two years later she landed a contract at MGM and remained with the studio for a decade. Of *Freaks*, she said, "This was certainly not the kind of picture MGM was known for. But they had no control over the director, Tod Browning, and until he showed them the final print I don't think they knew just how strange the film was. The studio was very embarrassed by it and I must admit I'm surprised that it is still popular. I never got to know the real freaks well but the midgets were delightful. They were great fun on the set and I had them to dinner in my home several times" (from *Whatever Became of ...?* by Richard Lamparski). Ms. Hyams also appeared in

Tod Browning (wearing beret and standing at right) directs his cast during the Wedding Feast scene in *Freaks* (1932). (Courtesy of Ted Okuda.)

Island of Lost Souls (1933) and was *almost* in *Tarzan the Ape Man* (1932) (she turned down the role of Jane). Retiring from acting in 1937, she talked of this early exit from film a few years before her death in 1977: "I was never stagestruck. Acting was to me simply the profession I was born into. I never developed the driving ambition which you really need if your goal is stardom. I did enjoy making movies at first but after talkies came in no one seemed to know what he was doing. It became more and more like hard work."

Myrna Loy was considered for the pivotal role of Cleopatra before the part ultimately went to Russian-born Olga Baclanova. In a 1964 interview with John Kobal (published in *People Will Talk*) Ms. Baclanova recalled her first meeting with her special co-stars and Tod Browning's accompanying admonition: "'Now I show you with whom you are going to play. But don't faint.' I say, 'Why should I faint?' So he takes me and shows me all the freaks there. First I meet the midget and he adores me because we speak German and he's from Germany. Then he shows me a girl that's like an orangutan; then a man who has a head but no legs, no nothing, just a head and a body like an egg. Then he shows me a boy who walks on his hands because he was born without feet. He shows me little by little and I could not look, I wanted to faint. I wanted to cry when I saw them. They have such nice faces but it is so terrible. They are so poor, you know. Now, after we start that picture, I like them all so much." Ms. Baclanova goes on to say how "it was very, very difficult first time. Every night I felt that I am sick. Because I couldn't look at them. And then I was so sorry for them. That I just couldn't ... it hurt me like a human being. How lucky I was. But after that, I started to be used to them."

Even during the course of the nine weeks of filming, this controversial picture caused quite a commotion, creating discord among the studio employees. Not all those on the MGM lot were as charitable as Ms. Baclanova professed to be, and many felt uncomfortable sharing their commissary with the real-life freaks, making little effort to hide it. (Harry Rapf probably overstated the case when he complained to Irving Thalberg that "people run out of the commissary and throw up!") Louis B. Mayer ultimately succumbed to the bigoted complaints and banned the "freaks" from the studio cafeteria.

Hans and Frieda, the two midget lovers in *Freaks*, were actually brother and sister in real life — Harry and Daisy Earles. Born Kurt Schneider in Germany, Harry and another sister, Frieda, came to America in 1916 accompanied by friend Bert Earles, whose name they took. After the death of their friend in the mid-thirties, the Earles changed their last name to Doll ("because they said we looked like dolls," explained sister Tiny[6]). Harry had a total of three midget sisters (who all eventually joined him in California) as well as three other normal-sized siblings who remained in Germany. Harry (co-star of both the silent and sound versions of Tod Browning's *The Unholy Three*) joined Daisy (often billed as "the midget Mae West") and his two other diminutive sisters (Tiny and Gracie) to dance and sing their way down the Yellow Brick Road as Munchkins in *The Wizard of Oz* (1939). After *The Wizard of Oz* the Doll family returned to Ringling Brothers and Barnum & Bailey Circus where they entertained as parade performers until their retirement in 1956. A close-knit family, the four siblings all remained single and worked and lived together throughout their adult lives. Daisy died in 1980 and Harry in 1985.

Thirty-four-inch tall Angelo Rossitto ("Angeleno" in the film) had originally planned to go into the legal profession until John Barrymore (Rossitto claimed that they were drinking buddies) introduced him to stage and silent film work. Rossitto's film career spanned six decades (1927–1987) and he appeared in over fifty films. He doubled for Shirley Temple, co-founded the Little People of America Association (an organization dedicated to help midgets and dwarfs find film work), and ran for mayor of Los Angeles in 1941 (he didn't win). Rossitto also operated a Hollywood newsstand for many years to supplement his income ("If it wasn't for my newsstand I would have never made a living out here," the diminutive actor told *Fangoria*'s Tony Timpone). In the 1940s Rossitto made several poverty-row pictures with Bela Lugosi. "Bela Lugosi once told me," remembered Rossitto, "that he wanted me in all of his pictures. And he gave [producer] Sam Katzman instructions to put me in them. Lugosi told me, 'Angelo, you are my greatest free advertisement. When they see you they've got to say to themselves, 'There's the little guy who works with the monster.'" Among Rossitto's credits are a number of horror and science fiction films: *Seven Footprints to Satan* (1929); *The Mysterious Island* (1929), *Spooks Run Wild* (1941; with Lugosi); *The Corpse Vanishes* (1942; with Lugosi), *The Spider Woman* (1944; one of the more macabre Sherlock Holmes entries); *Scared to Death* (1947; with Lugosi), *Mesa of Lost Women* (1953); *Invasion of the Saucer Men* (1957; as one of the bulbous-headed saucer men); *The Magic Sword* (1962); *The Wonderful World of the Brothers Grimm* (1962); *Brain of Blood* (1971); *Dracula vs. Frankenstein* (1972); *Lord of the Rings* (1978; voice only); *Galaxina* (1980); *Something Wicked This Way Comes* (1982); *Mad Max Beyond Thunderdome* (1985), and *The Offspring* (1987; his final film). Rossitto died in 1991.

Siamese twins Violet and Daisy Hilton

were born in 1908 in Brighton England to Kate Skinner, an unmarried barmaid. Their impoverished mother sold the twins to her employer, Mary Hilton, who began exhibiting the sisters before their third birthday. Touring throughout Europe and the United States brought Mary Hilton great wealth and Violet and Daisy great unhappiness. The twins' manager was more like their "master"—keeping the girls in a perpetual state of servitude, with beatings and confinement the order of the day. This state of affairs continued even after Mary Hilton's death, when Mary's daughter Edith (who had been assisting her mother in promoting and exhibiting the twins) announced to the sisters that Mrs. Hilton had bequeathed them, along with all her other worldly goods, to Edith. Finally, in 1931, the 23-year-old sisters confided in a lawyer and a trial in the 94th District Court in San Antonio won them their freedom. After their release from bondage, the Hilton Sisters became (along with dwarf Angelo Rossitto and the midget Earles) two of the more successful *Freaks* in real life. Shortly after the film's release, the twins were earning up to $5,000 a week in vaudeville-style stage shows. (To put this in perspective, Boris Karloff's weekly salary at this time was only about a third of this sum.) The Hiltons' fortunes did not hold, however, and at the time of their deaths in 1969 (from the Hong Kong flu), they were working as checkout girls at a supermarket near Charlotte, North Carolina.

The film's bearded lady, Jane Barnell, was first exhibited at age four. Appearing alternately as Princess Olga, Madame Olga, or Lady Olga, she continued in freak shows into the 1940s. For *Freaks*, she utilized the pseudonym Olga Roderick. Though the center of the picture's most humane and tender scene (the birth of the bearded lady's baby), she came to regret her involvement in the production. "Miss Barnell," reported her manager afterward, "thinks this picture was an insult to all freaks everywhere and is sorry she acted in it" (as quoted in *Freaks: Myths and Images of the Secret Self*, by Leslie Fiedler).

Peter Robinson, the "Living Skeleton," who played the husband of the bearded lady in the film, weighed only 58 pounds and was married in real life to Bunny Smith, a 467-pound circus "fat lady." The couple performed together in a dancing act.

Johnny Eck, "The Half Boy," was one half of a set of identical twins; identical with one exception—his brother was perfectly normal while Johnny's body ended just below the rib cage. He began in sideshows at the age of twelve and was eventually hailed as "The Most Remarkable Man Alive" by Robert L. Ripley. For his performances (which consisted of acrobatics, trapeze work, and musical numbers) he always wore formal attire (just as he did at the climax of *Freaks*). Eck told Richard Lamparski (in *Whatever Became of...?: Ninth Series*) that he was paid "about $35" for making *Freaks*. Still, by his own account, Eck was one of the lucky few who rated a dressing room. "I was the only one who could command—and get—a private dressing room, other than Daisy and Violet Hilton," he told Frederick Drimmer in *Very Special People*. "The rest of the group settled in one large building with long benches and tables ... Talcum powder hung in the air like a pink fog." Unlike the Bearded Lady, Eck felt no ill will towards the picture, stating that he enjoyed appearing in it and labeling Tod Browning "a prince." Seeing himself on the screen for the first time, however, did have an effect on him. "It made me very self-conscious," he recalls. "Until then I never realized just how horrible I look." Eck made only one other film, playing "The Bird Man" in *Tarzan the Ape Man* (1932). He collected the same salary for this production as well.

Slitzie, a 40-year-old microcephalic (or "pinhead") possessing a mental age of three, was exhibited in the 1920s as "Maggin, the last of the Aztecs." Though presented as a woman, Slitzie was actually male, wearing a simple sacklike dress for practicality sake. Slitzie appeared in one other film, *Meet Boston Blackie* (1941), a Chester Morris vehicle set at a carnival. After the demise of the Freak Show in the late 1940s, Slitzie ended up in a state institution.

With *Freaks* (1932), life imitates art: The Johnny Eck exhibit circa 1932.

Prince Randian, the Living Torso (whose name is misspelled in the film's credits as Rardion), was born in British Guyana in 1871. Brought to America by P. T. Barnum, he was billed as either "The Caterpillar Man" or "The Snake Man," and was a featured attraction at Coney Island for many years. His act included rolling and lighting a cigarette with his lips (as he does in the film) and shaving without benefit of hands. Randian spoke four languages, was married, and sired five children. He died in 1934. (For those who've always wondered just *what* Randian was saying in his single — and unintelligible — line of dialogue, the original continuity script has him reply to the bragging of one of the Rollo brothers with, "Can you do anything with your eyebrows?")

In an unlikely coincidence(?), Edward Brophy, who has a small part as one of the "Rollo Brothers" in *Freaks*, played an identically-named (and similar professioned) character in MGM's *Mad Love* three years later. In the later film he plays "Rollo" the circus knife-thrower (who is guillotined for murder and has his hands grafted onto the arms of the injured Stephen Orlac). Perhaps someone at MGM remembered Brophy's earlier character (or even Brophy himself suggested it) and thought it an amusing in-joke?

Clarence Aaron (Tod) Robbins, whose short story "Spurs" (published in "Munsey's Magazine" in 1923) served as inspiration for *Freaks*, was at one time married to Edith Hyde, the very first Miss America. They divorced shortly after she won the 1919 contest, and Edith turned her "gift" of clairvoyance into a profession, eventually adopting the name "Pandora." (No, she did not go to work in a circus sideshow, but in a New York City tearoom.)

While the general outrage leveled at *Freaks* certainly did not help Tod Browning's career in any way, it did not completely destroy it as some have intimated. The director made four more films (two of them major horror pictures — both for MGM again, no less) before he retired: *Fast Workers* (1932), *Mark of the Vampire* (1935), *The Devil-Doll* (1936), and *Miracles for Sale* (1939). So complete a failure of such a highly personal project as *Freaks*, however, could not have left Browning unfazed. A statement he made during his final horror film, *The Devil-Doll* (and printed in that picture's pressbook), illustrates the lesson Browning learned from *Freaks*: "A horror story told with a modicum of fantasy, which tinges the horror details with a sort of unbelief, will be entertainment. Whereas the same thing told too realistically proves unpleasant to the audience."

In 1967, David F. Friedman (a pioneer of nudie/sexploitation pictures and sometime partner of H. G. Lewis) produced an uncredited remake of *Freaks* entitled *She Freak*. "I saw *Freaks* in Birmingham when I was eight or nine years old, and never forgot it," remembered Friedman in *A Youth in Babylon*. "I remade the story as *She Freak* in 1967, but, by then, thanks to medical science and improved prenatal care, there were no freaks. I had to improvise." In this abysmal, excruciatingly dull cheapie (many scenes were shot without sound), a conniving woman marries the decent owner of a carnival freak show and contributes to his death, whereupon the loyal freaks take their terrible vengeance. Friedman (who wrote the screenplay in addition to producing) even steals the original's framing device of the carnival barker.

NOTES

1. From *Karloff and Company: The Horror Film*.
2. The original speech went as follows: Barker: "Just as they are represented on the banners outside, you've seen them in here, we didn't lie to you folks, we told you we had living, breathing monstrosities. Scientific and medical men have been amazed and mystified at these children of nature's cruel jokes. You laughed at them, shuddered at them, and yet, but for the accident of birth, you might be even as they are. They did not ask to be brought into the world, but into the world they came and lived. And yet, dear friends, there is not a hidden tear on these platforms. They accept their deformities and are proud of them. That's why I love them. Their bodies may be twisted and deformed but not their souls. Their code is a law unto themselves. Offend one and you offend them all. And now, folks, if you will just step this way, you are about to witness the most amazing, the most astounding living monstrosity of all times. (murmur of voices — scream) Friends, she was once a beautiful woman. A royal prince shot himself for love of her. She was known as the 'Peacock of the Air.'"
3. Once again, the poor Monster is confused with his creator, Frankenstein.
4. Critics have often harped upon the impossible nature of this bizarre transformation (*Variety* complained that "the author fails to explain the marvel of plastic surgery which converts the faithless wife into a legless bird-woman.") These critics missed the point, however, for it is not important to know the nuts and bolts of *how* the deed was accomplished, but *why*.
5. From *Mayer and Thalberg: The Make-Believe Saints*, by Samuel Marx.
6. *The Munchkins Remember*, by Stephen Cox.

VAMPYR
(THE DREAM OF ALLAN GRAY)
(1932; Carl Th. Dreyer Film Produktion; Germany/France)

Alternate Titles: *The Strange Adventure of David Gray*; *Castle of Doom*
Release Date: May 6, 1932

Running Time: 66 minutes (original English-language release); 72 minutes (recent "restored" version)

Director: Carl-Theodor Dreyer
Producers: Carl-Theodor Dreyer, Nicolas de Gunzburg
Screenplay: Carl-Theodor Dreyer, Christen Jul (based on the book *In a Glass Darkly,* by J. Sheridan Le Fanu)
Photography: Rudolph Maté
Art Directors: Hermann Warm, Dr. Hans Bittmann, Cesare Silvagni
Music: Wolfgang Zeller
Sound: Cesare Silvagni
Synchronization: Paul Falkenberg
Assistants to the Director: Ralph Holm, Eliane Tayara, Preben Birch
English Titles: Herman G. Weinberg
Cast: Julian West (Allan Gray*), Maurice Schutz (Bernard, the owner of the castle), Rena Mandel (Gisèle), Sybille Schmitz (Léone), Jan Hieronimko (Dr. Dorfarzt), Henriette Gérard (Old Mrs. vom Friedhof**), Albert Bras (Joseph, the manservant), N. Babanini (Jeanne, the housekeeper), Jane Mora (the nurse).

*In the film, he is called David Gray rather than Allan, though this discrepancy has been corrected in the restored version recently released on videocassette.
**In the film, she is referred to as Marguerite Chopin (the vampire). The restored version avoided this inconsistency by simply listing her as "The Old Woman from the Cemetery" in the credits.

> "The moonlit night was unique. Lights and shadows, voices and faces, seemed to possess a hidden significance." — narrative title card.

SYNOPSIS

"There are those predisposed to the fantastic and the supernatural," asserts the opening narrative card. "David Gray was one such, whose researches into age-old superstitions of Satanism and vampirism made him particularly susceptible to an encounter he once experienced. In one of his aimless wanderings, he found himself, on a late summer evening, before a secluded inn by the river in the village of Courtempierre." After securing a room, "David Gray felt a sense of the supernatural overpowering him," another narrative card informs us. "In vain was his resistance to the fright which engulfed him and his fear of inconceivable things that pursued him even in his agitated sleep."

Two loud knocks awaken David Gray from this "agitated sleep." His door opens and an old man enters. Inexplicably, the visitor says, "She mustn't die — do you hear?" and walks slowly to the desk. Pulling a small parcel from his pocket, the man writes "to be opened after my death" on it, leaves the package on the desk, and departs without another word.

Disturbed by the bizarre encounter, Gray dresses and goes out. In the moonlight he observes a number of shadows — moving of their own volition. A man's dark image is reflected in the water of the river but no one stands on the shore. The shadow of a gravedigger works methodically, but its actions are reversed — the earth *rises* from the ground to *meet* the shovel. Unattached to any owner, the shadow of a man with a wooden leg enters a building. Gray follows the one-legged apparition into an abandoned factory and observes the disembodied shadows of dancers whirling to music played by mere silhouettes. Gray also sees an old woman who is *not* a shadow. Her head held erect, her face hard and cruel, her features grimly set, she moves slowly through the building as if she belongs there among the spectral shapes.

Leaving the factory, Gray enters a nearby dilapidated house where he hears strange noises and the barking of dogs. An old man appears, a doctor, and ushers the trespasser out. Immediately after, the old woman arrives and hands the doctor a bottle of poison.

Out in the night, David Gray follows more disembodied shadows to a secluded chateau. "Here," a title card tells us, "lives the old chatelaine, whose desperate appeal reached him." Inside the castle, Bernard (the man who had left the parcel for Gray) looks in on his daughter, Léone, lying feverish in her bed, attended by a nurse. "The blood! The blood!" cries Léone and lapses into a stupor.

David Gray looks in through a window and recognizes Bernard. Just then, the shadow

The protagonist, David (sometimes Allan) Gray (Julian West; aka Nicolas de Gunzburg, the film's financial backer) moves through the hazy, dreamlike world of *Vampyr* (1932).

of the one-legged man creeps across the ceiling of the room. It raises a shadow-rifle and a shot rings out. Bernard falls to the floor.

Gray frantically runs around to the door of the chateau where Joseph, the manservant, lets him in. They rush into Bernard's room, but the old man dies. Gray remembers the package that Bernard had left with him. When Gray removes it from his coat, we see that the words Bernard had written have changed. It now reads: "Your help can free us from our affliction." The parcel contains a book, *The Curious History of Vampires*.

Gisèle, Léone's sister, observes Leone leaving the chateau, walking in a trancelike state. Gisèle and David Gray race out after her. Across a field they see the old woman, whom Gray had observed earlier with the disembodied shadows, bending over the now-prostrate form of Léone. As Gray and Gisèle rush toward the unconscious girl, the old woman rises and glides off into the night. Léone is carried back into the chateau.

Another title card (presumably a page from the book) tells us: "Like a polluted contagion, the vampire's blood-lust is transferred to his victim, thus an innocent human being becomes a vampire himself, seeking prey among his own kin...." Back in her sick-room, Léone revives. At first she is distraught, but a sinister change occurs in her demeanor and her face takes on a threatening animal intensity. Frightened, Gisèle moves away from her sister into the arms of the nurse, who ushers her out of the room.

David Gray sits down and begins to read the book. "Not only are the shades of executed criminals subservient to vampires.... A report from Hungary relates that the village doctor, who sold his soul to the devil, became a vampire's accomplice...."

The doctor (whom Gray had met earlier) arrives at the chateau. Leone is very weak and needs blood. The old physician presses Gray to donate his own blood. While the doctor performs the transfusion, Joseph (the manservant) picks up and reads the book on vampirism. "With the victim in his power, the vampire tries to push him to suicide, thus to deliver his soul to the devil." The book tells how to destroy a vampire, and recounts the tale of a Transylvanian village "where a vampire existed in the form of an old woman, whose nocturnal excursions had seeped a whole village in desolation...." The method of destruction was "to open her grave at dawn, where she appeared to be asleep. An iron stake was then plunged through her heart, thus nailing the repulsive soul of the woman to the earth ... the curse that was upon her and her victims was lifted." The book goes on to tell of a "murderous epidemic" which occurred eleven years before in the very village of Courtempierre. "Many still believe that only Marguerite Chopin, who is buried in the graveyard of Courtempierre, could be the vampire."

David Gray, recovering from giving blood, dreams of a skeletal hand gripping a bottle of poison. Joseph, sensing something is wrong, awakens Gray and the two burst into Léone's sick-room — just as she reaches for a bottle of poison left on her nightstand (presumably left by the doctor). The doctor disappears into the night and David Gray pursues him.

Joseph warns Leone's nurse that "she mustn't die — she must survive this night." He then collects some tools and leaves the chateau.

David Gray runs through the misty night and falls. He struggles to his feet and makes his way to a nearby bench to rest. Then, a curious thing happens. Gray seemingly splits into two entities. One entity, the phantom Gray, leaves his body slumped on the bench and walks on to the old house. Inside, he finds a coffin which contains — his own body! Recoiling from the frightening sight, he looks through a window into another room and sees Gisèle tied to an old bed (presumably kidnapped and brought there by the evil doctor). Before he can get the door open to release the captive, the doctor arrives, followed by the man with the wooden leg (the owner of the mysterious shadow). The phantom David Gray hides and watches as the one-legged man seals the coffin containing Gray's body. Gray's consciousness seemingly transfers into the body, for now he sees from *inside* the coffin through the tiny window set in the lid just above his face. The hideous, malevolent visage of the old woman — the vampire — looks down at Gray through the window, taking her last leave of him. A procession carries Gray in his coffin out of the house and through the village. Passing the spot where the corporeal David Gray rests on the bench, the coffin, the procession, and the phantom David Gray all vanish.

Gray recovers his senses and notices Joseph carrying his tools towards the churchyard. There Joseph uses a crowbar to pry off the stone lid over a grave and begins to remove the layer of boards covering the coffin inside. David Gray approaches and tentatively helps with the labor. Removing the coffin lid, they find the body of the old woman, her face ghastly white but perfectly preserved. Holding an iron bar, Joseph takes aim and plunges it into the chest of the old woman, whereupon the corpse turns into a skeleton.

Back at the chateau, Léone sits up in bed. "She's gone — I'm free!" she exclaims softly, a look of peace upon her face. She lies back, gives one final sigh, and dies, her soul now at rest.

At the graveside, Joseph replaces the covering stone and now we see the inscription carved there: "Marguerite Chopin ... Lord of Mercy, grant her eternal rest."

At the doctor's house (where Gisèle is imprisoned), the physician relaxes with a cigar while the one-legged man plays lazily upon a mandolin. Suddenly, a preternatural light streams in from outside the room's window. A gigantic face appears there — the face of Bernard, the murdered chatelaine. This sends the two men into a panic. Lights flicker, a scream is heard, and the one-legged man lies dead at the foot of the staircase. The doctor flees the house in terror.

We see a hand (David Gray's, we assume) locate the hidden key to Gisèle's impromptu cell and then loosen her bonds. Next we see Gisèle and Gray running across a field.

The doctor has fled to an old mill. He

In director Carl-Theodor Dreyer's world of illusion and shadow, Dr. Dorfarzt (Jan Hieronimko) seemingly conjures the old vampiress Marguerite Chopin (Henriette Gérard) out of thin air.

passes by the silent gears and wheels and steps into a cage-like room where the flour is sifted. As he looks about, the wire door swings shut, locking him inside. He spots Joseph moving above him and calls out, but Joseph makes no reply. Suddenly, the gears begin to move and flour descends upon the doctor in a suffocating cascade of white dust. Soon, only his head is visible above the white mass. While the doctor is being buried alive at the mill, Gisèle and Gray find a boat along the riverbank and set out into the fog. Reaching the opposite shore, they step onto the sunny bank where the fog has lifted. Arm in arm, they walk off into the sunlit landscape. At the mill, the white powder has completely engulfed the doctor and the gears and wheels grind slowly to a halt.

MEMORABLE MOMENTS

Vampyr possesses an exquisitely intense moment of malevolence when the vampire's influence takes hold of Léone after the attack outside the chateau. The nurse swabs the freshly opened wounds on Léone's throat. At this, the unconscious girl flinches and shudders. Her eyes open and all the horror of her situation floods in upon her. She brings her fingers up to her trembling lip and, sobbing, covers her face with her hand. "If I could only die! ... I'm lost...," she moans, her eyes tightly closed, her face a tortured mask of hopelessness. Upon this pronouncement, Léone's face relaxes and her expression goes blank. Then, a strange and terrible thing occurs — her nostrils flare almost imperceptibly, the corners of her mouth twitch, and her lips draw back from her tightly clenched teeth in a horrible rictus grin. "Léone?" asks Gisèle tentatively. In response, Léone's head falls to the side. Then her eyes open and she looks up. The hideous grin widens and her expression intensifies to one of animal hunger. Frightened, Gisèle slowly backs away. Staring upwards, wide-eyed and intent, her teeth still bared, her lips quivering, Léone follows Gisèle with her terrible, lustful gaze.

Up to now, Dreyer has shot Léone from above in extreme close-up, the camera looking down to reveal every nuance of her horrible transformation. He then cuts to a side view with her head in a vertical position. We watch, a bit disoriented and unnerved by the sudden shift in spatial position, as the frightening face turns slowly toward us. A cut-away shot shows the now-terrified Gisèle fleeing into the arms of the nurse (who is also a nun) for comfort. The camera cuts back to Léone, her face now turned completely towards Gisèle and the nun — towards us — and the hideous grin fades, her mouth and eyes taking on a hard, cold look of pure hatred. Suddenly, Léone sits up and thrusts her head forward. A cut-away to Gisèle shows the nun hurriedly ushering the terrified sister out of the room.

Sybille Schmitz as Léone is first convincing, then *frightening* to behold. She begins the scene in a state of abject abhorrence which deftly and naturally slides into hopeless despondency. When the vampiric change occurs, she transforms utterly. By gradual steps her expression takes on a terrifying feral intensity, inhuman and shudderingly convincing. Throughout the scene, the music adds a background tension. Beginning soft and low, it builds as Léone's face changes. A high-pitched note is added and held, the pitch increasing as the tension mounts while low, rhythmic tones throb in punctuation. Sybille Schmitz's subtle, inhuman expressions, Dreyer's disorienting camera placement, and the pulsing, mounting background music combine to create a scene of powerful intensity. Once seen, it is not easily forgotten.

Vampyr's most involving sequence comes when David Gray dreams/envisions that he is sealed inside the coffin. For the next two minutes we *become* David Gray and are placed inside the cramped box. The lid is placed over us, restricting our view to the small window in the coffin lid. This window now becomes our sole connection to the outside world. We experience a moment of panic as, through our narrow pane, we see the face and hand of the one-legged man, his screwdriver turning methodically to drill down the screws that will seal us inside our wooden tomb. We watch helplessly as he sets a candle down on the glass directly above our eyes, wishing — but unable — to push it away because it blocks our already restricted view. To our horror, the aged, sinister visage of the vampire enters our field of vision, picks up the candle, and peers down at us through our tiny window. She sets the candle down again and is gone, condemning us to our horrible fate. Disturbing views of the ceiling, the face of the doctor, and the doorway pass before our staring eyes as we are carried through the house out into the street. We can see only the towering tops of buildings or the overhanging branches of trees as our sarcophagus moves beneath them. All is silent in our two foot by six foot world save for the mournful ringing of bells — tolling our death? Throughout this singular sequence, Dreyer draws us into the film, allowing — no, forcing — the viewer to conjure up whatever personal feelings this terrifying, claustrophobic experience may provoke.

ASSETS

Vampyr is something of an enigma. Respected film historian William K. Everson feels *Vampyr* is the greatest horror film of the decade. Many viewers, however, consider it to be the *dullest*. It is a difficult picture to judge in a simple manner. Moments of exquisite beauty and mood alternate with excruciatingly dreary stretches. If one studies the film closely, however, its many assets readily emerge.

Vampyr is unique among horror films of the 1930s. It spurns the accepted genre conventions (indeed, it spurns simple *narrative* conventions). Rather than branching off from the Golden Age horror family tree, *Vampyr* sprouts alongside it like a creeper, entwining about the trunk but never truly joining with it. It is merely an accident of time that *Vampyr* began filming in the same year as *Dracula* and *Frankenstein*, for it resembles its contemporaries not at all. Director Carl-Theodor Dreyer creates an atmosphere so saturated with the supernatural that it becomes a nebulous dream-state. Shot only at dawn and dusk, *Vampyr* possesses a singular lack of clarity in its visuals. Under Dreyer's direction, cinematographer Rudolph Maté filmed through gauze to intentionally fog the image so that the figures and landscapes of *Vampyr* lack sharply defined edges. Everything seems slightly blurred and indistinct, as in that wavering state between dreaming and wakefulness.[1]

A supernatural aura permeates the film and nothing seems truly real. The visuals are ephemeral; the landscape is hazy; no one reacts with any naturalness — everyone behaves oddly, in a slightly off-kilter fashion. The limited dialogue is strange and disjointed, as if the speaker never quite finishes his thought or says what he truly means. It all combines to form a dreamlike world of shadows and nightmare. Dreyer creates a setting in which anything can happen and natural laws no longer apply — nor, in fact, do the laws of cinematic time and space. Events occur without explanation. People come and go seemingly without cause. Dreyer has subjugated the storyline and focused his camera on disconnected or ancillary imagery in order to create a new (sur)reality. Therein lies the strength of *Vampyr*—and its fatal weakness (at least according to the expectations of the general "horror audience"). *Vampyr* is difficult for American viewers. Hollywood filmmaking is firmly based on narrative — the story (and character) is the thing. Dreyer, however, sported a different set of cinematic sensibilities and sought to promote the *image* over the story. Choosing the role of "artist" over "entertainer," he sacrificed clear narrative and character involvement in order to create general unease and ethereal visions. He succeeded and, in so doing, alienated much of the traditional cinema audience.

Vampyr is filled with bizarre, macabre, and striking imagery, little of which is explained or even explicable. At the beginning, David Gray walks through the night and observes the shadow of a man digging a grave. Aside from the fact that this shadow is unattached to its owner, it also moves in *reverse*: defying all natural laws, earth flies up to *meet* the shade's shovel in mid-air! Later, when the old woman enters the doctor's study, the empty eye sockets of an infant's skeleton begin to glow with an eerie light while a skull sitting on the desk slowly turns toward her of its own volition. At this point we have no idea that the old woman is a vampire, or that a vampire even *exists* in the story. Yet these strange portents reveal that something unnatural is happening — and *will* happen. More mainstream horror films might include such surreal moments as well, but invariably they are explained when we learn the rules being followed. While this may satisfy our need for rationality, to some extent it disappoints by removing the mystery. In *Vampyr*, Dreyer dispenses with rules and lets the mystery remain with — and engulf— the viewer.

Everything in *Vampyr* is planned and executed to stress the supernatural and mysterious. Dreyer steadfastly refuses to use accepted establishing shots, so that we are unsure as to how a character has entered a building or even in *which* building he may be at the moment. Characters often simply appear in a locale without ever having been seen journeying there. Inside the buildings, the camera may move across a room to reveal a person standing there without our having known that he is even in the room, and certainly not how he got there. Thus, the various locations and internal spaces seem to blend together, their borders becoming indistinct and mysterious, adding to the disorienting, unnatural atmosphere.

Dreyer uses visuals to confound even simple physical realities. For instance, after the doctor ushers Gray out through the front door of his house, the back door at the opposite end of the hall slowly opens by itself. The doctor walks down the hallway toward the open portal. When he nears the opening, however, he unexpectedly turns to his right and faces the wall. He reaches out and grasps an arm appearing from *inside* the wall. The arm belongs to the old woman and her grim, malevolent countenance soon emerges into the hall along with her entire body. Only then do we realize that there is a doorway there. Dreyer places the camera at such an angle that we cannot see the doorway on the right side of the hallway, making it appear as if the old woman walks straight out of the wall or simply appears out of thin air. With this sleight-of-camera Dreyer intensifies the preternatural presence and power of the woman. He pulls a similar trick later on involving the man with the wooden leg. As the doctor stands by an old grandfather clock, the one-legged man seems to step out of nothing (or out of the clock itself). From our angle of vision we cannot see the doorway there.

Illustrative of the importance of the supernatural to *Vampyr* is the sequence in which David Gray, weakened from loss of blood, visualizes (or dreams of) a skeleton. The bony hand rises up and offers a bottle of poison. When Joseph shakes Gray awake, the scene switches to inside the bedroom where Leone reaches for an identical bottle of poison, which the doctor had brought. Aside from providing some obvious foreshadowing, this weird sequence with the skeleton emphasizes David Gray's affinity towards the strange and uncanny. Dreyer includes bizarre touches like this throughout the picture, indicating that the supernatural pervades everything. On the surface the moon may be shining and its light streaming down, but underneath flows an inescapable force which weaves its dark threads through all.

Dreyer and his cameraman Rudolph Maté utilize lighting to enhance the dreamlike tone of *Vampyr*. Throughout the film, changes in illumination embody preternatural portents or events. David Gray's first contact with the shadowy world of the vampire occurs when the old man enters Gray's room and leaves the parcel containing the tome on vampirism: After Gray is awakened by two knocks, a close-up of the door handle reveals the key turning in its lock. The room is dimly and uniformly lit, but as the door begins to open (the door to the supernatural?), a bright light creeps up the wall from below, adding a harsh contrast to the once placidly uniform scene. It's as if all the light from around the room gathers and concentrates in that one corner. Then, when the man wordlessly leaves, the concentrated light diffuses once again and returns to a dim uniformity.

Later, when the vampire enters the doctor's office, Dreyer cuts to a shot of the child's skeleton. Triggered by the presence of the unnatural being, the empty eye sockets in the skull begin to glow with an eerie inner light. Still later, after David Gray donates his blood, we see a close-up of his head resting on a pillow. The picture darkens and light plays violently on the wall behind him like the reflection of some mad lightning storm. He dreams, and a skeleton rises up into the frame with the same mad storm of light playing behind *it*. In the bony hand is a bottle of poison, an unearthly warning of Leone's impending suicide attempt. In all three of these instances, changes in lighting signify a transition from the natural world to the supernatural.

Rudolph Maté's extremely mobile and fluid camerawork does much to build a dreamlike (un)reality. With numerous tracking shots and nearly 360 degree pans, the camera follows David Gray much as Gray himself follows the uncanny proceedings. The fluid motion brings a connectedness to the visuals, suggesting a unified (supernatural) presence flowing throughout everything.

Dreyer uses sound well (if sparingly), as evidenced by the film's very beginning. While waiting at the door of the inn, David Gray sees a silhouette down by the river. A dark figure of a man with a scythe rings the bell at the ferry dock. This reaper-figure pulls slowly and rhythmically on the bell rope (summoning something more than a simple ferryboat?). As David Gray enters the inn, the bell continues to toll on the soundtrack. The camera follows Gray, gliding deeper into the house after him — almost pursuing him much as the mournful tolling of the bell pursues him. Through the pervading sound of the ringing bell it seems as if the reaper silhouette — the figure of death — has attached itself to David Gray and followed him into the house. The pursuing camera reinforces this impression by seeming to draw the sound in with it.

Wolfgang Zeller's moody musical score

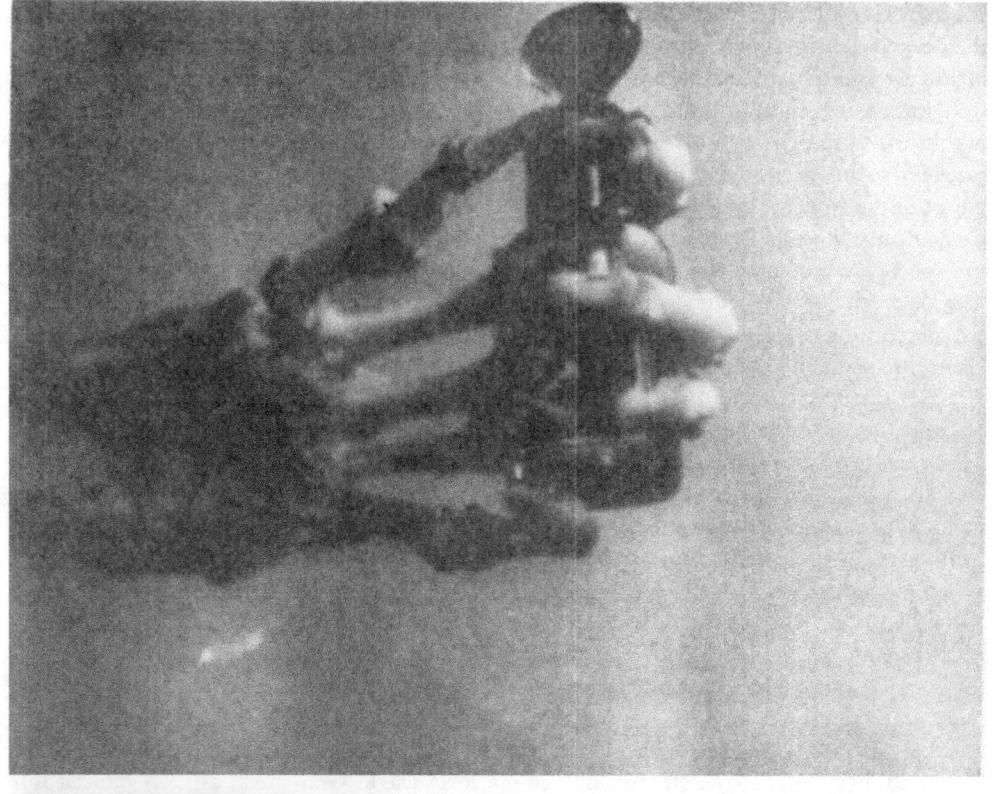

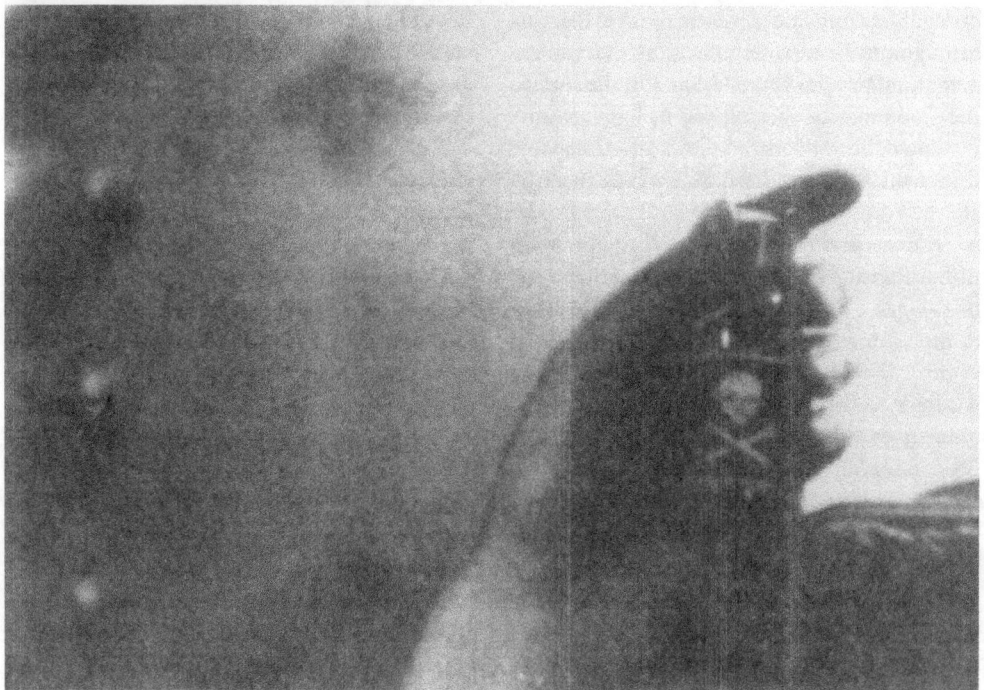

The line between reality and dreams blurs in *Vampyr* (1932) as David Gray envisions a skeletal hand offering up a bottle of poison (*top*) just as Léone reaches for an identical bottle in her bedroom (*bottom*).

emphasizes the unearthly quality of the picture. Strings play low and ominously, the tones ebbing and flowing like preternatural currents moving below the surface. The eerie music combines with the mobile visuals to create an impression of a dark underground sea whose surges and continual motion conjure up waves of blackness to engulf whoever stands (or watches) on the shore.

LIABILITIES

Vampyr is like a dream. Unlike one's own dreams, however, *Vampyr* relegates the viewer to the status of a simple observer and not a participant. One has no connection to the characters in the story. Their motivations are hazy at best, their actions and speech frequently inexplicable. *Vampyr* carries the surreal confusion often found in dreams, but it lacks the more personal, intimate aspect of one's own nocturnal chimera.

Dreyer focuses on general mood and atmosphere rather than exploring the emotions of his characters. Layer by layer he adds a visual richness and depth to his settings, building a mysterious mood and unearthly atmosphere with shadows, light, and movement. He sets his characters down in this heady ambiance — and then abandons them. Their thoughts, feelings, and motivations are *told* to us via title cards rather than demonstrated visually and verbally. We must *read* about "the fright which engulfed [David Gray] and his fear of inconceivable things that pursued him" rather than see the manifestation of this "fear" for ourselves. Without an emotional attachment between them and the viewer, the characters become unimportant, little more than animated furnishings which Dreyer utilizes to populate his carefully-constructed dream world. The audience has no connection with the characters, no reason to care about what happens to them or indeed what will happen next. Always watching detachedly, the viewer never becomes truly involved. In cinema, atmosphere without solid characters is like an abstract painting — it may generate feeling, but, unfocused, it ultimately becomes meaningless.

Dreyer's preoccupation with visuals is reflected in his cast — all, save two, are non-professionals. The director obviously chose his actors for their look (or their pocketbook, in the case of Julian West) rather than their emoting ability, for little emotion is forthcoming (nor undoubtedly was it required by Dreyer). As David Gray, Julian West (a.k.a. Nicolas de Gunzburg) moves through the film devoid of expression. He walks about observing events without any reaction, almost like a somnambulist (which by the end of the picture describes the majority of viewers, as well).

The sparse spoken dialogue is almost nonsensical, and does little to illuminate the emotions of the characters or explain the confusing narrative (a job that falls to the numerous, inadequate title cards). For instance, just before David Gray encounters the doctor, he hears the barking and howling of dogs while he prowls about the house. A moment later, when Gray approaches the physician, the doctor looks at him and asks, "Have you heard?" to which Gray answers, "Yes, a child" (though no children — just dogs — were heard on the soundtrack).[2] This brings the doctor up short. Staring intently, the old man says, "There's no child here," and walks toward Gray. "But there are — dogs," answers Gray. "There are no children here and no dogs," is the doctor's short reply. "No?" asks Gray. "No. Good night," says the doctor and ushers Gray out the door. The entire exchange is emotionless and utterly inexplicable. While this bizarre exchange effectively enhances the mood of mystery and unease, it further distances the viewer from David Gray. By denying the audience a character anchor, the viewer is left to drift alone on the sea of surrealism.

As shot, the characters' behavior often seems as unfathomable as the dialogue. When Bernard lies dying (or dead — we cannot be sure at this point) on the floor, for example, David Gray suddenly reaches over, takes a cup and saucer off a sideboard, and begins spooning its contents into the mouth of the prostrate man. This seems an extremely *odd* thing to do, to say the least. The screenplay explains it thus: "The dying man ... stammers: 'Water!'

[David Gray] gets up; on a table he finds a tray with cups and a jug of linden-tea. He pours out a little tea in a cup, which he lowers to the dying man. With a teaspoon he moistens the dying man's lips." In the film, however, we do not hear the cry for water, do not see Gray pour any tea, and are given no dialogue regarding the action. Dreyer shoots the scene in medium shot, without any close-up of the man's face, so we cannot tell that Gray is "moistening the dying man's lips." It just appears as if he's shoveling spoonfuls of some unknown substance into the mouth of an unconscious man (or, for all we know at the time, the mouth of a lifeless corpse!).

Very little happens in *Vampyr*—just a series of almost ephemeral occurrences loosely connected by the presence of David Gray. Gray glides through the supernatural proceedings like a sleepwalker (a condition which turns literal when his "phantom" self leaves his body and prowls about on its own). Nothing truly touches him and he truly touches nothing. At best, he acts as a vague, tenuous catalyst to the events. In the end, however, he makes very little impact (it is the old servant, remember, who reads the book left to Gray, learns what must be done, and dispatches the vampire while Gray simply looks on). Gray is the protagonist, the obvious audience identification figure (in fact the viewer takes on his point of view in the film's most memorable sequence), so this disconnectedness of character, coupled with Julian West's extremely flat affect, denies the viewer true access into the story. With the exception of the coffin sequence, we remain on the outside looking in, with no reason to care about the characters. We have no stake in the proceedings (pardon the pun), and are left with nothing more than a disjointed series of surrealistic images.

The film was made cheaply and one of the economy measures taken by Dreyer was to shoot the picture without sound and then add most of the dialogue later. For modern viewers (or even viewers of 1932), this makes for slow going. The film possesses many stretches of silence or near-silence. The absence of naturalistic sounds and background noises makes events seem distant and unreal, further distancing the viewer from the proceedings. One really must possess an affinity for silent films in general to obtain much enjoyment from *Vampyr*, since, essentially, *Vampyr* is just that—a silent film with some minimal sound and dialogue added later.

Vampyr also sports that bane of silents: the unwieldy title card. Narrative cards tell us what David Gray feels; what he does next; why he went here or why he went there. Sound films generally deliver these essentials through dialogue, emoting, and action. Not so *Vampyr*. In several instances the manservant reads through the book on vampires and we must read along on the cards. It becomes almost ludicrous as we see a shot of the reader, then the title card, then a brief shot elsewhere and back to the reader, then the next title card, once again to the reader, and back to *another* title card. Aside from breaking the picture's flow, these artificial intrusions remove us completely from the film's reality, reminding us that we are watching a film—a visual hoax. It would have been much less jarring to reveal the important information through dialogue sequences, which would not so devastatingly interrupt the flow of the picture and ultimately *suspend* our suspension of disbelief. Once again, we are kept at arm's length, forbidden to become a part of the proceedings.

By denying cinema conventions while at the same time brilliantly employing cinematic techniques, Dreyer has constructed a nocturnal dream world of mystery and unease, a laudable achievement which sets *Vampyr* apart from its horror contemporaries. Still, during much of the film I could not help wishing I was viewing Tod Browning's slow and stodgy *Dracula* (1931), which, despite its stagy plodding, is still faster paced and infinitely more watchable than *Vampyr*. True, *Vampyr* features striking, unique visuals and possesses an ephemeral, dreamlike quality. It also possesses a quality that many real dreams share—a disjointed, disconnected narrative thread. And that, in my view, is one of the *worst* qualities of dreams.

Vampyr is a picture that you really have to

work at to like. If one devotes patience and energy to the process, it can be a rewarding, eye-opening experience. For many casual viewers, however, it frequently turns out to be a rather somnambulistic one.

REVIEW

The Berlin correspondent for the *New York Times* (July 31, 1932) could not accept the film as a whole, but admitted that "although in many ways it was one of the worst films I have ever attended, there were some scenes in it that gripped with a brutal directness." Going on to praise "Charles" Theodor Dreyer's method of filmmaking, the reviewer noted that the picture's scenes "matured slowly" and "have depth and a simplicity of style which is seldom achieved in the hurried world of the film studio.

"But, for all that, it was a peculiarly irritating picture. The scenario was so bad that the author had to excuse it by pretending it was a dream. It was merely a tritely developed, muddled treatment of the old vampire theme ... And then the photography was always underexposed, evidently with the idea of it being ghostly. It succeeded only in looking muddy. And the dialogue, evidently dubbed in later on, was childish and was spoken unconvincingly."

Summing it up, the reviewer announced: "No, I could only recommend you to look at *Vampire* [sic] when it comes to New York, if you're willing to forgive everything else for a few scenes of unmotivated spinal titillation of fascinating dramatic tension."

PRODUCTION NOTES

Purportedly, *Vampyr* came about as a reaction to Tod Browning's *Dracula* (1931). "I could damn well make one of those too," Dreyer told Bjorn Rasmussen in a 1964 interview (as quoted in *The Films of Carl-Theodor Dreyer* by David Bordwell). The director and Christen Jul wrote the screenplay for *Vampyr* in Paris in the fall of 1931. Dreyer shot *Vampyr* silently in France, then later added a soundtrack in Berlin (though there is very little dialogue in the film, and much of the movie is still silent).

It took nearly a year to film *Vampyr*, for the picture was shot in fits and starts on location in Courtempierre. During production, Dreyer explained his approach to *Vampyr*: "Imagine that we are sitting in an ordinary room. Suddenly, we are told that there is a corpse behind the door. In an instant, the room we are sitting in is completely altered; everything in it has taken on another look; the light, the atmosphere have changed, though they are physically the same. This is because *we* have changed, and the objects are as we conceive them. That is the effect I want to get in my film."[3]

Financing for *Vampyr* came from Baron Nicolas de Gunzburg, a Dutch aristocrat who offered to back the production if he could play the male lead (using the alias Julian West). With two exceptions (Maurice Schutz and Sybille Schmitz) the entire cast was made up of nonprofessional actors. According to Dreyer's assistant, Ralph Holm,[4] the director sent him out to search for a cast in the streets of Paris. After looking under the bridges of the Seine and at the Salvation Army, Holm found Jan Hieronimko, a Polish journalist, to play the doctor, and Henriette Gérard, the mother of an actress, to play the vampire. The innocent heroine Gisèle was played by Rena Mandel, a nude model. The remainder of the cast was filled out by Dreyer's friends and acquaintances.

Born in Duren, Germany in 1909, Sybille Schmitz studied drama in Cologne. Catching the eye of Max Reinhardt, Schmitz signed with the Deutsches Theater at the tender age of 16. Shortly after completing *Vampyr*, Schmitz was given a five-year contract with the German film company UFA, where she appeared in their science fiction adventure, *F.P.1 Antwortet Nicht* (*F.P.1 Doesn't Answer*). Schmitz also starred in Frank Wisbar's haunting *Fahrmann Maria* (1936). Joseph Goebbels, the Nazi Minister of Culture and Propaganda, disliked Schmitz, as much for her less-than-Aryan dark looks as for her rather reticent demeanor and yearn for privacy. Though she continued to act throughout the thirties, she often had to overcome obstacles placed in her way by the powerful Nazi minister. (Gustav Grundgens, for instance, had to fight Goebbels in order to cast Schmitz in his *Tanz auf dem Vulkan* [*Dance on the Volcano*, 1938].) After a shaky return to films following World War II, Schmitz felt her acting days were over and attempted suicide. The actress died under mysterious circumstances in 1955 from an overdose of sleeping pills (the issue of poisoning was raised). Rainer Werner Fassbinder based his 1981 film *Die Sehnucht der Veronika Voss* (*Veronica Voss*) on her life.

As David Bordwell relates in *The Films of Carl-Theodor Dreyer*, *Vampyr*'s premiere in Berlin "was turmoil, with boos mixed with applause...." The picture received very little attention at the time and was given only a spotty release. The film was a commercial failure, and very few people saw, or even heard of, *Vampyr* upon its initial release.

When *Vampyr* was originally "translated" into English (utilizing an odd combination of dubbing in some spots and subtitles in others), the picture was shorn of over five minutes of footage in a desperate (and ultimately futile) attempt to quicken its slow, stately pace. For decades, this shortened version is the one which has been seen at theatrical revivals and on videotape. Recently, a restored version has been released to video which is largely taken from a more complete German print. This "new" *Vampyr* leaves the few dialogue passages initially dubbed into English in their original German and slightly alters the wording on the title cards (though retaining the same basic concepts presented in the original translation). More importantly, this new version contains a number of shots never before seen by American audiences. Among the restored scenes are: a shot of the Doctor advancing slowly down the stairs when he first meets David Gray; the dying Bernard taking a ring from inside his jacket and placing it in Gisèle's hand (no explanation for this incident is forthcoming, and the ring plays no other role in the film); an additional shot of the nurse attending to Léone just before the entranced girl takes her midnight stroll; and a few brief shots prefacing scenes existing in the original version such as the nurse placing Leone in bed after her nocturnal wandering and David Gray picking up the vampire book to read just prior to the appearance of an explanatory title card. In truth, these missing scenes are of minimal importance to the film and carry little impact, except perhaps in smoothing over a few abrupt moments and jump cuts.

After *Vampyr*, Dreyer had difficulty financing another film. In 1936, he prepared *Mudundu*, "to be shot in Somalia" with the backing of the Turin newspaper *La Stampa* and a Russian producer living in Paris. Dreyer filmed for several months in Africa but returned to Paris with the project unfinished, citing creative differences as the reason for his departure. It was not until 1942—ten years after *Vampyr*—that he completed another film.

Polish cinematographer Rudolph Maté worked with many of Europe's greatest filmmakers. He entered films in Hungary in 1919 as an assistant cameraman to Alexander Korda. He later apprenticed under Karl Freund in Germany, and went on to work with such luminaries as Erich Pommer, René Clair, Fritz Lang, and of course Carl Dreyer (for whom he photographed *The Passion of Joan of Arc* in 1928). Maté journeyed to Hollywood in 1935, where he continued his illustrious career in cinematography, garnering five Oscar nominations along the way. In 1947, Maté turned director. Among his directing credits is the 1951 science fiction classic, *When Worlds Collide*.

NOTES

1. This "look" came about quite by accident. In an interview with Michel Delahaye (published in *Cahiers du Cinéma*, September 1965, and translated in *Voices of Film Experience* by J. Leyda), Dreyer explained: "Generally, you find the definitive style for a film at the end of a few days. Here, we found it right away. We started to shoot the film—starting with the beginning—and, at one of our first screenings of rushes, noticed that one of the takes was gray. We asked ourselves why, until we became aware of the fact that it came from a mistaken light that had been shining on the lens. The producer of the film [and] Rudolph Maté and I thought about the take, in relation to the style we were looking for. Finally, we said that all we had to

do was to repeat, on purpose, every day, the little accident that had happened. Henceforth, for each take, we directed a false light on the lens by projecting it through a veil, which sent the light back to the camera."

2. The film's screenplay called for sounds of "hounds braying and a child weeping. Then a scream, a half-suppressed child's scream, as if a hand had closed over the mouth of the screamer." No child's scream made it onto the final soundtrack, however.

3. Quoted in *Classics of the Horror Film*, by William K. Everson.

4. From "Vampyren fra Courtempierre," *Berlingske Aftenavis*, April 16, 1942 (on file at Danish Film Archive), as cited in *The Films of Carl-Theodor Dreyer*, by David Bordwell.

WHITE ZOMBIE
(1932; United Artists)

Release Date: July 28, 1932
Running Time: 69 minutes
Director: Victor Halperin
Producer: Edward Halperin
Story and Dialogue: Garnett Weston
Photography: Arthur Martinelli
Editor: Howard McLernon
*Art Direction: Ralph Berger, Conrad Tritschler
*Dialogue Director: Herbert Farjeon
*Makeup: Jack Pierce, Carl Axcelle
*Special Effects: Harold Anderson
*Original Music: Guy Bevier Williams, Xavier Cugat
*Musical Arrangements: Abe Meyer
*Additional Music: Nathaniel Dett, Gaston Borch, Hugo Riesenfeld, Leo Kempenski, H. Herkan, H. Maurice Jacquet
*Production Assistant: Sidney Marcus
Assistant Director: William Cody
*Second Assistant Director: Herbert Glazer
Cast: Bela Lugosi (Murder), Madge Bellamy (Madeline), Joseph Cawthorn (Dr. Bruner), Robert Frazer (Beaumont), John Harron (Neil), Brandon Hurst (Silver), George Burr MacAnna (Von Gelder), Frederick Peters (Chauvin), Annette Stone (Maid), John Printz (Latour), Dan Crimmins (Pierre), Claude Morgan (Zombie), John Fergusson (Zombie), Velma Gresham (Maid), Clarence Muse (Driver).

Uncredited on film print or simply grouped together under "Art and Technical"

"I kissed her as she lay there in the coffin — and her lips were *cold*." — Neil.

SYNOPSIS

A young couple (Madeline and Neil) arrive at the wealthy Mr. Beaumont's Haiti plantation. "Madeline and I planned to be married the moment she arrived," explains Neil to Dr. Bruner (the parson who will marry the couple), "but Mr. Beaumont [whom Madeline had met on the ship from New York] persuaded us to come here. He promised to take me out of the bank at Port au Prince and send me to New York as his agent."

A moment later, we learn of Beaumont's *true* motive when he speaks privately with his servant and confidant, Silver. "Why, I'd sacrifice anything I have in the world for her. Nothing matters if I can't have her."

A carriage arrives and takes Beaumont to an eerie sugar mill, worked solely by zombies! A zombie servant shows the apprehensive visitor to Murder Legendre, voodoo-master.

"They're to be married tonight," wails Beaumont. "If she were to disappear — for a month…" Legendre whispers a suggestion, but Beaumont is aghast. "No, not *that*!" Undeterred, the sorcerer produces a small vial. "Only a *pinpoint*, Monsieur Beaumont," beams Legendre, "in a glass of wine or perhaps a flower." "I'll find another way," insists Beaumont, though he takes the vial with him when he leaves.

Back at the plantation, the nuptials begin. "I love you, Madeline," pleads Beaumont even as he escorts her down the stairs to the wedding march. When she demurs ("Don't —

Please—You've been so wonderful. Don't spoil everything now"), he offers her one last gift—a rose (tainted with Legendre's zombie powder).

Madeline weds Neil as planned, though outside in the garden lurks Legendre. The voodoo-master takes a candle from its lamp bracket and, wrapping Madeline's stolen scarf about it, begins to carve the wax with his dagger. When the sorcerer places the crude figure into an open flame, Madeline collapses at the banquet table—dead.

After placing his bride in her tomb, Neil drowns his sorrows at a cafe. Tormented by her image, he rushes back to the cemetery. To his horror, he finds the tomb empty. Beaumont and Legendre (with his zombie helpers) have already been there.

Dr. Bruner tells Neil that "Either the body was stolen by the members of a death cult that use human bones in their ceremonies or else—she's not dead." The sage doctor warns the distraught Neil that "Before we get through with this thing, we may uncover sins that even the Devil would be ashamed of."

In Legendre's clifftop castle overlooking the sea, Beaumont listens as Madeline plays the piano. Though her fingers move across the keys, her eyes only stare sightlessly ahead. Even when he places a diamond necklace about her pale neck, he cannot rouse her. "I was mad to do this," Beaumont tells her unheeding shell. "Forgive me Madeline, forgive me. I can't bear it any longer." To Legendre, he pleads, "You must put the life *back* into her eyes."

Legendre finally agrees and offers Beaumont a glass of wine to "toast the future." After taking a drink, Beaumont sniffs his glass suspiciously. "I have other plans for Mademoiselle," declares Legendre ominously, "and I'm afraid you might not agree." The sorcerer has placed the zombie drug in Beaumont's wine! As the paralyzing drug takes effect, Beaumont can only plead with his eyes and feebly move his hands in useless supplication, while the voodoo-master simply watches with detached interest.

Bruner and Neil ride through the jungle toward Legendre's clifftop aerie. When Neil suddenly grows weak from fever, Bruner leaves him to rest and goes on alone. In his fevered vision, Neil sees Madeline's image and staggers to his feet. In his weakened condition, however, he can only collapse upon reaching the great hall where Legendre sits carving a wax effigy to complete Beaumont's spell. Upon seeing the intruder, an evil thought possesses Legendre—he will have Madeline kill her lover. Legendre, locking his hands tightly together to focus his will, forces Madeline to raise a dagger to strike. Just then, a black-gowned hand emerges from behind a curtain and grabs the entranced girl's wrist. At this, Madeline, despite Legendre's further exertions to control her, moves across the hall and out onto the clifftop terrace. Neil revives and chases after her, grabbing her emotionless form just as she teeters on the brink. Legendre follows to the terrace and summons his zombies. "What are they?" shouts Neil. "To you, my friend," replies the sorcerer, "they are the angels of death." Neil shoots at the approaching figures—to no effect. As Legendre watches his zombie minions force Neil back toward the precipice, the black-robed Dr. Bruner creeps up behind and strikes the sorcerer on the head, knocking him cold. Neil ducks under the now-masterless automatons and the advancing zombies simply step over the edge and plunge into the sea far below.

Madeline begins to revive, but Legendre awakens and she again resumes her lifeless stare. The sorcerer explodes a gas pellet to keep Neil and Bruner at bay, but a shadow looms behind the evil voodoo-master. The forgotten Beaumont, half-paralyzed by the debilitating zombie-drug, makes a staggered lunge at Legendre and topples the sorcerer off the parapet to his death. Unable to recover his balance, Beaumont follows a moment later. "Neil, I—I dreamed," says Madeline wonderingly, restored by the zombie-master's death. The couple embrace.

MEMORABLE MOMENT

Perhaps the eeriest sequence in a film suffused with uncanny atmosphere comes when Beaumont visits Murder Legendre's unholy mill. Following the voodoo-master's zombie servant, Beaumont enters the drab stone building. Inside we see a large two-story expanse around which runs a recessed balcony. Men, half-dressed in rags, shuffle forward to their tasks in a lethargic, steady stream. Dominating the center of the hall is a round catwalk encircling what appears to be a large wooden vat. Underneath is a large spoked wheel with a man pushing against each spoke in order to turn the cylinder. The figures move slowly, silently; their unnatural stillness and emaciated frames too strange to be men — at least not *living* men. As Beaumont steps onto the balcony, the camera views him from low on the catwalk across the room so that half-naked, ragged legs pass back and forth in the foreground. Figures with baskets of sugar cane on their heads move in a slow, steady stream around the circular walkway to drop their load into the vat. The camera takes us inside the huge cylinder and we see large wooden and metal blades at the bottom rotating relentlessly to chop up the cane. One of the lumbering, silent figures stumbles and topples sideways into the vat. The camera pans down to show his fellow workers continue walking in their neverending circuit to power the grinding blades — their unseeing, dead eyes oblivious to their fellow's gruesome fate.

Throughout the sequence, the only sound heard is the almost unearthly groan of the straining wooden gears and grinding cane — a moan rising and falling like the very souls of the damned, speaking eloquently for those empty shells who no longer possess the will to cry out.

ASSETS

His ninth film as director, but only his third talkie, *White Zombie* is undoubtedly Victor Halperin's finest cinematic achievement. Like *Dracula* before it, Halperin's picture generates a powerful mood of eerie dread. *Un*like that earlier classic, however, *White Zombie* sustains and steadily builds upon that mood from beginning to end. Whether by design (unlikely), accident (possibly), or a combination of both (probably), the poverty-row director (undoubtedly led by cinematographer Arthur Martinelli's visual acumen) created the most atmospheric independent horror film of the decade, a darkly gothic shadowplay of good vs. evil. Halperin went on to direct seven more features after *White Zombie*, three of them horror films — *Supernatural* (1933), *Revolt of the Zombies* (1936), and *Torture Ship* (1939). None of his subsequent pictures, however (even *Supernatural*, which cost many times *White Zombie*'s budget to make), comes close to the atmospheric power generated by *White Zombie*. Garnett Weston's languorously macabre script; Bela Lugosi's iconographic evil; Conrad Tritschler's brooding matte paintings (which manage to simultaneously expand Ralph Berger's redressed Universal sets while intensifying the claustrophobic morbidity of its subject); and, above all, Arthur Martinelli's shadow-land lighting and fluid nocturnal photography all combine to produce a unique classic of the horror cinema. Much like Erle Kenton did with *Island of Lost Souls* a few months later, Halperin seemingly rose above his own limitations to serendipitously wring from the disparate talents at hand a cohesive masterwork.

Dramatic impact was the name of the game for Victor and Edward. In a pre-credit sequence (a novelty for the time), the picture opens on an eerie, dimly-lit long shot of a midnight burial in which tattered natives solemnly stand about an open grave while others shovel dirt into the gaping hole. On the soundtrack, a drum beats a dirge-like pattern in an almost subliminal rhythm. The word "WHITE" in stylish gothic/art-deco letters appears at the top of the scene. Then, in time with the drumbeats, translucent rays stream upwards from the bottom of the screen (seemingly from the open grave itself) to illuminate letters one by one, slowly spelling out Z-O-M-B-I-E and complete the title of this eerie production.

Shortly thereafter, a coach moves through the near-blackness of night. Suddenly, a pair of huge eyes, their whites shining as if from an inner fire,[1] appear superimposed over the traveling carriage. The scene shifts to another stretch of road alongside which a dark figure stands. As the coach moves into view and approaches the man, the following eyes dwindle in size, moving toward the motionless figure until they disappear altogether, seemingly absorbed into the blackness of the mysterious form just as the coach pulls abreast of him and stops. Via these orbs, Halperin visually evokes the near-omniscient power of Murder Legendre—*before* we've even met him—to generate an uneasy awe at this pivotal introduction.

Halperin then places Arthur Martinelli's camera on the opposite side of the carriage, looking *through* the coach to the diabolical stranger, so that we see the silent figure lean in the coach window, invading the safety of the interior while he slowly and deliberately places his long hand on the door—on the very *barrier* separating the heroine (and viewer) from the menacing figure. After the coach has sped away when the driver spies "zombies!" coming down the hill, Martinelli's camera views Legendre from a low angle (and slightly tilted to add an almost subliminal unease) so that the demoniacal figure looms menacingly large. With a smugly evil grin, Legendre tucks the scarf (ripped from around the neck of the heroine as the coach abruptly pulled away) into *not* his pocket as expected but into his shirt itself, as if desiring the garment next to his naked skin. The action thus becomes almost a violation—and a foreshadowing of worse ravishments to come ("It felt like hands clutching me," gasps the heroine as punctuation).

It is difficult (often impossible) to separate out the contribution of a director vs. cinematographer. Did Halperin carefully position Martinelli's camera to his own specification, or did he simply follow the cinematographer's advice in setting up the shots? More likely it was a combination of both, but based on the two men's quality of output, one strongly suspects that the latter was more prevalent than the former. In any case, their partnership bore some wonderfully strange fruit.

When Neil stumbles back to the cemetery and sees the door to Madeline's tomb flung wide, for instance, he hesitates at the threshold, the back of his hand pressed tightly to his mouth, fearful of what he may find. Neil finally steps into the mausoleum, but we (the camera) remain outside. After what seems a lifetime of tension (though only a few seconds in reality), the gentle nocturnal cacophony of croaking frogs and chirping crickets is shattered by an anguished scream reverberating off the vault's interior when Neil finds his beloved gone. The tense waiting and unseen cry make for a moment of drama both heartwrenching and frightening (and a moment almost "Lewtonesque" in its unseen import).

Martinelli took pains with his atmospheric lighting, enhancing mood and providing illuminating metaphors with his subtle shadings. When Madeline, cradled in Neil's arms, succumbs to Legendre's evil spell, she closes her eyes. With the camera focused on her luminous face, the light steadily darkens to a gray dimness—as if the light of her very soul had suddenly gone out.

Shooting almost entirely at night enhances the picture's sepulchral atmosphere. Even the few daylight scenes appear filtered, so that the moody gray light brings with it little illumination and no sense of warmth.

Enzo Martinelli, second assistant cameraman on *White Zombie* (and Arthur's nephew) recalled in the February 1988, issue of *American Cinematographer* the care with which Arthur Martinelli worked. "My uncle was always sure it was possible to recognize the source of the light in those scenes. In so many shows today they just ignore the light source. When working on the indoor sets he always gave them a little scope, a little depth. He kept the actors well *into* the set, not back against the walls. The sets were nicely lit for depth and mood."

Martinelli's camera moves often and with great purpose—drawing the viewer into the uncanny proceedings. In the funereal sugar mill, the camera moves in front of Beaumont as he crosses the infernal factory floor to Legendre's unholy lair. Retreating before him, the camera seemingly backs *through* a gate of ornate wrought-iron. The camera continues to recede, drawing Beaumont in after it, as the man opens the bars and steps through like the condemned entering a prison cell — or a fly entering the spider's lair. For a moment he stands, uncertain, the dark lines of the gate behind him reminiscent of an arachnid's web.

For Madeline's burial scene, the camera retreats in front of the casket as the silent pallbearers carry it slowly forward and the robed priest intones his liturgy. Moving ahead of the coffin, the camera seemingly backs into the sepulchral niche — carrying the viewer *inside* the dark tomb itself as they lift the coffin onto the lip of the opening. Our view narrows to a small rectangle above the invading casket so all we see are the silent, stunned forms of Beaumont and Neil hanging back at the mausoleum's steps. The only sound is the ominous grating of the coffin as it slides inexorably toward us, pinning us within the black crypt.

Though far from his most expensive production, Victor Halperin seemingly took more care with *White Zombie* than his subsequent projects. Within his unholy den of death, Legendre, in sepulchral tones, commands Beaumont to "Send me word — when you use [the poison]." Like an infernal vapor, wisps of steam punctuate the words exhaled from Lugosi's satanic lips. By taking the time to capture his icy breath for this one close-up (and single line), Halperin adds a bizarre, hellish flourish to the moment.

Halperin and Martinelli make inventive use of sound and shadows to visually evoke Neil's state of singular grief. Neil, the only person visible, sits at a table in a noisy cafe, while on the wall behind him move silhouettes of couples dancing or talking animatedly at tables. Though surrounded by the sounds of laughter and clinking glasses, Neil sits isolated from the gaiety, as removed from the spectral images of humanity as light from shadow. The moving shades cannot touch Neil and he cannot touch them, for he is utterly alone in his anguish.

The Halperins had the good sense (and good fortune) to borrow from Universal the services of makeup wizard Jack Pierce (with assistance from Carl Axcelle) to create the zombie faces as well as Lugosi's devilish countenance. Not until Karloff's Hjalmar Poelzig in *The Black Cat* (also a Jack Pierce creation) two years later would another human visage reflect such focused diabolism. Pierce's subtle makeup turns slow-moving actors into frightening gargoyles of living death. When Beaumont mounts the carriage sent him by Legendre, he looks over at the driver beside him. A close-up of the driver's hands holding the reins reveals two cadaverous claws, the spaces between the fingers and tendons darkened to create a bony skeletal impression. Halperin heightens the impression by showing the reins threaded tightly through the unmoving fingers — as if they have little power to grasp or move of their own volition and are as brittle as dried bones. When Beaumont looks away from the hands toward the driver's face, his eyes go even wider and he involuntarily draws back from what he sees. The camera pans left to show the upturned face of a corpse, its bony features made prominent by Pierce's subtle shadings while the eyes stare sightlessly ahead and a black hood frames the cadaverous visage.

Murder Legendre is the epitome of evil — vile for the sake of vileness. As such, Lugosi was the ideal choice for the role. Unrestricted by the constraints placed on other men, Lugosi's Legendre indulges his evil whims to the fullest, delighting in the suffering he causes. Lugosi's glowering expression reflects his diabolical intent while the actor keeps his movements slow and measured to intensify the impression of malevolent power. His hypnotic gaze and sardonically evil smirk speak volumes of the man's malignant character. Though Lugosi plays the part perfectly, it ultimately becomes limiting.

LIABILITIES

As Murder Legendre, "[Bela Lugosi's] portrayal even surpasses that former work of artistry [Dracula]," ballyhooed the *White Zombie* pressbook. While Lugosi-philes find it hard to disagree with such a grandiose assessment and have long held *White Zombie* up as one of that actor's finest vehicles (it *is*, after all,

"UNUSUAL TIMES DEMAND *UNUSUAL* PICTURES," announced the 1938 reissue pressbook for *White Zombie* (1932). Indeed, this "live, weird, strangest of all love stories" is one of the most unique and atmospheric films from the Golden Age of Horror.

difficult to envision anyone else in the role of the evil voodoo master), Murder Legendre simply fails to do justice to the actor. Much like Karloff's Fu Manchu of the same year, Lugosi's Legendre is a thoroughly evil entity, devoid of any grace-saving attribute or emotion. While this provides the actor with plenty of opportunities to exercise his particular brand of menace, the one-dimensional character severely limits him — moreso even than *Dracula*, who indeed possessed a sympathetic side (who can forget Lugosi's sad soliloquy ending with, "To die, to be really dead — that must be glorious").

Even so lowly a vehicle as 1935's *Murder by Television* (arguably Lugosi's *worst* film of the decade) allowed the actor more range of expressive emotion than did *White Zombie*. To his credit, Lugosi plays the diabolical Legendre splendidly, his powerful presence in fine form as he unleashes his malevolent hypnotic stare at an unwitting victim or leeringly strokes the heroine's hand with his spiderlike fingers while giving full sardonic weight to his mocking voice. Still, in the end, Legendre is merely a one-dimensional bogeyman, devoid of the romantic mystique of *Dracula*'s Count, the emotional pain of *The Black Cat*'s Vitus Verdegast, or the tortured obsession of *The Raven*'s Dr. Vollin. While Lugosi serves *White Zombie* admirably, if one examines his character closely, *White Zombie* fails to return the favor. Often thought of as the consummate Lugosi vehicle, in truth *White Zombie* simply took him for a ride further down the typecasting highway.

The single greatest fault found in *White Zombie* is the creaky, silent-era acting which permeates the picture. The cast constantly overplays. (In fact, the only natural performance in the film comes from Joseph Cawthorn's Dr. Bruner — a sort of Comedy Relief Van Helsing — whose easygoing manner remains free from the heavy theatricality of the rest.) Even Lugosi (never the most restrained of actors) succumbs to temptation and poor (or, by some accounts, *lack of*) direction from Victor Halperin and plays too broadly at times. Often, the actor's mastery of malevolent melodramatics allows him to pull it off.

When Legendre begins carving his wax voodoo doll outside Beaumont's mansion, for instance, a croaking caw splits the silence and the camera pans up from Legendre to reveal a vulture perched atop a stone pillar. Lugosi, with an evil, smug smile on his lips, cocks an appreciative eyebrow and gives a knowing glance toward the bird, whose hawkish eye seems to sparkle back at him. At other times, however, Lugosi simply goes too far. Upon casting his spell over Madeline by burning the wax effigy, Lugosi stares directly into the camera (no doubt at Halperin's [mis]direction), ludicrously bats his eyelashes several times as if coming out of a daze, and opens his eyes to their white-orbed, impossible widest before stalking directly toward the camera, his face coming so close that it ultimately blocks the screen. The painfully obvious theatrical expressions simply draw unwanted attention to themselves and serve to distance the viewer from the proceedings.

As the "white zombie" of the title, Madge Bellamy plays her role of mindless automaton perfectly. Unfortunately, the same cannot be said for her stint as a living character. Ms. Bellamy, a star of silent films trying to break through to talkies (before *White Zombie*, she hadn't made a picture in two years), appears soulless from the very beginning, with a vacant look in her large doe-eyes and little inflection in her high-pitched child-voice. She needed a director more versed in sound (and more comfortable with actors) than Victor Halperin (who'd only made two talkies previous to this picture) to transform her waifish pantomime into the more natural acting now required in this new age of sound pictures.

REVIEWS

Variety (August 2, 1932): "Now and then a tendency to overplay jars slightly, but in the main the atmosphere of horror is well sustained and sensitive picturegoers will get a full quota of thrills. The story is fairly steeped in gloomy mystery."

New York Daily News: "Bela (Dracula) Lugosi performs further hair-raising screen duties in the current picture. His Mephisto-like haircut ... and his penetrating eyes ... frighten the cash customer who's easily awed. The acting is heavy — except that of Joseph Cawthorn, who endeavors a little comedy relief."

PRODUCTION NOTES

The Halperin Brothers apparently received their inspiration for *White Zombie* from a Broadway play called "Zombie" which had opened on February 10, 1932, running for a scant 21 performances. The play (itself inspired by the 1929 book *The Magic Island*, W. B. Seabrook's fascinating account of his experiences with Haitian voodoo) is set in Haiti and features a plantation owner who suspects his wife of infidelity. When he drinks a potion concocted by his wife's suspected lover he seemingly dies but later rises up to stalk about and frighten the rest of the cast. The *Motion Picture Herald* announced on February 20, 1932, that the play would soon be made into a film (which never materialized). Meanwhile, the Halperin Brothers hired Garnett Weston to write a screenplay featuring a somewhat altered storyline.

When the play's author, Kenneth Webb, learned of the Halperin project, he filed suit in March against them for copyright infringement. Webb lost the suit, however, when the Halperins argued that the play was not a success and so its commercial viability would not be hurt, and that, more to the point, Webb did not have a copyright on the idea of zombies.

According to studio publicity, the Halperins intentionally kept the dialogue in *White Zombie* to a minimum, even trimming pages from the shooting script. "The producers decided that the public is tired unto death of 100 percent dialogue in pictures," reported an article in the film's pressbook. "In fact, it is their firm conviction that the public is tired of even 20 or 30 percent dialogue. The result is that only 15 percent of the length of 'White Zombie' is accompanied by dialogue. This was permitted because the story is all action, and stirring action at that." The two brothers had come to Hollywood from Chicago in the early twenties and begun their own production company.

Having produced over 30 previous features, the majority of them silents, the pair undoubtedly felt more comfortable with the silent medium (as evidenced from the heavy, melodramatic acting found not only in *White Zombie* but in their subsequent features as well, from *Revolt of the Zombies*[1936] to as late as *Torture Ship* in 1939).

Though (rightly) calling *White Zombie* "one of the eeriest and most fantastic stories ever pictured for the screen," United Artists promoted the movie as something of an exposé. "The story of 'White Zombie,'" announced the film's pressbook, "is based upon personal observation in Haiti by American writers and research workers, and, fantastic as it sounds, its entire substance is based upon fact." The picture's advertising and ballyhoo played up the apparent recognition of zombies by the Haitian Penal Code, encouraging theater owners to place in their lobbies blow-ups of "Article 249":

> Also shall be qualified as attempted murder the employment of drugs, hypnosis or any other occult practice which produces lethargic coma, or lifeless sleep. And if the person (**Zombie**) has been buried it shall be considered murder no matter what result follows."

As one might suspect, the bracketed word "zombie" was strictly a Hollywood inclusion, inserted to lend a supernatural air to Article 249's medical/legal emphasis.

White Zombie, shot for a mere $62,500 (less than *one-fifth* what *Dracula* cost), was filmed in two weeks, primarily at night, on the Universal backlot. "We never went off the Universal lot," recalled Enzo Martinelli. "Even the night exteriors on the backwoods roads were shot there." Standing sets from previous horror pictures were redressed and expanded (via the wizardry of realistic glass paintings flawlessly matted in with the physical settings) to produce the forbidding mountaintop fortress of Murder Legendre. The sorcerer's great

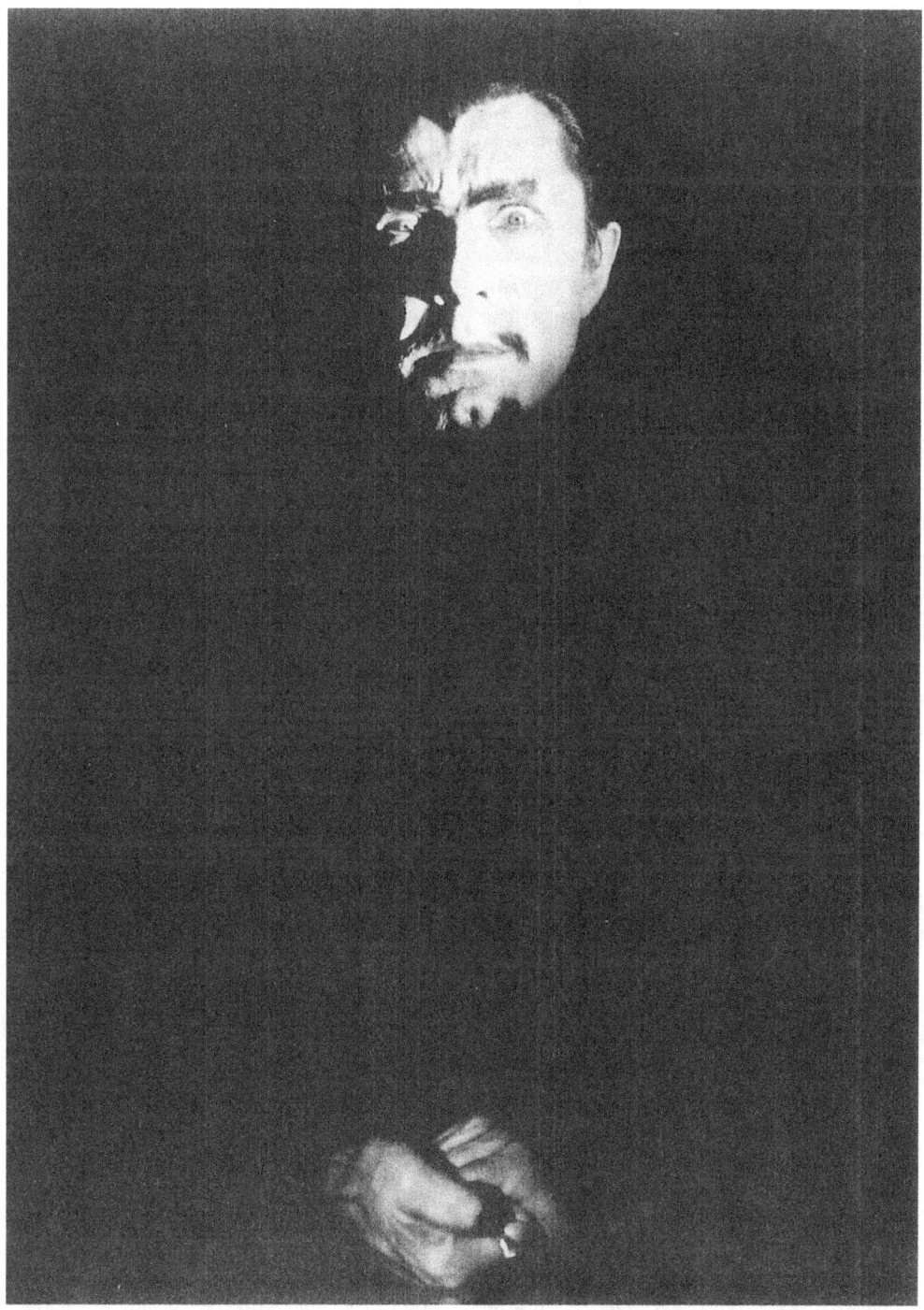

This shot of Bela Lugosi as Murder Legendre captures the intense, moody tone of *White Zombie* (1932).

hall is a rearranged Castle *Dracula* interior, and is furnished with the huge, ornate chairs from *The Cat and the Canary* (1927). Legendre's fateful terrace sports the impressive staircase from Castle Dracula while the basement of *Frankenstein* castle became the voodoo-master's subterranean vaults. A balcony from Universal's 1923 *Hunchback of Notre Dame* cathedral juts out from the magician's mountaintop aerie.

While *White Zombie* was a huge financial success for the Halperin brothers, the film only made around $800–$900 for its star, Bela Lugosi. Despite this sore point, Lugosi considered this picture along with *Dracula* to be two of his best according to film historian William K. Everson, who saw the actor often in the early 1950s. "He had great respect for the speed and efficiency with which the Halperin brothers made that minor classic," wrote Everson in *Castle of Frankenstein* #8, "and an envy for all the money they'd made out of it while he had only signed for a flat salary."

Lugosi's official biographer, Robert Cremer (in the book, *Lugosi, The Man Behind the Cape*), told a different story. According to Cremer, Lugosi was displeased with the way director Victor Halperin was handling the film and so took it upon himself to go about "reordering scenes, restaging some completely, rewriting others, and finally taking the director's baton in hand to mold the film to his personal specifications." Actor Clarence Muse (who played the coach driver) concurred: "Bela made a lot of changes in the script and directed some of the scenes himself."

Muse credited much of the picture's fine atmosphere to Lugosi. The film was shot in the dead of night, and Muse recalled, "Those guys on the set cut out a lot of lights they needed and they only used reflectors. I was driving the carriage with two wild horses and they just had the road marked out with reflectors. It was tough keeping those horses going in the right direction, but Bela knew what atmosphere he wanted to create and he never settled for anything less."

Clarence Muse graduated with a degree in international law from Fairleigh Dickinson University in 1911 but never practiced, opting instead to enter showbusiness by singing and dancing in traveling road shows and vaudeville. He turned to the legitimate stage in the 1920s and became one of the preeminent black actors of the theater.

Muse was lured into motion pictures by a then-princely salary of $1250 per week, making his screen debut in *Hearts of Dixie* (1928). He went on to appear in a total of 219 films, including the genre entries *Black Moon* (1934), *The Invisible Ghost* (1941; again with Lugosi), and *Flesh and Fantasy* (1943). His final film was *The Black Stallion* (1979), completed shortly before his death. Apart from his acting, Muse also composed songs, gave concerts, and worked extensively in radio. In 1973, he was among the first to be inducted into the Black Filmmakers Hall of Fame.

Female lead Madge Bellamy (born Margaret Philpott) saw *White Zombie* as her comeback vehicle. Ms. Bellamy was a supremely successful star of the silent screen, but hadn't made a picture in over two years. Her "comeback" didn't take, however, and she made only a handful of (minor) films after *White Zombie*. A decade after her failed "comeback," the actress' name once again became front-page news, though not because of her acting. In 1943, Madge Bellamy shot and wounded her millionaire lover of five years when the man suddenly married another woman. "Pistol Packin' Madge" (as one paper dubbed her) received a suspended sentence for the assault and was placed on probation. "I only winged him," the actress told Richard Lamparski (in *Whatever Became Of ... 11th series*) years later, "which is all I meant to do. Believe me, I'm a crack shot." After leaving motion pictures, she owned and operated a large junk yard in Ontario, California, for many years. "I've avoided all my life the romantic stuff which novels and movies are about," declared the former actress. "Never went in for that mush."

An amusing (and outlandish) publicity article printed in the picture's pressbook claimed that Ms. Bellamy's screen "death" greatly affected the actress. "Madge Bellamy Scared to Death by Own Portrayal in 'White Zombie'" announced the headline. When the actress viewed the day's rushes, reported the article, "that part of the sequence in which she is seen lying in a coffin was flashed upon the screen, and, after taking one look, Miss Bellamy let cut a piercing scream and bolted for the door.

And nothing could prevail upon her to return. Now Miss Bellamy is a convert to cremation."

As the Halperins' favorite cinematographer, Arthur Martinelli photographed both *Supernatural* (1933) and the brothers' zombie follow-up feature, *Revolt of the Zombies* (1936). According to *Variety*'s obituary (September 20, 1967), the 50 year veteran cameraman "is credited with having filmed the first pix of both Ethel and John Barrymore." One of Martinelli's last films was the Bela Lugosi Poverty Row potboiler, *The Devil Bat* (1942).

Former musical comedy star Joseph Cawthorn began his stage career at age four. At nine he went to England where he toured music halls for four years. Coming to Hollywood in 1926, he appeared in over 50 films in 15 years. According to his obituary (*Variety*, January 19, 1949), Cawthorn "was a favorite comedian of numerous famed persons, including the late President Woodrow Wilson."

Like fellow *White Zombie* actor Robert Frazer, John Harron achieved great success on the silent screen but was reduced to minor roles or minor films with the coming of sound. He appeared in one other (borderline) genre entry — *Midnight Warning* (1933). Harron died unexpectedly in 1939 at the age of 36.

"Musical Arranger" Abe Meyer also provided the background score (if cribbing snippets from the stock music library can be termed "scoring") for *The Vampire Bat* (1933), *Mystery Liner* (1934), *House of Mystery* (1934), *The Ghost Walks* (1935), *Condemned to Live* (1935), *The Rogues Tavern* (1936), and the Halperin brothers' follow-up zombie feature, *Revolt of the Zombies* (1936).

The "catch lines" used to advertise *White Zombie* ranged from suggestive to racist to downright amusing:

"What does a man want in a woman, is it her body or is it her soul?"

"They knew that this was taking place among the blacks but when this fiend practiced it on a white girl — all hell broke loose."

"Look around you, do your friends act queerly — strangely they may be ZOMBIES — living, breathing, walking, under the spell of the Master of the Living Dead."

NOTES

1. Enzo Martinelli, who worked as an assistant to Arthur Martinelli (his uncle), remembered how the inventive cinematographer achieved this effect (without expensive opticals): "Arthur just took a cardboard and cut two holes in it about as wide apart as Lugosi's eyes, placed it in front of Lugosi's face and put a light through it. It put two little spots right on his eyeballs when he started to become dangerous." (From *American Cinematographer*, February 1988.)

DOCTOR X
(1932; First National)

Release Date: August 3, 1932
Running Time: 77 minutes
Director: Michael Curtiz
Screenplay: Robert Tasker and Earl Baldwin (based on a play by Howard W. Comstock and Allen C. Miller)
Photography: Ray Rennahan
Art Director: Anton Grot
Editor: George Amy
Mask Effects: Max Factor Co.
Vitaphone Orchestra Conductor: Leo F. Forbstein
Photographed by Technicolor
Cast: Lionel Atwill (Dr. Xavier), Fay Wray (Joan Xavier), Lee Tracy (Lee Taylor), Preston Foster (Dr. Wells), John Wray (Dr. Haines), Harry Beresford (Dr. Duke), Arthur Edmund Carewe (Dr. Rowitz), Leila Bennett (Mamie, Dr. Xavier's maid), Robert Warwick (Commissioner Stevens), George Rosener (Otto, Dr. Xavier's butler), Willard Robertson (O'Halloran), Thomas Jackson (Editor), Harry Holman (Policeman), Mae Busch (The Madame), Tom Dugan (The Sheriff)

"The human mind will only stand so much; we are all a little strange up here." — Otto (pointing to temple).

SYNOPSIS

In the dead of night, a body arrives at the Mott Street morgue. There, Commissioner of Police Stevens squeamishly looks on as the coroner autopsies the corpse. The victim was strangled, announces Dr. Xavier upon completion of the procedure, and, incredibly, was also subjected to cannibalism.

Lee Taylor, a nosy reporter, sneaks into the morgue and overhears the confidential conversation. "I'm layin' ten bucks to a dime it's another moon-killer murder," Taylor relates when he phones his editor.

"This is the sixth murder in the same number of months," recounts the Commissioner to Xavier, "all committed in the full of the moon with no apparent motive, by means of strangulation and an incision with a strange surgical knife." Evidence indicates that this "strange surgical knife" is a special type of brain scalpel which can be found only at Dr. Xavier's own private Academy of Surgical Research. Moreover, all the murders occurred in the vicinity of Xavier's Institute. This convinces the Commissioner that Xavier's medical academy is tied to the "moon-killer," who indeed may be a member of Xavier's staff.

Wary of the bad publicity a full police investigation would bring to his Institute, Xavier pleads with the Commissioner. "If my Academy is under suspicion, give me a chance to conduct an investigation of my own. Surely with our knowledge of the human brain we have every facility to catch a madman."

At the Institute, Xavier introduces his staff to the Commissioner. First is Professor Wells, studiously at work on an experiment in which he has kept a human heart beating in a glass tank for three years via "electrolysis" (putting to shame Henry *Frankenstein*'s boast of keeping a heart alive for three *weeks*). The Commissioner's eyebrows arch when he learns that "Professor Wells is a student of cannibalism." The policeman soon chuckles at his own hasty conclusion, however, when Wells is revealed to have only one arm (and so could not possibly be the murderer). They next meet Professor Haines. "Dr. Haines and two other scientists were shipwrecked off Tahiti about a year ago," explains Dr. Xavier. When finally rescued after 24 days adrift, one of the men had disappeared. Though nothing was proven, cannibalism was suspected. The other survivor was Dr. Rowitz, another staff member who innocently tells the Commissioner of his "interest in the qualities of the moon." The final suspect is Professor Duke, a "hopeless paralytic" who goes about in a wheelchair or on crutches. (And let us not forget Xavier himself, who behaves rather suspiciously, moving about furtively and complaining at one point about the "ghastly" moonlight bothering him.)

"If you leave me alone," Xavier promises the Commissioner, "I can conduct a series of tests which within 48 hours will conclusively prove whether the killer is a member of this academy." The Commissioner agrees but warns Xavier that after the 48 hours have elapsed he would move in with his own, less discreet, investigation.

Meanwhile, Xavier's daughter, Joan, has caught Lee Taylor nosing about the Institute and orders him off. While lighting a cigar nearby, a cloaked figure with a hideous countenance creeps up behind the reporter. Just then, the cigar explodes (a trick gift from a jovial cop) and scares the moon-killer off.

The following day, Taylor goes to Xavier's residence looking for a photo of the doctor for his newspaper. When Joan confronts him and learns that Taylor wrote the story about her father's involvement printed in that morning's edition, she becomes angry. "Now, on account of that newspaper story, [my father] has to go some other place to carry on his investigation. He *hates* publicity."

To escape this hated publicity, Xavier removes himself and his staff to his remote manor house on Long Island. There, Xavier explains his intentions to his curious colleagues: "I want every one of you to submit to a psycho-neurological test, an experiment that

I have devised which I hope will prove each one of us innocent." Though some protest, they all eventually agree.

Never one to give up, Taylor arrives at the manor and sneaks into the house. While hiding in a storeroom (filled with bones and skeletons), an eye peers through a hole in the wall, immediately followed by a stream of sleep-inducing gas which knocks out the inattentive reporter.

In Xavier's private laboratory, the doctor hooks up each of his colleagues to a bizarre piece of equipment which works as a sort of emotional lie detector. "It is my theory," explains Xavier, "that one of us in the past, through dire necessity, was driven to cannibalism. The memory of that act was hammered like a nail into the mind of that man. Shrewd and brilliant, he could conceal his madness from the human eye, even from himself—but he can't conceal it from the eyes of the radio-sensitivity. Every time his heart beats from mental excitement, the thermal tubes will betray him."

Xavier then reveals, one by one, wax statues of the murder victims. Next, he presents a reenactment of the latest murder (with Xavier's own butler and maid acting the parts). As the quasi-killer grabs the throat of his pseudo-victim, a hand throws a switch which extinguishes the lights. Chaos ensues as chairs are overturned and panicked voices raise in shouts of alarm. A shaft of light penetrates the darkness and reveals one of the thermal tubes boiling over. Xavier triumphantly proclaims "The guilty man is—Rowitz!" When the lights come on, however, they find Rowitz dead, "stabbed in the base of the brain, murdered like all the other moon-killer victims."

Professor Wells, excluded from suspicion because of his missing arm, had been operating the equipment from the secluded recording booth. Xavier rushes to the small room and finds him dazed after being struck on the head when the lights went out.

As things quiet down after the failed experiment, Xavier finds the unconscious reporter in the closet and revives him. Joan talks with Taylor and (thanks to her coquettish charm) convinces him to stay the night and hold off on phoning in his story until the next day—*after* the investigation's conclusion. The following day, Joan keeps an eye on the willing Mr. Taylor and the two seem to hit it off.

That evening, the maid falls prey to her nerves and cannot reprise her role of victim in the deadly drama. Pressured by a call from the Commissioner, Xavier reluctantly agrees to let Joan take the maid's place as the moon-killer's victim during the macabre reenactment scheduled for that evening. Meantime, the troublesome reporter is nowhere to be found, having stumbled upon a secret passage and hidden room.

This time, the three remaining suspects (including Xavier) are handcuffed to their chairs. Wells goes off to prepare the equipment. As he stares out a window at the rising moon, he begins to gasp for breath. Going into a secret chamber, Wells produces a grotesque arm and hand made of "synthetic flesh." Placing the member in his empty sleeve, he holds it within the path of arcing electricity, galvanizing the hand to life! He then coats his face in the synthetic flesh until the horrible, distorted visage of the moon-killer emerges.

Via a secret passage, the madman sneaks into Otto's room, kills the hapless butler, and dons the black robes to assume his place as the quasi-killer. As he enters the stage, Joan looks up from her victim-bed and screams, "It's the killer!" As the three helpless spectators struggle vainly against their bonds, the hideously-transformed Wells hovers over the terrified Joan. "For years I've been searching to find the secret of a *living* manufactured flesh," exclaims the fiend, "and now I've found it!" Gloating in his triumph, the madman continues, "That's what I needed—living flesh from humans for my experiments. What difference did it make if a few people had to die?! Their flesh taught me how to manufacture arms, legs, faces that are *human*! I'll make a crippled world whole again!" As the fiend turns his attentions back to Joan, Taylor makes his way into the room and attacks the madman. The two struggle violently until Taylor grabs an oil lamp and hurls it at the monster. Before the fiend can recover, Taylor rushes at him and pushes him through a window to fall flaming to his death on the rocks below.

A few moments later, Taylor phones in his story. When Joan approaches him, he adds, "Take this to the society editor — It is rumored that on her return from Europe, Miss Xavier will have a very important announcement to make — concerning a very promising and prominent young newspaperman." The two embrace just before THE END.

MEMORABLE MOMENT

Helped by eerie lighting and precise editing, the sequence of the initial experiment becomes a tension-filled, chilling reenactment. With the lights dimmed, Xavier narrates the weird scene taking place on the impromptu stage set before the three experimental subjects hooked up to the baroque detection device. "She is passing through an alleyway," intones Xavier, "when suddenly, a terrible figure steals out — and starts creeping towards her." A shot of the black-robed Otto, arms raised menacingly, quickly gives way to a series of frantic, odd-angled close-ups of each of the observers, briefly revealing their heightened tension. "As old Annie stoops to pick up a newspaper," continues Xavier's voice as the scene shifts again to the drama on-stage, "the figure suddenly takes her throat in his powerful hands —" At this, Annie/Mamie lets out a shriek of terror. A quick cut to a hand throwing an electrical lever and the stage, the three spectators, the entire room, goes black — save for two glass globes glowing green on each side of the frame. As Mamie's continued shrieks are joined by alarmed shouts from the men, in rapid succession we see a close-up of hands struggling free from their equipment restraints, the tell-tale glass tubes, a shadowy pair of legs advancing, crutches crashing to the floor, and finally the blackness again — pierced only by the two green spheres. Suddenly, a shaft of light opens up between the two radiating orbs and Xavier steps into it to exclaim, "Look at that tube!" The camera then pans up the weird glass structure to reveal the liquid boiling up at the top. After three quick cuts of the suspects and their horrified reactions, the camera focuses on Xavier standing beside the glass tubes. "It's a success!" declares Xavier triumphantly. "The guilty man is —" A panicked scream of terror erupts before Xavier can name the culprit and we see Rowitz in close-up, his mouth open wide in horror as he emits a long, tortured shriek. Cutting back to Xavier, the undaunted doctor cries, "The guilty man is *Rowitz*!" Another shot of a hand closing the circuit switch and the lights come up to reveal Rowitz lying dead on the floor.

Editor George Amy employs 25 cuts in only 50 seconds to produce a sense of chaotic urgency and excitement. The near-hysterical shrieks and shouts uttered by the players ("Stop it!"; "I can't stand it!"; "The lights!"), along with the sounds of stumbling movements and falling objects, pierce the semi-darkness to augment the disordered intensity of the moment. Even during the few brief instances of ominous silence, the steady high-pitched hum of the machinery creates an impression of dire forces in motion.

ASSETS

"We are not here to preaching with pictures, to take political sides or bring a great message; we are here to entertain," opined Hungarian-born director Michael Curtiz in his trademark broken English.[1] The talented director brought this philosophy of movie-making to bear fully on *Doctor X*, creating a fast-paced, visually exciting gem of spine-tingling entertainment. No deep issues of facing death, responsibility, or rebirth here, just a plethora of surface thrills and chills centering around morgues, mad scientists, cannibalism, and "moon-killers."

A master filmmaker, Curtiz doesn't miss a trick in wringing every shudder from his lurid storyline. Even for simple introductions he plays up the bizarre, off-center qualities of his characters. Professor Wells is introduced sitting at a desk peering intently at a heart inside a glass jar while electricity crackles in the background. Professor Haines is first seen in silhouette, his profile (complete with satanic goatee) illumined by an eerie blue-green light flickering behind him so that the shadow creates a sinister, even diabolical impression. Dr. Rowitz, seen bending over a huge globe, looks up with a menacing slowness and forbidding expression as the door opens.

Curtiz makes good use of multiple camera angles — shooting from below, from above, at a slant (to create an impression of imbalance) — even within a single scene. Not only does this create a rich visual experience, but the varied viewpoints serve to instill a feeling of unease by keeping the viewer slightly off-kilter in his perspective.

Under Curtiz' skilled direction, Ray Rennahan's camera moves almost constantly, following the characters in a flowing rhythm that captures and enhances the mood of the moment. Warner's publicity department made much of the picture's deft camerawork (even going so far as to stick it with a painfully cute appellation). "The 'curious camera,'" states a *Doctor X* publicity piece, "is responsible for much of the feeling of suspense ... Director Michael Curtiz has named it that because he puts the camera in the place of an interested and curious person, poking it into dark hallways and mysterious closets, investigating this and running down that and trying as best it can to solve the mystery."

Carefully placed objects in the foreground add a visual depth to the camera movement. "The smells," taunts Otto, holding up the soiled garments of the moon-killer's victim for the frightened maid to see, "don't they remind you of an embalming parlor, eh Mamie?" As he steps closer to her, Mamie retreats and the camera pans with them so that the glass tubes of some peculiar device pass between the camera and the actors, creating a distorted vision of the characters and adding to the weird, uneasy feel of the moment. For a full 30 seconds the camera makes its slow pan, staying with Otto as he taunts the increasingly hysterical maid all across the cavernous room.

"The primary purpose of set designing," stated art director Anton Grot in the *Doctor X* pressbook, "is to establish the mood of the story." Grot (born Antocz Franciszek Groszewski in Poland) went on to explain the special needs of a horror picture: "When we design a set for mystery and melodrama we know that it must be of heavy construction with dark colorings and shadows. When we want to add menace to that, we put in a top-heavy effect over doors and windows, we build in low arches which give the feeling of overhanging danger. We design a set that imitates as closely as possible a bird of prey about to swoop down upon its victim, trying to incorporate in the whole thing a sense of impending calamity, of overwhelming danger." True to his word, Grot provides some marvelously eccentric sets and furnishings, creating a multi-textured canvas upon which Curtiz paints his cinematic portraits. Heavy stone pillars and recessed archways, high ceilings with oversized beams, massive carved wooden balustrades topped with gargoyle-like figures, and dark heavy wooden furniture surround all manner of strange machinery. Rounded glass pyramids held in metallic prongs hover above the raised seats, while rods of metal spark dangerously and dials swing wildly. The futuristic equipment, all sharp angles and glass tubing makes a striking contrast to the massive pillars and archways of the gothic sets. The forbidding surroundings serve to cloak the "scientific" experiments in a shroud of ominous mystery, inspiring thoughts more along the lines of medieval alchemy than of modern science.

Ray Rennahan's varied lighting increases the sinister menace of the sets. Shadows create mysterious pools of blackness while bands of light and dark add an uneven, disturbing quality to the surroundings.

Lionel Atwill (earning $2,000 a week for his turn as Dr. Xavier) steals the show by creating a quirky, complex, and *suspicious* character out of what could easily have been a more transparently benign role. When the apprehensive maid asks Xavier what part she'll play in the upcoming reenactment, Atwill replies forcefully, with a hint of impatience, "The scrubwoman of course," then adds, "the one who was *murdered* last night." Upon uttering "murdered" Atwill's lips curve upwards ever-so-slightly as if evincing a subliminal enjoyment in verbalizing the gruesome topic.

Fay Wray never looked lovelier than in *Doctor X*. Photographed in soft focus and gentle highlighting, her face nearly glows with an ethereal beauty. The character of Joan gives her a more complex and well-rounded role than most of her subsequent genre parts (including those in next year's *Mystery of the Wax Museum* and *King Kong*). As Joan Xavier, she ranges from righteous indignation to coquettish flirtation to genuine love and concern — not forgetting her famed screams of terror. Ms. Wray runs the gamut well and her natural innocence and charm make of Joan a genuinely likable character.

Underneath the more obvious (and ineffectual) comedic shenanigans runs a vein of sardonic humor in Robert Tasker and Earl Baldwin's script. "I don't believe Dr. Rowitz *could* commit a crime," opines Dr. Xavier. "He has such a *lovely* nature — why, he's the author of several volumes of poetry."

Finally, the two-strip Technicolor process, while appearing washed-out and unnatural compared to today's refined color process (or even the three-strip technique utilized later in the decade), becomes an effective asset in *Doctor X*. Dominated by subdued greens and reds, the muted coloring adds an otherworldly feel perfectly suited to the bizarre storyline and macabre characters.

LIABILITIES

Though thoroughly entertaining, the rather outlandish script contains a few suspiciously convenient lapses in logic. Where, for instance, did Xavier scare up four lifelike wax statues of the moon-killer's victims on only 24-hours notice? And how did Wells know about the secret lab — in Xavier's *private* home — and set up his own equipment so quickly? Luckily, Curtiz keeps things moving so briskly that one tends to overlook such contrivances in the excitement of the moment. Unfortunately, the picture's major liability remains painfully obvious, holding center stage throughout much of the film.

The only thing worse than arbitrarily inserting abrasive comedy relief into a horror movie is to saddle a main character with this burden. In *Doctor X*, the screwball reporter is the hero and as such receives a great deal of screen time. He is also the Comic Relief which means a thick layer of humor coats the picture. Admittedly, this can be very effective — but only if it is the right performer working with a witty script (Bob Hope in *The Cat and the Canary* or Glenda Farrell in *Mystery of the Wax Museum*, for example). Lee Tracy is *not* the right performer, and the series of lame insults and bland practical jokes (centering around a dime store hand buzzer) are far from witty. When Tracy is on-screen, the picture suffers, for the writers abandon their subtle, sardonic brand of humor for a more obvious (and awful) buffoonery. When Joan catches Tracy on the fire escape of the Institute and demands to know what he's doing there, Tracy lamely comes back with, "I'm a building inspector — I work nights so I won't get sunburned." When she brushes aside this "witticism," he tries, "I'm a somnambulist — I probably came up here to have my head examined."

Rather than endearing himself to the audience with his zany outlook and fun-loving attitude, Tracy becomes an annoying boor. Not only does this constant, prattling humor detract from the mood and tension of the film, it also dispels audience sympathy by turning the hero (the audience identification figure) into an irksome clown. Consequently, at the climax, while we feel definite concern for Fay Wray's character when menaced by the real moon-killer, once Tracy shows up interest declines as we watch the murderer wrestle with an irritating hero for whom we have lost all empathy. Thus the climax becomes nothing so much as a common brawl since we no longer have any real emotional interest vested in the proceedings. At this point, while it is a foregone conclusion that Tracy will somehow come out on top, one's mind begins to conjure up alternative endings which feature Our Hero dying in a variety of nasty ways.

REVIEWS

Reviewer Mordaunt Hall of *The New York Times* (August 4, 1932) had nothing but praise

Otto (George Rosener), Dr. Xavier's sinister butler, stands near the bizarre machinery which will put to the test Xavier's theory that "strong mental repressions, phobias hidden in the darkest corners of the subconscious mind, can be brought to the surface and made to register through certain reactions of the heart."

for this "production that almost makes 'Frankenstein' seem tame and friendly. That the audience which filled the theater was duly impressed was obvious from the nervous giggles and the sudden explosions of relieved laughter." Mr. Hall observed that the film possesses "some remarkable laboratory settings" as well as an effective director in Michael Curtiz "who always keeps his eyes open wide for chances for striking camera work, and here his penchant in that direction is assisted by the impressive settings, the more or less natural color effects, and also by the weird sounds emitted during Doctor Xavier's experiments."

Incredibly, the reviewer also found merit in the film's "vein of adroitly conceived comedy relief," calling Lee Tracy's portrayal "splendid" and noting that "the timing of his comedy is very shrewdly accomplished."

Variety (August 9, 1932) was also impressed with the picture as a whole: "A lot of 'Doctor X' is routine, including the love interest and the conventional murder mystery technique and background, but with material of three cycles involved, it does not become tedious."

This reviewer also noted the frequent bouts of laughter occasioned by *Doctor X*. Interestingly, however, this particular reviewer interpreted the audience laughter differently than the above-quoted Mr. Hall.

PRODUCTION NOTES

First National, former home of Charles Chaplin, was actually owned by Warner Bros., who had purchased the Culver City studio in the late 1920s. As a satellite operation, Warners continued to utilize the First National trademark for a number of years.

Doctor X began in 1928 as a play by Howard W. Comstock and Allen C. Miller called "Terror." When first produced, however (in January of 1931), the play was retitled "Doctor X" to avoid confusion with the better-known Edgar Wallace property, *The Terror*.

Though "Doctor X" played on Broadway and received some good reviews, it closed after 80 performances. Warner Bros. purchased the film rights for $5,000 in January 1932 and assigned writer/actor George Rosener to pen the screenplay. Dissatisfied with Rosener's work, the studio set Earl Baldwin and Robert Tasker to rework it and consoled Rosener by awarding him the rather juicy part of Otto in the film.

Shooting began on March 19th, and Curtiz worked his cast and crew mercilessly in order to finish within the production's tight 24-day schedule. Fifteen-hour days quickly became the norm, and with the formation of the Screen Actor's Guild still two years away, the workers had little recourse for complaint.

On one day (Saturday, April 2nd), the *Doctor X* company worked a grueling 24 hours straight as Curtiz completed an amazing 27 set-ups (which accounted for nearly eight minutes of screen time — one-tenth of the finished picture!). Despite the company's Herculean efforts, *Doctor X* wrapped two days *over* schedule. Upon viewing the finished product, however, Warners' brass stifled whatever complaints they may have had and (after an enthusiastic *Doctor X* preview) immediately began planning a follow-up feature, *The Wax Works* (ultimately to become *Mystery of the Wax Museum*).

Born Mihaly Kertesz in Hungary, director Michael Curtiz started his career as an actor at the Royal Academy of Theater and Art in Budapest at the tender age of 14. He entered films in 1912 and soon after journeyed to Sweden where he became a director. (He supervised the great Greta Garbo in only his second assignment, *History's Great Women*.) After World War I, Curtiz made films in Austria, Germany, Italy, France, and England before Harry Warner brought him to America in 1926.

Over the next three decades, Curtiz made close to one hundred features for Warner Bros. (*five* in 1932 alone). With *Doctor X*, Curtiz joined the studio's "A" director list, subsequently helming many of Warners' most prestigious successes, including *Captain Blood* (1935), *Angels with Dirty Faces* (1938), and *Casablanca* (1942; for which Curtiz won an Academy Award).

Doctor X was Fay Wray's first horror picture. Ms. Wray talked of her director, Michael Curtiz, in her autobiography, *On the Other Hand*: "Michael Curtiz was a machine of a person — efficient, detached, impersonal to the point of appearing cynical. He stood tall, militarily erect; his calculating, functional style made his set run smoothly, without humor. He had a steely intelligence and moviemaking know-how that made you feel there was a camera lens inside his cool blue eyes." The actress went on to relate several amusing anecdotes about Curtiz. "Looking through the finder one day at a group of extras," she recalled, "he called out to one, 'Move to your right ... more ... more ... more ... *now* you are out of the scene. *Go home*!' So wicked, it was almost funny."

On location for this picture's beach scene, remembered Ms. Wray, the director "paced back and forth in front of a crew and cast who were having the usual cold box lunch. He paced and muttered, 'Why should they eat? I don't eat! Why should we be wasting this time...?'"

Fay Wray commented on the film itself in *Starlog* #194: "I saw *Doctor X* in Minneapolis just a couple of years ago. I thought it was paced a little too fast, and everyone talked too fast, that would be a criticism of it. But that didn't seem to bother the audience — they were pretty fascinated."

Though shot in the two-strip Technicolor process, *Doctor X* was seen in color in only a handful of select first-run theaters, the majority of prints struck being in standard black and white.

In 1929 (when the color process was still in vogue) Warners had signed a hefty long-term contract with Technicolor (possibly in an attempt to corner the color market for their own product). Even though by 1932 the two-strip process had fallen out of favor with the public, Warners was still obliged to fulfill their contract (especially with a $25,000 *non-refundable* deposit already paid for each proposed feature staring them in the face).

Therefore, while Ray Rennahan filmed in color, another cinematographer, Richard Towers, manned a second camera unit to shoot simultaneously in black and white. The two outfits generally shot side by side, or, if the setup was more complex, Towers would shoot immediately after Rennahan. Though the lighting remained the same (with Towers utilizing filters and adjusted exposure to adapt to Rennahan's color-oriented illumination), the camera angles sometimes differ in the two versions.

Shooting in color posed its own unique technical difficulties. "Color photography requires about twice as much light as does black and white work," related the *Doctor X* pressbook, "and twice as much light on the set means twice as much heat. The wax figures provided for the setting of the demonstration began to look discouraged after the first few minutes of work under the heat of the lights used. At the end of a half hour their faces were longer than Director Curtiz' arm. Their hands hung to the floor and their noses began to rest on their chins." Curtiz solved the problem by sending to the Warners' casting office for four live extras to replace the melting dummies. (Unlike Francis Drake's futile attempts to impersonate a wax statue in *Mad Love*, the four players in *Doctor X* did a marvelous job of holding still.)

Doctor X's cinematographer, Ray Rennahan, was not an employee of Warners/First National but instead worked for the Technicolor Corporation, who supplied him to the studio for this specialized technique. (Rennahan also shot Warners' follow-up entry, *Mystery of the Wax Museum*, a scant six months later.)

Rennahan was the premier color cinematographer of his day, lensing the very *first* two-strip Technicolor feature (1921's *The Toll of the Sea*) and also the first *three-strip* Technicolor feature (1935's *Becky Sharp*). The cinematographer received nine Academy Award nominations over the course of his career, winning twice — for *Gone with the Wind* (1939) and *Blood and Sand* (1941). Like his contemporary, Karl Freund, Rennahan eventually turned to television, photographing over 500 features and series episodes from 1957 to his retirement in 1972.

Anton Grot, *Doctor X*'s talented art director, had been nominated for an Oscar the previous year for *Svengali*. As head of the Warners Art Department, Grot went on to design sets for *Mystery of the Wax Museum* (1933) and *The Walking Dead* (1936).

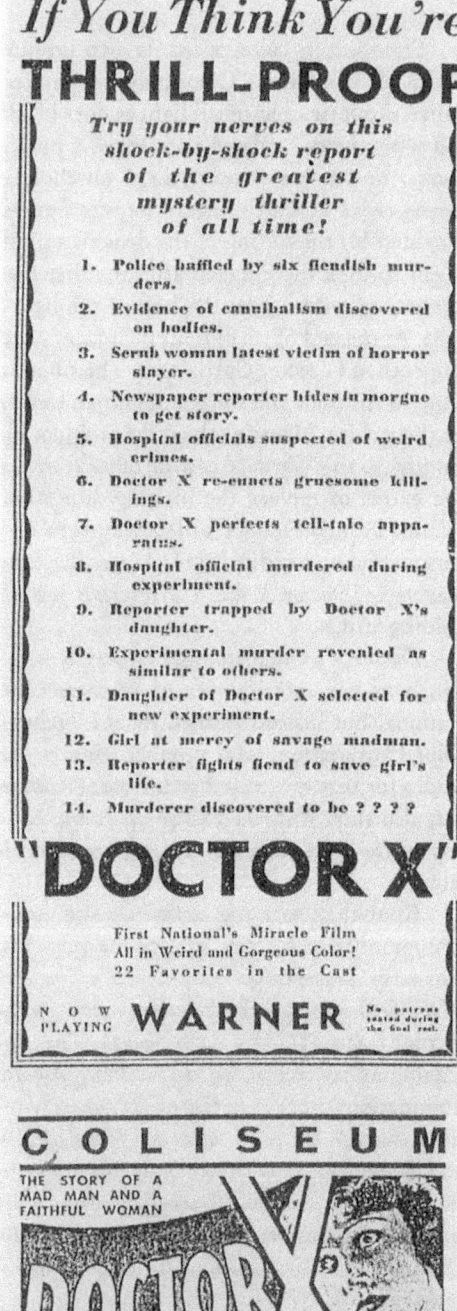

In advertising *Doctor X* (1932), Warner Bros. stressed mystery thrills over horror scares. (Courtesy of Ron Borst/Hollywood Movie Posters.)

In one *Doctor X* scene, Lee Tracy phones his editor from inside a brothel — a location which would have been forbidden to even mention (much less show) two years later, after the instigation of the revamped Production Code. The madam in charge is Mae Busch — frequent foil to Laurel and Hardy.

Lee Tracy became typecast early in his career as the ideal fast-talking reporter when he made the role of Hildy Johnson in Broadway's "The Front Page" his own. He played dozens of newspapermen in his subsequent film, theater, and television work.

Born William Lee Tracy, he worked for a time on the railroad before turning to the stage in 1921. By 1924, he was making a name for himself on Broadway. Tracy entered films in 1929 but constantly returned to his first love, the theater. Late in his film career, he received an Academy Award nomination for his role of Arthur Hockstader in Gore Vidal's *The Best Man* (1964), a part he'd made famous on the stage. Tracy died in 1968, leaving his $2,000,000 estate to his wife and upon her death to a number of charities, including the Motion Picture Relief Fund, the Salvation Army (because, said the actor, "they were the first ones on the job in both world wars"), and the Midnight Mission ("I couldn't leave that one out," said Tracy, who had been a heavy drinker in his day, "because there, but for the grace of God, go I").[2] Fay Wray (in *Starlog* #194) reported that her co-star "was just like you see him on the screen — kind of casual, easy-going and very snappy."

Preston Foster first entered the legitimate theater as an opera singer. After working as a bus driver, clerk, ad salesman, and professional wrestler(!), Foster finally won a spot with the Philadelphia Grand Opera. He quickly rose to operatic prominence and shifted over to Broadway where he was spotted by Mervyn LeRoy of Warner Bros., thus beginning his long career on the screen (over 100 films). *Doctor X* was one of Foster's first screen appearances.

Foster never gave up his music and published a number of songs over the years (including "To Shillelah O'Sullivan" recorded by

Bing Crosby and "Let's Go, Padres," the official song of the San Diego baseball team). Retired since 1966, *Variety*'s obituary (July 22, 1970) reported that "His chief interests in Pacific Beach, his wife said, were 'boats, music and baseball ... in that order.'" One of Foster's final films was the low-budget but imaginative science fiction outing, *The Time Travelers* (1964).

John Wray (no relation to Fay), born John Griffith Malloy, began his cinema career *behind* the camera — as a director of silent films. Becoming one of Thomas Ince's leading directors, Wray helmed 16 features (including the screen's first *Anna Christie* in 1923) before stepping in front of the lens at the advent of sound. When he switched to acting in 1929, he never went back to directing and continued working in front of the cameras up until his death in 1940 at the age of 52. Among the 75 films in which he appeared (in only a single decade) are *The Black Doll* (1938) and *The Cat and the Canary* (1939).

Lionel Atwill was arguably the screen's most effective mad doctor, a character type he excelled at throughout the 1930s and '40s. Atwill was born in Croyden, England, in 1885, five miles from Boris Karloff's birthplace. When he was a teenager Atwill had aspirations of becoming a real-life doctor until he found stage acting too fascinating to give up. Like Fay Wray, *Doctor X* was Lionel Atwill's horror debut.

Atwill, a Broadway matinee idol before abandoning the legitimate theater for the "bastard art" of films, put great stock in the motion picture industry. Returning to New York at the time of this film's release, the actor told *The New York Times*: "I am one of those few stage actors who really like the films, and admit it!" He went on to explain that, "There are two different techniques. That is why some stage actors are not good in the pictures and why some movie stars fail on the stage. It is easier for the former to learn the other mode than the latter."

Warners' publicity department stressed the "aura of mystery" surrounding *Doctor X*— and the dollars that could be wrung by ballyhooing its surprise ending. "Climax in 'Doctor X' Kept Secret from Cast," headlined one pressbook article, which related that "no visitor was allowed upon the stages or locations while this company worked and many members of the cast and crew were kept in the dark concerning the amazing denouement until the last moment when those scenes were made." In an "IMPORTANT NOTE" to theater managers, the pressbook advised, "Be sure to ask your patrons, via theatre front signs and the screen, not to reveal the exciting climax of 'Doctor X' to their friends." Even further, the pressbook suggested that theaters have their patrons sign the following pledge upon leaving the cinema: "Because I realize that to reveal the climax of 'Doctor X' might detract from the enjoyment others will get from the picture, I promise to keep the name of the murderer a secret."

Unconvinced of the viability of the fledgling "horror" genre, Warners further advised its exhibitors to soft-peddle the horror angle. "Sell its importance," counseled the *Doctor X* pressbook, "— its bigness — its novelty — its combination of mystery-thrills, love and comedy — its splendid technicolor effect. AVOID any suggestion of horror or shock. The picture contains more laughs and more romance than any mystery thriller ever made. It is important to get this over in your promotion." Catchlines like "The Most Mystifying Mystery in Years" and "It's the Miracle Film of 1932" were supplied to do just that.

The studio was less shy about their ballyhoo methods. The pressbook suggested "MYSTERY PHONE CALLS" be used to promote the picture. "Use the phone in your 'Doctor X' exploitations, calling up as many people as possible every day before and during your showing. Have a man with a mysterious voice, corresponding to that of 'The Shadow' on the radio, tell the people who answer the phone — 'You have an appointment with Doctor X — Do not slip up — he will be waiting — Remember because I do not forget — Ha! Ha! Ha! (dirty laugh) — The Phantom.'"

On a more sober (though no less ridiculous) note, the following letter was intended for doctors and scientists:

Dear Dr.____

As one medical man (scientist) to another, I feel certain you will find in my picture a brand of entertainment which will be particularly interesting to you, based as it is on scientific and medical happenings. You'll find plenty of comedy relief in the picture which is one of the most unusual pictures I have ever seen.

It's a real mystery. You'll enjoy it, I'm sure.

The four doctors appearing with me form a most interesting collection. You'll be interested in them and in our laboratory.

Sincerely,
"Doctor X"

NOTES

1. Quoted in *Hollywood Without Make-up*, by Pete Martin.
2. Quoted in *Star Quality*, by Arthur F. McClure and Ken D. Jones.

THE LODGER
(1932; Woolf and Freeman Film Service/ Olympic Pictures Corporation; Great Britain)

Alternate Title: *The Phantom Fiend* (American)
Release Date: September 8, 1932 (British); April 19, 1935 (American)
Running Time: 85 minutes (British); 65 minutes (American)
Director: Maurice Elvey
Producer: Julius Hagen
Scenario: Ivor Novello*, Miles Mander, Paul Rotha
Adapted for the screen by H. Fowler Mear (from the celebrated novel *The Lodger*, by Mrs. Belloc Lowndes)
Photography: Basil Emmott, William Luff
Art Direction: James Carter

Editor: Jack Harris
Musical Director: W. L. Tryte
Cast: Ivor Novello (Angeloff), Elizabeth Allan (Daisy Bunting), A. W. Baskcomb (Mr. Bunting), Barbara Everest (Mrs. Bunting), Jack Hawkins (Joe Martin), Shayle Gardner (Snell), Peter Gawthorne (Lord Southcliffe), P. Kynaston Reeves (Bob Mitchell), Antony Holles (Sylvano), Andreas Malandrinos (Rabinovitch), *Drusilla Wills (Mrs. Coles), *Molly Fisher (Gladys), *George Merritt (Commissioner).

**Uncredited on American film prints.*

"Nine million people in London at the mercy of some phantom fiend," — Lord Southcliffe (providing the inspiration for the American retitling).

SYNOPSIS

London is held in a grip of terror by a string of gruesome murders committed by a misogynisitic madman dubbed the "Avenger" by the press. The upstanding Bunting family, who live in the vicinity of the crimes, have fallen on hard times and are forced to take in a lodger. A man appears in answer to their sign and takes the room. He is a foreigner and a musician and he calls himself Michael Angeloff. He practices his music by day and at night ventures out into the fog. Daisy, the Bunting's grown daughter, and he strike up a friendship and, after many strolls through the park and impromptu concerts in his room, Daisy falls in love with Angeloff. The Avenger murders continue, however, and Daisy's former beau, a brash reporter named Joe Martin, becomes jealous and suspicious of the reticent Mr. Angeloff.

As the police pursue their hitherto ineffectual investigation, they receive testimony from

Ad for *The Phantom Fiend*, the American release title for *The Lodger* (1932). (Courtesy of Ron Borst/Hollywood Movie Posters.)

a Mr. Sylvano, who tells of a homicidal maniac named Stephen Rabinovitch, an escapee from an asylum in his home country. "His wife deserted him in a very — disgraceful manner," Sylvano explains, "and this apparently unhinged the poor young man's brain," resulting in an unreasoning "animosity against all women." Aside from being a mad killer, Rabinovitch is also an accomplished musician(!).

Back at the Bunting household, Angeloff attempts to rebuff Daisy's affections. "Stay away from me," he pleads. "Don't ever be alone with me." She trusts him, however, "no matter what you've done." In the face of such loving confidence, Angeloff cannot deny his own feelings. "Oh, why should I fight something that's too strong for me?" he asks and embraces her.

Angeloff continues to make his mysterious evening exoduses, arousing suspicion in Mrs. Bunting. When she asks him why he is going out on such a foggy, inhospitable night, he becomes angry. "I like to be left alone," he tells her coldly, "and I cannot stay in this house if I am — watched and spied on." After apologizing for his shortness, he walks out into the night. Shortly thereafter a shrill scream is heard in the streets, quickly followed by a constable's whistle.

The following evening, Angeloff is taking a late stroll with Daisy when they encounter Joe. The young man becomes belligerent and insists upon escorting Daisy home. Angeloff gallantly acquiesces and moves off into the fog. Soon after, another body is found. Mr. Bunting, out looking for Daisy himself, runs into Angeloff nearby. Angeloff drops his handkerchief and Bunting picks it up and hands it back. Angeloff accepts the cloth wordlessly and Bunting returns home. Washing his hands, he is alarmed to see the water in the basin turn red with blood — blood from the handkerchief he had picked up. Bunting calls the police and they issue a warrant for the arrest of Michael Angeloff, a.k.a. Stephen Rabinovitch. Arriving at the house later, the officers handcuff Angeloff, but he makes a break and escapes.

After eluding the police, Angeloff phones Daisy and asks her to meet him in the park that night. She goes to the fog-enshrouded, ill-lit spot to wait. There she sees Angeloff and calls to him, but when he turns, she sees that it is not her lover after all. Stuttering an apology (the stranger does bear a striking resemblance to Angeloff), she resumes her vigil. Suddenly, this stranger attacks her. As she screams, a figure rushes out of the dark and wraps a chain about the assailant's neck. The rescuer is Angeloff and, using his manacle chain as a garrote, he slowly strangles the madman. Sobbing, Angeloff relates that the phantom fiend is his unhinged brother, Stephen (whom Mr. Bunting had mistaken for Angeloff when he ran into him in the dark the previous evening). Angeloff (whose real name is Michael Rabinovitch) had tracked his brother to England. Daisy rushes to him and comforts her stricken lover, grieving at his dead brother's side.

MEMORABLE MOMENT

The film's most effective sequence (and its single exciting moment) comes at the very end, when Daisy goes to meet her lover in the park. By the weak illumination of an inadequate street lamp, she sees a tall man moving slowly through the darkness and goes up to greet Angeloff. As the man slowly turns towards her, however, she gives a start when she sees his face. There is a wild look in the man's eye and a half-crazed smile on his lips. "Oh, I'm sorry," she stammers, "I thought you were — you looked like —" She trails off and nervously moves back to the bench to wait. The stranger stares after her silently and his face hardens. Then he slowly turns away. Daisy is unsettled now, almost frightened, and she looks anxiously about her in the half-light. A figure walks up behind her in the dark. Unexpectedly, the camera furiously rushes towards her, then abruptly cuts to view a wild-eyed, grimacing face — a madman's face — filling the screen. The man lunges at her and she screams. As he grabs at her straining throat, a second figure enters the frame and wraps a chain around the attacker's neck. Using the chain to pull the madman off her, the rescuer drags him to the ground and tightens the chain. The rescuer is Angeloff, using his manacles as a garrote. "Stephen —" he says to the struggling figure, his voice pleading for recognition, "Michael — Michael." "Michael!" echoes the madman, his voice a high-pitched gurgle. As the terrified Daisy looks on, Michael tightens his grip and deliberately chokes the life out of the killer. As the madman gasps out his dying breath on the soundtrack, we see Daisy react first with wide-eyed disbelief, then with obvious horror, before the camera focuses once more on Michael. Tortured by his deed, he sobs, "Stephen — he was my poor, unhappy brother." Barely able to control his own grief and horror, he continues: "He was mad, he would have killed you. He's been mad for years. That's why —" his voice breaks, "That's why I had — I had to come here — to — to try to find him — before they hurt him." He finally breaks down into racking sobs. Rushing to his side, Daisy comforts him. "They can't hurt him now," she says then adds, "They can't hurt you now." As Michael, Ivor Novello's playing throughout the rest of the picture is generally too melodramatic, but in this powerful sequence his theatrical style effectively conveys the tortured anguish of the man. The realistic reaction shots of Elizabeth Allan as she watches her lover strangle a man (his own brother in fact) effectively conveys to us fellow spectators the sheer horror of the heinous (though necessary) fratricide. It makes for a moment both shocking and agonizing.

ASSETS

An obvious "Jack the Ripper" tale (though the names have been changed — to protect the guilty?), *The Lodger* makes good use of the traditional foggy London setting. Dark alleyways and fog-enshrouded figures abound. Most of the action takes place at night. Out in the street people become mere shadows, while a tall figure in a long coat and hat pulled down over his features is seen stalking through the misty darkness. Even such an innocent setting as a park, so sunny and peaceful by day, becomes an uneasy, dreadful place at night, with the fog swirling about and a single street lamp giving off only a dim circle of pale illumination which leaves the benches nearby in a sinister half-light.

Maurice Elvey directs with care. Working with cinematographers Basil Emmott and William Luff, he keeps the camera mobile, employing the movement to good effect. For instance, when Joe uses the Buntings' telephone to call in the most recent murder, the door opens and we see Angeloff enter the house unobserved. As Joe's voice is heard describing the ghastly "gash across her throat, [her] head almost severed," the camera moves past Joe and follows Angeloff as he quietly moves up the dim stairway. The camera tracks with him into the darkness in almost a visual accusation.

Elvey also carefully sets up some imaginative (and rather tricky) shots. In a dialogue sequence between the two leads, the camera focuses on Angeloff approaching a wardrobe with a mirrored front. When Daisy opens the cabinet, her reflection comes into view in the full-length mirror as she begins to speak. The obvious care and planning Elvey brings to the picture produces a high level of visual interest. Unfortunately, the story and his leading man are not nearly so intriguing.

LIABILITIES

Ivor Novello, playwright, screenwriter, romantic star of the British stage and silent screen, doesn't appear to have adapted well to the coming of sound. Hugely successful on the London stage, he retained much of his theatrical style and many of his mannerisms when performing in films. This was perhaps fine for silent pictures, but difficult to swallow after the advent of sound, when audiences came to expect more naturalistic performances. Novello's theatrical, modulated tones, pained expressions, and exaggerated gestures paint a picture canvassed on romantic melodrama.

Whether by accident or design, Novello's portrayal is definitely along romantic — and sympathetic — lines. His smooth, handsome face, suave, cultured demeanor, and soft, gentle voice point in the direction of a likable leading man. While it could be argued that this demeanor is true to his character (since he is NOT the mad "Avenger," after all), for 60 minutes we've been led to *believe* that he is a "homicidal maniac" and his presence should reflect this to some extent. There is no menace in his performance, no momentary lapses of control, and his attempts at cruelty or anger are feeble at best. When contrasted with the ostensible "hero" of the film — Joe Martin, who is obnoxious, callous, and insensitive (barking out things like "I hate foreigners" or "shut up!") — Novello is definitely the "good" protagonist of the piece, and there is little doubt that the Phantom Fiend must be someone else entirely.

The greatest fault *The Lodger* possesses is a general dullness. Taking its inspiration from the most enduring and fascinating murder spree in history (the "Jack the Ripper" killings), it fails to generate the thrills and excitement promised by the morbid material. Aside from Angeloff's quick escape from the police, nothing really happens until the film's final moments. None of the murders are shown onscreen; we are either simply told of their occurrence or, in one instance, briefly shown the body of a woman lying on the cobbles. There are no sequences of a caped figure stalking a frightened victim in a dark alleyway, no reaction shots of a friendly smile abruptly changing to a look of sheer terror on a victim's face.

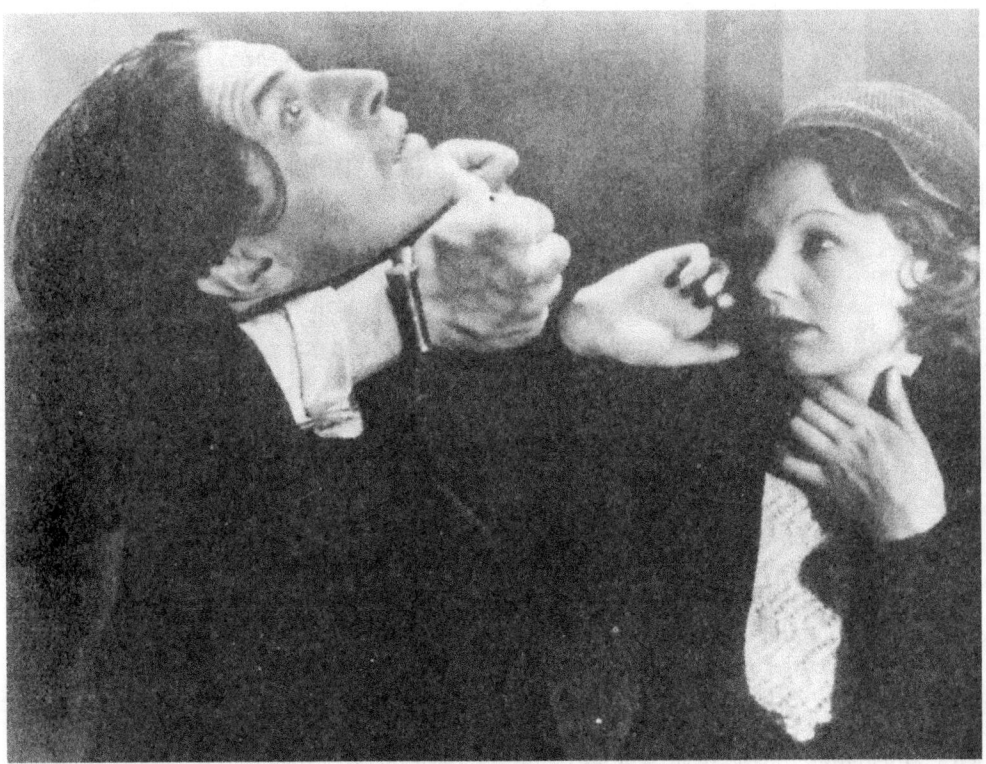

Using his manacled hands as a garrote, Angeloff saves Daisy (Elizabeth Allan) from the mad Rabinovitch (Andreas Malandrinos) in *The Lodger* (1932). (Courtesy of Freda Novello).

Unless such scenes were excised from prints when the film made its way across the Atlantic,[1] it appears as if director Maurice Elvey either let opportunities go unrealized or purposely downplayed the horror in favor of romance (possibly in deference to his star's status?). Instead of calling it *The Phantom Fiend*, perhaps Olympic Pictures Corporation *should* have renamed it *The Phantom* Lover.

The film desperately needs a musical score. In 1932, it was not uncommon to release a picture *sans melodie*. *The Lodger* is no exception, which is a pity. The proper mood music playing low in the background could have given Novello some much-needed sinister support. And, while there are some effectively photographed sequences along the darkened, fog-blanketed streets, a few ominous strains playing on the soundtrack would have added greatly to the feeling of unease and foreboding. W. L. Trytel is credited as "Musical Director," though his contribution barely deserves recognition. The only music heard in *The Lodger* are a few brief snatches of piano concertos played by Angeloff onscreen. Besides, according to the film's pressbook, these compositions were actually written by Ivor Novello(!), who, besides being a leading actor and playwright, "is a music composer of note." (Novello composed the popular World War I song, "Keep the Home Fires Burning.")

REVIEWS

Variety's London correspondent, "Jolo," was impressed (September 20, 1932): "Despite the subject of 'Jack the Ripper,' this is an eerie, absorbing story without being morbid.... The production is artistic, without being ostentatious; photography generally good, but lacking distinction, with the recording generally effective."

Curiously, when the picture finally made it to American shores in 1935, that same publication was not nearly so kind. *Variety*'s

"Odec" (April 24, 1935) stated: "'The Phantom Fiend' tries hard at kidding the audience into thinking it's a shocker. With the exception of a couple minutes toward the end, it offers a first-rate cure for insomnia."

The New York Times' (April 22, 1935) Frank S. Nugent, however, was laudatory, boldly stating that "for sheer, cold-blooded suspenseful and spine-chilling melodrama, nothing like it has been seen since the German picture "M" was shown here about a year ago…. Ivor Novello contributes a gripping performance…. The direction and photography contribute immeasurably to the macabre quality of the picture. One word of warning: leave the youngsters and impressionables at home."

PRODUCTION NOTES

Filmed and released in Great Britain in 1932, *The Lodger* took nearly three years to make its way to American shores. When it finally did arrive, it had lost 20 minutes of running time and gained the new title, *The Phantom Fiend*.

Shooting began in the summer of 1932, shortly after star Ivor Novello returned from Hollywood, where for the past year he'd worked as a screenwriter for MGM. While Novello toiled at Twickenham studios during the day, he trod the London stage at night starring in his own play, *I Lived with You*. His tremendous energy stood him in good stead, for even before *The Lodger* was completed, he began another film, *The Sleeping Car*, at Gaumont-British. Soon after finishing *that* picture, he made yet another—the film version of his play, *I Lived with You*, for which he also wrote the screenplay. If this wasn't enough, he *continued* to appear in the play at night while filming the same story during the day! Novello, whose first love had always been the stage, soon retired from films altogether (worn out perhaps?), making only one more picture before his death in 1951. Three further films were made based on his plays.

Born William Seward Folkard in 1887 and raised in poverty, director Maurice Elvey received no education and began working for a living at the age of nine. He became a stage actor in his teens and eventually a theatrical director. He turned to films in 1913 and directed a staggering total of over 300 features (plus numerous shorts) over the next 44 years, making him Britain's (indeed, the world's) most prolific film director. His credits include one other Golden Age (borderline) horror film, *The Clairvoyant*, as well as an early science fiction entry, *The Tunnel* (both 1935). Elvey retired in the late 1950s after losing an eye.

Co-cinematographer Basil Emmott photographed one other Golden Age (borderline) horror film—the excellent British entry *They Drive by Night* (1938). Emmott's final film was (sadly) 1965's *Curse of the Fly*.

Jack Hawkins, who plays the film's obnoxious reporter "hero," Joe Martin, began in the theater when only 13 years old. Rising to prominence on the London stage, he made his film debut in 1930. *The Lodger* was his second motion picture and his first substantial part. In his autobiography, *Anything for a Quiet Life*, Hawkins relates how he "suffered from terrible camera shyness." The actor remembered that "as soon as I went on the set I developed a frightful nervous twitch that made my face twist into fearful grimaces. I found that the only way to control this was to take aspirin. However, by the end of *The Lodger* I was able to control it unaided." Hawkins married fellow British stage star Jessica Tandy this same year, though the couple were divorced in 1940. He went on to a long film (and television) career in Hollywood. Among his acting triumphs were roles in *The Bridge on the River Kwai* (1957), *Lawrence of Arabia* (1962), and *Zulu* (1964). In 1966 Hawkins lost his voice to cancer of the larynx, but continued in films with his speaking parts dubbed by others (usually Charles Gray or Robert Rietti). In the last year of his life he appeared in two horror films—the uneven anthology, *Tales That Witness Madness* (1973), and the witty *Theatre of Blood* (1973).

Heroine Elizabeth Allan (described by co-star Jack Hawkins as "one of the most beautiful young women I have ever seen") began on the British stage in 1927, and moved to films

Maurice Elvey (holding lamppost) directs the climax of *The Lodger* (1932) at Twickenham studios. (Courtesy of Freda Novello.)

in 1931, doing seven pictures in her first year! She appeared in one other Golden Age horror film—*Mark of the Vampire* (1935). Elizabeth Allan starred in several other pictures for MGM, including the prestigious *A Tale of Two Cities* (1935), before a falling out with Louis B. Mayer prompted her return to England (where she successfully continued her career for a further 25 years of stage, screen, and television successes). Mayer had promised her the lead in *The Citadel* (1938) but changed his mind and awarded the part to Rosalind Russell. At this, Elizabeth Allan sued Mayer, who retaliated by blackballing Ms. Allan in Hollywood. Her last picture was *Grip of the Strangler* (1958; titled *The Haunted Strangler* in America), starring Boris Karloff. Ms. Allan's name is misspelled in *The Lodger*'s credits — as *Allen*. (This was not an unusual occurrence for the actress, even in her native England; on *Grip of the Strangler*, for instance, she is correctly called Allan in the main titles but *Allen* in the end credits!)

Even beyond Ms. Allan, Olympic, the American distributor, seemed to have great difficulty with names. Several other players suffered the same ignoble fate at the hands of careless technicians: Peter Gawthorne's name appears as Peter Gaw*throne*; and the colorful Greek character actor Andreas Malandrinos is labeled *Andre Malandrinas*.

Playing the concerned busy-body Mrs. Bunting, Barbara Everest (whose name, naturally, is misspelled — as *Everst*) worked in Hollywood as well as England. Among her numerous films are three other genre pictures: the opulent *Phantom of the Opera* (1943), the superior ghost story, *The Uninvited* (1944), and the downbeat radiation picture, *The Damned* (1961).

Kynaston Reeves (Bob Mitchell in the film) was yet another of *The Lodger*'s alumni who went on to a successful screen and television career. Among his 90 film credits are the classic British horror anthology, *Dead of Night* (1945); the early Hammer science fiction venture, *Four Sided Triangle* (1953); the somewhat silly but highly enjoyable *Fiend Without a Face* (1958); and the offbeat feline vengeance film, *Shadow of the Cat* (1961).

New Zealand-born Shayle Gardner (Snell in *The Lodger*) was an architect before becoming an actor. He began in films in 1922 and successfully made the transition to sound, continuing his movie career in Britain until 1939, when he retired from acting.

The Lodger is a remake of the 1926 Alfred Hitchcock silent film of the same name, which also starred Ivor Novello. Two more versions of the Mary Belloc Lowndes novel followed — a 1942 remake, again called *The Lodger* (the definitive version, featuring a superb performance by Laird Cregar) and *Man in the Attic* (1953, with Jack Palance giving a less subtle but still effective portrayal). Unlike the first two films, the lodger in these later entries truly *is* Jack the Ripper.

NOTES

1. This is a possibility, because in Britain the film ran 20 minutes longer than in America. It seems unlikely, however, that the English would allow scenes that the American distributors would not. However, since the picture did not hit American screens until 1935, a year after the Production Code was fully enforced, it is feasible that the Hays Office demanded excisions of the more "excitable" scenes.

THE MOST DANGEROUS GAME
(1932; RKO)

Alternate Titles: *The Hounds of Zaroff* (British release title); *Skull Island* (1938 reissue title)
Release Date: September 9, 1932
Running Time: 63 minutes
Directors: Ernest B. Schoedsack and Irving Pichel
Associate Producer: Merian C. Cooper
Executive Producer: David O. Selznick
Screenplay: James Ashmore Creelman (from the *O. Henry Prize Winning Collection* story by Richard Connell)
Photography: Henry Gerrard
Art Director: Carroll Clark
Editor: Archie F. Marshek
Music: Max Steiner
Makeup: Wally Westmore*
Recorded by: Clem Portman
Cast: Joel McCrea (Bob), Fay Wray (Eve), Leslie

Banks (Zaroff), Robert Armstrong (Martin), Noble Johnson (Ivan), Steve Clemento (Tartar), William Davidson (Captain), Dutch Hendrian. (Scar-face), Hale Hamilton* (Bill Woodman), Landers Stevens* (Doc), James Flavin* (First Mate).

*Uncredited on film print.

"Only after the kill does man know the true ecstasy of love."—Count Zaroff.

SYNOPSIS

A yacht bearing Robert Rainsford, a famous big-game hunter, and four companions returning from a hunting expedition makes its way through the treacherous Malay archipelago. While Rainsford and the men discuss the contradictions inherent in "civilized" hunting, the boat suddenly lurches as it hits a hidden reef. All is chaos when the sea water rushes in below deck and hits the hot boilers, ripping the ship apart in a spectacular explosion. Rainsford is the only one to make it safely through the shark-infested waters and reach the shore of the nearby island.

After wandering through the jungle, he looks across a steamy clearing and spies a castle-like structure in the distance. It is the home of Count Zaroff, a Russian aristocrat who fled the revolution with most of his fortune intact. "Welcome to my poor fortress," says the cordial Count, "built by the Portuguese centuries ago. I have had the ruins restored to make my home here." Rainsford soon meets two more of Zaroff's impromptu "guests," Eve and Martin Trowbridge, survivors of a previous shipwreck. There had been four survivors, but neither Eve nor Martin has seen their two sailor companions for three days. Zaroff claims they are out hunting, but Eve doesn't think so and relays her suspicions to Rainsford.

The Count is impressed by Rainsford, whom he considers to be a "kindred spirit" in his passion for hunting. Zaroff tells him, "God made some men poets, some he made kings, some beggars; *me* he made a hunter! ... Hunting is my one passion." That evening the conversation turns mysterious as Zaroff talks of his growing ennui, and how he rekindled his passion for hunting. "I have done a rare thing," he boasts. "I have invented a new sensation." But he prefers not to elaborate, saying only, "It is my one great secret."

Eve's suspicions are soon proven to be justified when she and Rainsford sneak into a secret trophy room. There they find a horror to shock the senses—a room filled with *human* trophies. The pair are discovered when Zaroff returns with his latest "trophy"—the body of Eve's brother, whom Zaroff had just "hunted." With fire in his eyes, Zaroff tries to enlist Rainsford in his sadistic sport of hunting "the most dangerous game." Our hero will have none of this and so becomes the Count's next prey.

While Zaroff's henchmen restrain Rainsford and Eve, the Count sets the ground rules for his game of "outdoor chess," as he terms it. Rainsford and Eve (who insists on going along) will be given a knife and a head start, and if they survive until 12:30 the following day they will be set free. (Of course, to date no one has met the challenge and won.) There then ensues a deadly game of wits as Rainsford uses his hunter's knowledge to set various traps for the pursuing Zaroff, but ultimately fails to kill his adversary. Finally there is nowhere left to run and the pair are cornered above a waterfall. Zaroff lets his hound loose, and as Rainsford struggles with the vicious brute, the Count fires his rifle. Man and dog topple over the cliff into the raging torrent. Stroking the scar on his forehead, Zaroff leers at Eve—his "prize."

Returning to his fortress, Zaroff plays the piano after ordering that Eve be brought to him. The door opens and Rainsford enters—torn, tattered, but alive. "You hit the dog, not me," he relates to the surprised Count. "You have beaten me," replies an admiring Zaroff, but the treacherous Count is not yet finished. When Zaroff reaches for a hidden pistol, Rainsford leaps at him. In the ensuing melee Zaroff grasps his bow, but Rainsford wins out and stabs the Count in the back with his own arrow. Rainsford grabs Eve and they rush to the launch. The Count is not yet dead, however, and he staggers to the window to raise his bow as the escaping boat moves into view. His strength is gone, though, and Zaroff collapses onto the window ledge, only to roll over and fall into the jaws of his own vicious hunting dogs waiting below. The boat, carrying our hero and heroine, speeds safely away.

MEMORABLE MOMENTS

In a film as good as this, it is difficult to select standout scenes. Rather than a series of individual moments, there are whole sequences which blend perfectly into a memorable whole. For instance, the preliminary scenes, in which Rainsford meets Zaroff and they expound upon the nature of hunting, form an unforgettable tableau of uneasy dread. Zaroff extols his obsessive view of the hunt, his words underlined with a Sadean, erotic meaning. "One passion builds upon another. *Kill*— then love…. Once you have known that, you have known ecstasy." The dialogue and Leslie Banks' delivery fill these scenes with an almost palpable foreboding.

One of the most startling moments comes when the two protagonists stumble upon the gruesome trophy room. Rainsford's light shines upwards into the darkness and illuminates a hideous sight — a human head preserved and mounted on the wall like some perverted deer trophy. As Eve backs away, she bumps into another human head, this one bobbing in a tank as the dim light silhouettes its grotesque twisting and turning. This was strong stuff for 1932, and a scene possessing enough gruesome style to unsettle a viewer even six decades later.

The chase through the jungle, as Zaroff pursues his human prey, is thrilling and full of action and suspense. As the two flee for their lives through the swamp, the dim, misty light turns them into silhouettes running in terror through this primordial hell of fog, rotted logs, and hanging vines. As the dogs howl at their heels, the music builds, builds, builds, until it becomes a symphony of frenetic terror.

ASSETS

The Most Dangerous Game is a film in two parts. The first half carefully builds the mood, creating a feeling of unease and dread, a feeling which is validated by the sheer fast-paced terror of the second half. From the moment we meet Count Zaroff, with his passion for hunting, his cultured yet cold manner, his cryptic talk of the "most dangerous game," and his sinister, sadistic views of love and sex ("What is woman, even a woman such as this, until the blood is quickened by the kill?"), we sense the sinister undertones to the seemingly innocuous events going on. The bizarre setting, Eve's vague fear, and Zaroff himself all set the stage for the symphony of terror and violence soon to commence, as the two protagonists are forced to flee for their lives, hunted as "the most dangerous game."

The storyline of *The Most Dangerous Game* is one of those timeless classics, like *Dr. Jekyll and Mr. Hyde* or *Frankenstein*, which continue to fascinate as the years go by. It is the tale of a man who takes an obsession to the extreme. James Ashmore Creelman's screenplay adapts Richard Connell's short story into a taut, intelligent, literary work of cinematic art. The characters are well drawn, the dialogue is excellent, and the screenplay's structure draws the viewer into this nightmare situation and holds him fast until the final reel. Of course, credit must be given to directors Ernest B. Schoedsack and Irving Pichel for their masterful pacing and camerawork, which find a base in the literate screenplay and leaps forward to create a rollercoaster ride of excitement.[1]

Scriptwriter Creelman wisely avoided falling into the age-old love-interest trap. The film's romance, what there is of it, is only implied (by the facts that the two protagonists are man and woman and that Rainsford is dedicated to protecting her). Rainsford and Eve never kiss or exchange any romantic banter; they are merely two people thrown together who must fight for their lives. The only talk of love comes from Zaroff himself, and it is a twisted, savage form of love. "First kill, then love," is Zaroff's credo. Other than this Sadean view of sex, there is no romantic interlude to intrude upon the terror and dark mood of the film, no moments of romantic respite to lessen the horror of the situation. This absence of romance strengthens the impact of *The Most Dangerous Game*, allowing the audience to identify with the two people caught in this horrible game without being distracted by their sudden romantic interest in each other (which often comes across as implausible and unconvincing).

One of the most striking aspects of *The Most Dangerous Game* is the literate and insightful dialogue. For instance, when Rainsford expresses how "incredible" the deaths of his companions seems, Zaroff counters with this sagacious observation: "Such things are always incredible. Death is for others, not for ourselves." The script is filled with juicy lines, particularly when Zaroff verbally spars with Rainsford or elucidates his sadistic theories of life, love, and the hunt. Screenwriter Creelman provides Zaroff with a diverse array of illuminating phrases, utilizing lines both blatant and subtle to reveal this man's warped and twisted character. Towards the beginning, as we first get to know Zaroff, he makes a revealing statement. "One night as I lay in my tent with this, this head of mine," he relates while unconsciously reaching up to stroke the scar on his forehead, "a terrible thought crept like a snake into my brain — hunting was beginning to bore me." "Is that such a terrible thought, Count?" asks Eve, her voice full of sarcastic reproach. "It is, my dear lady," Zaroff continues, "when hunting has been the whip for all other passions. When I lost my love of hunting I lost my love of life..." he says and, after a significant pause, adds "of love."

Later, when Rainsford and Eve discover the horror of the "trophy room," the true nature of Zaroff's cruelty and sadism is revealed with a few understated and euphemistic lines. "You see," Zaroff explains to his two horrified captives, "when I first began stocking my island, many of my guests thought I was joking, so I established this trophy room. An hour with my trophies and they usually do their best to keep away from me." Then, just before the hunt is to begin, a bit more of Zaroff's twisted perspective is revealed in this exchange: "I'm going to be hunted," an angry Rainsford tells the frightened Eve, but Zaroff interrupts to reassure her. "Oh no, no Miss Trowbridge — outdoor chess, his brain against mine, his woodcraft against mine, and the prize —" he trails off, with a pointed look at Eve. She insists upon going with Rainsford, but our hero protests that "He'll kill you too," to which Zaroff answers, "Not at all — one does not kill the female animal."

Underneath its exciting cinematic exterior, the film is one long treatise against the sport of hunting. While not necessarily a virtue per se (at least according to the NRA), it is a theme worthy of note and one put forth well enough to make a good case. From the opening, in which Rainsford and his companions discuss the morality of the sport, to the inexorable climax of human beings stalked for the thrill of the hunt (which, after all, is just the sport taken to its ultimate extreme), we are shown the folly and cruelty of this bloody pastime. At the film's beginning, one of Rainsford's companions makes a wry observation: "I was thinking of the inconsistency of civilization. The beast of the jungle, killing just for his existence, is called 'savage'; the man, killing just for sport, is called 'civilized.' It's a bit contradictory, isn't it." Rainsford responds with this poor argument: "What makes you think it isn't just as much sport for the animal as for the man?" His companion presses the issue by asking this Great White Hunter if "there'd be as much sport in the game if you were the tiger instead of the hunter?" "Well, that's something I'll never have to decide," is Rainsford's evasive reply. "This world is divided into two kinds of people, the hunter and the hunted. Luckily, I'm a hunter. Nothing can ever change that," he continues confidently, just as the ship lurches under him and his "hunter's world" is turned upside-down. In the end, even Rainsford, whose life is dedicated to the deadly pastime of hunting for pleasure, comes to realize the wasteful brutality of the sport. When treed like a wild beast by Zaroff, he learns what it's like to be on the

Armed with only a knife, Rainsford (Joel McCrea) and Eve (Fay Wray) are hunted as *The Most Dangerous Game* (1932).

other side of the gun barrel. "Those animals I cornered, now I know how they felt," he empathizes.

Directors Schoedsack and Pichel utilize the satyr motif, with all its bestial and sexual implications, throughout the film to underscore the dark themes of The Hunt and its brutal relationship to sex. Beginning with the opening credits, it is the first thing we see. Focusing on a heavy wooden door, the camera moves in to rest on the unusual and forbidding door knocker — a satyrlike figure holding a swooning girl in its arms. Suddenly a hand rises up into the frame, raps with the knocker, and the first credits appear. When we are introduced to Zaroff, this imagery also plays an important role. Rainsford, his head full of suspicions about his unusual host, walks up the massive staircase towards his room. On the wall he notices a gigantic mural. Again it is the satyr with the captured woman in his arms, but in much more revealing detail. Shocked, Rainsford stops his ascent and the camera closes in on the tapestry, revealing the swooning woman to be half nude, with one breast exposed. The camera then cuts to Zaroff gazing up at it, an unhealthy gleam in his eye and a cruel half-smile on his lips. The man obviously identifies with the brutal and amorous satyr. Schoedsack makes good use of this nice symbolic touch provided by art director Carroll Clark.

In his screen debut, Leslie Banks gives a wonderfully sinister performance as the sadistic yet cordial Count Zaroff. With his glaring eyes, his small but significant gestures and mannerisms (such as lovingly stroking the scar on his forehead when his bloodlust is aroused), and his exquisite dialogue delivery he makes a perfect villain. Banks is given all the best lines, and he takes full advantage. "One passion builds upon the other," he says, "Kill, then *love*." Banks rolls the word "love" on his tongue, stretching it out, changing its meaning into something dark and degenerate. Banks provides the film with its best performance.

Henry Gerrard's photography makes excellent use of the wonderfully medieval interiors of Zaroff's castle, with its huge stone fireplace, massive steps, and spectacular masonry, as well as the lush jungle sets, all towering plants, decayed logs, and hanging creepers. (This, by the way, is the same jungle seen in *King Kong*.)

In one of the most exciting sequences, Gerrard's mobile camera takes the viewer on a wild ride through this hellish setting. As Rainsford and Eve flee through the jungle, the camera moves in front of them, keeping pace with their panic-stricken flight. We are shown their faces in close up, each in turn. First comes Rainsford — grim, determined; then Eve — frightened, almost in a panic; and finally Zaroff — eyes bulging in a bloodlust frenzy. The camera then turns to the point of view of the fleeing protagonists as they rush through the jungle; leaves and plants slap our face as now we, the viewers, join the panicky flight. This use of the subjective camera brilliantly draws us into the characters' plight and inspires an exciting urgency and involvement not found in many films of the day (or of any day, for that matter).

LIABILITIES

In a film as strong as this, there is not much to be found on the debit side. One fault is the sometimes dated dialogue given to Rainsford. (Paradoxically, the rich dialogue written for Count Zaroff is one of the picture's strongest assets.) For instance, when Zaroff suggests that Rainsford join him in his deadly hobby, an incensed Rainsford answers with: "You murderous rat, I'm a hunter, not an assassin." While this line gets the point across, it conjures up images of an Edward G. Robinson gangster picture. Earlier, when Rainsford tells Zaroff of his shipwreck and the friends he'd lost, he describes them as "the swellest crowd on Earth" — a rather quaint thirtiesism.

Thankfully, only Rainsford utters these little slices of slang, which remind us that the film is indeed set firmly in the 1930s. However, this does set up a nice contrast between the two rival characters: Zaroff, sophisticated and proud in his mad obsession, and Rainsford, simple yet honest in his convictions, an Everyman for the times (who thus must speak like the Everyman of his time).

Overall, *The Most Dangerous Game* is an exciting, intelligent, involving film — a genuine classic from the Golden Age of Horror. The mobile camerawork, strong themes, timeless storyline, generally effective dialogue, and fast-paced direction make it a thrilling piece of cinema history which continues to delight after repeated viewings.

REVIEWS

Variety (November 22, 1932): "Fantastic would-be thriller whose efforts at horrifying are not very effective.... For his photography Henry Garard [sic] rates a big nod, despite that his efforts were wasted."

Critic Mordaunt Hall, of the *New York Times* (November 24, 1932) was much more charitable towards the production, calling it a "highly satisfactory melodrama" and noting that "it has the much-desired virtue of originality, which, in no small measure, compensates for some of its gruesome ideas and its weird plot." Impressed by Leslie Banks, he noted, "Mr. Banks makes this strange Count really interesting. In fact his portrayal is so good that both Joel McCrea and Fay Wray ... are quite overshadowed." He also found praise for the picture's exciting second half, stating that "the sequences dealing with the mad ... hunt are set forth in a peculiarly impressive fashion."

PRODUCTION NOTES

Richard Connell's 1924 short-story has, like many classic storylines, been filmed numerous times (though never as successfully as this first outing). *A Game of Death* (1945), *Run for the Sun* (1956), and *Bloodlust* (1961) are all true remakes, while *Kill or Be Killed* (1950), *The Black Forest* (1954), Cornel Wilde's African-set *The Naked Prey* (1966), Jess Franco's *The Perverse Countess* (1973), *Slave Girls from Beyond Infinity* (1988; a ridiculous no-budget sci-fi version), the 1991 made-for-cable *Deadly Game*, John Woo's *Hard Target* (1993), and the superior Rutger Hauer vehicle *Surviving the Game* (1994) all incorporate Connell's story to one degree or another. The first remake, *A Game of Death*, even borrows footage from *The Most Dangerous Game*, and the screams of star Audrey Long in *A Game of Death* are actually those of Fay Wray, taken from an old soundtrack recording.

The Most Dangerous Game was made by the team of Merian C. Cooper and Ernest B. Schoedsack, the men responsible for *King Kong* (1933). Another *Kong* alumnus was screenwriter James Creelman. (Cooper had promised the job of writing *The Most Dangerous Game* to Edgar Wallace after receiving his original treatment for *King Kong*, but Wallace's premature death in 1932 cut short his involvement in both projects.) Tragically, the talented Creelman took his own life in 1941 by leaping from a New York high-rise. He was 40 years old.

Though released before *King Kong*, *The Most Dangerous Game* was actually filmed *after* the start of that classic ape movie (which took close to a year to complete, mostly due to the time-consuming animation work). "We needed a project while the [*King Kong*] script was rewritten and while the animation for *Kong* was being done," recalled Cooper (in *David O. Selznick's Hollywood*, by Ronald Haver), "so I picked up this short story and got Jimmy Creelman to write the script. The title means when man hunts man, instead of animals, and I thought Monty [Schoedsack] and I could introduce all those things that we used in *Chang* [1927] — the traps and the dead falls, and all those things. None of them are in the original story, neither was the love story.... *The Most Dangerous Game* was a cheap picture to make — it only cost about $150,000.[2] We saved money by using Fay Wray and Robert Armstrong in between sessions on *Kong*. Since both films were laid in the jungle, we were able to use the same sets for both, switching back and forth; I'd be shooting *Kong*, then Monty would move in and do *The Most Dangerous Game*. There's a shot in *The Most Dangerous Game* where you see Leslie Banks, the villain, running through the fog; as soon as Schoedsack did that shot, I moved in and took the same set and did the shot in *Kong* where the sailor is being chased by the dinosaur. The same thing where *Kong* shakes the men off the log; when I was through doing the live action, Monty came in and shot a scene for *Dangerous Game* showing Fay and Joel McCrea, playing the hero, crossing the log trying to escape from the madman. We had a lot of fun, and

Rainsford (Joel McCrea) struggles with Zaroff (Leslie Banks) at the climax of *The Most Dangerous Game* (1932). (Courtesy of Ted Okuda.)

the picture was a hit, and it's been remade several times, but each time the people who did it used our concept, the traps and the love story and all."

As reported by film editor Archie Marshek (in *The Making of King Kong,* by Orville Goldner and George E. Turner), director Schoedsack didn't always see eye-to-eye with his producer and partner Merian C. Cooper while making *The Most Dangerous Game.* According to Marshek, Schoedsack would sometimes hide in the editing room when Cooper was on the set because the two each had their own ideas of how the chase scenes should be shot.

By avoiding Cooper, Schoedsack could do things his own way. Even so, Schoedsack was not at all convinced that they had a classic on their hands. The director later admitted that he "didn't think it would be very good so I just decided to keep it moving so fast that nobody would notice.... We didn't know what a good picture we had until it was finished."

Cooper and Schoedsack originally envisioned *The Most Dangerous Game* as a big-budget spectacular, but the RKO head office set strict limitations for the production. This demanded significant revisions in the script, including the elimination of *nine* actors (set to play Rainsford's fellow passengers) from the proposed cast. Among those lost before the yacht ever went down were Leon Waycoff (fresh from Universal's *Murders in the Rue Morgue*), Creighton Chaney (later Lon Chaney,

Jr.), and a young Ray Milland. Cooper and Schoedsack's reworking of the shipwreck sequence (which would have been much more expensive had it been shot as originally planned) is illustrative of their cost-cutting process.

In a note to production supervisor Val Paul, dated May 4, 1932, Schoedsack outlined the proposed alterations:

> Mr. Cooper and I have discussed and approved a change in the yacht sequence which should result in considerable economy, while improving and adding realism to the wreck with a more modern and convincing method...
>
> At the instant that the ship scrapes bottom, we leave the interior of the dining salon as the set rocks over, but before the water enters. We cut to the flash on the bridge as the officer discovers the water has reached the boilers. We cut to a miniature explosion of flash powder on our miniature hull and instantly dissolve to a series of overlapping and rapidly dissolving flashes such as falling wreckage (all in close-ups), a man being washed along a deck, falling spars and gear, drowning sailors, hissing steam, etc., accompanied by screams, crashes and the roaring of water. Over all will be exposed flashes of foaming and churning water, and the last flash might be the last of the masthead disappearing under the water. Inasmuch as these scenes are fast and impressionistic, I think they could be very cheaply made, or perhaps a great many found in stock. At the end of the series, we dissolve to the scene of the boy in the water, as in the present version.
>
> As you will see, this lineup eliminates the following items:
> 1. Building a salon set in tank, with water dumps.
> 2. Possibly eliminate rockers on both bridge and salon.
> 3. Eliminates deck set in tank entirely.
> 4. Simplifies miniature yacht work to some extent.
> 5. Eliminates costume changes for extras in cabin.

Irving Pichel, co-director of *The Most Dangerous Game*, worked in front of as well as behind the camera. As an actor he appeared in *Murder by the Clock* (1931), *Dracula's Daughter* (1936; in which he was unforgettable as Sandor, the slimy, evil, scheming servant of the title character), and *Torture Ship* (1939). Behind the camera he co-directed *She* (1935) with Lansing C. Holden and later helmed George Pal's milestone science fiction film, *Destination Moon* (1950).

"The front office was afraid I couldn't handle dialogue," stated Ernest B. Schoedsack (in *The Cinema of Adventure, Romance and Terror*, by George E. Turner), "so they sent Irving Pichel over and he just stood behind me and watched." Fay Wray, however, remembered Pichel as doing more than just standing and watching. She remembered that, while Schoedsack directed the action scenes in *The Most Dangerous Game*, it was Pichel who actively supervised the dialogue portions.

Along with Ms. Wray, three other actors from *Kong* were featured in *The Most Dangerous Game*. Robert Armstrong, who here plays Martin Trowbridge (Eve's besotted brother), had the pivotal role of Carl Denham in *King Kong*. Steve Clemento (a Yaqui Indian named Esteban Clemente who was known in vaudeville as the world's greatest knife thrower) appears as Zaroff's "Tartar" servant in *The Most Dangerous Game* and later as the "Witch King" in *Kong*. Noble Johnson, here playing Ivan, Zaroff's strong, silent henchman, was the imposing village chief on Kong's island. Johnson, a well-known local dog breeder, was originally contracted to provide several of Zaroff's hounds for the picture, but his stature and imposing presence earned him a spot in the film alongside his animals. Joel McCrea was *almost Kong* as well.

McCrea told John Kobal (for his book, *People Will Talk*) that Merian C. Cooper wanted McCrea for the role of Jack Driscoll in *Kong* but he turned the director down and instead recommended Jacques de Bujac (who became Bruce Cabot) for the role.

While working on *King Kong*, Bruce Cabot made a bid for the role of Count Zaroff in *The Most Dangerous Game*. Though he submitted portraits of himself made up as Zaroff, RKO passed him over in favor of English stage star Leslie Banks, then appearing on Broadway. Banks subsequently returned to England, where he continued his

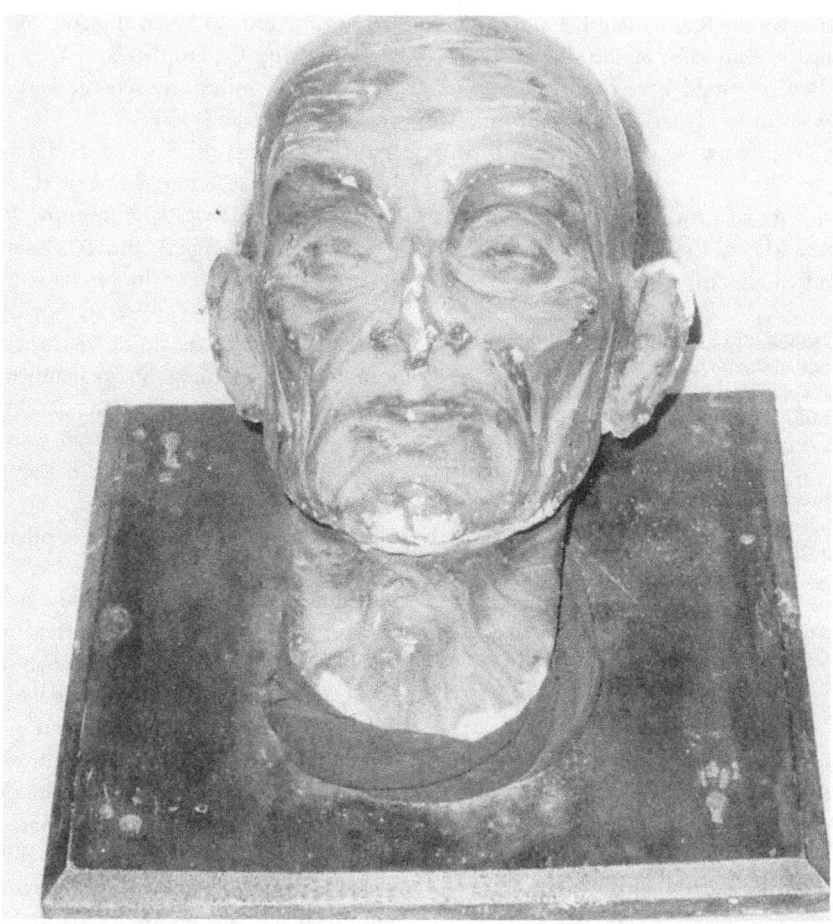

Original head prop seen on the wall of Zaroff's gruesome trophy room in *The Most Dangerous Game*. (Photo: Lynn Naron, 1993.)

film career, though he never made another picture in America.

Whether Leslie Banks' subsequent avoidance of American productions had anything to do with his experiences on *The Most Dangerous Game* is purely a matter of conjecture, though the English actor did suffer at least one embarrassing (and painful) mishap during filming. "Once, where we were working on the Fog Hollow set," remembered Ernest B. Schoedsack, "Leslie came bounding out of the fog, clutching his rear end, and told us, 'I say, one of those dogs bit me!' The lady from the training school [five of the 20 Great Danes used were provided by the Hollywood Dog Training School] said, 'Oh, no, it's impossible! None of those dogs would do that!' Leslie said, 'Well, perhaps it was a cameraman, but *something* bit me in the ass.' He was bleeding and had to have first aid and stitches."[3]

According to Joel McCrea, producer Merian C. Cooper had more than a professional interest in his star, Fay Wray, though he never acted on it. "He got me and Fay Wray," stated the actor, "because he loved Fay Wray ... he loved Fay Wray, but he married Dorothy Jordan, and she [Fay Wray] was married to John Monk Saunders, who wrote *Wings*."

Clarence Linden ("Buster") Crabbe earned $5 a day as Joel McCrea's stunt double on *The Most Dangerous Game*. An Olympic athlete-turned-stuntman-turned-actor, Crabbe is best remembered for his portrayal of *Flash Gordon* in the 1936 serial and its subsequent sequels. It is interesting to note that McCrea himself began his life in motion pictures as a stunt man in the 1920s. By 1932, however, he was much too valuable a star for the studio to risk his neck performing dangerous stunts, and so RKO hired Crabbe to take the risks.

NOTES

1. Director Ernest B. Schoedsack deliberately set out to achieve this effect. "When I read the script I felt that nobody would believe it," said Schoedsack. "I decided the main thing was to keep it moving so they wouldn't have time to think it over. I didn't know a damned thing about stage direction, but I tried one thing that worked: I brought a stopwatch to the stage and sometimes I'd say, 'That scene took 30 seconds; I think we could do it just as well in 20,' and we'd speed it up that way" (quoted in *The Cinema of Adventure, Romance and Terror*, by George E. Turner).

2. Actually, the production was budgeted at a more substantial $202,662 for a three-week shoot. Cooper and Schoedsack brought the picture in about $16,000 over budget and a week over-schedule.

3. Quoted in *The Cinema of Adventure, Romance and Terror*, by George E. Turner (ed.).

THE OLD DARK HOUSE
(1932; Universal)

Release Date: October 20, 1932
Running Time: 71 minutes
Director: James Whale
Producer: Carl Laemmle, Jr.
Screenplay: Benn W. Levy (from the novel *Benighted*, by J. B. Priestly)
Photography: Arthur Edeson
Art Director: Charles D. Hall
Editor: Clarence Kolster
Makeup: Jack P. Pierce
Assistant Director: Joseph A. McDonough
Sound Recorder: William Hedgcock
Cast: Boris Karloff (Morgan), Melvyn Douglas (Penderel), Charles Laughton (Sir William Porterhouse), Lillian Bond (Gladys), Ernest Thesiger (Horace Femm), Eva Moore (Rebecca Femm), Raymond Massey (Philip Waverton), Gloria Stuart (Margaret Waverton), Elspeth [John] Dudgeon (Sir Roderick Femm), Brember Wills (Saul Femm).

> Horace Femm: "You must stay here. The misfortune is yours, not ours."
> Rebecca Femm: "No beds! They can't have beds!"
> Horace Femm: "As my sister *hints*, there are, I'm afraid, no beds."

SYNOPSIS

Traveling through the Welsh mountains during a violent rainstorm,[1] Philip and Margaret Waverton and their friend Mr. Penderel narrowly escape a mudslide and are forced to seek shelter from the battering storm at a large stone house owned and occupied by the bizarre Femm family. After meeting the nervous, disdainful Horace Femm, his partially deaf and fanatically religious spinster sister, Rebecca, and their mute "brute" of a butler, Morgan, they all sit down to a rather uncomfortable supper.

During the meal, two other unexpected guests are forced to invade this "benighted household," the bluff Sir William Porterhouse and his cheery friend, Miss Gladys Ducane, whose car has been smashed by a falling tree.

After dinner, they sit around the fire and each reveals something about themselves. Penderel's amusing demeanor hides a cynical aimlessness: "My trouble is I don't think enough things are worthwhile." Sir William admits, "I don't admire meself too much.... Once you've started making money it's hard to stop, especially if you're like me — there isn't much else you're good at." And Gladys confesses that her name isn't Ducane but Perkins. "These people here know a chorus girl when they see one —

and incidentally not a very good chorus girl at that."

Penderel and Gladys go off to the stables to retrieve a bottle of whiskey from the car, while Philip accompanies Horace upstairs to find an oil lamp, and Sir William goes to Rebecca's room to help shut a window (which Margaret had left open earlier after a frightful encounter with Rebecca). Seeing Margaret alone in the parlor, a drunken Morgan attacks her. Philip returns, however, and fights him off, knocking the brute unconscious with the lamp. Philip then tells his wife of "a voice calling from behind a door upstairs, a tiny voice rather like a child's," and the two go to investigate. Opening the mysterious door, they find Sir Roderick Femm, aged 102, bedridden but still lucid. He tells the visitors that "this is an unlucky house ... we are all touched with [madness] a little, you see." Sir Roderick tells of the one Femm they have not yet met — Saul. "Saul is the worst, you know. He just wants to destroy, to kill." Saul is kept locked behind a double-bolted door at the very top of the house, tended to only by Morgan. If he managed to get out, relays Sir Roderick, "Saul would quite certainly set fire to the house," making it "a burnt offering."

Philip and Margaret leave the old man only to find Morgan gone from where he had lain at the foot of the stairs. Horace steps out from his room and tells them, "He's gone to let Saul out. Wait for him downstairs and kill him," then disappears back into his sanctuary.

As Philip informs the others about Saul, a hand appears on the banister above them — Saul's hand. Just then Morgan advances down the stairs and attacks the men. As Philip, Penderel, and Sir William wrestle the drunken butler into the kitchen, a scream from the two remaining women draws Penderel back to the parlor. Rebecca locks the door after him and scurries off to the safety of her bedroom. Penderel subsequently locks Gladys and Margaret in a large cupboard and faces the madman alone. Instead of a hulking maniac, however, Penderel sees only a small frightened man, a victim imprisoned by his own family simply for knowing that "they killed their sister, Rachel," as Saul tells it. But Saul's timidity is only a mask and soon gives way to an obvious madness. As Penderel nervously tries to humor him, Saul tells of his passion for flame. Ultimately, Saul attacks Penderel and knocks him unconscious. Grabbing a burning log from the fireplace, Saul races to the second floor landing to set the curtains alight. Penderel awakens and rushes to stop the lunatic. In the struggle, the two topple from the balcony, and both lie still. Morgan escapes his two remaining captors and breaks through the door into the parlor. Hearing the two women in the cupboard, Morgan releases them. After knocking Gladys unconscious, he advances on Margaret. Pointing out Penderel and Saul lying motionless on the floor, she pleads, "He's hurt!. I've got to look after him and the other man too — Saul." At that, Morgan turns and rushes to the prostrate forms. Pushing Penderel's body aside, he takes Saul into his arms, cradling the dead form before lifting the body and carrying it gently away. Finally, Philip and Sir William break through into the parlor as well. When they revive Gladys, she rushes to Penderel.

In the morning the floods have subsided and the Wavertons can now take the car and fetch an ambulance for the injured Penderel. "Good bye," waves Horace from the doorway, "so happy to have met you." From an upstairs window, Rebecca only scowls. Inside the house, Penderel awakens with his bandaged head cradled in Gladys' lap. "Perkins," he says, "will you marry me?" They kiss.

MEMORABLE MOMENT

In a film so full of import that nearly every moment becomes a memorable one (so much so that repeat viewings are necessary to fully absorb it all), one sequence surely stands out as the picture's signature scene. It occurs when Rebecca takes Mrs. Waverton to her room so the young woman can change out of her wet things. There the dour old woman tells of her sister Rachel who died in this room and of her wicked family. "They were all godless here," pronounces Rebecca sourly, "they used to bring their women here." At this the scene cuts from

The brutish Morgan (Boris Karloff) eyes the beautiful Margaret (Gloria Stuart) with menacing interest in *The Old Dark House* (1932).

Rebecca sitting on the edge of the bed to a shot of her face in a mirror, the image slightly askew as she continues her tirade. "Brazen, lolling creatures in silks and satins. They filled the house with laughter and sin, laughter and sin." Here the picture cuts to a close-up of Rebecca, her witchlike profile lit so that only her shadowy face stands out from the blackness around her. "And if I ever went down among them," she continues, "my own father and brothers, they would tell *me* to go away and pray." An abrupt cut shows her profile in the mirror, though now greatly distorted in the angled, beveled glass, as she continues, "They wouldn't tell Rachel to go away and pray — heh heh heh heh heh." Throughout the scene the isolating lighting and disintegrating imagery mirrors (literally) Rebecca's own distorted mind. But it is not over yet. As Margaret strips off her wet clothes, Rebecca circles her, looking her up and down. "You're wicked too," she pronounces, "young and handsome, silly and wicked. You think of nothing but your long straight legs and your white body and how to please your man. You revel in the joys of fleshly love — don't you!" Grabbing up a fold of the satiny gown Margaret has slipped over her head, Rebecca fingers the smooth material. "That's fine stuff," she observes, "and it'll rot." Pointing a gnarled finger at the young woman's chest, she accuses, "That's finer stuff still, but it'll rot *too* in time." With that, she places her hand abruptly on the young woman's breastbone. "Don't!" shouts the shocked Mrs. Waverton, backing away, "How dare you?!" A knock dispels the tension and as Rebecca exits, she pauses just a moment to adjust her hair in the mirror before leaving, ending this interpersonal nightmare with a brilliant touch of ironic (and illuminating) humor.

ASSETS

Of all the Golden Age horror films, *The Old Dark House* may be the most difficult to analyze, simply because it draws the viewer in so completely that one quickly loses any sense of detachment while watching, becoming so embroiled in the mood and the characters that a dispassionate third person analysis becomes difficult. While *The Old Dark House* is the least *seen* of James Whale's horror quartet (the others being *Frankenstein*, 1931; *The Invisible Man*, 1933; and *Bride of Frankenstein*, 1935), it is by no means the least. More than any other picture from the Golden Age of Horror, *The Old Dark House* improves with each successive screening. Its potent atmosphere, perverse humor, thematic depth and, above all, richness in character reward repeat viewings.

"In *The Old Dark House*, Whale presented what is perhaps his finest personal distillation of the bizarre," wrote Roy Edwards in *Sight and Sound* (Autumn 1957) shortly after the director's death. Indeed. James Whale places a cadre of talented actors within the confines of Benn Levy's penetrating script to create the finest, wittiest, most effective character study of horror's Golden Age.

For a setting, art director Charles D. Hall's Old Dark House itself is a wonderfully ominous structure, its interior dominated by a huge, forbidding staircase that branches off in two directions, adding an almost Lady-or-the-Tiger ambiance. The banister's long, pointed, spearlike balustrades bespeaks of imminent danger. Whale uses the sets, particularly the staircase, as a brush with which to paint his study of eccentricity and outright madness. When Philip and Horace are sent by Rebecca to fetch an oil lamp from the top landing after the lights have failed, Horace ducks out at the second floor, obviously terrified of continuing on up to the top. Philip goes on alone, armed only with a single inadequate candle. The camera follows behind him as he mounts the dark staircase. The stairs make a slight turn so that the dreaded landing abruptly comes into view above. At that very instant, a flash of lightning from an unseen window makes the landing seem to glow eerily, our angle of vision turning the space into the gaping maw of a tunnel. Philip stops, momentarily startled — as are we, following close behind. Through the use of sets, lighting, camera movement, and sound (nothing is heard except the howling wind outside and Philip's solitary footsteps), Whale creates a startling moment of unease and tension — one of many.

Even during simple scenes, Whale brilliantly joins the many disparate elements at his disposal into an atmospheric whole. Towards the beginning, when Penderel mentions casually that "the road below is underwater and for that matter this place itself may be underwater soon or even buried," Horace abruptly drops the vase he'd been holding which shatters violently, the harsh sound startling in the silence. Whale then cuts to a close-up of the shards at Horace's feet and then quickly pans upward, moving up his body to stop on Thesiger's anxious, almost panicked visage and nervously wringing hands. The lighting is such that the black background and Horace's dark clothing make Thesiger's cadaverous white face and bony hands stand out starkly, accentuating the character's isolation and fear. Then Horace turns suddenly and moves to his sister, his eyes darting like a startled bird. "We're trapped, we're trapped!" he quails. "You're afraid Horace," answers Rebecca contemptuously. "You're afraid aren't you. You don't believe in God and yet you're afraid to die." Eva Moore's hard voice quickens with the strength of fanaticism, "You've seen His anger in the sky and you've heard Him in the night, and you're afraid — afraid — afraid." Through lighting, sound, acting, and dialogue, Whale constructs moment after exquisite moment of moody fascination and character revelation.

Working with cinematographer Arthur Edeson (*Frankenstein*, *The Invisible Man*), Whale uses lighting and movement to heighten a mood or highlight a character. For Horace Femm's pivotal introduction, for example, Edeson's camera, stationed below, tracks forward as Ernest Thesiger descends the stairs, making his approach seem quicker than normal. The low angle of the camera and Horace's unhurried yet unnaturally rapid advance accentuate the unease inspired by Thesiger's sharp features and bony countenance. (Aided by Jack Pierce's dark makeup around the actor's eyes, Edeson's lighting nearly makes of Thesiger's visage a living death's head.) Then, as Horace pauses at the bottom of the stairs to make his introduction, the rippling shadow of heat waves rising from the room's huge fireplace plays on the wall behind him, adding an almost Mephistophalean touch to the moment. (Whale utilized this same satanic-shadow technique for Thesiger three years later when he played Dr. Pretorius in *Bride of Frankenstein*.)

Rich in thematics, *The Old Dark House* (under Whale's direction) takes a satirical swipe at religion. Here, however, unlike his near-random mockery in *Bride of Frankenstein*, the director does so with purpose. Through Rebecca Femm, Whale exposes the traps of dogma and hypocrisy. Rebecca has become a sour, embittered old woman who clings to her rituals yet has dispensed with the feeling behind them. She has twisted religion to suit her own dour personality. After chastising Horace for his "blaspheming" when she orders him to hold his hungry hand until after she's said grace, her subsequent benediction is delivered impossibly fast and without inflection—a mere ritual without meaning. Throughout the perfunctory prayer, her sour, bored expression never alters, and upon her abrupt conclusion she reaches for the bread without pause. Earlier, Rebecca had lectured Mrs. Waverton about the evils of vanity and "fleshly love," but, upon exiting the room, the old dowager pauses just a moment to adjust her hair in the mirror before leaving, her own sense of vanity exposing the hollow sanctimony of her words. With Saul Femm, Whale seemingly ties religion to outright madness. "Did you know my name is *Saul*," asks the madman of Penderel, while fingering a large knife. "Saul, my friend—and Saul *loved* David. But Saul was afraid of David because the Lord was with him and was departed from Saul.... And there was a javelin in Saul's hand and Saul *cast* the javelin." At this, Saul stabs his knife into the table in front of Penderel with a startling thud. "—and he said I will smite David even to the wall with this." And smite this lunatic does, hurling the weapon to imbed itself in the wall mere inches from Penderel's head. Through Saul's identification with the biblical tale, Whale uses dialogue and characterization to link religious mania to homicidal insanity.

Beyond such religious revelations, *The Old Dark House* explores the broader theme of hidden nature. So much lurks below the surface of this "benighted household," that one fairly gets lost in a miasma of uneasiness and half-revealed truths. From the very beginning, when Horace Femm picks up a bouquet and explains "My sister was on the point of arranging these flowers" before tossing them into the fireplace, the viewer senses that unhealthy undercurrents simply rage beneath the exterior of this bizarre family. Ultimately, it becomes clear that none of these strange characters are quite what they seem. Horace Femm's disdainful imperiousness masks a sniveling cowardice. As discussed, Rebecca Femm's religious mania (not to mention her *selective* deafness) hides a self-serving hypocrisy. Morgan, the focus of menace for much of the film, turns out to be a relatively benign force (Saul's handler in fact), or at worst a rather ambivalent danger. No character, however, brings the concept so powerfully home as Saul. After giving the unseen Femm a tremendous buildup (a glimpse of Saul's double-locked door, Horace's obvious terror at even approaching Saul's room, and even Rebecca seeming to quail at the idea of Saul set loose), Whale completely confounds the viewer's expectations. Nothing presented could possibly fulfill our anticipation of this fearsome creature, so Whale cleverly takes another tact. Saul's introduction begins suspensefully enough (further whetting the viewer's appetite) with a hand coming into view on the banister—and nothing more. Then, after the men have muscled Morgan away into the kitchen and Penderel is left alone to face the unseen horror that is *Saul*, the unmoving hand finally advances. But out of the shadows emerges not a ghastly, hulking maniac, but a small, timid man, whose frightened eyes dart about anxiously. Coming down the stairs, he jumps back in fear at Penderel's approach. "Please, please, don't touch me," he

Those trapped in *The Old Dark House* anxiously await the approach of the madman, Saul. From left to right: Charles Laughton, Gloria Stuart, Lillian Bond, Eva Moore, Raymond Massey, Melvyn Douglas.

pleads. "Listen, don't put me back," he implores, "Don't let them put me back. I'm not mad, I swear before heaven I'm not mad. It's just that they've locked me up, here. They're all wicked." When Penderel asks why they imprisoned him, he answers, "They're frightened of me; I know something about them. Years ago they killed their sister Rachel." He continues, almost in tears, wailing, "Morgan—I tell you he's the devil. Morgan *beats* me." Just as we begin to believe that this poor wretch is indeed the victim of his mad siblings, his expression changes. He slowly tilts his head, his gaze intensifies, and a cruel smile turns up the corner of his mouth, while a dry, unhealthy, barely audible laugh reveals Saul's madness. With a start we see his true nature cut through his masklike exterior. Obviously, you can't judge a madman by his cover. Whale has pulled yet another switch, lulling us into a false security with Saul's benign surface only to subsequently intensify the terror by abruptly pulling the thematic rug out from under us.

Whale expands this theme of deception further, going beyond a single individual to encompass whole situations. When Mrs.

Waverton, after the frightening encounter with Rebecca in the old woman's bedroom, races in near hysteria back to the parlor, Mr. Penderel sees the beautiful gown she's changed into and remarks cheerily, "Good for you, Mrs. Waverton, you make it look like a party," totally oblivious to the barely-contained consternation on her face. Through this juxtaposition, Whale underscores the irony of surface illusion (echoing Horace's earlier toast, "I give you — illusion"), the idea of superficial gloss obscuring a very different nature underneath — in this case the nature of a situation.

The acting in *The Old Dark House* is strictly top-drawer. Ernest Thesiger's waspish Horace Femm, Eva Moore's sour Rebecca, Brember Wills' changeable, psychotic Saul, and even Elspeth Dudgeon's ancient, bedridden Sir Roderick all come fascinatingly alive through the actors' quirky performances. The remainder of the cast perform nobly as well, their diverse portrayals providing stark contrast to the frightful Femm family. Though Universal awarded Boris Karloff top billing and promoted *The Old Dark House* as a follow-up Whale/Karloff vehicle to *Frankenstein*, the actor really plays a secondary (though still important) role in Morgan. More of a physical, menacing presence than a fully rounded personality, Karloff still manages to imbue the brutish butler with human qualities. The climax sees Karloff stealing the show as he cradles his dead friend's head on his breast, gently rocking back and forth while sobbing softly in a touching display of emotion.

LIABILITIES

None. Though it may not measure up to the loud exuberance of *King Kong* or the flashy brilliance of *Bride of Frankenstein*, *The Old Dark House* remains the one truly flawless picture from the Golden Age of Horror.

REVIEWS

Variety's "Abel" (November 1, 1932) was unimpressed, calling it "a somewhat inane picture." Of course, this particular reviewer had no time for horror films, nor did he think too highly of their audience. It is unfortunate that so many reviewers of the time took this holier-than-thou attitude and generally dismissed the blossoming horror genre — and its audience — out of hand.

The reviewer for *Film Weekly* (October 21, 1932) shared Abel's disdain for the horror product (as well as his appreciation of the fine cast), though he seemed to be more receptive to the offbeat storyline: "The vexed question of the horror film again rears its ugly head (and rears is the word) with the arrival this weekend of the latest James Whale–Boris Karloff excursion into the realms of the unnatural. To give them their due, Messrs. Whale and Karloff have progressed since the day when they dabbled in the crude though diverting sensations of *Frankenstein*. There is a new and welcome restraint about their work in the respective roles of director and star. They have the advantages, moreover, of a story which does not depend entirely on lurid thrills (J. B. Priestly's *Benighted*), and of a supporting cast composed of as fine a company of players as one could wish to see in any picture."

Harrison's Reports, however, was openly enthusiastic: "This should certainly please the followers of horror melodramas for it has everything to send chills up one's spine.... The individual performances are so excellent that the story is believable."

PRODUCTION NOTES

Though Benn Levy, a London playwright friend of James Whale, received sole screenplay credit for *The Old Dark House*, several other writers worked on the script as well. F. Hugh Herbert had provided a framework through an early, incomplete draft while Jack B. Clymer made a few revisions to Levy's screenplay (as did Whale). When shooting began in April 1932, Levy had returned to England so Whale's friend R. C. Sherriff provided whatever on-set dialogue adjustments were needed.

The Old Dark House marked Charles Laughton's American film debut, though this was something of a surprise to the actor himself. He had originally journeyed from England to star in *The Devil and the Deep* for

Paramount, but when Laughton arrived he found that the script was not yet ready, so the studio loaned him out to Universal for this James Whale production (at Whale's request). "Charles was very pleased to get the camera experience for the larger part to come [in *The Devil and the Deep*]," remembered his wife, Elsa Lanchester, in *Charles Laughton and I*. "He knew he had to bridge a large technical gap in one giant stride." While Laughton quickly grasped the difference in playing on stage and on screen, he "at first suffered agonies in controlling his gestures." Though appreciating the chance to develop his film acting in "a small part" at Universal before being thrust into the spotlight at Paramount, Laughton wasn't completely satisfied with his debut vehicle. "Paramount pushed Charles into the arrangement on the condition that *The Devil and the Deep* would be released first," wrote Elsa Lanchester in *Elsa Lanchester, Herself*. "[When it wasn't,] Charles was very irritated." This irritation extended to the picture's cast as well, according to Laughton biographer Simon Callow[2]: "Laughton had no very warm feelings for any of the cast (though of course he had previously been directed by,[3] and was later himself to direct, Raymond Massey). He never cared for Karloff..."

Co-star Raymond Massey also made his American film debut in *The Old Dark House* (as did both Ernest Thesiger and Eva Moore). A respected stage actor and director, Universal originally signed Massey as a writer/director (despite no motion picture experience in either of these), with no mention of acting in his contract. After a number of fruitless, wasted weeks in his guise as writer, Junior Laemmle finally assigned him to *The Old Dark House*—as an *actor*. Massey realized his was the least interesting role in the picture, calling it a "colorless juvenile part," but having signed the rather ambiguous contract with Universal, he buckled down and made the best of it. Of the picture itself, Massey felt that "It turned out to be a good one," though he admitted, "Or so I was told. I never saw it" (from his autobiography, *A Hundred Different Lives*). Throughout most of the picture, Massey was hiding a bandaged finger. About a week into filming, the actor broke up a fight between two small dogs at a cocktail party, with the end result being that the tip of the second finger of his left hand was bitten off at the base of the nail. "Gary Cooper found the missing fingertip at once," related Massey in his autobiography. "'Get a cocktail glass and put it in,'" [Dr.] Sam [Hirshfield] said. 'I've got some alcohol in my bag.' Sam did a deft job of cauterizing and fixing me up, assisted by Justine Wanger. 'It's a good thing that little beast wasn't hungry,' he said. 'Now, where's that glass, Coop?' Gary Cooper looked embarrassed. 'The bartender says he threw a half-finished Gibson down the drain. That must have been it.'"

Playing the "savage brute" Morgan, *The Old Dark House* was Karloff's first horror film after *Frankenstein* (1931), and Universal was quick to play up their new horror star in their publicity. The studio even tacked on this caption at the film's beginning: "PRODUCER'S NOTE: Karloff, the mad butler in this production is the same Karloff who created the part of the mechanical monster in 'Frankenstein'. We explain this to settle all disputes in advance, even though such disputes are a tribute to his great versatility." Though not his first starring role (*Frankenstein* provided him with that), *The Old Dark House* was the first film to give the actor top star billing (he was billed fourth in *Frankenstein*). Like Raymond Massey, Karloff also realized the picture's excellence. "I haven't seen it in years," the actor told director Curtis Harrington in 1968, "but that *was* a good film."[4]

On the British stage from age 14, Lillian Bond came to Hollywood in 1926 where she made over two score films until her final screen bow in the mid-fifties. In 1935 she married millionaire Sidney Smith, but continued her acting career. She appeared in one other horror classic, *The Picture of Dorian Gray* (1945), as well as two lesser (but still solid) entries of the 1950s: *The Maze* (1953) and *Man in the Attic* (1954).

Eva Moore (Rebecca Femm), a former London stage beauty, was the mother of Jill Esmond, Lawrence Olivier's first wife. "She

Mourning the death of his charge, Morgan (Boris Karloff) carries off the lifeless body of Saul (Brenber Wills) while Sir William (Charles Laughton) and Philip (Raymond Massey) look on.

was lovely," remembered co-star Gloria Stuart, "she was a wonderful actress." James Whale used her again for *Bride of Frankenstein*. (When editing necessitated the shooting of one additional sequence to bridge a continuity gap, Whale cast Moore as an old pipe-smoking gypsy woman.)

The Old Dark House is one of only four film appearances by British stage actor Brember Wills (who played the dangerous Saul to such chilling effect). Undoubtedly, Wills' participation was expedited by James Whale's theatrical background and reputation.

The role of the 102-year-old family patriarch, Sir Roderick Femm, was actually played by a *woman*, a 60-year-old actress named Elspeth Dudgeon (who graciously accepted a billing of "*John* Dudgeon" in the film's credits to uphold the charade.) Whale kept his little casting joke secret even from his players. "We all thought that James Whale had a man stuck up there," remembered Gloria Stuart. "None of the scenes with her were shot with other actors around and we didn't know it until about the cast party. And it was James' secret and he enjoyed it." *The Old Dark House* marked the sexagenarian stage actress's (credited) screen debut.[5] Ms. Dudgeon made more than 35 subsequent pictures over the following two decades, including the borderline horror entry, *Sh! The Octopus* (1937).

Gloria Stuart remembers *The Old Dark House* as her favorite of the three Golden Age horror pictures she made (the other two being *The Invisible Man* and *Secret of the Blue Room*, both 1933). In 1993, she commented on how very British the production seemed. "Melvyn Douglas [a last minute replacement for Russell Hopton], and I were the only two Americans. I remember the first day on the set at 11 o'clock the prop man brought in tea and it was spread out and all the English, including our director, sat down and had "elevenses" and left Melvyn and me on the sidelines.... They were very very clannish. They were very nice but very clannish." The leader of this clan was not Whale, according to Ms. Stuart: "I would say it was Ernest Thesiger. He was the oldest one and a brilliant character actor, brilliant."

Ms. Stuart had nothing but praise for her English director: "I consider James probably the top director in Hollywood. He had a very unfortunate career that went downhill after four or five brilliant films like *Frankenstein* and *The Old Dark House*. He was the most meticulous of all the men that I worked for. He would come on in the morning, and he has plotted all of the camera moves, where everyone is going to be, how long the scene should take and so on and so forth. He went over it with you as an actress, and with the cameraman, and with the prop man; he went over every prop on the set, where it was, why it was, so forth and so on. For example, he put me in what we used to call a Jean Harlow dress—a biased-cut, pale pink, satin velvet dress, sheath, with spaghetti straps, crystal earrings, pearls. And I said to him, 'James, we just arrived an hour ago sopping wet in the wind and the mud. Nobody else is dressed, they're all still wet and muddy at the dinner. Why me, why do I get dressed?' He didn't like to be questioned. He said, 'Because that's the way I feel.' And I said, 'But James, *why*?' And he said, '*Because*, Gloria, Boris is going to chase you up and down the corridors and I want you to appear like a white flame.'"

In his later years, James Whale was rather self-effacing about his film work. In 1951 the British Film Institute honored Whale by producing a tribute to the director at which they screened *The Old Dark House*. Curtis Harrington, a friend of Whale's, accompanied the guest of honor: "I remember sitting there and watching the scene where Eva Moore talks and her face becomes more and more distorted with those wonderful cuts. That was very imaginative filmmaking, and I would say to him, 'Oh, that's so wonderful, Jimmy.' And he would sit there and say, 'Don't you think it's a little dated and kind of corny?'" (from *James Whale*, by James Curtis).

As with all of Universal's Golden Age horror pictures, Jack Pierce provided the makeup.

"He was very fussy—a martinet," recalled Gloria Stuart, "enormously talented and liked his way of doing it." Pierce naturally was much more interested in the unusual character makeups for Karloff and Wills and co. than in the glamour makeup for the women. "In those days I was very young," remembered Gloria Stuart, "and I figured ... it's not going to be 45 minutes in the chair with Jack. So I said to him very early on, 'Jack, I think I can do my own makeup.' He said, 'Be my guest.' So I put my own makeup on all the rest of the time. But he was wonderful with Karloff and Claude [Rains (in *The Invisible Man*)] and the others. He was great with men. He didn't really want to work with women."

William Castle remade *The Old Dark House* in 1963 for Hammer Films as an (abysmal) straightforward comedy. Boris Karloff was approached to star in it but turned it down. As he told William F. Nolan in *Famous Monsters of Filmland* (April, 1963): "The new version was simply not to my liking. I sent back the script. Wanted no part in it. After all, I've been in the acting profession for more than half a century. High time to pick and choose my vehicles."

NOTES

1. Of this opening sequence, actress Gloria Stuart remembered: "It was shot on the back lot from about six o'clock [in the evening] until about five the next morning, with wind machines and rain machines and mud machines—close-ups and longshots. It was my first experience on what we call location and it was horrendous. They wrapped us in blankets in-between each shot, with portable heaters and so on."
2. Simon Callow, as well as being a writer, is an accomplished actor/director in his own right, appearing in such films as *Amadeus* and *A Room with a View*.
3. A play entitled *The Silver Tassie*.
4. From *Close-Ups: The Movie Star Book*, edited by Danny Peary. Curtis Harrington was responsible for finding *The Old Dark House* (then considered a lost film) in 1966 and arranging for its restoration.
5. Ms. Dudgeon appeared briefly (and uncredited) in *Murders in the Rue Morgue* (1932) as a riverbank crone who, when the gendarmes pull a woman's corpse from the water, sagely observes, "Life is hard. The river is *kind*. The river is *soft*. It rocks them to sleep, heh heh heh heh, and asks no pay."

THE MASK OF FU MANCHU
(1932; MGM)

Release Date: November 5, 1932
Running Time: 72 minutes
Director: Charles Brabin
Screenplay: Irene Kuhn, Edgar Allan Woolf, and John Willard (from the story by Sax Rohmer)
Photography: Tony Gaudio
Art Director: Cedric Gibbons
Editor: Ben Lewis
Recording Director: Douglas Shearer
Gowns: Adrian
Cast: Boris Karloff (Dr. Fu Manchu), Lewis Stone (Nayland Smith), Karen Morley (Sheila), Charles Starrett (Terrence Granville), Myrna Loy (Fah Lo See), Jean Hersholt (Von Berg), Lawrence Grant (Sir Lionel Barton), David Torrence (McLeod).

"Should Fu Manchu put that mask across his wicked eyes and take that scimitar into his bony cruel hands, all Asia rises!"—Nayland Smith.

SYNOPSIS

In London, Sir Lionel Barton is planning an archeological expedition to search for the hidden tomb of Genghis Kahn, located "on the edge of the Gobi desert." Sir Nayland Smith of the British Secret Service (and also a friend of Sir Lionel) summons the archeologist to warn him of the evil Asian villain Fu Manchu's interest in the expedition. "Sir Lionel," Nayland tells him, "you *must* find that tomb, we cannot allow for any failures. And you must be the *first* to find it." He goes on to warn that if Fu Manchu should obtain the sacred sword and mask of Genghis Kahn, "he'll declare himself Genghis Kahn come to life again, and he'll lead hundreds of millions of men to sweep the world." But before Sir Lionel can begin the expedition he disappears, kidnapped by Fu Manchu's men.

Nayland Smith induces Sir Lionel's associates, Von Berg and McLeod, to go through with the planned expedition anyway and attempt to locate the tomb before Fu Manchu can torture the secret of its location out of Sir Lionel.

Sir Lionel's daughter, Sheila, insists upon going along for she, along with her father, is privy to the tomb's location and can be of great value to the expedition. While Fu Manchu indeed tortures Sir Lionel, the British party succeeds in their quest and retrieves the sacred sword and mask of Genghis Kahn. Smith then journeys from London to join the group, which is secretly camped at a local abandoned compound. Several of Fu's agents steal into the house to try to obtain the sword and mask, but are unsuccessful.

The following day, a severed human hand is thrown over the wall, and on its finger is a ring belonging to Sir Lionel. A messenger (a servant of Fu Manchu) knocks at the gate and instructs Terry Granville (Sheila's fiancé and a member of the expedition) to bring the sword and mask to a certain nearby shop. At Sheila's hysterical urgings, Terry agrees to go—without telling Smith. He takes the relics to Fu Manchu, but, unknown to Terry, Nayland had substituted duplicates of the mask and sword before leaving England. Fu discovers the fakes and, in a rage, hands Terry over to his daughter for torture (and worse, for it seems the sadistic, lascivious Fah Lo See has developed an unhealthy interest in the handsome Westerner).

Things look grim as Sir Lionel is unceremoniously dumped outside the compound—dead. Nayland follows one of Fu's minions to his secret lair, where he ends up as Fu's prisoner. Meanwhile, Terry is strapped to a table while Fu Manchu (in full surgeon's gown and mask) prepares a special drug. "This serum," explains Fu Manchu, "distilled from dragon's blood, my own blood, the organs of different reptiles, and mixed with the magic brew of the sacred seven herbs will temporarily change you into the living instrument of my will. You will do as I command!"

Fu, now in complete control of Terry,

sends him back to the camp in order to lure the others into a trap. The ploy works and the real sword and mask are now in the hands of the dreaded Fu Manchu, as are Sheila, Terry, Smith, and Von Berg. Fu sends them off to their various tortures while "the new Genghis Kahn" makes his plans to sweep the world with his "teeming hordes." While Fu Manchu, wearing the mask and wielding the sword, incites his collected group of Asian leaders and warriors into a bloodlust frenzy ("Conquer and breed! Kill the white man and take his women!"), Nayland manages to break his bonds and helps to free Terry and Von Berg.

The three discover Fu's secret weapon — a death-ray machine capable of delivering "a million volts." They turn it on the screaming warriors as Terry rushes in and slays Fu Manchu with the villain's own sword just as Fu Manchu is about to use it to sacrifice Sheila.

On the boat back to England, they dump the relics into the sea. As Smith states: "We cannot afford to take any chances. There may be other Fu Manchus in the future." (For MGM, at least, this did not turn out to be the case).

MEMORABLE MOMENTS

"The Frankenstein of the Orient" (as Metro's publicity labeled the nefarious Fu Manchu) received an appropriately sinister and very memorable introduction in *The Mask of Fu Manchu*. The first time we see Fu, his evil visage is huge and distorted, reflected in a large curved mirror. The sadistic villain is drinking some kind of bubbling potion and smiling evilly, with electricity crackling noisily in the background and sinister shadows playing across his face. It is a startling vision and truly a fitting introduction to one of the most loathsome madmen ever to cross the screens of the Golden Age.

A rather tasteless but effective moment comes when the expedition enters the undisturbed tomb of Genghis Kahn and finds the skeleton of the great warrior seated upon a regal throne. The camera closes in on the skeletal legs and then pans upwards to show the sword laid across the bony knees. Then it moves up to the grinning skull, wearing an exquisitely-carved gold mask. When Terry removes the mask, a large black spider crawls out from one of the empty eye sockets — a chilling and rather gruesome sight for that time.

Whenever Boris Karloff as the wicked Fu Manchu is onscreen, there are memorable moments aplenty. One in particular comes early on, when Fu tortures Sir Lionel in an effort to obtain the secret of the tomb's location. Strapped underneath a gigantic bell, Sir Lionel listens as Fu asks, "Seems harmless doesn't it? Just a bell ringing. But the percussion and the repercussion of sound against your eardrums will soften and destroy them until the sound is magnified a thousand times." This last is said with a cheerful smile and with almost good-humored anticipation in his voice.

Smiling cruelly, Fu continues: "You can't move, you can't sleep. You will be frantic with thirst, you will be unspeakably foul." Fu's smile disappears and his voice hardens. "But here you will lie day after day until you tell." Then, for good measure, Fu brings a bowl of fruit and sadistically waves a luscious bunch of grapes over the face of the suffering Sir Lionel. Later he returns again, this time with a goblet of cool water.

As he stops the maddening ringing of the bell, Fu lovingly strokes Sir Lionel's brow with his long, bony fingers. "Rest and quiet," he promises, and smiles. "Now for a nice long drink," he says, gently holding Sir Lionel's head up to the cup. The desperately thirsty man drinks, then suddenly turns his head away in renewed torment. Fu laughs wickedly. "Oh, I forgot to tell you," he says with mock remorse. "It was *salt*." "Fiend," gasps the weakened Sir Lionel, and the audience can only agree.

ASSETS

The first thing to strike the viewer about *The Mask of Fu Manchu* are the lavish sets and costumes, which MGM was able to bestow upon this "A" production with its usual glitter and polish.

The beautiful, exotic Asian gowns worn by Fu's daughter are only surpassed in splendor by those flowing garments worn by Fu Manchu himself. The huge, modernistic, almost art deco sets of Fu's laboratory and operating theater contrast sharply with the myriad snakes, spiders, and assorted vermin he keeps within them. As Fu Manchu, Boris Karloff (borrowed from Universal at a $3,500 fee) gives a larger-than-life portrayal of the sadistic, brilliant villain. With his false smiles, wicked dialogue delivery, and frequently sinister (almost perverse) gestures, he creates an unforgettably vile creature. Unlike many of Karloff's characters, Fu is thoroughly evil. He does not have a good side. He is not an innocent gone bad through no fault of his own (as in *Frankenstein*), nor is he a dedicated scientist transformed by vengeance into a madman (à la *The Invisible Ray* or *The Man They Could Not Hang*). Karloff's Fu Manchu is simply a sadistic beast, whose thin veneer of education and civility makes it all the more startling when it drops away to reveal the brutal megalomaniac underneath.

Karloff, who can be both subtle and broad in his acting technique, was a perfect choice for this larger-than-life villain. His wonderful dialogue delivery (one of his true strengths as an actor) serves him well as he invests each delightful line with sinister nuances. (Fu Manchu is the first leading horror role in which Karloff exercised his excellent command of dialogue, since his two previous major parts, in *Frankenstein* [1931] and *The Old Dark House* [1932], are mute.) When Fu Manchu tells the captive Terry of his plans to inject him with a mind-controlling serum, he states (with sinister amusement): "I am only going to give you the smallest amount which will pass off in a short time, because I want you to be your very self when I hand you over to my *gentle* daughter." Karloff's subtle emphasis on the word gentle leaves no doubt as to the diabolical double-meaning he's invested in that innocuous word. Later, Fu holds a gun on the captured Nayland Smith and tells him, "Why, my dear Sir Nayland Smith, I will show you the sword myself ... just before I dispatch you to your cold, saintly *Christian paradise*." Karloff begins the line with good-humored civility and ends with a withering tone of sarcastic contempt.

Of course, it helps Karloff's performance greatly that he has so many juicy lines to work with. Screenwriters Irene Kuhn, Edgar Allan Woolf, and John Willard have invested their admittedly flawed screenplay with enough witty and shocking lines to delight the ears nearly as much as the lavish sets and costumes delight the eyes. Some choice dialogue: When Sir Lionel, outraged at being kidnapped, snaps "You're Fu Manchu aren't you?" the poised villain responds, "I'm a doctor of philosophy from Edinburgh, I'm a doctor of law from Christ College, I am a doctor of medicine from Harvard. My friends, out of courtesy, call me 'doctor.'" Later, when Fu takes Nayland unawares, he warns, "The slightest move will send a bullet crashing through your *stiff British spine*."

Myrna Loy, as Fu's sadistic, lascivious daughter Fah Lo See, provides a perfect complement to Karloff's Fu Manchu. This "worthless daughter," as Fu calls her, is a chip off the old block when it comes to torture and cruelty, with an added bit of perverted nymphomania thrown in for good measure. Loy's exotic beauty (highlighted by the Asian makeup she wears) and cruel half-smile serve her well in the role. When she first sees the handsome Terry, the wicked expression on her face lets one almost see the blood quicken in her icy veins. "The whip!" she orders, barely able to control herself in delicious anticipation. Then, as the whip is applied, she trembles and cries out in an almost orgasmic shudder, shouting "Faster, faster, faster, faster!" before finally grabbing the whip herself to apply it first-hand in an uncontrollable burst of frenzied sado-sexuality.

Not the least of this film's assets (some would say) are the tortures and brutal episodes which run throughout this rather daring production and which give it much of its exciting, lurid (and, others would say, exploitative) appeal.

Evil incarnate: Boris Karloff at work as the diabolical Fu Manchu. (Courtesy of Ted Okuda.)

The film is filled with vicious tortures (Sir Lionel becoming "frantic with thirst [and] unspeakably foul" under the torture of The Bell; Nayland Smith strapped to one end of a monstrous teeter-totter with the sand running out on the other end, lowering him head-downwards into a pit of hungry alligators; Von Berg held between two walls of sharp spikes moving ever closer and closer to his corpulent, sweating form) and shots of creeping spiders and slithering snakes. Couple this with the general air of sadism exuded by the laughing Fu Manchu and the wanton sado-eroticism of his wicked daughter, and *The Mask of Fu Manchu* contains enough horrific sensationalism to keep most viewers engrossed. Whether this trait is an asset or a liability depends wholly on the sensibilities of the individual viewer, though credit should be given to production supervisor Hunt Stromberg and director Charles Brabin for courageously not pulling their punches to weaken the shock value, and for allowing their performers to play their parts to the fullest.

LIABILITIES

While *The Mask of Fu Manchu* is handsomely mounted, frequently shocking, and at times even thrilling, it is also a rather disappointing film overall. One of the picture's major problems is the overly-theatrical acting which permeates the production. While Fu Manchu is admittedly a larger-than-life character Karloff has the ability to combine subtlety with his grand acting style to keep this character rooted in reality and believable within the context of the film. Unfortunately, the same cannot be said for many of the other key players.

Lewis Stone is one dimensional as the no-nonsense Nayland Smith, and as such comes off as a humorless cardboard caricature — a disappointing adversary for such a fascinating villain as Karloff's Fu Manchu. Charles Starrett as Terry, the film's hero/love-interest, possesses a large bulk but no real physical presence. He is unconvincing, frequently overplaying his lines and emotions, and he produces one of the most lackluster fight scenes ever filmed (detailed below). But Karen Morley as Sheila is probably the biggest detraction. Her exaggerated acting, full of melodramatic hysterics and tearfully heartfelt speech, comes across as insipid and grating. It is unfortunate that two such wonderful (and delightfully wicked) performances as Karloff's and Loy's should be given such inadequate support.

A second disappointment is the "thrill-a-minute" cheap serial feel the film frequently exhibits. Filled with scientific gadgets, hordes of henchmen, and speeded-up fight scenes, this picture begins to resemble a sci-fi serial more than the lavish MGM production it truly is.

As mentioned above, the climax contains one of the most poorly staged and apathetic fight scenes ever filmed. As Terry is about to be strapped down for further ministrations of Fu's "serum," he breaks free and fights with two hulking black guards. His weak punches, feeble kicks, and pitiful flailing (often missing his target) wouldn't slow down a grammar-school bully, and yet the huge, muscular guards are laid low. (One would think that the rich and powerful Fu Manchu could find some better hired help!) To make matters worse, high-speed photography is employed to quicken the action at the fight's end, reinforcing the feeling of a crude (and poorly staged) serial cliffhanger.

A final (and perhaps most damning) criticism of *The Mask of Fu Manchu* is the overt racism which runs throughout the picture (a trait more insidious than Fu himself is purported to be). In this film, the "Eastern races" (as Nayland Smith once refers to Asians) are portrayed as either superstitious savages lusting after Caucasian blood and white women or comical dolts happily taking the brunt of an unkind joke. Lines like "A Chinaman beat me?—he couldn't do it!" or "You hideous yellow monster!" abound. And running throughout the film is an unhealthy vein of racial paranoia, a "Yellow Menace" panic. Admittedly, *The Mask of Fu Manchu* was filmed 60-odd years ago, before our country's "racial enlightenment" (such as it is), but there is still no excuse for such a blatantly racist attitude.

Despite these liabilities, *The Mask of Fu Manchu* is still a solid horror picture (containing two wonderfully wicked central performances [by Karloff and Loy] and enough lurid excitement for two such films) and one that is unafraid to take risks by serving up the horror in ample portions.

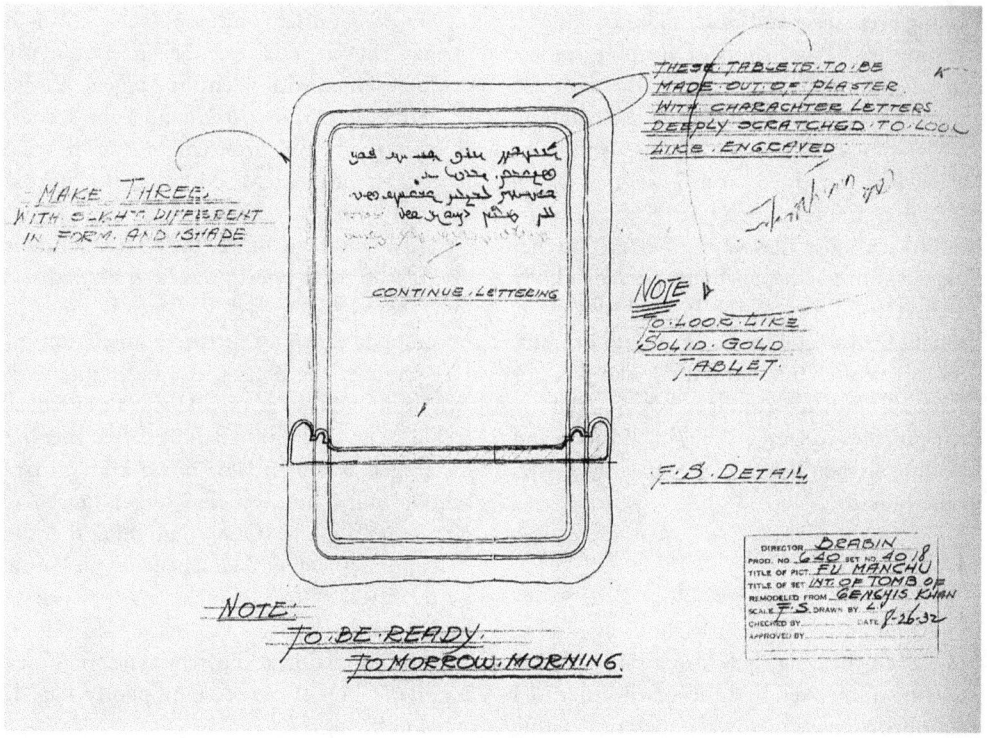

Prop design request for three gold tablets ("to be ready tomorrow morning"!) with which to dress the Tomb of Genghis Khan set in *The Mask of Fu Manchu* (1932). (Courtesy of Lynn Naron.)

REVIEWS

Variety's "Bige" (December 6, 1932) laughed off the proceedings as so much hoke, lamenting the horror emphasis and failing to appreciate either Karloff's or Loy's performance: "The diabolical stuff is piled on so thick at the finish, audiences are liable to laugh where they oughtn't. ... Everybody is handicapped by the story and situations."

The reviewer for *Film Weekly* (March 17, 1932), however, disagreed, calling the film "a blood and thunder thriller of nightmare dimensions." He went on to hail Karloff's terror talents: "Boris Karloff, the new Fu Manchu, is given every opportunity of living up to the reputation for frightfulness he has acquired in several horror films. Equipped with three-inch fingernails and a mustache which nearly meets below the chin, he is allowed to indulge in an orgy of organized torture that would have been the envy of any medieval monarch."

PRODUCTION NOTES

Early on in filming, this MGM production ran into some difficulties when the picture's original director, newcomer Charles Vidor (making only his second picture), was replaced by Charles Brabin and much of the footage already shot by Vidor was scrapped and reshot.

In the process, numerous changes were made. For instance, originally it was Nayland Smith (Lewis Stone) who was to be crushed between the two walls of spikes, not the rotund Von Berg (Jean Hersholt). Apparently, someone felt that a fat victim would be more horrific in this particular torture and so the corpulent actor Jean Hersholt was placed in this predicament, while the slender Lewis Stone was sent to the alligator pit.

Charles Brabin could certainly commiserate with the ousted Charles Vidor, having been the recipient of a similar humiliation (also inflicted by MGM!) on *Ben-Hur* (1926).

A scant year after *The Mask of Fu Manchu*, Brabin was once again on the receiving end of a pink slip when Metro removed him from *Rasputin and the Empress* (1932) and replaced him with director Richard Boleslawski. The following year, Brabin (only in his early fifties) said enough was enough and retired from films altogether, moving to Manhattan with his wife, former silent star Theda Bara.

Shooting from August 6 to October 21, 1932 (including a full month of "retakes and added scenes"), *The Mask of Fu Manchu* cost a hefty $327,600 to produce. Fiscally, it was worth it, for *Mask* turned a modest net profit of $62,000 for MGM.

In a 1959 radio interview,[1] Boris Karloff remembered the filming of *The Mask of Fu Manchu* as "a shambles" and "simply ridiculous."

The actor went on to note the frequent script changes that plagued the production: "I shall never forget, about a week before we started, I kept asking for a script—and I was met with roars of laughter at the idea that there would be a script. On the morning that we started shooting, I went into the makeup shop and worked there for about a couple of hours getting this extremely bad makeup on, as a matter of fact, for Fu Manchu. It was ridiculous. And, as I was in the makeup chair, a gentleman came in and handed me about four sheets of paper which was one enormous, long speech. That was to be the opening shot in the film and I was seeing it for the first time, then and there. It was written in the most impeccable English. Then, I said, 'This is absolute nonsense. I can't learn this in time to do it,' and he said, 'Well, it will be all right. Don't worry.' So I got my makeup on and, on my way to the stage from the makeup shop, I was intercepted by somebody else who took those pages away from me and gave me some others that were written in Pidgin English! They had about five writers on it and this was happening all through the film. Some scenes were written in beautiful Oxford English, others were written in—God knows what!"

According to Peter Underwood in his book *Karloff*, author Sax Rohmer (the creator of Fu Manchu), while never having seen the film, felt that "Boris Karloff would be an ideal choice for Fu Manchu." Arthur Sarsfield Ward (a.k.a. Sax Rohmer) first introduced his inscrutable villain Fu Manchu in a series of short stories published in a single volume in 1913. Rohmer wrote another 11 books featuring his Asian villain over the next four decades, earning an estimated two million dollars from these works alone (the Fu Manchu books were only a fraction of the prolific author's voluminous output).

Karloff's makeup took two and a half hours to apply, much of that time spent on creating his Asian eyes. This was not the first time Boris Karloff played an Oriental character (he was "Nikko," a Chinese tavern owner in *The Miracle Man* released earlier in 1932), nor was it the last. He donned the false eyelids again for *West of Shanghai* (1937) and the five "Mr. Wong" films for Monogram in which he played a Chinese sleuth.

Heroine Karen Morley (born Mildred Litton) secretly married Charles Vidor (the initial director ousted from *The Mask of Fu Manchu*) the same month in which the film was released. They were divorced in 1943. Ms. Morley was very active in left-wing causes and in 1951 was blacklisted when she invoked the Fifth Amendment before the House Un-American Activities Committee. She never worked in films again (her final big-screen appearance was in the 1951 remake of *M*). Three years later she turned to politics when she ran for the office of New York State's lieutenant governor on the American Labor Party ticket.

She did not win. Ms. Morley returned to acting briefly in the early 1970s as a regular on the short-lived television series, "Banyon," starring Robert Forster.

Oscar-nominated Lewis Stone (for *The Patriot*, 1928) became a full-time contract star at MGM in 1928 at the age of 50! On stage since before the turn of the century, Stone had been in motion pictures since 1915. Among his over 150 films are the silent Willis O'Brien dinosaur epic, *The Lost World* (1925), and the borderline Golden Age horror, *The Thirteenth*

Chair (1937). A veteran of both the Spanish-American War and World War I, the 73-year-old actor finally succumbed to a heart attack in 1953 while chasing three teenage vandals off his Hollywood estate.

Myrna Loy commented (to Rex Reed for his *New York Times* article, "Myrna's Back — And Boyer's Got Her") on the lascivious nature of her character: "I carried around a pet python[2] and whipped a young man tied to a rack and all sorts of dreadful things. Now I had been reading a little Freud around that time, so I called the director over one day and said, 'Say, this is obscene. This woman is a sadistic nymphomaniac!' And he said, 'What does *that* mean?' I mean, we did it all before these kids today ever thought of it, and we didn't even know what we were *doing*!"

In her autobiography, *Myrna Loy: Being and Becoming*, Ms. Loy noted both her and Karloff's contributions to the film: "That was a crazy part, yet when Roddy McDowall tricked me into seeing it recently, it astonished me how good Karloff and I were. Everyone else just tossed it off as something that didn't matter, while Boris and I brought some feeling and humor to those comic-book characters." She went on to further praise her co-star, adding, "Boris was a fine actor, a professional who never condescended to his often unworthy material."

Boris Karloff, while the consummate professional, was not above succumbing to the humorous side of an absurd situation. His co-star, Charles Starrett, related this amusing incident (quoted by Cynthia Lindsay in her book *Dear Boris*): "Boris was a subtle, good-humored man — an actor's actor, a most adaptable man — he could think himself into any part. Never blew a line — except once — in *Mask*. I, the hero, was lying face down strapped to a table; he as Fu Manchu was about to do me in by injecting a hypodermic needle into the back of my neck. We couldn't get it right — it never looked like the real thing. So the director, I think it was Charles Brabin, suddenly yelled, 'I've got it!' He sent to the commissary for four especially baked potatoes. He tucked one of them into the collar of my shirt and said to Boris, 'Go ahead, jab it in, you can't hurt him. It will only go into the potato.' We started the scene, Boris plunged the needle into (allegedly) my neck — the potato exploded with a great pop, got all over Boris and all over me. The two of us couldn't stop laughing. We went through three more takes, using up the rest of the potatoes with the same results until we were hysterical. Finally the director said, 'You two just go home — you're no use — we'll shoot it in the morning.'"

Less than a year after these vegetable vagaries, Karloff and Starrett turned serious when they took a rather dangerous stand (professionally speaking) as two of the 15 founding members of the Studio-opposed Screen Actor's Guild.

NOTES

1. Radio interview by Colin Edwards, Carmel, California, as cited by Scott Allen Nollen in *Boris Karloff, A Critical Account of His Screen, Stage, Radio, Television, and Recording Work*.

2. Ms. Loy, overcoming her initial reluctance to handle the large snake, eventually became rather enamored of her reptilian co-star. In her autobiography she wrote: "After much cajoling, I allowed them to put the snake in my lap. I touched it, expecting a cold, clammy body. Instead, it was warm and doped within an inch of its life so that it wouldn't harm me. Well, my heart went out to that poor creature. They all mumbled, 'Crazy woman,' on the set, but I was very attentive to my pet python after that."

THE MUMMY
(1932; Universal)

Release Date: December 22, 1932
Running Time: 72 minutes
Director: Karl Freund
Producer: Carl Laemmle, Jr.
Screenplay: John L. Balderston
Story: Nina Wilcox Putnam and Richard Schayer
Photography: Charles Stumar
Film Editor: Milton Carruth
Special Effects: John P. Fulton

Cast: Boris Karloff (Imhotep), Zita Johann (Helen Grosvenor), David Manners (Frank Whemple), Arthur Byron (Sir Joseph Whemple), Edward Van Sloan (Doctor Muller), Bramwell Fletcher (Ralph Norton), Noble Johnson (The Nubian), Kathryn Byron (Frau Muller), Leonard Mudie (Professor Pearson), James Crane (The Pharaoh), Henry Victor[1] (The Saxon Warrior).

"You will not remember what I show you now. And yet I shall awaken memories of love, and crime, and death."—Imhotep to his reincarnated love.

SYNOPSIS

In 1921, the British Museum Field Expedition uncovers a secret tomb in the Egyptian desert. The leader of the expedition is Sir Joseph Whemple, renowned archeologist. Inside the tomb they find the mummy of Imhotep, the contorted muscles and lack of an embalming scar revealing that he was buried alive. They also discover a small casket housing the Scroll of Thoth which contains "the magic words by which Isis raised Osiris from the dead." Ralph Norton, Sir Joseph's assistant, cannot contain his curiosity and begins to read and translate the parchment. The mummy comes to life and disappears with the sacred scroll, leaving Norton a laughing madman. "He went for a little walk. You should have seen his face... Ha, ha, ha, ha, ha...."

Eleven years later, Sir Joseph's son, Frank, is on another expedition—this one unsuccessful. A strange man approaches and tells them where to dig to find the tomb of Princess Anck-es-en-Amon. The man calls himself Ardeth Bey, but he is, in fact, the living mummy Imhotep, who had been condemned to "a nameless death" when he attempted to use the scroll to revive his lover, Princess Anck-es-en-Amon, 3700 years before.

Later, Imhotep goes to the Cairo museum where he attempts to restore the Princess' mummy to life with the scroll. His incantations fail, however, for Anck-es-en-Amon's soul has been reincarnated as Helen Grosvenor. Helen is staying with Dr. Muller (who happens to be an expert on the occult) and has fallen in love with Frank Whemple.

Exorcising his mystical powers, Imhotep wills Helen to come to him, intending to sacrifice her body in order to make her a living mummy like himself. He reveals their past together and brings forth memories of Princess Anck-es-en-Amon. She resists: "No, I'm alive. I'm young. I won't die. I loved you once but now you belong with the dead." Rushing to a statue of Isis, she pleads, "Save me now, teach me the ancient summons, the holy spells I have forgotten."

Imhotep raises his knife to strike, but as Helen/Anck-es-en-Amon intones some archaic rite, the statue's arm rises. In a blinding flash of light Imhotep crumbles to a pile of ancient bones and dust, while Frank and Dr. Muller rush to Helen's prostrate form. "Call her," urges Dr. Muller. "He has dragged her back to ancient Egypt. Call her; her love for you may bridge the centuries." Frank softly speaks her name, she opens her eyes, and all is well.

MEMORABLE MOMENT

The sequence in which the mummy first comes to life is an unforgettable introduction to one of the screen's classic monsters. As Ralph Norton silently mouths the words while he translates the Scroll of Thoth, the camera moves from him to the still form of the mummy, then back again to Norton. The next shot focuses on the mummy's desiccated head. After a moment of pregnant stillness, the eyes slowly open. The camera pans down the mummy's torso and the arms, crossed on its chest, slowly slide down its body, breaking free of the rotted bandages which held them for 3700 years. The camera cuts to Norton, still engrossed in his translation, and then pans down to the scroll on the table. A hand enters the frame, a long, bony, withered hand which briefly touches the scroll, almost in a caress, before drawing it away. Norton looks up, gives a startled yell, and backs away. He begins to laugh, starting low but gaining in intensity until it becomes a horrible, uncontrollable laugh of madness. The camera pans to the floor and we see two trailing bandages drawn out the door as Norton's mad laughter continues — the only sound punctuating an otherwise silent soundtrack. This subtle scene, fraught with tension and terror, is truly one of the most memorable scenes of horror ever filmed. Though we never see the Mummy walk, the bits and pieces revealed let our own imaginations create a more striking and terrifying scene than if we'd seen him stalk in full view from his sarcophagus.

ASSETS

Often when one thinks of "The Mummy" an image comes to mind of a bandaged monster sent out to do the evil bidding of a sinister high priest. The creature's face is wrinkled and blank as it inexorably limps toward an intended victim, its single good arm outstretched to strangle the life out of anyone who stands in its way. This is the mummy of Universal's four sequels made to the original 1932 Karloff vehicle: *The Mummy's Hand* (1940), *The Mummy's Tomb* (1942), *The Mummy's Ghost*, and *The Mummy's Curse* (both 1944). They are sequels in name only, for they create their own separate history (though not above borrowing much of the impressive flashback sequence from the original), and have little to do with the first picture. They also fail to come close to the quality and power of *The Mummy*, which is a subtle, intelligent masterpiece of horror presided over by Boris Karloff in the title role, giving one of the most memorable performances of his career. Karloff's mummy is not a shambling, inarticulate monster; he is an intelligent being of power, a master of the black arts. He does not kill through physical violence, but through the mere exertion of his indomitable will. Unlike those lumbering impostors that followed, he is more man than monster, a creature consumed by loneliness and love — monstrous, yes, but also distinctly human in his longings.

This film billed Boris Karloff as "Karloff the Uncanny," and his performance lives up to every adjective the Universal publicity department could dream up. With his imposing height, penetrating gaze, and slow, measured speech, he creates a forceful, and at times frightening, figure. Aided by Jack Pierce's exquisite makeup, he truly does look "uncanny" — his face a mass of tiny cracks and lines, eyes deep set, cheeks hollow and withered. At the same time that Karloff projects an air of unholy menace and malignant power, he brings forth the pathos that made his Frankenstein Monster so memorable, investing his living mummy with enough humanity to lift him out of the category of "monster" and into the realm of tragedy.

Karloff is ably supported by Edward Van Sloan as the occult expert, Professor Muller. Van Sloan essentially reprises his role of Professor Van Helsing, the arch-nemesis of *Dracula* (1931). He lends an air of calm authority to the part of chief antagonist to Imhotep, creating a knowledgeable foe leading the fight against evil. Likewise, Zita Johann, with her exotic beauty and wry charm, is ideal as the reincarnated princess torn between two worlds, bringing an inner strength and conviction to her role. (Perhaps Ms. Johann's sincerity is due in part to her personal beliefs. A self-proclaimed "mystic," she was a firm believer in reincarnation. In fact, according to writer/interviewer Greg Mank, she vividly recalls her own death in 1793 in the same 200-year-old house which she occupied at the end of her life.)

The Mummy was the directorial debut of Karl Freund, a cinematographer turned director (he had photographed *Metropolis* [1926] and *Dracula* [1931], among others). He later directed the 1935 classic, *Mad Love*. With *The Mummy*, Freund, aided by his total control of the camera and its movements, creates a moody, tense, muted tale of obsessive love and understated horror.

Freund effectively employs the camera as a thematic device. For instance, instead of utilizing a simple dissolve to get from the scene of Ardeth Bey gazing at the sarcophagus of Anck-es-en-Amon at the Cairo Museum to Helen Grosvenor at a modern party, Freund lets motion bridge the gap of space—and time. From the painted visage of Anck-es-en-Amon embossed upon her sarcophagus, the camera suddenly whirls away to focus on a moving panorama (unfortunately, a less-than-convincing curved diorama). As the exotic city rapidly unspools before us, the camera whirls again and comes to rest on the contemplative countenance of Helen, gazing as if into the abyss of time itself. The quick camera movement effectively masks the break between shots, making it appear as if the camera has spun from one side of the ancient city to the other in one rapid motion. This rushing movement creates a connection between the two scenes and, more importantly, between Ardeth Bey and Helen Grosvenor.

In another scene, the camera prowls waist-high through the shadowy exhibit room of the closed museum, moving slowly and unsteadily like a creeping sneak-thief. Rounding the corner of a display case, we come upon the kneeling form of Ardeth Bey, intently hunched over the Scroll of Thoth. The camera movement sets the tone of the scene and enhances its theme—one of a secretive, forbidden presence.

Freund worked with his cameraman, Charles Stumar to combine fluid movement, a rich depth of field, and moody lighting into an atmosphere of supernatural antiquity. (Stumar was a talented cinematographer in his own right whose work enhanced both *Werewolf of London* and *The Raven* before his career was

Boris Karloff ("now one of the most treasured actors that Universal Pictures have at command," declares this English cigarette card) as *The Mummy* (1932).

cut short by a fatal plane crash in 1935.) When the men open the forbidden box containing the Scroll of Thoth, for instance, the actor placement, camera movement, and lighting enhance the ominous anticipation of the scene. The camera "stands" behind Sir Joseph Whemple and his assistant, Ralph Norton, peering between their shadowy forms which frame the shot on either side. At the bottom of the picture lies the small box, well-lit so we can see the hieroglyphics carved upon its lid. When Whemple begins reading the inscription, the camera smoothly tracks forward, pulling our building curiosity with it, until the casket's lid fills the bottom third of the screen. The framing and movement create an increasingly claustrophobic feel which combines with Whemple's halting translation of the hieroglyphics ("Death, eternal punishment — for — anyone — who — opens — this — casket") to inspire unease in the viewer. "Good heavens, what a terrible curse," states the momentarily shaken Sir Joseph. While the rather generic curse itself doesn't seem so very terrible, the feeling of dread one gets from the general scene *does*.

Soon after, when Whemple and Muller go out "under the stars of Egypt" to discuss the curse, Stumar employs a dim light which casts the two men mostly in shadow. Only their hands and their profiles are highlighted to give definition, while the background consists of uneven pools of darkness and light reflected off the craggy desert rocks. The predominant blackness and selective lighting create a dark, ominous mood, so one can well believe Muller when he claims that "the gods of Egypt still live in these hills."

The Mummy is one of those rare horror pictures of the Golden Age (or *any* age, really) that builds its foundation on a firm bedrock of mysticism. An aura of the supernatural permeates this passion play as otherworldly forces ebb and flow across its surface. Only a few films, such as *Vampyr*, have managed to immerse themselves so successfully in a supernatural dream world. *The Mummy* is a coherent *Vampyr*, however, one possessing a linear narrative and a heart full of tragedy and pathos. Rather than providing the startling shocks and jolts of terror à la *Frankenstein* (1931), *The Mummy* takes a subtle approach in weaving its cinematic tapestry of the strange and terrible. Touching on life, love, and death, *The Mummy* is poetic horror and truly one of the greatest, most original fantasy films of all time.

LIABILITIES

Unfortunately, David Manners, as the nominal hero Frank Whemple, truly lets the side down. His annoyingly affected delivery and almost puppyish demeanor as he fawns over the heroine turn him more into a caricature than a character. Manners, while never the most exciting of leading men (he did his regular milquetoast routine in *Dracula*, 1931, and — not as obtrusively — in *The Black Cat*, 1934), here manages to outdo himself in blandness. His near-whining tones make some scenes almost painful to watch, as he prattles on like a love-sick puppy to the heroine. With more conviction and less artless naiveté, the scenes could work, but David Manners is basically a pretty face who learns his lines and is not up to the job.

The way Helen immediately falls in love with Frank is too pat a plot device to be convincing. Even given a decent amount of time for the two to interact (which they are denied), it is doubtful that the intelligent, thoughtful Helen would fall for an empty-headed pratt like Frank. Young Whemple seems to have inherited none of the wisdom or dedication of his serious-minded father, and displays his wit by making pointless comments about the weather or answering a legitimate query as to how he can be so blasé about defiling the ancient dead with offhand inanities like, "Had to — science, you know!"

While not a particularly serious flaw, several mismatched stock shots tend to draw attention to themselves, creating unsightly ripples in the smooth flow of the film. Early on, when Helen takes time out from dancing at the society gala, she looks out over a balcony and we see a shot of the pyramids surrounded by open desert. The nearness of the monoliths makes it seem as if her balcony in downtown Cairo rests only a few hundred yards from the Pharaohs' tombs. Then Helen turns her gaze downwards and we see a shot of the bustling metropolis at her feet, the exotic buildings and crowded streets stretching out as far as the eye can see. The two vistas create a geographic impossibility which momentarily pulls the viewer out of the film's cinematic illusion. Also, the diorama used in one scene transition becomes rather obvious when the same shot of a domed mosque unspools *twice*, again disrupting the film's world. Fortunately, the horrific poetry and sheer power of *The Mummy* quickly plucks

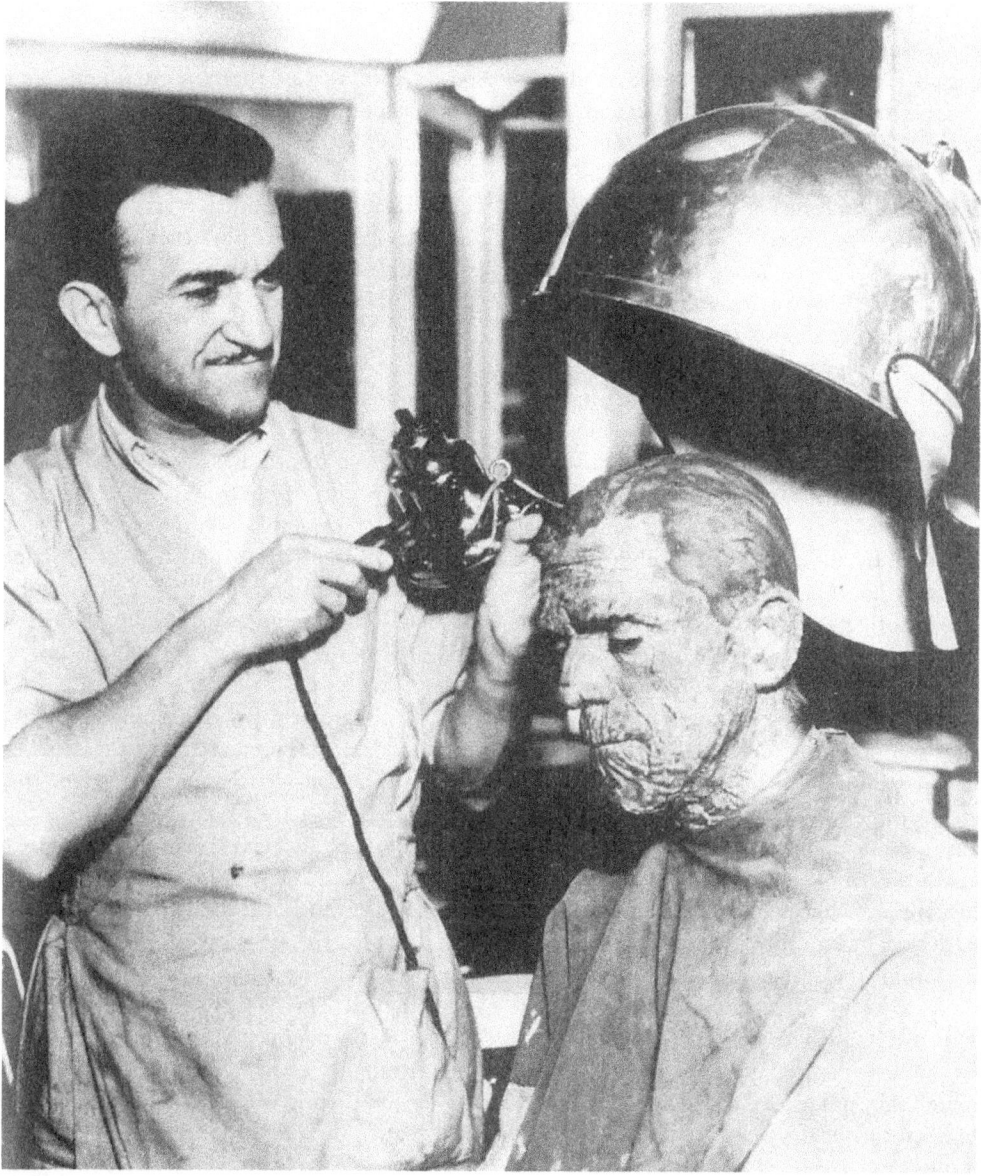

Jack Pierce working on Boris Karloff's eight-hour makeup ("the most trying ordeal I have ever endured") as *The Mummy* (1932). (Courtesy of Ted Okuda.)

the floundering viewer from the waves of mundane reality and carries him/her away on the dark, dreamlike waters of the ancient Nile.

REVIEWS

Britain's *Kinematograph Weekly* (January 19, 1933) called the film "wildly incredible," but observed that "the brilliant acting of Boris Karloff, together with some very notable technical work and imaginative direction, invest it with a realism which rivets the attention and excites grim suspense. An unusual offering, one which by reason of its novel theme and amazing star, cannot fail to win full box-office honors. Boris Karloff's makeup is remarkable and the coming to life of the mummy is an amazing piece of transformation."

Variety's "Waly" (January 10, 1933) felt

that "There are more reasons than not why 'The Mummy' should show a nice profit. It has an excellent title, some weird sequences and it is the first starring film for Karloff." (Apparently Waly missed the Karloff starring vehicles *The Mask of Fu Manchu* and *The Old Dark House*, released one and two months before this, respectively.)

The New York Times' Andre Sennwald (January 7, 1933) was less impressed and took issue with the picture's slow and steady pace. "Karloff stalks out of his winding cloths after 3,700 years of restless sleep, and that is a hideous enough theme to freeze the most callous imagination. But the fable thereafter depends on mystic incantations, which are only words." (Possibly Mr. Sennwald would have preferred the more action-packed but less engrossing Lon Chaney, Jr., follow-ups to this elegant original.) He did go on to state that "for purposes of terror there are two scenes in 'The Mummy' that are weird enough in all conscience. In the first the mummy comes alive and a young archeologist, going quite mad, laughs in a way that raises the hair on the scalp. In the second Im-Ho-Tep is embalmed alive, and that moment when the tape is drawn across the man's mouth and nose, leaving only his wild eyes staring out of the coffin, is one of decided horror. But most of 'The Mummy' is costume melodrama for the children."

PRODUCTION NOTES

When the project was originally announced by producer Carl Laemmle, Jr., it was under the name *Cagliostro*, which was based on a nine page treatment by Nina Wilcox Putnam and Richard Schayer. *Cagliostro* followed the exploits of an Egyptian magician who achieves immortality through the injection of nitrates. Throughout the centuries he destroys all those who resemble the woman who betrayed him, even resorting to such modern contrivances as radio and television rays.

The title of *The Mummy* wasn't finalized until halfway through production. The film was started under the title *Imhotep*. Rookie director Karl Freund brought *The Mummy* in *under* schedule and *under* budget (at a final cost of $196,000), even after an incredibly rushed beginning (he received the final script on a Saturday, cast the film on Sunday, and began shooting on Monday).

Screenwriter John L. Balderston named his two principal characters after historical Egyptian figures. Imhotep was a high priest, author, architect, and physician who served in the court of the Pharaoh Djoser. Anck-es-en-Amon was the queen of the 18-year-old Pharaoh, Tutankhamen, commonly known as King Tut. Of course, in reality, Imhotep and Anck-es-en-Amon never met, having lived 1300 years apart — in the third dynasty (c2600 B.C.) and eighteenth dynasty (c1300 B.C.) respectively. *The Mummy* was in fact an outgrowth of the public's interest in Ancient Egypt aroused by the magnificent discovery of Tutankhamen's tomb in 1922 — and the subsequent deaths or curse surrounding those involved with the discovery.

In his script, Balderston noted that the role of the heroine was a demanding one, writing that "an emotional actress of high caliber is needed" and suggesting Katherine Hepburn. The Broadway actress was unavailable at the time, though, and Universal offered the part to Zita Johann. Ms. Johann, however, was less-than-enthusiastic about the production. She accepted the assignment only at the urging of her then-husband, John Houseman, who argued, "It's more money than you could ever make in the theatre."[2]

A number of Ms. Johann's scenes ended up on the cutting room floor, including several sequences which spotlighted her character in various (re)incarnations. Scenes of her as an eighth-century Saxon queen, a medieval princess, a French aristocrat, and a Christian martyr fed to the lions were excised at the request of producer Carl Laemmle, Jr. Years later, Boris Karloff told his producer Richard Gordon that the scenes were edited to avoid slowing the film's pace.

According to Ms. Johann, Freund was something of a sadist. In an interview with author Gregory William Mank (quoted in his book *Karloff and Lugosi*), the actress related how Karl "Papa" Freund "threatened to have

This scene in which Imhotep (Boris Karloff) shows Helen (Zita Johann) her past incarnations in a mystic mirror was cut before *The Mummy*'s release.

her pose nude from the waist up; how he saw to it she didn't get a chair with her name on it, as did the other leading players; how he worked her so sadistically that, late on a Saturday night, as Karloff was playing a scene with her, she collapsed. 'I was out for an hour — dead. They couldn't get a doctor — it was 11 o'clock at night — so the crew prayed me back to consciousness.'" Ms. Johann felt that the insecure Freund (untried as a director) "needed a scapegoat in case he didn't come in on schedule,"[3] and that *she* was that scapegoat. In fact, Freund brought the picture in *ahead* of schedule.

Ms. Johann was not alone in feeling that Freund was "a monster," "a sadist," and "a pig." Francis Drake, the leading lady of Freund's *Mad Love*, called him "a wretched, big, fat man," while Hume Cronyn (who appeared in 1943's *The Seventh Cross*, for which Freund was cinematographer) characterized him as "an absolute bastard."[4] Despite these detractors, Freund still managed to win the affectionate appellation "Papa."

"Karloff the Uncanny" had to endure eight hours in the makeup chair for Jack Pierce to transform him into the mummy. The actor remembered it as "the most trying ordeal I have ever endured." Pierce based his mummy make-up (having no previous cinematic precedent) upon photographs of an actual mummy — that of King Seti II — which he obtained from the Cairo museum. The talented makeup artist considered *The Mummy* to be his finest achievement.

Bramwell Fletcher was no better at choosing wives than he was at choosing which forbidden caskets to open. The "man-who-laughed" married the troubled Helen Chandler (the heroine who survived *Dracula* was not so fortunate with chemical dependency) in 1935. After divorcing her, Fletcher wed Diana Barrymore, daughter of John, and the Princess of Hollywood's "Royal Family." That didn't last either and Fletcher married twice more before his death in 1988. Apart from *The Mummy*, Fletcher appeared in several other genre entries—*Svengali* (1931), *Daughter of the Dragon* (1931), and *The Monkey's Paw* (1933). Fletcher left films in the early forties and concentrated on stage and television (playing over 200 lead roles on the small screen).

Many parallels can be drawn between *The Mummy* and *Dracula*, of the previous year. John L. Balderston wrote both, and *The Mummy* is a veritable retelling of *Dracula*'s storyline. Both concern a small group of mortals banding together to battle an ancient fiend possessing supernatural powers who is intent upon claiming a young woman for his own. Both feature an occult expert (Dr. Muller here and Professor Van Helsing in *Dracula*) who uses his supernatural knowledge (along with the forces of good) to defeat the evil monster. The parallels are even underlined by the film's casting, which brings David Manners back as the ineffectual hero and Edward Van Sloan as the Egyptologist version of Professor Van Helsing.

Universal's publicity department was shameless in its ballyhoo, even suggesting stunts that teetered on the edge of legality. "Get up a fake mummy and case," suggested the pressbook. "Now, arrange for a delivery truck to carry the mummy to the busiest section of town and DROP IT FROM THE TRUCK.... The mummy, of course, should carry no advertising or identification. The police, mystified, will report the occurrence to newspapers, and headlines will announce the finding of a mysterious mummy. Then it is your cue to step in, announce that 'The Mummy' was being delivered to your theatre as a display and claim it!"

NOTES

1. Though listed in the credits, Henry Victor does not appear in the film. All of his scenes were cut when it was decided to excise the numerous reincarnation sequences detailing Helen Grosvenor's past lives.
2. Quoted in *Whatever Became Of...? Fourth Series*, by Richard Lamparksi.
3. *Films in Review*, interview with Gregory William Mank.
4. Quoted in "Gift of Gab," by Gregory William Mank, *Scarlet Street* no. 10.

ISLAND OF LOST SOULS
(1933; Paramount)

Release Date: January 11, 1933
Running Time: 72 minutes
Director: Erle C. Kenton
Screenplay: Waldemar Young, Philip Wylie (from the novel "The Island of Dr. Moreau" by H. G. Wells)
Photography: Karl Struss
Art Direction: Hans Dreier
Special Effects: Gordon Jennings
Makeup: Wally Westmore

Cast: Charles Laughton (Dr. Moreau), Richard Arlen (Edward Parker), Leila Hyams (Ruth Thomas), Bela Lugosi (Sayer of the Law), Kathleen Burke (Panther Woman), Arthur Hohl (Montgomery), Stanley Fields (Captain Davies), Paul Hurst (Donohue), Hans Steinke (Ouran), Tetsu Komai (M'ling), George Irving (the Consul); also: *Robert Kortman, *Alan Ladd, *Duke York, *John George, *Randolph Scott

*Uncredited on film print.

"What is the law? Not to run on all fours, are we not men?"—the "Sayer of the Law."

SYNOPSIS

Island of Lost Souls opens as Edward Parker is rescued at sea by the SS *Covena* after his own ship went down. Parker was headed for Apia where he was to marry his fiancée, Ruth. Onboard the *Covena* is Montgomery, a disgraced

Erle C. Kenton (holding script, back to the camera) directs Charles Laughton and Kathleen Burke in *Island of Lost Souls* (1933).

physician and current assistant to Dr. Moreau. Montgomery is overseeing the transportation of a load of exotic animals bound for Moreau's private island.

After Parker regains his strength, he confronts the drunken captain when the man cruelly attacks Montgomery's strange servant, M'ling. Later, when the cargo ship nears the island, Dr. Moreau meets the boat with his schooner and takes possession of the animals. Just as the large ship pulls away, the disgruntled captain spots Parker and throws him over the side onto Moreau's boat, despite both Parker's and Moreau's protestations. With no other options, Moreau and Montgomery take Parker to their island. Once there, Parker catches glimpses of the strange, misshapen inhabitants which populate the island. "Strange-looking natives you have here," comments the innocent Parker, with his only answer a slight sardonic smile from Dr. Moreau.

Moreau decides he can use the handsome Parker to his advantage and introduces him to Lota, "the only woman on the island." Unknown to Parker, Lota is one of Moreau's "manimals"—the humanlike creatures which populate the island and which Moreau has created from animals. Lota is his most perfect creation and Moreau wishes to observe her reaction to this man. "Will she be attracted," the Doctor muses, "has she a woman's impulses?"

Later that night, Parker learns the horrors behind the mysterious "House of Pain" (the name given Moreau's laboratory by the pitiful beast-men who have endured countless sessions of painful vivisection as Moreau shapes and molds them under the knife). Disgusted, Parker attempts to flee with Lota. They are accosted by the manimals but saved by Moreau, who then tells Parker the whole story. "With plastic surgery, blood transfusions, gland extracts, with x-ray baths ... with what I have discovered in my own work among the cellular organisms—MY work, MY discoveries, mine alone—with these I have wiped out hundreds of thousands of years of evolution."

With Parker set to leave the following day, Moreau has his own sailing sloop scuttled so Parker is forced to remain. Meanwhile, Ruth learns that Parker was dropped off (literally) at Moreau's Island. The American Consulate arranges for Captain Donohue to take his ship to the island, with Ruth going along.

Back on the island, Lota is attracted to Parker and he momentarily succumbs to her "animal charms." But Lota's hands give away her true nature ("the stubborn beast flesh creeping back," laments Moreau) and Parker learns the truth of her origin (she was created from a panther). In a fury of indignation, he assaults Moreau. Despite this, Moreau still plans to keep Parker on the island and continue his "experiment" with him and Lota.

"He is already attracted," reasons Moreau, "time and monotony will do the rest."

When Captain Donohue and Ruth arrive on the island, Ruth is reunited with Parker. However, darkness has fallen and the three must spend the night at Moreau's compound. After the trio has retired, the manimal brute called Ouran attempts to break into the house to get at Ruth, apparently with the sanction of Moreau, who views it as another "experiment" in attraction. Ruth's screams rouse Parker and Donohue, causing Ouran to run off into the jungle. Montgomery finally confronts Moreau: "I'd have stood for anything," he disgustedly tells Moreau. "I HAVE stood for plenty. But not this!" Montgomery helps Captain Donohue leave the compound, intending to bring back his crew in force. Moreau observes this and orders Ouran to kill the captain: "I want you to follow him and put your hands around his throat—" Ouran succeeds in his mission and takes the body back to the manimal village. This puts the beast-men in an uproar and they set fire to the village. The Law Sayer and leader of the manimals confronts Ouran with what he has done. "What is the law? Not to spill blood. Are we not men? YOU broke the law," he cries, pointing at Ouran. "Law no more," is Ouran's response. "HE tell me spill blood." This is the beginning of the end of Moreau's godlike control over these creatures.

Moreau goes out to subdue them but the beast-men no longer fear his whip and "The Law." As the creatures advance, chasing Moreau back to the house, Montgomery, Ruth, Parker, and Lota sneak out the back and head for the boat. Ouran follows, but Lota, trailing behind, gives her own life to defend the three from the beast-man.

The manimals carry Moreau to the "House of Pain" where they pin him to the operating table. Clawed hands reach for knives and scalpels as a hideous wail of agony issues from the center of the slashing creatures gathered around the table. While Moreau meets his fate at the hands of his creations, the three protagonists row away from the now-burning island. "The fire will destroy all of Moreau's work."

The "manimals" rebel at the climax of *Island of Lost Souls* (1933), chasing the whip-wielding Moreau (Charles Laughton) from his own fortress-like house. Under all the hair in the center is Bela Lugosi as the "Sayer of the Law."

MEMORABLE MOMENTS

One of the most frightening and brutal moments in this very frightening film comes when Moreau confronts the manimals at their village for the final time, only to find he can no longer control them. As the creatures steadily advance, the camera becomes Moreau and focuses on the lead beast-man advancing towards him (and the viewer). Moreau cracks his whip and it winds about the beast-man's neck — to no effect, and the creature continues his inexorable advance. Then another of the creatures has the whip wrap around *his* neck — again to no effect — as Moreau futilely continues trying to stop them. Finally, one more creature advancing towards the camera is struck by the whip, which this time winds about its *face*, but it keeps coming. The combination of the low lighting and surrounding darkness with the manimals' constant wailing and murmuring and the sight of the whip cracking futilely across their hate-filled countenances creates a frightening tableau, drawing the viewer in to feel Moreau's own panic and terror.

A second memorable sequence comes a few minutes later when the advancing beastmen have forced Moreau back to his house. In desperation, Moreau shouts at them: "Have you forgotten the House of Pain?!" This

A study in animal magnetism: Kathleen Burke as Lota, the Panther Woman. (Courtesy of Ted Okuda.)

momentarily stops the manimals and, in an overhead shot, we see the creatures huddled and cowering in remembered fear. Suddenly, the Law Sayer stands up and cries, "You — You made us in the House of Pain!" and the camera tracks downward to close in on him. "You made us THINGS!" he wails as the camera moves in tight on his bestial form. "Not men!" he shouts and takes a step towards the camera. "Not beasts!" he adds and takes another step closer. The camera abruptly cuts to the terrified Moreau, then back to the beast-man. "Part man, part beasts..." continues the Law Sayer, moving still closer. "THIIIINGS!" he screams and the hideous hairy face fills the screen. Then in quick succession a half dozen creatures rush at the camera one at a time until they too fill the screen with their hideous bestial visages, echoing "Things!" "Part man!" "Part beast!" "Things!" The claustrophobic effect is both powerful and horrifying.

Even the power and ferocity of these scenes pale in comparison to the climactic demise of Dr. Moreau — the most chilling fate ever to befall a villain in the Golden Age of Horror. The sequence is truly horrific and once seen is not soon forgotten. While no overt bloodshed is seen (as would be the case in a modern film version), the sights and sounds and feel of the sequence are terrifying. Carrying Moreau into the laboratory, a dozen bestial hands hold him down while a dozen more shatter a glass cabinet to grab at knives and scalpels. Soon a hideous wail of agony emanates from the center of the monstrous forms huddled around the operating table. As the camera pulls back and the scene dissolves into a shot of the laboratory entrance, the frantic screams from Moreau are almost too much to bear. This is undoubtedly the most horrific, certainly the most sickeningly exciting, and arguably the greatest climax in the Golden Age of Horror, comparable only to the shuddery ending of Tod Browning's *Freaks* (1932).

ASSETS

Any way you look at it, *Island of Lost Souls* is strong stuff, particularly for 1933. So strong was it, that for 35 years the film was banned outright in England (a country known for its sensitivity to animal rights and vivisection). H. G. Wells, on whose novel the film is based, heartily denounced the picture (and eagerly endorsed the British ban). With the subjects of vivisection, sadism, and implied bestiality running throughout the film to assault the sensibilities of puritanical censors and critics, it's not hard to fathom such outrage. But even beyond these ostensibly offensive elements, *Island of Lost Souls* was met with hostility because it simply worked too well as a horror film — it actually *horrified* people.

The frightening "manimals," the claustrophobic jungle setting, the hideous experiments, the painful wails from the "House of Pain," and Moreau himself — devoid of compassion, sadistic in his work; all these add up to an unrelenting 72 minutes guaranteed to disturb even the most jaded film viewer. The film is relentless. No comedy relief softens the harshness. The standard love-interest is minimal, with most of the focus instead on the relationship between the hero and the blossoming panther-woman. The implication of bestiality is clear, and the film doesn't hold back or apologize for its subject matter. Dr. Moreau even spells it out for the hero (and the audience): "Lota [the panther woman] is my most nearly perfect creation," beams Moreau. "I wanted to prove how completely she was a woman, whether she was capable of loving, mating, and having children. She was afraid of Montgomery and myself. Then *you* came. Well, she was very much attracted to you. You can see, of course, the possibilities that presented themselves."

Charles Laughton (in his sixth American film in a little more than a year) gives us the greatest mad doctor of them all. Moreau is *not* experimenting for the good of science, *nor* is he a wronged man using his genius for revenge. No, he knows what he is doing and he knows why. "Mr. Parker," he asks, more to himself than to his guest, "do you know what it means to feel like God?" (A line similar to this was cut from *Frankenstein* soon after its initial engagements. While Universal did not want its Dr. Frankenstein uttering such blasphemy, apparently Paramount had no such compunction about their Dr. Moreau.) Unlike Colin Clive's impassioned, high-strung Henry Frankenstein, Laughton's Moreau is a cool, calm creator, reveling in the monstrosities he lords over. As the "Law Sayer" intones the ritual phrase, "HIS is the hand that makes. HIS is the hand that heals. HIS is the House of Paiiiiiin," Moreau beams down at the beastmen like a god accepting homage. In another revealing scene, Moreau examines one of his monstrous creations strapped to an operating table. He casually turns the thing's head this way and that, examining his handiwork, while the pitiful beast-man screams in pain — a wail that starts low and grows steadily until it becomes an unbearable cry of agony — but the preoccupied doctor pays no attention. Laughton's Moreau can also be lascivious (in a somewhat detached manner, anyway). When he spies Lota saying goodnight to Parker in a rather tender fashion, he comments, "How that little scene spurs the scientific imagination onward." Laughton's low, intense delivery leaves little doubt that more than *scientific* imagination has been inflamed. Laughton's Moreau characterization is a brilliant study in control and composure — a sinister, perverse composure with an underlying power strong enough to hold his island in a grip of fear.

The bulk of the film takes place on Moreau's private jungle island and the setting creates a moody oppressiveness, a growing claustrophobic feeling of unease. On-location shooting at Catalina Island lends a great deal of authenticity to the production, and the realistic setting is lush and dark, with overripe foliage and decaying greenery closing in on all sides. Moreau's weird house, made of stone blocks and iron bars (almost prisonlike), overgrown inside and out with the decay of the jungle creeping in, only adds to this trapped, closed-in feeling, and mirrors the moral decay of Moreau himself.

Island is filled with memorable performances. Aside from Laughton's Moreau, Lugosi turns in a weird, tortured portrayal as the "Sayer of the Law." His pronounced accent, halting speech, and odd inflections add further texture to this unusual — and unnatural — character, perfectly complementing his bizarre hirsute appearance. Lugosi's innate authoritative presence, coupled with his anguished emoting as he recites his litany of "The Law" or wails at Moreau ("You made us THINGS!"), make his character a brutally eloquent spokesman for the pitiable beast-men.

Newcomer Kathleen Burke creates an unforgettable character in Lota, the pantherwoman. The combination of her odd, angular, yet very attractive face and her unaffected body language (as she languorously lounges against the hero, almost purring in satisfaction) creates a heady mixture of animal sensuality and primitive innocence.

Karl Struss' camerawork is impeccable. The Oscar-winning cinematographer makes good use of foreground placement, framing, and the mobile camera. Perhaps the film's most distinctive cinematic feature, however, is the relatively little-used subjective technique of keeping the camera steady and having the actors advance straight at the camera (and at the audience). Director Kenton and Struss used this procedure with the manimal monsters, accentuating the shock appeal of Wally Westmore's grotesque makeups. The resulting impact felt by viewers as the bestial creatures rush straight at them is one of a fierce claustrophobic head-on charge.

Director Erle C. Kenton handles the directing chores admirably, bringing each element together to form a powerful, frightening whole. While Kenton's work is effective, not a small portion of the picture's success stems from the cast and technical crew. Struss' camerawork, Hans Dreier's atmospheric jungle sets, Wally Westmore's gruesomely original makeup, Waldemar Young and Philip Wylie's no-holds-barred screenplay, and Laughton and Burke's excellent characterizations give the picture its power and impact. Kenton continued to work both within and outside of the horror genre, but his subsequent output (efficient but undistinguished) indicates that for *Island of Lost Souls* Kenton became something of an overachiever.

LIABILITIES

Richard Arlen as the hero delivers a very ineffective performance which weakens this otherwise compelling production. Arlen alternates between obvious overdramatics (which don't gel with the very subtle performances of Laughton and Burke and the solid playing of the rest of the cast) and toneless acting. His supposedly "revealing" expressions of disgust (particularly when he learns the truth about Lota) and anger are unconvincing on his wooden countenance. His voice generally does not carry the conviction of his words. When Arlen confronts the doctor, for instance, saying,

"Moreau, you don't deserve to live," his words are fierce but his tone is bland and unconvincing. It is unfortunate that this classic film suffers from the same "ineffectual lead" syndrome that mars *Dracula* (1931), *The Mummy* (1932), and to a lesser extent *The Black Cat* (1934).

Nevertheless, *Island of Lost Souls* stands up and dares to be counted among the handful of films that were unafraid to break ground and walk on American cinema taboos. It pulls no punches and makes no apologies. It is powerful, enthralling, and (much like its contemporary, *Freaks*) was ahead of its time.

REVIEWS

The New York Times' Mordaunt Hall (January 13, 1933) was reservedly impressed: "Although the attempt to horrify is not accomplished with any marked degree of subtlety, there is no denying that some of the scenes are ingeniously fashioned and are, therefore, interesting. The general effect of the film is enhanced greatly by Mr. Laughton's urbane impersonation.... Richard Arlen portrays Parker acceptably. Arthur Hohl does quite well as Moreau's agent, Montgomery...."

Variety's "Waly" (January 17, 1933) noted the exploitability of what he termed "a freak picture": "Paramount will make money with this picture, and so will every exhibitor, including the first big runs, who pays some attention to its exploitation." He also noted that "...While the action is not designed to appeal to other than the credulous, there are undoubtedly some horror sequences which are unrivaled."

The reviewer was not so appreciative, however, of Ms. Burke: "The extra billing given Kathleen Burke as Lota, Panther Woman, is strictly for the marquee. Girl is too much like a girl to even suggest transformation from a beast. Her part is little more than a 'White Cargo' bit."

PRODUCTION NOTES

Director Erle C. Kenton went on to direct other notable (but far less effective) genre films, including *Ghost of Frankenstein* (1942), *House of Frankenstein* (1945), and *House of Dracula* (1945). A workmanlike director who got his start directing two-reel comedies for Mack Sennett, Kenton never lived up to the promise shown on *Island of Lost Souls*. In 1950 he left films for the new (and profitable) field of television, directing many episodes of "Racket Squad" and "Public Defender."

Cinematographer Karl Struss was one of the greatest in the business. His illustrious career spanned four decades and included films such as *Ben-Hur* (1926), *Sunrise* (1927; for which he received an Academy Award), *Dr. Jekyll and Mr. Hyde* (1931), and *The Great Dictator* (1940). After leaving Paramount in the early 1940s, Struss worked primarily on independent "B" films, including half-a-dozen science fiction entries: *Rocketship X-M* (1950), *Mesa of Lost Women* (1953), *She Devil* (1957), *Kronos* (1957), *The Fly* (1958), and *The Alligator People* (1959) (his next-to-last film). Throughout the sixties, Struss turned exclusively to photographing television commercials. He retired in 1970. Struss was impressed with Erle C. Kenton, claiming the director "had a greater command of the English language than anyone I ever worked with" (*Hollywood Cameramen*).

According to William Brown in *Charles Laughton: A Pictorial Treasury of his Films*, Laughton modeled his mad Dr. Moreau after an oculist he visited (to correct a minor eye malady) shortly before production on the film began. The actor was fascinated by the man's appearance, particularly by his small, satanic-looking beard.

Laughton felt a bit overwhelmed by the various "manimal" monsters. He later recalled, "I remember each horror and monster had more hair than the one before. Hair was all over the place. I was dreaming of hair. I even thought I had hair in my food." (From *The Laughton Story*, by Kurt Singer.) According to author Charles Higham in *Charles Laughton, An Intimate Biography*, the actor "was disgusted by the story. His love of animals welled up; he felt a deep-seated repulsion at what he felt to be a crude exploitation of the theme of vivisection." (Laughton was not alone in these feelings, judging by the public outcry against

"PANTHER WOMAN TO MARRY" reads the official tag to this Paramount publicity still. "Kathleen Burke will marry Glen A. Rardin, who followed her to Hollywood from Chicago following her selection from among 60,000 candidates throughout the nation for the role of the Panther Woman in Paramount's *Island of Lost Souls*, she announced today. Miss Burke announced the marriage would take place following the completion of her screen debut." What the publicity blurb failed to mention was that Rardin became such a nuisance that Paramount eventually banned him from the set, particularly after the jealous suitor reportedly tried to beat up director Erle C. Kenton. Burke and Rardin did marry shortly after the completion of *Island of Lost Souls*, but they divorced a year and a half later.

in *Charles Laughton: A Difficult Actor*). Higham noted that Kenton "insisted on acting out scenes dressed up in the evil doctor's white tropical suit and hat, and even offered to teach Charles how to handle a whip," though the actor was already quite proficient with the prop. Karl Struss concurred that Kenton "played every scene through for the actors, even for Laughton, who was superb as Dr. Moreau." The cinematographer failed to characterize the director as bullying, however — far from it. "I admired Kenton," admitted Struss.

A disgruntled actor was not the worst of the problems faced during filming. William Brown (in *Charles Laughton: A Pictorial Treasury of His Films*) tells of a serious accident that occurred when one of the "manimal" extras ran too close to the tiger's cage on the ship and received a vicious swipe of the animal's claws which nearly tore his arm from the socket.

Two of Moreau's manimals were played by *one* man — stuntman Joe Bonomo. For the first creature, Bonomo merely sported fangs and Fredric March's fright wig from *Dr. Jekyll and Mr. Hyde* (1932). The second manimal required a more complex makeup application, however, for as the "Tigerman" Bonomo's hirsute countenance resembles that of Oliver Reed in Hammer's *Curse of the Werewolf* (1961). "All of us who played beasts in that picture wore animal suits," remembered Bonomo in his autobiography, *The Strongman*, "constructed with the torso built down nearly to the knees, with a fifty pound sack of sand in the crotch, making

the picture which culminated in a complete ban from the British Isles.) "I was never able to enjoy a zoo again," complained the actor himself. "The very smell of caged animals reminded me of the picture, and made me sick."

Apparently, Laughton's troubles did not end there, for he took issue with the intrusive hands-on directorial style of Erle C. Kenton (who was characterized as "pompous and bullying" by Laughton biographer Simon Callow any effort to walk exceedingly clumsy and grotesque." Bonomo's screen career began when he won a 1921 "Modern Apollo" contest sponsored by the *New York Daily News* which included a film contract. Bonomo's first assignment was doubling for none other than Lon Chaney in *The Light in the Dark* (1922).

Square-jawed screen hero Richard Arlen (born Richard Cornelius van Mattimore) worked variously as a sports writer, swimming coach, and Texas oil field laborer before journeying to Hollywood. Arlen (quite literally) broke into motion pictures while employed at the Paramount film laboratory. He fractured his leg while on the job and ended up in the studio hospital where he was spotted by a director who promised him a film part once he recovered. While the high point of Arlen's career, perhaps, came in 1927 with a starring role in *Wings* (the film which received the first Academy Award for Best Picture), Arlen continued acting for a full five decades. Specializing in actioners and westerns, Arlen also appeared in three further fantastique films (though the latter two are far from "fantastic" in quality)—*The Lady and the Monster* (1944), *The Crawling Hand* (1963), and *The Human Duplicators* (1965).

According to Paramount's publicity department, Kathleen Burke was a Chicago dental assistant before winning a much publicized, nationwide "Search for the 'Panther Woman'" contest to obtain this, her debut role. (The film's pressbook claimed that she was chosen over *60,000* other entrants!) As reported by the Los Angeles *Examiner* (September 30, 1932), "The contest was decided by a board of judges composed of Ernst Lubitsch, Cecil B. DeMille, Rouben Mamoulian, Norman Taurog, Stuart Walker and Erle C. Kenton. A $200 a week contract with a five-week guarantee is the prize."

Paramount's director of recording, Loren L. Ryder, created the unnerving "manimal" sounds by combining recordings of animal noises and foreign languages played backwards, then alternately speeding them up and slowing them down to produce a suitably bizarre and otherworldly cacophony. Ryder's innovative use of sound earned him twelve Academy Award nominations and netted him five Oscars over the course of his career.

Working as assistant director on *Island of Lost Souls* was Charles T. Barton. Barton graduated to full director a year later and embarked upon a prolific career, directing over 70 features (predominantly for Columbia and Universal). Among them were 11 Abbott and Costello vehicles (including *Abbott and Costello Meet Frankenstein* [1948] and *Abbott and Costello Meet the Killer, Boris Karloff* [1949]).

Three remakes of H. G. Wells' story have appeared on the big screen: *Terror Is a Man*, an interesting, small-scale version filmed in 1959; *Twilight People*, a cheap 1972 Filipino co-production; and *The Island of Dr. Moreau*, a much bigger (though even less effective) production released in 1977.

THE VAMPIRE BAT
(1933; Majestic)

Release Date: January 17, 1933
Running Time: 62 minutes
Director: Frank Strayer
Producer: Phil Goldstone
Screenplay: Edward T. Lowe
Photography: Ira Morgan
Art Direction: Daniel Hall
Editor: Otis Garrett
Sound Engineer: Dick Tyler
Cast: Lionel Atwill (Otto von Niemann), Fay Wray (Ruth Berlin), Melvyn Douglas (Karl Bretschneider), Maude Eburne (Gussie Schnappman), George E. Stone (Kringen), Dwight Frye (Herman Gleib), Robert Frazer

(Emil Borst), Rita Carlisle (Martha Mueller), Lionel Belmore (Gustav Schoen), William V. Mong (Sauer), Stella Adams (Georgianna), Harrison Greene (Weingarten).

"I have lifted the veil. I have created life, wrested the secret of life *from* life!" — Dr. von Niemann.

SYNOPSIS

The story opens in the European village of Kleinschloss (literally "little castle"), where the burgermeister and his "Grand Council" are discussing a recent rash of murders. Six people have been "drained of their life's blood, found dead in bed — lifeless skeletons of skin and bones." The burgermeister shouts, "Vampires are at large I tell you, VAMPIRES!" In steps Karl Bretschneider, the local law, who injects a voice of reason. "I'm looking for a human fiend," he states as he good-humoredly scoffs at their superstitious fears.

The stage set, we're now introduced to kindly Dr. von Niemann and his lovely assistant Ruth, who is Karl's fiancée. We also meet Herman, the village half-wit with an affinity for bats (of which there seem to be an overabundance in this little hamlet). "Bats good. They not hurt Herman," he claims in his pitiful broken speech. Herman is generally well-intentioned and kind (bringing flowers to an old sick woman, for instance), but he's not above having a bit of ill-advised fun with the superstitious villagers who fear him a little because of his close association with bats. At one point he playfully pushes his pet bat (which he keeps inside his coat) at the villagers and laughs as they shrink away. Inevitably, the locals soon suspect poor Herman of being a bloodsucking monster.

An old woman named Martha falls victim to the mysterious fiend. Despite Karl's outrage ("Has the whole village gone mad?! Herman wouldn't hurt a baby and you know it!"), suspicions regarding the unfortunate Herman intensify. Yet another villager is found dead and still another disappears, and the baffled Karl has nary a clue to go on. When the burgermeister storms in and confronts Karl about these recent crimes, the harried law officer has little choice but to deputize the villagers and order them to find Herman and bring him in *unharmed*. "I hate to think of that poor misfit being hunted down like a dog," sympathizes Karl, and he makes it clear that there shall be no stakes driven through anyone's heart tonight. Despite Karl's firm admonitions, the overzealous villagers chase the frightened Herman into a cave where the terrified wretch half leaps, half falls to his death from a cliff edge.

Meanwhile, Georgianna, Dr. von Niemann's housekeeper, has found Martha's crucifix in Emil's room. "He must be the one," she concludes about von Niemann's loyal manservant, and takes it up with the doctor. Curiously, von Niemann advises her not to tell anyone while he looks into the matter.

Von Niemann then warns Emil, "You've got to be careful." With an unpleasant glint in his cold eye, the doctor concludes, "she's no better than the rest." A shadow falls across the sleeping form of Georgianna. When next we see the unfortunate woman, she is dead in von Niemann's lab, her body connected by tubes to a living, pulsing lump of artificial flesh!

When Georgianna's body is later discovered (strategically placed back in her bed), an exasperated Karl decides to search the house. Fearing discovery, von Niemann suggests a different course of action: "Take my advice young man, go home and go to bed. Get a good night's sleep and if there are any clues they'll be here in the morning when your nerves are calm and your mind is — clear." The doctor offers Karl some "sleeping tablets" to help. Of course, these tablets were taken from a bottle marked "poison." Karl stupidly takes the doctor's advice, goes home, and reaches for the pills while a dark figure crawls across his roof. It is Emil.

At von Niemann's house, Ruth comes upon the doctor seemingly talking to himself, urging Emil on from a distance: "Handle him like the others. You are strong Emil, very strong." She unwisely confronts him, and he ties her up in the lab, intending to "immortalize" her in his "great work" alongside Karl,

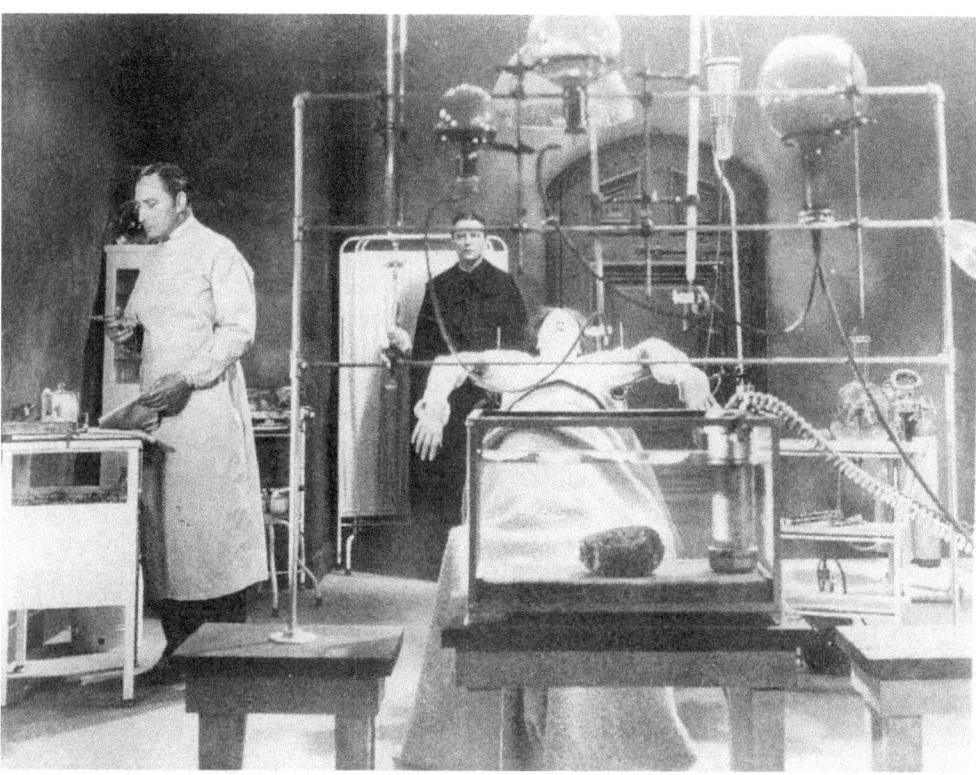

A rare chilling moment from *The Vampire Bat* (1933) as Dr. von Niemann (Lionel Atwill) drains the blood of his own maid, Georgianna (Stella Adams), to feed his vampiric sponge-monster (in tank). Atwill's faithful servant Emil (Robert Frazer) looks on.

who has been brought back by Emil. When the doctor lifts the sheet covering Karl's body, however, he finds Emil's face underneath. Karl, in Emil's hat and cloak, now steps forward with a gun and states the obvious: "I didn't take your sleeping pills, doctor." In a panic, von Niemann tries to place the blame on Emil, then lunges at Karl. In the ensuing struggle, Karl drops the gun. Emil regains consciousness and, having overheard von Niemann's accusations, picks up the gun. "I'll take care of von Niemann!" shouts the enraged Emil. "Get HER out of here." As Karl leads Ruth out of the room, we hear the sounds of a struggle and then two shots. Karl returns to the lab, where he finds von Niemann and Emil dead, each having killed the other.

MEMORABLE MOMENTS

It is rather disappointing that a film of this caliber should be so *un*memorable. There are, however, a few standout moments. The scene in which we discover the first on-screen victim of the fiend is a masterful use of camerawork and shadows to produce a true *frisson*. It begins as the camera fluidly pans down from the town clock striking the ominous hour of midnight, and a quick dissolve takes us into a small cottage. We prowl slowly through the room, finally coming to rest on the peacefully sleeping form of the old woman, Martha. Suddenly her eyes open wide and she utters a stifled cry as a sinister shadow moves across her terrified form. When the shadow has passed, the camera is still on her body, but the scene has changed. She is not sleeping but dead, lying on a slab in a makeshift morgue. The sudden appearance of the ominous shadow and the disorienting transition from a live woman in her bed to a dead body in the morgue is startling.

The film's high point comes when we

learn the terrible truth behind the diabolical murders. While Georgianna, who knows too much for her own good, sleeps peacefully in her bed, the dreaded shadow falls across her sleeping form. The next shot is a close-up of a pulsing, spongy mass of tissue in a glass tank. The camera's focus changes and suddenly we see *through* the tank to the prostrate body of Georgianna, arms outstretched in a crucifixion pose, her life blood running out through tubes connected to that grotesque parody of life in the tank. It makes for a chilling tableau, as the camera pulls back to reveal the whole malevolent milieu — the mad doctor, Emil, and the lab. The effective staging of this sequence gives the film its one truly horrific moment involving the disappointing sponge-monster, which we soon come to view with derision.

ASSETS

For what is essentially a "B" picture, the filmmakers have assembled a group of players that would be the envy of many "A" productions. Melvyn Douglas, Lionel Atwill, Fay Wray, and Dwight Frye are all excellent in their respective roles. Douglas shows the promise of the sterling career to come as he flexes his acting muscles in the role of Karl Bretschneider. In his spirited performance we see his good-humored skepticism dissolve into self-doubt, turn to anger at his own ineffectuality, then surge again in renewed determination. His self-effacing and human portrayal helps keep the fantastic proceedings believable. Lionel Atwill, in another of his many mad doctor roles, again shows why he worked so steadily in the 1930s and '40s. His authoritative presence and solid delivery add conviction to the frequently banal and awkward dialogue. Miss Wray, though given little to do but look beautiful and scream in the right places, still makes her character warm and appealing. And Dwight Frye, so underused throughout his career, takes the stock role of a village idiot and makes of him a sensitive, frightened human being.

Ira Morgan's fluid cinematography, under Frank Strayer's direction, draws us into the film to involve us directly in the bizarre proceedings. Through subjective camerawork, the viewer becomes a *participant* rather than just an observer. In the film's opening sequence, the camera moves slowly through the house until it finally comes to rest on the old woman's sleeping form. Only then do we realize that WE, in fact, are the murderer — or at least we share his point of view. Later, when von Niemann warns Emil (the killer) to be careful, the doctor looks directly at the camera — at *us*. Again we have become the murderer (and this is 45 years before the point-of-view shot was turned into a horror movie cliché by the grisly doings of a madman on *Halloween*).

The sets, though sparse, effectively create an atmosphere ready to embrace whatever horror is presented. (Unfortunately, nothing too horrific ever materializes.) Thanks to Ira Morgan's effective lighting, what we see of the village is all shadowy archways and dark, forbidding recesses. The doctor's lab, full of bubbling beakers and glass fixtures, seems designed for the most modern of scientific research, but the oversized wooden tables and cold stone walls make it seem more suited to the pursuit of confessions by the Inquisition than the pursuit of knowledge by scientists.

LIABILITIES

The film's dialogue is often stilted and awkward. Even the obligatory you-think-I'm-mad speech is poorly worded and unwieldy: "I have lifted the veil. I have created life, wrested the secret of life *from* life! Now do you understand?" Not really. In addition, the script contains plenty of pointless passages like: "She'll be all right. If she isn't, let me know."

The tedious romantic interludes between Douglas and Wray do nothing to endear their characters to us as intended. Instead, their silly patter and frivolous love games only disrupt the dark mood of the rest of the picture.

Likewise, the comic relief, in the form of the hypochondriac aunt, is much too drawn out and intrusive to be effective. Ideally, comedy in a horror film is used sparingly and at just the right intervals to produce some small relief from the terror and suspense, and so lessen the danger

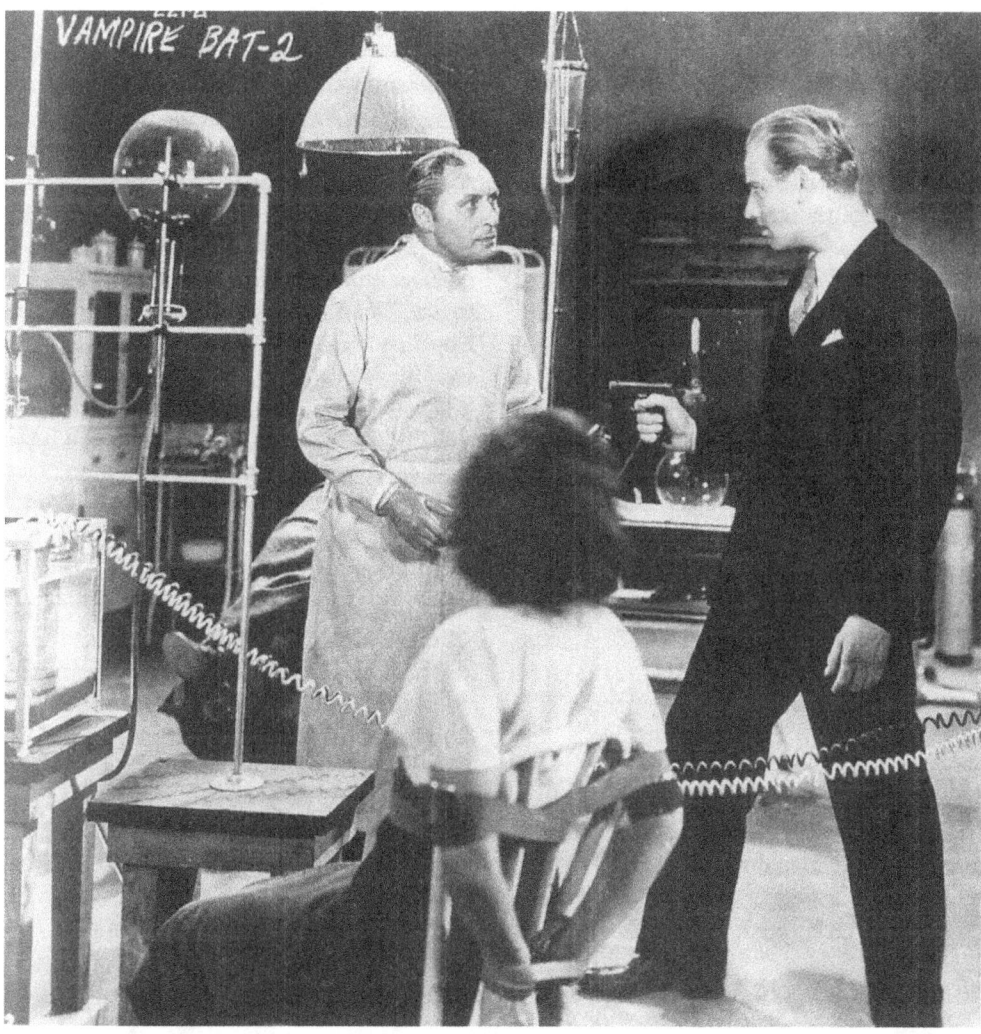

Holding Dr. von Niemann (Lionel Atwill) at bay, Karl Brettschneider (Melvyn Douglas) prevents his fiancée, Ruth (Fay Wray), from becoming the next victim of *The Vampire Sponge* ... uh ... *Bat* (1933). (Courtesy of Ted Okuda.)

of desensitization. By contrasting the comedic with the horrific, those terrors that follow will then be intensified. In this picture, there is very little horror to relieve in any case, and the comedy sequences are so frequent and drag on so long that they actually detract from any scare possibilities that do arise.

The film's "monster" is laughable. With all the buildup, and eight murders to warrant its existence, a pint-sized sponge in a glass tank does not quite deliver the impact needed when a bloodsucking creature is finally revealed to an eagerly waiting audience. The thing looks like nothing but a misshapen, pulsing sponge, and one wonders what all the fuss was about and why Lionel Atwill makes such grandiose claims over it. The whole purpose of this silly blob's existence is rather vague, as is the process and reasoning behind its creation.

Most disappointing of all is the climax, what there is of it. It begins with a weak and listless struggle between Atwill and Douglas. Then, with Douglas out of the picture, the two villains (Dr. von Niemann and Emil) simply shoot each other—*off screen*. A more unexciting and mundane ending for a mass murderer and his mad doctor master has yet to be conceived.

Despite a strong cast, a few good sets, and an occasional bit of effective camerawork, *The Vampire Bat* ultimately fails to overcome its myriad script weaknesses, intrusive comedy, weak climax, and lack of monster/menace, remaining a decidedly minor effort from the Golden Age of Horror.

REVIEWS

Variety's "Rush" (January 24, 1933) reacted favorably but likened the idea of making another horror picture to beating a dead horse: "Shiver picture, well enough done but coming along too late in the cycle to figure in the money.... Graveyard-at-midnight cycle has passed like any number of given cycles.... So a painstaking and well-made production misses, despite no little technical and acting merit."

Like *Variety*, the *New York Times* (January 23, 1933) also singled out the cast: "The film is acted somberly by Mr. Atwill, heroically by Mr. Douglas and in the conventional feminine pattern for these matters by the heroine, Fay Wray. Dwight Frye wins a few mild chills with his sinister portrait...." Overall, however, the reviewer felt that "familiarity, in the case of these operating-room idylls, has bred indifference, and it is difficult to achieve any considerable state of alarm over the things that are happening."

PRODUCTION NOTES

The Vampire Bat made use of several standing sets at Universal City. The village is the same one used in *Frankenstein* (1931), which was originally constructed for *All Quiet on the Western Front* in 1930. In addition, the makeshift village morgue is actually the wine cellar set from *Frankenstein* and Dr. von Niemann's mansion is the original, mysterious *Old Dark House* (1932). The production went on location to shoot the cave sequence in nearby Beachwood Canyon in Los Angeles.

During the filming of *The Vampire Bat*, Lionel Atwill told reporters that he was happier doing horror films than stage plays. "So long as I've got something definite and picturesque to get my teeth into I feel I can have a field day and enjoy myself, whether the role is equal to Hamlet or not" (as quoted in *Famous Monsters* #59). At about this time, Atwill (once a Broadway star) received an offer to appear in a play which, according to the New York producer, would establish him once more as Broadway's #1 actor. Atwill turned it down. "Frankly," he explained, "I've had my fill of art. It's all very well in its way, but there's an entirely different fascination to pictures that I haven't gotten over yet. No doubt I never will. It may be a little childish, but the sheer mechanical ingenuity of the whole thing gets under my skin the way a mechanical toy fascinates a boy. I've been having a tremendous good time and I don't see why I should stop." True to his word, *The Vampire Bat* was the first of eight films released in 1933 to feature Lionel Atwill. (Among them were the genre films *Mystery of the Wax Museum*, *Murders in the Zoo* and *Secret of the Blue Room*.)

Lionel Atwill and Fay Wray had been paired in two earlier horror films—*Doctor X* (1932) and *Mystery of the Wax Museum* (1933; filmed before but released after *The Vampire Bat*). Ms. Wray appeared in the staggering total of 11 features in 1933. She had the highest regard for her two co-stars, Lionel Atwill and Melvyn Douglas, more so than for the film itself.

In her autobiography, *On the Other Hand*, she relates, "We had the good fortune to add Melvyn Douglas in *The Vampire Bat*. He wondered, I'm sure, what he was doing in such a film. Probably making money, just as I was." Douglas had appeared a year earlier in the James Whale classic, *The Old Dark House* (1932).

In *See You at the Movies: The Autobiography of Melvyn Douglas*, the actor confirmed Ms. Wray's suspicions when he laughed off his participation in the film, noting dryly that "in *The Vampire Bat* I exposed a faked monster—and let a breathlessly waiting world know that Epsom salt has a scientific name." Summing up his cinematic experience so far, Douglas concluded that "the artistic product which resulted from the whole process of getting up in the morning and 'turning it on' for the studio fell far short of the hopes I had had when moving west." Shortly after completing *The Vampire Bat*, Douglas asked for and received a release of contract from Samuel Goldwyn and abandoned Hollywood for the New York stage (his true love).

The talented Dwight Frye, typecast by Hollywood as the perennial ghoulish assistant after *Dracula* (1931) and *Frankenstein*, lamented his ignoble fate at the hands of unimaginative producers. *The Vampire Bat* pressbook quoted him as saying: "If God is good, I will be able to play comedy in which I was featured on Broadway for eight seasons and in which no producer of motion pictures will give me a chance! And please, God, may it be before I go screwy playing idiots, halfwits, and lunatics on the talking screen!" Frye died in 1943 at the age of 44 from a heart attack, his prayer unanswered, for he was still typecast as "idiots, halfwits, and lunatics." (His last horror role, in 1943's *Dead Men Walk*, saw Frye as the crazed servant of vampire George Zucco.)

Director Frank Strayer had earlier helmed the vapid poverty row mystery/horror film, *The Monster Walks* in 1932. He later directed the equally disappointing *Condemned to Live* and *The Ghost Walks* (both 1935) before making many *Blondie* comedies for Columbia.

The Vampire Bat's screenwriter, Edward T. Lowe, had penned the 1923 Lon Chaney classic, *The Hunchback of Notre Dame*, and later wrote the Universal monster rallies *House of Frankenstein* (1944; also featuring Lionel Atwill) and *House of Dracula* (1945). Retiring from film writing in 1946, Lowe "burned all his scripts, clippings and mementos accumulated through his 35 years in the industry in what he called 'the great cleansing,'" reported *Variety* (May 23, 1973 obituary), and "kept his vow never to write again."

Though cinematographer Ira Morgan had worked for the major studios in the 1920s, he spent most of the subsequent two decades on poverty row shooting low-budget independent features (though occasionally landing an assignment at one of the "minor majors" like Columbia or Universal — where he helped shoot their 1938 borderline horror entry *The Black Doll*). Morgan's final picture was the awful Bert I. Gordon (Mr. B.I.G.) film, *The Cyclops* (1957).

MYSTERY OF THE WAX MUSEUM
(1933; Warner Bros.)

Release Date: February 16, 1933
Running Time: 79 minutes
Director: Michael Curtiz
Screenplay: Don Mullaly, Carl Erickson (from the story by Charles S. Belden)
Photography: Ray Rennahan
Camera Operator: Dick Towers*
Art Director: Anton Grot
Editor: George Amy
Makeup: Perc Westmore*
Gowns: Orry-Kelly
Wax figures by: L. E. Otis*
Assisted by: H. Clay Campbell*

Vitaphone orchestra conducted by: Leo F. Forbstein
Cast: Lionel Atwill (Ivan Igor), Fay Wray (Charlotte Duncan), Glenda Farrell (Florence), Frank McHugh (Jim the editor), Allen Vincent (Ralph Burton), Gavin Gordon (George Winton), Edwin Maxwell (Joe Worth), Holmes Herbert (Dr. Rasmussen), Claude King (Golatily), Arthur Edmund Carewe (Professor D'Arcy), Thomas Jackson (Detective), DeWitt Jennings (Police captain), Matthew Betz (Hugo), Monica Bannister (Joan Gale), Bull Anderson* (Janitor), Pat O'Malley* (Plainclothes man).
*Uncredited on film print

"I am going to give you immortality. You will *always* be beautiful!" — Ivan Igor.

SYNOPSIS

London 1921: A storm rages outside the sidestreet "Wax Museum." Master wax sculptor Ivan Igor receives an after-hours visit from two important art critics, who, impressed by his beautiful wax creations, propose to submit his work to the Royal Academy. After the pair leaves the grateful artist, Ivan's business partner, Joe Worth, enters. The museum has run out of funds (Worth blames Ivan's refusal to pander to morbid tastes and create a chamber of horrors) and the unscrupulous man intends to burn down the building for the insurance money. When Worth sets some papers alight, Ivan attacks the arsonist. The two struggle while the museum goes up in flames around them, Ivan's exquisite statues burning and melting. Worth overpowers Ivan and leaves his unconscious partner to die in the conflagration. Ivan awakens but can only stand helplessly watching his "children" burn.

New York 1933 (New Year's Eve): A visibly aged Ivan Igor peeks out from his curtained window at the nighttime revelers only to see the body of a young woman, a suicide, being loaded into the morgue wagon. Later, in the quiet of the small hours, two morgue orderlies attend to their cold charges before leaving for the night.

Upon their departure, one of the sheet-covered corpses abruptly sits up[1] — revealing a cloaked man with a hideously scarred face. The mysterious figure lowers one of the (real) cadavers out a window to his confederates waiting below.

Next we see Professor D'Arcy, a drug addict, deliver a large, coffin-sized box to a secluded storehouse, where it's received by none other than Joe Worth, Ivan's treacherous ex-partner!

The police feel the young suicide, Joan Gale, may actually be the victim of murder and they hold Ms. Gale's former beau, "millionaire playboy" George Winton, for questioning. Florence, a brassy young female newspaper reporter following the story, visits Winton in jail, where she becomes convinced of his innocence.

Later, at the morgue, the coroner prepares to autopsy Gale's body when it's discovered that the socialite's corpse is missing! Though Florence tells her scoffing editor that "eight bodies have been stolen in New York in the last 18 months," he pooh-poohs any connection with the Gale case.

The following day, the "London Wax Museum" opens in New York City; its proprietor: a wheelchair-bound Ivan Igor. Charlotte, Florence's roommate, visits the museum to see her fiancé, Ralph, a young sculptor working for Igor. Florence tags along and there sees the recently-completed Joan of Arc exhibit which she recognizes as the very image of Joan Gale. Florence is not the only one to receive a shock of recognition, for Igor sees in Charlotte the face of his long-lost masterpiece, Marie Antoinette. "You are that figure come to life," the crippled artist (whose hands are scarred beyond use) tells Charlotte, and asks her to pose sometime for one of his sculptors.

That evening, Igor conducts a tour of his marvelous creations. "The originals were destroyed twelve years ago in London in a fire," explains Igor to the rapt crowd, "and were reproduced only after *years* of arduous toil. To reproduce the figures destroyed, I had to train men for years to do the work that *I* could no longer do."

Florence learns that Professor D'Arcy (who Igor says "has been my hands for years") sculpted the Joan of Arc statue. Accompanied by Winton (so smitten with Florence that he has asked her to marry him), she follows D'Arcy to an old building where the nervous addict meets Joe Worth. Sneaking into the building, Florence finds a wooden box in the cellar — just large enough to hold a body — before she's forced to hide when the hideously scarred figure from the morgue enters the basement.

Rushing out when the coast is clear, Florence runs to the police. "I found the body!"

she cries. When the cops break into the building, they seize D'Arcy and open the dread box—only to find it full of illegal whisky! Worth, Igor's ex-partner, is a bootlegger (and he's nowhere to be found).

The next day, Charlotte goes back to the museum looking for Ralph. Igor tricks her into his basement laboratory (complete with a huge vat of bubbling wax). Rising from his confining wheelchair with surprising ease, Igor suddenly grabs the startled girl. Just then, Florence, sensing something amiss at the museum, arrives at the entrance where she meets Ralph.

At the police station, the sergeant finds on D'Arcy a watch belonging to the recently-vanished Judge Ramsey. D'Arcy, suffering horribly from withdrawal, breaks down. "All right, I'll talk, I'll tell you all I know! Ramsey was murdered because he looked like Voltaire.... It was Igor at the wax museum. You'll find your Judge embalmed in wax.... I tell you the whole place is a morgue!"

Back at the museum, an obviously mad Igor informs the frightened Charlotte of the death—and artistic rebirth—awaiting her. "I am going to give you immortality," he avows, "you will *always* be beautiful." The terrified girl strikes out with her fists—and Igor's face cracks beneath her blows, revealing the scarred wreck of a countenance belonging to the morgue fiend. Igor's "normal" face was simply a wax mask!

Now completely unhinged, Igor crows triumphantly of how he'd finally achieved his just revenge and unveils to the cowering girl the waxen body of Joe Worth, his old partner and enemy. Charlotte's screams draw Florence and Ralph to the laboratory. Florence goes for help while Ralph rushes at the fiend, but Igor knocks the young man unconscious.

With Charlotte now strapped beneath a filling nozzle of molten wax (ready to have her beauty "immortalized"), a squad of police arrive and break into the lab. After a vicious struggle, one of the officers shoots the madman and Igor falls from a catwalk into his own cauldron of boiling wax. Ralph regains his senses just in time to move Charlotte's gurney out from under a cascade of molten death. The two lovers embrace.

Back at her desk, Florence finishes her scoop and storms into her editor's office. When he puts her success down to luck, she shoots back, exasperated, "Listen stupid, could I possibly ever do anything that would meet with your approval?!" He immediately responds, "Yes you could. Cut out this crazy business, act like a lady, marry me." Glancing out the window to Winton (and a fortune) waiting just outside, she answers, "I'm gonna get even with you, ya dirty stiff. I'll do it," and they clinch.

MEMORABLE MOMENT

While the famous "unmasking" scene remains a powerful moment fraught with both terror and pathos, the picture's most striking sequence (so to speak) comes near the very beginning, when fire consumes Ivan Igor's museum. When Joe Worth (Igor's *worth*less partner) suggests they burn down the museum to collect the insurance money, an outraged Igor calls him insane. "Let me show you how *easily* it can be done," replies Worth, undaunted. Taking out his lighter, he sets a piece of paper alight. When Igor sees his intent, the outraged sculptor grabs at the paper, but Worth, a large bull of a man, muscles Igor over toward a female statue, the flaming paper clutched in his outstretched hand. In a mirror we see the two locked together as in a violent, desperate dance before the camera pans to show Worth force the flaming paper beneath the figure's dress, setting the delicate material ablaze. Worth then strikes Igor in the face, sending him crashing backward against a wall. A tongue of flame shoots up into the foreground and Igor lunges at his enemy. As the two struggle, we see shots of Igor's creations—his children—burning, their angelic, innocent faces bubbling in ugly blisters, their wax skin oozing and running in a horrible parody of death. While the two men fight, silent and desperately intent, flames continue to mount all around them. Worth grabs a lamp and hurls it a Igor. The missile shoots past its target to explode at the feet of Igor's masterpiece—his Marie

Mystery of the Wax Museum (1933): The wheelchair-bound Ivan Igor (Lionel Atwill) confers with his two sculpting assistants, Professor D'Arcy (Arthur Edmund Carewe, at left) and Ralph Burton (Allen Vincent).

Antoinette. With a violent jerk, Igor frantically shrugs off his weighty antagonist and sprints to her side, but Worth pursues and pulls him away. Worth sends the sculptor reeling against a heavy balustrade, but the banister gives way and Igor crashes to the floor. Dazed, he struggles to rise but falls again, mounting a few steps only to collapse backwards and lie still. Worth steps past Igor's prostrate form and looks back to take in the raging inferno the museum has become. As the villain strides away, huge roof beams collapse and land at Igor's very feet. Worth moves to the side door and the scene switches to the blessed, quiet coolness of the rainy, dark alley outside. Almost immediately, a thin line of blinding red and yellow splits the dimness of this tranquil respite to reveal Worth opening the door. He steps out and turns to close it again, the entire doorway now a wall of orange flame. He locks it.

Throughout this furiously paced and perfectly orchestrated sequence, the only sounds heard are the deafening, thundering *hiss* of the hellish fire, the intermittent *crack* as fists strike flesh, the *snap* of wood as a body falls against a shelf or banister, and the crashing *thud* of ceiling beams collapsing to the floor below. The human combatants remain silent, mute as Igor's martyred "children," adding an eerie note of quiet desperation to the scene.

Igor's obvious love for his "children" generates a powerful compassion in the viewer which turns to fiery anger at Worth's callous betrayal, adding a deeper dimension to the almost sickening excitement felt while watching the statues "die," their lifelike bodies burning and twisting as the agony spared the unfeeling figures is reflected a hundredfold in Igor's anguished face. This collision of emotions makes for a powerful moment, both thrilling and saddening.

ASSETS

Warner Bros., wishing to repeat the earlier success of their gruesome shocker *Doctor X* (1932), again placed the horror reins in the deft hands of Michael Curtiz for *Mystery of the Wax Museum* (and also granted the director Lionel Atwill, Fay Wray, *and* the two-strip technicolor process from the earlier picture). Given a better script in *Mystery*, a superior lead in Glenda Farrell (as opposed to a boorish Lee Tracy from *Doctor X*), and once again allotted Anton Grot's marvelous art direction, Curtiz creates a witty, exciting, frightening tale of the macabre which rises above even the high standards set by *Doctor X*.

Curtiz, a gifted, hard-working filmmaker (seven of his films were released by Warners this same year!), set down his views on filmmaking for the *Mystery of the Wax Museum* pressbook: "Odd, unusual camera angles should never be used for their own sake though the temptation to do so is often great, especially to the man who has an aptitude for thinking in them. The only reason for using an angle, in presenting a scene that would not seem the usual one to the onlooker, is to obtain a definite effect upon the spectator, which can be gained in no other way. You wish to arouse at that point a feeling of surprise, of terror, of repulsion, of admiration—and to emphasize it, the person or thing you are photographing must be presented from a special angle. Otherwise the natural, straightforward method of recording a scene in pictures is the one that holds the spectator's interest, keeps the story moving and preserves the flow and tempo of the action. It is very easy, in a story like The [*sic*] *Mystery of the Wax Museum*, for instance, to overdo the use of bizarre, startling angles. That is why I used them throughout the picture sparingly, and always with a definite purpose in mind. Unless one is wary of the employment of them, their effect is very quickly blunted, and thereafter they become a nuisance instead of a help." In *Mystery*, Curtiz succeeded in utilizing these "odd, unusual camera angles" both judiciously and brilliantly.

Just as he did in *Doctor X*, Curtiz (with the help of Ray Rennahan's mobile cinematography) makes the camera an active participant rather than simply a passive recorder, creating mood, shocks, and thematic parallels with his use of varied set-ups and angles. At the picture's very beginning, before we've ever met the unscrupulous Joe Worth, Curtiz shows us Igor's partner lurking near the corner of a building. In medium close-up, an off-kilter camera angle generates an uncomfortable impression of this unsavory character. Near the climax, when Igor abruptly rises from his wheelchair to threaten the heroine, Curtiz reveals the astonishing action via a low-angle shot so that the madman appears to tower menacingly as he stands. When Charlotte strikes out at the fiend, shattering his wax mask into fragments to reveal the twisted death's head beneath, Curtiz shoots from behind the terrified girl's shoulder, placing the viewer almost literally in her shoes so it seems as if it is *our* fists which lash out again and again to expose the horrid ugliness underneath. Thus, the viewer experiences first-hand the shock of the moment.

In another sequence, the camera picks up a dark-clothed figure and follows the retreating back all the way across a litter-strewn street, the mobile camera keeping pace with the mysterious figure until it enters a building. Once inside, the camera again picks up the unknown individual and continues to track a few paces behind. As the shape walks into a room, the camera chases, moving ever closer until the figure sits down and finally turns to reveal the unexpected profile of Joe Worth. By turning the viewer (via the camera) into an unseen pursuer, Curtiz increases the impact of the final startling revelation.

When the police find the missing Judge Ramsey's watch on D'Arcy, they usher the cowering addict into an office, hold up the watch, and ask accusingly, "That yours?" The scene dissolves to a close-up of a liquid boiling away furiously. The camera quickly tracks back to reveal the huge vat of bubbling liquid wax in Igor's laboratory—an amusing visual representation that D'Arcy, in fact, truly is in "hot water."

Macabre touches do abound. For an

establishing shot of the morgue exterior, Curtiz places the camera at a high angle looking down on the ill-lit street and shadowy morgue entrance below. He then moves the camera slowly forward to take us in closer to the dread entryway only to stop short as two menacing shadows creep across the threshold, their owners left unseen to exacerbate the unease of the moment.

Shots of the wax statues melting in the fire add a genuinely gruesome touch, the eye sockets widening into corpselike stares as the wax dissolves and runs, the melting wax sloughing off the face like layers of leprous skin, the head finally folding in upon itself and dropping sideways from the neck as if from a guillotine blade (with which Curtiz ends the scene as the fire burns through the execution exhibit rope, sending the blade slicing downward to sever the wax neck below with a shuddery *thunk*).

Curtiz went on to direct one other Golden Age horror classic, *The Walking Dead* (1936), as well as completing over a hundred other features for Warner Bros. With three horrific triumphs to his credit (*Doctor X*, *Mystery*, and *The Walking Dead*) Michael Curtiz can truly be called a grand master of horror's Golden Age, second perhaps only to James Whale in his stylishly macabre accomplishments.

Art director Anton Grot even surpasses his brilliant work in *Doctor X*, melding shadowy gothic with angular modernism to provide settings that underscore mood and create an eerie stage upon which the bizarre passion play can unfold. The morgue interior, for instance, is a quirky circular space in which the walls curve upward and inward to suggest the confining cap of a vaulted dome. The pillars set at regular intervals and arching toward the center create an aura of oppression, as if the massive supports were hovering just above us and could drop like the Sword of Damocles upon our unprotected heads at any moment. A cluster of heavy, conical lamps hang down like metallic vultures. Strange red and green-hued shadows lay along the recessed walls and among the shrouded gurneys. The oh-so-still occupants spread out along the circular room point toward the center to create a ghastly fence of (thankfully covered) cold flesh enclosing the viewer.

Igor's basement laboratory creates a very different impression, all angular modernism with suspended metal catwalk and curved staircase encircling and dominating the pit-like space below. Huge metal girders serving as pillars stand uneasily at weird angles, while banks of esoteric machinery, dials and switches along one wall testify to technological terrors. On the staircase above, huge metal bars for railings conjure up images of a stifling prison cell. The room's centerpiece, a gigantic cauldron filled with molten wax, its fumes and light casting a nightmarish hue throughout the chamber, creates a modernist's vision of Hell.

Don Mullaly and Carl Erickson's screenplay thankfully replaces the puerile humor (usually involving a hand-buzzer) found in *Doctor X* with witty dialogue delivered with rapid-fire precision by Glenda Farrell. Farrell tosses off lines like, "I'm fired — I have to make news if I have to bite a dog," and "I've been in love so many times my heart's callused," with a rat-a-tat delivery that brings her character to vivacious life. A lively bickering and comedic tension defines her relationship with her hard-nosed editor. When she gives him a raspberry over the phone, her boss quickly comes back with "a cow does that and gives milk besides" before hanging up.

While *Doctor X* was a fast-paced carnival ride of macabre thrills, *Mystery* adds that element so important in creating a lasting impression in a horror tale — pathos. Ivan Igor is an eccentric, likable, even kindly man. We smile as he lovingly talks of (and to) his beautiful wax creations — his "children" — and share his subsequent anguish as he helplessly watches them "die" in the consuming flames. We understand his bitterness at the slow, painful, imperfect recreation of his art (and life) through the hands of others, and can comprehend (if not entirely condone) his short temper and irate outbursts at those less deft than he. And finally, while we gasp in horror at his ghoulish activities, we can still find pity for this "fiend," so painfully wronged and only longing to recapture the beauty — the life — that was once his. His innate humanity has been twisted and blackened along with his mangled face and hands, yet it remains; and our shudders and cheers at the climactic demise of the fiend and rescue of the heroine is tempered with a pang of sympathy.

Lionel Atwill imbues Ivan Igor with a genuineness and passion that brings the character fully to life. Atwill is charming at the beginning as the humble sculptor proudly showing off his "children." The hint of an accent, his surprised delight and gratitude at the critic's praise, and his genuine affection demonstrated toward his work makes him a warm, affecting character. When the fire consumes his work — his life — Atwill displays real rage at the act and when all is lost, the helpless anguish on his face as he stands aghast, watching the flames engulf his "children," is truly heartrending.

A consummate actor, Atwill can inspire terror just as effectively as he elicits compassion. At the climax, when Igor rises from his wheelchair and grasps Charlotte with an impassioned "My Marie Antoinette!," Atwill's eyes go wide with a mad ardor and fix her with a searing stare so painfully intent it seems capable of burning a hole through mere mortal flesh. Little wonder that she screams under the crazed scrutiny of the agonizing glare.

Yet even at the height of his menace, Atwill still evokes a certain sympathy. Atwill's intense sincerity when he promises Charlotte "immortality" as a wax statue — as though offering his greatest gift — is pitifully touching. Then, after she cracks his mask to reveal the loathsome ugliness beneath, Atwill turns his head away and bows it slightly, averting his eyes to avoid the look of horror which would cut into his heart like a knife. When she recovers her shocked voice and finally screams, his head droops even lower in dejection at the reaction he inspires.

Igor's indomitable passion refuses to be extinguished and flares again under Atwill's fierce command. "There *was* a fiend," he answers heatedly when Charlotte affronts him with the hated appellation, "and this is what he did to me." Atwill suddenly whirls and stalks determinedly across the room toward an upright box resting against the wall, quickening his pace to violently rush the final few steps with one fist raised in anger to bitterly shout, "You! You did this!" at the heedless box. A stinging anguish shows through his madness and we pity him.

"I don't know what he was but he made Frankenstein look like a lily!" exclaims Florence when describing the ruined visage of Ivan Igor. Ms. Farrell's misappellative observation aside,[2] Perc Westmore's disfiguring makeup for Igor's grotesquely burned countenance is both unique and shocking, the gnarled walnutlike skin appearing hard and twisted, almost like petrified wood — or wood warped and blackened by fire. The ghastly visage inevitably draws the eye in horrible fascination. Many took note of Westmore's handiwork — not least of all the British censors, who labeled Atwill's horrific makeup "the most nauseating and by far the worst of its type."[3] The offended Britons even demanded that the picture's establishing title of "*London* 1921" be removed from their prints in an attempt to distance their country from the vile production. (The English public, however, held a different opinion from the outraged bluenosed bureaucrats; after *Forty-Second Street*, *Mystery of the Wax Museum* was Warners' biggest overseas hit of 1933.)

LIABILITIES

While scripters Don Mullaly and Carl Erickson create several fascinating characters (Ivan, Florence, her editor, Professor D'Arcy), they fail to bring to life the two juvenile leads (hero and heroine). Ralph comes across as a weak, dreary drone, little more than a whipping-boy for Ivan's bitter artistic disappointments. Charlotte is a silly, bloodless character, all-too-easily startled by the smallest of things. Fortunately, the snappy go-getter Florence provides the viewer with someone to focus on (and admire).

Mixing live actors posing as statues with actual wax dummies was a mistake. The actors

In *Mystery of the Wax Museum* Ivan Igor (Lionel Atwill) offers Charlotte (Fay Wray) "immortality"—as a wax statue.

do well enough in holding still to convince the viewer of their authenticity and add credence to Ivan's waxing poetic (so to speak) about their realistic beauty. However, the real wax images look ridiculously phony in contrast, making one wonder if Ivan had one hellaciously bad sculpting day to produce such obviously inferior works. It would have been better had Curtiz utilized only actors throughout (as he did in *Doctor X*) to represent the statues.

REVIEWS

If one listened to the bulk of reviewers, the film would be better titled Misery *of the Wax Museum*. Thornton Delehanty of the *New York Evening Post* felt that the film "never achieves anything but a waxlike imitation of horror. The newspaper scenes are filled with painfully unfunny dialogue, so that even such good actors as Glenda Farrell and Frank McHugh are made to seem bad. The picture, incidentally, is photographed in Technicolor, which leaves it about where it would have been in black and white."

Variety's "Abel" (February 21, 1933) was a bit kinder, noting that the cast "struggle about as effectively as did Mike Curtiz, the director, with a loose and unconvincing story, to manage a fairly decent job along the 'Frankenstein' and 'Dracula' lines." Impressed by Perc Westmore's work, he added, "Makeups are about the last word in gruesomeness." Less impressed by the wise-cracking reporter angle, he commented, "Like most newspaper stuff, the flippant, cynical and hardboiled manifestations in the role essayed by Miss Farrell rarely convince. The studious cynicism of the character creates a theatrical artificiality..."

The timorous Mordaunt Hall, reviewing for *The New York Times* (February 18, 1933) had his sensibilities shocked by the "ghastly details" of a film "going too far." (Apparently "glimpses of covered bodies in a morgue and the stealing of some of them by an insane modeler in wax" was simply too horrifying.) Grateful for any relief from the horror, Mr. Hall continued, "As an antidote to the abhorrent scenes, there is some good comedy afforded by Glenda Farrell ... and by Frank McHugh.... It is a relief to hear Miss Farrell wise-cracking to Mr. McHugh, and she gives a vivacious and clever performance." The reviewer concludes by saying, "After witnessing this unhealthy film it is very agreeable to gaze upon a short subject dealing with the wonders of Yellowstone Park."

PRODUCTION NOTES

Early in July of 1932, Warner Bros. loosed their legal eagles to track down and acquire the rights to an unpublished story entitled "The Wax Works" written by a former reporter-turned-screenwriter named Charles Belden.[4] The studio paid Belden $1,000 for his story before they discovered to their fiscal chagrin that in February Belden had sold a play (obviously based upon his short story) entitled "The Wax Museum" to independent producer Charles Rogers. To further complicate matters, Rogers was threatened with a copyright infringement suit by Ralph Murphy, co-author of the Broadway play "Black Tower" (in which a mad sculptor creates statues by injecting victims with embalming fluid). Though this element was the only (tenuous) connection between the two stories, Rogers dropped his option on "The Wax Museum" to avoid legal entanglements — happily leaving the way clear for a more intrepid Warner Bros. On the one hand, studio attorney Ralph E. Lewis advised Warners' head office that "there is a closer analogy between these two scripts than there was between *Wings* and *The Dawn Patrol* and we only got clear on *The Dawn Patrol* by the skin of our teeth,"[5] while on the other hand citing Thorne Smith's novel "Night Life of the Gods" (later filmed by Universal) as safe evidence that the idea of turning people into statues was nothing original. Warners went ahead with their property and apparently encountered no further legal difficulty (or at least left no record of such).

The studio handed *The Wax Works* (an initial working title which gave way to *Wax Museum* during shooting and finally transformed into *Mystery of the Wax Museum* a scant two weeks before its premier) to Hollywood newcomer Don Mullaly, a moderately successful playwright recently awarded a contract at the studio. *The Wax Works* was his first assignment. Mullaly turned in his initial treatment on July 27, and the studio immediately set one of their contract writers, Carl Erickson, to create an "optional outline" (adding a few ideas and refinements to Mullaly's scenario). Pleased with both contributors, the head office assigned them to continue work on the screenplay as a team.[6] Four collaborative re-writes later and *Wax Museum* was ready to go before the cameras.

Like *Doctor X* (1932), its predecessor and model, *Mystery of the Wax Museum* was shot in the two-color Technicolor process. This red and green process, which was unable to reproduce the full range of the spectrum, originated in the mid-twenties (utilized for select insert sequences in silents) but achieved its greatest popularity in the early talkies, specifically in musicals. As early as 1931 this process' popularity had waned with the public and *Mystery of the Wax Museum* became the final significant feature to be shot utilizing this technique. The year 1934 brought the development of the more natural-looking three-color process and color films were once again a viable (and profitable) option.

Director Michael Curtiz, in the *Mystery of the Wax Museum* pressbook, extolled the virtues of color (and lighting) in building mood in a picture of this type: "Much more effective is the specialized type of lighting we used to establish and build up a mood that we wished to communicate with the spectator. This was particularly true of the sequences laid in the two wax works — the London one and the New York museum.[7] In each, without being too obvious in our lighting, we tried to arouse in the spectators' minds a vague, intangible feeling of uneasiness, mystery, a sinister something lurking in the shadows, never shown but only suggested. The use of color is an asset in creating such moods in a story of this type. To be sure, stories of the fantastic, the horrible, the bizarre have been told with fullest success in black and white photography. But it has always been a question in my mind whether those very stories would not have been more gripping, more realistic, if they had been photographed in color such as we have employed with such unusual success in *The Mystery of the Wax Museum* and previously in *Doctor X*."

Art director Anton Grot had also designed the sets for *Doctor X*, and the similarities are clearly evident, even to the point of his reusing some of the laboratory equipment from the earlier film (the nozzle of Igor's wax dispensing machine, for instance, is a piece from the bizarre lie detector machine from *Doctor X*).

Glenda Farrell's wisecracking reporter served as a blueprint for her later "Torchy Blane" series in which the actress played the nosy newshound in seven pictures. Farrell began in stock theater at the tender age of seven (playing Little Eva in "Uncle Tom's Cabin") and made it to Broadway in 1928 (at age 24). After a bit part in 1929's *Lucky Boy*, she gained her first prominent screen role in Warners' *Little Caesar* (1931). Ms. Farrell "preferred stage and TV" to film work, according to *Variety*'s obituary (May 5, 1971), and she guest-starred in a number of television series in the fifties and sixties in-between stints on Broadway (including "Bonanza," "Wagon Train," "The Fugitive," and "Dr. Kildare"). Her small screen work culminated in an Emmy for an appearance on "Ben Casey" in 1963.

Francis Curray ("Frank") McHugh was born into show business, the son of actors Edward A. and Catherine McHugh, owners and managers of the McHugh Stock Company. After making his stage debut at the age of six in blackface in "For Her Children's Sake," Frank pursued his theatrical career to Broadway in 1925. Turning to films in 1930, McHugh appeared in over 150 motion pictures (mostly for Warner Bros.). He appeared in one other genre film — *Mighty Joe Young* (1949).

Fay Wray, in her autobiography, *On the Other Hand*, related how she experienced one of the hazards of working in a horror picture. "There is a scene in *The Mystery of the Wax Museum* when, in self-defense, I hit the face of Lionel Atwill. His face cracks and falls away, revealing horrible scarring underneath. This couldn't be rehearsed. Only two wax masks had been made. When the mask broke and I saw the repulsively scarred face, I absolutely froze instinctively, wanting not to touch that face again." The actress, having never seen the makeup before, was genuinely shocked (a testament to Perc Westmore's work) and the scene had to be reshot using the second mask. She continues: "Curtiz, with his camera-eyes watching over my shoulder, wanted to see the whole revolting visage at the first strike. 'You should have kept on hitting!' So we did it again with the second mask. Now that I knew what to expect, I could do it technically."

Ms. Wray acted in *Mystery of the Wax Museum* and *King Kong* simultaneously. She remembers the making of *Kong* as "just doing little bits and pieces all the way through that whole year; when I was at Warner Bros. doing *The Mystery of the Wax Museum* [*Kong* director Merian C.], Cooper would wait for me, so I'd go over to RKO and work on a weekend. It was kind of a paradox; here it was the middle of the depression, and it seems in retrospect that for me, it was a period of an enormous amount of work."[8]

In the 1970s, after viewing the "rediscovered" *Mystery of the Wax Museum* at a midnight showing at Grauman's Chinese Theatre (for years *Mystery* was a lost film until located and released to television in 1975), Ms. Wray commented on the merits of the picture: "I loved the color and Lionel Atwill's schmaltzy delivery and wisecracking Glenda Farrell."

"Schmaltzy" star Lionel Atwill reveled in his villainous roles, and worked hard to perfect his characterizations (sometimes *too* hard, as the actor revealed): "They fooled me in the *Wax Museum* thing, or rather, they let me fool myself. I'd been practicing before a mirror for weeks, learning how to keep my face as stiff as a board and just wiggle my jaws in talking, eyes set and staring — a grand effect. But then, in the finished picture, I looked so much like a stone image that they had to cut all those close-ups for fear of giving away that fact that my face was supposed to be a wax mask!"

Atwill, a complex man both in front of and behind the camera, enjoyed playing villainous roles—so long as they were not one-dimensional. While still a matinee idol on the Broadway stage, he began acting in early silents. In a 1919 interview for *Motion Picture Classic*, Atwill commented on the future of moving pictures, and his views on screen villainy: "I honestly think pictures have possibilities, but not until some of these old-fashioned ideas are combed out of them. For instance, to the picture director, a character is either a hero, who is all good, or a villain, who is all bad.... No one is wholly good or evil.... I, for one, will never play in pictures again until I am assured that the director is broad-minded enough to present a villain who has lovable qualities, or a hero who has a few weaknesses." While not holding true to this vow on every occasion, his role of Ivan Igor in *Mystery of the Wax Museum* proved to be just such a complex and rewarding one.

Later, in 1933, after becoming an established screen star, Atwill further expounded upon his convictions as to the duality of man (and himself) in *Motion Picture* magazine: "See, one side of my face is gentle and kind, incapable of anything but love of my fellow man. The other side, the other profile, is cruel and predatory and evil, incapable of anything but the lusts and dark passions. It all depends on which side of my face is turned toward you—or the camera. It all depends on which side faces the moon at the ebb of the tide."

NOTES

1. This bit of ghoulish shockery was lifted directly from *Doctor X*.
2. Florence fell into that age-old trap of referring to the Monster as "Frankenstein," when in fact, Colin Clive (as Frankenstein) was considered quite attractive. Even a mere 15 months after its cinematic birth, this unjust misidentification dogged the Monster's heavy footsteps.
3. MPPDA case file, April 15, 1933, as cited in *The Monster Show* by David J. Skal
4. Belden's rather unremarkable screenwriting career climaxed with a series of Charlie Chan pictures for Fox in the mid-thirties, the best being *Charlie Chan at the Opera* with Boris Karloff. Married to actress Joan Marsh in 1938, Belden died in the Motion Picture Country Hospital in 1954 at the age of 50.
5. Interoffice communication from Lewis to executive Morris Ebenstein in Warners' New York office (Warner Bros. legal files of the Wisconsin Center for Film and Theater Research).
6. Sadly, tragedy soon engulfed the two screenwriters. Mullaly died of tuberculosis a mere six months after completing the final script for *Mystery*, while Erickson committed suicide a scant two years later at the age of 27, reportedly despondent over his upcoming divorce.
7. Color worked particularly well in the fire sequence. The predominant reddish color-scheme of the two-strip process adds a hellish quality to the conflagration, turning the blazing museum into a livid purgatory as shades of fiery red and orange dance and blend together.
8. From *David O. Selznick's Hollywood*, by Ronald Haver.

KING KONG
(1933; RKO)

Release Date: March 2, 1933
Running Time: 100 minutes
Directors/Producers: Merian C. Cooper and Ernest B. Schoedsack
Screenplay: James Creelman and Ruth Rose (from an idea conceived by Merian C. Cooper and Edgar Wallace)
Photography: Eddie Linden, Vernon Walker, J. O. Taylor
Chief Technician: Willis O'Brien
Art Technicians: Mario Larrinaga, Byron L. Crabbe
Technical Staff: E. B. Gibson, Marcel Delgado, Fred Reese, Orville Goldner, Carroll Shepphird

Settings: Carroll Clark, Al Herman
Editor: Ted Cheesman
Music: Max Steiner
Sound Effects: Murray Spivack
Production Assistants: Archie F. Marshek, Walter Daniels
Recorded by: Earl A. Wolcott

Cast: Fay Wray (Ann Darrow), Robert Armstrong (Carl Denham), Bruce Cabot (John Driscoll), Frank Reicher (Captain Englehorn), Sam Hardy (Charles Weston), Noble Johnson (Native chief), Steve Clemento (Witch king), James Flavin (Second Mate), and King Kong (The Eighth Wonder of the World).

"Listen, I'm goin' out and make the greatest picture in the world, something that nobody's ever seen or heard of! They'll have to think up a lot of new adjectives when *I* come back!"—Carl Denham.

SYNOPSIS

According to *TV Guide*, *King Kong* is the second most often shown film on American television (beaten only by *Casablanca*). In any case, it's hard to imagine that any reader of this volume is *not* intimately familiar with *King Kong*'s storyline. But, as a refresher, here's a brief recap. Adventure filmmaker Carl Denham journeys to the remote and uncharted Skull Island to investigate the legend of "Kong" and hopefully capture it on film. He brings along a young woman, Ann Darrow, as the lead for his proposed picture. The island natives (whose village lies in front of a colossal wall which isolates them from the rest of the island) kidnap Ann and offer her as a sacrifice to their god, "Kong." Denham's rescue attempt is foiled when Kong himself, a gigantic ape, appears to carry off his prize. When Denham and his men pursue the monstrous simian, they fall prey to the dinosaur inhabitants of the island and Kong himself, leaving only Denham and Jack Driscoll (the ship's first mate) alive. After battling several dinosaurs, Kong carries Ann to his mountaintop lair. Driscoll follows and manages to sneak Ann away from the huge ape and make it back to the village. Kong chases after them and is only stopped when Denham subdues the leviathan with gas bombs. Denham takes Kong back to New York in chains, but the giant beast escapes during his premier exhibition. Rampaging through the city, Kong seeks Ann. Finding his prize, he finally heads for the tallest spot in the city, the Empire State Building. Climbing to the top, he must face down a squadron of biplanes, whose relentless barrage of bullets tear into his flesh. Setting Ann down one last time, Kong succumbs to his wounds and falls to his death.

MEMORABLE MOMENT

Very little happens in *King Kong* that is *not* memorable. Who can forget the mighty ape's first appearance, as he crashes through trees to claim his screaming prize tied to the two altar pillars; or the moment when Kong realizes his "golden woman" is escaping down a vine from his clifftop aerie and the gargantua begins hauling up the makeshift rope with the two humans kicking helplessly at the end of it; or Kong's thrilling encounter with the elevated train in New York when he sees it as some gigantic snake and deals with it accordingly; or finally, his fateful battle with the biplanes atop his new island home's tallest peak (Manhattan's Empire State Building)?

Yet, undoubtedly the most exhilarating sequence in a film full of excitement is Kong's titanic battle with the Tyrannosaurus. Arguably the most thrilling three-and-a-half minutes ever committed to celluloid, this amazing contest was one of the first bits of animation shot by Willis O'Brien and his technicians. This sequence, along with Kong's encounter with the sailors on the giant log (and a few bits from O'Brien's earlier aborted project, *Creation*), made up the ten-minute test reel which convinced David O. Selznick and the other RKO executives to back *King Kong* to the tune of $600,000 (three times the budget allotted a typical RKO "A" production).

The scene begins with Ann sitting atop the upright dead tree where Kong had placed her before going back to deal with his pursuers at the ravine. A huge Tyrannosaurus Rex steps

Marcel Delgado and his brother Victor construct the full-sized hand of *King Kong* (1933).

into the background and Ann screams. At this, the gigantic saurian charges. Hearing Ann's shrieks, Kong leaves his quarry (Driscoll trapped in a shallow cave in the cliff wall) and races back to his golden-haired Beauty, leaping over a fallen log in his haste. He reaches the clearing before the reptile can reach Ann and the two primordial combatants face off for a moment, measuring each other. Suddenly, Kong rushes forward to leap upon the T-Rex's back. There ensues a vicious melee of titanic proportions as the Rex shakes off Kong and fastens its huge jaws around the ape's protecting forearm. Kong breaks free and swings at his foe; the dinosaur leaps at Kong who grapples with the monster, grabbing its tree-sized leg to bring it crashing to the jungle floor. Its tail and legs move and kick furiously, sending Kong reeling back into Ann's tree which slowly but inexorably topples to the ground, taking Ann *and us* (as the camera tilts and seemingly goes over) with it. Kong finally wrestles the Tyrannosaur to the ground where he grabs the two halves of the snapping jaws and pulls. With a sickening crack, the Rex abruptly goes quiet and blood oozes from between its broken jaws. Kong moves the lifeless mandibles to make sure, then roars his triumph as he pounds his massive chest.

Bar none, this is indeed the most exciting dinosaur battle ever created and, even to this day, the single most impressive endorsement for the magic of stop-motion animation.

ASSETS

Nearly 50,000 people viewed *King Kong* on March 2nd at its twin-premier at New York's Radio City Music Hall and its sister theater, the RKO Roxy, and it's a safe bet that not one went away feeling cheated. King Kong, like Dracula and Frankenstein, has become an institution in modern culture, an oversized icon personifying the Beauty-and-the-Beast theme. Undoubtedly the greatest adventure film of the decade (and possibly of all time), *King Kong* is undeniably the most *exciting* production from the Golden Age of Horror.

But is *King Kong* truly a horror picture — or should it be taken simply as a fantasy film? Does *King Kong* contain moments of horror? Certainly. The natives fleeing in terror only to be grabbed by a huge hairy hand and chewed alive in Kong's gaping maw or crushed to death under a gargantuan foot; or the hapless sailor chased through the swamp only to be seized (head-first) by gigantic saurian jaws are each moments of pure terror. And let's not forget the shocking moment when Kong realizes he has hold of the wrong girl in New York and simply tips her upside down and drops the screaming unfortunate to her death on the street far below. Scenes don't get much more horrific than that. Does *King Kong* frighten? I'd challenge any viewer to sit through the log sequence and not feel a twinge in the pit of his or her stomach as the sailors cling for their lives before they roll off and fall screaming into the dreaded ravine below. Whatever else it might be (the ultimate adventure movie, for instance), *King Kong* is *definitely* a horror film.

James Creelman and Ruth Rose's straightforward screenplay is brilliantly constructed into three acts. The initial portion of the picture provides not only an efficient, no-nonsense character introduction, but a steady buildup to the all-out excitement of the second act. The script is full of dark hints about the terrors to come. When Denham finally lifts the veil of secrecy and tells the Captain and Driscoll about Skull Island, he tells them, "The natives keep that wall in repair — they *need* it." "Why?" asks Driscoll, to which Denham replies, "There's something on the other side of it — something they *fear*." Then, when Denham conducts a film test with Ann aboard the ship, he directs her "Look up slowly, Ann ... Now look higher, still higher. Now you see it ... It's horrible, Ann, but you can't look away. There's no chance for you Ann, no escape. You're helpless Ann, helpless ... Throw your arms across your eyes and scream Ann, scream for your life!" At the actress' ear-piercing shriek, Driscoll, watching from the upper deck, unconsciously grasps the skipper's arm and asks, "What's he think she's *really* gonna see?" What indeed? The middle section, and the film's centerpiece (in more than just a temporal sense), is the adventure on Skull Island which fully exploits the excitement (and terror) of the exotic — including the monstrous indigenous fauna. The final section brings the horror home to a more identifiable environment — back to civilization. No longer is the danger safely held on a faraway island, it now comes crashing into our own back yard. Once Kong appears, the film becomes a rollercoaster ride of cinematic excitement, taking us up peaks and plummeting into valleys, but never once stopping until the final frame.

"Put us in it," co-producer/director Merian C. Cooper told scripter Ruth Rose. "Give it the spirit of a real Cooper-Schoedsack expedition." Ms. Rose (wife of Cooper's partner, Ernest B. Schoesdack) did just that, capturing the filmmakers' spirit of adventure and excitement brilliantly, even going so far as to make Carl Denham a composite of Cooper and Schoedsack. "Makes me sore," complains Denham at the film's beginning, "I go out and sweat blood to make a swell picture and then the critics and the exhibitors all say, 'If this picture had love interest it would gross twice as much!'" Schoedsack, after the release of *Rango* in 1931 (his last picture before *Kong*), told the press, "Everyone seems to think that stories, to be vital, must have a love interest. A picture can't be good unless it's built around a throbbing scene between a male and a female. That's a mistake, as Cooper and I tried to show with *Grass* and *Chang*. We focus our lenses, not on silly close-ups of love-sick females, but on the elemental clashes between nations and their fundamental problems, between man and nature." Later, Denham explains why he always operates his own camera. "I'd have got a swell picture of a charging rhino but the cameraman got scared. The darned fool, I was right there with a rifle. Seems he didn't trust me to get the rhino before the rhino got *him*. I haven't fooled with cameramen since, I do it myself." While shooting *Chang* in the jungles of Siam, Cooper often stood by with a rifle — and on more than one occasion had to use it.

What makes *King Kong* so captivating, even 60-plus years *after* it created a worldwide sensation? Beyond its excitement, its exotic locale, and its amazingly lifelike dinosaurs, *King Kong* possesses an appealing grandeur. It is a film truly larger-than-life in more than just the obvious sense. Creelman and Rose's script cleverly lets the viewer participate in this epic adventure through the characters, which (including Kong himself) are simple, honest — likable. The tough Jack Driscoll, who never once hesitates in the face of danger, is not above admitting he's scared. Carl Denham, equally intrepid, displays a sense of humor about himself. "You're a pretty tough guy," Denham cautions Driscoll, "but if beauty gets ya —" Here Denham breaks off with a self-deprecating half-smile and wryly snorts, "Huh, I'm goin' right into a theme song here."

Robert Armstrong lives up to his surname as the strongest player in the cast. His boisterous enthusiasm and genuine bravado is downright contagious, drawing the viewer in to carry them along on his adventure. When, eyes sparkling, he promises Ann that "It's money and adventure and fame; it's the thrill of a lifetime and a long sea voyage that starts at six o'clock tomorrow morning!," Armstrong's overt excitement extends the exhilarating prospect to the viewer as well, so that we, too, can't wait for that six A.M. call.

Then there's Kong. From the very beginning, "The Eighth Wonder of the World" captures our emotions. At first he inspires awe, tinged with fear. But, almost immediately, he also engenders some measure of sympathy, as his monstrous hand gently, solicitously lifts up his golden-haired prize in a very *un*monster-like manner. Yes, Kong is a terrifying figure — as the hapless men on the log learn to their (short-lived) regret, but he also possesses a grand nobility. In Kong's very first battle, for instance, he literally saves the heroine from the jaws of death (in the form of a rampaging Tyrannosaur). When Kong's wrath is aroused, such as when his "Beauty" has been stolen from him, he shows no mercy and sows death and destruction indiscriminately, but he also possesses a tender side, as evidenced when he gently "unwraps" his prize on his mountaintop lanai, peeling away Ann's outer clothing with as much care as a child undressing a fine porcelain doll.

"I've always believed that over-civilization destroys people," philosophized Cooper. "All of Schoedsack's and my pictures have had one basic theme: that of man's fight against nature for survival." With *King Kong*, the filmmakers added an additional twist — Kong's (or nature's) fight against *civilization* for survival. On Skull Island, it's man (Denham and his sailors) against nature (Kong and the dinosaurs). On the island of Manhattan, however, Kong can be seen as Man's representative, man as Nature's child (or "noble savage" if you will) — now hemmed in by the constraints of civilization. In Cooper's terms, "over-civilization" certainly destroyed Kong. The conflict in *Kong* comes not from the clash of good and evil, or villain vs. hero, but of nature against civilization. There are no antagonists, no "bad guys," in *King Kong* (hungry dinosaurs excepted), just three protagonists whose desires clash — Kong simply wants to be left alone with his beautiful prize, whereas Jack wants Ann back and Denham wants Kong himself. One of the most poignant points about *King Kong* is how the tables turn on the mighty gorilla so that he loses his prize and *becomes* the trophy of someone else, his proud nobility now put on display to anyone with a ten-dollar ticket. As Denham relates to his gawking Broadway audience, "He was a king and a god in the world he knew. But now he comes to civilization merely a captive, a show to gratify *your* curiosity." When the curtain rises and we see the magnificent beast trussed up, crucified to a metal stanchion, our heart goes out to him.

So much praise has been heaped upon Willis O'Brien's contribution to *King Kong* that few superlatives remain. A consummate technician, O'Brien adds complex and delicate touches which makes the unreal real and brings the impossible to life. The Tyrannosaurus scratching his ear before attacking (perhaps a reaction to Fay Wray's piercing screams?); a barely noticeable ripple in the pool behind Kong as he sets Ann down on a ledge in his cave — indicating that they are not alone; steam continuing to rise up in the background during Kong's struggle with the Plesiosaur; Kong's shadow on the wall behind him moving with the behemoth as he steps back into his cave — all these extra touches and attention

Denham and company watch the progress of a Brontosaurus in this posed publicity shot from *King Kong*. In the film itself, the mighty saurian chases the men through the swamp, killing several along the way. *Bottom*: Willis O'Brien's brontosaurus model today. (Photo: Lynn Naron, 1993.)

to detail go a long way towards creating the film's convincing realism.

Beyond his innovative and brilliant technical achievements, O'Brien supplied his title character with a heart as well as lifelike movement. Thirty years later, O'Brien's widow, Darlene O'Brien, remarked, "King Kong *was* Obie. It was his personality. I could just see Obie in Kong's every movement, every gesture."[1] Though billed in lights as "Carl Denham's Giant Monster," Kong is more than that — he's a sympathetic character with his own personality and near-human traits. Our hands go to our own throats as Kong struggles with the coils of the snakelike Plesiosaur wrapped about his neck. We see the suffering and desperation in his face and demeanor, his mouth open, gasping, and his head reflexively thrown back. Later, when one of Denham's gas bombs goes off at his feet, Kong rubs his eyes and grasps his throat in an all-too-human mannerism, then struggles valiantly to crawl slowly forward even as the gas overcomes him. Though Denham has stopped Kong's rampage, we feel more than a twinge of sadness at the mighty Kong's first defeat. And finally, at the thrilling climax atop the Empire State Building, Kong flinches as the planes strafe his body. He feels his chest, then looks at the blood which comes away on his fingers. As the repeated gunfire takes its toll, Kong's head droops and he wipes his brow with the back of his hand as if trying to rub away the life-draining fatigue. He can barely hold on now. His eyes are half closed and he gives a last, half-hearted snarl in a final, defiant gesture which conjures merely a shadow of his former ferocity. Through O'Brien's effective characterization, we've come to respect, even *like* this character so that what could have easily been a simple man vs. monster ending becomes a bittersweet moment of poignancy.

One simply cannot overestimate the musical contribution of Austrian-born composer Maximilian Raoul Walter Steiner. "*King Kong* was made for music," recalled Steiner. "It was the kind of film that allowed you to do anything and everything from weird chords and dissonances to pretty melodies." Originally, RKO, wishing to save money, had ordered Steiner to simply recycle old music tracks from some of the composer's previous horror/mystery scores — *The Most Dangerou Game, Secrets of the French Police,* and *The Monkey's Paw.* With the backing of Cooper, however, Steiner ignored the front office and created one of the greatest scores of the Golden Age of Horror. Steiner's innovative score, in which he imitated action with his music whereby every movement has a corresponding musical figure (the sound department dubbed it "Mickey Mousing") expands Kong's personality and adds tremendously to the larger-than-life, fairy-tale feel of the picture. Amazingly, with a pre-set March release date, Steiner had only *two weeks* to compose the entire score and two more weeks to record it! Ray Bradbury, in writing the liner notes for the *King Kong* original score record album (United Artists Records, 1975), opined that "If you lopped Steiner's music from the film and substituted the usual early thirties thin-skinned one drum, two flutes and four violins treatment you might well end up with the comedy of the century!"

LIABILITIES

As brilliant as it is, *King Kong* possesses its share of technical flaws. The full-scale Kong head seen in close-ups does not quite fit in with O'Brien's facial movements on the animated model. The mockup's face is too flat, lacking the sloping forehead of the model, and, worst of all, it seems to wear a perpetually benevolent smile — even while chewing on a hapless extra. The large prop looks unwieldy and phony whereas the animated Kong seems alive with expressive snarls and roars. The lighting and texture of the two never quite seem to match up either.

The sailors scooped out of the water by the jaws of the Brontosaurus (actually an Apatosaurus for the paleoentological purists) are obviously small dolls that bend and flap about unnaturally. Likewise, the sailors falling into the dreaded ravine and Ann and Driscoll taking that long drop into the river look just like what they are — rag dolls.

Denizens of the primordial ravine: When Kong knocks the sailors off the huge log spanning the chasm, the victims plunge into this canyon to be devoured by a myriad of gigantic creatures, including this spider. The sequence in the ravine was cut before release because of pacing and (unlike a number of other excised scenes) has remained lost.

Some 60 years after *King Kong* was produced, some of the dialogue (particularly the sexist remarks) has become high camp. In this politically correct day and age, some of the lines make the characters seem hopelessly out-of-date. Early on, Jack Driscoll tells Ann that "Women just can't help bein' a bother — made that way I guess," and Ann simply swallows and accepts it! (When heard today, this bit of misogynistic "wisdom" never fails to bring down the house.)

In a 1969 article for *The New York Times*, Fay Wray explained how she managed her penetrating trademark scream. "I made myself believe that the nearest possible hope of rescue was at least a mile away and my only chance of survival was to be heard loud and clear!" While Ms. Wray performs brilliantly in the vocal department (not to mention adding a capitol "B" to "beauty"), her starry-eyed playing, heaving bosom, and wide-eyed innocence in the more mundane scenes make her character seem a bit unreal. Fay Wray was a good actress (she held her own against Claude Rains in 1935's *The Clairvoyant*, for instance), but too often filmmakers simply relied upon her beauty rather than her thespian talents. *King Kong* is no exception. Though undoubtedly her most famous role, it is by no means her best. Her romantic exchanges with Bruce Cabot are the picture's weakest points. In his first starring role, Cabot fares little better. Though he puts over the tough-guy heroics well enough, his tender line "I uh — say, I guess I love you," complete with a nasal emphasis on the word "love," is the most painful moment in the film.

The above are just minor quibbles, however, tiny scratches on the celluloid surface of the greatest adventure film ever made. No amount of time, shoddy knock-offs, or terrible "remakes" can erase the magic of the original *King Kong*. On February 10, 1933, Willis O'Brien participated in a half-hour promotional radio broadcast on the National Broadcasting Company network. "Speaking for myself," the animator said, "*King Kong* represents the goal of more than 20 years. For that long a time — and that is a long time in motion pictures — I have delved into bygone periods, studied the life of animals long before the descent of man, preparing myself for the day when someone would dare to reproduce on the screen the giant beasts that once ruled the world. Without knowing it, I was waiting for *King Kong*. That is the picture for which I have studied 20 years. I feel it has been worth the long years of research. And I hope you, too, will feel the same way after seeing *King Kong*." Standing tall atop his mountain aerie, *King Kong* sets astride the very pinnacle of the Golden Age of Horror.

REVIEWS

The New York Times (March 3, 1933): "The narrative is worked out in a decidedly compelling fashion, which is mindful of what was done in the old silent film 'The Lost World'.... The producers set forth an adequate story and furnish enough thrills for any devotee of such tales.... Needless to say that this picture was received by many a giggle to cover up fright. Constant exclamations issued from the Radio City Music Hall yesterday.... Miss Wray goes through her ordeal with great courage. Robert Armstrong gives a vigorous and compelling impersonation of Denham."

Variety (March 7, 1933): "So purely an exhibition of studio and camera technology — and it isn't much more than that — 'Kong' surpasses anything of its type which has gone before it in commercial film-making. The work has many flaws, but they're overcome by the general results. [The reviewer, 'Bige,' obviously thought Kong was a man in an ape suit.] 'Kong' mystifies as well as it horrifies, and may open up a new medium for scaring babies via the screen."

PRODUCTION NOTES

King Kong creators Merian Caldwell Cooper and Ernest Beaumont Schoedsack had specialized in jungle adventure documentaries such as *Grass* (1925) and *Chang* (1927). In 1931, Cooper was given the job of sifting through various unfinished projects at RKO to see what was salvageable, and he came across a test reel for an unrealized project called *Creation*. *Creation* was a film proposed by Willis O'Brien following his success with *The Lost World* (1925) which would feature various dinosaurs on an island rising out of the sea during an earthquake. While Cooper felt *Creation* lacked sufficient commercial punch, he did see in O'Brien's wondrous technique of stop-motion animation a way to bring to life his own pet project — the tale of a huge gorilla pitted against both prehistoric reptiles and modern man. Upon conceiving his Giant Ape movie, Cooper had originally thought of using a live gorilla, then later envisioned an actor in a gorilla suit as the giant ape, with live Komodo dragons standing in for the dinosaurs. (A friend of Cooper's, W. Douglas Burden, had told the filmmaker of his adventures on the island of Komodo in Malaysia, on which he had seen these gigantic reptiles which grew to lengths of ten feet.) But the idea was deemed too expensive by studio heads and Cooper had been unable to sell the project. Enter Willis O'Brien. Obie (as his friends called him) was, in Cooper's words, "A true genius. The only way he could communicate an idea was by sketching it out. He could sketch animals, particularly prehistoric animals, better than any man who ever lived. He was certainly the most brilliant trick and special effects man that Hollywood had ever seen; not only that, he was as good an animation sculptor as Walt Disney was an animation cartoonist."[2] Ultimately, Cooper conceded that "*Kong* is as much his picture as it is mine."

With only a rough storyline to go by, O'Brien set about filming and assembling a test reel (titled simply *The Beast*) which Cooper

King Kong's creators: Merian C. Cooper, Ernest B. Schoedsack, and Willis O'Brien (foreground) pose with Fay Wray and Skull Island extras on the RKO-Pathé backlot village set.

could show to the RKO brass. After receiving the green light, Cooper then commissioned mystery writer Edgar Wallace to write a script for *The Beast*. Wallace constructed a 110-page scenario, though he credited Cooper with the majority of the story element. Donald F. Glut, in his book *Classic Movie Monsters*, gives a capsule synopsis of Wallace's treatment: "Carl Denham, an explorer, circus man and once friend of P. T. Barnum, is aboard a tramp steamer when he rescues the survivor of a shipwreck on an uncharted island. Denham laughs at the man's tale of sea serpents. Meanwhile, Shirley and John, the heroine and hero of the story, and crew of ex-convicts are in a lifeboat which is overturned by an Apatosaurus. The survivors reach the island where prehistoric monsters abound. Shirley becomes the intended rape victim of the crew when Kong appears, rescuing her from one "fate worse than death" and carrying her through the jungle to one considerably worse. In his cave Kong displays his affections for Shirley by gently caressing her cheek and offering her a pterodactyl egg. Later a drugged Kong is exhibited to the public in Madison Square Garden. But when the giant ape sees his beloved Shirley menaced by Denham's circus tigers, he escapes his cage and kills them. His final stand atop the Empire State Building occurs during a storm. After being riddled with bullets fired by airborne policemen, Kong is electrocuted by a bolt of lightning."

The project was now titled *Kong*. (Burden remembered that Cooper "especially liked the strength of words beginning with K, such as Kodiak Island and Komodo, and it was then, I believe, that he came up with the word 'Kong' for a possible gorilla picture."[3]) The name was shortlived, however, for the studio executives objected to "*Kong*" (thinking it too Oriental sounding and too similar to Cooper and Shoedsack's earlier *Chang*), and Wallace suggested *King Ape*. Eventually, the two were combined, and *King Kong* became the project's immortal moniker.

David O. Selznick had this to say about Wallace's involvement (and his own) in the project: "As to *King Kong*, I would say I was simply executive producer. RKO, when I took it over, had a big investment in an animation process of Willis O'Brien's. I brought back into the business as my Executive Assistant Merian C. Cooper, with whom I had been associated at Paramount on *The Four Feathers*, and assigned to him as one of his jobs a study of this animation process, and Cooper conceived the King Kong character idea." (Cooper had actually conceived of Kong in 1929, but it was not until December of 1931 that he decided to apply O'Brien's stop-motion animation technique to the project after investigating the process at Selznick's request.) "I had signed up and sent for Edgar Wallace," continued Selznick, "and brought him to California, where unfortunately he died in consequence of getting pneumonia and refusing to have a doctor since he was a Christian Scientist. But while he was in California, I assigned him to work with Cooper on *King Kong*. I have never believed that Wallace contributed much to *King Kong*, but the circumstances of his death complicated the writing credits. The picture was really made primarily by Cooper and Ernest Schoedsack, under my guidance; and one of the biggest gambles I took at RKO was to squeeze money out of the budgets of other pictures for this venture." (From *Memos from David O. Selznick*, by Rudy Behlmer.) Cooper was grateful for Selznick's "gamble" and for his non-interference. "[Selznick] didn't have the slightest idea what I was doing," remembered Cooper, "but he said that Schoedsack and I had only made three films and they had all been smashes, so he'd back me all the way. And he did too. He never interfered, never tried to tell me what to do."[4]

After Wallace's death, Cooper handed the treatment over to screenwriter James Creelman, who punched it up into a filmable format. Cooper was still unsatisfied, however, and found his solution in the wife of his longtime partner, Ernest B. Schoedsack. Ruth Rose (Mrs. Schoedsack) was far from a professional writer (her sole experience consisting of a few articles about an exploratory expedition and one romantic short story printed in the *Ladies' Home Journal*). But she had been on far-flung expeditions herself and knew the type of men that journeyed to the remote corners of the earth and how they talked. "I had read the stuff she wrote when she was on expedition in South America," remembered Cooper, "she wrote simply and descriptively and I liked it. I had no way of telling whether she could write a script or not, but I gave her all the outlines and drafts and asked her if she could combine all the things I liked from each one. Well, she quickly showed she could write scripts like nobody's business. She changed the characters; she made Denham and Driscoll very much like Schoedsack and myself, and most importantly, she rewrote all the dialogue. I asked her to keep hitting the Beauty and Beast theme again and again, before we saw Kong, which she did brilliantly and nonchalantly. I don't think another human being in the world could have given me the simple, direct, fairy-tale dialogue that she did. It was just what I wanted."[5]

After viewing the impressive test reel for the project, RKO's New York executives gave the production the go-ahead with a budget of $600,000 (which included the $100,000 already spent on O'Brien's aborted *Creation* project). The film's final cost was $672,000, but the front office had little reason to grumble. On its initial release *King Kong* netted RKO over $2 million, giving the studio a clear profit of $690,000—going a long way towards staving off RKO's impending bankruptcy.

The film opens with a title card quoting an "Old Arabian Proverb": "And the Prophet Said—And lo, the beast looked upon the face of beauty. And it stayed its hand from killing. And from that day, it was as one dead." In reality, this Beauty and Beast-minded proverb was concocted by Cooper himself, though much like the oft-quoted poem from *The Wolf Man* ("Even a man who's pure in heart..."), its Hollywood origins have given way to accepted authenticity.

Cooper's sense of the fantastic overpowered his sense of reality in *Kong*, sometimes to the consternation of O'Brien and his staff.

O'Brien had scaled his miniatures and sets an inch to one foot, meaning Kong would always remain a constant 18 feet tall. Cooper would have none of this constraining measuring: "I was a great believer in constantly changing Kong's height to fit the settings and illusions. He's different in almost every shot; sometimes he's 18 feet tall and sometimes 60 feet high or larger. This broke every rule that Obie and his animators had ever worked with, but I felt confident that if the scenes moved with excitement and beauty, the audience would accept any height that fitted into the scene. For example, if Kong had been only 18 feet high on the top of the Empire State Building, he would have been lost, like a little bug; I constantly juggled the height of trees and dozens of other things. The one essential thing was to make the audience enthralled with the character of Kong so that they wouldn't notice or care that he was 18 feet high or 40, just as long as he fitted the mystery and excitement of the scenes and action."[6] This poetic license extended to the dinosaurs as well. The Stegosaurus is over 50 paces long — or about 150 feet (Denham and Driscoll carry on an entire conversation as they walk the length of it), making it larger than any dinosaur known to exist!

Once the production got rolling in earnest, it took nearly a year to complete the principal photography. In her autobiography, *On the Other Hand*, Fay Wray commented on the schedule: "The pattern of work [on *King Kong*] had been established: Animation and special effects would be prepared, then there would be a few days of shooting with me.... The film took about ten months once they got into this on-again-off-again rhythm and I would be able to do other films while Kong and the prehistoric animals were performing together. I began to believe it was the rumored scariness of Kong that stimulated producers to offer other "scary" movie roles to me: *Dr. X* [sic], *The Mystery of the Wax Museum*, *The Most Dangerous Game*, and *The Vampire Bat*—all these in the same year as the making of *King Kong*."

Much speculation has surrounded the scene on the giant log in which Kong knocks the sailors off into the canyon below. Legend has it that O'Brien shot footage of the sailors being devoured by a myriad of creatures lurking on the ravine floor, including an octopus-like monster, huge lizards, and a giant spider. According to author Donald Glut, who had the opportunity of speaking with Cooper in 1966, it is no legend but fact. Frequent references have been made as to why the spider sequence was deleted — it was too gruesome. Not so. Cooper related (in Glut's *Classic Movie Monsters*) that he removed it (after gauging audience reaction at preview screenings) because "it slowed down the action." "O'Brien was heartbroken," Cooper remembered,[7] "he thought it was the best work he'd done, and it was, but it worked against the picture, so out it came." Author Ray Bradbury remembered having seen the lost spider sequence as a boy at an Arizona theater, so perhaps some prints *were* released with the scene intact (or maybe he caught a rare sneak preview screening). The missing spider finally popped up in O'Brien's 1957 film, *The Black Scorpion*, where it chases a small boy before falling prey to a giant scorpion. It can also be seen (along with a number of other creatures from *King Kong* and *Son of Kong*) sitting on the shelf of a movie studio set in the RKO production, *Genius at Work* (1947). The final appearance of this ill-fated spider was in *Women of the Prehistoric Planet* (1965), though rather than being animated, it is simply jerked around on an all-too-visible string.

Beyond this excised sequence, a number of damaging cuts (Kong peeling off Fay Wray's clothing; his various stompings and chewings; his casual dropping of the "wrong woman" in New York) were demanded by the Production Code Administration for the film's 1938 re-release. Cooper, understandably, was incensed. For nearly five decades, this altered version played in moviehouses and on television sets across the nation, with the missing footage considered "lost." Thankfully, it has been found and restored, and the true Kong now chews, stomps, sniffs and drops in all his glory.

The sense of mystery and menace which

Merian C. Cooper finally tells Fay Wray about her "tallest, darkest leading man in Hollywood" in this gag publicity shot for *King Kong* (1933).

fills the jungle landscapes of *King Kong* can be attributed to the works of Gustave Dore. Cooper insisted that O'Brien and his team copy Dore's engravings for Milton's *Paradise Lost*. Recalls Cooper: "The lighting, the jungle, the foliage we stole direct from Dore. But we had great difficulty getting a sense of depth on the miniature jungle; it just didn't have the quality of receding mystery to it that jungles have, the semi-darkness, the shadows, and the sense of hidden dangers." To achieve the desired effect, O'Brien and Cooper "devised what we called 'arial perspective,' whereby the jungle sets were built on three large tables. On those tables were a series of plate-glass panes on which [O'Brien's artists] Larrinaga and Crabbe painted sections of the jungle and skies, all copied directly from Dore."[8]

The monstrous roars emanating from Kong (which sometimes lasted 30 seconds) were actually the sounds of a lion recorded at half speed and printed in reverse. His mighty footfalls were made by two toilet plungers covered in sponge rubber tromping across gravel.

On any elaborate action-oriented production, accidents are bound to happen and *King Kong* was no exception. Stuntman Gil Perkins, who worked for over a month on the project, related how Fay Wray's double was injured during the vine-escape scene. "I was just hanging onto the liana (that's what *they* called the vine)," Perkins told Tom Weaver in *Starlog* #194, "and the ape was lifting it up and down and shaking it. Actually, it was being hoisted by special FX guys, off camera. Fay Wray had a stunt double there also, of course; I can't think of her name now. We had pads down below us, 'cause sometimes we were up as high as 45 feet on this cliff set. She wasn't one of the best stunt gals that I knew. There *were* some great gals, but she wasn't one of 'em; she was a gal who didn't take very good care of herself— she smoked and all. She was trying her best, but at one point she couldn't hang onto me any more, and she fell about 20 feet onto the pads. She hit the wrong way and started to cough up blood, which scared the bejeezus out of everybody, because she had injured her lungs."

Joel McCrea was director Merian C. Cooper's first choice for the heroic role of Jack Driscoll. McCrea told John Kobal (for his book *People Will Talk*) that when Cooper offered him the role, the actor answered, "Well, doesn't sound like the way I want to go," feeling that his upcoming participation in *The Most Dangerous Game* was enough of "that kind of adventure-dream idea." Cooper then asked McCrea to "think of somebody who will be good." Shortly after, McCrea went out to dinner. "On the way in," recounted McCrea, "I saw the bouncer, the guy on the door, and it was Jacques de Bujac, who later became Bruce Cabot.... I got him to write out his name and address and phone number, gave it to Irene [wife of David O. Selznick] and she gave it to David Selznick. The next thing I knew, they had made a test of him, and they decided to do it, and he did the thing and became Bruce Cabot."

Cooper and O'Brien often differed in their view of Kong's character. Obie felt that Cooper was making Kong too brutal to be sympathetic (what with viciously stomping and chewing on natives). Schoedsack agreed with O'Brien. "They were both convinced that I could never get any sympathy for the ape at the end if I had him doing all these brutal things," said Cooper, "but I knew that people would cry at the end when he was killed, so I overrode them all on this."[9]

While Schoedsack directed much of the live action, particularly the complicated crowd and panic scenes, Cooper supervised O'Brien and in fact "directed" some of the animation scenes—by painstakingly going through the motions he wanted in each of the characters (including the dinosaurs), acting them out for the animators to copy. "The only way I could do it was to get up in front of the animators and act the whole thing out, first in regular speed, man-speed, then do it again in slow, slow motion for them while they were animating." Cooper wryly observed that "the ape wasn't too bad, I got that down pretty good, but I sure as hell didn't look like a dinosaur." Cooper had some trouble with Kong's death scene, however. "The first time I did it, I was too broad, too hammy, and they did it just like that. Well, it was the funniest damn thing you ever saw, that ape, pop-eyed, rolling, writhing, and clutching. We all had a good laugh and then I did it again for them, this time toning everything down, and this time they got exactly what I wanted."

Ironically, it was not the airplanes, it was *Cooper and Schoedsack* who killed the beast! When it came time to film the live action close-ups of the biplanes strafing Kong, Cooper told Schoedsack, "Let's kill the son-of-a-bitch ourselves." So the two directors doffed flying caps, climbed into the cockpit mock-ups and sent their beloved Eighth Wonder of the World toppling to his death. Cooper was no stranger to a biplane cockpit, having served as a combat pilot in World War I (he was shot down — *twice*).

According to production assistant Archie Marshek, we have Cooper's superstitious nature to thank for one of *King Kong*'s most exciting sequences. When the film was finally put together in a rough cut, remembered Marshek, "it ran 13 reels and Coop had a fit. 'No picture of mine is going out in 13 reels,' said Cooper. 'I'll shoot an extra sequence and bring it up to 14.'"[10] This extra sequence is the exciting and terrifying destruction of the mid–Manhattan elevated train by Kong.

All the sexual, racial, religious symbolism read into *King Kong* over the years was categorically rejected by Cooper. To the end of his life, he maintained that *"King Kong* was never intended to be anything more than the best damned adventure picture ever made. Which it is; and that's all it is."[11]

It was Merian C. Cooper (a founding member of David O. Selznick's new production company) who later convinced Selznick to utilize the expensive Technicolor process for *Gone with the Wind* (1939). The great wall on Skull Island was destroyed in the burning of Atlanta climax of *Gone with the Wind*. The massive gate was utilized in the 1935 fantasy/adventure film *She*; and the Skull Island sets appeared in the 1934 Bela Lugosi serial, *The Return of Chandu*. Actually, this massive wall set was not built for *King Kong*, but was a standing set on the RKO-Pathé studio lot, having been constructed for the Cecil B. DeMille biblical epic, *The King of Kings* (1927).

In the early 1950s, Merian C. Cooper became head of production for the Cinerama Organization, and briefly considered remaking *King Kong* using the Cinerama process. Titled *The Eighth Wonder* (Cooper's first shooting title for the original *King Kong*), the project never went past the planning stages.

In 1961, Willis O'Brien planned a further adventure for Kong in the form of a tongue-in-cheek meeting between the giant ape and a new version of the Frankenstein Monster. The project was originally titled *King Kong vs. Frankenstein*, though O'Brien changed the name to *King Kong vs. the Ginko* ("Ginko" being a humorous combining of the words "King" and "Kong"). O'Brien wrote a scenario, prepared a series of drawings and watercolor paintings, and took his proposed project to producer John Beck. (In O'Brien's various sketches, Ginko looked like an 18-foot tall vaguely apelike homunculus.) O'Brien's story has Carl Denham explaining that Kong never really died but was smuggled, after his plunge from the Empire State Building, back to Skull Island. Denham's idea is to retrieve the mighty gorilla and stage a boxing match between him and some other monster in San Francisco. That "other" monster (dubbed "Ginko") is created by Dr. Frankenstein's grandson from the organs of African animals. Beck, however, eliminated O'Brien from the project and turned the concept over to writer George Worthing Yates, whose new treatment was titled *King Kong vs. Prometheus*. Unable to raise financing for the project, Beck went to Toho International in Japan. Toho was interested in the idea, but for the Frankenstein creature they substituted their own "King of the Monsters"— Godzilla. Toho released *King Kong vs. Godzilla* in 1962, the year Willis O'Brien died.

Of course, in 1976 Dino ("Money means never having to say you're sorry") De Laurentiis attempted to further sour the *Kong* mystique by sinking 24 million dollars into a regrettable remake. In an interview printed in *The London Times* in 1978, Fay Wray related that she had been sent the script in hopes that she might appear in the picture, but she found it so appalling that she declined even to see the finished film.

The brown-haired Fay Wray related (in *Return Engagement* by James Watters) that the reason she donned a blonde wig was that "they didn't want a brunette opposite a brunette" (Kong, of course). Cooper told her, "Of course you'd have to be a blonde. We've got to have that contrast. We thought about Jean Harlow, then we decided you could wear a blond wig." Of her *Kong*-induced fame, Ms. Wray commented that "And the damned thing is around me all the time. *King Kong* just has a life of its own, and if I ever got tired of it, then I'd be tired all the time. But what a creation of imagination and exuberance!" What a creation, indeed.

NOTES

1. From *Famous Monsters of Filmland*, Vol. 5, No. 4.
2. From *David O. Selznick's Hollywood*, by Ronald Haver.
3. *Ibid.*
4. *Ibid.*
5. *Ibid.*
6. *Ibid.*
7. *Ibid.*
8. *Ibid.*
9. *Ibid.*
10. *Ibid.*
11. *Ibid.*

MURDERS IN THE ZOO
(1933; Paramount)

Release Date: March 31, 1933
Running Time: 61 minutes
Director: Edward Sutherland
*Associate Producer: E. Lloyd Sheldon
Screenplay: Philip Wylie and Seton I. Miller
*Additional Dialogue: Milton H. Gropper
Photography: Ernest Haller

Cast: Charlie Ruggles (Peter Yates), Lionel Atwill (Eric Gorman), Gail Patrick (Jerry Evans), Randolph Scott (Dr. Woodford), John Lodge (Roger Hewitt), Kathleen Burke (Evelyn Gorman), Harry Beresford (Professor Evans), *Edward McWade (Dan).

*Credit not appearing on film print.

"If I had lacked the courage to *kill* for you, I couldn't expect you to go on loving me."—Eric Gorman.

SYNOPSIS

The film opens in the jungles of French Indo-China where Eric Gorman (a millionaire sportsman and patron of the Municipal Zoo) leaves his friend Taylor to die—after binding him and sewing his mouth shut! Back at his camp, Gorman passionately embraces his wife, Evelyn. She inquires after Taylor, but Gorman only tells her that he went on ahead. At this point, a native approaches bearing a pistol holster and a mangled belt. They belong to Taylor and the native relates how the white man was eaten by tigers.

On the ocean-liner home, Evelyn confesses her fear and suspicions of her sadistic husband to Roger Hewitt, a family friend who is also in love with Evelyn. "I'm going to have it out with him," the determined Roger tells her, for he wants to take her away from this life of fear and degradation. "Oh, you can't!" pleads Evelyn. "I know him, I know what he'd do! On the expedition, a man named Taylor tried to kiss me. Eric saw him. Later that night, he was found in the jungle—*dead*."

Back in America, Peter Yates (a publicity man with a drinking problem) applies to the Municipal Zoo curator, Professor Evans, for the job of zoo press agent. Yates' first assignment is to cover the arrival of Gorman's ship which carries a number of new animals captured by Gorman and intended for the zoo. On the way, Yates meets Dr. Woodford, the zoo's "very clever young biochemist and toxicologist," and Professor Evans' daughter, Jerry, assistant to and fiancée of Dr. Woodford.

Among the new animal acquisitions is a specimen of the deadly green mamba, a snake possessing "the swiftest-acting venom there is." Woodford begins study on the animal right away. After the various beasts are transferred from the ship to the zoo, Professor Evans tells Gorman of the zoo's recent financial problems.

"Since you've been gone, our budget's been cut four times." Gorman's solution is to "get together the most influential men in the town and make up the deficit by private subscription." Yates suggests holding the fund-raising dinner at the zoo itself for novelty and publicity value.

At Roger Hewitt's apartment, Roger and Evelyn plan her escape to Paris and ultimate divorce from Gorman so that she can marry Roger. The suspicious Gorman arrives unexpectedly at the apartment on the pretext of inviting Hewitt to the upcoming zoo dinner. Though Evelyn hides in another room, Gorman sees evidence of her presence.

At the much-ballyhooed dinner party (held in the building housing the big cats) Roger suddenly gasps and then collapses. An examination reveals a snake bite on his leg—and the green mamba has disappeared from its cage in Woodford's lab. With no known antidote, Hewitt is dead within five minutes.

Back at Gorman's house, Evelyn accuses her husband of somehow killing Hewitt. Gorman only laughs, and, his passion aroused, forces her to kiss him. Full of loathing, Evelyn breaks away and locks herself in her room. As the amorous Gorman pounds on her door, she sneaks across the balcony and into Gorman's study. There, in Gorman's desk, she finds a dried snake head wrapped in a handkerchief, venom dripping from its fangs. Evelyn races out of the house with the incriminating object, closely followed by Gorman who has discovered the snake-head missing. Evelyn heads for the closed zoo, intending to present the evidence to Dr. Woodford. Before she can reach Woodford's lab, however, Gorman catches up with her on the bridge spanning the alligator pond. Gorman wrests the snake-head from her grasp. Evelyn threatens to "tell them all," yelling "You're a murderer!" Gorman smothers his wife's shouts and quickly drops her over the railing into the jaws of the waiting alligators.

When a few scraps of Evelyn's dress are found floating in the alligator pond the next day, Gorman puts on a show of anguish and rage. "You were responsible for Hewitt's death—" Gorman accuses Dr. Woodford, "your carelessness and stupidity. And now my wife has died here, died *horribly*—again because of carelessness! I'm *through* with this zoo, Evans, it's a public menace. I'm going to see that the city closes it before there are any more of these *ghastly* incidents. As for you Woodford, I'm going to have you prosecuted for criminal negligence, but the charge *ought* to be manslaughter!" True to his prediction, the city council permanently closes the zoo.

While helping out around the zoo after most of the staff have been let go, Peter Yates stumbles across the missing green mamba. Dr. Woodford then compares the bite width of the recovered snake to the measurements taken from the wound on Hewitt's leg. The two measurements do not match.

Woodford calls Gorman and induces him to come to the lab. When the doctor confronts Gorman and accuses him of murdering Hewitt with a second mamba, Gorman strikes Woodford with his poisoned snake-head. Gorman then kills the real mamba and places it near the dying doctor to make it appear as if the snake bit him before Woodford could dispatch it. As Gorman is leaving, Jerry arrives and Gorman pretends he's just coming in to see Woodford. They "find" the unconscious Woodford and Jerry runs for the newly-discovered anti-toxin. "He just finished it today," she shouts from the next room to the stunned Gorman. As Jerry prepares the serum, Gorman approaches her menacingly. Realizing his intent, she hits him with a large mixing rod and rushes back into the lab, locking the door behind her. While Gorman pounds on the door, Jerry injects Woodford with the life-saving serum. She then phones Yates, who sounds the alarm.

Gorman makes a run for it but finds his exit blocked by incoming police. He rushes into the big cat building and pulls the lever to open all the cages, releasing the animals as a diversion. While most of the ferocious felines fight among themselves, several lions spot Gorman and chase him out through the door. He takes refuge behind the bars of a cage, not

Lurid ad for Paramount's *Murders in the Zoo* (1933).

realizing that the cell is already occupied. As Gorman waits for the lions to depart, a huge python rears up and strikes before wrapping itself about Gorman, choking the life out of the villain.

With the excitement over, Dr. Woodford recovers in bed and a fallen-off-the-wagon Peter Yates staggers about the zoo. In the final scene, Yates assumes that an overlooked roaming lion is simply a drunken delusion and comically thumps the big beast on the head. The lion turns and walks docilely away while Peter totters blissfully off in the other direction.

MEMORABLE MOMENT

Murders in the Zoo contains arguably the strongest opening from the Golden Age of Horror. In a small jungle clearing, an unidentified man lies on the ground, pinned by two native bearers. Another man (whom we later learn is Eric Gorman) bends over the captive's head, earnestly engaged in what at first glance appears to be *embroidery*. The bodies of the natives partially obscure the figure on the ground so we cannot be sure of what is really happening, though an occasional sharp grunt or sudden moan of pain issuing from the prostrate man (accompanied by a quick, spasmodic jerk of his legs) tells us that all is certainly not well.

As Gorman works, sleeves rolled up, hands drawing back thread with a careful flourish again and again, he begins to speak. "A Mongolian Prince taught me this, Taylor — an *ingenious* device for the right occasion," Gorman states coldly. "You'll never lie to a friend again — and you'll never kiss another man's wife." Gorman finishes, wipes his hands on a handkerchief, and stands. He and the two natives walk off and now we can see the man stretched out on the ground, his hands tied behind his back. The man struggles painfully to his knees and then finally up to his feet, turning away from the camera to stumble off into the jungle. The scene shifts to Gorman mounting an elephant and moving away. Suddenly, the victim emerges from the brush and staggers toward the camera. In shocking close-up we see his face for the first time and observe that his lips have been crudely *sewn shut*! His sweat-drenched countenance, the bloody lips closed unnaturally tight, and, most of all, the panicked, tormented look in the man's eyes shock the senses with the cruelty of this act. This harsh, horrific sequence, dwelling intently on barbarous torture so coldly and callously inflicted, could never have made it past the revamped Production Code a mere year later.

ASSETS

Fall of 1932 was a time of uncertainty for Hollywood horror. The mammoth successes of *Dracula* and *Frankenstein* (and to a lesser extent, *Dr. Jekyll and Mr. Hyde*) were a year old. The handful of Hollywood's follow-up pictures were a mixed bag of success and failure. While *Doctor X* was doing fair business and *White Zombie* cleaning up, Universal's *Murders in the Rue Morgue* was a box-office disappointment and MGM's *Freaks* an outright bomb. Most studios (Universal excepted) were still on the graveyard fence as far as horror was concerned. One can easily envision the Paramount top brass sitting in the inner sanctum conference room debating what to do with their unwholesome little horror property, "Murders in the Zoo." Their success with *Dr. Jekyll and Mr. Hyde* had encouraged them to mount a second horror film, *Island of Lost Souls*, then currently in production. "Still, it might be better," we can almost hear them say, "if we hedge our bets until we know if this horror-thing will last." Paramount had no such reservations about comedy, however, a tried and true box-office glamour gown. A solution: top-line one well-known and well-liked comedian in the form of Charlie Ruggles[1] and place a director well-versed in comedy at the helm (Edward Sutherland). Paramount brass could now rest easy that their "baby-scarer" would also be a "laugh-riot."

Though the emphasis on comedy in general (and the casting of Ruggles in particular) turned out to be a mistake, the choice of directors was a fortuitous one. While untried in the horror arena (the marginally mystical *Secrets of the French Police* being his only [small] step into the Dark Cinema), Sutherland brought a technical expertise and a sure knowledge of the medium to the production. Sutherland chose to eschew the standard gothic trappings and Germanic leanings of the genre and present his horrors in a straightforward, head-on manner befitting the picture's modern day metropolis setting (a thinly disguised New York). Midnight moonlight and graveyard atmosphere give way to unflinching daylight and stark realism. In this way, *Murders*

Paramount Publicity Department: The *Mamba* Kings?

in the Zoo became one of the first films to take horror out of the nebulous land of mists and shadows and bring it into the everyday world of Joe Public. In *Murders in the Zoo*, horror was not the far-removed province of Eastern Europe or bizarre tropical islands or even the nineteenth century; the terror was right here and right now, pounding the pavement of our greatest city. This gives the picture an immediacy and realism (even to the more farfetched elements) which strikes a contemporary chord even today.

The opening credits herald *Murders in the Zoo* as something special. No standard static backdrops here as the camera tracks fluidly back along a junglelike zoo path while the technical credits swipe across the screen. Then, each of the major players are introduced by shots of wild animals. A circus seal clapping its flippers dissolves into a shot of top-billed Charlie Ruggles clapping *his* flipp — er, hands. A cuddly black bear dissolves into the equally cuddly Harry Beresford; a split-screen image of a dove and owl precede Gail Patrick (placid heroine) and Randolph Scott (intelligent hero), while two panting cougars presage would-be lovers Kathleen Burke and John Lodge. Finally, a solitary tiger dissolves into the image of Lionel Atwill staring intently as he takes a drag on his cigarette and blows smoke through his predatory nostrils. Sutherland cleverly uses animals as visual metaphors to give the viewer a foretaste of the various characterizations and foster an immediate interest in the characters.

Through his technical expertise, Sutherland employs sequencing and motion to enhance the film's immediacy by bringing the viewer directly into the thick of things in the very first scene. The sequence opens with a shot of a contoured map of French Indo-China. The camera zooms closer and dissolves into a shot of a lush mountain range. Then, through a series of further dissolves (mountain range to valley to section of trees to specific foliage and finally into the clearing itself) coupled with the seemingly continual forward motion of the camera, Sutherland visually draws the audience into the picture and sets the viewer down in the steaming jungle right alongside his characters.

The director also knows when to keep the camera still for its greatest impact. After utilizing motion to bring the audience into his jungle setting, Sutherland then traps the viewer there by refusing to move the camera at a crucial moment. The moment comes when a man stumbles out of the brush to reveal that his mouth has been sadistically sewn shut. By keeping the grisly process a mystery during the awful operation and then having the victim stagger forward toward the stationary camera until his bloody, anguished countenance nearly fills the screen, Sutherland adds claustrophobic impact to the gruesome shock. We want to back away from the horrific sight — indeed, from the whole idea of this terrible deed — but the unmoving, unrelenting camera will not allow us to turn and flee, forcing us to see and learn what we do not wish to by crowding the screen with this hideous sight.

Sutherland utilizes transitional dissolves and horizontal wipes to create a smooth continuity between scenes. For instance, upon leaving the jungle setting, the camera focuses on a large round drum on which a native beats out a rhythmic sound. This dissolves into the similarly-shaped image of a life-saving ring mounted on the rail of an ocean liner. The visual unity provides a connection between the two diverse locales.

Ernest Haller's fluid camerawork enhances the picture's involving visuals. As Evelyn strolls along the ship deck in one scene, the camera tracks beside her past deck chairs, passengers, and doorways to add a visual expansiveness to the cramped set. Later, she relates the terrible fate of Taylor to Roger Hewitt. The camera focuses in medium close-up on the couple as Evelyn concludes that "there was no way of proving any—" She stops before verbalizing this last suspicion and stares past Hewitt's shoulder. When Hewitt turns his head, the camera tracks right to follow (and become) Hewitt's gaze, finally coming to rest on the figure of Eric Gorman, who momentarily stands there before advancing toward the couple. This type of personalized movement helps bond the viewer with the characters.

That Sutherland and Haller took great care with their visuals is evident from the marvelous composition and framing of scenes. When Roger Hewitt talks with Evelyn on the deck of the liner, for instance, they stand at the rail, their bodies framing the shot on either side of the screen. "Please don't let [Gorman] see us together again," pleads Evelyn. In the background between the two figures is a window, the curtains half drawn. The nature and placement of this background detail adds further anxiety to the scene, suggesting that Gorman at any minute could easily spy them together. Evelyn glances over her shoulder (toward, and then past, the window) adding, "He'll be out any minute." The window becomes a metaphor for the couple's exposed position.

Philip Wylie and Seton I. Miller's intriguing screenplay works on a number of levels. From the opening sewing sequence, one knows this film has bite. This bite is further barbed with a liberal dose of black humor. When Gorman tells his wife that her would-be lover had left, she asks what he said before departing. "He didn't say anything," is Gorman's sardonic reply. Later, when Evelyn accuses Gorman of killing Roger Hewitt at the zoo dinner, Gorman answers innocently, "Evelyn, you don't think I sat there all evening with an eight-foot mamba in my pocket, do you?" then quips, "Why, it would be an injustice to my tailor." Unfortunately, Wylie and Miller, whether by studio dictate or misplaced design, nearly bury these shining moments of subtle humor under a pile of lusterless sledgehammer comedy bits involving Charlie Ruggles (see Liabilities section, page 192).

The plot clips along at a fast pace, with the cruel murders evenly spaced to generate ever higher peaks of intensity. The final climax, in which all the big cats are let loose, resulting in a ferocious feline free-for-all pitting lions against leopards and panthers against pumas, is exciting in its feral intensity (but something that filmmakers could only get away with in the pre–Code days; it is too vicious to get past post–1933 censors). By releasing the caged animals, Gorman creates a veritable orgy of violence, paralleling the release (discovery) of his own previously secret savagery — only to have it turn and destroy him.

The screenplay pulls no punches in regards to sex, either. After Gorman cleverly murders another rival for his wife's affection, for instance, he focuses his amorous attention on his appalled spouse. Full of loathing, she exclaims disgustedly, "Now you want to make love to me!" Strong stuff for 1933. Undeterred, Gorman continues his ministrations, his hand slowly inching upwards as he holds her fast, crawling up her arm like a sensual snake. As his hand moves from arm to shoulder, Gorman brings it around to hover a moment over her breast, the hand *almost* touching, before moving sinuously up to grasp her shoulder. Then, overcome by his lust, he grabs her firmly and his right hand actually rests on her breast as his left arm crushes her unwilling form to him. This scene of blatant sexuality is a rarity, even *before* the enforcement of the Production Code, particularly considering the undercurrent of brutality which runs throughout the sequence. It makes for a powerful, disturbing moment.

Murders in the Zoo was produced during the worst of the Great Depression and Wylie and Miller's screenplay effectively reflects the mood of the time through its characters. Gorman, the picture's sadistic and despotic antagonist, is a millionaire. The two other wealthy characters, Evelyn and her would-be paramour Roger Hewitt, both display, if not outright immorality, then a decided lack of propriety by scheming to run away together behind the husband's back. (While this may seem defensible given the circumstances, it still technically smacks of faithlessness.) All three of these moneyed characters meet gruesome fates, even the two more-or-less innocents (Evelyn is punished for allowing herself to have been seduced by Gorman's power and wealth, while Hewitt is destroyed for simply belonging to the same vile class as Gorman).

The hero, on the other hand, has no such bloated wealth. While a doctor, he still must worry about financing for his work and making enough money so that he can marry his sweetheart (new funding, he laughingly tells Jerry, will "let you quit stalling about marrying me"). This protagonist occupies the same sinking financial boat as the bulk of Middle America at the time.

Gorman becomes a metaphor for the wealthy elite, a symbol of responsibility for the financial ruin of the average American. In this light, the zoo, plagued with fiscal difficulties and teetering on collapse, is the American economy. The devious dealings (murders, in fact) of Gorman (the unscrupulous financier) cause the closing and ruin of the zoo (the economy). The scene in which a regretful Dr. Woodford must lay off a group of zoo workers brings the scenario powerfully home. "I know you boys have families," Woodford apologizes while handing out their final paychecks. "I *hate* to let you go but there's nothing else I can do." Gorman eventually pays the ultimate price for this disregard for others when a giant python slowly strangles the life out of him (much as the Depression slowly choked the financial life from millions of Americans). For audiences of the time, this could be (at least on a subconscious level) a most cathartic release. While often helpless in their fiscal reality, the Depression-era viewers could see the symbol of their financial misery receive his just deserts up on the silver screen — and watch an entertaining horror yarn at the same time.

Eric Gorman is a fascinating character. Civilized and generous on the outside, inside he is little better than a wild beast himself— worse, in fact, for he is infinitely more dangerous. Gorman identifies more with the animal he hunts than with fellow human beings. "I love them," he says of the beasts. "They're honest in their simplicity, their primitive emotions. They love, they hate, they *kill*." Atwill adds a pointed emphasis to this last word by drawing the corners of his mouth back in the briefest of grimaces. Gorman revels in the "primitive emotions" about which he speaks. Immediately after his first two murders, Gorman's passion spills over and he embraces Evelyn, his blood quickened by the kill. Sharing an obvious kinship with Count Zaroff of *The Most Dangerous Game* (1932), the jealous and sadistic Gorman draws a close link between sex and death.

While Gorman may espouse an admiration for the animals' "simplicity," this devious and complex man is anything *but* simplistic. His words are full of double meanings, and he invests his phrases with hidden messages. When Gorman comes to see Hewitt in his apartment and realizes that Evelyn had been (or still is) there, Gorman tells him, "You know, I was rather surprised to find that a man like you should take such an interest in something which is, shall we say, outside his province. I mean, on the boat you and I seemed to have a — mutual interest." Gorman's almost subliminal emphasis on key words further enhances the hidden meaning — and menace — of the dialogue. "I'm afraid I don't quite understand," replies Hewitt cagily, playing along with Gorman's game of civility. "I was referring to my animals," lies Gorman, who obviously means "my wife." Gorman hides behind his animals in his words just as he makes use of them in his murderous deeds.

The role of Eric Gorman was tailor-made for Lionel Atwill, one of the screen's best "cultured" villains. Atwill relishes his part, imbuing lines like, "I can promise you a really *unusual* evening," with deliciously sinister undertones. After marking Roger Hewitt as a potential victim, Gorman states, "It'll be a great *pleasure* to show Mr. Hewitt through the zoo." Atwill takes the word "pleasure" and draws it out ever so slightly, giving it an unwholesome sound pregnant with dark, hidden menace.

Atwill utilizes gestures and expressions to further add depth and illumination to his character. When discussing his newly delivered green mamba, Gorman relates how "it kills hundreds of natives every year —" with the trace of a smile forming at the corners of his mouth at this tragic thought before continuing, without pause, "— and no anti-toxin has ever been developed for it." While subtle, his expression conveys an image of sublimated sadism. The versatile Atwill can utilize broad expressions to great effect as well. As the crate containing the deadly mamba wheels away, the camera moves back onto the face of Gorman. Atwill then narrows and hardens his gaze, the half-lidded eyes conjuring up images of the serpent itself. Though a rather obvious ploy, Atwill's cold authority makes it an effective one. As emphasis, the picture then fades from Gorman's snake-eyed countenance to a close-up of the real snake as Woodford extracts venom from its fanged mouth. This juxtaposition drives home the slithery metaphor.

Kathleen Burke does well in the role of Gorman's wife, a woman bound to him by fear of this jealous and sadistic man. Her emotions spill forth when she finally rebels against his cruelty. "Oh, you're not human!" she cries, appalled and disgusted when he tries to kiss her after Hewitt's death. As he pulls her to him, she pushes away with a final, "Oh, I *hate* you!" Given the expression of loathing on Ms. Burke's face, the words become almost superfluous. Later, when she discovers the false snake head in her husband's study, she looks up with a cold hatred in her eyes. At her fateful confrontation with Gorman on the bridge, she finally overcomes her fear. Gathering strength, she excitedly, almost breathlessly, warns him, "You can't frighten me anymore. I'm going to tell them all — that you're a murderer, that you've no right to live!" The actress' shoulders shake with each word, her voice rising in pitch to near hysteria, her whole demeanor speaking of long-suppressed hatred and horror boiling to the surface. (Unfortunately, while Kathleen Burke's effective performance is perfectly timed, the timing of her character wasn't quite so well thought out — much to the delight of the hungry gators.)

LIABILITIES

When Atwill is absent from the screen, the picture slows considerably. During these lulls, Sutherland focuses on unfunny bits of "humor" with Charlie Ruggles, or simply inserts stock shots of zoo animals as time filler.

One tedious sequence follows a messenger boy looking at the various zoo exhibits for a full two minutes!

Aside from Gorman (and to a lesser extent his wife, Evelyn) none of the other characters are fleshed out enough to generate much interest, nor do the players attempt to overcome this shortcoming.

Professor Evans is alternately gullible (duped by the fast-talking inanities of Peter Yates) and bumblingly ineffective (unable to act on the zoo's financial difficulties until Gorman arrives to take a hand). Harry Beresford simply walks through the part, investing just enough energy to keep it at the level of caricature. Hewitt and Dr. Woodford, though miles apart in their financial and social strata, could be interchangeable (the same can be said for actors John Lodge and Randolph Scott), both being rather stiff, brave, upstanding hero-types (the only difference being that one was bright enough to rely on brains — developing an anti-toxin — rather than dollars and so was able to save himself). As a heroine, Jerry simply hovers about the periphery, almost unnoticed, making little impact until her brief moment of heroism at the climax. Compared to Kathleen Burke, Gail Patrick appears lifeless and lackluster.

The film's most serious flaw, however, takes the form of the painfully intrusive "comic relief" of comedian Charlie Ruggles. He wastes many of the film's precious few 61 minutes variously cringing from caged lions, taking fright at his own reflection, or even soiling himself when he inadvertently traps the missing mamba with a pitchfork ("Is there a good laundry in this town?" he asks tremulously).

His comical highlights include cutting himself shaving every time a nearby lion roars or repeatedly tugging painfully on his ears while making an interminable dinner speech as an (unheeded) signal for the photographers to snap their pictures. Ruggles' dialogue consists of repeated inanities like "That's just a small idea of my ideas." Too bad this type of blatant, lowest-common-denominator humor was felt to be obligatory by Paramount at the time (Ruggles even received top billing). With more emphasis on the infrequent but effective *dark* humor rather than on the copious sledgehammer-style *light* humor, *Murders in the Zoo* could have joined the ranks of such hard-hitting classics as *Freaks* (1932), *Island of Lost Souls* (1933), and *Mad Love* (1935). Even so, it remains an effective, unique, and entertaining shocker from the Golden Age of Horror.

REVIEWS

Variety's "Char" (April 4, 1933) noted that "this picture has what it takes to chill and entertain. A horror film compact in subject matter and action, it is also exceedingly well played and directed," though he adds, "...but the snakes in this one are apt to be more than some can stand." (Perhaps "Char" possessed a touch of ophidiophobia?)

Andre Sennwald, reviewer for *The New York Times* (April 3, 1933), labeled *Murders in the Zoo* "a particularly gruesome specimen," and (incredibly) claimed to be "thankful for the generous footage given to Charles Ruggles as a timid and bibulous press agent for the zoo." Noting that "Lionel Atwill as the insanely jealous husband is almost too convincing for comfort, and Kathleen Burke as the wife suggests the domestic terrors of her life capably," Mr. Sennwald concludes that "judging by its ability to chill and terrify, this film is a successful melodrama."

PRODUCTION NOTES

According to the film's pressbook, "An entire zoo, complete in every detail, was constructed for the filming of the new thrill picture."

While the "entire" claim can be put down to publicity department exaggeration, Paramount did construct several zoo sets on their lot specifically for this production. These included the Alligator Pit and Carnivora House. Four professional animal trainers (headed by Chubby Guilfoyle) were employed to control the 19 big cats released during "one of the most dangerous motion picture scenes ever filmed." "Three weeks of preparation" were necessary, claimed the pressbook, to allow the animals "to get accustomed to each other in neighboring cages." Noting that "sturdy fences were placed around the setting to give the crew space for cameras," Paramount's publicity writers dramatically described the hazardous scene: "Four animal trainers, who, according to the script, were to drive the beasts back into cages, entered the enclosure, and for an hour, while cameras ground, they sweated at the task. They had to work almost back to back to guard against attack from the rear. Three leopards and one puma found hiding places in dark corners, however, and would not return to their cages without a vicious struggle."

Paramount obtained most of the animals for their film from the nearby Selig Zoo. Transportation of the beasts required 16 trucks (six for the alligators alone). The film's pressbook reported that "the caravan passed through Los Angeles at about 4 o'clock in the morning, so that danger of automobile collision and resultant possible escape of the animals was most remote." The pressbook also claimed that 50 alligators were employed, though this seems doubtful since only a fraction of that number are seen onscreen. In any case, once they arrived, the reptiles proved to be too torpid to "act" due to the recent cool weather (alligators tend to sleep long and heavily through the winter months). To rouse them, the crew had to warm the water in their tank at the steady rate of a quarter degree an hour. It took a week of gradual warming before the animals were once again wide awake and fully active.

Much of director Edward Sutherland's childhood was spent in vaudeville and on the "legitimate" stage. In 1914, the 19-year-old Sutherland entered films as a stuntman, graduating to actor in a number of Keystone comedies and feature-length silents. He served as apprentice director to Charlie Chaplin on *A Woman of Paris* (1923) and became a full-fledged director shortly thereafter. Sutherland gravitated toward comedies, directing several W. C. Fields pictures (including 1933's *International House* which featured a rare Bela Lugosi nonhorror appearance); Laurel and Hardy's *The Flying Deuces* (1939); and Abbott and Costello's screen debut, *One Night in the Tropics* (1940). Though *Murders in the Zoo* was the director's only true horror picture (he was originally slated to direct *Dracula's Daughter* for Universal in 1935 but studio delays forced him off the project), he journeyed into the land of cinematic fantasy on two other occasions, exposing the mesmeric *Secrets of the French Police* (1932) and capturing the comical antics of *The Invisible Woman* (1942).

Renowned cinematographer Karl Struss, who photographed Sutherland's *Up Pops the Devil* (1931) and *Every Day's a Holiday* (1938), remembered that "working with Eddie Sutherland was always a lot of fun." Struss also recalled that the director possessed a unique method of demonstrating his personal industry to the studio executives. "To show how efficient he was, he always watched everything sitting directly under the camera lens, and whenever he was satisfied, he would yell 'cut' and immediately jump up, blocking out everything, just to show the producers watching the rushes that he's right there on the job and alert."[2]

Murders in the Zoo cinematographer Ernest Haller lensed 160 films over a career that spanned four decades, including such mainstream classics as *Dark Victory* (1939) and *Gone with the Wind* (1939; for which he won an Academy Award). Haller lent his considerable talents to two other horror productions (late in his career)—*Back from the Dead* (1957) and *What Ever Happened to Baby Jane?* (1962).

California native Charlie Ruggles began acting with a San Francisco stock company in 1905, eventually playing on Broadway. Entering films in 1915, Ruggles quickly rose to popularity as a likable, comedic "average-man." Apart from *Murders in the Zoo*, he also appeared in *Terror Aboard* (1933) and *The Invisible Woman* (1940). Ruggles was one of the first film stars to enter the fledgling medium of television, starring in "The Ruggles" in 1949 and several subsequent live TV shows. Charlie Ruggles' brother, director Wesley Ruggles, helmed *The Monkey's Paw* (1933).

Beauty and the Beast: The allure of Kathleen Burke and the leer of Lionel Atwill in *Murders in the Zoo* (1933).

Atwill's first snake-bite victim, lawyer-turned-actor John Lodge, retired from acting after serving in World War II and turned to politics, eventually becoming governor of Connecticut in 1950. After serving his term as governor, his political career took a diplomatic turn when he became US Ambassador to Spain and then later ambassador to Argentina. *Murders in the Zoo* was only his second film.

In a bit of ironic casting, Paramount awarded Kathleen Burke the role of Atwill's terrified wife who is ultimately eaten by animals (alligators). Earlier this same year she had played "Lota" the Panther Woman, who was *created from* an animal in *Island of Lost Souls*.

Born Margaret LaVelle Fitzpatrick, Gail Patrick studied law at the University of Alabama intending to go into politics (with her sights set on the governorship of Alabama). Before completing her education, however, she entered and won a newspaper contest which sent her on a week's trip to Hollywood as Birmingham's "Panther Girl." (This contest was a publicity ploy orchestrated by Paramount to promote their upcoming production of *Island of Lost Souls* by searching the nation for the right young ingenue to play the mysterious Panther Woman in the film.) Though not chosen as their "Panther Girl" (as mentioned above, Kathleen Burke won the role), Paramount did offer Ms. Patrick a contract at $50 a week. "My dad never made more money than $175 a month in his life," the actress told Richard Lamparski in *Whatever Became Of... Fifth Series*. "I got them up to $75 a week and grabbed that contract." Among her over 60 screen credits is the Golden Age fantasy, *Death Takes a Holiday* (1934). When she married prominent literary agent Cornwall Jackson in 1947, Gail Patrick retired from acting. In 1956, however, she returned to the entertainment industry as Executive Producer of the popular and long-running "Perry Mason" television series. Of her career in front of the camera, she stated, "I always felt self-conscious as an actress because I'm tall. I see that it came over as haughtiness. I just don't have an actress' soul. I think mine has a dollar sign on it."

The 25-five foot, 360-pound python that puts the stranglehold on Lionel Atwill at film's end was named "Oswald." Fascinated by the creature, Atwill refused a stunt double (over the objections of director Edward Sutherland), and so the actor himself is seen wrapped in the giant snake's smothering coils. Atwill was so taken with Oswald that he reportedly bought the reptile from its owner ("Snake" King, operator of a Texas snake ranch) and took him home after the film wrapped.

Lionel Atwill, with roles in *Mystery of the Wax Museum*, *The Vampire Bat*, and *Murders in the Zoo*, was fast becoming one of Hollywood's foremost screen villains. In 1933,

Motion Picture magazine dubbed the actor "The MENTAL Lon Chaney," going on to say, "Here is a *handsome* man who makes women's hearts beat faster —*until he stops them*. Here is a charming and very polished gentleman who makes women's blood run warmer —*until he chills it*. This man murders with a smile, violates with a chilling laugh.... Here is a man with the most sardonic mouth I have ever seen, the coldest and most merciless eyes ever set in a man's skull."

Co-screenwriter Philip Wylie was well versed in the gruesome and macabre (not to mention animal stories), having previously co-scripted *Island of Lost Souls*.

When *Murders in the Zoo* opened in New York at the famed Paramount Theater, the picture shared the stage with a live comedic stageshow — headlined by a young vaudevillian named Bob Hope.[3]

NOTES

1. Paramount had just pulled a similar trick by casting Ruggles as a cowardly steward in their rather gruesome murder melodrama *Terror Aboard* (1933).

2. From *Five American Cinematographers* by Scott Eyman.

3. Bob Hope was no stranger to gala movie premiers, having emceed another live stage show (starring Bing Crosby, no less) four months earlier for the Big Apple premier of MGM's *The Mask of Fu Manchu* at the Capitol Theatre.

SUPERNATURAL
(1933; Paramount)

Release Date: April 21, 1933
Running Time: 65 minutes
Director: Victor Halperin
Producer: Edward Halperin
Screenplay: Harvey Thew and Brian Marlow (based on the story and adaptation by Garnett Weston)
Dialogue Direction: Sidney Salkow
Photography: Arthur Martinelli

Cast: Carole Lombard (Roma Courtney), Alan Dinehart (Paul Bavian), Vivienne Osborne (Ruth Rogen), Randolph Scott (Grant Wilson), H. B. Warner (Dr. Houston), Beryl Mercer (Madame Gourjan), William Farnum (Robert Hammond), Willard Robertson (Warden), George Burr MacAnnon (Max), Lyman Williams (John Courtney).

"You're not going to get within reach of those — hands of hers?"— Madame Gourjan.

SYNOPSIS

RUTH ROGEN, NOTORIOUS STRANGLER, DOOMED TO DEATH reads a newspaper headline. "Rogen Killed Men Who Loved Her" tops the text, reporting, "Ruth Rogen yesterday confessed she killed each of her three lovers after a riotous orgy in her sensuous Greenwich Village apartment."

At the prison at which Ruth Rogen awaits her impending execution, Dr. Houston ("one of the world's greatest psychologists") talks with the warden. "Have you ever noticed that when a criminal is executed for some — unusual crime, there's frequently an epidemic of similar crimes?" The Warden simply puts this phenomenon down to "imitators," but Dr. Houston has a different theory. "Perhaps they've been possessed by another personality, a powerful, malignant personality without, well — without a body of its own," conjectures the doctor. Dr. Houston then requests that Ruth's body be brought to him after the execution, explaining, "I've been experimenting lately with mitrogenic rays ... ultraviolet rays given off by the body. Now if my experiments are correct, I *might* be able to prevent her personality from escaping after death — and committing other crimes."

Needing the subject's permission, the warden agrees to talk to Ruth, during which he intimates that Houston's proposed "experiment" *might* bring her back from death. (Obviously the Warden is unconcerned with such trivial issues as truth and ethics.) The idea appeals to Ruth (as it would to anyone): "If I could use my hands just for a few minutes —" she ponders then laughs maniacally and crushes a metal cup in her strong grip.

In the middle of the night, a man steals into a darkened mansion where the body of a young millionaire, John Colton, lies in state before burial. The solitary figure begins some clandestine preparation on the corpse resting in its casket. We soon learn that the man is a phony "spiritualist" named Paul Bavian, and that he has secretly made a death-mask of John Colton.

A letter arrives for Bavian from Ruth Rogen: "Don't let me die without seeing you. I forgive you everything — even for betraying me to the police. Make my last moments happy. Come to see me." Fearful of coming within Ruth's strangling grasp, however, he stays away from his former lover.

In the meantime, Bavian sends a note to John Colton's grieving twin sister, Roma, claiming that he has been contacted by her brother's spirit and that John is in "great distress and urgently requested me to contact you."

When Bavian's snooping landlady, Mrs. Gourjan, learns of his nefarious intentions, she tries to blackmail the charlatan (threatening to expose his fraudulent tricks). Bavian plays up to her but then uses a special ring he wears to prick her hand with a poisoned needle.

Roma goes to see "Paul Bavian, spiritualist," accompanied by her skeptical beau, Grant Wilson. Utilizing the fresh death-mask and a bevy of other fraudulent techniques, Bavian conjures up the spirit of John Colton, who warns Roma that Robert Hammond, the manager of their joint estate, wants their money and in fact *murdered* John!

Leaving Bavian's place, a shaken Roma and a still-skeptical Grant go to see Dr. Houston (an old family friend) at his penthouse apartment/laboratory. They walk in on Houston just as his experiment with the body of Ruth Rogen concludes. As they talk with the doctor, the room suddenly grows cold and a mysterious wind begins to blow. Roma clutches her throat. Dr. Houston, alarmed, urges Grant to take her out of there quickly for "there's danger of contagion." Marks on Roma's neck convince Houston that Ruth Rogen "tried to get possession of Roma's body. Thank heavens she failed!"

The supernatural crisis now behind them, Dr. Houston turns his mind towards Roma's problem. He suggests that Roma have Bavian come to her house for a second session attended by himself, Hammond, and Grant.

At the séance, Bavian utilizes more tricks to repeat his bogus message that Hammond murdered John Colton. Bavian also uses his poisoned ring to strike down Hammond and slips a vial of poison into the victim's pocket to make it look like suicide.

Also during the seance, Roma collapses and the spirit of Ruth Rogen enters her body. Roma/Ruth leaves with Bavian as the others are busy attending to the dying Hammond. She leads the bewildered Bavian to Ruth Rogen's apartment, answering Bavian's queries by telling him she knew Rogen well. When Bavian makes a pass at her, she embraces him. As they kiss, Roma/Ruth brings her hands up to his neck — but is interrupted by Max, the apartment concierge, who orders them out of the flat. The possessed woman becomes enraged and lunges at the man's throat. When he threatens to call the police, Bavian suggests that they go to Roma's yacht docked in the harbor.

Meanwhile, Dr. Houston and Grant trace Roma to Ruth Rogen's apartment. When Houston finally realizes that the spirit of the murderess has entered Roma's body, he collapses (presumably from fear and anguish). As Grant tends to the debilitated doctor, the image of John Colton appears (though unseen by Grant). Suddenly, a wind blows through the room and a glass sculpture of a ship inexplicably falls off its stand and shatters. The startling event triggers the idea in Grant's mind that Roma has gone to her yacht. Leaving the doctor in Max's care, he races off to the docks.

In one of *Supernatural*'s few memorable moments, Dr. Houston (H. B. Warner) seemingly animates the body of executed murderess Ruth Rogen (Vivienne Osborne) for one brief instant. Though his experiment was intended to "prevent her personality from escaping after death and committing other crimes," it has accomplished just the opposite.

On the yacht, Ruth/Roma plies Bavian with liquor. When they embrace, Roma's hand moves up to his throat. At this Bavian draws away, spooked by her resemblance to his dead lover. "Why did you take me to [Ruth Rogen's] place?" he demands. "Why is it that sometimes you look like her?!"

The now-nervous Bavian tries to leave but Roma insists on one last drink. Suspicious, Bavian fingers his deadly ring but Roma (Ruth) is wise to his murderous trick. With a protective handkerchief she grabs his hand and forces him down on a couch, her other hand around his throat. "Now do you recognize me?" she taunts, staring intently into his frightened face. "I *am* Ruth Rogen. I'm going to *kill* you before I leave this body you like so much."

At this moment, Grant arrives and breaks into the locked stateroom, allowing Bavian to escape. With Grant holding back what he thinks is Roma, Ruth's spirit leaves the girl's body. Hysterical, evil laughter follows the terrified Bavian as he tries to unfasten the line securing a small launch to the yacht. As he struggles with the rope, he becomes entangled. Turning to look back, Bavian's eyes go wide and he falls backwards off the deck — and is strangled by the rope wrapped about his neck.

At that instant Roma faints. She awakens a moment later with no memory of the supernatural events. As Grant and Roma gaze into each other's eyes, a familiar wind wafts through the cabin and the image of John Colton appears (again unseen). The wind flutters the pages of a magazine which opens to reveal a romantic ad, whose catchline reads "GO TO BERMUDA FOR YOUR HONEYMOON." The lovers embrace.

MEMORABLE MOMENT

Few memorable scenes, "supernatural" or otherwise, can be found in this picture. Perhaps the film's eeriest moment comes when Roma and Grant interrupt Dr. Houston in his experiment. With the doctor momentarily out of the room, the couple approaches the figure of a woman seated in a chair on a raised platform. Lightning flashes from the storm outside while strange electrical sounds emanate from the machinery around the dais. With the camera placed behind them, Roma and Grant advance toward the figure and we see framed between them the corpse of Ruth Rogen. The camera then cuts to a close-up of Ruth's pallid face. As the electricity hums, the cadaver's dead eyes open ever so slowly and stare, blank and unseeing, at the couple — at us. Suddenly, the lids drop and the body collapses, slumping over in its chair. This scene chillingly captures the connection (and ambiguity) between life and death which subsequently becomes the very theme of the picture.

ASSETS

After eyeing the considerable financial success of *White Zombie*, Paramount signed the Halperin Brothers to produce the studio's next horror entry, *Supernatural*. Director Victor Halperin opens his film with a dramatic flourish. The credits flash on the screen, superimposed over a dark, forbidding sky and punctuated by flashes of lightning and peals of thunder. On the soundtrack, a chorus of voices rings wild and shrill. Three quotations appear, charging out from the background one after another, each preceded by a jagged bolt of lightning and rumbling crash of thunder:

TREAT ALL SUPERNATURAL BEINGS WITH RESPECT — BUT KEEP ALOOF FROM THEM! — CONFUCIUS.

WE WILL BRING FORTH THE DEAD FROM THEIR GRAVES — MOHAMMED.

...AND HE GAVE HIS TWELVE DISCIPLES POWER AGAINST UNCLEAN SPIRITS TO CAST THEM OUT — MATTHEW 10:1.

These decidedly unsettling quotations from hallowed religious sources immediately generate an anticipation for the macabre while at the same time adding a legitimacy to the subject of "spirits" and the "supernatural."

Following the trio of prophetic sayings, Halperin then opens with a series of newspaper headlines superimposed over a multi-layered montage of images. Shots of a jury, the working gears of a printing press, and Ruth Rogen herself (sometimes even double-imaged, her face imposed over her own profile) speaking lines like "He's lying; I'll *kill* him!" and "I'd do it again — and again and *again*" and "Men — I hate the whole brood" flash past. The chaotic, swirling montage continues with Ruth voicing, "One week more. Six days — five days — it goes fast, doesn't it?" In urgent tones, the condemned woman speaks of Paul Bavian: "Why doesn't he come?!" The montage finally concludes with an intense close-up of her eyes, the whites lit so that they almost glow (a trick Halperin borrows from his earlier *White Zombie*) as she screams in anger and frustration and fear. Throughout the sequence, music plays frantically on the soundtrack while Ruth Rogen's hard-edged voice speaks quickly, urgently. The fleeting, ever-changing glimpses of layered images effectively set the story background, laying the groundwork for the film's scenario much more quickly and more excitingly than a series of mundane courtroom and jail cell scenes would have done. This concise montage allows Halperin to jump immediately into the most intriguing aspect of the story — the weird, supernatural element — while also pulling the audience into the plot with fast-moving visuals and a sense of urgency. By transforming the credits into a series of striking visuals and following this up with a fast-paced collage of images, Halperin grabs his audience right at the start, throwing everything he's got at them to reel the viewer in like a thrill-hungry fish on a hook baited with sensationalized dramatics. (As it turns out, Halperin needs every barb he can find to latch onto his audience, for he soon asks them to swallow a stomach full of ridiculous dialogue and outlandish theories.)

On the technical side, Halperin directs adequately, evincing solid judgment with his choice of unique visuals and unusual shots. In one sequence the camera pans up the side of a skyscraper (an effective model) through a driving rainstorm to reveal the brightly lit section of penthouse windows belonging to Dr. Houston. The camera then tracks forward toward the band of illumination and the scene dissolves to a shot, still seen through the pouring rain, of Houston working around the corpse of Ruth Rogen. The camera seemingly hovers outside the windows looking in, heightening the macabre voyeurism of the scene and thus emphasizing the forbidden, dangerous nature of the terrible tableau.

Halperin handles the critical possession sequences with an understated subtlety appropriate to the spiritual (rather than physical) nature of the transformation. When Ruth possesses Roma's body at the seance, for instance, Carole Lombard's rather light cosmetic makeup suddenly darkens—her lips and eyes become darker and more defined, giving her delicate face a hard edge absent a moment before. The effect, while subtle, is startling and quite effective at conveying the unearthly change without resorting to a monstrous Jekyll-and-Hyde-style makeup. This result did not come cheap, however, costing much in terms of patience and strain on star and director alike.

Dialogue director Sidney Salkow, writing in *Close Ups: The Movie Star Book* by Danny Peary, reported on the friction this time-consuming procedure caused: "Particularly painful to both Victor and Carole were those times when facial transformations had to be filmed. It was a painstaking process that required Carole to remain motionless for what seemed an eternity while the transformation was achieved with makeup and stop-frame photography. For Carole, whose internal combustion machine was never at rest, this was the final indignity. She came down hard on Victor. 'God, this bastard's trying to paralyze me. Victor, God'll punish you for this…,' she moaned." (If only Halperin had been cognizant of the makeup/filter technique employed by Rouben Mamoulian for his 1931 *Dr. Jekyll and Mr. Hyde*, the beleaguered director might have saved himself much aggravation and abuse.)

Arthur Martinelli moves his camera frequently, adding interest and efficacy to the visuals. (Though Martinelli was under the direction of Victor Halperin, the static and mundane look of the director's later films such as *Revolt of the Zombies* and *Torture Ship* leads one to suspect that much of the credit for *Supernatural*'s visuals belongs to the veteran cinematographer.) When Paul Bavian breaks into the Colton mansion, the camera moves away from the silhouetted intruder to prowl about the darkened house in an effective point-of-view perspective. As we, the audience, *become* Bavian, we creep from the shadowy foyer past pillars and into a large room where the camera (our vision) scans across the chamber until we spy a coffin resting on a pedestal. The camera steadily and stealthily approaches the macabre, unexpected object until we can see the name of John Colton engraved on its opened lid. Only then does the viewpoint change back to "third person" and we watch Bavian conduct his ghoulish business with the corpse.

In another sequence, Roma enters her brother's room after his funeral. The "spirit" of John Colton is briefly glimpsed looking on. The camera then follows Colton's faithful dog, King, as he retrieves his master's favorite slippers from the closet and places them on his owner's empty chair. Turning to Roma, the camera follows her as she moves dejectedly from place to place about the room, fingering her beloved brother's personal effects. The almost continual camera movement creates a definite sense of presence—as if a third party were in the room and moving alongside the other two, effectively making the viewer a part of the unseen spirit world.

Perspective and movement can generate amusement as well. One scene begins with a close-up of a floral print. The camera then tracks backwards to reveal the flowery dress covering the nosy Mrs. Gourjan's generous backside as she peeks through the keyhole of Bavian's door!

While Harvey Thew and Brian Marlow's script ultimately comes up short, it does feature some sparse but genuinely droll humor. When Bavian suddenly opens the door on Mrs. Gourjan in the afore-mentioned scene, the corpulent snooper tumbles unceremoniously into the room. Looking up at him from the floor, she remarks, "I just dropped in to see if you got your phone message." Bavian answers dryly, "Yes I did, thank you very much. Now drop out again."

Ultimately, *Supernatural* proves rather comforting in its theme, becoming a validation of the Judeo-Christian belief in the hereafter. "Roma, my dear," assures the "famous doctor," "life does continue after death — there's not a doubt of it." This is something many viewers love to hear.

The sets for *Supernatural* reflect the considerable resources of Paramount, making this the best-dressed picture produced by the Halperin Brothers (who generally worked outside the major studios). The plush, well-furnished penthouse of Dr. Houston, the lavish mansion of Roma Colton, the opulent seediness of Paul Bavian's seance room help to legitimize the proceedings. And such extravagant details as setting a single scene in a beautiful private aviary adds a rich visual elegance to the production.

Sound plays an important role in *Supernatural*. Beginning with the cracks of lightning and sharp bursts of thunder during the opening credits, the various sound effects add immeasurably to key scenes. When Bavian takes the plasticine death mask of the corpse, for instance, he dollops several spoonfuls of the substance into the open casket at about where the corpse's face should be. With his fingers he then prods and pats at the concoction on the cold countenance — all kept unseen by our perspective.

The moist *plop-plop* and wet slapping sounds add a gruesome note to the unwholesome business. The sound alone inspires revulsion and even a ghoulish curiosity in the viewer's mind which would have been lost had the camera shown the action full view. Then, of course, the ghostly visitations are always preceded and accompanied by a disharmonious noise like a low, unearthly chiming, doing much to solidify the often unseen presence of the supernatural.

Even the more mundane sounds add emphasis: A clock tolling the hour of two while Bavian works feverishly at his clandestine task becomes a startling interruption in the deadly silence. Later, an unseen train going by as Bavian walks through the darkened streets adds a disturbing, almost deafening background noise.

Vivienne Osborne as Ruth Rogen delivers the picture's one animated performance. One can feel the hate rolling off her in waves as she stares off into some inner space that no one but herself can see, her eyes glittering with evil emotion and her strong hands clenching and unclenching unconsciously or even crushing a metal cup. Ms. Osborne speaks at a quicker and louder rate than normal conversational tones, giving her hard voice an air of bitter urgency and convincing power. Her laugh — cold and without mirth — is frightening in its cruelty. Due to Ms. Osborne's intensity, the screen's first female serial killer becomes a frightening "monster" (another female first).

Supernatural features one other performance of note. Beryl Mercer as Paul Bavian's landlady is a delight as she taunts her tenant and giggles gleefully at her observation that "You're not going to get within reach of those — hands of hers, are you dearie?" Spying through the transom, listening at the keyhole, she presents a decidedly unwholesome character who yet remains likable in her quirky antics (smashing a cockroach with her bottle of wine, for instance, and then frantically trying to salvage what liquid is left in the shattered bottle).

Madame Mercer contributes a fine character bit worthy of James Whale himself. Unfortunately, she plays only a minor part and is onscreen for too little time before her character is "removed" from the scenario.

LIABILITIES

Harvey Thew and Brian Marlow's screenplay ultimately proves too shallow and uneven to be convincing. To begin with, it fails to bring the intriguing conflict and contrast between the spiritualistic trickery and the genuine supernatural events to the fore. Revealing Bavian's chicanery before the audience has a chance to see it in action robs the film of an opportunity to promote eerie chills. *After* the viewer has shuddered at the spectral figure and ghostly voice, the hoax could have then been exposed as such. Not only would this have generated more supernatural atmosphere, it would have provided an effective juxtaposition to the genuine article when it finally arrived.

After the promising opening, the picture bogs down in long stretches of dialogue and inactivity as it follows Bavian and Roma to the apartment where they talk, drink, and embrace, then to the yacht where they drink, embrace, talk, embrace again, drink, etc. Neither Carole Lombard nor Alan Dinehart possesses enough magnetism to sustain interest during these long periods of inactivity. In addition, other scenes of Randolph Scott chasing about after them, trying to track down the errant couple to learn what the viewer already knows, slows the pace even further.

With few exceptions, director Victor Halperin fails to coax effective performances from his players. On the whole, they deliver professional yet perfunctory performances which fail to sell the supernatural scenario. This same failing can be seen even in the director's "masterpiece," *White Zombie*. Fortunately, that earlier production featured Bela Lugosi, who possessed a natural intensity and could exude menace even without specific direction.

The preposterous dialogue spouted by Dr. Houston requires a sincere and even enthusiastic delivery. H. B. Warner, however, is so blasé and dull in his manner that never once can he be taken seriously. Warner lacks the conviction and zeal of a Karloff, Lugosi, Atwill, or Rathbone which could have made the outrageous ideas seem plausible (at least in the character's eyes). Warner speaks of his wild theories as if talking of a new strain of fertilizer.

Alan Dinehart as the villain Paul Bavian speaks quickly and tersely, sounding very much like Edward G. Robinson. Unfortunately, he lacks that actor's expressiveness or charisma and so remains a dull, flat, and ultimately unconvincing villain. Randolph Scott performs an uncanny David Manners impersonation as the ineffectual hero. His handsome face remains bland and unmoving throughout most of the picture and he makes little impact in *any* scene.

Carole Lombard, while physically right for the part (her delicate beauty makes her a fragile, vulnerable heroine), creates too passive a presence for the dual role. She remains too placid and expressionless, even after her "possession" by the evil spirit. There is nothing sinister in her eyes, and so her mild facial contortions and smirks fall flat.

Overall, *Supernatural*, while featuring an intriguing premise and good production values, fails to convince due to poor pacing, some risible dialogue, and ineffectual acting.

REVIEWS

Variety's "Bige" (April 25, 1933) called it "a 65-minute ghost story that dies after the first hour," and was unimpressed with Ms. Lombard. But Bige seemed most concerned with the picture's believability: "The villain is a phony spiritualist, and he's painted with a pretty broad brush all the way. On the other hand there's a prominent scientist whose ideas are equally far-fetched.... But audiences won't believe in the scientist any more than the spiritualist, and that's 'Supernatural's' weakness."

The *Motion Picture Herald* (April 29, 1933) also had trouble swallowing the film's premise: "If the so-called supernatural were made rather less inconceivable, less obviously a machination than a manifestation of something beyond ordinary ken, it doubtless would have more entertainment value. Such comment may well be registered with respect to Paramount's *Supernatural*. The too obvious effort to appear mystical, mysterious and weird causes it at times to descend of its own weight to something approaching absurdity."

Mordaunt Hall, of the *New York Times* (April 22, 1933) gave the film one of its few good reviews: "Notwithstanding the incredibility of many of its main incidents, 'Supernatural' ... succeeds in awakening no little interest in its spooky doings. It not only depicts the various tricks of a charlatan spiritualist but also undertakes through camera wizardry to show the spirit of a dead murderess entering the body of a wholesome girl...." The usually more discerning Mr. Hall was also pleased with the cast, saying "Mr. Dinehart does very well by his role. Miss Lombard's portrayal is also praiseworthy. Vivienne Osborne makes the most of the part of Ruth Rogen and Randolph Scott is pleasing as Roma's sweetheart."

PRODUCTION NOTES

According to Paramount publicity, "Followers of spiritualism throughout the world deluged Edward and Victor Halperin, young movie producers, with advice and comment when they announced plans for production of 'Supernatural.'" The film's pressbook even recounted how the Halperins received a scenario sent in by a woman who claimed it had been written while under spirit control. "Edward Halperin read it," reported the article, "then sent it back with the following note: 'Have this produced and distributed 'under spirit control.' It will be easier for all concerned.'"

Another publicity article reported that the Halperins asked "the noted British psychic," Sir Oliver Lodge, to serve as technical advisor for the film. He declined. Fortunately, "numerous other spiritualists volunteered their advice and services on the picture," assured the pressbook, "for it is the first in which spiritualism has been given sympathetic treatment, even though one of its principal characters is a 'phoney' spiritualist."

Though the film was supposedly "sympathetic" to spiritualists, not all spiritualists felt sympathetic toward the film. Paramount's publicity department reported that "not a day passed without the arrival of a flood of telegrams, letters and other messages from 'cranks,' many of whom delivered thinly veiled threats." One, signed "Occulta," read: "There's nothing more dangerous to human progress than misleading information pertaining to supernatural phenomena. Watch your step, or else—."

Another, from "Spiritual Worker," warned: "Unnecessary exposure of spiritualistic ritual will not be tolerated." Still, "numerous spiritualists," continued the article, "who understood that the film dealt sympathetically with the subject, sent friendly invitations to attend seances and demonstrations, or offered aid and advice."

The elegant, well-liked, delicate beauty, Carole Lombard, was anything but delicate in her everyday manner and speech. Edith Head, who designed many gowns for her over the course of her career, stated (in *The Dress Doctor*) that "she actually used the most colorful language of any human I've ever met, with a purpose, I'm sure. It was part of her individualism." Ms. Head also noted that she was extremely well-liked by the staff ("the girls in the workroom worshipped her, the fitters begged to work with her").

Carole Lombard fulfilled the small-town-girl-makes-good dream of many a Hollywood starlet. Born Jane Alice Peters in Fort Wayne, Indiana, in 1908, she received her first motion picture role at age 12 when Allan Dwan spotted her playing ball in the street and cast her as Monte Bule's sister in *A Perfect Crime* (1921). After high school she studied drama and received a contract from Fox in 1925, taking the stage name of Carol (sans the "e") Lombard.

When her contract expired she became one of Max Sennett's "bathing beauties" in two-reel comedies. At the advent of talkies, she moved over to Pathé and finally Paramount. In her first movie there, the studio misspelled her name, adding the "e." "Since they're paying me so well," stated Carol(e), "I don't care how they spell my name."[1] In 1931 she married one of her leading men, William Powell. The union ended in an amicable divorce in 1933, and the two remained fast friends. Lombard achieved true stardom when Paramount loaned the actress out to Columbia for *Twentieth Century* (1934), emerging as one of the industry's top comedy stars. In 1939, Carole remarried, wedding romantic screen idol Clarke Gable. Then, in January 1942, while returning from Indianapolis during a war bond tour, her plane crashed into the side of a mountain. "No tragedy has struck the theatrical field with such widespread sorrow since the death, also by airplane disaster, of Will Rogers, in August 1935," observed *Variety*. She was 33.

During the late thirties (long *after Supernatural*), Carole Lombard was listed as the world's highest paid actress, with yearly earnings totaling $465,000. (Ironically, fallen silent star William Farnum, playing the small supporting role of Hammond in *Supernatural*, was the world's highest paid actor nearly a decade earlier.)

Back in 1933, however, Carole Lombard ranked a low ninety-fourth on the *Motion Picture Herald*'s rating of movie box-office personalities, and *Supernatural* did nothing to improve her standing at the time.

Ms. Lombard was very unhappy about her assignment to *Supernatural*. In Danny Peary's *Close Ups: The Movie Star Book*, future director Sidney Salkow wrote of the actress' antipathy toward the project. "She read the script, met the director Victor Halperin, and then promptly threatened to kill herself, Halperin, and everyone in Paramount's front office in order to avoid the assignment. Finally, worn out by her agent and Paramount's threats to suspend her, Carole acquiesced." As filming proceeded, she became highly critical of Victor Halperin's direction and "bridled at Halperin's every suggestion." Never one to keep thoughts to herself, she let fly with barbs like "This guy ought to be running a deli" and "Who do you have to screw to get off this picture?"[2]

"Matters were not helped much," remembered Salkow, "when Halperin, a sweet mild-mannered gentleman, consistently managed to place Carole on the wrong side of the camera, revealing her scar. [An auto accident at age 17 had left a one inch scar on her left cheek; proper makeup and lighting would render it invisible.] Poor Victor, subject to Carole's pithy and never-ending verbal assaults from morn till night, seemingly could no longer tell her right side from her left. Each time he bumbled, Carole would erupt. As Carole girded herself to deal shot by shot with the absurd story, her profanities came more regularly and her appeals for help wracked the stage walls."

During production, it took an "Act of God" to temporarily halt the *Supernatural* proceedings. "At 5:10 P.M., March 10, 1933," recalled Salkow, "the set suddenly started to rumble; a deep roar drowned out the clatter of lights, props, furniture, and sets rattling and crashing while the ground swayed and the earth buckled and writhed. In panic everyone ran shrieking from the set in wild flight. To all of us it was the Long Beach earthquake (it took 52 lives). To Carole it was 'Lombard's Revenge.' I watched her, mindless of everyone's preoccupation with the moment, stride to Victor Halperin huddled outside the still-swaying stage and point a finger at him, 'Victor—*that was only a warning!*' "[3]

Born in Des Moines, Iowa, Vivienne Osborne began her stage career in 1902 at the tender age of five. She broke into pictures in 1920 but attained her greatest fame as a leading lady on the Broadway stage. Her final screen appearance was in *Dragonwyck* in 1946, playing opposite Vincent Price. She died in 1961.

B-western star Randolph Scott made appearances in several of Paramount's Golden Age Horror productions, co-starring in *Murders in the Zoo* (released only three weeks prior to *Supernatural*) as well as making an unbilled appearance in *Island of Lost Souls* a mere two months before that. By the following year, the handsome Scott had gained widespread popularity. A 1934 publicity poll in which 50 popular actresses were asked to list their ten favorite male stars saw Randolph Scott listed alongside the likes of Ronald Colman, Clarke Gable and Joel McCrea.

The son of famous nineteenth-century British actor Charles Warner, H. B. (Henry Byron) Warner studied medicine in London before the lure of the theatre caused him to abandon his studies and begin a long, distinguished career on both the British and American stage. *Supernatural* notwithstanding, Warner entered films in 1914 and brightened such prestigious pictures as *Lost Horizon* (for which he received an Oscar nomination), *You Can't Take It with You* (1938), *Mr. Smith Goes to Washington* (1939), and *The Ten Commandments* (1956). Warner also appeared in one other Golden Age (semi)horror, *The Phantom of Crestwood* (1932).

Alan Dinehart, as Paul Bavian, plays the very same piano piece as a prelude to his seance in *Supernatural* that Boris Karloff later played when he gave his first recital as *The Walking Dead* (1936).

Though he made over 100 motion pictures (the popular actor once appeared in 33 films in only 27 months), Dinehart's first love was Broadway, to which he returned periodically throughout his career.

British stage star and character actress Beryl Mercer went to Hollywood in 1922 and made a career out of playing charwomen and long-suffering mothers (in fact, *Variety* called her "the screen symbol of respectable motherhood" in their August 2, 1939, obituary). Her 53 film credits include the borderline horror pictures *Six Hours to Live* (1932), *Night Must Fall* (1937), and *The Hound of the Baskervilles* (1939; her final film before her death). She was married to character actor Holmes Herbert (of *Dr. Jekyll and Mr. Hyde*, 1931; *The Invisible Man*, 1933; and many other horror films).

"The stage and screen veteran [William Farnum], who has been in practical retirement since 1925 when he suffered an injury, makes his comeback in a leading role in 'Supernatural,'" claimed the film's pressbook. On stage from age ten, Farnum became a silent screen star with his very first motion picture, *The Spoilers*, in 1914. Starring in dozens of films over the next decade, Farnum commanded the highest salary in Hollywood, earning $520,000 a year. During the filming of *A Man Who Fights Alone* in 1925, he was seriously injured and could only accept minor parts for the remainder of the decade. Farnum reportedly lost $2,000,000 in the 1929 stock market crash, a misfortune largely responsible for his "comeback" attempt. Paramount's publicity proclamation aside, Farnum launched his comeback long before his seventh-billed role of Hammond in *Supernatural* (he appeared in three films in 1931, for instance, including playing King Arthur in *A Connecticut Yankee*). Farnum's popularity had waned, however, and the once-wealthy actor eventually had to trade his former $10,000 a week salary for a $25-a-day paycheck for bit parts. The same year he appeared in *Supernatural*, the actor filed for bankruptcy, claiming $500 in clothes as his only asset. Farnum continued to work in pictures up until his death in 1953, appearing in one other horror film, 1944's *The Mummy's Curse*.

"Dialogue Director" Sidney Salkow studied law at Harvard but ultimately turned to the theater, directing several successful Broadway plays before coming to Hollywood as a screenwriter. He began directing in 1937 and embarked on a prolific career making second feature "action" pictures for the next three decades. Among his final films are *Twice Told Tales* (1963) and *The Last Man on Earth* (1964; U.S. version), both starring Vincent Price.

NOTES

1. Quoted in *The Hollywood Death Book*, by James Robert Parish.
2. Quoted in *Carole Lombard: A Bio-Bibliography*, by Robert D. Matzen.
3. From *Close Ups: The Movie Star Book*, by Danny Peary.

THE GHOUL
(1933; Gaumont-British Picture Corp. Ltd.; Great Britain)

Release Date: July 24, 1933 (British); January 26, 1934 (American)
Running Time: 80 minutes
Director: T. Hayes Hunter
Producer: Michael Balcon
Screenplay: Roland Pertwee, John Hastings Turner
Adaptation: Rupert Downing(based on the novel by Frank King and Leonard Hines)
Photography: Gunther Krampf
Musical Score: Louis Levy
Art Direction: Alfred Junge
Film Editors: Ian Dalrymple, Ralph Kemplen
Makeup: Heinrich Heitfeldt
Unit Manager: Geoffrey Boothby
Assistant Director: R. Lyons
Recordist: A. Birch
Production Personnel: Angus MacPhail, George Gunn
Cast: Boris Karloff (Professor Morlant), Cedric Hardwicke (Broughton), Ernest Thesiger (Laing), Dorothy Hyson (Betty Harlon), Anthony Bushell (Ralph Morlant), Kathleen Harrison (Kaney), Harold Huth (Aga Ben Dragore), D. A. Clarke-Smith (Mahmoud), Ralph Richardson (Nigel Hartley), Jack Raine (Chauffeur).

"When the full moon strikes the door of my tomb, I will come back, you hear?! I will come *back*—to *kill*!"—Professor Morlant.

SYNOPSIS

A mysterious Egyptian, Aga Ben Dragore, enters a seedy house to confront another man who has stolen The Eternal Light, a sacred jewel. The thief no longer has the jewel, having sold it to Professor Morlant, a prominent British Egyptologist who believes in the power of the ancient gods. Upon learning this, the Egyptian determines to retrieve the sacred stone at all costs.

In England, the aged professor is on his deathbed. Morlant calls his servant, Laing, to his bedside in order to deliver his final instructions: "You will place the figure of Anubis at the west of the inner chamber, and on the night of the full moon, at the first hour, I will make my offering of The Eternal Light to Anubis, Opener of the Way. If I have done well in his sight, those fingers will close over the jewel and he will open to me the gates of immortality…. Bandage my hand. The Eternal Light must lie with me in the tomb." Morlant then issues this terrible warning: "If this [jewel] should leave me, then you'll have reason to fear. For when the full moon strikes the door of my tomb, I will come back—to *kill*!" With the order given and the curse uttered, Morlant dies.

Morlant's body is placed in his Egyptian-style burial tomb built on the grounds of his estate. The key to the mausoleum is left *inside*, as per his instructions. Soon the intrigues start. Mr. Broughton, Morlant's devious solicitor, questions Laing about the jewel, but Laing shrewdly feigns ignorance, having stolen the jewel from Morlant's bandaged hand and hidden it inside a coffee tin. Laing intends that the valuable object should go to the Professor's heirs—Betty Harlon and Ralph Morlant, his niece and nephew. To this end, Laing takes a note to Betty warning her that "there's something of value" at the old house and that "others are after it, so come." Betty (accompanied by her ditzy roommate) and Ralph decide to investigate together, despite the fact that the two cousins loathe each other.

Upon arriving, the two put aside their differences when they discover Broughton is already there (rooting around for the jewel) as is as a local parson. In addition, Aga Ben Dragore soon arrives, along with a companion, who claim to be old friends of the deceased.

On his way home from town, Laing passes the mausoleum and in the moonlight sees the crypt door open. The vengeful Morlant emerges, just as he had promised to do! Terrified, Laing rushes back to the house, retrieves the jewel, and hides it in Betty's suitcase. Morlant follows and, encountering Dragore's companion, strangles the man. Morlant then breaks into the house (by bending iron bars covering a window) and grabs Laing, who in his terror tells the walking dead man that Betty has the jewel. Leaving Laing to faint, Morlant stalks off in search of the girl. Meanwhile, Broughton has seen this confrontation and reports Morlant's horrific resurrection to the others—who do not take the account seriously. Soon Morlant is stalking about the house while the various characters alternately drink, search, and generally make nuisances of themselves.

Morlant finally finds Betty just as she discovers the hidden jewel in her case. He attacks her and grabs the stone. While the shocked Betty slips away, Morlant takes The Eternal Light back to his tomb. There he invokes a ritual in which he opens up his shirt, takes a knife, and carves an ancient symbol upon his chest.

Laing leads Ralph and Betty to the tomb to investigate. There they find Morlant prostrating himself in front of the idol of Anubis and offering up the jewel. When he places it in the statue's hand, the stone fingers miraculously close about the sacred object. Morlant gives a cry of triumph and suddenly falls dead.[1] Then the statue's "hand" is withdrawn and out from behind the idol steps the parson. "Hartley," shouts Ralph, "so you're not a parson, just a dirty crook!" Hartley picks up Morlant's knife, but Ralph quickly throws an urn and knocks him unconscious. Just as suddenly, Aga Ben Dragore arrives on the scene with a gun and grabs the jewel from Ralph's hand. Ralph disarms him and struggles with the Egyptian, who retrieves his gun and shoots Ralph a glancing shot to the temple. Making his escape with the jewel, Dragore closes the tomb, sealing in Ralph and Betty. Ralph had earlier phoned the police, however, and as Dragore staggers away with his prize, two officers are speeding toward the house. Here we are offered a natural explanation behind the seemingly supernatural resurrection of Morlant: "The doctor in charge didn't understand the case," one officer tells the other. "I'm afraid of catalepsy. Morlant was buried alive."

The fleeing Dragore runs into Betty's overly romantic roommate who ends up accidentally ripping the Egyptian's coat pocket, dropping the jewel onto the ground. Now Broughton appears on the scene, having hidden in Dragore's car, and demands he hand over the valuable object. "That woman," shouts Dragore when he realizes his pocket is ripped and empty, "There she is! She's got it!" But "that woman" keeps the pair at bay by holding the jewel out over a deep well, threatening to drop it into the unfathomable depths.

Back in the tomb an oil lamp has fallen and started a fire. Although the police finally arrive and end the standoff at the well, the fire reaches the tomb door and detonates the dynamite which the "Parson" had previously planted there (presumably to blow open the massive door of the tomb). The explosion does indeed blow open the door, releasing the tomb's two captives. Carrying Betty in his arms, Ralph walks out of the crypt to a happy ending.

MEMORABLE MOMENTS

Morlant's attack on Betty is one of the picture's most shuddery sequences. As Betty discovers the jewel hidden in her suitcase, Morlant violently swings open the door. Spying his sacred jewel in her hand, he approaches Betty from behind. When Betty turns and sees his horrible visage, she panics and tries to flee. Morlant grabs her arm, swings her around and grasps her throat. Terrified, she finds the strength to break loose, but he catches her again and forces her slender body backwards while his hands shake her by the throat until she drops the jewel. Morlant's weird, corpselike appearance, highlighted by the luminescence of the flickering firelight, makes this sudden and ferocious violence especially startling.

The picture's most gruesome scene comes when Morlant returns to his tomb after retrieving the jewel. Prostrating himself at the foot of the statue of Anubis, Morlant suddenly rises to his knees and violently rips open his shirt. Taking up a knife, he draws the blade across his bare chest while his face and body go rigid with pain. As the unseeing idol of Anubis looks on, Morlant rises again and spreads his arms wide, revealing a bloody Egyptian cross which he's carved in the living (dead?) flesh of his chest as a symbol of devotion to his heathen god. This bloody act of fanatical self-mutilation was strong stuff for 1933 and even today remains a rather shocking scene. This is one of the few instances in Golden Age horror films (or any films of the 1930s, for that matter) when filmmakers did not pull their punches in regard to the red stuff. Gunther Krampf's camera unabashedly reveals Morlant's bloody handiwork and boldly refuses to shy away from the oozing, moist flesh. While perhaps not in the best of taste (particularly for more tradition-minded British audiences), it *is* effective.

ASSETS

The Ghoul contains many of the elements necessary for an engaging and even spine-tingling horror picture. A good initial buildup involving the morbid topics of death and returning from the grave establishes an expectant air of dire things to come. A solid foundation in mysticism and the supernatural is laid with the introduction of exotic ancient gods and unholy supernatural powers (reminiscent of *The Mummy*, 1932). There is an Old Dark House occupied by a potentially sinister servant, and a weird tomb filled with various objects of unknown, archaic purpose. Presiding over the macabre proceedings is the master of menace himself, Boris Karloff, suitably made up in a subtly horrific guise. Although these elements are for the most part nullified by a convoluted script, too many characters, and a sluggish pace, some assets remain.

Heinrich Heitfeldt's effective makeup for Boris Karloff received the lion's share of praise in the reviews, much more so than the film itself. *Kinematograph Weekly* called the makeup "clever" and the *New York Herald Tribune* observed that "Mr. Karloff ... does resemble, even before his demise, something dead rather than alive." With deep-set eyes, hollow cheeks, and a ragged hairline to accentuate the forehead (and remind one of the Frankenstein Monster), Karloff indeed looks the part of a resurrected dead man. Director T. Hayes Hunter makes good use of the makeup, filming Karloff stalking head-on into the camera for maximum effect. This makes it doubly disappointing that Karloff is given so little time on screen, and so little to do once there.

Ernest Thesiger, as Laing, gives the picture its one memorable performance (as well as a convincing Scottish accent). The waspish thespian excelled in eccentric roles such as Horace Femm, occupant of *The Old Dark House* (1932), and Dr. Pretorius, co-creator of the *Bride of Frankenstein* (1935). While deprived of the wonderful dialogue and eccentricities possessed by these other unique characters, Thesiger still manages to make an impression as the concerned servant. He shines in one scene in particular, when he's down on his knees pleading with his returned master, who has risen from the dead. "When you told me you'd come back from the grave, how could I believe you?" he asks, his voice filled with awe. "I never knew such things could be!" Thesiger's tortured expression and tremulous voice reveal the terror and anguish in his very soul.

The Ghoul has a very effective musical score (surprisingly so, because this was 1933 and film scoring was still a fledgling art form, with many pictures having little or no musical emphasis whatsoever). The score, dominated by the low tones of an oboe and the rhythmic beating of base drums, adds an air of expectancy and dread to key scenes. When Morlant stalks toward the camera in one sequence, the oboes play low in the background while the low rolling of the drums intensifies as the hideous dead man's face looms near, adding an ominous, urgent note to the scene. For the sequence in which Morlant confronts Betty, the music quickens and becomes almost frantic as he attacks the girl, matching and emphasizing the sudden ferocity of the attack. Overall, the score efficiently sets the tone and pace and greatly enhances what little mood and excitement the picture possesses.

LIABILITIES

If the plot synopsis seems hard to follow at times it is not surprising, since the film itself shares this problem. With an overabundance of secondary characters (who are given very little in the way of true characterization), and a very fragmented storyline which tries desperately to squeeze in some *raison d'être* for each of its myriad players, *The Ghoul* takes on the characteristics of a poorly constructed, overcrowded mystery, with characters coming and going for the arbitrary convenience of the scriptwriters (and to the utter confusion of the viewers). This results in a plodding pace during the central portion of the picture which completely neutralizes any anticipation inspired by the first two (admittedly effective) reels. When the resurrection finally comes, and Karloff is stalking about, it is too little and too late. The few chills and moments of excitement that follow cannot overcome the tedium and disinterest of the previous half hour.

To make matters worse, Karloff's character, about which the picture revolves, is disastrously underdeveloped. At the film's beginning, we are given a brief introduction to Professor Morlant, who utters a curse or two and then dies. With Karloff absent from the screen for an interminable amount of time, the film then follows the various comings and goings of assorted uninteresting characters until Morlant finally returns as a vengeance-seeking killer. Given no further dialogue and saddled with a single-minded purpose, Karloff's Morlant simply becomes a one-dimensional monster who inspires no empathy or even sympathy for his plight (even though Morlant IS the injured party, having had the jewel stolen from him in the first place). Unlike Karloff's Frankenstein Monster, his various Mad Doctors, or even his similar zombie-like character in *The Walking Dead* (1936), this role offers very little for the actor to build upon.

Since the film is ostensibly centered around Morlant, this lack of characterization robs the production of a center of focus and weakens it almost to the point of collapse. The tepid plottings and scattered machinations of the secondary characters cannot generate enough interest to carry the picture until Karloff/Morlant returns. An alternative center of focus would have been Ralph Morlant, the film's nominal hero. But Anthony Bushell as Ralph is so rude and obnoxious, continually barking out his words or engaging in high-pitched shouting, that he becomes an annoying bore. (Bushell was capable of better, as evidenced by his effective portrayal of the cowardly lieutenant in *Journey's End*, 1930.) So the picture must rely upon Karloff's weird appearance (coupled with a few brief moments of that actor's effective pantomime) and his sinister intentions to hold audience interest. The structure is simply too weak.

The Ghoul suffers from a drawn out ending that comes off as an *anti*climax. After Morlant is killed for the final time by simply having him drop dead,[2] there ensues an entire reel of common fisticuffs and the various villains playing jewel-jewel-who's-got-the-jewel until the police arrive and the tomb is torched. By dispatching Karloff's character so early, the film dispenses with what little horror element existed and resorts to mundane action sequences for a wrap-up. It is not even an effective ending in terms of a mystery, for everything has already been revealed and the script simply drags out the inevitable. The weight of too many superfluous characters drags the film down as the script scrambles to tie up each and every loose end for the final fade out, taking much too long after the bubble of mystery and horror has been burst. [Incidentally, the rug had been pulled out from under the film's supernatural feet when Morlant's promised return from the dead was explained away in one throwaway line about catalepsy—but if that is the case, then how was Morlant able to obtain entry into the house by bending iron bars with his bare hands in a show of superhuman (or *supernatural*?) strength?]

REVIEWS

Britain's *Kinematograph Weekly* (July 27, 1933) dismissed *The Ghoul* as a "picture devised on lines similar to that of *The Mummy*, but lacking its plausibility in presentation, treatment and dramatic construction."

Clutching a sacred Egyptian jewel, the dying Professor Morlant (Boris Karloff) orders his servant Laing (Ernest Thesiger) to "Bandage my hand. [This jewel] must lie with me in the tomb."

The New York Times (January 27, 1934) was no more charitable: "Karloff the Uncanny, Hollywood's great authority on the art of spine-chilling, has had the misfortune in his new picture to fall among amateurs at the game. 'The Ghoul,' which is British-produced, has nothing like the hearty terror that the uninhibited script writers in Hollywood piled into 'Frankenstein' and 'The Mummy.' Not one scream was torn from the reverent congregation at the Rialto yesterday, not one hysterical giggle ... A newsreel of a Sunday school picnic would have been more thrilling."

Variety (January 30, 1934) also saw little of merit. "So imperfect a production as 'The Ghoul' cannot win universal favor ... Characters, altogether too unrelated to the action or the dialog, constitute a major weakness in the plot."

PRODUCTION NOTES

In 1933, Universal had planned to star Boris Karloff in their adaptation of *The Invisible Man*. When it came time to cast the picture, however, the studio decided that they would cut Karloff's salary (against the terms of his contract). The actor, who would soon become a founding member of the Screen Actors Guild, refused to be intimidated and walked out on Universal. During this hiatus from his home studio, Karloff was offered the lead in *The Ghoul*, only the second sound horror film to be produced in Great Britain (1932's *The Lodger* being the first). Accepting the role allowed the actor to return to his native England for the first time in 23 years. Though Karloff was at the height of his popularity, *The Ghoul* was the only film the actor made in 1933 (a result of his difficulties with Universal and the ensuing trip to

Ernest Thesiger (pictured here on an English cigarette card from the early 1930s) was primarily a stage actor whose theatrical career spanned half a century. He was also an expert in needlepoint and authored a book entitled *Adventures in Embroidery*.

England), compared to nine pictures in the previous year.

The Ghoul was long thought to be a "lost" film until a single print was unearthed in Czechoslovakia in 1969. The print itself had deteriorated somewhat and had the distinct disadvantage of bearing Czech subtitles. Thus, *The Ghoul* received almost no exposure even after its miraculous resurfacing. Recently an intact British print was located and now *The Ghoul* is available for reassessment.

During its absence, the film had developed a near-legendary reputation among film fans and scholars, based solely on a few enticing stills and aging memories. Unfortunately, as with many "lost" films that are finally found, the actual picture does not live up to the legend. Such was the misconception about the film that author Peter Underwood, in his 1972 book, *Karloff*, claimed *The Ghoul* to be "regarded by many film students as one of Karloff's best films." It is difficult to believe that Underwood had any firsthand knowledge of the picture, since he went on to describe it as "exciting and fast-moving" and "a truly memorable film." He claimed that "*The Ghoul* is generally regarded as outstanding by film-critics and the filmgoing public alike" [though certainly not by the critics of the day, as evidenced by their reviews]. Even more damning is Underwood's inaccurate plot synopsis: "Karloff played a dual role of the half-mad recluse, Professor Morlant, and a master criminal known as 'the Ghoul,' an expert at disguise who impersonates the Professor after murdering him."

Director T. Hayes ("Happy") Hunter, an American, had a generally undistinguished career, though he did succeed D. W. Griffith as the resident director of Biograph Studios after Griffith's departure in 1913. There he directed the early thrillers *The Vampire* (1913) and *The Vampire's Trail* (1914). (Despite their titles, neither one was a horror picture.) After relocating to London in 1927, Hunter directed another 14 unimportant features before giving up film production in 1934 to concentrate on the *business* end of movies. Creating Film Rights, Ltd., Hunter founded England's leading theatrical and motion picture agency, expanding to open a Hollywood office in 1937. Among his many clients were Robert Morley, Flora Robson, Sabu, and Roland Pertwee (co-scripter of *The Ghoul*).

In *Michael Balcon Presents ... A Lifetime of Films*, *The Ghoul*'s producer recalled that Hunter's moniker "Happy" was well deserved. "He was as gentle as a golden Labrador," wrote Balcon, "always smiling ... and it was impossible to feel depressed in his company. Actors and technicians alike loved working with him and I used to tease him by saying that his assistant director's first job on any film was to arrange the collection for the farewell present to be given to him at the end of shooting. I have never known a director who was so invariably given a presentation by the people working with him, and it was a sincere tribute to the fact that it had been a happy experience all round." Of Hunter's work, Balcon stated simply that "Hayes was not a great film director," but added that "part of his charm was that he knew it." Two of the principals from *The Ghoul*, however, did not hold the same "Happy" opinion of Hunter. When William K. Everson screened *The Ghoul* in the early '70s for cast members Dorothy Hyson and Kathleen Harrison, Everson noted that "they were quite vehement in their description of Hunter as being something of a combination of von Stroheim and Lang—without of course the extraordinary talents that those gentlemen possessed to make up for their lack of diplomacy in dealing with actors."

Cinematographer Gunther Krampf came from a background in the German Expressionism of the silent era, having worked on such early horror classics as *Nosferatu* (1922), *The Hands of Orlac* (1925), and *The Student of Prague* (1926). What little visual interest there is in *The Ghoul* can undoubtedly be credited to Krampf's shadowy cinematography rather than to Hunter's drab direction.

Co-screenwriter Roland Pertwee was a novelist, playwright, and also an actor, appearing in a baker's dozen of British films from 1916 to 1947. He is the father of Jon Pertwee, best known to horror fans as the actor-turned-vampire in "The Cloak" segment of *The House That Dripped Blood* (1971).

Eighth-billed Ralph Richardson made his screen debut as the devious "Parson" Nigel Hartley in this picture. He went on to receive an Oscar nomination for his performance in *The Heiress* (1949). Richardson's long and successful career included appearances in two prominent horror/science fiction films of the 1970s, *Tales from the Crypt* (1972) and *Rollerball* (1975).

Newcomer Richardson and his co-star Cedric Hardwicke became good friends, with Richardson often weekending at his colleague's stately home. Hardwicke (in *A Victorian in Orbit*) claimed his compatriot was obsessed with "the internal combustion engine," said obsession taking the form of Richardson "buzzing [my] house in an airplane" or "racing whatever car he owned on the London road." Both men ultimately received a knighthood for their inestimable contribution to English theater.

Ernest Thesiger, while appearing in over two dozen films over the course of his career, was first and foremost a stage actor. His theatrical career spanned half a century, beginning in 1909 and ending only a few weeks before his death in 1961. (At the time of his death, Thesiger, age 81, was Britain's second oldest practicing actor.) Thesiger's last part was in Enid Bagnold's play, "The Last Joke," appearing opposite another survivor of *The Ghoul*—Sir Ralph Richardson.

Anthony Bushell, cast as the young hero Ralph Morlant, later became Sir Laurence Olivier's general manager and associate producer on *Hamlet* (1949). Bushell also turned director (while continuing as an actor) on such films as *The Long Dark Hall* (1951) and *Richard III* (1955; associate director with Olivier); he later helmed *Terror of the Tongs* (1961) for Hammer Films.

In 1961, a British film company named Embassy remade *The Ghoul* as an outright comedy in the "Carry On" mode called *No Place Like Homicide*. It was retitled *What a Carve Up!* for American distribution. Filmmaker Alex Gordon planned to produce (and direct) a second remake of *The Ghoul* in 1968. According to Forrest J Ackerman (who was scheduled to play the Ernest Thesiger part), Karloff was contracted to reprise his original role. Unfortunately, when the actor died later that year so did the project. On February 21, 1973, a made-for-television movie called *The Norliss Tapes* aired on NBC. Though this Dan Curtis production failed to credit any prior source, it is rather obvious that scripter (and self-professed Karloff fan) William F. Nolan took his inspiration from the 1933 version of

The Ghoul. The picture's plot follows a dying man who obtains an Egyptian scarab ring purported to possess life-restoring powers. He's buried with it and then returns from the grave to terrorize people in and around his own estate, killing an art dealer with designs on the ring (a counterpart of the original Broughton character). At the end, the walking dead man prays to a grotesque statue which comes to life (just as the Egyptian statue in *The Ghoul seemed* to come alive).

NOTES

1. Morlant is NOT shot by the phony parson as some sources have erroneously claimed; he simply (and inexplicably) drops dead.
2. *Ibid.*

THE INVISIBLE MAN
(1933; Universal)

Release Date: November 13, 1933
Running Time: 71 minutes
Director: James Whale
Producer: Carl Laemmle, Jr.
Screenplay: R. C. Sherriff
Photography: Arthur Edeson
*Retake Photography and Miniatures: John J. Mescall
Art Director: Charles D. Hall
Editor: Ted Kent
Special Effects: John P. Fulton

*Music: W. Franke Harling
*Makeup: Jack P. Pierce
Cast: Claude Rains (Dr. Jack Griffin), Gloria Stuart (Flora Cranley), William Harrigan (Dr. Kemp), Henry Travers (Dr. Cranley), Una O'Connor (Jenny Hall), Forrester Harvey (Herbert Hall), Holmes Herbert (Chief of Police), E. E. Clive (Police Constable Jaffers), Dudley Digges (Chief of detectives), Harry Stubbs (Police Inspector Bird), Donald Stuart (Inspector Lane), Merle Tottenham (Milly).

Credit not appearing on film print.

"We'll begin with a reign of terror, a few murders here and there. Murders of great men, murders of little men, just to show we make no distinction."—The Invisible One.

SYNOPSIS

During a violent snowstorm, a mysterious stranger arrives at the Lion's Head Inn in the small village of Iping. "Bandages right up to the top of 'is 'ead all 'round his ears," observes the landlord's wife. The stranger sets up a veritable "chemist's shop" in his room where he feverishly conducts experiments.

Meanwhile, at Dr. Cranley's private home/laboratory, Flora (Cranley's daughter) talks concernedly with her father about Jack Griffin, Cranley's assistant. Griffin has been gone a month now, to work on his own secret research, and Flora (who loves Griffin) is worried. Her worries prove well founded when we learn that it is Griffin under those bandages in Iping—and he's made himself invisible. He's holed up in this out-of-the-way village to try and find a way back to visibility.

When the landlord, Mr. Hall, tries to turn him out (Griffin's outbursts have disturbed Mrs. Hall), Griffin pushes the man out the door and down the stairs. They send for the police, but when the constable leads a group of men into Griffin's room, Griffin removes his clothing to show he's invisible and eludes their grasp. "An invisible man can *rule* the world," he tells the terrified onlookers, "Nobody will see him come, nobody will see him go. He can hear *every* secret, he can *rob* and *rape* and *kill!*" With that he makes his escape, wreaking (harmless) havoc along the way.

Back at Cranley's lab, Cranley and Kemp (another assistant) discover that Griffin was experimenting with monocane, a terrible drug that "draws color from everything it touches." It also possesses the side effect of inducing madness. "I only pray to God that Griffin hasn't been meddling with this *ghastly* stuff," states the concerned Cranley.

That evening, Griffin visits Kemp at his home. "The drugs I took seemed to light up my brain," he tells the frightened man. "Suddenly I realized the power I held, the power to *rule*, to make the world *grovel* at my feet!" Obviously, the monocane has affected his mind. Griffin plans a reign of terror and he needs a partner, "a *visible* partner—to help me with the little things." Terrified, Kemp knuckles under and agrees to take Griffin back to the Lion's Head Inn to retrieve his notebooks. When they arrive, the police are conducting an inquiry into the afternoon's events. Griffin slips upstairs and drops his ledgers out a window to Kemp and then goes down and breaks up the inquiry—by frightening off the people and finally killing a policeman.

The police throw out a dragnet and send men to comb the countryside for 20 miles around. Kemp becomes jittery and calls Dr. Cranley to tell him about Griffin. Cranley intends to try and find a cure for Griffin, but Kemp ("a dirty little coward," as Griffin labels him) calls the police. Flora, having overheard her father's conversation, insists on going to Griffin. When they arrive at Kemp's home, she speaks with Griffin alone but he answers her offer of help with ravings about ruling the world. His ranting is interrupted by the arrival of a squadron of police, who surround the house. Removing his clothing, Griffin confronts Kemp. "I've no time now," he informs the terrified Kemp, "but believe me, surely as the sun will set and the moon will rise I shall *kill* you tomorrow night ... At ten o'clock tomorrow night I shall kill you!" At that, he makes his escape through the police barrier.

The next day, Griffin goes on a terror spree, which includes wrecking a train. "Twenty men in the search parties have been killed," laments the police chief, "and one hundred in the train disaster."

The police concoct a plan to catch the invisible man. Using Kemp as bait, they escort him to the police station at 9:30 that evening. Then, armed with spray guns loaded with black paint, they wait for Griffin to come while Kemp slips out a secret entrance disguised as a policeman. Driving away into the countryside, Kemp is startled to find Griffin in the car with him. "I came with you to keep my promise," he says ominously. "I went into the police station with you, Kemp. I stood by while you changed into that coat. I rode on the running board of the car that took you home again." Griffin overpowers Kemp, ties him up, and then sends his car, with Kemp inside, careening over a cliff.

The manhunt continues. Griffin seeks shelter in a barn, where he settles down to sleep in a pile of hay. A farmer hears him moving about and reports to the police that "there's breathing in my barn." The weather is on their side, for it's begun to snow. The police surround and then set fire to the barn. When Griffin emerges from the burning building, the inspector tracks his footprints in the snow and shoots. (In a minor continuity gaff, a close look reveals that these prints are made by someone shod rather than barefoot, as Griffin must be.)

At the hospital later, Griffin is dying. "The bullet passed through both lungs," reports the doctor. "It's impossible to treat the wound." At Griffin's bedside, Flora watches. "I meddled in things that man must leave alone," says Griffin quietly. With a sigh, he dies, his body gradually becoming visible again as life goes.

MEMORABLE MOMENT

The sequence in which Flora visits Griffin at Kemp's home is a brilliant moment of chilling illumination which reveals both sides of Jack Griffin—the man *and* the monster. It begins when Griffin tenderly takes Flora's hands and leads her over to the window seat. "How beautiful you look," he says softly as they sit together. "That funny little hat," he continues, "I've always liked it." His voice is quiet, tender. "You've been crying!" "I want to help," Flora answers, her eyes moist. "Why did you

The Invisible One (Claude Rains) becomes despondent over his inability to find the path back to visibility in *The Invisible Man* (1933).

do this?" she asks. "For you, my darling... I was so pitifully poor. I had nothing to offer you, Flora. I was just a poor struggling chemist..." Griffin's voice changes subtly and becomes harsher, while both his breathing and speech quickens. "There *is* a way back, Flora. And then I shall come to you. I shall offer my secret to the world, with all its *terrible* power! The nations of the world will bid for it — thousands, *millions*!" Griffin's chest rises and falls violently as his hand, bunched into a fist, pounds on his leg in rhythm with his speech. While Flora insists that her father can help him, Griffin's hand goes to his head as if he's confused — or in pain. Her plaintive words fall on deaf ears. "Don't you see what it means? *Power*, power to *rule*—" his clenched fist rises, "to make the world *grovel* at my feet!" At that he extends his arm out and looks down, like a monarch accepting homage from a kneeling subject. His frame shakes with the violence of his emotion. Flora, near tears now, leans toward him and pleads, "[My father] knows something about monocane even *you* don't know. It alters you, changes you, makes you feel differently ... We'll fight this thing out together." Though he looks at Flora, Griffin pulls back, his body language drawing him away from her promise of salvation. Without even acknowledging her pleadings, he suddenly turns from her and rises to his feet. "*Power*, I said! Power to walk into the gold vaults of the nations, into the secrets of kings, into the holy of holies. Power to make multitudes run *squealing* in terror at the touch of my invisible finger!" At this, he extends his hand toward the camera, whose low angle makes him appear huge and terrifying. He turns and looks past his shoulder out the window. Folding his arms defiantly across his chest, he announces, "Even the Moon's frightened of me — frightened to death! The whole world's frightened to death!" At this moment, that includes the viewer. Thanks to R. C. Sherriff's grandiose dialogue, Claude Rains' brilliant inflection and physical acting, and James Whale's perfect staging, this becomes a scene both illuminating and chilling in its intensity.

ASSETS

With four bonafide genre classics to his credit, James Whale is undisputedly *the* most important director from the Golden Age of Horror. Though the quantity is quite impressive, it's the quality that sets Whale apart — and above — his contemporaries. (*Frankenstein*, *The Old Dark House*, *The Invisible Man*, and *Bride of Frankenstein* are all included among the top ten horror films of the decade — see Appendix B.) Tod Browning also gave us four (*Dracula*, *Freaks*, *Mark of the Vampire*, and *The Devil-Doll*), but while they all possess a significant level of merit, several fall well short of the classic mark. And let's not forget that stubborn independent, Victor Halperin, who contributed one genuine gem (*White Zombie*) and then finished out *his* quartet with a trio of dismal failures (*Supernatural*, *Revolt of the Zombies*, and *Torture Ship*). Several other directors have provided us with multiple classics (Michael Curtiz with *Doctor X*, *Mystery of the Wax Museum*, and *The Walking Dead*; Karl Freund with *The Mummy* and *Mad Love*; the Cooper/Schoedsack team with *The Most Dangerous Game* and *King Kong*), but no other of the decade's filmmakers possesses such a prolific — and perfect — record as James Whale. His third, *The Invisible Man*, is yet another "Whale of a Picture." Of the director's four genre ventures, it may be the most balanced — it's more sophisticated than *Frankenstein*, less idiosyncratic than *The Old Dark House*, and avoids the heavy-handed symbolism and directorial grandstanding of *Bride of Frankenstein*. Deftly blending humor and horror, Whale places his stamp on every portion of *The Invisible Man* (from his trademark jump cut introduction of the title character — à la *Frankenstein* — to his mocking sense of humor) to facet yet another cinematic jewel.

Whale selects varied angles — shooting from on high to show the timid townspeople scurrying down the tavern stairs or shooting *up* at Griffin to turn Rains' rather short personage into a towering figure. Each perfectly framed shot is unique as Whale takes care not to repeat himself, even altering the angle or distance slightly when he goes back to an earlier shot in order to add a visual variation and keep the viewer slightly off-balance. Whale never settles for the mundane. For example, in place of the standard newspaper headline montage one would expect (in a 1933 production) to illustrate the manhunt for the invisible man, Whale relays his information with a rich visual flair. It begins in a dance hall when the music stops and an announcer's voice states, "I must interrupt the dance music for a moment. I have an urgent message from Police Headquarters." The camera moves us forward through the bewildered dancers while the bulletin continues until we stop momentarily before the old-style victrola speaker. The camera then moves forward again until the round cone fills the screen and the image dissolves to an elderly couple listening by their radio. The camera continues tracking smoothly forward in each successive scene as one image dissolves into the next — the old couple to a group of children gathered around the wireless to a middle aged pair in their home... As the special broadcast finishes, the image dissolves once more into the original dance hall radio and the camera backs away in reverse. In every shot the camera continually moves forward, taking us along as the information and subsequent panic flows through the radio from person to person.

Whale immediately follows this sequence with a series of extreme close-ups of people frantically locking their doors, throwing their deadbolts, and even nailing up boards. With the camera at tilted, odd angles and a babble of agitated voices in the background, Whale creates an air of panicked urgency.

Whale builds upon Sherriff's script to infuse the film with a wicked sense of humor which sometimes bubbles up into near-hilarity. Once having seen it, who can forget the priceless moment when a seemingly disembodied pair of trousers comes skipping down a country lane jauntily singing "Here We Go Gathering Nuts in May"?

R. C. Sherriff's clever screenplay sports enough rich dialogue to make *The Invisible Man* one of the most quotable films from Horror's Golden Age. Memorable lines like "Look, e's all eaten away!" and "Even the Moon's frightened of me!" and "How can I handcuff a bloomin' shirt?!" proliferate.

The characters are delightfully drawn, particularly Jack Griffin. Though his transformation from beleaguered scientist into maniacal killer comes fairly quickly, it is nonetheless believable. Frustrated to the point of distraction, he initially lets loose with a volley of malicious pranks — tipping over a grandfather clock, tossing glasses around the pub, throwing an old man's hat into a pond. Among these impish acts, however (like some evil omen of the dire things to come), Griffin also callously tips over a baby carriage, causing the distraught mother to rush around to rescue her spilled — and possibly injured — bundle of joy. Later, when Griffin disrupts the inquest at the tavern, he begins comically enough by throwing ink in the face of the doubting policeman and tossing various flagons and pitchers at the screeching Mrs. Hall and scrambling locals. He ends it, however, with a brutal blow to the bobby's face with a wooden stool — killing the man. Griffin has now crossed the line completely — our worst fears have been realized and the madness seizes him fully as he embarks on his reign of terror. Even when Griffin becomes a truly frightening figure, however, he never completely loses his humanity. He can still manage a moment of tenderness with Flora, and he keeps his manners — rewarding Kemp with a polite "thank you" for a pair of gloves and bandages. Ultimately, we still care about Griffin's condition and feel genuine sorrow at his plight and (admittedly deserved and necessary) death.

Through his intelligent, powerful voice and expressive body language, Claude Rains creates a character who, though faceless, becomes more real (indeed, more *visible*) than many other star portrayals. After Mrs. Hall bursts in and interrupts Griffin, Rains holds up a vial of liquid and growls, "a whole day's work *ruined* by a foolish ignorant woman!" and savagely hurls the beaker into a corner. Then, grabbing up a notebook, he strides to the table and slams the journal purposefully down on the surface. Dropping into a chair, he suddenly places his elbows on the open pages and brings his fists up to his temples in a position of abject frustration. "There *must* be a way back," he exclaims. "If only they'd leave me alone!" The anger mixed with desperation in Rains' voice generates a deep sympathy and immediately places the viewer firmly on his side. If only they'd leave him alone, indeed. This empathy gives the film a more powerful resonance so that when Griffin turns into a dangerous megalomaniac, the change inspires an anxious sympathy as well as fear.

A few moments later, when told to leave by Mr. Hall, Rains clasps his hands in front of him and explains, entreats really, "I came here for quiet and secrecy. I'm carrying out a difficult experiment. I *must* be left alone." The plaintive pleading in Rains' voice, his hands gripped tightly in front of him as he looks up, creates an attitude of supplication that makes us yearn to hear the landlord capitulate. When that does not happen, and Griffin does violence to the man, we simultaneously applaud and abhor the action. We come up short, however, when Rains' high-pitched, hollow laughter—a chilling, unhealthy sound—raises the hackles.

Rains' body language expresses a cold, matter-of-fact ruthlessness which conveys his character's megalomania as much as if it's spoken aloud. Though much smaller than his co-star, William Harrigan (playing Kemp), Rains uses body language to make Griffin tower over the bigger man. His confident, precise steps and ramrod posture speak of assured superiority which overcomes any barrier as trivial as mere size. One can certainly empathize with Kemp's near-debilitating terror.

John P. Fulton's amazing special effects add the finishing touches that bring the scenario to realistic life. When we see a shirt running around the room on its own, arms waving in mockery at the dumbfounded spectators, or a cigarette and box of matches rise and light themselves (complete with a subsequent exhalation of smoke issuing out of thin air), we have no doubts that invisible hands really are manipulating these objects. Even the more mundane gags involving simple props (with no matting techniques), such as a chair pulled forward on its own and turning to face the fire before the cushion indents under the weight of an invisible backside, are so flawless and natural that suspension of disbelief never becomes an issue. From what we *do* see, we have no doubt that what we do not see is truly there.

A reissue poster from 1948 for *The Invisible Man* (1933). The figure pictured at bottom left is actually Vincent Price from the 1940 sequel, *The Invisible Man Returns*. (Courtesy of Lynn Naron.)

LIABILITIES

Only once does Whale fall into the directorial extravagance which threatened to overpower his later *Bride of Frankenstein* at times. When Kemp follows Flora from the adjoining lab into the house proper, Whale takes the camera smoothly *through* the wall (as he did — to good effect — in *Frankenstein*). It fails to work this time, however, since the camera tracks too far back from the wall's end and angles so that we get a clear view of both rooms at the same time. Strangely, Whale also places a small table with a (large) plant conspicuously at the end of the wall — like the structure is *supposed* to stop there. If so, it's not a wall at all but a bizarre half-partition sporting an (unnecessary) door. This odd bit of architectural (or directorial) confusion calls attention to itself and distracts the viewer (though, fortunately, only momentarily) from the proceedings. This admittedly minor quibble, whose adverse effects last no more than a few questioning seconds, is Whale's sole misstep.

The only other blemish on this otherwise flawless film is a bit of unconvincing modelwork. During Griffin's reign of terror, he knocks out a signalman and throws a switch which sends a train roaring off a cliff. The obvious miniature model which crashes down a papier-mâché mountainside serves to date this otherwise timeless classic. Fortunately, Whale keeps the shots brief, and we quickly forget about the technical faux-pas.

REVIEWS

Variety (November 21, 1933) called *The Invisible Man* "a picture that develops something new and refreshing in film frighteners." The reviewer had nothing but praise for the picture, summing it up this way: "In production, story handling and direction, 'Invisible Man' needs nothing which it hasn't got."

Mordaunt Hall, of *The New York Times* (November 18, 1933) was equally impressed, calling it "a remarkable achievement." He also made special note of the effective comedic element: "Although various incidents may be spine-chilling, it is a subject with a quota of well-turned comedy."

PRODUCTION NOTES

The Invisible Man, like many film projects, traversed a rather winding route from novel to screen. As early as 1931 the film was announced as a starring vehicle for Universal's new "King of Horror," Boris Karloff, with Robert Florey (of *Murders in the Rue Morgue* fame) set to direct. While this initially came to naught, the concept kept evolving. In addition to H. G. Wells' book (the author was paid $25,000 for the film rights), Universal had purchased the rights to the Philip Wylie novel *The Murderer Invisible*, intending to merge the two works in order to incorporate Wylie's more gruesome elements into Wells' story. Over the next two years numerous writers (among them Garrett Fort, John Balderston, and Gouverneur Morris) worked on the project and various treatments emerged. The film's final screenwriter, R. C. Sherriff, described some of the earlier screenplay variations in his autobiography, *No Leading Lady*: "The man who had turned it out no doubt had the original H. G. Wells book beside him, but to justify his employment he had got to improve on it. If he had stuck to the original story and made a faithful adaptation the studio would probably have said he hadn't got any initiative or imagination of his own; that they weren't paying him good money merely to copy out what Wells had written.[1] So he had set aside the original story and given the invisible man adventures from his own imagination.

The studio had no doubt felt there were good ideas in it but not enough, and passed it on to another writer. The second writer had got to go one better and invent a lot more new ideas. The third writer had to trump the one before, and so it went on, each new effort becoming more extravagant and fantastic and ridiculous. One writer [Preston Sturges] took the scene to Tsarist Russia at the time of the Revolution and turned the hero into a sort of invisible Scarlet Pimpernel. Another made him into a man from Mars who threatened to flood the world with invisible Martians, and all of them envisaged him as a figure of indescribable peril to the world, threatening to use his unique invisibility to reform it or destroy it, as he felt inclined. One thing stood out clearly in every page I read. The charm and the humor and the fascination that had established the original Wells story as a classic had been utterly destroyed." Sherriff ended up ignoring all the previous treatments and discarding the Wylie novel altogether when he based his screenplay strictly on the Wells novel, sticking as closely to it as possible within the confines of a screen adaptation. Ironically, Universal did not even *possess* a copy of the book for which they'd purchased the rights, so when Sherriff decided to return to the source, he had to comb the junk markets of downtown Los Angeles before finally locating a secondhand copy of the Wells book in a Chinese market.

The independent-minded Sherriff found it difficult to conform to Universal's rigid work regime. Studio head Carl Laemmle insisted on all his writers clocking onto the lot at 9:00 every morning, but Sherriff did his best work at night and in hotel rooms. So James Whale suggested that the writer report to the lot at the scheduled hour, spend the day visiting sets, then return to his hotel to do the real work in the evenings. This arrangement seemed to work and Sherriff rapidly fulfilled his assignment while keeping "Uncle Carl" happy at the same time (and justifying the writer's $1,500 a week salary).

Long before Sherriff's involvement, Universal "ace" director James Whale took an interest in the project and in fact worked up a story treatment of his own (dated January 3, 1932). In it, a kindly doctor, his face horribly mutilated in a research accident, discovers the secret of invisibility in order "to remove from the eyes of mortal man the harmful sight of this frightful face." In the process of becoming invisible, however, his mind is unhinged and he "now has only a longing to kill those very people he had healed and befriended." The project (set to star Boris Karloff) was shelved by the front office, however, when Whale was assigned to direct *The Kiss Before the Mirror*. Finishing up that romantic melodrama, Whale returned his attentions to *The Invisible Man* and apparently decided to discard his storyline (along with all the other varied screen treatments) when he asked his friend R. C. Sherriff to tackle the final screenplay.

According to stuntman/novelist/screenwriter John Weld (the last writer to turn in a scenario before Sherriff was hired), it was H. G. Wells himself who suggested Sherriff for the assignment, not Whale. In addition, Weld reported that Wells held veto power over the script. Writing in his autobiography, *Fly Away Home*, Weld also stated that Sherriff was not the first to go back to the original source, and intimated that he was *not* the sole author of the final screenplay, screen credit notwithstanding. "It was logical to assume that Wells would approve his own story line, and his approval was mandatory.... When I had finished [the adaptation]," wrote Weld, "it was sent to Wells in England and to Laemmle's surprise and delight he approved it.... Wells followed his cable [of approval] with a letter stating that the screenplay was to be written by his friend, R. C. Sherriff, author of *Journey's End*, a highly successful play about World War One, and that Sherriff was to get full screen credit. This meant that my name would not appear on the film as the adaptor. Such injustices were common in the movie industry at the time, and it was to correct these abuses that the Screen Writers' Guild was founded. I became a charter member."

H. G. Wells was much more satisfied with this particular cinematic treatment of his work than with *Island of Lost Souls* (which he condemned outright) released earlier this same year. While fascinated by the technical process of cinema, Wells had nothing but contempt for the short-sighted filmmakers themselves, stating in a symposium on "The Novelist and the Film" in *John o'London's* (August 4, 1923), that "cinema people" were "utterly damned fools, beneath the level of a decent man's discussion." The author later revised his opinion and held at least two of these "cinema people" in high regard—James Whale and R. C. Sherriff. In 1934's *Experiment in Autobiography*, Wells called *The Invisible Man* "a tale, that thanks largely to the excellent film recently produced by James Whale, is still read as much as ever it was," adding, "to many young people nowadays I am just the author of *The Invisible Man*." Upon the film's release, a pleased

Wells told the London Press: "Here I do find my narrative sequences respected and the interest gathered together and brought to a climax in competent story-telling style. That is, I suppose, because the synopsis was made by Mr. R. C. Sherriff, himself a competent dramatist and story-teller. I am told that Mr. Sherriff's version was the thirteenth prepared. I should be amused to see the other twelve versions." Wells' satisfaction was not quite complete, however, for he criticized Sherriff's use of the drug monocane to turn Griffin insane. "If the man had remained sane," Wells explained, "we should have had the inherent monstrosity of an ordinary man in this extraordinary position. But instead of an Invisible Man, we now have an Invisible Lunatic!" Whale, also at the press party, countered by wryly observing that "If a man said to you that he was about to make himself invisible, wouldn't you think he was crazy already?"[2]

When Boris Karloff walked out on Universal on June 1, 1933, after to a contract dispute (the studio refused to award the actor a salary increase promised six months earlier), Whale was left without an Invisible Man. (Some sources claim that this suited the director right down to his jodhpurs. Biographer James Curtis claimed, "Whale was dead-set against using Karloff," feeling the actor "was simply wrong for the part.") Colin Clive's name came up in the studio's search for "The Invisible One," but Whale had already set his sights on a stage actor named Claude Rains. Rains had never acted in motion pictures before. (He had done a screen test for RKO, playing scenes from the plays *A Bill of Divorcement*, *The Man Who Reclaimed His Head*, and *Man of Destiny*, but nothing had come of it. "And they were terrible!" admitted Rains. "I was all over the place! I knew nothing about screen technique, of course, and I just carried on as if I were in an enormous theatre. When I saw the test, I was shocked and frightened...." Over the protestations of producer Carl Laemmle, Jr., Whale managed to locate the "terrible" screen test and show it to a gathering of Universal executives. "Along came a test of a man called Claude Rains," recounted the actor. "Well, they howled with delight! But, Whale said, 'I don't give a hang what he looks like. That's how I want him to sound — and I want HIM!"

"Claude was what we call an 'actor's actor,'" recalled co-star Gloria Stuart. "You know that when you say, 'well, he's an actor's actor' it's a little deprecating. It means enormous ego, enormous concentration on oneself and *death* to the rest of the actors. Claude was an actor's actor's *actor*! He used to back me into the scenery. And I would say 'James!' And he'd say, 'Now Claude, be nice to Gloria. You know it's not the stage, we can do it again, so be nice to Gloria, don't do it.'" Even so, Ms. Stuart still regarded Rains as "a very nice person and a brilliant actor."

Upon the completion of *The Invisible Man*, Universal (which had awarded the first-time screen actor a long-term contract) promptly dropped Rains from their roster, and the disappointed actor returned to his New Jersey farm and more work on the Broadway stage (though it was not long before Hollywood beckoned again and transformed him from an invisible actor into a highly visible star). During his subsequent career, the illustrious actor received four Oscar nominations (*Mr. Smith Goes to Washington*, 1939; *Casablanca*, 1943; *Mr. Skeffington*, 1944; and *Notorious*, 1946), but never won.

Also slated to appear in *The Invisible Man* was American star Chester Morris. When Morris learned that the newcomer Claude Rains was to be given star billing above himself (Rains insisted on it), Morris left the production rather than settle for second billing, and William Harrigan took his place.

The astounding special effects by John Fulton were usually attained with the use of the fledgling traveling matte process. Fulton clothed Rains' stunt double in black velvet tights and helmet over which were worn the clothes of the invisible man. The stuntman then completed the actions required (disrobing, moving about, etc.) on a set also cloaked in black velvet. "This gave us a picture of the unsupported clothes moving around on a dead black field," revealed Fulton to *The American*

Cinematographer (September 1934). "From this negative, we made a print, and a duplicate negative, which we intensified to serve as mattes for printing." When combined and reprinted with a positive background, the composite created the startling sight of clothing walking about on its own.

Fulton encountered many problems in his efforts to create his invisible man. Curiously, most of the difficulties stemmed not from the techniques themselves, "but had to do with acting and direction — getting the player to move naturally, yet in a manner which did not present, for example, an open sleeve-end to the camera. This required endless rehearsal, endless patience — and many 'takes.'"

"In nearly all of these scenes," Fulton continued, "though they were made silent, it was difficult — sometimes impossible — to direct the actor, for the helmet muffled the sound from outside, and the air-tubes [necessary to let the actor breathe inside the sealed helmet] made a roaring rumble in his ears, which drowned out any sounds which might filter through the padding. When I used a large megaphone, and shouted at the top of my voice, he could just barely hear a faint murmur! Accordingly, we had to rehearse and rehearse — and then make many 'takes'; as a rule, by 'Take 20' of any such scene, we felt ourselves merely well started toward getting our shot!"

According to Gloria Stuart, the effects work was kept secret even from the actors. "We were not allowed to see it and nobody knew for years how it was done."

Among those appearing in *The Invisible Man* in brief walk on parts are Walter Brennan (who loses his bicycle to The Invisible One), John Carradine (then called John Peter Richmond), who phones in a suggestion on how to capture an invisible man, Dwight Frye (as a reporter), and Violet Kemble Cooper, who played Karloff's mother three years later in *The Invisible Ray*.

The Invisible Man was a huge success, both critically and financially. *The New York Times* placed it at number nine on their "Ten Best" list of 1933, and the picture broke two years' worth of attendance records at New York's Roxy theater.

NOTES

1. One of the subsequent writers, Preston Sturges, confirmed this front-office attitude. According to Sturges' biographer, James Curtis (in *Between Flops*), producer Carl Laemmle, Jr., told Sturges to ignore H. G. Wells' original story, as it "stunk." Eager for a vehicle to showcase Universal's most bankable star at the time, Boris Karloff, Junior Laemmle sent daily memos to both Sturges and intended director James Whale to spur them on. "I am making Karloff's part in *The Invisible Man* just as important as I possibly can," Sturges wrote to Laemmle. "The strange thing about these horror characters is that their effectiveness grows in inverse ratio to the amount of time we see them. Familiarity breeds contempt and too much gruesomeness becomes funny. Karloff will curl your back hair in every scene I've got him in to date, and you ain't seen nothin' yet."

2. Quoted in *The H. G. Wells Scrapbook*, edited by Peter Haining.

THE SON OF KONG
(1933; RKO)

Release Date: December 20, 1933
Running Time: 70 minutes
Director: Ernest B. Schoedsack
Executive Producer: Merian C. Cooper
Associate Producer: Archie Marshek
Screenplay: Ruth Rose

Photography: Eddie Linden, Vernon Walker, J. O. Taylor
Settings: Van Nest Polglase and Al Herman
Editor: Ted Cheesman
Music: Max Steiner
Sound Effects: Murray Spivack

Recording: Earl A. Wolcott
Chief Technician: Willis O'Brien
Art Technicians: Mario Larrinaga, Byron L. Crabbe
Technical Staff: E. B. Gibson, Marcell Delgado [models], Carroll Shepphird, Fred Reese, W. G. White
Cast:
Robert Armstrong (Denham), Helen Mack (Hilda), Frank Reicher (Englehorn), John Marston (Helstrom), Victor Wong (Chinese Cook), Ed Brady (Red), *Clarence Wilson (Peterson), *Lee Kohlmar (Mickey), *Noble Johnson (Native chief), *Katherine Ward (Mrs. Hudson), *Gertrude Short (Reporter), *James L. Leong (Trader), *Frank O'Connor (Process Server), *Gertrude Sutton (Servant Girl), *Steve Clemento (Witch king), *Constantine Romanoff (Bill), *Harry Tenbrook (Tommy), *Leo "Dutch" Hendrian (Dutch).

*Uncredited on film print.

"Good boy, Little Kong. Say, can he scrap, just like his old man!" — Carl Denham.

SYNOPSIS

It is one month after King Kong took his fatal fall from the Empire State Building. Carl Denham (the man responsible for capturing the giant ape and bringing him to New York) resides in a seedy boarding house, dodging various creditors and process servers who've descended upon him in the wake of the massive destruction wrought by Kong. "I thought I had him safe," the remorseful Denham tells a brash young reporter, "don't you suppose I'm *sorry* for the harm he did. I wish I'd left him on his island. Old Kong, I'm sure paying for what I did to you."

With a grand jury indictment only hours away, Denham manages to escape his predicament along with Captain Englehorn on the *S.S. Venture*. It was Englehorn's ship which had transported Kong from his island home, and the captain decides to get out before they come looking for him as well. For the next few months, the captain and Denham eke out a living shipping freight amongst the smaller island ports of the East Indies.

While in one such port, Dakang, they run across a cheap monkey act featuring "La Belle Helene" — a pretty but tuneless songstress named Hilda. After the show, her drunkard father invites a seedy Norwegian ex-captain named Helstrom over to their tent to share a drink. They argue and Helstrom hits the old man over the head with the bottle, knocking over a lantern. The tent catches fire and everything burns while Helstrom flees. Hilda drags her father out of the blaze but, sadly, he dies in her arms.

Later, in a local bar, Denham and Englehorn run into Helstrom. "Say, do you know who this is?" Denham asks Englehorn by way of introduction, "the man who gave me the map of Kong's island." (Nils Helstrom was mentioned but never seen in *King Kong* as the man who sold Carl Denham the Skull Island map).

Helstrom, desperate to get away from Dakang (afraid of what the murdered man's daughter might say to the local magistrate) concocts a story about a treasure on Kong's island and convinces Denham and Englehorn to take him along as a partner in a search for this mythical fortune.

Just before they sail, Denham visits Hilda and gives her what little money he has so that she can book passage on the next ship out of Dakang. She pleads with Denham to take her with him on his own ship, but he will not expose her to the dangerous voyage they're about to undertake. Once out to sea, however, Denham discovers that the strong-willed young lady has stowed away onboard.

The scheming Helstrom incites the crew to mutiny but his plan backfires once they reach Skull Island. The sailors mutiny all right, forcing Denham, Englehorn, Hilda, and the loyal Charlie (the Chinese cook) over the side into a lifeboat. The turncoat crew then throws Helstrom over the side as well ("Do you think that we got rid of a good captain so we could have a bad one?" laughs one crew member).

The stranded band make for the island's one accessible beach, but they are chased off by the angry natives who blame Denham for the destruction of their village by Kong's rampage.

Finding a narrow passage through the sheer cliffs which rim the rest of the island, the intrepid group finally lands. Climbing up the rocks, Denham and Hilda spot a small-scale (12 foot tall) albino version of Kong stuck in some quicksand. "Well if it isn't a little Kong," marvels Denham, "I never knew that old Kong had a son!" Feeling guilty over the death of the 'father', Denham pushes over a dead tree to help the giant ape get out of the quicksand. Pulling himself free, a happy Little Kong goes merrily on his way.

Meanwhile, Englehorn, Helstrom, and Charlie, who've gone off to hunt for food, are chased into a cave and cornered by an enraged Styracosaurus (a spike-frilled variation of the Triceratops). At the same time, Denham and Hilda are menaced by a giant cave bear. Hearing the girl's screams, Baby Kong rushes to the rescue and battles the larger mammal. The ape wrestles and pummels the beast into submission, but his finger(!) has been hurt in the fracas. Denham then makes a friend for life when he wraps a makeshift bandage about the giant ape's wounded digit.

With Little Kong's help, Denham and Hilda break into an ancient temple and discover a huge idol holding a primitive necklace dripping with diamonds. (Helstrom's wild yarn notwithstanding, there truly *was* treasure on Kong's island.) While inside, the trio are besieged by a dragonlike giant lizard which Baby Kong must battle to the death to protect his newfound friends.

Englehorn and the rest escape the Styracosaurus and make it back to the temple. When the nervous Helstrom catches sight of Little Kong, he panics and flees in terror, heading for their lifeboat. At the boat, however, the traitorous coward is met (and eaten) by a giant sea serpent. Suddenly, an earthquake rocks the island and the very ground begins to crumble. Englehorn, Hilda, and Charlie make it to the boat and take it out into the open water (Denham having gone back for the treasure). The island literally sinks beneath them as Denham and Little Kong continually climb for their lives to the very pinnacle of the mountain — now only a few feet above the water and sinking fast. Then, as the last trace of Skull Island sinks beneath the waves, the loyal Little Kong holds Denham aloft in his huge hand until the lifeboat can pick him up. Finally, his hand slips beneath the waves and is gone forever (an ironic end for the Son of Kong — sacrificing his own life to save the man responsible for his father's death). Later, a passing ship rescues the castaways and all live happily ever after as Denham and Hilda clinch while they split the treasure among them.

MEMORABLE MOMENT

The picture's most exciting (and effective) moment occurs when Captain Englehorn, Charlie, and Helstrom encounter the Styracosaur. The scene begins with a flawless profile long shot of the three humans to the left of a gigantic vine-choked tree and the prehistoric animal to the right. In an instant, the behemoth roars and charges its tiny prey. Simultaneously, the captain hurriedly fires a shot at the beast which slows the creature for a brief moment. As the three humans run out of the frame, the Styracosaur regains its balance and chases after them, passing behind the tree and trampling over the ground our protagonists just vacated. In the next shot (again in profile), we see the three sprint into a cleft in the rock wall of the mountain with the charging dinosaur not ten feet behind. Once again, strategically placed trees in the foreground allows O'Brien to integrate the actors and the monster perfectly, so that we can almost feel the creature's fetid breath on our own necks. With a crunching thud and a horrendous cry the angry animal crashes headlong into the cliff face, its bony frill too wide to fit through the crevice. It draws back and shakes its mammoth head from side to side, roars, and butts into the cleft a second time. Then we see the horrible predicament our protagonists face — their sheltering cave is only a few yards deep! From over the back of the behemoth we watch the horned head as it pounds again and again at the rocks, trying to get at the tiny humans cringing just beyond its reach. On the

Though "he isn't a patch on his old man," *The Son of Kong* can still defend his human friends, Denham (Robert Armstrong) and Hilda (Helen Mack), against marauding dinosaurs.

soundtrack, its enraged bellows alternate with the crunching jolts of its furious assaults. The scene fades as Charlie desperately strikes out at the monster's horny snout with his hopelessly small cleaver, the beast tossing its head as if annoyed by a stinging insect. Though lasting less than a minute, the superb integration and tense excitement makes this saurian sequence a scene (the *only* one) worthy of *King Kong* itself.

ASSETS

Literally volumes have been written over the years on *King Kong* but very little has been said about that film's offspring, except perhaps for a dismissive sentence or at best a denigrating paragraph. Long looked upon as a bastard son, *The Son of Kong* has its merits and deserves better than its relative obscurity. If its name did not inspire such high expectations, the picture would undoubtedly be better received, since it possesses a cast of likable characters, a cadre of fine performances, and, particularly, an excellent story (up until the arrival on Skull Island, at least). So, for the moment anyway, let us forget that there ever was an "Eighth Wonder of the World" and look at this *Son* on its own merits.

Surprisingly, the most effective aspect of *Son* is also the one many viewers complain about the most — the lengthy human drama and character development which takes up the bulk of the picture. *The Son of Kong* is really two films in one — or, more precisely, one picture broken up into two parts, each possessing its own distinct character. The first (and lengthiest) is an excellent adventure/budding romance/down-on-your-luck/underdog story constructed like a precision instrument so that everything fits together smoothly. Denham and Englehorn's escape from their financial/legal plight in New York; their barely successful attempts to make a living in the dirty backwaters of the East Indies ("It's a dull life, Skipper," resignedly admits the once-adventurous showman); the pitiful local "show" (a sad parody — and painful reminder — of Denham's past); Denham's innocent yet charming encounters with Hilda (who now has nowhere, and no one, to turn to); the appearance of the murderous Helstrom, desperate to flee the island, who provides Denham with a reason to return to Skull Island — all these disparate elements cleverly intertwine to draw the protagonists toward the picture's ultimate goal (and second half) — the return to Kong's island. Unfortunately, after 40 minutes of carefully constructed buildup and character development, the arrival on Skull Island heralds the arrival of the picture's most dire liabilities as well. Up to this point, however, a number of assets shine through.

A gentle humor peppers Ruth Rose's screenplay, giving *Son* a dimension lacking in the original (though, admittedly, the epic *King Kong* did not really need it). "It was a case of 'if you can't make it bigger you'd better make it funnier,'" explained Rose. During La Belle Helene's tuneless musical number, for instance, Denham sees potential in the vivacious girl. "You know, she's got something," he tells Englehorn, to which the bored captain replies, "It certainly isn't a voice." Later, Denham runs across Hilda trying to coax her trained monkeys down from the trees:

Denham: "You'll never catch a monkey that way."

Hilda: "Did you ever catch a monkey?"

Denham: "Did I ever—?" (chuckles) "Lady, you'd be surprised."

Denham has obviously kept his sense of humor — it's all he has left. When Helstrom encounters Denham in the bar, the ex-captain tries to wrangle some money out of him:

Helstrom: "I'm down, Denham. Don't you think you owe me something?"

Denham: "Well sir, you certainly came to the right man. How 'bout a fifty-fifty split?"

Helstrom: "You mean that?"

Denham: "Sure I mean it. I'll give you half of everything I made out of King Kong."

Helstrom: "How much would that come to?"

Denham: "Well, let's see" (looking up as if performing computations in his head), "Ten — no, 11 lawsuits and the privilege of being indicted by the Grand Jury too."

Helstrom (despondently): "You're broke too."

Denham (wryly): "Broke? I'm shattered."

This self-deprecating humor helps make Denham a much more charming and approachable character. The gusto and reckless enthusiasm he showed in *King Kong* has been tempered, making *Son of Kong*'s Carl Denham a more down-to-earth figure than the previous film's seemingly human force-of-nature. Like the sequel's version of Kong himself (and the film as a whole), Denham has shrunk in stature — if not physically, then in spirit. Gone is the energetic, fearless showman of *King Kong*, replaced by a saddened, almost haunted man seeking escape rather than adventure. One of the most satisfying aspects of *Son* is to follow this once-indomitable man as he regains his enthusiasm and thirst for adventure.

Robert Armstrong's demeanor perfectly suits his now more well-rounded character. Armstrong is quieter, his delivery gentler. Gone is the grandiose shouting, replaced by a voice full of introspection and concern for others. "For me personally," recalled the actor, "the role was better than before. It gave me a great deal more character, swell dialogue and love scenes."[1] Armstrong welcomed the chance to play the great showman again. "Denham was a character audiences could identify me with; many actors work all their lives without getting that."

Armstrong's co-stars lend able support. Helen Mack makes the most of what proves to be the most capable heroine of horror's Golden Age. No simple clinging vine, the plucky Hilda has "got personality" as Denham observes. Alone after the dreadful but sincere show, Hilda removes the little monkeys' costumes. Ms. Mack's sad smile and wistful expression reveal much about her unfortunate plight — and her stoicism. Later, after dragging her father from the burning tent, she demonstrates both courage and a cool head by running back into the inferno to salvage her dress and a trunk before the whole tent is consumed. Racing back to her father, she cradles his head and watches him die. The painful anguish in her face quickly gives way to a hard stare as she gazes upon the fire and remembers its villainous cause. When Helstrom meets Hilda in the street the next day, the actress' face goes rigid, her eyes stony as her steely voice tells him with a calm conviction, "You killed my father." When Helstrom protests, she responds with "How do you know *what* my father said to me before he —" she pauses momentarily, then as her resolution returns, "— before he died." Ms. Mack's voice and face are a study in control, the only slip her momentary hesitancy at speaking her father's death aloud. Unfortunately, upon reaching Kong's island her once-strong character becomes little more than Denham's shadow, another example of the mounting liabilities found in the film's second half.

As Helstrom, John Marston's shifty eyes and dour face add an untrustworthy look to his character, particularly when his eyes go wide and nearly glitter with greed as Denham leads him on about sharing the wealth. Add to this a harsh yet effectively subtle accent and a demeanor which shifts between brutal bullying, an obvious deviousness, and outright cowardice, and Marston's Helstrom becomes a thoroughly despicable (and convincing) human villain.

Alongside Carl Denham's character development, *The Son of Kong* allows Captain Englehorn further character expansion as well. The solid, unflappable captain has learned a thing or two from his previous unhappy experiences, and the returning Frank Reicher's rather stolid portrayal in the first picture gives way to a more human characterization here. When told by Denham that a Little Kong inhabits the island, Reicher sputters an alarmed "What?! A little K —." Reicher stops without finishing the dreaded word and half swallows before asking in a voice pitched a little higher, "*How* little?" The actor's subtle change in face and voice perfectly conveys the effect the news has on this sturdy character.

Ernest B. Schoedsack directs with his usual eye toward action and excitement, even during the more sedate first half of the picture. "We're off again," pronounces a jubilant Denham, pouring a drink in celebration after learning of the island's "treasure" from Helstrom. Schoedsack opens the next scene with a shot of Denham's legs walking through the darkened streets, his white trousers and shoes a stark contrast against the almost black ground. Denham's steps are light and quick and he leaps lithely over a bit of foliage, showing us the renewed excitement and spring in his step now that adventure once again looms on the horizon. With this simple yet ingenious scene, Schoedsack subtly and effectively reveals a character's mood without a lot of unnecessary exposition.

When an opportunity for more robust excitement presents itself, Schoedsack takes full advantage. He shoots the fire scene, for instance, in a fast-paced, thrilling manner. The camera follows Hilda as she dashes into the burning tent, frantically throws open the cage doors to release the monkeys, then grabs her father under the arms and drags his unconscious form out through the door, kicking aside obstacles as she goes. Menacing flames rise up in the bottom of the frame as Hilda hurls crates out of the way to reach the man, adding a sense of danger and urgency. All the while, Schoedsack keeps his camera on Hilda, pacing alongside her as she drags her prone father out of the flames, in front of the stage, through the tent anteroom, and finally out into the safety of the night air. The camera tracks beside her during the whole ordeal, exposing her struggle and her fortitude and deftly drawing the viewer into her terrible plight to feel the dreadful excitement of the moment. Then, much to our alarm, Schoedsack takes us *back into* the inferno as Hilda rushes in to grab what she can before the fire totally consumes the tent. Schoedsack's careful staging and camera movement effectively enmeshes the viewer in the young girl's plight. (Afterwards, one very nearly needs a handkerchief to mop the sweat from one's brow.)

Max Steiner reused much of his score from *King Kong* to rekindle the excitement of the original. In addition, he creates a number of new melodies, including a leitmotif for Hilda (emphasizing the increased importance of this picture's *human* characters) based on "The Runaway Blues" which she sings so earnestly during her first scene. Steiner cleverly changes the tune's tempo and tone to reflect a scene's particular mood (adding an ominous low note as Hilda wakes to find the tent ablaze, or slowing the tune until it becomes a dirgelike reflection of Hilda's sadness as Denham bids her good-bye). Regrettably, once Little Kong arrives, Steiner saddles him with a kazoolike comical theme reminiscent of the buzz of an annoying housefly, proving that even the genius of Max Steiner was not infallible.

LIABILITIES

Unfortunately (for the sequel), the gigantic shadow of *King Kong* looms so large that *The Son of Kong* cannot escape its bedimming presence. Comparisons are inevitable and certain to favor the mighty father rather than the modest son.

RKO did not further their sequel's cause when they filled their ballyhoo with such grandiose but empty claims as "'Son of Kong' is more elaborately staged, its photography is much smoother than in the former production, and it is far more convincing and thrilling." Setting themselves up for an Empire State Building-sized fall, the studio flatly stated in their pressbook that "RKO-Radio has actually produced a sequel more appealing than its predecessor."

Publicity articles with delusions of grandeur aside, *The Son of Kong* (in the words of Carl Denham) "isn't a patch on his old man." Allotted little more than a third the time and money by a studio eager to cash in on their *King Kong* success, the producer/director team of Merian C. Cooper and Ernest B. Schoedsack wisely decided to emphasize completely different aspects than those featured in *King Kong*. Since, given the reduced resources, there was no way to top their previous creation in terms of scope, adventure, and sheer excitement, the filmmakers resolved to play up and expand upon the human characters from their mammoth monster movie. Yes, they were obliged to include the expected dinosaurs and the titular titan (though both in scaled-down versions), but these are *not The Son of Kong's* main focus, title notwithstanding (in fact, a more accurate moniker might be *Road to Skull Island*, since the story's primary concern is the teaming of, and interaction between, Denham, Englehorn and Hilda).

To give them credit, RKO's publicity department at least recognized the picture's new direction and incorporated it in their press releases. "According to Ernest B. Schoedsack, who directed 'King Kong' and who holds the same post for 'Son of Kong,' the terrors dominating the first fantasy have been given a different application in the sequel, the plot of which gets down to a more romantic basis. 'Son of Kong,' it is said, has more thrills but they are treated in a more sympathetic theme than in 'King Kong.'" (The "more thrills" they allude to but fail to specify must be of a decidedly human rather than monstrous variety.) Another article notes that *The Son of Kong* "is an entirely different yarn than its startling predecessor.... The theme of the story tends to romance with adventure, rather than toward unmitigated terrors, which, in 'King Kong,' reached a high peak."

Cold statistics tell the comparative story. At 70 minutes, *Son* is a full half-hour shorter than its illustrious predecessor. The character of Kong dominated *King Kong*, with the title terror onscreen for nearly 25 minutes (or 25 percent of the picture's 100-minute running time). Thus, Kong enjoyed more screen time than most of his human co-stars! In *Son*, however, Little Kong must make do with a mere 11 minutes onscreen. This works out to only 16 percent of the film's running time. *Son* lags behind *King* in terms of dinosaurs as well. *King Kong* features nine minutes of dinosaur footage whereas *Son* only contains four minutes of monster mayhem. Beyond that, dinosaur purists will be sorry to see that the bulk of this footage is taken up by a mammal (cave bear) and mythical beasts (dragon, sea serpent) rather than true thunder lizards. Only two factual dinosaurs appear — a Styracosaurus (for

37 seconds) and an Apatosaurus (for a barely glimpsed three seconds), making *Son*'s saurian screen time a sorry one percent! Obviously, Little Kong is not the featured attraction his papa was; nor are the prehistoric inhabitants of Skull Island a prominent feature in *Son* as they were in *King*.

Once our intrepid band land on Kong's island, things rapidly go awry. What should have been the sweet fruit of the first half's well-crafted labor turns out to be sour apples. The single most disappointing aspect of the picture's second half is the handling of Little Kong, for *The Son of Kong* turns out to be a comical rather than prodigal son. Never do we feel the menacing awe inspired by his father, nor do we feel much of anything but derision for this puppyish progeny, whose continual simpering inspires more annoyance than affection. (If studio publicity can be believed, Little Kong's various whimpers and squeals were the product of "the first recording of a conversation between two gorillas for talking picture purposes." According to a pressbook article, a sound crew journeyed to the San Diego Zoo where they recorded the noises made by two baby gorillas. "Their voices later become utterances of the 'Son of Kong.'")

The disappointment sets in with the ape's very first (non)appearance. Little Kong's all-important introduction carries absolutely no buildup or fanfare. Gone are the impressive native ceremony, the gong-sounding, the roaring and smashing of trees. Instead, a jump cut takes us abruptly from the captain and company to the sight of Little Kong with only his (bowed) head and shoulders visible between some rocks — no terror, no suspense, no excitement. It is as if the filmmakers used up all their artistic energies simply getting their characters to Skull Island and now, too creatively exhausted to complete the work, opt for the dull, easy way out. Undoubtedly, time and money dictated what could be presented, but something so important as the title attraction's entrance should not be so casually thrown away.

From this banal opening, the focus is on "cute" mannerisms, as Little Kong engages in all manner of comical and "endearing" gestures such as rubbing his eyes when sleepy, or scratching his head when confused, or brushing off his hands after completing a job, or even turning to the camera and giving an open-handed shrug (for no apparent reason). This anthropomorphic buffoonery reaches its height (or, more accurately, plumbs its depth) when Denham watches over Hilda in front of the fire at night. Little Kong peeks from behind the rocks, spies the romantic couple and places his hand over his mouth in modesty as he moves back out of sight. He quickly peeps out again, however, smiles, and touches his finger to his lips like some large, furry cupid. Not only is this a colossal waste of animation time and money, it also makes the son of the mighty Kong into a ridiculous figure. This juvenile approach sat well with neither audiences nor critics. *The New York Times* labeled Little Kong "a vaudeville buffoon" while *Variety* went so far as to call the giant ape "a bit of a pansy."

Such clowning marred even the prehistoric battles. When Little Kong defends Denham and Hilda against the cave bear, the confrontation begins as an exciting, even vicious, struggle, with the bear's fangs and claws flashing while Little Kong desperately grabs and pummels the beast with his fists. The thrill quickly evaporates, however, when Baby Kong takes a fall against the rocks, goes cross-eyed, and holds his head (while comical music on the soundtrack hits viewers over *their* heads). Little Kong recovers and comes out roaring, but the scene has been shattered by the injection of puerile humor into what should be a colossal fight to the death. Just as the battle seems to get serious again, with the bear on top of Little Kong viciously trying to bite and claw his throat, the giant ape goes into a big-time wrestling mode to twist and gnaw his opponent's leg before grabbing him in a headlock. The crowning indignity comes when the defeated bear revives and attacks again, and Little Kong ends up crawling out from between the bear's legs! Then, after chasing the mammoth mammal off with a big stick, Little Kong sits down and nurses his battle wound — *a sore finger*!

The subsequent encounters with the island

denizens become a lackluster parody of *King Kong*'s mighty struggles on his island home, with the filmmakers failing to come up with anything even remotely original. The previously-described Little Kong vs. cave bear episode is a lamentably farcical stand-in for Papa Kong's battle with the Tyrannosaur; the three protagonists chased into a cave by the Styracosaurus is a small-scale replacement for the sailors' flight from the angry Apatosaurus in the original; and Little Kong defending Denham and Hilda from the dragon in the temple is the counterpart to Kong's defense of Ann from the Plesiosaur in his mountaintop retreat. With the exception of the Styracosaurus sequence, each of these thinly-disguised parallels are merely pale imitations of Kong's classic confrontations and ultimately conjure up unfavorable comparisons in the mind of the viewer. Rather than mimic scenes they could not hope to equal, much less surpass, O'Brien and his team would have done better to try for something new and unusual.

While the animation is technically up to *King Kong*'s standards (Orson Welles even commandeered a background scene from *Son* featuring animated birds for his 1941 classic, *Citizen Kane*), the heart is missing. Willis O'Brien imbued the original Kong with a wealth of personality without stooping to silly antics and foolish expressions. For Kong, Jr., however, the filmmakers work so hard to make him an adorable figure that they completely supplant personality with witless humor. O'Brien himself balked at this approach, and the lack of verve in the animation may be a result of O'Brien's limited participation. According to Ray Harryhausen (O'Brien's pupil and successor to his title of "King of Stop-Motion Animation"), "O'Brien objected strongly to the story and the concept and really had very little to do with the film," and was averse to even discussing the picture in later years.[2] Darlene O'Brien (the animator's second wife) elaborated: "Obie was unhappy about the making of *Son of Kong*. He felt it was too soon to follow *King Kong* and that there was not going to be enough money to make it good. He asked them to not put his name on it and he didn't do any more than put in appearances each day, so that he would get his check. He did no animation and was a little unhappy with some of the humor—supposedly that was put in to it, and especially laughed at the idea of bandaging the little finger of a big creature like that. He never wanted to do anything that would make Kong or [Mighty] Joe [Young] look ridiculous."[3]

The climax to *The Son of Kong* typifies the film's second half—technically adept but hurried and ill-conceived. Right after Denham secures the treasure and the two groups are reunited, all hell breaks loose when blocks of stone rain down as an earthquake rocks the island. Incongruously, the very next shot shows a violent hurricane buffeting a handful of panicked natives. (Not only does the storm suddenly appear as if by magic, the natives *dis*appear just as abruptly, for this is the last we see of any of Skull Island's indigenous human inhabitants.) Driving rain beats down as the earth literally crumbles and huge rocks topple about our protagonists. From out of nowhere a seething hurricane has engulfed the island with gale force winds and a violent rain. Earthquakes do not normally have such an *instantaneous* effect on atmospheric conditions, and this is certainly the only time on the screen (or in recorded history) when both an earthquake and hurricane hit *simultaneously* in one spot. One can only suppose that the filmmakers decided it was time to wrap it up and thought-what better way than to simply destroy the entire island in a two-minute special effects extravaganza? It makes for an impressive spectacle but hardly any sense. Shots of the jungle seemingly folding in upon itself to be swallowed up by the foaming seas, the temple sinking beneath the roiling waves, and the very mountain crumbling under the onslaught of wind and rain, rank among the decade's best scenes of cataclysmic destruction. While visually spectacular, however, this abrupt wrap-up fails to satisfy story-wise and does further injustice to the careful buildup and character development of the picture's first half.

RKO (and Kong, Jr.) paid for their mistakes. Audiences responded poorly to this

As this behind-the-scenes shot shows, *The Son of Kong* has one gigantic grip for a primate only 12 feet tall. (Courtesy of Ted Okuda.)

hastily rushed-out sequel and it scored only moderately at the box office, squelching any further sequel plans. O'Brien toyed briefly with the idea of yet a third film which would focus on the time before Denham transports Kong back to New York. The giant ape was to escape into the Malay Archipelago for another adventure, but, of course, the story remained untold.

Though possessed of expanded characterizations and some isolated stellar moments, *The Son of Kong* was not the "Ninth Wonder of the World" it might have been. In the end, one cannot help but think that this kinder, gentler *Son* was a deep disappointment to his old man.

REVIEWS

Variety's "Bige" (January 2, 1934) was unimpressed: "This is the sequel to and wash-up of the King Kong theme, consisting in salvaged remnants from the original production and rating as fair entertainment.... But the punch is no longer there, and in this rehash the same qualities that thrilled on the first trip are likely to impress now as being too much for anybody to swallow." Bige also noted the change in giant ape demeanor from the first: "Where Old Man Kong was a menace all the way, the Kid is more inclined to comedy relief."

B. R. Crisler of *The New York Times* (December 30, 1933) went even further, stating that "the Prince of the celebrated house of Kong is a vaudeville buffoon alongside of his old man," while at the same time lamenting that "to its leading player the film devotes a regrettably small portion of its story." Mr. Crisler failed to appreciate the picture's expanded character development, feeling that "The introduction is a long and windy account of Carl Denham's preparations for the trip [which] goes to unnecessarily trying lengths to plant the villain and the girl."

PRODUCTION NOTES

The same month that *King Kong* premiered to record-breaking crowds, Cooper, Schoedsack & Co. were hard at work on a mysterious new project called *Jamboree*. Budgeted at $250,000 (little more than a *third* of *King Kong*'s final $650,000 cost), *The Son of Kong* was a small-scale comedic follow-up rushed out to capitalize on the monstrous success of *King Kong*. The misleading *Jamboree* title was utilized to keep the sequel a secret during production. "We called it *Jamboree* to keep people from visiting the set," explained Schoedsack. "If they'd known we were making another Kong picture they'd have driven us crazy trying to find out how it was done." *The Son of Kong* reached theaters by December of 1933.

Economy was the production's watchword, even extending to recycling two of *King Kong*'s dinosaurs and ultimately to the mighty King himself. In order to build the three working models of Kong, Jr., Marcel Delgado cannibalized the metal armatures that served as the skeletal structures for his progenitor. Delgado's models of the spike-frilled Styracosaurus and the long-necked Apatosaurus (briefly glimpsed rising up out of the turbulent waters at the climax of *Son*) were borrowed for the sequel as well. (Ironically, even though this was the Styracosaurus's second film, it was its first screen appearance, since all scenes featuring that particular dinosaur were trimmed from the original *King Kong* before its release.) Delgado augmented the two borrowed dinosaurs by constructing a few mythical creatures of his own for this production, including the dragonian lizard which Little Kong battles in the temple and the sea serpent that devours the treacherous Helstrom. As originally planned, all the island's dinosaurs were to stampede and run amok in a spectacular sequence at the film's climax, but the concept was dropped when deemed too expensive. (Apparently, RKO failed to notify their publicity department of this fact, for *The Son of Kong* pressbook promises that "The amazing spectacle of hundreds of prehistoric monsters, many of them as big as two-story buildings, all engaged in a snarling, hissing, roaring free-for-all battle to live, is one of the photographic treats offered in RKO-Radio's new adventure film, 'Son of Kong.'")

Though common knowledge today, the pioneering stop-motion animation techniques devised by Willis O'Brien for *King* and *Son* were akin to magic in 1933. (Even two decades later, people conjectured that Kong was actually a man in a suit!) RKO labeled O'Brien "Hollywood's mystery scientist who revives denizens of prehistoric ages" in their *Son of Kong* pressbook. The studio shamelessly exploited this technical mystery angle with misleading publicity and, in the case of *The Son of Kong*, boldfaced lies. "The activities of the gigantic snow-white ape..." wrote RKO publicists in the film's pressbook, "made it necessary to bathe it each morning. A fire hose and ten pounds of strong soap were used for each ablution." (Ten pounds of soap and a fire hose seems like overkill for an 18-inch model made of rubber and rabbit fur!) Another publicity snippet described six-foot-six director Ernest B. Schoedsack as "the only man connected with the production who could shake hands with the film's gigantic hero, a snow-white ape, without climbing a stepladder." Beyond intimating that Little Kong was a real (and exceedingly tall) gorilla, the pressbook also claimed the various dinosaurs were actually full-sized gargantuas! "Six gigantic prehistoric monsters, the smallest almost thrice as large as an elephant, were towed through the ocean from the Port of Los Angeles to Catalina Island, 20 miles off shore, for sequences in RKO-Radio Pictures' current fantasy, 'Son of Kong.'" While Catalina did serve for some location shooting, it was live actors rather than "gigantic prehistoric monsters" which journeyed to the island. The article finally turns truthful when it blithely closes with "Residents [of Catalina Island] did not see the invasion [of monsters]."

A horrible tragedy occurred in stop-motion animator Willis O'Brien's life near the finish of *The Son of Kong*. His wife, who had a history of mental illness, was stricken with both tuberculosis and cancer at the time. On October 7, 1933, the despondent woman shot both of O'Brien's sons and herself. The two boys died, but she survived for a full year. O'Brien remarried in 1934 to Darlene Prenette, this second union happily lasting until his death in 1962.

A musical prodigy, Austrian-born Max Steiner graduated from Vienna's Imperial Academy of Music at age 13 after completing the four-year program in a single year. At age 16 he began conducting professionally while continuing his music studies with Robert Fuchs and Gustav Mahler. In 1914 Steiner emigrated to the U.S. where he conducted and orchestrated musicals on Broadway. He began working on films in 1929 and ultimately scored over 300 motion pictures, including the genre entries *The Most Dangerous Game* (1932), *The Phantom of Crestwood* (1932), *The Monkey's Paw* (1933), *Secrets of the French Police* (1932), *She* (1935), *Arsenic and Old Lace* (1944), and *The Beast with Five Fingers* (1947). Steiner received 15 Academy Award nominations, winning three times. Few musicians have had as much of an effect on films as Max Steiner. Upon Steiner's death in 1970, it was Merian C. Cooper who delivered his funerary eulogy.

Robert Armstrong (born Donald Robert Smith) studied law at the University of Washington before making a name for himself as an actor on the vaudeville circuit and then the legitimate stage. He made his screen debut in 1927 in *The Main Event*. Armstrong reprised his characterization of Carl Denham yet a third time in *Mighty Joe Young* (the new name of Max O'Hara does not fool anyone — he's still the same old Denham). The actor also starred in two other genre pictures, *The Most Dangerous Game* (1932) and *The Mad Ghoul* (1943). Coincidentally, Robert Armstrong died only one day before his frequent producer, Merian C. Cooper, who passed away on April 21, 1973.

Born Helen McDougall in 1913, Helen Mack entered the theater and movies at an early age, becoming a child star of both Broadway and East Coast-produced silents. After a seven year hiatus, Mack returned to the screen in 1931 as an adult (though *The Son of Kong* pressbook touted their 20-year-old star as a "new discovery"). Besides *The Son of Kong*, she lent her lively presence to two other genre pictures — *She* (1935) and *Strange Holiday* (1945; her final film). She retired from the screen after marrying Thomas McAvity, who later became an executive at NBC.

Born in Munich, Germany, Frank Reicher emigrated to the U.S. in 1899 and quickly became a popular stage actor and director. He entered films in the latter capacity, directing numerous silent pictures for the likes of Metro and Paramount before returning to the theater in 1921. He reentered pictures five years later, this time as an actor, and appeared in nearly 200 films over the next three decades. In addition to the two *Kong*s, his many credits include *The Crooked Circle* (1932), *Secret of the Chateau* (1934), *The Great Impersonation* (1935), *The Invisible Ray* (1936), *The Florentine Dagger* (1936), *Dr. Cyclops* (1940), *The Mummy's Tomb* (1942), *Night Monster* (1942), *The Mummy's Ghost* (1944), and *House of Frankenstein* (1945).

John Marston learned his craft on the stage, playing leading roles on Broadway in the 1920s (including the stage production of *The Bat* which ran for two and a half years) before turning to films.

Aside from the principals Robert Armstrong, Frank Reicher, and Victor Wong (Charlie, the Chinese cook), Noble Johnson also returns from *King Kong* (in a brief cameo) to add his statuesque presence as Skull Island's native chief. Johnson had been a pioneering producer (and star) of "all-colored" films in the silent era, joining with his brother George to help form the Lincoln Motion Picture Company and produce such all-black features as *A Negro's Ambition* and *Trooper of Troop K* (both 1916). In front of the camera, Johnson was one of the first black actors to break into the Hollywood mainstream, debuting in 1914 (as an Indian!) when he filled in for an injured actor. By 1918, Johnson was receiving featured billing in a successful string of serials at

Universal. At this point, the studio demanded that "the race's daredevil movie star" (as the black press referred to the actor) cease starring in his own all-black features since Johnson's pictures for Lincoln were doing better business with black audiences than their white-made competition. Forced to choose between his hard-won Hollywood success and the more doubtful future of independent black features, Johnson went with the studio and resigned as president of the Lincoln Motion Picture Company. Johnson subsequently became one of the busiest black actors in Hollywood, appearing in over 60 silents and remaining in the industry for over 30 years. Among his early film roles were Friday in *Robinson Crusoe* (1922), a cannibal in Buster Keaton's *The Navigator* (1924), and a bit in *The Thief of Bagdad* (1924). Johnson appeared in a number of other genre entries, including *Murders in the Rue Morgue* (1932; as "Janos, the Black One," though he wore white face!), *The Most Dangerous Game* (1932; again in white face as a Russian Cossack), *The Mummy* (1932; as Karloff's Nubian slave), *She* (1935; a native), *The Ghost Breakers* (1940; an imposing zombie), and *The Mad Doctor of Market Street* (1942; as a native chief again).

Among the publicity ploys suggested by RKO to promote their picture was a "'Son of Kong Klub' for the Kids" in which "the basis of the Klub is the kindness and understanding and sacrifice of the 'Son of Kong' ... The youngsters should write to the newspapers telling of kind deeds to humans done by their small pets or larger animals, and vice versa." Another "stunt" was to have a screening at the zoo! "It would be a wow of a newspaper story to have some local scientist study the reactions of the lions, apes or other beasts to the fights of 'Son of Kong.'" On the literary front, the pressbook suggested a Limerick Contest tied in with the local newspaper and supplied several sample starter limericks to which the contestants were to add the final line:

"The Allosaurus bragged it could escape

From 'Son of Kong,' the giant ape;

'Til the colossal Jocko

Swung at it — *Socko!* —"

Whereas *King Kong* has been reissued many times over the years, always to great critical (re)assessment and financial success, *Son* never enjoyed any such revival. After its initial run, the best it ever did was to ride on the coattails of *Dracula* and *Frankenstein* as the bottom third of a triple-bill desperation ploy undertaken in 1938 by a near-bankrupt Hollywood theater owner named Emil Ulmann. Moviegoers flocked to see the monsters again and Ulmann's theater was saved. More importantly, the program's unparalleled success caught the eye of Universal, who were smarting financially with their money-making monsters in limbo. The studio then reissued *Dracula* and *Frankenstein* themselves nationwide to phenomenal business. This in turn led to their producing *Son of Frankenstein*, which started the horror ball rolling again in 1939. So, at least superficially, *The Son of Kong* was part of the great horror revival which this triple-bill's success sparked in the industry, and helped to launch the second wave of screen horror (whose seas had lain becalmed for nearly two years). Undoubtedly, *Son*'s contribution was little more than incidental, but it *was* there. In any case, RKO showed no renewal of interest in their progeny and never bothered to reissue *The Son of Kong* on its own. Thus, it remained largely unseen until the American Movie Classics cable channel began showing it regularly in the early 1990s, exposing a whole new generation of viewers to Kong's forgotten offspring. For horror historians, anyway, *The Son of Kong* occupies, if not a full niche, than at least a wall-plaque in the museum of cinema history.

NOTES

1. As quoted in *The Making of King Kong*, by Orville Goldner and George E. Turner.
2. *Film Fantasy Scrapbook*, by Ray Harryhausen.
3. Letter from Darlyne O'Brien to Mike Hankin dated March 16, 1982, as quoted in *Willis O'Brien*, by Steve Archer.

THE BLACK CAT
(1934; Universal)

Alternate Titles: *The House of Doom* (British release title); *The Vanishing Body* (reissue title)
Release Date: May 7, 1934
Running Time: 65 minutes
Director: Edgar G. Ulmer
Producer: Carl Laemmle, Jr.
Screenplay: Peter Ruric (from the story by Edgar G. Ulmer, Peter Ruric
"Suggested by the immortal Edgar Allan Poe classic"
Photography: John J. Mescall
Art Director: Charles D. Hall
Musical Director: Heinz Roemheld
Editor: Ray Curtiss
Cast: Karloff (Hjalmar Poelzig), Bela Lugosi (Dr. Vitus Werdegast), David Manners (Peter Alison), Jacqueline Wells (Joan Alison), Lucille Lund (Karen), Egon Brecher (the majordomo), Harry Cording (Thamal), Henry Armetta (the sergeant), Albert Conti (the lieutenant).

"We shall play a little game, Vitus, a game of death if you like."—Hjalmar Poelzig.

SYNOPSIS

While on a train trip through Eastern Europe, Peter and Joan Alison, a honeymooning couple, meet a strange, tortured man named Dr. Vitus Werdegast. After debarking, they share a bus with him which, during a violent storm, has an accident in which the driver is killed. Fortunately for them (or *un*fortunately as it will turn out), they are near the house of Hjalmar Poelzig, which was Dr. Werdegast's destination.

After treating Joan's superficial injuries, Werdegast confronts his host and demands to know what has become of his wife and daughter. Here we learn of Poelzig and Werdegast's long and hate-filled history. Poelzig's treacherous actions during World War I were responsible for Werdegast's being captured and sent to prison "where I rotted for 15 years." Now Werdegast has returned to seek his revenge and find his wife and daughter whom his rival had stolen.

Poelzig takes his old adversary down into the bowels of the old fortress upon which the house was built. There he shows Werdegast his wife's body—perfectly preserved and suspended upright in a weird glass sarcophagus. In a rage, Werdegast pulls a gun, but the sudden appearance of Poelzig's black cat unnerves him. (Werdegast has an overpowering fear of cats.)

Then begins their "game of death." Poelzig, the leader of a satanic cult, intends to sacrifice Joan as "the chosen maiden" at "the Dark of the Moon." Werdegast, who has taken on the role of the couple's protector, challenges Poelzig to "fight it out alone," with the fate of the young house guests hanging in the balance. Poelzig chooses to play a game of chess instead, and the two sit down to play for the life of the girl.

Peter, sensing something is very wrong, determines to leave. But Werdegast has lost the game and so Peter is knocked unconscious and thrown into the old gun turret room by Werdegast's servant (who has been ordered by his master to obey Poelzig until the time is right to move against their enemy).

Joan is taken upstairs to be prepared for the ceremony. Karen, Werdegast's grown daughter—and Poelzig's wife—enters the room. She believes that her father is dead, and Joan tells her the truth. "Your father has come for you," exclaims Joan, but Poelzig has overheard. Entering, he forces the protesting Karen out of the room and a terrified scream is heard.

Soon the Satanists arrive for the ceremony and Poelzig dons his high priest's robes. During the course of the proceedings, Werdegast manages to steal Joan away and flee to the vaults. Once there, Joan tells Werdegast the truth about Karen: "Your daughter—she's alive, here in this house. She's Poelzig's wife!" Enraged, Werdegast begins a frantic search for his daughter. He finds her in Poelzig's private embalming room — dead. Poelzig has murdered Karen, his own wife, to keep her from her father.

Poelzig, who has pursued him into the catacombs, now attacks Werdegast. With the aid of his servant, Werdegast overpowers the Satanist and straps him to his own embalming rack. "Do you know what I'm going to do to you now?" asks Werdegast, with a glint of madness in his eyes. "Flay the skin from your body, slowly, bit by bit." As Werdegast begins his grisly work, Peter regains consciousness and rushes to the chamber. The door is locked, however, and the key is in the hand of Werdegast's dead servant (shot by Poelzig's butler). Werdegast leaves his gruesome task to help Joan pry the key from the dead man's hand, but Peter mistakes his actions as menacing and shoots him. The wounded Werdegast begs the couple to go and then approaches a bank of instruments. "It's the red switch, isn't it Hjalmar?" he asks. "The red switch ignites the dynamite." Pulling the lever which sets off the explosives left there from the war, Werdegast proclaims the two men's epitaph: "It has been a good game." While the Allisons flag down a car on the road below, the house, the Satanists, Poelzig, and Werdegast are all destroyed in the ensuing explosions.

MEMORABLE MOMENTS

The very essence of *The Black Cat* is captured in what is perhaps the film's finest sequence. When Werdegast discovers the fate of his lost wife, he threatens to kill Poelzig for what he's done. Poelzig responds with this monologue: "Come Vitus," he softly intones, "are we men or are we children? Of what use are all these melodramatic gestures? You say your soul was killed, that you have been dead all these years. And what of me? Did we not both die here in Marmorus 15 years ago? Are we any the less victims of the war than those whose bodies were torn asunder? Are we not *both* the living dead? And now you come to me, playing at being an avenging angel, childishly thirsting for my blood. We understand each other too well. We know too much of life. We shall play a little game Vitus, a game of *death* if you like." Director Ulmer underscores this revealing passage by changing the camera's point of view. As Poelzig starts to speak, the camera *becomes* Poelzig, and begins moving slowly along the stone passage, toward the stairs which spiral upwards in a symbolic promise of events to come, a portent of all the darkness buried below finally rising to the surface. By doing this Ulmer takes us *inside* Poelzig, *inside* the story and its melancholy emphasis on death. It is a moment not to be missed.

ASSETS

The Black Cat is a totally unique film. There has never been another quite like it, either in mood or in execution. This is a rare thing in the often unimaginative copy-cat system of Hollywood, even during its Golden Age.

Though the film is "suggested by the immortal Edgar Allan Poe classic" (according to the film's credits), screenwriter Peter Ruric (with story help from director Ulmer) delivered a script that is about as far from Poe's short story as one could get. Of the many adaptations (in most cases the better word would be "suggestions") of "The Black Cat," Ruric and Ulmer's vision is perhaps the least faithful to the storyline, but the most faithful to the *spirit* of Poe. A spirit of melancholy, sadness, and — most of all — death, permeates this film, just as these feelings are embedded in the brilliant, tortured works of the nineteenth century author.

Nearly the whole of the film takes place within the walls of the fascinating, ultra-modern house of Hjalmar Poelzig. This house is built upon the very foundations of the World War I Fort Marmorus, "the greatest graveyard in the world." Early on in the film Werdegast confronts Poelzig: "You sold Marmorus to the Russians. You scurried away in the night and left us to die. Is it to be wondered that you should choose this place to build your house? A masterpiece of construction built upon the ruins of the masterpiece of destruction — a masterpiece of murder." Werdegast gives a

In the guise of Satanist Hjalmar Poelzig, Boris Karloff sits upon the neo-expressionistic altar set created by Charles Hall and director Edgar G. Ulmer for *The Black Cat* (1934).

sardonic laugh and adds, "The murderer of 10,000 men returns to the place of his crime." From the start there is a brooding, dark atmosphere, as the drama unfolds upon those very graves of 10,000 men; "It may well be an atmosphere of death," observes Werdegast. The intriguing art-deco sets were designed by Ulmer himself (the director began his career as a set designer for Max Reinhardt in Germany). Consisting of square panels, interior-lit walls, sliding doors, and stark white furniture, this setting exists above the massive stone vaults and cold iron doors of the cellars of the fort. Consequently, underneath the modernistic exterior is a tomblike structure in which you can "still sense death in the air." This reflects the very essence of the film — the idea of things lurking below the surface, the feel of death and decay—painted over but still there and exerting its brooding influence. Nothing is quite as it seems. Even the outward cordiality of Poelzig and Werdegast is merely a thin disguise for the loathing and animosity that exists between them, and their seeming innocuous words drip with hidden meaning.

This is the first time Karloff and Lugosi were paired together (they appeared jointly in a total of seven films) and it is the most powerful. It is the only one of their appearances in which they meet as true equals. (Lugosi took a subordinate role in succeeding films, with the exception of 1935's *The Raven*, which is decidedly a Lugosi vehicle despite the fact that Karloff receives top billing.) In *The Black Cat* both men were at the peak of their acting prowess and they gave two very different but very fine performances. It is fascinating to watch the two "Titans of Terror" face off against each other—both very civilized yet both equally dangerous.

Karloff is the embodiment of all things evil and sinister. From his black flowing garments to the sharp widow's peak on his forehead, even to the black makeup around his eyes and lips, malevolence nearly oozes from his person. Karloff's extraordinary use of body language comes into full play here. For instance, he does not simply walk, he *stalks*— stiffly and forcefully moving his body, bent slightly forward as if meeting a great resistance. His movements are slow, measured, without waste, and very forceful. Karloff's delivery is equal to his movements. His wonderful control of the English language imbues every line of dialogue with deep hidden meanings. No words are wasted or simply pleasant. Even a phrase as innocuous as "sleep well" takes on sinister connotations coming from Karloff's lips.

Lugosi is cast in a very different role. He is a man tortured in spirit, driven almost mad by circumstance, and returning to seek justice or at least find retribution. While Karloff is the evil antagonist, Lugosi is the good protagonist. But the struggle between the two characters is not a struggle of good and evil, not black versus white, but more one of black versus gray, for Werdegast's motivations and actions are themselves twisted. (As originally written and shot, Werdegast intended to rape the heroine rather than set her free! This was omitted from the final release print and some new scenes filmed to maintain the continuity. Despite this omission, the character is still far from benign since Werdegast is motivated solely by vengeance and ultimately slips into the madness of his obsession.) This makes for a much more interesting conflict than a simple good versus evil scenario. Here Lugosi rises to the challenge and delivers one of the best performances of his career. One scene in particular should put to rest those critics who have claimed that Lugosi was strictly a one-dimensional actor. It comes when Poelzig takes Werdegast down to the underground vaults to show him the macabre sight of his dead wife, whom Poelzig had stolen and made his own. Her body is preserved and suspended upright in a weird glass case. Subtle emotions play across Lugosi's face as he tearfully demands, "Why is she like this?" With a tremor in his voice, his eyes misting with sadness and sorrow etched into the lines of his face, Lugosi's performance is genuinely moving. Such a tender, emotional portrayal is something far above a "one-shot Dracula."

Another of the film's many assets is the wonderfully dark dialogue. The choice of words adds tremendously to the brooding, unearthly feel of the film. Werdegast does not merely have a fear of cats; he has, as Poelzig explains it, "an intense and all-consuming *horror*" of them. Later, when the hero tries to send for aid and discovers the phone doesn't work, Poelzig turns to Werdegast and declares, "You hear that Vitus, the phone is dead. Even the *phone* is *dead*." The emphasis on darkness and death is again underscored by the dialogue.

Even the obligatory comedy relief works to the benefit of this film. Unlike many movies from the Golden Age of Horror, the comedy element found in *The Black Cat* is brief, self-contained, and effective rather than obtrusive. The moment comes directly after the two rivals agree to play chess for the lives of the innocent couple. The high level of tension in that scene would have been difficult to maintain throughout the rest of the picture, so the brief comedic sequence comes at a perfect time to relax the viewer and then allow the film to start building towards the climax. The comedy is subtle in approach, as well, befitting the moody nature of the film. It starts with the hero and heroine engaging in some romantic by-play, which leads to them lightly poking fun at Poelzig's name. This segues directly into a more overtly comic scene involving two gendarmes who extol the merits of their respective villages. And that is it — short and sweet. We never see the jolly gendarmes again, nor do we need to, for they've served their purpose and the film moves on.

Throughout the picture, Ulmer's brilliant direction and visual flair prevails. For instance, the shot in which we first see Poelzig (an important scene because it gives us our first impression of this pivotal character) makes masterful use of light and shadow and movement. In silhouette, we see his upper body rise stiffly from a bed, as if rising from a coffin. He reaches out to touch a lamp, but instead of the lamp lighting up to illuminate the room, the entire wall behind him lights up. This only deepens the blackness of his silhouette, emphasizing the mysterious, dark nature of the man.

In another scene, Ulmer's use of foreground and focus transforms an ordinary moment — a kiss — into a passionate, sinister sequence. As Joan ardently kisses Peter in front of their host, Ulmer changes the camera focus to the foreground and a figurine of a reclining naked woman. At the height of Joan's passion, Poelzig's hand reaches into the frame and grasps one naked arm of the figurine, as though he shares the couple's intensity. The foreground, the suggestive statue, and the change in focus combine to give the scene a connotation that is both sexual and sinister. Of course, the contribution of cinematographer John J. Mescall cannot be underestimated. The fact that Ulmer never again achieved quite the level of artistic success he did with *The Black Cat* suggests that much of the merit of this picture is due at least in part to Mescall and the other technicians Ulmer utilized.

The Black Cat has held up very well over the years, losing very little of its power and mood. Filled with marvelous touches, such as the modernistic sets, the point-of-view camerawork, the prevalence of contrasting black, white, and shadowy grays, and the timeless subjects of love, hate, and death, *The Black Cat* is a true classic.

LIABILITIES

In a film as good as this, there really are no true liabilities, only a few points of lesser achievement.

Aside from Karloff and Lugosi, the remainder of the cast are merely adequate. The rather unremarkable performances of David Manners, as the nominal hero, and Jacqueline Wells, as the endangered heroine, do not significantly detract from the film, however. After all, their characters are merely pawns in Poelzig and Werdegast's game of death (a concept brought symbolically home when the two sit down to play their life-and-death game of chess). The insubstantial presence of bland leading man David Manners even becomes an advantage, serving to emphasize the power and control of the two leads.

Most complaints against *The Black Cat* have been aimed at its story and (in)coherence. While there does appear to be an occasional lapse in continuity, and the motivations of the characters at times seem hazy (Werdegast's manservant seemingly aiding Poelzig, for instance), these incongruities actually add to the perverse appeal of the picture and enhance its dark, otherworldly texture. While having a character behave in a seemingly oppositional manner would stand out as a jarring liability in most movies, in this extraordinary picture these perverse actions only serve to heighten the mystery and macabre undertones which run throughout the film. Nothing is quite as it appears on the surface, and that includes the characters' motivations.

One should point out that this picture may not be for all tastes, however. It is *not* an action film, even by 1930s standards, and its

"Fifteen years I've rotted in the darkness, waiting," Vitus Werdegast (Bela Lugosi) tells his hated enemy Hjalmar Poelzig (Boris Karloff), "not to kill you — to kill your *soul*."

slow, brooding pace may not be to everyone's liking, particularly in today's MTV-style, quick-cut cinema world. But for anyone who loves and can appreciate the great Golden Age of Horror films, *The Black Cat* is a unique gem to be treasured and savored over and over again.

REVIEWS

Variety (May 22, 1934) was uncharacteristically blind to the picture's macabre merits: "Because of the presence in one film of Boris Karloff, that jovial madman, and Bela Lugosi, that suave fiend, this picture probably has box office attraction. But otherwise and on the counts of story, novelty, thrills and distinction, the picture is sub-normal." They also took issue with the general air of sadism which permeated the film that culminated with the skinning alive sequence: "This skinning alive is not new. It was done in a Gouverneur Morris story, 'The Man Behind the Door,' filmed during the war. A truly horrible and nauseating bit of extreme sadism, its inclusion in a motion picture is dubious showmanship."

Most reviewers of the time were no more astute. *Film Weekly* (March 15, 1935), for instance, observed "Boris Karloff and Bela Lugosi piling horror upon horror until it all becomes just silly. Lots of screams, but neither rhyme nor reason."

The *New York Times* (May 19, 1934) admitted that "the staging is good and the camera devotes a proper amount of attention to shadows and hypnotic eyes," but ultimately called it "more foolish than horrible."

Despite these critical lambastings, the picture was a box-office success, doubling Universal's investment during the film's initial run.

PRODUCTION NOTES

The Black Cat was awarded a paltry budget of $91,125 (by comparison, *Frankenstein* was budgeted at $262,000) by the Universal head office and slated for a hectic 15-day shooting schedule (less than half the time usually

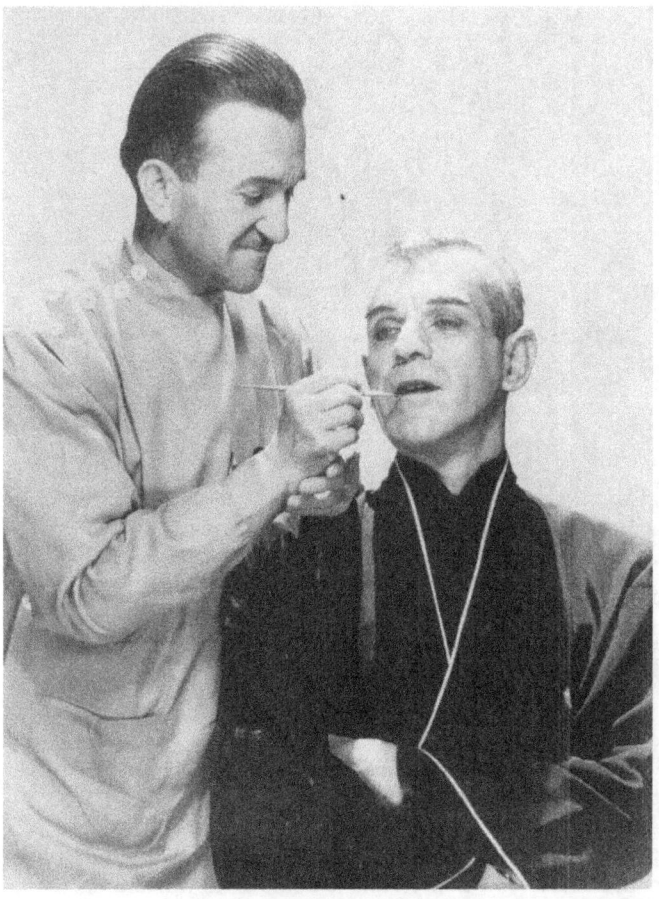

Jack Pierce touches up Boris Karloff's satanic countenance for *The Black Cat* (1934). (Courtesy of Ted Okuda.)

Amazingly enough, a mere $3,700 was spent on the sets, reflecting the less-is-more (re: cheap) attitude the front office took towards the entire production.

Three previous (and ultimately ignored) treatments of *The Black Cat* existed in Universal's story department: One (from 1932) by Universal story editor Richard Schayer, was relatively true to Poe's story; a second (also from 1932) by Stanley Bergerman (an in-law of producer Carl "Junior" Laemmle) and Jack Cunningham was called "The Brain Never Dies" and featured a cat with half a human brain; and a third (from 1933), written by Tom Kilpatrick and Dale Van Every (a team that later created 1940's *Dr. Cyclops*) which featured an evil Count intent on driving a young girl mad with tortures.

The Black Cat came in one day over schedule, but was deemed by the Universal head office to be too sadistic and perverse to release to the public and (more to the point) make it past the all-important censors. Three and a half days of reshoots were ordered and significant changes made in Lugosi's character. As originally shot, Werdegast was driven mad by the sight of his wife's preserved body, becoming a dangerous fiend who lusted after the heroine, intent on rape and torture. By all accounts, Lugosi was quite pleased when these scenes were deleted and the retakes placed his character in the more benign light seen in the finished film.

The character of Hjalmar Poelzig was fashioned by Ulmer and Peter Ruric (who shared story credit) after the infamous Aleister Crowley, a real-life Satanist labeled by the sensational press of the day as "The Wickedest

allotted an "A" production). Director Edgar Ulmer received a total of $900 for his services (while Universal's "Ace" director James Whale pulled in three times that amount *per week*). The screenwriter, Peter Ruric, made more than double Ulmer's salary, earning $1,966.

By his own account, director Edgar Ulmer not only designed the sets (along with Charles D. Hall) for that "way out" house (as the director referred to it), but also designed Karloff's wardrobe, from his black flowing robe to his satanic pajamas. Ulmer (in an interview for *Modern Monsters*, August 1966) claimed that "one of the things [Karloff] found most exciting in the film was the wardrobe ... his outfits in particular. He knew he would be playing 'Karloff,' but also felt in these duds, he could employ a sort of 'out of this world' appearance."

Man in the World." Ulmer named his character after Hans Poelzig, a celebrated architect and set designer Ulmer worked under while in Germany in the 1920s. Poelzig designed the medieval sets haunted by *The Golem* in 1920.

For the first time in his career, Boris Karloff was given the honor of being billed by surname only — simply as KARLOFF. This was also the first time Karloff was paired with Bela Lugosi and the union was indicative of things to come. As well as being top billed over Lugosi, Karloff earned nearly twice the salary of his co-star: $1850 per week compared to Lugosi's $1000. Throughout their careers, Karloff would continue to dominate in both billing and salary, a fact that caused more than a little resentment and jealousy in his colleague.

According to Edgar Ulmer, Karloff "never took himself seriously." "My biggest job," the director told Peter Bogdanovich in 1970, "was to keep him in the part, because he laughed at himself." Calling Karloff "a very fine actor — five star," Ulmer related how the actor's sense of humor often got the better of him. During the bedroom scene, in which Karloff is seen for the first time, "he got into bed, we got ready to shoot, and he got up, he turned to the camera, after he put his shoes on, and said 'Boo!' Every time I had him come in by the door, he would open the door and say, 'Here comes the heavy…'" (from *Kings of the Bs*, by Todd McCarthy and Charles Flynn).

While Karloff "laughed at himself," his co-star did not share in this self-deprecating humor. "You had to cut away from Lugosi continuously," stated Ulmer, "to cut him down."

Lugosi, whose character has an "intense and all-consuming horror of cats," shared Werdegast's fear in real life. According to Hope Lugosi, his fifth wife, "he was afraid of cats, he hated them."

The organist in the black mass scene is John Peter Richmond, in one of his early bit parts. John Peter Richmond later changed his name to John Carradine.

Cinematographer John Mescall went on to lens what many consider to be the greatest film from the Golden Age of Horror — *Bride of Frankenstein* (1935).

The Black Cat was reissued in 1953 under the new title of *The Vanishing Body* so as not to confuse it with Universal's "new" 1941 version called *The Black Cat* starring Basil Rathbone (and featuring Bela Lugosi in a supporting role) reissued about that time as well.

Recalling *The Black Cat* three decades later, Boris Karloff laughingly lamented: "The things we did to Poe when he wasn't around to defend himself—!" (*Famous Monsters* #47). These "things" ultimately proved quite lucrative; with the final cost a mere $95,745, *The Black Cat* made over $140,000 profit for Universal, making it the top grosser of the studio's 35 films released in 1934.

The many (and varied) incarnations of "The Black Cat" include: the apparently "lost" 1932 German anthology film titled *The Living Dead*; the exploitative and tasteless *Maniac* of 1934; Universal's tepid 1941 mystery; Roger Corman's entertaining and often humorous *Tales of Terror* (1962); the all-but-forgotten 1966 version called *The Black Cat*; Lucio Fulci's gory 1981 interpretation of *The Black Cat*; Luigi Cozzi's incoherent 1990 version, *The Black Cat*; and most recently, Dario Argento's half of *Two Evil Eyes* (1991).

DRUMS O' VOODOO
(1934; International Stageplay Pictures)

Alternate Titles: *Louisiana*; *Voodoo Drums*; *She Devil* (1940 reissue)
Release Date: May 1934

Running Time: 70 minutes
Director: Arthur Hoerl
Producer: Lou Weiss

Screenplay: J. Augustus Smith (by arrangement with George L. Miller)
Photography: Walter Strenge, J. Burgi Contner
Editor: Adrian Weiss
*Art Director: Sam Corso
*Production Manager: Ben Berk
*Sound Effects: Lyman J. Wiggin and Verne T. Brayman
Recorded by Cineglow Sound

Cast: Laura Bowman (Aunt Hagar), Edna Barr (Myrtle Simpson), Lionel Monagas (Ebenezer), J. Augustus Smith (Amos Berry), Morris McKinney (Thomas Catt), A. B. Comathiere (Deacon Dunson), Alberta Perkins (Sister Knight), Fred Bonny (Brother Zero), Paul Johnson (Deacon August), Trixie Smith (Sister Marguerite), Carrie Huff (Sister Zuzan).

*Credit not appearing on film print.

"Beat dem drums... Beat dem drums... Beat dem drums... The ancient god Voodoo commands you... Beat... Beat... Beat... Beat!"—Aunt Hagar.

SYNOPSIS

In a rural Louisiana black community, Voodoo and Christianity exist side by side. "The choral processions," the opening written narration tells us, "the sacred chants and the incessant beating of the voodoo drums on the eve of a sacrifice, are horrible and wonderful embellishments of a religion that is practiced as fervently today in certain communities as Christianity."

The old voodoo priestess Aunt Hagar presides over "the ancient worship of the jungle gods" while Elder Berry(!) ministers to his Christian flock. Into this peaceful coexistence comes the evil, unscrupulous Tom Catt(!!), who wants the parson's niece, Myrtle, for his "jook joint" across the river (a den of liquor, gambling, and loose women). Ebenezer, Aunt Hagar's grandson, loves Myrtle and so goes to his grandmother and begs her to keep the innocent girl from Tom Catt's claws. To this end, the voodoo witch intones a curse and assures Ebeneezer that no harm will come to the girl.

The whole god(and voodoo)-fearing community wants the vile Tom Catt gone, but are afraid to act. Catt tries to blackmail the parson into sending Myrtle to him. (Many years ago, before he had found God, Reverend Berry was with Tom Catt on a chain gang and Catt has been periodically extorting money from Berry by threatening to tell all to the congregation.) When the minister refuses to sacrifice his niece, Tom Catt first tries to charm Myrtle and then force himself upon her. A group of passing townspeople rescue Myrtle and Aunt Hagar warns Catt that "if the sun goes down in this community on your worthless carcass, I'm gonna *blind* ya—I'm gonna *blind you*, ya hear me?!" The swaggering rogue puts no stock in the old woman's threats, however.

That night, Tom Catt breaks into the church revival meeting to tell the congregation that "Amos Berry ain't the man you think he is." Amos rises and stops Tom Catt with his own confession: "I go over to his place to pay him money not to tell you all that I—was on the chain gang once—for murder." This puts the congregation in an angry uproar. Tom Catt takes advantage of the confusion and pulls out his razor to threaten the crowd. "I told you that anything I wants I gets," he tells them menacingly. "I want that gal," he demands, motioning to Myrtle. Before he can act, however, he's suddenly struck blind. This section of the film is so choppy that it is difficult to tell exactly what happens. In the next scene, Aunt Hagar tells Pastor Berry that Ebeneezer has taken the stricken Tom Catt home, "but it ain't over yet." The print currently available for viewing abruptly ends here, but reviews of the day indicate that Tom Catt stumbles out into the swamp and is swallowed up by (off-screen) quicksand.

MEMORABLE MOMENT

The picture's opening is quite promising—a promise which sadly remains unfulfilled. As a rhythmic voodoo chant and drumbeat (reminiscent of the native ceremonial chant from *King Kong*) plays on the soundtrack, the scene begins with the camera tight on a steaming cauldron. Lit from inside, the devilish pot seems to glow. As the camera pulls back (in the film's *only* tracking shot), we see a group of half-naked black men, their bodies glistening with sweat, dancing around the cauldron, their forms twisting and turning rhythmically with the drumbeat. Tending the voodoo vessel in the center is a black-robed, hooded figure who, lit from the fire below the bubbling kettle, conjures up images of a hellish devil-crone. In a circle around the dancers sit the chanters, their arms rising and falling along with their primal voices. A near-solid curtain of Spanish moss surrounds the scene, the wispy tendrils almost glowing in the eerie light cast upon them. Unfortunately, this all-too-brief scene quickly dissolves to a lengthy, mundane sequence at "A Louisiana Jook" (as the on-screen title informs us). When the picture again returns to the cryptic voodoo ritual, all hopes of uncanny mystery immediately vanish when the crone reveals herself to a be a benign elderly Aunt Hagar (who's more than a little comical in her overacting). Never again does *Drums o' Voodoo* generate anything even approaching a spine-tingle.

Original ad mat for the rare all-black horror film, *Drums o' Voodoo* (1934).

ASSETS

The poor condition of the one surviving print (distributed on video by Sinister Cinema) makes a complete assessment of *Drums o' Voodoo* impossible. The print is so choppy that dialogue often ends in mid-sentence and whole scenes are missing (including all but a snippet of the picture's climax). Still, the butchered remains of *Drums o' Voodoo* can give us some idea of the film's merit.

Despite its crude production values, slow pacing, and missed opportunities, *Drums o' Voodoo* remains a worthy entry in the Golden Age of Horror because of the unique perspective it affords us. *Drums o' Voodoo* portrays a time and place in which the religion of voodoo is just as real as Christianity (in fact, more so, since it is voodoo rather than Christian prayer which accomplishes the aims of the community). Rather than the evil black magic seen in

White Zombie (1932) or the destructive fanaticism holding sway in *Black Moon* (1934), voodoo is here portrayed as a benign, helpful force. Voodoo ceremonies are as commonplace — and just as valid — as weekly church services. Every member of the community knows of, tolerates, and acknowledges the ancient religion. Even the minister himself admits, "I believe [Aunt Hagar] is the only one 'round here that can drive Tom Catt out of this community." While some have turned away and tried to forget their religious heritage, in the end they must come back to the fold to save their town from the earthly evil (in the form of the violent — and ungodly — Tom Catt) that threatens their physical — and spiritual — selves. This stress on voodoo as a primal religion rather than a perverted sorcery gives *Drums o' Voodoo* a unique, refreshing atmosphere and affords us a glimpse into an alternative spirituality.

Screenwriter J. Augustus Smith peppers his meandering screenplay with colorful dialogue that brings to life the colloquial time period and superstitious subject. Aunt Hagar's curse upon Tom Catt, for instance, is a rhythmic whammy at once amusing *and* chilling:

> "Jungle gods, I makes a spell
> to cast this imp back to hell.
> In a pit of bile and sand,
> let him join his hellish band.
> Let no mercy stay thy heart,
> jungle gods make him depart.
> Plunge him, crush him — like a crumb,
> for you Voodoo, I beats dem drums."

Later, when Hagar restrains the townspeople from attacking Tom Catt for what he tried to do to Myrtle, she unleashes this invective: "Don't stain your hands with his worthless blood. *I'll* fix him. I'll fix him [turning to Tom Catt] — you creepin', crawlin', hissin', lizard-eatin', poisonous black Catt... Your soul is as black as the soot on a skillet!"

LIABILITIES

The juxtaposition of voodoo and Christianity makes a fascinating springboard for a tale of spiritual conflict which, sadly, fails to materialize in Smith's story. The written narration at the film's beginning informs us that "a struggle between the White God and the Black Gods still goes on — to the steady beat of the voodoo drums." While *Drums o' Voodoo* indeed exposes us to plenty of voodoo drumming in the ritual ceremony scenes (the only visually interesting sequences in the picture), the only "struggle" takes the form of several of the Christian congregation complaining about the noise of the drums keeping them up at night. Smith chooses to fill the running time with lengthy scenes of bible-thumping revival meetings, complete with noisome spirituals and enraptured "Amen"s. In the end, very little conflict arises and very little happens in the picture, with most of the film's 70 minutes filled with time-killing songfests or dull exchanges between the parishioners.

On the technical side, *Drums o' Voodoo* is without a doubt the most primitive entry in the Golden Age of Horror. A filmed play, the whole production is completely stagebound with the exteriors represented by a few unconvincing stage sets. The pedantic photography and direction emphasize the picture's static nature. All cinematic considerations seem to have fallen by the wayside, for the camera never moves after the opening scene. Director Arthur Hoerl (helming his fourth — and final — feature) fails to exploit the mystery or horror in his subject and chooses to simply anchor the camera and film his players moving in front of it. The only indication the viewer has that this is a motion picture are the infrequent close-ups which Hoerl grudgingly inserts every few minutes.

With one exception, the performances lack conviction. Laura Bowman's (in awful makeup that makes the black actress look as if she's a white woman wearing blackface!) doomful, singsong delivery and swaying gestures inspire more titters than shudders, and the story's author, J. Augustus Smith, appears so stiff and uncomfortable in the role of the persecuted minister that it is almost a relief when he finally loosens up and goes on a long and ridiculous tirade at the climactic revival meeting. The picture's one good performance comes from Morris "Chick" McKinney as Tom

Catt, whose swaggering attitude is balanced by an easygoing charm, making his vile villain dangerously seductive.

REVIEW

"Bige" of *Variety* (May 15, 1934) called this "all–Negro feature" "cheaply produced and looking it; also badly acted. Fails to rate either as a film laboratory experiment in racial traits or as an entertainment." Bige had nothing good to say technically either: "So shallow are the settings, picture appears to have been produced in one room, not too large. Besides shallow they are too phony in appearance to fool any audience.... Poor lighting as well as the unfortunate scenery combine to make the photography look bad, while jerky cutting doesn't help either." On the plus side, the reviewer did admit that "the sound is satisfactory and the dialog exceptionally good."

Reissue poster from 1940 bearing a new title for *Drums o' Voodoo* (1934).

PRODUCTION NOTES

During the mid-thirties, there were between 200 and 600 black theaters in the United States (the estimates vary) which catered strictly to the "colored" population. By contrast, over 35,000 cinemas served white patrons. So, while a market *did* exist for all-black films, it was extremely limited. Consequently, producers were forced to work within minuscule budgets to guarantee a profitable return on their investment. (The average cost of an "all-colored" production in the early 1930s was an incredibly low $6,000.)

When J. Augustus Smith's stageplay *Louisiana* closed after only one week on Broadway in 1933, Smith turned his one-act play into a movie script and took it to independent producer Louis Weiss. The cost-conscious producer utilized nearly the entire stage cast (including Smith himself, who played Amos Berry in the play just as in the movie) to save money since they already knew their lines and were in costume. Thus *Drums o' Voodoo* became the first film based on the work of a black dramatist.

Director Arthur Hoerl shot Smith's story at New York's Atlas Soundfilm Recording studios in late March of 1933. Even during production, the picture went through a confusing series of retitlings. Filmed under *two* working titles, *Louisiana* and *Voodoo*, the New York State Censor Board approved the picture (after substantial cuts) in 1934 as *The Devil*. When the film finally saw general release in May of 1934 (over a year after completion), it carried the moniker *Drums o' Voodoo*. Later reissues added *Louisiana*, *Voodoo Drums* and *She Devil* to the roster. So, while *Drums o' Voodoo* may be the cheapest production of the Golden Age of Horror, it certainly sports the most impressive array of names.

J. Augustus ("Gus") Smith ran away from home at age 14 to join the Rabbit's Foot Musical Comedy troupe. After touring with traveling minstrel shows throughout the South for a number of years, Smith finally made it to Broadway by starring in his own play, *Louisiana*, produced by George Miller for the Negro Theater Guild. The play garnered several good reviews, but the powerful theater critic Brooks Atkinson savaged the production in his critique, leading to the play closing after only eight performances.

Laura Bowman's acting career spanned nearly half a century, most of which she spent touring the U.S. and Europe in theater companies. "The Negro Barrymore" (as the press sometimes labeled her) frequently appeared on Broadway, supporting the likes of Tallulah Bankhead, Helen Hayes, and Miriam Hopkins, and once gave a command performance at Buckingham Palace before King Edward VII. In 1935, the 54-year-old actress married LeRoi Antoine ("the first Haitian singer-actor to come to the U.S." according to *Variety*), a man 28 years her junior. Ironically, Ms. Bowman was deathly afraid of voodoo in real life. Her husband recalled that during a trip to Haiti, Bowman was fearful that she might die and be transformed into a zombie.

Lionel Monagus emigrated to the United States from his home country of Venezuela at an early age. He began acting with the Lafayette Players in Harlem (appearing in plays such as *Old Man Satan*, *Roll on Sweet Chariot*, and *Blackbirds of 1933*), where he met and worked with Laura Bowman and the majority of the *Drums o' Voodoo* cast.

Though at this time a few blacks produced their own films (Oscar Micheaux being the best-known example), most "all-colored" pictures were made by whites. *Louisiana* was no exception and, while starring black actors, carried an all-white crew.

After acquiring the screen rights from Edgar Rice Burroughs in 1918, producer Louis Weiss was the first to bring Tarzan to the silver screen. Throughout the twenties, Weiss supervised a number of lower-berth pictures, specializing in westerns and comedies. At one point, he headed Columbia Pictures' serial division, producing the Frank Buck "Jungle Menace" series, among others. With the advent of television, Weiss adapted to the new medium and produced the "Craig Kennedy, Detective" series. Weiss remained active in the industry through film distribution up until his death in 1963.

Having trained as a newsreel cameraman in New York, cinematographer Walter Strenge began working in Hollywood movies only a year previous to his *Drums o' Voodoo* assignment. Over the next four decades, he carved out a distinguished career in the industry, culminating in an Academy Award nomination for *Stagecoach to Fury* (1958). That same year he became president of the American Society of Cinematographers and eventually co-authored the *American Cinematographer Manual*, the primary textbook of film photography.

Strenge's co-cameraman, J. Burgi Contner, also went on to bigger and better things, particularly in television, working on shows such as "You Are There," "Naked City," and "The Defenders." Also an engineer, Contner is credited with several important inventions, including the Academy Aperture used in theater projectors, the Cineglow sound system, an early color film process, and the Cineflex combat camera (for the U.S. Army Air Corps).

THE SECRET OF THE LOCH
(1934; Associated British Film Distributors; Great Britain)

Alternate Title: *The Loch Ness Mystery*
Release Date: June 1934
Running Time: 80 minutes
Director: Milton Rosmer
Producer: Bray Wyndham
Screenplay: Billie Bristow, Charles Bennett
Photography: James Wilson
Camera: Cecil Cooney
Underwater Photography: Eric Cross
Production Manager: Keith Horan
Decor and Technical Director: J. Elder Wills
Assistant Art Director: L. Fisher-Smith
Editor: David Lean

Music: Peter Mendoza
Assistant Directors: Hector Elwes, B. Graham Soutten
Sound Recordist: Eric Williams
Continuity: Lilian G. Day
Cast: Seymour Hicks (Professor Heggie), Nancy O'Neil (Angela Heggie), Gibson Gowland (Angus), Frederick Peisley (Jimmy Andrews), Eric Hales (Diver), Rosamund John (Maggie), Ben Field (Piermaster), Hubert Harben (Professor Fothergill), Rob Wilton, F. Llewellyn, *D. J. Williams (Judge), *Stafford Hilliard (Macdonald), *John Jamieson, *Elma Reid.

*Uncredited on film print.

"There's things it's best *not* to know."—Angus.

SYNOPSIS

The picture opens on an "Extract from *Daily Mail* of Oct. 19th, 1933": "Whether people believe in the existence of a Loch Ness 'Monster' or not, Highlanders are convinced that the watery depths harbor some fantastic and abnormal creature." Hands sift through a pile of newspaper headlines reading LOCH NESS MONSTER REAPPEARS and SEEN WITH LAMB IN ITS MOUTH and finally PEOPLE ALARMED. The scene dissolves to a man running through the night while people flee inside and bolt their doors. Bursting into the local pub, the frantic man proclaims, "Boys, boys, I've seen it!" Some of the locals believe his "monstrous" tale while others put it down to the house scotch. All stop short, however, when a low rumbling roar pierces the babble of voices. Just then, Professor Heggie enters, accompanied by his burly servant, Angus. Heggie too believes in the "monster," but shows his acquaintances what the London papers say of their conviction: "Mass Hallucination." The monster is "a danger to the fishin'" proclaims one man, "to the sheep," adds another, "to all of us," finishes the professor.

Professor Heggie speaks to a gathering of "the finest scientific brains in the country" at the Museum of Natural History in London. "Your monster, sir, is a floating log of wood," concludes one unconvinced scientist. Heggie persists: "Gentlemen, to the best of my knowledge and belief, the monster which is haunting the waters of Loch Ness is nothing more or less than a reptilian survivor of prehistoric ages, a giant *dinosaur*—Diplodocus!" The gathering responds with indignation at this far-flung theory. "You're making fools of us, sir. The dinosaur has been extinct for millions of years!" With the meeting in an uproar, Professor Heggie finally shouts down his detractors. "For years past," he explains, "blasting operations have taken place in Loch Ness. I believe that there has lain in the rock foundations a dinosaur egg. I believe that blasting operations have disturbed it and that the abnormal heat of last summer has somehow hatched it out." To shouts of "charlatan," the professor is unceremoniously ejected from the meeting.

Young reporter Jimmy Andrews observes the tussle and approaches the departing professor with a promise of publicity. Professor Heggie, however, is in no mood to be laughed at by the papers and warns the lad to stay away.

Undeterred, Jimmy follows the professor up to Loch Ness only to find a whole flock of his fellow journalists gathered at the local inn like vultures feeding on the story. When one of the reporters tries to interview the professor, however, Angus sets the dogs on him.

Jimmy notices the professor and Angus returning from some mysterious nocturnal voyage on the Loch and overhears them speak of finally discovering "the great cave." Jimmy follows the pair to the Heggie ancestral manor. There the eager reporter sneaks into the house via an open window — and right into the bedroom of the professor's granddaughter, Angela, where he's immediately smitten with the wholesome young woman.

The ruckus alerts the household and the professor orders Angus to chuck the intruder out. As the big Scotsman manhandles the reporter down the stairs, he notices Jimmy's tartar tie (which the lad had purloined from a secretary back at his London office). The tie convinces Angus that Jimmy is a fellow member of the "Macknockie" clan. Jimmy now has a friend for life in Angus, though the big man still warns his newfound 'kinsman' to "forget what you've heard about the great cave."

Using the information he'd overheard from the professor and later gleaned from Angus, Jimmy phones in an "exclusive interview" to his editor. While the article slants favorably toward the professor, the unwanted publicity only infuriates the man further (though it seems to charm his granddaughter).

Now somewhat taken with the brash young reporter, Angela runs across him as he spies on her grandfather and his men loading a boat with mysterious equipment. Angela's loyalty to her grandfather proves stronger than her attraction to the young man, however, when she takes Jimmy on an evening drive and then leaves him out in the middle of nowhere. "You shouldn't have spied on Grandpa," she yells to him before driving off, adding apologetically, "This is for *your* sake as well as his."

While trudging down the road, Jimmy meets Jack Campbell, a deep-sea diver hired by Professor Heggie. "Seems the professor thinks this monster's living there," snorts Campbell, "down below the surface in a sort of cave. I've gotta go down and see if it's possible to fix nets over the mouth."

When Jimmy gets back to the inn, he receives a call from his editor telling the young reporter that he's fired for not dropping the story and returning to London as ordered. "What? I'm fired?" echoes Jimmy into the phone. "And the only thing that'll save me is an interview with the monster himself—with photographs?!"

This only fires Jimmy's determination further. From the shore, he watches as the professor lowers Campbell down into the depths. At the bottom, a huge shadow passes over the rocks and Campbell yanks frantically on his tether to be pulled up. When the crew reels in the air hose and rope, however, they find no diver on the end — the lines have been severed.

Professor Heggie is charged with negligence in the tragedy and brought to trial. During the hearing, Jimmy testifies on the professor's behalf, stating that he too believes the "fantastic" claim that the monster was responsible for the diver's demise. Still, the jury's "death from misadventure" verdict carries a rider stating "Professor Heggie has been guilty of gross and culpable negligence." In spite of Jimmy's support during the hearing, Heggie still refuses to cooperate with the young reporter and orders him never to set foot in his house again — especially after Jimmy blurts out that he wants to marry Angela (who exhibits as much surprise as her grandfather at the request, though not nearly so much anger). Angela urges Jimmy to leave, fearing that her grandfather has been driven to the brink of madness by his failure to prove his claim and all the attendant vitriolic press. "I'm frightened," admits the worried Angela, "It's making him — dangerous."

Jimmy determines to prove himself both to the professor and to Angela by finding the monster. Secretly enlisting Angus' aid, Jimmy sets off for the boat just before dawn. The professor, now in an almost permanent state of agitation, sees the pair from a window and rushes out after them, armed with a shotgun. Angela awakens and chases after her grandfather, stopping at the inn to get help (and arousing the curiosity of the reporters gathered there).

Out on the boat, Angus and the crew pack Jimmy into a second diving suit (Jimmy had previously done some amateur diving for "a newspaper publicity stunt"). Lowered down into the depths, he finds the mouth of the great cave — and the helmet of the missing diver half buried in the sandy bottom. Suddenly, a gigantic lizardlike beast rises up from behind the rocks. Upon seeing the behemoth, Jimmy draws his pitifully inadequate diver's knife and tugs frantically on his guide line. At that moment topside, the deranged professor arrives in a skiff. Brandishing his shotgun, he orders the crew not to touch the lines. "That man most of all ridiculed me — wants to prove that I'm wrong — that the cave is empty," raves the professor. "Let those ropes alone! He shan't come back!" While down below the prehistoric creature approaches the retreating Jimmy, on the surface Angela reaches the boat and distracts her grandfather enough so that Angus can wrest the gun from his hands. With the monster nearly upon Jimmy, the crew rapidly hauls on the ropes, snatching him away from the creature's gaping jaws and to the safety of the ship. The prehistoric leviathan rises to the surface and swims peacefully away, allowing the reporters on the shore to get all the photographic proof they need. Angela kisses Jimmy, and the professor (having recovered his reason) gratefully shakes the brave lad's hand.

MEMORABLE MOMENT

The monster's first "appearance" is an effective use of shadow and editing to create a moment of suggestive terror. As the diver approaches a rocky outcropping at the bottom of the loch, he wheels around suddenly to see a great shadow rise up over a rocky cliff face until the dark shape fills the screen. The diver then tugs frantically on his guide line as a signal to be pulled up. Topside, the crew strain and heave furiously on the ropes, but encounter a resistance as if something has hold of the line. When they finally break the rope free of its obstruction and haul it in, they find a frayed tether and no diver. The suggestive shadow and near-panicked reaction of the diver, coupled with the tense, frenzied activity of those above on the ship, lets the viewer's imagination conjure up all manner of horrific visions (ones much more exciting than the eventual garden-variety iguana seen at the film's end).

ASSETS

Ask any movie buff, even an aficionado of fantastic films, to name the dinosaur pictures of the Golden Age, and nine times out of ten said buff will list two titles: *King Kong* and *The Son of Kong* (both 1933). Yet, a third exists, an obscure cousin spawned some 6,000 miles away from the formative father and son pairing. In 1934, Great Britain released its own contribution to dinosaur cinema, challenging Willis O'Brien's supremacy of the subgenre. The challenge, however, went unanswered, for *The Secret of the Loch* came and went generally unseen outside its native Britain — even to this day. Wags will say that this is just as well, for, rather than featuring O'Brien's lifelike animals designed (to the best scientific knowledge of the day) to resemble real dinosaurs and made to breathe and move and act like living prehistoric beasts, the "Secret of the Loch" turned out to be a photographically-enlarged lizard passed off as an antediluvian monster. Still, this gives *The Secret of the Loch* the admittedly dubious distinction of being the first film to utilize this unsatisfactory dinosaurian technique (a technique "perfected" six years later in *One Million B.C.* and copied in countless subsequent pictures — whose makers often simply stole footage from *One Million B.C.* itself rather than wrangle their own baby alligator or miniature iguana). In addition to utilizing a leviathan lizard, *The Secret of the Loch* holds several other "firsts" as well. It is the first *British* dinosaur in cinema history (remaining the only one for a quarter century until the U.K. uncurled its stiff upper lip and deigned to share *The Giant Behemoth* as a 1959 co-production with the U.S.). More importantly, however, the real "Secret of the Loch" is the screen debut of none other than the *Loch Ness Monster*!

Historical perspective aside, does *The Secret of the Loch* deserve to be raised from the watery depths or should it remain hidden away at the bottom of a lake—*loch*—of obscurity? The consummate cineast will cry "viva la découverte!" while the disappointed dinosaurian will sadly moan "bury the beast!" *The Secret of the Loch* works well as an amusing, even witty, human drama but makes a rather poor specimen of saurian cinema. Still, there is plenty in this *Secret* worth discovering.

The picture's success begins with its screenplay. Billie Bristow and Charles Bennett's charming script is sprinkled with colorfully incorrigible characters and wry bits of subtle humor seldom found in American genre product of the time. One example occurs when Jimmy first arrives at the pub and a crusty old-timer overhears the young man inquiring about the monster and professor:

> Old man: "Was it the professor you was speakin' of, sir?"
> Jimmy: "Yes, do you know him?"
> Old man: "Aye, ah do, sir."
> Jimmy: "When did you last see him?"
> Old man: "Uh—monster or professor?"

The old curmudgeon goes on to tell Jimmy that the professor "lives in a terrible house—it's haunted ... the district's *full* of spirits." Looking down into the depths of his empty glass, the thirsty geezer adds ruefully, "supposed to be—mine's a whiskey."

Director Milton Rosmer knew how to utilize the camera for punctuation and took full advantage of the script by wringing the best of the biting humor from it. When Professor Heggie takes his case to the distinguished body of doubting scientists, for instance, the camera moves from the speaking professor up to a stuffed walrus head mounted on the wall. Then, as the professor addresses the gathering as "the finest scientific brains in this country," the camera pans down to a corpulent bald man sitting to the professor's right who sports an enormous walrus mustache. The comical comparison immediately establishes the stuffy state of these "fine scientific brains" which only deepens when the fleshy face blows out its cheeks and sends the great mustache fluttering outwards on a puff of air. Then, when the professor punctuates his point that "steps must be taken!" with a forceful rap of his cane on the floor, the same fellow suddenly bellows in pain as the stick strikes his unwary foot—sounding very much like a wounded walrus.

Rosmer continues to mine this satirical vein and poke fun at the haughty scientific establishment. Immediately after one blustery scientist protests that "every one of us here present has some pretensions to being considered above the level of the mentally deficient," the camera pans to the speaker's left and reveals one of his esteemed colleagues playing "catch-the-finger."

The Secret of the Loch is no mere comedy, however, and Rosmer wisely never strays too far from the dark, dangerous thread which holds the film together. Between the amusing dialogue and biting satire, Rosmer periodically interjects night shots of the forlorn loch, the threatening clouds brooding overhead and craggy rocks sitting dark and sinister along the water's edge reminding us of the story's more ominous subject matter. Occasionally, the loch's surface ripples suddenly—as if something huge had just passed underneath.

Just as Rosmer's direction enhances the comedic elements, he also takes care when emphasizing the picture's more dire aspects as well. In one sequence, Jimmy and Angela stare out the window and speak of the monster. Rosmer begins the scene with a shot of the forbidding loch, the baleful clouds and silhouette of hills (uncomfortably monster-shaped) causing Jimmy to realize that "there might be anything under that water." Angela adds, "it's so deep that in some places they've never found the bottom." The scene then shifts to show the couple standing at the open window with the camera placed outside looking in. As Jimmy shivers "brrr" at the thought, the tip of a bush at the very bottom of the frame waves slightly in the wind. The rustling foliage adds a cold creepiness to the moment and draws the viewer into the scene by conjuring up his or her own dark night when an innocent breeze turned the tips of a tree into monstrous fingers on the windowpanes.

Under Rosmer's direction, a veteran cast of British (and one Australian) stage stars and players handles all the dinosaur delving quite expertly. Leading the cast as Professor Heggie is Seymour Hicks. In *The Secret of the Loch*, Hicks utilizes all his stage presence and theatrical techniques (properly subdued for the more intimate camera, of course) to make the rather broadly drawn professor a likable and believable character. His stern, deep, fatherly voice, measured speech, and rolling tones are almost comforting, inspiring a genuine respect and affinity for the man. Hicks' considerable talents come to the fore in one scene in particular, when the professor first speaks of the mysteries of the loch to a rapt audience of locals at the inn. "My father believed it, and his father did before him. So do we —," states Hicks firmly, "right back to the beginning of things. And yet these clever people, they think we're superstitious. Well — maybe we *are*. But they can never know the loch —" at this, Hicks' eyes stare straight ahead, unseeing in his suddenly grim countenance, before his forceful voice grows quiet, almost hushed as he finishes "— as we know it." He continues, "On dark winter nights when the mist hangs over it as it does now, we've known —" his voice lowers again so that we must almost strain to hear as he solemnly intones, "— death come in many ways to the honest folk who've been claimed by that dark stretch of water — and whose bodies have never been found again. That's not superstition, that's hard *facts*. As for this *creature* — we know that those waters go down, down, deeper than man has ever plumbed." Hicks' voice rises and falls, quickens and slows to make his ominous words come alive and his tale take on a dread conviction. Like the best storytellers, he speaks with total confidence yet with just the right amount of hesitancy, as if almost unwilling to say aloud the full, ominous truth. With his pauses for dramatic effect and his gaze fixed as if he's forgotten his listeners and focuses on something only he can see, Hicks erases all trace of doubt in the viewer's mind. There IS something down there!

Frederick Peisley as Jimmy makes an eager, audacious, and winning hero. Good-humored and fun-loving in the bar with his colleagues, he exhibits no compunction about breaking and entering to pursue a story. When Angela confronts him after he climbs through her bedroom window, Peisley turns on the boyish charm and shows a likable aplomb in the awkward circumstance, telling the startled girl as an introduction: "It's all right, I'm not the monster." Then, as he quickly becomes captivated by her wholesome innocence, his bravado gives way to a polite sincerity. "Oh, don't be annoyed," he says, "I mean, I'm terribly sorry to come bursting in on you." Unable to contain himself, however, he brashly blurts out, "I mean — I'm not sorry now that I've seen you." Peisley's friendly tone is eager and sincere and anything *but* apologetic.

As Angela, Nancy O'Neil presents a self-possessed young woman with a wry sense of humor who can exchange barb for barb with her brash beau-to-be. She also shows genuine tenderness toward her grandfather, the obvious concern allowing her an appealing humanity.

Rounding out the principals is Gibson Gowland as the hulking Scotch servant, Angus. A huge, bearded bear of a man, Gowland creates a strong, gruff, even menacing Scotsman. Yet at the same time, his obvious loyalty and forthright demeanor make him an appealing character. (Besides, it's difficult to dislike a man in a kilt.)

James Wilson's lighting and camerawork add a rich visual texture even to the more mundane proceedings. When the terrible roar is heard at the pub, for instance, the camera raises up over the now-hushed group gathered at the bar and steadily moves toward the door until only the solitary portal remains in the shot. The door suddenly opens and Professor Heggie steps in. The advancing camera, excluding all the people from the frame by its movement, creates both a sense of isolation and dread expectancy, making for a dramatic entrance to the story's main character ("Nessie" excepted). The camera then tracks back before the advancing professor to again include the various patrons and finally settles down

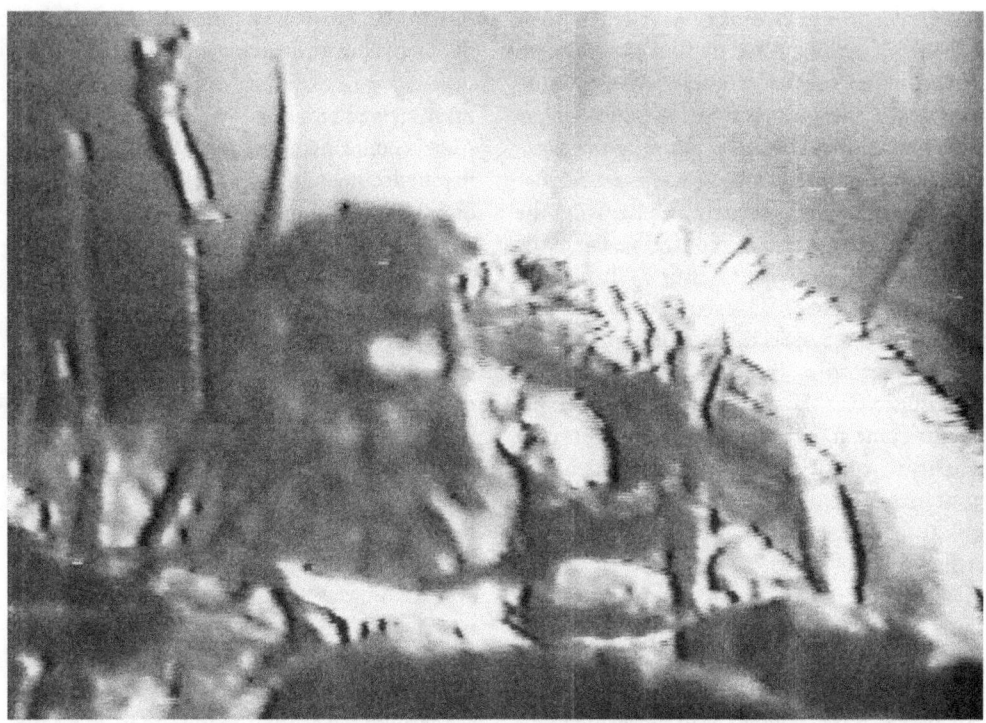

The Secret of the Loch (1934) turned out to be a photographically enlarged iguana. (Photo: Lynn Naron)

behind the bar to resume its original position — all in one smooth fluid motion. In another scene, the camera follows Jimmy as he breaks into the professor's house by moving alongside the young man and going right *through* the window with him as he climbs into Angela's bedroom, effectively drawing the viewer into the room as well.

Wilson photographed the loch-haunting lizard as best he could, utilizing a macro lens to make it look huge on the miniature set. Then, by suddenly shifting the focus from seaweed in the foreground to the hideous monster advancing toward us, he fills the screen with its scaly visage, emphasizing the beast's menacing ugliness.

The submerged sequences are photographed to good effect as well (by underwater specialist Eric Cross). In one shot, the camera moves from left to right with various ragged rocks, swaying seaweed, and spindly plants like huge twisted fingers passing by in the foreground to add a depth and breadth to the obvious (though well-dressed) studio tank.

Editing plays a key role in *The Secret of the Loch* and Rosmer was fortunate enough to have David Lean on his production team. Lean's judicious editing enhances scene after scene and does much to augment the admittedly disappointing special effects. During the professor's solemn speech about the loch, for instance, Lean expertly inserts shots of the professor's spellbound listeners at just the right moments to emphasize a point and play up the dire nature of his words.

Jimmy's climactic escape from the (literal) jaws of death is a masterful use of editing to create suspense. Lean utilizes 21 shots in a mere 40 seconds as follows: 1) Close-up of the beast; 2) The men on the boat pulling frantically on Jimmy's guide ropes; 3) Angus restraining the struggling professor; 4) Close-up of beast rising up with Jimmy now in foreground, knife raised; 5) Close-up of men hauling on ropes; 6) Jimmy starting to rise; 7) Men pulling; 8) Professor struggling against Angus; 9) Long shot of Jimmy rising with beast raising itself off the loch floor to follow; 10) Men pulling;

11) Jimmy, suspended by the rope, lashing out with his knife at the creature's gaping jaws; 12) The crew working furiously to get Jimmy up; 13) Jimmy still rising as the creature's body passes in front of him; 14) The worried Angela looking on as crew works; 15) Angus finally wresting gun away from the professor; 16) Crew pulling for all they're worth; 17) Jimmy rising between underwater rock cliffs; 18) Angela, almost frantic, looking on; 19) Close-up of depth gauge, the needle moving; 20) Angela looking questioningly at crewman who gives a reassuring smile in answer; 21) Jimmy's helmet breaking the surface. By breaking up the longer shots into brief snippets, the quick, strategic cuts add a frantic immediacy to the sequence, building the excitement and wisely not over-exposing the creature. The brief, teasing glimpses of the beast make its slow movements and now too-familiar lizard look more menacing and exotic.

Peter Mendoza's effective musical score aids in building the general mood and adds a punctuation to specific moments (the appearance of the monster, for instance). When the frightened man runs through the night at the film's opening, the music plays fast and frantic, the frenzied melody itself seeming to pursue the hapless fellow in his wild flight. Later, when the ill-fated diver descends into the loch at night, bassoons play low and ominous on the soundtrack, the eerie music enhancing the scene's uncanny qualities.

LIABILITIES

While the screenplay entertains with various bits of droll dialogue, nothing much really happens for the first hour, making it rather slow going until the professor's diver finally descends into the murky depths. Even at this point, all we see is a vague, formless shadow; the titular titan does not actually appear until the film's final five minutes! Admittedly, screenwriters Billie Bristow and Charles Bennett worked under obvious constraints dictated by the (brief) special effects, but this lack of dinosaur activity (never once does it leave the loch, even for the briefest of rampages) or any significant action at all cannot be completely overcome by snappy dialogue and agitated characters.

This absence of significant action led Bristow and Bennett to overdo their characterizations in an attempt to provide an(y) attention-grabber. Jimmy, while a likable lad, sometimes goes overboard with his antics (performing a ridiculous jig in his newspaper office, for instance) and crosses the line from energetic eagerness to silly buffoonery. After attending the scientific meeting, the professor literally becomes a walking blood-pressure bomb. In nearly every subsequent sequence, he shouts and raves and looks as if he's about to blow a vessel. His aggressive tirades become rather tiresome after awhile.

The most damning thing about *The Secret of the Loch*, however, is the (not so) special effects. The technique itself is executed fairly well, and Rosmer employs a variety of (blessedly quick) trick shots to transform his lizard into a leviathan, but one simply cannot gloss over the inevitable disappointment felt by today's viewers. Lacking the unique services of Willis O'Brien, the production was denied the superior dinosaur effects technique of stop-motion animation (O'Brien was the only stop-motion animator around at that time and guarded his secrets carefully), and so had to do the next best thing—trick photography with a live animal (itself a nascent technique). Though at times uneven, on the whole the creature scenes are actually rather well done and about as good as one could expect from them. One long shot in profile has Jimmy retreating down a rocky slope with the behemoth advancing toward him, the dim lighting casting the beast almost in silhouette, adding a dark, sinister quality to the spectacular scene. Other shots are not so effective, however. With Jimmy frantically tugging on the rope in one sequence, the monster coming at him is obviously rear projection, the mismatched lighting and disparate focus giving away the cheap trick. The creature becomes most effective in extreme close-up (showing off the ugly lizard's alienlike countenance) or in shadowy silhouette; Rosmer (with considerable help from editor David Lean) wisely concentrates on these types of shots. Lean never holds on one shot for more than a few seconds, shrewdly keeping each creature exposure brief by cutting away frequently to the turmoil topside (the professor brandishing his shotgun, the men frantically tugging on the rope, Angus wrestling the gun away from the professor, etc.). (Actually, the worst effects in the picture are the more mundane ones. The scenes of Angela driving her roadster feature inexcusably sloppy rear-projection; the discordant lighting and jumpy scenery rolling behind her studio-bound car makes the trick look shoddy and unconvincing.)

Unfortunately (for the filmmakers), every child knows that a modern-day iguana looks nothing like the mighty long-necked Diplodocus, a close cousin to the Brontosaurus. Iguanas, like all of today's reptiles, possess a sprawling posture — their legs stick out at right angles from their sides. Diplodocus, however, possessed an upright posture with its legs fully under its body, similar to the modern elephant's. This laughable impersonation is nearly as ludicrous as screenwriter Charles Bennett's other dino "epic," *The Lost World* (made 26 years *later*), in which Claude Rains as Professor Challenger labels a lizard with a frill a "Brontosaurus" and a baby alligator with horns glued to its head a "Tyrannosaurus Rex"!

Speaking of saurians, *The Secret of the Loch* falls short not only in quality but in quantity as well. To begin with, *Secret* features a single dinosaur whereas its cinematic brethren boast multiple thunder lizards — six in *King Kong* and four in *The Son of Kong* (though two of the latter's dinosaurs are based more on modelmaker Marcel Delgado's imagination than archeological accuracy). Plus, *Secret*'s "Diplodocus" is only seen onscreen for a total of 54 seconds whereas *The Son of Kong* gives us over two minutes of dinosaur screentime and *King Kong* delivers over *nine* minutes of prehistoric presence.

Furthermore, aside from the ultimate exposure to the world of the dread "secret of the loch," no real resolution occurs by film's end. Rather than being captured or even dispatched, the beast simply swims away unperturbed after menacing our hero for a few moments. What about the aforementioned "danger to the fishin'—to the sheep—to all of us"? Perhaps the professor and associates feel that merely unmasking the beast's existence will nullify this danger (much like unveiling Batman's true identity would destroy his crimefighting career?). Or maybe the final disposition of the monster was to take place in the sequel? Unlikely. Whatever the reasoning, the live-and-let-live ending wraps up the human drama nicely but leaves the dinosaur saga sorely unfulfilled.

As dinosaurs go, *The Secret of the Loch* cannot compare favorably to its two Cretaceous colleagues, *King Kong* and *The Son of Kong* (but then, how many films *can*?). Even so, thanks to a cadre of talent both behind and in front of the camera, it remains a fine example of a well-executed, witty British drama spiced with an occasional chill and morsel of suspense.

PRODUCTION NOTES

Producer Bray Wyndham borrowed contract actor/director Milton Rosmer from Gaumont-British to expose *The Secret of the Loch*. Rosmer began his show-business career before the turn of the century as a stage actor, often playing major parts in the classical works of Galsworthy, Ibsen and Shaw. His theatrical career reached its zenith when he served as artistic director of the Shakespeare Memorial Theatre at Stratford-on-Avon for the 1943-44 season. Beginning in films in 1915, Rosmer acted in over 50 pictures while simultaneously continuing his prosperous stage career well into the 1950s. Making a successful transition to sound, Rosmer also occasionally directed. His one other genre credit is the 1948 version of *The Monkey's Paw* (though in it Rosmer works in front of, rather than behind, the camera—as an actor). Rosmer's wealth of acting experience stood him in good stead when he stepped behind the camera, and it is no wonder that he was able to coax effective performances from his actors in *The Secret of the Loch*.

Co-screenwriter Charles Bennett wrote or co-wrote many of Alfred Hitchcock's early thrillers, including *The Man Who Knew Too Much* (1934), *The Thirty-Nine Steps* (1935), and *The Secret Agent* (1936). Bennett also co-scripted another Golden Age (borderline) horror, *The Clairvoyant* (1935), starring Claude Rains and Fay Wray. "I wrote a thing called *The Secret of the Loch*," Bennett remembered (in *Backstory: Interviews with Screenwriters of Hollywood's Golden Age* by Pat McGilligan) "because the Loch Ness monster had been sighted, and I went up to the Scottish highlands and searched out Loch Ness. I never met the monster, but I found a wonderful Scotch whiskey." Bennett recalled that *The Secret of the Loch* was one of ten movies he wrote during this period, devoting about a month to each screenplay and collecting 300 pounds Sterling for them ("which wasn't bad in those days"). When asked by interviewer Tom Weaver (in *Attack of the Movie Makers*) if he believed in the Loch Ness Monster, Bennett responded, "Of course I do! I think too many people have seen it *not* to believe in it. It's been seen by thousands of people now. I wouldn't say that I necessarily believed in it at the time I wrote that crappy picture about it, but I believe in it now!" Toward the end of his career, Bennett dealt with the realm of horror and science fiction almost exclusively, co-writing the classic *Curse of the Demon* (1956), the juvenile 1960 version of *The Lost World* (another dinosaur "epic"), the overblown *Voyage to the Bottom of the Sea* (1961), and the intriguing misfire, *War Gods of the Deep* (1965; his last screenplay). In 1964, 30 years after *The Secret of the Loch*, Bennett wrote six episodes for the "Voyage to the Bottom of the Sea" television series. Apparently, he still had not completely forgotten his early dinosaur film, for he titled one episode "Secret of the Loch" (which, of course, sent the *Seaview* chasing after none other than the Loch Ness Monster)!

Director of photography James Wilson began shooting features in 1930 and continued in the British film industry for 36 years. Though probably best known for lensing the supremely successful *Old Mother Riley* films (he shot 11 of them), Wilson also worked on the low-budget sci-fi entry *Satellite in the Sky* (1956) and the gruesomely effective Poe adaptation, *The Tell-Tale Heart* (1960).

Editor David Lean began in films as a "tea boy" for Gaumont-British in 1928. After such illustrious jobs as messenger and clapperboy, he graduated to editing newsreel footage in 1930, ultimately working his way up to feature film editor in 1934 (with *The Secret of the Loch* as one of his first assignments). Lean turned to directing in 1942, earning critical acclaim with films like *Great Expectations* (1946) and *Oliver Twist* (1948). Lean won a Best Director Oscar in 1957 for *The Bridge on the River Kwai* and garnered a second Academy Award five years later for *Lawrence of Arabia*. And to think that it all began by splicing together dinosaur footage...

Assistant director B. Graham Soutten also worked in front of the camera, as *Ben* Soutten (or even *Graham Ben* Soutten). As an actor, he appeared in three Golden Age horror (or near-horror) pictures: as a sailor in *Mystery of the Mary Celeste* (1935), as "the Beadle" in *Sweeney Todd, the Demon Barber of Fleet Street* (1936), and as "Nathaniel" in *The Crimes of Stephen Hawke* (1936). Aside from his professional versatility, Soutten also possessed an unusual physical characteristic—he was missing a leg. In films he often wore an artificial appendage to disguise this handicap (as in *Sweeney Todd*).

Actor, screenwriter, playwright, producer, director, author, and recipient of the Legion of Honor, Sir Seymour Hicks was a giant of the British stage for nearly half a century (he died in 1949). After a handful of sporadic silent pictures (including a 1913 version of *Scrooge*), Hicks appeared in a score of talkies in as many years, and wrote the screenplays for many of his films. Hicks even collaborated with Alfred Hitchcock in 1922, sharing the directorial chores on *Always Tell Your Wife*, a picture Hicks also produced. Perhaps Hicks' most famous film appearance is as *Scrooge* in the 1935 version (which he also co-scripted).

Nancy O'Neil, a 22-year-old Australian actress, made her film debut as the granddaughter of the man seeking to discover *The*

Secret of the Loch. Aside from a good supporting role in the 1935 version of *Brewster's Millions*, O'Neil generally appeared in lower berth pictures which are all but forgotten today. She retired from the screen in 1962.

Gibson Gowland appeared in a number of prestigious silents, including *Birth of a Nation* (1915; his screen debut at age 43!), *Greed* (1924), *Phantom of the Opera* (1925) and *Mysterious Island* (1929). A reliable character actor, his presence enhanced pictures on both sides of the Atlantic. Gowland appeared in two other genre films before his death in 1951: *Mystery of the Mary Celeste* (1935) and *The Wolf Man* (1941).

After starring in an even dozen films in the 1930s (*The Secret of the Loch* was his third picture), Frederick Peisley essentially abandoned the screen and devoted himself to a successful stage career. He appeared in only four more films (the last in 1968) before his death in 1976.

MANIAC
(1934; Roadshow Attractions)

Alternate Title: *Sex Maniac*
Release Date: September 1934
Running Time: 67 minutes
Director/Producer: Dwain Esper
Story and Continuity: Hildegarde Stadie
Photographer: William Thompson
Editor: William Austin
Assistant Director: J. Stuart Blackton

Cast: Bill Woods (Maxwell), Horace Carpenter (Dr. Meirschultz), Ted Edwards (Buckley), Phyllis Diller (Mrs. Buckley), Theo Ramsey (Alice Maxwell), Jenny Dark (Maizie), Marvel Andre (Marvel), Celia McCann (Jo), J. P. Wade (Embalmer), Marion Blackton (Neighbor).

"You and your weird ideas!"—Maxwell.

SYNOPSIS

In a bizarre amalgam of Edgar Allan Poe,[1] Universal's *Frankenstein*, and early stag films, the story begins in a seedy basement laboratory where two men dressed in surgical smocks are diligently at work. "Tonight, my dear Maxwell," announces Dr. Meirschultz to his assistant, "I'm ready to try my experiment on a human. In the morgue there is a lethal gas suicide—an *ideal* specimen." Maxwell balks at the idea of stealing a human body, but a quick reminder by the doctor that "the police would be very glad to find you" changes his mind.

A vaudeville impersonator-turned-fugitive, Maxwell puts his stage skills to work and gets Meirschultz and himself into the morgue by impersonating the coroner. Finding the body they seek, the doctor injects his experimental fluid into the neck of the corpse of a young woman. As the two work over the cadaver, signs of life appear! "I must get her out of here," whispers the excited doctor.

Later, at the Bureau of Missing Persons, Captain Jones questions the morgue attendant and the *real* coroner about the two impostors. "[The] description is very much like your friend Meirschultz," observes the captain. The coroner defends the learned doctor, however. "Dr. Meirschultz is really a great research scientist ... he's no *body snatcher.*" The captain remains suspicious. "Well, doctors and scientists often have some queer things on their minds. Anyway, I'll look into it." The captain also sends one of his men to check the files on the elusive Don Maxwell.

Back at the lab, Meirschultz, though pleased with the results of his experiment, raves at Maxwell. "This is but a step. Cases like this has [*sic*] the element of doubt. What I want is a victim with a *shattered* heart. Yes, a heart—[and he looks down at an organ pulsing within a glass jar]—that I can replace with this beating thing that I have forced life back into! You will get me such a victim Maxwell!"

To this end, Maxwell breaks into the local funeral parlor, but a pair of house cats viciously fighting in the mortuary frightens off the startled resurrectionist. When the doctor learns of Maxwell's failure, he breaks down into angry tears. The mad medico's lamentations abruptly cease, however, when he is struck with an idea. Laughing hysterically, the doctor grabs a gun from his desk. "You know my powers," he shouts at Maxwell. "You have worked with me, you have faith *in* me." Handing the gun to his cringing assistant, the doctor commands, "Take this! Take it—and take your life—and I shall give it *back* to you! My beating heart shall beat in *your* body!" Holding the gun in horror, Maxwell panics and shoots the raving Meirschultz, killing him.

A title card suddenly appears, and with soft music playing in the background, informs us about DEMENTIA PRAECOX. "This is the most important of the psychoses," reads the text, "both because it constitutes the highest percentage of mental diseases and because recovery is so extremely rare…"

The abrupt pseudo-psychiatric lesson eventually concludes and we're back with Maxwell and Dr. Meirschultz's corpse again. Overcoming his initial remorse, Maxwell decides to hide the body. Just then, the doorbell rings. It is Mrs. Buckley come about her husband's "positively alarming hallucinations." "Why," she explains, "he thinks he's the orangutan murderer in Poe's 'Murder of the Rue Morgue [sic].'" Though Maxwell tells her the doctor is out, Mrs. Buckley insists on fetching her hallucinating husband.

Maxwell has a brainstorm. "Meirschultz would be missed," he reasons, "Maxwell never would." With his handy makeup kit, Maxwell quickly transforms himself into the image of the dead doctor. "Not only do I look like Meirschultz," raves an obviously unhinged Maxwell, "I *am* Meirschultz! I will be a *great man*!"

Here the second instructional card appears, informing us about PARESIS: "General paralysis of the insane or paresis, is the most serious disorder for the criminologist…"

When Mrs. Buckley returns with her husband, Maxwell (masquerading as the doctor) mistakenly injects Mr. Buckley with a dose of "super adrenaline" instead of the harmless water he'd intended to administer. The drug triggers a violent reaction in Buckley. At that instant, the resurrected girl wanders out into the office in a zombielike state and the now-uncontrollable Buckley grabs the waif. Rushing out of the house, the madman carries her into the woods where he rips off her clothes (exposing her breasts) and begins to strangle her.

Back in the lab, Mrs. Buckley sees the body of Meirschultz, but not its face. Maxwell/Meirschultz tells her it's the body of Maxwell who committed suicide and that he'll bring his assistant back to life with his experimental technique. This gives the scheming Mrs. Buckley the idea that the doctor can do the same thing to her deranged husband, reasoning (oddly) that then she can "control him."

When Mrs. Buckley leaves, Maxwell determines to carry out the operation as planned and restore the doctor to life with the living heart. Satan, the doctor's black cat, however, has a different aim and knocks over the jar to get at the pulsing (and obviously tantalizing) heart. With his hopes of restoring Meirschultz dashed along with the nibbled organ (as if he, a vaudeville performer with no medical training, had much chance of success anyway), Maxwell decides to wall up the body in the cellar. Distracted by Satan, however, Maxwell goes into a mad rage and gouges out the hapless animal's eye—and then eats it!

As Maxwell continues to wall up the corpse, the third textbook lesson appears on the screen to tell us about the PARANOIAC. Unnoticed by Maxwell, Satan has leapt up and scampered through the opening in the false wall before Maxwell sets the final brick.

"Maxwell had forgotten all about his wife," announces a title card, "and she him until…" In a seedy boarding house, Alice (Mrs. Maxwell) and her three roommates bathe, dress, and complain about men. One of them reads in the paper that Maxwell has inherited some money. "Say," says Alice, the dollar signs lighting up her eyes, "I wonder if he's still with that goofy professor."

After yet another title card explains about MANIC-DEPRESSIVE PSYCHOSES, a few scenes show Maxwell lecherously eyeing his female "patients," affording us viewers another glimpse of nudity.

Maxwell reacts to Alice's sudden arrival with suspicion and determines to do away with his annoying wife by enlisting the aid of Mrs. Buckley (while at the same time plotting the demise of his reluctant cohort). Telling each of the two women that the *other* is crazy and must be subdued, Maxwell lures them down into the basement together and locks them in. The two terrified women panic and viciously attack each other while Maxwell cackles with glee.

At that moment, the police (who have been asking pointed questions of Meirschultz's neighbors) arrive with a search warrant. Hearing the women's screams, they grab Maxwell and break up the fight in the cellar. A howling from behind the wall alerts the police to Meirschultz's hidden body. Maxwell ends up behind bars, raving about "the gleam!"

MEMORABLE MOMENT

While *Maniac* contains a number of memorable moments (generally notable for the wrong reasons), one sequence in particular stands out as the epitome of gruesome bad taste. It begins with a creepy shot of the vengeful Maxwell, his eyes wild and his face determined, crawling slowly up the cellar stairs after the cat, Satan. Suddenly, the scene cuts to the cat scrambling across a table with Maxwell lunging in pursuit. A violent chase ensues until Maxwell falls to his knees and grasps the cornered feline. Then, in extreme close-up, we see Maxwell's hands clasped about the animal's head and neck. As the beast gives a wailing cry, Maxwell's thumb painfully pries out a dark object from the cat's eye socket. He has *gouged out the animal's eye*! After a brief close-up of Maxwell's insane face, the hands release the screaming animal and we next see a dark shape flit across our line of vision, knocking aside pans and shattering vials as the cat flees in a frenzy of pain and terror. Maxwell then looks down and for a split second we see the orb itself lying on the floor. Maxwell reaches down and picks up the grisly trophy. Chuckling to himself, he observes, "Why, it's not unlike an oyster — or a grape." His unhealthy laughter suddenly stops as he hisses, "But, the *gleam* is *gone*!" Laughing evilly, he tilts his head back, raises his arm, and drops the ghastly thing into his mouth. Chewing heartily, he resumes his mad laughter. Looking around, Maxwell abruptly stops laughing (as if realizing the horror of his revolting actions) and swallows hard as the scene fades.

Though the object pried out of the cat's eye socket looks like a dark button on closer scrutiny, and the eyeball on the floor is obviously a glass eye with a slimy tail stuck onto it, the shots are quick enough that the nauseating impact of the horrendous act remains undimmed (unlike the eye itself). Once seen, the astonished viewer is unlikely to forget the sight.

ASSETS

The year 1934 was a lean one for screen horror, with only four genre pictures released in the 12-month period. In addition, only one of them, *The Black Cat*, is a bonafide Hollywood terror film which received general distribution in the U.S. Great Britain uncovered *The Secret of the Loch* (and kept the secret *inside* their borders); the "Negro circuit" offered an all-black voodoo voyage to *Louisiana* (a.k.a. *Drums o' Voodoo*); and Dwain Esper unleashed his *Maniac* on unwary roadshow patrons.

Though technically crude, this lurid independent production holds many points of (admittedly unhealthy) interest. Shot on a budget considered inadequate even by poverty row standards (a mere $7,500 according to Dan Sonney, whose father financed the picture), director/producer Dwain Esper managed to create a mildly grotesque, moderately risible, but extremely intriguing film; one that holds more interest than many of its more "professional" contemporaries.

Battling the budget, Esper and cinematographer William Thompson at least attempt (and partially succeed) to create some visual interest in the generally static milieu by placing objects in the foreground to add a sense of depth (even shooting *through* glass tubes and beakers to the wild-eyed actors beyond). And though the camera rarely moves, Esper manages to break up the visual monotony with frequent inserts and reaction shots. The director even employs some rather inventive scene transitions. A shot of the doctor exhorting Maxwell to procure him a body fades to black, when all of a sudden the black screen itself seems to split open as Maxwell opens the lab door, allowing the light from inside the room to spill out and illuminate the scene behind. Then, when the hesitant Maxwell finally comes to a decision and steps determinedly over the threshold toward us, the screen goes black as the door closes and shuts out the light from inside. Admittedly, for the most part the picture looks ill-lit and static; but, while no Orson Welles, the few flashes of imaginative technique suggest that Dwain Esper was no Ed Wood either.

As Maxwell, Bill Woods gives an overripe but still rather affecting performance. His mad ravings do nothing if not startle. While lacking the screen presence of a Lugosi or Carradine, Woods' enthusiasm and wild intensity grab the viewer's interest. Though his uneven acting often veers dangerously close to the ridiculous, he remains enjoyable to watch (if nothing else, simply to see what in the hell he'll do next!).

By creating an adults-only entry shown strictly in burlesque houses and adult theaters, Esper deftly circumnavigated the censorial body lording over the Hollywood product. This freedom from the recently revamped Production Code (indeed, even from the basic restrictions of good taste) allowed for much more gritty (and gruesome) realism in the production. A human heart, for instance, suspended in liquid inside a glass jar, the organ grotesquely pulsing with a life of its own, was a singularly shocking sight in 1934 (over two decades before the famed exposed brain scene in *The Curse of Frankenstein* startled viewers in 1957).

"It's horrible I tell you — workin' on the dead — tryin' to bring back life!" shouts Maxwell (Bill Woods, at right), the unstable assistant to the equally cracked Dr. Meirschultz (Horace Carpenter), in *Maniac* (1934).

While Esper exploited much of this realism simply for shock or titillation value (the heart and eyeball, the brief nudity), it also provided opportunities for less blatant and more subtly effective shocks. As Maxwell finishes up his disguise as Dr. Meirschultz, he casually reaches down to Meirschultz's body and retrieves the doctor's spectacles, plucking them from in front of the *open* eyes of the corpse. The eyes wide open in a sightless stare of death add a shuddery shock of reality to the moment. In mainstream Hollywood productions, corpses invariably rest with their eyes closed, as if merely in peaceful slumber. Here, the sightless gaze hammers home the finality of death (Maxwell's grandiose dreams of restoration aside).

Then, for emphasis, Esper has Maxwell notice the wide-eyed glare and reach down to close the eyes with a half-mad muttering of "the *gleam*." Later, when Maxwell takes Meirschultz's body down into the basement, the corpse's heels bang on each step—thump, thump, thump—as Maxwell drags the lifeless body after him. The jarring noise creates yet another subtle shudder. Esper's attention to gruesome details such as these creates a more quiet brand of horror and shock which juxtaposes nicely with his more lurid moments of gore.

Esper lifted scenes from the Swedish witchcraft "exposé" *Haxan* (1920; a.k.a. *Witchcraft Through the Ages*) and the German epic *Siegfried* (1923) to signify madness. Superimposing images of bony fingers clawing and wriggling or horned devils laughing and cavorting over shots of Maxwell thinking aloud creates a crude but effective visual subtext. The bizarre images lend an optical emphasis to the madman's words and add a chaotic sense of urgency to his blossoming psychosis.

LIABILITIES

"Once a ham, always a ham!" taunts Meirschultz when an outraged Maxwell raves at the doctor. Obviously Horace Carpenter (playing Meirschultz) never heard the old adage about throwing stones in glass houses. Carpenter comes off as a second-rate version of a Bela Lugosi mad doctor—a full six years before that actor began unconsciously parodying himself in a string of cheap poverty-row productions in the 1940s. (In some twisted way Carpenter's performance may give a warped perspective on how Lugosi *might* have played Henry Frankenstein—as once was announced—before Universal switched him to the role of the monster and conducted their famous screen test.) In one scene, Carpenter states indignantly, "You know I do not vurk—under *prying* eyes," his back stiffening and his eyes going wide for emphasis. Carpenter comes complete with odd accent and slowed speech, punctuated by dreadfully pregnant pauses and glowering looks while employing gestures like clasping his hands together over his head in triumph and even pulling his hair in anguish. When Maxwell fails to bring him a body, Carpenter bursts into angry tears, though he manages to shout "You fool! You have failed me!" through his violent sobbing.

Maniac is a film of extremes, and the production's cast reflect this. Esper was definitely not an actor's director (nor did he have much to work with here). On the one hand we have Horace Carpenter's volatile Dr. Meirschultz, Bill Wood's hysterical (though admittedly likable) Maxwell, and Ted Edwards' violent Buckley; while at the other end of the acting spectrum, the remaining cast members range from a deadpan, inflectionless policeman to a goofy, dim-witted neighbor. The generally amateurish level of acting in the supporting players is typified when one of the morgue attendants repeatedly looks directly at the camera and delivers his (blessedly short) lines as if reading them off a cue card (which may very well have been the case).

Even Bill Woods, who gives the picture its most memorable (if not altogether good) performance, careens about wildly in his acting quality. "Think of it," he says, almost in awe, "*life*—back in the body that sought oblivion. Uncanny. The possibilities *terrify* me." After a long, sincere pause, he raps his knuckles on the table—then slowly, deliberately, does it *again*! Rather than providing emphasis, the poorly timed gesture merely suggests that he cannot quite remember his next line.

Laughable, outrageous dialogue abounds. "It's horrible I tell you—working on the dead, trying to bring back life," shouts Maxwell at the doctor before adding in all seriousness, "It's not natural!" Or how about this dialogue exchange when the police captain asks a neighbor about Meirschultz and Maxwell:

> Neighbor: "They're sorta queer, I'd say. There's lotsa queer goin's-on up there. Why, they even brought a dead dog back to life once.
> Captain: "Why, that sounds remarkable to me."
> Neighbor: "It may be, but to my notion, those that monkeys with what they got no business to gets queer sooner or later."

Exploitationeer extraordinaire Dwain Esper (maker of *Maniac*, 1934) often attempted to legitimize his roadshow productions with virtuous propaganda like this piece used to promote his 1936 birth-of-a-baby opus, *Modern Motherhood*.

Maxwell's final scene has him behind bars. "The gleam, they drove me to it, I tell you," he pleads. Almost sobbing, he adds, "They drove me with hunger, with misery and humiliation. I only wanted to amuse, to entertain, but here I am."

Some dialogue passages border on the nonsensical. Maxwell, after having shot Meirschultz: "Why should the unconscious peace of the dead — be disturbed? Isn't the spark that moves the maggot the selfsame spark that moves the man? Preserving that spark in the individual is not important. What we *do* with the spark while we have it *is* important. In Meirschultz the spark is gone, in Maxwell it *lives*!"

Fortunately, like in the best of "bad" movies, the dialogue often transcends its awkwardness to become a source of amusement. "Hey Mazie," chides one woman to another taking a bath, "we know you're hard-boiled; you don't have to stay in the water 30 minutes to prove it." Mazie's answer: "Oh let me alone; I may not be decent but I'm sure gonna be clean."

The picture's worst dialogue passages are not even spoken. They come in the form of awkwardly written "lectures" on mental illness (in an obvious attempt by Esper, who promoted his questionable films by taking a virtuous stand [see illustration above], to justify the unwholesome "thrills" found in *Maniac*). These "educational passages" scroll down the screen at inopportune moments in the film to relate to the viewer such brilliant insights as "There are three phases of the manic-depressive psychoses, the manic phase, the depressed phase, and the mixed phase" or, "The brain, in, and of its physical self, does not think any more than a musical instrument can give forth a melody without the touch of a musician's hand. The brain is indeed the instrument of thinking, but the mind is the skillful player that makes it give forth the beautiful harmony of thought." At times, these tangential messages become downright bizarre: "It is because of the disastrous results of fear thought not only on the individual but on the nation, that it becomes the duty of every sane man and woman to establish a quarantine against fear... Fear thought is most dangerous when it parades as forethought. Combat fear by replacing it with faith. Resist worry with confidence." Beyond their overt ludicrousness, the arbitrary insertions of these pseudo-educational platitudes disastrously disrupt the film's pace and completely dispel whatever tension has been built up, while their scholarly, moralistic tone jars painfully with the noxious flavor of this unsavory tale. Also, the presence of these title cards make this crude production seem even more primitive by conjuring up images of the silent film. Esper even goes beyond the psychiatric mumblings to toss in a simple narrative card (about Maxwell's estranged wife) to move the story along — a technique straight out of the silent era. (Esper was very familiar with silent filmmaking, having produced a number of features in the 1920s, primarily no-budget westerns.)

About the best that can be said of William Thompson's static camerawork is that he keeps things in focus and adequately centered. His gloomy, uneven lighting, however, is amateurish at best, making this no-budget production look even cheaper. The interiors are frequently underlit; and this becomes a near-debilitating distraction as the viewer strains hard to see the proceedings. The mundane exteriors (consisting of an ordinary house porch, suburban sidewalk, and backyard full of cat cages) are uniformly murky. To add to the visual confusion, the haphazard lighting inexplicably changes from one shot to the next, the same location seen in *almost* adequate light at one moment and a nearly impenetrable dimness in the next. (Thompson, who lensed a handful of forgotten low-budget silents and early talkies, abandoned cinematography soon after *Maniac*. He resumed his sporadic career in the early 1950s — by photographing Ed Wood films. *Glen or Glenda?* [1953], *Bride of the Monster* [1956] and *Plan Nine from Outer Space* [1959] all feature the "Thompson Touch.")

A leering, sleazy aura permeates the picture, due not only to the gratuitous flashes of female nudity but primarily to the sick, mean-spirited attitude of the film. Buckley's vicious attack on the zombielike girl smacks of violent rape. A dialogue exchange between two morgue attendants suggests a lascivious necrophilia: "Say, did you see the *beaut* that come in today," asks one to the other, "she's the one that has the coroner doin' the night watch." A vicious fight between two women shows one beating the other with a stick (no coy shadows here but full-view violence) in a blatantly brutal display. Even the comedy relief (in the form of the dimwitted neighbor) possesses a nasty, distasteful tone. "You see," boasts the neighbor, "I figured that rats breed faster than cats, and cat skins makes good fur. Cats eat rats, and rats eat raw meat — that is, they eat the carcasses of the cats. So, the rats eat the cats, the cats eat the rats, and I get the skins." While these unwholesome elements add to the film's fascination, it makes the picture more of a guilty curio than a meritorious movie. (*Maniac* offers up a choice morsel of amusing irony when one title card warns us that "unhealthy thought creates warped attitudes which in turn creates criminals and manias." *Maniac* is simply *bursting* with "unhealthy thought" and "warped attitudes"!)

Speaking of cats, for some inexplicable reason Esper seems obsessed with the animals, periodically cutting to shot after shot of cats: a cat chasing a mouse as Maxwell and Meirschultz enter the morgue; two cats spitting and fighting while Maxwell breaks into the funeral parlor; endless shots of the neighbor's caged kitties. One may conjecture that the cat motif is Esper's thematic device to represent some sort of triggering device (a *catalyst* for madness?) since it *was* a cat who ate the all-important heart and later revealed the body; but more likely these intrusive and incongruous shots simply join with the numerous tangential explanatory cards in stretching the running time out to an acceptable length.

Maniac is filled with scenes of titillation; some shock (Buckley violently ripping off the girl's clothing and viciously attacking her) while others simply slow the picture to a standstill (the lengthy sequence of Maxwell's wife and her roommates prattling on in various stages of undress). While the scene with Mrs. Maxwell and her floozy friends may be a voyeur's delight (at least for the 1930s), it slows the pace terribly and brings the weird-but-intriguing proceedings to a grinding halt. For over three minutes we're subjected to shots of the chippees bathing, ironing their undergarments, lounging in lingerie, performing a 1930s version of aerobics, and babbling on about men ("In his day men were men, but today they're too scared to be anything but honest."[?!])

Though it may be bad, *Maniac* is seldom boring (unlike the technically superior but entertainment-*inferior Condemned to Live* or *Revolt of the Zombies*). Watching with a slack jaw and numbed brain, one gets the feeling that *anything* can — and will — happen. This offbeat, audacious, shocking mishmash is the Golden Age of Horror's very own combination *Plan Nine from Outer Space* and *Blood Feast*.

REVIEWS

Apparently, no trade publication ever reviewed the picture, making *Maniac* the Golden Age of Horror's sole recipient of this signal (dis)honor.

PRODUCTION NOTES

Upon its initial release, *Maniac* failed to pull in the dollars as expected, even on the undiscriminating roadshow circuit. So Dwain Esper added a *Sex* to the title and worked up new ads and promotional material. The old adage "sex sells" worked, and *Sex Maniac* cleaned up at the grindhouse box offices. (*Film Daily* reported in January 1936 that *Sex Maniac* was the first "adults only" picture to play in New Orleans since the "advent of the Legion of Decency," though the local *Times-Picayune* ultimately refused to run ads for this "breakthrough" film.)

This first-ever sexploitation horror movie was created by the "father of modern exploitation," Dwain Esper, and his screenwriter-wife Hildegarde Stadie. The husband-and-wife-team went on to make *Marihuana, Weed with Roots in Hell* (1936), *Modern Motherhood* (1936, an early birth-of-a-baby epic), *Narcotic* (1937), and *How to Undress in Front of Your Husband* (1937; starring Elaine Barrie, wife of John Barrymore), taking them around the country to show at burlesque theaters and grindhouses.

A World War I veteran, Dwain Esper left a successful career as a building contractor to break into movies in the mid-twenties by producing and distributing cheap features, mostly low-end oaters. (Esper once boasted to David F. Friedman that he could churn out a 60-minute silent western in two days for only $1,200.) Ever the opportune showman, Esper made his real mark after the advent of sound by producing controversial educational features for adults. In them, he would slip in bits of nudity and tastelessly lurid sequences (such as *Maniac*'s eye-gouging/eating scene) and get away with it by taking a high-handed moral tone with the subject matter. He was able to circumnavigate the Hays Office by showing his pictures in burlesque theaters and roadshow houses rather than in the more mainstream movie palaces.

After taking a hiatus from roadshowing during World War II (to "work on inventions," as reported by *Variety* in Esper's obituary), Esper returned to the circuit in 1947 when he reissued *Freaks* (which he had purchased from MGM and slapped with exploitative retitlings like *Nature's Mistakes* and *Forbidden Love* to draw in the roadshow rubes). Esper toured the country with his "new" feature, often accompanied by his very own live "freakshow" to promote the picture.

The only "name" actor in *Maniac*'s cast was Horace Bernard Carpenter, who began his thespian career before the turn of the century. He entered early silent films as a member of the Famous Players–Lasky Co., made a name for himself in westerns (both silent and sound), and even worked behind the camera as a screenwriter, penning scenarios for Douglas

Fairbanks, Sr. Fortunately, *Maniac* was not seen widely enough to seriously damage Carpenter's career, and he kept active in pictures up until his death in 1945. His final screen appearance was in RKO's *Belle of the Yukon* (1944).

Though *Maniac*'s epicurean eyeball was a phony, the one-orbed feline was the genuine article. Louis Sonney, another patriarch of cinema exploitation, provided the financing for *Maniac*, and his son, Dan Sonney, helped out by wrangling cats for the production, including finding a one-eyed tom.

NOTES

1. Hildegarde Stadie filled her screenplay with references (some subtle, some blatant) to Edgar Allan Poe, stealing shamefully from (and without crediting) the Grand Master of the Macabre. The "gleam" Maxwell continually raves about is lifted from "The Tell-Tale Heart." The grisly eye-gouging, the entombment of the corpse, and the subsequent betrayal by the yowling cat walled up with the body are blatant plot points stolen from Poe's "The Black Cat." And Mr. Buckley's thinking he's "the orangutan murderer" is obviously from "The Murders in the Rue Morgue" (*not* "Murder of the Rue Morgue" as Mrs. Buckley misnames it).

MARK OF THE VAMPIRE
(1935; MGM)

Release Date: May 2, 1935
Running Time: 61 minutes
Director: Tod Browning
Screenplay: Guy Endore, Bernard Schubert
Photography: James Wong Howe, A.S.C.
Editor: Ben Lewis
Art Director: Cedric Gibbons
Associates: Harry Oliver, Edwin B. Willis
Recording Director: Douglas Shearer
Gowns: Adrian

Cast: Lionel Barrymore (Professor Zelen), Elizabeth Allan (Irena), Bela Lugosi (Count Mora), Lionel Atwill (Inspector Neumann), Jean Hersholt (Baron Otto), Henry Wadsworth (Fedor), Donald Meek (Dr. Doskil), Jessie Ralph (Midwife), Ivan Simpson (Jan), Franklyn Ardell (Chauffeur), Leila Bennett (Maria), June Gittelson (Annie), Carroll Borland* (Luna), Holmes Herbert (Sir Karell), Michael Visaroff (Innkeeper).

*Note: Carroll Borland's name is misspelled in the credits as "Carol."

"There is no more foul or relentless enemy of man in the occult world than this dead-alive creature spewed up from the grave."—Professor Zelen.

SYNOPSIS

In a small Balkan village, Sir Karell Borotyn, one of the landed gentry, is found dead, his body completely drained of blood. The superstitious villagers all cry vampire, as does the local doctor. "These little wounds on his throat are the bite of the vampire. I have seen such marks in these parts," the timorous physician tells Inspector Neumann. The peasants believe the vampires to be Count Mora and his daughter, both long dead. The matter remains unresolved and the coroner's inquest can only conclude that Sir Karell "met his death from cause or causes unknown."

A year passes and Sir Karell's daughter, Irena, now lives with her legal guardian, Baron Otto, a kindly friend of her father's. While Irena discusses her upcoming wedding, Fedor, her fiancé, staggers into the room and collapses. He cannot remember what has happened but he's very weak and sports two marks on his neck.

At the now-ruined estate of Sir Karell, the vampiric Count Mora and his daughter, Luna (wearing her funeral shroud), glide through the dismal interior. Luna, under the malevolent eye of her undead father, lures Irena out onto the terrace and descends on her insensate form. When Irena is found the next morning, the two marks on her throat tell all.

Prompted by Inspector Neumann, the anxious doctor sends for professor Zelen, an expert in the occult. The learned Professor orders bat-thorn (obviously this region's answer to wolfsbane) placed at all the windows to ward off the undead fiends.

Baron Otto finds a document with Sir Karell's signature on it, dated *after* his death, and Irena hears her father's voice calling to her. Sir Karell, a victim of the vampires, has obviously joined the ranks of the undead. Inspector Neumann, however, remains unconvinced. The inspector and Baron Otto go to Sir Karell's tomb where they find the coffin open and empty. From the shadows peer the luminous faces of Count Mora and Sir Karell, watching … waiting.

Inspector Neumann and Baron Otto hear ghostly organ music coming from the ruined castle. Peering through a window, they observe an eerie tableau — while the resurrected Sir Karell plays, Count Mora and another, unidentified cadaverous figure watch as Luna, her luminous shroud outstretched like huge wings, descends batlike to the castle floor. There can be no doubt now, and the professor, Neumann, and Otto discuss their plans.

Meanwhile, despite the professor's precautions of bat-thorne, a sinister shadow[1] enters Irena's room and attacks her sleeping form. "I heard a sound like wind at the casements," the revived Irena later tells the concerned men. "I felt a draft. Then I saw *her* … I fought to keep my eyes open, but they closed. I felt again that deadly cold breath. The horror of it — made me feel faint."

Professor Zelen counsels his compatriots that to save Irena "we must break the spell" she is under, warning, "If we don't succeed in destroying those *monsters* by sundown, it may be too late."

The trio spend most of the day searching the castle. Finding nothing, they finally get around to investigating the vaults beneath the old ruins. There they find the corpse of Sir Karell. "We must find the others," instructs Zelen, but Baron Otto panics and grabs a sword to strike at the slumbering monster. Neumann restrains the Baron while Zelen warns that they must destroy all the vampires together rather than "expose ourselves to the vengeance of the others. Why, their fury would follow us to the ends of the Earth!" In their agitation, the trio accidentally extinguish their candles, plunging them into darkness.

With the sun now down, Count Mora and Sir Karell watch as Luna glides out through the garden to give some silent command to her thrall, Irena. Turning to Fedor, who has remained to watch over her, Irena puts on a false air of gaiety and suddenly runs from the room, locking the door behind her. Fedor rushes out through another door in pursuit.

Below, Professor Zelen and Baron Otto seem to have lost Inspector Neumann, while upstairs, Luna leads Irena to the gathered vampires. As Irena stares, frightened, Sir Karell suddenly speaks: "Be brave my child … go with Luna."

In the cellar, Zelen and Otto hear organ music. Zelen starts up the stairs but the terrified Baron refuses to follow. "But don't you see," entreats Zelen, "if Sir Karell was in life the kindly, benevolent person you described, your lifelong and devoted friend, you could go to him, you could *appeal* to him." The baron is petrified. "No, no, I *can't*," he pleads.

Upstairs, Luna is about to bite Irena when Fedor sees them through a window and breaks in. With a vicious animal hiss, Luna grabs Irena and whisks her through the chamber door. The pursuing Fedor runs straight into the clutches of Count Mora.

Zelen hypnotizes Baron Otto. Now the jig is up, the game afoot.

Upstairs, Irena approaches her vampiric father. Staring at him, she suddenly loses her nerve. "I can't do it," she quails. Enter the missing Inspector Neumann. Now we learn that the vampires had been a ruse, with actors playing the parts, including a man who looks *exactly* like the late Sir Karell! "But you said Baron Otto would break down and confess if you confronted him with this gentleman pretending to be my father," protests the distraught Irena. The plan has failed, however, and now they must make one final desperate ploy to try and trap their suspect.

"It's one year ago," Zelen instructs the entranced Baron, "You're going to see Sir Karell." The pseudo-Karell then repeats the murdered man's actions at his last meeting with Baron Otto on that fateful night a year before. As the inspector and the professor watch, the hypnotized baron proceeds to reenact the crime. After drugging the phony Sir Karell, the baron moves to puncture his victim's neck. The inspector restrains him, Zelen releases him from his hypnotic state, and they arrest Baron Otto for the murder of Sir Karell. The motive: Baron Otto secretly loved Irena and killed his friend to prevent Irena's impending marriage. With everything revealed, Irena apologizes to Fedor for keeping him in the dark: "They were afraid that you wouldn't let me go through with it."

In a castle chamber-cum-dressing room, Count Mora, Luna, and the unnamed third bloodsucker remove their makeup. For the first time we hear Mora speak. "This vampire business, it has given me a great idea for a new act. Luna, in the new act *I* will be the vampire. Did you watch me? I gave *all* of me. I was greater than any *real* vampire!" he announces grandly with a flourish of his cape. "Sure, sure, but get off your makeup," is Luna's amused response while the third partner pipes in with "yes, and help me with some of this packing." The music rises and it is THE END.

MEMORABLE MOMENT

Along with the gruesome beginning of *Murders in the Zoo*, this picture features one of the strongest openings from the Golden Age of Horror. In a gypsy camp, lit by flickering firelight, an old woman hangs a charmed weed on her wagon while a matron mutters a protective prayer over her newborn babe and the men sing a melancholy dirge in the background. The scene then switches to a dank and dark graveyard full of blackened trees and swirling mists. An old snaggled witch-creature gathers up a mysterious weed which grows on the graves (to what unwholesome purpose we cannot say). As she scurries among the tombstones, a carriage races past the massive cemetery gates, the driver obviously fearful of even passing this unhallowed spot. The noisy, frenetic passage is startling in the otherwise slow, moody scene. As the old crone reaches down for another sprig, a bat flies toward her out of the darkness. She shrieks in fright and turns to flee, but her ragged gown catches on a gravedigger's hoe carelessly left there. In mortal terror she tugs at the garment until it finally tears and, while a wolf howls in the distance, she makes her panicked escape and scuttles off among the gravestones.

This macabre opening chills the very marrow with its full-blooded atmosphere ripe with horrific imaginings. While nothing supernatural or even truly frightening occurs, we can almost feel the cold mists around our ankles and share the old woman's hysterical horror at the clutching hand from the grave.

ASSETS

Mark of the Vampire simply reeks of atmosphere. From the opening sequence at the gypsy camp, the stage is set for supernatural terror. The atmospheric settings exude gothic menace, beginning with the best graveyard set of the era. Blackened, dead trees reach out with their spiny branches. Rank weeds poke up along the forbidding iron railings and broken tombstones which mark the unkempt graves. A light fog, dank and mysterious, moves sluggishly over the tenements of the dead. Brrrrrr! No wonder the old woman nearly collapses from fright at her own clumsiness. Each and every set possesses its own eerie touches. The primitive country inn is steeped in shadows; the expansive drawing rooms of Baron Otto feature medieval wood-and-iron doors and forbidding suits of armor; the "exteriors" consist of shadowy trees shrouded in layers of mist. Even the room holding the officious coroner's inquest contains a macabre occupant. As the head investigator responds to the witnesses' tales of vampires with a claim of "superstitious twaddle," a skeleton (obviously belonging to Dr. Doskil) stands in the background, casting a sinister shadow upon the wall.

The picture's stunning centerpiece, however, is the ruined "castle" of the deceased Sir Karell. Art directors Harry Oliver and Edwin B. Willis (supervised by department head Cedric Gibbons) transform this dilapidated manor house into a scaled-down version of Castle Dracula. Though smaller, it is just as atmospheric and nearly as effective. Director Tod Browning obviously felt that his vampires should have suitable quarters and ordered a duplication of his earlier success. Just as in Dracula's castle, massive stone archways enclose a wide balcony and staircase, while dust and cobwebs cover all. Moonlight streams through the huge broken windows to cast the castle's recesses in sinister shadows. The stairway sports a similarly oversized spider web stretching across its path (and Count Mora and Luna seemingly pass through the web without disturbing it just as Dracula had). The same phony spider from *Dracula* scuttles up the wall (pulled on a string), and that out-of-place Transylvanian opossum makes an encore appearance. Browning goes even further, however, and enlarges his legion of fauna from the earlier film. *Dracula*'s solitary wasp climbing from within a coffin-shaped box is supplanted by a whole swarm of beetles. Thankfully leaving his duo of armadillos back in Transylvania, Browning replaces them with a trio of bats clinging to a wall covering—a nice (and refreshing) touch of realism.

Going beyond mere window dressing, Browning utilizes his fauna for more direct effect. When Inspector Neumann and Baron Otto enter Sir Karell's crypt only to find the dead man's coffin open and empty, a live bat suddenly drops down onto the satin lining. Then, as the two men recoil and retreat from the desecrated sepulcher, we see what appears to be a large white wolf moving among the tombstones in the misty background. This attention to eerie detail enhances the macabre mood.

James Wong Howe's camera takes full advantage of the creepy sets, as well as exploiting the frightening figures of Count Mora and Luna. When we first see the vampiric pair in their ruined castle, for instance, a long shot shows us the whole eerie, crumbling interior, establishing the setting and its mood of decay. Howe's camera then follows in front of the unholy pair as they move silently down the staircase. The camera reveals devilish details as it moves, lingering on the gigantic spider web and huge balustrade surmounted by a macabre statuette.

Beyond simply enhancing a mood, Howe's canny camera often generates a scene's power. In one sequence, two servants drive their carriage through the night only to come upon the figure of Luna standing by the road in front of the cemetery gates. From an elevated angle— about the height of a horse-drawn wagon, in fact—the camera approaches steadily closer to the macabre figure. While the *rate* of approach is smooth, Howe wisely jostles the camera as it tracks closer (just as if it were riding on the bumpy cart), creating a sense of immediacy and an air of realism. Luna simply stands still, performing no action whatsoever. The elevated camera angle and rushing, unsteady movement place the viewer in the driver's seat and so create the terror as we move inexorably toward this frightful figure.

Howe lights the sets with an eye toward texture and mood, often choosing to illuminate a room as if it were lit by a single lamp, leaving the edges and even some of the actors in dimness and shadow. Howe allows shadows to fill the corners—even, for instance, in the relative normality of Irena's chambers. A single table lamp is seemingly the only source of illumination for her bedroom, so that a maid placing bat-thorne on the French doors becomes a mere silhouette in the background. Howe's choice of dim lighting becomes a visual reminder that the darkness—the evil— creeps into even the safest of sanctuaries. For the scene in which Luna attacks the entranced Irena on the terrace, light coming through the windowpanes casts bars of shadow across Irena's form, creating layers of light which blend with the layers of fog in the background, giving Irena an insubstantial, ephemeral

Bela Lugosi in his Count Mora makeup smokes one of his beloved cigars between takes. Note the prominent bullet wound in his temple. The original screenplay stipulated that Count Mora carry on an incestuous relationship with his daughter Luna before murdering her and then killing himself with a revolver (thus condemning the pair to eternal damnation as the undead). No mention of these sacrilegious acts made it to the finished film, however.

presence—a visual metaphor for the darkness engulfing her by degrees.

Later, Howe utilizes light to turn a potentially awkward transformation scene into a moment of eerie horror. The camera looks down a hallway through an open set of French doors onto a balcony. Out of the foggy darkness flies a bat, slowly flapping its wings as fog seems to emanate from its very body. The dim, diffuse lighting quickly but steadily goes dark so that for a moment we can just barely make out the outline of the scene. The light quickly comes up again, but it has changed—transformed as the subject it highlights has transformed. Now a more concentrated illumination focuses on the startling sight of Count Mora standing on the balcony, his spotlighted white face seemingly floating above his black cloak. The surrounding edges of the scene can now only barely be perceived as all the light appears drawn to that ghastly white face. The changing illumination first heralds, then parallels the supernatural transformation, effectively focusing the viewer on the eerie vision.

"I think that James Wong Howe really was a genius," Carroll Borland told this author, and she credited the film's success to Howe rather than Browning.

While *Mark of the Vampire* lacks a full musical score, sound becomes a perfect compliment to the atmospheric sets and moody lighting/photography. Whenever we step into the fog-enshrouded night or the vampires are prowling about the ruined castle or graveyard, an eerie symphony of sound effects presages their presence. The low moaning of wind rises and falls while crickets play their staccato rhythms alongside the almost subliminal howling of dogs in the background. The sounds come together to create a weird, unsettling harmony. This cadence of the damned raises the already upright hackles yet another quarter inch.

With one notable exception, the acting in *Mark of the Vampire* is first rate. Without uttering a word, Bela Lugosi, as Count Mora, takes command of the picture. This was the first time since *Dracula* that he played a vampire, and Lugosi projects his full demonic presence into this vampiric cousin. ("There was never any question but that Lugosi was replaying his then-famous Dracula part," recalled Carroll Borland in *The Castle Dracula Quarterly*.) Lugosi's eyes and face deliver all the expression needed; his ghastly visage and intense stares become evil personified. While denied his powerful voice, and generally limited to leering from the shadows or frightening maids, Lugosi's imposing presence lends a macabre authenticity to the eerie surroundings. In one scene, for instance, he watches intently as Luna approaches Irena. As the vampiress suddenly spreads her arms and descends on her victim's prostrate form, Lugosi's slight, nearly imperceptible turning upwards of the mouth speaks of the depravity and evil of his character. This subtle, almost subliminal movement on his glowering countenance turns what could be a warm half-smile into a cold, chilling, hateful leer.

Carroll Borland, as Luna, compliments Lugosi's Count Mora perfectly. Her odd, angular beauty (made odder still by ghostly makeup and high-fashion grave shroud) is a magnet for the eyes. Utilizing exceptional physical acting, she contrasts her slow, measured movements — gliding through the mists almost without touching the ground — with a sudden ferocity as she abruptly descends on her victim or gives forth an animalistic hiss at her enemy.

Lionel Atwill is authoritative as the no-nonsense Inspector Neumann. With his quick speech and commanding presence, he has no tolerance for incompetence or foolishness. Early on, the cowardly Dr. Doskil makes excuses for why he waited until morning to examine Sir Karell's body: "It was night and I knew there was nothing I could do." The inspector mocks the timid physician with, "Oh, I see, you're no *moon flower*, you're a *morning glory*."

Atwill's sardonic tones hold nothing but contempt. Atwill plays the inspector as a man of decisive action, bringing an element of immediacy to the occasionally lethargic proceedings. Neumann even becomes terse with Professor Zelen. "Don't let's stand here *talking*!" interrupts Neumann, his impatience boiling over as Zelen launches into another of his lengthy vampire lectures.

Ivan Simpson as Jan, the nervous butler, and Leila Bennett as the simpleton maid both play their comedy relief roles straight, adding a further dose of conviction to the dire doings. Their fear seems genuine and they both suppress the urge to go over the top. Thus their comical antics carry an undercurrent of unaffected terror which enhances believability. We are amused at their frequently unwarranted panic, but at the same time are a bit uneasy at their fearful sincerity, so it seems as if there really *is* something to fear at every turn. Thus, simple comedy relief becomes amusement tinged with fear — an effective combination achieved in few films (the Bob Hope vehicles *The Cat and the Canary*, 1939, and *The Ghost Breakers*, 1940, being prime — and rare — examples).

LIABILITIES

Two things *mark* this *vampire* as sub-par and keep it from joining the (un)holy pantheon of bonafide Golden Age Horror Classics.

The first and most obvious liability is the cheat ending which few horror fans can forgive and no one can forget. The second devastating detraction comes in the form of an untethered Lionel Barrymore, He of the Impossibly Arching Eyebrows. Barrymore acts without restraint and seriously damages the tone of the picture. Director Tod Browning obviously left the actor to his own devices, which consisted largely of over-dramatic gestures, continual bowing and bobbing, and a slow yet oddly breathless delivery, as if he's constantly been taken by surprise. Barrymore is simply awful and one just cannot take him seriously. While the players around him display sincerity, Barrymore displays his acrobatic eyebrows. In one scene, Professor Zelen chases after the disturbed Baron Otto and calls to his retreating back: "I must speak to Inspector Neumann before he leaves." Barrymore raises the pitch of his voice and draws out the word "leeeeeaves" so that he sounds like a whining child on the verge of a tantrum. Then, turning his head, Zelen spots Irena standing at the open window. Suddenly, Barrymore's eyebrows shoot upwards, his hands come up convulsively, and his mouth pops open in a large O while he loudly sucks in his breath. Barrymore transforms what was supposed to be a look of consternation into the equivalent of a comic double-take.

The 56-year-old Oscar-winner obviously felt the picture was all hokum and played it accordingly. It takes sincerity to pull off lines like, "Sir Karell is dead. Miss Borotyn and her fiancé lie within the shadow of worse than death. The vampire is a pestilence that grows ... a corpse by day, at night it leaves its coffin to sustain its unnatural life on the blood of the living." Edward Van Sloan possessed such sincerity; Lionel Barrymore did not. Barrymore places untimely emphasis on his words and adopts an almost sing-song tone while delivering these lines, destroying the illusion of believability which is so vital to the scene.

Pressbook cover for *Mark of the Vampire* (1935). (Courtesy of Lynn Naron.)

roll Borland agreed that her co-star overdid it. "Lionel Barrymore is ... muttering and peering and scratching and bumping and making these noises so much of the time during the picture that they lost their value."

A solid script and good production values can offset even a bad Barrymore performance, as proven a year later by Browning himself with *The Devil-Doll* (though, in truth, Barrymore did give *half* of a good performance in that production). While possessing the proper production values, however, *Mark of the Vampire* tries to sell an outlandish plot more unbelievable than any *real* vampires. It is simply ludicrous to think that Inspector Neumann went to the expense and trouble of engaging three actors (and finding one who is the spitting image of the murder victim, no less!) to wander about in character, frightening the populace for an indeterminate length of time, hoping against hope that someone will peek in a window or drive by a country road and observe their ghoulish charade. "We all thought our vampire scheme was so simple, so certain of success," relates the disappointed Inspector Neumann. This convoluted scheme was anything *but* simple.

Professor Zelen is trying to convince others, but cannot seem to convince himself— or the audience. "It's only in its corpselike state that it can be destroyed," proclaims Barrymore, happily rocking backward and forward on his heels with one thumb hooked into his vest and a grin on his face. His lilting voice and smug tone belie the macabre, weighty nature of his words. Barrymore's overall demeanor does not help either. He alternates from overly-solicitous father figure (continually placing his hands and arms around whomever he talks to in a smarmy manner) to contemptuous schoolmaster (either talking down to his listeners as if they were second graders or dismissing them outright with, "bah, the fool!"). While showing great respect for the man, Car-

When the supernatural rug is pulled out from under the plot, logic seems to fly, bat-like, out the window. If the pseudo-vampires have no supernatural power after all, then how do Count Mora and Luna walk through a giant spider web without breaking its strands; and how does Luna fly on giant bat-wings down from the castle rafters; and why do doors open of their own accord to allow the vampires passage? Plus, if there truly were no vampires, then what accounts for the victim killed prior to Sir Karell's murder? At the inquest, Dr. Doskil testifies that earlier a peasant farmer had been found dead, "the corpse drained of blood. There were the same marks that I found on Sir Karell's throat."

Even if one chooses to overlook these lapses in logic, one cannot ignore the boredom engendered by the final reel. Once the deception is revealed, the picture's pace comes to a screeching halt as we are treated to a tedious anticlimax consisting of a reenactment of scenes we've already witnessed. All the carefully built up mood and horror have vanished and the only mystery left is just exactly *how* the baron drained Sir Karell's blood (a "hot glass over the wound creates a powerful suction")—not much to sustain the film's final ten minutes.

Carroll Borland remembered that Browning's ending, in which all the supernatural elements are explained away, incensed the actors—when they were finally allowed to read it. "You see," she explained, "Browning didn't give any of us the final scene, so neither Bela nor I knew exactly how it would end. We were playing it as straight horror—which is exactly what Browning wanted us to do, but when he gave us the ending everyone protested. We didn't like it at all, because we felt that *Mark of the Vampire* was a fine horror story in its own right. No one wanted to use the gimmick ending, but Browning insisted. We talked about rewriting the ending, and there was even a nefarious plot afoot to add still another twist: Barrymore, after solving the crime, would receive a telegram from the vaudeville artists he thought were already there, saying, 'Sorry we couldn't make it. Stop. Train delayed. Stop. Signed, The Flying Moras.' That would have established the realism of the story, but Browning was against it, so it ended with a gimmick."

Mark of the Vampire parallels *Dracula* in a number of ways. While possessing many of *Dracula*'s strongest attributes (eerie sets, Van Helsing-type character, Bela Lugosi as Count Drac—uh, Mora)[2], it also features *Dracula*'s weakest liability—Tod Browning as director.

Once again, Browning exhibits poor placement of his players. For instance, in one scene Professor Zelen hurries over to Irena to prevent her from going out to answer "the voice" she hears calling her. As Zelen approaches her, the entranced, weakened Irena is a good head taller than the professor because she stands on the bottom step of the stairway while he stands below her on the floor. Though Zelen is the authority figure and Irena the weakened invalid, their positioning places Irena in the place of power and has her tower over the professor. (Browning made this very same mistake in *Dracula*.)

When asked by this author what kind of a director Tod Browning was, Carroll Borland answered, "Nonexistent. I mean that almost literally. He would say to me, 'Get out there, walk down to the corner and you turn right,' and that's what I did. He expected us to know our jobs. He was used to working with stage people and he simply gave his stage directions and that was it.... He was a very charming, quiet gentleman who expected us to know our business.... His direction was very low-key."

Browning's "low-key" direction even extended to something so simple as names. Confusion reigns among his actors regarding the proper pronunciation of Professor Zelen's name. Donald Meek, as Dr. Doskil, calls him Professor *Zaylent*; to Lionel Atwill he is Professor *Zaylen*; and Elizabeth Allan refers to him as Professor *Zellen*.

Overall, Browning seemed to be striving to recreate his four-year-old success with *Dracula* while at the same time hedging his bets and laughing away the supernatural at the end by turning the horror into hokum (perhaps in reaction to the vicious reception of his previous, all-too-real horror picture, *Freaks*). To most modern viewers, he has performed the cinematic equivalent of shooting himself in the foot.

REVIEWS

Mark of the Vampire generally received good notices. *Variety*'s "Char" (May 8, 1935) called it "a blood curdler which deftly combines murder mystery, chiller and novelty elements for pretty good entertainment results." "'Vampire' is sufficiently eerie in background to satisfy the more demanding of the spine-shivering clan. At the same time it is unique murder mystery fare, admirably developed under careful scripting and direction, with the suspense neatly keyed and sustained. It also has a strong dash of novelty in that the characters suspected of being human vampires, rising from graves at night to attack, are actually a troupe of actors..." The reviewer also singled out both Lugosi and Caroll Borland for their atmospheric performances: "Bela Lugosi is particularly effective as one of the vampires.... [Caroll Borland] almost takes the picture away from Lugosi on the chiller end, her performance being exceptional. Miss Borland's makeup is tops."

Frank S. Nugent of *The New York Times* (May 3, 1935) noted that the film "manages, through use of every device seen in Dracula and one or two besides, to lay a sound foundation for childish nightmares. Even the adults in the audience may feel a bit skittery.... For all its inconsistencies, 'Mark of the Vampire' should catch the beholder's attention and hold it, through chills and thrills, right up to the moment when the mystery of the vampires of Visoka is solved. Like most good ghost stories, it's a lot of fun, even though you don't believe a word of it."

Mark of the Vampire was well received by both critics and audiences alike. So perhaps Browning's assessment of what moviegoers (of the time) truly wanted was not far off after all.

PRODUCTION NOTES

As director Tod Browning's "comeback film," *Vampires of Prague* (*Mark of the Vampire*'s original production title) was budgeted at a modest $208,000 with a 24-day shooting schedule. Despite two recent flops for MGM — *Freaks* (1932) and *Fast Workers* (1933) — the alcoholic, armadillo-loving Browning still commanded a hefty fee; he was paid $31,023 for *Mark of the Vampire* (compared, for instance, to Universal "Ace" James Whale, who earned $24,640 for *Bride of Frankenstein* shot the same year). Browning took *Mark of the Vampire* $96,000 over budget and ten days over schedule, though the film earned a modest net profit of $54,000 for MGM on its initial release.

The first cut of *Mark of the Vampire* ran 75 minutes, 14 minutes longer that the final release print. The trimmed footage includes a sequence with the old witch (seen at the film's beginning) chastising her albino daughter over a bubbling cauldron back at their tumble-down shack; the nervous Dr. Doskil treating a peasant woman and hurrying away from the farm before nightfall; a superfluous "comedy relief" sequence involving Porkpie, "the fat man," trying to teach the village children to dance for Irena's upcoming wedding; an introduction of the mysterious third vampire following the first entrance of Count Mora and Luna; and numerous (lengthy) lines of dialogue — cut, no doubt, to unburden the already dialogue-heavy film and keep the picture's pace from slowing to a crawl.

Heroine Elizabeth Allan, who (whether by coincidence or design) is made up to bear a striking resemblance to Helen Chandler in *Dracula*, played the female lead in 1932's *The Lodger* (in which she was menaced by a *real*—though human—monster). Bela Lugosi held a rather low opinion of his co-star, even forbidding his young protégée, Carroll Borland, from fraternizing with Ms. Allan. "[Bela] was sort of like a big uncle to me," admitted Ms. Borland. "He didn't want me to be around Elizabeth Allan because Elizabeth Allan had a bad reputation."

Carroll Borland had appeared with Lugosi in the stageplay, *Dracula*. The young actress answered the MGM casting call for *Mark* without revealing that she had previously worked with Lugosi (and in fact was his protégé). "Bela and I pulled one on them," recalled the actress in Robert Cremer's *Lugosi, the Man Behind the Cape*. "I called Bela and told him what part I was being considered for and said that they thought I wasn't tall enough. I was only 5'4" and Bela was well over 6'. I told him that I didn't want him to let on that we had worked together, because I wanted to get the part on my own and make them think that

Professor Zelen (Lionel Barrymore) examines the *Mark of the Vampire* on Irena's (Elizabeth Allan's) neck.

our mannerisms meshed perfectly because I was a terrific actress. He said, 'Okay, I won't let on that I have ever seen you before.' On the set the next day, Browning said, 'You know, Bela, this is not a dress call, so you don't have to get into costume. It really is unnecessary.' With that, Bela became flustered and said almost indignantly, 'I never play Dracula without my cape.' When we finally ran through some movements, everyone was amazed that I mirrored Lugosi's movements perfectly. Little did they know!"

While he cooperated with his young friend, Bela Lugosi tried to dissuade Carroll from playing in the film. "He was afraid I'd get typed," recalled Ms. Borland, "which I certainly did."

Lugosi designed his own costume for the part — a variation on his formal attire from *Dracula* (1931). Carroll Borland's voluminous flowing shroud, however, was created by the famous fashion designer Adrian. "I am sure that I was the first person in the world to have a *shroud* designed by Adrian," claimed the amused actress. Though beautiful in appearance, her costume was none-too-practical. "I had to have the thing cleaned after every day on the set," recalled Ms. Borland, "and Bela just broke up every time the shroud came back from the cleaners because it had shrunk. I swear that it was only half the original length by the time that the picture was finished. Bela started calling it my 'nightie' after a while."

The scene in which Luna (Carroll Borland) makes a dramatic 50-foot descent through the air (via piano wire) was intended to be shot with a stunt double. When her double became airsick from hanging so high above the stage while the shot was readied, however, Ms. Borland stepped in and eventually completed the stunt herself. By her account it was a long, expensive (about $10,000 worth) process. "They took two weeks to build a harness for me," the actress recalled to Forrest J Ackerman. "I had to be fitted in various places all over Hollywood. Other gowns had to be made that would fit over this harness, and these were Adrian designs, so each time it had to be redesigned. And then they built a track on the ceiling of a big sound stage ... they'd hoist me, and I hung up there for about three days, till they got this thing settled." The actress had more to do than just hang around, however, as she quickly (and painfully) learned. "Then they practiced for another couple of days landing me, and this was a nice, tricky thing. I had a bar that went from the back of my neck down to my ankles, and was strapped to this thing. And they had to learn to lower the tail-wires first, so I could land, and you know, talk about three-point landings ... I had a very raw, rubbed tummy before they finally got on to this thing! 'Cause they'd land me and Shhhh! — right across the floor ... it was covered in dry ice anyway." With the technical difficulties finally mastered, directorial deviations caused further delays. "Then, when they got all this done, after about a week's work," recalled Carroll Borland, "Tod Browning decided that he didn't like to have me fly this way; he wanted to have me fly that way, which meant rebuilding the track, and the track was in the wrong place, so they tore the wall out of the side of the sound stage and built it out!"

Lugosi received good notices for his sinister performance as Count Mora. Critic Edith Dietz wrote in the *Oakland Tribune*: "While his makeup is not nearly so horrifying as that of Karloff, he depends more upon a certain sinister, occult atmosphere, derived from a long cape, a scar, a menacing expression of countenance and his long, threatening hands. His effects are more mental than physical." The actor himself boasted "I was such a success in that movie that they gave me top billing instead of Lionel Barrymore" [wishful thinking on Lugosi's part, perhaps, for he was billed third, behind Barrymore *and* Elizabeth Allan][3].... "It made me a top star again."

One may wonder why Count Mora sports a bullet hole mark on his temple throughout the film. The explanation for this in Guy Endore's original scenario was that Count Mora murdered his daughter/lover Luna and then committed suicide by shooting himself in the head. All references to this incestuous relationship and sacrilegious act failed to make it into the final cut, however.

Makeup man Jack Dawn utilized an apprentice on this picture named William Tuttle. This assistant eventually became head of MGM's Makeup Department and went on to win a special Oscar for his brilliant work on *The Seven Faces of Dr. Lao* (1964). "I had a face that used to be considered so bizarre," remarked Carroll Borland, "so they sent me to the men's makeup department every morning; I never got near the women's makeup department.... Bill Tuttle was an apprentice so they sicced him on me. And Bill and I did a version of Lugosi's makeup on my face and it worked beautifully. That's how Bill got his start, making me up." Tuttle was still creating vampire makeup 44 years later, when he transformed George Hamilton into Dracula for *Love at First Bite* (1979).

Ms. Borland related an amusing incident that happened during the filming of *Mark of the Vampire*, illuminating just how effective their vampire makeup turned out to be. Lugosi's wife Lillian picked up both her husband and Carroll after a day's shooting. With both of them still in full ghoulish makeup, they drove off the MGM lot. "We pulled up to a light," remembered Carroll, "still looking like death warmed over, when a truck loaded with wooden crates filled with live chickens pulled up alongside. As the driver sat there waiting for the light to change, he glanced over casually at the car. He did a Harry Langdon triple take at both of us sitting in the car like tombstones and then drove off through the light. He lost control of the truck just a little way along the street and drove up onto a sloping lawn, causing all the crates of chickens to fall off the back of the truck. As we drove by, we saw an explosion of feathers. Luckily no one was injured, but it just goes to show you how Bela could affect people. The driver was spooked by it."

Director Tod Browning was reportedly a very demanding man to work for. According to William Tuttle, "The crew and I didn't like to work for director Tod Browning. We would try to escape being assigned to one of his productions because he would overwork us until we were ready to drop from exhaustion.... He was determined to get everything he could on film. If the crew did not do something right, Browning would grumble: 'Mr. Chaney would have done it better.' He was hard to please. I remember he gave the special effects men a hard time because they weren't working the mechanical bats properly." (From *The Films of Bela Lugosi*, by Richard Bojarski.)

Cinematographer James Wong Howe assessed Browning as "one of the old school who did not know much about the camera. He had the actors play 'at' the camera instead of moving around it, so the picture was very stagy, and he used cutting to get him through" (from *Hollywood Cameramen*, by Charles Higham).

An atmospheric publicity shot of Carroll Borland as the vampiric Luna.

Of the film's star, Howe only said, "Bela Lugosi was funny; he lived the part of the vampire."

Howe claimed that Rita Hayworth(!) was one of the young girls who tested for the part of Luna, the female vampire. Had she won the part, the career of Rita Cansino (at the time she was using her real name) might have taken a very different turn.

Innkeeper Michael Visaroff was no stranger

to vampiric doings. The Russian-born actor also ran the Transylvanian inn at which Renfield stopped in *Dracula* (1931). Even after four years, he was still trying to persuade travelers to stay indoors after dark and beware "the demons of the castle."

This was the second time director Tod Browning chose to remake one of his own silent films into a talkie version. In 1930, Browning remade *Outside the Law* (1921) and *Mark of the Vampire* is, of course, a sound remake of Browning's earlier *London After Midnight* (1927). Both the silent pictures were Lon Chaney vehicles.

NOTES

1. The shadow is distinctly recognizable as that of Count Mora, complete with short hair, cape, and large collar, though Irena curiously claims it was Luna who attacked her.

2. In fact, Universal threatened an injunction to block *Mark of the Vampire*'s release, claiming the picture was a thinly disguised *Dracula*. While stylistically this was true, MGM's legal department held up *Mark*'s trick ending as evidence of the two films' dissimilarity and won the argument.

3. To be fair, Lugosi *was* listed first in a *few* select ads — though most advertising material heralded Elizabeth Allan as the premier thespian attraction.

BRIDE OF FRANKENSTEIN
(1935; Universal)

Release Date: May 6, 1935
Running Time: 75 minutes
Director: James Whale
Producer: Carl Laemmle, Jr.
Screenplay: William Hurlbut
Adaptation: William Hurlbut, John Balderston (suggested by the original story written in 1816 by Mary Wollstonecraft Shelley)
Photography: John J. Mescall
Film Editor: Ted Kent
Art Director: Charles D. Hall
Photographic Effects: John P. Fulton
Musical Score: Franz Waxman

Orchestra Conductor: Bakalenikoff
Cast: Karloff (The Monster), Colin Clive (Henry Frankenstein), Valerie Hobson (Elizabeth), Ernest Thesiger (Doctor Pretorius), Elsa Lanchester (Mary Wollstonecraft Shelley), Gavin Gordon (Lord Byron), Douglas Walton (Percy Bysse Shelley), Una O'Connor (Minnie), E. E. Clive (Burgomaster), Lucien Prival (Butler), O. P. Heggie (Hermit), Dwight Frye (Karl), Reginald Barlow (Hans), Mary Gordon (Hans' Wife), Ann Darling (Shepherdess), Ted Billings (Ludwig).
*The Monster's Mate...?

*Elsa Lanchester

"Alone you have created a man. Now together, we will create — his mate." — Dr. Pretorius.

SYNOPSIS

"It was a dark and stormy night..." in the Villa Diodati on Lake Geneva in 1816 as Lord Byron, Percy Shelley, and Mary Wollstonecraft lounge in an elegant drawing room. The conversation comes round to Mary's story of *Frankenstein* and Byron briefly recalls moments from the first film. "I do think it a shame, Mary, to end your story so suddenly," remarks Shelley, to which Mary replies, "That wasn't the end at all. Would you like to hear what happened after that? ... Imagine yourself standing by the wreckage of the mill. The fire is dying down..." The scene dissolves to the burning wreckage of the old windmill. As the fire finally burns itself out, the mob of villagers wander back to their homes — all but Hans and his wife, the parents of poor little drowned Maria from the first film. Hans falls through the unstable wreckage into the underground millpond below. There in the waist-deep water, the monster lurks, scarred by the fire but still very much alive. The creature kills Hans and his wife and stalks off into the countryside.

Englishman Colin Clive and Boris Karloff break for tea during the filming of *Bride of Frankenstein* (1935). (Courtesy of Ted Okuda.)

After the villagers bear Henry's "corpse" home to Castle Frankenstein, Elizabeth finds that he's not dead after all. Recuperating under Elizabeth's tender care, Henry has a rather sinister late night visitor — Dr. Pretorius, Henry's former teacher who was "booted out" of the university "for knowing too much" (as the doctor puts it).

Pretorius shows Henry his own experiments in creating life — six miniature homunculi in glass jars — and entreats Henry to join forces with him. "Think what a *world*-astounding collaboration we should be, you and I — together."

Meanwhile, the monster, roaming the countryside, comes upon a young shepherdess.

When she catches sight of him, she loses her balance and topples into a stream. The monster rescues her but is shot by a passing hunter for his troubles. The hunter alerts the villagers and they pursue him through the forest. Capturing the creature, the burgomaster has him chained in a dungeon. The monster quickly breaks his chains, however, and escapes, going on a rampage of murder through the town. Fleeing to the safety of the forest, the monster stumbles upon the hut of an old blind hermit. The lonely man befriends the creature and even teaches him some rudimentary speech before their idyll is shattered by two hunters who run across the cabin. .

With the townspeople after him again, the monster takes refuge in an underground crypt, where he meets Pretorius (there to procure "materials" for the upcoming experiment). Pretorius befriends the monster. "I think you can be very useful," says the doctor, thinking aloud, "and you will add a little *force* to the argument if necessary."

When the vacillating Henry refuses to complete his part of the experiment (as expected), Pretorius has the monster kidnap Elizabeth and secure her in a mountain cave. "If you can bring her back," a beaten Henry tells Pretorius, "I'll do anything you want."

What Pretorius wants is to create a woman. "Male and female created He them," quotes Pretorius suggestively. With the aid of a murderer-cum-graverobber named Karl (who, unbeknownst to Henry, kills a young girl to obtain a fresh heart for the monster's "Bride"), the scientists set about constructing their woman. (Karl comes to a sticky end when the monster inexplicably stalks up to the roof and hurls the little ghoul to his death during the experiment's climax.) During a calamitous storm, Henry and Pretorius harness the lightning and imbue their new creature with life. As the two bask in their triumph, the monster enters, seeking his new "friend." This wild, grotesquely beautiful creature rejects the ugly monster, however, responding to his awkward affection with a piercing shriek. "She hate me — like others," declares the creature bitterly. In angry despair, the monster stalks forward, bent on destruction. "Look out," yells Henry, "the lever!" as the creature's hand brushes a large switch. "Get away from that lever," warns Pretorius, "you'll blow us all to atoms."

In the meantime, Elizabeth has slipped her bonds and raced to the laboratory. Bursting in, she entreats Henry to come away with her. "I can't leave them, I can't," protests Henry. "Yes, go!" urges the monster, "You *live*." Turning to Pretorius, he orders, "You stay. We *belong* dead." With a tear rolling down his misshapen cheek, the monster pulls the fateful lever which rocks the laboratory with explosions. As the stone building crumbles to its foundation, burying the monster, the Bride, and Pretorius under tons of rubble, Henry and Elizabeth embrace on a nearby hillside.

MEMORABLE MOMENT

Director James Whale and editor Ted Kent create one of the most exciting sequences from the Golden Age of Horror when they call down the bolts from Heaven to bring the Bride to life. The entire six-minute sequence (beginning when Henry and Pretorius remove the sheet covering the bandaged body and ending with Pretorius' feyly proud pronouncement, "The bride of Frankenstein" upon revealing the creature in all her grotesque glory) utilizes 130 edits. The height of the excitement comes when Henry hurries back down from the roof after releasing the metal kites to throw that all-important switch, setting a bizarre array of electrical devices in motion. Glass cylinders hum and glow, electricity jumps between metal rods, a bank of conductors sparks violently, a circular generator shoots electricity around its perimeter, rows of contacts emit small explosions and plumes of white smoke. The whole laboratory seems to come alive with sparks, light and smoke while a steady thump, thump, thump, like the beat of a cosmic heart, pounds underneath the crackling and booming of the machinery and the violent storm raging outside. Using 26 cuts in as many seconds, Whale and Kent suffuse the moment with a frantic energy. "The Special Effects and

Electrical Departments made up numerous meaningless gadgets, switches, indicators and the like," recalled Ted Kent (in *James Whale*, by James Curtis), "and Whale chose the most interesting.[1] In a sequence of this sort, where so many cuts are required, the burden of constructing it has to be the editor's. Procedure is slow and one has to feel his way through an abundance of film. The length of the cuts is important. The gadgets and paraphernalia interspersed with the subject must be interestingly used so as to avoid repetition. The effect is made to hold the audience's attention to the extent that they forget that they are watching nothing but film." Forget we do indeed, as we're caught up in the thrill of the moment.

ASSETS

Director James Whale uses *Bride of Frankenstein* as his personal showcase, bringing all his considerable directorial powers to bear on the bizarre story. (Whale himself even designed the Bride's distinctive beehive-gone-mad hairstyle.) A master of shadows and angles, Whale works with cinematographer John Mescall to create a brilliant collage of visual imagery and mood. Upon Pretorius' introduction, the gaunt doctor stalks into Henry's bedroom where the lighting casts a huge, forbidding shadow of the invader upon the wall. Whale then cuts to a medium close-up of the cadaverous Pretorius in which the shadows cast by the smoke rising from the room's huge fireplace ripple across the intruder and the wall behind, conjuring up a hellish, demonic connotation. Later in the same scene Pretorius proposes, "We must work together." At this, Henry leaps out of bed, protesting, "I'm through with it. I'll have no more to do with this *hellspawn*!" Agitated, Henry walks a few paces, wringing his hands. He stops abruptly, right in the spot where a shadow of the window's crosshatching forms a weblike pattern on the wall behind him. With Pretorius hovering at his shoulder like a great black spider, Henry seems caught in Pretorius' web, held fast by his own curiosity as the demented doctor talks of his own experiments.

In *Bride of Frankenstein*, Whale (alongside cinematographer John Mescall) raises the science of camera angles to a fine cinematic art. In preparation for the Great Experiment, Henry and Pretorius set everything in place. As they move their large gurneys of instruments and equipment, the titled camera makes it look as though they're struggling to push the cart *uphill*. The next shot shows them shoving another cart directly toward the camera, but this time the angle makes it appear as if the gurney is coming *downhill*, so that if they let go the surgical instruments would come crashing into the camera—into the viewer. With a strategic use of angles, Whale adds an unsettling feel to this key anticipatory moment.

Whale angles his camera to draw parallels between Frankenstein and Pretorius as well. In a close-up of Henry working in the lab, the angle makes it appear as if he looks upwards to the right, while in the next shot the camera tilts in the opposite direction to show Pretorius looking upwards to the *left* in a mirror image that emphasizes the two characters' connection. With this visual link established, Whale then cleverly makes a distinction between the two very different personalities in the next shot. With both of them now together, Whale has Pretorius standing behind some equipment, his face seen through the opening of a gigantic gear wheel, while Henry stands in the open. The dark wheel shape forms a barrier between the two men to underscore the difference and distance between the idealistic Henry and the sinister Pretorius. With this point made, Whale again jumps back into their dichotomous relationship by returning to the tilted angles mirroring one another as the two scientists take up the discussion of their work—and Henry's scientific zeal (their bond) surges again.

While *Frankenstein* harbors subtle subtexts beneath its gothic surface, *Bride of Frankenstein* simply *explodes* with thematic allusions involving individuality, sexuality, and religion.

Whale's insistence on including the Mary Shelley prologue and casting the same actress in the two roles of author and creature (i.e., creator and creation) is perhaps a specific

A study in sinister: Ernest Thesiger as Dr. Pretorius.

Just as the sensitive, high-strung Henry Frankenstein possesses a doppelganger in the monster, so the perceptive, elegant Mary Shelley possesses a secret double in the monstrous Bride.

No doubt James Whale identified more with Dr. Septimus Pretorius than any of his other characters. As Thesiger plays him, Pretorius' prissy manner and obvious disdain for women reflect a decidedly alternative sexuality. "My business with you, Baron," he says to Henry and looks toward Elizabeth, "is private." Thesiger's hawkish nose turns up in the air while his mouth nearly puckers with distaste when contemplating the negligee-wearing female. Later, when Pretorius' miniature King escapes his jar and runs over to the tiny Queen, Pretorius remarks acidly that "Even royal amours are a nuisance." Then, of course, there's a backhanded stab at conjugal bliss with Minnie's tearful observation, "Oh what a *terrible* wedding night."

reflection of the homosexual director's distrust of women, or, more generally, a revelation of the-monster-in-us-all. "James' feeling was that very pretty, sweet people, both men and women, had very wicked insides ... evil thoughts," remembered Elsa Lanchester (in *It's Alive!*, by Gregory William Mank). "These thoughts could be of dragons, they could be of monsters, they could be of Frankenstein's laboratory. So James wanted the same actress for both parts to show that the Bride of Frankenstein did, after all, come out of the sweet Mary Shelley's soul." Though Mary is afraid of storms and cannot stand the sight of blood, beneath the surface of "that bland and lovely brow" lies a soul that "conceived a Frankenstein." Mary, in fact, IS the monster.

Through Pretorius, Whale not only pokes fun at conventional sexuality but at religion as well. While much of this irreverence stems from William Hurlbut and John Balderston's witty script, Whale expands upon it with his (sometimes overdone) visual references and particularly with his direction of Ernest Thesiger. "I also have created life—" boasts Pretorius before adding disdainfully "— as we say, in God's own image" (a blasphemous remark which Pennsylvania's censor board demanded be excised). Later in the same scene, Pretorius toasts "To a new world of gods and monsters," obviously placing himself in the first category. If considering himself something of a deity,

Pretorius definitely leans more toward the devilish end of the spectrum than the holy. Upon revealing his Mephistophelian miniature creature to Henry, Pretorius observes, "There's a certain resemblance to me don't you think? Or do I flatter myself?"[2] He follows this up with, "Sometimes I have wondered whether life wouldn't be much more *amusing* if we were *all* devils, and no nonsense about *angels* and being *good.*" Pretorius urges Henry to "Leave the charnel house and follow the lead of *nature*—" adding with a slight sneer, "—or of God if you like your *bible* stories."

Even Thesiger's dress (supervised by Whale) carries a perverse religious inference. When first seen, Pretorius wears a black cloak and hat with a white collar visible only as a thin band encircling the neck—looking very much like a priest's collar. Of course, when he doffs his coat, we see that this collar is simply a regular ascotlike garment, but the first impression is unmistakable. Later, when Pretorius takes Henry to his lodgings, Thesiger sports (for no discernible reason) a black yarmulkelike skull cap. (Apparently, Whale aimed his sharp lampoons at the entire Judeo-Christian spectrum.)

Beyond such backhanded satirizing, the script features one passage which rationally and intelligently answers the age old caveat about men meddling in God's domain. When Henry goes on about finding the secret of life, Elizabeth admonishes, "Henry, don't say those things, don't *think* them. It's blasphemous and wicked. We are not *meant* to know those things." To this Henry answers, "It may be that I'm *intended* to know the secret of life. It may be part of the Divine Plan," giving an obvious and truly sensible response to such an irrational argument.

Ernest Thesiger steals every scene he's in—an amazing accomplishment considering he must frequently vie for attention with Karloff's monster. Universal originally announced Claude Rains for the role of Dr. Pretorius, but when Rains began work on *The Mystery of Edwin Drood* instead, Whale, in an inspired bit of casting, recruited his old friend Ernest Thesiger for the part. "I've had a terrible lesson," whines Henry Frankenstein, to which Pretorius mocks, "That is *sad,* very *sad.*" Thesiger's slight sneer and subtle emphasis on "sad," his tilt of the head and smug mouth all make it obvious how truly sad he feels. When Pretorius makes his macabre toast "to a new world of gods and monsters," Thesiger's eyes widen slightly and his mouth momentarily twists into an off-kilter grin before he gives a dismissive half-laugh and returns to his precise speech and pinched expression, allowing us a glimpse of the subtle madness lurking beneath his cultured exterior. Alone in a crypt, he later toasts, "I give you the monster," to a skull he's set up on a coffin. Thesiger's mirthless, unwholesome laughter at his macabre joke becomes truly disturbing, though it soon pales in perversity to the actor's smirking leer when the monster joins him and requests, "Woman—friend—*wife.*"

John Mescall's lighting augments Thesiger's unwholesome demeanor, emphasizing the actor's sharp, pinched features to conjure up images of a leering death's head. Low-key lighting sets his eyes so deeply in shadow that they appear to be empty sockets. At times, Pretorius looks even more cadaverous than the monster, whose original corpselike appearance has given way to a softer, fleshier grotesqueness lacking the hollow cheeks and dark, deep-set eyes seen in the first film.

For *Bride,* Colin Clive's Henry Frankenstein has become a sniveling, self-pitying wretch who never shows any backbone. He exhibits little of the drive and sheer force of will which led him to create the monster in the first place, and his helpless whining about not hearing from Elizabeth or not being able to work with the monster around does little to engender sympathy. While on the surface this may seem a liability, it serves to increase the focus on the monster and makes of Henry's creation a more sympathetic figure by contrast. Thus, our allegiance has shifted from Henry (with whom we sided in the first *Frankenstein*) to the monster.

Bride of Frankenstein gives Boris Karloff more range than he had in the original, allowing the full pathos of the monster's pitiable existence to shine forth. The monster has now outgrown his initial innocence in the first film and become "wise in his generation." Seeing his hideous reflection in a pool, Karloff's face hardens and anger flares in his eyes as he growls and strikes the water to erase the hated image. He now knows that it is his ghastly appearance which separates him from the world of men. Even so, he still approaches people with a hopeful, pleading demeanor—only to be spurned and shot at. "I love dead, hate living," the monster finally admits to Pretorius with a dull sadness. Despite this, Karloff still manages to evince a childlike joy when he finally does find a friend (the blind hermit) and even compassion for his new friend's loneliness (comforting the crying man with an awkward pat and a tear of his own). When the world once more intrudes on this peaceful idyll in the form of two hunters, the monster's bearing changes abruptly. Karloff rises ominously and growls low, his face set in an expression of chilling menace. Then, after the hunters have removed the hermit and the hut has caught fire, Karloff stumbles through the door with his pleading hands held out, calling "friend" in a soft, heartbreaking voice. Though Karloff often complained of the decision to have the monster speak, the few words he utters add much to the character, and Karloff's insightful delivery makes the most of them. When confronting his creator for the first time, Karloff growls, "Frank-en-stein," his guttural voice deep and hard, edged by the obvious hatred he feels in that single word. Just as he does with his brilliant pantomimic gestures and body language, Karloff uses his few brief lines to express a full range of emotion, from joy to anger, from heartfelt pain to fleeting pleasure.

Given $37,500 to work with, art director Charles D. Hall created a series of detailed sets to match and surpass even those of *Frankenstein*. While his interiors fit the story perfectly, it is actually his *exteriors* for this studio-bound production which create the most impact on tone and mood. The first time the monster enters the woods, he walks through a sunlit forest filled with lush underbrush, a placid stream, and contented sheep. Seeking only companionship, the monster is attacked in this beautiful setting, once more rejected by humanity despite his efforts to save a young girl from drowning (obviously having learned a lesson from his fateful meeting with little Maria in the first film). When next we see the monster, the bloodthirsty villagers are hot on his trail. The woods have changed, however, and the monster flees through an almost surreal landscape of stark, limbless tree trunks, jutting rocks, and dark, denuded forest floor. The change in environment reflects the change in the monster—from hopeful innocent to beleaguered prey.

"It was a 'super horror' movie and demanded hauntingly eerie, weird and different music," observed composer Franz Waxman, whose music for *Bride* adds immeasurably to the picture's overall success by brilliantly evoking a scene's mood. When the villagers carry Henry's "corpse" home, a slow rhythmic dirge conjures up images of a funeral march. For the monster's first appearance, ominous drums build as the creature's hand and arm move into view, coalescing into the harsh, five-note "Monster Theme" when the creature steps full into the frame. Waxman's magnificent score brilliantly utilized leitmotifs to evoke the personalities and mood of key characters such as the monster, Pretorius, and the Bride. So effective was the music that it became a keynote of Universal's stock library, and was reused for serials such as *Flash Gordon*, *Buck Rogers*, and *Radio Patrol*. The score later became the object of a lawsuit when Waxman sued Oscar Hammerstein for stealing his wonderful "Wedding Theme" for the song "Bali Ha'i" in *South Pacific*. Waxman was awarded a substantial settlement.

LIABILITIES

Long thought of as the absolute pinnacle of the Golden Age of Horror, *Bride of Frankenstein* slips just a bit under close scrutiny.

As Elizabeth, the young (aged 17) and inexperienced Valerie Hobson comes off as silly and flighty with vapid comments like, "It's the *devil* that prompts you," and her bizarre fit when she imagines "a strange apparition ... a

Dr. Pretorius exhibits his tiny creations. Left to right: Queen (Joan Woodbury), Mermaid (Josephine McKim), Devil (Peter Shaw), Baby (Billy Barty), Ballerina (Kansas DeForrest), Bishop (Norman Ainsley), King (Arthur S. Byron).

figure like death" that reduces her to weeping hysteria (sounding more like *laughter* than crying). Why such a brilliant scientist as Henry Frankenstein would put up with such nonsensical pabulum is a wonder.

Why does the monster stalk up to the laboratory roof and, unprovoked, arbitrarily murder Karl (Dwight Frye), who's just then engaged in the very process of bringing about the monster's one desire? Obviously, the Production Code could not allow Karl to go unpunished for his murderous deeds (having killed a woman to provide a needed heart), but to have the monster kill him at that moment makes little sense and becomes a jarring incongruity. Luckily, the character of Karl is so vile that we feel no pity for him and so his murder does not damage our sympathy for the monster. But it does generate some confusion as to his motivations — and his intelligence.

In 1935, James Whale was Universal's own "creative genius." With Junior Laemmle as the front office "Crown Prince," Whale was the undisputed "King" of the studio's directors. As such, he very nearly received carte blanche to do anything he wanted, and the studio brass took a hands-off policy towards their ace filmmaker. This resulted in a film both brilliant in its eccentricities and outrageous in its excesses. Of Whale's four fabulous Golden Age horrors (*Frankenstein*, *The Old Dark House*, *The Invisible Man*, and *Bride of Frankenstein*), *Bride* is the most self-indulgent.

Una O'Connor's shrieking harpy marks James Whale's most significant lapse in judgment, for she ruins nearly every scene she's in. At the monster's first appearance after climbing from the millpond, he stalks up behind Minnie (O'Connor). When she turns and sees him, O'Connor gives a long, noisy, comical buildup to her panicked shriek, her body and face twisting and turning as her screech builds. Throughout her lengthy, overplayed antics, the monster simply stands there like a buffoon until she finally scurries off. One cannot take *her* seriously so why should we feel any different about the monster standing stupidly beside her. Later, when Henry's "corpse" moves, O'Connor lets out a long, ear-piercing shriek and *screams* out, "Look, milady, he's alive!!" in a painful parody of Henry's own excited observation from the first film. O'Connor's performance is better suited to one of the later "Carry On" pictures than to a classic horror tale. When the burgomaster, fed up with her wretched caterwauling, finally tells her "Oh, shut up," we can only applaud. O'Connor's noisy harridan seems to be everywhere, continually popping up to get in her shrewish two cents worth. She's there at the monster's capture, then among the gawkers at the dungeon; she's there at the creature's escape (and even bullies a man into standing his ground — only to get his head bashed in for his effort), and it is O'Connor who discovers the monster's victims, the Neumanns. She seems to dog the monster like some screeching bloodhound. Fortunately, after the first 30 minutes, she largely disappears from the film. Obviously, Whale held a special fondness for Una O'Connor (he even remembered her in his will). "She amused James very much," Gloria Stuart (who worked with both O'Connor and Whale on *The Invisible Man*) told this author in 1993. "He just loved her work and everything she did; she was very creative. We were all so impressed and frightened of Whale that we *always* knew our lines and we *always* did what we were told; we didn't question him at all. But Una was flying all over the set and so creative it was wonderful." For *Bride of Frankenstein*, however, Whale's indulgence of this "creativity" proved more painful than "wonderful."

Technically, the film is a brilliant collage of cinematic techniques, and James Whale flexes his full visual genius throughout the picture; but Whale also loads it down with heavy-handed religious symbolism — often to no great purpose. Whale makes his monster a Christ icon, trussing him up in a crucifixion pose (with an obvious look of suffering on his face as the Romans — villagers — jeer and throw stones), having him dine on bread and wine (the Sacrament), or lingering on a crucifix (with Christ attached) on the wall above the monster during a prolonged fadeout. The heavy-handed mockery becomes more of a distraction than revelation. Rather than the symbolism making a point or underscoring some irony, it all seems a rather snide conceit. Through this misplaced emphasis, Whale ("who had no religious convictions of any kind"[3]) simply indulges his own prejudices rather than sharing any insight or subtle context with the viewer.

The scene with Pretorius' tiny creations veers so wildly into near-juvenile fantasy it becomes painfully ludicrous and jars with the mature nature of the rest of the picture. Pretorius dresses up his Lilliputian creations in silly costumes — the Henry the Eighth–styled "King" (an in-joke referring to Elsa Lanchester's husband, Charles Laughton, who played the title role in 1933's *The Private Life of Henry VIII*) complete with turkey drumstick, a queen, an archbishop (waving his finger and sternly lecturing the amorous king), a pirouetting ballerina in tutu, a mermaid, and "the very devil." To complete the ridiculous picture, the creatures rave in high-pitched gerbil-like squeaks and carry on as if they truly *were* a king, queen, or archbishop. While John Fulton provides flawless effects (far superior to the uneven matting techniques seen a year later in *The Devil-Doll*, for instance), one simply cannot take it seriously. The silly sequence becomes so farcical it detracts from the story itself. "But this isn't science," observes Henry, disturbed, "It's more like black magic," — or, more like a farcical fantasy.

Variety's review of *Frankenstein* on December 8, 1931, observed that, "The feeling of horror is not once let go past the point at which it inspires disbelief, where out of excess it would create a feeling of make-believe." In *Bride*, Whale races past that point like a charging thoroughbred. Where *Frankenstein* creates its own harsh — and believable — reality, *Bride* concocts a near-comedic fairy-tale ambiance.

The monster's mad
And I'm glad

And I know what'll please him—
A gift divine
From Frankenstein
A little mate to squeeze him!

This sample ditty appearing in the film's pressbook to promote a *Bride of Frankenstein* "Jingle Contest" may well echo James Whale's whimsical attitude toward his new horror project. "*The [Bride] of Frankenstein* was approached by its director as a 'hoot,'" wrote Whale biographer James Curtis. By including a plethora of parodic touches, Whale seems to be continually winking at the audience. Even the director's insistence on the Mary Shelley prologue (which editor Ted Kent advised be cut completely) reinforces the idea that this is just a fanciful story after all. Add such bizarre touches as Una O'Connor's shrewish Minnie and Dr. Pretorius' miniature goblins and the break from reality is complete. Where *Frankenstein* brings a shudder and a tear, *Bride* elicits a smile and a sneer.

"The whole of the theatre, both stage and screen, is unreal," stated Whale in the *Bride of Frankenstein* pressbook, "and if for an hour and a half the audience can be transported into a strange atmosphere in which unnatural things happen—but appear to happen naturally and believably—the object of the film producer is accomplished." On *Bride of Frankenstein*, Whale apparently abandoned his self-professed "object."

"Many people like *The Bride of Frankenstein* better than the first one," observed the monster himself, Boris Karloff (in *Movie Monsters #3*), a few years before his death, "but I don't know. I've always preferred the original film. In that picture the monster didn't speak, you remember. But when we made the sequel about the bride, they had me speaking all sorts of dialogue. Time and time again I argued that the monster shouldn't speak. If he spoke, he would seem too much more human, I thought. But the director won his argument." Indeed he did, though it's not so much the monster's speech that detracts from the film but the overplayed parody.

While *Bride* possesses touches of undeniable brilliance and moments of exquisite excitement and depth, it also sports several seriously marring liabilities which pull the audience away from the story, reminding the viewer that, indeed, this gothic fairy tale is simply a movie. As a directorial showcase, *Bride* outstrips its progenitor, but as a horror film it comes in a definite second.

Thankfully, *Bride*'s liabilities come predominantly during the picture's first third (in a reversal of *Dracula*'s strong opening and flagging end). Once past the regrettable homunculi sequence, *Bride* finally becomes the near-flawless masterpiece of its vaunted reputation.

REVIEWS

The Hollywood Reporter (April 6, 1935), after viewing a special preview screening, called the 92-minute film "one of the finest productions that has come off the Universal lot for many a day. Mounted extravagantly, gorgeously photographed, excellently cast..." Despite laudatory reviews like this one, 17 minutes were shorn from the picture before its official release on May 6.

The New York Times (May 11, 1935): "...Mr. Karloff is so splendid in the role that all one can say is 'he is the Monster.' James Whale ... has done another excellent job; the settings, photography, and the make-up ... contribute their important elements to a first-rate horror film." The reviewer also expressed his wish that "the Monster should become an institution, like Charlie Chan"—a wish granted in the six successive sequels (and beyond).

Variety (May 15, 1935): "And now Frankenstein's monster has a bride and Universal has another money-maker. While there may be a few things about this film to quibble about, the net total is the same—an imaginative and outstanding film sure to rake in the shekels.... And, of course, all due credit to James Whale for welding the component parts into a homogeneous whole."

PRODUCTION NOTES

Universal planned *The Return of Franken-*

"Friend?" (*Bride of Frankenstein*, 1935).

stein, a sequel to their 1931 blockbuster, as early as the summer of 1933, with James Whale to direct and Karloff (naturally) to star. Whale, however, resisted the idea, telling his friend R. C. Sherriff (who was scripting *The Invisible Man* at the time), "If they score a hit with a picture they always want to do it again. They've got a perfectly sound commercial reason. *Frankenstein* was a gold-mine at the box office, and a sequel to it is bound to win, however rotten it is. They've had a script made for a sequel and it stinks to heaven. In any case I squeezed the idea dry on the original picture, and never want to work on it again" (from *No Leading Lady* by R. C. Sherriff). Whale avoided the dreaded sequel assignment by seizing upon Sherriff's just-completed script for *The Invisible Man*. "I'm not just using your script as a way of getting out of this horrible *Frankenstein* sequel," the director assured his friend. "It's a lovely job, and I'd do it if I had a hundred scripts to choose from."

The Laemmles then passed the Frankenstein project on to German director Kurt Neumann, but the production stalled due to Universal's fiscal difficulties (the studio saw red that year to the tune of over one million dollars). At one point, Bela Lugosi's name became entangled with the project (along with Karloff's). A press notice of 1933 reported that Lugosi's "current role is opposite Karloff in *The Black Cat*. Following this it was planned to co-star the two in Robert Louis Stevenson's *The Suicide Club*[4] and *The Return of Frankenstein*."

In early 1934, Whale proposed to direct *A Trip to Mars* (a story in which the leader of an underground Martian civilization captures

Earth astronauts) from a script by his friend R. C. Sherriff. Set to star Boris Karloff, it was to begin as soon as that actor finished up *The Black Cat*. The project failed to take off (much less make it to the Red Planet) due, according to Whale's biographer, James Curtis, to Carl Laemmle, Sr.'s objections over the script and its proposed costs. Finally, Whale agreed to be the director of the Frankenstein sequel and thereupon sat down with John Balderston to shape and refine playwright William Hurlbut's ("Lilies of the Field") initial draft into the Swiftian screenplay that became *Bride of Frankenstein*.

Budgeted at $293,750 (just $2,000 more than *Frankenstein*'s final cost), Whale began filming *The Return of Frankenstein* (the picture's working title) on January 2, 1935, on a 36-day shooting schedule. The director's meticulous methods, however, took the picture ten days over schedule and more than $100,000 over budget. The final cost was $397,023.

Just as initially intended for the original *Frankenstein*, the monster's creator was to die at the end of the sequel (along with Elizabeth, who was banging at the door trying to get in when the explosion erupts). At the last minute, however, Universal opted to let the scientist live, and Whale reshot scenes of Henry fleeing with Elizabeth to the safety of a nearby hillside. The climactic laboratory destruction sequence was too expensive to redo, however, and if one looks closely, one can still see Henry against the wall at the left of the screen in longshot as the building comes crashing down.

Bride of Frankenstein was trimmed of 17 minutes between its preview screenings and general release. The deleted scenes include the monster's murder of the burgomaster (one shot of which shows up among the flashbacks from *Frankenstein* seen at the film's beginning!), an entire subplot involving Karl (Dwight Frye) murdering his wealthy aunt and uncle and blaming the monster, and yet another of Pretorius' tiny homunculi — a baby (played by midget actor Billy Barty) described in the script as "already twice as big as the Queen, and looking as if it might develop into a Boris Karloff" ("I think this Baby will grow into something worth watching," quips Pretorius at the in-joke).

"Who will be the Bride of Frankenstein? Who will *dare*?" asked Universal's publicity department. Among the names bandied about in the press were Arletta Duncan (one of Mae Clarke's bridesmaids from *Frankenstein*) and Brigette Helm (of *Metropolis* [1926] fame). Publicity-generating prognostications aside, James Whale had his mind set on an elfin actress he had worked with during his early days on the London stage — Elsa Lanchester. "I have an odd face," the actress told Greg Mank in *It's Alive*, "and James was absolutely dead set that my face was the face for the Bride of Frankenstein!" Not only did Whale envision Ms. Lanchester in the role of the monster's mate, but as Mary Shelley as well. "James Whale in his production of *Bride of Frankenstein* did deliberately use me to play both 'Mary Shelley' and the monster's bride," wrote the actress in a letter to *Life* magazine (April 5, 1968), "because he wanted to tell that Mary Shelley indeed had something in common with the dreadful creature of her imagination." While Ms. Lanchester received credit for playing Mary, the actress gamely went along with the studio's ploy of billing "The Monster's Mate" with a "?" in the opening and closing credits.

Though top-billed in the original, Colin Clive had to settle for second billing here — the top position going to one of Universal's biggest stars of 1934 and 1935, Boris Karloff. The actor was enjoying so much popularity and prestige at the time that Universal billed him by surname only, simply as "KARLOFF" (an honor awarded to only a handful of actors over the years). The monster surpassed his creator in terms of salary as well—KARLOFF received $2,500 a week while Colin Clive earned $1,500 weekly.

Nominated for Best Sound Recording (but losing to MGM's *Naughty Marietta*), *Bride of Frankenstein* became the only entry in Universal's Frankenstein series to rate an Academy Award nomination.

NOTES

1. Kenneth Strickfaden spent an additional $2,000 on these "meaningless gadgets, switches, and indicators" which he revamped and expanded from the original *Frankenstein* laboratory equipment.

2. Indeed there was, for this "little devil" was played by Peter Shaw, Ernest Thesiger's double (though the *Bride* pressbook erroneously reported that Thesiger himself donned the costume).

3. James Curtis writing in *James Whale*.

4. Though this proposed Karloff/Lugosi pairing failed to materialize, MGM filmed an adaptation of Stevenson's story in 1936 as *Trouble for Two*.

WEREWOLF OF LONDON
(1935; Universal)

Release Date: May 9, 1935
Running Time: 75 minutes
Director: Stuart Walker
Executive Producer: Stanley Bergerman
Associate Producer: Robert Harris
Screenplay: John Colton
Original Story: Robert Harris
Photography: Charles Stumar
Art Director: Albert S. D'Agostino
Editor: Russell Schoengarth
Musical Score: Karl Hajos
Musical Supervision: Gilbert Kurland
Special Effects: John P. Fulton
Cast: Henry Hull (Dr. Glendon), Warner Oland (Dr. Yogami), Valerie Hobson (Lisa Glendon), Lester Matthews (Paul Ames), Lawrence Grant (Sir Thomas Forsythe), Spring Byington (Miss Ettie Coombes), Clark Williams (Hugh Renwick), J. M. Kerrigan (Hawkins), Charlotte Granville (Lady Forsythe), Ethel Griffies (Mrs. Whack), Zeffie Tilbury (Mrs. Moncaster), Jeanne Bartlett (Daisey).

"The werewolf is neither man nor wolf, but a *satanic* creature with the worst qualities of both."—Dr. Yogami.

SYNOPSIS

British botanist Dr. Wilfred Glendon journeys to Tibet in search of the rare flower *mariphaisa lumina lupina*, whose blossoms bloom only by the light of the moon. Abandoned by his superstitious native bearers, Glendon presses into a forbidden mountain valley. Glendon's perseverance is rewarded, but as he begins to dig up his trophy he is attacked by a strange creature—neither man nor wolf but part of each. Glendon manages to stab the creature, sending it scurrying away with a howl of pain, but not before the beast has bitten him on the arm.

Back in England, Glendon has little success in making the rare specimen bloom in his laboratory. At a gathering of the Botanical Society, he meets Dr. Yogami, who shows a keen interest in the plant. Yogami tells of the plant's connection with what he calls "werewolfery." "In modern London today, at this very moment there are two cases of werewolfery known to me," he tells the incredulous Glendon. "These men are doomed but for this flower." According to Yogami, the blossom of the mariphaisa is the only cure for lycanthropy.

Later on, Glendon finally makes the flower bloom—and none-too-soon, for just then he notices to his horror that his hand is darkening and sprouting hair. Remembering Yogami's words, he breaks off one of the flowers and rubs the sap from it onto his hand. It works and his hand returns to normal.

Yogami returns and pleads for one of the blossoms, since he was the creature in Tibet, himself searching for the precious plant. "Two blossoms of the mariphaisa flower in there would save two souls tonight," Yogami tells Glendon. Despite his recent "hair-raising" experience, Glendon will not believe Yogami's "superstition" and refuses the request (though he is inwardly alarmed to learn that the plant is *not* a cure, but merely "an antidote, effective only for a few hours"). Yogami leaves him with this warning: "The werewolf instinctively seeks to *kill* the thing it loves best."

That night, Glendon transforms completely, though he still retains the power of reason. Going to his lab for the flower, he discovers that the two remaining blooms have been stolen. Thinking of his wife Lisa (the "thing he loves best"), the werewolf dons his hat and coat and goes out after her. (She has innocently gone to a party with her former beau, Paul, since Glendon has been shamefully neglecting her.) Not finding Lisa, the werewolf murders a young girl on the street.

The next day, Glendon feels intense remorse over what he's done and determines to distance himself from Lisa, since the one remaining mariphaisa bud will not be ready by dark. Taking a dingy room in the seedy Whitechapel district, he prays that the transformation will not happen again. It does and the werewolf commits another murder.

Returning to London, the miserable Glendon discovers that the stubborn mariphaisa *still* refuses to bloom. This time he goes to his wife's old family estate (now deserted except for a caretaker) and has himself locked in a tower room.

Lisa, out for a moonlight drive with Paul, unfortunately decides to visit the old homestead. The now-transformed Glendon, spying them together, furiously breaks the bars on the window. When the werewolf attacks Lisa, Paul stuns him with a stick and the pair escape.

Paul goes to Scotland Yard and informs them that "there was something grotesquely familiar about it. Then it suddenly struck me — it was Wilfred Glendon." The inspector is not convinced and Paul's case is not helped when the inspector learns of yet another "werewolf" murder 150 miles away from Paul's attack. Of course, this was the handiwork of Yogami — the second werewolf.

Paul and the inspector go to the murder scene which turns out to be Yogami's hotel room. Finding the spent mariphaisa blooms Yogami had stolen, Paul makes the connection and the search is on for both Yogami and Glendon.

Avoiding the police, both men make it back to Glendon's laboratory just as the plant's final bud blooms. While Glendon's back is turned, Yogami sneaks in and snatches up the precious blossom, using it on himself. The two men struggle and the untreated Glendon transforms. No match for the ferocity of the werewolf, Yogami is killed.

Now the werewolf sets his sights on Lisa. Paul and the inspector finally arrive, and just as the werewolf has Lisa cornered, the inspector shoots him. Collapsing to the floor, the lucid lycanthrope speaks: "Thanks, thanks for the bullet. It was the only way. In a few moments now I shall know why all of this had to be. Lisa, good-bye — good-bye Lisa. I'm sorry I couldn't have made you happier." He dies and transforms back to his human appearance.

MEMORABLE MOMENTS

The first transformation, though brief, is a moment of sheer beauty and drama, as well as exquisite technical precision. Sitting in his study, Glendon looks at his hands as they grow dark and hairy. Rushing out of the room in consternation, he glances at his hands again and covers his face in anguish. Regaining his composure, he moves through the garden towards his laboratory, passing behind a pillar. The camera moves with him, and when Glendon steps from behind the pillar he has changed. His face is now hairier, more bestial, and his ears are pointed. With a look of tortured confusion he continues walking and passes behind a second pillar. When he emerges his face has become the full satanic visage of a werewolf. Accomplished in seemingly one continuous, fluid camera movement, the effect is striking. John P. Fulton's near-flawless effects work affords the scene an elegant simplicity, while the visual movement emphasizes and heightens the metamorphosis, creating a more intense impact than any static transformation.[1]

A brief but memorable moment comes during the climactic fight between the werewolf Glendon and the human Yogami. After the werewolf has overcome Yogami, the camera focuses in on the lycanthrope. For a few seconds his devilishly feline visage fills the

A half-sheet poster giving fair warning to all "hysterical women" watching *Werewolf of London* (1935).

screen as it ever-so-slowly moves closer to the camera. One has a chance to study the frightening countenance, noticing the pointed ears, the wicked creases around the hollowed eyes, the stained (bloody?) lower fangs protruding upwards from the bestial mouth. Suddenly the eyes widen, the chin and fangs are thrust forward, and from the bestial mouth comes a sharp half bark/half growl. This sudden change in expression occurs in a split second and is startling.

ASSETS

As the enigmatic Dr. Yogami, Warner Oland comes off quite sympathetic as a man trying to spare Glendon the torment he himself has endured (as well as attempting to prevent an epidemic of lycanthropy from overrunning London). Reading of the brutal murders committed by his counterpart, Oland demonstrates genuine sorrow and remorse for what he has brought about (for it was he who attacked and infected the now-rampaging Glendon). Yet Yogami's motives are not altogether altruistic, for he desperately wants the antidote for himself and in the end is not above sacrificing Glendon to get it. This adds complexity to Yogami's character. While distanced from the tragedy he can demonstrate concern and sympathy (even going so far as informing the police of what is happening, though of course they put no stock in his claim), but when the terror becomes personal, and his own individual demon is involved, he turns cold and willing to forfeit his fellow unfortunate.

The makeup, while not as hairy and bestial as Lon Chaney, Jr.'s in *The Wolf Man*, has a satanic look to it which makes it equally effective, if not moreso. The sharp widow's peak, the pointed ears, and the jutting fangs suggest a demon more than a wolf (unlike Chaney's more straightforwardly hirsute version). While *The Wolf Man* may appear more savage, the werewolf of London is definitely the more evil-looking of the two. Makeup man Jack Pierce deserves high praise, particularly considering the difficulties posed by a less-than-cooperative Henry Hull, who reportedly objected to an earlier hairier design, so Pierce had to come up with this more streamlined — and satanic — version.

The direction is adequate — but only just, with Walker's straightforward approach revealing little inspiration. Technically, the picture has merit, with effective lighting, particularly in the early Tibetan sequence, full of menacing shadows, and in the later low-key illumination of Hull's werewolf visage, which enhances its satanic quality. There are some wonderful sets, such as Glendon's private botanical garden, genteel and pleasant on the surface — all glass partitions and orderly rows of leafy greens — which also contains its fair share of savagery in the form of a carnivorous frog-eating plant and a gigantic *Madagascar carnalia* waving its octopuslike tendrils in hope of snatching some unwary creature.[2] This private Garden of Eden can almost be seen as a metaphor for Glendon's own bipolar condition — civilized and proper on the outside, but deadly and savage under the surface.

LIABILITIES

Werewolf of London blunders into the same pitfall that traps many horror pictures from the Golden Age — Comedy Relief (with a capital C and not much relief). The unfunny comedic scenes between two drunken old ladies at the Whitechapel lodging house go on far too long to do anything but deaden the pace of an already slow picture. After Glendon transforms in his dingy upstairs room and hurls himself out the window, the tension is thick and expectations are high. This horrific anticipation is promptly deflated, however, by a full minute and a half of Mrs. Whack and Mrs. Moncaster hitting each other over the head for a drink of gin. Then, after a brief incident at the zoo (in which the werewolf claims his second victim), we are "treated" to yet another two minutes of if-you-saw-what-I-saw with the two drunken sots. Ideally, comedy relief in a horror picture relieves tension at just the right moment and so lets the film build again and lead up to yet *another* horrific moment. This creates a balance and keeps the audience moving back and forth between the tension of fright and the release of laughter. Unfortunately, this is such a difficult balance to achieve and maintain that it takes both a skilled screenwriter and an insightful director to find it. This picture possessed neither. It is so much easier to simply insert a comedy scene periodically than actually plan out the peaks and valleys, and the *Werewolf of London* lopes lethargically down this path of least resistance.

When one sees a werewolf don a cape and cap to go out "on the town" (as the transformed Glendon does on several occasions), the first response is to chuckle rather than shiver. While a bestial werewolf wearing a hat and slinking about the streets with a collar pulled up to disguise his hairy countenance seems a little ridiculous now, it must be remembered that in the pre–*Wolf Man* (1941) days there was no precedent (and no cliché) yet established for werewolf behavior. It was not until six years later that *The Wolf Man* revealed what a snarling, savage brute a werewolf truly is, and (with the various sequels and variations over the years) established the lycanthropes' credo in cinematic mythology. So, while one might wish for a bit more snarl and savagery from Hull's too-civilized werewolf and feel disappointment at how easily the characters chase off the rampaging lycanthrope with a knife or a big stick, one cannot come down too hard on this first of all werewolves. Unfortunately, as time has passed and this film has been *sur*passed by its progeny, *Werewolf of London* has dated badly. One cannot critique in a vacuum and as such this original comes up short in the monster department.

It is especially lamentable that the two opposing werewolves never meet in lycanthropic form — *that* would have been a climactic fight worth seeing. As it is, the final confrontation between the werewolf Glendon and the human Yogami is a less-than-satisfying exhibition. Even more disappointing is the fact that so little is made of the potential soul-wrenching conflict between the two damned men, each struggling for some brief salvation via the magical plant. Despite ample opportunity for tragic confrontation, the solitary instance consists of one brief line at the very end, when Glendon yells accusingly at Yogami: "You brought this on me!"

Apart from Warner Oland, the general

Henry Hull as the *Werewolf of London* (1935), the first (and only) werewolf of the decade. Jack Pierce designed the rather sparse but effective makeup to accommodate Hull's antipathy towards long makeup sessions.

acting level is low. Henry Hull is stiff and formal in his demeanor. While initially this suits his rather cold, aloof character, Hull is *too* stiff to be sympathetic. This does nothing to engender empathy for him and so denies the film much of the power inherent in its tragic situation. His humorless manner, continually furrowed brow, and rapid, clipped speech serve to distance the audience from him. Letting Hull play his character in such a cold fashion was a near-fatal error on the part of director Stuart Walker, since it precludes the pathos so crucial for a story of this kind. Simply put, *Werewolf of London* lacks heart. (These elements — tragedy and pathos — are what make *The Wolf Man* such a success. Lon Chaney, Jr., is infinitely more approachable and likable in that picture than Hull is in this one, and so his fate disturbs the viewer more).

The two secondary leads — Valerie Hobson as Glendon's neglected wife and Lester Matthews as her former (and still-interested) suitor — also fail to convince. Hobson is too melodramatic, constantly staring off into space and overdoing the lost, tragic look. Matthews alternately strains and stamps with indignation at her neglect while following her about with moon-eyed adoration. Both make very poor audience identification figures.

Despite these liabilities, there is enough general competence, story interest, and occasional flourish in *Werewolf of London* to make it a somewhat stolid but still dependable second-string player on the Universal horror team.

REVIEWS

Variety's "Bige" (May 15, 1935) observed that "A gripping shocker might have been made of the wholecloth that serves as the story foundation for 'Werewolf of London,' but this is neither sufficiently gripping nor more than moderately shocking..."

The reviewer singles out the acting prowess of Henry Hull, noting that the actor "is required to do too many fantastic things for any actor's own good, yet Hull surmounts most of the handicaps with a sterling performance."

The *New York Times* reviewer (May 10, 1935) was a little less discriminating, noting that "designed solely to amaze and horrify, the film goes about its task with commendable thoroughness, sparing no grisly detail and springing from scene to scene with even greater ease than that oft attributed to the daring young aerialist. Granting that the central idea has been used before,[3] the picture still rates the attention of action-and-horror enthusiasts."

PRODUCTION NOTES

As early as 1932 Universal had begun planning a werewolf film, initially titled *The Wolf Man* and set to star Boris Karloff under the direction of Robert Florey. Despite the presence of a completed script, the project never went into production. In 1934 the idea (but not the script) was revived, with Kurt Neumann slated to direct. Playwright John Colton (author of the Broadway smash "Rain") was commissioned to write a new screenplay, earning a then-significant sum of $8,150 for his efforts. Stuart Walker eventually landed the directing job (at a hefty salary of $12,500), after his successes with *Great Expectations* (1934) and *Mystery of Edwin Drood* (1935).

Reportedly, Bela Lugosi was briefly considered for the role of Dr. Yogami. Had Lugosi played Yogami, Universal could have saved a good percentage of the film's $159,000 budget. Lugosi's standard fee at the time was $1000 a week which would have run up a bill of $3000 on *Werewolf of London*'s twenty-day shooting schedule. Warner Oland, on the other hand, earned a total of $12,000 for three weeks' work, *four times* Lugosi's cost! Stuart Walker eventually brought *Werewolf of London* in four days over schedule and $36,000(!) over budget (with a final price tag of $195,393.01).

In a studio publicity article, Robert Harris (the author of the original story and the picture's associate producer) explained why he chose to concoct a werewolf story: "One of the most prolific fields for motion picture stories has scarcely been scratched [in 1935]. This untapped field is found among the legends and folk tales of the people in the back countries of Europe. These stories have been handed down from generation to generation, stories so weird and bloodcurdling as to send cold chills along the spine.... They are the greatest source for picture stories that exists today, only the film people seem to have passed them by." This last is a rather ironic statement in that one short year later these "film people" would truly abandon this source *entirely* with an unofficial ban on horror product in 1936.

Harris went on to ask (and rightly so — at least according to most horror fans), "Why struggle with problem plays and gangster stories when you have this untapped field of stories that are simply packed with all the tense human drama plus almost unbelievable thrills? I believe these folk stories and legends are clean and thrilling entertainment. That's why I decided to write this werewolf story." Unfortunately, this enlightened view of "clean and thrilling entertainment" was not shared by most of the British and American film community of the time.

Jack P. Pierce created Henry Hull's werewolf makeup, the first (and only) werewolf of the 1930s. Originally, Pierce's design resembled the more hairy countenance he later applied to Lon Chaney, Jr., in 1941's *The Wolf Man*.

Pierce was forced to modify and tone down the wolfishness of the makeup at the demand of prominent stage actor Henry Hull, who refused to sit for a sufficient amount of application time. It has also been intimated that Hull thought the heavier-style makeup too concealing of his handsome face, as well as too painful to wear and remove.

Warner Oland, on the other hand, experienced no such difficulties with makeup chores. The only time his character, Yogami, is seen in wolf form is at the film's beginning, and stuntman Alex Chivra was the man behind the makeup during that scene. Though of Swedish birth, Oland was frequently cast by Hollywood as an Oriental and is best remembered as Charlie Chan, whom he played in a long string of films up until his death in 1938 at the age of 57.

In a curious coincidence, the two stars shared the same birthdate — Warner Oland and Henry Hull were both born on October third (though ten years apart — 1880 and 1890, respectively).

The young Valerie Hobson (only 17 at the time) was frightened to the point of hysterics

In *Werewolf of London*'s disappointing climactic confrontation between the two lycanthropes (Warner Oland and Henry Hull), only one (Hull) is in hirsute form.

by Pierce's modified-but-effective makeup. The actress revealed to the readers of *Famous Monsters of Filmland* (#86) that, "I knew Mr. Hull was supposed to look horrible, but I had no idea he would look like that. I took one look at him and then started to scream. I couldn't stop. He thought I was joking so he ran towards me and let out an unearthly yell while he reached out a hairy hand as though to grasp my throat. Suddenly he and director Stuart Walker discovered I was in the middle of a fit of hysterics. They rushed me to the studio hospital where they gave me a sedative. When I quieted down I was so weak I could not walk. I had to go home for the remainder of the day." Ms. Hobson had to contend with yet another horrible visage that same year while playing the *Bride of Frankenstein* (*Doctor* Frankenstein, that is). No further screaming incidents were reported.

"So pleased was Carl Laemmle, Jr., at Miss Hobson's work in this thriller," reported an article in the *Bride of Frankenstein* pressbook, "that she was given the feminine lead opposite Henry Hull in "The Werewolf" which will soon be ready for release in this country." Born in Northern Ireland, Valerie Hobson first appeared in pictures at the tender age of 16. In 1935 she was invited to Hollywood, but returned to England the following year after making seven films. She continued her career in Britain, becoming one of the foremost leading ladies of the English screen. She retired in 1954 after marrying politician John Profumo. The elegant British Lady stood by her husband during the infamous Christine Keeler sex scandal which rocked the British government in 1963, forcing Profumo to resign from his post as Minister of War after perjuring himself before the House of Commons. Upon leaving public office, Profumo worked tirelessly at Toynbee Hall, a welfare organization for the poor and victims of alcohol and drugs. In 1975, Ms. Hobson was gratified to see her husband honored by the Crown, receiving the title of Commander of the British Empire from the queen in recognition for his service to the poor.

In a 1964 newspaper interview, Henry Hull revealed that he had never seen *Werewolf of London* in its entirety. "I saw snatches of the film shortly after we shot it almost 30 years ago, and I saw perhaps the first ten or 15 minutes of it on television Saturday night. Then I went to bed. Sleep means more to me than any movie, even my own. It was a pretty good get-up, wasn't it? Jack [Pierce] had a special talent for turning men into freaks. I got out of the monster mold while the getting was good. The studio liked the job I had done ... and they wanted me for similar roles but I declined because I didn't want to be limited to work in horror films."

During production, studio head Carl Laemmle supposedly offered a $50 incentive to studio employees who could come up with a better title. Some of the (frequently amusing) entries included *Bloom, Flower, Bloom*; *Moon Doom*; *The Whelp from Tibet*; and *What Price Curiosity*. No one collected the reward, however, for the original title was retained.

In April of 1935, the studio's publicity department released an article aimed at distributors and theater owners entitled "A Message from the President of Universal Pictures." In it, Carl Laemmle made some rather grandiose claims about his newest horror product:

> When we produced *Werewolf of London* we gave it all the shock and goosepimples we could jam into it.
>
> Human nature is still the same as it has been for a thousand years. We love the thing that shocks us or sends a chill down the spine.
>
> We fear it. We dread it. But we love it. *Werewolf of London* is a bloodcurdling thing...
>
> It is as gruesome as *Dracula*—as startling as *Frankenstein*—as much of a soul-shocker as we know how to make.
>
> But it is a glorious change from the Pollyanna pictures which you may have been using as a steady diet...
>
> *Werewolf of London* is a freak of a shocker. We warn everybody to stay away—then watch them come in droves.

Ah, Uncle Carl, if only it were true....

NOTES

1. David Horsley, assistant to John P. Fulton, discussed this sequence with *Photon*'s Paul Mandell. "John and I pondered a lot on how this shot was actually going to get done in the pre-production stages of the film. It was obvious to us from the outset that a series of cuts would be a bit too obvious as it would entail breaks in an otherwise smooth piece of camera movement. It was decided to photograph Hull against a black velvet background and matte his figure onto the normal background scene. The pillars were separately photographed and further matted onto this composite, masking the precise instant where the alteration in make-up occurred, so that in its final stage there appeared to be no break in camera movement."

2. The script called for a small boy to be grabbed by this huge plant during the Botanical Society party scene. Indeed, this sequence was probably filmed, since a surviving shot shows a frightened boy whimpering in the arms of his mother while a crowd gathers around the exotic plant as if something exciting had just happened.

3. Here the reviewer is alluding to the supposed parallels with *Dr. Jekyll and Mr. Hyde* (the transformation idea) and (incredibly) *The Invisible Man*, which features "a man who realizes in his moments of sanity that he may be driven to the murder of his wife and others 'whom he loves best.'"

THE RAVEN
(1935; Universal)

Release Date: July 4, 1935
Running Time: 61 minutes
Director: Louis Friedlander
Associate Producer: David Diamond
Screenplay: David Boehm (suggested by Edgar Allan Poe's immortal classic)
Photography: Charles Stumar
Art Director: Albert D'Agostino
Dialogue Director: Florence Enright
Dance Arrangement: Theodore Kosloff
Editor: Albert Akst
Music Supervision: Gilbert Kurland
Cast: KARLOFF (Edmond Bateman), Bela Lugosi (Dr. Richard Vollin), Lester Matthews (Dr. Jerry Halden), Irene Ware (Jean Thatcher), Samuel S. Hinds (Judge Thatcher), Spencer Charters (Geoffrey*), Inez Courtney (Mary Burns), Ian Wolfe (Col. Bertram Grant*), Maidel Turner (Harriet).

*Note: In actuality, Spencer Charters played the part of Col. Bertram Grant while Ian Wolfe played the role of Pinky Geoffrey. In a curiously careless error their names were switched in the credits.

"What torture, what a delicious torture, Bateman. Greater than Poe! Poe only conceived it, I have *done* it, Bateman. Poe, *YOU ARE AVENGED*!" — a raving Dr. Vollin.

SYNOPSIS

"When a man of genius is denied of his great love he goes mad. His brain, instead of being clear to do his work, is tortured. So he begins to *think* of torture." This line sums up the basic plot of *The Raven*. Bela Lugosi plays Dr. Vollin, a brilliant surgeon who has an intense obsession with the works (and torture devices) of Edgar Allan Poe. "The raven is my talisman," he states, "Death is my talisman." Vollin, though retired from active practice and now devoted solely to research, is the only man who can save a young woman critically injured in a car accident. The woman is Jean Thatcher, a professional dancer and daughter of the prominent Judge Thatcher. The judge calls Vollin from the hospital, but the doctor refuses to participate. The desperate Thatcher then goes to Vollin's home to plead with him. Vollin is immutable until Thatcher admits that "[Drs.] Cook and Hemmingway and Halden, they say that you're the only one." This admission appeals to Vollin's sense of importance. "So they *do* say that I am the only one," muses an obviously satisfied Vollin. "Very well, I will go."

One month after the successful surgery, a recovered Jean visits with Vollin while he plays the organ for her. "You're not only a great surgeon, but a great musician too," she marvels. "Extraordinary man, you're almost not a man, almost—" "A god?" suggests Vollin, adding, "a god with the taint of human emotions." Vollin, who has become obsessed with Jean, expresses his powerful feelings for her, but she feigns ignorance, and invites him to an interpretive dance recital she has choreographed in his honor. The surprise dance turns out to be a version of Poe's "The Raven."

Judge Thatcher, concerned over Vollin's connection with his daughter, goes to see him. When he learns that Vollin is set upon having her, Thatcher warns him to stay away from his daughter. Vollin demands that Thatcher send Jean to him, at which the outraged father calls him mad and stalks out.

Meanwhile, Edmond Bateman, an escaped criminal, arrives at Vollin's house to see the doctor. "I want you should change my face," he tells the surgeon and offers him money. It is not money Vollin has need of, however. "First, you must do something for me... It's in your line ... torture, murder." As if trying to atone for, or at least explain, his past misdeeds, Bateman says, "I'll tell you something, Doc, ever since I was born, everybody looks at me and says, 'You're ugly.' Makes me feel mean. Maybe because I look ugly — maybe if a man looks ugly he does ugly things." This brings Vollin up short. "You are saying something profound. A man with a face so hideously ugly—" he trails off, obviously inspired. Bateman presses him, "Don't ask me to do this job for you, Doc, I don't want to do them things no more."

Vollin agrees and performs the procedure in his operating theater located in the secret cellar of his mansion. He makes the change by manipulating the nerve endings of Bateman's face, explaining, "If something happens to these nerve ends it alters your expression. In other words, I, who know what to do with those nerve ends, can make you look any way I choose." But Vollin tricks Bateman, and instead of making him look good as he'd promised, Vollin transforms half of his face into a hideous death-mask. "Bateman," taunts Vollin from a safe distance, "You're monstrously ugly. Your monstrous ugliness breeds monstrous hate. Good, I can use your hate. You will do this for me, Bateman." When Bateman balks at what Vollin wants him to do, the doctor threatens, "Do you wish to remain the ugly monster that you are?"

Vollin then invites Jean and Jerry (her fiancé), along with four of their friends, to his house for a weekend party. He also invites Judge Thatcher, who only comes to try and persuade Jean to leave. While the houseguests are engaged in frivolous parlor games, Judge Thatcher finally arrives. Vollin offers his apology to Thatcher for the harsh words spoken during their earlier confrontation.

The group encounters the now-hideously disfigured Bateman, whom Vollin passes off as his servant. Jean, who had earlier been startled by Bateman, apologizes for her previous behavior and shows kindness towards the unfortunate man.

After being shown to their rooms, the unpacified Judge Thatcher tries to get Jean and Jerry to leave at once, but the young people laugh off his concerns.

Bateman tries to warn Thatcher, but is interrupted by Vollin. That night, Vollin sends the reluctant Bateman to grab Judge Thatcher and take him down to the secret basement which Vollin has filled with torture devices, including Poe's legendary pendulum.

Jerry sees Bateman drag the struggling Thatcher through the secret panel, but is knocked unconscious when he tries to interfere.

In the torture chamber, Vollin places Thatcher on the table beneath the deadly swinging pendulum, torturing the man with the knowledge that he has only 15 minutes before the massive blade reaches his heart. "Torture, waiting, *waiting*!" taunts Vollin. "Death will be sweet, Judge Thatcher!"

Vollin then throws a lever and Jean's entire bedroom drops down like an elevator into his dungeonlike cellar.

Jerry awakens and rouses Geoffrey and his wife (two of the other houseguests). They try to telephone for help, but another lever thrown by Vollin cuts out the phone and drops steel shutters over all the windows, sealing the guests in "as if we were all in a tomb."

Leading them down to the dungeon by opening the secret panel, Vollin forces Jerry and Jean at gunpoint into a room with moving walls, planning to crush them to death—together. "You will live in this place forever and ever. It will be the perfect marriage, the perfect *love*," he mocks. "You will never be separated, *never*!"

Remembering the kindness Jean had shown him earlier, Bateman finally rebels, determined to let the girl go. Ignoring Vollin's threats, Bateman pulls the switch to release the couple from the room. Vollin shoots Bateman. Though fatally wounded, Bateman overpowers Vollin and drags the madman into the death chamber. With his dying breath, Bateman pulls the lever to set the walls in motion. Ignoring Vollin's terrified screams, Jerry and Jean rescue Thatcher from the descending blade of the pendulum.

MEMORABLE MOMENTS

The transformation of Bateman from bearded fugitive to disfigured henchman forms the film's centerpiece. As Vollin removes the bandages following the brief operation, the soundtrack music builds steadily until finally the wrappings are stripped away and the music crescendos as we see the hideous handiwork of

Dr. Vollin. One half of Bateman's face is paralyzed into a repulsive death mask. As the unfortunate man grins (with the one half of his mouth that still works), thinking he's been helped, Vollin looks on and smiles evilly, relishing the sight. "Do — Do I look — different?" asks the unknowing Bateman. "Yes," replies Vollin with a sardonic grin and nod of his head. Vollin then leaves. Bateman, now concerned, gets up. Suddenly, a row of curtains automatically draws back to reveal full-length mirrors. The now-horrified Bateman, seeing the monster he has become, grabs his gun and shoots the mirrors, shattering his multiple reflections one by one. The music crescendos again, with Vollin's maniacal laughter riding the waves of the melody. Karloff's pathetic anticipation, coupled with Lugosi's obvious glee at his diabolical deed creates a heartbreaking contrast which only intensifies when Bateman's impotent rage culminates in the destruction of his own image.

When Vollin first shows the disfigured Bateman his reconstructed torture chamber (which he plans to put into gruesome operation later that night), he proudly reveals the prize of his collection — Poe's pendulum. Walking over to the massive metal table, Vollin begins his loving lecture. "This device is from one of Poe's stories, 'The Pit and the Pendulum.' A man was thrown into a pit and tied to a slab like this." Vollin reaches down and flips a switch. "Suddenly, he hears a peculiar noise coming from above his head. He looks up —" (as does Bateman, letting us see the swinging blade for the first time) "and sees the knife flashing, swinging rhythmically as it gradually descends." Gesturing, Vollin continues, "These things here are manacles which are controlled by that lever. Clasped 'round the wrist and ankles," he goes on, smiling and obviously enjoying showing off his ingenious torture device, "they hold a man on the slab; helpless, he cannot move. In 15 minutes, the knife reaches his heart." As Vollin talks, he demonstrates by carefully laying out on the table. As Vollin finishes talking, Bateman glances at the lever, an idea forming. Suddenly, Bateman flips the switch. "Got you!" he cries. The now-shackled Vollin is startled and momentarily panicked. Then, uttering an uneasy laugh, he says in a friendly tone, "C'mon Bateman, release me." His amicable request unheeded, Vollin then shouts his command: "Release me Bateman!" Eyeing the swinging blade, Bateman stands fast. Recovering his composure and friendly tone, Vollin gently prods his underling with this reminder: "And please try to remember, should anything happen to me, you remain the hideous monster that you are." Bateman still doesn't move. "C'mon Bateman," presses Vollin with a little more uncertainty and an uneasy laugh. For one tense moment, Bateman holds his hand on the lever as he ponders his predicament. His hand briefly relaxes as if to draw away and leave the madman to his fate, and the viewer feels a moment of triumph for the unfortunate Bateman. Suddenly, Bateman grasps and pushes the lever, releasing the doctor. Vollin sits up and exhales heartily, a victorious smile on his face. Bateman has lost. The scene generates a palpable tension as the previously self-assured and masterful Vollin vacillates between near-panic, confidence, renewed uncertainty, nervous laughter, and finally triumph.

ASSETS

Over the years *The Raven* has taken a lot of critical heat, probably more so than any other of Universal's Golden Age entries (with the exception of *Dracula*). Much of the criticism has been doled out unfairly, though, since many detractors' viewpoints tended to peek out from behind the shadow of Universal's previous Poe entry (and Karloff/Lugosi vehicle), *The Black Cat* (1934). Often looked upon as the poor relation of *The Black Cat*, *The Raven* certainly cannot stand beside it and compare favorably with the sheer elegance and macabre intensity of that earlier classic. Taken on its own, however, *The Raven* is an exciting, fast-paced horror film which sports a quintessential Lugosi performance and ranks among the more successful Poe adaptations (or more accurately inspirations) on the screen.

The most obvious and readily seen asset possessed by *The Raven* is LUGOSI, who finally

"The raven is my talisman," announces Dr. Vollin (Bela Lugosi), "*death* is my talisman." From *The Raven* (1935).

achieves the honor of billing by surname alone (alongside his more illustrious colleague, KARLOFF) for the first and only time in his career. (This was only a partial victory for the actor, however, for while he was billed as "LUGOSI" above the opening title, the more mundane "Bela Lugosi" was listed in both the opening and closing credits; whereas Karloff kept his singular moniker throughout.) Thousands of words have been written extolling the talent of the Hungarian actor named Bela Lugosi and an equal number have been written deriding the same. Lugosi is a matter of taste. Unlike his "rival" (and superior) in the horror field, Boris Karloff, who played many different types of roles over the course of his long career, Lugosi was predominantly cast as "Lugosi." Whether this was due to acting limitations or to unfair typecasting has been a point of hot contention. Personally, I feel that Lugosi was never given a real chance to prove his worth and was much more versatile than Hollywood would allow him to be — just look at his performance in *Mystery of the Mary Celeste* (1935) for evidence of his ability. It boils down to this: Karloff was an actor and Lugosi was a personality. Possessing an immense screen presence, unique dialogue delivery, and a riveting stare, Lugosi commands all attention when onscreen. While he frequently overplayed his part, he was never boring; his presence filled the screen. In later years he became something of a caricature of himself, but in 1935, at the height of his cinematic prowess, Lugosi was in fine and forceful form, and nowhere is it more evident than in *The Raven*.

Lugosi pulled out all the stops for *The Raven* and delivered a full-blooded performance unchecked by director Louis Friedlander (who obviously gave free reign to Lugosi's theatricality). Consequently, while Vollin does not seem quite believable, he also appears somehow more than human, almost — "a god?" One's first reaction is to chuckle at the actor's deadly dramatics, but Lugosi's sheer power and sincerity choke the welling laughter. Shortly after completing *The Raven*, Lugosi commented on his sincere approach to horror roles: "You can't make people believe in you if you're playing a horror part with your tongue in your cheek. The screen magnifies everything, even the way you are thinking. If you are not serious, people will sense it. No matter how hokum or highly melodramatic the horror part may be, you must believe in it while you are playing it" (Interview in the *New York Times* as quoted in *Karloff and Lugosi* by Greg Mank). In Lugosi's hypnotic hands, Vollin transcends normality and becomes a larger-than-life character fascinating in his excesses and obsessions and to which mundane measures of normalcy no longer apply. Though Lugosi delivers a rather obvious performance for the most part (when, at the film's beginning, the museum representative comments on Vollin's "curious hobby" of building Poe's torture devices, Lugosi responds with "It's more than a hobby," and stares intently off into space before turning with a quick, theatrical motion to come back to earth), the actor does not forego subtlety entirely. When Vollin examines Jean's healing neck on her visit after the operation, he smilingly notes that "the scar is almost gone. When I touch it, does it hurt?" Lugosi's voice and face are expectant as he leans close, anxious to hear of the pain. When Jean answers "no," his face falls ever so slightly and he draws back, disappointed. Lugosi's odd, forceful delivery of a snippet of "The Raven" adds more subtle shading to his character. Forcing the words out in an almost painful manner, Lugosi transforms Poe's lyrical poem into something tortured and grotesque.

It takes an actor of Lugosi's stature to make the most of such juicy yet dangerously ponderous lines like "The restraint that we impose upon ourselves can drive us mad." Not only does Lugosi add emphasis by breaking up the line with his patented pregnant pauses, he also adds a tortured tone of believability by injecting a note of torment into his commanding voice.

When Thatcher confronts Vollin about his daughter, Lugosi displays yet another aspect of the fascinating Vollin. "Listen Thatcher," Lugosi begins forcefully, his tone harsh, commanding, "I'm a man who renders humanity a great service. For that — my brain must be clear, my nerves steady and my hand sure." Then his voice changes, softens, as he confesses, almost pleading, "Jean torments me. She has come into my life, into my brain." At this, Lugosi truly does sound like a man in torment. The actor's tortured, tremulous tone actually inspires pity for this sadistic yet obviously tormented man. Thatcher's compassionate urging to "Forget it man, forget it," only reinforces the sympathy. This charitable emotion quickly evaporates, however, as Lugosi recovers his cold, commanding demeanor and orders Thatcher to send Jean to him (resulting in Thatcher labeling him as "stark, staring mad").

Boris Karloff, though receiving top billing, plays strictly a support role as the unfortunate (though far from innocent) Bateman, Vollin's victim and unwilling henchman. The actor brings his considerable skill at evoking pathos to his role and provides a striking contrast to the haughty, self-assured Lugosi. The following exchange at their first meeting captures the dynamics of Karloff-vs.-Lugosi and highlights their respective skills:

> Lugosi, his voice hard, accusing: "You shot your way out of San Quentin. Two guards are dead. In a bank in Arizona, a man's face was mutilated, *burned*, a cashier of the bank."
>
> Karloff, defensively: "Well, he tried to get me into trouble. I told him to keep his mouth shut. He gets the gag out of his mouth and starts yellin' for the police—" Karloff pauses and his eyes look away and then down. Though obviously shamed by the memory, he continues, "I had the acetylene torch in my hand—"
>
> Lugosi, interrupting excitedly: "So you put the burning torch into his face—" and adds with a cruel half-smile, "into his *eyes*."
>
> Karloff purses his lips and offers, "Well, sometimes you can't help—things like that." Throughout his explanation, Karloff carries a hangdog look and is unable to maintain eye contact, obviously not proud of the incident. Karloff's hunched shoulders and bowed head (so that he has to look *up* at Vollin, like a chastised child) contrasts with Lugosi's ramrod, proud demeanor and unflinching, controlling voice.
>
> At the end of the conversation, Karloff makes a final plea: "Don't ask me to do this job for you, Doc. I don't want to do them things no more." His remorse-filled eyes and pleading voice convince us of his sincerity.

Lugosi and Karloff are ably supported by the steadying presence of Samuel Hinds as Judge Thatcher. Hinds' fixed gaze and rock-solid delivery make him the voice of reason which serves as a strong counterpoint to Lugosi's dramatics. Then, when the assured Hinds finally loses his composure under the swinging pendulum blade at the end of the film, it becomes doubly effective. Irene Ware makes an attractive, likable and intelligent heroine, whose overall good humor and kindness (shown towards Bateman) make her a thoroughly sympathetic identification figure.

First-time director Louis Friedlander worked alongside veteran cinematographer Charles Stumar (*The Mummy*; *Werewolf of London*) to make good use of the camera and choose his shots carefully. Toward the beginning of Jean's operation sequence, when Vollin first catches sight of his beautiful patient, Friedlander goes to a close-up of Lugosi's face, masked except for the eyes, the soft-focus underscoring the furtive intensity in the actor's gaze and hinting at the obsessive madness brewing there. At the end of this brief scene, the anesthesiologist places the mask right over the camera lens, blocking out all light. This visual trick places the audience in Jean's position and firmly aligns the viewer with the heroine (even before meeting her).

Next, the darkness lifts to reveal a roaring fire while sinister organ music plays in the background. The camera draws back from the massive fireplace to finally show Vollin at the organ, playing for Jean. Disorienting and a touch surreal, the shift from darkness to fire to recital, coupled with the movement and music, creates an almost dreamlike moment — reminiscent of the groggy awakening from a deep anesthetic. Friedlander also shoots Vollin at the organ through a row of banister posts, intimating the prisonlike obsession he has been trapped in (Vollin pictured behind the bars of his own madness, so to speak).

Friedlander positions both the players and the camera to convey mood and even underscore relationships. When Judge Thatcher, hat in hand, pleads with Vollin to operate on Jean ("I — I *beg* you for my daughter's life"), Friedlander places the camera at a low angle. With Vollin in the foreground, the forced perspective makes him appear twice the size of the beseeching Thatcher, who gazes seemingly heavenwards at this godlike man. Thus, Friedlander extends all the power of the scene to Vollin. Veteran filmmaker Tod Browning, who often exhibited poor placement of his actors, could have benefited from a lesson or two from *The Raven*'s fledgling director.

David Boehm's script provides an excellent contrast in characterization between the inherently evil Lugosi character and the evil-only-by-circumstance Karloff portrayal. Bateman is the simple creature of impulse. He only kills in anger, in the heat of the moment when the opportunity presents itself. Vollin, on the other hand, is cold and calculating in his murderous deeds, orchestrating events to bring about the desired results. Later, after Bateman's change, a line of dialogue underscores the contrast. In speaking of the "torture and murder" he wants Bateman to do for him, Vollin explains, "I can't use *my* hand to do it. My brain, your hand." This indeed sums up the difference between the two men. Bateman, despite his occasional violent and cruel impulses, still has his humanity whereas Vollin has denuded himself of his compassion, his emotion, and indeed feels "I am a law unto myself." Up until he meets Jean, he feels content in this world of his own making, in which he has withdrawn from the human race and busied himself with his own esoteric research. There he finds his escape in the works and life of Poe. Living apart from — and above — other men, however, has cost Vollin his humanity and this loss is manifest in his mania for Jean — and for Poe.

While possessing a few suspect passages, the script generally features excellent dialogue, such as this illuminating monologue delivered by Vollin as he expounds upon his interpretation of "The Raven." "Poe was a great genius," explains Vollin, "and like all great geniuses there was in him the insistent will to do something big, great, constructive in the world. He had the brain to do it. But, he fell in love. Her name was Lenore. Something happened; someone took her away from him. When a man of genius," intones Lugosi, almost as if he were reciting an immutable law, "is denied of his great love, he goes mad. His brain, instead of being clear to do his work, is tortured. So *he* begins to think of torture, torture for those who have tortured *him*."

Sardonic humor often permeates the dialogue, humor black enough for the very spirit of Poe himself. One gem occurs when Vollin straps Judge Thatcher to the table under the pendulum.

Thatcher (looking up): What's that thing?
Vollin: A knife.
Thatcher: What's it doing?
Vollin: Descending.

This comedy of the obvious quickly gives way to a darker mood as the exchange continues:

Thatcher: What are you trying to do to me?
Vollin: Torture you.
Thatcher: Oh, *try* to be sane, Vollin.
Vollin: I'm the sanest man who ever lived. *I* will not be tortured. I tear torture out of myself by torturing *you*!

Through dialogue, an amusing moment suddenly becomes an horrific one. Later, when Bateman forces the struggling Judge Thatcher into the torture chamber, the waiting Vollin delivers a wry apology: "My servant is a — little uncivilized, so I ask your forgiveness." Then, in an amusing tone of mock concern, Vollin continues, "Now I see you can hardly stand on your feet. Bateman, see that Judge Thatcher—" [glancing down at the slab]— "lies down." And as Bateman throws Thatcher onto the stone under the deadly pendulum and violently subdues him, Vollin adds, "Make him comfortable, Bateman." The saturnine humor gives the unpleasant proceedings an even sharper edge.

Tight editing builds tension and greatly enhances *The Raven*. Toward the climax, for instance, quick cuts flash back and forth between the couple trapped in the Death Chamber with the walls moving ever closer; a shot of the clock revealing the time slipping away; and the terrified Judge Thatcher strapped underneath the swinging blade, moaning in terror. The quick flashes of these images effectively create an air of immediacy and frantic anxiety.

Ballet master Theodore Kosloff provides an excellent dance interpretation for Poe's poem (performed by dancer Nina Golden doubling for Irene Ware), which is enhanced by Albert D'Agostino's excellent theatrical sets — a study in stylized minimalism. An oversized portal stands on the far side of the stage while a huge window, flanked by eight-foot candlesticks, reaches up to the rafters behind, tree limbs silhouetted through the oversized panes. On the opposite side, at a high writing desk, sits Edgar Allan Poe himself (an actor made up to resemble the famous author), reciting in sepulchral tones his timeless poem while the moody orchestral music rises and falls. On stage, diaphanous black cloth flowing out behind her like macabre gossamer wings, Ms. Golden bends and spins and leaps in an energetic yet strikingly somber dance. The surreal, flowing costume and lithe quick movements of the dancer contrast with, yet oddly compliment, the rhythmic poem read above the moody background music.

LIABILITIES

While the general plot of *The Raven* is quite good, and the obsessive love theme (coupled with the elements of torture and madness) creates a part tailor-made for Lugosi, the scenario possesses some serious flaws. Boris Karloff himself labeled the screenplay "an attempt to pile on the thrills without much logic" (*Karloff*, by Peter Underwood).[1] Bateman's medical transformation, for instance, is patently ridiculous. "The operation is very simple," explains Vollin, "in ten minutes it's done." This "operation," centers around "the seventh cranial nerve which has its root here [Vollin touches the base of Bateman's neck]. From this comes the nerves which control the muscles of the face. If something happens to these nerve ends, it alters your expression." The idea that simply pressing on some nerves can create the withered skin and pancake eyeball which Bateman later sports is absurd. And why does Vollin bandage Bateman's countenance (indeed, nearly his entire head)? Since no cutting or physical manipulation of the face was necessary, it seems a superfluous gesture (though it *does* increase the drama of the unveiling).

The picture strains credibility further when Vollin reveals his wondrous control panel with levers manipulating not only the numerous mechanized torture devices (like the room with moving walls) but also the phone line and automatic steel shutters over the windows. While we *may* be able to swallow this unlikely exhibition of electronic gadgetry if we lean toward a generous suspension of disbelief, presenting a bedroom which turns into an elevator chokes us on its own lack of logic. This final indulgence is just too much. These fantastical devices add an unnecessary, everything-but-the-kitchen-sink element reminiscent of a cheap serial.

Further, why an obviously brilliant man planning a series of tortures and murders would invite four extraneous people (each a potential *witness*) to his house is a wonder. The obvious reason they are present is to provide Comic Relief, most of which proves unsuccessful, as evidenced by the following exchange:

> Pinky: "You know, I *like* horses. I grew up with them."
> Mrs. Grant: "Yes, I can see that when I look at you."

Still, one of the intrusive characters (the hypochondriac colonel) *does* provide one moment of sublime humor when he requests a sleeping draught from his sadistic host, Dr. Vollin. As the blissfully ignorant colonel drowsily wanders off with his sleeping powder in hand, he opines, "Such a nice man, so thoughtful."

While Lugosi's heavy and flamboyant dramatics generally fit the tone of this dark, unrestrained picture, the actor goes too far in one instance. For the scene in which Vollin gloats over his "delicious torture," Lugosi waves his arms wildly (one of which holds a gun which he flails about to a decidedly dangerous degree) and throws his head back in an explosion of maniacal laughter. For today's horror aficionado, Lugosi's unrestrained over-the-top histrionics at this point conjure up images of that actor's later Ed Wood films. (The original shooting script called for an even sillier display of melodramatics by having Lugosi say in a sing-song voice, "The Raven — Symbol of Death — Nevermore — Nevermore — The lost Lenore." Fortunately, these ludicrous lines, which would have lengthened and *worsened* the already embarrassing scene, were cut.)

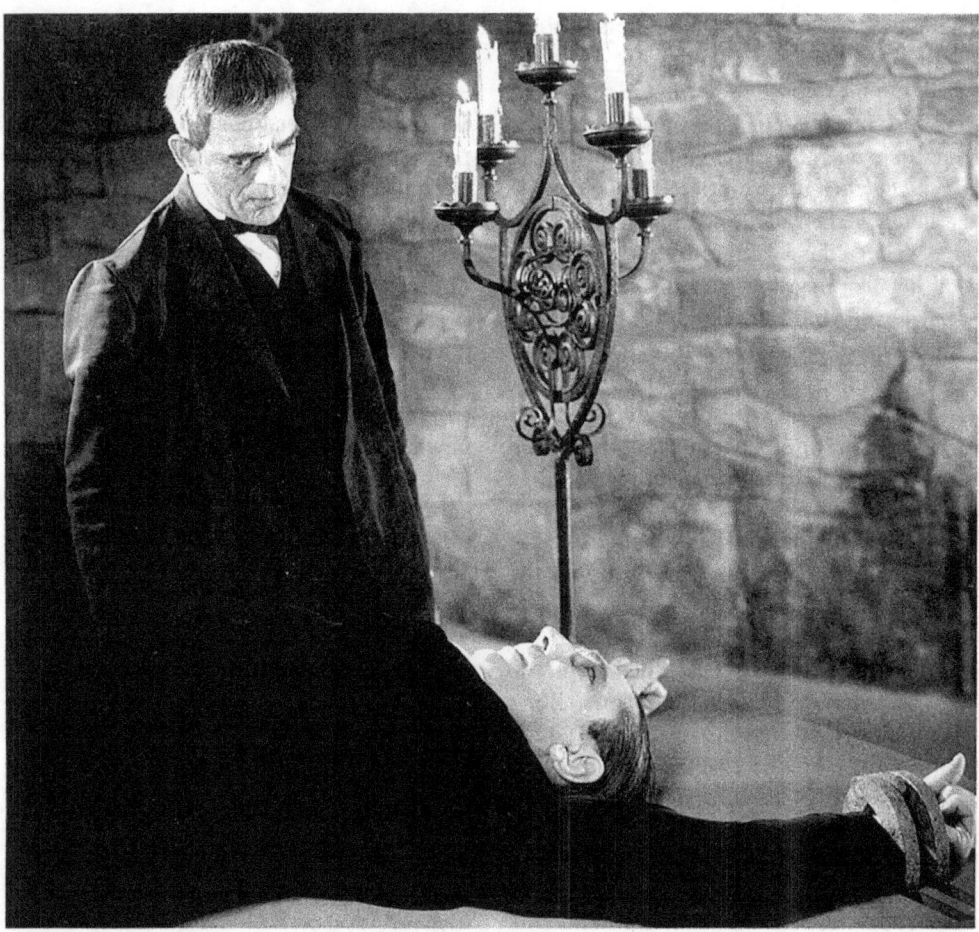

For an instant, the tables are turned as Bateman (Boris Karloff) straps his Poe-obsessed master, Dr. Vollin (Bela Lugosi), to his own torture device in *The Raven* (1935).

Karloff performs a bit of image-conjuring himself, borrowing mannerisms from an earlier classic portrayal. Unfortunately, Karloff's growls and gestures aping the Frankenstein monster sound ridiculous coming from a relatively articulate "normal" human being. Once again, the script included much more in the way of growling than actually survived on-screen (thankfully) in a rather too obvious attempt to conjure up the image of Karloff's monster. The effect is achieved, and the vision of the cadaverous creature is planted in the brains of the audience. Rather than frightening further, however, this merely serves to point out the poor comparison Bateman in his pitiful makeup makes to the immortal monster. Shaking his fists impotently, growling like the inarticulate creature he's not, Bateman cuts a more comical figure than a frightening or sympathetic one. We keep waiting for him to turn toward the ceiling and hold out his hands looking for the sunlight.

One of the picture's greatest detracting elements, however, is the awful makeup applied to Boris Karloff (specifically, the fake, flat-looking papier-mâché eyeball). During the revelation sequence, Bateman becomes concerned when he cannot see out of one eye. "Something's the matter —" he says and brings up his hand toward his disfigured visage, adding, "— my eye." This scene has always inspired in me the irrational urge to shout at the confused Bateman, "It's the cardboard!" The phoney makeup calls attention to itself, severely damaging the pathos and power of the scene (even more than it damages Bateman's countenance). Universal publicity claimed that Pierce fashioned the makeup after Conrad Veidt's horrific grin in *The Man Who Laughs*. If that were the case, then Universal's makeup genius fell well short of the mark. In actuality, the script itself delineated Bateman's look: "Certain muscles have been paralyzed through cutting of the nerve ends. Certain others have been permitted to remain — giving life to the part of the face they control, so that here is a face — a crazy quilt of death and life. One part of his face remains fixed in a horrible dead grimace, while the other remains alive — side by side with the corpse. One eye remains open, unblinking — staring straight ahead." Friedlander dwells in loving close-up on the unconvincing mess, and we can only stare and wonder at what Jack Pierce must have drunk the night before to become so uncharacteristically careless in his (previously perfect) judgment. Granted, the wrinkled, ruined skin is effective enough (as a toned-down version of Pierce's *The Mummy*), but that awful, painted, two-dimensional eye completely negates the makeup's effectiveness. This is the only instance during the Golden Age of Horror in which the legendary Jack Pierce failed to convince with his grotesques.

There is nothing very "deep" or "significant" in *The Raven*, no hidden messages or great truths revealed. Instead, we are given an exciting, action-packed 61 minutes of solid horror entertainment presided over by the Golden Age of Horror's most charismatic individual — Bela Lugosi.

REVIEWS

Variety's "Abel" (July 10, 1935) called *The Raven* "a good horror flicker. With both Karloff and Lugosi in the cast, it should scare 'em into the b.o.'s [box offices] in spades. 'The Raven' maintains Universal's high batting average with the shockers, only this one looks the least costly of 'em..."

The *New York Times* (July 5, 1935) reviewer, however, did not agree with *Variety*'s assessment, labeling *The Raven* "the season's worst horror film. Not even the presence of the screen's Number One and Two Bogymen, Mr. Karloff and Bela (Dracula) Lugosi, can make the picture anything but a fatal mistake from beginning to end.... Of course, it must be said that Lugosi and Karloff try hard, even though, both being cultured men, they must have suffered at the indignity being visited upon the helpless Edgar Allan."

PRODUCTION NOTES

The Raven's rather tortuous flight to the screen began on August 31, 1934, when Guy Endore submitted a 19-page scenario (ostensibly based on Poe's poem) to Universal's head office. (Incidentally, Endore had written the novel *The Werewolf of Paris*, published in 1933, which was eventually made into a film itself by Hammer Studios in 1961 and retitled *The Curse of the Werewolf*.) Endore later co-wrote the screenplays for MGM's *Mad Love* and *Mark of the Vampire* (both 1935). Nothing further came of *The Raven* until November when two other writers, Michael Simmons and Clarence Marks, turned in a full screenplay. When their effort was deemed unsatisfactory, another screenwriter (Jim Tully) took a hand and submitted a second full-length screenplay. Still lacking, a final writer took over, David Boehm, and wrote not one but *three* separate finished scripts. One was accepted and production began on March 2, 1935.

Next to *The Black Cat*, *The Raven* was Universal's most economical horror picture of the Golden Age. Awarded a brief 15-day shooting schedule and a paltry $109,750 budget (which included over $10,500 "wasted" on the various discarded screenplays), director Louis Friedlander brought the production in right on schedule but slightly over budget at $115,209.

Reaction to *The Raven* in England was swift and terrible. With its themes of lust, sadism and torture, *The Raven* was a major contributor to the banning of horror films in the British Isles (which contributed to a cessation of horror production in Hollywood for nearly two years).

This new British ban on horror set in

Despite the attitudes of Karloff and Lugosi in this gag publicity shot, *The Raven* (1935) contains enough murder, madness and mayhem to keep any viewer awake.

help it if they made a type out of me. The kind of role in which I have to work is completely foreign to my human and dramatic nature, but for the time being I put up with my fate resignedly; I wear this clown's cap that I did not want at all." He went on to hope that "Some day I will get back the old roles that I played before *Dracula*, or, at least, roles similar to them where I will be allowed to appear on the stage as a human being and speak with a human voice. Until, then, I carry and bear this heavy cross." It was a burden that throughout his career he was never able (or allowed) to put down.

Though Lugosi has the starring role and almost double the screen time of Karloff, Karloff received top billing and twice the salary ($10,000 for Karloff vs. $5,000 for Lugosi). Contrasting the two stars, character actor Ian Wolfe (Geoffrey in *The Raven*) remembered to Roger Hurlburt in *Filmfax* #39 that "[Karloff] was a real nice guy and a pussycat, not at all like the characters he played. But Lugosi ... no one could get to know him. Very distant." Lugosi's co-star and rival, Boris Karloff, outlined his relationship with, and respect for, Bela in a 1967 interview at Hollywood's Magic Castle (as reported in *Famous Monsters of Filmland* #47): "We really didn't socialize. You see, our lives, our tastes,

motion by *The Raven* affected Bela Lugosi in the most severe fashion. So closely was the actor tied to horror roles, that he was not offered a film part for nearly a year and a half during the horror hiatus. Lugosi lamented his total identification with horror as early as 1933 when he stated: "I am a victim of the success of *Dracula*. That horror drama and, along with it, myself have stumbled onto such great fame that producers and theater directors cannot even imagine that I could appear with a human face, too, and that I feel and believe that real art means talking with a human voice. I can't were quite different. Ours was simply a professional relationship. But I have warm recollection of him as a fine actor and a great technician."

After Karloff and Lugosi (earning $2,500 and $1,000 a week respectively), lawyer-turned actor Samuel Hinds was the highest paid player in *The Raven*, taking home $500 per week (as opposed to $461.50 a week for toupee-wearing leading man Lester Matthews and $250 a week for heroine Irene Ware). After 35 years as a practicing lawyer (and amateur thespian), the loss of his considerable fortune during the stock market crash served as catalyst for a career change. Hinds made his professional acting debut in 1932 at age 58, going on to appear in over 150 films, including such genre entries as *The Ninth Guest* (1934), *She* (1935), *Man Made Monster* (1941), *The Strange Case of Dr. RX* (1942), *Son of Dracula* (1943), *Cobra Woman* (1944), and *Jungle Woman* (1944).

Director Lewis Friedlander made his feature film debut on *The Raven*, having previously directed only serials for Universal. He was paid a mere $900 for directing the picture. Friedlander changed his name to Lew Landers when he went to work for RKO the following year. Friedlander/Landers directed Karloff again in *The Boogie Man Will Get You* (though this time the "King of Horror" was *sans* Lugosi, paired instead with alternative screen bogeyman Peter Lorre). Landers did cross paths with Lugosi again, however, when he oversaw that actor's final big studio "straight" starring vehicle, *Return of the Vampire* (1944).[2] Landers directed one other excursion into the macabre, *The Mask of Diijon* (1946; with Erich von Stroheim and Edward Van Sloan) before his death in 1962, having amassed an amazing total of 125 feature films to his credit.

Art director Albert D'Agostino designed and dressed the sets for two other Universal horror productions, *Werewolf of London* (1935) and *The Invisible Ray* (1936). D'Agostino later left Universal and went to RKO where producer Val Lewton utilized his talents on all nine of his atmospheric horror pictures, beginning with *Cat People* (1942) and concluding with *Bedlam* (1946). D'Agostino worked on one further genre classic, Howard Hawks' *The Thing* (1951).

D'Agostino redressed some of Universal's standing sets for *The Raven*. The stone entryway into Vollin's dungeon, for instance, is the same spot to which the monster was chained when briefly captured in *Bride of Frankenstein* (1935).

Universal's publicity department, aside from suggesting the usual "Chamber of Chills" and "Curtain Teaser Stunts" to theater owners, also aimed their ballyhoo at the more literary-minded, shamelessly extolling the film's (nearly nonexistent) connection with Poe. The pressbook for *The Raven* offered a form letter which could be sent to various high school and college English teachers:

> Dear Sir (or Madam): We feel that your students will be interested in seeing on the screen a remarkable entertainment, inspired by Edgar Allan Poe's literary classic, *The Raven*. Karloff and "Dracula" Lugosi are the featured players ... the pit yawns, the pendulum swings.... The great writer's lines are frequently quoted throughout the picture, and you and your students will feel a new interest, and appreciate more keenly the dramatic power of this famous verse...."

NOTES

1. Karloff was not only less than satisfied with his current assignment, he also expressed a growing disillusionment with his home studio in general (understandable after their extortive treatment of him in 1933 over *The Invisible Man*). Ian Wolfe related an amusing and illuminating anecdote about the actor. "Wolfe arrived at Universal extra-early his first day," reported Greg Mank in *Karloff and Lugosi*. "In fact, so early was Wolfe that, upon his arrival at the studio, the only person he could find was Karloff, who had also arrived early so to have his face prepared for the makeup. The makeup assistant hadn't shown up. As Karloff waited, Wolfe approached him. 'Mr. Karloff,' asked Wolfe, 'could you please direct me to a toilet?' 'This whole place,' said Karloff, waving at the studio-at-large, 'is a toilet!'"

2. With the exception of RKO's comedic *Zombies on Broadway* (1945), Lugosi's few subsequent appearances for the majors cast him strictly in supporting roles (even for his swan song as Dracula in Universal's comedic *Abbott and Costello Meet Frankenstein*, 1948).

MAD LOVE
(1935; MGM)

Alternate Title: *Hands of Orlac* (British release)
Release Date: July 12, 1935
Running Time: 68 minutes
Director: Karl Freund
Producer: John W. Considine, Jr.
Screenplay: P. J. Wolfson and John L. Balderston
Screen Adaptation: Guy Endore (from the novel *Les Mains D'Orlac* by Maurice Renard)
Translated and Adapted by Florence Crewe-Jones
Photography: Chester Lyons, Gregg Toland
Musical Score: Dimitri Tiomkin
Musical Director: Oscar Radin
Recording Director: Douglas Shearer
Art Director: Cedric Gibbons
Associates: William A. Horning, Edwin B. Willis
Wardrobe: Dolly Trent
Editor: Hugh Wynn
Cast: Peter Lorre (Doctor Gogol), Frances Drake (Yvonne Orlac), Colin Clive (Stephen Orlac), Ted Healy (Reagan), Sarah Haden (Marie), Edward Brophy (Rollo), Henry Holker (Prefect Rosset), Keye Luke (Dr. Wong), May Beatty (Françoise).

"Each man kills the thing he loves." — Dr. Gogol.

SYNOPSIS

Yvonne Orlac is an actress at "Le Théatre Des Horreurs," a Grand Guignol theater in Paris which specializes in torture plays. Her most ardent admirer is Dr. Gogol, a famous surgeon who has rented the theater's best box for every performance. The doctor makes advances to Yvonne, but his attention is unwanted because Yvonne is happily married to a brilliant young pianist, Stephen Orlac. Gogol, undaunted in his obsessive love, goes so far as to buy the wax statue of Yvonne which the theater had used for advertising in its lobby. A compassionate doctor and healer of children by day, at night the obsessed Gogol sets the wax statue up in his private study and plays the organ for it.

On the way back from a concert tour, Stephen Orlac is in a train wreck and the pianist's hands are crushed beyond saving. Desperate, Yvonne takes advantage of Gogol's attraction to her and has Stephen brought to the great surgeon, but even Gogol cannot save his hands. Suddenly, Gogol is hit by an inspiration. With a phone call the influential doctor has the body of an executed murderer brought to his house. The unfortunate was Rollo, a knife-thrower in a circus, who was guillotined earlier that day. Gogol had attended the execution (it seems he never misses one). The brilliant doctor attempts an experimental operation and grafts the hands of Rollo onto the arms of Stephen Orlac. The operation is a success, except now Stephen seems unable to play the piano. Worse still, his hands have a newfound penchant for throwing knives (Gogol did not tell him that he now possesses the hands of a murderer).

In the face of mounting debt, Stephen goes to his estranged stepfather for help. When the old miser rebuffs his stepson, Stephen becomes angry and his newly acquired hand picks up a knife and throws it at a wall. Though his stepfather is unhurt, Stephen is nearly unhinged by the event and rushes out in confusion and despair.

After being finally and utterly rejected by Yvonne, the now-mad Gogol plans to completely destroy Stephen, who is already in a weakened mental state because of his inability to play and resulting money troubles. Gogol dresses in a bizarre neck brace and a set of metallic hands to convince Stephen that he is Rollo, brought back to life with his head restored by Gogol, and the murderous hands that were once his are now on the arms of Stephen (this last part being true). He plants the suggestion that Stephen has killed his stepfather (a crime Gogol has committed and framed Stephen for).

Stephen is arrested for the murder of his stepfather and Yvonne, suspecting the truth, goes to Gogol's house in search of proof. She is forced to impersonate her own statue, however, when the madman returns home laughing his triumph. When she is discovered, Gogol thinks the statue has come to life: "My love has made you live!" Yvonne tries to escape but is trapped by the madman, and just as he is about to strangle her with her own hair, the police arrive with Stephen. Using his new talent, Stephen throws a knife to kill Gogol before he can strangle Yvonne. The two lovers are reunited.

MEMORABLE MOMENTS

In one of the movie's most literate and revealing sequences, Gogol plunges deeply and irrevocably into madness. After being spurned a final time by Yvonne, Gogol is forced to leave an operation when her words come back to torment his tortured mind: "Liar! Hypocrite! You disgust me!" In a mirror, his reflection speaks to him: "They are laughing at you in there, go back." Then suddenly, from another mirror, his second reflection answers: "Let them laugh. Nothing matters to you but one thing — Yvonne, Yvonne in your arms." As he approaches the second mirror, he approaches this other side of his psyche and the reflection changes from that of the white-gowned doctor — a surgeon, healer, bringer of mercy — to that of the black-suited Gogol — obsessed madman. Through his deft direction, Freund brilliantly visualizes the two sides of this man's nature, the inner struggle of the tormented Gogol.

The film's most macabre moment comes when Gogol dons a bizarre disguise to convince the confused Stephen that he has killed his stepfather. Entering a seedy hotel room, Stephen faces a shadowy figure across a rough table. The room is illuminated by a single lamp, which serves to keep the stranger in near-darkness. The camera is placed behind the figure, so that all we see is a dark silhouette. When Stephen implores him to tell what he knows about Stephen's hands, the figure answers in a sinister, rasping whisper: "They throw knives, ha!" "How do you know that?" demands the shocked Stephen. The camera moves in on the table and the stranger brings up his hands — or what serve as his hands — a pair of bizarre metal gauntlets. "I have no hands," hisses the figure, "Yours — they were mine once." Suddenly stabbing a knife into the table, he exhorts Stephen to "use it — when they try to arrest you." "Who are you?" demands Stephen. "I am *Rollo*, the knife thrower," is his answer. "They cut off my head." The figure suddenly stands. "But that Gogol," he continues in his hideous, gravelly voice, "he put it back — here." For the first time we see the figure from the front as he opens his coat to reveal a medieval-looking neck brace, all stiff leather and gleaming metal, which obscures the whole of his lower jaw and neck. The evil-looking brace, combined with dark wraparound goggles and slouch hat, makes him a grotesque, terrifying figure. The camera moves in on the weird, frightening countenance, and the upper lip moves upwards in an unpleasant sneer while a dry cackle, devoid of all mirth, issues from the mouth. It is a shuddery moment, subtly gruesome in its implications.

ASSETS

Cinematographer-turned-director Karl Freund (who had directed *The Mummy*, one of the greatest horror films of all time, three years earlier) again creates one of the best entries from Hollywood's Golden Age of Horror. With *Mad Love*, his only other horror picture as director, Freund shows us that his earlier success was not merely a fluke. While not as fluid as *The Mummy*, and lacking the iconographic presence of Boris Karloff, *Mad Love* is still a literate, powerful, darkly beautiful film deserving of the title classic.

Freund uses the camera like a brush, painting shadows and light upon a celluloid canvass to create mood and meaning in every frame. Nothing in this picture is flat, there are always layers upon layers of dark and light. Gogol's house, for instance, is not simply a collection of rooms and stairways, but a series of oversized shadows, mysterious spaces, and pools of darkness in the vein of the German Expressionist cinema (not surprisingly, since

"Peter Lorre and Frances Drake in a scene from a gruesome horror film, 'Hands of Orlac,'" reads the back of this English cigarette card sporting the British release title for *Mad Love* (1935).

Freund had worked as a cinematographer for such famed German directors as Fritz Lang in the 1920s).

Freund never settles for the ordinary or mundane. From the opening credits, when we see a fist rise up and smash through the glass on which the credits are printed (a startling harbinger of dire events to come) to the climactic moment when Gogol is about to strangle Yvonne with her own hair, the film reeks of the macabre. Freund continually uses striking visuals to enhance a scene or explore a character. Even an act as simple as answering the telephone is turned into a macabre visual treat. Instead of the camera viewing Gogol's housekeeper pick up and answer the phone, we are shown her shadow on the wall performing this task. And then the shadow delivers this little gem of dialogue: "The Professor isn't 'ere," she states and gives an unpleasant little laugh before adding, "If you want to know, 'e's visiting 'Madam Guillotine.' He never misses one o' those head-choppin's."

When we first meet Dr. Gogol, he is sitting in a theater box, watching Yvonne (the object of his "Mad Love") on stage. Gogol's face is bisected by a line of shadow from the box curtain. By placing the subject's face half in and half out of darkness, Freund creates a visual introduction to the duality of the man. On the one hand Gogol is a kind, compassionate doctor, capable of affectionately comforting a sick child. On the other hand, he is a demented, obsessed madman with a sick passion for death and a woman he cannot have. Gogol is indeed a man half in and half out of the darkness.

Mad Love was Peter Lorre's first American film, and he gives a bravura performance as the obsessed Dr. Gogol—a performance which won him accolades from the critics.

Andre Sennwald of the *New York Times* wrote (August 5, 1935): "Mr. Lorre, with his gift for supplementing a remarkable appearance with his acute perception of the mechanics of insanity, cuts deeply into the darkness of the morbid brain. It is an affirmation of his talent that he always holds his audience to a strict and terrible belief in his madness." Lorre's great passion was psychology, and in fact he studied for a time under Sigmund Freud. "An actor," Lorre said, "to be good, must be a psychologist. He must outstrip the professional psychologists, who concern themselves only with a few phases of a subject's mind. An actor must be *a hundred percent psychologist*—for he takes his character apart and reconstructs all his emotions. Then he takes those emotions into himself, becomes that character, be the character mad or not. The actor must be the character, utterly" (*Famous Monsters Yearbook*, 1966). Lorre's deep knowledge of the mind stood him in good stead for his role in *Mad Love* and indeed over the course of his entire career.

Also well cast are Francis Drake as Yvonne (a last-minute replacement for Virginia Bruce) and Colin Clive as Stephen Orlac. The fresh, wholesome beauty of Francis Drake contrasts strikingly with Peter Lorre's Gogol, who, with his bulging eyes and fleshy lips and completely shaved head makes a decidedly *un*wholesome figure. A very talented actress, Drake makes good use of her large expressive eyes and subtle movements and gestures to create a tragic figure of innocence. Colin Clive is perfectly cast as the nervous, high-strung, highly suggestible pianist. His Stephen Orlac is a direct outgrowth of his classic role in *Frankenstein* (1931)—a tortured, brilliant man on the verge of nervous collapse.[1]

Mad Love is a stylish, rich, dark fantasy which lets us look into the mind and soul of a madman. It is a *Dr. Jekyll and Mr. Hyde*, but less fantastic, with the evil being released not by a magic potion, but by the magic of a human mind lost in obsession and madness. With the talent evident in this and his earlier effort, one can only wish that Freund had stayed with directing (he went back to cinematography after this feature), and that while directing he had taken more forays into the realm of the macabre.

LIABILITIES

Mad Love is not a perfect film. First of all, the concept of the hands of a murderer being grafted onto the arms of a normal man, only to have the limbs retain their murderous skill, is patently absurd.[2] But it is treated here with such serious care, and we are so drawn in by the fascinating characters, that it ceases to be a problem as the film builds its own reality with a superb sense of gothic style.

Given that, even after the happy ending, there are plenty of concerns left — Stephen still is unable to play the piano, and, of course, there's the problem of his new hands still "wanting to throw knives" (a rather dangerous hobby).

Gogol's death is too abrupt. Gogol, now completely mad, gets a knife in the back and promptly dies without a word. When so many choice words had been issuing from his mouth throughout the rest of the picture, it is rather disappointing to have him end in silence.

Finally, there is the wax statue. At times it is indeed a wax figure (in a not-so-good likeness of Ms. Drake), and at other times, particularly in close-ups, it is obviously Francis Drake herself trying to hold her breath and keep perfectly still. This substitution is not convincing and detracts from the scenes' realism by calling attention to the deception (Is it live or is it memorwax?).

REVIEWS

Variety's "Char" (August 7, 1935) called this production "ideal starring material for the foreign actor, Peter Lorre," before adding, "the results in screen potency are disappointing..." However, "Char" detailed no specific faults to back up his broad criticism and in fact lavished nothing but praise on the film: "No complaint can be raised against the production given the story by John W. Considine, Jr., producer, and the director Karl Freund. Although the script situations are wildly fantastic, yet essential in telling the story, every ounce of horror has been wrung from the 'Hands of Orlac' property.... Lorre's fine performance does the rest..."

Andre Sennwald, of *The New York Times* (August 5, 1935), began by calling *Mad Love* "not much more than a super-Karloff melodrama, an interesting but pretty trivial adventure in Grand Guignol." He went on to commend newcomer Peter Lorre, however, and his ability to hold his audience. "He is one of the few actors in the world, for example, who can scream: 'I have conquered science; why can't I conquer love?'—and not seem just a trifle silly."

Mr. Sennwald was unimpressed by the picture's comedy relief, complaining about what he terms "one of those absurd movie newspaper men, whose behavior is so inappropriately foolish as to cast a pall of burlesque over several of the most striking excursions in terror.... Ted Healy, a highly amusing comedian, has gotten into the wrong picture."

"But even if it is not quite what we might have looked for in Mr. Lorre's first American picture, 'Mad Love' is an entertaining essay in the macabre..."

PRODUCTION NOTES

Mad Love is based on the novel *Les Mains D'Orlac* (The Hands of Orlac) by French author Maurice Renard. Four versions of the novel have been filmed to date. While not the first, *Mad Love* is the best and definitive one. The initial adaptation of Renard's novel was a dull, static German film made in 1925 (as *The Hands of Orlac*), with silent screen star Conrad Veidt agonizing over his new appendages. *Hands of a Stranger* was a weak American remake from 1962, and the British *The Hands of Orlac* was a slight improvement in 1965.

The filmgoing public of 1935 expressed little love (mad or otherwise) for this macabre picture. Costing $257,000 to produce, *Mad Love* suffered a net loss at the box office of $39,000.

Even MGM's own discarded stepchild *Freaks* (1932) did better at the domestic box office than *Mad Love* (which fared better abroad than at home—due, no doubt, to European star Peter Lorre's name value).

After previewing *Mad Love* in Hollywood, MGM cut nearly 15 minutes of footage before its official release. Among the rejected scenes: Gogol encountering a blind man begging in front of the theater whom the doctor had cured ("Being blind is my trade!"); additional footage of the hair-raising stage tortures at the Théatre des Horreurs; an encounter between a street girl (intent upon robbery) and Stephen's miserly (and apparently lascivious) stepfather; and the picture's gruesome centerpiece—Gogol restoring the guillotined Rollo to a modicum of life in order to facilitate the transplant operation's success. "The room is fitted up with glass pipes," described the screenplay, "tubes, wires, coils, all the appliances of scientific experiment. Camera pans slowly around until it catches Gogol and Wong in center of room. In front of them, on table propped against wall, is body of Rollo. His head is fastened by means of straps and iron braces to trunk. A glass tube is in his neck. This is attached by long rubber tube to beaker which holds blood fluid, under which gas flame is burning." With the revamped Production Code hovering above the production like the Sword of Damocles (not to mention the easily shocked sensibilities of Louis B. Mayer), it is no surprise that this graphic, blasphemous sequence fell before the editor's censorial scissors.

After viewing Lorre's bravura performance in *Mad Love*, legendary comedian and director Charlie Chaplin declared him "the greatest living actor." This was Lorre's American debut. Following *Mad Love*, Lorre did one other film in America (*Crime and Punishment*, 1935) before journeying to England for Alfred Hitchcock's *Secret Agent* (1936). There, Lorre was contacted by Adolf Hitler and invited to join the German film industry. Der Fuehrer professed to admire Lorre's portrayals of murderers. Lorre's written reply was short and to the point: "Thank you, but I think Germany has room for only one mass murderer of my ability and yours." According to Ted

Sennett in *Masters of Menace*, Hitler apparently had a long memory, for during World War II the FBI reportedly captured eight Nazi assassins possessing a hit list of 100 names. Peter Lorre was listed third.

Many great actors were rather vain, and Peter Lorre was no exception. According to Francis Drake, Lorre insisted on meeting his leading lady *before* his head was shaved so that she could see him with hair. Also, Lorre would occasionally upstage his co-star by intentionally ruining a scene ("He didn't want you to be too good!" laughed the actress), ad-libbing "Don't you know me? I'm your little Peter!" (from *Karloff and Lugosi*, by Greg Mank).

Born Frances Morgan Dean in New York City in 1913, Frances Drake had no aspirations to a career in acting — or a career in anything for that matter. The daughter of a wealthy mining magnate, she was educated (including finishing school) in Canada and England. It was only the loss of her family's fortune in the 1929 stock market crash that sent Frances looking for employment. She began as a ballroom dancer in fashionable London clubs and then graduated to the legitimate theater. She only entered movies because "they paid even better than the stage" (*Whatever Became Of...* by Richard Lamparski). Ms. Dean received several offers from Hollywood (including one from Universal), and ultimately chose Paramount because "they offered the most money."

The studio then changed her name to Drake (and publicized that their new "find" was actually related to the famous pirate!). In 1939 she married Cecil Howard, son of the Earl of Suffolk and Berkshire. At her husband's behest, Ms. Drake retired from acting in 1942, continuing as long as she did only because her husband had not yet come into his inheritance. Of her career and early retirement, she said: "From beginning to end my career was because of money. Yet, I did miss it a bit for a while. I consoled myself that at least I'd not have to be anywhere near such coarse, crass people as [studio executives] Al Kauffman and Harry Cohn."

Portrait in obsession: Peter Lorre as Dr. Gogol in his American film debut, *Mad Love* (1935).

Mad Love was Karl Freund's last film as a director, a career that spanned only three years and eight films. Freund dismissed directing, claiming, "anyone can make a good cake if he has the right ingredients. It all depends on story, cast, and circumstances." After *Mad Love*, Freund returned to cinematography, shooting such classics as *Pride and Prejudice* (1940) and *Key Largo* (1948). He also won an Academy Award for cinematography for *The Good Earth* (1937) and, according to a studio memo, was considered by David O. Selznick for the job of photographing *Gone with the Wind*. In the 1950s, Freund accepted the job of chief cinematographer at Desilu Studios, where he developed the three-camera technique while working on *I Love Lucy*, a process which became the standard for television sitcoms.

It is interesting to note that Freund both began and ended his directing career with horror films (*The Mummy* and *Mad Love*, respectively), and that out of his eight credits it is only these two that are remembered.

While Freund demonstrated intense visual acumen, he was not what one would call an "actor's director." According to Frances

Drake (as told to Greg Mank), Freund was too concerned with the camera to give much direction to the actors, leaving them largely to their own devices. Fortunately, these actors were all thorough professionals who could perform effectively without detailed direction.

Co-cinematographer Gregg Toland went on to become one of the most respected and influential cinematographers in film. His innovative use of high-key photography and the deep-focus technique set industry standards. Toland won an Academy Award for his work on *Wuthering Heights* (1939), and shot such classics as *The Grapes of Wrath* (1940), *Citizen Kane* (1941; for which he won a second Oscar), and *The Best Years of Our Lives* (1946). On *Mad Love*, Toland was forced into the role of simple cameraman rather than creative cinematographer by dictatorial director Karl Freund. "And Gregg Toland was a marvelous cameraman!" remembered Frances Drake. "Such a dear little man, and he looked rather hunted when this wretched big fat man [Ms. Drake's unflattering term for her director] would say, 'Now, now, we'll do it *this* way!'"

NOTES

1. By all accounts this characterization was not far from reality. "I remember that Clive was a very talented actor," recalled Ian Wolfe, who played Orlac's stepfather in *Mad Love*, "but a noticeably high-strung and nervous one." (Interview with Roger Hurlburt in *Filmfax* #39.)

2. Updated for the science of the 1990s, the idea still seems ludicrous. Watch *Body Parts* (1991) for confirmation of the concept's absurdity.

THE BLACK ROOM
(1935; Columbia)

Release Date: July 15, 1935
Running Time: 68 minutes
Director: R. William Neill
Producer: Robert North
Screenplay: Arthur Strawn, Henry Myers
Story: Arthur Strawn
Photography: Allen G. Siegler, A.S.C.
*Assistant Cameraman: Gert Anderson
Editor: Richard Caboon
Art Director: Stephen Goosson

Musical Director: Louis Silvers
Costumes: Murray Mayer
*Sound Technician: Edward Bernds
Cast: Boris Karloff (Anton/Gregor), Marian Marsh (Thea), Robert Allen (Lt. Lussan), Thurston Hall (Col. Hassel), Katherine DeMille (Mashka), John Buckler (Benic), Henry Kolber (Baron de Berghman), Colin Tapley (Lt. Hassel), Torben Meyer (Peter).

*Uncredited on film print.

> "Principio et finem Similia — I end as I began." — Baron de Berghman, reciting the fateful family motto (and curse).

SYNOPSIS

At the beginning of the nineteenth century, in central Europe, twins are born to the aristocratic House of Berghman. "No, do not toast this birth," admonishes the worried Baron de Berghman. "Do you all know how our family began? With twins, Brand and Wolfram, and it will end with twins. Brand, the younger, murdered his brother. This House began with murder and it will end the same way." The baron is convinced that the age-old curse that hangs over his family will be fulfilled by his own twin sons, Gregor and Anton. "This murder will happen again," he predicts, "in the Black Room — just as it did before." The Black Room is a curiously constructed chamber inside the Berghman castle, with walls of onyx and a deep pit at its center. Attempting to circumvent the curse, the Baron orders the Black Room sealed up forever.

Years pass and it is now 1834. The brothers' parents are both dead and Gregor, the elder twin, is now the baron. He is a cruel and heartless ruler, hated and feared by the populace. "The baron is a tyrant," declares one villager. "He's worse than that — he's a fiend!" exclaims another.

Fearing for his life, Gregor sends for his twin brother, the kindly Anton, who has been away for the past ten years in self-imposed exile. After Gregor murders another of the local women, the townsfolk storm the castle. Gregor, anticipating this action, is prepared. He proposes to hand his title over to his respected brother Anton and then leave the country. This satisfies the villagers, but Gregor has a secret plan. He lures his benign brother into the Black Room (which Gregor has secretly reopened) and topples Anton into the pit to his death. Gregor then assumes the role of his murdered brother. There is one difficulty with the deception, however. Anton was born with a paralyzed right arm, and so now Gregor must remember never to use this limb while carrying out his impersonation.

Setting his sights on marrying Thea (the niece of family friend Colonel Hassel), Gregor murders the colonel when the old gentleman discovers the baron's deception. The wily baron blames the crime on a young lieutenant, Thea's true love. With the lieutenant awaiting execution, Gregor forces Thea into a betrothal. On the day of the wedding, Tor, Anton's faithful hound, escapes his lead and races to the cathedral. There he attacks Gregor, who raises his right arm to defend himself, revealing to all his true identity. A chase ensues, and Gregor races back to his castle and the safety of his secret Black Room. Tor follows and knocks him into the pit — right onto the upturned knife of his dead twin. Thus, the family prophecy has been fulfilled.

MEMORABLE MOMENT

The picture's most literate moment is also a most revealing one. Back at the castle after dining with Colonel Hassel and his niece, the baron is being serenaded by the serving wench Mashka, who sings the same song which Thea had earlier offered. Propped casually in an oversized chair, Gregor slices and eats a pear, absorbed in the fruit and giving scant attention to the woman. Finishing her song, Mashka looks for approval. "Don't I play as good as she does? Didn't you listen?" she asks, but gets no reply from the preoccupied baron. Going to his side, she bends down to kiss him but Gregor brings his hand up to cut another slice and brush her away. "Don't you *want* to kiss me?" she asks. "A pear's the best fruit," is Gregor's only reply, admiring the fruit in his hand.

Mashka is angry now. "Every time you see *her* you want to be rid of *me*," she says sharply. "Lots of juice in a pear," states the baron enthusiastically, as if he had not heard her tirade. "You'll find I won't be got rid of so easy," demands Mashka, infuriated by the baron's indifference. "Do you hear what I say?!" "Adam should have chosen a pear," says the baron heartily, slicing off another bite. Spitefully, Mashka continues: "You've got it all planned, don't you. You're going to marry *her*. You're going to make *her* your wife, your *baroness*." Finishing his fruit, Gregor declares, "I like the feel of a pear; and when you're done with it —" he terminates his sentiment by tossing the fruit aside.

Undeterred, Mashka announces, "Well, you're not going to marry her; I'll put a stop to it." Gregor, still chewing his last bite and licking his fingers, finally acknowledges her presence. "You will?" he asks disinterestedly, not deigning to look up, "How?" Mashka then makes a fatal error and threatens him with her knowledge of the Black Room. At the mention of that infamous chamber, Gregor suddenly stops picking his teeth. His air of indifference evaporates and his face becomes hard, ugly, dangerous. Mashka presses the point. "[I've] seen you carry *heavy* things in there late at night." Then she notices his face and realizes her mistake as he grabs her wrist. Her venomous recriminations die on her lips and her forceful demeanor abruptly changes to terrified supplication. "Oh, I didn't mean it!" she blurts out quickly, her fear bringing her close to tears. She breaks free from his grasp and as he approaches her again she impulsively grabs at his hand and presses her face to it, while sobbing, "Oh, I didn't mean to, really." Gregor's face, however, is hard and unmoving. He grabs both her wrists and, holding them in one hand, forces her down, out of frame. Gregor holds a knife in his other hand and there is no doubt of Mashka's fate.

This sequence captures the baron's attitude perfectly, and Karloff's offhanded indifference-turned-menace is startlingly effective. The bit with the pear is a brilliant allusion which reveals much about the man's character. The nihilistic baron sees people not as human beings but as "fruit" for his own pleasure — something to be consumed and digested and the remnant tossed aside as so much offal.

ASSETS

The Black Room showcases two major assets — Boris Karloff and Boris Karloff. As Anton and Gregor, Karloff is able to stretch his acting ability (an opportunity often denied the pigeon-holed actor) and deliver two very different characters. These roles were tailor-made for Karloff, who built a career out of alternately playing kindly (though often misguided) men (his numerous mad doctor roles) and heartless, menacing fiends (as in *The Mask of Fu Manchu* or *The Black Cat*). Despite the two characters' similar appearance, one quickly comes to see Anton and Gregor as two wholly different people with distinct mannerisms, modes of speech, and outlooks on life. Karloff's Gregor is coarse-mannered, loutish, arrogant. He is unkempt, with disheveled hair and loose clothing. His voice is harsh and his face hard and scowling. Karloff's Anton, on the other hand, is genteel, polite. He is well-groomed and fastidiously dressed. Anton's voice is soft and kind, and his face smooth and gentle.

Karloff takes the dual role a step further when he plays Gregor impersonating Anton. Employing subtleties of variation, Karloff creates yet a third character: Gregor-as-Anton. The distinction is evident immediately after Gregor murders his brother in the Black Room. Walking up to look at himself in the reflective wall, Gregor smoothes his hair back and erases (almost) the scowl from his face. Straightening up and tilting his head back slightly to mimic Anton's upright posture, he practices the impersonation. "Will you announce Baron Anton," he says cheerily, smiling. The smile is false, however, and the good cheer rings hollow. While the mouth turns upwards in a grin, the eyes remain hard and there is an underlying sardonic quality about the countenance. By briefly stretching out a word here and adding an undertone there, Karloff gives his voice a subtle tone of insincerity. He puts on the mask of Anton while still retaining the essence of Gregor underneath. In this third guise, the actor delivers a performance sincere in its insincerity. *The Black Room* is a joy for Karloff admirers, for the picture is a testament to Karloff's acting prowess and, as such, arguably his finest vehicle.

Karloff is given first-rate sets to stalk through. The baron's castle is filled with ornate arches, massive stone pillars, and oversized fireplaces. Yet the large chambers are so meticulously and realistically furnished as to make it a believable, even livable, place. (The film's pressbook claimed that, in order to achieve authenticity on his sets, art director Stephen Goosson "spent days studying old prints and paintings of medieval castles, as well as photographs of the ruins of the few still existing feudal fortresses.") The notorious Black Room, about which much is heard at the film's beginning, does not disappoint once we're allowed inside. Its "onyx" walls (after the dust of decades has been wiped away) are darkly, ominously reflective. The deep pit dominating the room's center is surrounded by medieval machinery. The impressive gears and wooden levers and massive stone covering raised by thick metal chains conjure up images of the horror and pain of the Inquisition. The village appears to be right out of the Tyrolean Mountains. Columbia decks it out sumptuously and fills it with scores of costumed extras, giving it every bit the scope of a Universal Frankenstein picture. (In fact, it *is* the famed "Frankenstein" village — Columbia rented and redressed the standing set on the Universal backlot.)

Allen G. Siegler's cinematography deserves

Mashka (Katherine DeMille) has said too much and now Gregor (Boris Karloff) will introduce her to *The Black Room* (1935).

high praise. His fluid camerawork makes the most of the shadowy castle, the lofty cathedral, the authentic village. The shots are always carefully framed and meticulously planned to provide a maximum of visual interest. Fluid tracking shots create an excellent depth of field by moving past pillars, archways and fences placed in the foreground. Siegler and director Roy William Neill avoid lengthy static shots and transform the camera from a simple recorder of events into a purveyor of thoughts and emotions. For instance, toward the beginning of the picture the camera tracks in on a cemetery, passes two twin boys kneeling at a graveside, and focuses on the gravestone itself. After a dissolve, the camera pulls back from a similar tableau and we now see two young men standing there — 20 years later. The camera motion not only creates visual interest but becomes a metaphor underscoring the passage — the movement — of time.

Siegler and Neill also utilize the camera for emphasis. When Colonel Hassel glances in a mirror and sees the reflection of Anton surreptitiously signing a document with his right hand, he realizes that Gregor is putting over a deception. This key moment is emphasized by the camerawork. First there is a shot of the shocked colonel. Next, a cut to Gregor shows him resuming the deceptive posture. The camera then suddenly and rapidly tracks away from Gregor and back towards the colonel, just as the awful realization sets the colonel's mind reeling.

Character emphasis aside, at other times Neill uses the camera for just plain thrills, as in the scene in which the colonel's body is discovered. The camera focuses on a hallway mirror across from the door to the colonel's study. We watch the reflection of the maid carry a tray through the study door. We hear a crash and a scream and suddenly the camera whirls round to focus on the door itself as the woman comes racing out in terror. While we know what she will find when she enters the room, the swift, almost disorienting camera movement combines with the maid's horrified shrieks to inject excitement and surprise into the expected scene.

Neill's attention to detail includes a nice bit of visual foreshadowing. Upon Anton's return to the family castle, he reads the fateful family motto on the de Berghman crest carved in stone above the doorway. In a subjective shot, the camera first focuses on the crest, then pans down and tracks back to take in the entire doorway. Through the opening we see Gregor sitting and waiting — waiting for the fulfillment of the prophecy, perhaps?

Visual acumen aside, Roy William Neill also directs with an eye towards subtext. He often utilizes mirrors not only for their unique visuals but to underscore a theme. When Gregor murders Mashka, we see him force her down out of frame. Neill then cuts to a servant knocking on the door. Going back to Gregor, we view him rise up from Mashka's body, but he is now reflected in a mirror. Since the glass is tilted at an angle, Gregor's image is slightly off-kilter. This crazy, off-balance image points toward the warped monstrousness of the crime and the killer. Also, the fact that Gregor is in the mirror, and not seen in "reality," removes him somewhat—distances his presence—which emphasizes his cold aloofness and general disregard for the rest of humanity. In addition, firelight flickers in the background behind him—possibly a subtle inference to the damnable, *hellish* nature of the crime?

LIABILITIES

The Black Room is basically a costume melodrama with horror overtones. As such, it often comes across as stiff and formal, though still handsome to look at. Fortunately, Karloff, upon whose shoulders (both sets) the film rests, breathes life into the proceedings and overcomes this facade of formality (particularly in the role of Gregor, whose insolence and swaggering attitude is a breath of fresh air in the frequently stuffy Victorian-style atmosphere).

Also, the technical difficulties inherent in shooting a film about twins in which both siblings are played by the same actor can be a distraction. While generally well done, the awkward cuts, split screen techniques, and use of a double draw attention to themselves at the beginning. Fortunately, Karloff's two very different performances, which bring these two distinct characters to life, eventually make one forget all the camera trickery necessary to pull it off. The viewer becomes caught up with these characters and no longer sees them as the same actor.

The most readily visible and disappointing flaw of *The Black Room* is the carriage chase at the climax. The obvious rear-projection shots and speeded-up photography of the racing carriage accompanied by an intrusive, "rousing" musical score give the sequence the artificial look and sound of a thrill-a-minute serial. This cheapens the grand scale of the film, which the art direction, photography, and acting had been at such pains to create in the previous 65 minutes. While *The Black Room* appears as a genuine dyed-in-the-wool "A" production up to this point, this frenetic climax only serves to expose the picture's B-movie roots. (Columbia, the least of the eight "Major" studios and often looked upon as a "poor relation," built its foundations on the B product which was at this time becoming indispensable with the growing popularity of double-features.)

Overall, however, *The Black Room* is still a slick, handsomely mounted production which showcases a bravura performance from the Golden Age of Horror's greatest on-screen contributor—Boris Karloff.

REVIEWS

Variety (August 21, 1935): "Karloff fans get a load of their favorite to the saturation point here, but the picture will not get much at the box-office. Its best qualities are scenic investiture and photography, which do not excite dollars to elope from people's pokes...."

Britain's *Kinematograph Weekly* (September 5, 1935): "For once in a while Boris Karloff appears with no enormity of disguise and, in consequence, he is able to thrill even more effectively in this ingeniously devised story of fratricide. He differentiates well between the twin brothers and gives a sound performance, but he is badly served with dialogue which is generally stilted."

Famed novelist and highbrow film critic Graham Greene, writing in Britain's *The Spectator* (September 20, 1935), was pleased to see that "Mr. Boris Karloff has been allowed to act at last.... Karloff is not quite at ease with virtue, suavity and good looks, but he gives a very spirited performance as the wicked Count and carries the whole film, so far as acting is concerned, on his own shoulders." Mr. Greene audaciously compares *The Black Room* to *Frankenstein*—and *The Black Room* comes out ahead (!): "The direction is good: it has caught, as Mr. James Whale never did with *Frankenstein*, the genuine Gothic note."

PRODUCTION NOTES

In May 1934, Boris Karloff signed a one-picture contract with Columbia. Though the studio made several announcements over the next few months regarding their acquired star, nothing came of it until a year later when "*The Black Room Mystery*" began production on May 6, 1935. (In the interim, Karloff had scored further success at his home studio in *Bride of Frankenstein* and *The Raven*.)

The Black Room was originally shot as *The Black Room Mystery*, though the "*Mystery*"portion of the title was dropped before release (presumably so that Columbia could market it as a horror picture rather than a mystery melodrama—a wise decision since it is definitely *not* a mystery). "My recollection," remembered sound technician Edward Bernds (in an interview with Gregory William Mank from *Hollywood Cauldron*), "is that *The Black Room* was treated considerably better than the typical Columbia 'B,' and I guess it shows in the film."

Veteran director Roy William Neill (born Roland de Gostrie in 1886) entered show business as a child stage actor. After a stint as a war correspondent in China in 1912, Neill went to work for Thomas H. Ince, for whom he began directing motion pictures in 1916. After helming nearly 60 silent films (in only 13 years), Neill successfully adapted to sound production and directed over 50 more films up until his death in 1946. Among his credits are the borderline horror entries *Black Moon* (1934) and *The Ninth Guest* (1934). Neill is probably best known for guiding Basil Rathbone through his prolific Sherlock Holmes series, though horror fans will best remember him for directing Bela Lugosi's belated (and unfortunate) turn as the monster in *Frankenstein Meets the Wolf Man* (1943).

"Roy Neill was soft-spoken and gentlemanly," recalled Edward Bernds, "unlike most of the 'loud-speaker' directors at Columbia—Lew Landers, Lambert Hillyer, Ross Lederman, Al Rogell, C. C. Coleman, and the like. And this made him an ideal director for Karloff.... Karloff liked and respected Roy Neill. I think Karloff recognized the 'try-for-quality' that Neill made.... But there was one thing about Roy Neill—I didn't like to work with him for one very good reason. On the Columbia 'quickies,' we always worked long, dreary hours. In the morning, Roy was a meticulous, artistic director, taking pains with every scene—so, we'd fall behind schedule for the day's work. The production office would get on him, tell him to get the scheduled day's work or else, and Roy was too gentle and submissive to argue. So he'd try to speed up. But he was genuinely incapable of shooting anything really sloppy—and we'd often work far into the night. We knew him—not in his presence—as 'rocking chair' Neill. That was because he had to have a rocking chair on the set, and the prop man always provided one for him. He sat there and rocked, and we worked far into the night—that was Roy Neill."

The Black Room was Boris Karloff's first

Gregor or Anton? Actually, it is Gregor *impersonating* Anton in order to retain his power and wed Thea (Marian Marsh) in Columbia's *The Black Room* (1935).

horror film in which he appeared relatively normal—*sans* special makeup (even in *The Black Cat* he sported a bizarre, satanic haircut, dark eyeliner, and black lipstick). "An actor's most versatile tool is his own face," recalled Karloff in *Fantastic Monsters of the Films* #3 (1962). "I felt I could handle any type of role without elaborate makeup." The lack of grotesquerie in his guise for *The Black Room* let him utilize this "versatile tool" to create two distinct and impressive characters. In fact, Karloff was so pleased with the finished product that in 1936 he called *The Black Room* "my favorite picture so far." Despite this brief respite of normality, the actor remembered that "there was no living down this reputation for horror that I seem to have built up since the outset of my screen career. The demand for monstrous characterizations kept recurring, so there remained nothing to do but satisfy it." He was back to the grotesques for the majority of his remaining Golden Age horror films, playing a horribly disfigured criminal in *The Raven*; a hollow-eyed zombie in *The Walking Dead*; the bald-domed Neanderthal Mord in *Tower of London*; and the Monster once more in *Son of Frankenstein*. Karloff's face was not his own again until the end of the decade when *The Man They Could Not Hang* began his string of Mad Doctor portrayals and he was allowed to play scientists who were at least normal *looking,* if not so normal in their actions.

Leading lady Marion Marsh became quite friendly with her co-star Boris Karloff and was a frequent dinner guest at the actor's Coldwater Canyon home. In Gregory William Mank's *Karloff and Lugosi*, Ms. Marsh painted an amusing picture of the screen's greatest bogeyman as one of the world's greatest animal lovers: "Boris had a pet pig, whose name was Violet.... And the pig had a playpen, with little rails, and a spread over the floor, inside the house.... Boris would be late from the studio ... when the pig heard his car, it would start bouncing, forward and back, forward and back.... It was amazing—just like a dog who knew the master's car!... So, in would come Boris. 'How's my little Violet today?' he'd ask, and with his long legs, he would climb into the playpen with the pig, and they would romp together. It was really a sight to be seen."

Marian Marsh was born Violet Krauth (sharing the same Christian name as Boris' beloved pig—though the actress never let on, thinking "it might upset him") in 1913 on the island of Trinidad, though she came to America with her parents at age seven. Beginning on the stage at the tender age of 16, she made her screen debut in *Hell's Angels* (1930), but is best remembered for playing Trilby opposite John Barrymore's *Svengali* (1931). She appeared with Barrymore again (*and* a then-unknown Boris Karloff) in the similarly plotted *The Mad Genius* later that same year.

Born Katherine Lester in Vancouver, Canada, Katherine DeMille was the adopted daughter of filmmaker Cecil B. DeMille. "Determined to succeed on the screen despite the handicap of a famous father" (as *The Black Room*'s pressbook noted), Ms. DeMille paid her dues as an extra and bit player before working her way up to supporting roles like the fallen "Mashka" in this production. Her main ambition, claimed the pressbook, lay behind the camera, for she intended to become a producer. Her last film (*as an actress*) was in 1947 and her ambition remained unrealized. Ms. DeMille was married to Anthony Quinn from 1937 to 1965, when they divorced.

Celebrity product endorsements are far from a modern phenomenon. Back in 1935, both top-billed stars of *The Black Room*—Boris Karloff and Marian Marsh—were plugging something or other. Karloff was hawking the new Dodge and Ms. Marsh was publicizing Max Factor (the makeup "used exclusively at the Columbia studios"). "Contact local distributor immediately and have him inquire at Dodge factory or agency regarding local advertising plans!" *The Black Room* pressbook urged theater managers. And do not forget that "newspaper ads and display pieces are available" which feature Marian Marsh utilizing "the new Lovli-Lash Flipstick (brushless) mascara."

"Tor," the Great Dane who reveals the evil deception and chases Gregor to his death, possessed the similarly brief moniker of "Von." According to studio publicity, the massive dog consumed four and a half pounds of raw meat each day (one and a half pounds per meal). The old Hollywood axiom "never work with children or animals" hit home for director Roy William Neill. Whenever Neill would shout "action" during the scenes which featured the huge dog, the canine would let go with threatening growls and booming barks. This happened again and again, ruining each take. Apparently, Von had been trained to bark on cue from a speech which contained the word "action," and the dog took his job seriously. Neill ultimately had to forego the time-honored vocal command and resort to hand signals.

According to a studio article, Boris Karloff discovered one day that a flintlock pistol contained in a cabinet decorating one of the sets for *The Black Room* was not merely a prop-department mock-up, but an authentic sixteenth century weapon (dated 1764) "brought to America by a Hessian officer during the Revolutionary War." Karloff arranged to purchase the firearm from the rather unobservant (or uncaring) Columbia property department.

Continuing in this vein of authenticity, the production employed a number of extras of Czechoslovakian descent (35, claimed the studio) for the picture's wedding scene. These "Old World" extras furnished their own personal authentic national costumes from their homeland ("Many of them one hundred and more years old [which have] been in families for half-dozen generations"). "'Some of these costumes represent the work of years,' claimed the technical expert at Columbia studios. 'The fine embroidery and artistic choice of colorings are made by peasant women without any knowledge or study of art. It is part of their training, handed down from generation to generation.'"

Columbia's publicity strategies for this production were rather dignified (as befits the staid nature of *The Black Room*) compared to most studio ballyhoo schemes. The publicity boys suggested nothing more outlandish than sponsoring an essay contest on "family superstitions, traits, habits, etc." or "asking readers to send in — in from one to two hundred words — their conceptions of exactly what goes on in 'The Black Room.'"

CONDEMNED TO LIVE
(1935; Invincible)

Release Date: September 15, 1935
Running Time: 67 minutes
Director: Frank R. Strayer
Producer: Maury M. Cohen
Story and Screenplay: Karen De Wolfe
Photography: M. A. Andersen, A.S.C.
Recording Engineer: Richard Tyler
Art Director: Edward C. Jewell
Film Editor: Roland D. Reed
Assistant Director: Melville Skyer
Production Manager: Lon Young
*Musical Director: Abe Meyer

Cast: Ralph Morgan (Professor Paul Kristan), Pedro De Cordoba (Dr. Anders Bizet), Maxine Doyle (Marguerite Mane), Russell Gleason (David), Mischa Auer (Zan), Lucy Beaumont (Mother Molly), Carl Stockdale (John Mane), Barbara Bedford (Woman), Robert Frazier (Doctor), Ferdinand Schuman-Heink (Father), Hedi Skope (Anna), Marilyn Knowlden (Maria), *Harold Goodwin (Villager), *Charles "Slim" Whittaker (Villager), *Dick Curtis (Villager), *Frank Brownlee (Villager), *Horace B. Carpenter (Villager).

*Uncredited on film print.

"You were born that night —*condemned to live*!"— Dr. Anders Bizet.

SYNOPSIS

In the "darkest depths of Africa," drums beat rhythmically outside the mouth of a cave where three white people — a pregnant woman, her husband, and a doctor — have taken refuge from hostile tribesmen. The natives will not enter the unholy cavern because it is lorded over by the dreaded vampire bat. Suddenly, a huge bat descends upon the prostrate woman and fastens itself to her throat. She screams and the picture fades. A written narrative informs us that "Years later the mark of the Bat brings tragedy and terror to a peaceful village in another land."

A bell tolls mournfully as a group of torch-bearing villagers (in an unspecified locale, possibly puritan New England) view the body of the latest blood-drained victim of this "tragedy and terror." The frightened people fear it is the work of a giant bat-monster. Realizing that the attacks "never happen in the light," the villagers call in their most respected and learned citizen, Professor Paul Kristan. This saintly man, "who lives for the poor," can shed little light on the mystery and so pleads with the people to look to their safety and remain indoors after dark.

Enter Marguerite, a wholesome beauty who is engaged to Professor Kristan. The young innocent doesn't really love Kristan, but, thinking it "an honor," she is determined to "be worthy of him [and make him] a good wife." David, a young medical man, is unhappy about the impending marriage for he loves Marguerite and it seems that she secretly shares his feeling.

Leaving the budding romantic triangle for a moment, we learn that the professor himself is actually the vampiric killer. After falling asleep at his desk, Kristan awakens in darkness. He raises his head and his expression changes and distorts into that of a madman. The fiend creeps into the bedroom of a sleeping woman; his hands reach for her — and next we see Dr. Kristan's loyal manservant, the hunchbacked Zan, carrying the woman's body to the local cave (where all the victims have been found).

Dr. Anders Bizet, Professor Kristan's old friend and mentor (and foster father), arrives. Kristan confides to Bizet that he's "had a strange malady of late," describing "strange headaches followed by vagueness and exhaustion." A thoroughly good and kindly man, the professor does not connect his ailment with the murders.

Meanwhile, Dr. Bizet advises Professor Kristan that perhaps Marguerite is not truly in love with him but merely "in awe" of him. Determined to find out the truth from his fiancée, the professor sets out after dark to Marguerite's house. Kristan trips over a log along the wooded path and his lamp is extinguished. In the dark he transforms and once again rises as the mad fiend. Continuing to Marguerite's house, the madman murders a maid and then flees.

Still, none of the villagers suspects, though the professor is now more concerned than ever about his blackouts and vows that "until this malady is passed, I cannot marry Marguerite." Dr. Bizet, however, is beginning to form his own suspicions. Confronting Zan, he finally learns the awful truth.

Meanwhile, Professor Kristan has once again trudged back through the woods to Marguerite's house (without stumbling this time) to release her from her promise. As the couple talk, Marguerite blows out the lamp to ease the professor's growing headache. This upsets the professor, but one candle still illuminates the room. He confides, "I'm afraid *I* am the fiend," but Marguerite cannot believe this. "If I only knew, if I only can be sure," laments the tortured professor. Marguerite blows out the last candle to prove his fears are unfounded. Of course we know better and the professor's pounding headache immediately grows worse. A cloud passes over the moon and the room is plunged into total darkness. As he changes, Marguerite screams and Zan (who had followed his master) rushes in and wrestles the professor/fiend to the floor. The villagers, who had been searching for Zan (their number one human suspect) break in and, thinking Zan has attacked the professor, chase the hunchback to the cave.

Back at the house, Professor Kristan, his old self once again, pleads with Dr. Bizet to tell him the truth. "It started nearly 40 years ago," begins Bizet. "A monstrous bat had fastened to your mother's throat. They beat it off, but the harm was already done. You were born that night..." His worst fears confirmed, the kindly professor's first thoughts are for his persecuted servant and he rushes off with Bizet to try and help the hapless Zan.

As the mob corners Zan at the cave, David arrives and voices Zan's innocence. The enraged villagers will have none of it, however, and determine to burn the "blasphemer" along with Zan. Fortunately, Professor Kristan arrives in time and tells all to the stunned villagers. "I have only one thing left to do," he sadly tells Bizet. Walking alone into the back of the cave, he leaps from a ledge to his death. Zan, ever the faithful servant, follows him into the abyss — faithful even unto death.

MEMORABLE MOMENTS

There is nothing very memorable about *Condemned to Live*. Even immediately after viewing, one is hard-pressed to recall a single intriguing image. The most obvious candidates are the three transformation scenes. To a one, however, they are handled so haphazardly as to make no impact whatsoever. In the first, Professor Kristan wakes up at his desk to find the candle is out. Going to the window, he sees the moon pass behind the clouds. He lowers his head and when he lifts it again, he is grimacing and wheezing — he has (abruptly) become "The Fiend." This sequence contains background music, but the low, monotonous string melody inspires nothing but ennui. For the second transformation (devoid of music — monotonous or otherwise), Kristan gingerly steps over a log in the woods and then awkwardly trips, extinguishing his lantern. His approach and clumsy pratfall are viewed in a single long shot. The camera angle then (finally) changes, switching to a medium close-up of the professor's face. After rubbing his head, he lowers his hand and gives a "hard" stare while puffing out his cheeks. That's it! No music, no camerawork, no acting. The third and final

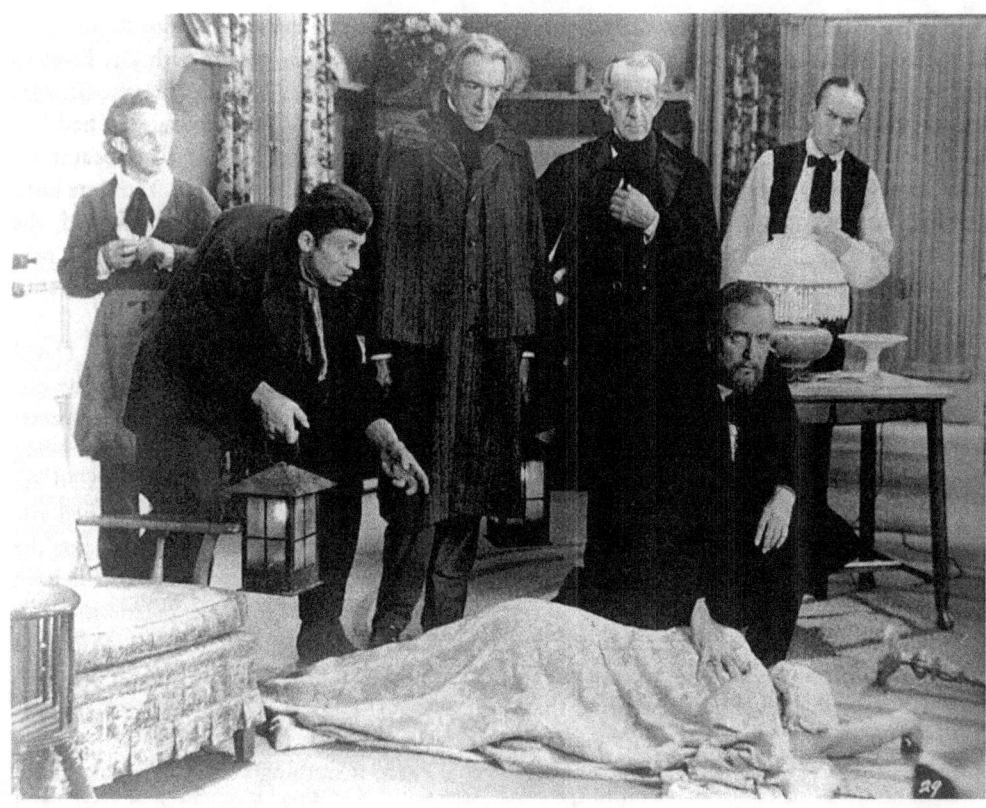

Zan (Mischa Auer, holding lantern) and Professor Kristan (Ralph Morgan, kneeling) discover the latest victim of the vampiric fiend in *Condemned to Live* (1935).

changeover, also lacking music, is even less dramatic (if that is possible). Whining, "A light, a light!," Kristan stands up with his back to the camera. When he turns, there's that "hard" stare again. These key scenes are so poorly staged (both technically and histrionically) that they become almost non-scenes (or is that non-sense?), along with the rest of the mundane picture.

ASSETS

For an admirer of the Golden Age of Horror, *Condemned to Live* is one of those hard-to-find entries for which one has high hopes while searching for the picture — which only sink to low contempt when it is finally found. The tantalizing combination of the vampire and Jekyll/Hyde themes, the presence of such standout character actors as Mischa Auer and Pedro De Cordoba, and the guidance of director Frank Strayer (who made such intriguing use of the camera in *The Vampire Bat*) all serve to whet one's horror appetite and build up an anticipation for, if not a first-rate horror picture, then at least an entertaining lower-birth thriller. Alas, for those who hope to discover an overlooked gem, *Condemned to Live* is condemned to disappoint. The themes are bungled, the players are wasted, and Strayer's direction is dull and lifeless (leading one to suspect that credit for the visual interest of *The Vampire Bat* is due primarily to that picture's cinematographer, Ira Morgan).

So many potential assets are left untapped that it becomes tiresome attempting to locate the silk in this cinematic sow's ear. The picture's only real interest comes from Mischa Auer's portrayal of the unfortunate hunchback, Zan. While Ralph Morgan's white-washed Professor Kristan is completely unconvincing in his too-saintly-to-be-true demeanor, Auer's Zan is more down-to-earth in his self-sacrificing, silent, single-minded loyalty to his master. This unfortunate hunchback, who is shunned even by the innocent Marguerite (though she eventually realizes her error), is not bitter, not cruel, but only wishes good for others and protection for his unfortunate master. Russian-born Mischa Ounskowsky (taking the screen name of Auer), who so frequently played villainous roles at this early stage of his screen career, turns in a heartfelt portrayal in what is an unfortunately underdeveloped part.

LIABILITIES

Cinematically speaking, *Condemned to Live* is a lifeless desert. Most scenes are filmed in medium shot with few cuts (not even to an occasional reaction shot), creating a visual sameness which only adds to the picture's dry, stuffy dullness. While the camera is not completely static, it might as well have been, for instead of building mood and atmosphere, it does nothing more than occasionally follow a character from one side of a room to another. What little visual movement is present is perfunctory and holds no dramatic impact. In the hands of director Frank Strayer and cinematographer M. A. Andersen, the camera becomes more of a dentist's drill than an artist's brush.

Screenwriter Karen De Wolfe's characters are all so colorless and shallow that the picture fails to draw the audience in and establish any empathy, leaving the viewer cold. The only character who seems even human is the poor hunchback, Zan. The two young leads — the audience identification figures — are ineffective; Marguerite is silly and foolish while David is persistent to the point of being boorish and petulant. Poor Pedro De Cordoba, while sincere in his portrayal of Dr. Bizet, cannot overcome the pedantic dialogue and lack of characterization. Worst of all, Professor Kristan, about whom the film revolves, continually spouts platitudes like "pride goeth before a fall" and "beauty or ugliness is only of the soul"; pompous and dull and impossibly-good, he becomes a ridiculous whitewashed caricature.

The stilted dialogue is so deadly serious that it soon becomes laughable (inspiring titters of the derisive variety, rather than guffaws of real enjoyment). Odd, unwieldy lines proliferate: "You're right old woman, 'tis ungodly not to be afraid" or "She's incapable of dissimulation." Everyone is so lofty in their manner and speech that the viewer begins to suspect he is listening to a Victorian sermon rather than a horror picture.

Even the film's plot construction works against it. After a few moments of mystery revolving around the ghastly murders and supposed giant bat-creature, we immediately learn that it is Professor Kristan who unknowingly becomes this blood-drinking fiend. This revelation comes much too soon to be anywhere near effective since we've barely even met the saintly Professor, much less come to know him as a character. At this point in the narrative, all we really know is that he speaks in tired platitudes, helps children with their letters, and is rather dull. No connecting link with the audience has been established, so this potentially shocking and tragic revelation is thrown away.

The picture also suffers from an almost total lack of music. (The few strains heard are snippets of a melodramatic theme lifted from *The Vampire Bat*, 1933). An effective musical score could have added some much-needed impact to key sequences, particularly the transformation or "mad fiend" scenes. Since so little is done with the camera (or the actors, for that matter), an appropriately sinister musical background could have beefed up the menace to some degree. Alas, these scenes are almost silent (as is the near-dozing audience).

Like a number of films from this era, *Condemned to Live* has aged badly. Unlike many of its contemporaries, however, it possesses none of the charm or enthusiasm which can make even a dated picture enjoyable today. *Condemned to Live* is condemned to die a quiet death in deserved obscurity.

REVIEWS

Variety (October 9, 1935) conjectured that "*Condemned to Live* probably read much better

Professor Kristan (Ralph Morgan), backed by his friend and mentor, Dr. Anders Bizet (Pedro De Cordoba, far left), protects the frightened Zan (Mischa Auer) from the wrathful villagers in this lobby card scene from *Condemned to Live* (1935).

than it screens. In picture form it is neither much of a chiller nor a romance.... Takes about two reels to get the story going. And then it lacks conviction.... Much of the dialogue is meaningless and element of romance mostly incidental and never intriguing." The only good thing the reviewer (Char) had to say was regarding two of the cast members: "Ralph Morgan gives a smooth performance as the Jekyll-Hyde character.... A hunchback is well done by Mischa Auer."

"'*Condemned to Live*' Condemned to Die," announced *The Hollywood Reporter* (October 26, 1935). "*Condemned to Live* is a classic of errors in every department. True, it is full of laughs, in the wrong spots, and will be greeted with tremendous applause, satirically, throughout its showing and by a grateful audience at its fadeout.... Ralph Morgan has seldom been seen in such a comedy of errors and poor direction."

PRODUCTION NOTES

Being a poverty row outfit without their own facilities, Invincible Pictures Corporation rented not only the sets from Universal (including Universal City's Tyrolean village, still dressed from *Bride of Frankenstein*, and the bell tower from their Notre Dame cathedral replica) but also that studio's wardrobe (primarily the costumes from their two Charles Dickens pictures, *Great Expectations*, 1934, and *Mystery of Edwin Drood*, 1935). Interiors for *Condemned to Live*, however, were shot at nearby Talisman Studios rather than at Universal. According to the *Hollywood Reporter* (July 15, 1935), Universal could not spare the space because it had six of its own companies hard at work on its home soundstages.

Ralph Morgan (born Raphael Kuhner Wupperman) earned a law degree from Columbia University but abandoned a career in the legal profession to become an actor. His move into show business was emulated by his younger brother Francis, who changed his name to Frank Morgan (and is best known for playing the title role in 1939's *The Wizard of Oz*). According to the *Condemned to Live* pressbook, "the Morgans are fussy about the pictures they appear in, and, they can well afford to be. For they are independently wealthy...", receiving an annual income from a family-owned corporation. (One suspects that Ralph's dividends were rather light the month he was offered *this* picture.) Ralph Morgan's other genre credits are *Rasputin and the Empress* (1932), *The Mad Doctor* (1941), *Night Monster* (1942; in which he contributes a particularly effective portrayal), *Weird Woman* (1944), *The Monster Maker* (1944), and *The Creeper* (1948).

The aristocratic-mannered (though American-born) Pedro De Cordoba appeared in a number of significant horror pictures, including *The Devil-Doll* (1936), *Before I Hang* (1940), *The Ghost Breakers* (1940), *The Picture of Dorian Gray* (1945), and *The Beast with Five Fingers* (1946).

Labeling Mischa Auer "one of the best horror-men in Hollywood" (despite the fact that the actor never appeared in a full-blown horror picture before — or since[1]), the film's pressbook claimed that "even the production crew at the Invincible Pictures Corporation studio was frightened when they beheld Mischa Auer in his make-up for the role of Zan, the hunchback." Perhaps this "best horror-man" label wasn't completely unwarranted, for the following year Auer received an Academy Award nomination for his work in *My Man Godfrey* (1936), in which he played a man who impersonates a gorilla! The bogus "horror-man" appellation immediately fell by the wayside, however, as Auer quickly became known for his comical characterizations (such as the hilarious Russian balletmaster in *You Can't Take It with You*, 1938). Mischa Auer was born Mischa Ounskowski in St. Petersburg, Russia. Fleeing the Bolshevik Revolution as a teenager, he escaped to Italy. Mischa's maternal grandfather, celebrated violinist Leopold Auer, then brought the boy to the US. Taking his grandfather's surname, Mischa began his acting career on the stage in 1925, entering films three years later. Though he appeared in nearly two-score previous pictures, it was not until *My Man Godfrey* that Auer finally became a character star. "That's when I hit the Hollywood mother lode," said Auer. "That one role made a comedian out of me. I haven't been anything else since. It's paid off very well."[2] Auer continued acting (often appearing in European productions, for which he utilized his fluency in French, German, Spanish, and Russian) up until his death in 1967 at age 61.

Russell Gleason was born into show business. Both of his paternal grandparents were actors as were his mother and father (renowned actor/director/playwright James Gleason). Following in his familial footsteps, Russell played supporting roles and even leads in a number of pictures until his career was cut short at age 39 by a bizarre tragedy. After serving three years in the Army (despite his advanced age), Gleason was two months away from discharge. In late December, 1945, Gleason was at the Hotel Sutton in New York City when he plummeted out of a fourth-story window to his death. The police ruled the fall accidental. "Gleason had been given sulfa drug to clear up a bad cold," reported *Variety* (January 2, 1946), "and it's believed that he became groggy and fell. His body was found on a parapet outside a second-story window."

The picture's prologue features two fallen stars of the silent screen — Robert Frazer (as the doctor) and Barbara Bedford (as the woman who gives birth to the monster "condemned to live"). Frazer, a romantic hero in the teens and twenties (appearing in over 60 silents), was forced into supporting roles in grade B (through Z) talkies. He was awarded a much meatier role in the low-budget (but infinitely better) *White Zombie* three years earlier, playing the tragic, love-smitten Beaumont. The next year he played the rather thankless part of Emil, Lionel Atwill's murderous servant in *The Vampire Bat* (1933). Frazer appeared in one other (semi-)horror film when he fell prey to Bela Lugosi in *Black Dragons* (1942). He died in 1944 at the age of 52. It is a rather sad commentary that Mr.

Frazer's name is misspelled in the credits of *Condemned to Live*.

In addition to this picture, Frank Strayer also directed *Murder at Midnight* (1931), *The Monster Walks* (1932), *The Vampire Bat* (1933), and *The Ghost Walks* (1935). With the exception of *The Vampire Bat*, none of them are any better than *Condemned to Live*. He is perhaps better known as the director of the seemingly endless *Blondie* series, begun in 1938.

One studio-penned article attempted to promote this film by taking a "scientific" angle: "Pro and con arguments by learned psychiatrists have brought forth no conclusive decisions of the question of prenatal influence affecting the afterlife of a child, and, if there is such a thing, does it lie dormant for a period and then make itself manifest in later years. An argument on the pro side of this problem is offered along with thrills and chills in the new Invincible picture, 'Condemned to Live.'" The article goes on to claim that the film "reveals a true case history which though seemingly too horrible to be believable is none the less fact." (No further details about this "true case history" were offered.)

Some of the more outrageous selling angles suggested by Invincible's publicity department include sponsoring an essay contest entitled "Do Human Vampires Really Exist?"; dressing the local hypnotist ("there must be a hypnotist in your town") as a vampire bat and having him operate in the outer lobby; and caging live bats in the lobby or offering "free admission to anyone who brings a live bat to the theatre."

NOTES

1. The closest Auer had previously come to a horror film was a small part in the borderline entry *Rasputin and the Empress* (1932) (also with Ralph Morgan), while the nearest he came *after Condemned to Live* was appearing opposite Abbott and Costello in *Hold That Ghost* (1941).

2. Quoted in *Comic Support*, by Ron Smith.

THE CRIME OF DOCTOR CRESPI
(1935; Liberty/Republic)

Release Date: October 21, 1935
Running Time: 63 minutes
Producer/Director: John H. Auer
Associate Producer: Herb Hayman
Screenplay: Lewis Graham, Edwin Olmstead
Story: John H. Auer (suggested by Edgar Allen [sic] Poe's *The Premature Burial*)
Photography: Larry Williams
Art Director: William Saulter
Editor: Leonard Wheeler
Recording: Clarence Wall

*Makeup: Fred Ryle
*Production Supervisor: W. I. O'Sullivan
*Musical Director: Milton Schwarzwald
Cast: Erich von Stroheim (Dr. Crespi), Harriet Russell (Mrs. Ross), Dwight Frye (Dr. Thomas), Paul Guilfoyle (Dr. Arnold), John Bohn (The dead man), Geraldine Kay (Miss Rexford), Jeanne Kelly (Miss Gordon), Patsy Berlin (Jeanne), Joe Verdi (Di Angelo), Dean Raymond (Minister).
*Credit not appearing on film print.

"In your frenzy you will *pound* and *scratch* and you will gasp and *suffocate*!"—Dr. Crespi.

SYNOPSIS

The famed Taft Clinic, a private hospital, is run with an iron hand by the formidable chief surgeon, Dr. Andre Crespi. When a car accident critically injures Dr. Stephen Ross, Ross' wife Estelle telephones the clinic. "Dr. Crespi is one of the few men—perhaps the only man—who can save him," advises Ross' attending physician. Though Ross is a former assistant, Crespi rudely refuses to speak with his worried wife.

Determined to talk with the great doctor,

Estelle goes to the hospital. She pleads with him ("You are the only one that can save him!") but he remains unmoved. "Oh why can't you forgive — forget," she says despairingly. At this Crespi becomes angry. "I understand how he turned you away from me," he hisses, "after I treated him like one would a brother. I understand how he made love to you — right under my own *eyes*!" Evelyn defends her husband, admitting that "Stephen never knew you cared for me in that way.... Stephen never dreamed you wanted to marry me."

Crespi finally acquiesces and, assisted by doctors Thomas and Arnold, saves Stephen with a brilliant operation. Back in his office, though, Crespi pulls out a blank death certificate and fills in Stephen's name *and* the time of death — at 15 minutes from now! Placing the prognosticating paper under his desk blotter, Crespi goes to see his recovering patient and there administers an injection. Suddenly, Ross' respiration grows weaker and in a moment he is dead. When Dr. Thomas asks for a death certificate back at Crespi's office, the doctor pulls out the already completed form from under his desk blotter. Thomas' eyebrows raise in suspicion but he says nothing.

After ordering Ross' body taken to the morgue, Crespi, the soul of conciliatory comfort, goes to Estelle's house. There he gives solace to the grieving widow and suggests she go away for awhile.

At midnight Crespi creeps into the clinic morgue and uncovers Ross' body. "Hello Stephen my friend," he says, "my *dear* friend — my *dead* friend. No, you are not dead are you? They just *think* you're dead." Suddenly, we see the muscles in the corpse's face twitch. "The potency of this drug," continues Crespi in a triumphant whisper, "lasts only for about 24 hours. You're *juuust* coming out of it." Crespi then gives Stephen another injection. "You've made me suffer for five long years," accuses Crespi, "by marrying Estelle.... Ever since then I've hoped and prayed for the chance to pay you back someday *with compound interest*.... Tomorrow around midnight your muscles will be alive again — but it will be too late. You will be encased in a casket which I myself have picked out for you and eight feet of heavy earth above you."

The following day, Dr. Thomas confronts Crespi. "Ross was poisoned," accuses Thomas, "and you can't get away with it." Crespi attacks Thomas and chokes him into unconsciousness. Tying him up, Crespi locks Thomas in his office closet.

After Ross' burial services, Crespi returns to the clinic and lets Thomas out. "Sorry I had to treat you so rough," apologizes Crespi as he unties the shaken man. "You know, if I wouldn't have locked you up today, you would have blurted your ideas all over. I think I'm going to let you go back to work, but in the future, Thomas, I wish you would keep your ideas to yourself."

Thomas tells Dr. Arnold of Crespi's attack on him and his suspicions regarding Ross' death. Reluctantly, Arnold finally agrees to help Thomas dig up Ross' body and perform an autopsy. While Crespi drinks and gloats in his office over his triumph, the two doctors unearth Ross' body and bring it back to the clinic. As they begin the procedure, Stephen revives. Stephen slowly staggers away from the astonished Thomas and Arnold into Crespi's office, where he collapses in a chair. Just then Estelle arrives (Crespi was going to "see her off" before her impending trip) as do the two doctors, now recovered from their shock. Estelle rushes to Stephen's side and Crespi pulls a gun from his desk drawer. Facing them all down, Crespi finally lowers his weapon. "Don't worry," he says resignedly, "I'm not going to hurt any of you. It's all finished. I'm through." In a sadly sardonic tone he adds, "the *great Dr. Crespi*." Suddenly, the scene switches to the shocked reaction of Dr. Thomas who yells "Don't!" as a shot rings out. We then see Crespi collapse, having shot himself.

Later, Dr. Arnold enters his office as the new chief surgeon to meet his wife (presumably the nurse he'd been romancing) while a smiling Dr. Thomas makes time with Miss Gordon, the duty nurse outside.

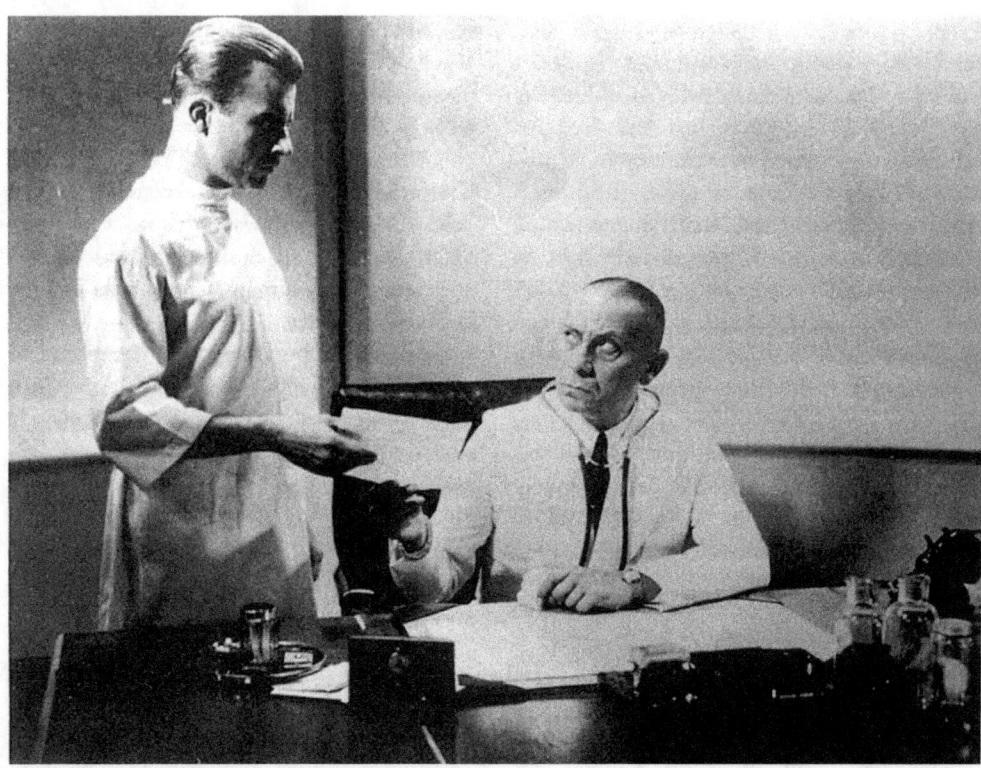

The glowering Dr. Crespi (Erich von Stroheim) hands a death certificate to a suspicious Dr. Thomas (Dwight Frye) in *The Crime of Doctor Crespi* (1935).

MEMORABLE MOMENT

"Fair warning to the tender-hearted!" heralded the picture's pressbook. "'The Crime of Dr. Crespi' will make you shiver, shudder, shout and shriek!" Surprisingly, the studio ballyhoo was not far off—at least for one or two scenes. Ross' move from the dead to the living is a case in point. In the autopsy room, we see the clock strike 12 as Dr. Arnold begins to make his incision on the bare chest of the corpse. With the camera focused on the head of the body, Dr. Thomas gives a terrified, almost incoherent yell offscreen. The shot then changes to between the feet of the cadaver, looking down the length of the body at the level of the table. Slowly, ever-so-slowly, Stephen's corpse sits up, the low-key lighting making dark, empty sockets of his eyes and casting his form in a cadaverous hue. Throughout the shuddery scene, the clock strikes slowly and relentlessly, tolling the midnight hour.

The scene then shifts to the corridor outside the operating room where the night nurse sits at her desk talking on the phone, her back to the hallway. In the background we see Stephen emerge from a door and advance slowly, unsteadily, along the wall behind her. As he moves closer and closer with a zombie-like shuffle, she talks on, complaining that "there hasn't been any excitement since the quintuplets." Placing a hand on her shoulder, Ross slowly and painfully gets out the words, "Where is Dr. Crespi?" Recognizing his hollow-eyed countenance as belonging to a man dead and buried, she screams.

Ross' slow, silent shuffle toward the oblivious nurse, his deathly pallor and sunken eyes (When Ross finally makes it to Crespi's office, the doctor insultingly observes that "as a ghost, you're just as hideous as that rotten *carcass* of yours"), and the silent (save for the midnight tolling), dimly lit surroundings of a nighttime hospital all combine to create a moment of true *frisson*.

ASSETS

Under John Auer's effective direction, Larry Williams' lighting and camerawork almost single-handedly save the picture, raising it above the dross of its poverty-row contemporaries like *Condemned to Live* and *Revolt of the Zombies*. Frequent tracking shots keep the visuals alive and create a sense of movement (something sorely lacking in the story itself), while numerous camera set-ups and varied angles keep the shots from growing stale. As Estelle pleads with Crespi for the life of her husband, for example, Williams and Auer bring the camera in for an extreme close-up (only the actors' heads visible) to hear Crespi's bitter reply. With Estelle's profile shadowed on the edge of the frame, von Stroheim's glowering, hate-filled countenance fills half the screen as he spits out his venomous answer. The stark-white background lends an air of blank detachment, letting no background distraction break the intensity of the moment. For Estelle's retort, the camera cuts back to a medium close-up (heads *and* shoulders now visible) so that some background details can now be seen. Finally, as the tense scene concludes with Crespi's acquiescence, the camera shows his capitulation in a full-bodied medium shot. With the varied visual distance at the proper moments, the camera seemingly retreats as the scene's intensity dissipates.

Williams avoids static uniformity in his lighting just as he avoids a static camera. Via low-key illumination, he casts intricate shadows across his subjects' faces, particularly that of von Stroheim (visually suggesting his character's intensity and complexity of emotion). Williams also creates much variation in the background, throwing patches of light and dark against the walls to give a depth of perspective lacking in most poverty-row productions of the time. Through his careful lighting, Williams generates a three-dimensional visual sense, a sense heightened when the actors move in and out of the pools of light and shadows. When Crespi torments the paralyzed Stephen with his imminent premature burial, von Stroheim's shadowy face looms out of a pitch black background. The low-key lighting upon his countenance adds to the macabre gloom of the scene while the surrounding darkness conjures up the enveloping blackness of the very grave about which Crespi speaks.

Kept busy throughout the 1920s, Williams lensed a handful of early talkies for Paramount before quitting cinematography in 1931. How Liberty Pictures lured him out of semiretirement for *The Crime of Doctor Crespi* is anybody's guess (though every viewer's gain). Sadly, Williams only photographed one further film (*Tevya* in 1939).

Fortunately, *The Crime of Doctor Crespi* possessed a director astute enough to recognize and take full advantage of his cinematographer's talents. John H. Auer selects his shots to emphasize Williams' compelling camerawork and suggestive lighting. Rather than simply showing us the funeral procession moving along, Auer includes a brief *Vampyr*like[1] shot of the trees passing by overhead as the camera looks straight up into the leafy canopy in a coffin's-eye-view shot. With the mournful tolling of bells punctuating the background organ music, the viewer feels a moment of disorienting anxiety — as if we, too, have suddenly awakened to find ourselves trapped in a coffin on its way to the grave. Auer then goes a step further. As the casket is lowered into the grave the camera again becomes the coffin and we look up at the mourners gathered around the edge of the enclosing pit while we descend slowly into the earthen tomb. Finally, inevitably, we watch helplessly from inside the grave as earth cascades down upon the camera lens — upon *us*.

Auer rarely shoots against a flat background or wall, choosing instead to show a corridor stretching behind or an open door revealing the depth of space beyond. By choosing angles that emphasize space and depth, the director makes the most of the few sets he has to work with.

Auer also fills his sparse sets with activity. As the principals walk down a hall, a man pushes a wheelchair across the corridor in the background. While we watch Crespi scrub up for an operation, his assistants prepare the instruments in the room behind him. For one key dialogue sequence Auer has his two surgeons stand at sinks and wash vigorously before an operation to deliver their lines rather than simply letting them sit in an office discussing the matter. This keeps the action going by including at least *some* activity in the scene. Small (and sometimes complicated) touches such as these add a visual interest to the frequently flagging story.

Editor Leonard Wheeler assembles the many shots and varied angles provided by Auer and Williams with an eye to further augment a mood or induce an emotion. When Crespi taunts the helpless Stephen in the morgue, Wheeler cuts to different angles of von Stroheim's face — cutting even while in midsentence — to create a disjointed, disorienting feeling of unease as Crespi talks calmly but intently of burying his victim alive. These quick and frequent cuts help create a feeling of helplessness and anxiety in the viewer, just as Crespi's victim experiences these same emotions.

In the operation sequence, Wheeler cuts quickly from one shot to another, never allowing the visuals to rest (just as the doctors themselves cannot rest), to add a sense of urgency to the scene. As the operation reaches its critical stage, the cuts become faster, almost frantic. Wheeler utilizes 33 shots in a sequence lasting little more than a minute, never holding on one scene for more than a few seconds.

Wheeler even contrasts different scenes to draw parallels and generate suspense. At one point, he intercuts shots of the bound Dr. Thomas struggling desperately to get out of the closet with scenes of the casket being lowered into the grave. By this juxtaposition Wheeler cleverly reminds the viewer of the hopeless struggle soon to come *inside* that very coffin.

The only truly interesting character in *The Crime of Doctor Crespi* is Crespi himself, and the production was fortunate to have such a strong presence as Erich von Stroheim to fill the mad medico's shoes. Auer seemingly realized this and took great care with the Crespi character. Crespi's first appearance, for instance, sees the doctor step off an elevator after allowing an attractive nurse to exit ahead of him. As she turns to go off down a corridor, Crespi's head casually turns and von Stroheim looks intently after her, even as he walks off in the other direction. Immediately, we get a feel for the less-than-healthy, even lecherous, nature of the character.

Working with art director William Saulter, Auer even manages to make the few limited sets reflect the character of this complex (and disturbed) individual. On one side of Crespi's office rests a large lab table covered in the glass tubes and bubbling beakers one expects from a mad doctor. On the other side sits Crespi's mammoth, imposing desk, with his large leather chair standing thronelike behind it. The room is cold, austere, perfectly fitting Crespi's commanding, aloof, arrogant demeanor. The opaque window/wall behind his desk suffuses the room in a harsh, white light, bringing everything out in stark relief. A macabre detail here and there adds to the (character) illumination. Against one bare wall of Crespi's inner sanctum stands a liquor cabinet — with a baby's skeleton perched atop it. In one scene, Crespi pours himself a drink, nonchalantly flicks the small skull with his finger, throws his head back and tosses down his shot of liquor.

Von Stroheim vacillates wildly in his portrayal, making Dr. Crespi a volatile, even unstable, man — though, oddly, one that exudes an aura of complete control. (Even when the inebriated Crespi sees the corpse of his victim stagger into his office, he remains unperturbed — thinking perhaps it is an alcoholic hallucination — and hurls an insult at the daunting specter.) Soft-spoken and placating one moment, von Stroheim barks out orders and shouts clipped commands the next. Von Stroheim's powerful presence and sense of control make each varied mood believable while demonstrating the dangerous complexity of his character. Though appearing sincere on the surface, von Stroheim's face betrays an inner core of coldness that his false and fleeting moments of exterior warmth fail to melt. One shudders when von Stroheim laughs low, almost giggling with an excited glee, and tells his victim to look for carnations on the casket — "They'll be from me."

Dwight Frye's sincere performance almost brings the lackluster character of Dr. Thomas to life. Almost. When Crespi slaps Thomas after he calls Crespi a murderer, we see the defiant determination mixed with barely checked anger on Frye's face as he spits back, "Go on! Hit me again, I don't care! I *still* say you poisoned him!" Frye finally gets to exhibit his talents at portraying genuine emotion (shock at the vicious slap, flaring anger, and a desperate determination) rather than simple (though admittedly effective) lunatic grins and giggles. Still, he cannot quite overcome the script's underdeveloped characterization of sniveling underling handed to him, and his screen time remains brief.

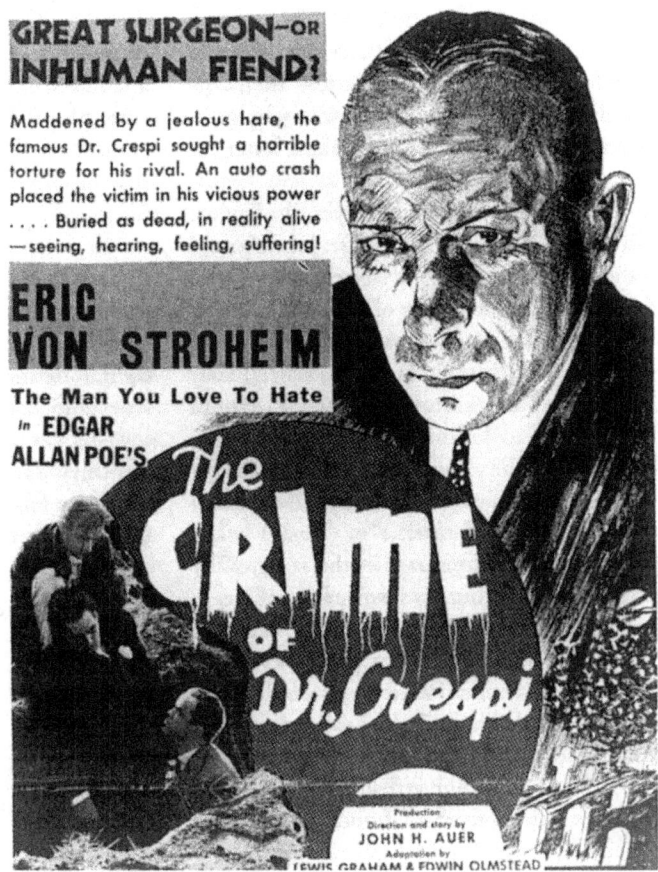

Trade ad for *The Crime of Doctor Crespi* (1935). (Courtesy of Ron Borst/Hollywood Movie Posters.)

LIABILITIES

All the above assets remain surface dressing, however, for there is little substance to this petty *Crime*. Lewis Graham and Edwin Olmstead's hastily written screenplay (from a story by director John Auer) *barely* fits the bill for a feature length film (even at a scant 63 minutes). Auer was forced to pad the picture's running time with innumerable fillers to cover the frequent dead spots in the script. For instance, in one sequence we watch Crespi at his desk filling out a form (we later learn it is Ross' death certificate) — for a full 40 seconds — the only action being the scratching of his pen. In another scene, we observe Crespi thoroughly scrubbing up at a sink. While a few moments before we witnessed an important dialogue exchange at this same spot, absolutely nothing happens here (except we get a long, loving look at Crespi's hand washing technique).

Nothing much occurs to warrant the film's running time, except that someone (whom the viewer has never met and has no invested interest in) is buried alive. Aside from a few key moments (Crespi's visit to the morgue, Stephen's burial, Thomas' confrontation with Crespi, and Stephen's revival) little happens to hold the viewer's interest. Instead of suspenseful action, much needed character development, or atmospheric set-pieces, the screenplay pads out the slim scenario with uninteresting subplots and scenes about a doctor romancing a nurse or a mother lying to her little girl about her dead father.

The inconsequential romance between Dr. Arnold and Nurse Jeanne is silly and poorly written (its lengthy scenes creating more precious time filler). Arnold lures her away from her post to "take a letter," then cannot think of anything to say. Consequently, Jeanne has him sit down and take a letter for *her*.

Staring dreamily into his eyes, she begins: "Your petition sets forth that Dr. John Arnold is the most competent physician in the world, that he has the nicest way of laughing with his eyes and crinkling his nose..." The budding romance goes abruptly (and pointlessly) sour in another time-killing scene when Arnold later whines to Jeanne like a jealous schoolboy: "This is the second time you've broke our date — and it's always Dr. Crespi. Dr. Crespi *this* and Dr. Crespi *that*!...."

Logic plays little part in the story. Why would Crespi fill out his former friend's death certificate ahead of time — unless he wanted to present an opportunity for prying eyes like those of Dr. Thomas? And why would Crespi brutally attack his underling (who knows at least a part of the truth), lock him in a closet, and then let him out a few hours later and *send him back to work* as if nothing had happened?!

Perhaps Graham and Olmstead were squeamish about allowing a real murder in their story and so concocted this lame, nonsensical plot point to smooth it over.

The picture suffers acutely from a lack of likable — or realistic — characters. With the exception of Crespi (thanks largely to the powerful presence of von Stroheim), the picture is populated with underdeveloped ciphers. There is no real hero figure, no one with whom the viewer can truly identify (unless it's the corpse, perhaps).

Dr. Thomas comes off as a sullen, second-rate snooper almost as unstable as Crespi himself. Dr. Arnold's selfish and cowardly attitude does little to ingratiate him with the viewer. When Thomas attempts to enlist Arnold's aid, his hypocritical reply is merely, "Count me out. It may be true, but you're never going to prove anything on the old man, even if he did poison him." Only when Thomas threatens to go to the D.A. directly does Arnold reluctantly agree to help, only because "if it ever gets out, it'll put us *all* under a cloud of suspicion." Estelle spends the picture pleading and grieving while Jeanne, Arnold's love interest, alternately engages in silly flirtation and grows petulantly tearful at his jealousy.

It is a tribute to director Auer, cinematographer Williams, editor Wheeler, and players like von Stroheim and Frye that *The Crime of Doctor Crespi* is watchable at all. With a tighter, better-developed script to work from, Auer and company could have produced a low-budget macabre gem rather than the substanceless fools gold it became. Though von Stroheim felt *The Crime of Doctor Crespi* was really "the crime of Republic, the screenwriter, and the director," the blame for this cinematic felony rests squarely with screenwriters Graham and Olmstead.

REVIEWS

Variety (January 15, 1936) observed that "Eric [*sic*] von Stroheim's entrance into the field of horror pictures does not get him very far. Overaction and overstress in a creaky adaptation of Edgar Allen [*sic*] Poe's 'The Premature Burial' brings laughs where none are sought." Of the picture itself, *Chic* called it a "cheap melodrama crudely played and while it occasionally shocks, it is a feeling of disgust rather than of horror." "The idea is there," the reviewer concluded, "and could probably have been developed into something effective in a macabre way, but in this practically every opportunity has been muffed.... As a baby scarer this is a weak entry."

The New York Times' (January 13, 1936) B. R. Crisler took a typically condescending view of the subject matter when he began: "Even as 'horror pictures' go, which is pretty far South as a rule, *The Crime of Doctor Crespi* ... is an almost humorously overstrained attempt at grimness." Calling von Stroheim's performance "unconvincing," Crisler finds praise for his co-star (who so frequently was unfairly overlooked in the praise department): "The only redeeming presence in the picture is that of Dwight Frye ... Mr. Frye, once chosen as one of the ten best legitimate actors on Broadway, makes the best of a bad situation..."

PRODUCTION NOTES

Taking a cue from Universal's recent money-makers, *The Black Cat* (1934) and *The Raven* (1935), Liberty Pictures decided to create their own horror tale nominally based on the works of Edgar Allan Poe.[2] (*The Crime of Doctor Crespi* was produced by Liberty but released by Republic Pictures Corporation, who, in 1935, bought up the completed productions of the financially-shaky Liberty and Majestic companies and distributed them under the Republic banner.) The poverty row studio exhibited even *less* respect for Poe than Universal did, as evidenced by the film's credits which read: "Suggested by Edgar Allen Poe's 'The Premature Burial,'" *misspelling* the famous author's middle name.

The Crime of Doctor Crespi was filmed at the old Bronx Biograph studio (the final home of D. W. Griffith) in only eight days. Erich von Stroheim remembered that he was contacted on Saturday and had to fly out to New York by that Monday when the incredibly rushed production began shooting. "I worked literally day and night and met myself at the gate coming in and going out," complained the actor.[3]

This was Erich von Stroheim's first horror film, and he was generally well received by the critics. *The Hollywood Reporter* opined that he "out-Karloffs Karloff without a make-up," and gives "such a cruel, cold, malignant and malevolent portrayal of a fiend in human flesh, that one gets an insane urge to up and let him have it." Despite the occasional laudatory reviews, von Stroheim was less than pleased with the picture himself, commenting caustically that *The Crime of Doctor Crespi* "was also the crime of Republic, the screenwriter, and the director!"[4]

He went on to appear in three other horror pictures — *The Lady and the Monster* (1944), *The Mask of Diijon* (1946), and *Unnatural ... The Fruit of Evil* (1952) — before his death in 1957. Vera Ralston, who co-starred with von Stroheim in *The Lady and the Monster*, recalled that "he was a little on the hard side to work with; he was very precisioned."[5] It was this very precision which proved to be his undoing as a filmmaker and effectively ended his career *behind* the camera, where his true genius lay (for in the 1920s von Stroheim had gained more recognition as a director, producer, and writer of films than from his acting credentials).

Born Erich Oswald Stroheim in Vienna to Jewish parents, he emigrated to the United States in 1909. He began in Hollywood as an actor, even appearing in D. W. Griffith's *Birth of a Nation* (1915; playing six different "Negro" extras). Rising to prominence in roles of villainy (usually as a ramrod-backed, monocled Prussian), the studios began ballyhooing him as "The Man You Love to Hate." He started directing pictures in the 1920s and soon earned another label due to his spendthrift attitude and explosive temperament — "Hollywood's *homme terrible*." Von Stroheim quickly became known for his directing extravagance and his insistence on authentic detail (which drove Universal's Irving Thalberg to distraction on the expensive 1922 film, *Foolish Wives*). Von Stroheim's greatest achievement was directing the MGM classic, *Greed* (1923). The initial print was a seven-hour, 42-reel epic which was hailed as one of the cinema's best works by those critics who were fortunate enough to see it. The studio eventually wrestled it away from von Stroheim and cut it down to a more playable ten reels. "In my opinion," declared Fritz Lang in 1977, "there were only two directors in Hollywood who made films without regard to box-office success: Von Stroheim and myself."[6]

It was von Stroheim who was responsible for "discovering" the reigning scream queen of the Golden Age of Horror. Though Fay Wray had been in pictures since 1923, she was a relative unknown until von Stroheim made her a star by choosing her as the lead opposite himself in *The Wedding March* (1928). After this film, however, von Stroheim was never allowed to make another picture (though he continued in vain to seek out directing projects throughout the remainder of his life and even began several uncompleted projects) and was forced to remain *in front of* the cameras. (Von Stroheim did eventually land a job as an MGM staff writer in the mid-thirties, receiving $150 a week from the same studio that had paid him $5,000 weekly just a few years earlier; his 20-month stint included punching up the script for *The Devil-Doll* in 1936.) Ever the frustrated filmmaker, von Stroheim the actor could be hard for other directors to handle. Anne Baxter recalled (in *Forties Film Talk* by Doug McClelland) that "Billy Wilder was the director on *Five Graves to Cairo* [1943] and highly competent in his own right. But he did not count on the incessant advice he got from Erich von Stroheim. Erich would take me aside to coach me and I appreciated it, until I realized he wanted the scenes to go his way."

Among the cast was newcomer Jeanne Kelly (real name Ruby Kelly), playing Miss Gordon (the night nurse who screams at the sight of the resurrected Dr. Ross). She later changed her name to Jean Brooks and starred in two Val Lewton classics—making memorable appearances first as the heroine of *The Leopard Man* and then in the title role of *The Seventh Victim* (both in 1943). "It was Erich von Stroheim who helped Jean get into show business," recalled Mary White, Jean's first cousin.[7] Apparently, von Stroheim saw her singing at a New York nightclub and began a brief affair with the ambitious young starlet. He was probably instrumental in securing for her the brief part in *Doctor Crespi*.

Hungarian immigrant John Auer began his directing career in 1933 by working on Spanish-language films. He soon came to Republic, however, and began a long and profitable association with the studio, turning out low-budget actioners. After *The Crime of Doctor Crespi* (Auer's fifth film), he went on to make nearly 50 more (largely forgotten) movies over the next 30-plus years.

The Crime of Doctor Crespi pressbook aimed its ballyhoo squarely at the horror audience, promoting catch-lines like "Horrors as you've never dreamed in your wildest nightmare!" and "You shuddered at 'Dracula'— shrieked at 'Frankenstein'—you'll yell at 'The Crime of Dr. Crespi.'" Republic's publicity department also featured a number of articles on Dwight Frye which played up that actor's close association with horror. After the name value of "von Stroheim" and "Poe," Republic felt that "Frye" was the next biggest draw for their intended audience.

The Crime of Doctor Crespi was a rare departure for Dwight Frye, allowing him to play something other than "idiots, halfwits, and lunatics" (as the actor referred to his usual screen assignments). Studio publicity played up this angle, headlining a pressbook article with DWIGHT FRYE LIVES AT LAST IN HORROR EPIC, "DR. CRESPI." The publicity plug continues: "'The man who has died a thousand deaths' is at last permitted to live! The man is Dwight Frye, famous screen portrayer of halfwits, lunatics and moon-maddened neurotics who has come to a violent end in every film he has made." Dwight Frye, Jr., remembered that his father "felt *The Crime of Doctor Crespi* was the beginning of a possible break from typecasting. Unfortunately, as you know, it didn't work out that way."[8] Frye never escaped his maniacal henchman persona and was generally relegated to small supporting roles throughout his career. It is a testament to his ability that he created so many memorable and enduring characters from the limited material offered him. In the words of Dwight Frye, Jr.: "It's a shame he wasn't appreciated when he was alive, and he would be astounded if he knew how he was appreciated now."

Stage actor Paul Guilfoyle (Dr. Arnold) made his film debut in *The Crime of Doctor Crespi*. He subsequently acted in nearly 100 films, generally "B" crime dramas or mysteries (including several of the "Saint" and "Whistler" series) with an occasional "A" production like *The Grapes of Wrath* (1940). Guilfoyle appeared in one other genre picture, *Mighty Joe Young* (1949). His final film was Bert I. Gordon's *The Boy and the Pirates* (1960).

As promotional gimmicks, Republic suggested a "DOPE" CAPSULE ("a transparent medical capsule is used, and in it a strip, 6" × 7", carrying effective teaser copy, is inserted;

every person who receives a capsule is sure to be curious enough to examine the contents"), a PRESCRIPTION THROWAWAY ("the usual prescription blank is used, headed by your medical Rx, recommending 'The Crime of Dr. Crespi' for relief from boredom, low-blood pressure, etc."), and "DR. CRESPI'S" CARD ("imitate the usual business card ... beneath the name of Crespi print the line, 'Specializing in Chills, Thrills and Shivers'").

NOTES

1. It would be unfair to cry plagiarism for this borrowing, since it is extremely unlikely that either Auer or Williams had seen Carl Dreyer's 1932 film, which received such poor distribution in the United States that it remained virtually unseen in this country for decades.

2. Republic seemed to take more than a cue from Universal's recent Poe release. The main tenants of *The Raven* and *The Crime of Doctor Crespi* are suspiciously similar: A brilliant surgeon, who is the only one that can save a life, then plots torture and murder to avenge himself for the love he cannot have.

3. From *Hollywood Scapegoat*, by Peter Noble.
4. Ibid.
5. From *Poverty Row Horrors*, by Tom Weaver.
6. *Movie Talk*, by David Shipman.
7. Interview with Gregory William Mank in *Midnight Marquee* #46.
8. Interview in 1993 with the author.

THE INVISIBLE RAY
(1936; Universal)

Release Date: January 10, 1936
Running Time: 82 minutes
Director: Lambert Hillyer
Producer: Edmund Grainger
Screenplay: John Colton
Original Story: Howard Higgin, Douglas Hodges
Photography: George Robinson
Art Director: Albert S. D'Agostino
Musical Score: Franz Waxman
Special Cinematographer: John P. Fulton
Editor: Bernard Burton
Sound Supervisor: Gilbert Kurland
Production Assistant: Alfred Stern
Gowns: Brymer
Cast: Karloff (Dr. Janos Rukh), Bela Lugosi (Dr. Felix Benet), Frances Drake (Diane Rukh), Frank Lawton (Ronald Drake), Violet Kemble Cooper (Mother Rukh), Walter Kingsford (Sir Francis Stevens), Beulah Bondi (Lady Arabella Stevens), Frank Reicher (Professor Meiklejohn), Paul Weigel (Monsieur Noyer), Chief of the Surete (Georges Renevant).

"I believe that this city is at the mercy of a madman whose body is an engine of *destruction*." — Dr. Felix Benet.

SYNOPSIS

"Every scientific fact accepted today once burned as a fantastic fire in the mind of someone called mad," states the picture's written prologue, which finishes with, "That which you are now to see is a theory whispered in the cloisters of science. Tomorrow these theories may startle the universe as fact." Indeed. High up in the Carpathian castle home of Dr. Janos Rukh, four visitors arrive to witness the scientist's demonstration. The four are Sir Francis Stevens, his wife Lady Arabella Stevens, their nephew, explorer Ronald Drake, and the distinguished astro-chemist, Dr. Felix Benet.

"Years ago, Sir Francis," begins Rukh, "I voiced the belief that a great meteor, bearing an element even more powerful than radium, struck an uncharted spot somewhere in the continent of Africa." Then, to his guests' amazement, Rukh uses his special equipment to capture a ray from Andromeda upon which this very event is recorded. "Everything that has ever happened has left its record on nature's film," he explains. The overwhelmed Stevens asks Rukh and his young wife, Diane, to join their upcoming expedition to Africa.

Once on the Dark Continent, however, Rukh soon separates from his colleagues and goes off to search for "Radium X" on his own, leaving Benet, with the backing of Sir Francis, to carry on his own experiments in astrochemistry. Rukh also leaves behind Diane. Though Diane resists, she and Drake fall in love.

Rukh discovers a fiery pit in the side of a mountain. Wearing a protective suit, he descends into the crevasse and takes a sample of the flaming rock. Placing it within a special, cannonlike device, he creates a ray which can disintegrate boulders (much to the terror of his apprehensive "safari boys").

Rukh soon learns his discovery has taken its toll, however, when his face and hands begin to glow in the dark. He has become contaminated by Radium X and his very touch has become lethal to all living things.

Just then, Diane, determined to stay loyal to her husband, arrives at his camp. Afraid to let her see him, however, Rukh gruffly orders her away.

Rukh secretly makes his way back to the main camp to see Benet. "I've discovered an element a thousand times more powerful than radium," he tells his colleague, "but it's done something to me — something *horrible*." Benet analyzes a sample of the element and creates a counteractive. "Nothing can ever cure you," warns Benet. "At best, your state of poisoning can only be checked, suspended. And now that the counteractive has gone into your bloodstream, you can only live if you use a small amount of it at regular intervals each day — all the days of your life." Benet also cautions, "I don't know enough yet to say what effect the violent surcharge of poison and antidote will have on the *brain*." Rukh swears Benet to secrecy and goes back to complete his work.

More weeks pass without Rukh's return and Benet journeys to Janos' camp. "I've harnessed it at last, Benet," Rukh gloats. "I could crumple up a city a thousand miles away." Benet answers with, "You have harnessed its power to destroy. Have you harnessed its power to heal?" At Rukh's dismissive, "That will come later," Benet states, "Stevens and I felt that would be your attitude. That is why we decided your discovery was too important to be in the hands of one man." Benet then reveals that Stevens has taken the Radium X specimen Rukh had left with Benet to the International Scientific Congress in Paris. "Thieves, thieves!" shouts Rukh. Benet further reveals that Diane has been ill and has returned to Europe with the Stevenses. He delivers a note from her which says that she feels Janos no longer loves her and that she loves another — Drake.

Rukh eventually returns to his Carpathian laboratory where he uses his ray to cure his mother's blindness, while, in Paris, Dr. Benet has been using "the miraculous healing power of Radium X" to treat hundreds at his clinic.

Rukh goes to confront Benet in Paris, where his colleague tells Janos, "All Paris is waiting to pile honors on you." Benet also relates how Diane has become Lady Stevens' secretary and wishes to marry Drake — but not before hearing from Janos. Rukh is not pleased.

Janos fakes his own death by murdering a man and planting his clothing and papers on the charred corpse. Later, Diane and Drake marry. Watching secretly, Rukh catches sight of six stone statues on the cathedral. "Six," he spits, "six of *us*," and visualizes each of the expedition members in place of the figures.

Soon, Rukh kills Sir Francis and symbolically melts one of the six statues with his ray. Benet, by means of an ultraviolet photograph of the dead man's eye, discovers that Rukh was the last thing Sir Francis saw before he died. Before Benet can act upon his knowledge, however, Rukh strikes again, this time killing Lady Stevens.

Benet and Drake go to the police and reveal what they know. Setting a trap for the madman, they announce a late night scientific gathering at Benet's clinic to lure Rukh out into the open. Along with a few select scientists (admitted by invitation only), the house will be stocked with incognito police. Rukh sneaks in unobserved, however, and manages to kill Benet with his deadly touch.

Janos then goes up to Diane's room. "No, I can't kill you, I can't," he laments, "but *he* must die" (meaning Drake). Leaving her room,

Rukh runs into his mother, just arrived at Benet's house. Startled, Janos pulls out his antidote, realizing he has not the time to finish off Drake before he must take his next life-saving dose. Before he can take the counter-active, however, Madam Rukh smashes the precious vials of serum with her cane. "It's better this way," agrees Rukh, momentarily regaining his sanity. "Good-bye mother," he whispers and jumps from a window, his poisoned body consumed in a blast of Radium X fire before it reaches the ground below. "Janos Rukh is dead," pronounces his mother, "but part of him will go on in eternity — working *for* humanity." Drake and Diane embrace.

MEMORABLE MOMENT

The Invisible Ray's most memorable moment is one of technical achievement, accomplished by John P. Fulton and his assistants. When Rukh's native bearers in Africa threaten to leave his camp, Rukh provides a little demonstration of his new discovery's power. "You see that rock," he asks his head man, pointing to a large outcropping. "I want you to keep your eyes on that rock. Tell the boys to do so too." Rukh then loads a metal box into the top of his megaphone-shaped ray device and swivels it toward the target. When he turns a dial, the machine emits an ominous electric hum. We now see the rock suddenly begin to melt before our very eyes. Liquid pours forth in rivulets just before the outer layers crumble and fall. After a brief glimpse of the natives cowering in awe and fear while Rukh gives a brief smirk of satisfaction, we see the rock seemingly implode, collapsing in upon itself as chunks disintegrate and run off in streams of molten rock while a white smoke erupts and billows from its center as jets of magma spurt from within. Not only are the natives impressed, but so are we.

ASSETS

Under Lambert Hillyer's journeyman direction, George Robinson's (*Dracula's Daughter*, 1936, *Son of Frankenstein*, 1939, *Tower of London*, 1939) camera moves infrequently but to good effect when it does. For Diane's introduction, the camera tracks forward past a tabletop statue of an angel into the huge castle drawing room to reveal the white-robed Francis Drake gazing out the window, her position and uplifted arm mirroring the statue's pose in a striking visual parallel. Towards the end of the picture, when Rukh steps out of Diane's room at Benet's house, the camera pans quickly from Rukh closing the door to Madam Rukh standing on the landing. The sudden camera movement reflects Janos' own startled surprise upon seeing his mother there.

Art director Albert S. D'Agostino provides some impressive sets that add an expansive look to the film. Rukh's laboratory, with its vaulted dome (a convincing matte painting), gigantic pillars, curved stone staircase, and some of the same intriguing devices seen in the previous year's *Bride of Frankenstein*, sets the tone (one which, sadly, the picture soon abandons). When Frances Drake strides across an open connecting walkway between the vast living quarters and Janos' lab, the half wall of massive stone blocks topped by solid pillars creates a caged, oppressive impression which is intensified by George Robinson's shadowy lighting.

As Dr. Felix Benet, Bela Lugosi gives an extremely restrained performance, one no less effective for its subtlety. When left to his own devices (as in most of his later poverty row assignments) or working under lesser directors (or those, like Robert Florey, who simply lacked an affinity for actors), Lugosi tended to chew the scenery unmercifully. Admittedly, this often proved effective and nearly always entertaining. Under Lambert Hillyer's direction in *The Invisible Ray*, however, Lugosi uses subtle facial expressions (a wry smile or a raised eyebrow) along with a more natural dialogue delivery to ground his character firmly in reality. When asked by the police chief what will happen to anyone touched by the poisoned Rukh, Lugosi answers softly, almost apologetically, "They die." Perhaps the rare opportunity of playing a benign character gave the actor a more relaxed outlook. Though die-hard Lugosiphiles may miss the evil grins and hypnotic hand-waving, his calm performance

This English cigarette card shows a rare moment of tenderness between Janos Rukh (Boris Karloff) and his wife Diana (Frances Drake) before Janos succumbs to the madness of *The Invisible Ray* (1936).

here shows a different (and welcome) side of Lugosi the actor.

While most of the cast perform well (including the ever-dependable Frances Drake and the genuinely likable Frank Lawton), the other thespian standout is Violet Kemble Cooper as Mother Rukh. John Colton's script has cast her as a stable, almost omniscient force, something like a Greek chorus. Her voice of humanity among all the scientific (and ill-advised) enthusiasm adds some much needed balance to the screenplay. Ms. Cooper brings a forceful, steady presence to her role (effectively hiding the fact that the camera-shy actress "was so nervous that the moment the camera started, she started shaking — very, very nervous," according to Frances Drake — in *Karloff and Lugosi*, by Gregory William Mank). Cooper's trembling joy upon being able to see again is quickly tempered by her restrained strength which keeps her from breaking down (though Rukh himself nearly does) and allows her to warn her son of the "tragedy" to come if he persists in his pursuit of vengeance. At the climax, after smashing Rukh's counteractive (and thus condemning her own son to death), Cooper's strong voice becomes soft and tremulous as she declares, "My son," making the simple statement both an admonishment and a declaration of love. Her voice regains its strength as she continues, "You have broken the first law of science," the actress' sincerity bringing dignity even to this hoary line.

LIABILITIES

John Colton's disjointed screenplay seemingly got away from the writer and took on a wild life of its own. The story begins as gothic horror (complete with a shadowy castle in the storm-shrouded Carpathians) but quickly becomes a tour-of-the-universe astronomy program, switches to an African jungle safari adventure, then takes a sci-fi "death ray" tack followed by a "forbidden love" romance, and ends with a "madman-on-the-loose" theme. The frequent changes in locales (Transylvania, Africa, Transylvania again, Paris) and shifting of gears casts the proceedings in a disjointed, even bewildering light. Though with *The Invisible Ray* Colton managed to avoid the intrusive comedy relief which mars his earlier *Werewolf of London* script, he failed to bring the relative tightness of that earlier screenplay to bear on his second genre foray.

In addition, inconsistencies crop up at an alarming rate during the final reel. Why would Benet, expecting a visit from a madman bent on his destruction and whose very touch will kill, go *alone* to his laboratory and actually *open* an outside door? And why do the two police officials stationed at the house's main gate fail to recognize Janos Rukh (the very man they are there to spot) when, wearing no disguise other than a slouch hat, he hands them an invitation stolen from another scientist? Further, why, once inside, does Rukh seemingly have the run of the house and can wander slowly up the stairs to Diane's unprotected room? Where are the guards one would expect? Such hastily glossed-over incongruities may serve expediency but they also serve to weaken the story's structure.

The Invisible Ray shares a similar problem with *Dracula* (1931) in that Hillyer and company opt to talk about key events rather than show them, wasting grand opportunities to create some chilling and dramatic moments. For instance, we never see the death-dealing Rukh confront any of his victims (until he finally faces Benet at the end). We only see Sir Frances' lifeless body *after* the fact and can only wonder along with Lady Arabella, "what hideous thing did he see?" Lady Stevens' murder only comes to us via newspaper headlines. Likewise, the melting of the statues could have become a thrilling (and frightening) spectacle but, once again, we can only *read* about how "TERROR GRIPS CROWD AS STATUE MELTS." (The original script included a scene of this nature, in which a gendarme raises his sword only to have the weapon disintegrate in his hand, but it was never filmed.)

While some of John Fulton's visual effects are striking (such as the melting boulder sequence costing nearly $700, and Rukh's eerie glow), others fail to convince. During Rukh's demonstration showing a huge meteor crashing into the Earth, the revolving planet is an all-too-obvious papier-mâché globe which whirls so rapidly one feels it might spin right off its axis and drop to the floor. When the supposed meteor impacts upon the globe, the resultant explosion (complete with a miniature jet of flame and puff of smoke) looks terribly phony—almost "Ed Woodian."

Though Karloff outshines Lugosi in terms of salary and billing (with the singular "KARLOFF" appearing in letters nearly twice the size of "Bela Lugosi"), it is Lugosi who provides the prime thesping while Karloff goes overboard in his melodramatics. Director Lambert Hillyer must have spent all his time and energy coaxing a low-key performance from Lugosi, for he lets his co-star flail about wildly. From his very first scene, Karloff overplays terribly. His eyes go impossibly wide and his voice grows to theatrical proportions when he grandiosely pronounces, "I'll take them somewhere they've never been before—back into time!" Then his mouth forms an awkward grimace as he grates "They'll never laugh at me again," his eyebrows furrowing to an exaggerated degree. It's a much too theatrical performance, particularly considering how natural and restrained Lugosi and Frances Drake appear. Karloff's overstated "intensity" is too melodramatic, too obvious to be effective on the big screen. (It's almost as if Karloff, tiring of his repeated bogeyman roles, decided to spice up his latest assignment by laying on some of the theatrical mannerisms gleaned from 20 years of stock theater.) Later, when Rukh learns of Benet and Stevens' "treacherous" actions, Karloff goes into a veritable paroxysm of melodramatics, his strangled noises and wringing hands almost becoming an embarrassment. Dr. Benet appears incredulous at Rukh's (over)reaction and the viewer can only share the doctor's astonishment at Karloff's misplaced histrionics. Granted, Karloff is not *all* bad. The actor's innate warmth shows through in a few scenes when his eyes soften at Diane's tears of rejection, mirroring the pain he feels at this necessary cruelty, but these moments of subtlety come few and far between. Though Karloff arguably provided more good work during the Golden Age of Horror than any other single actor, *The Invisible Ray* shows that even he was not infallible, as Dr. Janos Rukh easily ranks as

Karloff's worst genre performance of the decade. (Coincidentally, *The Invisible Ray* marked the last time Karloff would be billed by surname alone.)

Unlike many a Golden Age horror, *The Invisible Ray* fails to improve with age or repeated viewings (particularly for Karloff fans), remaining Universal's least-satisfying principal horror entry of the 1930s. It certainly falls well short of the studio's other 1936 release, *Dracula's Daughter*.

The Invisible Ray is also one of the poorest of the seven[1] treasured Karloff/Lugosi pairings (superior only to *Black Friday*, 1940, and the dismal mystery/musical/comedy *You'll Find Out*, 1940). Despite efficient cinematography and art direction, and an effectively subtle performance from Bela Lugosi, *The Invisible Ray* shines its light from the *bottom* of Universal's Golden Age barrel.

REVIEWS

Variety (January 15, 1936) opined that this latest entry in "Universal's cycle of horror pictures … isn't blood-curdling to the point achieved in some Hollywoodian efforts but it is different and fairly entertaining…. Backgrounded familiarly and photographed for eerie effect, the story doesn't make quite the effort to chill that 'Invisible Man' and the 'Frankenstein' series have."

Of the cast, the reviewer (Char) singled out the two Titans of Terror: "[Karloff] and Lugosi stand away out in an otherwise average cast." Char had no patience with Violet Kemble Cooper as Janos' mother, calling her performance "over-theatrical."

The Cinema (February 12, 1936) was more overtly enthusiastic: "It is this combination of laboratory possibility with film studio extravagance that makes the picture—finely staged and powerfully portrayed as it is—of considerable appeal to the masses…. Boris Karloff makes a curiously sympathetic figure of the stricken Rukh, and gives us not small insight into the tortured brain responsible for his later atrocities."

The New York Times (January 11, 1936) reviewer (who apparently sneered at "films of this sort") noted that "Universal … has made its newest penny dreadful with technical ingenuity and the pious hope of frightening the children out of a year's growth."

PRODUCTION NOTES

Following their completion of *The Raven*, Universal planned to star Karloff in an adaptation of *Bluebeard*. When this ran into scripting troubles, however, the studio quickly put into production a story property they had recently purchased for $1,250. *The Death Ray*, which became *The Invisible Ray*, was a tale by Howard Higgin and Douglas Hodges of a Belgian scientist whose very touch becomes deadly due to contamination by a radioactive meteor. Universal assigned successful playwright John Colton, fresh from scripting *Werewolf of London*, to draft the screenplay for the hefty final fee of $7,791.60.

Universal, deciding at the last moment to turn their Karloff vehicle into another Karloff/Lugosi pairing, cabled Lugosi in London where the actor and his wife were about to embark on a vacation to his native Hungary. In a terse telegram, the studio *ordered* Lugosi to return to Hollywood immediately. "They really made a stink about it," recalled Lillian Lugosi to Greg Mank (in *Karloff and Lugosi*). Then, after reporting to the studio as instructed, an incensed Lugosi learned that financing difficulties had delayed the project for three weeks! In the end, Bela would never make his intended triumphal return to his homeland.

Universal's first choice for director was Stuart Walker, who had previously helmed *Werewolf of London*. Walker, though not on the level of James Whale, still commanded a substantial fee of $2,000 a week. Trading on the expected prestige that goes along with a hefty paycheck, Walker insisted upon a further three-day delay to polish the shooting script which he deemed unsatisfactory. Universal balked at the delay and the final result was that Walker walked off the picture and ultimately walked out on Universal. "I am very enthusiastic about the story and the cast," Walker reported to the trades (cited in *Universal Horrors* by Brunas,

"A ray from [Andromeda] will be caught here and electrically transferred to the projector in my laboratory," explains the brilliant but unstable Janos Rukh (Boris Karloff) to Dr. Felix Benet (Bela Lugosi) and Sir Francis Stevens (Walter Kingsford). "There I will *recreate* what is recorded by that beam of light." From *The Invisible Ray* (1936).

Brunas, and Weaver), "but I did not feel that I could do the studio or myself justice under the conditions that came up suddenly. So far as I was concerned I needed more time and, as this could not be arranged, I suggested that some other director would be better for the assignment. It was not a matter of 'walking out'...." During the remaining five years of his life (he died in 1941) Walker never directed another film.

As a replacement, the studio chose veteran director Lambert Hillyer, whose undistinguished career (spanning two decades and over 80 films) centered around B-westerns. Though the choice may seem an odd one for an important horror picture, the price was right — Hillyer performed his task for the relatively low fee of $3,750. Hillyer served a similar function on Universal's next horror project, *Dracula's Daughter*, by filling the vacancy left by originally intended director Edward Sutherland (who departed that picture due to production delays). Hillyer's two successful forays into the horror genre failed to make an impression, so he quickly returned to the wide open spaces of frontier filmmaking; he directed another 81 films (in only 13 years!) after *Dracula's Daughter*, 70 of which were westerns.

Universal's contractee Gloria Stuart (*The Old Dark House, Secret of the Blue Room, The Invisible Man*) was the studio's first choice for the role of Diane. After four years at Universal, however, Ms. Stuart had had enough. "I finally got tired of making those lousy movies," she told Greg Mank in *Karloff and Lugosi*, "and I told my agent to get me out of my contract." Her agent managed it and she eventually transferred over to 20th Century–Fox.

Without a leading lady, Universal cast

After Rukh fakes his own death, Diana (Frances Drake) and Ronald (Frank Lawton) wed in this scene which was significantly shortened before *The Invisible Ray*'s release. Dr. Benet (Bela Lugosi), Sir Francis (Walter Kingsford), and Lady Arabella (Beulah Bondi) look on.

their net outside their gates and landed Frances Drake, borrowing her from Paramount. At $500 a week, she signed for the pivotal role of Diane. Ms. Drake was quite taken with both her "horrific" co-stars. "Both Karloff and Lugosi were delightful!" she told Greg Mank (in *Karloff and Lugosi*). "Boris was a darling man ... a very charming man, and a quite brilliant man. He was very busy with the Screen Actors Guild, of which he was a founder, on the set." The actress went on to relate an amusing incident which occurred during filming. "Remember when he's in Africa in the film, up on that sort of 'lift,' the platform which lowers him into the radium pit? They played a trick on him, while we were shooting out on the back lot. I was not in on it, because I don't really like those sorts of jokes; but after they raised him up, very high on the platform, they went off, during the lunch hour — and left Boris up there! And he was such a good sport about it! Absolutely charming! He never punched anyone, he never roared at anyone, he was so darling about it. I thought, 'I wouldn't have been quite so pleasant!'" Of Lugosi, Ms. Drake remembered him as "a charming man, very soft and very congenial." She saw none of the supposed rivalry between the number one and number two horror stars. "They worked well together. I thought they were probably friends. I like them both very much!"

A scene in which Ronald Drake saves Diane from an attacking lion (a judicious replacement for a charging rhinoceros — which the script suggested could be realized by stock footage) was cut before release. Frances Drake was quite taken with the ferocious feline set to imperil her life. "The lion was a darling," remembered the actress to Greg Mank. "I think her name was Margie, and she was from MGM, where the children used to ride on her back. I didn't mind being chased by her at all — in fact, I hoped she would catch up with me, so I could pet her!"

Once again, Karloff outshone Lugosi in terms of billing and salary, this time earning nearly 2½ times his co-star's fee ($3,125 a week for Karloff vs. a flat $4,000 for Lugosi which worked out to about $1,333 per week). The single largest expenditure on the film's $166,875 proposed budget was the cast, whose combined cost totaled an estimated $46,700. Among the higher-priced cast members were Frank Lawton ($1,250 per week), Violet Kemble Cooper ($1,150 a week), Beulah Bondi ($1,000 a week) and Walter Kingsford ($850 a week). (Kingsford [1881–1958] is probably best remembered for his recurring role as Dr. Carew in the "Dr. Kildare" series, appearing in all nine of the Lew Ayers/Kildare pictures as well as in five of the spin-off "Dr. Gillespie" films starring Lionel Barrymore. Among Kingsford's 102 screen appearances are *The Mystery of Edwin Drood*, 1935, *Fingers at the Window*, 1942, and *Ghost Catchers*, 1944.)

John Fulton was allotted a meager budget of $4,500 to provide all the pictures' rather elaborate special effects. The effects wizard's perfectionism eventually more than doubled this amount. Fulton worked long and hard to create a glow-in-the-dark makeup for Karloff. In the end, however, he abandoned the endeavor and instead added the glowing effect directly to the film's negative during post-production.

Rukh's magnificent laboratory cost Universal about $4,000, with an extra $550 for the observatory apparatus. The studio also made use of a number of their free-standing-horror landmarks. In addition to *Dracula*'s Carfax Abbey staircase set (redressed for Rukh's lab), *The Invisible Ray* incorporated the ever-present backlot Tyrolean village seen recently in *Bride of Frankenstein* (and countless other pictures) and the famed Notre Dame cathedral replica erected for Lon Chaney's *The Hunchback of Notre Dame* (1923). (The cathedral received $850 in renovation for the wedding sequence in *The Invisible Ray*.)

The Invisible Ray required 36 days of shooting to complete (running 12 days over schedule) at a final cost of $234,875 (a whopping $68,000 over budget!). Apart from the previously mentioned special effects increase, the cost overruns included $14,004 extra in actors' fees and an additional $4,895 for set construction.

NOTES

1. There are actually *eight* Karloff/Lugosi films, but the "Twin Titans of Terror" put in only the briefest of cameo appearances in the little-seen and all-but-forgotten *Gift of Gab* (1934). The remainder of the pairings are: *The Black Cat* (1934), *The Raven* (1935), *Son of Frankenstein* (1939), and *The Body Snatcher* (1945).

THE WALKING DEAD
(1936; Warner Bros.)

Release Date: February 29, 1936
Running Time: 66 minutes
Director: Michael Curtiz
Producer: Lou Edelman
Screenplay: Ewart Adamson, Peter Milne, Robert Andrews, and Lillie Hayward
Photography: Hal Mohr, A.S.C.
Art Director: Hugh Reticker
Editor: Thomas Pratt
Dialogue Director: Irving Rapper
Gowns: Orry—Kelly

Cast: Boris Karloff (John Elman), Ricardo Cortez (Nolan), Edmund Gwenn (Dr. Beaumont), Marguerite Churchill (Nancy), Warren Hull (Jimmy), Barton MacLane (Loder), Henry O'Neill (Werner), Joseph King (Judge Shaw), Addison Richards (Prison Warden), Paul Harvey (Blackstone), Robert Strange (Merritt), Joseph Sawyer (Trigger), Eddie Acuff (Betcha), Kenneth Harlan (Stephen Martin), Miki Morita (Sako), Ruth Robinson (Mrs. Shaw).

"Can't you remember anything that happened—before you died?"—Dr. Beaumont.

SYNOPSIS

John Elman, a mild-mannered musician, has just been released from prison after serving 10 years for second degree murder. "It was my wife," he explains, "I struck a man, but I didn't mean to kill him." Elman has been dealt a rather harsh hand by the deck of fate and now only wishes to find a job and resume what is left of his life. Unfortunately for him, he's taken in by four powerful (and ostensibly "respectable") racketeers who frame him for the murder of an honest judge causing trouble for them.

Elman is convicted and sentenced to die. On the eve of the execution, two witnesses who can clear Elman, Jimmy and Nancy, finally overcome their fear of the racketeers and come forward—but it is too late and Elman is put to death in the electric chair.

Jimmy and Nancy both work for an eminent researcher named Dr. Beaumont. Beaumont, who'd been working on the restoration of life in animals, performs an experimental procedure on Elman's body and brings him back to life. Elman has changed, though, and is only the shell of the man he once was. He has very little memory and is almost an invalid. However, at certain times he gains some mysterious access to knowledge denied him in life—namely, the identities of his hidden enemies, those who had secretly framed him. "I'm positive Elman has some knowledge not given to him by Man," declares Dr. Beaumont.

One by one Elman confronts his enemies. Elman's very presence unnerves each of the racketeers, and their own guilt and terror leads them to their deaths. One man (the group's hitman) falls backwards in fright and shoots himself with his own gun; another flees into the path of an oncoming train; a third backs through an upper story window.

Finally, Elman retreats to a cemetery. "I belong here," he says quietly. The two remaining racketeers follow him there and shoot him, but receive their just reward when their fleeing car careens off the road and crashes into a power pole—sending them to their own impromptu electric chair.

As Elman lies dying (for the second—and final—time), Dr. Beaumont questions him: "John, look at me, try to remember, you must.... Try John, try, that's why I brought you back from death.... Tell me, what is death?" Suddenly, everything seems to become clear to Elman. "I think I can," he says. "After the shock I seemed to feel peace and—and—"and he dies, taking his mysterious knowledge with him as he rejoins his Maker. As Elman had said earlier, "The Lord our God is a jealous God."

MEMORABLE MOMENT

The heart and soul of *The Walking Dead* is found in the first scene of retribution, when Elman confronts "Trigger" Smith, the racketeers' hired gun. Instructed to eliminate Elman, Trigger loads his weapon. The door to his room opens and he sees the figure of his intended victim. The scene quickly takes an unsettling turn when the camera views Elman from a slightly off-kilter low-angle. Although startled, Trigger quickly recovers himself: "Funny ... here I been thinkin' of payin' you a visit and—you save me the trouble by walkin' in." Elman stands unmoving, his face a stone mask. With the camera peering up at his shadowy, cadaverous visage, Elman intones, "Why did you kill Judge Shaw?" His voice is flat and hollow, yet with a frightening certainty and subtle force behind it. Trigger's facade crumbles. "Lay off that stuff!" he barks angrily. "That night, I thought you were my friend," Elman continues. Trigger panics and pulls his gun, shouting, "Put 'em up!" Elman slowly raises his hands. "You can't kill me again," he states, the flat monotone of that unearthly voice carrying a conviction that leaves no room for doubt. Arms upraised, Elman begins to advance. The dangling chain of the room's overhead lamp catches on his hand and the room is plunged into darkness. Moving steadily forward, the shadowy figure issues a statement: "You can't use that gun." Near hysteria, Trigger shouts, "Keep back, keep back!" Elman steps into a patch of light and stops.

With a subtle, almost sorrowful, shake of his head, he says simply, "You can't escape what you've done." This stark statement of fact is the core of the picture — one must answer for one's actions. Trigger is now thoroughly terrified and, in trying to cheat fate, stumbles backwards and falls violently over a table. The gun fires accidentally and Trigger is dead. The killer has died by his own hand, his unthinking actions leading him on to his fatal destiny.

ASSETS

The Walking Dead is an often overlooked classic that frequently gets unfairly lumped in with Karloff's "Mad Doctor" and "Back-from-the-Dead" films (*The Man They Could Not Hang*, 1939; *Before I Hang*, 1940; etc.). These later horror films are basically low-budget potboilers, albeit with a touch more class than most of their contemporaries. It is a mistake, however, to dismiss *The Walking Dead* as simply another of Karloff's "Mad Monster Movies."

One point that sets *The Walking Dead* above its fellows is a very strong and literate script, which possesses a greater thematic depth than most. The confirmation of an afterlife, the revelation that the guilty WILL be punished, and the assurance that there is indeed a God watching over us, ready to take a hand, touch some very real and basic human needs. Screenwriters Adamson, Milne, Andrews, and Hayward utilize these needs in order to draw the viewer into their story. They deliver the goods in the end, for the film's message is one of reassurance, and as such is rather appealing and, ultimately, satisfying.

Also appealing is the character of John Elman. He is a likable but rather naive man who trusts people and the system but is betrayed by them. It's easy to empathize with Elman, because most of us have been taken advantage of at one time or another (though, it is hoped, not to the extent of Elman's case). The sympathy engendered by Elman's plight gives each viewer an emotional stake in the proceedings, and draws each viewer into the story. At the end, Elman (and, through him, the audience) receives assistance from, and finds solace in, a higher court than the American judicial system.

Elman is always a sympathetic figure. Even after he's brought back to life and sets out to bring retribution to the guilty, he is no monster; he's merely an innocent victim who, through some higher power, has become an instrument of justice. He never actually kills the guilty men; he merely confronts them with their guilt and lets their consciences press them on to their own deaths. This is an important distinction, one that separates him from — and sets him above — his enemies, for he could never intentionally kill as they did, even if in his case it might be justified. (Ewart Adamson and Joseph Field's original story for *The Walking Dead*, dated November 19, 1935, painted Elman in a drastically different light than the gentle being seen in the finished film. According to the original treatment, "Dopey" Elman is "a nervous wreck" due to drug and alcohol addictions. Even worse, after his resurrection, Elman "is a repulsive, vicious thing without the power of speech, which makes one recoil in horror." Thankfully, subsequent script revisions turned this vicious monster into a sensitive man.)

Warner Bros. signed Boris Karloff to a one-picture contract at a princely $3,750 per week. Out of the $217,000 spent on *The Walking Dead*, the actor's salary may very well have been the best $18,700 investment Warners made, for Karloff's performance here is among his best. His pleading at the trial, for instance, is heartbreaking: "You can't kill me for something I didn't do I tell you, you can't, you can't!" Later, as he's about to be executed, we see his despair turn to bitterness. When the Warden offers him a last request, Karloff's sardonic reply is, "Take away my life and grant me a favor in return — now that's what I call a *bargain*." This momentary rancor is never directed at another person, however; it is simply a result of his unjust circumstance — and it does not last long. The actor's natural soft-spokenness and humanity shines through his performance, and no animosity or baseness is allowed to creep into the character. A kindness and innate belief in his fellow man shines through Karloff's eyes. Throughout the film Karloff inspires sympathy and the audience is behind him 100 percent.

After his miraculous revival from the dead, Elman presents a striking figure: cadaverous cheeks, half-veiled eyes, a streak of white in his hair, his left arm turned up tight at his side. His movements are slow and at first glance he puts forth an image of frailty. At the same time, however, his inexorable advancing gait and determined voice give an impression of strength and undeniable power. Karloff's body language is superb.

The character of Dr. Beaumont is quite fascinating. He is a good man, a kind man, who becomes obsessed with finding the elusive knowledge so far denied mankind. "Dr. Beaumont has changed," complains Jimmy. "He's forgotten everything we started out to do. All he thinks of now is trying to find out what Elman experienced when he was dead, trying to put his soul under a microscope." Unlike the whiny and unimaginative Jimmy (some scientist!), we can certainly identify with this quest for knowledge, in wanting to KNOW for sure, and only wish Dr. Beaumont would work faster in preparing those microscope slides.

Technically, the film is superior as well. The direction is purposeful and effective. There are varied viewpoints within a scene and good use is made of unusual angles and setups. In the memorable sequence in which Elman takes the long walk to the electric chair, the camera creates a moving tableau of sadness. In a slightly off-kilter angle we see the shadows of bars on the wall and a slowly rotating fan overhead. The camera moves in as Karloff swallows and raises his head upwards. In a low, soft voice he says, "He'll believe me."

Director Michael Curtiz utilized much of the skill and expertise for *The Walking Dead* that would later bring him such acclaim for classics such as *The Sea Wolf* (1941) and *Casablanca* (1942). Few directors are as adept at drawing their audiences into the action as the Hungarian-born Curtiz. One standout feature in *The Walking Dead* is the varied use of low-key lighting from the side, which effectively highlights the emotional changes in the characters. Curtiz would occasionally shift the lighting emphasis from the side to the front, thus emphasizing a new understanding on the part of a character or underscoring the fear in the faces of Elman's adversaries. An interesting example of these subtle but effective changes in lighting occurs at the climax, when Karloff describes his experience in the heavenly realm. Just as Elman utters his last words, the lighting shifts from the side to the front, illuminating his entire face. This subtle change, combined with a very soft focus, suggests an awareness of a supreme force at work and also conveys a sense that Elman himself has been absolved and can finally rest in peace and wholeness.

Along with Curtiz, much of the credit for the technical superiority of *The Walking Dead* must go to Hal Mohr, the film's ace cinematographer. This highly skilled craftsman, fresh from his Oscar-winning work a year earlier on *A Midsummer Night's Dream* (1935),[1] plays an integral part in the dreamlike visual quality of *The Walking Dead*. Mohr's extensive use of lens focusing as a means of transition is smooth and fluid. In addition, his placement of objects and people in the foreground of the scene creates three-dimensional images which hold one's visual interest, perfectly complementing the story and actions unfolding onscreen. Mohr's varied use of unusual camera angles is equally outstanding. One fine example (of low-angle positioning) occurs as Karloff takes that long walk towards his fated electrocution. The camera is set at such an angle that Karloff appears to be walking at an upward slant, symbolizing his impending ascent to the heavenly beyond. This sequence, which normally could be a very tense and suspenseful moment, is given a very different mood, one that is not at all frightening but more like the feeling of a sad but peaceful passing. Another effective use of camera perspective comes after Karloff is revived from the dead. Now that he has become the instrument of justice, he is photographed exclusively from below, as if he were a deity looking down in judgment.[2] Concurrently, the racketeers are usually viewed from a higher

Dr. Beaumont (Edmund Gwenn), "positive Elman has some knowledge not given to him by Man," studies his zombielike charge (Boris Karloff) while the concerned Nancy (Marguerite Churchill) looks on. From *The Walking Dead* (1936).

camera position so they appear smaller and not as powerful as Elman. All of these cinematic tools, combined with Karloff's ability to evoke sympathy and pathos, contribute to the dramatic impact of these scenes.

LIABILITIES

The Walking Dead did not escape the seemingly obligatory comedy relief. This time it comes in the form of an annoying character named "Betcha," who tries to wager on just about anything (including Elman's conviction). This coarse, unsuccessful comedy is so out of step with the serious, weighty tone of the film that it becomes a jarring intrusion rather than a smooth relief from tension.

Though the script is well fashioned (the comedy relief notwithstanding), it has one troublesome area. The characters of Jimmy and Nancy (the intended audience identification figures) are too sketchily drawn. We do not really know WHY they did not come forward until the eleventh hour (other than base cowardice), and their feelings are never fully explored. When they finally do present themselves (too late, of course), it happens in an abrupt way. There is no build-up revealing their change of heart (or acquisition of courage), no scenes of moral torment or conscience wrestling — just bam! they're suddenly in Dr. Beaumont's office pleading with the doctor to help them stop the execution. In many films, this injudicious use of plot expediency would easily slide by, but *The Walking Dead*'s generally superior level of writing makes the lapse quite noticeable and rather disappointing.

REVIEWS

Variety's "Odec" (March 4, 1936) was unimpressed by this Warner Bros. foray into the realm of the macabre: "Those with a yen for shockers will get limited satisfaction from the story that has been wrapped around Boris

Karloff's initial stalking piece under the Warner Bros. banner. The director and the supporting cast try hard to give some semblance of credibility to the trite and pseudo-scientific vaporings of the writers, but the best they can produce is something that moves swiftly enough but contains little of sustained interest."

Britain's *Kinematograph Weekly* (April 30, 1936) saw some merit in the production, however, calling it a "High voltage melodrama linking gangsterdom with the supernatural through the macabre histrionics of Boris Karloff," stating that "this picture hands out holding entertainment for the masses, those who never tire at nibbling at the eerie.... Boris Karloff gives a human and sympathetic performance in the fantastic role of Ellman [*sic*]; acting ability rather than grotesque make-up invests his portrayal with conviction."

The *New York Times*' Frank S. Nugent (March 2, 1936) noted that "there is no denying that he [Karloff] makes an impressive zombie. With a blaze of white streaking his hair, with sunken mournful eyes, hollow cheeks and a passion for Sindling's 'Rustles of Spring,' Karloff is something to haunt your sleep at nights. We didn't even dare laugh when he sat down to play the piano..." Of the production itself, the only thing the reviewer had to say was that "horror pictures are a staple commodity, and this one was taken from one of the better shelves."

PRODUCTION NOTES

The laboratory equipment featured in *The Walking Dead* was of a more authentic nature than the usual "Mad Medico" apparatus seen in the films of the time. Several experimental devices in the picture were supposedly based on innovative medical inventions, including the "Lindbergh Heart" (a mechanical circulating system designed by famed flyer Charles A. Lindbergh and Dr. Alexis Carrel) and a motor-controlled, tilting operating table utilized by Dr. Robert E. Cornish in his experiments in the reanimation of dead dogs. According to the film's pressbook, "the studio built a working model [of the Lindberg Heart] from blue-prints sent from the Rockefeller Institute." The pressbook also claimed that "this is the first time either of these reanimating mechanisms have [*sic*] been shown on the screen." Warners' publicity department conveniently forgot about (or simply had not seen) Universal's *Life Returns* released a year earlier, a banal boy-and-his-dog tale built around actual footage of an experiment conducted by Cornish on May 22, 1934, at the University of Southern California.

The sequence which employed these devices—Elman's resurrection scene—was not easy to shoot.

According to the pressbook, it took 12 tries before everything went right: "The call for action was heard and the actor played his part. Something went wrong—a light flickered out, necessitating another take. Again and again Karloff rose from the dead only to be told that some important object in the scene was not recorded properly." After eight hours, Curtiz was finally satisfied. Karloff, however, was a bit the worse for wear. After see-sawing up and down for hours on end strapped to the tilting table, the actor could not bring himself to eat his dinner. Worse, he returned later that evening to play a scene "and had to eat, for the benefit of the cameras, six hotdogs smeared with mustard and drink six cups of coffee. He got them down, but they refused to stay."

"*Film Revives Controversy Over Capital Punishment*" read the headline in a *Walking Dead* publicity piece. "*Members of Cast of 'The Walking Dead' Divided in Opinion.*" According to the article, both Karloff and Barton MacLane were against the death penalty, but their enlightened viewpoint was not shared by the remainder of the cast. Henry O'Neill, Marguerite Churchill, Warren Hull, Edmund Gwenn, and Ricardo Cortez were all in favor (though Cortez limited it to men over 45, since "men over 45 haven't a chance to reform"). Director Michael Curtiz was "on the fence," believing "people should not be killed to pay a debt to society unless they have definitely committed a cold-blooded, premeditated murder."

Beyond intellectual arguments over capital punishment, Warner Bros. ran into a bit of legal difficulty over *The Walking Dead*. According to *The Hollywood Reporter* (October 3, 1936), a writer by the name of Ferdinand Voteur charged that *The Walking Dead* plagiarized his story, "Resurrection Morning." The studio answered that the film's four screenwriters concocted their screenplay from yet another script by Ewart Adamson and Joseph Fields. Nothing further seems to have come of Voteur's accusation.

Ricardo Cortez (born Jacob Krantz) entered films in the 1920s as a potential successor to Rudolph Valentino. In 1925, he appeared opposite Greta Garbo in her first American film, *The Torrent*. Cortez was top billed in the production, making him the only performer who ever received better billing than the great Garbo in any of her American pictures. When sound came, Cortez successfully changed his "Latin Lover" image to that of a suave heavy, becoming one of Hollywood's busiest villains (appearing in a total of 49 films in the 1930s). While continuing his acting career, he also directed, helming seven features between 1938 and 1940. Sensing that as a director he was fated to remain in the realm of the B's, he once again concentrated fully on his thespian abilities. Cortez eventually retired from film work and became a stockbroker. His brother, Stanley Cortez, was a successful cinematographer (*The Black Cat*, 1941; *The Magnificent Ambersons*, 1942; *Flesh and Fantasy*, 1943; *Night of the Hunter*, 1951; *The Angry Red Planet*,

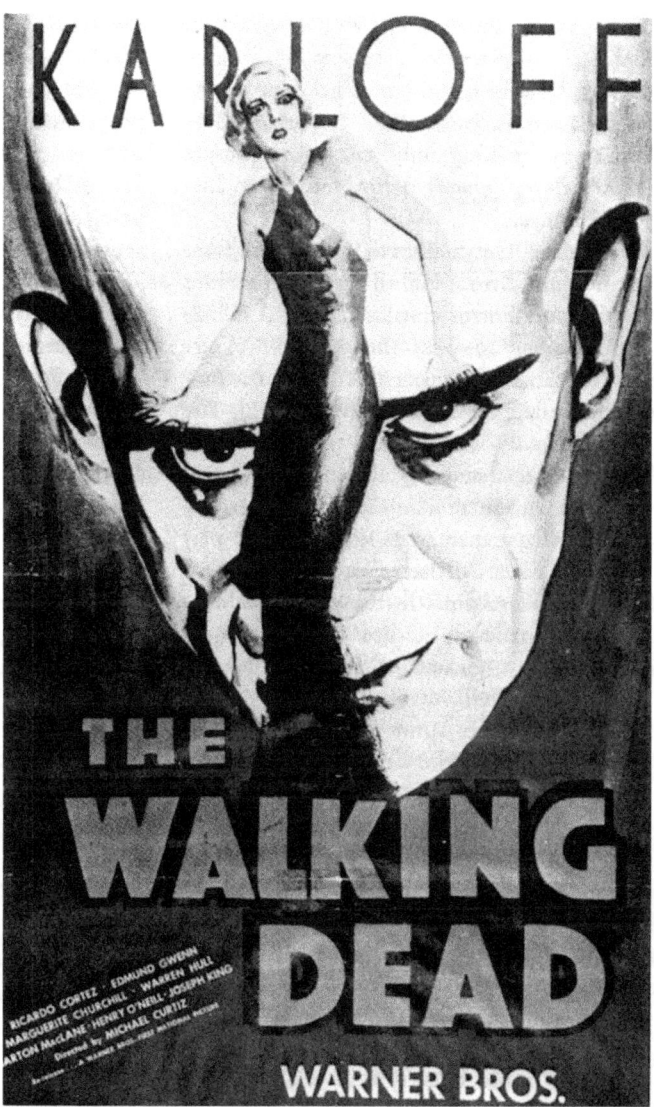

Striking reissue poster for *The Walking Dead* (1936).

1960; *The Ghost in the Invisible Bikini*, 1966; etc.).

Trained at New York's Professional Children's School and Theatre Guild Drama School, Marguerite Churchill made her Broadway debut at 13. Six years later she made her first film, appearing opposite Paul Muni in *The Valiant* (1929). In 1933 she married cowboy star George O'Brien and retired from pictures. Ms. Churchill resumed her career only a few months prior to the start of *The Walking Dead* (and only a few months *after* the birth of their daughter). She also starred in *Dracula's Daughter* the same year. Marguerite Churchill's cinematic comeback was short-lived, however, for in 1937 she returned to Broadway, making only one more picture (1950's *Bunco Squad*) before retiring to Lisbon, Portugal.

Michael Curtiz directed nearly 100 films for Warner Bros., including two previous Golden Age horror classics, *Doctor X* (1932) and *Mystery of the Wax Museum* (1933). Curtiz, an established Warners "A" director, commanded a hefty $17,660 fee for directing *The Walking Dead*—a salary nearly equal to that of his high-priced star. By all accounts, Curtiz was quite an outspoken character. Warners' publicity department was never slow to play this up: "When Michael Curtiz ... saw Karloff for the first time in the ghastly yellow-and-green make-up he uses in portraying a man who's just got out of his grave, he said: 'Swell! Now I'll tell you of another job you can have. Go out and haunt the houses of those tenants of mine who are not paying their rent!'"

The Walking Dead was cinematographer Hal Mohr's only Golden Age horror film, though he photographed two in the 1940s: the lavish 1943 Claude Rains remake of *The Phantom of the Opera* (for which he won an Oscar) and the tepid *Phantom* follow-up, *The Climax* (1944). Mohr also shot such varied classics as *Destry Rides Again* (1939) with Jimmy Stewart and *The Wild One* (1954) with Marlon Brando. The talented director of photography finished up his illustrious career shooting two low-budget sci-fi features: *Creation of the Humanoids* (1962) and *The Bamboo Saucer* (1968; his final film as cinematographer).

Various clips from *The Walking Dead* popped up in the 1964 Warner Bros. war comedy, *Ensign Pulver* (1964), under the guise of *Young Dr. Jekyll Meets Frankenstein*, a picture being shown on the deck to a crew of discontented sailors "hypnotized by despair."

It was not only the poverty-row outfits that came up with outlandish selling slants for their pictures; even a studio as prestigious as Warner Bros. could generate some downright bizarre suggestions: "Think you can hold a screening at the morgue?" asked *The Walking Dead*'s pressbook. Or how about this angle: "Newspapers have been devoting considerable space to doctors who are conducting experiments on bringing dogs back to life after asphyxiation. If there's a local medico who ever conducted such an experiment or would be likely to try it, hop around to see him and see if he'll cooperate by working it—with proportionate tie-in for film." Imagine: Bring Rover to the Roxy on Friday to be gassed and restored to life at intermission!

NOTES

1. Mohr was not even nominated that year but won on a write-in vote, becoming the only person to ever win an Oscar in that fashion. After Mohr's surprise victory, the Academy changed the rules so that no one could vote for anyone other than the official nominees.

2. To "heighten" the effect even more, Karloff was made four inches taller. "According to prison authorities," reported the film's pressbook, "a man 'grows' an inch or two after taking the 'jolt' in the electric chair. It was necessary to increase Karloff's stature four inches to produce the effect."

DRACULA'S DAUGHTER
(1936; Universal)

Release Date: May 11, 1936
Running Time: 69 minutes
Director: Lambert Hillyer
Associate Producer: E. M. Asher
Screenplay: Garrett Fort (based on a story by Bram Stoker)
Suggested by Oliver Jeffries
Photography: George Robinson
Special Cinematographer: John P. Fulton
Editor: Milton Carruth

Sound Supervisor: Gilbert Kurland
Gowns: Brymer
Cast: Otto Kruger (Jeffrey Garth), Gloria Holden (Countess Marya Zaleska/Dracula's Daughter), Margeurite Churchill (Janet), Edward Van Sloan (Professor Von Helsing*), Gilbert Emery (Sir Basil Humphrey), Irving Pichel (Sandor), Halliwell Hobbs (Hawkins), Billy Bevan (Albert), Nan Gray (Lili), Hedda Hopper (Lady Esme Hammond), Claude Allister (Sir Aubrey), Edgar Norton (Hobbs), E. E. Clive (Sergeant Wilkes).

*The character's name inexplicably changes from the original "Van Helsing" in Dracula to "Von Helsing" here.

"She was beautiful when she died—a hundred years ago."—Professor Von Helsing citing *Dracula's Daughter*'s epitaph.

SYNOPSIS

Dracula's Daughter begins right where *Dracula* left off. Two constables walk down the stairs at Carfax Abbey (the *Frankenstein* watchtower set standing in for the lofty, curved staircase of the original *Dracula*) to find Renfield's broken body (his face coyly covered by an arm to avoid paying Dwight Frye for a return day's work). In the cellar, Professor Von Helsing leaves the coffin of Count Dracula (containing a wax dummy in the general likeness of Lugosi) and comes out to meet the policemen. The sergeant promptly arrests the professor for murder.

At the Whitby Jail, the two constables keep a watch over Dracula's and Renfield's corpses while awaiting the arrival of Scotland Yard. A mysterious woman dressed all in black arrives and, using a reflective ring, hypnotizes the policemen on duty and steals Dracula's body.

Out in the woods, the woman's servant, Sandor, stands guard as Dracula's daughter (for that is who she is) consigns her father's body to the flame. "Be thou exorcised, O Dracula," she intones, then rejoices, "Free, free forever. Free to live as a woman, free to take my place in the bright world of the living—instead of in the shadows of the dead." As it turns out, her joy was premature, for she cannot fight the bloodlust of her birthright and must go forth into the London fog to claim yet another victim.

While being held at Scotland Yard, Von Helsing calls upon his friend and former student, renowned psychiatrist Jeffrey Garth, for help. "You must convince them of my sanity." Though Garth hasn't the faintest idea where to start, he agrees that "if there's a way to clear you, I'll do it."

Later, at a London social gathering, Garth meets a painter named Countess Marya Zaleska (actually Dracula's daughter). During the course of the evening, Garth talks of treating mental illness. "Sympathetic treatment will release the mind from any obsession," he concludes. This piques Countess Zaleska's interest.

When Zaleska invites Garth to her apartment to speak privately, she asks for his help. "Could you conceive of a superhuman mentality influencing someone from the other side of death?" she asks Garth. "There is such a one," she continues. "Someone—something—that reaches out from beyond the grave and fills me with horrible impulses." She finally pleads with him to "use my brain, my will, as an instrument, as he has used them—but for *release*." Garth assures Zaleska that her strength comes from within and advises her to put it to a test.

Later that night, she does just that. Hiring a young girl to pose for a portrait at her Chelsea studio, Zaleska succumbs once again to the bloodlust.

The young victim is brought to St. Mary's Hospital for "loss of blood and apparent amnesia." Garth, on staff at the hospital, examines her. When he sees two puncture marks on the patient's neck, Garth goes to see Von Helsing (who has been released since the disappearance of the corpus delicti). At Von Helsing's warning that vampires cast no reflection in mirrors, Garth remembers that Countess Zaleska's apartment was completely devoid of mirrors.

The next night, Zaleska goes to see Garth at his office. She states that she's leaving for the Continent and pleads with him to go with her.

"You're a great doctor of minds, of souls. I need you, Dr. Garth. I need you to save *my* soul." Garth refuses and orders the countess to remain in his office (and "sit down very calmly and make up your mind how you're going to tell me the truth, the *entire truth*") while he goes to treat the vampire victim. Placing her under hypnosis, Garth learns of the studio in Chelsea, but the girl dies before she can say more.

Meanwhile, the countess calls Sandor up to Garth's office and they abduct Janet, Garth's beautiful and feisty secretary, in order to compel Garth to go with Zaleska to her homeland. Janet loves Garth and vice-versa (though the astute psychiatrist has not yet realized it).

Finding Zaleska gone from his office, Garth rushes to the Chelsea studio. There he finds the countess waiting. When he confronts her with his knowledge, she admits, "I am Dracula's daughter." She tells him that she now holds Janet hostage. While he checks on this, she slips away.

Garth follows her to Transylvania (as planned by Zaleska). At Castle Dracula, Sandor questions his mistress. "What do you want of Garth? Release, still release?" She answers "No, I know that's impossible now. I want *him*... His life in exchange for hers." Sandor becomes angry. "Have you forgotten your promise that I was to have eternal life? There is *death* for Garth if he comes here, death *not* life — and *destruction* for you." Zaleska coldly orders him away.

When Garth arrives, he finds Janet lying helpless in a hypnotic coma. "She's under a spell that can only be broken by me — or death," Zaleska tells him and offers to free her if he "remain here — with me, among the undead as one yourself." Unable to help Janet, Garth agrees. Just as Zaleska steps toward Garth to consummate the unholy union, the bitter Sandor fires an arrow into his mistress' heart. With Sandor drawing a second arrow intended for Garth, a policeman (just arrived with the commissioner and Von Helsing) shoots the villain.

Janet comes out of her unnatural trance and the two embrace.

MEMORABLE MOMENT

The night after Dracula's daughter has burned her father's body to "exorcise" his unholy evil, she retires to her Chelsea loft, thinking herself free from the undead influence. The scene that follows reaches a height of intensity unmatched throughout the rest of the picture and captures perfectly the theme of inner conflict which powers the story.

As Zaleska sits at the piano, Sandor enters. "The night is here," he intones. "You think this night will be like all the others, don't you?" replies the countess. "Well, you're wrong," she continues, a hint of triumph in her soft voice. "Dracula is destroyed, his body's in ashes. The spell is broken." Zaleska's speech quickens, as if saying the words aloud will make it true. "I can live a *normal* life now," she continues, "*think* normal things, even play normal music again. Listen —" she begins to play, an almost sweet smile of innocence on her face, "— a song my mother once sang to me long long ago, rocking me to sleep as she sang in the twilight." "Twilight," echoes Sandor eagerly. "Quiet. Quiet, you disturb me," commands Zaleska, though softly, her eyes and thoughts obviously far away as she plays her gentle melody. "Twilight," she continues her reverie, "long shadows on the hillside." "*Evil* shadows," injects Sandor. "No, no," responds Zaleska, a look of concern now clouding her brow, "*peaceful* shadows —" Even as she makes this almost desperate contradiction, her playing subtly changes, the tempo increasing and the melody becoming harsher. "— The flutter of wings in the treetops," she persists, speaking quicker now, almost urgently. "The wings of *bats*," smiles Sandor evilly. "No, no," answers the now-troubled Zaleska, "the wings of birds — from far off the barking of a dog." The pleasant half-smile on her face has now given way completely to a disturbing anxiety. "Barking because there are *wolves* about," interjects Sandor. "Silence," commands Zaleska harshly, "I forbid you!" At this Sandor rises from his chair and moves to her side. "Forbid?" he asks, "*Why* are you afraid?" "I'm not," she pleads, even as the pace of her playing increases. Her voice takes on a frantic urgency as she insists,

"I'm not, I found release." "That music doesn't speak of release," points out Sandor. At this, Zaleska's eyes dart from side to side while the almost discordant tempo of her playing increases yet again. "No —" she answers with a desperate realization, "No —*you're right*!" Sandor presses: "That music tells of the dark — evil things — shadowy places." "Stop — stop — stop!" protests Zaleska as her playing halts suddenly and she rises abruptly. With a tortured, hunted look, she turns away from the piano. Slowly, silently, Sandor moves off. "Sandor," she asks despondently, and he turns, "Look at me. What do you see in my eyes?" After a pause, Sandor simply replies, "Death," and moves to get her cloak.

ASSETS

In *Dracula's Daughter*, screenwriter Garrett Fort (*Dracula, Frankenstein*) has created a "monster" of a very different stripe. Not only does the picture focus on a *female* vampire in a male-dominated arena[1] but on a *sympathetic* one as well. Gloria Holden's Countess Marya Zaleska is much more than a bloodsucking demon, she is a tortured soul, a pitiable "victim" (of her own despised heritage) as much as a vicious victimizer. This sympathetic characterization adds a fascinating "monster-as-victim" subtext (a theme which makes the Frankenstein films so intriguing) to what could otherwise have become just another straightforward vampire yarn. Admittedly, Frank Strayer's *Condemned to Live* (1935) touched on the topic to some extent, but Karen De Wolfe's screenplay separated out the two halves — normal human and bloodsucking fiend — in a Jekyll and Hyde manner. Thus, until the very end, the afflicted soul in *Condemned to Live* remained ignorant of his evil side and so lacked the tortured conflict which rages through *Dracula's Daughter*.

Fort makes no bones about this picture's sequel status, but he cleverly avoids the trap of repetition without expansion. While grounding *Dracula's Daughter* solidly in the proven Transylvanian soil of her father by repeating familiar scenes (an autopsy sequence plays out nearly identical to one in *Dracula* — and even steals an establishing long shot from the earlier film) and exact lines of dialogue (when offered sherry, Countess Zaleska declines with, "Thank you, I never drink — wine"), Fort takes his characters in new directions.

Fort creates a fascinating being in Countess Marya Zaleska. Though her very nature has made her cold and aloof, the haughtiness carries a decidedly hollow ring. While her face may remain passive, her voice can readily quicken with excitement to betray the hope and longing lurking beneath the cold countenance. Fort gives his tortured countess wonderful lines which not only illuminate her nature but her wit as well. When Garth makes a skeptical comment at a party, Zaleska cleverly disarms him with, "Possibly there are more things in heaven and Earth than are dreamed of in your — psychiatry, Mr. Garth."

Gloria Holden brings this tormented spirit to life with her restrained-yet-earnest performance, revealing the living being beneath the undead exterior. Holden truly uses her eyes to mirror her character's soul. She keeps her gaze almost unfocused at times, as if her inner self were concentrating elsewhere, attempting to escape from her own nightmarish existence. At other times her staring eyes dart about, almost desperately, as if searching for the escape she craves. When she talks of living "a normal life" in which she'll "think normal things," the faraway look in her eyes and half-smile on her lips speak of the hopeful expectations stretched out before her. After her moral defeat during the piano scene, Sandor holds up Zaleska's black cloak and ring (the symbols of her nocturnal cravings) so she can go out to find another victim. Holden hesitates, gazing at the despised garment in ambivalent fascination. Unable to resist the lure, she finally turns and allows Sandor to drape the damning cloak on her shoulders. Holden's face remains outwardly impassive, but her eyes and slight, downward turn of expression betray sadness at her defeat.

While not Universal's first choice as Sandor (Herbert Marshall was that), the role fits Irving Pichel like a demonic glove. Like an evil

"What do you see in my eyes?" asks Countess Marya Zaleska (Gloria Holden). "Death," answers Sandor (Irving Pichel). From *Dracula's Daughter* (1936).

albatross hung about the tormented Zaleska's neck, Sandor's presence constantly hovers in the background to weigh her down and prevent her flight from the shadow-world she inhabits. Pichel's sepulchral tones, delivered in a slow, resonant baritone, augment the aura of inevitability permeating the picture. Pichel, never the most expressive of actors (see his petrified performance in *Torture Ship* [1939] for a [non]demonstration) gives a measured, dour, unnervingly calm performance which embodies the story's gloom and doom thematics. *Dracula's Daughter* proved Pichel's finest hour (and nine minutes)—at least in *front* of the camera (Pichel also worked as a director).

Scripter Garrett Fort handles his comedy much better in the sequel than he did in the original by relying on subtle, dry humor rather than the damp silliness which nearly drowned the comedy relief character in *Dracula*. When Zaleska arrives at an elite social gathering, the unknowing hostess whispers to the countess that "You know, my guests are *dying* to meet you." Later, the skeptical commissioner disdainfully tells his butler to get his hat and coat because, "I'm going out after vampires!" "Vampires?" asks the butler, quizzically. "Vampires! Ha Ha Ha!" shoots back the scornful commissioner, to which the butler dryly retorts, "But I always understood you went after them with checkbooks, Sir."

Cinematographer George Robinson's subtle lighting does much to illuminate (so to speak) the characters and theme. In close-ups, Robinson provides an intense lighting for Gloria Holden to give her face an almost ethereal luminescence (which he augments with an occasional soft focus). When combined with Ms. Holden's soft, melancholy voice and the script's plaintive, fateful dialogue, it completes the picture of sadness and tragedy—a portrait more angelic than satanic. In contrast, the thoroughly evil Sandor is always heavily shadowed, the low-key illumination giving his character a very different cast and leaving little doubt as to which side of heaven Sandor aspires to.

Though Edward Van Sloan takes a back seat to Otto Kruger in *Dracula's Daughter*, he manages to make more of his Von Helsing in the limited screen time allowed here than he did in *Dracula*. For the sequel, Von Helsing has subtly changed, as if his earlier battle with the Lord of the Undead had deeply affected this venerable sage. Van Sloan shrugs off much of the affected slowness and awkward posing he exhibited in *Dracula*, while still retaining his unshakable authority and rock-steady presence. His voice, low and steady, possesses a touch of resigned sadness (particularly in the early scenes with the policemen). With his gruesome task now finished, the full weight of his efforts seems to have caught up with him. "Who is he?" asks the sergeant, pointing to the crumpled body of Renfield. "A poor, harmless imbecile who ate spiders and flies," answers Van Sloan evenly but with a note of deep sadness. Still, he speaks with an authority impossible to contradict. While perhaps a bit wearier now, Von Helsing has not completely lost his inner fire. When the commissioner labels his story "unbelievable," a spark ignites in Van Sloan and he answers, "The strength of the vampire, Sir Basil, lies in the fact that he *is* unbelievable," his voice becoming animated with the zeal and conviction which powered him through the previous film.

Top honors belong to Otto Kruger, who makes psychiatrist Jeffrey Garth a likable, intelligent, and *human* protagonist. *Dracula's Daughter* is one of the few pictures in which the hero is nearly as interesting as the villain. Kruger exhibits both self-assurance and a wry sense of humor, making his character grand enough to make confident sweeping statements about the human mind yet human enough to show frustration and annoyance at his inability to tie his own tie. Kruger speaks rapidly but smoothly, in a very natural manner filled with subtle inflections and small nuances (a far cry from David Manners' puppyish playing in *Dracula*). Lacking the overt melodramatics which mark most of the decade's thesping, Kruger's performance has aged better than most. Thanks to Fort's characterization and Kruger's acting, Jeffrey Garth becomes the most likable and intelligent protagonist from the Golden Age of Horror.

Kruger and Marguerite Churchill (as the feisty Janet) play off each other superbly. There is real chemistry between the two, a pleasant friction which generates sparks of annoyance tempered with affection. It makes for a refreshing change from the usual pretty-boy hero/wallflower heroine relationship seen in many a Golden Age horror.

LIABILITIES

The biggest disappointment delivered by *Dracula's Daughter* is a general lack of atmosphere (something her progenitor possessed in abundance). Aside from a few moments at the very beginning and end, the picture spends most of its time in well-lit modern settings. Castle Dracula, Carfax Abbey, and even Seward's Victorian-style mansion from the original give way to contemporary offices, hospital rooms, and luxury flats, giving a decidedly small-scale cast to the proceedings. Even the montage sequence (when the commissioner orders a dragnet thrown over London to head off the escaping Zaleska) consists of a series of modern images (telephone wires, electrical towers, modern printing techniques, radio announcers) which emphasize the "technological efficiency" angle. Even when the picture *finally* returns to Charles Hall's original Castle Dracula sets at the very end (with gigantic spider web intact), the pursuing police pull up right in front of the castle in a *car*—with brakes squealing. Thus, the daughter loses the atmospheric grandeur of the father.

Scenes occasionally play too long, slowing the film's pace considerably. One sequence of Garth attending to Zaleska's victim at the hospital lasts over three and half minutes—only to have the unfortunate (under hypnosis) repeat lines we've already heard and relive moments we've already seen.

While Garrett Fort manages to bring some effective humor to his story, he did not *completely* escape the hamfisted comedy which marred his original *Dracula*. The blatantly (and pointless) comedic interlude with the two cowardly constables at Whitby Jail goes on for much too long, and it jars with the more quickly paced, low-key comedy (the playful bickering between Garth and Janet, for instance) which spices the rest of the picture.

Lambert Hillyer's straightforward direction is competent but uninspired (much like that offered in Hillyer's other Golden Age horror film, *The Invisible Ray* [also 1936]). While Hillyer adds an occasional flourish, such as employing a skillful dissolve to bridge scenes or utilizing a well-timed cutaway (the camera suddenly panning upward to a stone death mask as a victim screams), he fails to bring a cohesive mood to the film. It's rather telling that the picture's most significant and memorable sequence revolves around dialogue and thematic content rather than visuals or atmosphere. For *Dracula's Daughter*, Hillyer seemingly steps aside and lets the actors and script carry the show — which, admittedly, is an ability some self-conscious directors never master (to the detriment of their films). For *Dracula's Daughter*, this works adequately enough — though one cannot help but wonder what *might* have been. While far above a Victor Halperin or Frank Strayer (and certainly *steadier* than Tod Browning), Hillyer proved himself to be no Karl Freund or James Whale.

Though perhaps a bit unfair to label Hillyer's no-frills approach a liability, it certainly is no asset either. One can only wonder at what Whale might have done with *Dracula's Daughter*, a tantalizing "what if" made a bit more substantial by the fact that early preproduction publicity for *Dracula's Daughter* cited Whale as the picture's intended director. Alas, as the poet John Greenleaf Whittier wrote, "For of all sad words of tongue or pen, the saddest are these — 'it might have been.'"

No, *Dracula's Daughter* is not as "good" as *Dracula*. Still, while lacking the overpowering presence and almost palpable atmosphere of its father, this *Daughter* can well take pride in its *own* thematic and thespic accomplishments. *Dracula's Daughter* remains an entertaining, solid member of the genre's pantheon and presents a fitting close to Universal's horror heyday. To borrow from a competitor (Columbia's *The Black Room*): "Principio et finem Similia — I end as I began."

REVIEWS

The New York Times' (May 18, 1936) Frank S. Nugent seemed to be impressed by the picture's chilling aspects but took an irritatingly condescending attitude in his review: "Quite terrifying it all is, to be sure, and we strongly recommend your stopping off at a nearby florist to buy a few sprays of bat-thorn to hold protectingly over your head as the wolves howl on the screen and hooded figures drift through the eddying fog." (Note: Mr. Nugent seems to have confused the original *Dracula* with the more recent *Mark of the Vampire* of the previous year, since "bat-thorn" was the vampire-repellent of choice in the latter picture whereas wolfsbane was the weed employed to battle *Dracula* — or perhaps he simply felt that one vampire picture was the same as another.)

Apparently unable to decide whether *Dracula's Daughter* was indeed "terrifying" or simply titillating, Mr. Nugent called Gloria Holden "a remarkably convincing bat-woman" while finishing up by labeling *Dracula's Daughter* "a cute little horror picture," adding "be sure and bring the kiddies."

Variety (May 20, 1936), however, exhibited no such ambivalence: "This is a chiller with plenty of ice; a surefire waker-upper in the theatre and a stay-awake influence in the bedroom later on. Rates tops among recent horror pictures and, as such, figures to deliver nice grosses. Entire E. M. Asher production rates bows, from the scenario groundwork up through the acting, direction and photography. For a change, this is a picture that is quite entertaining along with its shocks...."

PRODUCTION NOTES

Universal's last horror production of the initial Golden Age (released just before horror's two-year hiatus) was originally proposed as a high-profile vehicle for Boris Karloff, Bela Lugosi *and* Colin Clive to be scripted by writer John L. Balderston (*The Mummy*). After the studio rejected Balderston's screenplay, however, they dropped Karloff (and Clive) from the project and opted to scale the production back to an inexpensive horror programmer. (Ultimately, even Lugosi was dropped.)

While *The Black Cat* and *The Raven* had both received smaller budgets than *Dracula's Daughter*, these previous Universal "babyscarers" also possessed the considerable drawing cards of the Karloff and Bela Lugosi tandem. The biggest name in *Dracula's Daughter* was to be Otto Kruger, and his box-office draw was less than weighty. Ironically, while intended as a modest production, *Dracula's Daughter* turned out to be one of Universal's most expensive horror films, largely because of costs incurred by of delays and revisions. R. C. Sherriff (screenwriter for *The Invisible Man*), for instance, received a whopping $16,650 for his (rejected) treatment. Another writer, Peter Dunne, was paid $2,350 for his services. Neither man's name appears on the final credits. Garrett Fort (co-screenwriter of *Dracula* and *Frankenstein*) received sole screenplay credit and $6,375 for his efforts. The production's original director, Edward Sutherland (*Murders in the Zoo*, 1933), was paid $17,500 for "retained time" while waiting out the studio's delays. Sutherland ultimately had to abandon the project (but not his healthy paycheck) due to time constraints, and was replaced with Lambert Hillyer (charging up an additional $5,400 expense for Universal). The studio paid Marguerite Churchill

This atmospheric publicity pose captures both the allure and torment of *Dracula's Daughter* (1936). (Courtesy of Ted Okuda.)

an extra $750 for "accumulation" time incurred by the delays. Universal also shelled out $4,000 to Bela Lugosi (who was originally called upon to reprise his role of Dracula) for time retained before his character was dropped altogether from the final script (thus Lugosi earned more by staying *out* of the sequel than he did from *starring* in the original!). All in all, Universal wasted $41,250 in "accumulation," "retention," and discarded screenplay fees — nearly *one fifth* of the film's final $230,425 budget!

Along with the script revisions came cast changes as well. Aside from the ultimate exclusion of Bela Lugosi, Jane Wyatt was replaced by Marguerite Churchill (on loan from Warner Bros.) and the film's original hero, Cesar Romero, gave way to Otto Kruger.

If one judges by salary, the star of *Dracula's*

As shown by this preproduction herald, Universal "Ace" James Whale was an early candidate to direct *Dracula's Daughter* (1936). Note the superimposed likeness of Bela Lugosi to the left. Universal signed the actor to reprise his role of Dracula in the sequel, but the part was ultimately dropped from the film during early script revisions.

Daughter was Otto Kruger, earning $2500 weekly, compared to Gloria Holden's (the picture's *true* star) meager $300 per week. Supporting player and seasoned vampire hunter Edward Van Sloan commanded $600 a week.

Otto Kruger, a grandnephew of Oom Paul Kruger, president of South Africa during the Boer War, was born in Toledo, Ohio, in 1885 and educated in music at Columbia University. Kruger trained for the concert stage, becoming an accomplished musician on the piano, cello, and viola, and even conducting a symphony orchestra at age 12! At Columbia, however, he was bitten by the acting bug and gave up his musical aspirations to pursue a career in the theater. He made his way to Broadway in 1915 and quickly rose to become one of the leading matinee idols of the theater. MGM brought him to Hollywood in 1932 and Kruger appeared in over 100 pictures until his retirement in 1965 (though he frequently returned to the stage). A look at Kruger's other genre appearances (the awful *Jungle Captive*, 1944 ; the mildly interesting *Woman Who Came Back*, 1945; the fairly good *Colossus of New York*, 1958; and the juvenile *Wonderful World of the Brothers Grimm*, 1962) shows that

Kruger's first horror film was also his best. Politically active, Kruger became a board member of the Motion Picture Relief Fund in 1937 and was eventually elected to the office of Vice President of the Fund, a post he maintained up until his death in 1974.

Star Gloria Holden was none too enamored of her one and only foray into the realm of horror. In later years, her general response when queried about *Dracula's Daughter* was a terse "I hated that thing."

Universal borrowed Irving Pichel from Republic, who held his actor-director term contract in abeyance while he played the heavy in *Dracula's Daughter*. Pichel's show business career was a series of progressions: stage actor to screenwriter to film actor to director. After graduating from Harvard, Pichel tried a variety of short-term jobs before becoming a stage actor. In 1927, MGM offered him a position as a scenarist. After about six months in the writers' bullpen, however, he returned to acting. In 1932, he stepped behind the camera, co-directing *The Most Dangerous Game* and *She* among others, while still acting in films. In 1940, he stepped behind the camera completely to concentrate solely on directing. Among his later directorial credits are *Mr.*

Peabody and the Mermaid (1948), *The Great Rupert* (1950), and *Destination Moon* (1950).

Nan Grey (born Eschal Miller), who so effectively played the victim of Countess Zaleska's bloodlust, received a larger, though less memorable, part in Universal's *Tower of London* (1939). Her other genre credits are (the borderline) *The Black Doll* (1938), *The Invisible Man Returns* and *The House of the Seven Gables* (both 1940). She began in films in 1934 and quit the big screen in 1941 to concentrate on radio where, for seven years, she played the female lead of Kathy Marshall on the popular soap opera, "Those We Love." In 1950 she retired from show business altogether when she married singer Frankie Lane (though she did make one guest appearance opposite her husband in a 1960 episode of "Rawhide"). "In the mid–1960s," reported her obituary (July 27, 1993, issue of *The Seattle Times*), "Miss Grey marketed a special cosmetic mirror for nearsighted women, and numbered among her customers Princess Grace of Monaco."

Before becoming one of Hollywood's top gossip columnists ("whose newsprint bite was more feared than her reportorial ability was admired," remembered *Variety*'s obituary, February 2, 1966) and arch-rival to Louella Parsons, Hedda Hopper was a Broadway stage actress and popular screen player. "After her acting career petered out" (*Variety* again) shortly after the release of *Dracula's Daughter*, she turned journalist (though not above making the occasional screen appearance all the way up until her death). She is the mother of William Hopper, who achieved fame as detective Paul Drake on television's "Perry Mason" (not to mention as antagonist of *The Deadly Mantis*, 1957).

Shooting on this reticent production finally began on February 4, 1936, over two years after Balderston delivered his original treatment in January of 1934. Lengthy delays were not the only problems plaguing the picture. Nine days into filming, a large lamp fell over — right onto the head of director Lambert Hillyer, who was then rushed off to the Universal City infirmary. Fortunately, his injury proved minor, though the studio publicity department took full advantage of the incident by noting with a delicious shudder the date of the accident — Friday the 13th. *Dracula's Daughter* ran seven days over schedule and nearly $50,000 over budget, wrapping with a final cost of $278,380, making this modest thriller one of Universal's most expensive horror properties.

Studio owner Carl Laemmle and chief production executive Carl Laemmle, Jr., never got to reap the (considerable) benefits of their final horror production, for *Dracula's Daughter* was released in May, nearly two months after the Laemmle regime was sent packing by the usurping antihorror owners of "The New Universal."

NOTE

1. The few female nosferatu seen prior to *Dracula's Daughter*, such as *Dracula*'s wives or *Mark of the Vampire*'s "Luna," had been decidedly subordinate to their male counterparts (the single exception being Carl Dreyer's *Vampyr* [1932] — a film definitely *outside* the Hollywood mainstream).

REVOLT OF THE ZOMBIES
(1936; Academy)

Alternate Title: *Revolt of the Demons*
Release Date: June 4, 1936
Running Time: 65 minutes
Director: Victor Halperin
Producer: Edward Halperin
*Screenplay: Howard Higgin, Rollo Lloyd, Victor Halperin

Photography: Arthur Martinelli, A.S.C.
Cameraman: J. Arthur Feindel
Art and Technical Direction: Leigh Smith
Editor: Douglas Biggs
Sound Technician: G. P. Costello
Musical Direction: Abe Meyer
Production Manager: John Hicks

Coiffeurs: Phillip Scheer
Studio Executive: Leon d'Usseau
Special Effects: Ray Mercer
Cast: Dorothy Stone (Claire Duval), Dean Jagger (Armand Lauque), Roy D'Arcy (General Mozoia), Robert Noland (Clifford Grayson), George Cleveland (General Duval), E. Alyn (*Fred*) Warren (Dr. Trevissant), Carl Stockdale (MacDonald), William Crowell (Priest Tsiang), Teru Shimada (Buna), Adolph Millard (General von Schilling), Sana Rayya (Dancer).

*Uncredited on film print

"Tsiang still insists his gods say he must create zombie soldiers." — Armand Lauque.

SYNOPSIS

The picture opens with this written prologue: "Many strange events were recorded in the secret archives of the fighting nations during the World War — But none stranger than that which occurred when a regiment of French Cambodians from the vicinity of the lost city of Angkōr arrived on the Franco-Austrian front—"

During World War I, a priest from this "lost city of Angkōr" directs a troupe of zombie soldiers against the Axis powers. This squadron of "human automatons" proves unstoppable by the enemy's bullets.

An envoy from the "Central European Powers" (i.e., Axis) pleads with the Allied leaders: "In the name of humanity, you must not go further with your experiment. It may mean the destruction of the white race!" This rather racist argument proves unnecessary, however, for the ungrateful (and fearful) Allies have already placed the priest under arrest and ended his "experiment." While confined, the priest is murdered by those seeking his power for themselves.

An international expedition journeys to Angkōr to find the secret of the zombies and destroy it. Among the party members are mild-mannered translator Armand Lauque, his rough-and-ready soldier friend Cliff Grayson, and the beautiful Claire, daughter of the expedition's leader, General Duval. Armand falls in love with Claire, and she agrees to marry him. This is just a ruse, however, for she really loves Cliff and simply uses Armand to "excite his jealousy." Though shocked when he learns of this deception, Armand still loves Claire but the experience has made him colder, more ruthless.

The expedition turns up nothing at Angkōr and, after an accident which leaves one of their members, MacDonald, crippled, they return to the Expedition Base Headquarters in Phnom Penn.

While Claire and Cliff enjoy their courtship, Armand discovers a clue in a photo of the temple at Angkōr. Journeying back to the "lost city" alone, he stumbles into a secret passageway under the temple. There he follows a priest through a swamp to a hidden vault, upon whose wall is written the secret of the zombie formula.

Back at his lab in Phnom Penn, Armand mixes up a batch of zombie powder and tests it on his native servant. It works. Armand also learns the means by which he can exert his will over anyone at seemingly any distance.

Armand remembers what Cliff had once said to him: "Be ruthless. Forget all sentiment. Get to your objective, take it, and hold it." With his newfound power, Armand heeds his friend's innocently given advice and proceeds to enslave the entire camp to his will. With a company of obedient zombie soldiers to make his control total, he sets his sights on Claire — his "objective."

Armand induces Claire to marry him by promising to allow Cliff's safe return to England. He reneges on his word, however, and (unknown to Claire) makes Cliff another of his zombie slaves.

Claire still pines for Cliff, and Armand soon becomes dissatisfied with possessing her "gratitude" (for sparing her lover) rather than her love. In a moment of conscience, Armand tells her: "I'd give up everything I have if you could just find it in your heart to think kindly of me." To prove his love for her, he vows to "give up this power" and "release these people."

This he does, and all the zombies return to normal. "We are free again, we can think," exclaims Armand's servant. "The madman who did this to us must die, so he can never do it again!" His rage is echoed by the other-recovered zombies.

As Armand prattles on to Claire ("I love you, I love you"), the angry soldiers storm the house. Breaking in, they shoot down their former controller. While Claire and Cliff embrace, MacDonald looks down at Armand's body and delivers this eulogy: "Whom the gods destroy, they first make mad."

MEMORABLE MOMENT

This disappointingly dull picture has only one moment of note, and it is memorable more for its gruesome nature than its emotional power or cinematic quality. It comes near the beginning, when the Cambodian priest intends to "show how a handful of zombies can take an entire enemy trench." On a mock-up battlefield stand half a dozen unmoving zombie soldiers. As a rear-projection battle rages in the background, the face of the Cambodian priest is superimposed over the eerie tableau, then fades into a pair of glowering eyes (Bela Lugosi's eyes, to be precise — Halperin lifted the shot from his earlier *White Zombie*). As the undead platoon advances, a German soldier fires his Luger repeatedly at one of the ragged zombies. In quick succession, five bloodless holes appear in the naked, bony chest, unnoticed by the weird recipient. Continuing his slow advance, he and his undead comrades move up and over the edge of the enemy trench with their bayonets poised to strike down the terrified enemy.

The sight of these bullet holes appearing one after the other (via crude stop-motion photography) is gruesome and shocking, and the rat-a-tat background sound of machine gun fire and exploding bombs creates an air of panicked urgency which contrasts sharply with the slow, inexorable movement of the zombies. Unfortunately, this is the only sequence in the entire picture which makes even a marginally effective use of the zombies; the rest of the film matches the pace of the plodding zombies rather than moving with any sense of urgency.

ASSETS

None.

Except for the intriguing idea of using invulnerable zombie soldiers during wartime, there is nothing of merit offered by this *Revolt*. Even *this* tantalizing concept, so ripe with possibilities, is left unexplored after the brief sequence described above. It is not through lack of opportunity, however, for after Armand creates his own zombie battalion, there are ample occasions to explore and exploit the frightening concept of an unfeeling foe which cannot be killed. But Halperin chooses to ignore any potential encounters with the undead and instead focuses interminably on a ridiculous love triangle. Consequently, the picture's one fascinating notion remains as lifeless as the zombies themselves.

LIABILITIES

This follow-up by the Halperin brothers to their hit Bela Lugosi film *White Zombie* (1932) is a disappointment in all departments. Most immediately apparent are the shoddy production values. The interiors consist of a few cheap, bleak sets, while a plethora of enlarged photographs of Eastern temples and such combine with a few potted palms to create the "exotic" exteriors. Halperin's overuse of rear-projection emphasizes the stagy cheapness of the production, and quickly becomes laughable. A sparse tent interior with a photo of an ancient temple seen through the doorway, for example, is no more convincing than the cityscape behind a talk show host's desk. In some instances, the shot is so cheap that people pass in front of a backdrop and we're not even shown their feet! (thus saving on floor "decoration"). Poor Dean Jagger looks ridiculous while walking through a rear-projected swamp. Rocking back and forth in place in some tiny studio tank to simulate slogging through the water, arms held up and shoulders rhythmically moving side to side while the projected film unreels behind, he looks absurd — as if performing some slow-motion

Watusi. Surprisingly, some live (though invariably static) shots of figures actually moving through the swamp are periodically inserted, so why use the ridiculous rear-projection when the set was obviously available? Perhaps it was the time factor, or maybe Halperin just has some perverse love for rear-projection, à la Alfred Hitchcock. (If so, then this is the *only* thing Halperin shared in common with the great director.)

Victor Halperin's direction is unimaginative at best and devastatingly dull at worst. The picture opens well enough, with an extreme close-up of a military cap resting on a desk. The camera smoothly pulls back to reveal the cap's owner speaking behind the desk. Aside from this shot (and a nearly identical one 15 minutes later), the subsequent camera movements exist strictly for practical rather than aesthetic reasons (a 20-degree pan to follow a character as he crosses a room, for instance). Even these basic movements are rare, occurring fewer than a dozen times over the course of the film's 65 minutes. It is difficult to believe that this picture was directed by the same man who made the wonderful *White Zombie* four years earlier.

It is a poor choice indeed to use the same shots of the zombie soldiers streaming by again and again, drawing undue attention to the shoddy production values. The same two shots of zombie soldiers marching up stairs and shuffling past a fountain is used two and three times respectively within the space of a few minutes! Halperin (or editor Douglas Biggs) even takes one distinctive shot of the zombies marching along a path and uses it again *after* they've supposedly been returned to normal, and he uses the close-up of Bela Lugosi's eyes borrowed from *White Zombie* a total of nine times!

The script is tedious and rambling. Instead of utilizing the zombies in any suspenseful manner, the story focuses on the bland romantic triangle, meandering through one melodramatic encounter after another: Armand professing his love for Claire, Claire confessing her love for Cliff, Cliff admitting his love for Claire — and so on). Each of these episodes comes complete with pained expressions, dramatic gestures, and overstated emotion. The zombies, having faded into the background, serve merely to bracket this soap-opera romance. The potential menace generated by the zombies' presence totally dissipates under the crushing weight of the romantic triangle, which takes up the bulk of the film.

Inconsistencies abound when it comes to the unfortunate zombies. As explained (and demonstrated) in the story, these "zombies" are not reanimated corpses, but simply *living* people placed under the hypnotic control of a "zombie-maker." However, when the zombie soldier is shot at the film's beginning, the bullets have no effect. If these beings were truly just normal people placed in a trance, would being shot through the heart not kill them regardless of their hypnotic condition? Also inconsistent is the mechanism by which zombies are created. Although Armand needs his new-found zombie powder to transform his servant into a mindless slave, he performs the same transformation in others (even over long distances) simply by willing it. But, after all, this zombie business is a trifling matter; obviously what really counts is the juicy romantic angle!

The picture's cause is not helped by the script's flowery, awkward dialogue and maudlin love-talk:

Claire: "It isn't easy to give up the one thing in the world one loves."
Armand: "No it isn't, is it? I too love only one thing in the world, but cannot give it up. Our difference is — I haven't your courage."
Or: "He did try, by sundry means, to win her love, but she, as women will, could not care for him."
Or this: I have been made somewhat ridiculous, it's true, but — I still love you."

The formality and archaic construction of these verbal passages belong in an eighteenth-century gothic romance, not in a 1936 motion picture striving for some modicum of believability.

The actors (with the exception of Dean Jagger) fail to rise above the tedious plot, archaic dialogue, and dismal (non)direction, choosing instead to wallow in melodramatic

Armand Lauque (Dean Jagger, at left) uses the fumes from his zombie powder to turn his servant (Teru Shimada) into a "living automaton" in *Revolt of the Zombies* (1936).

histrionics. Jagger, however, simply sinks *below* it all. He seems to have chosen the opposite tack and underplays (or, more precisely, *non*-plays) his role, walking through his part with toneless delivery, blank looks (ostensibly passing for "dreamy"), and a few feeble hand gestures. His countenance is often so wooden and expressionless that one forgets that he is actually the zombie *master* and not one of the emotionless subjects. To be fair, however, Jagger does occasionally give a hint of the talent that would later flourish under more astute direction. For instance, when Armand first tests the zombie powder on his servant, Jagger has a wild look in his eye and his hand visibly shakes while spooning out the powder and lighting the burner, which reflects both Armand's excitement and his trepidation. Unfortunately, Jagger's flat delivery and monosyllabic tones undermine this nice touch of physical acting.

The haphazard musical score is applied to the picture in a slap-dash, often inappropriate manner. One of the worst examples of film scoring occurs during the sequence in which the Cambodian priest prays before the multi-armed statue of the goddess Shiva. A rather somber melody of rhythmic horns plays on the soundtrack. Lost in his ministrations, the priest does not notice a human arm, grasping a dagger, appear from behind the statue. Suddenly, the priest rises up from his prayer and the arm is hastily withdrawn. We are now fully aware of the imminent danger to the priest, but light strings rise to an airy, frolicking motif, evoking a decidedly happy and wholesome mood! This poor choice of music completely negates the suspense of the sequence, confusing the viewer by undercutting a moment of tension with a pleasant, light-hearted mood (should we be *happy* about this dire situation?).

One would never suspect that this atmospheric ad is promoting the Golden Age of Horror's *worst* film, *Revolt of the Zombies* (1936). (Courtesy of Ron Borst/Hollywood Movie Posters.)

nearly three full minutes the viewer is treated to shot after shot of the two men slowly slogging through waist deep water in the (rear-projected) swamp. Back and forth the shots go — from the priest to Jagger, from Jagger back to the priest — ad infinitum, ad nauseam. For exciting variety, Halperin occasionally has Jagger duck behind a swamp bush. Editor Douglas Biggs (given an impossible job, judging from the footage he had to work with) probable saw this as the closest the picture came to possessing an action sequence, and so milked it for all (and much more) than it was worth.

The film features a singularly unexciting climax. Armand, finally realizing that Claire does not care for him, releases his hypnotic hold on the zombies in order to prove his love to her. The zombie subjects simply return to normal, break into Armand's house, and shoot him. These final scenes are given such poor build-up and played with such little conviction that instead of becoming poignant or tragic they just come off as silly — which pretty much sums up the whole film.

Revolt of the Zombies is truly the nadir of the Golden Age of Horror.

Poor pacing makes an already tedious picture collapse under the weight of its own inertia. For instance, the sequence in which Armand follows the native priest through a swamp to the secret temple drags out for an interminably long time. Though the film's pressbook singled this episode out as "tense with excitement," it is anything but. For

REVIEWS

Critic Frank S. Nugent, of *The New York Times* (June 5, 1936) was comically appalled at the poor treatment zombies received at the hands of the Halperin brothers: "Under any code of fair practice, a zombie is entitled to be authentically dead but revived horrendously by some sorcerer to do his evil bidding. Too, he must render thanatoid service to an utter villain, not to a shilly-shallyer who cannot decide between a necrologic career and blue-eyed blonde.... To hint that they [the zombies] are not really zombies at all, but sleep-walkers or something, is to imperil the very foundations of a grand spook legend. No wonder the zombies revolted, turned upon their lovelorn master and shot him down: he was their conjur' man and he done them wrong."

In a more serious vein, Mr. Nugent also took issue with the three-sided romance, noting that "where romance comes in ... that is where the picture deflates itself rather pitiably into a crudely produced and generally ridiculous melodrama."

Variety's "Chic" (June 10, 1936) was no more kind, calling it "a stab at the horror stuff from a new angle, but opening no new treatment.... There is so little to the real story that the action stalls terribly at times.... The action moves tediously to the final revolt, brief and rather unexciting. The dialog is trite, sometimes boring, the speeches written in the flowery style of the old-fashioned melodramas. There is never the thrill and suspense that might well have been created from the material. Faulty direction seems to extend to the acting..."

PRODUCTION NOTES

According to the film's pressbook, "An entire camera crew was sent to Cambodia by the Halperin Brothers to secure interesting native material and records of the architectural splendor of lost Angkor..." Right. Also, the Halperins reportedly spent nearly two years "gathering important facts and data concerning this mystic kingdom." If this source can be believed, production was often delayed by such authenticity-driven practices as searching "high and low throughout the country for a life-sized image of ... the mythical, green-eyed, blue-throated, moon-god, Siva." An authentic statue was finally located in "an out of the way antique shop in New York City."

Revolt of the Zombies ran into some legal difficulties during its initial release. Amusement Securities Corporation, which had financed and now held the reissue rights to the Halperins' earlier *White Zombie*, brought an injunction suit against Academy Pictures for "Unfair Competition By Use of Name 'Zombie' in Title."

After a 14-day trial, the court ruled that the word zombie had become so suggestive of the earlier picture that the title *Revolt of the Zombies* did indeed constitute unfair competition. Therefore, the Halperins were forced to retitle their picture *Revolt of the Demons*. Fortunately for the filmmakers, the ruling was ultimately overturned and the picture could reassume its original moniker.

Dean Jagger taught school before turning to acting. In 1949 he received an Academy Award for Best Supporting Actor (*Twelve O'-Clock High*). Jagger made one other horror picture, *So Sad About Gloria* (1973), as well as three science fiction films — *On the Threshold of Space* (1956), *X the Unknown* (1956), and *End of the World* (1977).

Co-screenwriter Howard Higgin began writing motion picture scripts in 1917. Under the tutelage of Cecil B. De Mille, he became an assistant director, production supervisor, and finally full-fledged director. He continued directing (mainly low-to-medium budget action pictures like 1931's *The Painted Desert* and 1933's *Carnival Lady*) up until 1937, when he turned exclusively to screenwriting. It seems inconceivable that Higgin also shared story credit for Universal's *The Invisible Ray* the same year as *Revolt of the Zombies* (but then, on *Invisible Ray*, Higgin had the benefit of the talented John Colton to complete the shooting script).

"Coiffeur"-provider Phillip Scheer moved from hairdressing to monster makeups in the 1950s, creating the creatures for *I Was a Teenage Werewolf* (1957), *I Was a Teenage Frankenstein* (1957), *Attack of the Puppet People* (1958), *How to Make a Monster* (1958), and *Invisible Invaders* (1959).

THE DEVIL-DOLL
(1936; MGM)

Release Date: August 7, 1936
Running Time: 70 minutes
Director: Tod Browning
Executive Producer: E. J. Mannix
Screenplay: Garrett Fort, Guy Endore, Erich von Stroheim
Story: Tod Browning (based on the novel *Burn Witch Burn!* by Abraham Merritt)
Photography: Leonard Smith, A.S.C.
Art Director: Cedric Gibbons
Associates: Stan Rogers, Edwin B. Willis
Editor: Fredrick Y. Smith
Musical Score: Franz Waxman
Recording Director: Douglas Shearer
Wardrobe: Dolly Tree
Cast: Lionel Barrymore (Lavond), Maureen O'Sullivan (Lorraine), Frank Lawton (Toto), Rafaela Ottiano (Malita), Robert Greig (Coulvet), Lucy Beaumont (Mme. Lavond), Henry B. Walthall (Marcel), Grace Ford (Lachna), Pedro de Cordoba (Matin), Arthur Hohl (Rodin), Juanita Quigley (Marguerite), Claire du Brey (Mme. Coulvet), Rollo Lloyd (Detective), E. Allyn Warren (Commissioner).

"You'll never know how happy it makes me to leave one of my beautiful dolls in your home." — Madame Mandelip (aka Paul Lavond).

SYNOPSIS

Two men, Paul Lavond and his cellmate Marcel, escape from a French island prison. Eluding their pursuers, the pair make their way to an old house hidden away deep in a swamp. Marcel is a scientist who, along with his companion Malita, had been developing a process to shrink living beings. Malita has continued the work while Marcel was in prison. "Lavond, my friend," explains Marcel, "millions of years ago the creatures who roamed this world were gigantic. As they multiplied, the Earth could no longer produce enough food. Think of it, Lavond — every living creature reduced to one-sixth its size, one-sixth its physical needs. Food for six times all of us!"

While Marcel and Malita have managed to shrink living dogs down to the size of hamsters, the experiment has not met with complete success. "In reducing the brain," explains Marcel, "all records are wiped off, no memory left, no will of its own." The subjects are dormant, "creatures capable of responding only to the force of another will."

Marcel, however, believes he has solved the problem during his long stay in prison. That night, Marcel and Malita test their process on a human being — their half-wit servant girl, Lachna. Unfortunately, she turns out like all the rest. The disappointment is too much for the elderly Marcel, and his heart gives out.

We learn of Paul Lavond's history. "I was once a very successful banker," he tells Malita. "Three men, my partners, lied and tricked me into prison. Well, three lives are going to pay for it."

Undeterred by neither the failure nor Marcel's death, Malita entreats Lavond to help her carry on the work. "We can make the whole world small!" she exclaims, her eyes alive with a mad excitement. "We can go to Paris. There are many people there —" she says eagerly. While Lavond initially wants no part of her mad dream, he begins to see the possibilities of utilizing the process to carry out his vengeance and agrees to go with her.

In Paris, Lavond's three ex-partners, Coulvet, Matin, and Rodin, are a little nervous now that the man they had framed is at large. They place a 50,000-franc reward on his head. ("There's a certain amusing irony in offering a man's *own* money for his capture," observes Matin dryly.) Soon the whole city is on the lookout for Paul Lavond. They search in vain, however, for Lavond is cleverly disguised as Madame Mandelip, "a poor, toddling old woman" (as Lavond characterizes her) who runs a small toy shop in Montmartre. Only Malita and Lavond's aged, blind mother (whom he occasionally visits) know the truth.

Madame Mandelip goes to see Rodin, ostensibly seeking financial backing for her shop. She presents a miniature horse, which prances around on his desk. This arouses both Rodin's amazement and his greed. Madame Mandelip takes him back to her shop and there paralyzes him. After revealing his identity to the horrified but helpless captive, Lavond shrinks Rodin down to a foot-tall automaton, thus (with the previously shrunk Lachna) completing a his-and-hers set of devil-dolls.

Lavond has a daughter, Lorraine — a pretty young girl who, because of her family's financial ruin, is forced to work in a laundry sweatshop. Embittered by the infamy of her family name, she has "grown to hate her father's memory." As Madame Mandelip, Lavond sometimes visits Lorraine and her grandmother, though he never reveals his true identity to the girl.

Lorraine is in love with Toto, the young owner/driver of a fledgling taxi company. She thinks of herself as the daughter of a murderer, however, and so is reluctant to pledge herself in marriage. When Toto presses her, she tells him, "I can never escape from the fact that I'm *his* daughter. I could never ask any man to share that with me."

Now Lavond chooses victim number two — Coulvet. Madame Mandelip pays a visit to Mrs. Coulvet and sells her a doll, the miniaturized Lachna. Lavond sneaks back to the house that night and, standing outside, uses his will to activate Lachna. The tiny creature first retrieves Mrs. Coulvet's jewels from the dresser and drops them off a window ledge into Lavond's waiting basket. Lachna then goes to Coulvet's bed and stabs him with her tiny stiletto, the poisoned blade leaving him paralyzed for the rest of his life ("a brilliant mind imprisoned in a useless body").

The final conspirator, Matin, is unnerved by the dire fates of his two compatriots. He receives a note from Lavond which warns him to confess or die at ten o'clock that night. Matin calls the prefect of police and soon a half-dozen men are stationed within his palatial home.

On Matin's Christmas tree hangs a doll, unnoticed, wrapped in a bow.

As the appointed hour draws nigh, Matin becomes more and more agitated: "Two minutes — I can't stand much more of this." Controlled by Lavond, the diminutive "doll" Rodin creeps up under Matin's chair. As the clock strikes ten, Rodin raises his tiny stiletto but the intended victim's nerves fail him and Matin breaks down and confesses. Matin is arrested and Lavond's name is cleared.

Back at the toy shop, Lavond burns his wig, having mailed a letter in the name of Madame Mandelip to the police confessing responsibility for the disappearance of Rodin and the demise of Coulvet. Malita is ecstatic: "We can go on with our work without being bothered by the police." Lavond feels differently. Thinking of the crimes he has committed as Madame Mandelip, Lavond informs her they must destroy the shop and the backroom laboratory. "I never had any plans beyond the vindication of my name, and I only wanted *that* because of my family," he tells her. "We can't go on. Why, our work is hideous, we're cruel and it's *got* to come to an end tonight!" Malita is incensed. While Lavond changes out of his Madame Mandelip clothes for the last time, Malita goes to the back room. Talking to the brainless Rodin doll, she schemes, "Reduced to your size, I'll control him as easily as I control you." Malita activates Rodin and sends him to strike. Fortunately, Lavond notices Malita's intent stare in time and turns a chair over onto the devil-doll. Desperate, Malita grabs a vial from the lab and brandishes it overhead. "Malita," yells Lavond, "put that down, you'll blow yourself to atoms!"[1] Spitefully, she throws the vial and it explodes. Lavond makes it out the door but Malita, the lab, and the devil-dolls all go up in flames.

Lavond then tracks down Toto and introduces himself. Going to the Eiffel Tower to talk, Lavond tells Toto the whole story, concluding that "now that I have my freedom, my exile must commence all over again." He explains that he can never see Lorraine: "Even when I was innocent, her hatred of me hurt a good deal. Now that I'm guilty, her *belief* in me would hurt even more."

Just then, Lorraine comes out of the elevator, for she was to meet Toto there at sundown. Lavond, posing as a friend of her father's, delivers his love and blessing to her in the form of a "message" from her father, whom he says died in his arms while escaping from prison. Taking his leave, Lavond descends in the elevator, having clearly implied that he will commit suicide to atone for his crimes (however justified they might have been).

MEMORABLE MOMENTS

It is appropriate that the film's two most outstanding moments reflect the picture's nature—that of sentimental tragedy overlaid with horror/sci-fi trappings. The first moment is a triumph of special effects, most evident in some spectacular set design from Academy Award winner Cedric Gibbons and his associates, Stan Rogers and Edwin B. Willis. It begins as the inanimate "devil-doll" Lachna suddenly awakens. Answering the will of Lavond stationed outside, Lachna disentangles herself from the arms of Coulvet's sleeping child and crawls out between the slats of the crib, her actions mirrored by the shadow cast on the wall. She moves across the floor past oversized toy blocks to the huge door of the parents' room, opened only a crack. Pulling at the mammoth (to her) portal, the door slowly begins to open. Viewing from a high angle, the camera perspective emphasizes the immensity of Lachna's surroundings. The camera then cuts to the other side of the door and we watch her straining to push it further open. As she creeps across the threshold, the inertia of the gigantic door swings it open a few more inches. Colossal shadows, presumably thrown from the windowpane, are cast across the door and move as it opens, adding depth and realism to the scene.

Lachna creeps noiselessly past the mountain-sized bed to the vanity across the room. Not able to reach the top of the footstool, she cleverly retrieves one of Mrs. Coulvet's high-heeled shoes. Lugging it across the floor she uses it as a stepladder to gain the top of the footstool. From there she climbs up to the divan seat and finally crawls up the drawers as if she's scaling a cliff. Attaining the top of the vanity, she opens the coffin-sized jewel box and pulls out what must be the world's largest pearl necklace prop. Dragging it across the vanity to the second-story windowsill, she drops it into the waiting basket of Madame Mandelip. After retrieving a second piece of jewelry, Lachna descends to the floor and tiptoes across to the monstrous bed where she shimmies up the bedclothes. Creeping along the gigantic sleeping form of Monsieur Coulvet, she draws out her tiny stiletto and raises it to strike. The camera then cuts suddenly to Madame Mandelip waiting outside while an off-screen strangled cry tells us that the deed is done. The colossal sets are so detailed and realistically lit, and the athletic acrobatics of the tiny Lachna so fascinating as she cleverly surmounts ordinary objects and furniture which have been transformed into looming mountains, that we cease to wonder at the trickery and become absorbed in the *reality* of the moment. This is truly the best reaction which a special effects scene can hope to attain.

The second moment is one of simple humanity, which, due to the sincere playing of Lionel Barrymore and Maureen O'Sullivan, avoids becoming mere maudlin sentimentality. It comes at the very end, when Lavond accidentally meets his daughter at the Eiffel Tower and poses as a friend of her father's. Lavond begins by telling Lorraine that her father has passed away. Upon hearing this she closes her eyes and leans her head back in grief. Touched, Lavond continues: "He sent me with a message to you." At this her eyes open expectantly, and we notice they are shining with moisture. "He told me," says Lavond gently, "if I ever saw you—to take your hand—" (this he does) "to tell you that he loved you very dearly, and that all those years in prison he watched you grow, talked to you, laughed with you, dined with you. And that he sent you a kiss." After a poignant pause, she leans forward to receive the kiss on her forehead, her

"Look at me and see what 17 years in the grave has done to me," orders Paul Lavond (Lionel Barrymore) as he reveals himself to a terrified Rodin (Arthur Hohl), paralyzed by poison and soon to become one of *The Devil-Doll*s (1936).

eyes closed once again. "And then—" Lavond continues softly, his voice a little rougher with emotion, "he said, uh—" Lavond stumbles for words, then continues forcefully, "This was the most important thing of all. He told me to tell you to *forget* him, to find happiness and keep it, to marry and to give your children all the love you might have given him if he hadn't been taken away from you." Throughout this exchange we ache to reveal the truth, to see them embrace and know all is well. Lavond knows in his heart, however, that all can never be well. We can only imagine the pain he feels at having to disguise his love for his daughter in this manner, and Barrymore's kindly face is tinged with sorrow. Both Barrymore and O'Sullivan betray their anguish and emotion in a stoically subtle manner, which ultimately is more effective than had they gushed forth with obvious tears and affected lamentations. Thus, the scene is exquisitely bittersweet without being cloying, and it becomes the most genuinely touching moment in the Golden Age of Horror.

ASSETS

The Devil-Doll is a rather sentimental film which seems to be at odds with itself. On the one hand it wants to be a horrific special effects picture. On the other, it strains for sentimental tragedy. At times it comes perilously close to being maudlin. Fortunately, Lionel Barrymore is there to add substance to the sympathetic scenario. As the grievously wronged Paul Lavond, Barrymore's kindly, stoic, and likable portrayal lends an air of dignity (yes, even while in drag) and sincerity to the film. Lavond is a tragic figure, one who could easily become both insipid and ridiculous in his self-pity, female disguise, and fantastic scheme of vengeance. Barrymore's genuine and heartfelt performance anchors a picture which continually threatens to fly off in opposing directions.

Barrymore's fellow actors ably support him on all sides. As Lorraine, Maureen O'Sullivan balances the bitterness and the love felt by Lavond's daughter, creating a complex and realistic character. Frank Lawton, while given the rather thankless juvenile lead role of Toto, makes the best of his brief (but well-written) scenes, infusing his portrayal with compassion and down-to-earth common sense. (This makes *The Devil-Doll* one of the few Golden Age horror pictures to feature a good performance by the juvenile male lead.) The ever-reliable Pedro de Cordoba (as Matin) slips from suave urbanity to concerned nervousness to near-hysterical anxiety with an effective smoothness. His mounting tension and ultimate breakdown would make even Basil Rathbone envious; De Cordoba's increasing irritability and nervousness is steadier, less violent, more subtle, and ultimately more effective than Rathbone's Wolf von Frankenstein (in *Son of Frankenstein*), adding a sharp edge to the suspenseful scene.

The top honors, however, should be reserved for Rafaela Ottiano. She takes her unsubtle, rather one-dimensional character of Malita and delivers a convincing portrayal of obsessive madness. With her eyes wide and wild, her eyebrows arched, her visage contorted with a mad zeal, she forces her words out with breathless excitement and insane conviction. Malita's physical appearance adds to the effect. Walking with a limp and leaning on a crutch, her unkempt dark, wiry hair sporting a shock of white (à la *Bride of Frankenstein*), the gleam in her eye and her animated face paint a convincing picture of mad enthusiasm. The staid Barrymore is no match for her vibrant presence and she steals nearly every scene she's in. Malita reminds us that this picture is indeed a horror film, and in their scenes together, Ms. Ottiano's zealous energy completely overpowers Barrymore's sedate stodginess. She is truly the decade's best (albeit only) female mad scientist.

The Devil-Doll is definitely the best *acted* of Tod Browning's horror pictures. Browning has been characterized as giving little direction to his actors (perhaps stemming from his close association with Lon Chaney, who was a near-autonomous thespian entity), so possibly the major credit for the excellent acting in *Devil-Doll* should lie with the players themselves, professionals all. In any case, the supporting performances do much to ground the fantastical film in reality.

Aside from the actors, much of the film's effectiveness stems from the excellent special effects, specifically the incredible realism of the oversized props and sets. When the miniaturized Lachna crawls out of a gigantic crib, climbs a three-story dresser, or pushes open a mammoth bedroom door, the colossal surroundings leave no doubt that she is truly only a foot tall. Stan Rogers and Edwin Willis' sets (with supervision from MGM art department head Cedric Gibbons) are intricately detailed and convincingly scaled. To Browning and cinematographer Leonard Smith's joint credit, they are well-photographed and realistically lit, with oversized shadows adding depth and realism while high-angle camerawork adds to the illusion of diminutive size.

Screenwriters Garrett Fort, Guy Endore, and Erich von Stroheim provide *The Devil-Doll* with some excellent dialogue. With three such unique talents involved, this is not surprising (nor is it surprising that the film goes off in so many different directions). A telling exchange occurs at the film's very beginning when Lavond and Marcel flee through the swamp:

> Marcel: "I've dreamt only of my work."
> Lavond, sourly: "My work is no dream—I've been away for 17 years."
> Marcel: "But you have only hatred in your heart—My work will help the world to *live*."
> Lavond: "My work will help three men *die*."

The interlocking dialogue cleverly connects the two characters while at the same time underlining their two very different defining characteristics (scientific altruism vs. selfish vengeance).

LIABILITIES

The Devil-Doll is a strange combination of horror, science, and heartrending tragedy which never quite meshes and so ultimately bleeds together into an unsatisfying hodgepodge of fantasy and drama. The film reveals its uncertainty early on, in one of the first sequences. We see a gloomy old dark house situated in a swamp, complete with a dead tree silhouetted in front. This eerie shot dissolves to the candle-lit interior where a woman plays an ominous tune on an organ. Suddenly, this moody scene switches to a brightly lit modern laboratory outfitted with gleaming bottles and a shining, sterile table. The change from a menacing atmosphere ripe with dread possibilities to one of bright, sunny science is jarring and ill-conceived.

The picture having passed the baton from horror to science, Marcel gives a brief, grade-school lecture on the building blocks of matter (and even finds time to pithily explain away the demise of the dinosaur — a hotly contested issue even to this day — in one sentence by implying that they all starved to death because of their great size). This scientific focus quickly blurs into pure fantasy, however, with the notion that Marcel's scientifically shrunken beings can be controlled by hypnotic willpower — a "beam of thought." This mesmeric angle makes the diminutive creatures seem more alchemic homunculi than an achievement of modern science. The picture has now slid into the realm of fantasy.

Rather than focus on this (admittedly intriguing) fantasy aspect, however, the film shifts gears yet again, driving toward something akin to Greek tragedy (though mainly just spinning its wheels in neutral). The fantasy is relegated to secondary status, a mere tool to be used briefly in the scenario of injustice, revenge, and atonement which is played out in the remaining hour. For the rest of the film, horror rarely rears its ugly head, science is all-but-forgotten, and fantasy pops up only briefly as a mere tool of revenge. These elements are left sadly untapped and unexplored in the midst of the human drama.

While Barrymore does well with the sentimental aspects of the tale, he fails to round out his character with the very necessary dark elements of bitterness and hate Paul Lavond is purported to possess. In discussing his burning hatred and thirst for vengeance, Barrymore's manner is flat and devoid of the feelings he professes to have. At the film's beginning, he explains himself to Malita. "You see, when a man saves an ambition in a dirty dungeon for 17 years," he says while casually putting his hands in his pockets and rocking back on his heels, "it becomes almost an insane obsession." At this last, Barrymore takes his hands back out and waves them in front of him while moving his shoulders from side to side in a rhythmic motion, as if imitating the rocking of a boat. Barrymore continues: "With Marcel it was science. With me it was hate — hate and vengeance." The actor puts absolutely no emphasis on these last three emotional words. In fact, he delivers them in a lazy, lackadaisical manner. Throughout this potentially charged and revealing soliloquy, Barrymore's attitude is one of almost casual detachment, as if he's explaining the workings of a combustion engine rather than the workings of a combustible state of mind. Lavond then relates how his partners railroaded him to prison and how "three lives are going to pay." Barrymore's grandfatherly tone is devoid of any anger or conviction and his casual stance (hands in trouser pockets, stomach thrust forward in a comfortable slouch) makes one think he's speaking of three rambunctious grandchildren who've just broken the basement window, rather than three ruthless enemies who've stolen 17 years of his life. Barrymore is so easygoing that one just cannot take him seriously. (He so downplays any sinister or even angry aspect of character that it appears Lavond is just going through the motions of his revenge out of habit, without any real conviction behind it.) This weakens the whole structure of the picture, which revolves around Lavond's justified thirst for retribution. If Barrymore does not seem to believe it, why should we? (The actor is much more animated as Madame Mandelip and seems to enjoy playing the elderly female, showing much more spark as the "poor, toddling old woman" than as the supposedly hate-filled Paul Lavond.)

Besides this, Barrymore appears uncomfortable with the fantasy elements of the picture. In the initial shrinkage sequences, he simply stands about with his mouth open, his eyes staring dully, looking more foolish than amazed. Barrymore obviously did not possess the conviction that the scenes required and seems to be saving his sincerity for the more natural moments of ordinary human drama. (Perhaps he felt the picture's fanciful concepts beneath his exalted actor's station, and so allotted only a cursory nod to the more implausible scenes.)

While *The Devil-Doll* is frequently praised for its amazing special effects, a careful scrutiny reveals them to be uneven at best. The scenes involving the oversized sets are impeccable. The remaining miniature effects, however, are not. The matte shots are particularly weak in places (and nowhere near the standard set by *King Kong* three years earlier). The shots of the tiny creatures (dogs, horses, humans) moving about on table tops are quite obviously matted in. Their movements across the background never seem quite three dimensional and the lighting never matches convincingly, with the overbright living subject standing out conspicuously from the more naturally lit background.

Franz Waxman's sentimental musical score tends to play up the more mawkish aspects of the picture. While frequently pleasing to the ear, the music sometimes works against the more sinister moments. For instance, when Marcel experiments on his shrunken servant girl, he is animated with a kind of scientific madness. Malita's eyes also stare hugely with an insane gleam. The beakers bubble, and mysterious steam spews from the apparatus to envelop the tiny figure. On the soundtrack, however, we hear a smooth and soothing violin and harp melody. The excitement, the intensity, the *insanity* of the moment is undercut and nullified by the poor choice of "mood" music.

Tod Browning's direction is straightforward but uninspired. Once again, he fails to make full use of the camera. It moves occasionally, but never to any great purpose (usually just following a character from one end of a room to the other). Most often the camera is static and Browning relies on different set-ups within a scene for variety. Rather than utilizing the camera for emphasis or interest, Browning counts on his editor to keep the scenes moving visually. Admittedly, Browning shoots enough varied footage to make this work adequately, but one comes to expect something more than "adequate" from someone of Browning's stature (a stature that is quickly being cut down to its proper size in the more recent reassessments of his work). Still, at least for *The Devil-Doll*, Browning did not make the downright *poor* decisions which nearly ruined *Dracula* (1931).

REVIEWS

Frank S. Nugent of *The New York Times* (August 8, 1936) called the picture "a photoplay which is grotesque, slightly horrible and consistently interesting" and "an entertaining exhibition of photographic hocus-pocus." Mr. Nugent had kind words to say about Tod Browning, observing that the director "has invested [a series of] essentially ridiculous episodes with a menacing, chilling quality which makes it impossible for you to consider them too lightly. That, naturally, is as it should be in a horror film."

Variety (August 12, 1936) also found this "illustration of the photographic art ... interesting, although not very practical. The technical aspects may provide diversion to the limited number of people who are interested in such things, but in general appeal the picture is lacking. Through its basic 'idea,' the picture is in the horror category, and it has about everything an adult-scarer needs except story. The fault lies with the failure of the scenarists to fortify the fantastic 'idea' with a helpful and credible plot...."

PRODUCTION NOTES

As reported by David J. Skal in *The Monster Show*, Tod Browning's *The Devil-Doll* began as a voodoo property called *The Witch of Timbuctoo*. The story was severely altered to pacify the British censors, with *The Hollywood*

In the guise of Madame Mandelip, Paul Lavond (Lionel Barrymore) talks with his own unknowing daughter, Lorraine (Maureen O'Sullivan), while Malita (Rafaela Ottiano) looks on. From *The Devil-Doll* (1936).

Reporter (December 10, 1935) noting that "once again a foreign government has stepped in to censor a Hollywood script for political reasons." Apparently, Great Britain was concerned that the voodoo sequences would "stir up trouble" among their black subjects throughout the British empire and requested that all black characters be dropped. MGM not only removed all the black characters, they erased all traces of voodoo as well and basically started over with a new (scientific) storyline.

Browning lifted several elements from his earlier film, *The Unholy Three* (1925) for the story of *The Devil-Doll*. Most obvious is having the protagonist disguise himself as an old woman running a specialty shop (a toy shop here and a bird shop in the earlier film). Also repeated is a tense scene in which stolen jewels are hidden inside a toy which the police inspector casually handles, unaware of its contents.

According to MGM's publicity mill, these jewels were *real*. "Motion Picture Realism is Carried to Nth Degree," announced a pressbook article, claiming that "$172,000 worth of precious stones were merely 'props' on 'The Devil-Doll' set." These "props" (watched over by two "brawny detectives") were loaned to the studio by "a Los Angeles firm of jewel brokers." "No one," continued the article, "but members of the Tod Browning company were permitted to enter or leave the stage until the baubles were safely on their way back to the downtown vaults from which they came."

After *Dracula* (1931), *The Devil-Doll* was Tod Browning's most successful film of the decade (financially speaking), earning a modest $68,000 profit for his home studio, MGM.

The film is based on the novel *Burn Witch Burn* by Abraham Merritt, which bears no relation to the 1962 film of the same name based upon Fritz Leiber's novel, *Conjure Wife*.

Star Lionel Barrymore lent his voice to a radio adaptation of *The Devil-Doll* performed on Louella Parsons' radio show "Hollywood Hotel" in order to promote the film. Parsons called the picture "eerie and creepy," and one that "will intrigue any audience with its sheer novelty."

In the film's pressbook, Barrymore complained of the hazards of playing a man disguised as an old woman, a part ballyhooed as "the strangest role of his screen career." "I never realized how difficult it was to change sex," began the actor. "The make-up alone was an ordeal. I was never meant for wigs and dresses! When my false hair wasn't slipping out of place, my feet were getting entangled in the hem of my skirt."

The Production Code forbade the portrayal (or even mention) of suicide, so the film's screenwriters had to skirt the issue by dropping hints and intimations (Lavond commenting that "where I'm going, Toto, I won't need any money" or "death doesn't frighten me; why, it's been part of my plan").

Maureen O'Sullivan is best known for her recurring role of Jane to Johnny Weismuller's Tarzan. The Irish-born actress arrived in Hollywood in 1930 under contract to Fox, but shortly thereafter switched to MGM, where she remained until 1942, when she retired from films to raise a family with her husband, writer-director John Farrow. She had seven children, two of which followed in their mother's footsteps—Mia Farrow (*Rosemary's Baby*, 1968) and her less successful sister Tisa Farrow (*Zombie*, 1980). Ms. O'Sullivan returned to the screen in 1948 and continued to make an occasional picture; she also appeared in several Broadway productions in the 1960s.

Henry B. Walthal (Marcel) studied law but abandoned his chosen profession when he came to New York and became an actor. After making a name for himself on Broadway, he joined D. W. Griffith's acting troupe at Biograph and starred in many of the pioneering director's early classics, often playing opposite Mary Pickford. Even as late as the 1940s Griffith spoke of Walthal's portrayal of the Little Colonel in *The Birth of a Nation* as the greatest male performance in the history of films. Walthal appeared in nearly 100 silent films, including the lost Lon Chaney/ Tod Browning collaboration, *London After Midnight* (1927) and over 50 sound features, including one other Golden Age (borderline) horror film, *Chandu the Magician* (1932). Walthal succumbed to a chronic illness, however, two months before *The Devil-Doll*'s release.

Frank Lawton (Toto) also played the juvenile lead (and again got the girl) in Universal's *The Invisible Ray*, released earlier in 1936.

The Devil-Doll owes much to its art direction, which was supervised by Cedric Gibbons. This is unsurprising considering Gibbons has been labeled "the most celebrated and possibly the most important and influential production designer in the history of American films."[2] Not only did Gibbons win 11 Academy Awards over the course of his career, he also *designed* the Academy statuette—'Oscar.' He created the atmospheric sets for one other Golden Age horror film, *Mark of the Vampire* (1935), again directed by Tod Browning and again starring Lionel Barrymore. Gibbons' only other foray into the genre was a prestigious one, the classic and definitive 1945 version of *The Picture of Dorian Gray*.

Co-screenwriter Garrett Fort was a horror veteran of the first rank. Since he wrote or co-wrote the screenplays for both *Dracula* (1931) and *Frankenstein* (1931), it is likely that what little horror can be found in *The Devil-Doll* is attributable to Fort. While under contract to Universal, Fort also scripted the last horror picture produced by the Laemmle regime—*Dracula's Daughter* (1936). In addition to these ventures, the busy writer produced drafts of both *The Invisible Man* and *The Black Cat*, though neither of them was used.

French novelist and screenwriter Guy Endore was no stranger to horror either, having co-authored two other Golden Age horror scripts—Browning's earlier *Mark of the Vampire*

(1935) and Karl Freund's final film as director, *Mad Love* (1935). Endore also worked up a treatment for *The Raven* (1935), but his contribution was passed over. In 1961, Endore's novel *The WereWolf of Paris* (published in 1933) was brought to the screen (without his active participation) by Britain's Hammer Films as *The Curse of the Werewolf*.

The Devil-Doll's third screenwriter was Erich von Stroheim, the fallen "homme terrible" of Hollywood. Von Stroheim had been an actor/director of the first order in the 1920s (with lavish pictures like *Greed*, 1924, and *The Wedding March*, 1928) but had been denied the chance to direct in the 1930s due to his legendary extravagance and volatile temperament. He returned to acting and screenwriting. Having acted in only a handful of films in the first half of the decade, von Stroheim jumped at the chance of a regular salary when MGM offered him a position as a staff writer. The formerly great director who had commanded budgets upwards to a million dollars ten years previously was offered the low-end salary scale of $150 per week—and took it. MGM did not hire von Stroheim to write complete scripts, however, but to serve as a collaborator on works in progress by adding his own particular touches. William K. Everson, in *Classics of the Horror Film*, conjectured that these von Stroheim "touches" in *The Devil-Doll* most likely included "the idea of having tragedy and evil played out against a Christmas tinsel motif" and the detective's crack about the Christmas season bringing out all the religious fanatics.

E. J. Mannix, a high-ranking Metro executive and member of Hollywood's "Old Guard," served as executive producer on *The Devil-Doll*, a position he also filled on both of Tod Browning's earlier MGM horrors, *Freaks* (1932) and *Mark of the Vampire* (1935). One suspects that Mannix, who was only infrequently assigned to supervise individual films, played the role of Metro watchdog on these pictures, sent to keep an eye on the alcoholic, semireliable Browning. While an important figure in Hollywood history, Mannix has also become something of a macabre footnote. In the book *Deadly Illusions: Jean Harlow and the Murder of Paul Bern*, author Samuel Marx (former Metro producer) claimed that Howard Strickling (one-time Metro PR chief) finally confirmed the long-standing rumor that Mannix had murdered George "Superman" Reeves in 1959. Reeves' death was officially labeled suicide at the time, though the actor's mother (and many others since then) insisted it was murder. Apparently, Reeves was the third point of a romantic triangle involving Mannix and his wife. (Reeves, in fact, willed his estate to Mrs. Mannix.)

NOTES

1. This exclamation is an almost plagiaristic "borrowing" from the climax of the previous year's *Bride of Frankenstein*.
2. *The Film Encyclopedia*, by Ephraim Katz.

THE MAN WHO CHANGED HIS MIND
(1936; Gaumont-British; Great Britain)

Alternate Titles: *The Man Who Lived Again* (American title); *Dr. Maniac* (1940s reissue title); *The Brain Snatcher* (TV title).
Release Date: September 11, 1936 (British); December 15, 1936 (American)
Running Time: 65 minutes
Director: Robert Stevenson

Producer: Michael Balcon
Associate Producers: P. Edward Black, Sidney Gilliat
Screenplay: L. du Garde Peach, Sidney Gilliat, John L. Balderston
Photography: Jack Cox
Art Director: Alex Vetchinsky

Editor: R. E. Dearing, Alfred Roome
Makeup: Roy Ashton
Musical Director: Louis Levy
Recordist: W. Salter
Dresses: Molyneux
Cast: Boris Karloff (Dr. Laurience), John Loder (Dick Haslewood), Anna Lee (Dr. Clare Wyatt), Frank Cellier (Lord Haslewood), Donald Calthrop (Clayton), Cecil Parker (Dr. Gratton), Lyn Harding (Professor Holloway), *Clive Morton (Newspaperman), *D. J. Williams (Innkeeper).

*Uncredited on film print.

"I shall show you strange things about the mind of man." — Dr. Laurience.

SYNOPSIS

Dr. Clare Wyatt leaves her London hospital position to go work for "mad brain specialist" Dr. Laurience (as her colleague calls him). "Eccentric," corrects Clare. Once at Laurience's dilapidated country house, she learns of her mentor's strange research. "I can take the thought content from the mind of a living animal," explains Laurience, "and store it as you would store electricity." That very night he proves his claim by taking two chimps, one docile and the other aggressive, and switching their minds.

Clare's persistent suitor (reporter Dick Haslewood) follows her and prints an unauthorized story on Laurience. Lord Haslewood, owner of the newspaper (and Dick's father), comes down himself to offer Laurience the use of the Haslewood Institute of Modern Science, "the biggest thing of its kind in Europe." At Clare's urging, the eccentric Laurience reluctantly accepts the offer, taking Clayton (a bitter cripple living on borrowed time and serving as Laurience's helper) and Clare with him to the new lab. Haslewood splashes headlines like "Wonder Doctor to Work at Our Expense" all over his newspaper. "We must never rest until we've made 'Laurience' a household word," Haslewood instructs his editors.

Despite Laurience's protestations ("I dislike having to publish before the work is finished"), Haslewood insists on an early conference to spotlight Laurience's research. When "the flower of English science" laughs Laurience and his claims off the podium, however, the pompous Haslewood feels cheated and withdraws his support from Laurience, threatening to seize his papers and destroy his equipment (which was paid for by Haslewood). At this, Laurience traps Haslewood in his experimental chair. "Let him change bodies with *you* Clayton," suggests Laurience excitedly and the cripple readily agrees. The experiment works and Clayton's body, with Haslewood's mind, collapses from the strain and dies. Assuming the role of newspaper magnate Lord Haslewood, Clayton orders that "Laurience must continue to work under my protection."

Clare goes back to the lab to collect her things, for she objects to Laurience's intention to experiment on human beings (unaware the first attempt has already been completed). Laurience tries to stop her. "You're not going to leave me. This new power, I can share it only with you for you alone are worthy to receive it." Laurience wants Clare, but the feelings are not reciprocal. "I understand, I'm old," presses Laurience. "But with this power I needn't remain old. I can take a new body, a young body and keep my own brain... Think of it, I offer you eternal youth, eternal loveliness." Clare rushes out of the lab back to Dick waiting below in the car. As Laurience watches from the window, she agrees to marry him. Laurience now knows whose "new body" he wants.

Later that night, Dick tells Clare that his father seems changed, almost "like a different person." At this, Clare becomes suspicious and goes to confront Laurience. Though the doctor admits to nothing, Clare tells him that tomorrow she'll take Dick to his "father" and make sure.

Worried, Laurience goes to see Clayton/Haslewood, but the man has discovered that his new "sound body" is not so sound after all, for Haslewood was afflicted with a bad heart. Clayton comes up with a plan to have Laurience transfer his mind from

Haslewood to his son, Dick, and thus inherit his own fortune. To this end, Clayton calls Dick and asks to meet him at the institute. Laurience has another idea, however, and strangles Clayton. "I've no further need for you," Laurience tells his victim as he chokes the life out of him. "*I'll* take his body and he'll take mine — a body which will be hanged for *murder!*"

Before Clare can reach Dick, he arrives at the institute. Laurience uses chloroform to overpower the young man and then straps him into the apparatus and makes the switch.

Clare learns where Dick has gone and arrives at the lab just after Laurience (now in Dick's body) smashes a beaker of chemicals to create a choking gas which will kill his old body. Clare realizes what's happened and rushes into the lab only to see Dick (in Laurience's body) grope blindly through the fumes toward the window and topple to the street below.

Just then the police arrive and apprehend Laurience. Dick, in Laurience's battered body, only has a short while to live, and Clare convinces the police to let her attempt to "undo what he's done." The reversal works and Dick's mind is restored to his rightful body. In a final repenting speech, Laurience asks that his work die with him. "Clare," gasps Laurience painfully, "please forgive me. You were right, the human mind *is* sacred."

MEMORABLE MOMENT

The picture's most emotionally charged sequence is also the film's cinematic centerpiece. It comes when Haslewood confronts Laurience in his lab after the doctor's disastrous presentation to the Scientific Society. In a heated shouting match, Haslewood rails, "Now you're *finished* here, and your apparatus is mine to do exactly what I like with!" When Laurience shouts back "You shant touch it!," Haslewood sends a stand of beakers and test tubes crashing to the floor in defiance. At this Laurience's hands fly to his head in shocked consternation. Suddenly, the room begins spinning. Images appear, superimposed over Laurience's confused countenance: Haslewood proclaiming over and over, "I paid for everything! I paid for everything!"; Clayton condemning, "Finest laboratory in the world and you sold yourself for it"; the members of the smug Scientific Society laughing at him; Clare warning, "You can't do that! You can't do that!" The phantoms appear at odd angles to mirror Laurience's off-kilter state of mind, while Karloff's haunted eyes dart this way and that in a vain attempt to escape the hated memories. Finally, as bouts of ridiculing laughter chase through the soundtrack, Laurience's dazed visage dissolves into a blur. When the picture slowly comes back into focus, we see Laurience slumped in a chair, head bowed and totally drained, with Haslewood standing over him asking, "Dr. Laurience, do you feel better?" The montage of images and spinning surroundings superimposed over and around Laurience's face brilliantly reflects the man's disturbed, confused state as the jumble of hostile sights and sounds finally pushes him over the brink into madness.

ASSETS

The Man Who Changed His Mind is one of those little-seen British horror films which has not been officially released on video and seemingly never makes it to television or into revival houses. Unlike most others in this category (*The Ghoul*, for instance), *The Man Who Changed His Mind* does not disappoint once the determined fan finally gets a look. Not only does it feature a full-blooded Karloff performance, but its intriguing blending of gothic atmosphere and mad science makes it a welcome addition to the Golden Age of Horror.

The story begins in a modern, brightly lit hospital as we witness the story's heroine — a strong-willed, good-humored, young female surgeon — leaving to go work with Laurience in a rural village. When she disembarks from the train, rather than getting into a modern taxi at the station, she steps into a horse-drawn carriage (and then the fearful coachman refuses to take her to Laurience's creepy doorstep). It's as if she steps out of the modern world of operating theaters and powerful locomotives into a dark tableau of forbidding

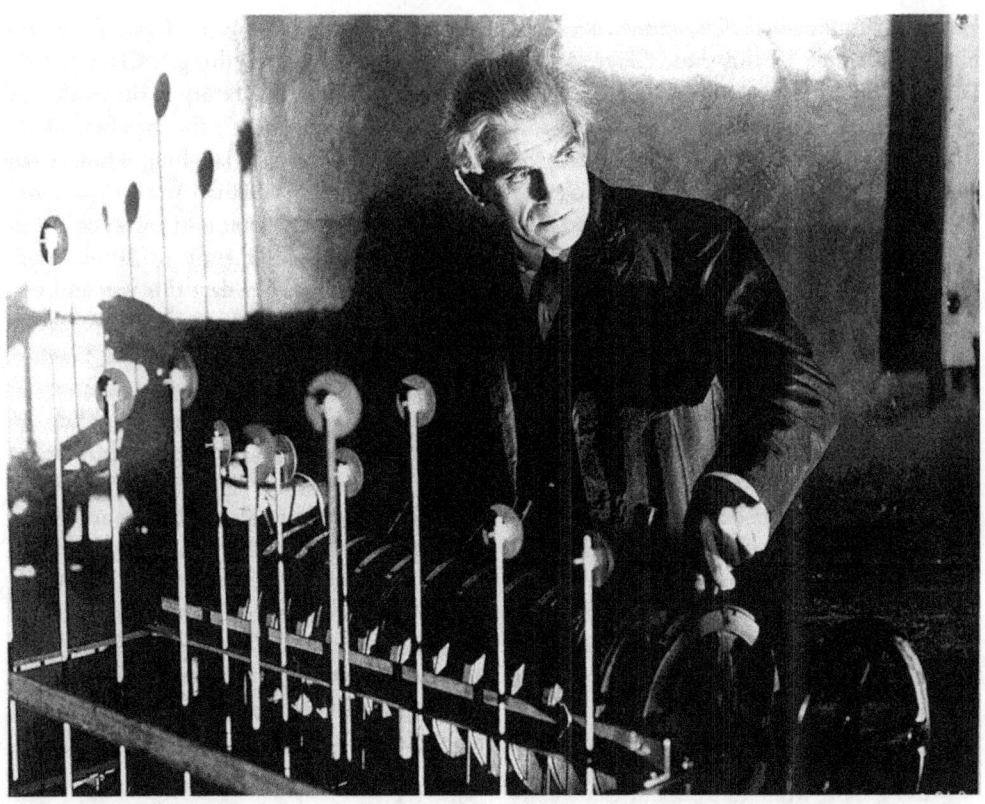

Dr. Laurience (Boris Karloff) works his mind transference device in *The Man Who Changed His Mind* (1936).

mansions, horseless carriages, and superstitious coach drivers. The sudden switch from bright modernism to a shadowy gothic makes a striking contrast which serves to heighten the ominous atmosphere. Though its subject may be science, *The Man Who Changed His Mind* is first and foremost a *horror* film.

Along with *The Invisible Ray* released earlier in 1936, *The Man Who Changed His Mind* was Karloff's first stab at a mad scientist role. Fortunately, the actor turns in a much more effective performance in this picture than he did in *The Invisible Ray*. (Karloff and mad science proved to be such a successful character match that a substantial portion of his subsequent career was spent among the tell-tale test tubes and Bunsen burners.) While Dr. Laurience may not be Karloff's most subtle characterization, the actor convincingly portrays a man driven half-mad by his obsession. During his introductory scene, Laurience turns away from Clare to stare at his own reflection in the mirror. "The leading surgeon in Genoa," he observes, his tone low and bitter, "the greatest authority on the human brain—" Karloff's voice quickens with anger as he finishes, "—until I told them something about their *own* brains!" He turns back and runs his hand through his hair in frustration. "Then they said I was *mad*." His eyes flash and he looks up as if suddenly remembering Clare's presence. He stares at her a moment, then breaks into a smile. "Look at me," he says benignly. "Am I mad?" Before she can answer, Clayton (thankfully) interrupts. While he may not be mad exactly, Karloff's mannerisms and volatile mood change let us know that Laurience is not far from it.

Witty dialogue peppers the clever screenplay by L. du Garde Peach, Sidney Gilliat, and John L. Balderston. In one scene, Lord Haslewood reluctantly sits in the chair offered by Laurience. "You must understand that once my mind is made up—" begins Haslewood, but Laurience finishes with "You will not change it." With a quick motion, Laurience shackles Haslewood to the chair. "Perhaps I can do it for you," Laurience offers in a bit of darkly ironic humor (since he intends to literally change Haslewood's mind with that of another). When Clare asks, "Haven't you a housekeeper?" Laurience answers, "Only Clayton, and you've seen him," at which Clayton chimes in with, "And she was not amused." Many of the choicest lines go to Clayton. "I wonder which revolts you most," wonders the wheelchair-bound cripple, addressing Clare, "my miserable body or my perverted mind." Later, after breakfast, Haslewood offers his institute's scientific services but Laurience objects that "I must work in my own way." Looking around the dingy house and makeshift lab, Haslewood asks, "How can you work in this atmosphere?" to which Clayton snidely pipes up, "If you refer to the smell of bacon, it is no obstacle to scientific research."

Clayton is indeed the film's most eccentric — and interesting — character. "Most of me is *dead*," he remarks acidly. "The rest of me is *damned*. Laurience manages to keep the residue alive. *Why* is his own affair." As the cynical, misanthropic paraplegic, Donald Calthrop delivers a performance arch enough even for Ernest Thesiger. "Having been a cripple for 30 years," he remarks, "I've a rather nasty nature." Calthrop's sour expressions, biting tones, and clipped speech leave no room for anything but bitterness — and an acerbic sense of humor. Later, while briefly playing Haslewood in Clayton's body, Calthrop barks out a chilling, ugly laugh before his character drops dead. The harsh, mirthless, *evil* sound raises the very hackles. Only later do we learn of the ironic joke (that, unknown to its new occupant, Haslewood's body is itself diseased).

The remainder of the cast admirably bring to life their well-formed characters. Not only is *The Man Who Changed His Mind* one of the decade's better written horror pictures, but it is also one of the better *acted* entries. Anna Lee makes an intelligent, headstrong heroine while John Loder plays Dick as a likable, good-humored young man. Best of all is Frank Cellier's dual portrayal of the arrogant, self-important Haslewood and the bemused Clayton-as-Haslewood, who possesses a whole new set of mannerisms — along with a sense of humor. "Oh what a pompous ass I am," he remarks cheerfully, amused at reading that Haslewood lists "hard work" as his hobby.

Under Robert Stevenson's deft direction, cinematographer Jack Cox's camera draws the viewer into the story and creates a rich visual interest, utilizing forward as well as lateral movement to keep things from getting static. The camera frequently glides smoothly forward to bring the characters into close-up or punctuate an important moment, even following its subject upstairs while peering past posts and pillars to add depth. In addition, Stevenson and Cox take care in setting up their shots. Rather than taking the easy way out and filming two characters in conversation side-by-side in a flat manner, the filmmakers opt to create depth and visual interest by shooting past the shoulder or arm of one to the other to place the listener (and the viewer) in the foreground.

Alex Vetchinsky's sets add much to the film's careful blend of gothic/scientific. Laurience's dilapidated house, for instance, sports heavy pillars topped with bizarre crenellations reminiscent of the paws of some gigantic art-deco beast. Jack Cox's careful lighting creates a maze of angular shadows and dark recesses, while bands of light and dark add an almost expressionistic feel to the sinister surroundings. This moody lighting extends to the characters themselves. During close-ups, for instance, blocks of shadows seemingly surround the figures to create an ominous milieu perfectly suited to the strange story.

LIABILITIES

While *The Man Who Changed His Mind* features an intelligent storyline revolving around an intriguing premise, the authors fell into the trap of expediency at certain points. Having Laurience suddenly fall in love with Clare so that he now wants to inhabit the body of her fiancé seems too pat a plot device. Its artificial abruptness does not jibe with the rest of the cleverly constructed story.

Also, the picture glosses over a rather important continuity problem involving Laurience switching bodies with Dick. When Laurience places Dick inside the experimental chamber, Dick is securely strapped into the chair, helpless and yelling "Let me out!" After setting the equipment to work automatically, Laurience goes to the other booth and simply sits in the chair. After the switch, however, Dick's body (now housing Laurience's mind) easily gets up and walks out of the booth while Laurience (with Dick's mind) must struggle to free himself from the chair's restraints. Apparently, the steel clasps transferred along with the minds?

Finally, three full-blown transference sequences (not even counting the original monkey-switching scene) — Clayton/Haslewood; Laurience/Dick; and the Laurience/Dick reversal — proves to be at least one too many. While the various shots of the laboratory equipment glowing, flashing, and sparking are impressive enough for the first experiment scene, they become a bit tiresome by the third go-round. It is a redundancy which adds nothing to the climax and only serves to eat up a little time before it winds down to its foregone conclusion. More stringent editing would have gone a long way to stem the viewer's growing complacency regarding this all-important moment.

While *The Man Who Changed His Mind* may not exactly be a household title (even to the horror fan), it remains Britain's best contribution to the Golden Age of Horror and surpasses many of the decade's Hollywood entries as well.

REVIEWS

Variety's (September 22, 1936) unnamed London reviewer had nothing but praise for this "spine tickler", calling the production "painstaking and realistic and, indeed, the whole thing seems all too feasible." Of the cast: "Nothing very horrific in Karloff's performance, his manner at most times being almost gentle. Frank Cellier as the magnate and Donald Calthrop as the cripple give splendid characterizations."

Two months later, however, when the picture made it to New York, *Variety*'s American reviewer ("Char" in the December 23, 1936, issue) felt just the opposite, stating the "plot construction of *Man Who Lived Again* offers nothing very original nor exciting, let alone anything that is very believable." Char singled out Frank Cellier just as his British counterpart did ("a standout performance") but claimed that Donald Calthrop "evoke[s] no more than passing notice."

PRODUCTION NOTES

The Man Who Changed His Mind came about more by default than by intent. In late 1935, Gaumont-British contracted with Boris Karloff to come to England and make a horror picture. As noted by *The Hollywood Reporter* (January 13, 1936), however, the "Middlessex County Council restrictions of horror pics" (which would severely limit a horror film's audience by slapping it with an "adults-only" tag) changed the studio's mind about the project. Gaumont-British then entered into negotiations with Karloff about a cash settlement over the aborted $30,000 contract. Failing to reach an arrangement with the actor, the British studio decided to bring Karloff to London after all, to star in a different type of picture than the straight horror film intended. On March 5, 1936, *The Hollywood Reporter* revealed that Gaumont had chosen *The Man Who Changed His Mind*, "a story relying on the thrills of a scientific experiment," as their Karloff project in order "to avoid the prejudice of local licensing committees against horror pix." L. du Garde Peach, Sidney Gilliat, and John L. Balderston then wrote *The Man Who Changed His Mind* specifically as a vehicle for Boris Karloff with a (supposedly) more scientific rather than horrific emphasis.

The picture was Karloff's first British film since making *The Ghoul* three years earlier (also for Gaumont-British). A founding member of America's newly-formed Screen Actors Guild, Karloff was appalled at the actor's lot

Dr. Laurience (Boris Karloff, center) plays mind games with Clayton (Donald Calthrop, left) and Lord Haslewood (Frank Cellier, right) in this lobby card sporting the American release title for *The Man Who Changed His Mind* (1936).

in nonunion England. He refused to work on Saturdays as the studio wished and, as reported by Anna Lee (in Tom Weaver's *Science Fiction Stars and Horror Heroes*), "he lectured us all quite firmly on the fact that we must have a union."

In the film's pressbook, Boris Karloff expounded upon the appeal of his terror films: "My roles generally provide the kind of thrills which transcend human emotion. The fear generated is synthetic, but the movie-goer vicariously endures the tortures of the terror-smitten fictional character. His mind wanders into the unlimited and unbounded world of imagination where anything can and does happen. And then the escape — the grateful realization that, like a bad dream, the thing isn't real."

Of Karloff, Ms. Lee had nothing but kind words, calling him "the kindest, sweetest, nicest, quietest man I think I've ever worked with." The two passed the frequent bouts of inactivity on the set by reciting poetry. "He would start a poem, like, 'Between the dark and the daylight, when the night is beginning to lower,' and I'd go on, 'Comes a pause in the day's occupation, which is called the Children's Hour.' We went on for hours and hours doing this, seeing if we could stump each other!"

Ms. Lee did not have such a favorable opinion of her nonhuman co-stars. "Right next door to me, practically sharing my dressing room, were the monkeys — the chimpanzees that you see in the film. And they smelled awful! I remember holding my nose whenever I had to go into my dressing room!" Sam and Gonette's (the chimpanzees) odiferous nature was not their only undesirable trait. For the filming of Karloff's death scene, complete quiet was necessary on the set while the microphone sensitivity was increased to record the actor's whispered last words. As the cameras rolled, the sound man picked up a dull, thumping noise coming from somewhere in the building. It was soon discovered that the annoying noise was caused by the two chimps wildly jumping up and down in their cages. According to the film's pressbook, "the only way they could be effectively quieted was by getting Momo, the black boy who looks after them, to take them out of their cages, put on their dressing gowns, and lead them onto the set where, in the glare of the arc lamps, they remained happily silent, under the impression they were once more appearing before the camera."

Born Joan Boniface Winnifrith, Anna Lee took her stage name from such diverse sources as Leon Tolstoy and the American Civil War. "I was reading Tolstoy at the time and I thought Anna — from *Anna Karenina* — was very romantic, a lovely name. Then I was also reading American history and I thought Robert E. Lee was a rather good chap, so I decided to take the name Lee." Ms. Lee's other genre outings include *Bedlam* (1946), *Jack the Giant Killer* (1962) and *Picture Mommy Dead* (1966). Still acting (she has been a regular on TV's "General Hospital" for years), Anna Lee reassessed *The Man Who Changed His Mind*: "I saw the picture again recently ... and I thought it was very well done, that it stood up remarkably well. I think it is one of Karloff's better pictures."

Anna Lee was the real-life wife of *Man Who Changed His Mind* director Robert Stevenson. They met in Egypt in 1934 while working on a picture and were married upon returning to England. "They were both on location for my film *The Camels Are Coming*," remembered producer Michael Balcon, "and Bob was struck down by some form of desert fever which made him delirious. Anna, like everyone else on the unit, felt very sorry for him and came into his tent one day to ask if she could do anything for him. Just then — according to Anna — Bob was so far gone in his delirium that he was trying to climb up the pole of his tent. '*In that one instant*,' Anna solemnly declares, '*I knew I loved Bob*.' She persisted in this story, even though I asked her if she thought that this explained the popularity of the Tarzan films!"[1]

Born in Buxton, England, in 1905, Stevenson never even saw a motion picture until he was 22 years old, upon which he immediately decided upon a career in the industry. Beginning as a reader at Gaumont-British, he quickly rose from dialogue director to editor to production supervisor to screenwriter and finally to full director in 1932. According to *Variety*'s obituary (May 7, 1986), "his first major hit was *The Man Who Lived Again*." This hit was also Stevenson's first (and only) venture into the horror genre; in 1956 he turned exclusively to family entertainment with Walt Disney Studios, directing such Disney classics as *Old Yeller* (1957), *Darby O'Gill and the Little People* (1959; a picture possessing some effectively horrific content); and *Mary Poppins* (1964; for which he was nominated for an Academy Award). His final film was *The Shaggy D.A.* in 1976. In 1977, *Variety* reported that Stevenson was the most commercially successful director of all time, having placed a record 17 films (all of them Disney productions) on the *Variety* all-time box office hits list, earning over $250,000,000 in worldwide rentals.

Producer Michael Balcon started in films in 1919 as a distributor. He produced his first picture in 1922 (*Woman to Woman*) on which he employed a young Alfred Hitchcock as screenwriter, art director, and assistant director. Balcon provided Hitchcock with his first opportunity to direct and thereafter supervised Hitchcock's early masterworks. Balcon also produced Gaumont-British's earlier Karloff vehicle, *The Ghoul* (1933). As recognition for his services to the British film industry, he received a knighthood in 1948. Sir Michael Balcon is the father of actress Jill Balcon and grandfather of Daniel Day-Lewis.

Co-screenwriter John L. Balderston was educated at Columbia University as a journalist. During World War II he worked as a war correspondent. After the war he became the London correspondent for the *New York World* before turning his hand to play and later screen writing. Balderston contributed to more

Driven to the brink of madness, Dr. Laurience (Boris Karloff) menaces his beautiful colleague, Dr. Clare Wyatt (Anna Lee) in *The Man Who Changed His Mind* (1936).

Golden Age horror classics than any other writer; his credits include *Dracula* (1931), *Frankenstein* (1931), *The Mummy* (1932), *Bride of Frankenstein* (1935), and *Mad Love* (1935).

Though having photographed such prestigious British productions as Alfred Hitchcock's *The Lady Vanishes* (1938), cinematographer Jack Cox was not above filming the arrival of *The Devil Girl from Mars* (1954) (and her giant toaster-oven robot) in his later years.

The son of a British general, John Loder served as a lieutenant at Gallipoli in World War I, where he was captured and became a prisoner of war. After appearing in a number of German silents, Loder came to Hollywood in the late twenties where he played in early talkies. Returning to his native England in 1931, he became a star of the British screen. Loder went back to Hollywood during World War II and appeared in a score of pictures over the next seven years (including *A Game of Death*, the 1945 remake of *The Most Dangerous Game*; and the intriguing poverty-row witchcraft entry, *The Woman Who Came Back*, 1945). Failing to attain the level of screen stardom he had achieved in Britain, Loder turned to Broadway and then finally returned to England where he made several more pictures before retiring to his fifth wife's ranch in Argentina. Hedy Lamarr was among his previous wives.

Frank Cellier made his stage debut in 1905 and quickly rose to prominence in the theater. Though he made nearly 40 films from 1931 up until his death in 1948, Cellier was best known for his theatrical work. *Variety*'s obituary (September 29, 1948) called him "the stage's most polished murderer." Making an unbilled appearance in *The Man Who Changed His Mind* was Frank Cellier's future son-in-law, Bruce Seton (*Sweeney Todd, the Demon Barber of Fleet Street*, 1936; *Love from a*

Stranger, 1937). Seton later married Cellier's daughter, actress Antoinette Cellier.

Donald Calthrop began on the stage at about the same time as Frank Cellier and also quickly rose to prominence in the theatrical community, acting alongside Sir Henry Irving and even running his own theater in which he acted and produced. Unlike Cellier, however, Calthrop turned to films early, making his screen debut in 1916. Among his nearly 70 films are two borderline horror pictures, *The Clairvoyant* (1935) and *Love from a Stranger* (1937). He died in 1940 at the age of 52.

NOTES

1. From *Michael Balcon's 25 Years in Films*, by M. Danischewsky (ed).

SON OF FRANKENSTEIN
(1939; Universal)

Release Date: January 13, 1939 (Friday the 13th)
Running Time: 96 minutes
Director/Producer: Rowland V. Lee
Screenplay: Willis Cooper (suggested by the story written in 1816 by Mary Wollstonecraft Shelley)
Photography: George Robinson, A.S.C.
Art Director: Jack Otterson
Associate: Richard H. Riedel
Editor: Ted Kent
Musical Director: Charles Previn
Musical Score: Frank Skinner
Assistant Director: Fred Frank
Sound Supervisor: Bernard B. Brown
Technician: William Hedgcock

Set Decorations: R. A. Gausman
Gowns: Vera West
Cast: Basil Rathbone (Baron Wolf von Frankenstein), Boris Karloff (The Monster), Bela Lugosi (Ygor), Lionel Atwill (Krogh), Josephine Hutchinson (Elsa von Frankenstein), Donnie Dunagan (Peter von Frankenstein), Emma Dunn (Amelia), Edgar Norton (Benson), Perry Ivins (Fritz), Lawrence Grant (Burgomaster), Lionel Belmore (Lang), Michael Mark (Ewald Neumuller), Caroline Cooke (Mrs. Neumuller), Gustav Von Seyffertitz (Burgher), Lorimer Johnson (Burgher), Tom Ricketts (Burgher).

"This is place of the dead. We're all dead here."—Ygor.

SYNOPSIS

Many years have passed since the monster's demise (at the close of *Bride of Frankenstein*). Wolf von Frankenstein (Henry's son) comes to the village of Frankenstein to claim his inheritance, bringing with him his wife and small son. Excited by the new surroundings ("A new life lies before us!"), they take up residence in the ancestral castle. The villagers, however, are not too keen on having another Frankenstein in their sorrow-laden village, and show no kindness or hospitality to the new arrivals.

Inspector Krogh, the commander of the local constabulary, visits Wolf to assure him of protection in case of need (and also to make certain that the son will not follow in his father's footsteps). The inspector has even more cause for concern than most, for, as a boy, he had his arm "torn out by the roots" by the monster and he now wears a wooden prosthesis in its place.

Wolf, a doctor and scientist like his father, goes to explore the ruined laboratory. There he finds not only the old equipment, but an exposed bubbling sulfur pit which over the years has risen to a temperature of 800 degrees Fahrenheit. He also encounters Ygor, an unwholesome character who years earlier had been hanged for the crime of graverobbing.

"You see that?" asks Ygor, pointing to the broken bone which bulges out from his neck. "They hanged me once, Frankenstein. They broke my neck. They said I was dead. And they cut me down."

Ygor has found the monster, Henry Frankenstein's creation, and has befriended him. But the creature walks no more. A short time before, while out "hunting," the monster was struck by lightning and has since lain in a coma. Ygor entreats Wolf to "make him better," and, his scientific curiosity aroused, Wolf sets about reviving the monster. "I, as a man, should destroy him," reasons Wolf, "but as a scientist I should do everything in my power to bring him back to conscious life, so that the world can study his abnormal functions. *That* would vindicate my father, and his name would be enshrined among the immortals." The die is cast.

Wolf succeeds in reanimating the monster, but Ygor has other, decidedly *un*scientific, plans for his huge friend. Ygor had been using the monster to dispatch those men of the council who had condemned the graverobber to death, and with the creature walking again, Ygor resumes his spree of murderous revenge.

Meanwhile, the villagers have become more and more suspicious of Wolf and the crates of scientific equipment he's been receiving at the castle. An unruly mob forms outside the castle gates. Inspector Krogh arrives to place Wolf under house arrest, telling him it is "for your own protection." But Krogh too is convinced that Wolf is somehow involved in the mysterious deaths plaguing the village, and possibly even in the revival of the monster. The two men square off, matching wits over a game of darts.

Later, Wolf goes to confront Ygor. When Ygor attacks him with a hammer, Wolf shoots, killing the monster's only friend. The monster finds the body of his dead companion, and his initial sorrow soon turns to rage. He goes berserk and wrecks the laboratory. In the midst of his rampage, the creature stumbles across a picture book given to him by Wolf's innocent son, Peter (whom the monster had visited earlier via a secret passage). A diabolical plan to take revenge on Wolf forms in the monster's misshapen brain.

The monster kidnaps Peter, arousing the household, and Wolf, Krogh, and the servants rush to the laboratory. The monster finds he cannot harm Peter, however, for the boy had been kind to him.

When Krogh reaches the laboratory, the monster once again rips off Krogh's arm (this time his artificial one) and brandishes it above his head while holding little Peter down under his huge boot heel. Krogh fires his gun, but the bullets have no effect. Wolf climbs up to the ruined roof, grabs a chain hanging there, and swings out, kicking the monster in the chest and knocking him backwards to fall screaming into the lethal bubbling sulfur pit.

Soon afterwards, Wolf and his family bid farewell to the cheering villagers at the train station. "May happiness and peace of mind be restored to you all," says a cheery Wolf before leaving the village of Frankenstein forever.

MEMORABLE MOMENTS

Boris Karloff, as the monster, provides the film with several memorable moments. Perhaps the best comes when the monster first walks.

Taking Wolf unaware in the laboratory, the monster catches sight of himself in a large mirror. With a sweep of his arm and a growl from his throat, he tries to erase his own hideous reflection. Touching his own face, the monster turns towards Wolf and opens his hands to him, pleading for some help and understanding. When Wolf fails to respond, the monster grabs him and pulls him in front of the mirror. Looking at the reflection, he bring Wolf's handsome face next to his own ugly visage and compares the two. The monster's eyes droop and he turns away, thrusting his reflection from him in sad disgust with a push of his hand.

Another fine scene occurs when the monster finds the body of Ygor. Climbing up out of the pit, the creature notices his fallen friend. Filled with concern, the hulking figure rushes to Ygor and kneels by his side. Grabbing his friend's limp hand, the monster clutches it to him while he rocks from side to

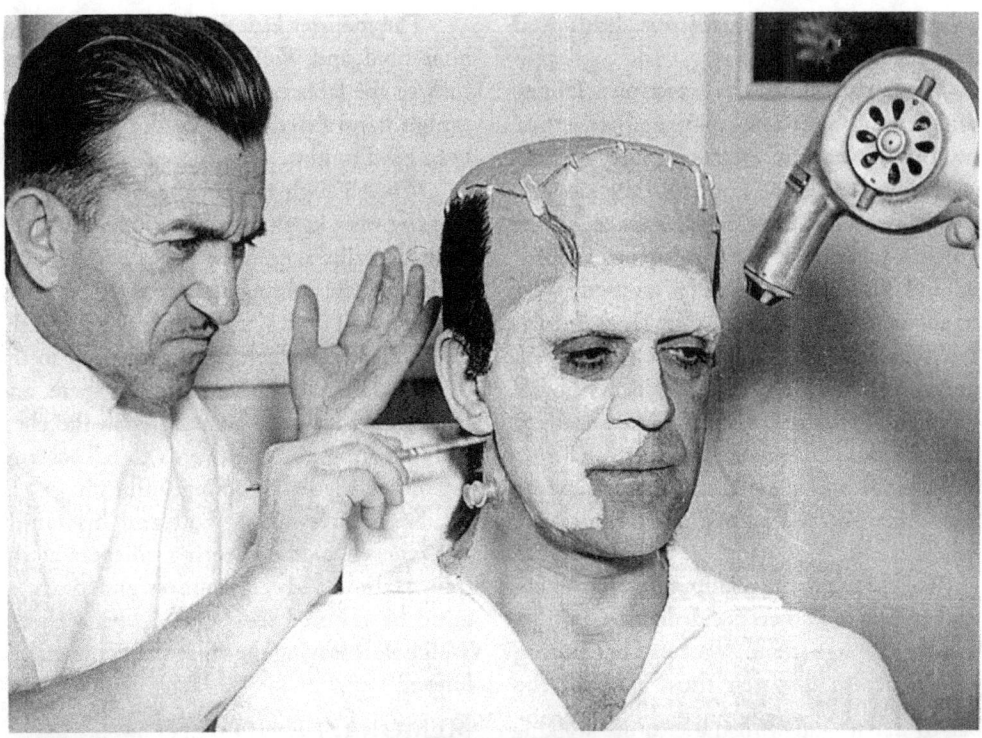

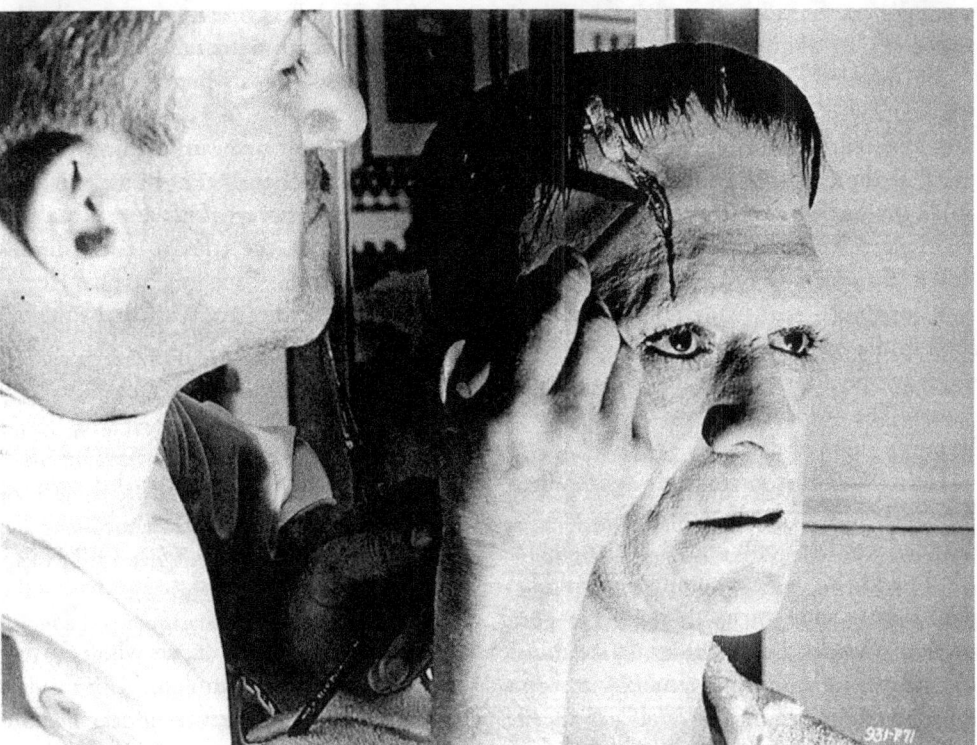

Jack Pierce making up Boris Karloff for his third and final turn as the Frankenstein monster in *Son of Frankenstein* (1939). (Courtesy of Ted Okuda.)

side, confused by his companion's stillness. When the creature's hand brushes Ygor's stomach, he stops suddenly and looks down. Seeing the blood on his hand — his friend's blood — the monster emits a heartrending howl of anguish.

With scenes such as these, Karloff's wonderful physical acting and wordless emoting transform what could have been simply a living prop into a real character who inspires sympathy as well as fear.

The fast-paced climax makes for an appropriately exciting finale. The sequence builds and builds until it explodes into frantic action as all the principals converge on the laboratory.

While the monster towers menacingly above little Peter, whirling Krogh's prosthetic arm wildly above his head (a priceless bit of black humor), Krogh kneels and fires desperately while Wolf swings out in the best Errol Flynn tradition to consign the monster to a bubbling grave. Throughout it all, the quick-step music adds further urgency to the thrilling sequence.

ASSETS

Son of Frankenstein is the third and final "classic" in the Universal Frankenstein series. Five more sequels were to follow: *The Ghost of Frankenstein* (1942), *Frankenstein Meets the Wolf Man* (1943), *House of Frankenstein* (1944), *House of Dracula* (1945), and *Abbott and Costello Meet Frankenstein* (1948). While all are entertaining (to varying degrees), they fail to capture the power and excellence of the original three.

The first thing to strike the viewer of *Son of Frankenstein* is the bizarre, unsettling set design. Gone are the brightly lit pastoral landscapes of *Bride of Frankenstein* (1935), and in their place is a land perpetually shrouded in fog and shadow. The nights are filled with raging storms and violent lightning. The days are gray and bleak and gloomy. In the opening scene, in which Wolf and his wife ride by rail through the "strange-looking country" to start their "new life," the desolate countryside rushing past their window is a portent of the horror that awaits them. The dark, foggy landscape is filled with blackened, leafless trees, looking dead and broken. The twisted limbs are devoid of greenery, and there is no sign of life to be seen anywhere.

The film's interiors, particularly the castle, are even more ominous in their bleak, overpowering presence. Everything is huge, oversized, on a massive scale. Everywhere you look there are immense windows, high ceilings, and huge open spaces in the rooms — dwarfing the beds in the bedrooms, for example — and dwarfing the humans inhabiting them. Even the furniture is oversized. It's as if the castle were made not for ordinary mortals, but for beings of monstrous size and form, subtly reminding us of what this story revolves around.

Remember, as Inspector Krogh points out, there is "only one [giant hereabouts] that I ever heard of." To complete this picture of unease, Jack Otterson built his sets so that "the angles and masses were calculated to force an impression of a weird locale without intruding too strongly into the consciousness," as the brilliant art director later related. These wonderful sets are also lit in such a way as to accentuate their size and ominous presence. The wide, wooden staircase, which dominates the castle's main hall, sports massive banister posts and stair slats which, when (ostensibly) illuminated by the immense walk-in fireplaces, throw huge shadows on the wall. These shadows resemble the bars of some mammoth cell, bringing to mind a colossal prison from which there is no escape.

Willis Cooper's script (with input from Rowland V. Lee — pages were rewritten daily by the director) is as solid as they come, filled with wonderful dialogue and just the right blend of dark graveyard humor. For instance, when the village council summons Ygor to inquire about his recent activities, Ygor becomes agitated when one of the council members threatens to hang him again. "All that's been settled. You were hanged and pronounced dead," states the chief justice. "But he was NOT dead," objects a councilman, to which the justice peevishly replies, "He was

PRONOUNCED dead by Dr. Berger, and all the others Berger has pronounced dead for the last 30 years have BEEN dead, haven't they?! If Ygor came to life again it is the Devil's work and not the court's!"

Later in the same scene, Ygor gets up to leave and suddenly coughs — right on Councilman Neumuller.

> Neumuller: "Hey, you spit on me!"
> Ygor: "I'm sorry, I cough. You see [pointing to his protruding neckbone], bone gets stuck in my throat."

Sprinkled in with the black humor are some grand, epic passages which fit in well with the towering sets and noble themes (of science, creation, etc.). "What a dreadful storm, what awful lightning," cries a frightened Mrs. Frankenstein. "It's magnificent!" is the baron's breathless, defiant response. "Nothing in nature is terrifying when one understands it. Think of it, darling, my father drew that very lightning from the heaven and FORCED it to his own will, to bring life to a being he created with his own hands. Why should WE fear anything?!"

The most significant aspect of *Son of Frankenstein*, and that which makes the film work so well, is the stellar cast assembled by producer/director Rowland V. Lee. Basil Rathbone, Boris Karloff, Bela Lugosi, Lionel Atwill — rarely in horror films has such a cast been gathered together and utilized so well. All of these often misused horror stars are here given roles worthy of their talents. The four characters they play are all complex and fascinating, and these thoroughly professional actors rise to the occasion, providing performances both unique and memorable. *"The Menace of Basil Rathbone! The Fright of Boris Karloff! The Horror of Bela Lugosi! The Hate of Lionel Atwill!"* promised the ads, and these stars did not disappoint.

Rathbone, as Wolf von Frankenstein, brings a very different tone to the role of "maker of monsters" than did Colin Clive as Henry Frankenstein. Instead of Clive's high-strung, tortured scientist, Rathbone's Frankenstein is forceful, self-possessed, and determined. Rathbone's aristocratic bearing and energetic delivery create a character both likable and fascinating. When the circle of events starts to close in on Wolf, Rathbone's true genius shines through. As Inspector Krogh and Wolf face off against each other, Rathbone becomes a bundle of nerves and restless energy, his anxiety showing in his raised voice and quick, restless movements. He is like a caged animal, seemingly ready to explode into action at any moment. Yet at the same time he keeps his civilized aplomb on the surface. "I don't mind telling you, Inspector," he states after being placed under house arrest, "that as a *guest* in my own house you'll find me extremely disagreeable!"

The scenes between Rathbone and Atwill, as these two forceful personalities spar with each other, contain a unique energy. The chemistry between the actors sends sparks flying. While on the surface the two adhere to the social graces and good manners required of them, sometimes the veneer slips, as when Atwill, frustrated by Wolf's denials, warns, "I'll stay by your side until you confess. And if you don't, I'll feed you to the villagers like the Romans fed Christians to the lions!" The tension between these two actors is a one-of-a-kind occurrence, and truly a high point in a movie filled with high points.

Rathbone's high-pitched performance here has provided a topic for heated debate by Universal horror aficionados. One either loves it or hates it. Such literary luminaries as Paul M. Jensen (*Boris Karloff and His Films*) noted Rathbone's "embarrassingly hysterical acting," and William K. Everson (*Classics of the Horror Film*) stated that "Rathbone, sad to say, hams it up rather badly." On the other side, Greg Mank (*It's Alive!*) maintained that "a great blessing of *Son* ... is the presence of Basil Rathbone," who brought to the film "that Rathbone charisma, but also zeal and a most welcome comic timing." John Brunas (*Universal Horrors*) concluded, "Basil Rathbone's high-strung performance, undeservedly lambasted by historians over the years, is in perfect harmony with the picture's larger-than-life melodramatics." Whatever one's personal taste, there's no denying that Rathbone, at the very least, provides an attention-getting focal point.

Lionel Atwill takes his role of the one-armed inspector and makes it his own. Just as Rathbone IS Sherlock Holmes, Karloff IS Frankenstein's monster, Lugosi IS Dracula, so Atwill IS Inspector Krogh. With his forceful, formal bearing, clipped speech, and wide array of quirky mannerisms, Atwill creates a character totally unique and unforgettable. He provides one of the film's most vivid passages when he tells of his personal encounter with the monster. "Do you honestly know of one criminal act that this poor creature committed?" a defensive Wolf demands of Krogh. "I was but a small boy," begins Atwill. "The monster was ravaging the countryside, killing, maiming, terrorizing. One night he burst into our house.... He grabbed me by the arm..." and Atwill suddenly pushes his wooden arm downwards to hit the wall with a punctuating thud before adding, "One doesn't easily forget, Herr Baron, an arm torn out by the roots." It is the little things, the eccentric mannerisms, often tinged with deadpan humor, which Atwill does that make the character stand out: studiously polishing his monocle while relating this story; his habit of responding with a cryptic "Perhaps," giving this simple word all sorts of deeper connotations; clicking his heels together and giving a slight bow whenever he leaves a room; or sticking the extra darts into his wooden arm as he plays a strained game with the nervous Wolf.

Perhaps even more impressive a performance than Atwill's is Lugosi's characterization of the broken-necked blacksmith-cum-graverobber Ygor. With a twinkle in his eye, a rasp in his voice, and a spring in his sinister step, Lugosi takes this hairy, snaggle-toothed, misshapen, decidedly unwholesome character and makes of him an irrepressible rogue who gleefully goes about seeking his revenge. Lugosi displays an infallible sense of timing in his delivery and mannerisms, his uneven modulation and pregnant pauses implying hidden meanings in the most innocuous of phrases. For instance, when he first shows Wolf the dormant monster and explains, "He's my friend. He, he *does* things for me," there is no doubt that the word "does" holds all sorts of nasty connotations.[1] Then, in the same scene, he adds further dimension to his character when he switches from sinister menace to affectionate concern, at one point saying, "He walks no more," with a genuine tremor of sor-

"He, he *does* things for me." Bela Lugosi as Ygor and Boris Karloff as the monster in *Son of Frankenstein* (1939).

row in his voice. Awarded many of the juiciest lines, Lugosi manages to make them still juicier; and difficult as it is in a group of characters so rich and in a cast of actors so talented, he manages to steal the show, giving the second greatest performance of his career (*Dracula* being the first).

Now we come to the monster. Karloff again displays his masterful use of pantomime, gestures, and facial expressions to turn an inarticulate hulk into a poignant, expressive being—both fearsome and pitiable. This is the last time Karloff was to play the monster on the silver screen (he donned a modified version of the makeup one more time for a comic 1962 Halloween episode of TV's *Route 66*), and that is just as well. The monster had been so thoroughly presented by Karloff and James Whale in the first two pictures that there was little more for him to do than become just what he was in the later films—a monstrous oaf. Here Karloff's screen time is limited, and he must make do with mostly lying on a table or committing the odd murder (which are very effectively—and shockingly—presented). He is given few scenes in which to shine, but Karloff takes those scenes and forges another unforgettable performance with them. Once again, Karloff makes his monster live.

Director Rowland V. Lee does an admirable job of bringing everything together and instilling a larger-than-life feel into the proceedings (just as he did with the wonderful period horror film, *Tower of London*, again with Rathbone and Karloff, released later this same year). *Son* is filled with fine details and neat touches, such as a scene shot from inside one of the oversized fireplaces during which Rathbone actually walks *into* the huge fireplace and towards the camera. Moreover, Lee was not afraid to exploit the humor in the horror. The scene at the climax, in which Krogh confronts the monster only to have his arm ripped off a second time—this time his artificial arm—with the monster bellowing his rage and waving the wooden appendage above his head like some weird club, is priceless in its macabre humor—a bit worthy of James Whale himself.

LIABILITIES

Son of Frankenstein is not altogether perfect, however. As mentioned before, the monster is not treated terribly well, and what's worse, he is forced to wear that ridiculous sheepskin vest—replacing his original ghoulish graveyard appearance with sheer hairy bulk.[2] With so many other fascinating characters to fill up the screen, however, the brevity of the monster's appearances can be excused.

What cannot be excused, however, is the obnoxious performance of little Donnie Dunagan as Wolf's son, Peter. His screeching "Well hellllo" and constant baby talk are grating and intrusive. Director Lee should have toned down this little hellion and saved us all some auditory aggravation. As written, the part of Peter is quite good. For instance, when Inspector Krogh explains that "I only have one real arm, this one isn't mine," Peter asks the obvious question, "Well, whose is it?" The part just needed a more natural, more realistic performance to make it work.

Though lacking the unique raw power of the original *Frankenstein*, and not quite up to the macabre, fairy tale brilliance of *Bride of Frankenstein*, *Son* is still a grand epic of horror filled with memorable performances and quirky, brilliant touches. It marks a fitting end for Boris Karloff's "monster."

REVIEWS

Variety (January 18, 1939): "For offering of its type, picture is well mounted, nicely directed, and includes cast of capable artists.... Universal has given 'A' production layout to the thriller in all departments. Story is slow and draggy in getting under way prior to first appearance of Karloff, but from that point on, sustains interest at high pitch."

Most reviewers were a bit more lavish in their praise than *Variety* for this "offering of its type." *Motion Picture Herald*: "Artistically, *Son of Frankenstein* is a masterpiece in the demonstration of how production settings and effects can be made assets emphasizing literary melodrama. Histrionically, the picture is outstanding because of the manner in which Basil Rathbone, Boris Karloff, Bela Lugosi and Lionel Atwill, as well as the members of the supporting cast, sink their teeth into their roles."

The Hollywood Reporter (January, 1939) called it "a knockout of its type for production, acting, and effects.... Rowland V. Lee's direction creates and keeps a chillingly sombre mood, and the grim humor that's in it, he handles very well indeed..."

There are always a few sour grapes, however, and *The New York Times* (January 30, 1939) outrageously claimed that if *Son of Frankenstein* "isn't the silliest picture ever made, it's a sequel to the silliest picture ever made, which is even sillier." Apparently silly is not all bad, however, since the reviewer goes on to amend his insult: "But its silliness is deliberate—a very shrewd silliness, perpetrated by a good director in the best traditions of cinematic horror, so that even while you laugh at its nonsense you may be struck with the notion that perhaps that's as good a way of enjoying oneself at a movie as any."

PRODUCTION NOTES

After 1936, horror in the movies was on the wane, so much so that not one horror film was released in 1937 or 1938. To illustrate the extent of the horror drought, Bela Lugosi (who was so closely tied to "horror" that he rarely appeared in any other genre) had not worked for 15 months prior to *Son of Frankenstein*. Toward the end of 1938 there was little sign of improvement until Universal re-released the original *Dracula* and *Frankenstein* together on a double bill, which did so well that it even outgrossed the originals' box-office receipts in many cities. Thus began a revival of horror, and Universal's springboard was *Son of Frankenstein*. As *Variety* related on October 13, 1938: "*Son of Frankenstein* ... will be hurried through to cash in on the interest stirred in this type of fare by current reissue of chillers, including *Frankenstein* and *Dracula*." Note that Peter Lorre was Universal's initial choice for Wolf von Frankenstein, but, on director Rowland V. Lee's insistence, high-priced ($5,000 a week) Basil Rathbone was signed for the part. Rathbone was not altogether pleased with his involvement in the film, however, and referred to it as a "penny dreadful." Despite his personal feelings, Rathbone gave an excellent performance, as befitted a professional of his stature.

Originally, Universal had planned to reap a quick profit with *Son*. To that end, they allotted only the modest budget of $250,000 to the film, a sum less than that spent on the original, made nearly eight years earlier! Lee, who at that time was a power to be reckoned with at the studio, pushed hard for *Son* and managed to get the budget increased by $50,000.

What is more, *Son of Frankenstein* was to be shot in Technicolor, which would have made it the *first* full-color horror film ever produced. The idea was abandoned, however [after much of the scenery and the monster's new sheepskin costume was designed just for that purpose], when the monster's makeup proved ineffective in the color screen tests.

Universal's front office wanted a quick start on *Son*. Willis Cooper's original script, however, was deemed unsatisfactory by Lee, who demanded a complete revision. The studio executives would brook no delays, and so *Son of Frankenstein* was rushed into production without a completed screenplay. Throughout the shoot, rewritten pages of the new script were rushed to the set daily, sometimes mere minutes before the scene was to be shot. Universal eventually paid the price for their haste, since under such difficult circumstances Lee was unable to keep the cost of production from skyrocketing to a final tab of $420,000. (This *Son* outdistanced its parents, costing $23,000 more than *Bride* and a full $129,000 more than the original, making *Son* the most expensive of Universal's Frankensteins). In addition, the film ran 19 days over schedule. Lee shot the final scenes for *Son* in the early morning hours of Thursday, January 5—a mere *two days* before Universal's planned preview date! The editing and musical scoring had already begun and composer Frank Skinner and orchestral leader Hans J. Salter worked literally around the clock to complete the film's music. "I remember," related Salter to *Cinefantastique* (Vol. 7, no. 2), "there was one stretch, pretty close to the recording date, where we didn't leave the studio for 48 or 50 hours." The film finally premiered on Friday, January 13, only eight days after Lee completed the picture.

Despite the cost overruns, it turned out to be money well spent. Thanks to the popularity of *Son of Frankenstein* (along with a few other hits such as the W. C. Fields vehicle *You Can't Cheat an Honest Man* and Bing Crosby's *East Side of Heaven*) Universal's front office stopped seeing red for the first time in years when the studio went into the black to the tune of $1,000,000 for 1939!

As originally planned, Lugosi's role of Ygor was much smaller and less important. Universal, in an opportunistic attempt to take advantage of Lugosi's financial plight (remember, the actor had not worked in 15 months), decided to cut Lugosi's salary from $1,000 a week to $500 and planned to shoot all of his scenes in one week. As Lugosi's then-wife, Lillian Lugosi Donlevy, later related: "When Rowland V. Lee heard about this, he said, and I quote, 'Those God-damned sons of bitches! I'll show them. I'm going to keep Bela on this picture from the first day of shooting right up to the last!' And he did" (Interview with Gregory William Mank in *It's Alive!*). Lee expanded Lugosi's part with additional dialogue and scenes, and thus created one of horrordom's most endearing characters. Lugosi even reprised his role of Ygor in the series' next entry, *The Ghost of Frankenstein* (1942), making a miraculous recovery from the numerous, supposedly fatal, bullet wounds he received in *Son*.

Boris Karloff had received top billing in *Bride of Frankenstein* (1935), but had to settle for second billing on this picture (under Basil Rathbone). (Ironically, in *Bride*, Karloff had previously ousted Colin Clive from the top spot.) This is the third and last time Karloff played the Frankenstein monster on the silver screen. He later explained his reasons for not continuing with the character (in *Shriek*, October 1965): "There was not much left in the character of the monster to be developed; we had reached his limits. I saw that from here on, he would become rather an oafish prop, so to speak, in the last act or something like that, without any great stature." And that is exactly what happened.

While celebrating his fifty-first birthday on the set of *Son of Frankenstein*, Karloff learned that he had became a father for the first time. His daughter, Sara Jane, was born on his own birth date.

Dwight Frye (who also appeared in the first two Frankenstein films) played an angry villager in this entry. He is not seen in the final print, however. All of Frye's scenes were edited out in order to shorten the film's excessive 100-minute running time, and the actor, much to his dismay, ended up on the cutting room floor instead of on the screen.

Two *Frankenstein* (1931) veterans who survived the editing (aside from Karloff) were Lionel Belmore (Burgomaster Vogel from the original) and Michael Mark (little Maria's grief-stricken father). Both actors played members of the town council in *Son*.

Rowland V. Lee had an unusual method of coaxing performances from his actors. As Josephine Hutchinson recalled to Greg Mank (in *It's Alive!*): "I do remember that the director had a theory that dialogue learned at a moment's notice would be delivered more naturally. For actors like Basil and Pinky [Lionel Atwill] and myself, trained in theatre technique, this is not true. Nevertheless, Mr. Lee did some rewriting on the set. We spent a lot of time in separate corners pounding new lines into our heads, which, of course , one can do, but it adds pressure." Lee's "theory," was undoubtedly born of necessity, since new script pages were being written daily.

Son of Frankenstein was the first horror movie to be presented in comic book form (a common occurrence these days). An eight-page adaptation of *Son* appeared in the very first issue of *Movie Comics*, published by Picture Comics (later to become National Periodical Publications) in 1939. Also included in the issue were versions of *Fisherman's Wharf*,

The Great Man Votes, *Gunga Din*, and the serial *Scouts to the Rescue*.

NOTES

1. Indeed, the word held even humorous connotations, as Karloff related: "In the scene where Bela slowly tells Basil, 'He — does things for me,' — and there I am, all stretched out on this dais — well, we all just doubled up, including everyone else on the set — the entire crew, cast and even Rowland, who said he didn't mind the extra takes for the chuckles it gave everyone" (from *Heroes of the Horrors*, by Calvin Thomas Beck).

2. In an interview for *Castle of Frankenstein* (#9), Karloff expressed a definite opinion on the monster's new attire: "I didn't like it because they changed his clothes completely ... wrapped him up in furs and muck, and he just became nothing. I mean the makeup, like the clothes, had become part of him."

THE MAN THEY COULD NOT HANG
(1939; Columbia)

Release Date: August 17, 1939
Running Time: 65 minutes
Director: Nick Grinde
Producer: Wallace MacDonald
Screenplay: Karl Brown
Story: Leslie T. White, George W. Sayre
Photography: Benjamin Kline, A.S.C.
Film Editor: William Lyon
Musical Director: M. W. Stoloff

Cast: Boris Karloff (Dr. Henryk Savaard), Lorna Gray (Janet Savaard), Robert Wilcox ('Scoop' Foley), Roger Pryor (District Attorney Drake), Don Beddoe (Lt. Shane), Ann Dorian (Betty Crawford), Joseph De Stefani (Dr. Stoddard), Charles Trowbridge (Judge Bowman), Byron Foulger (Lang), James Craig (Watkins), John Tyrrell (Sutton).

"I offered you life. You gave me death." — Dr. Savaard.

SYNOPSIS

Dr. Henryk Savaard, a brilliant research doctor, has developed an artificial heart which can revive a subject from death. As the doctor explains, "If we can revive a man who's been scientifically put to death, then we have the perfect anesthetic. And in that moment, the art of surgery will have advanced a thousand years." The procedure has been successful with animals and all that remains is to test it on a human being. Savaard's young assistant, Bob (a medical student), has volunteered. Bob's fiancée, Betty, protests, but he persists in his faith in Savaard and the experiment. While Savaard and Lang, his other assistant, prepare Bob for the experiment, Betty rushes out to bring back the police and stop the proceedings.

The police arrive just after Bob has been put to death in preparation for his revival, so Savaard sends Lang away to hide the artificial heart pump and he faces the police alone. Despite Savaard's heartfelt pleadings, the police lieutenant refuses to let him continue the experiment and the young man remains dead.

Savaard goes on trial for murder. The jury, despite Savaard's explanation, convicts him and the judge sentences him to death by hanging. While in prison awaiting execution, Savaard arranges for Lang to obtain his body afterwards. Using the artificial heart pump, Lang restores Savaard to life, but it is evident that he has somehow changed.

Months pass and six of the jurors in the Savaard trial have died; they apparently hanged themselves, though in truth they were victims of the vengeful doctor. A reporter, "Scoop" Foley, starts digging and attempts to contact the remaining jurors. He finds that they (along with the arresting lieutenant and police coroner) have all been summoned to Savaard's old

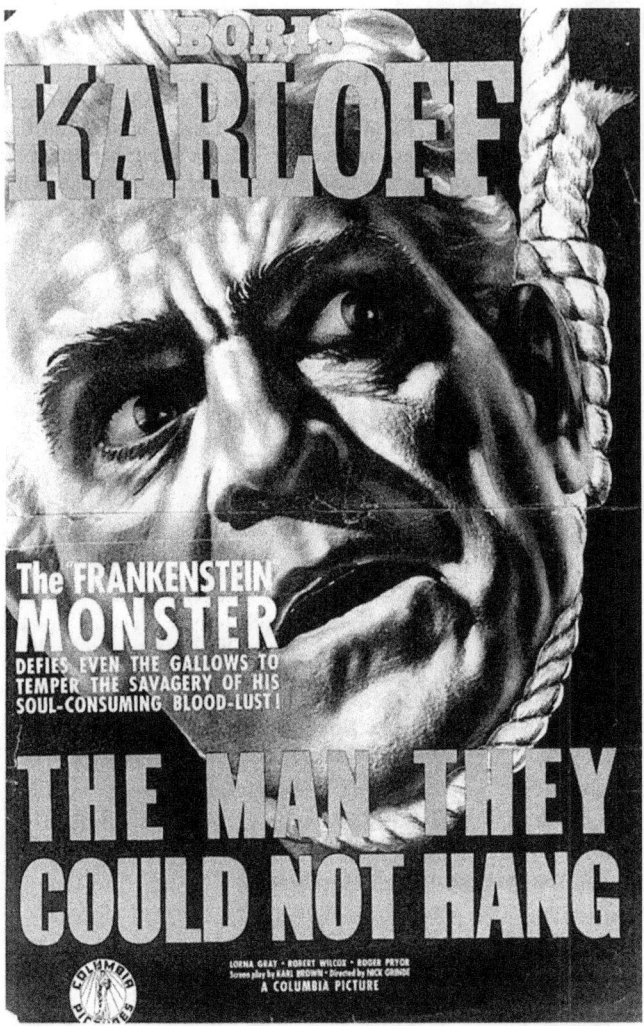

Over a year and a half after Boris Karloff's final turn as the Frankenstein monster, studios continued to capitalize on his most famous role (as evidenced by this trade ad for *The Man They Could Not Hang*, 1939).

house (closed since his death) that very day, supposedly by Judge Bowman, who presided over the trial. Once all the "guests" have arrived, they discover they've been lured to the house under false pretenses. Savaard then makes his appearance before trapping them within the house, which is fitted with metal shutters and an electrified grill. He intends to kill them one by one.

Each of the terrified captives is given a place card stating the exact time of his or her impending death. Savaard slips away and then announces over a loudspeaker: "It will do no good for you to search for me. You can never reach me where I am, but I can and will reach you — every 15 minutes." After two victims are murdered, Savaard's daughter, Janet, arrives at the house. (Scoop had phoned her earlier with his suspicions.) The jurors, trapped behind the grill, tell her what is happening. She goes upstairs to confront her father. Savaard, who can still feel warmth towards his only child through his cold, consuming hatred, begs her to leave him to his retribution. She refuses to go and Savaard locks her in a closet for her own safety, while he resumes his game of death.

Hysterical, Janet begs to be let out. Opening the door, Savaard tells her, "Janet, I wanted to spare you all this ... will you go now?" She agrees to leave, but on the way out she approaches the electrified grill. "Dad," she calls up, "can you see my hands? I'm going to open this grill. You only have to throw a switch to save my life." Before Savaard can reach the switch, however, she grabs the handles. Frantic, Savaard turns off the power and rushes downstairs to his daughter's side. The lieutenant shoots him as he kneels by her prostrate body.

Unlocking the grill, the wounded Savaard gasps, "Save Janet — get her upstairs — the laboratory — the heart will save her." The experiment works and Janet is revived. While the others tend to his daughter, Savaard grabs a rifle and shoots his miraculous machine, obliterating his work. "Why did you destroy it?" asks the reproachful coroner, but Savaard dies of his wound, leaving the question unanswered.

MEMORABLE MOMENTS

One of the most illuminating and sensitive moments in the film comes when Savaard, awaiting execution, is visited by the prison chaplain. The following exchange allows Savaard to express his dedication to science, and reveals to the audience the character's sense of wonder and his noble thirst for knowledge, even in the face of his own death:

> Chaplain: It seems strange to see you in such good spirits.
> Savaard: Is it strange that I should have no fear of dying? Well, I've lived for so long questioning the unknown that this plunge into its depths is only the last and, perhaps, the greatest of my experiments.
> Chaplain: Have you no faith?
> Savaard: As a scientist, I'm afraid I'm a professional skeptic who doubts everything, even the certainties.
> Chaplain: But do you not recognize certain great truths that all men accept?
> Savaard: I've never found one that would bear analysis.
> Chaplain: Can't you conceive of a truth too great for the human mind to analyze?
> Savaard: Tonight, no. But tomorrow — I may know better.

The insightful scripting coupled with Karloff's sensitive, subdued delivery, makes this scene one of the picture's highlights.

The high point of the film's second half comes after Savaard begins exacting his revenge on the jurors he's trapped in his house. Following the unexpected death of Judge Bowman, they are wary and frightened, especially Mr. Kearney, the jury foreman, whom Savaard has announced will be the next to die — at exactly 7:15 P.M. "And now Mr. Kearney, time is *flying*," declares Savaard's disembodied voice over a hidden loudspeaker. "May I draw your attention to the clock?" he continues, sadistically taunting his victim-to-be, who is now almost hysterical with fear. The group forms a circle around the terrified man in an effort to protect him — from what, no one is sure. The tension is thick when suddenly — the phone rings. Such a seemingly innocuous occurrence is transformed into a startling event by the anxiety and nervous tension built up beforehand, and indeed, it turns out to be a not-so-innocuous occurrence after all.

ASSETS

The Man They Could Not Hang is a well-constructed film, deftly split into two parts. The first half revolves around the noble Dr. Savaard and his earth-shaking medical breakthrough. As the plot moves from his tragically interrupted experiment to the mockery of a trial stacked against him and finally to his unfair execution, Savaard is portrayed as a kind, noble, rational individual who has fallen victim to the small minds of others. The script, direction, and Boris Karloff's genuine performance all paint a picture of a caring forward-thinker to be admired and supported. Conversely, his accusers and prosecutors are shown to be ignorant and overly emotional, with an almost moblike mentality ("Hanging's too good for him!"). This firmly aligns audience sympathy with Savaard. After he's been found guilty, Savaard addresses the jury and spells out their ignorance for them (and the audience): "You who have condemned me, I know your kind. Your forebears poisoned Socrates, burned Joan of Arc, hanged, tortured all those whose only offense was to bring light into the darkness." Now there is no doubt as to with which side the audience will identify.

The second part of the film begins with Savaard's resurrection. No longer the noble humanitarian, he has become a vengeful, cold-blooded killer, poisoned by the suffering and persecution he has endured. "They killed the man I was," he tells his daughter. "All that's left is the will to hate and to destroy."

The transition to this second half is appropriately sinister. We first see the resurrected Savaard in a long shot taken from above. He is strapped to a table, with a weird brace on his neck (reminiscent of Dr. Gogol in *Mad Love*, 1935), and the edges of a foreground skylight frame the picture in darkness. This opening shot sets a dark, eerie tone for the weird, macabre happenings to come.

When Savaard begins to systematically kill off the jurors he has lured to his house, the audience is in a quandary. Having been so firmly

Dr. Henryk Savaard (Boris Karloff) and his assistant Lang (Byron Foulger) check to make sure their volunteer subject is dead before utilizing Savaard's experimental artificial heart device to revive him. From *The Man They Could Not Hang* (1939).

aligned with this man throughout the first half of the film, it becomes very disturbing to see the object of their admiration and identification transformed into a cold-blooded murderer. This two-part construction sets up an emotional ambivalence in the audience which quite neatly draws them into the murderous proceedings. The film's excellent first half build-up, which enmeshes the audience in Savaard's character and plight, allows the viewers to ally themselves emotionally with the doctor as he commits his vicious acts in the second half of the picture. While on the surface they abhor the violent vengeance Savaard is administering, the ground has been well laid to encourage them to identify with him and even condone these killings as a just retribution. Ultimately, however, Savaard (and the audience) lets reason win out over the madness of vengeance. This makes for a very enjoyable, rewarding, and arguably cathartic, experience for the viewer.

Much of the film's success is due to the convincing dualistic performance of Boris Karloff. His sincere, heartfelt delivery in the picture's first half builds a warmth and trust in the audience. After his revival from death, however, all warmth is drained away and Karloff turns cold and cruel. It is a shocking contrast and a testament to his acting ability. This transformation is brought home in the very first scene following his resurrection. His head bandaged and wearing a metal neck brace, Karloff begins to speak, "They won't come to learn," he tells his assistant in a weary, almost resigned tone, "only to stare." Karloff's eyes open suddenly and his face hardens as he continues. "I'll be a freak in a sideshow. 'Lazarus the Second'— 50 cents to look, a dollar to touch!" Karloff's inflection, tone, and expression reflect the change in Savaard's soul just as surely as the doctor's machine effected the change in his body.

Director Nick Grinde and veteran cinematographer Benjamin Kline make good use of lighting right from the start. In Savaard's lab, for instance, the myriad glass vials, odd-shaped jars, and intriguing instruments cast an intricate pattern of shadows both on the wall and across the players, creating a textured tableau of light and dark. Shadows play an important role in establishing mood and theme throughout the rest of the picture, as well.

After the guilty verdict is returned, the doctor begins his address to the jury while seated in front of a wall upon which the shadows of window blinds create a prison cell of light and dark. Later, when we first see Savaard in his (actual) cell awaiting execution, it is not the man but his *shadow* on the wall which paces back and forth; Savaard, at his lowest ebb, has become the shadow now. Add to this deft use of lighting the frequent smooth tracking shots and the excellent use of depth (with objects such as medical instruments, flowers, tables, and even a character's shoulder placed in the foreground), and *The Man They Could Not Hang* delivers a three-dimensional visual quality usually reserved for "A" productions, which have the extra time and money to spend on such cinematic luxuries.

LIABILITIES

Apart from Dr. Savaard, the characters in the film are generally shallow and underdeveloped. "Scoop" is a brave and guileless cardboard hero; Lang is merely a lackey with no motivation or character of his own; and Janet is simply the standard "Scientist's Daughter" character (though, to be fair, she is given one illuminating scene in which she challenges her father to kill her along with the others). Truly, the film rests on Karloff's stooped shoulders, and fortunately he is able to bear the weight. When Savaard is on screen the film is involving; when he's not, interest wanes considerably.

Despite the many possibilities inherent in the concept, *The Man They Could Not Hang* totally skirts the issue of what happens after death. Before the execution, the chaplain asks Savaard if he believes in an afterlife. "Tonight, no," is his thoughtful reply. "But tomorrow — I may know better." Though the script looks down this avenue of wonder, it ultimately backs off and refuses to step onto this controversial path to Ultimate Knowledge. Nothing more is said of this intriguing issue, and Savaard never addresses the question of where he was and what happened in the many hours during which he was clinically dead. "Tomorrow" came and went, and if indeed he did "know better," he never let on. It is as if screenwriter Karl Brown pulled the pin on a live grenade and then ignored it. This is an unfortunate oversight (or sidestep, if intentional), and one that blows up in Brown's face as far as audience expectation goes.

It is also unfortunate that the film ends as it does, with Savaard deliberately destroying his life-saving machine. One can only assume this action is one of sheer spite, a mean-spirited final act which undermines the audience's sympathy that was so carefully built up in the first half and then reestablished at the end when he saves his daughter. No final words of explanation or rationale are given Savaard to speak. He just dies, his last act robbing humanity of a great boon. Earlier, Savaard had gone on about how "Every gift that science has given them has been twisted into a thing of *hate* and *greed!*" He continued, "But not this one. That instrument is perfect, the secret of eternity. It dies with me — after I've made them pay for all they made me suffer." This was the reasoning of the madman he had become, but at the end Savaard regains his sanity. His character should have been treated better at the finale and allowed to regain fully his humanity before that last, *final* death. As it is, the spiteful ending merely confounds the audience and makes their earlier sympathetic view of the man a cheat. "Why did you destroy it?" is the last question uttered in the film. Indeed, Savaard's once-noble character and the audience that backed him deserve to be given an answer.

This lobby card shows Lt. Shane (Don Beddoe) arresting Savaard (Boris Karloff) before he can revive his subject, thus sentencing the brave young volunteer to a permanent death. Newspaperman "Scoop" Foley (Robert Wilcox) and Savaard's daughter Janet (Lorna Gray) look on.

Despite these faults, and while not wholly satisfying, *The Man They Could Not Hang* is still quite entertaining and a solid blueprint for the myriad "Mad Medico" movies to come.

REVIEWS

Variety (September 27, 1939): "Boris Karloff looks less menacing than he has been in the past, but while he is a complacent, kindly type of character a part of the way, in 'The Man They Could Not Hang' he ends up on a rather sinister note. The unexpected and implausible revenge doesn't jell, but Karloff turns in his usual good performance. His daughter is played moderately well by Lorna Gray..."

Kinematograph Weekly (October 19, 1939): "The initial experiment and trial scene are impressive, it is during the second half that the picture falls foul of conviction. Savaard's campaign of revenge is carried out in circumstances that not only defy intelligent acting and direction, but outstrip the most lurid serial. However, Karloff is the key to the film's macabre appeal, and his presence, augmented by ambitious technical presentation, enables the thriller to be given the benefit of the doubt..."

PRODUCTION NOTES

The story of *The Man They Could Not Hang* was inspired by actual experiments conducted by Dr. Robert Cornish involving the supposed reanimation of dead dogs. In 1934, Dr. Cornish restored life to dogs that he had killed with nitrogen gas. Cornish (like any good *screen* scientist) wanted to take that final step and try his experiment on humans — executed criminals to be precise. He was denied permission.

Actress Ann Dorian (Betty in *The Man*

They Could Not Hang) remembered her co-star Boris Karloff as "the sweetest man that God ever made on this earth.... We worked very, very late hours on that one, and this man never lost his good humor. It didn't bother him to go over and over and over something, because he always wanted to do a good job."[1]

The success of *The Man They Could Not Hang* prompted Columbia to star Karloff in a string of similar "Mad Doctor" vehicles, all released within a span of 18 months: *The Man with Nine Lives* (1940), *Before I Hang* (1940), and *The Devil Commands* (1941). In each he plays a sympathetic scientist attempting to solve some great mystery for the benefit of mankind, only to have the experiment go awry through outside interference or unfortunate circumstances. While all three are entertaining (if small scale), none of them matches the technical expertise or story freshness of *The Man They Could Not Hang* (with the arguable exception of *The Devil Commands*, whose rich atmosphere and weird storyline makes for a truly striking film).

While Karloff was not particularly happy with the repetitive quality of the series, Columbia was more than willing to cash in on their successful formula. In a 1962 interview (*The Motion Picture Guide*), Karloff related a revealing discussion he had had with the series' producer, Wallace MacDonald: "Once, during the crazed-scientist cycle, I said wearily to the producer: 'These things are all right, but don't you think we should perhaps spend a little more in the writing or change the format?' He was in an expansive mood. He opened his desk drawer and pulled out a great chart. 'Here,' he said, 'here's your record. We know exactly how much these pictures are going to make. They cost *so* much. They earn *so* much. Even if we spend more on them, they wouldn't make a cent more. So why change them?'"

Producer Wallace MacDonald began his showbiz career as a stage actor, entering motion pictures in the early silents (appearing in such films as the 1924 version of *The Sea Hawk*) and starring in a string of westerns. At the advent of sound he went behind the camera and ultimately rose to the position of supervisor of writers at Republic. In 1936 he left Republic to become a producer at Columbia where he supervised over 100 films (including the Karloff "Mad Doctor" series).

Harry A. (Nick) Grinde directed nearly two-score films from the late twenties to mid-forties, mostly comedies or crime dramas. Ann Dorian characterized her director as "a great guy" who possessed an "uplift — always an 'up' feeling. Even when he was angry or upset, he never let his actors see it — unless he was upset with *them*!" Pleased with Grinde's work on *The Man They Could Not Hang*, Columbia tapped him for their two follow-up Karloff pictures as well, *The Man with Nine Lives* and *Before I Hang*. In 1945 Grinde left motion pictures to work in the expanding television industry, eventually becoming a producer of commercials.

Longtime Columbia sound technician Edward Bernds worked on the second Grinde/Karloff vehicle, *The Man with Nine Lives* (1940). In an interview with Gregory William Mank (in *Hollywood Cauldron*), Bernds opined that "Grinde was not a bad director — I think he was a cut above a lot of the Columbia directors — but he was more preoccupied with getting it done on budget, on schedule, satisfying the bosses, getting another assignment." Of Grind's relationship with his star, Bernds remembered that "Karloff was professional, of course, but he didn't confer with Grinde as much" (as the actor had with *The Black Room* director Roy William Neill).

Screenwriter Karl Brown entered films in 1912 as a lab assistant and still photographer. He quickly rose to the rank of assistant cameraman and worked on a number of D. W. Griffith's films, including *The Birth of a Nation* (1915) and *Intolerance* (1916). In 1927 he graduated from cinematographer to director, helming over a dozen "B" pictures over the next decade. Brown also wrote screenplays, again generally for "B" pictures, which he sometimes directed as well. In addition to *The Man They Could Not Hang*, Brown scripted *The Man with Nine Lives* and provided the story for *Before I Hang* (the second and third in the "Mad Doctor" series, respectively).

Cinematographer Benjamin Kline photographed nearly 200 feature films over his four-decade career. Though *The Man They Could Not Hang* was his first foray into the horror genre, he lensed a number of subsequent entries, including Columbia's two follow-up Karloff vehicles, *The Man with Nine Lives* and *Before I Hang* (1940). His other genre credits are: *Island of Doomed Men* (1940), *The Giant Claw* (1957), *The Man Who Turned to Stone* (1957), and *Zombies of Mora Tau* (1957).

Editor William Lyon went on to win two Academy Awards (for *From Here to Eternity* in 1953 and *Picnic* in 1956), both for his home studio, Columbia, where he worked for over 30 years.

NOTES

1. Interview with Richard Valley (*Scarlet Street* #17).

TORTURE SHIP
(1939; Producers Pictures Corporation)

Release Date: October 22, 1939
Running Time: 62 minutes
Director: Victor Halperin
*Associate Producer: Sigmund Neufeld
*Screenplay: George Wallace Sayre (suggested by the Story "A Thousand Deaths" by Jack London)
Photography: Jack Greenhalgh, A.S.C.
Art Director: Fred Preble
Editor: Holbrook Todd
Sound Engineer: Hans Weeren
Musical Director: David Chudnow

*Uncredited on film print.

Cast: Lyle Talbot (Lt. Bob Bennett), Irving Pichel (Dr. Herbert Stander), Jacqueline Wells (Joan Martel), Sheila Bromley (Mary Stavish), Anthony Averill (Dirk), Russell Hopton (Harry), Julian Madison (Paul), Eddie Holden (Ole Olson), Wheeler Oakman (Ritter), Stanley Blystone (Briggs), Leander de Cordova (Ezra), Dmitri Alexis (Murano), Skelton Knaggs (Jesse), *Adia Kuznetzoff (Krantz), *William Chapman (Bill), *Fred Walton (Fred).

"If you guys wanna be tortured like rats, that's your business." — Ritter.

SYNOPSIS

"Is it true that through your experiments with endocrine glands you can cure crime?" asks one of the reporters dogging the steps of the beleaguered Dr. Herbert Stander, who is waiting to hear if he will be indicted for his experiments. These unauthorized experiments involved the harboring of criminals, among other things (though all in the name of science, of course). When news of the impending indictment comes, Stander forms a plan. "I intend to go on with my experiments regardless," the determined doctor tells his assistant, Dirk. Dr. Stander helps a number of notorious killers escape and makes them an offer they cannot refuse: "In return for helping me with my experiments, I'll give you safe passage to another country." Among the murderers are "Harry the Carver," "Machine Gun Slayer" Jesse, "Bluebeard Killer" Ezra Matthews, and "Poison Mary." Captained by his innocent nephew, Navy man Bob Bennett, the doctor's yacht hastily departs with its cargo of criminal guinea pigs. Once safely out to sea, the murderers ask what exactly the doc plans to do to them. When they discover it involves an untested serum and a delicate operation, they collectively balk. "On shore you haven't a chance to live," retorts the doctor. "Here, it's fifty-fifty." This does nothing to reassure the thugs, but they do not have much of a choice since the doctor and

Bob (Lyle Talbot) becomes a homicidal maniac after Dr. Stander (Irving Pichel) injects him with an experimental serum in *Torture Ship* (1939). From left to right: Talbot, Jacqueline Wells, Pichel, Anthony Averill, Julian Madison, Stanley Blystone, unidentified.

his loyal crew hold all the cards (and all the guns).

Bob finally learns just what type of pleasure cruise he's captaining and, while not entirely pleased, he goes along with it. However, his view quickly changes when he meets Joan. Joan was the secretary of "Poison Mary" Stavish, and, though innocent, was convicted along with her employer. "I swear I didn't know she was poisoning people to collect their insurance," Joan tells Bob. "As her secretary, I believed she was in a legitimate insurance business."

The experiments begin, and the first subject, Ezra (the "Bluebeard Killer"), dies from the treatment. Bob, who has begun to fall in love with Joan, worries that the doctor will choose her for his next guinea pig. Hoping to keep her out of the doctor's sight, he lets her into his own cabin and instructs her to lock the door and stay there.

Undaunted by his initial failure, the doctor chooses a second subject from among the criminal ranks. This one reacts violently to the treatment, breaks free of his restraints, kills a sailor, and attacks Bob, knocking him unconscious. At this point, the doctor comes to a realization: "To go on I must change my procedure. As you know I've obtained in this synthetically the active ingredients of the endocrine glands governing criminality—*synthetically*. That's just the trouble; I've been trying to duplicate nature's work in the test tube. It just can't be done. I must let nature do this for me in the body of a normal person."

Inspired, the doctor goes to where Bob lies unconscious. When his two assistants are slow to obey his commands, he explains, "I know what you're thinking—Bob is my nephew. I've sacrificed everything to prove my theory. Bob is free from criminal taint, a perfect subject."

Stander injects Bob with the serum (presumably to let "nature do it" and then extracts the "endocrine gland ingredients" later). Awakening shortly after the treatment, Bob gets up and, in a daze, moves mechanically out into the room where Joan is sleeping. She wakes and smiles when she sees him, but her smile fades as she sees his blank expression. Just as his hands reach out for her throat, the doctor enters and Bob knocks him unconscious. Joan slips out, but is quickly followed by Bob.

The doctor's assistants come to his aid and, with several members of the crew, break into the cabin where Bob has cornered Joan. As they gain entry, Bob, a chair raised over his head like a club, collapses. Joan is shaken but unhurt. While this is taking place, Harry "The Carver," Mary, and Ritter (another killer) sneak into the untended office. They find a gun — but, feeling it is not yet the right time, they hide the weapon.

Bob wanders about the ship in a zombie-like state — now harmless, but seemingly mindless as well. Despite Dr. Stander's reassurance ("There's no cause for alarm, he'll recover"), Joan is distraught. When Bob enters the radio room it becomes evident that he has indeed recovered and is faking his condition to keep the doctor and his men off guard. Intending to send an S.O.S., he is interrupted and must resume his dazed act. Wandering down to the ship's hospital ward, he learns that the doctor intends to administer his "treatment" to Joan. Desperate to keep Joan from harm, Bob asks Ritter and the rest of the thugs to help take over the ship. He obtains a gun from Ole, the Swedish cook, and the criminals retrieve their own hidden weapon. Ritter promises not to harm the doctor and crew. Of course, the first thing the new gang does is plug the doctor and his assistant, Paul. They then turn on Bob and disarm him, but he manages to lock Joan, the wounded doctor, his other assistant, Dirk, and himself in the ward. Leaving them there, the ship's new captain — Ritter — and his men celebrate with a hearty meal and plenty of booze.

In the midst of their revels, the doctor's voice comes on over the loudspeakers: "Men, now that you've had your little repast, I must tell you something of serious importance. That last injection I gave each of you was only temporary. Unless you have another one immediately you are due to experience a complete paralysis of heart action. Remember what happened to the unfortunate Ezra." This is Bob disguising his voice, since the doctor is out of commission, but the thugs do not know that and, while not buying it completely, they become a little uneasy.

Just then, "Poison Mary," who was the most recent recipient of the doctor's treatment and is recovering in the ward, awakens and calls Joan over to her. "Joan," she begins (as soft music starts), "it's hard to explain, but something has come over me. I don't know, but a short time ago I hated you. Now, I'm sorry. Please forgive me, Joan. You know, it's funny, but I want to give myself up now." Mary has been cured of her criminal tendencies — the doctor's experimental treatment has worked!

The gravely wounded Dr. Stander overhears Mary's heartfelt speech and manages to whisper, "She'll live to prove that I was right" (unlike his other unfortunate subjects). "They'll heap honors on you now, doctor," Dirk respectfully replies. But it is too late for the doctor, and while a beaming Mary reveals, "I feel as if I've been born again," the doctor dies, content that he was indeed proven right.

Meanwhile, the now-drunk killers are getting more and more nervous, as the psychology of Bob's trick works on their minds. Jesse goes looking for wine and runs into the Swedish cook, who is taking the last bottle to Harry. Grabbing the bottle, Jesse takes a belt and demands more. "Dat's all der is," the cook explains. "I yust found dat hiding in Miss Mary's luggage." "Poison Mary's?!" exclaims Jesse and throws the bottle down as if bitten by it. Joining the others in the stateroom, Jesse has just enough time to hear another phony warning over the loudspeaker ("May I remind you men your time is almost up") before dropping dead in front of the others. That does the trick and the thugs give themselves up.

"Three days and we're home, Bob," says Joan up on deck. After Bob adds: "Returning the guinea pigs back to the authorities," the picture fades out on their embrace.

MEMORABLE MOMENTS

There is really only one standout moment in *Torture Ship*, and that comes when Bob revives after being given the experimental treatment. Upon awakening, he staggers out of the ward and through the door of the doctor's office. Straightening up as if suddenly given a purpose, he begins to advance. He moves slowly and we see a blank, hollow look on his face. In medium close-up the camera retreats in front of him, holding his face in the frame as he passes through shadows while low-key lighting transforms his countenance into a sinister visage. Finally we see his purpose as the camera cuts to Joan sleeping peacefully on the office couch. The camera pulls back to reveal Bob's menacing shadow falling across her, growing ever bigger as he comes closer and closer and finally bends over her. Joan awakens and then we see what she sees — Bob towering over her. Suddenly his blank face hardens and twists in anger, and his hands reach out for Joan's throat.

It must be noted, however, that even this sequence is more mediocre than "memorable." It is only elevated above the rest of the picture by the general lack of any truly significant scenes. While possessing a few frightening flourishes, the sequence is a typical example of an opportunity wasted. For instance, the shot of Bob's expression changing from blankness to rage — a potentially powerful and terrifying moment — is so short that it barely registers. (To be fair, this may be the fault of Lyle Talbot's general inexpressiveness — Talbot looks more constipated than enraged and perhaps the astute editor, realizing this, cut the shot to a mere flash.) Aside from the opening movement, in which shadows and low-key lighting set the tone, the sequence is generally overlit, greatly diminishing its impact. Throughout, the music, rather than heightening the tension, works against the horror and suspense of the scene. Instead of building slowly and steadily to a climactic crescendo, the music plays at one continually frantic pace from the beginning to the end, which is completely at odds with the scene's construction and style. With more attention to detail and to the inherent horror of the scene, this could have been a truly memorable moment instead of merely the best of the bland.

ASSETS

A few worthwhile ideas can be found on this *Torture Ship*. The concept of forcing criminals to participate in experiments to cure their criminality is rife with ethical and moral possibilities. (Too bad these potential ethical conflicts are left unexplored.) The characterization of criminal behavior as resulting from a "mental disorder" (as Dr. Stander calls it) is rather progressive for the time (and is ultimately proven correct when Stander finally cures Poison Mary).

By far the most intriguing idea in the story is the concept of a hero-turned-monster. By transforming Bob into a monster (albeit temporarily) and having him menace the very person he has vowed to protect, a unique conflict arises that becomes perversely satisfying. Along the lines of Jekyll and Hyde, this transformation suggests that even the most noble and courageous individual has something inside him which is dark and violent. The fear of losing control over one's own behavior, over one's very nature — to have it changed against one's will — is at the heart of the matter. The fact that this film's most overt moment of horror stems from this theme only underscores the potential inherent in the concept.

This becomes the most effective moment in the film because of the ambivalence it generates in the mind of the viewer. On the one hand, it appeals to our baser instincts, as we watch the transformed Bob approach the sleeping heroine with bad intent. (Exactly *what* form this intent might take — violent or sexual or both — is left to the viewer's imagination.) On the other hand, we know that Bob is actually good and kind, and while we can excuse this behavioral lapse since it is due to something beyond his control, we fear for Bob (and the lasting effect this will have on him) as well as for Joan. So, while we wait in delicious anticipation for the dire deed to be done, at the same time we dread it.

(Uncredited) screenwriter George Sayre

must be lauded for providing a few intriguing ideas — and then condemned for the script's frequently awkward dialogue and generally scattered construction.

There are several good characterizations among the criminals, and able performances to go with them. Ritter, the "big-shot killer" and self-proclaimed leader of the impromptu gang, is a big-fish-in-a-small-pond, intent on ordering his cohorts about and talking tough. Wheeler Oakman plays the part well, with Ritter attempting to be suave and charming while the brutality and coarseness underneath show through. The aptly named Skelton Knaggs, always interesting to watch (he was fascinating in Val Lewton's 1943 thriller, *Ghost Ship*), is quite convincing as the slimy killer Jesse. Knaggs' skeletal face, cold eyes (here magnified by thick glasses), hard mouth, slicked-back hair, and slow but pregnant dialogue delivery create a chilling psychopath. Director Victor Halperin (in one of his few good decisions) makes the most of Knaggs' creepy appearance and intonation by introducing him shrouded in darkness, with only half of his face visible and his eyes staring ahead, as he chillingly states, "I got about as high as I could in my profession here," and agrees to go with the doctor in order to "build up a reputation all over again" somewhere else. Unfortunately, Jesse is a minor character and Knaggs is given only a few scenes. (Ironically, Knaggs was *not* Halperin's first choice for the role. According to the Call Bureau Cast Service, John Miller was to have played Jesse, and Knaggs only came on board at the last minute.)

Another effective character, this one a bit more important, is knife-killer Harry. Russell Hopton makes of Harry a thug who is almost likable, due to his genuine enthusiasm for his "profession" and his rather sick sense of humor. Whether he's smiling with unpleasantly genuine glee at the prospect of adding another victim to his "scrapbook," or caressing the tools of his "trade," or recognizing the black humor of the Swedish cook innocently asking him for a shave, this is a fun-loving killer. Sadly, Harry Russell Hopton ("Harry" was actually his Christian given name) died of a sleeping pill overdose six years later, a suspected suicide.

In its use of humor (so often a sore spot in horror films), *Torture Ship* comes off rather well. One bit in particular is quite amusing. While the Swedish cook sits in Harry's impromptu barber chair, innocently prattling on while awaiting a "close shave," Harry goes over to the porthole to measure if Ole's body will fit through. Coming back, Harry casually shows Ole his scrapbook detailing his crimes, while he begins to wield the straight-razor. Ole unfolds a clipping, reads the headline, and bolts for the door, leaving the amused but disappointed Harry standing by an empty chair. This gallows-type humor fits in well with the murderous characters and general theme of the film. It is also rather refreshing to have the Comedy Relief Character be someone other than the usual cowardly black servant or wisecracking reporter/sidekick. Rather than being a distracting annoyance (as so many Comedy Relief Characters become), Eddie Holden as the Swedish cook turns out to be quite likable with his ridiculous accent and naive demeanor.

The above are all minor points of achievement, however, and they quickly sink beneath the waves of a sea of liabilities.

LIABILITIES

This all-but-forgotten independent production (it is not even listed among star Irving Pichel's credits in some sources) is one long string of missed opportunities. While few have seen it (either at its original release or in the ensuing years), there is nothing much in the picture to belie its deserved obscurity.

While the production values and photography are generally adequate for a low-budget "B," the picture needed more than a minimal technical competency to hold it together. The film consists of a series of standard medium shots, with an occasional (though minimal) camera movement or close-up. While adequate for the more mundane dialogue scenes, such uninspired shooting does not suffice for the more important moments of suspense and horror. Time after time, director Victor

Halperin fails to exploit the sinister quality of a scene and elects to shoot it straight on as if filming a drawing-room melodrama. Mr. Halperin shows none of the macabre flourish found in *White Zombie*. Perhaps, seven years after that film's success, he did not feel like making another horror picture and so decided to go for straight melodrama, though why he would consciously decide this is a mystery, for in 1939 the horror revival was in full swing and the terror picture a very lucrative product.

Perhaps there was just too tight a stranglehold on the film's budget, and so no time or money for any extras was provided. Often, however, a bit of creativity is worth more than its weight in gold (and, besides, *White Zombie* was itself a low-budget production.) Granted, Halperin did not have the benefit of so magnetic a personality as Bela Lugosi for *Torture Ship* as he did on *White Zombie*, and so perhaps remained uninspired. (Lugosi's influence on *White Zombie* cannot be overestimated. Actor Clarence Muse even reported that Lugosi, dissatisfied with Halperin's direction, took over the director's chair himself for some key sequences.) However, the most likely explanation for Mr. Halperin's poor direction on *Torture Ship* is that he was basically not a very good director.

A list of his credits bears this out, with such disappointing genre fare as the unconvincing misfire *Supernatural* (1933) and the devastatingly dull *Revolt of the Zombies* (1936). *White Zombie*, perhaps, was one of those happy accidents in which talent and circumstances come together to create a whole greater than the sum of its parts. In any case, on *Torture Ship*, Victor Halperin was back to his old unimaginative self.[1]

Aside from the introduction of "Machine Gun Slayer" Jesse and the Bob-Gone-Bad sequence, the picture is poorly lit. Scenes are constantly overlit and there is a decided lack of dark corners, dim corridors, and menacing shadows which could have made the mundane interior sets so much more interesting. The lighting does nothing to create any kind of menace or atmosphere, making the film feel more like a crime drama than a horror picture or even a suspense thriller.

Alas, the film also takes no advantage of the unique setting — a large yacht out in the middle of the boundless ocean, its occupants alone and with no hope of escape from this private prison ship. There are only a few minor scenes on deck, with most of the action taking place in the cabins. Below-deck the rooms are unremarkable, with nothing to distinguish them from any apartment or hotel room anywhere.

The sinister possibilities of menace on a ship are ignored: no noisy engine-room sequence; no narrow corridors; no mysterious reflections of water on the cabin walls; no rocking or sudden lurches at just the right (or wrong) moment. For all the use made of the setting, the picture might just as well have taken place on land.

The slipshod screenwriting shows through in several sequences of obvious unbelievability. Poison Mary's miraculous cure is a case in point.

Screenwriter Sayre did not bother with any buildup or development, or any lead-in scenes which might give an inkling of the change to come. Instead, this thoroughly evil, self-centered woman simply wakes up as a sweet, thoughtful angel. It was as if Sayre could not let the doctor die in vain, and so this bone of unbelievability was thrown to him (and *at* the audience). The sugary sweet scene (complete with the painfully obvious heart-tugging violin strains swelling on the soundtrack) is insipid.

The silly ending, in which the frightened criminals give themselves up, is no better. "Come in one at a time with your hands up," orders Bob. As each man enters, Dirk slugs him on the chin and lets him fall in the corner, with each successive crook piling up on top of the others. At any moment you expect Curly of the Three Stooges to come through the door and take *his* rap on the chin.

Even with all these faults and wasted opportunities, the picture might have salvaged some entertainment value had the resident mad doctor been played by the likes of Karloff,

Lugosi, Lionel Atwill, or George Zucco. Instead, we are given the staid acting of Irving Pichel. Pichel was not a bad choice for the pivotal part (having shown in *Dracula's Daughter*, 1936, his propensity for villainy), but whether through (mis)direction or simply a lack of interest, he plays Dr. Stander in such a soft-spoken, bland manner that he becomes a non-presence.

There is no fire, no conviction, not even when he delivers the obligatory mad medico speeches. Never becoming excited, he keeps his tones modulated, with little inflection. Walking through the role, Pichel is more kindly uncle than obsessed scientist, and the film suffers for it.

While containing some intriguing ideas, a few good supporting characters and performances, and a setting ripe with possibilities, *Torture Ship* is sunk by mundane direction, poor lighting, bland acting, and a complete lack of atmosphere, as well as suffering a bad case of wasted opportunities. What could have become an interesting above-average horror picture instead sails off into low-grade — even cheesy — melodrama.

REVIEW

Variety (November 29, 1939): "Quickie action thriller that misses fire all the way on its possibilities. There can be no quarrel with the acting of the principals, it being of a rather superior grade than the story. Yarn has so many unreasonable and unexplainable points that it will annoy even the most juve-minded. Production is fair, not revealing the film's cheapie nature. It's rather slow in getting started, however, and the minor members of the cast are going to win no Apollo contests or femme trade."

PRODUCTION NOTES

Torture Ship, only the second production of the fledgling independent company called Producers Pictures, began shooting in late August of 1939 at a rented soundstage at Grand National Studios.

With their next film, *Buried Alive* (also directed by Victor Halperin), a dull prison yarn made later that year, the upstart outfit became Producers Distributing. A few more pictures and it evolved into PRC (Producers Releasing Corporation — or, in the eyes of the more acerbic critics, "Poverty Row Cinema"). PRC became a mainstay of "B" horror in the forties, producing and/or distributing such memorable low-budget fare as *The Devil Bat* (1941), *Strangler of the Swamp* (1945), and *The Brute Man* (1946; discarded by Universal and picked up by the less-proud PRC).

Prolific cinematographer Jack Greenhalgh was poverty row's busiest cameraman, lensing an amazing 100+ low-budget features in 15 years! His credits include *Reefer Madness* (1939), *The Mad Monster* (1942), *Dead Men Walk* (1943), *The Flying Serpent* (1945), and *The Lost Continent* (1951). Greenhalgh's final film was the atrocious (though highly entertaining) *Robot Monster* (1953). "We end as we begin."

Hero Lyle Talbot (born Lisle Henderson) began his showbusiness career right out of high school — as a tent-show magician. Leaving magic behind, he turned to acting and toured with a variety of stock companies before forming his own acting troupe, The Talbot Players, in Memphis. In 1932 he entered films, appearing in both A and B pictures for the next three decades, including one borderline horror entry, *The Thirteenth Guest* (1932). In the late forties and early fifties he became popular in serials, starring in the likes of *Batman and Robin* (1949) and *Atom Man vs. Superman* (1950; as Atom Man). Turning to television, Talbot appeared in over 100 different programs, including an 11-year stint on the "Ozzie and Harriet Show" and lengthy runs on such series as "Burns and Allen" and "The Lucy Show." Talbot's eldest son, Stephen, followed in his father's acting footsteps at age eight, appearing regularly on television's "Leave It to Beaver" (as Beaver's friend, Gilbert Bates). (Lyle himself guest-starred in two episodes.)

Though an actor of some fame, Irving Pichel is best known for working behind the camera.

Pichel directed or co-directed over three

dozen features, including *The Most Dangerous Game* (1932; co-director), *She* (1935; co-director), and George Pal's landmark science fiction film, *Destination Moon* (1950). By 1940, Pichel had stopped acting completely and concentrated entirely on directing.

Heroine Jacqueline Wells (born Jacqueline Brown) was the leading lady in one other horror film of the Golden Age — the 1934 Karloff/Lugosi vehicle *The Black Cat*. Descending from the moody brilliance of *The Black Cat* to the dull melodrama of *Torture Ship* was rather indicative of her flagging career, and so it came as no surprise that in 1941 Ms. Wells changed her name to Julie Bishop and began her career anew at Warner Bros.

A former Miss California, beautiful, blonde-haired Sheila Bromley entered films quite late (for an ingenue, anyway) at age 26. Between 1937 and 1942, she appeared in over two dozen (generally bad) motion pictures (though one of her first assignments was in Warner Bros.' entertaining B-picture, *West of Shanghai*, with Boris Karloff). Realizing her movie career was going nowhere, she left Hollywood for the stage. After a decade in the theater, Ms. Bromley returned to films as a character actress and later worked in television, where she appeared fairly regularly in dramas such as "Adam-12." Over her long and varied acting career, Sheila Bromley has employed several different stage names, including Sheila Manners, Sheila Mannors, and Sheila Fulton.

The Catholic Legion of Decency placed *Torture Ship* in their dire "B" category ("objectionable in part for all"). Their complaint: "A scientist acting on the false principle 'end justifies the means' operates on criminals without authorization and without their consent."

NOTES

1. *The Hollywood Reporter* announced that Rex Hale was originally to have directed *Torture Ship*. Whether Hale (whose negligible directing career was even less distinguished than Halperin's) would have done any better is questionable — though it's difficult to imagine anybody doing *worse*.

TOWER OF LONDON
(1939; Universal)

Date of Release: November 16, 1939
Running Time: 92 minutes
Director/Producer: Rowland V. Lee
Screenplay: Robert N. Lee
Photography: George Robinson
Art Director: Jack Otterson
Associate: Richard H. Riedel
Set Decorations: R. A. Gausman
Editor: Edward Curtiss
Musical Director: Charles Previn
Orchestrations: Frank Skinner
Sound Supervisor: Bernard B. Brown
Technician: William Hedgcock
Gowns: Vera West
Assistant Director: Fred Frank
Technical Advisors: Major G.O.T. Bagley and Sir Gerald Grove, Bart.

Cast: Basil Rathbone (Richard, Duke of Gloucester), Boris Karloff (Mord), Barbara O'Neil (Queen Elyzabeth), Ian Hunter (King Edward IV), Vincent Price (Duke of Clarence), Nan Grey (Lady Alice Barton), Ernest Cossart (Tom Clink), John Sutton (John Wyatt), Leo G. Carroll (Lord Hastings), Miles Mander (King Henry VI), Lionel Belmore (Beacon), Rose Hobart (Anne Neville), Ronald Sinclair (Boy King Edward), John Herbert-Bond (Young Prince Richard), Ralph Forbes (Henry Tudor), Frances Robinson (Duchess Isobel), G. P. Huntley (Prince of Wales), John Rodion (Lord DeVere), Walter Tetley (Chimney Sweep), Donnie Dunagan (Baby prince).

"I've never killed in *hot* blood. It must be different, more — more exciting!" — Mord the executioner.

Boris Karloff demonstrates his professional technique to co-stars Basil Rathbone and John Rodion (Rathbone's real-life son) during a break in filming *Tower of London* (1939). (Courtesy of Ted Okuda.)

SYNOPSIS

"No age is without its ruthless men," begins *Tower of London*'s written prologue, "who, in their search for power, leave dark stains upon the pages of history. During the Middle Ages, to seize the Tower of London was to seize the throne of England. In 1471 this has been done by Edward IV—who has violently deposed the feeble Henry VI and holds him prisoner. Within the deep shadows of the Tower walls lives the population of a small city—some in prison cells and torture chambers—some in palaces and spacious lodgings—but none in peace. A web of intrigue veils the lives of all who know only too well that today's friends might be tomorrow's enemies..."

In the Tower courtyard, Lord DeVere, betrayed by Richard (King Edward's favorite brother), is executed for supporting the deposed King Henry. John Wyatt, DeVere's cousin (and also cousin to the queen), stands at the condemned man's side, raising the ire of Richard.

That evening, Richard opens a locked cabinet to reveal a set of tiny figures arranged around a miniature throne. "I have plans for you all, my little ones," he intones, touching them each in turn. "Paper crown Henry, Wales—you robbed me of the only woman I ever loved, my nephews, brother Clarence, myself. I will not always be sixth in succession to the throne."

John Wyatt seeks King Edward's permission to marry Lady Alice Barton, the queen's handmaiden. On Richard's suggestion, however, Edward orders Wyatt into an arranged marriage to obtain a favorable financial alliance and "bring the Norfolk tribe into the fold." When Wyatt refuses, Edward banishes him to France, where Wyatt seeks refuge with the exiled Henry Tudor, a strong contender for the crown.

Meanwhile, the Prince of Wales (son of the ousted King Henry) lands in England with a large force. Richard instructs his henchman, Mord the executioner and chief torturer, to have his pack of beggars "play on the temper of the people" and "spread the word that King Henry has renounced all claims to the throne and is supporting King Edward" (thus squelching any lingering support for the old king). Richard tricks the feeble-minded Henry into accompanying them to the battle of Tewksbury in hopes he'll be struck down—by his own son's men. Though Edward and Richard's forces win the day and Richard slays his rival,

Wales, Henry survives and returns to triumphant cheers. Richard rectifies the situation, however, by ordering Mord to murder the old king.

With Wales dead, Richard then schemes with Edward to put on a show of protection in order to convince Wales' widow, Anne Neville ("The only woman I ever loved," Richard claims) to marry him — her husband's killer. Richard next goads his wine-loving weaker brother Clarence into plotting against Edward. Then, with Mord's help, Richard drowns Clarence in a vat of wine. Now, only Edward and his two young sons block Richard's path to the crown.

Years pass and Edward lies dying. On his deathbed, he pardons John Wyatt, allowing him to return from exile. He also appoints Richard guardian and protector of his two under-age sons — despite objections from the queen (who always feared Richard). Soon, using Mord's rumor-mill, Richard generates mob sentiment espousing "Richard for King!"

When John Wyatt returns from France, the queen (in sanctuary at Westminster Abbey) entreats his help. "Richard's plans must be blocked," she tells him. "He's assumed power over both my sons, and with the exception of Lord Hastings, he has the entire council in the palm of his hand." Wyatt answers that Tudor has laid plans to raise an army but lacks the funds. "John," says the queen, "you must steal the treasure from the Tower. In the hands of Henry Tudor it will serve as a weapon strong enough to overcome even Richard." Wyatt does just that, by employing a group of sailors to tunnel into the vaults. Richard, however, learns who was behind the theft and arrests Wyatt, turning him over to Mord for torture. Despite the brutal torments, Wyatt refuses to divulge the treasure's whereabouts until Alice, aided by a sympathetic chimney sweep, sneaks into the Tower and engineers her beloved's escape.

Richard is incensed. "The queen and Tudor have been hand in glove, with Wyatt as go-between. That woman has stopped me at every turn! She's in sanctuary where I can't touch her — but I can crush her spirit for all time. Take the young princes to the bloody Tower," he orders Mord. Employing three hired thugs, Mord murders the boy-king and his brother.

Now Richard finally sits upon the throne, but his hold is uncertain. "Henry Tudor himself means nothing," he tells Mord, "but the combination of Tudor and royal treasure means *war*." The executioner begs Richard to take him into battle and Richard agrees. "I may need every friend I have," he says ominously. Tudor lands his forces and the two armies meet at Bosworth field. During the battle Richard and Tudor come face to face, and after a furious sword fight, Tudor runs Richard through. Seeing this, Mord tries to flee, but Wyatt spots his misshapen enemy and gives chase, killing the chief torturer and sending his body crashing over a cliff. Henry Tudor then assumes the throne and Wyatt and Alice finally marry.

MEMORABLE MOMENT

Tower of London opens with a macabre bang that sets the tone for the gruesome story to follow. It begins with a close shot of Mord sharpening his huge headsman's ax on a stone grinding wheel, a black raven perched malevolently on his shoulder. As Mord concentrates on his work, a vein across his forehead stands out grotesquely against his bald pate. The camera then slides back to show a scruffy man standing next to Mord's elevated platform, working hard to turn the huge lever that spins the grinding wheel. As Mord, satisfied with the razor-sharpness of his executioner's friend, gets up and strides through the stone-walled torture chamber, the camera tracks with him. Though his gait is purposeful, Mord pauses long enough to lift up and add another heavy weight onto a board under which lies a suffering victim. The torturer's diligence is rewarded with an agonized, breathless groan as the air is pressed further out of the unfortunate's lungs. Moving on, Mord pauses again, this time to lift a ladle of cool water to his lips while a chained man, tortured by thirst, strains and pleads. Mord then throws the ladleful onto the ground next to the pitiable figure, sending the victim to his hands and knees in a pathetic attempt to lap up the moisture from the dirty flagstones. Like some demonic master craftsman, Mord moves through his shop tending to an item of business here and there — only Mord's craft is pain and his "shop" the torture chamber.

ASSETS

An historical melodrama with horror trappings, *Tower of London* has been included in the genre more from tradition than actuality. Since it's a Universal film starring Basil Rathbone and Boris Karloff, and because it sports a plethora of tortures and murders, *Tower of London* has fallen by default into the horror realm. Much more than your average chiller, however; it's one of the best historical dramas of the age. Superb acting, grand spectacle (as well as some chilling, intimate moments of horror), precise photography, a classic storyline, and deft direction make *Tower of London* one of the most impressively mounted productions from the Golden Age of Horror.

Almost immediately, the viewer is whisked inside Jack Otterson's magnificent castle sets, whose authenticity is only matched by their size and grandeur. Immense walls and towers rise 75 feet above the castle courtyard while the spacious yet forbidding interiors are made even more ominous by the huge stone fireplaces, stone-block walls, mammoth pillars, and massive wooden doors. Otterson even built an authentic replica of the watery Traitor's Gate which leads to the Thames, an imposing structure which opens and closes like the mouth of a great beast to devour the characters.

Robert N. Lee's excellent screenplay is full of well-drawn, contrasting characterizations, the most notable being the strong King Edward (ebulliently played by Ian Hunter) and his cunning brother, Richard. Edward is a hearty, guileless, even good-humored man, whose misdeeds arise not from malice or forethought, but from the weight of leadership and the willingness to take the most expedient route. With an engaging impishness, he plays along with Richard's ploys, failing to see his sibling's darker motivations. Richard, however, schemes and plots to achieve his ends, drawing his brother in when necessary but never revealing to anyone but himself his true intent. One truly likes Edward, and wishes that he had a more noble advisor than Richard. Though Richard is definitely the villain of the piece (with Mord as a physical extension of his antagonism), he is not thoroughly evil. He exhibits genuine love for Ann Neville, and while we abhor his vile deeds (including his callous manipulation to win back his one love), we also admire his cunning and even feel a pang of pity for this brilliant but misguided man.

Lee peppers his script with some wonderful, incisive dialogue, such as when Mr. Clink, the local chimney sweep tries to shield his young apprentice from the sight of an execution:

> Apprentice: "Please Mr. Clink, please wait. I wants to see the 'ead fall in the basket."
> Clink: "A body would think your 'eart was as black as yer face. People thinks now us sweeps is black all through instead of black all over."
> Apprentice: "It won't make me no cleaner to miss the fun."
> Clink: "I says you can't see it! Better have a black face than be worryin' about black deeds."

Later, when John Wyatt refuses to abide by an arranged marriage, King Edward angrily pronounces, "You've made a choice between head and heart, but I assure you your heart will not be worth much once your head falls!"

Little fault can be found with Rowland V. Lee's grand direction. Though creating a lavish spectacle filled with costume extras, Lee does not neglect any attention to detail. As the herald mounts the execution platform, for instance, the man casually reaches out to the body-sized wicker basket lying on the stage's corner to flip open the lid, readying the container for its imminent use. With a small but forbidding gesture, Lee adds a subtle shudder to the somber scene.

Working with cinematographer George Robinson, Lee frames his shots carefully. When we see Richard and Mord together for the first time, Mord kneels before his seated master and the camera frames them together with a lit candelabra in the background to form a circular composition — Mord's head and shoulders on the lower left, the candelabra at the top, Richard's head and upper body on the right, his arm extending left across the bottom of the frame to keep the viewer's eyes moving in a circular pattern from one man to the next, tying the two together. The candles hovering above them are like the living flame of their unholy bond.

Lee handles the various murders beautifully, showing little while capturing much. Just as old King Henry leaves Richard and passes through the doorway to the chapel, a shadow moves into the frame while the music takes an ominous turn. The camera then swings left to reveal Mord standing near Richard, his countenance grim. Taking the dagger from his belt, Richard hands it to the executioner who disappears through the doorway into the chapel. Through careful staging, Lee brilliantly wrings every ominous ounce from the moment.

Spanish herald for *Tower of London* (1939). (Courtesy of Lynn Naron.)

Tower of London sports more than its fair share of thrilling battle sequences, all wind and rain and clashing swords. Lee utilizes a montage of images — men swarming over the hill, knights battling hip-deep through a muddy stream — appearing one after the other to create a sense of chaotic urgency, heightened by the driving rain and sounds of trumpets mixed with the clang of metal and the screams of dying men.

Basil Rathbone gives another vibrant performance to bring the character of Richard to full malevolent life. Rathbone's steely gaze and black eyes are like the stare of a snake. In the early execution scene, his gaze never wavers as the headsman's ax falls, though his eyes seem to glitter evilly and flicker with excitement while a barely detectable half-smirk deepens on his cold countenance.

Though for the most part a forbidding figure, Karloff gives Mord a soul nonetheless. With gestures and hesitations at the murder of the young boy king and his brother, for instance, Karloff imbues his character with some small sympathy. When Mord picks up the young prince fallen asleep at his devotions, the sleeping child's arm trustingly goes around the executioner's neck. At this, Karloff's face softens slightly and one can almost see the compassion struggling behind his eyes — before he again sets his face grimly and forcibly hardens his heart.

For a brief moment, Karloff shows the man beneath the brute, adding a key dimension to his despicable character. The final death scene becomes that much more horrific, for we're aware of the hesitation behind it. Director Rowland V. Lee brings this out fully when he has the three thugs, backed by Mord himself, hesitate at the threshold as if afraid of what they must do, before they suddenly rush forward at Mord's forceful command of "Go!," closing violently on the children while we hear their high-pitched screams and cries.

Jack Pierce's clever makeup beautifully accentuates the characters' traits. Mord's bald head and bushy eyebrows make him a medieval Neanderthal, the muscle behind his master's brain.

Rathbone's black hair is cut straight across his forehead and diagonally across his ears so that they appear sharp and pointed — like a devil's ears.

LIABILITIES

After King Edward dies, the film's pace slows considerably as the story focuses on the worrying queen and the romance between Alice and Wyatt. Compared to the sequences involving the intrigues of Richard and Mord, this stretch feels dull and slow. Fortunately, this lull does not last long and we're soon back among Mord's torture chamber and Richard's battlefields.

The entire *Tower of London* principal cast performs admirably, with one exception — John Sutton as Wyatt. As the romantic male lead, he's pleasant enough to look at but seems vacuous and uninteresting, his tone and expression rarely changing. His eyes remain dull and lifeless. He certainly exhibits none of the fiery passion necessary to accomplish his character's heroic deeds, opting instead for a flat stoicism. His through-the-motions performance is unworthy of such a superior production.

Finally, Richard's group of dolls which represent those that stand in the way of his ascension to the Crown is an unnecessary, banal device.

Should one believe that such a cunning Machiavellian as Richard would needlessly possess such damning evidence — or that he just cannot *remember* who and how many he needs to murder and so needs this visual aid? Beyond that, it tends to make Rathbone look a bit silly as he spends far too much time (in too many scenes) manipulating his dolls. This childish bit of visual expediency is out of place in an otherwise effective picture.

Despite these minor detractors, *Tower of London* remains a grand historical epic with enough blood and thunder to please most genre fans.

REVIEWS

Variety (November 22, 1939) observed that, "As a horror picture, [*Tower of London* is] one of the most broadly etched, but still so strong that it may provide disturbing nightmares as aftermath.... Script provides a more than passable interest in the court pageantry and continual intrigue of the period, neatly dovetailing with display of the various instruments of torture in vogue at the time.... Reminiscence of the Frankenstein series is present here, with Karloff a clubfooted and misshapen giant who is chief executioner and torturer for the conniving Basil Rathbone.

Britain's *Kinematograph Weekly* (February 22, 1940) noted that *Tower of London* "commends itself to the masses as a colorful, hair-raising entertainment. Authentic crime is robustly catalogued and there is also ample evidence of the torture, refined and otherwise, of the period, wholesale executions, spectacular escapes, exuberant hand-to-hand conflict, and battles on a big scale, to prevent any flagging of interest."

The *New York Times'* (December 12, 1939) reviewer, Frank S. Nugent, was unimpressed with this "gory business of wading through slaughter to a throne," calling the picture "less than stunning as pageantry, less than thrilling as drama and less than satisfactory as entertainment," adding "it is more than rich in murder and all the sinister appurtenances thereof."

While the reviewer obviously did not approve of Boris Karloff, he inadvertently pays the actor a great backhanded compliment: "Karloff is the man who robs it of dignity, of course. Karloff can't be taken seriously — else he would drive one insane of fright." (Perhaps Karloff is a bit too effective at his job for the timid Mr. Nugent?)

PRODUCTION NOTES

Problems plagued the *Tower of London* production, which finally wrapped ten days over its 36-day shooting schedule and nearly $80,000 over its already hefty $500,000 budget.

For example, director Rowland V. Lee had great difficulty in shooting the battle scenes. Three hundred extras were there ready for battle only to have their cardboard helmets and shields disintegrate when the rain machines were turned on. Lee finally overcame these obstacles by shooting small bands of men fighting and transposing them against a background of battle scenes already shot to create a montage effect.

The picture originally possessed a unique musical score consisting of authentic fifteenth-century English compositions. After preview screenings in early November, however, the studio brass demanded a more conventional score. Under severe time constraints, Charles Previn and Frank Skinner had to crib selections from Skinner's earlier *Son of Frankenstein* music (which, admittedly, fit the bill nicely).

Vincent Price, in one of his first substantial roles (as Clarence), had great respect for his two horror costars. "Boris was a great professional," Price told interviewer Gregory J. M. Catsos in *Filmfax* (#42), "I was very fond of him. He was a man who loved his work and knew exactly what he was doing. Off the set, he was a very funny man." Basil Rathbone "was an intelligent person and a brilliant actor."

In a letter to Cynthia Lindsay (a close friend of the Karloffs), published in her book *Dear Boris*, Vincent Price wrote a tribute "to one of the few (very select) of my Hollywood life I'd even care to mention. Boris came into it early on — my second or third film, *Tower of London*, and he and Basil Rathbone introduced me to a kind of joyousness of picture-making I too seldom encountered in the hundred films that came later."

This "joyousness" frequently ran to the form of practical jokes. Price (the newcomer among the three) related one particular incident in *Basil Rathbone: His Life and His Films*, by Michael B. Druxman: "It was the scene where Basil and Boris drown me in the vat of wine. Being young and foolish, I insisted on going into the vat myself. The stunt co-ordinator instructed me to grab onto a bar at the bottom of the vat, count ten, then come up for air. The ten count would allow Basil to finish the take and, also, give the crew enough time to reopen the lid of the vat. Anyway, while I was down at the bottom of that tank ... holding onto the bar and counting ... I heard the crew breaking into the vat with axes. It seems that my friends, Boris and Basil, had sat on top of the lid and the thing was stuck. Luckily for me, they got it open before I was in any serious danger."

Price went on to speak of his other co-star: "The crew on that picture loved Basil. There was one grip, who would always be making good-natured insults about England. Basil would feign anger and chase the man up into the catwalks."

Rathbone, who was forced to decline a principal role in RKO's upcoming remake of *The Hunchback of Notre Dame* due to his Universal commitments, had to divide his time between two productions during the first week of filming *Tower of London* since he also played a lead role in *Rio* which had not quite finished shooting.

At the film's beginning, actor John Rodion falls under the blade of Mord's ax, providing top-billed Basil Rathbone with the dubious pleasure of watching the execution of his own offspring — John Rodion is Rathbone's real-life son.

Director Rowland V. Lee took his job very seriously. "Every time a director looks through his camera lens," theorized Lee in a studio publicity piece, "he is looking directly into the eyes of millions upon millions of people all over the world.... The vast audience is countless times greater than all the persons who saw and heard Moses, Buddha, Jesus, Mohammed and all other prophets combined. What a privilege! What an obligation!"

Lee began his career as an actor in stock companies and on Broadway. At one point he gave up acting to become a stock broker on Wall Street, but after two years returned to the stage.

In 1915 he entered films, acting for the Thomas Ince Company. After serving in World War I, he returned to Ince where he became a director in 1920. In addition to *Tower of London*, Lee heralded the revival of Hollywood horror by directing *Son of Frankenstein* earlier the same year.

Rowland V. Lee hired his own brother, screenwriter Robert N. Lee, to pen *Tower of London*'s screenplay.

Working for most of the majors over the course of his lengthy career, Robert N. Lee contributed to such classics as *Little Caesar* (1930) and *Captain Kidd* (1945; also directed by brother Rowland).

George Robinson was Universal's busiest cinematographer. Among his 150 films (nearly all of them for Universal) are a number of genre entries: *Dracula's Daughter* (1936), *Son of Frankenstein* (1939), *Tower of London* (1939), *The Mummy's Tomb* (1942), *Frankenstein Meets the Wolf Man* (1943), *Captive Wild Woman* (1943), *Son of Dracula* (1943), *House of Frankenstein* (1944), *House of Dracula* (1945), *The Cat Creeps* (1946), *The Creeper* (1948), *Abbott and Costello Meet the Invisible Man* (1951), *...Meet Dr. Jekyll and Mr. Hyde* (1953), *...Meet the Mummy* (1955), and *Tarantula* (1955).

Beautiful, stately Broadway actress Barbara O'Neil entered films in 1937 and achieved her greatest fame playing Scarlett O'Hara's mother in *Gone with the Wind* (the same year she appeared as Queen Elyzabeth in *Tower of London*). In 1940 she received an Academy Award nomination for Best Supporting Actress in *All This and Heaven Too*.

South African-born Ian Hunter had played a king the previous year in *The Adventures of Robin Hood* (as King Richard the Lionhearted)[1] before donning the crown once again as King Edward IV in *Tower of London*. Hunter appeared in one other horror film over his 100-picture career, the 1941 version of *Dr. Jekyll and Mr. Hyde* (as Lanyon).

Roger Corman remade *Tower of London* in 1962, but filmed his version as a small-scale ghost story rather than an historical horror epic.

Ironically, Vincent Price, who played the supporting role of the Duke of Clarence in the original, graduated to the role of Richard himself in Corman's low-budget remake.

NOTES
1. Ian Hunter named one of his two sons "Robin." Coincidence?

THE DARK EYES OF LONDON
(1939; Pathé/Monogram; Great Britain)

Alternate Title: *The Human Monster* (American)
Release Date: November, 1939 (British); March 2, 1940 (American)
Running Time: 75 minutes
Director: Walter Summers
Producer: John Argyle
Screenplay: Patrick Kirwan, Walter Summers, John Argyle (adapted from the novel by Edgar Wallace)
Additional Dialogue: Jan Van Lustil
Photography: Bryan Langley
Camera: Ronald Anscombe

Music Composed and Arranged by: Guy Jones
Organ Music: C. King Palmer
Production Manager: H. G. Inglis
Production Assistant: George Collins
Recording Supervisor: H. Benson
Sound Recording: A. E. Rudolph
Film Editor: E. G. Richards
Art Director: Duncan Sutherland
Assistant Director: Jack Martin

(*The producers gratefully acknowledge the co-operation of the National Institute of the Blind*)
Cast: Bela Lugosi (Dr. Orloff), Hugh Williams (Inspector Holt), Greta Gynt (Diana Stewart), Edmon Ryan (Lieutenant O'Reilly), Wilfred Walter (Jake), Alexander Field (Grogan), *Julie Suedo (Secretary), *Arthur E. Owen (Dumb Lou), *Gerald Pring (Henry Stewart), *Charles Penrose (Drunk).

*credit not appearing on American prints.

> "I wanted to devote my life to the healing of mankind. I wanted to be a doctor. But they got together, those narrow-minded, prejudiced medical men, to see how they could *ruin* me. Brilliant but unbalanced—that was their verdict." — Dr. Orloff.

SYNOPSIS

A body, floating in the Thames River, washes ashore. In the Criminal Investigation Department of Scotland Yard, the chief berates his men: "Five insured persons have been found drowned in the last eight months and not one of you has brought in a scrap of evidence as to who benefited, though all the claims, heavily underwritten, have been met." Inspector Holt is given the assignment of checking out an insurance company run by a certain Dr. Orloff.

At Orloff's office, Mr. Stewart borrows money from the doctor. Orloff, a philanthropist at heart, tells Stewart of his charity work: "I wanted to be a doctor but ... Brilliant but unbalanced—that was their verdict. And so I serve the blind. In Greenwich, Mr. Dearborn, himself blind, runs a home for blind vagrants." Orloff urges Stewart to go and visit the institute, which Orloff supports and there "learn the joy of giving charity."

When Inspector Holt arrives at Orloff's office, he learns that two of the five deaths under investigation involved Orloff's insurance business. After the inspector leaves, Orloff types out a message in Braille and tosses it out the window to a blind violinist playing on the sidewalk below. The blind messenger takes the note to Dearborn's Home for the Destitute Blind, where the white-haired, soft-spoken Mr. Dearborn reads the Bible (a Braille Bible, of course) to his many charges. Among them is Dearborn's deformed assistant, an ugly, hulking brute named Jake, who is also blind.

Later, Stewart makes his promised visit to Dearborn's institute and is greeted by Dr. Orloff himself; Dearborn is out. Lou, the blind (and mute) violinist seen earlier, drops a note—unseen—into Stewart's pocket. Orloff shows Stewart upstairs, where Jake is waiting to murder the man!

Meanwhile, a Chicago detective, Lieutenant O'Reilly delivers to Scotland Yard an English crook and forger named Grogan. Inspector Holt suspects that Grogan has some connection with Orloff.

O'Reilly is assigned to work with Holt on the case in order to "learn something of our antiquated methods" (as Holt's sour superior puts it).

Stewart's body is found floating in the river, just like all the others, and Holt discovers a note in the dead man's pocket—a note in Braille. The lab report later reveals that the water in Stewart's stomach was ordinary tap water and not river water from the muddy Thames. "Stewart wasn't drowned in the Thames," reasons the inspector. "He was drowned somewhere else and dumped there afterwards." In short, it was not suicide or an accident, but murder.

Grogan is bailed out by Orloff, who then forces the crook to forge Stewart's signature on an insurance policy naming Orloff as the beneficiary. Inspector Holt returns to Orloff's office with more questions. Orloff explains that

Stewart was experiencing financial difficulties and Orloff had lent him some money. When the inspector learns that Stewart had a life insurance policy with Orloff's company, he asks if Stewart's daughter was the beneficiary. "I'm the beneficiary," replies Orloff. "You see, Stewart made over the policy to me when he couldn't meet the premiums, in return for the loan of 2,000 pounds."

Orloff sends Jake out to murder Grogan, in order to make sure the forger will not talk. He then contacts Stewart's daughter, Diana, who had recently returned to England. The doctor, claiming to be a concerned benefactor, arranges for the girl to take a job with Mr. Dearborn as his secretary. Inspector Holt learns of this new development and forms a plan with Diana, who desperately wants to solve her father's murder. "Somewhere between Orloff's office and the Dearborn place is the answer," Holt tells her. "That's all I know. Now, you go there, keep your eyes open, and keep in touch with me. I'll never be far away from you."

Back at the institute, Orloff learns of Lou's treacherous note and straps the unfortunate to a cot in the upstairs hospital room. Holding him up to a weird machine, Orloff tells him, "You have been very foolish, Lou. You have been writing on little bits of paper. The police have been here. They might come back, Lou, they might ask you questions. You're blind and you can't speak, but you can hear — and that will *never* do!" As he finishes speaking, Orloff places a sinister electrical device over Lou's ears and the man screams.

Down in Dearborn's office, Diana has run across a check from her father, a donation to Dearborn's institute. With it is a note stating that Orloff is arranging for him to come for a visit — on the evening he was murdered. Orloff enters the office and sees Diana with the incriminating note, but says nothing. Moments later, Orloff sends Jake to silence her.

Back at the Yard, the inspector has now figured it all out and relates his deductions to O'Reilly. "[Orloff] runs an insurance company," begins Holt. "He takes out bogus policies, forges the signatures of carefully selected people and lays off the sum to the underwriters. He waits a reasonable time in paying the premium and everything is above board..." "Then neatly bumps them off," interjects the fascinated O'Reilly. "[He] collects the money from the underwriters," continues Holt, "and makes a fictitious entry in his books saying the money has been paid out to people that don't exist!"

Diana places a call to Holt from her flat, just as Jake breaks in. The two investigators, hearing her screams over the phone, rush to the house and scare Jake off before the deed can be done.

Scotland Yard puts out a warrant for Orloff's arrest, but somehow the murderer manages to elude this "nation-wide search." Holt and O'Reilly visit Dearborn to question him about Orloff. The inspector tells the incredulous Dearborn (who claims that Orloff was the "kindest man I'd ever met") that "[Orloff] used you. He gave money to your institute in order to get the blind men here as dupes." Holt also wants to question Lou but finds he cannot get through to the ailing man, who is now deaf as well as blind and dumb. The inspector has a solution, though, and he instructs Dearborn: "I want the man to answer some questions. If the poor devil can't see, hear, or speak, he can still feel. So if you have these [questions] transcribed into Braille he can write down the answers."

Shortly thereafter, Diana (who had gone back to work at Dearborn's on the off-chance of learning something more) discovers a cufflink in a cupboard in Dearborn's office. "This cufflink belonged to my father," she tells Dearborn, "how did it get into *this* house?" The blind man replies, "I don't recall ever seeing this before," and *looks down* at the object in her hand. "You're no more blind than I am!" declares Diana. "You're a fake, and you're shielding the man who killed my father." But Diana is wrong. Dearborn is not shielding the murderer, for he IS the murderer. Dearborn removes his dark glasses and wig and drops his disguised voice to reveal — Dr. Orloff!

Orloff ties Diana up and forces her to watch as he drowns Lou in a tub of water

The monstrous Jake (Wilfred Walter) is about to carry out Dr. Orloff's orders to drown heroine Diana Stewart (Greta Gynt) in Britain's *The Dark Eyes of London* (1939). Note the lobby card bears the picture's American release title.

(insuring that he cannot even "write down the answers") and then dumps his body out the window into the Thames. Orloff summons Jake and orders him to eliminate Diana and "this time make no mistake." Diana, desperately kicking and screaming as Jake is about to immerse her, frantically asks, "Where's Lou, Jake? He's gone, Jake. Orloff got rid of him, like he got rid of all the others." The ploy works, and Jake, who had genuinely loved the blind violinist, goes on a rampage. Orloff enters and Jake moves to attack him, but Orloff shoots his former henchman. "I will have to settle with you myself," he tells Diana. Before he has a chance to "settle" with her, however, the police arrive and Holt breaks into the institute. Orloff mixes a few chemicals and sets up a smokescreen downstairs. Bolting up the stairs to the "hospital," he locks the door and starts to climb to the roof. Jake is not quite dead, however, and he grabs Orloff's leg. Staggering to his feet, the mortally wounded giant struggles with Orloff and finally pushes him out the window—to be sucked into the mud flats of the river below. Holt arrives, Diana is freed, and O'Reilly goes home, telling the embracing couple to "put me down for a couple of bucks for a wedding present."

MEMORABLE MOMENTS

A startling moment occurs when Dr. Orloff shows Mr. Stewart around Dearborn's institute. Beaming out his beneficence, the doctor leads Stewart up the wooden stairs to their "little hospital." Smiling benignly, Orloff opens the door and they step in, with the camera remaining outside and shooting through the door. Stewart suddenly stops. Then as he turns to look at Orloff in confusion, we see past him to the hulking figure of Jake, a straitjacket raised in his hands, advancing menacingly toward Stewart. As both Stewart and the audience sense danger, the man turns to flee, but a quick move from Orloff causes the door to slam shut in his face (and ours). Looking at the now-closed door, we hear Stewart's terrified scream. This scene makes good use of surprise, catching the viewer off-guard by Lugosi's easy, smiling manner, and by having the menace initially hidden by the bodies of the two men as they open the door. Then the sudden slamming of the door, shutting us off from the horror within, coupled with the awful single scream, lets our imaginations do the rest.

The sequence in which Diana is attacked by Jake in her apartment is the picture's most effective set-piece. While Diana talks on the phone, the door opens behind her. At the same moment, the lights go out. She turns to see a dim, hulking figure, and screams. Jake, growling, lunges for her in the dark. Desperately trying to elude his outstretched arms, Diana makes it into the bedroom and locks the door. She turns on the lights with a sigh of relief, but her relief is short-lived as the homicidal madman beats and tears at the door with animalistic fury until it finally bursts opens. He swipes at the light switch and plunges the room into terrifying darkness. Backing toward the wall, Diana frantically grabs a lamp and turns it on, holding it in front of her in a pitiful attempt to ward off the monstrous brute. Jake stumbles into it and grabs the lamp. Almost absentmindedly, he rips off the shade and grasps the bare bulb, screaming in pain when his hand touches the hot object. Venting his sudden fury, Jake crushes the bulb in his hand and grabs Diana's throat, meaning to crush it too. At that instant Inspector Holt rings the doorbell and Diana is saved.

Throughout this sequence, Diana's terror is intertwined with the darkness itself. She is terrified when the lights go out and temporarily relieved when she escapes to the light of the bedroom lamp. Terror again surges when the lamp is violently extinguished and darkness (death) closes in. The fact that Diana's brutish attacker is blind, familiar with a world of perpetual darkness, only underscores the terror of the situation. Darkness is made out to be a frightening thing, full of violence and horror, thus effectively evoking (and exploiting) the viewer's own primal fear of the dark and ultimately intensifying the horrific mood of the scene.

ASSETS

For what is essentially a crime-drama decorated with horror trappings (it IS a Lugosi vehicle after all, and so the producers felt it MUST be a horror picture), *The Dark Eyes of London* possesses some nice macabre touches. The tone is set in the opening credits, which begin with a shot of London Bridge and the Thames. Suddenly, Lugosi's unmistakable eyes are superimposed over the image and zoom towards us out of the foggy background. Perhaps director Walter Summers had seen *White Zombie* (1932) and felt that if the actor's trademark stare was good enough for that film, it was good enough for his picture. In any event it makes for a promising introduction. Following this, the pledge of macabre thrills is extended further with the startling sight of a body floating face up near a pier. In a series of quick cuts we follow the bloated corpse as it drifts out into the open water and finally washes up along the shoreline in a crumpled heap. Yes indeed, Summers wastes no time in getting to the chills and this whets our appetite for the gruesome doings to come. Unfortunately, because this film IS structured like a crime-thriller, we must labor through long stretches of detective work before any other shivers are forthcoming.

Summers, with the invaluable aid of cinematographer Bryan Langley, makes sure things move briskly, even through the less-active stretches. The fluid camera movements and varied set-ups draw the viewer into even the more mundane expository scenes. The camera is never left stationary for long — it moves almost constantly, though not to the point of intrusion. This roving eye not only looks from side to side, following a character across a room, but it also moves forwards or backwards at the same time, tightening or opening up the frame as desired. This adds a depth to the visuals which a simple linear, left-to-right motion lacks. Nor is all this movement without purpose. Summers utilizes these techniques to introduce or include characters in a shot. Instead of simply cutting from one character to another as they talk, for instance, the camera will pull back to reveal the second speaker, or follow the movement of one as he approaches another until they both stand within the frame.

Summers even utilizes the camera to create shocks, as in the introduction to Jake (the "Human Monster" of the American title). When the doorbell to the institute rings, our vision rests on Dearborn, a mild-looking, white-haired, elderly gentleman sitting peacefully in an overstuffed chair. In a gentle, pleasant-sounding voice, he says, "Answer it, Jake." The camera suddenly moves up and away from Dearborn and over to a large figure standing beside the chair. Then, in one fluid motion, the camera quickly zooms in to a close-up of Jake's hideous countenance. Lit from below, his face is seen in high-contrast with the shadows emphasizing his ugliness. The suddenness of the motion from the harmless-looking Dearborn to the shadowy, ugly Jake transforms a simple introduction into a startling shock. Of course, nothing shocking happens—Jake just answers the door—but this brief, almost inconsequential moment becomes an ominous portent of horrors to come.

Lugosi is excellent. At ease as the quick-thinking Orloff, he speaks glibly and easily with Holt while periodically injecting that patented Lugosi treatment (malevolent stare, odd inflections) to remind the audience of what's in store. His facial expressions and pregnant pauses work wonders. "Find me poor Stewart's number in the phone book," he tells his secretary. "I want to *communicate* with his daughter." Lugosi's odd inflection on "communicate" and his drawn out "dauuughter" invests this simple statement with hidden, sinister meaning. Summers took full advantage of Lugosi's talent for menace: As the actor speaks, the camera moves in ever-so-slowly—almost subliminally—to augment Lugosi's delivery and imbue it with even more malevolent intensity. Later, when Orloff drowns poor Lou, Lugosi's cruel, satisfied smile speaks volumes about the sadistic nature of his character. On the basis of Orloff and Ygor (in *Son of Frankenstein*), it is evident that Lugosi was in fine form during his first year back after a 15-month exile from the screen. This makes it all the more regrettable that *The Dark Eyes of London* was Lugosi's last truly worthy starring vehicle. With few exceptions (*Ghost of Frankenstein*, 1942; *Return of the Vampire*, 1944; and *Abbott and Costello Meet Frankenstein*, 1948), it was leads in poverty-row potboilers or red-herring bits in Major films from here on out.

Shakespearean actor Wilfred Walter (in his third of only six screen appearances) is quite good as Jake, lending pathos to the inarticulate brute by demonstrating a crude love and rough affection in his scenes with Lou. As Karloff had with his Frankenstein monster, Walter transcends the role of murderous brute and makes of this creature a truly human monster (thus validating the film's American title—though undoubtedly not in the sense held by Monogram, the American distributor). The makeup (partially devised by Walter himself) is quite effective, with his overlarge lower teeth exposed, his eyes rolled up in his head to show their whites and to remind us of his blindness, and a crop of short hair. It all adds up to create a rather simian countenance reminiscent of Fredric March's Mr. Hyde.

Hugh Williams, as Inspector Holt, appears capable, intelligent, and self-assured. He is quite likable and possesses a wry sense of humor. His crisp, no-nonsense character is still human enough to evince sympathy for Diana after her father is killed, and British enough to be forever ordering tea.

Greta Gynt gives a very convincing, natural performance as the heroine. For instance, when she is interrupted by Orloff after discovering the incriminating note in Dearborn's office, she hurriedly gathers up her things—panic-stricken and wanting badly to escape, but knowing she mustn't bolt outright. Later, her obvious terror when cornered by Jake and her near-hysterical pleadings as Orloff drowns Lou add a realistic sense of horror to the sadistic deeds.

"You're blind and you can't speak," Dr. Orloff (Bela Lugosi) tells the terrified Lou (Arthur E. Owen), "but you can hear — and that will *never* do!" From *The Dark Eyes of London* (1939). (Courtesy of Lynn Naron.)

LIABILITIES

As mentioned before, *The Dark Eyes of London* is basically a crime-drama dressed up as a horror picture for the benefit of its star. To that end, Lugosi is not only a criminal, but a mad medico possessing ominous-looking apparatus in his upstairs "laboratory." He is given a hulking, deformed brute of an assistant whom he can send out to do his nefarious bidding. These elements aside, the film retains the crime-thriller structure and, as such, the viewer must wade through scene after scene of detectives at work trying to crack the case and discover for themselves what the audience already (at least partially) knows. Although these middle sequences are well done and benefit from sharp pacing and a truly likable lead, the horror-minded viewer will wish for more shudder and less sleuthing. While the film succeeds admirably as a crime drama, it does not quite fulfill its promise in the horror department.

Continuity gaffes arise occasionally as a result of the attempted Orloff/Dearborn deception. Toward the beginning, Orloff writes a message to his henchman, Jake, and tosses it out the window to Lou, the blind violinist waiting below. Lou heads off with his note and Inspector Holt immediately arrives at Orloff's office, where the two converse for several minutes. The next scene shows Lou arriving at Dearborn's Institute with Orloff's message — and Orloff is *already there* in the guise of Dearborn! Now, it's not inconceivable that Orloff could have beaten the blind man to his destination, but it *is* rather unlikely, especially since Orloff has to sneak in, change his clothes, apply a false wig and mustache, and then settle down before the blind messenger arrives. And why send a message through Lou which Orloff could just as easily have given to Jake directly? Of course, we do not know at the time that the two men are one and the same, but in retrospect it becomes something of a cheat to throw the audience off-track.

Since Bela Lugosi's distinctive voice and accent would have immediately given away his identity as the kindly Mr. Dearborn, his voice was dubbed by British actor O. B. Clarence. The lip-synching is quite good. Unfortunately, the effect is betrayed by a technical sound problem. Dearborn's voice has an isolated, hollow ring to it, as if coming from inside a drum (or studio sound room). Also, it is just a bit too loud compared to the other performers.

REVIEWS

Variety (March 27, 1940) was impressed: "'The Human Monster,' patently a British-made picture, is not only reminiscent of 'Frankenstein,' but contains numerous horror scenes no longer permitted under the Haysian code. Additional asset is the presence of Bela Lugosi in a more villainous characterization than he's been in for some time. Film won't disappoint for theatres going in for sheer grotesque chills.... Too much is made of the scenes where the blind are shown at work and the anti-climax is too heavily prolonged after the story apparently is concluded.... Despite these flaws and a tendency to elaborate too much early in the vehicle, director Walter Summers has done surprisingly well to hold suspense.... Lugosi acts with more relish than in recent times on the screen.... Hugh Williams, as the Scotland Yard inspector, and Edmond Ryan ... are competent in the chief supporting roles...."

The New York Times' critic B. R. Crisler (March 25, 1940), however, seemed positively aghast: "Even connoisseurs of the horror film will doubtless be constrained to admit that nothing quite so consistently horrid as 'The Human Monster' ... has ever befallen this hapless city. Brooded over by the batlike spirit of Bela Lugosi, it comes like an evil visitation compared to which the hunchback of Notre Dame (first and second string); the two Doctors Jekyll and Messrs. Hyde, and both King Kong pere and fils are about as intimidating as Ferdinand the Bull." Stuffed-shirt critic Crisler quickly recovered his innate condescension, however, remarking that "all Mr. Lugosi has to do is to look at people and they either get hypnosis or cramps from laughing. Our personal reaction was more hysterical than horrified, but that's a matter of taste."

PRODUCTION NOTES

The Dark Eyes of London was the first English film to receive the British Censor's new "H" rating for "Horror" (which prohibited persons under 16 years of age from seeing the film). The reactionary rating had been created in 1937, largely as a response to the 1935 Lugosi picture, *The Raven*.

When released in America as *The Human Monster*, the Catholic Legion of Decency gave the film a "B" classification ("objectionable in part for all") for "excessive brutality and gruesomeness" and "explicitness in depicting methods of committing crime."

Bela Lugosi's trip to England to work on this production in April of 1939 brought him close to the machinations of Hitler and the war looming upon the horizon. Returning to New York, an impassioned Lugosi told a reporter for *Az Ember* (a New York publication for the Hungarian community): "Seeing all the horrors overseas, we have to stick to this country fanatically. Here we can live in human peace and love while over there countries disappear overnight. After what Adolf Hitler has recently done to the people of Czechoslovakia, I wonder if there is still an American of Hungarian descent who can nurture anything but hate for the Nazis. The lie about liberation has been revealed, and honest people point their fingers at Herr Hitler, the land robber and conqueror of nations."

Norwegian-born Greta Gynt began her stage and film career in England in 1934. She appeared in nearly 50 features (including James Whale's *The Road Back*, 1937) before retiring in 1964. Her one other foray into the cinema of the macabre was opposite George Sanders in *Bluebeard's Ten Honeymoons* (1960).

The Dark Eyes of London was adapted from the book of the same name by prolific English crime novelist Edgar Wallace. Between 1905 and 1930, Wallace wrote 175 novels, 17 plays, and several hundred short stories. It generally took him about nine days to dictate a novel, but on one occasion he managed to complete a book over a single weekend! According to Margaret Lane's *Edgar Wallace: The Biography of a Phenomenon*, Wallace held no illusions as to the lasting literary merit of his works, yet he was determined that he would be remembered for his unusual storylines. His final project was to be the screenplay for *King Kong*. Unfortunately, he died of pneumonia before the production could really get under way. Wallace posthumously received co-story credit on the film.

For its U.S. release, *The Dark Eyes of London* was retitled *The Human Monster*. The picture was later reissued on a double bill with another British horror/mystery, *Chamber of Horrors* (1941), which is also based on an Edgar Wallace story.

In 1961, the film was remade in West Germany as *Die toten Augen von London* (released in the United States as *Dead Eyes of London*). Filmed in Hamburg, with the Elbe standing in for the Thames, this dull, overlong version separates the Orloff and Dearborn characters into two persons (brothers, in fact).

THE RETURN OF DR. X
(1939; Warner Bros.–First National)

Release Date: November 22, 1939
Running Time: 62 minutes
Director: Vincent Sherman
*Associate Producer: Bryan Foy
Screenplay: Lee Katz (based on the story "The Doctor's Secret" by William J. Makin)
Photography: Sid Hickox
Editor: Thomas Pratt
Dialogue Director: John Langan
Art Director: Esdras Hartley
Sound: Charles Lang
Gowns: Milo Anderson
Technical Adviser: Dr. Leo Schulman
*Music: Bernhard Kaun
*Makeup Artist: Perc Westmore
*Assistant Director: Dick Mayberry
*Unit Manager: Louis Baum
Cast: Wayne Morris (Walter Garrett**), Rosemary Lane (Joan Vance), Humphrey Bogart (Caine/Xavier†), Dennis Morgan (Michael Rhodes), John Litel (Dr. Francis Flegg), Lya Lys (Angela Merrova), Huntz Hall (Pinky), Charles Wilson (Detective Ray Kincaid), Vera Lewis (Miss Sweetman), Howard Hickman (Chairman), Olin Howland (Undertaker), Arthur Aylesworth (Guide), Jack Mower§ (Detective Sgt. Moran), Creighton Hale (Hotel Manager), John Ridgely (Rodgers), Joe Crehan (Editor), Glenn Langan (Interne), DeWolfe Hopper‡ (Interne).

*Uncredited on film print.
**Though the onscreen credits list Wayne Morris as playing "Walter Barnett," he is called Walt Garrett in the film (as well as in newspaper headlines).
†Strangely, Bogart's character is listed as "Marshall Quesne" in the credits, though he's always referred to as Caine or Xavier in the film itself.
§Though the onscreen credits list Cliff Saum as Detective Sgt. Moran, studio publicity and reviews credit Jack Mower in the role.
‡Though credited as "DeWolfe" Hopper, this was not the famous matinee idol and silent movie star (who died in 1935) but his son, William DeWolfe Hopper, Jr., who later simply went by the name William Hopper.

"My experiments have turned into madness; I've created a monster." — Dr. Flegg.

SYNOPSIS

Reporter Walt Garrett goes to stage actress Angela Merrova's hotel suite for an interview but finds her stabbed to death, her body drained of blood. When the police arrive some time later, however, the body has disappeared.

The next day, Ms. Merrova turns up at Garrett's newspaper office — very much alive. As a result, his editor fires him. Garrett goes to his friend at the local hospital, a young doctor named Mike Rhodes. Rhodes mentions the incident to hematology specialist Dr. Flegg, but the learned doctor merely suggests that Garrett "change his brand of liquor."

When a professional blood donor, Mr. Rodgers, fails to show up at the hospital for that morning's operation, student nurse Joan Vance (who possesses the same rare "Group 1" blood type as Rodgers) volunteers to donate her hemoglobin. Rhodes and Joan are attracted to one another and make a date for that evening.

After the operation, the police call Rhodes to Rodgers' apartment and Garrett tags along. Rodgers has been murdered — and drained of blood. Rhodes takes a bloodstain sample and finds that it's not Rodgers' blood. Moreover, "it doesn't even look like human blood." Taking his sample to Dr. Flegg at his home, Rhodes encounters Caine, Flegg's assistant. "His interest in blood almost equals my own," remarks Flegg. Caine looks very strange, "like a piece of white marble, like something dead." Garrett observes that Merrova's got "that same cold graveyard look." To Rhodes' surprise, Flegg denies anything unusual about the blood sample.

Garrett and Rhodes go to question Angela Merrova. She agrees to tell them all she knows but Caine arrives, standing in for Dr. Flegg, her regular doctor. Soon after, Merrova is found dead "of natural causes."

Garrett remembers seeing Caine's picture somewhere and sneaks back into his (former) newspaper office to dig back through the files. He discovers that Caine is actually Dr. Maurice Xavier (or "Dr. X") who died in the electric chair two years earlier for a "child slaying" during his experiments. The body was claimed by one Dr. Flegg!

When Rhodes and Garrett go to confront Flegg, he finally admits that "Caine and Dr. Xavier are one and the same." Flegg takes them into his private laboratory and, using a dead rabbit, demonstrates how he brought Xavier back to life. "He was a medical genius and I felt that he had been a martyr to science," explains Flegg. Besides, Flegg needed Xavier "for further research." Flegg continues: "After we've recreated life, the second and greater problem is to sustain it. In order to do that we must be able to give the person a new bloodstream. For six years in that laboratory I've been striving to create a usable, workable synthetic blood." Flegg has not entirely succeeded, however. "It's true that my formula will sustain life for a short period, but, unlike human blood, it fails to recreate itself." Therefore, Caine must have fresh human blood of the Type 1 group to live. Angela Merrova was Type 1 and fell victim to Caine. When Flegg learned of this, he brought the unfortunate woman back to life, but of course could not *keep* her alive. Caine is determined to hang onto his second life as long as possible. "Caine will continue to kill until destroyed," laments Flegg.

Caine/Xavier, who had overheard Flegg's confession, shoots the doctor and makes off with Flegg's list of Type 1 blood donors. Joan's name is on the list. Xavier kidnaps Joan and heads for the site of his earlier experiments/crimes — an abandoned shack out in the woods. Rhodes, Garrett, and the police deduce where Xavier has gone and chase after him. With Joan strapped to a table, Xavier engages in a gun battle with the police. He tries to flee across the rooftop, but is shot by a policeman. Rhodes frees Joan, Xavier dies (this time permanently), and Garrett receives his own daily column from his grateful editor.

MEMORABLE MOMENT

The climax of *The Return of Dr. X* contains a brilliantly staged moment of pure terror as Xavier prepares to add Joan to his list of victims. It opens on a shot of Joan, bound and gagged, strapped to a table inside the old

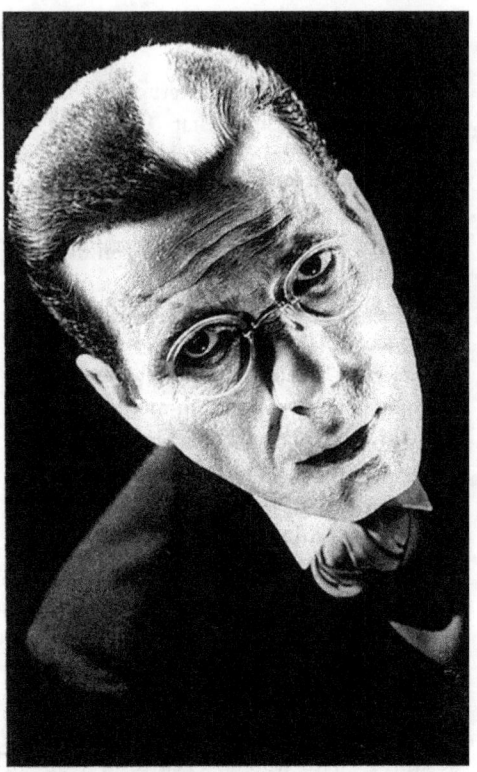

Humphrey Bogart (sporting makeup by Perc Westmore) in his only horror film, *The Return of Dr. X* (1939).

shack. Deep shadows fill the room, which seems to be lit solely from a single oil lamp. Xavier stands over an ancient stove as the flames from within cast a hellish glow over his already ghoulish countenance. Smoke rises up around him to complete the diabolical portrait. He steps over to his captive, whose eyes go wide with fear. The corner of Xavier's mouth turns up in an evil half-smirk and he turns to retrieve his medical bag. Removing Joan's gag, he advises, "I wouldn't scream," his voice low and menacing. "No one can hear you." A close-up shows Xavier taking up a scalpel. Eyeing the lethal instrument, he turns back toward Joan. At this, the camera turns with him to bring Joan into the frame and then zooms in tight on her terrified face so that her ear-piercing shriek fills the frame. During the scene the music builds and builds until it climaxes, blending with her scream into a horrifying crescendo of terror.

ASSETS

As the last Hollywood horror film of the decade, *The Return of Dr. X* features the screen's very *first* scientific vampire (the pint-sized pulsing sponge from *The Vampire Bat*, 1933, aside) in a rather intriguing storyline. Lee Katz's fast-paced screenplay is well constructed to keep the viewer guessing for the film's first half while providing plenty of menace during the picture's latter stages. Katz peppers his snappy script with clever bits of humor, such as when Garret bids a polite good-bye to the helpful undertaker with "I hope to see you again sometime," only to have the solemn mortician reply knowingly, "I'm sure you will."

Though definitely a "B" picture, one can find little fault on *Return*'s technical side. "We had to rush it right through with no special effects," remembered director Vincent Sherman (in *Films in Review*). "But I had a first-class cinematographer, Sid Hickox, to guide me." Indeed he did. Hickox's fluid camera and varied lighting bring a rich visual sense to the strange proceedings. Hickox always places objects in the foreground of his shot to add depth, tracking smoothly past rows of test tubes and beakers or shooting past lamps and even skulls. As Dr. Flegg sits at his desk, a skull resting on his desktop grins up at him from the lower left hand corner of the shot. Then, later, when Rhodes revives a swooning Angela Merrova at her apartment, she reclines on her divan. Her out-of-focus face in the lower right hand foreground gazes up at Rhodes in a mirror image of the earlier death's head. Through angles and placement, Sherman and Hickox draw a visual parallel between the dying Merrova and the very symbol of death itself.

With careful composition and precise set-ups, Hickox uses his camera to generate an unsettling mood. For Caine's important introduction, the camera, set at a low angle, retreats before his steady advance while low-key lighting intensifies his bizarre appearance. By forcing the viewer to look *up* at the character while at the same time backing away as he moves towards us, Sherman and Hickox create a threatening atmosphere and inspire an immediate uneasiness about the character. The next shot has Caine coming face to face with Rhodes, the two standing in front of a double door so that the doorway's seam creates a dividing barrier between the two — the hero and the villain, the living and the living *dead*. Then the portal suddenly opens and Flegg steps into the shot, breaking into their wary conversation to effectively obliterate their dividing line and thus tie the two characters together.

As the pasty-faced, living-dead zombie needing periodic fixes of fresh blood, Humphrey Bogart cuts a strikingly unwholesome figure. With darkened eyes, clammy white skin, hollow cheeks, a shock of white streaking through his black hair, and dark lips that accentuate the unnatural pallor of his skin, Bogey's craggy good looks succumb to Perc Westmore's makeup ministrations and become the features of a walking corpse. "When I shook his hand," remembers Rhodes, "it was cool and lifeless like a dead person's." From Caine's creepy appearance, we have no trouble believing this. Bogart completes the illusion by adopting a limping, shambling gait and holding a useless, clawed left hand tight across his abdomen. The actor's low, even tones and evil, smirking half-smiles add the finishing sinister touches to this macabre characterization. Far from Boris Karloff's sympathetic Elman from Warners' earlier resurrection tale, *The Walking Dead* (1936), Bogart's Caine/Xavier exudes pure malevolence.

John Litel's steady, powerful performance adds credence to the character of the brilliant scientist, Dr. Flegg. Litel's hawkish face (complete with devilish goatee, widow's peak, and eye monocle), shifty glances and clipped, forceful speech paint a portrait of intelligence and consuming obsession. Flegg is no madman, however, and he finally realizes the horror he has wrought. At this point, Litel's commanding voice takes on an air of resigned sadness and, as he sits slumped in his chair, his body language speaks of great weariness. When he admits that "somehow, somewhere, the magic element of life has eluded me," a note of almost desperate sorrow creeps into his voice. Then, when he lowers his head and quietly says to no one in particular, "May God forgive me," Litel effectively shows the character's humanity, and the viewer truly feels the burden of his failure.

LIABILITIES

Apart from Litel and Bogart, the film is not particularly well acted. Top-billed Wayne Morris fails in his bid to become ingratiating or charming with his puppyish pleadings and pouting demeanor. His cub reporter comes off as a shallow, peanut-popping version of Lee Tracy from the original *Doctor X*. Dennis Morgan's sober portrayal makes the young Dr. Rhodes a dull nonentity with an almost perpetual expression of quizzical concern on his bland face. One wonders why Joan falls so hard and so fast for the lusterless character. Rosemary Lane receives little to do in the thankless role of Joan and never makes her presence felt. She's literally just along for the ride as Rhodes and Garrett drag her all over town chasing down leads.

The film also suffers from an unfortunate anticlimax. After Caine dies (his dying line, "Tell Dr. Rhodes we'll have to postpone our talk on blood composition," is laced with a chill black humor), the picture's final loooong sequence has Garrett's editor trying to induce the now-smug reporter to sign a contract and stay on at the paper. Garrett, however, is only concerned with his new pipe-smoking image and the Great American Novel he intends to write. When he gets a look at his boss's attractive new secretary, however, he suddenly drops his grandiosity and signs on the dotted line. This protracted bit of silliness only serves to reinforce the character's shallowness and leaves a bad taste of fluff in the viewer's mouth.

Still, as a fast-paced, visually engaging horror thriller, *The Return of Dr. X* marks an effective end to the moody style of the Golden Age of Horror and serves as a fitting transition into the quicker-paced, action-oriented craftsmanship of the 1940s.

REVIEWS

The Return of Dr. X was well received by

As the screen's first scientific vampire, Dr. Xavier (Humphrey Bogart) holds the police at bay so that he might drain heroine Joan Vance (Rosemary Lane) of her blood in *The Return of Dr. X* (1939).

the critics. *Variety* (November 29, 1939) opined that "Addicts of the gory and the macabre should get a kick out of this chip off the Frankenstein block. Even though the course of the plot can easily be anticipated and the general pacing isn't so strong, the film packs enough dramatic sock to sustain the interest...."

The *New York Times* (November 23, 1939) gave little in the way of specifics, but (utilizing a rather odd choice of adjectives) informed their readers that "all in all you're going to find 'The Return of Dr. X' a cheerful little picture."

The *Hollywood Reporter* (November 24, 1939) was positively *aglow*: "*The Return of Dr. X* is a weirdly fascinating thing, a horror picture, to be sure, but one so intelligently presented that it will delight all classes of audiences.... It has a definite plot, an extremely novel and interesting one, and relies on high class productions for startling effect.... Dennis Morgan is the picture's standout with his sincerely fine work. Unusually excellent performances are turned in by Wayne Morris, John Litel, and Humphrey Bogart as well."

PRODUCTION NOTES

Though a sequel in name only, Warner Bros. touted *The Return of Dr. X* as a direct follow-up to their previous horror hit, *Doctor X*. "Dr. Xavier made his first breath-taking appearance in the summer of 1932," stated *The Return of Dr. X* pressbook, "in a shocker which Warner Bros., in his honor, gave the simple title of 'Dr. X.' At that time, Dr. Xavier's forbidding visage assumed its camera form in the features of Lionel Atwill." The studio publicists noted that "film audiences like to have their favorite horror characters return to the screen in series of stories such as the Frankenstein, Dracula, and Doyle's Dr. Moriarty yarns." Having either forgotten (or conveniently ignored) the plot of the previous picture, the pressbook article lamented that "Warners made it hard for themselves when they had Lionel Atwill killed in the original 'Dr. X' seven years ago." Of course, Atwill's Dr. Xavier turned out to be a sympathetic character rather than the villain and finished the picture very much *alive*!

Warner Bros. may have had second thoughts about their cash-in publicity campaign, for at one time during preproduction the project's moniker changed to *The Doctor's Secret* (the nondescript title of William J. Makin's story upon which the screenplay was based). The lure of surefire publicity proved too strong, however, and the PR department tied the picture to *Doctor X*'s coattails after all.

Warners originally announced (in February 1939) *The Return of Dr. X* as a vehicle for Boris Karloff. When the actor instead began shooting *Enemy Agent* (released as *British Intelligence*) for Warners in mid–March, the studio entered into negotiations with Universal to contract the services of Bela Lugosi. When that fell through, James Stephenson stepped in but was quickly snatched away by Michael Curtiz for *The Private Lives of Elizabeth and Essex*. In the end, Jack Warner & Co. filled the void with their troublesome contract player, Humphrey Bogart (as a rumored punishment for refusing too many assignments). *The Return of Dr. X* began shooting on May 24, 1939.

"I knew Humphrey Bogart pretty well," remembered director Vincent Sherman (in a *Films in Review* interview), "and Jack Warner called me into his office and said, 'I can't do a thing with Bogey. All he can play is gangsters.' So I tried him out in this very belated sequel to the original 1932 *Doctor X*."

Bogart was less than pleased with this assignment. Richard Gehman, in *Bogart*, quoted the actor as saying: "This was one of the pictures that made me march into Jack Warner and ask for more money again. You can't believe what this one was like. I had a part that somebody like Bela Lugosi or Boris Karloff should have played. I was this doctor, brought back to life, and the only thing that nourished this poor bastard was blood. If it'd been Jack Warner's blood, or Harry's, or Pop's, maybe I wouldn't have minded as much. The trouble was, they were drinking mine and I was making this stinking movie."

Having to wear Perc Westmore's effective-but-restricting corpse-like makeup did not help Bogart's disposition any. Because of the flammable nature of the makeup, the chain-smoking actor was forced to smoke his beloved cigarettes through a 12-inch cigarette holder.

The Return of Dr. X earns the title of "Most Unusual Cast in a Golden Age Horror Picture." Besides Humphrey Bogart (in his only horror appearance), the film featured a variety of off-beat players. Female lead Rosemary Lane was one of the popular "Lane Sisters," while Huntz Hall (before becoming one of the "Dead End Kids"), Lya Lys (French actress of *Un Chien Andalou* and *Confessions of a Nazi Spy* fame), Glenn Langan (destined to stand tall as *The Amazing Colossal Man* in 1957), William Hopper (son of silent screen star DeWolfe Hopper and famous Hollywood gossip columnist Hedda Hopper), and George "Superman" Reeves all appear in supporting roles or bit parts.

A graduate of the famed Pasadena Playhouse, Wayne Morris (born Bert de Wayne Morris) received a Warner Bros. contract in 1936. His career was interrupted by World War II, in which Morris became a decorated Navy flyer. Credited with shooting down seven Japanese fighters as well as sinking an enemy gunboat and two destroyers, Wayne received two Air Medals and four Distinguished Flying Crosses. After the war he returned to films, but his career was cut short by a fatal heart attack at age 45.

Fourth-billed Dennis Morgan was a radio announcer, small-time opera singer, and minor stage player before breaking into pictures in 1936 under his real name of Stanley Morner. In 1938 he changed his professional moniker to Richard Stanley but quickly altered it again to Dennis Morgan when offered a Warner Bros. contract. He soon became one of Warners' most popular leading men and ultimately the studio's highest-paid star, holding that financial honor for nearly a decade. Morgan left films in 1956 but starred on television in the late 1950s series, "21 Beacon Street." In the 1960s Morgan retired from acting altogether to devote himself full-time to his volunteer work for the American Cancer Society (even turning down an offer of $10,000 a week to star in a production of "The Vagabond King").

Though born in Wisconsin, John Litel joined the French army in World War I, receiving two military decorations for bravery.

Returning to the US after the war, he studied acting and toured with various companies before becoming an acclaimed fixture on Broadway. Litel made his screen debut in 1929 but did not abandon New York for Hollywood until 1937. Among his more than 200 subsequent films are *Invisible Agent* (1942), *Murder in the Blue Room* (1944), *Flight to Mars* (1951), and *Voyage to the Bottom of the Sea* (1961).

Producer Bryan Foy earned the amusing moniker "Keeper of the B's" by heading up the Warner Bros. B-picture unit from the mid-thirties to the beginning of World War II (when he went over to 20th Century-Fox after Warners de-emphasized their quickies in favor of more "A" pictures). The eldest son of vaudeville headliner Eddie Foy, Sr., Bryan grew up on the stage as one of the "Seven Little Foys." Bryan Foy entered pictures in 1918 as a director of comedy shorts and later graduated to full features with the coming of sound. In fact, Foy directed *Lights of New York* (1928), ballyhooed as "the first 100 percent all-talking picture." (1927's *The Jazz Singer* featured dialogue in select key sequences only.) Foy continued directing through the early 1930s (including helming the 1931 version of *The Gorilla*), when he became supervisor of the B-unit at Warner Bros. *Variety*'s obituary (April 27, 1977) quoted a Foy colleague as saying, "He'd make anything. Brynie didn't care what he made as long as it made a buck," and quoted Foy himself exclaiming, "I hate dialog! Any picture with dialog is an A-picture!" No project could be too topical or too gimmicky for Foy. *Variety* recounted how "at one point in the 1930s Foy flew to Spain to try to sign up fascist dictator Francisco Franco as star of a pic, but that scheme fell through after liberal groups vehemently protested"(!) Among his many films as producer, Foy supervised *The Loves of Edgar Allan Poe* (1942), *The Lodger* (1944), *House of Wax* (1953), and *The Mad Magician* (1954).

A former stage actor and playwright, director Vincent Sherman began in films as an actor, appearing in such productions as *Counselor-at-Law* (1933) and *One Is Guilty* (1934). In 1937 Warners placed Sherman under contract as a screenwriter, where he collaborated on *Crime School* (1938) and *King of the Underworld* (1939) among others. With *The Return of Dr. X*, his debut, Sherman graduated to director, and subsequently turned out a number of melodramas for Warner Bros. over the next two decades.

Cinematographer Sidney Hickox had worked before with both Bryan Foy (on *The Gorilla* in 1931) and Vincent Sherman (on *King of the Underworld* in 1939). The veteran cameraman began shooting motion pictures in 1915 at American Biograph and worked for Warner Bros. throughout the 1930s and forties (lensing over 125 features in 25 years for his home studio). In 1954 Hickox's crisp, almost documentarylike photography did much to insure the success of *Them!*, the seminal nuclear mutation/Big Bug film. Shortly thereafter, Hickox gave up features to work in television.

Appendix A: Borderline Horrors, "Lost" Films, and Foreign Exclusions

THE BLACK DOLL (1938; Universal) Director: Otis Garrett. Producer: Irving Starr. Screenplay: Harold Buckley (from the novel *The Black Doll* by William Edward Hayes). Photography: Stanley Cortez and Ira Morgan. Cast: Donald Woods, Nan Grey, Edgar Kennedy, C. Henry Gordon, Doris Lloyd, John Wray, Addison Richards, Holmes Herbert, William Lundigan, Fred Malatesta, Inez Palange, Syd Saylor, Arthur Hoyt.

The Black Doll is the second entry in Universal's "Crime Club" series begun in late 1937 with *The Westland Case*. Universal had contracted with Crime Club, publishers of pulp mysteries, to option four of their novels per year. In a two-year period the studio produced seven of these low-cost whodunits. *The Black Doll* is the only one to feature any element (though decidedly slight) of horror. At an isolated country house, the rich, ruthless Marian Rood is disturbed by the inexplicable appearance of a black doll impaled with a knife—a dire portent ("In my country," warns the Mexican butler, "it often means *death*"). This particular doll is connected with a man murdered by Rood years earlier and there's talk of the dead man returned from the grave. This is quickly dismissed, however, when two murders, a violent storm, and one bumbling sheriff later, the picture settles down to a comfortable Old House mystery as the hero (a vacationing private eye) sets about unraveling the plot. A mobile camera, effective acting (with the painful exception of Edgar Kennedy as the stoogelike sheriff), and a few well-staged sequences (the heroine attacked by a dark figure out in the driving rain, for instance) sets *The Black Doll* above many of its contemporaries. Unfortunately, the nearly continuous buffoonery of the blustering, incompetent sheriff quickly overwhelms and engulfs the picture, dragging it back down to its bargain-basement, lowest-common-denominator roots.

Heroine Nan Grey played the victim of *Dracula's Daughter* in 1936 and near-victim of the *Tower of London* in 1939. Musical director Charles Previn shamelessly raided the Universal vaults to create a patchwork (though not unpleasing) score made up of snippets from *The Invisible Man*, *Werewolf of London*, *Bride of Frankenstein*, *The Raven*, and *Dracula's Daughter*.

BLACK MOON (1934; Columbia) Director: Roy William Neill. Screenplay: Wells Root (based on the 1933 novel *Black Moon* by Clements Ripley). Photography: Joseph August. Cast: Jack Holt, Fay Wray, Dorothy Burgess, Cora Sue Collins, Arnold Korff, Clarence Muse, Lumsden Hare.

"*Black Moon* is a film I've almost erased from my consciousness," admitted Fay Wray (in *Starlog* #194). So has the moviewatching world in general since, until recently, the picture belonged to that shamefully neglected subgroup, the "lost film." Sadly, *Black Moon* is not much of a rediscovery. "I've never seen it," stated Ms. Wray, "but I think it was supposed to be a pretty interesting story." Indeed it was. Juanita (Dorothy Burgess) takes her small child back to visit the tiny West Indian island where she was raised. There, lured by the jungle drums, she resumes her old role of voodoo priestess and participates in a human

Ad mat for *Black Moon* (1934), one of the most recent (and disappointing) "rediscoveries."

sacrifice. When her unknowing husband (Jack Holt) arrives, he discovers her involvement in the local voodoo cult and tries to take his daughter and leave the island. Juanita incites the natives to rebel and marks him and his attractive secretary (Fay Wray) for death. When they escape the natives' clutches, the voodoo high priest demands that Juanita sacrifice her own daughter in her husband's place. Just as Juanita succumbs to her fanaticism and shakily raises the ceremonial knife over her daughter, her husband arrives and shoots his wife, saving the child.

Those seeking a horror rediscovery in *Black Moon* are destined for disappointment. Despite the involvement of voodoo and human sacrifice, nothing is made of the mystical (much less horrific) aspects of the West Indian religion. No zombies, no hexes or curses, no talk of vengeful spirits or voodoo gods, not even a single ceremonial snake rears its sacred head. The story might just as well have taken place in the wilds of India as a tale of religious upheaval or in darkest Africa as some Tarzan movie subplot. The film's main interest comes from the themes of fanaticism and love and the moral dilemma posed when the two conflict, rather than from any voodoo trappings. "Out of the inferno of tropic madness comes the weirdest romance of our time!" shout the ads for *Black Moon* in a bit of revealing ballyhoo.

The players generally acquit themselves well. Jack Holt, as the husband and father, exhibits an unselfconscious, ebullient affection for his young daughter and, later, a bitter shock when he learns of his wife's savage activities. Fay Wray, beautiful as always, does well with the few significant scenes given her, showing tender concern for the child and a wistful, pained stoicism in submerging her true — and forbidden — feelings for her married employer. As Juanita, Dorothy Burgess is too cold to elicit much sympathy from the viewer and so denies the film much of its potential power. Also, the screenplay provides little insight into Jaunita's character. We never see the ties that bound her to this brutal sect as she matured on the island — we're simply *told* that she was raised to it. The viewer shares no common base with her and subsequently cannot empathize with her compulsion. At the end, however, when she chooses to sacrifice her own child, Ms. Burgess effectively displays an emotional turmoil which at least momentarily draws the viewer into her plight.

The picture moves at a painfully slow pace. Scenes often drag on far too long to be effective (including the tedious ceremonial dancing) and very little happens over the course of the film's 68 minutes. Much of the picture focuses on the husband discovering what the viewer already knows. Roy William Neill's straightforward but uninspired direction generates only paltry suspense while Joseph August's adequate but frequently static camerawork creates little mood. One expects more from the director of *The Black Room* and the cinematographer from *The Hunchback of Notre Dame* (1939) than a barely average melodrama.

Black Moon received a lukewarm reception from the critics. *Variety*'s "Shan" commented (July 3, 1934) that "direction in 'Black Moon' is commendable and the acting is good, but the scenario possesses dubious elements. Studio has made a strong effort to weave an interesting white romance around the black magic of the Negroes of the West Indies, but unsuccessfully." Thornton Delehanty of the *New York Post* (June 28, 1934) labeled *Black Moon* "a humid melodrama ... put together hastily on a formula that has frequently done service for the cinema and pulp magazines."

THE CAT AND THE CANARY (1939; Paramount) Director: Elliott Nugent. Producer: Arthur Hornblow, Jr. Screenplay: Walter DeLeon, Lynn Starling (based on the stage play by John Willard). Photography: Charles Lang. Cast: Bob Hope, Paulette Goddard, John Beal, Douglas Montgomery, Gale Sondergaard, Elizabeth Patterson, George Zucco, Nydia Westman, John Wray.

While arguably the best mystery/horror film of the Golden Age, *The Cat and the Canary* is undeniably the premier mystery/*comedy* of the decade. With enough reaching hands, hidden passages, and unusual plot twists to keep any Old Dark House mystery fan happy, some genuine suspense, a hideous killer, and Bob Hope one-liners make this stellar production a "streamlined, screamlined" winner (as the *New York Times* reviewer so colorfully put it). Bob Hope is likable, funny, and even heroic, but he's at his best when making fun of his own fears — a sort of comedic whistling in the dark — something that audiences can identify with and admire. When told by the sinister housekeeper that "There are spirits all around you," Hope nervously quips, "Well, could you put some in a glass, I need it badly." Paulette Goddard makes a likable, strong-willed heroine, a pleasant and intelligent change from the standard window dressing screamer. And the supporting players all do well, headed by the cultivated, urbane George Zucco and the mysterious Gale Sondergaard. Production values are high, and the climax, though brief, is unexpected and edge-of-the-seat material.

John Willard's successful 1922 Broadway play *The Cat and the Canary* (starring Henry Hull, the

Paulette Goddard is menaced by "The Cat" in a publicity photo for *The Cat and the Canary* (1939).

Werewolf of London himself) had originally been filmed in 1927 by Universal and was first remade with sound in 1930 as *The Cat Creeps* (now a "lost" film). In 1938, Universal considered yet another remake, but subsequently sold the rights to Paramount, who mounted this production. The two previous versions were both straight thrillers, whereas this 1939 film was tailored to the comedic talents of Bob Hope.

"I had suggested that story to Paramount," remembered director Elliott Nugent to interviewer Leonard Maltin on the genesis of this version of *The Cat and the Canary*. "It was a play that had been a moderate melodramatic success in New York, and I had played it in stock, and they were looking for a mystery story, a fright-wig story. One of their producers said, 'Do you know any stories about an old haunted house?' and I said why not get *The Cat and the Canary*?"

With *The Cat and the Canary* Paramount finally provided a starring vehicle for their stage-trained contract player, Bob Hope, who had been working in the shadow of comedienne Martha

Raye in pictures like *College Swing* and *Give Me a Sailor*. (Interestingly enough, a preproduction announcement in the *Hollywood Reporter* included Martha Raye in the cast. She did not appear in the finished film.) In his autobiography, *The Road to Hollywood*, Hope referred to *Cat* as "the turning point for my movie career." *Cat* also provided Hope's co-star, Paulette Goddard, with her first starring role and thus began an impressive career for the glamorous yet down-to-earth star-to-be. The film proved to be an able vehicle to launch the two stars into their "glory years" in the 1940s.

Elliot Nugent recalled that "[Bob Hope] had his gag writers and when the producer and I were satisfied with the writers' script, then Hope's writers would take over and they would submit to us various gags to be spotted here and there. He would take maybe half of them, and reject the other half. But he had two writers on the set at all times, and every once in a while they would come up with an idea, sometimes for a gag and sometimes a little directorial suggestion. Quite often they were good."

Charlie Chaplin, married to Paulette Goddard at the time, was impressed by Bob Hope's work in the film. When Ms. Goddard first introduced a star-struck Hope to Chaplin, the great comedian/director told him: "Young man, I've been watching the rushes of *The Cat and the Canary* every night. I want you to know that you're one of the best timers of comedy I have ever seen" (from *Paulette*, by Joe Morella and Edward Z. Epstein).

Co-star John Beal (born James Alexander Bliedung) appeared in one other genre feature (nearly two decades later)—playing the title role in *The Vampire* (1957). Apart from films, Beal worked in radio, television, and on Broadway. Critic Brooke Atkinson hailed him as "one of the best actors in our theatre" and Emory Lewis called Beal "the most significant actor in New York" after his performance in "Long Day's Journey into Night." Beal retired from the big screen in 1960, though he continued to act on stage and in television, guest-starring on a variety of shows as well as playing a recurrent role on the daytime soap opera "Another World."

Gail Sondergaard's career was effectively ended in 1949 by the communist witch-hunts of the House Un-American Affairs Committee. Sondergaard's husband, writer-director Herbert Biberman (founder of the Director's Guild) went to prison (cited for contempt) as one of the "Hollywood Ten" who defied the committee. Subpoenaed herself in 1951, Sondergaard took the Fifth Amendment and voiced a defense of her political rights. She subsequently did not work in Hollywood again for nearly two decades.

The success of *The Cat and the Canary* (1939) led to an even more successful (and even better) follow-up vehicle for Hope and Goddard with *The Ghost Breakers* the following year.

Bob Hope later reprised his nervous hero role of Wallie Campbell on radio in the April 3, 1949, "Screen Directors Playhouse" broadcast of *The Cat and the Canary*. On television, NBC-TV's "Dow Hour of Great Mysteries" presented *The Cat and the Canary* (starring Collin Wilcox, Andrew Duggan, George Macready, and Telly Savalas!) on September 27, 1960. Finally, in 1978, *The Cat and the Canary* made it to the big screen once more as an English production directed by soft-core filmmaker Radley Metzger (going "legit").

CHANDU ON THE MAGIC ISLAND (1935; Principal Pictures) Director: Ray Taylor. Producer: Sol Lesser. Screenplay: Barry Barringer. Photography: John Hickson. Cast: Bela Lugosi, Maria Alba, Clara Kimball Young, Deane Benton, Phyllis Ludwig, Murdock McQuarrie, Wilfred Lucas, Josef Swickard, Jack Clark.

This patchwork afterthought created from the last seven episodes of the 1934 12-chapter serial *The Return of Chandu* and released as a feature in 1935 offers little to either the horror or the serial fan, even given the presence of Bela Lugosi as the title character. As the mystical hero, Lugosi has little to do except creep about trying to avoid capture, contact his spiritual mentor (the Yogi), or lament the loss of his hypnotic powers (due to an "invisible barrier of black magic"). At one point, the villain traps Chandu in an underground maze and gloats, "You may walk the passages for years and find no way out." With the amount of footage devoted to Lugosi moving slowly through these tunnels, one fears this may indeed become a dreary reality. Lugosi appears listless and less enthusiastic than in the previous feature made from the first five chapters (called simply *The Return of Chandu*). Perhaps he grew tired of the lackluster role after making the first half-dozen episodes. The plot features the Eastern-taught magician protecting his lady love, the Princess Nadji of Egypt, from the evil clutches of a cult of cat-worshippers on the "lost island of Lemuria." The Lemurians intend to sacrifice the princess to their deity and thereby resurrect their beloved high priestess. Despite the picture's serial origins, very little actually happens. The characters generally stand about waiting for the next scheduled disaster to strike (kidnapping, shipwreck, etc.)—which, more often than not, arrives with a whimper rather than a bang. Despite an occasional bit of bizarre interest (as when Chandu's grown nephew writhes beneath a scimitar/pendulum torture device), the crude, static photography, melodramatic acting, hollow sound, and terrible musical score (which pays no attention whatsoever to the events taking place onscreen) serve to create a dull, lifeless pastiche. About the only thrill found in *Chandu on the Magic Island* is in seeing (in full daylight) the mammoth gate from *King Kong* (used to represent the temple of Lemuria) and the Dakang port set from *The Son of Kong* (utilized as the town of Suva) which producer Sol Lesser borrowed from RKO. (See also *The Return of Chandu*.)

CHANDU THE MAGICIAN (1932; Fox) Directors: Marcel Varnel, William C. Menzies. Screenplay: Barry Conners, Philip Klein (from the radio drama by Harry A. Earnshaw, Vera M. Oldham, and R. R. Morgan). Photography: James Howe. Cast: Edmund Lowe, Irene Ware, Bela Lugosi, Herbert Mundin, Henry B. Walthall, Weldon Heyburn, June Vlasek, Nestor Aber, Virginia Hammond.

Though this was intended as a feature film from the start, *Chandu the Magician* might just as well be another condensation of a serial (much like the later 1934 and '35 releases, *The Return of Chandu* and *Chandu on the Magic Island*). The story follows Chandu, a westerner who has just attained the rank and power of "Yogi." "The world needs thee," proclaims Chandu's aged mentor. "Go forth in thy youth and strength and conquer the evil that threatens mankind." This evil takes the form of Roxor, a megalomaniac scientist who has kidnapped Chandu's brother-in-law, Robert. Robert has perfected a death ray and Roxor intends to pry the secret from his captive and use its destructive powers to rule the world. What follows is 72 minutes of rescues, escapes, and confrontations in which Chandu utilizes his Yogi powers of hypnosis and illusion to perform all manner of daring-do. This gives *Chandu the Magician* the feel of a simplistic serial — with the added advantage, however, of a feature-film budget and the production staff to go with it. The sets and photography are excellent, not surprising considering that famed set designer William Cameron Menzies co-directed and James Howe served as cameraman. In smooth tracking shots, Howe explores the imposing temple sets filled with huge columns, forbidding statues, and dark corners. While the picture *looks* good, little can be said for the one-dimensional characters or the melodramatic acting. As Chandu, Edmund Lowe falls flat and fails to bring his character to mystical life. Lowe studied for the priesthood at one time, though perhaps not *well* for he neglected to imbue Chandu with any semblance of spiritualism. Bela Lugosi, on the other hand, goes overboard and makes his over-ripe Roxor *bigger* than life. Lugosi draws out his enthusiastic rule-the-world speeches with such relish that one simply can't take this madman seriously. Still, while no more convincing than Edmund Lowe, Lugosi is infinitely more *fun* to watch. Though the raw materials were present to make *Chandu the Magician* an all-out horror film à la *The Mask of Fu Manchu* (world-hungry madman, threatened captives, death ray, exotic locale, etc.), *Chandu* focuses on romance and adventure rather than the darker elements of sexual deviance and torture. In so doing, *Chandu the Magician* becomes a hokey, mildly entertaining adventure fantasy pleasing to the eye but bland to the palate.

Chandu the Magician began as a children's radio program in 1931. Noting the program's popularity, Fox purchased the screen rights to the character and cast their contract player and all-around leading man, Edmund Lowe, in the title role. Fox originally intended to do a series of Chandu pictures, but the returns on this first one were disappointing and so no further installments materialized. Two years later, independent producer Sol Lesser obtained the character rights and filmed *The Return of Chandu* as a 12-chapter serial. Ironically, Bela Lugosi, the arch-villain in the original picture, was cast as Chandu — the hero — in this serial.

THE CLAIRVOYANT (1935; Gaumont-British; Great Britain) Alternate Title: *The Evil Mind* (American Release Title). Director: Maurice Elvey. Screenplay: Charles Bennett and Bryan Edgar Wallace (adapted from "The Clairvoyant," a novel by Ernest Lothar). Photography: G. Mac Williams. Cast: Claude Rains, Fay Wray, Mary Clare, Ben Field, Jane Baxter, Athole Stewart, Jack Raine, Margaret Davidge, Denier Warren, Donald Calthrop.

Maximus (Claude Rains) is a fake mind-reader who suddenly develops the power of true prophecy. He cannot control these spells, however, which seem to come upon him only when Christine, the daughter of a newspaper magnate, is nearby. Maximus is torn between Christine (Mary Clare), who encourages Maximus to exploit his "gift," and his wife (Fay Wray), who fears the toll the power takes on her husband. Maximus predicts a train wreck (and disembarks just in time), the winner of a horse race, and even the death of his own mother before he sees disaster waiting for the men working in an underground tunnel. Though he warns the workers, they head down into the shaft anyway, afraid of losing their jobs. When a nervous workman sets off a charge too early, the shaft collapses. Two hundred are killed and 110 remain missing. Maximus goes on

As *The Clairvoyant* (1935), Claude Rains receives solace from Fay Wray (cigarette card).

trial, accused of being a publicity-seeking charlatan. "This terrible tragedy in the Humber Shaft," states the prosecutor, "was brought about by *panic*— panic which is directly traceable to the so-called prophecy of the prisoner of the bar." On the stand, however, the power takes hold of Maximus one last time and he is vindicated (and acquitted).

Claude Rains makes Maximus an engaging, likable character whose breezy outlook quickly becomes heavy with the burden of his gift. "With those burning eyes of his, he made everything ring true," remembered Rains' co-star, Fay Wray. Cinematographer G. Mac William's pinpoint lighting helps along "those burning eyes" by making Rains' eyes seem to glow from within during the eerie "second sight" moments. Fay Wray takes full advantage of playing a strong-willed character and gives a convincing performance as Maximus' devoted wife determined to fight (even against forces beyond her ken) for the life and happiness of her husband. The screenplay by Charles Bennett (*The Secret of the Loch*, 1934) and Bryan Edgar Wallace (son of Kong-creator Edgar Wallace) raises some intriguing questions about moral responsibility and the unforeseen consequences of one's own actions. When, during the trial, the prosecutor points out that "had the prisoner not stopped the train, it would have cleared the points and the collision would have been avoided," it poses a painful conundrum. Maurice Elvey's (*The Lodger*, 1932) surehanded direction keeps things moving and the disaster sequences boast a gritty realism.

Though it's unsurprising to find English-born Claude Rains (a relative newcomer to the screen) in a British production, one may wonder what Fay Wray, an established American (though Canadian-born) star, was doing making movies on the British Isles. Trying to escape the far-reaching clutches of King Kong, that's what. "My first important role had been in *The Wedding March*, with Erich von Stroheim as writer, director and actor," wrote Ms. Wray in a 1969 *New York Times* article. "The film was rich with realism, perception and sensitivity. Naturally, I had hoped for a continuation of the particular values I found in such filmmaking. Instead, because of the enthusiastic reception given *Kong*, more horror films were offered me. By the time I had finished *The Mystery of the Wax Museum* and *The Vampire Bat*, I was desperately in need of escape and welcomed an invitation to go to England, to make pictures there. It seemed an irony to be met, upon my arrival, by a representative of the BBC who asked that I come to their studios and broadcast a sample of my scream."

THE CRIMES OF STEPHEN HAWKE (1936; MGM; Great Britain) Alternate Title: *Strangler's Morgue* (American release). Producer/Director: George King. Screenplay: Frederick Hayward (scenario: Paul White; dialogue: Jack Celestin and H. F. Maltby). Photography: Ronnie Neame. Cast: Tod Slaughter, Marjorie Taylor, D. J. Williams, Eric Portman, Ben Soutten, Gerald Barry, George M. Slater, Charles Penrose, Norman Pierce, and Flotsam and Jetsam.

In his follow-up vehicle to *Sweeney Todd, the Demon Barber of Fleet Street* (also 1936), Tod Slaughter ("The Horror Man of Europe") eschews his razor for the "sinews of steel" in his bare hands. Kindly moneylender Stephen Hawke (Slaughter) leads a double life as the notorious "Spine-Breaker," a fiend who snaps his victims' spines in his crushing grip. Though a ruthless murderer/thief, Hawke exhibits a real love for his adopted daughter and in the end even sacrifices his own life and liberty to prevent her unwanted marriage to a blackmailing police chief. The character of Stephen Hawke allows Slaughter to step beyond his stock slimy villain characterization and portray a more multi-faceted character. While the Spine-Breaker is a thoroughly loathsome killer (even snapping the spine of a young — though admittedly obnoxious — boy), Slaughter manages to inspire some pathos for the man via his unceasing love for his daughter and even (for a short time) place the viewer squarely on his side so that he might complete his murderous mission and eliminate the unscrupulous blackmailer. Director George King (who also helmed Slaughter's earlier *Sweeney Todd* and later *The Face at the Window*, 1939) makes the most of the realistic period settings. Like most Tod Slaughter films, however, the acting is flowery and melodramatic and there are numerous slow points when Slaughter is absent from the screen. Still, *The Crimes of Stephen Hawke* possesses a few macabre thrills, such as the agonized screams of the fiend's victims as their life runs out through his vicelike fingers (accompanied by Slaughter's chilling chuckles), and one shuddery sequence in which a young man poses as his father's corpse come back to life in order to frighten Hawke into revealing himself. Also, in the best tradition of horrific henchmen, Hawke's ghoulish assistant is a one-eyed, one-legged (this infirmity belonging to actor Ben Soutten himself) hunchback. *Stephen Hawke* also allows Slaughter some priceless dialogue, rife with black humor. When the unsavory police chief approaches the reluctant Hawke about marrying his daughter, the following exchange occurs:

> Chief (unaware he is addressing the "Spine-Breaker"): "So, further discussion is in order, Sir?"
> Hawke: "Naturally. Then, we can come to *grips* with the matter."
> Chief: "Good. Then we can clinch the bargain, eh?"
> Hawke: "'*Clinch*' is the word, Sir."

Of course, Hawke ultimately snaps the spine of this expectant suitor.

Don't be confused when the film opens on two tuxedoed radio performers named "Flotsam and Jetsam" singing a silly duet. This is the picture's novel hook — the story is actually part of a radio broadcast related by Tod Slaughter who appears as himself and elucidates with relish upon his earlier murderous screen deeds.

The Crimes of Stephen Hawke is Slaughter's best film of the decade, and it received good reviews upon its initial release in England. *Kinematograph Weekly* (May 21, 1936) cited the film's "gripping story, disarming treatment, great work by Tod Slaughter, good title, rousing comedy relief, and first-rate exploitation angles," while the *Monthly Film Bulletin* (May, 1936) noted that "Tod Slaughter throws himself with zest into his part; the supporting cast is adequate, and the period settings are effective."

THE CROOKED CIRCLE (1932; World Wide) Director: H. Bruce Humberstone. Producer: William Sistrom. Screenplay: Ralph Spence. Photography: Robert B. Kurrle. Cast: Zasu Pitts, James Gleason, Ben Lyon, Irene Purcell, C. Henry Gordon, Ray Hatton, Roscoe Karns, Burton Churchill, Spencer Charters, Robert Frazer, Ethel Clayton, Frank Reicher, Christian Rub, Tom Kennedy.

"The Crooked Circle" refers to a secret band of "counterfeiters and thieves deluxe," whose nemesis is a group of amateur sleuths called The Sphinx Club. The Circle has marked one of the Sphinx members for death, so his fellow sleuths journey with him to his recently purchased Long Island mansion, which legend has it is haunted. There they encounter a creepy, hunchbacked neighbor, secret panels, ghostly violin music, and a skeleton in the attic. There's even a sinister Hindu, who ends up using some mystic art to place a man in a state of suspended animation ("We of India frequently practice it").

After much pointless running about and unfunny humor ("Beware!" warns the creepy neighbor, to which the dimwitted housekeeper asks, "Be — where?"), the villains are finally rounded up in their secret hideout under the crypt. The various ghostly trappings are quite superfluous to the plot of this substandard crime/mystery. "Hey, you know this thing is turning into a mystery," observes the goofy cop, to which the hero replies, "It's worse than that, it's a nightmare." We can only agree.

World Wide was an independent studio which operated for a short three-year period between 1930 and 1933. With product such as *The Crooked Circle*, it's a wonder they lasted as long as they did. The film's greatest claim to fame is one of pure novelty. *The Crooked Circle* was the first motion picture to be broadcast on television. The *Los Angeles Times* reported that on March 28, 1933, KHJ (a radio station in Hollywood) transmitted *The Crooked Circle* to a television set placed in the window of Barker Bros. department store on Hollywood Boulevard across from Grauman's Chinese Theatre. "A crowd of interested spectators gathered to look at this first experimental transmission," noted the article, "and many voiced wonder at how it was done."

DAUGHTER OF THE DRAGON (1931; Paramount) Director: Lloyd Corrigan. Screenplay: Lloyd Corrigan and Monte M. Katterjohn (dialogue: Sidney Buchman); from Sax Rohmer's "Daughter of Fu Manchu." Photography: Victor Milner. Cast: Anna May Wong, Warner Oland, Sessue Hayakawa, Bramwell Fletcher, Francis Dade, Holmes Herbert, Lawrence Grant, Harold Minjir, Nicholas Soussanin, E. Allyn Warren.

"As everyone knows," begins the opening written narration, "twenty years ago Dr. Fu Manchu terrorized London. Demented by the accidental death of his wife and son during the Boxer Rebellion in China, he wrongly placed the blame on General Petrie, and swore to wipe out the entire Petrie family." Now, after two decades, Fu Manchu (long thought dead) returns to wreak his vengeance on the late General Petrie's descendants (which consists of Sir John Petrie and his son Ronald). Sneaking into the Petrie mansion, Fu places Sir John in a hypnotic trance through the use of a special poison. In an eerie and rather startling scene, Fu orders Sir John to advance, zombielike, to the top of the stairs, below which are gathered his family and friends. "My first victim now descends toward you," Fu calls out, "his life hanging by a strained thread—which my vengeance now *severs*." At that, Fu claps his hands and the entranced Sir John groans, clutches his throat, and plunges down the stairs, dead. A police inspector (visiting the Petries at the time) shoots the madman, but Fu makes his escape to the house next door where his long-lost (and unknowing) daughter, Ling Moy, awaits him. The dying Fu reveals himself to her and extracts a promise that she'll "deliver the soul of Ronald Petrie to me—to our ancestors." She responds with an appropriately bloodthirsty oath of filial piety: "The *blood* is mine, the *hate* is mine, the *vengeance* shall be mine." Ling Moy then makes the acquaintance of Ronald and, according to plan, induces him to fall in love with her. Contrary to plan, however, *she* falls in love with *him* as well. "I can't kill him, I love him. I would rather kill myself." Before she can translate these words to action, however, Fu's former servant intervenes. At the house altar, Ling Moy calls out to her dead father for a strengthening of her resolve. Suddenly, the mournful, ghostly voice of Fu Manchu answers back: "We are not resting. We shall never rest until you kill him who remains. Ling Moy, you must kiiiill." Bolstered by her dead dad, Ling Moy continues with her nefarious plans until an appropriate running time has elapsed and she receives her just desserts in the end.

Comparisons between *Daughter of the Dragon* and *The Mask of Fu Manchu* (1932) are inevitable. While *Daughter* contains some regal set dressing and gowns beautiful in their Eastern splendor, the picture cannot match the grandeur of the later MGM production. (Nor could it quite match *Mask*'s $327,600 budget—though at a respectable $268,000, this *Daughter* was no poor relation.) Compared to Boris Karloff, Warner Oland's Fu is strictly second-rate. (This was Oland's third and final outing as Sax Rohmer's Asian villain, the first two being *The Mysterious Dr. Fu Manchu*, 1929 and *The Return of Dr. Fu Manchu*, 1930.) Oland's chubby face and almost kindly voice lacks the evil sarcasm of Karloff's interpretation, and his short, portly frame speaks not of diabolical power but of too much chow mein. After Fu dies, the film slows terribly with various roundabout, overelaborate plots and "tragic" romance dragging out the running time. Anna May Wong, as Fu's daughter, lacks the presence to carry the remainder of the picture, and plays the role with a decided lack of menace (where is Myrna Loy when you need her?). *Variety* dismissed the film as "Chinese blunderings, murders, and silly acting. Best for the combos where the kids may get a kick out of it." The picture saves one final chill for the end, however. With Ronald held captive, Ling Moy threatens to torture Joan, an occidental rival for Ronald's affection (played by Frances Dade, the doomed "Lucy" from *Dracula*). Before Ronald is to die, the diabolical daughter tells him, "You will first have the torture of seeing beauty eaten slowly away by this hungry acid." Of course, they are saved in the nick of time. Alas, Fu's daughter has found her true self too late both for her plan of vengeance *and* for the near-dozing audience.

THE DEVIL'S DAUGHTER (1939; Sack Amusement Enterprises) Alternate Title: *Pocomania*. Director/Producer: Arthur Leonard. Screenplay: George W. Terwilliger. Photography: Jay Rescher. Cast: Nina Mae McKinney, Jack Carter, Ida James, Hamtree Harrington, Willa Mae Lane, Emmett Wallace.

In early 1939, screenwriter George Terwilliger reworked the script he wrote, produced and directed in 1935 as *Ouanga* for independent filmmaker Arthur Leonard. Leonard then took an all-black cast to Jamaica to film *The Devil's Daughter*. In a much altered (and much *softened*) version of Terwilliger's original tale of vengeful voodoo on a Haitian plantation, Nina Mae McKinney plays Isabelle, whose position of plantation head is usurped by her half sister, Sylvia (Ida James), returning from New York. Though Sylvia is willing to share the plantation with her sibling, Isabelle wants "all or nothing." While Isabelle really possesses no magical powers, she plans to frighten her sister off the island with "obea." "I'm gonna put that sweet sorority sister of mine in the obea sacrifice," she says, "that's gonna make her so scared that she'll leave this island and never come back. And when she's gone I can resume my rightful place again." To that effect Isabelle drugs Sylvia, takes her out into the jungle, and performs a mock voodoolike ceremony over her semi-conscious form. John Lowden (Emmett Wallace), a neighboring planter who loves Sylvia, arrives to put a stop to the malicious plot. Sylvia revives from the drug, agrees to marry John, and forgives Isabelle, turning over the family plantation to her.

Taken as a genre film, *The Devil's Daughter* is even less horrific than its tepid model, *Ouanga*. No one ever mentions voodoo, using instead the less-than-sinsister sounding term "obea" when talking of the jungle drums and ceremonies. Beyond that, nobody takes it seriously, including Isabelle, the supposed high priestess, who freely admits that she has no special powers and must drug and disorient her victim before conducting her sham ceremony. The picture's main focus is on a romantic "square" involving Sylvia, Isabelle, John and Philip (Sylvia's overseer). Looong scenes of tedious "native" dancing and a silly subplot about a gullible servant searching for a little pig which he believes houses his soul round out the proceedings. Everything takes place in bright sunshine, robbing the story of whatever sense of mystery or menace it might have generated. Director Arthur Leonard shoots everything in dull medium shot and rarely asks Jay Rescher to move his camera. Fortunately, the authentic jungle settings occasionally provide something interesting to look at. Apart from Nina Mae McKinney, who sometimes manages to breathe a little fire into her performance, the principles are as stiff and lifeless as zombies (which this film sorely lacks).

(White) Producer/Director Arthur Leonard was a former assistant director for Warner Bros. in New York. When the company closed its East Coast facilities, Leonard turned to the burgeoning low-budget black film industry. In explaining his career choice, the director's own words illustrate the white film establishment's attitude toward black films: "I figured there wasn't a chance in the Hollywood market and ... the best thing I could do was to enter some freak field." *The Devil's Daughter* was Leonard's directorial debut. He personally helmed only three more pictures (*Straight to Heaven*, 1939; *Boy! What a Girl!*, 1946, and *Sepia Cinderella*, 1947).

The MGM front office was so impressed by Nina Mae McKinney's sexy portrayal of the sassy vamp, Chick, in King Vidor's *Hallelujah* (1929) that the studio signed her to a five-year contract. Unfortunately, they didn't know what to do with the screen's first black love goddess, and so used her in only two films — *Safe in Hell* (1931) and *Reckless* (1935) in which she appeared onscreen in only a small role (though she dubbed all of Jean Harlow's songs). McKinney left her stagnant film career to sing in nightclubs and cafes across Europe, becoming "the Black Garbo."

DOUBLE DOOR (1934; Paramount) Director: Charles Vidor. Screenplay: Gladys Lehnan, Jack Cunningham (from the play by Elizabeth A. McFadden). Photography: Harry Fischbeck. Cast: Evelyn Venable, Mary Morris, Anne Revere, Kent Taylor, Sir Guy Standing, Colin Tapley, Virginia Howell, Halliwell Hobbes, Frank Dawson, Helen Shipman, Leonard Carey.

Victoria Van Brett (Mary Morris), domineering matriarch of the distinguished Van Brett family, objects to her much younger half brother, Rip (Kent Taylor), marrying a common nurse (Evelyn Venable). (Coincidentally, the name of Rip's new bride is Anne Darrow, the same moniker sported by *King Kong*'s love interest.) With Victoria's almost hypnotic control over the household, the bitter spinster sets out to intimidate the new bride and dissolve the marriage. When Victoria's false accusation of infidelity results in Rip finally defying his hateful half sister, Victoria locks the new bride in a secret soundproof vault to suffocate. After a fruitless search, the rescue finally comes just in time — along with ironic retribution for Victoria.

Despite ad-lines touting "Mary Morris as the Female Frankenstein of Fifth Avenue," *Double Door* is predominantly a drawing room melodrama which takes a sideswipe at horror during the last few minutes. The terror arises from the idea of being "buried alive" (as Victoria's terrified sister puts it) in the empty blackness of the tomblike vault. Mary Morris, reprising her role from the stage play (and making her sole screen appearance), inspires a few chills with her commanding witchlike demeanor and evil intent. "You'll never find her —" she says venomously to her unsuspecting brother, pausing ever so slightly before amending "— in this house." Though only his third picture, director Charles Vidor (the man who began — but failed to finish — *The Mask of Fu Manchu*) establishes an effectively claustrophobic atmosphere inside the gloomy Van Brett mansion — but then fails to control his actors sufficiently enough to sustain the mood. Aside from the sinister intensity of Mary Morris and the suppressed hysteria of Anne Revere (repeating her stage role as the subservient sister), the picture's acting creaks more than the mansion's stairs, with the principals suffering paroxysms of plaintive yearnings and stoic martyrdom. Evelyn Venable and Kent Taylor (reunited, along with Sir Guy Standing, from the romantic fantasy *Death Takes a Holiday* released earlier the same year) engage in such unlikely melodramatics that one nearly comes to share Victoria's disdain.

In 1947, *Double Door* provided the basis for an episode of *Kraft Television Theatre*, starring Eleanor Wilson.

DRACULA (Spanish language version) (1931; Universal) Director: George Melford. Associate Producer: Paul Kohner. Screenplay (Spanish adaptation): B. Fernandez Cue. Photography: George Robinson. Cast: Carlos Villarias, Lupita Tovar, Barry Norton, Pablo Alvarez Rubio, Eduardo Arozamena, José Soriano Viosca, Carmen Guerrero, Amelia Senisterra, Manuel Arbó.

In the burgeoning sound era (before the advent of practical dubbing), studios would occasionally produce foreign language versions (most often Spanish) of their more prestigious pictures to sell in the lucrative foreign markets. By utilizing the same sets and low-cost foreign actors, the studio could create a second version for a fraction of the cost of the original. At the suggestion of producer Paul Kohner, Universal slated their upcoming "Terrific Vampire Thriller" (as the pressbook labeled it) for the foreign-language treatment. Shooting at night on the same sets after the American cast and crew had gone home, Kohner and director George Melford filmed this alternate version for a mere $66,000 (about one seventh the cost of the English language *Dracula*). Melford ("a wonderful man," according to female lead Lupita Tovar), whom the cast affectionately dubbed "Uncle George," directed through an interpreter to create a vision parallel yet *superior* to Browning's version. Though lacking the (truly essential) iconographic presence of Bela Lugosi (Carlos Villarias makes a poor substitute), Melford's visual acumen outshines Browning's haphazard direction at nearly every turn. With the long-thought-lost Spanish version now released on video, devotees of the Golden Age of Horror can see what *Dracula* truly *might* have been.

THE DYBBUK (1937; Foreign Cinema Arts; Poland) Director: Michael Waszynski. Screenplay: Sz. A. Kacyzne, Andrew Marek (Synopsis by A. Stern); from the play by S. Ansky. Cast: A. Morewski, R. Samber, M. Libman, Lili Liliana, Dina Halpern, G. Lamberger, L. Libgold, M. Bozyk, S. Landau, S. Bronecki, M. Messzinger, Z. Katz, A. Kuro, D. Lederman.

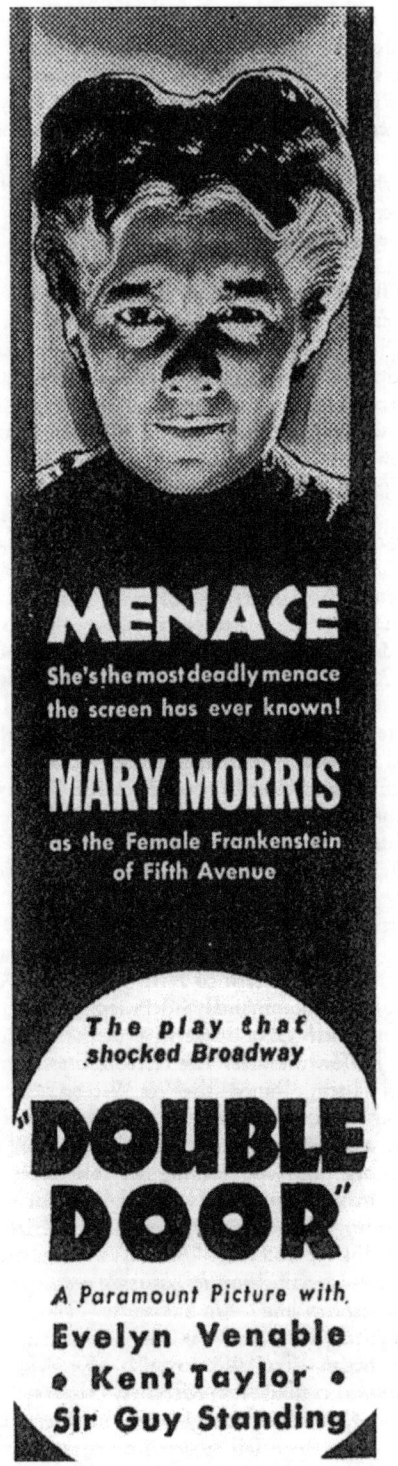

Though not quite "the Female Frankenstein of Fifth Avenue," Mary Morris nevertheless manages to induce a few shudders in *Double Door* (1934).

Carlos Villarias and Lupita Tovar in Universal's Spanish language version of *Dracula* (1931).

Filmed in Warsaw, this Yiddish production tells the tragic tale of thwarted love and spiritual possession. "All creatures are drawn to the source of the Divine Being," states the written prologue. "In these migrations it may happen that a wandering soul — a *Dybbuk* — enters a human being which once it loved." Two friends, Sender and Nison, make a sacred pact that their unborn offspring, if they be boy and girl, will marry each other. Nison, however, dies on the night of his son's birth. Eighteen years later, Sender is a miserly money-counter with a beautiful daughter named Leah. Channon, Nison's son, journeys to Brainitz to study the Yashiva. He is directed to Sender's house by a mysterious stranger, the "Messenger," who literally appears and vanishes at opportune moments. Sender forgets his 18-year-old pledge and betroths his daughter to a wealthy young man, though Leah has fallen in love with Channon. A penniless student, the desperate, misguided Channon calls on Satan to secure Leah for himself. In the process, however, he dies. Leah is heartbroken and during her wedding ceremony, rushes to Channon's grave. "Come my bridegroom," she tells the cold tombstone, "I shall bear both our souls — like unborn children." The spirit of Channon enters Leah's body and so becomes a Dybbuk. Sender takes his possessed daughter to a famed Rabbi who exorcises the phantom. The disconsolate girl, however, offers up her soul to the spirit, who claims it and leaves the father grieving by his dead daughter's side.

At 122 minutes, *The Dybbuk* is overlong, particularly as much of the running time consists of mournful religious songs, pious ceremony, and repetitive folkdancing ("The Dance of the Poor," "The Dance of Death," "The Dance of the Wealthy," "The Dance of the Beggars," "The Tap Dance"...). In spite of its length, an almost oppressive aura of inevitability pervades the picture as tragedy and resignation become the central themes. In addition, the principals are so consumed by weighty religious issues that the line between the temporal and spiritual blurs beyond recognition, allowing the viewer to take the (omni)presence of the supernatural "Messenger" and the reality of wandering spirits as a matter of course. The horror fan is bound for disappointment, however, since the ghostly proceedings contain no element of terror — merely a note of inevitability. While the production boasts adequate production values, this Yiddish take on Shakespearean tragedy can easily lose the viewer in a miasma of ceremony.

THE FACE AT THE WINDOW (1932; Real Art; Great Britain) Director: Leslie Hiscott. Producer: Julius Hagen. Screenplay: H. Fowler Mear (from the play by F. Brooke Warren). Cast: Raymond Massey, Isla Bevan, Claude Hulbert, Eric

Poster for the 1939 Tod Slaughter vehicle, *The Face at the Window*. (Courtesy of Lynn Naron.)

Maturin, Henry Mollison, A. Bromley Davenport, Harold Meade, Dennis Wyndham, Charles Groves.

In this apparently "lost" 52-minute British "Quota Quickie," Raymond Massey plays a Paris detective who fakes the revival of a murdered man in order to expose the respectable Count Fournal as a notorious killer and bank robber. In 1939, George King remade the story as a vehicle for Tod Slaughter. This later version *has* survived (see next entry).

THE FACE AT THE WINDOW (1939; British Lion; Great Britain) Producer/Director: George King. Screenplay: A. R. Rawlinson, Ronald Fayre (based on the play by F. Brooke Warren). Photography: Hone Glendinning. Cast: Tod Slaughter, Marjorie Taylor, John Warwick, Leonard Henry, Aubrey Mallalieu, Robert Adair, Wallace Evenett, Kay Lewis, Billy Shine, Margaret Yarde, Harry Terry.

A British murder melodrama with horror overtones, *The Face at the Window* is a vehicle for Tod Slaughter, the self-proclaimed "Horror man of Europe." Slaughter plays a rich gentleman who is really the evil murderer known as "The Wolf." This killer's nefarious crimes are always preceded by a horrible countenance staring in at the victim through a window (hence the title) just before the unfortunate receives a knife in the back. Add an innocent ingenue (Marjorie Taylor) and a young hero framed for the Wolf's crimes (John Warwick), and it's vintage melodramatics. The hero is courageous, the heroine bravely defiant, and the villain suave yet slimy. As expected, Slaughter plays his role to the hilt, and you're just waiting for him to tie the girl to the railroad tracks. The first two thirds of this already brief (65 minutes) film move rather too slowly and predictably as Slaughter makes advances to the heroine and goes about framing her lover, but the final 20 minutes hold the viewer's interest with glimpses of the horrible, drooling face in question and Slaughter's final surprise revelation as to his relationship with this face. There's a clever twist (borrowed from the earlier Slaughter film, *The Crimes of Stephen Hawke*) in the way the hero forces the Wolf to reveal himself, and Slaughter's final ravings as we learn The Whole Truth are chilling in an over-the-top way. If you like British melodramas (along with ample arm-waving and prodigious posturing), this will adequately fit the bill; if on the other hand you're looking for some suspenseful horror, you'll have to look elsewhere.

Heroine Marjorie Taylor's short (four-year) screen career included three other Tod Slaughter vehicles: *The Crimes of Stephen Hawke* (1936), *It's Never Too Late to Mend* (1937), and *Ticket of Leave*

Man (1937). "I have been dodging a fate worse than death for years," laughed Ms. Taylor in the *Face* pressbook. "Tod is always on my track trying to marry me, or trying to kill my screen-sweetheart but, fortunately, I have been saved in the nick of time in each instance."

Director George King, known in industry circles as England's "King of the Quickies," is credited with the discovery of Laurence Olivier, according to the *Face* pressbook. (King *did* direct Olivier at the beginning of his film career in 1930's *Too Many Crooks*).

F. Brooke Warren's turn-of-the-century stage-play, "The Face at the Window," had been filmed twice before—first in 1920 starring C. Aubrey Smith and next in 1932 with Raymond Massey.

A FACE IN THE FOG (1936; Victory) Director: Bob Hill. Producer: Sam Katzman. Screenplay: Al Martin (from "The Great Mono Miracle" by Peter B. Kyne). Photography: Bill Hyer. Cast: June Collyer, Lloyd Hughes, Lawrence Gray, Jack Mulhall, Al St. John, Joack Cowell, John Elliot, Sam Flint, Forrest Taylor.

A sinister hunchbacked figure dressed in a slouch hat and black cloak hobbles about in the night to murder his victims. A woman reporter, her amorous male colleague, and their thick-witted staff photographer become embroiled in the search for this mysterious maniac. "He's about as elusive as a gust of wind," their exasperated editor informs them. The police have discovered no motive for the murders (despite the fact that several of the victims were members of a current musical play), nor do they even know "the Fiend's" (as the press unoriginally labels him) method. "They were poisoned all right, but the mystery is —*how*. The coroner's so confused that he almost did a postmortem on himself," cracks the editor. This mysterious method of murder is unwisely given away at the very beginning when we see the fiend load a special gun with a strange-looking bullet made of frozen poison. Add an amateur sleuth, a handful of mystery clichés (one victim dies just as he's about to finger the murderer: "His name is —"), and the forgettable concoction is complete. Sadly, *A Face in the Fog* doesn't even hold up well as a mystery, much less a horror film. Despite its title, there is no face (we never see the fiend's visage until the final denouement) and definitely no fog. In fact, there seems to be no attempt to generate any atmosphere or mood whatsoever. Director Bob Hill seemed satisfied with an ambiance of contemporary realism (or as much realism as could be achieved with cheap sets and sub-par acting). Dull, static photography, uniform lighting, and listless direction deprive the film of whatever mood and suspense might have been generated by a sinister, cloaked figure performing dire deeds in the dead of night.

Female lead June Collyer (born Dorothea Heermance) also appeared in *The Ghost Walks* and *Murder by Television* in 1935. She retired from films soon afterwards, though she later returned to acting (on the small screen), co-starring in the TV series "The Trouble with Father." Canadian-born director Robert F. ("Bob") Hill churned out numerous serials and low-budget features from 1919 to 1941. In the 1921 serial *The Adventures of Tarzan*, Hill directed the screen's first "Lord of the Apes." He later directed Buster Crabbe in the role (for *Tarzan the Fearless*, 1933). Undoubtedly, Hill's most remembered work is the serial *Flash Gordon's Trip to Mars* (1938). Hill helmed one other near-horror, *The Rogue's Tavern*, the same year as *A Face in the Fog*. As well as directing, Hill sometimes worked as a screenwriter, even collaborating on Paul Leni's excellent *The Cat and the Canary* (1927).

FAHRMANN MARIA (1936; Pallas Film G.m.b.H.; Germany) Director: Frank Wysbar. Screenplay: Hans Jurgen Nierentz, Frank Wysbar. Photography: Franz Weihmayr. Cast: Sybille Schmitz, Aribert Mog, Peter Voss, Carl de Vogt, Karl Platen, Gerhart Bienert, Eduard Wenck.

Translated as either *Ferryboat Woman Maria* or *Ferryboat Pilot Maria*, this German romantic fantasy film never made it to American shores. (Not so the picture's director/co-writer, Frank Wysbar, who emigrated to the U.S. in 1939. Coming to Hollywood in 1943, he resumed his interrupted film career and eventually remade this dark fantasy as a more straightforward [and more entertaining] horror picture for PRC in 1946 called *Strangler of the Swamp*.)

The story of *Fahrmann Maria* is set in a small village surrounded by marshes. An elderly man runs the single ferryboat connecting the hamlet to the outside world. Just after midnight one evening, he ferries across a man dressed all in black. This dark figure is Death himself, and the old ferryman's time has come. A young woman named Maria (played by *Vampyr*'s Sybille Schmitz) arrives in the village and, desperate for work, takes the job of ferryboat pilot (which nobody seems to want). Soon after, she rescues a young man from a group of mounted pursuers and nurses him back to health. The two fall in love, but the young revolutionary develops a fever. That night, Maria is summoned to ferry across a man dressed all in black. Death has returned—this time for her newfound lover. With her paramour lying in the cottage, Maria tricks Death by telling him that the man he seeks is at the village festival. When Death cannot find him there, Maria overcomes her terror and delays the shade by dancing with him. Finally, Maria can stand it no longer and flees Death to take refuge in the village church. The Grim Reaper observes no religious boundaries, however, and follows her in. The night wears on and Death demands to be taken to his intended charge. Maria offers herself in place of her lover, but the specter refuses, having laid his claim. Desperate, Maria leads Death into the swamp, ready to sacrifice herself to delay the dire phantom. As they walk through the treacherous marshland, Death is caught in quicksand and sinks below the mire while Maria miraculously walks safely on into the arms of her waiting lover. Her love and self-sacrifice has overcome Death itself.

Much of *Fahrmann Maria* takes place at night, and the pervading twilight creates an eerie atmosphere. The occasional daylight scenes and the natural settings, however, are far too bright and harshly realistic to accommodate the mystical aspects of the picture's theme. The film moves rather slowly, its leisurely pace a result of the many romantic sequences. Wall-to-wall music carpets the picture, laying a tune for every mood. While this works in several specific instances, the continual (and obvious) music ultimately becomes intrusive. Wysbar's direction is careful and deliberate (as is the acting). He makes good use of Franz Weihmayr's mobile camera and creates some imaginative framings and dissolves. For instance, one sequence featuring a classroom full of singing children is shot through an open window with the edges framing the picture. This smoothly dissolves into the next shot of a man singing and playing the guitar — again seen through a window with its edges similarly framing the scene. Overall, *Fahrmann Maria* succeeds as a stately and sometimes otherworldly fantasy.

Released on February 7, 1936, in Berlin, the picture received generally favorable reviews. It also attracted some bizarre criticism as a result of the repressive, Aryan-oriented climate of the times. One Dr. Lemme, writing in the periodical, *Volk und Rasse* (*People and Race*), felt the film failed to meet the proper "standards of racial hygiene," and complained about the ambiguous nature of the brunette Maria's national and ethnic origins!

THE FLORENTINE DAGGER (1935; Warner Bros.) Director: Robert Florey. Screenplay: Tom Reed (story: Ben Hecht; additional dialogue: Brown Homes; dialogue director: Greville Collins). Photography: Arthur L. Todd. Cast: Donald Woods, Margaret Lindsay, C. Aubrey Smith, Henry O'Neill, Florence Fair, Frank Reicher.

Juan Cesare (Donald Woods), the last descendent of the murderous Borgia clan, feels an irresistible urge to kill. "The ghosts of the Borgias still walk in me," laments the tortured Juan to a sympathetic psychiatrist (C. Aubrey Smith). In order to conquer this compulsion, the psychiatrist suggests Juan write a play about Lucretia and family and so rid himself of this "Borgia complex." Juan does just that and the play is a hit. In addition, the now-recovered Juan falls for his leading lady, the daughter of the play's producer. When the producer turns up dead, stabbed with a Florentine dagger once owned (and wielded by) the dreaded Borgias themselves, Juan thinks he has lapsed back into his mania and viciously acted upon it — or is his intended bride a split-personality? (or is there yet a third mysterious suspect)? Director Robert Florey (*Murders in the Rue Morgue*, 1932) imbues this rather unlikely tale of "mania and murder" with a rich visual interest, making his usual excellent use of shadows, angles, and camera setups to create a dark, almost expressionistic atmosphere. Unfortunately, the picture is marred by a slow pace and (much like *Murders in the Rue Morgue*) some inane dialogue ("If there's one thing more useless than a talkative woman, it is one determined not to talk.").

THE GHOST WALKS (1934; Invincible) Director: Frank R. Strayer. Producer: Maury M. Cohen. Screenplay: Charles S. Belden. Photography: M. A. Anderson. Cast: John Miljan, June Collyer, Richard Carle, Henry Kolker, Johnny Arthur, Spencer Charters, Donald Kirke, Eve Southern, Douglas Gerrard, Wilson Benge, Jack Shutta, Harry Strang.

A young playwright and his producer are stranded in a storm and forced to spend the night at the nearby mansion of Dr. Kent. At dinner, the lights go out and a ghastly face floats through the darkness to frighten the guests. It all turns out to be a stunt staged by the playwright to demonstrate a new play to his producer, though it soon becomes apparent that something stranger than fiction is going on when one of the household turns up dead — for real. Sliding panels, portraits with shifty eyes, a bed that collapses upon itself, and one escaped mental patient later, *The Ghost Walks* finally stumbles its way out of mystery cliché purgatory for the wrap-up. The obligatory comic relief speaks volumes about the picture's level of sophistication: "I don't like that fellow Caraway," warns the producer, to which his secretary replies, "Oh forget it, he's just a *seedy* butler." With little suspense, unimaginative camerawork, sparse sets, and absolutely *no* action (at the climax, two sanitarium guards simply *talk* the escaped lunatic into giving up and coming with them), this *Ghost* doesn't walk, it crawls.

Director Frank Strayer supervised several horror and near-horror films of the Golden Age: *The Monster Walks* (1932), *The Vampire Bat* (1933), and *Condemned to Live* (1935). With the exception of *The Vampire Bat*, however, none of these lifeless productions were to Strayer's credit.

THE GOLEM (1936; Metropolis/A-B Film; France/Czechoslovakia) Alternate Title: *The Legend of Prague*. Director: Julien Duvivier. Screenplay: Andre Paul Antoine, Julien Duvivier. Photography: Vich and Stallich. Cast: Harry Bauer, Roger Karl, Gaston Jacquet, Germaine Aussey, Aimos, Roger Duchesne, Charles Durat, Jany Holt, Ferdinand Hart.

This first sound version of *The Golem* ("Inspired by the celebrated legend that originated in the ghetto of medieval Prague") is long on petty subplots but short on horror. Indeed, the titular titan (a statue of clay brought to life by magic to save the persecuted Jews of Prague) only appears in the film's final ten minutes. When it does finally awaken, this gargantuan (played by Ferdinand Hart who, like Karloff's Frankenstein monster, wears asphalt-spreader boots) resembles nothing more terrifying than a tall, broad man with balding head and brown complexion. The final reel does present an impressive spectacle as the clay creature topples columns, gates, and entire buildings on his rampage, but the destructive proceedings lack the more intimate personal element necessary to inspire terror. (And the living statue's final demise features some of the most inept special effects of the era. To simulate the clay Golem disintegrating, technicians simply took a still plate of the creature — background included — and broke it apart!) The picture's prior 80 minutes revolve around the mad King Rudolph II's (well played by Harry Bauer) overwhelming fear that Rabbi Jacob will revive the Golem and the monarch's tedious attempts to retrieve the slumbering statue or coerce the Jewish populace into giving it up. Various trivial subplots involving Rudolph's scheming mistress, an amorous French antiques dealer, and the king's slimy chancellor keep the picture sidetracked onto uninteresting courtly intrigues. The settings for this reportedly $300,000 production filmed on location in Prague are sumptuous, and Duvivier directs with an impressive visual flare, utilizing movement, shadows, and unique angles to draw the viewer into his historical world. Even so, he cannot overcome the rambling storyline and lack of horrific content.

This 1936 production was not the first, nor the last, of The Golems. The clay man first walked on the screen in 1915, when Germany's Paul Wegener directed himself as *The Golem* (a.k.a. *The Monster of Fate*). After a Danish company released their version of *The Golem* in 1916, Wegener followed up with his comedic *The Golem and the Dancing Girl* (1917). Three years later, Wegener teamed up with director Carl Boese and the resources of UFA to produce the best-known version of *The Golem* (1920). After one more silent adaptation (Austria's *The Golem's Last Adventure* released in 1921), Julien Duvivier introduced the first talking-cinema Golem in 1936. Subsequently, the supernatural statue would walk through a number of productions. The 1943 compilation film *Dr. Terror's House of Horrors* featured footage from Duvivier's version; Czechoslovakia produced a political satire in 1951 called (among other things) *The Emperor and the Golem*; France made a television version of *The Golem* in 1966 (released as *Mask of the Golem* theatrically); the same year Britain gave us *It* with Roddy McDowall animating a Golemlike statue which proved impervious to the atom bomb(!); the Golem legend became part of the framing device of a three-part Czech film called *The Nights of Prague* in 1968; and France produced one more version in 1971 called *The Golem's Daughter*.

THE GORILLA (1931; Warner Bros.) Director: Bryan Foy. Screenplay: B. Harrison Orkow (based on the play by Ralph Spence). Cast: Lila Lee, Joe Frisco, Harry Gribbon, Walter Pidgeon, Purnell Pratt, Edwin Maxwell, Rosco Karns, Landers Stevens, William Philbrick.

No print of this first sound adaptation of Ralph Spence's 1925 Broadway hit play, "The Gorilla," is known to exist. If one believes the reviews of the day, it is no great loss (*Variety*, for instance, called it "a goofy and unreasonable burlesque on a murder mystery in which neither the acting nor the action may be seriously considered"). The story involves two detectives assigned to protect a zoologist from attack by a mysterious gorilla which has been killing people indiscriminately. *Variety* reported that star Joe Frisco (a famous vaudeville headliner) "got around $40,000 to make this picture and a couple of shorts."

THE GORILLA (1939; 20th Century–Fox) Director: Allan Dwan. Associate Producer: Harry Joe Brown. Screenplay: Rian James and Sid Silvers (based on the play by Ralph Spence). Photography: Edward Cronjager. Cast: Jimmy Ritz, Harry Ritz, Al Ritz, Anita Louise, Patsy Kelly,

Lionel Atwill, Bela Lugosi, Joseph Calleia, Edward Norris, Wally Vernon, Paul Harvey, Art Miles.

Like *The Cat and the Canary* released later the same year, *The Gorilla* is an adaptation of a hit play. Ralph Spence's popular "Old Dark House" story had already been filmed twice (in 1927 and 1931) before 20th Century–Fox transformed it into a vehicle for the Ritz Brothers. The comedy team is a trio of bumbling private eyes (from the Acme Detective Agency, naturally) called in to protect Lionel Atwill, who has been threatened by a "maniac murderer" known as "The Gorilla" ("Is It Man or Beast?" asks a newspaper headline). At Atwill's gloomy mansion they encounter strange noises, sliding panels, mysterious notes, clutching hands, a sinister servant (Bela Lugosi no less), and even a real gorilla (named "Poe") before a series of unlikely twists and turns leads to the happy ending.

Just like *The Cat and the Canary*, *The Gorilla* possesses a wonderfully sinister old mansion setting, fine supporting players, and solid production values. What *The Gorilla* lacks, however, is a strong female lead (the bland Anita Louise is no Paulette Goddard) and effective comedy — three Ritzes don't even come *close* to one Hope. The tepid threesome's brand of low-brow mugging and inept silliness quickly becomes tiresome, and the only truly funny comedy comes from a sharp-tongued maid (Patsy Kelly). Bela Lugosi is a welcome presence as the unflappable, enigmatic butler, and it's always a joy to watch Lionel Atwill play (as he does here) a shifty, slightly sinister character. Too bad Atwill disappears (literally) after a couple of reels and Lugosi puts in only sporadic appearances throughout. Physiology aside, in this instance *The Cat* rates much higher on the intelligence scale than *The Gorilla*.

THE GREAT IMPERSONATION (1935; Universal) Director: Alan Crosland. Producer: Edmund Grainger. Screenplay: Frank Wead, Even Greene (based on the novel by E. Phillips Oppenheim). Photography: Milton Krasner (Special Cinematographer: John P. Fulton). Cast: Edmund Lowe, Valerie Hobson, Wera Engels, Murray Kinnell, Henry Mollison, Esther Dale, Brandon Hurst, Ivan Simpson, Spring Byington, Lumsden Hare, Charles Waldron, Leonard Mudie, Claude King, Frank Reicher, Harry Allen.

As yet another of Universal's pseudo-horror entries, *The Great Impersonation* features a spy story decked out with a few horror trappings. Set on the eve of World War I, an agent for an evil "international munitions ring" impersonates the alcoholic, unstable Sir Everard Dominey in an attempt to "cripple the effectiveness of England's mighty war machine" and thus enrich the coffers of the crooked cartel which "owes allegiance to no country." The horror element comes from the "Black Bog" on the grounds of Dominey Hall, from which emanate wild, horrible screams at night — the ghostly wailings of a man supposedly murdered by Sir Everard a year earlier. The plot twists and turns through several neat complications and surprises before everything comes out right — and the ghost is exposed as a very-much-alive madman. (This unfortunate is none other than a long-bearded Dwight Frye collecting his $100 paycheck for a day's work.) Edmund Lowe (who made considerably more — $16,700 more to be exact) makes for a likable double (or is that *triple*?) agent and cuts a rather dashing figure, while the lovely Valerie Hobson serves adequately as the beautiful wife driven to the brink of insanity by the hideous screams. Said screams provide the occasional chill as they echo throughout the ominous, castlelike rooms and stone corridors of Dominey Hall (which include standing sets from *Frankenstein* and *The Old Dark House*). With good production values, a likable cast and a fairly intriguing story, *The Great Impersonation* slips by as a painless, at times even enjoyable, 64 minutes. Audiences in 1935 didn't think so, however, for *The Great Impersonation* "flopped" at the box office according to the *Hollywood Reporter*, which noted the film did only 70 percent of usual business at the theaters the publication canvassed.

HELLAVISION (1937; Roadshow) Producer: Louis Sonney.

Pioneer roadshowman Louis Sonney (a contemporary of Dwain Esper, whom he sometimes partnered with) returned to his native Italy and bought the American rights to an Italian film called *Dante's Inferno*. Sonney eventually sold the footage to 20th Century–Fox who incorporated the hellish visions into their 1935 Spencer Tracy vehicle of the same name. Sonney also produced his *own* picture utilizing the footage, calling it *Hellavision*. In it, a scientist invents a machine dubbed the Helivision which could look into the future and show a person whether he was going to heaven or hell. According to David F. Friedman (in *Cult Movies* #8), "The Sonneys had this film on roadshow for three or four years and did very well with it." Unfortunately, Dan Sonney (Louis' son) reported that the negative has completely deteriorated and no prints of the film now exist.

THE HOUSE OF FEAR (1939; Universal) Director: Joe May. Associate Producer: Edmund

Grainger. Screenplay: Peter Milne (based on the 1922 play *The Last Warning* by Thomas F. Fallon adapted from the 1916 novel *Backstage Phantom* by Wadsworth Camp). Photography: Milton Krasner. Cast: William Gargan, Irene Hervey, Dorothy Arnold, Alan Dinehart, Harvey Stevens, Walter Woolf King, Robert Coote, El Brendel, Tom Dugan, Jan Dugan, Donald Douglas.

Broadway actor John Woodford collapses and dies on-stage during the opening performance of his new play. In the confusion, the body disappears from his dressing room. A year passes and the police are no nearer a solution to Woodford's death/disappearance, so a detective poses as a producer and stages a revival of the play at the same theater with many of the same cast. Soon, ghostly phone calls from John Woodford on disconnected phones, menacing notes, and falling stage props set the company on edge as the ghost of Woodford seems intent on preventing the play from opening. Throughout it all, however, it is evident that a human rather than supernatural hand is behind the mystery.

Despite the spooky trappings, the picture (taking place entirely within the theater dressing rooms, cellar, offices, and stage) never generates much atmosphere, and the story just seems to be going through the ghostly motions without any real conviction. Aside from one instance when an eerie, glowing face glides through the darkness of the empty theater, no chills are forthcoming. Still, thanks to clever dialogue ("All I know is that some person or persons is playing ghost — and doing an *uncanny* job of it"), some effective satire on the theatrical business in general and "act*ors*" in particular, and the crisp, ingratiating playing of William Gargan as the producer/detective, *The House of Fear* becomes a diverting (if not altogether satisfying) 65 minutes.

Abandoning his thriving German film career in 1934, Austrian-born director Joe May fled to America to escape the Nazi regime. Though *The House of Fear* went well over its 15-day schedule and $100,000 budget, Universal subsequently entrusted May with two of their more prestigious (i.e., expensive) horror projects of 1940 — *The House of the Seven Gables* and *The Invisible Man Returns*.

House of Fear is a remake of Universal's silent *The Last Warning* (1929), which was directed by the great Paul Leni (*The Cat and the Canary*, 1927, *The Man Who Laughs*, 1928) and starred Laura La Plante (Universal's top female lead of the time) and John Boles (*Frankenstein*). Leni would make only one more film before his untimely death (of blood poisoning) in 1929.

HOUSE OF MYSTERY (1934; Monogram) Director: William Nigh. Producer: Paul Malvern. Screenplay: Albert De Mond (from the play by Adam Hull Shirk). Photography: Archie Stout. Cast: Ed Lowry, Verna Hillie, John Sheehan, Brandon Hurst, Laya Joy, Fritzi Ridgeway, Clay Clement, George Hayes, Dale Fuller, Harry Bradley, Irving Bacon, Mary Foy, Samuel Godfrey.

"Nowhere in this world can you escape the Curse of Kali," relates a weary Mr. Prendergast to his houseguests. Twenty years earlier, Prendergast had led an expedition to Asia where he defiled the temple and rituals of Kali (by killing a sacred monkey) and stole the god's treasure, earning the dreaded "curse." Now a wheelchair-bound recluse, Prendergast lives in constant fear of sounds and shadows, particularly the shadow of an ape. The investors in the expedition have finally tracked him down and now demand their share of the treasure. Prendergast had hoped to spare the others his fate and so makes one demand. "I'll give you all your shares on one condition — that you come here and live in this house with me for a week and learn what happens to the possessor of it." During the first night, one of the guests conducts a seance. Mysterious tom-toms begin beating and the shadow of a gorilla passes over the wall. When the lights come up, the medium is dead — strangled. The police are called but that doesn't stop the beastly shadow from claiming another victim (again accompanied by the rhythmic beating of the tom-tom — as well as a bowl of smoking incense). Now the film, after having built up a fine atmosphere ripe with dread, settles down to a typical drawing room mystery. The buffoon of a detective in charge and his two stooges begin questioning each of the guests, which include an absent-minded professor, his overbearing wife, a slow-witted plumber, a Hindu housekeeper, a typical young ingenue, and a hero who keeps annoying everyone (including the audience) by trying to sell them all insurance. (Radio and vaudeville headliner Ed Lowry made his screen debut as the pestering hero — and never made another picture afterwards.) At this point, the film slows to a crawl and never regains its feet. In the end, a Scotland Yard detective (whose British accent is conspicuous only in its absence) shows up to solve the whole riddle and finally trap the (obvious) guilty party responsible for the killings. Yes, the ape is real: "The ape was trained to go immediately to the incense when it heard the tom-tom and break the neck of the first person it met." (This particular idea was later borrowed and adapted for the infinitely more enjoyable Bela Lugosi vehicle, *The Devil Bat*, in 1941.) Slow-paced and slow-witted ("No son of an ape is going to make a monkey out of me!" exclaims the dim detective), this *House of Mystery* quickly becomes a house of boredom.

Heroine Verna Hillie, a young radio actress from Detroit, got her start in Hollywood as one of four finalists of Paramount's "Search for the 'Panther Woman'" contest, a shameless studio ploy to scare up publicity (as well as a new contractee) for their upcoming production, *Island of Lost Souls* (1933). "Paramount publicized the Panther Woman Contest in every newspaper in every major city in the United States," Ms. Hillie remembered to Greg Mank in 1994. "I thought it was demeaning! However, my mother sent my picture in, and the Paramount people contacted me to make a test for the Panther Woman." Though she did not win the role, the actress did secure a brief contract and began acting in films such as *College Humor* (1933) and *Duck Soup* (1933). Monogram borrowed Ms. Hillie from Paramount for their production, which carried the working titles of *The Ape* and *Curse of Kali* before the studio settled on the final (unilluminating) moniker *House of Mystery*. Verna Hillie left motion pictures in 1938, but her daughter, Pamela Lincoln, carried on the family acting tradition (appearing in 1959's *The Tingler*).

Director William Nigh also helmed *Mystery Liner* this same year and *The Mysterious Mr. Wong* in 1935. A success in silents (Nigh began his directing career making Mack Sennett comedy shorts), he slipped into "B" status during the talkies, working steadily for Monogram in the 1930s and forties, directing, among others, their "Mr. Wong" series starring Boris Karloff (no relation to the 1935 Lugosi picture). In 1940 Nigh directed *The Ape* for Monogram which (the credits claimed) was also based on the same Adam Hull Shirk play. *The Ape* (a mad scientist vehicle for Boris Karloff), however, does not resemble *House of Mystery* at all (save for the fact that it also features a man in a gorilla suit).

THE HUNCHBACK OF NOTRE DAME (1939; RKO) Director: William Dieterle. Producer: Pandro S. Berman. Screenplay: Sonya Levien (adapted by Bruno Frank). Photography: Joseph H. August. Cast: Charles Laughton, Sir Cedric Hardwicke, Thomas Mitchell, Maureen O'Hara, Edmund O'Brien, Alan Marshal, Walter Hampden, Harry Davenport, Katherine Alexander, George Zucco, Fritz Leiber, Etienne Girardot.

When a beautiful gypsy girl named Esmeralda (Maureen O'Hara) refuses the advances of an infatuated chief high justice (Sir Cedric Hardwicke), the powerful judge frames her for a murder he himself has committed. Quasimodo (Charles Laughton), the ugly hunchback who works as bell-ringer at Notre Dame, rescues Esmeralda and provides sanctuary at the cathedral. When the Beggar's Guild marches out to save the girl from the noble's intent on hanging her, Quasimodo mistakes them for a lynch mob and hurls stones and molten lead down upon them. In the finale, the girl receives a pardon from the king (after the monarch learns of his chief justice's treachery) and leaves with her poet lover (Edmund O'Brien), while the heartbroken Quasimodo is left sitting atop his beloved Notre Dame, alone with the mute gargoyles, lamenting "Why was I not made of stone like thee?"

"One shrinks from the ugly yet wants to look at it. There's a *devilish* fascination in it. We extract pleasure from horror," observes King Louis upon seeing the deformed Quasimodo. While a spectacular costume drama exuding both an expansive "cast of thousands" grandeur and a grimy, medieval backalley authenticity, *The Hunchback of Notre Dame* offers very little "devilish fascination" in terms of *horror*. The only moment in the picture even approaching terror comes when a frightening array of menacing beggars seemingly materialize from nowhere to crawl forth from the blackness and surround Esmeralda's lover. (Douglas Fairbanks, Jr., was originally set to play this part, but the romantic role ultimately went to Edmond O'Brien). Charles Laughton's heartrending Quasimodo, a misshapen "monster" ostracized by the world, inspires the pathos generated by Karloff's Frankenstein monster — but without the terror. Horror or no, *The Hunchback of Notre Dame* remains a mesmerizing tale of human weakness and strength, wisdom and folly, pettiness and grandeur, set against the squalid, boisterous life of fifteenth-century Paris.

Though the 1923 epic starring Lon Chaney is often considered the first film adaptation of Victor Hugo's novel *Notre-Dame de Paris*, there had been numerous screen incarnations of Hugo's famous character previous to Chaney's. The first was a ten-minute French short entitled *Esmeralda*, released in 1905 and directed by a woman (a very rare instance in early cinema — or *later* cinema for that matter). At least eight other cinematic adaptations, borrowings, or outright thefts popped up in various countries, including France, Great Britain, Germany and America (*The Hunchback*, 1909; *Hugo the Hunchback*, 1910; *The Darling of Paris*, 1916; etc.). All of these earlier versions, however, were completely eclipsed in 1923 when Universal produced their lavish spectacle (at a then-unheard-of price tag of $1,250,000) which rocketed the magnificent Lon Chaney from mere star to superstar status. It is difficult to say which is the better production, the 1923 or the 1939 film. Both are considered classics and both feature a masterful performance from its star (Chaney's Quasimodo was the more acrobatic and energetically alive of the two while Laughton's hunchback exuded more pathos).

Universal announced as early as 1931 that they would remake their 1923 epic—with Bela Lugosi in the title role (the "next best" now that Chaney was dead, according to the July 14th *Variety* announcement). Like many a proposed project, however, nothing came of it. Irving Thalberg briefly considered taking on the story in 1934, even discussing it with his choice for Quasimodo—Charles Laughton. Then, in 1936, Universal again became interested. *The Hollywood Reporter* (September 19, 1936) noted that "a fan poll has determined Universal to go ahead with plans to remake *The Hunchback of Notre Dame*." The "fan preferences" for the title role included Fredric March, Paul Muni, Ronald Colman, Lionel Barrymore, and Peter Lorre. "The studio favors Lorre," and in fact began negotiations with the Hollywood newcomer, but again it came to naught.

In 1937, producer Carl Laemmle, Jr. (who had recently come to MGM after his father was forced to sell Universal) persuaded Metro to buy the property from "The New Universal" as a starring vehicle for Paul Muni. "Junior," however, only lasted two months at MGM and the studio decided against the remake, eventually selling the rights to RKO.

The up-and-coming Lon Chaney, Jr., reportedly sought the title role in RKO's *The Hunchback of Notre Dame*, but the studio (thankfully) denied him this opportunity to follow in his father's footsteps by casting Laughton in the part.

An air of secrecy surrounded Laughton's Quasimodo makeup, with the RKO publicity department refusing to release any advance photos of the

Quasimodo (Charles Laughton) ponders his wretched existence for a moment in the lavishly produced 1939 version of *The Hunchback of Notre Dame*.

hunchback's visage. The studio was determined that audiences should receive the full shock of this frightening yet believable countenance when first seen in the sudden full-face close-up in the film. The development of this makeup was a long and lugubrious process. Makeup innovator Perc Westmore ("borrowed" from Warners for the princely sum of $10,000) worked on it for months, producing one version after another before finding just the right face to suit both the actor and director. Laughton then had to endure three hours in the makeup chair while two-thirds of his face was covered in latex to transform him into the unfortunate Quasimodo. Laughton, however, experienced very little physical discomfort compared to his illustrious predecessor. To achieve the look of humped deformity he desired, Chaney had outfitted himself with a harnesslike device and various pads that weighed in at a whopping 70 pounds, whereas Laughton's aluminum and foam rubber hump added a mere six pounds to his rather corpulent mass. Despite the improvement in makeup technology, Laughton was determined to bring as much, if not more, suffering to his role as had the "Man of a Thousand Faces" a decade and a half earlier. Laughton endured numerous welts and bruises as a result of the "realism" of the lashing Quasimodo took on the wheel. To further add to this realism, Laughton at one point asked the makeup assistant to grab his foot and twist it, screaming "More, more, twist it more," to achieve that extra bit of painful sincerity in his performance.

While it took a joint effort to bring Quasimodo to life, the two principal creators did not get along. Perc (pronounced "Purse") Westmore and Charles Laughton were in constant struggle over the character. Their first clash was over the hump itself. According to Frank Westmore (in *The Westmores of Hollywood*), Laughton was dismayed at how light the new hump was, deciding that he "couldn't possibly work effectively unless he was suffering under the same weight Chaney had carried." When Westmore suggested that Laughton simply conjure up the pain ("You know, *act* as if you're in agony"), the actor was outraged at the makeup man's perceived insolence and went storming out to producer Pandro S. Berman, demanding that Westmore be fired. "He is going about this makeup all wrong," Laughton complained to Berman. "You see, I must look like a pig with a very heavy hump." Westmore's reply: "Don't give it another thought. You look like a pig *without* a very heavy hump." Despite the insults, Berman was able to placate the two.

The mutual animosity finally boiled to a head one day, however, as witnessed by Perc Westmore's younger brother Frank. In *The Westmores of Hollywood*, Frank related the incident: "[Perc] laughed when he told me that in order to put on the hump, with its complicated arrangement of straps to hold it in place on Laughton's back, the dignified actor had to get down on all fours on the floor. 'He sweats,' Perc said unkindly, 'like the pig he is, and he grunts like one, and the whole process makes him very thirsty.'" Following his brother to Laughton's bungalow, Frank watched as Laughton "got off the couch and dropped to his hands and knees" to have the hump attached. "I watched as Perc unwound the straps from around the hump. For the first time I noticed he was carrying a bottle of quinine water. As he began to put on the hump, sure enough, Laughton started to sweat. Beads of perspiration dripped on the floor. Without looking up, he said, 'Give me a drink, Perc.' 'Yes, Mr. Laughton,' said my brother. Deliberately he squatted down right in from of Laughton's face and vigorously began to shake that bottle of quinine water. 'No, Perc, no! You wouldn't!' 'Yes, Mr. Laughton, I *would*,' Perc said, and he shot the whole fizzy bottleful right into the face of one of England's most distinguished actors. For good measure Perc then stood up, walked to the other end of his captive on the floor, and kicked him squarely in the ass. 'That's for all the grief you've given me,' said Perc. 'I brought my brother today because I needed a witness to say this never happened, if you try to say it did. But you won't, Mr. Laughton, you won't.' Laughton didn't." After the film wrapped, Perc Westmore and Charles Laughton never worked together again.

The full-scale replica of the Notre Dame square cost RKO $250,000 (nearly one-seventh the film's final $1,826,000 budget), making it one of the most expensive sets ever constructed. Built at the studio's 88-acre ranch at Encino, the standing set showed up (in various guises) in dozens of subsequent pictures.

John Eastman, in his book, *Retakes: Behind the Scenes of 500 Classic Movies*, relates an important event that occurred during the filming of this picture, one which had a deep effect on star Charles Laughton. Eastman writes, "A moving moment occurred following the sequence when Quasimodo rings the bells in the tower for the gypsy girl Esmeralda (played by Maureen O'Hara). It was the day, filled with intense emotion and anguish for all the British residents in Hollywood, when England went to war against Germany. After the sequence ended for the camera, Laughton continued ringing the bells with almost frenzied abandon, and everyone knew why." Later, in his dressing room, Laughton could only say: "I couldn't think of Esmeralda in that scene at all. I could only think of the poor people out there, going in to fight that bloody, bloody war! To arouse the world, to stop that terrible butchery! Awake! Awake! That's what I felt when I was ringing the bells!"

The Hunchback of Notre Dame received two Academy Award nominations — Best Sound Recording and Best Score. It did not win in either category. It *did* win at the box office, however, earning $3,155,000 in film rentals for RKO. Even so, the RKO corporation went on to show a net *loss* of $185,495 for the year 1939.

J'ACCUSE (I ACCUSE) (1937; Forrester-Parant; France) Alternate Title: *That They May Live*. Director/Producer: Abel Gance. Screenplay: Abel Gance, Steve Passeur. Photography: Roger Hubert. Cast: Victor Francen, Line Noro, Marie Lou, Marcel Delaitre, Jean Max, Renee Devillers.

With this powerful film, Abel Gance exposes the horrors of war by exposing its victims — 20 years after their deaths. The story begins in the rubble, mud, and filth of a bombed-out French village during World War I, around which a squadron of soldiers fight and die. Inventor Jean Diaz (Victor Francen), the single survivor of the last patrol of the war, vows that his comrades will not have died in vain and works for the next 16 years toward preventing further war by developing a form of impenetrable "steel glass." His obsession with the dead proves too much for his mind, however, and he goes insane, slipping into an almost cataleptic state. In 1936, Europe is again on the brink of war, and Diaz suddenly awakens from his lethargy only to find that his inventions have been stolen and twisted by the warmongers. With war inevitable, Diaz calls upon the dead to stop the folly of the living. "My 12,000,000 comrades killed in the war, you who were ignored and trampled on for 20 years, arise, all of you! The living are at war again!" As if in a collective nightmare, the graves disgorge their occupants, who march forth to remind the world of the horror it must not create again. "The dead will save you in spite of yourselves," Diaz tells a terrified mob. "Fear has seized you because you betrayed your dead. Fear the death rattle in those millions of throats — 'I accuse, I accuse, I accuse!'" The film's original ending showed the nations of the world suing for peace and the dead, their mission accomplished, returning to their graves. When the film was released in America and Britain in 1939 (when war was indeed inevitable), however, it was reedited so that the picture ended abruptly with the dead marching out in an appeal for peace.

With *J'Accuse*, Gance uses actual war footage (some of which he shot himself during World War I for a similarly titled antiwar film released in 1918) and authentic rubble-strewn, muddy settings to depict the chaos and blood and fear that make up modern warfare. His battle scenes become both intimate and horrendous, so that we can fully understand Diaz's subsequent zealous conviction. As Diaz, the Belgian actor Victor Francen gives such a passionate, utterly convincing performance that his character's emotions soon become the viewer's own. For the climactic mass resurrection scenes, Gance brilliantly employs tilted angles and warped lenses to make the ocean of crosses seem to stir and the ground heave while the stone monuments appear to stretch and come alive. For the dead themselves, Gance employed a number of actual veterans disfigured by the war, their ruined countenances serving as shocking testimonials. Unfortunately, Gance relies almost solely on superimpositions (no doubt due to budgetary restrictions) so that the dead legions never quite integrate with the world of the living. Still, the overall effect remains a powerful one, making *J'Accuse* one of the most unique — and effective — of message pictures.

Unsurprisingly, this antiwar film was banned in Germany.

LIFE RETURNS (1935; Universal) Director: Eugen [Eugene] Frenke. Screenplay: Arthur Horman and John F. Goodrich (dialogue by Mary McCarthy and L. Wolfe Gilbert; original story by Eugen [Eugene] Frenke and James Hogan). Photography: Robert Plank. Cast: Dr. Robert E. Cornish, Onslow Stevens, George Breakston, Lois Wilson, Valerie Hobson, Stanley Fields, Frank Reicher, Richard Carle, Dean Benton, Lois January, Richard Quine, Maidel Turner, George MacQuarrie, Otis Harlan.

On May 22, 1934, Dr. Robert Cornish and his team of assistants conducted an experiment at the University of Southern California in which he restored "life" to a dead dog (asphyxiated by nitrogen gas). Movie cameras captured the moment for posterity. German filmmaker Dr. Eugene Frenke apparently contacted Cornish, obtained the rights to the experimental film, and struck a deal with Universal to split production costs and profits of a movie centered around the story and footage. (Dr. Cornish must have driven a hard bargain, for his name appears *above* the film's title and before any other cast member, despite his playing a relatively minor role in the picture. Apart from the few minutes of the experiment footage at the end, he appears in only a few scenes and has minimal dialogue.)

Though a plethora of writers worked on the screenplay, *Life Returns* is a hopeless, jumbled mess, a gimmick film built around the few (dull) minutes of real-life footage. (While this actual footage may be authentic, it's completely devoid of drama.) The reanimation angle simply wraps up a tepid boy-and-his-dog tale. It begins with three young doctors working together on a means to restore life. One of them, Dr. Kendrick (Onslow Stevens), goes to work at a commercial lab, while doctors Stone (Lois Wilson) and Cornish (himself) continue working on their own. Kendrick loses his job because his research is deemed impractical, neglects his private practice, and devotes everything to his experiments. This leads to his financial ruin, the death of his wife, and his son, Danny (George Breakston), remanded to the court. Danny runs away with his dog Scooter and hides out with a gang of boys his own age. The dogcatcher nabs Scooter and gasses the dog. Danny comes to his father to beg him to try his experiment on Scooter, but Kendrick has failed in his work as well as his life. Finally, Kendrick finds some resolve and takes Scooter's corpse to his former colleagues, Stone and Cornish, and the three succeed in restoring life to the dog. Life returns to Scooter, Kendrick's dream has finally come true, and Danny's faith in his father is restored.

Kendrick, about which the film revolves, is such a spineless, whiny dreamer that the viewer quickly loses all sympathy for the pathetic man who can't seem to rouse himself enough out of his glassy-eyed stupor of self-pity to function as a human being. Poor Onslow Stevens (whose alternately sympathetic and maniacal Jekyll/Hyde-type character proved the greatest asset of 1945's *House of Dracula*) can do little more than run his hands through his disheveled hair and lie about on the couch. The film's other main focus is on Danny and the Little Rascal-like gang of clubhouse kids he falls in with. It all makes for an excruciatingly dull 60 minutes.

According to a piece in *The Hollywood Reporter* (October 23, 1934), only a few of the people involved with the real-life restoration experiment knew that it was being recorded on camera. Though the film's opening written narration claims that "Dr. Robert E. Cornish of California has recently astounded the world with his amazing experiments in this field," the doctor and his accomplishment seems to have been forgotten by the world in general and the medical field in particular (apparently no corroboration or repetition of his procedure has ever been reported). Therefore, it seems unlikely that Cornish fully accomplished what had been implied or succeeded in doing anything with practical, far-reaching effects.

THE LIVING DEAD (1932; Hoffberg; Germany) Original Language Title: *Unheimliche Geschichten (Unholy Tales)*. Director: Richard Oswald. Producer: Gabriel Pascal. Screenplay: Heinz Goldberg, Eugen Szatmari. Photography: Heinrich Gaertner. Cast: Paul Wegener, Harald Paulsen, Bert Reisfeld, Roma Bahn, Mary Parker, John Gottowt, Pal Henckels, Ilse Feurstenberg, Viktor de Kowa.

The American release poster for this German production promised that this "story of strange people based on the stories of Edgar Allan Poe and Robert Louis Stevenson," was a "fantastic adventure into the macabre." Just *how* fantastic and *how* macabre remains to be seen — as does the picture itself, for, at the moment, *The Living Dead* seemingly belongs in the forgotten fold of "Lost Films." Cinema's first horror anthology, *The Living Dead* stars Paul Wegener (*The Golem*, 1920) as a mad scientist who walls his wife up in the cellar (à la Poe's *The Black Cat*) and thereafter, dogged by a determined reporter, shows up in a series of vignettes.

One story, based on Poe's "Doctor Tarr and Professor Fether," has Wegener imprisoning the guards of an insane asylum and setting the inmates free to run it themselves. The final tale is based on Stevenson's "The Suicide Club," which MGM filmed in 1936 as *Trouble for Two*. Note: *The Living Dead* should not be confused with the 1933 British-made picture of the same name, a mundane melodrama (titled *The Scotland Yard Mystery* in its native country) involving insurance fraud and a serum which induces catalepsy.

LOVE FROM A STRANGER (1937; United Artists; Great Britain) Alternate Title: *A Night of Terror* (1945 reissue). Director: Rowland V. Lee. Producer: Harry E. Edington. Screenplay: Frances Marion. Photography: Philip Tannura. Cast: Ann Harding, Basil Rathbone, Binnie Hale, Bruce Seton, Jean Cadell, Bryan Powley, Joan Hickson, Donald Calthrop, Eugene Leahy.

Basil Rathbone plays a Bluebeard-type killer who marries Ann Harding, a young woman who has just come into a fortune by winning the French national lottery. For the first half hour, the picture looks like a straight romance, with Ms. Harding throwing over her rather stodgy beau for the elegant charm of Mr. Rathbone. Soon, however, her new husband begins acting strangely (carefully developing a photograph of his wife only to deliberately and brutally crumple it in his fist, for instance), and little by little his cunning madness is revealed.

The film's final 20 minutes are an exquisite study in mounting terror as she uncovers his secret and enters into a tense and deadly game of wits with the madman. The suspense mounts into near hysteria until the clever climax, one twist building upon another. Both Ann Harding and Basil Rathbone are superb. Harding becomes a study in controlled hysteria, holding herself in check as she tries to think and reason and scheme for her very life. Rathbone is a cracked mirror — calm and clear until one gets close in the right light and the broken shards of his madness begin to show. Toward the end, his carefully concealed anticipation slips as his sharp voice and agitated speech betray his barely contained mad excitement. Rathbone delivered a similarly pitched performance toward the end of *Son of Frankenstein* two years later (once again under the guidance of Rowland V. Lee).

Love from a Stranger is based on the play by Frank Vosper, itself derived from a novel by Agatha Christie. The picture was remade in 1947 with John Hodiak as the madman.

M (1931; Nero; Germany) Director: Fritz Lang. Screenplay: Thea von Harbou, Fritz Lang. Photography: Fritz Arno Wagner, Gustave Rathje. Cast: Peter Lorre, Fritz Odemer, Karl Platen, Ernst Stahl-Nachbaur, Georg John, Paul Kemp, Inge Landgut, Theo Lingen, Theodor Loos, Franz Stein, Hertha von Walther, Otto Wernicke, Rosa Valetti, Ellen Widmann.

While the majority of film historians exclude *M* from the horror genre, most have recognized the horrific nature of the picture. *M*'s subject matter is undoubtedly horrific — the film, however, is not. *M* follows the structure of a crime thriller, focusing on a mammoth manhunt (both by the police and by the underworld) for the child killer who holds Berlin in a grip of fear. Only at the very end of the picture are we exposed to any horror — and this is strictly psychological — when the tortured psyche of the abhorrent murderer is laid bare. Even then, Lang and Lorre work to present a pitiable wretch whose heinous actions are an almost unconscious manifestation of his sad psychopathology. As Carlos Clarens observed in his seminal work, *An Illustrated History of the Horror Film,* "the very theme of the picture excluded the introduction of fantasy and whatever horror there was derived from the pathology of its murderer." When this pathology is finally exposed, however, the pitiful killer ultimately inspires more sympathy than terror. Nevertheless, *M* is a powerful film, the power arising from the picture's realism. *M* does not deliver the "safe" terrors of impossible creatures such as vampires, werewolves, and zombies. It forces us to face the horror of reality (the monster within our own society and thus within ourselves) and denies us the opportunity to contain, explore, and purge our fears within the comforting framework of the impossible. Refusing to allay our anxieties, *M* does not neatly dispatch some supernatural monster in the end. Instead, it shows us that the monster among us cannot always be so easily recognized nor so easily destroyed.

M is a landmark film in several respects. It is the first picture about a true serial killer (and a *child murderer* at that). The film courageously delves into the mind and motivations of the fiend to expose not a monster but a human being tormented beyond endurance by the inner demons of his insanity. Lang and Lorre accomplish the near-impossible by eliciting sympathy for this wretch while intimating that "there but for the grace of God…" *M* marked the screen debut of Peter Lorre, whose brilliant, tortured performance as the killer who can't help himself received critical acclaim and catapulted him to international stardom (as well as type-casting him for life). *M* was Fritz Lang's first talkie, and the director broke new ground in the fledgling art of cinema sound. Lang was one of the first directors to really make sound an integral, irreplaceable part of the narrative itself (by including off-screen sound effects in addition to the standard on-screen variety, and by employing sound — whistling, for example — as a thematic device).

The film carried the preproduction title of *Murderers Among Us* and this led to great difficulties with the Nazi authorities. Lang was refused permission by Nazi officials to use an old zeppelin hangar as a studio and had even received threatening letters. The director finally discovered that these brownshirt bureaucrats believed the title was referring to their beloved Nazi party. When Lang explained to them that the reference was to child molesters and not politics, the relieved officials gave him their full cooperation and granted all permits. (Lang, a pillar of the German film community, despised the Nazis and eventually left his homeland in 1934 to escape their tyranny.) Ironically, though perhaps not unexpectedly, Peter Lorre's final confession in *M* was lifted out of context by the Nazis in 1940 and added to their anti-Semitic "documentary" entitled *The Eternal Jew.*

Many sources have claimed that *M* is based on the case of Peter Kurten, "the Vampire of Dusseldorf," whose last victim was an eight-year-old girl. According to *Variety,* however, screenwriter Thea von Harbou (wife of director Fritz Lang) wrote the script before Kurten was ever caught (in May of 1930), proving, claimed *Variety,* "that her vision foresaw the problem of this human beast." Lang himself denied that Kurten was any source of inspiration. *M* was Fritz Lang's personal favorite of all his films. Lorre's whistling, which played such a crucial role in the story, was actually the whistling of Fritz Lang himself, since Lang's star had never learned to whistle. For the kangaroo-court climax, in which the captured killer is tried by members of the criminal underworld, the director recruited real-life criminals to add realism to the scene. By the end of filming, two dozen of Lang's extras had been arrested.

THE MAN WHO COULD WORK MIRACLES (1936; United Artists; Great Britain) Director: Lothar Mendes. Producer: Alexander Korda. Screenplay: H. G. Wells. Photography: Harold Rosson. Cast: Roland Young, Ralph Richardson, Edward Chapman, Ernest Thesiger, Joan Gardner, Sophie Stewart, Robert Cochran, Lady Tree, Lawrence Hanray, George Zucco, Wally Lupino, Joan Hickson, Wally Patch, Mark Daly, George Sanders, Ivan Brandt, Torin Thatcher.

This "film of imaginative comedy," as screenwriter H. G. Wells described it, was shot before, but released *after*, Wells' other hands-on picture, *Things to Come* (1936). Unlike the cold, preachy *Things to Come*, however, Wells allows some characterization in his *Miracles* screenplay and keeps the socialist speech-making limited to a few characters toward the picture's end. Wells adapted his own short story (written back in 1898) of a mild-mannered middle-aged shopworker who receives the gift of ultimate power from a godlike being conducting a social experiment on "pitiful" humanity. Roland Young gives an excellent performance as the timid George McWirter Fotheringay, who is first uncertain, then self-serving, and finally repentant of his unlimited power. Both George Sanders and George Zucco, early in their respective film careers, appear in small parts — Sanders as a deity scoffing at "these silly, greedy human scabs," and Zucco as a butler. Sanders brings his patented disdainful superiority to his character while Zucco manages to balance his innate urbanity with an effective working-class accent. Ernest Thesiger is given a bigger role but can do little as the pedantic clergyman extolling the virtues of brotherly love. Production values are good, but some of the camera tricks, including the more mundane appearances and disappearances of objects and people, are not as seamless as one would expect, often calling attention to themselves with their awkwardness. Since the story deals with real humans as well as issues and ideas, *Miracles* avoids the lapses into boredom which mars *Things to Come*, and Wells presents his theories on man and social structure in a more palatable concoction, with Young's personable performance making it that much easier to swallow and digest.

(In 1967, the RCA Victor Record Division intended to finance a remake of *The Man Who Could Work Miracles* as a *musical*, along with distributing the picture's sound track album, but the project never went past the preproduction stage.)

THE MAN WHO RECLAIMED HIS HEAD (1934; Universal) Director: Edward Ludwig. Producer: Carl Laemmle, Jr. Associate Producer: Henry Henigson. Screenplay: Jean Bart [Marie Antoinette Sarlabous] and Samuel Ornitz (from the play by Jean Bart). Photography: Merritt Gerstad. Cast: Claude Rains, Joan Bennett, Lionel Atwill, Baby Jane [Juanita Quigley], Henry O'Neill, Henry Armetta, Wallace Ford, Lawrence Grant, William B. Davidson.

False advertising and Universal's misleading publicity aside, *The Man Who Reclaimed His Head* is *not* a horror film. Instead, it is a well-acted, mostly effective antiwar message picture. Told in flashback by its protagonist, Paul Verin (Claude Rains), the story follows the brilliant but shy pacifist Verin as he is manipulated and used by the unscrupulous publisher Henri Dumont (Lionel Atwill). The sole horrific moment comes when Verin finally snaps and attacks Dumont with a bayonet. Though never explicitly stated, it is implied that the black satchel the distraught Verin subsequently carries to his lawyer friend contains the severed head of his enemy. "And then it seemed to me that Henri Dumont was I," explains Verin, "that my love, my life, were his — because my *brain* was his. I wanted back what was mine. That's all."

Universal, who had so quickly dropped the fledgling screen actor Claude Rains after his completion of *The Invisible Man* (1933), offered the now-established Rains $2000 a week to return to Universal City and star in *The Man Who Reclaimed His Head*, reprising the role the actor had portrayed with such critical success on the Broadway stage. (In the short-lived play, which opened September 8, 1932, and closed after only 28 performances, the character of Paul Verin was quite different physically from the normal, attractive man seen in the filmed version. On Broadway, Rains' Verin was deformed and asthmatic, whereas in the film he possesses none of these defects.) *The Man Who Reclaimed His Head* was the first part of a two-picture deal Rains made with Universal. For the second film, the studio intended to star him in a *real* horror picture, *Bride of Frankenstein*, but ended up casting him in another straight melodrama (*Mystery of Edwin Drood*) instead.

MENACE (1934; Paramount) Director: Ralph Murphy. Producer: Bayard Veiller. Screenplay: Anthony Veiller (Adaptation: Chandler Sprague; story: Philip MacDonald). Photography: Benjamin Reynolds. Cast: Gertrude Michael, Paul Cavanagh, Henrietta Crosman, John Lodge, Raymond Milland, Berton Churchill, Halliwell Hobbes, Forrester Harvey.

Freddie Bastion (a very young Ray Milland — fifth-billed as "Raymond" Milland) operates a dam in East Africa. On a night of heavy rains, Milland's fiancée (Gertrude Michael) and two friends induce him to leave his post and come to a bridge party. The storm picks up and the dam bursts. Feeling responsible, Bastion commits suicide, for he knows that the deluge has drowned his two sisters. Bastion had one other relative, a brother in England who is "not quite right in the head." News of his siblings' deaths drives this brother over the edge and he is committed. Now a homicidal maniac, he escapes the asylum and determines to take revenge on the three people whom he feels are responsible for the tragedy—Bastion's fiancée and two friends. He sends each of the three threatening messages like "My brother's death will be punished" and "The debt you owe must be paid." He even tells them *when* they will die ("You have ten more days," states one communiqué). Well staged, this initial portion of the film provides an effective build-up for the dire doings to come. The opening scenes of the storm are excellent, all howling rain, thunderous lightning, and windows blown open. All we see of the mysterious madman are his hands typing the threatening messages and throwing knives into an outline of a person crudely drawn on the wall (each knife whizzing through the air to land with a resounding thud). A shot of a train engine barreling down the tracks tells us that the *Menace* is coming. As the train wheels move round and round, the chug chug of the engine becomes the sound of a man's voice: "I'm on my way!—I'm on my way!—I'm on my way!" Growing ever louder in rhythm with the engine noise, the edge of madness in the bizarre sound is full of macabre promise. Unfortunately, the film then settles down into a rather far-fetched mystery. As the three human targets gather at the (ex)fiancée's house, we're introduced to a number of suspicious characters (new butler, eccentric old lady neighbor and her young actor friend, newfound beau of the younger sister, etc.), each of whom may be the clever maniac. Soon the search begins, as the phone lines are cut, the cars disabled, and the murders commence. The contrived screenplay has characters behaving in the most unlikely manner. For instance, as soon as they realize that the murderer is one of them, they *split up* to search the

Atmospheric ad for *Menace* (1934).

house, thus providing ample opportunity for the killer to wreak further mayhem. At one point, a man gets a knife square in the back (just like the first fatality), but after a quick bandaging he's up and about and "good as new." The characters are thinly drawn, and in fact it's difficult to tell the three young male leads apart—they all act in the same stereotypical "fearless" manner. A few nice touches provide some interest, however. Not once, but *twice* we are "treated" to the gruesome sight of a knife thrown full into the back of a victim (entering their flesh with a hearty "thwack"!). Then, when it seems as if the madman has finally been found out, one final (and truly unexpected) twist shakes things up a bit. Overall, though, this *Menace* fails to live up to its title.

Menace was shot in 18 days (from August 13 to September 4, 1934). According to the trade papers, Mitchell Leisen (*Death Takes a Holiday*, 1934) was originally slated to direct the film before he was assigned to another production and replaced by Ralph Murphy. Fledgling director Charles Barton (*Abbott and Costello Meet Frankenstein*, 1948) was also briefly considered for the job. Also, the beautiful Frances Drake was at one time announced as one of the leads.

Halliwell Hobbes (the butler) played supporting roles in both *Dr. Jekyll and Mr. Hyde* (1931) and *Dracula's Daughter* (1936), as well as appearing in the borderline horrors *Six Hours to Live* (1932) and *Double Door* (1934). John Lodge (one of the young heroes) was previously a victim of the *Murders in the Zoo* (1933).

THE MISSING GUEST (1938; Universal) Director: John Rawlins. Associate Producer: Barney A. Sarecky. Screenplay: Charles Martin, Paul Perez (Story: Erich Philippi) Photography: Milton Krasner. Cast: Paul Kelly, Constance Moore, William Lundigan, Edwin Stanley, Selmer Jackson, Billy Wayne, George Cooper, Patrick J. Kelly, Florence Wix, Harlan Briggs, Pat C. Flick.

Universal's first remake of their *Secret of the Blue Room* (1933) is a painful 68 minutes of lowbrow, unfunny "comedy" sprinkled with a few hoary Old House gags (pianos playing by themselves, mysterious voices moaning "ooo-ooo-ooo," faces peeking in windows, etc.). Of the three versions (Universal filmed the old chestnut again in 1944 as *Murder in the Blue Room*), *The Missing Guest* is without a doubt the worst. During a costume party, a reporter (named "Scoop," of course) worms his way into the Baldrich mansion which houses the mysterious "Blue Room." Twenty years earlier, this supposedly haunted chamber was the site of a mysterious murder and disappearance. A fresh murder (and disappearance) puts Scoop onto the mystery. As if the smug, wise-cracking reporter/hero was not bad enough, a pair of bumbling ex-cons passing themselves off as private detectives arrive. It is simply too much and the silliness quickly overwhelms whatever atmosphere could be found in the story or Jack Otterson's Old House sets. Between the pair of Olsen and Johnson rejects, the cocky, condescending hero, and the wallflower ingenue, there's no room left (not even a blue one) for suspense or mood. "Now we find out what's happening in this house," says one character, to which the viewer can only think, "Not much!" Tightfisted director Jack Rawlins didn't even spend the picture's full $80,400 budget (a pittance), bringing *The Missing Guest* in for an even cheaper $72,000. The economy shows.

THE MONKEY'S PAW (1933; RKO) Director: Wesley Ruggles (additional scenes directed, uncredited, by Ernest B. Schoedsack). Associate Producer: Pandro S. Berman. Screenplay: Graham John. Photography: Leo Tover (additional photography, uncredited, by Jack MacKenzie, Edward Cronjager, J. O. Taylor, and Harold Wellman). Cast: Ivan Simpson, Louise Carter, C. Aubrey Smith, Bramwell Fletcher, Betty Lawford, Winter Hall, Herbert Bunston.

In 1932, RKO executive producer David O. Selznick purchased the rights to W. W. Jacobs' popular story and Louis N. Parker's one-act play version of "The Monkey's Paw," beating out Universal who had just announced its own plans to film the tale. Unfortunately, the resultant RKO picture was a dismal failure both financially and with the critics and went largely unseen by the public. The merits of the film remain a mystery today for no complete prints are known to exist. *The Monkey's Paw* joins the ranks of *London After Midnight* (1927) and *The Cat Creeps* (1930) as another tantalizing "lost" film.

The loss of *The Monkey's Paw* borders on tragedy for several reasons. First, the timeless tale has become something of a folk classic and deserves its day in the (halogen) sun. Second, the picture features a rare "horror" appearance by that fascinating British actor, Bramwell Fletcher, who laughed so horribly when he saw *The Mummy* go "for a little walk." Finally, half of the picture was directed by an uncredited Ernest B. Schoedsack (co-creator of *King Kong*) at the behest of the film's executive producer, Merian C. Cooper (*Kong*'s other co-creator).

The Monkey's Paw was the last film directed by Wesley Ruggles to fulfill his contractual obligations to RKO before the director moved over to Paramount. With a modest budget of $153,574.46, Ruggles shot British author Graham John's screenplay in 13 days, then moved on to his new job. After Ruggles' departure, the RKO front office learned, to their horror, that the picture (filmed exactly as written by John) ran just over half an hour! The studio shelved their expensive "featurette" until John could complete an 18-page prologue based on suggestions by Merian C.

Cooper. Cooper borrowed Ernest B. Schoedsack during a lull in *King Kong*'s production schedule to direct the prologue sequences and shoot a few retakes and voice-overs for continuity purposes. This took *The Monkey's Paw* well over budget, but, more importantly, brought the picture up to (nearly) feature length at 58 minutes.

The diabolical paw was constructed by *King Kong* model-maker Marcel Delgado and animated via stop-motion by another *Kong* technician, Orville Goldner. The prologue battle sequences were shot at Bronson Canyon, which later became the site of innumerable alien invasions and monster maraudings in the 1950s.

W. W. Jacobs' classic story was first filmed in 1915 as a British short. A second British version followed in 1923. After Ruggles' 1933 film, *The Monkey's Paw* made it to the screen once more, in 1948, under the direction of Norman Lee. The story also became an *Alfred Hitchcock Hour* episode starring Jane Wyatt.

THE MONSTER WALKS (1932; Action) Director: Frank Strayer. Producer: Cliff Broughton. Screenplay: Robert Ellis. Photography: Les Cronjager. Cast: Rex Lease, Vera Reynolds, Sheldon Lewis, Mischa Auer, Martha Mattox, Sidney Bracey, Sleep n' Eat (a.k.a. Willie Best).

The body of Dr. Earlton lies in state at the old Earlton mansion. The family (the deceased's daughter, Ruth, her fiancé, Earlton's paralyzed brother, a housekeeper, her sullen son, and the family lawyer) all gather for the reading of the will. The dead doctor was a researcher and as such kept a pet ape named Yogi in the cellar. This ape hates Ruth (jealous for his master's affection is the reason given), and she lives in terror that Yogi should get loose. Soon, a clutching hairy hand emerges from a secret panel and makes for Ruth's throat. The incident is dismissed as a nightmare, but the housekeeper later (mistakenly) dies by that very hand while sleeping in Ruth's bed. The servants skulk around the house suspiciously, and the paralyzed brother's hard stares and surprise at seeing Ruth alive cast doubts upon him as well. Something fishy is going on here, for the ape is obviously a red herring. After the murder of the housekeeper, Ruth's fiancé spells it out: "I don't think it was the ape. His animal instinct would have told him it was not Ruth." After an (overlong) 57 minute running time, the guilty (human) culprit meets his fate at the hands of the (innocent) ape.

A lifeless production, *The Monster Walks* has little going for it. The sparse sets are cheaply furnished and show little of the expansiveness evident in many of its contemporaries. Frank Strayer's dull direction and Les Cronjager's static photography add nothing to the dreary settings. (Cronjager's camera moves a total of 12 times over 57 minutes — that's an average of once every five minutes! Eleven of these are simple left/right pans following a character across a room — only once does he move his camera in a forward-tracking motion.) Still, the film might be watchable with some solid characterization and believable acting. Alas, the characters are all stock and the acting is forced and overly theatrical. If it wasn't for sound, one would think the picture was from the previous decade (*Variety* wryly observed that "'Monster' happens along about three years too late"). Particularly awful is Rex Lease as Ruth's fiancé, whose stiff demeanor and stilted delivery make for a dull hero indeed. Even the usually reliable Mischa Auer is disappointing. At times he seems to be doing a bad Bela Lugosi impression (slow speech, pointed looks, [over]long pregnant pauses). At others, Auer emulates the Karloff shuffle — body bent forward, arms hanging akimbo, hands open, fingers spread, neck craning. He even wears a dark coat with the sleeves too short — just like the Frankenstein monster. Aside from one solitary scene of surprise (when a hand enters the frame and extinguishes a candle, we notice that it is covered in hair like an *ape's* hand) there is little action and no excitement. By the way, the "ape" is really a large chimpanzee.

The Monster Walks was 17-year-old Willie Best's second film. Billed as "Sleep n' Eat", he plays "Exodus," the hero's slow-witted, cowardly black chauffeur. The following dialogue exchange typifies the insultingly racist tone of the film:

> Wilkes (the lawyer): "Dr. Earlton was an exponent of the Darwinian theory. He believed [apes] were our ancestors."
> Exodus: "You mean [this ape] is related to me? Well, I don't know. I had a grandpappy that looked somethin' like 'im, but he wasn't this active."

Best made a career out of such stereotypical characters, who only seemed to want to "sleep 'n' eat." The actor kept this demeaning moniker until 1934, when he switched to using his own name. Though *The Monster Walks* does not show it, Best was often able to invest some warmth or spark into his nonsensical racist parts, as he did in *The Ghost Breakers* (1940). (Bob Hope once called Willie Best "the best actor I know.") Best continued working on into the 1950s (often appearing in genre films like *Mummy's Boys*, 1936; *The Smiling Ghost*, 1941; *The Body Disappears*, 1941; *A-Haunting We Will Go*, 1942; and *Face of Marble*,

1946) and even turned up as a semi-regular on two television shows, "The Trouble with Father" and "My Little Margie."

MUMMY'S BOYS (1936; RKO) Director: Fred Guiol. Producer: Les Marcus. Screenplay: Jack Townley, Philip G. Epstein, Charles Roberts (story: Jack Townley and Lew Lipton). Photography: Jack MacKenzie. Cast: Bert Wheeler, Robert Woolsey, Barbara Pepper, Moroni Olsen, Frank M. Thomas, Willie Best, Francis McDonald, Frank Lackteen, Charles Coleman, Mitchell Lewis, Frederick Barton.

Beginning in 1929, the vaudeville comedy team of Wheeler and Woolsey made 21 features for RKO until Woolsey's death in 1938. Coming at the end of their partnership (the pair made only two more films together), *Mummy's Boys* makes a shoddy swan song. In this poorly scripted vehicle, the two play ditch diggers who join up with an archeological expedition to Egypt. Mr. Browning (Frank Thomas) heads the expedition, whose purpose (in all absence of logic) is to *return* the priceless artifacts taken from a recently excavated tomb. Ten of the original party have died, victims of the supposed "Curse of King Pharatime's Tomb," and so Browning intends to appease the "unearthly force" threatening himself and his daughter by replacing the treasure. Of course, the "unearthly" force turns out to be a decidedly human (and uninteresting) one. A series of painfully silly shenanigans and pointless "comic" episodes do absolutely nothing to advance the thin plot, whose threadbare story serves as nothing but an excuse for the babbling Woolsey and the dumb-as-a-post Wheeler to present their unfunny shtick (usually centering around Wheeler's inability to remember anything unless he takes a nap first). About the best the pair can offer in terms of witticisms comes when Woolsey studies a map. "We take this road here," he observes, "until we reach the Sudan," to which Wheeler asks, "Two door or four door?" So much for sophisticated comedy. At the climax, they meet a fake (and badly wrapped) mummy who momentarily chases them around the tomb. Willie Best plays "Catfish," serving both as their lackey and the butt of racist jokes:

> Best: "I won't go in there—too dark, might be ghosts."
> Woolsey: "Ghosts? Well what about it? They couldn't see *you* in the dark."

Noble Johnson (*King Kong*'s native chief) puts in a brief appearance as an Egyptian tattoo artist who tattoos a "secret map" onto Wheeler's back.

On the plus side, *Mummy's Boys* sports some decent production values and sophisticated camerawork by Jack MacKenzie (shooting from inside a fireplace, for instance), who also provides some eerie lighting. Unfortunately, there's really nothing *worth* shooting in *Mummy's Boys*—at least not with a camera.

MURDER BY TELEVISION (1935; Cameo/Imperial) Director: Clifford Sanforth. Producer: Edward M. Spitz. Screenplay: Joseph O'Donnell (from an idea suggested by Clarence Hennecke and Carl Coolidge). Photography: James Brown and Arthur Reed. Cast: Bela Lugosi, June Collyer, Huntly Gordon, George Meeker, Henry Mowbray, Charles Hill Mailes, Claire McDowell, Hattie McDaniel, Allan Jung, Charles K. French, Larry Francis, Henry Hall, William (Billy) Sullivan, William Tooker.

"The mad monarch of the laboratory waves his mighty hands and death-dealing rays strike down his hapless victims," promised the ads for *Murder by Television*—a promise left sadly unfulfilled in terms of execution (so to speak). Interesting only as a novelty, *Murder by Television* is a dismal little mystery involving the emerging technology of television. Professor Howland creates a new process by which he can tune into any place around the globe through his television device. Of course every communication corporation in the world (as well as numerous foreign powers) are intensely interested. A group of people gather at Howland's home/laboratory to witness the first public demonstration of his miraculous device. In the middle of the transmission, the professor collapses while onscreen—dead—and a vital tube is stolen from the apparatus. The police chief (who was present at the demonstration) now sets about sorting out the various suspects, motives, and opportunities—without much success. Bela Lugosi plays an assistant to the inventor and does his best to draw suspicion upon himself by skulking about and looking guilty. He is, of course, merely a red herring, for he's promptly murdered himself. Never fear, however, there's a *second* Lugosi on hand—the man's twin brother—who ultimately cracks the fantastical case and gets to explain it all with this ridiculous scientific hokum: "Dr. Scofield's equipment radiated waves to Professor Howland's laboratory. When these waves came in contact with those the professor's equipment was radiating, they created an interstellar frequency—which is—the death ray." Of course—the professor was *televised to death*! In there somewhere is another bit of science fiction involving a doctor who has perfected a machine that can differentiate a criminal brain from a normal one (too bad Henry Frankenstein didn't possess such a device):

> Doctor: "If part of the skull were resting on the medulla oblongata, it would materially diminish the faculties of perception."
> Police Chief: "Does that indicate a criminal tendency?"
> Doctor: "Undoubtedly."

Static photography, a leaden pace (complete with tepid time-filling song "I Had the Right Idea" and unending scenes of the inspector questioning each and every person in the house), puerile, racist humor (black "mammy" ["Oh, Lordy Lordy I knows I seen a ghost!"] and pidgin-spouting Chinese servant with "a penchant for quoting Confucius and *Charlie Chan*"), and acting stiff enough to break your teeth on make *Murder by Television* nearly murder to sit through. Fortunately, Bela Lugosi is on hand to generate at least *some* degree of interest.

For Lugosi's dual role, (doubtful) pressbook advances claimed that Bela created his own makeup for the film, utilizing 43 different shades of grease paint on his face to achieve the desired look for this black and white production. Multilayered makeup aside, Lugosi does manage to bring a differential depth to his twin characters (no mean feat, for Joseph O'Donnell's script gives the actor very little to work with). For the first half of the picture, Lugosi acts almost furtively, with an air of uncertain hesitancy rarely found among the actor's standard barnstorming performances. In the film's second half, Lugosi (now playing the murdered man's brother) creates a more commanding presence, one self-assured (all sardonic smiles and arching eyebrows) in contrast to his deceased brother's circumspect demeanor. Lugosi takes the rather dry, stale characters and wrings from them all the juice he can. In one sequence he flirts with the heroine, allowing an almost coquettish smile to play across his lips, while in another scene he expresses a tightly controlled grief over the death of his long-lost brother. When asked "With you here and alive, who was it that was killed?," Lugosi gives a long pause in which he half-closes his eyes in anguish and hardens his jaw as if steeling himself against the painful reply, "My brother." While Lugosi's twins can hardly compare favorably to Karloff's powerhouse Anton/ Gregor of *The Black Room*, the dual role at least provided a modicum of range for the actor.

The picture contains several bits of dialogue which, in hindsight, hold a humorous irony. "It is my hope," states the sincere inventor of the new television process, "to be able to prove that television is the greatest step forward we have yet made in the preservation of humanity." He goes on to claim that TV "will make of this Earth a paradise we have always envisioned but have never seen." Obviously he hadn't envisioned TV sitcoms. Dreadfully dull and abysmal on all counts, *Murder by Television* is a nonsensical mixture of (bad) science fiction and drawing room mystery, with the only point of interest in the picture being Lugosi's (dual) presence and his few sinister expressions (and the fact that resourceful art director Louis Rachmil managed to dress his sets with $75,000 worth of borrowed television equipment — an amount *double* the picture's meager $35,000 budget!).

Filmed at the old Tiffany Studios on Sunset Boulevard, this production (which carried a shooting title of *The Houghland Murder Case*) was Bela Lugosi's fifth picture (of six) released in 1935 — and definitely the worst of the lot. Poorly distributed (a single print sufficed for all of New York state), *Murder by Television* died a quick (and deserved) death at the box office. The picture's closing line (delivered by Lugosi) serves as an appropriate epithet: "As Ah-Ling would say, 'even though the eyes may see, the mind will not believe.'"

MURDER BY THE CLOCK (1931; Paramount) Director: Edward Sloman. Screenplay: Henry Meyers (from the novel *Murder by the Clock* by Rufus King and the play *Dangerously Yours* by Charles Beahan). Photography: Karl Struss. Cast: William Boyd, Lilyan Tashman, Irving Pichel, Regis Toomey, Sally O'Neil, Blanche Frederici, Walter McGrail, Lester Vail, Martha Mattox, Frank Sheridan, Frederick Sullivan.

"We're up against a murderer whose mind works like a clock," admits Lt. Valcour while pondering the convoluted series of killings at the Endicott mansion. The beautiful (and thoroughly ruthless) Laura Endicott uses her wily charms to induce her weak-willed drunkard of a husband, Herbert, to murder his old aunt, matriarch of the Endicott fortune. With Phillip, the old woman's half-witted (and potentially dangerous) son in jail for the crime, Laura next beguiles her would-be paramour, Tom, into strangling her troublesome husband. Beyond this, she then bewitches Phillip into escaping and dispatching Tom! Finally, when it appears that Herbert isn't dead after all and may revive after Tom's brutal attack, Laura dons the clothing and death mask of the old woman (who was mortally afraid of being buried alive) and finishes the job by frightening her recovering husband to death (this time permanently). It all catches up with this villainous vamp in the

The slow-witted but dangerous Philip (Irving Pichel) seeks sanctuary in the family graveyard in Paramount's slick horror/mystery, *Murder by the Clock* (1931). (Courtesy of Ted Okuda.)

end, however, when a skeptical police lieutenant uncovers the one flaw in her near-perfect plan.

The first thing to strike the viewer watching this early mystery laced with horror trappings is its excellent set design. Karl Struss' mobile camera makes good use of the macabre settings, from the decaying cemetery (all thin, denuded trees and massive tombstones) to the expansive-yet-claustrophobic family vault (its immense spaces crowded with columns and archways) and the stuffy old mansion honeycombed with secret passageways. Director Edward Sloman augments the creepy atmosphere by employing shadows to suggest menace and to silhouette the heinous killings.

Irving Pichel, as Phillip, provides a frightening portrayal of a being strong of hand but weak of mind, whose bestial nature rises through his civilized appearance when he shows off his immense strength and talks excitedly about killing with his bare hands. In Phillip, Pichel presents a better-dressed—and thoroughly dangerous—Lennie Small.

Lilyan Tashman (as Laura), however, plays her role of subtle schemer too broadly to convince, utilizing a plethora of melodramatic gestures and expressions. Though this serves her well in one scene (while watching Phillip strangle Tom, a wicked, almost frenzied, look of passion twists across her face as she forms her hands into murderous talons), such an obvious acting style jars with the subtle deviousness of her character. Though not quite convincing, the picture still entertains today and remains one of the decade's better horror/mysteries.

THE MYSTERIOUS MR. WONG (1935; Monogram) Director: William Nigh. Producer: A. George Yohalem. Screenplay: Lew Levenson, Nina Howatt, James Herbuveaux (suggested by the story "The Twelve Coins of Confucius" by Harry Stephen Keelor). Photography: Harry Neumann. Cast: Bela Lugosi, Wallace Ford, Arline Judge, Fred Warren, Lotus Long, Robert Emmet O'Connor, Edward Peil, Luke Chan, Lee Shumway, Etta Lee, Ernest F. Young.

"There is a tradition," reads the opening narration, "that twelve coins given by Confucius on his deathbed to twelve trusted friends will some day come to the possession of one man and give him extraordinary powers in the province of Keelat." The nefarious villain Mr. Wong (Bela Lugosi) is just such a power-hungry man. Posing as the old herb seller, Li See, in San Francisco's Chinatown, Wong and his minions torture and murder their way to 11 of the precious coins. It falls to ace reporter Jason Barton (Wallace Ford) and Chinese secret service agent Tsung (Fred Warren) to discover Wong's identity and stop the evil madman from obtaining the final coin which would make him overlord of China's Keelat province.

Like every film era, the Golden Age had its share of fool's gold. Attempting to pass itself off as a successor to *The Mask of Fu Manchu* (1932), this picture is simply another nugget of iron pyrite. Cheesy, spartan sets, overlong scenes invariably seen in medium shot, static camerawork, and muddy lighting place this picture firmly in the decade's bargain basement. The cast does little to alleviate the tedium. Wallace Ford quickly wears out his welcome as the smug, condescending reporter who spouts racist wisecracks like, "I'm supposed to bring in real live news and the best I can do is run down dead Chinamen." Bela Lugosi (who provides the sole reason for watching many a poverty row production) is oddly subdued, bringing little of his trademark flourish to his role.

Beyond skimping on production values, *The Mysterious Mr. Wong* is short on horror as well. Even the solitary torture sequence (*The Mask of Fu Manchu* featured nearly half a dozen!), when Wong threatens heroine Arline Judge's dainty fingernails with a heated bamboo spit, carries little tension since we know the good guys are just outside the door. The only true terror comes from facing scene after scene of excruciatingly dull filler as Barton and a variety of characters endlessly creep about to no great purpose. The jumbled storyline makes little sense, so it comes as no surprise when we find that Wong's secret torture chamber comes equipped with a handy telephone with which our imprisoned hero can simply dial up a rescue. *The Mysterious Mr. Wong* is not the worst of Lugosi's six pictures released in 1935 (*Murder by Television* wins that honor), but it comes in a close second.

While Lugosi may have been slumming in the fall of 1934 (at the apex of his career) by starring in Monogram's *The Mysterious Mr. Wong*, it was a taste of things to come. In the early 1940s, Lugosi worked almost exclusively on Poverty Row. In fact, he returned to Monogram *nine* times between 1941 and 1944, starring in *Invisible Ghost* (1941), *Spooks Run Wild* (1941), *Black Dragons* (1942), *The Corpse Vanishes* (1942), *Bowery at Midnight* (1942), *The Ape Man* (1943), *Ghosts on the Loose* (1943), *Voodoo Man* (1944), and *Return of the Ape Man* (1944).

It should come as no surprise that Bela Lugosi would speak longingly of his National Theater days in Hungary while working on this no-budget assignment. "Though it is egotism," said Lugosi in the film's pressbook, "it is, I hope pardonable when an artist has achieved recognition in his own country, to take it for granted that his name is not entirely strange in other centers of culture, and perhaps to resent it when he finds out that he is quite unknown and must begin again."

Once more lamenting his typecasting in pictures, the actor continues: "In spite, however, of the predominance of romantic roles in my repertoire, when I came to this country I found that because of my speech and pantomime with which most Europeans accompany their speech, that I was catalogued as a 'heavy.'"

Wallace Ford's great ambition was to become a train engineer. Growing up in England and then Canada, he left home to take a position in a railroad roundhouse as a laborer. When Ford's request to learn the trade of engineer drew only derision from the railway powers-that-be, he quit and went to New York where he fell in love with the Broadway stage and set his sights on becoming an actor.

Bela Lugosi as Fu Manchu–wannabe *The Mysterious Mr. Wong* (1935). (Courtesy of Ron Borst/Hollywood Movie Posters.)

Fast-talking heroine Arline Judge began her showbiz career as a dancer (on Broadway at age 15) and nightclub singer (appearing at Jimmy Durante's famous New York nightspot). The feisty actress devoted more time to her pursuit of husbands than film roles, however, marrying a total of seven times. Among her many husbands was director Wesley Ruggles (*The Monkey's Paw*, 1933). Ms. Judge's last picture featured her being strangled by *The Crawling Hand* (1964).

According to Monogram publicity, Caucasian actor E. A. Warren (Tsung in *The Mysterious Mr. Wong*) had played a Chinese character in 40 pictures (more even than Warner Oland—Charlie Chan himself!). Warren "has visited China twice," reported the film's pressbook, "and has lived there approximately two years, studying its culture, literature and customs."

Prolific Poverty Row director William Nigh was responsible for several other low-budget horrors: *Mystery Liner* (1934), *The Ape* (1940), *The Strange Case of Dr. RX* (1942) and *Black Dragons* (1942), as well as all five of Monogram's "Mr. Wong" detective films (no relation to the above) starring Boris Karloff as an Asian sleuth.

MYSTERY LINER (1934; Monogram) Director: William Nigh. Producer: Paul Malvern. Screenplay: Wellyn Totman. Photography: Archie Stout. Cast: Noah Beery, Astrid Allyn, Edwin Maxwell, Gustav von Seyffertitz, Ralph Lewis, Cornelius Keefe, Zeffie Tilbury, Boothe Howard, Howard Hickman, Jerry Stewart, George Hayes, George Cleveland, John Maurice Sullivan.

This dismal, forgotten Monogram programmer (a "Monogrammer"?) includes one slight science-fiction angle. The story revolves around a new invention—the S505 tube which "controls the energy which will operate [a ship] by radio." A test of this radio-control (which would revolutionize Naval warfare) takes place on a passenger liner(!). Other curious elements include a former captain who's gone mad and a control room containing weird electrical equipment which wouldn't be out of place in Dr. Frankenstein's lab. Unfortunately, the film quickly settles down to a mystery/spy drama as various murders occur and suspicious characters ("agents for a foreign power") creep about the ship. Production values are nil, and Monogram regular William Nigh (*The Mysterious Mr. Wong*, 1935) directs with a heavy hand and closed eyes. The camera is invariably stationary (the little visual movement present is due solely to the cameraman's carelessness as he jostles about trying to center his subject!). The players are painfully stiff and their expressions blank. A screenplay crammed with filler slows an already leaden pace. Particularly unctuous are scene after scene of a silly old lady insulting her dumb grandson and chasing after younger men. *Mystery Liner* is a poor vessel even for Monogram.

Austrian stage actor Gustav von Seyffertitz came to the United States in the early 1900s where he continued his successful theatrical career and entered motion pictures. During World War I, he utilized the screen pseudonym of G. Butler Clonblough to disguise his Teutonic origins. Von Seyfferititz also directed films for Vitagraph in the 1920s. He appeared in one other Golden Age (borderline) horror entry, RKO's *She* (1935). Von Seyfferititz retired in 1939 at the age of 76.

Mystery Liner is based on the Edgar Wallace novel, *The Ghost of John Holling*. (One "true" Golden Age horror picture was inspired by a Wallace book—1939's *The Dark Eyes of London*). Wallace is probably best known as the man who conceived of *King Kong* (though he died before the film was truly underway, earning only a story credit for the final production).

MYSTERY OF THE MARY CELESTE (1935; Hammer/General Film Distributors; Great Britain); Alternate Title: *Phantom Ship* (American release). Director: Denison Clift. Producer: M. Fraser Passmore. Screenplay: Charles Larkworthy. Photography: Geoffrey Faithfull, Eric Cross. Cast: Bela Lugosi, Shirley Grey, Arthur Margetson, Edmund Willard, Dennis Hoey, George Mozart, Johnnie Schofield, Gunner Moir, Ben Weldon.

This is a very early production by Hammer (in fact only their second), the British film company which single-handedly revived gothic horror in the 1950s and '60s. The film takes its inspiration from a true incident in 1872 in which a clipper ship, the Mary Celeste, was found adrift with no sign of the crew, remaining a real-life enigma to this day. *Mystery of the Mary Celeste* revolves around Captain Briggs and his new bride sailing on the Mary Celeste with various unsavory crew members, many holding grudges against the captain or his brutal first mate, Mr. Bilson. There's a sailor who was shanghaied and none too happy about it, another man who is secretly in the employ of the devious Captain Morehead (Briggs' old rival for his wife), and a grizzled, one-armed sailor named Anton Lorenzen (played by Bela Lugosi) who six years earlier had been shanghaied by Mr. Bilson on this same ship and as a result lost his arm to a shark. Soon crew members are murdered or disappear one by one until ... well, that would be giving it away. The direction and camerawork are unspectacular but adequate. The acting is melodramatic (not unusual for a British "thriller" of this period), the dialogue rough, and the characterizations shallow—with the exception of top-billed Lugosi. This is one of the more infrequently seen Lugosi performances and that is a pity because it's also one of his best. For the most part his is a sympathetic character, and Lugosi deftly handles the pathos while occasionally balancing it with his more usual chilling delivery. He has several standout scenes, foremost among them the one in which he kills a man while

Sporting the film's American moniker, *Phantom Ship*, this title lobby card for Britain's *Mystery of the Mary Celeste* (1935) utilizes a rather romantic image of Bela Lugosi — a far cry from the broken-down sailor he plays in the picture itself. (Courtesy of Lynn Naron.)

defending the captain's wife. He reacts to this heroic deed with horrified remorse, and his tortured lamentation, "I've killed my fellow man," is subtly effective. In another scene he explains that once he was "full of the hope of living" but, because of the brutal treatment he received, is now only a shell of his former self. "Now look at me," he invites, "My hair white, my arm — gone. Look at me now, derelict — like that ship" (pointing to a painting). Lugosi's delivery is perfectly timed, with pregnant pauses and pointed emphasis, and his demeanor effectively evinces anger coupled with self-pity, inspiring sympathy in the viewer. These scenes and Lugosi's performance in general show that perhaps the actor was a bit more versatile than his critics and film assignments allowed.

One other point of note — this picture contains two lines of dialogue unusual for a production in 1935. The first occurs when the captain seeks a crew in a sleazy waterfront bar. The proprietor states, "And here's your cook," pointing to a small white man in a dirty bowler hat. "If you don't like the look of his face I'll get you a chink or a nigger." Though filmed over 60 years ago, such a blatantly racist comment was shocking even by 1935 film standards. The second "scandalous" bit of dialogue comes when the captain, after having some trouble with the crew, orders his mate to "Find out what the *hell* is happening,"— and this a full four years before Clark Gable shocked the industry with his "Frankly my dear..." soliloquy. Though no classic, and not really a "horror film" per se (yet containing isolated moments of terror), *Mystery of the Mary Celeste* is noteworthy for its realistic settings and ship (the *Mary B. Mitchell*, a rented schooner), the air of dread laced with horrific undertones hanging over the doomed vessel, and most of all for Lugosi's controlled, excellent performance.

Bela Lugosi was so well received for his return to a more straight dramatic role that British Independent Pictures offered him a two-picture contract at $12,500 per film. However, when the actor learned that his four prized dogs would have to be quarantined for six months before they would be allowed to join him in England (due to that country's strict animal import laws), he turned down the offer and returned to Universal to eventually work on *The Invisible Ray.*

Ever looking to escape his role of Dracula and break out of the horror mold, Lugosi was encouraged by his success in *Mystery of the Mary Celeste* to make plans to start his own independent production company. The actor made no secret of his dissatisfaction in being passed over for non-horror parts, telling Eleanor Barnes of the *Illustrated Daily News* (Sept. 1935): "Every time I get my thoughts centered on a role that I believe fits me, some other actor — always a great actor — gets there first. So what am I to do? I'll finance my own company and star in pictures that I want to play in."

Cagliostro (a tale of an eighteenth-century wizard) was to be the first production of his new company, but the project (and the company) never fully materialized. An amusing remark made by Robert Montgomery (related by actress Audrey Totter in *Forties Film Talk,* by Doug McClelland) illustrates Lugosi's inescapable image: "One day while filming *The Saxon Charm* [1948] we were in the [Universal] commissary and Bela Lugosi was there, with a young boy [undoubtedly Bela Junior]. Bob Montgomery said, in a melodramatic voice, 'I see that Bela Lugosi is having a small boy for lunch!'"

NIGHT LIFE OF THE GODS (1935; Universal) Director: Lowell Sherman. Producer: Carl Laemmle, Jr. Screenplay: Barry Trivers (based on the novel by Thorne Smith). Photography: John J. Mescall. Cast: Alan Mowbray, Florine McKinney, Richard Carle, Peggy Shannon, William Boyd, Robert Warwick, Gilbert Emery, Phillips Smalley, Douglas Fowley, Henry Armetta, Wesley Barry, Irene Ware, Ann Doran, Ferdinand Gottschalk, Theresa Maxwell Conover, Pat DeCicco, Paul Kaye, George Hassell, Marda Deering.

Night Life of the Gods is a glossy, well-mounted production that fails to capture the bouncy, screwball tone so necessary for this sort of comic fantasy. While the film isn't a total disaster, its sluggish pace and meandering plotline result in tedium, making it seem longer that its 73-minute running time. Eccentric scientist Hunter Hawk (Alan Mowbray) invents a device which transforms people into stone statues. After testing his machine out on assorted annoying family members, he meets up with a woman who claims to be Megaera, one of the Furies from ancient Greece. Together they go on a petrifying spree before turning the machine on several statues of Greek gods at the Metropolitan Museum of Art. The process works in reverse and the stone statues come to life. After various madcap misadventures with their newfound Greek friends, the pair restore the Olympians to their former stony state and, with a knowing look, turn the machine on themselves. Suddenly, Hunter Hawk awakens in an ambulance. He'd received a bump on the head and it had all been an injury-induced dream! Once the plot gets underway, we're presented with one outlandish comic scene after another, all of which were apparently intended to strike the viewer as hilariously outrageous. Unfortunately, for a "riotous" comedy, nothing that occurs in *Night Life* is really all *that* funny. Furthermore, it simply isn't enough to present a series of loosely connected gags; in the most successful farces, one event logically (within the context of the film's tone) leads to the next, creating a progression of mayhem that culminates in a climactic payoff. In *Night Life*, however, things occur for no express purpose other than for sheer "wackiness." Accordingly, these contrived events don't build, they merely unfold, and the film fails to achieve any kind of momentum. Also, comedy is always dependent upon how characters react to what's going on around them.

In *Topper* (1937) and *I Married a Witch* (1942), two superior adaptations of Thorne Smith stories, the humor springs from the characters' behavior as they struggle to cope with situations beyond their comprehension. In *Night Life*, however, Hunter Hawk isn't fazed by anything. His attitude is mainly one of addled complacency, and he's not overly surprised or concerned when he turns human beings into stone and vice versa. Ultimately, this laid-back approach backfires; how can an audience take an interest in the hero's escapades when he doesn't seem to express any real interest in them himself? Although Alan Mowbray was a fine actor and welcome addition to nearly every film he appeared in, he was, in retrospect, miscast in the role of the eccentric Hunter Hawk. Mowbray was at his best playing snooty, upper class types; he was often ideally cast as arrogant aristocrats and pompous comic foils. Here, he's never entirely convincing as the off-kilter scientist. Still, he and his fellow actors struggle gamely and do what they can given the limitations of the script (and Lowell Sherman's direction). The handsome production values are easily the film's greatest assets. (Universal spared no expense — even hiring 20 artists to create 50 plaster statues at a cost of $35,000!) The gargantuan sets are genuinely impressive, the cinematography is sparkling, and the special effects are first-rate. The dream ending may be considered a letdown by some viewers, but by the time the disappointing *Night Life of the Gods* arrives at its final moments,

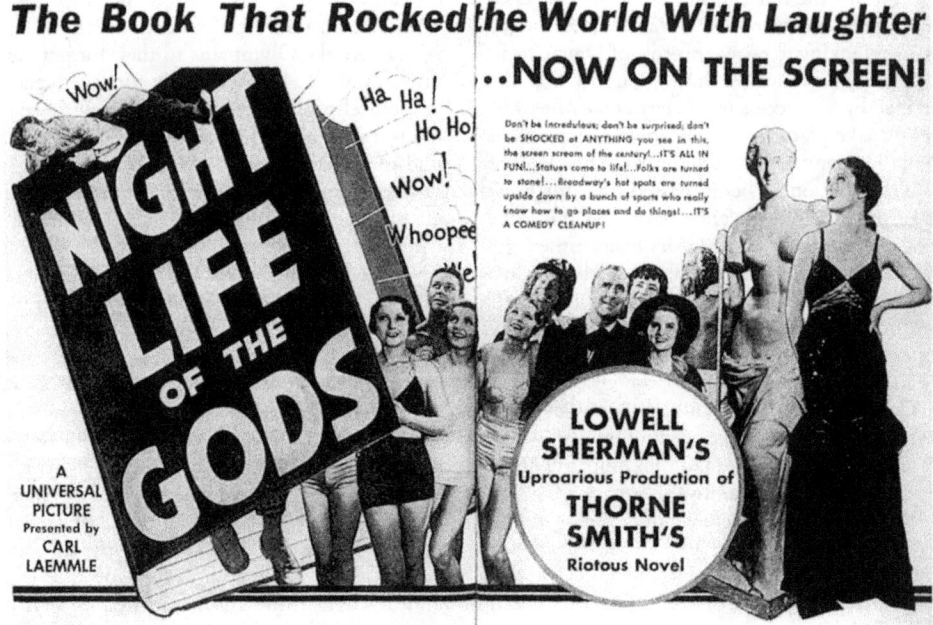

Ad for Universal's comic fantasy, *Night Life of the Gods* (1935), for all intents and purposes a "lost" film. (Courtesy of Ted Okuda.)

any conclusion is most welcome. (Note: Thanks to Ted Okuda for his assessment of this rare picture which, for all intents and purposes, has become a "lost" film. No 16mm or even bootleg video prints are currently available and, to my knowledge, the picture has never appeared on television. A few 35mm prints are purported to exist (in private collections), but the only screening in recent years occured at the Art Institute in Chicago in conjunction with Cinecon — as an unannounced "surprise" feature. Fortunately, Okuda was present and so could provide a firsthand evaluation.)

NIGHT MUST FALL (1937; MGM) Director: Richard Thorpe. Producer: Hunt Stromberg. Screenplay: John Van Druten (from the play by Emlyn Williams). Photography: Ray June. Cast: Robert Montgomery, Rosalind Russell, Dame May Whitty, Alan Marshal, Merle Tottenham, Kathleen Harrison.

Time magazine labeled *Night Must Fall* "easily the most interesting item in the year's cinema file on criminology." Indeed, this tight, handsomely mounted psychological thriller is certainly an engrossing, even chilling, character study. Robert Montgomery plays a charming sociopath named Danny who worms his way into the house and confidence of a wealthy old dowager (Dame May Whitty, reprising her role from the successful stage play and making her talking-picture debut at age 72). A young woman has disappeared in the vicinity and later turns up dead in the woods — minus her head. Among Danny's luggage is a battered hatbox, a *locked* hatbox... Rosalind Russell plays Olivia, the old woman's repressed niece, who so craves excitement in her dull existence that, despite her suspicions, she's caught up in a web of fascination with Danny at its center.

The brilliantly drawn and well-acted characters draw us into their cozy cottage of hidden natures and complex relationships while director Richard Thorpe adds the occasional shiver with the odd glimpse of the sinister hatbox or a shot of the gloomy woods at twilight. Rosalind Russell delivers a morbid, almost wistful soliloquy which sets the picture's tone and captures its subtle, frightening essence: "Here we all are, perfectly ordinary English people. We woke up this morning thinking 'it's another day.' We got up, looked at the weather, talked — here we are *still* talking. And all the time — all the time there may be something lying in the woods, hidden, under a bush, the feet showing, perhaps a high heel catching the sunlight with a bird perched on the end of it. And the other, the other's a stockinged foot — with blood that's dried in the stocking. Somewhere,

somewhere there's a man walking about, talking, just like us. He got up this morning. *He* looked at the weather—and he killed her." Unfortunately, rather than ending with a thrilling climax, the picture simply runs out of steam. Danny raves for a few moments, threatens Olivia, and then the police show up to slap on the handcuffs. Despite the disappointing finish, however, *Night Must Fall* remains a high spot of almost-horror in the *very* lean year of 1937.

As reported by author John McCarty in *Movie Psychos and Madmen*, playwright Emlyn Williams based his lead character on a real-life murderer "who also charmed his victim to death." McCarty relates that Williams "modeled Danny after Patrick Mahon, a 33-year-old married man, whose neighbors thought him a good husband and father until he was hanged in 1924 for killing and dismembering his mistress, whose body parts he had stuffed in a hatbox and other containers."

By 1936, MGM star Robert Montgomery was fed up with the continual stream of prim leading roles given him by the studio. The actor had a long-standing feud with MGM executives (even refusing the lead in *It Happened One Night* because he felt being sent to a "minor" studio like Columbia was a punishment from the front office; the role ultimately went to "lesser" star Clarke Gable who garnered an Oscar for his work). Montgomery began to badger the Metro brass incessantly about breaking out of this tepid happy-go-lucky mold. *Night Must Fall* was the result of his persistence, which paid off in an Oscar nomination for his portrayal of the demented Danny (he lost to Spencer Tracy in *Captains Courageous*). Understandably, Montgomery considered Danny the favorite of his many screen roles.

NIGHT OF TERROR (1933; Columbia) Director: Ben Stoloff. Screenplay: Beatrice Van, William Jacobs (story: Willard Mack). Photography: Joseph A. Valentine. Cast: Bela Lugosi, Wallace Ford, Sally Blane, Bryant Washburn, Tully Marshall, Gertrude Michael, George Meeker, Mary Frey, Matt McHugh, Edwin Maxwell.

Though *Night of Terror does* take place at *Night*, it lacks anything even remotely resembling *Terror*; the film would be better named *Night of Boredom*. The cliché-riddled Old House storyline features a killer dubbed "The Maniac" on the loose (and committing several murders), a pack of money-hungry relatives, two Hindu servants (one of which goes into a trance at the drop of a hat and the other of which is Bela Lugosi), a wisecracking reporter chasing not only a story but the murdered man's daughter as well, a gaggle of inept flatfoots, secret passages, a cowardly black chauffeur, an "and the murderer is..."-knife in the back scene, and an experimental serum which supposedly allows a character to be buried alive for eight hours.

Despite all these elements, *Night of Terror* remains a painfully dull 64 minutes. Not only must the viewer wade through scene after interminable scene of the caped "Maniac" creeping around the house and grounds, but several of the suspicious principals do their fair share of skulking about as well. An overabundance of players leaves no time for any significant characterization beyond the stock reporter, cop, sinister servant, et al. Technically, the film looks rushed, with little in the way of cinematic extras. Bela Lugosi, given nothing better to work with than lines like "I've come to warn you" and "Death is *always* very close," arches his eyebrows and scowls for all he's worth— to no avail. The only point of interest comes at the film's end when, in a bit of good-humored self-spoofing, the "Maniac" himself rises from the dead to stare directly at the camera. "If you dare tell how this picture ends—," he warns in a malevolent gravel-voice, "if you dare reveal who the murderer really is, I'll climb into your bedroom window tonight and tear you limb from limb! I'll *haunt* you. Goodnight, sleep tight, pleasant dreams, heh, heh, heh, heh, heh!"

Night of Terror featured "one of Hollywood's top cameramen" (as *Variety*'s May 25, 1949 obituary labeled Joseph A. Valentine). Valentine died only two months after receiving an Academy Award for his work on *Joan of Arc* (1948). Though nominated three times before, this was his first win. He began as assistant cameraman in 1918 and graduated to full cinematographer in 1924, working steadily up until his death. Valentine later applied his talents to help make *The Wolf Man* (1941) a classic and worked for Alfred Hitchcock on *Shadow of a Doubt* (1943) and *Rope* (1948). A few weeks before his death, Valentine announced that he was turning director on three pictures to be filmed in Mexico City starring Delores Del Rio.

The story for *Night of Terror* was reportedly inspired by a European scientist who claimed to have discovered a drug which would revive a person buried alive for seven days. Though originally announced in February of 1933 as *He Lived to Kill*, then later as *Terror in the Night*, the lurid title fell by the wayside and the picture finally made it to screens in June of 1933 with its new, more generic moniker, *Night of Terror*.

Having resisted for a full two years, *Night of Terror* was Columbia's first foray into (quasi)horror (and the only one of the studio's 36 pictures that year to fall within the genre). They waited *another* two years before making their next horror

In the first of what was to become a string of red-herring roles, Bela Lugosi (held at gunpoint by Wallace Ford) plays a sinister Hindu named Degar in *Night of Terror* (1933).

picture, *The Black Room* (perhaps not surprisingly, considering how poorly the first one turned out). Even these two films dealt more with mystery and melodrama than traditional supernatural terrors. Obviously, the studio was not interested in (or simply not adept at) the genre. It's odd that Columbia elected not to jump on the horror bandwagon along with most of the other majors in 1932/33, since this "minor major" (like Universal) thrived on quickly produced low-end pictures made for little money. Columbia's only other 1930s horror entry came in 1939 when the studio,

overcoming their horror of Horror, launched their Karloff/Mad Doctor series with *The Man They Could Not Hang*.

Apart from 1935's *Best Man Wins* (a deep-sea melodrama), this was the only time Columbia cast Bela Lugosi in one of their pictures during the 1930s. He didn't work at the studio again until 1944 when he returned as Dracula—er, Armand Tessla—in *Return of the Vampire*.

Though it has been reported that Lugosi was filming another movie (*The Devil's in Love*) concurrent with *Night of Terror*, this was not the case.

Night of Terror began shooting on March 1, 1933, and wrapped 12 days later on March 13, while *The Devil's in Love* didn't begin production until June. Lugosi lamented his typecasting woes in the studio press sheets for *Night of Terror*, complaining "I can blame it all on that play ['Dracula']." The actor continued his protestations by stating that he'd like to retire from acting soon and settle down on a small farm, though this surprising revelation from the continental stardom-seeker was not taken in a serious vein.

THE NINTH GUEST (1934; Columbia) Director: R. William Neill. Producer: Robert North. Screenplay: Garnett Weston (from the stage play by Owen Davis and the novel by Gene Bristow). Photography: Benjamin Kline. Cast: Donald Cook, Genevieve Tobin, Hardie Albright, Vince Barnett, Edwin Maxwell, Edward Ellis, Samuel S. Hinds, Helen Flint, Sidney Bracey, Nella Walker.

This intriguing mystery/suspense film begins with a group of eight people invited to a penthouse party. Though all eight know one another, they are not exactly on friendly terms. Once they realize there is no host present and they are trapped (by electrical gates) in the luxurious apartment, the bickering begins. It soon comes to light that they must engage in a battle of wits with their unseen host, who communicates with them only over a special radio. "You are about to meet my guest of honor —" warns the disembodied voice, "— the ninth guest. His name is *death*." According to the voice, one will die each hour, and sure enough, one by one their own weaknesses and shortcomings lead them to their doom. The film is well shot, the characters are realistic, and the acting is excellent. The well-constructed screenplay emphasizes the tension as they each try to avoid their seemingly inevitable fate.

This plot served as a blueprint for the Karloff vehicle *The Man They Could Not Hang* (1939), though *The Ninth Guest* lacks the fantastical element of scientific resurrection contained in that later film.

OUANGA (1935; Paramount; Great Britain) Alternate Titles: *Drums of the Jungle*; *Crime of Voodoo*; *The Love Wanga*. Director/Producer/Screenwriter: George Terwilliger. Photography: Carl Berger. Cast: Fredi Washington, Philip Brandon, Marie Paxton, Sheldon Leonard, Winifred Harris, Sid Easton, Babe Joyce, George Spink.

This "story of voodoo filmed entirely in the West Indies" (as the film's title card heralds the production) centers around Clelie Gordon (Fredi Washington), a plantation owner and voodoo priestess on the island of Haiti. When her neighbor, Adam Maynard (Philip Brandon), spurns her advances and becomes engaged to Eve Langley (Marie Paxton), Clelie sends a charm called an "ouanga" (pronounced "wanga") to cast a death spell over Eve. When this plan is thwarted, she sends two zombies to kidnap Eve and bring her to a voodoo ceremony for sacrifice. Maynard's foreman, Le Strange (Sheldon Leonard), whose love Clelie had rejected, tries to rescue Eve. Clelie shoots Le Strange, but the wounded man manages to snatch Clelie's protective ouanga from around her neck before she takes Eve off to the ceremony. As Clelie lifts the sacrificial knife above Eve's form, Le Strange staggers into the clearing and sets Clelie's charm on fire. Terrified at losing her protective ouanga, Clelie races off into the jungle with Le Strange in pursuit. Cornering her by a huge tree, Le Strange strangles Clelie before he dies of his wound, while Maynard shows up with the local gendarmes to rescue Eve from the voodoo cult's clutches.

Ouanga was an independent production picked up by British Paramount for distribution outside the U.S. Apparently the film was not shown in America until January of 1942, when states-rights distributor J. H. Hoffberg exhibited it briefly under the new title of *The Love Wanga*. *Variety* (January 1942) called it correctly when they asserted that "this quickie meller ... is badly lighted, photographed, acted and directed." Director George Terwilliger makes little attempt to infuse atmosphere into his story, relying heavily on static medium shots with an occasional mundane close-up for visuals. He also spends too much time aboard well-lit ships or focusing on silly subplots (such as a flighty maid trying to slip a love ouanga to her dim-witted beau). Though ads played up cinematographer Carl Berger's participation ("First Camera on *Bring 'Em Back Alive*"), the trumpeting rings hollow for Berger's flat lighting is amateurish at best (garishly over-illuminating a scene so that all semblance of shadows or depth disappears) and downright unwatchable at worst (occasionally lighting so poorly that one can barely see through the muddy darkness). Under Terwilliger's (mis)direction, the acting harkens back to the silent era, full of false smiles, vapid melodramatics, and gross parodies of emotion. (Though some references have claimed otherwise, *Ouanga* does indeed star *the* Sheldon Leonard, perennial screen gangster/thug and later TV mogul who produced such hits as "The Dick Van Dyke Show," "The Andy Griffith Show," and "I Spy.") The best part of this tepid film comes at the very beginning, when the off-screen narrator unwittingly provides a moment of high camp. Over the image of a silly-looking voodoo doll, he solemnly intones, "Wanga, wanga, that's *voodoo!*" *Ouanga, Ouanga,* that's awful!

Unlike similar voodoo entries like *Black Moon* (1934), *Ouanga* at least sports a pair of zombies (two half-naked black men with no special makeup). Unfortunately, Terwilliger makes no attempt to make them the least bit frightening. He shoots the scene of Clelie supposedly raising them from the dead in brightly lit sunshine, and her frantic arm waving and intense stare look ridiculous in the full light of day. And Clelie herself then refers to these creatures as "men." Apart from their kidnapping Eve, these zombies pose no menace whatsoever. In the end Maynard simply tells them to come with him back to the police station and they readily comply. So much for horror.

To his credit, producer/director/screenwriter George Terwilliger took his American cast to the West Indies to shoot his screenplay *Drums of the Night* in an authentic Haitian setting. Though he initially won the confidence of the locals, he quickly raised the ire of their religious leaders when the director asked to film their actual ceremonies. After several warnings (including an ouanga in the front seat of his car), Terwilliger had to move his production to Jamaica, shooting in the hills and jungles around Kingston to complete his picture.

Arthur Leonard (loosely) remade *Ouanga* in 1939 as *The Devil's Daughter*, again filming on Jamaica, though this time with an all-black cast.

THE PHANTOM CREEPS (1939; Universal). Directors: Ford Beebe, Saul A. Goodkind. Producer: Henry MacRae. Screenplay: George Plympton, Basil Dickey, Mildred Barish (story: Willis Cooper). Photography: Jerry Ash, William Sickner. Cast: Bela Lugosi, Dorothy Arnold, Robert Kent, Edwin Stanley, Regis Toomey, Dick C. Smith, Edward Van Sloan.

In 1939, Universal signed Bela Lugosi, fresh from his success in *Son of Frankenstein*, for a 12-chapter serial called *The Phantom Creeps*. In addition to supplying theaters with the weekly episodes, the studio also edited the serial down into a 75-minute feature. Lugosi plays Dr. Zorka, an amazingly prolific mad scientist who has developed not only the world's most powerful explosive (from a "secret element" taken from a meteorite), but an invisibility belt, a method of suspended animation, a revolutionary healing process, a death ray, and a clunky, sour-faced robot! With these various devices, he alternately plots to sell his secrets to a nefarious spy ring (headed by Edward Van Sloan in a nothing role) or rule the world himself. Dogging his invisible footsteps are Captain Bob West of the War Department (Robert Kent, giving what is perhaps the most toneless performance of the decade) and a female reporter (Dorothy Arnold). At the climax, Zorka ends up in a biplane, tossing his "world-destroying" explosives at any target he comes across—barns, battleships, even the Hindenberg (courtesy of actual newsreel footage).

As one might expect from a three-and-a-half hour program crammed into 75 minutes, continuity is not *The Phantom Creeps*' strong suit. (At least Lugosi's earlier serial-derived features, *The Return of Chandu*, 1934, and *Chandu on the Magic Island*, 1935, were culled from a mere seven and five chapters respectively, rather than the full 12.) *Phantom*'s slip-shod special effects, though plentiful, do nothing to improve matters. Despite being a Universal production, *The Phantom Creeps* was not deemed prestigious enough (nor awarded a big enough budget) to employ John P. Fulton's exquisite special effects techniques developed for *The Invisible Man* (1933). Instead, the standard (and awkward) use of wires and such was employed for the various pedestrian invisibility gags—and none-too-carefully at that. At one point, the shadow of the invisible Dr. Zorka steps inside a plane *before* he opens the outer door.

Logic seemingly remains as invisible as Dr. Zorka is supposed to be. Shots of an unconvincing model plane spiraling downward while spinning wildly out of control alternate with interior scenes of the occupants standing up, walking about, and donning parachutes—when they should be thrown about mercilessly inside the plummeting plane. Then, when the aircraft crashes nose first into the ground (and simply topples over rather than explodes), Captain Bob walks away unhurt, still wearing his hat!

Characterization and acting are strictly from the minimalist school, though Bela Lugosi turns in his usual ripe performance, reveling in his character's diabolical dealings. Sadly, the actor is forced to spout such ridiculous hoke as "One by one my enemies will be disposed of until I am master of the *universe!*"

The Phantom Creeps sports laboratory equipment from *Frankenstein*, music from *Bride of Frankenstein*, and footage (of Boris Karloff descending into a crater to accumulate radioactive material from a meteorite) from *The Invisible Ray*. (Ironically, Lugosi seemingly could not escape from Karloff's shadow even when his rival wasn't really in the film.)

THE PHANTOM OF CRESTWOOD (1932; RKO). Director: J. Walter Ruben. Producer:

Merian C. Cooper. Screenplay: Bartlett Cormack (Story: Bartlett Cormack and J. Walter Ruben). Photography: Henry Gerrard. Cast: Ricardo Cortez, Karen Morley, Anita Louise, Pauline Frederick, H. B. Warner, Mary Duncan, Sam Hardy, Tom Douglas.

The Phantom of Crestwood is an effective murder-mystery sprinkled with a few horrific moments. The plot concerns a scheming mistress (Karen Morely) who plans to "retire" to Europe after collecting sufficient blackmail funds to finance her retirement. To this end she induces four of her former beaus (each a "respectable pillar of society") to gather at an isolated mansion (though it is more like a castle — complete with secret panels and underground passages). There she reveals herself and her demands and is promptly murdered for her troubles. The horror comes from the killer wearing a death-mask, appearing out of the dark to terrify the intended victim with its frightening luminous countenance. This macabre sight, coupled by the victim's terrified reaction does indeed induce a chill or two. A respectable running time allows for more solid characterization than usual, and there are plenty of likely suspects and subplots to keep one interested. Much of the story is told via flashback as each suspect relates his or her part in the proceedings leading up to the murder. This keeps things cleverly moving along at a brisk pace as all the pieces fall together. Towards the middle, however, it becomes a bit obvious who-done-it, but the unique characters and the fluid direction and camerawork sustain interest. The theme itself is rather daring, and the many references to the fallen woman's "profession" are definitely pre-Code. Her alluring presence and revealing gowns add a great deal of decadent sensuality to her character, making her that much more intriguing. The film is filled with good, realistic dialogue and features an unusual ending: The racketeer-turned-self-appointed-detective gives the rather sympathetic guilty party an "out" by allowing the culprit to step off a cliff and commit suicide before the police arrive.

The Phantom of Crestwood started as a radio program. Beginning in August, the NBC radio network broadcast *Phantom* over a six week period. The final episode was not aired, however, and listeners were encouraged to take part in a "write-your-own-ending" contest. In order to find out what really happened, the faithful had to go see the movie. This scheme seemed to have worked, for the film was a modest success, turning a $100,000 profit for RKO (in a year in which the studio lost over ten *million*!). Later this same year, Karen Morley (the doomed mistress) played a more innocent role as the heroine of *The Mask of Fu Manchu*. Ricardo Cortez (the heroic racketeer) played yet another mobster in *The Walking Dead* (1936), though this time an *un*sympathetic one, for he frames an innocent Boris Karloff for murder.

RASPUTIN AND THE EMPRESS (1932; MGM) Director: Richard Boleslawski. Producer: Irving Thalberg. Screenplay: Charles MacArthur. Photography: William Daniels. Cast: John Barrymore, Ethel Barrymore, and Lionel Barrymore, Ralph Morgan, Diana Wynyard, Tad Alexander, C. Henry Gordon, Edward Arnold.

"It's his *smile*— it's like a man-eating shark with a bible under its fin."— Prince Chegodieff describing Rasputin in *Rasputin and the Empress.* Irving Thalberg pulled off the casting coup of the decade when he persuaded all three members of Hollywood's "Royal Family" to star in MGM's historical melodrama, *Rasputin and the Empress.* This was the first and only time John, Ethel, and Lionel Barrymore appeared together in a single picture. No expense was spared on the lavish production. The expansive sets, breathtaking costumes (one of Ethel's court robes alone cost $4800) and regal art direction added a larger-than-life quality to the story of an ambitious peasant monk who gains power at the Russian Court through his mesmeric hold over the young Prince Nikolas and his mother the Czarina. One would think that John Barrymore would have been the logical choice to play the evil, compelling Rasputin. Having assayed a similar role the previous year as *Svengali*, however, the Great Profile chose the heroic part of the faithful Prince Chegodieff, the one steadfast opponent of the conniving holy man, and left the villainy to his brother Lionel. While lacking the tragic depth of his sibling's *Svengali* (1931), Lionel Barrymore paints a vile yet commanding portrait of the infamous historical figure, Rasputin. According to William Darien (writing in *The Candlelight Room*, Vol. 1, no. 1), Bela Lugosi was originally considered for the role of Rasputin. After John Barrymore was cast for a part, however, "they decided *Ethel* Barrymore could play the Czarina in the film. One thing led to another. The big wheels at the studio started thinking. They thought about John Barrymore, Ethel Barrymore — and *Lionel* Barrymore."

The picture contains one scene of genuine horror — the murder of Rasputin. Facing his antagonist, Rasputin refuses to succumb to the virulent poison he's ingested. After a vicious struggle, Chegodieff strikes Rasputin again and again with a metal poker, but with an inhuman tenacity, the fiend will not die. His face awash in rivulets of blood, the unholy man staggers to his feet and advances toward his attacker. Finally unnerved, the nearly hysterical prince drags the monk out into the swirling snow and throws him into a half-frozen river where the monk finally surrenders to the icy water. The violent, gruesome struggle, coupled with the demonic stamina of the victim, creates a chilling moment of terror in this otherwise stately historical drama. The powerful scene took a full week to shoot ("It is commonly alleged that the fight took so long because each of us was battling for the limelight," Lionel wryly noted in his autobiography, *We Barrymores*).

The production was plagued with problems right from the start. Shooting began without a finished script in order to accommodate Ethel Barrymore's contractual stage commitments. The picture's original director, Charles Brabin, was fired (some accounts blame conflicts with supervisor Bernie Hyman and others state Ethel Barrymore had him removed for being too slow). Upon its release, the film won both financial and critical acclaim — until Prince Youssoupoff, the real-life slayer of Rasputin, and his wife, Princess Irena (the Czar's niece), brought a libel suit against the studio — and won. After paying the couple an out-of-court settlement amounting to nearly one million dollars (about half the cost of the picture itself), MGM basically washed their hands of the painful production. From then on, many subsequent Hollywood films carried the following disclaimer: "The events and characters in this film are fictional and any resemblance to persons living or dead is purely coincidental."

THE RETURN OF CHANDU (1934; Principal Pictures) Director: Ray Taylor. Producer: Sol Lesser. Screenplay: Barry Barringer. Photography: John Hickson. Cast: Bela Lugosi, Maria Alba, Clara Kimball Young, Lucien Prival, Deane Benton, Phyllis Ludwig, Cyril Armbrister, Murdock McQuarrie, Wilfred Lucas, Josef Swickard, Jack Clark.

When independent producer Sol Lesser proposed to film a 12-chapter serial entitled *The Return of Chandu*, he began searching for the ideal actor to fill the mystical/romantic shoes of this popular radio character. "By a surprisingly easy process of elimination," stated Lesser in his film's publicity material, "I reached the conclusion that Bela Lugosi, the Hungarian star, was the ideal I sought. On his own native stage — at the National Theatre of Budapest — his greatest successes had been achieved in romantic roles, such as Cyrano de Bergerac, Romeo, Hamlet and Petruccio in 'Taming of the Shrew.' Yet in America he had been 'typed' as a 'heavy', as in *Dracula* for instance. His voice, I found, could assume the modulations of Chandu as heard in all those countless homes throughout America where a radio was installed, and of course, his skill as an actor could be depended upon to complete the realization of what Chandu looks, acts, and talks like." Lugosi, fresh from a more-or-less benign characterization in Universal's *The Black Cat*, welcomed the chance to play a more romantic (though still mysterious) character. "*The Black Cat*," stated the actor in a *Return of Chandu* publicity article, "was the picture that secured for me my present stellar part in which I am at last permitted to appear before American audiences in a distinctly romantic characterization." *The Return of Chandu* wrapped on August 4, 1934, after a hectic three-week shooting schedule. A *Hollywood Reporter* item (August 15, 1934) noted that Lugosi, having finished *Chandu*, was checking in at Universal "for a top spot in *Daughter of Dracula*" (which ultimately evolved into *Dracula's Daughter*—without Lugosi).

An innovative (and enterprising) filmmaker, Sol Lesser released *The Return of Chandu* in two forms, offering the standard 12-chapter serial to those theaters who played such fare, and also creating a seven-reel film condensed from the first five chapters for cinemas whose venue required features. (Lesser also later hired editor Carl Himm to create a "sequel" feature out of the remaining seven chapters, calling it *Chandu on the Magic Island*.) The plot (of both features) has Frank Chandler (a.k.a. Chandu) use his mystic Yogi powers to foil the plans of a strange cat-worshipping sect located on "the lost island of Lemuria." The Lemurians need a sacrifice to restore their dead high priestess to life. Using their agents throughout the world, they attempt to kidnap the beautiful Princess Nadji of Egypt, a friend (and, ultimately, love-interest) of Chandu. Thus the picture consists of numerous kidnapping attempts (some successful, some thwarted) and rescues of the fair princess by Chandu and his nephew Bobby.

Of the two "features" culled from the serial, *The Return of Chandu* is by far the superior entry. Lugosi's hypnotic talents (complete with his patented *Dracula* gestures) and forceful presence are fully exploited here. In the second feature, *Chandu on the Magic Island*, his character loses his mystical powers and so Lugosi's hypnotic battle of wills with the evil villains is supplanted by endless dreary stretches of Chandu ineffectually skulking about trying to get out of one mess after another.

Sol Lesser's serial/feature ploy did not impress the critics (or moviegoers, for that matter) and the planned series of Chandu features and two-reel shorts the producer had proposed for Lugosi failed to materialize. In its review of *The Return of Chandu*, *Variety* observed "some action in this, but it is neither fish nor fowl. This might be expected when a serial of some 12 episodes is trimmed and pasted together for feature length. The trimming is good at times, but some of the padded stuff remains. And there are several yawning gaps in the continuity that spoil whatever effect was intended... Little or no production value. Technique is strictly serial. Bela Lugosi is wasted. Even at that he stands shoulders above the rest."

THE ROGUES TAVERN (1936; Mercury Pictures) Director: Bob Hill. Production Manager: Ed W. Rote. Screenplay: Al Martin. Photography: Bill Hyer. Cast: Wallace Ford, Barbara Pepper, Joan Woodbury, Clara Kimball Young, Jack Mulhall, John Elliot, Earl Dwire, John W. Cowell, Vincent Dennis, Arthur Loft, Ivo Henderson, Ed Cassidy, Silver Wolf.

The bare-bones plot of this film has a group of jewel smugglers lured to the titular inn under false pretenses and trapped there by a vengeful person or persons unknown. Wallace Ford (who just happens to be a detective) and his intended bride (Barbara Pepper, who in later years became a robust regular on television's "Green Acres") innocently stumble into the murderous mess. *The Rogues Tavern* does contain several macabre elements which set it apart from the standard mystery. For one thing, the murders appear to be committed not by any human but by some vicious, unkillable wolf/dog. This is soon proven to be a hoax, however, when the hero discovers that the murderer "used a set of false dog teeth." For another, the "Red Rock Tavern" is more along the lines of *The Old Dark House* (complete with secret panels and shadowy cellar) than a friendly

Independent producer Sol Lesser took his 12-chapter serial and condensed it into two features, *The Return of Chandu* (1934) and *Chandu on the Magic Island* (1935). The scene pictured here actually appears in the second feature.

pub. Finally, the killer, once revealed, turns out to be a raving lunatic who pronounces the sentence of death with a chilling hysteria. The screenplay offers up a few offbeat characters such as an exotic "card-reader" (who becomes nearly hysterical when the murders begin) and wise-cracking heroine ("I hate mysteries—I don't even like hash!"), but the action drags during long stretches where nothing really happens. These filler bits are made even more painful by the complete lack of music. Excruciating scenes lacking either dialogue or action (someone slowly walking downstairs and leisurely looking through a trunk, for instance) sink the film under a wave of boredom. Director

Gloria Stuart, star of *Secret of the Blue Room* (1933), with the author in 1993.

Bob Hill tries to invest some visual creativity into the production, adding some (often elaborate) camera motion and depth of field (shooting through doorways, fireplaces, car windows, etc.). Unfortunately, his attempts are frequently nullified by Bill Hyer's amateurish, jerky camerawork which becomes more of a distraction than an enhancement.

Prolific poverty-row screenwriter Al Martin began in film by writing subtitles for silent pictures (averaging 200 films a year over a period of ten years). The same year he penned *Rogue's Tavern*, he wrote a second pseudo-horror, *A Face in the Fog* (also directed by Bob Hill). Martin went on to script many low-budget potboilers, including *The Invisible Ghost* (1941), *The Mad Doctor of Market Street* (1942), and *Invasion of the Saucermen* (1957).

SECRET OF THE BLUE ROOM (1933; Universal) Director: Kurt Neumann. Producer: Carl Laemmle, Jr. Screenplay: William Hurlbut (story: Erich Philippi). Photography: Charles Stumar. Cast: Lionel Atwill, Gloria Stuart, Paul Lukas, Edward Arnold, Onslow Stevens, William Janney, Robert Barrat, Muriel Kirkland, Russel Hopton, Elizabeth Patterson, Anders Van Haden, James Durkin.

A storm rages outside Castle Helldorf while Robert von Helldorf, his daughter Irene, and her three would-be suitors celebrate Irene's birthday within. The talk turns to ghost stories and von Helldorf reluctantly reveals the castle's secret, a "haunted" chamber called the Blue Room. Twenty years earlier, "three persons met death there — under strange, peculiar circumstances," von Helldorf warns. Since then it has remained locked. To prove his courage to Irene, the youngest of the suitors, Tommy, proposes that each of the three spend a night in the haunted room to try to unravel the mystery. Tommy disappears, the second suitor is murdered, and it is up to the surviving Romeo (with the aid of a police inspector) to unlock the "secret" of the Blue Room. *Secret of the Blue Room* never tries very hard to be a horror film. While the principals initially talk of ghosts, sinister *human* characters are soon seen creeping about. The butler, chauffeur, and even von Helldorf behave suspiciously, indicating that the "secret" of the room has an earthly rather than supernatural basis. Besides, ghosts don't usually pack pistols (the victims are found shot to death). Once the police inspector arrives, all ghostly pretense is promptly dropped as the no-nonsense, intelligent detective alternately questions, bullies, and deduces his way towards the solution. Charles Stumar's mobile camera, coupled with the effective and likable cast (Atwill, Stuart, Lukas, and Arnold are all excellent) make *Secret* one of the decade's more watchable horror/mysteries.

Gloria Stuart, who plays Irene, entertains her suitors at the film's beginning with a rather lengthy song. The actress told this author that it was not her voice, but that of an unidentified professional singer which is heard on the soundtrack. Of Lionel Atwill, Ms. Stuart commented that he was "a very accomplished stage actor," who was "considerate and vain — as are a lot of actors."

Hungarian actor Paul Lukas (a member of the Hungarian wrestling team at the 1912 Olympics in Stockholm) was "discovered" by Paramount's Jesse Lasky while visiting Budapest. The powerful production executive saw Lukas' performance in the play "Antonia" and afterwards offered him a contract (through an interpreter) to come to America and make motion pictures. The actor arrived in the States not knowing a word of English. He went on to win a Best Actor Oscar in 1943 for *Watch on the Rhine*. Lucas appeared in one other genre effort — Walt Disney's *20,000 Leagues Under the Sea* (1954).

Universal remade *Secret of the Blue Room* twice, first in 1938 as *The Missing Guest* and later in 1944 as *Murder in the Blue Room*. Though *Secret* cost only $69,000 (making it the cheapest of the three — and the cheapest film of the entire year for Universal!), it stands head and shoulders above the two later pretenders.

SECRET OF THE CHATEAU (1934; Universal) Director: Richard Thorpe. Producer: L. L. Ostrow. Screenplay: Albert DeMond, Harry Behn (story: Lawrence G. Blochman). Photography: Robert Planck. Cast: Claire Dodd, Alice White, Osgood Perkins, Jack La Rue, George E. Stone, Clark Williams, William Faversham, Ferdinand Gottschalk, Dewitt Jennings, Helen Ware, Frank Reicher, Alphonz Ethier.

Despite ad lines like "Shadows Come to Life!" and "Trunks Swallow Men!," *Secret of the Chateau* is a straightforward (and rather uninteresting) mystery, though Universal's P.R. department would have us believe otherwise. No shadows come to life (the sets are so overlit that no shadows even *appear*), and there are certainly no man-eating trunks. The story revolves around a rare Gutenberg bible targeted by the mysterious book thief/murderer known as Prahec. Various characters gather at the bright and sunny chateau which houses the priceless book. Murders are committed, an inspector arrives, and the criminal is finally unmasked — all without much suspense or excitement. The picture becomes bogged down in unfunny humor dealing with toupee-snatching, fly-catching, and insulting "dames." Director Richard Thorpe adds little invention and no atmosphere to the mundane proceedings, showing little of the talent he later evinced on *Night Must Fall* (1937). The only real point of interest comes from third-billed Osgood Perkins (father of Anthony Perkins) playing the droll, contemptuous butler.

MGM house director Richard Thorpe made 179 feature films (66 of them at Metro) over the course of his long but undistinguished career, making him the most prolific studio director in the history of cinema. Only William ("One Shot") Beaudine directed more movies (182), though many of them were grade-Z independents. While the efficient, workmanlike Thorpe was usually assigned standard B features and series films (Tarzan and Lassie entries, for instance), he occasionally landed a few prestige pictures like *The Prisoner of Zenda* (1952), *Ivanhoe* (1952; Oscar-nominated for Best Picture), and *Knights of the Round Table* (1953). Despite his voluminous output, Thorpe is all but forgotten today. (James Mason once caustically observed that "his reputation for only one take is why we don't remember his films.") Aside from directing Elvis Presley's screen debut (*Jailhouse Rock*) in 1957, Thorpe's main claim to fame might be that he *almost* directed *The Wizard of Oz*. He began as the film's director but was replaced after only two weeks. None of his footage survived.

SECRETS OF THE FRENCH POLICE (1932; RKO) Director: Edward Sutherland. Screenplay: Samuel Ornitz, Robert Tasker (based on the *American Weekly* series by H. Ashton Wolfe). Photography: Alfred Gilks. Cast: Gwili Andre, Gregory Ratoff, Frank Morgan, John Warburton, Rochelle Hudson, Christian Rub, Murray Kinnell, Arnold Korff, Kendall Lee, Lucien Prival, Guido Trento.

In Paris, the evil General Moloff kidnaps a young flower girl and sequesters her in his private chateau because she is "a perfect hypnotic subject and also looks like a Romanoff." Moloff (a man with "an extremely magnetic personality") hypnotizes her into believing she is the lost Princess Anastasia, heir to the Russian throne. It falls to the Paris Surete, with help from the girl's lover (an elegant, likable thief) to foil Moloff's plans and rescue the entranced girl. After nearly an hour of romance, police procedures, and royal plottings, the picture abruptly switches gears and takes a stab at the horrific for its climax. Up until the final two minutes, even the potentially shuddery elements of hypnotism and Moloff's mysterious castle had been handled in a straightforward, mundane manner. The ending, however, takes us into Moloff's previously unseen basement lab in which we learn that he covers the bodies of his female victims (of which there have been several) in a special plaster to create beautiful death statues. Also, he possesses a dangerous, arcing electrical device (of unspecified purpose) which ultimately proves the evil man's demise during his climactic scuffle with the police. While only 55 minutes long, the picture tends to be slow-moving and overly talky, though the lively characters and opulent settings help hold one's attention. Once the hero breaks into the chateau toward the end, however, actions finally speak louder than words as he makes a daring escape from Moloff's guards; and the picture's swift but shocking ending never fails to make an impression.

Murray Kinnell (playing Bertillion, the French detective) also appeared in *Freaks* this same year as the carnival barker who assured us that he indeed had "living, breathing monstrosities." In *Mad Love* (1935), he played the small role of Charles, one of Yvonne's fellow actors in Le Théatre de Horreurs. Shortly thereafter, Kinnell became involved with the administration of the newly formed Screen Actors Guild and eventually left acting altogether to devote all his professional energies to SAG, ultimately becoming administrator of the Guild's agency division. If the all-but-forgotten *Secrets of the French Police* looks vaguely familiar, one should not be too surprised. Director Edward Sutherland utilized the impressive castle interior sets from the recently released *The Most Dangeorus Game* to create Moloff's chateau and dressed Moloff's henchmen in Count Zaroff's Cossack costumes.

SH! THE OCTOPUS (1937; Warner Bros.) Director: William McGann. Screenplay: George Bricker (from plays by Ralph Spence and Ralph Murphy and Donald Gallaher). Photography: Arthur Todd. Cast: Hugh Herbert, Allen Jenkins, Marcia Ralston, John Eldredge, George Rosener, Brandon Tyman, Eric Stanley, Margaret Irving, Elspeth Dudgeon.

Sh! the Octopus is another variation of Ralph Spence's play, "The Gorilla," only with a cephalopod standing in for the title primate and a lonely lighthouse supplanting the eerie mansion setting. In nearly all areas, *Sh!* fails to measure up to *The Gorilla* (1939), with the one exception being the exclusion of the Ritz Brothers. (Though the unfunny Hugh Herbert and Allen Jenkins inspire few laughs, at least they're less annoying than Jimmy, Harry, and Al proved to be.) Not only does *Sh!* sorely miss the presence of Lionel Atwill and Bela Lugosi, it also lacks anything even *resembling* logic. It starts out fairly well with the arrival at the abandoned lighthouse and an encounter with the grizzled, frightening "Captain Hook" (George Rosener) who, when he hears the ticking of a clock, "goes plumb out of his mind and wants to kill somebody," but the picture quickly bogs down in endless creeping about, octopus tentacles appearing out of secret passages to grab people or turn out the lights(!), and just plain silliness. After half-a-dozen characters arrive, the story becomes a pointless, jumbled mess involving a secret "radium ray" formula, the master criminal known as "The Octopus," and a submarine which never seems to arrive. "We're out in the ocean under a lighthouse with a lot of screwballs," sums up one character. Nearly everybody (besides the two bumbling detectives) turns out to be an undercover law officer (a fed, an intelligence officer, an agent of the "International Police," and even a woman from something called "The Peace League"). All the nonsense and loose ends don't really matter much, however, since the it-was-all-a-dream ending makes everything moot. The only really effective moment in the film's 54 minutes (which feels *double* that amount) is when Elspeth Dudgeon (Sir Roderick from *The Old Dark House*) reveals herself as The Octopus by removing her wig to transform from a kindly old lady into a hideous crone (via the same filter technique used in 1931's *Dr. Jekyll and Mr. Hyde*). Of course, just *how* her normal face suddenly becomes a mottled mass (or *why* her previously perfect teeth abruptly transform into a blackened, snaggletoothed mess) is a bit of horrific license designed to chill the blood rather than satisfy logic. Sadly, it's the *only* chill in an otherwise tepid picture. *Variety* hit the mollusk on the head when they observed that "this bit of grist for the double-feature bills is so feeble even the actors seem embarrassed."

SHE (1935; RKO) Directors: Irving Pichel, Lansing C. Holden. Producer: Merian C. Cooper. Screenplay: Ruth Rose (additional dialogue by Dudley Nichols; from the novel by H. Rider Haggard). Photography: J. Roy Hunt. Cast: Helen Gahagan, Randolph Scott, Nigel Bruce, Helen Mack, Gustav von Seyffertitz, Samuel Hinds, Jim Thorpe, Noble Johnson.

She, like *Lost Horizon* (1937), is predominantly an adventure fantasy, or (as the ads put it) an "astounding romantic spectacle." Unlike *Lost Horizon*, however, which focused on lofty moral and spiritual issues and is completely devoid of horrific content (or any significant *conflict*, for that matter), *She* features a few terrors along the way. Human sacrifice, death by "hot-potting" (placing a white-hot cauldron over the head of a victim), reincarnation, and the aging of centuries in a few seconds all fall into the realm of She-Who-Must-

Tanya (Helen Mack) about to be sacrificed to She-Who-Must-Be-Obeyed in *She* (1935).

Be-Obeyed. (While *Lost Horizon* also features a woman whose great age catches up to her in mere moments, the picture downplays the horrific aspect by hiding the transformation and playing the scene for sympathy rather than horror.)

Leo Vincey (Randolph Scott) and his friend Holly (Nigel Bruce) follow the clues left by Leo's fifteenth-century ancestor to a lost city near the Arctic Circle where they encounter an immortal queen (Helen Gahagan) known only as "She-Who-Must-Be-Obeyed." She believes Leo to be a reincarnation of her former lover (Leo's ancestor). Leo, who has fallen in love with their guide's daughter (Helen Mack), refuses the queen's advances and She, attempting to entice him with the promise of eternal life, steps into a magical fire that unexpectedly causes her to age rapidly.

She features some of the most impressive art direction from the Golden Age. Van Nest Polglase and Al Herman's towering sets (including the re-dressed great wall and gate from *King Kong*) are a fascinating mix of primitive savagery and art deco modernism. Directors Irving Pichel and Lansing Holden stage the various action sequences (battling savages, heroic rescue from the pit of fire, etc.) with an exciting verve but fail to bring any plausibility to the more mundane sequences. In fact, the overlong ceremonial scenes become an exercise in tedium, and the frequent overhead shots of the choreographed dancers lend a ridiculous Busby Berkeley-ish feel to the proceedings. Screenwriter Ruth Rose (*King Kong*, *Son of Kong*) provides only shallow characters and trite sentiment to battle the lure of immortality and She-Who-Must-Be-Obeyed. The principals fail to breathe life into their superficial characters and become mere ciphers. Why the all-powerful queen would fall for such a wooden, colorless, and humorless personage as Randolph Scott is the real mystery of *She*. Producer Merian C. Cooper wanted Joel McCrea (star of Cooper's *The Most Dangerous Game*, 1932) for the role of Leo Vincey, but when McCrea proved unavailable Cooper had to settle for Scott. Randolph Scott "seemed to think acting was memorizing lines and remembering when to repeat them," observed Frances Drake (who co-starred with Scott the following year in *And Sudden Death*). From his lackluster performance in *She*, one can only agree. In the end, *She* stands as a spectacular visual triumph that rings hollow for most viewers due to a weak script, bland characters and dull acting.

Reviewers generally praised *She* for its sumptuous art and technical direction, but lambasted its juvenile plotting. *Variety* (July 31, 1935) predicted that "'She' will be a spotty grosser on the basis of the gulf between its production values, which are excellent, and its story, which places a heavy load on the capacity of literate adults to indulge in make-believe," though admitting that "kids will probably go for the picture in a big way." *The New York Times* reviewer (July 26, 1935) agreed that *She* "is likely to find its greatest favor with the younger generation. The adult reaction, we fear, will be decidedly lukewarm." *She* failed at the box office, losing $180,000 for RKO. Even so, the studio showed profits of nearly $700,000 for 1935 (due to hits like *Top Hat* and *Star of Midnight*). It was the first year RKO made money since 1930.

H. Rider Haggard's 1887 novel first came to the screen in 1899 as a George Méliès one-minute short aptly called *Column of Fire* (since it focused solely on the story's climactic episode). The Edison Company filmed a longer, 17-minute treatment in 1908 entitled *She*. Four more silent versions appeared—in 1911, 1916 (with Henry Victor of *Freaks* fame), 1917, and 1925—before Merian C. Cooper decided to tackle the story in 1935. This Golden Age version was by no means the last. Filmmakers in India produced their own adaptation in 1953 titled *Malika Salomi*. Then in 1965, Britain's Hammer Films took time out from their Dracula and Frankenstein series to produce a variation with Peter Cushing and Christopher Lee (and, unfortunately, the lifeless Ursula Andress in the title role). This picture was successful enough to spawn a direct (and awful) sequel, *The Vengeance of She*, in 1968. A final *She* (1985), a futuristic sword and sorcery picture starring Sandahl Bergman, borrowed the name but little else.

The 1935 first-ever sound version was for all intents and purposes a lost film until located and revived in 1976 for Radio City Music Hall's Art Deco Week. The *Los Angeles Times* labeled the picture's set design as "a kind of Art Deco Barbaric," while *The New Yorker* called it, "the Art Deco style of Radio City Music Hall ... you keep expecting the Rockettes to turn up."

This version strayed significantly from the original novel. Haggard set his lost city of Kor in uncharted Africa, while the film placed it in Asia, above the Arctic Circle. In the book, Leo Vincey was thought to be the reincarnation of an Egyptian priest named Kallikrates, who lived 2000 years before. The film portrays Vincey as the (possible) reincarnation of his English ancestor, John Vincey, who died a mere 500 years past. Leo's native love-interest, Ustani, in the book, is replaced in the film with an anglo girl (a *safer* choice in the Hollywood of 1935), the daughter of a British trader/guide. No mention is made in the film of Haggard's ancient, powerful civilization upon whose ashes and throne She rules the primitive native people. (The 1965 Hammer version was actually much closer to Haggard's story, though it did alter the original ending by having Leo bathe in the fire and achieve immortality at the climax.)

Among cinematographer J. Roy Hunt's 150-plus films (most of them for RKO) are several worthy genre entries: *I Walked with a Zombie* (1943; arguably the best of the Val Lewton pictures), *A Game of Death* (1945; a fairly good remake of *The Most Dangerous Game*), and *Mighty Joe Young* (1949; a sentimental but still affecting Willis O'Brien feature).

She's star (and title character), Helen Gahagan, was a supremely successful stage actress and opera singer. Wooed away from Broadway, *She* was Ms. Gahagan's film debut. It became her big screen curtain call as well for she never accepted another movie role. Ms. Gahagan later went into politics, serving as a member of the U.S. House of Representatives from 1945 until 1949. In 1950 she lost a bid for a seat in the U.S. Senate—to Richard Nixon. Helen Gahagan was married to Melvyn Douglas (in 1931) and even authored a book entitled *The Eleanor Roosevelt We Remember*. Apparently, Ms. Gahagan looked back on her single screen role with something less than fondness. While running for the Senate, she reportedly attempted to buy up and supress all existing prints of the film.

She cast members Helen Mack, Samuel Hinds, and Noble Johnson all appeared in other Golden Age horror productions. Mack starred in *The Son of Kong* (1933), Hinds offered support in *The Raven* (1935), and Noble Johnson appeared in (among others) *Murders in the Rue Morgue* (1932), *The Mummy* (1932), and *King Kong* (1933).

In reactionary Great Britain, *She* failed to earn a "Universal" rating from the Board of Film Censors, which would have allowed children to see the picture unrestricted. Critic Graham Greene (writing in *The Spectator*, October 25, 1935) chided the board for their seemingly arbitrary decision: "The Wag of the Week is Mr. Shortt, [Chairman] of our Board of Film Censors, who has granted to [*Top Hat*], a quite pleasantly bawdy film, the Universal Certificate he has refused to the earnest manly Boy Scout virtues of Rider Haggard's *She*."

SIX HOURS TO LIVE (1932; 20th Century-Fox) Director: William Dieterle. Screenplay: Bradley King (from the original story "Auf Wiedersehen" by Gordon Morris and Morton Barteaux). Photography: John Seitz. Cast: Warner

Baxter, Miriam Jordan, John Boles, George Marion, Sr., Halliwell Hobbes, Irene Ware, Beryl Mercer, Edward McWade, John Davidson, Edwin Maxwell, Dewey Robinson, Torben Meyer.

Predating *The Walking Dead* by four years, *Six Hours to Live* centers around a man scientifically brought back from death who uses his newfound preternatural knowledge to (among other things) bring justice to the guilty. Unlike the later Karloff vehicle, however, *Six Hours to Live* utilizes this fascinating concept merely as a framing device, refusing to explore the fantastic (or horrific) aspects of the situation and instead focuses on a romantic subplot. Paul Onslow (Warner Baxter), representative for the mythical country of Sylvaria, opposes the unjust trade agreement concocted by the greedy attendees of the International Trade Conference. Of all the delegates, Onslow is the single holdout (the deal would mean ruin for his country) and, as a result, has received a number of death threats. The last day of the conference arrives, and the participants have until 11:00 P.M. to sway (one way or another) their solitary opponent, without whose vote of unanimity the treaty will fail. Sure enough, while Paul prepares for a dinner party at the home of his newly-pledged sweetheart (Miriam Jordan, making her screen debut), he is strangled. Fortunately, one of the house guests happens to be Professor Otto Bauer (George Marion), who has found a way to restore life to dead animals. The scientist had planned to demonstrate his miraculous invention (which generates a ray "more potent than all the radium in existence") on the morrow by restoring life to a dead rabbit. With Paul's untimely death, however, he pleads with the skeptical police inspector (Edwin Maxwell) to let him attempt the process on a human being. It works and Paul is brought back to life — with one hitch. "The vital energy generated by my ray lasts only six hours," admits the apologetic professor. After his miraculous revival, Paul appears normal (unlike Karloff's zombielike state in *The Walking Dead*) except that the former agnostic now firmly believes in God (presumably having seen Him first-hand). Paul knows who murdered him but refuses to divulge the information, insisting he must confront the guilty party himself. This he finally does, but only after the bulk of the film is taken up with Paul's numerous "noble" activities: breaking off his romance to make room for his friend and rival for the girl (who, unlike himself, will still be around in six hours), allaying another friend's debilitating fear of death, saving a streetwalker, giving money and solace to a little flower girl whose sister has died, and delivering comfort to a grieving mother (not to mention making a last-minute entrance at literally the eleventh hour to cast the all-important "no" vote and save his country from ruin). When Paul finally confronts his killer (one of the emissaries), it is brief, disappointing, and inconclusive. The scene is over before we know what Paul has done to the man (if anything). Instead, the picture finishes as it began — focusing on romance as Paul takes his (final) leave from his beloved (and from this world). Technically, the film is superior, with well-dressed sets, believable exteriors, and rich visuals (the result of John Seitz's fluid camerawork). The acting, however, is heavy on melodramatics, particularly between Paul and his lover who engage in starry-eyed cheek-pressing and maudlin love talk. In fact, the whole romantic triangle (which takes up the first third of the picture) quickly becomes tiresome. The impressive resurrection sequence, however, adds a much-needed jolt of interest. Inside a huge glass tube surrounded by gleaming bands and connected to strange apparatus lies the body. As the machinery hums and crackles, the form begins to glow and pulse until it becomes a blur of blinding light. Energy sparks out from its center like lighting bolts trapped inside the tube. As we watch the amazing scene, the camera cuts to inside the glass enclosure, drawing us into the riot of light and sound. Unfortunately, after this thrill the picture once again settles down to straight drama as Paul goes about his various missions of mercy. In the end, these *Six Hours* contain precious few minutes of excitement.

Early drafts of the screenplay revolved around the more volatile issue of disarmament rather than trade. Jason S. Joy, the director of the Studio Relations Office of the AMPP, however, advised 20th Century–Fox that "The important thing is not to undermine public confidence in disarmament conferences in which our country and other countries right now are very much interested." The studio obliged and changed the nature of Paul Onslow's conference.

John Boles (who plays the third point of the picture's romantic triangle) is best remembered by horror film fans as the concerned friend of Henry *Frankenstein* (1931). Boles began his career as a singer, studying for two years in France with the famous operatic tenor, Jean de Reszke, but soon turned to acting. He retired from films in the mid–1950s, moved to Texas, and went into the oil business. Boles once summed up his philosophy about acting this way: "Why attempt to kid the public? When a screen actor tells you his art, business, profession, or whatever he chooses to call it, is a serious, dignified pursuit, he is either spouting 'poppycock' or just taking himself too seriously."

German-born director William Dieterle had the rather odd idiosyncrasy of always wearing white gloves — a new pair every morning — while on the set. It has also been claimed (by Stuart Jerome in *Those Crazy Wonderful Years When WE Ran Warner Bros.*) that he was a superstitious man, "starting production only on a date deemed to be propitious by his astrologer." Dieterle began his career as an actor, appearing in such prestigious German productions as Paul Leni's *Waxworks* (1924) and *Faust* (1926). His greatest contribution to the Golden Age of Horror is the grand direction he brought to another borderline entry, *The Hunchback of Notre Dame* (1939).

SVENGALI (1931; Warner Bros.) Director: Archie Mayo. Screenplay: J. Grubb Alexander (based on the novel *Trilby* by George Du Maurier). Photography: Barney McGill. Cast: John Barrymore, Marian Marsh, Donald Crisp, Bramwell Fletcher, Carmel Myers, Luis Alberni, Lumsden Hare, Paul Porcasi.

Set in Paris, the story follows the unsavory singing teacher/pianist Svengali who becomes enchanted with a young artist's model named Trilby (Marian Marsh). Svengali hypnotizes Trilby and is subsequently able to control her through his thoughts. Though Trilby has fallen in love with Billee, a handsome young artist, Svengali uses his mesmeric powers to induce her to fake her own suicide and go away with him. Five years later, "Madame and Maestro Svengali" are the toast of Europe. With his hypnotic power, Svengali has turned Trilby's ordinary voice into that of an operatic diva. When the couple's concert tour brings them back to Paris, Billee sees Trilby and from then on dogs their footsteps. Svengali's love for Trilby is not reciprocated, and so he must use his hypnotic powers to bind her to him. The constant mesmeric exertion has taken its toll on Svengali and he falls ill. Finally, the maestro collapses on-stage. "Oh God," he pleads, dying, "Grant me in death what you denied me in life — the woman I love." As if in answer, Trilby also collapses and dies.

Though more a love story than a horror tale, *Svengali* remains a fascinating borderline entry in the Golden Age of Horror thanks to John Barrymore's intense performance, Anton Grot's intriguing art direction, and Barney McGill's fluid camerawork. Barrymore's Svengali, with his long, forked beard (like the split tongue of a serpent), lanky hair, and tight-fitting black clothes, is a smiling spider of a man. From Barrymore's hypnotic gaze and penetrating voice (not to mention the chilling, milky-white contact lenses worn over his eyes or the pinpoint lighting during the hypnotism scenes), one never doubts that he indeed has the power. Yet, to the actor's credit, Svengali also inspires a grudging sympathy, particularly when he sadly admits that Trilby's artificial "love" for him is "just Svengali talking to himself again." Barney McGill's mobile camera prowls about Anton Grot's wonderful sets (made up of equal parts dark expressionism and fairy-tale fantasy) to generate the occasional shudder. When Svengali exerts his evil influence to call Trilby to him for the first time, the camera creeps around Svengali's garret, winding about the man like some sinuous snake. It then retreats before him to flow out the window just as his hypnotic power reaches out, seemingly gliding across the rooftops of Paris to finally invade Trilby's bedroom.

Unlikely as it may seem, it was the role of Svengali that ultimately won John Barrymore his fourth (and final) wife. Elaine Barrymore related in her autobiography *All My Sins Remembered* that, after seeing *Svengali* at the age of 15, her "hero worship" of John Barrymore became "a real crush." Barrymore's Svengali, despite being "a maniac with a filthy heart and cataracts" (as described by Elaine's worried mother), so captivated Elaine that she determined "we're going to meet someday and mean a great deal to each other." "Barrymore was going on to different roles," wrote Elaine, "*Topaze, Councilor at Law, Dinner at Eight, Grand Hotel*, but I could never forget his wicked and witty Svengali. Perhaps his conversion by hypnosis of Marian Marsh from Trilby, the poor artist's model, into a glamorous opera star sowed a seed of hope in me. I can't be certain. I only know that I had already decided to be on the stage and had secretly made rounds of the theatrical agents after school." Elaine eventually did meet her idol and determinedly courted him, marrying the 54-year-old Barrymore when she was 21. (Speaking of marriages, in 1941 John Barrymore's daughter, Diana, married his *Svengali* co-star — and rival for Trilby's affection — Bramwell Fletcher.)

Svengali received good critical notices (and adequate box office receipts) so Warners tried to repeat their success with a hasty follow-up Barrymore vehicle, *The Mad Genius*, which hit the screens a mere five months later. Using much of the same cast (Marian Marsh, Carmel Myers, Louis Alberni) and production crew (scripter J. Grubb Alexander, art director Anton Grot, and cinematographer Barney McGill), this parallel-picture casts Barrymore as a scheming ballet master who shapes and molds a young peasant boy into "the greatest dancer of all time." Barrymore is Svengali again, though minus the forked beard and hypnotic powers. (Consequently, the picture doesn't even qualify as borderline horror.) While

The Mad Genius features yet another great Barrymore performance and good production values (not to mention Boris Karloff in a bit part as a brutal peasant), it proves less satisfying than *Svengali* due to a rambling storyline, leisurely pacing, and bad comic relief with Charles Butterworth as a tepid Stan Laurel-like assistant. *The Mad Genius* failed at the box office and Barrymore never again worked at Warner Bros.

SWEENEY TODD, THE DEMON BARBER OF FLEET STREET (1936; MGM [Great Britain] / Select [U.S.A.]; Great Britain) Alternate Title: *The Demon Barber of Fleet Street* (American release title). Director: George King. Screenplay: H. F. Maltby. Photography: Jack Parker. Cast: Tod Slaughter, Stella Rho, Johnny Singer, Eve Lister, Bruce Seton, D. J. Williams, Davina Craig, Jerry Verna, Ben Soutten, Billy Holland, Norman Pierce, Aubrey Mallalieu.

Tod Slaughter made a career out of villainous stage roles, the most famous being the murderous barber which he here plays on-screen. Slaughter was a stage actor of the old school, harking back to the great villains of Victorian melodrama. While he rarely made it to London's posh West End theaters, he became one of the most popular actors of the blue-collar East End stages and provincial playhouses. Newspaper accounts of the 1920s claimed that no actor in England had a bigger following than Tod Slaughter. According to *Who Was Who in Theater*, he appeared in over 500 different plays, sketches and farces. His many stage plays include "Maria Marten, or, the Murder in the Red Barn," "The Monkey's Paw," "Jack the Ripper," and "Dr. Jekyll and Mr. Hyde." Slaughter's greatest success, however, came as the dastardly villain Sweeney Todd. The actor gave more than 4,000 performances as "The Demon Barber of Fleet Street" over the course of his 50-year stage career. Though he achieved great success trodding the provincial boards, his mustache-twirling, hand-rubbing style of acting frequently failed to translate well to films so that Slaughter, the self-proclaimed "Horror Man of Europe," could be better named the "Melodramatic Man of Europe." Even so, his following was large enough to support a string of villainous film appearances from 1935 to 1952. According to his own publicity (for 1939's *The Face at the Window*), Tod Slaughter "admits to at least 200 murders on the screen and also confesses that he has never appeared in a picture in which, he too, like his victims, hasn't met violent death."

As the title character of *Sweeney Todd, the Demon Barber of Fleeet Street*, Slaughter kills and robs sailors and gives their bodies to the nasty bakerwoman next door as filling for her tasty meat pies. To accomplish this, Todd uses a special barber chair which, upon pulling a concealed lever, tips upside down to dump the unsuspecting patron through a trap door into the cellar below. Then Mr. Todd saunters downstairs to "polish off" his victim with his finely honed razor. Todd's nefarious activities are finally discovered when he attempts to kill a young sea captain in order to reduce the competition for the sailor's sweetheart, who's caught Todd's eye. The young man escapes, the heroine is saved, and the villain comes to a sticky end.

Sweeney Todd looks much older than a film produced at the close of 1935, due primarily to its rather primitive production values. The straightforward direction and standard cinematography are unremarkable. The players' melodramatic acting also stems from an earlier time, though this fits in well with the style of the film's star. Slaughter's broad performance may lack subtlety, but his gleefully enthusiastic villainy is quite entertaining to watch.

In its native country, *Sweeney Todd* was treated fairly well by the critics. The *Monthly Film Bulletin* (March, 1936) noted that "Direction and much of the acting belong to the stage, and there are several inconsistencies in the development of the plot, but a certain amount of the necessarily gruesome atmosphere has been caught and the story itself is so good that the film has some success." *Kinematograph Weekly* (March 5, 1936) called the film a "Colourful period thriller, smoothly adapted from the perennial provincial stage success. Approached mainly in a tongue-in-the-cheek manner, the old-time shocker mellows its hearty picture of diabolical villainy with plenty of robust comedy, thereby cultivating family as well as mass appeal." A butchering barber and cannibal cook the subject of "family" appeal?!

When the film finally made it to America three years later, however, the critics were not so generous. *Variety* (October 11, 1939) predicted that *Sweeney Todd* "will find the pickings none too certain in this country, although title may prove b.o. in some cases.... From the action and dialogue to the direction by George King the picture is stamped by mediocrity.... Slaughter is a sinister enough type but the way he overacts creates new highs among Britishers.... Technically, including photography, the film is away below standard."

Among co-star Sir Bruce Seton's 76 films are two other Golden Age genre appearances — *The Man Who Changed His Mind* (1936; uncredited) and *Love from a Stranger* (1937). Born a British baronet in 1909, Seton's first career was as a soldier, turning to acting in 1932 and making his

Tod Slaughter as *Sweeney Todd, the Demon Barber of Fleet Street* (1936), whose boast, "I promise to polish you off quicker than any other barber in London," holds a double-edged meaning as sharp as his razor. (Courtesy of Lynn Naron.)

film debut three years later. Seton received his greatest renown on television, starring in the long-running British series "Fabian of the Yard." After the show ended, Seton found himself typecast and his career waned, culminating in bankruptcy in 1962. He died in 1969.

D. J. Williams appeared in several borderline British horrors from the Golden Age. He acted opposite Bela Lugosi in *Mystery of the Mary Celeste* (1935) and joined Tod Slaughter again for *The Crimes of Stephen Hawke* (1937). In fact, Williams was something of a Slaughter regular, appearing in two of "The Horror Man of Europe's" straight murder melodramas — *Murder in the Red Barn* (1935) and *It's Never Too Late to Mend* (1937).

The Slaughter film was not the first time Sweeney Todd sliced his way across the screen; two earlier cinematic adaptations came in 1926 and 1928, but it is Tod Slaughter's portrayal which makes this 1936 version the definitive (and remembered) one. In America, *The Demon Barber of Fleet Street* (the American distributor dropped the *Sweeney Todd* from the title) was released on a double bill with a straightforward mystery called *Return of the Frog*. Advertisements promoted it as "Europe's double-thrill horror show."

Stephen Sondheim adapted "Sweeney Todd: The Demon Barber of Fleet Street" into a musical in 1979. The New York show ran throughout the eighties and even enjoyed an acclaimed Broadway revival in 1990. It's hard to keep a good barber down.

THE TERROR (1938; Associated British Pictures; Great Britain) Director: Richard Bird. Producer: Walter C. Mycroft. Screenplay: William Freshman (from the story by Edgar Wallace). Photography: Walter Harvey. Cast: Wilfred Lawson, Bernard Lee, Arthur Wontner, Linden Travers, Henry Oscar, Alastair Sim, Iris Hoey, Lesley Wareing, Stanley Lathbury, John Turnbull, Richard Murdoch, Edward Lexy.

Yet another Edgar Wallace crime thriller (*Mystery Liner*, 1934, etc.), *The Terror* revolves around a criminal mastermind perpetrating an audacious gold heist and then hiding out at an old manor house playing the part of a ghostly monk. There's a violent storm, mysterious organ music, secret panels, plenty of deep-voiced maniacal laughter, and "a man half-sane, half mad" who entombs his victims alive. Possessing good production values and excellent camerawork, the picture ultimately proves overlong, however, due to shallow characterization and a sluggish pace. While slow-moving and meandering, *The Terror* does possess an occasional moment that lives up to its name. One in particular raises a hackle or two: As the criminal madman plays his organ, a victim manages to free himself from his living tomb. The stone slab slides slowly outward and two bloody hands emerge, pushing and grasping. Then, from the darkness of the opening, a hideous face moves toward the camera. Eyes stare wildly from deep eyesockets and low-key lighting casts ominous shadows on the livid countenance spotted with dirt and blood to create a chilling sight. In addition, it's rather refreshing to finally find a mystery that features a serious murder investigation conducted by a realistic inspector who's backed up by a *team* of investigators (instead of a pair of bumbling "dicks" or a solitary amateur sleuth working on his own). The investigators' solid procedures (taking photographs, collecting fingerprints, taking measurements at the crime scene, etc.) don't insult the viewer's intelligence as most lame-brained mystery-solvers do.

The film's hero (who for the majority of the picture pretends he's drunk) is played by Bernard Lee, best known as "M" in the James Bond films. Among Lee's 131 features are the excellent 1965 anthology, *Dr. Terror's House of Horrors* and Hammer's final Frankenstein entry, *Frankenstein and the Monster from Hell* (1973).

TERROR ABOARD (1933; Paramount) Director: Paul Sloane. Screenplay: Harvey Thew, Manuel Seff (story: Robert Presnell). Photography: Harry Fischbeck. Cast: Charlie Ruggles, John Halliday, Neil Hamilton, Shirley Grey, Jack La Rue, Verree Teasdale, Stanley Fields.

This murder melodrama begins promisingly

Advertisement for Paramount's rather gruesome murder melodrama, *Terror Aboard* (1933). A young Neil Hamilton ("Batman"'s Commissioner Gordon) plays the hero.

enough with the discovery of a derelict yacht in the middle of the Pacific manned only by two corpses—a frozen woman and a hanged man. A flashback reveals a series of convoluted and extremely unlikely murders committed by the ship's ruthless owner who is determined to dispose of each and every person onboard (so that he can cleanly disappear from the world onto some remote island). The inane humor of Charlie Ruggles is (almost) balanced out by several well-staged and unnerving murder sequences, complete with spreading bloodstains and gruesome death rattles. The film's high body count was too much for some contemporary critics, as evidenced by an outraged

P. S. Harrison writing in *Harrison's Reports*: "It should sicken even the most morbid follower of horror melodramas, for there is one killing after another. One man is poisoned; another is shot; a woman is shoved into a refrigerator; a man is incited into killing another one and then himself; still another is stabbed; and as a final stroke of homicidal genius, a boatload of sailors are thrown into the sea and drowned." Neil Hamilton ("Batman"'s Commissioner Gordon) plays the hero, and, for the umpteenth time, Leila Bennett is the dim-witted maid (just as she was in *Doctor X* this same year and again in *Mark of the Vampire*, 1935).

The project was first announced under the title *Dead Reckoning* with "a possible cast" that included Richard Arlen, Cary Grant, Ricardo Cortez, and Carole Lombard! Obviously, something went *horribly* wrong.

DAS TESTAMENT DES DR. MABUSE (*The Testament of Dr. Mabuse*; 1933; Nero; Germany) American Title: *The Last Will of Dr. Mabuse* Director/Producer: Fritz Lang. Screenplay: Thea von Harbou. Photography: Fritz Arno Wagner. Cast: Rudolf Klein Rogge, Gustav Diessl, Otto Wernicke, Oscar Beregi, Vera Liessem, Camilla Spira.

Completed ten years after Lang's highly acclaimed *Dr. Mabuse der Spieler* (*Dr. Mabuse the Gambler*), *Das Testament des Dr. Mabuse* opens with the mad criminal genius a near-catatonic occupant of an insane asylum. Via his indomitable hypnotic will, the madman continues to direct his nefarious gang of criminals through an agent, his attending psychiatrist, Dr. Baum. After Mabuse's death, Baum is possessed by the spirit of Dr. Mabuse (or simply goes mad and believes himself Mabuse) and carries out the dead man's plans. In the end, pursued by Inspector Lohmann, Baum retreats to Mabuse's old cell where he gives in completely to his insanity.

Much like Lang's *M* (1931), *Das Testament* is more crime thriller than horror film, focusing on the destructive workings of Mabuse's criminal organization and the concerted efforts of Inspector Lohmann's police force to find and stop them. The single fantasy element, the specter of Mabuse appearing before, and entering the body of, Professor Baum, is brief and shot in a straightforward manner devoid of horror trappings. It can even be taken as merely a visual manifestation of Baum's own degenerative madness, particularly in light of the picture's ending. The director himself later dismissed any supernatural implication. "Today Lang feels that he would no longer use phantomatic superimpositions for a film essentially realist in style," wrote the director's confidant, Lotte Eisner, in *Fritz Lang*, "but would represent the voice of the subconscious that dominates the professor, by voice-off. The fantastic element of the superimposition, he considers, offsets the reality." Lang achieved his realism by utilizing authentic interiors, creating gritty characters, and punctuating his intricate plotting with exciting spectacle such as a bomb exploding in a room filling with water or the sabotage of a chemical factory (in which Lang blows up a real abandoned munitions plant). At nearly two hours long, the picture's pace flags in places, but the fascinating and realistic characters carry the viewer over the slow spots.

In 1932, Lang had the picture completed and ready for its premier. He was informed by the Nazi officials that they found the film objectionable. (In the picture, Lang denigrated the rising Nazi party by holding up the psychopathic Dr. Mabuse as a Nazi symbol. "I put all the Nazi slogans into the mouth of the ghost of the criminal," Lang told Peter Bogdanovich in *Fritz Lang in America*. "I remember one in the film — 'The belief of the normal citizen in the powers he has elected must be destroyed — on this we will build the realm of crime.' Which is exactly what the Nazis said.") On March 29, the newly-formed Nazi censorship board rejected the picture. Goebbels summoned Lang to his office in the Ministry of Propaganda. Once there, a wary Lang was greeted by a friendly and conciliatory Goebbels, who told the director that the only thing they really objected to was the picture's ending, feeling that the mad professor should have been destroyed by the collective will of the people rather than just succumbing to madness. Since Hitler thought of Lang's *Metropolis* as his favorite film, Goebbels then offered Lang a position as head of the new National German Film Industry (perhaps feeling that they could "redirect" Lang's talent into a healthier Aryan-oriented avenue). Lang left the meeting on an agreeable note, then boarded the next train for Paris, leaving his home, his considerable wealth, and his wife, Thea von Harbou (ex-wife of Rudolf Klein Rogge — Dr. Mabuse himself!), behind. Lang's wife promptly divorced her absent husband and became a full-fledged member of the Nazi party.

Das Testament des Dr. Mabuse, shot simultaneously in both German and French, debuted in Paris and Budapest in April of 1933. The picture didn't make it to the United States until ten years later.

THEY DRIVE BY NIGHT (1938; Warner Bros.—First National; Great Britain) Director: Arthur Woods. Producer: Jerome J. Jackson. Screenplay: Paul Gangelin, James Curtis, Derek Twist (based on the novel by James Curtis). Cast: Emlyn Williams, Anna Konstam, Allan Jeaves,

Ernest Thesiger, Jennie Hartley, Ronald Shiner, Anthony Holles, Billy Hartnell, Kitty de Legh, Joe Cunningham, Volande Terrell, Julie Barrie.

Sadly, this exquisite film noir-styled British thriller failed to make its way to American shores (even on television). Warners' Hollywood division borrowed the title and the truck-driving theme to produce their Raft-Bogart vehicle in 1940, and subsequently never released the British film to the U.S. market. (The Bogart picture was retitled *The Road to Frisco* when shown in Britain to avoid confusion with their 1938 home-grown product.) *They Drive by Night* is a study in realism, with naturalistic acting, everyday common dialogue, and authentic exteriors creating a gritty sense of honesty in both the characterizations and the story. It begins with small-time crook "Shorty" Matthews released from prison after serving a brief sentence. He goes to look up an old flame and finds her murdered. Losing his head, he flees the scene and becomes the object of a nationwide manhunt. The first half of the picture follows Shorty as he heads to the north country, moving from truck stop to truck stop by hitching rides with the lorry drivers. In a dark, driving rainstorm, Shorty is pursued through the rain-soaked woods in a thrillingly realistic chase scene. Eluding his pursuers, Shorty makes his way back to London and the picture's more horrific connotations begin. While Shorty hides out in an abandoned house, Molly, a friendly dance hostess, tries to find the killer among the murdered girl's regular dance clients. The murderer finds *her*, however, and Shorty must rescue Molly from the psychopath's stranglehold. In his best role since *Bride of Frankenstein* (1935), Ernest Thesiger gives another brilliant, eccentric performance as the "silk-stocking murderer." A self-professed "student of abnormal psychology," Thesiger's Mr. Hoover provides both the (black) humor and the chills. A gentleman fond of holding forth on his pet theories to his bar cronies, Thesiger's false friendliness belies the condescension—and the psychosis—just beneath the surface. "The man who killed that girl," explains Hoover to his skeptical listeners, "enjoyed for a moment the sensation of power over life and death. Now he has the sense of power that comes from knowing something that nobody else in the world knows." Thesiger starts out speaking quickly and brusquely but slows toward the end as if savoring that very sense of power. Direction and photography are first-rate, the use of angles, foreground, and movement enhancing the mood, tension, or excitement of a scene. It all combines to make *They Drive by Night* one of the best British thrillers of the decade (now thankfully available on video).

THINGS TO COME (1936; United Artists; Great Britain) Director: William Cameron Menzies. Producer: Alexander Korda. Screenplay: H. G. Wells. Photography: Georges Perinal. Cast: Raymond Massey, Edward Chapman, Ralph Richardson, Margueretta Scott, Cedric Hardwicke, Maurice Braddell, Sophie Stewart, Derrick de Marney, Ann Todd, Pearl Argyle, Kenneth Villiers, Ivan Brandt, Anne McLaren, Patricia Hilliard, Charles Carson.

Things to Come is pure science fiction (or, more aptly, pure *social* fiction) without a trace of horror. H. G. Wells' 100-year vision was brought to the screen as cinema's first Science Fiction Sound Spectacular, not to mention Britain's first $1,000,000 production. H. G. Wells adapted his own book *The Shape of Things to Come* into a screenplay loosely structured into three acts. Beginning on Christmas Eve 1940 as the world teeters on the brink of war and then slides over the edge, the film follows the fate of Everytown and those who reside in it through the 30-year conflict and resulting pestilence. In 1970, Everytown is a ruin with its people in a state of near-barbarism ruled by an aggressive warrior "Boss." A group of scientists and engineers who have preserved and improved upon the world's technology arrive to clean up the petty warlords and restore order and civilization. Finally, after nearly a hundred years, Everytown in 2036 is a place of peace and plenty as technology provides Man with Eden on Earth. Now it is time to explore the unknown and send a rocket to circle the moon. Even in this enlightened age, however, there are those who scoff at "progress" and want none of it. Led by a reactionary artisan, a mob attempts to stop the launching. They fail, and as the rocket moves out of sight, the president of this new age poses a question: "If we are no more than animals, we must snatch our little scraps of happiness and live and suffer and pass, mattering no more than all the animals do or have done. Is it *that*—or *this*? All the universe—or nothingness? Which shall it be? Which shall it be?"

Not since *Metropolis* (1926) had the screen seen such a sweeping spectacle of science fiction. In its epic scope, *Things to Come* surpassed that earlier classic. The special effects alone are a marvel. The sets are stupendous and the model work, while not always convincing, is imaginative and a wonder for the time. The sequences of destruction as the bombs fall and civilization crumbles are realistic and gripping. The middle third of the picture (by far the best) shows how easily people can slide back into a form of feudal barbarism. Still, impressive production values and far-seeing prophesies aside, *Things to Come* is a grand failure.

This cigarette card of Raymond Massey displays the futuristic garb seen in *Things to Come* (1936).

The problem with *Things to Come* arises from its tone. The film does not demonstrate, does not explore — it preaches. Rather than creating characters, Wells fashions ideologies, turning the people into walking pamphlets spouting sociological slogans. No one simply talks in the picture, they lecture and pontificate. It all becomes highly theatrical as the characters strike poses to deliver their "message." Though it deals with the fate of mankind, *Things to Come* lacks humanity. This left the audience cold and, as a result, the film failed at the box office. Star Raymond Massey, while impressed by the original novel, was appalled by Wells' screenplay. "Every trace of wit, humour and emotion, everything which made the novel so enthralling had been cut and replaced by large gobs of socialist theory," he wrote in his autobiography, *A Hundred Different Lives*. (Even this final, unsatisfactory adaptation was no easy matter for Wells — it took him three tries before he could fashion his book into a filmable script.)

THIRTEEN WOMEN (1932; RKO) Director: George Archainbaud. Screenplay: Bartlett Cormack, Samuel Ornitz (from the novel by Tiffany Thayer). Photography: Leo Tover. Cast: Irene Dunne, Ricardo Cortez, Jill Esmond, Myrna Loy, Mary Duncan, Kay Johnson, Florence Eldridge, C. Henry Gordon, Peg Entwhistle, Harriet Hagman, Edward Pawley, Blanche Friderici, Wally Albright.

Thirteen Women is the rather unlikely tale of a half-caste Hindu woman (Myrna Loy) who, many years after the fact, takes revenge on the 12 sorority girls who snubbed her at finishing school. She does this by sending each of the women a horoscope from a famous "swami," whom she controls with some sort of mystical hypnotic power (even inducing him to jump in front of a speeding train when it serves her purpose). Through the Hindu's own machinations and the power of suggestion planted by the doomful predictions, the women fall prey one by one to their own fears. In turn, they each fulfill the dire destinies laid out in the horoscopes until one of them finally fights back with the aid of a police detective. Though the picture is blessed with solid performances from Irene Dunne (as the strong-willed survivor), Ricardo Cortez (as the steady detective), and especially Myrna Loy, the indifferent direction and photography fail to take advantage of the atmospheric possibilities. At 59 minutes, *Thirteen Women* is brief enough to keep things moving steadily from one accident/suicide/murder to the next, but overall it remains a mildly diverting disappointment.

When the film was panned after its sneak preview in August, RKO delayed the picture's official release until it could be recut. The newly edited version finally released in October, however, fared no better with the critics. *Variety* [October 18, 1932], for instance, labeled it "an unreasonably far-fetched wholesale butcher shop drama which no amount of good acting could save."

MGM loaned Myrna Loy out to RKO to make this picture. Ms. Loy, while "recall[ing] little about that racist concoction" in her autobiography, did note that she was quite the prolific murderess. "The only one who escaped me in that picture was Irene Dunne," she wrote, joking, "and I regretted it every time she got the parts I wanted."

RKO originally assigned Zita Johann to the picture, but the actress, who had just signed a five-year contract with the studio, wanted nothing to do with the production and asked for her release instead. She finally *did* star in a horror picture (for another studio) later that year — opposite Boris Karloff in Universal's *The Mummy*.

Though a respected stage actress, this was Peg Entwistle's only major role in motion pictures. Despite her appearances in a number of successful Broadway plays, she is generally remembered as the woman who committed suicide by leaping off the Hollywood sign on September 18, 1932. *Variety* carried this headline two days later: "LEGIT-PIC ACTRESS, PEG ENTWISTLE, COAST SUICIDE", and went on to report, "According to the police, she had evidently jumped off the letter 'H' on the 'Hollywood' sign. With her was found this note: 'Afraid I am a coward and I am sorry for many things. If I had only done this long ago I could have saved a lot of pain.'" That same year, besides appearing in *Thirteen Women*, Ms. Entwistle had played leads in two Broadway productions, "Alice Sit-By-the-Fire" and "Getting Married." Shortly before her death, Radio Pictures declined to pick up her option, though to what extent this affected her decision is purely a matter of conjecture.

TROUBLE FOR TWO (1936; MGM) Director: J. Walter Ruben. Producer: Louis D. Lighton. Screenplay: Manual Seff, Edward E. Paramore, Jr. Photography: Charles Clarke. Cast: Robert Montgomery, Rosalind Russell, Frank Morgan, Reginald Owen, Louis Hayward, David Holt, Virginia Weidler, E. E. Clive, Walter Kingsford, Ivan Simpson, Tom Moore, Robert Greig, Guy Bates Post, Pedro de Cordoba, Leland Hodgson.

Based on Robert Louis Stevenson's "The Suicide Club," this tale of a secret society who metes out death becomes lost in a maze of farfetched coincidences, political intrigues, and romantic kingdom-saving. The scenes of the club meetings generate tension and a few chills, but the picture's main focus is on princely heroics and energetic sword-fights.

THE WITCHING HOUR (1934; Paramount) Director: Henry Hathaway. Screenplay: Anthony Veiller (adaptation: Salisbury Field). Photography: Ben Reynolds. Cast: Sir Guy Standing, John Halliday, Judith Allen, Tom Brown, William Frawley, Olive Tell, Richard Carle.

John Halliday (a paternal Ronald Colman-type) plays a good-hearted owner of a high-class gambling establishment who just happens to possess sporadic telepathic and hypnotic talents. He accidentally hypnotizes his future son-in-law and the boy unknowingly commits a murder. The film then quickly evolves into a courtroom drama in which the lad's "only defense is that under a hypnotic spell he killed." The picture's foundation is built upon the following statement delivered by Halliday: "Hypnotism is a great and powerful force and through hypnotism a person could be made to do things they'd never dream of doing otherwise." (Realistically speaking, however, this is a wholly inaccurate claim, since hypnosis cannot truly force anyone to do anything against his or her nature or inclination.) Aside from the hypnotism angle, the picture introduces another fantasy aspect when the spirit of the boy's dead grandmother briefly appears to Judge Prentice (Sir Guy Standing), an old beau of hers, to convince the retired legal eagle to accept this impossible case. These elements, however, are played for drama rather than horror.

The players are sincere and give a good accounting of themselves (with the exception of Tom Brown, whose whining and melodramatic histrionics makes his part as the unfortunate defendant an annoying bore). The direction, camerawork, and production values are adequate though unspectacular, but the near-nonexistent musical score is limited to a few strains of "Beautiful Dreamer" thrown in seemingly at random throughout the picture. Though outlandish and mildly entertaining, this courtroom drama is certainly no *Inherit the Wind*.

Based on the play by Augustus Thomas, this 1934 production is a sound remake of Paramount's earlier silent, *The Witching Hour* (1921).

THE WIZARD OF OZ (1939; MGM) Director: Victor Fleming. Producer: Mervyn LeRoy. Screenplay: Noel Langley, Florence Ryerson, Edgar Allan Woolf (adaptation by Noel Langley; from the book by L. Frank Baum). Photography: Harold Rosson (Associate: Allen Davey). Cast: Judy Garland, Frank Morgan, Ray Bolger, Bert Lahr, Jack Haley, Billie Burke, Margaret Hamilton, Charley Grapewin, "and the Munchkins."

Though undeniably one of the most beloved fantasies of all time (it seems as if *everybody*'s gone off to see the Wizard at one time or another), I personally do not find the film appealing. In fact, heretical as it may sound, if I had to describe *The Wizard of Oz* in a single word, that word would be "silly." Now that I've admitted what many would consider to be a serious character flaw on my part, the less said the better.

The most interesting points about the film (in my view) are found behind the scenes. During the project's genesis, MGM approached 20th Century–Fox about borrowing their star, Shirley Temple, for the role of Dorothy. When negotiations failed, Metro chose Judy Garland for the part. Garland began the film wearing a blond wig and heavy "baby-doll" makeup.

For the Cowardly Lion, the first idea was to use a real lion with an actor dubbing in a voice.

This would have beneficially (in my opinion) cut down on this character's dancing. Alas, it was not to be.

Gale Sondergaard was originally cast as the Wicked Witch. Instead of the traditional storybook ugly visage Margaret Hamilton finally sported, Sondergaard was to be beautiful and glamorous — though thoroughly evil. Just before filming began, however, the MGM powers-that-be decided that a beautiful evil witch was too far removed from the character in Baum's story, so Sondergaard donned the makeup and tested as an ugly witch. Displeased with the results, however, she declined to play the part and Margaret Hamilton was cast in her stead.

When shooting began, it was Richard Thorpe, not Victor Fleming, calling the shots. After two weeks, dissatisfied producer Mervyn LeRoy removed Richard Thorpe as director and replaced him with Victor Fleming. Fleming immediately discarded Garland's wig and heavy makeup and encouraged the youngster to just be herself. He also softened the Scarecrow's makeup and altered the Witch's appearance still further.

Thorpe was not the only principal to lose out. After a week of filming, Buddy Ebson experienced a violent reaction against his Tin Man makeup and had to be hospitalized. He was eventually replaced by Jack Haley.

Accidents plagued the production. Margaret Hamilton received severe burns when her fiery disappearance scene misfired. Her stand-in was also injured in another sequence when the Witch's broom exploded. Toto was stepped on by one of the Witch's Winkie Guards, putting him out of action for several days. And two actors playing winged monkeys came crashing painfully down to earth when their support wires snapped. Finally, after three and a half months of six-day-a-week shooting (and, amazingly, no fatalities), *The Wizard of Oz* was in the can and ready to make fantasy/musical history.

Appendix B: The Ten Best Films from the Golden Age of Horror

The following is a collective Ten Best list derived from the combined ratings of 30 writers, editors, critics, and filmmakers. Each participant was asked to choose what they consider to be the ten greatest horror films from the Golden Age of Horror and rank them in order of merit.

THE TEN GREATEST HORROR FILMS OF THE GOLDEN AGE (1931-1939)
1. BRIDE OF FRANKENSTEIN (1935)
2. KING KONG (1933)
3. FRANKENSTEIN (1931)
4. DR. JEKYLL AND MR. HYDE (1931)
5. THE INVISIBLE MAN (1933)
6. THE MUMMY (1932)
7. THE BLACK CAT (1934)
8. ISLAND OF LOST SOULS (1933)
9. THE OLD DARK HOUSE (1932)
10. FREAKS (1932)

THE FIVE RUNNERS-UP
11. SON OF FRANKENSTEIN (1939)
12. DRACULA (1931)
13. THE MOST DANGEROUS GAME (1932)
14. THE BLACK ROOM (1935)
15. MAD LOVE (1935)

The following is a list of the participants and their individual *TEN BEST (along with comments, if any):*

Forrest J Ackerman, founder and long-time editor of *Famous Monsters of Filmland* magazine, has contributed countless books and articles to the body of Fantastic Cinema literature and is reverently held to be the genre's original champion.

1. THINGS TO COME (1936)
2. KING KONG (1933)
3. FRANKENSTEIN (1931)
4. BRIDE OF FRANKENSTEIN (1935)
5. DR. JEKYLL AND MR. HYDE (1931)

6. THE INVISIBLE MAN (1933)
7. ISLAND OF LOST SOULS (1933)
8. DRACULA (1931)
9. THE MUMMY (1932)
10. WEREWOLF OF LONDON (1935)

Edmund G. Bansak has written articles for *Midnight Marquee* and is the author of *Fearing the Dark: The Val Lewton Career*.

1. KING KONG (1933)
2. BRIDE OF FRANKENSTEIN (1935)
3. DR. JEKYLL AND MR. HYDE (1931)
4. NIGHT MUST FALL (1937)
5. THE MUMMY (1932)
6. FREAKS (1932)
7. FRANKENSTEIN (1931)
8. THE WALKING DEAD (1936)
9. SON OF FRANKENSTEIN (1939)
10. MAD LOVE (1935)

The late **Robert Bloch**, author of *Psycho* and many other novels and short stories, was a frequent screenwriter whose credits include *Strait-Jacket* (1964), *Torture Garden* (1967), and *Asylum* (1972).

1. MAD LOVE (1935)
2. MURDERS IN THE ZOO (1933)
3. FRANKENSTEIN (1931)
4. THE MOST DANGEROUS GAME (1932)
5. THE MUMMY (1932)
6. DRACULA (1931)
7. ISLAND OF LOST SOULS (1933)
8. MYSTERY OF THE WAX MUSEUM (1933)
9. DR. JEKYLL AND MR. HYDE (1931)
10. KING KONG (1933)

"If horror *per se* is a criterion, then some of your listings seem invalidated. There are at least three fine titles on this list which I have not selected — because they are not really "horror films." *M* is a memorable movie with a memorable performance by Peter Lorre, but it doesn't horrify; nor does *Freaks*, which evokes sympathy for its sideshow performers except in their scene of revenge. And while *Bride of Frankenstein* is outstanding, I found nothing horrifying in it."

Ted A. Bohus is an independent film producer and special effects artist whose credits include *The Deadly Spawn*, *Metamorphosis: The Alien Factor*, and *The Regenerated Man*.

1. KING KONG (1933)
2. BRIDE OF FRANKENSTEIN (1935)
3. ISLAND OF LOST SOULS (1933)
4. THE INVISIBLE MAN (1933)
5. FREAKS (1932)
6. THE HUNCHBACK OF NOTRE DAME (1939)
7. THE MOST DANGEROUS GAME (1932)
8. THINGS TO COME (1936)
9. SON OF KONG (1933)
10. WEREWOLF OF LONDON (1936)

Ronald V. Borst has contributed articles to numerous magazines, including *Photon* and *Famous Monsters of Filmland*, and is the author of *Graven Images*.

1. KING KONG (1933)
2. BRIDE OF FRANKENSTEIN (1935)
3. FRANKENSTEIN (1931)
4. THE INVISIBLE MAN (1933)
5. DR. JEKYLL AND MR. HYDE (1931)
6. THE BLACK CAT (1934)
7. DRACULA (1931)
8. ISLAND OF LOST SOULS (1933)
9. WHITE ZOMBIE (1932)
10. THE MOST DANGEROUS GAME (1932)

"My ten 'best' horror films of the thirties are not necessarily my 'favorite' ten from the same decade. I don't think there's any doubt that either *King Kong* or *Bride of Frankenstein* are the two finest horror films from the thirties when one considers everything relating to their productions, but having been exposed to them so many times over 30 years, much of what is great about them fails to excite me as much as watching my favorite performer in the genre, Bela Lugosi, in his most famous films."

Ray Bradbury's short stories and novels have been adapted for the screen (sometimes by Bradbury himself) many times. Films from his works include *The Beast from 20,000 Fathoms* (1953), *It Came from Outer Space* (1953), *Fahrenheit 451* (1966), and *Something Wicked This Way Comes* (1982). Ten best in no order:

BRIDE OF FRANKENSTEIN (1935)
DRACULA (1931)
FRANKENSTEIN (1931)
THE INVISIBLE MAN (1933)
KING KONG (1933)
THE MAN WHO COULD WORK MIRACLES (1936)
THE MUMMY (1932)
MYSTERY OF THE WAX MUSEUM (1933)
THE OLD DARK HOUSE (1932)
THINGS TO COME (1936)

John Brunas is the co-author of *Universal Horrors*.

1. BRIDE OF FRANKENSTEIN (1935)
2. KING KONG (1933)
3. FRANKENSTEIN (1931)
4. THE INVISIBLE MAN (1933)
5. THE BLACK CAT (1934)
6. THE MUMMY (1932)
7. DR. JEKYLL AND MR. HYDE (1931)
8. THE OLD DARK HOUSE (1932)

9. SON OF FRANKENSTEIN (1939)
10. THE HUNCHBACK OF NOTRE DAME (1939)

Michael Brunas is the co-author of *Universal Horrors*.
1. BRIDE OF FRANKENSTEIN (1935)
2. DR. JEKYLL AND MR. HYDE (1931)
3. FRANKENSTEIN (1931)
4. THE BLACK CAT (1934)
5. KING KONG (1933)
6. THE HUNCHBACK OF NOTRE DAME (1939)
7. THE MUMMY (1932)
8. THE INVISIBLE MAN (1933)
9. M (1931)
10. THE BLACK ROOM (1935)

Joe Dante, a fan-turned-filmmaker, has directed numerous genre pictures, including *The Howling* (1981), *Gremlins* (1984), and *Matinee* (1993). Ten best in no order:
BRIDE OF FRANKENSTEIN (1935)
THE BLACK CAT (1934)
THE OLD DARK HOUSE (1932)
KING KONG (1933)
ISLAND OF LOST SOULS (1933)
FREAKS (1932)
THE INVISIBLE MAN (1933)
FRANKENSTEIN (1931)
DR. JEKYLL AND MR. HYDE (1931)
MAD LOVE (1935)

William K. Everson is a consultant to the American Film Institute and the British Film Institute and the author of (among others) *The Bad Guys*, *Classics of the Horror Film*, and *More Classics of the Horror Film*.
1. VAMPYR (1932)
2. BRIDE OF FRANKENSTEIN (1935)
3. THE OLD DARK HOUSE (1932)
4. FRANKENSTEIN (1931)
5. DR. JEKYLL AND MR. HYDE (1931)
6. WHITE ZOMBIE (1932)
7. THE MUMMY (1932)
8. THE BLACK CAT (1934)
9. THE MAN WHO CHANGED HIS MIND (1936)
10. KING KONG (1933)

"*King Kong* is in tenth place because I don't really consider it a horror film. Yet is has to *be* there. Consider it non-ranked but given 'guest star' billing."

Richard Gordon is a film producer (and scholar) whose long list of production credits include *Fiend Without a Face* (1958), *The Haunted Strangler* (1958), *Corridors of Blood* (1958), *Island of Terror* (1966), and *The Cat and the Canary* (1978). Ten best in no order:
THE BLACK CAT (1934)
BRIDE OF FRANKENSTEIN (1935)
DR. JEKYLL AND MR. HYDE (1931)
DRACULA (1931)
FRANKENSTEIN (1931)
THE INVISIBLE MAN (1933)
KING KONG (1933)
THE MOST DANGEROUS GAME (1932)
THE MUMMY (1932)
THE OLD DARK HOUSE (1932)

"I find it impossible to create an order of preference. Each of these films is, to me, of equal merit. Each has varied and different elements that make it so."

Bruce G. Hallenbeck is an author, screenwriter and filmmaker. He has written for *Fangoria*, *Femmes Fatales*, and *Little Shoppe of Horrors*, among others. He is the writer/director of the feature films *Vampyre* and *Black Easter* as well as the documentary *Fangs*.
1. ISLAND OF LOST SOULS (1933)
2. THE OLD DARK HOUSE (1932)
3. KING KONG (1933)
4. THE MOST DANGEROUS GAME (1932)
5. FRANKENSTEIN (1931)
6. BRIDE OF FRANKENSTEIN (1935)
7. DRACULA'S DAUGHTER (1936)
8. THE INVISIBLE MAN (1933)
9. FREAKS (1932)
10. THE BLACK ROOM (1935)

Ray Harryhausen has long been considered the successor to stop-motion animation pioneer Willis O'Brien. He is the special effects wizard behind the wonders of *The Beast from 20,000 Fathoms* (1953), *Earth vs. the Flying Saucers* (1956), *The 7th Voyage of Sinbad* (1958), *One Million Years B.C.* (1967), *Clash of the Titans* (1981), and many others.
1. KING KONG (1933)
2. DR. JEKYLL AND MR. HYDE (1931)
3. BRIDE OF FRANKENSTEIN (1935)
4. SHE (1935)
5. THE OLD DARK HOUSE (1932)
6. THE MOST DANGEROUS GAME (1932)
7. THE MUMMY (1932)
8. MYSTERY OF THE WAX MUSEUM (1933)
9. THE INVISIBLE MAN (1933)
10. FRANKENSTEIN (1931)

Paul M. Jensen is the author of *Boris Karloff and His Films*, *The Cinema of Fritz Lang*, and the upcoming *The Men Who Made the Monsters*.
1. THE MUMMY (1932)
2. KING KONG (1933)
3. DR. JEKYLL AND MR. HYDE (1931)

4. BRIDE OF FRANKENSTEIN (1935)
5. THE INVISIBLE MAN (1933)
6. THE OLD DARK HOUSE (1932)
7. THINGS TO COME (1936)
8. THE HUNCHBACK OF NOTRE DAME (1939)
9. FRANKENSTEIN (1931)
10. ISLAND OF LOST SOULS (1933)

"Reviewing my finished list, I found that I could draw some interesting conclusions about it. For one thing, seven of the ten films were made before 1934; in other words, before the enforcement of the Production Code made filmmakers more conservative in their aims and approaches and also, in more general terms, before the horror genre had been fully defined and reduced to a formula. Worth noting, too, is the fact that these films were made by directors who were not specialists in the genre; perhaps as a result they brought a more subtle and varied sensibility to their work. Finally, they all bear the imprint of forceful creative personalities, of distinctive individuals rather than competent craftsmen. (Erle C. Kenton appears to be an exception to this, though I suspect that in 1933 and based solely on *Island of Lost Souls* I would have believed that that description would have applied to him as well. In that sense, I guess *Lost Souls* was a 'false alarm'.)"

John Johnson, film critic for the *Keizertimes* in Keizer, Oregon, is the author of *Cheap Tricks and Class Acts: Special Effects, Makeup, and Stunts from the Fantastic Fifties* and the co-author of *Fantastic Cinema Subject Guide*.
1. KING KONG (1933)
2. DR. JEKYLL AND MR. HYDE (1931)
3. THE INVISIBLE MAN (1933)
4. THE OLD DARK HOUSE (1932)
5. FRANKENSTEIN (1931)
6. BRIDE OF FRANKENSTEIN (1935)
7. ISLAND OF LOST SOULS (1933)
8. THE BLACK CAT (1934)
9. THE MUMMY (1932)
10. MYSTERY OF THE WAX MUSEUM (1933)

Tom Johnson is the co-author of *Hammer Films: An Exhaustive Filmography* and *Peter Cushing: The Gentle Man of Horror and His 91 Films*.
1. FRANKENSTEIN (1931)
2. BRIDE OF FRANKENSTEIN (1935)
3. THE BLACK CAT (1934)
4. KING KONG (1933)
5. THE BLACK ROOM (1935)
6. THE MUMMY (1932)
7. DR. JEKYLL AND MR. HYDE (1931)
8. MAD LOVE (1935)
9. SON OF FRANKENSTEIN (1939)
10. TOWER OF LONDON (1939)

Richard Klemensen is the editor of *Little Shoppe of Horrors* magazine.
1. ISLAND OF LOST SOULS (1933)
2. THE BLACK CAT (1934)
3. KING KONG (1933)
4. WHITE ZOMBIE (1932)
5. BRIDE OF FRANKENSTEIN (1935)
6. SON OF FRANKENSTEIN (1939)
7. MURDERS IN THE RUE MORGUE (1932)
8. FREAKS (1932)
9. THE CAT AND THE CANARY (1939)
10. FRANKENSTEIN (1931)

John Landis, like Joe Dante, is another successful genre fan turned moviemaker, who counts among his many credits *An American Werewolf in London* (1981), *Amazon Women on the Moon* (1987), and *Innocent Blood* (1992). Ten best in no order:

KING KONG (1933)
ISLAND OF LOST SOULS (1933)
FRANKENSTEIN (1931)
BRIDE OF FRANKENSTEIN (1935)
SON OF FRANKENSTEIN (1939)
THE OLD DARK HOUSE (1932)
DR. JEKYLL AND MR. HYDE (1931)
FREAKS (1932)
MAD LOVE (1935)
THE MUMMY (1932)

Tim Lucas, editor of *Video Watchdog* magazine, is author of *The Video Watchdog Book* and the horror novel *Throat Sprockets*.
1. BRIDE OF FRANKENSTEIN (1935)
2. J'ACCUSE (1937)
3. DR. JEKYLL AND MR. HYDE (1931)
4. KING KONG (1933)
5. THE BLACK CAT (1934)
6. THE INVISIBLE MAN (1933)
7. FREAKS (1932)
8. VAMPYR (1932)
9. WHITE ZOMBIE (1932)
10. DRACULA (Spanish language version) (1931)

Gregory William Mank is one of the most prolific writers in the field of cinema; his many articles and books include *It's Alive! The Classic Cinema Saga of Frankenstein*, and *Karloff and Lugosi: The Story of a Haunting Collaboration*, and *Hollywood Cauldron*.
1. BRIDE OF FRANKENSTEIN (1935)
2. FRANKENSTEIN (1931)
3. KING KONG (1933)
4. THE INVISIBLE MAN (1933)
5. THE MUMMY (1932)
6. THE BLACK CAT (1934)
7. THE BLACK ROOM (1935)
8. SON OF FRANKENSTEIN (1939)

9. THE WALKING DEAD (1936)
10. THE HUNCHBACK OF NOTRE DAME (1939)

Mark A. Miller has written for *Filmfax* magazine and is the author of *Christopher Lee and Peter Cushing and Horror Cinema: A Filmography of Their 22 Collaborations*.
1. THE BLACK ROOM (1935)
2. DR. JEKYLL AND MR. HYDE (1931)
3. BRIDE OF FRANKENSTEIN (1935)
4. THE MUMMY (1932)
5. SON OF FRANKENSTEIN (1939)
6. THE INVISIBLE MAN (1933)
7. FRANKENSTEIN (1931)
8. DRACULA'S DAUGHTER (1936)
9. ISLAND OF LOST SOULS (1933)
10. DRACULA (1931)

"Although the current trend in film comment seems to be to drive a critical stake full force through the heart of Bela Lugosi's acting style, his flamboyance has always appealed to me. Bela is never boring, and *Dracula* deserves its place among the top ten in spite of its flaws."

Lynn Naron, an avid collector and genre scholar/researcher, has written for *Collecting Hollywood*.
1. BRIDE OF FRANKENSTEIN (1935)
2. FRANKENSTEIN (1931)
3. THE INVISIBLE MAN (1933)
4. THE BLACK CAT (1934)
5. DRACULA (1931)
6. DR. JEKYLL AND MR. HYDE (1931)
7. THE MUMMY (1932)
8. THE RAVEN (1935)
9. WHITE ZOMBIE (1932)
10. KING KONG (1933)

Ted Okuda, managing editor of *Filmfax* magazine, is the author of *The Monogram Checklist* and *Grand National, PRC and Screen Guild/Lippert: Complete Filmographies*, and co-author of *The Columbia Comedy Shorts*; *The Soundies Distributing Corporation of America*, and *The Jerry Lewis Films*.
1. KING KONG (1933)
2. BRIDE OF FRANKENSTEIN (1935)
3. THE INVISIBLE MAN (1933)
4. THE MUMMY (1932)
5. FRANKENSTEIN (1931)
6. THE BLACK CAT (1934)
7. SON OF FRANKENSTEIN (1939)
8. ISLAND OF LOST SOULS (1933)
9. FREAKS (1932)
10. DRACULA (1931)

John E. Parnum, former editor-in-chief of *Cinemacabre* magazine, has contributed articles to a number of publications including *Photon, The Monster Times*, and *Midnight Marquee*.
1. BRIDE OF FRANKENSTEIN (1935)
2. DR. JEKYLL AND MR. HYDE (1931)
3. KING KONG (1933)
4. THE MUMMY (1932)
5. M (1931)
6. THINGS TO COME (1936)
7. FREAKS (1932)
8. FRANKENSTEIN (1931)
9. DRACULA (1931)
10. THE MOST DANGEROUS GAME (1932)

Fred Olen Ray is a prolific independent producer/director of horror and action films. His vast (over 40) list of credits include *Armed Response, Deep Space, Hollywood Chainsaw Hookers, Beverly Hills Vampire*, and *Dinosaur Island*. He has also written for *Midnight Marquee* and *Filmfax* and is the author of the book *The New Poverty Row*.
1. BRIDE OF FRANKENSTEIN (1935)
2. FREAKS (1932)
3. KING KONG (1933)
4. ISLAND OF LOST SOULS (1933)
5. SON OF FRANKENSTEIN (1939)
6. TOWER OF LONDON (1939)
7. THE INVISIBLE MAN (1933)
8. MURDERS IN THE RUE MORGUE (1932)
9. THE MOST DANGEROUS GAME (1932)
10. WEREWOLF OF LONDON (1935)

Bryan Senn, the author of the present work, is also the co-author of *Fantastic Cinema Subject Guide*.
1. KING KONG (1933)
2. FRANKENSTEIN (1931)
3. THE OLD DARK HOUSE (1932)
4. THE INVISIBLE MAN (1933)
5. BRIDE OF FRANKENSTEIN (1935)
6. THE BLACK CAT (1934)
7. DR. JEKYLL AND MR. HYDE (1931)
8. ISLAND OF LOST SOULS (1933)
9. THE MUMMY (1932)
10. MAD LOVE (1935)

Don G. Smith is the author of *Lon Chaney, Jr.*, and *The Cinema of Edgar Allan Poe*.
1. BRIDE OF FRANKENSTEIN (1935)
2. KING KONG (1933)
3. FRANKENSTEIN (1931)
4. DRACULA (1931)
5. THE BLACK CAT (1934)
6. THE BLACK ROOM (1935)
7. ISLAND OF LOST SOULS (1933)
8. DR. JEKYLL AND MR. HYDE (1931)
9. FREAKS (1932)
10. WHITE ZOMBIE (1932)

Gary Svehla is editor-in-chief of *Midnight Marquee* magazine.
1. BRIDE OF FRANKENSTEIN (1935)
2. DR. JEKYLL AND MR. HYDE (1931)
3. FRANKENSTEIN (1931)
4. ISLAND OF LOST SOULS (1933)
5. THE MUMMY (1932)
6. THE INVISIBLE MAN (1933)
7. SON OF FRANKENSTEIN (1939)
8. DOCTOR X (1932)
9. THE MASK OF FU MANCHU (1932)
10. THE BLACK CAT (1934)

Richard Valley is the editor of *Scarlet Street* magazine.
1. BRIDE OF FRANKENSTEIN (1935)
2. KING KONG (1933)
3. THE MUMMY (1932)
4. THE INVISIBLE MAN (1933)
5. THE BLACK CAT (1934)
6. DR. JEKYLL AND MR. HYDE (1931)
7. FRANKENSTEIN (1931)
8. FREAKS (1932)
9. SON OF FRANKENSTEIN (1939)
10. MAD LOVE (1935)

Tom Weaver has written numerous articles for *Fangoria, Starlog,* and *Filmfax,* and is the author of (among others) *Science Fiction Stars and Horror Heroes*; *Attack of the Monster Movie Makers* and *Poverty Row HORRORS!* and the co-author of *Universal Horrors.*
1. KING KONG (1933)
2. DR. JEKYLL AND MR. HYDE (1931)
3. FRANKENSTEIN (1931)
4. ISLAND OF LOST SOULS (1933)
5. THE MOST DANGEROUS GAME (1932)
6. THE INVISIBLE MAN (1933)
7. THE MUMMY (1932)
8. THE OLD DARK HOUSE (1932)
9. BRIDE OF FRANKENSTEIN (1935)
10. THE BLACK ROOM (1935)

Bibliography

Ackerman, Forrest J. *The Frankenscience Monster.* New York: Ace, 1969.

_____. *Famous Monsters of Filmland,* vol. 2. Universal City, Calif.: Hollywood Publishing Co., 1991.

Anobile, Richard J. *James Whale's Frankenstein.* New York: Avon, 1974.

_____. *Rouben Mamoulian's Dr. Jekyll & Mr. Hyde.* New York: Avon, 1975.

Archer, Steve. *Willis O'Brien: Special Effects Genius.* Jefferson, N.C.: McFarland, 1993.

Balcon, Michael. *Michael Balcon Presents ... A Lifetime of Films.* London: Hutchinson, 1969.

Barrymore, Elaine, and Sandford Dody. *All My Sins Remembered: The Story of My Life with John Barrymore.* New York: Appleton-Century, 1964.

Barrymore, Lionel. *We Barrymores.* New York: Grosset & Dunlap, 1951.

Beck, Calvin Thomas. *Heroes of the Horrors.* New York: Macmillan, 1975.

_____. *Scream Queens: Heroines of the Horrors.* New York: Macmillan, 1978.

Behlmer, Rudy (ed.) *Memo from David O. Selznick.* New York: Viking, 1972.

_____. *Behind the Scenes.* Hollywood: Samuel French, 1990.

Benson, Michael. *Vintage Science Fiction Films, 1896–1949.* Jefferson, N.C.: McFarland, 1985.

Bogdan, Robert. *Freak Show: Presenting Human Oddities for Amusement and Profit.* Chicago: University of Chicago Press, 1988.

Bogdanovich, Peter. *Fritz Lang in America.* New York: Praeger, 1967.

Bogle, Donald. *Blacks in American Films and Television.* New York: Garland, 1988.

Bojarski, Richard, and Kenneth Beals. *The Films of Boris Karloff.* Secaucus, N.J.: Citadel, 1974.

Bojarski, Richard. *The Films of Bela Lugosi.* Secaucus, N.J.: Citadel, 1980.

Bonomo, Joe. *The Strongman.* New York: Bonomo Studios, Inc., 1968.

Bordwell, David. *The Films of Carl-Theodor Dreyer.* Berkeley: University of California Press, 1981.

Brosnan, John. *The Horror People.* New York: New American Library, 1976.

Brown, William. *Charles Laughton: A Pictorial Treasury of His Films.* New York: Falcon Enterprises, 1970.

Brunas, Michael, John Brunas, and Tom Weaver. *Universal Horrors: The Studio's Classic Films, 1931–1946.* Jefferson, N.C.: McFarland, 1990.

Bushnell, Brooks. *Directors and Their Films: A Comprehensive Reference, 1895–1990.* Jefferson, N.C.: McFarland, 1993.

Callow, Simon. *Charles Laughton: A Difficult Actor.* New York: Grove, 1987.

Carney, Raymond. *Speaking the Language of Desire: The Films of Carl Dreyer.* Cambridge: Cambridge University Press, 1989.

Clarens, Carlos. *An Illustrated History of the Horror Film.* New York: Capricorn, 1968.

Cox, Stephen. *The Munchkins Remember: The Wizard of Oz and Beyond.* New York: E.P. Dutton, 1989.

Cremer, Robert. *Lugosi, The Man Behind the Cape.* Chicago: Henry Regnery, 1976.

Crow, Jefferson Brim III. *Randolph Scott: The Gentleman from Virginia.* Carrollton, Texas: WindRiver, 1987.

Curtis, James. *Between Flops: A Biography of Preston Sturges.* New York: Limelight Editions, 1982.

_____. *James Whale,* Metuchen, N.J.: Scarecrow, 1982.

Curtiss, Thomas Quinn. *Von Stroheim.* New York: Farrar, Straus and Giroux, 1971.

Da, Lottie, and Jan Alexander. *Bad Girls of the Silver Screen.* New York: Carroll & Graf, 1989.

Danischewsky, M. (ed.). *Michael Balcon's 25 Years in Films.* London: World Film, 1947.

Darby, William. *Masters of Lens and Light: A Checklist of Major Cinematographers and Their Feature Films,* Metuchen, N.J.: Scarecrow, 1991.

Dooley, Roger. *From Scarface to Scarlett: American Films in the 1930s,* New York: Harcourt Brace Jovanovich, 1979.

Douglas, Melvyn, and Tom Arthur. *See You at the*

Movies: The Autobiography of Melvyn Douglas. Lanham: University Press of America, 1986.
Dreyer, Carl Theodor (translated by Oliver Stallybrass). *Four Screenplays*. Bloomington: Indiana University Press, 1970.
Drimmer, Frederick. *Very Special People: The Struggles, Loves and Triumphs of Human Oddities*. New York: Bell, 1973.
Druxman, Michael B. *Basil Rathbone: His Life and His Films*. South Brunswick and New York: A.S. Barnes, 1975.
Dunn, Linwood G., and George E. Turner (eds.). *The ASC Treasury of Visual Effects*. Hollywood: American Society of Cinematographers, 1983.
Eastman, John. *Retakes: Behind the Scenes of 500 Classic Movies*. New York: Ballantine, 1989.
Eisner, Lotte H. *Fritz Lang*. New York: Oxford University Press, 1977.
Everson, William K. *Classics of the Horror Film*. Secaucus, N.J.: Citadel, 1974.
_____. *More Classics of the Horror Film*. Secaucus, N.J.: Citadel, 1986.
Eyman, Scott. *Five American Cinematographers*. Metuchen, N.J.: Scarecrow, 1987.
Fernett, Gene. *American Film Studios: An Historical Encyclopedia*. Jefferson, N.C.: McFarland, 1988.
Fiedler, Leslie. *Freaks: Myths and Images of the Secret Self*. New York: Simon and Schuster, 1978.
Fischer, Dennis. *Horror Film Directors, 1931–1990*. Jefferson, N.C.: McFarland, 1991.
Friedman, David F., with Don De Nevi. *A Youth in Babylon, Confessions of a Trash-Film King*. Buffalo, N.Y.: Prometheus, 1990.
Gardner, Gerald. *The Censorship Papers: Movie Censorship Letters from the Hays Office, 1934 to 1968*. New York: Dodd, Mead, 1987.
Gifford, Denis. *Karloff: The Man, the Monster, the Movies*. New York: Curtis, 1973.
_____. *A Pictorial History of Horror Movies*. London/New York: Hamlyn, 1973.
Glut, Donald F. *The Dracula Book*. Metuchen, N.J.: Scarecrow, 1975.
_____. *Classic Movie Monsters*. Metuchen, N.J.: Scarecrow, 1978.
_____. *The Frankenstein Catalog*. Jefferson, N.C.: McFarland, 1984.
Goldner, Orville, and George E. Turner. *The Making of King Kong*. San Diego/New York: A.S. Barnes, 1975.
Gottesman, Ronald, and Harry Geduld. *The Girl in the Hairy Paw*. New York: Avon, 1976.
Haining, Peter (ed.). *The H. G. Wells Scrapbook*. London: Clarkson N. Potter, 1978.
_____. *The Dracula Scrapbook*. London: Chancellor, 1992.
Halliwell, Leslie. *Halliwell's Film Guide*, 7th ed. New York: Harper & Row, 1989.
Hanson, Patricia King, and Alan Gevinson (eds.). *The American Film Institute Catalog of Motion Pictures Produced in the United States: Feature Films, 1931–1940*. Berkeley, California: University of California Press, 1993.
Hardwicke, Cedric Sir (as told to James Brough). *A Victorian in Orbit*. Garden City, N.Y.: Doubleday, 1961.
Hardy, Phil (ed.). *The Encyclopedia of Horror Movies*. New York: Harper & Row, 1986.
Harryhausen, Ray. *Film Fantasy Scrapbook*. South Brunswick and New York: A.S. Barnes, 1972.
Harvith, Susan, and John. *Karl Struss: Man with a Camera*. Bloomfield Hills, Mich.: Cranbrook Academy of Art/Museum, 1976.
Haver, Ronald. *David O. Selznick's Hollywood*. New York: Alfred A. Knopf, 1980.
Hawkins, Jack. *Anything for a Quiet Life: The Autobiography of Jack Hawkins*. New York: Stein and Day, 1973.
Head, Edith, and Jane Kesner Ardmore. *The Dress Doctor*. Boston: Little, Brown, 1959.
Heisner, Beverly. *Hollywood Art: Art Direction in the Days of the Great Studios*. Jefferson, N.C.: McFarland, 1990.
Higham, Charles. *Hollywood Cameramen: Sources of Light*. Bloomington: Indiana University Press, 1970.
_____. *Charles Laughton, An Intimate Biography*. Garden City, N.Y.: Doubleday, 1976.
Hogan, David J. *Who's Who of the Horrors and Other Fantasy Films*. San Diego/New York: A.S. Barnes, 1980.
Hope, Bob, and Bob Thomas. *The Road to Hollywood: My Forty-Year Love Affair with the Movies*. Garden City, N.Y.: Doubleday, 1977.
Huston, John. *An Open Book*. New York: Alfred A. Knopf, 1980.
Jacobson, Laurie. *Hollywood Heartbreak*. New York: Simon & Schuster, 1984.
Jensen, Paul M. *Boris Karloff and His Films*. South Brunswick/New York: A.S. Barnes, 1974.
Jerome, Stuart. *Those Crazy Wonderful Years When WE Ran Warner Bros*. Secaucus, N.J.: Lyle Stuart, 1983.
Jewell, Richard B., with Vernon Harbin. *The RKO Story*. New York: Arlington House, 1982.
Katz, Ephraim. *The Film Encyclopedia*. New York: G.P. Putnam's Sons, 1979.
Kisch, John, and Edward Mapp. *A Separate Cinema: Fifty Years of Black-Cast Posters*. New York: Noonday, 1992.
Klotman, Phyllis Rauch. *Frame by Frame — A Black Filmography*. Bloomington: Indiana University Press, 1979.
Kobal, John. *People Will Talk*. New York: Alfred A. Knopf, 1985.
Koszarski, Richard. *Mystery of the Wax Museum*. Wisconsin/Warner Bros. Screenplay Series. Madison: University of Wisconsin Press, 1979.
_____. *The Man You Loved to Hate: Erich von Stroheim and Hollywood*. New York: Oxford University Press, 1983.
Kotsilibas-Davis, James. *The Barrymores: The Royal Family in Hollywood*. New York: Crown, 1981.
_____, and Myrna Loy. *Myrna Loy, Being and Becoming*. New York: Alfred A. Knopf, 1987.

Lamparski, Richard. *Whatever Became Of...?* (various series). New York: Crown.

Lanchester, Elsa. *Charles Laughton and I.* New York: Harcourt, Brace, 1938.

_____. *Elsa Lanchester, Herself.* New York: St. Martin's, 1983.

Lane, Margaret. *Edgar Wallace: The Biography of a Phenomenon.* New York: Doubleday, Doran, 1939.

Larson, Randall D. *Musique Fantastique: A Survey of Film Music in the Fantastic Cinema.* Metuchen, N.J.: Scarecrow, 1985.

Lasky, Betty. *RKO, the Biggest Little Major of Them All.* Englewood Cliffs, N.J.: Prentice-Hall, 1984.

Leab, Daniel J. *From Sambo to Superspade: The Black Experience in Motion Pictures.* Boston: Houghton Mifflin, 1975.

Lennig, Arthur. *The Count: The Life and Films of Bela "Dracula" Lugosi.* New York: G.P. Putnam's Sons, 1974.

Leyda, J. (ed.). *Voices of Film Experience: 1894 to the Present.* New York: Macmillan, 1977.

Lindsay, Cynthia. *Dear Boris: The Life of William Henry Pratt a.k.a. Boris Karloff.* New York: Alfred A. Knopf, 1975.

McCarthy, Todd, and Charles Flynn (eds.). *King of the Bs: Working Within the Hollywood System.* New York: E.P. Dutton, 1975.

McCarty, John. *Movie Psychos and Madmen: Film Psychopaths from Jekyll and Hyde to Hannibal Lecter.* New York: Citadel, 1993.

McClelland, Doug. *The Golden Age of B Movies.* Bonanza, 1978.

_____. *Forties Film Talk: Oral Histories of Hollywood, with 120 Lobby Posters.* Jefferson, N.C.: McFarland, 1992.

McClure, Arthur F., and Ken D. Jones. *Star Quality: Screen Actors from the Golden Age of Films.* New York: A.S. Barnes, 1974.

McGilligan, Pat (ed.). *Backstory: Interviews with Screenwriters of Hollywood's Golden Age.* Berkeley: University of California Press, 1986.

Mandelbaum, Howard, and Eric Myers. *Screen Deco.* New York: St. Martin's, 1985.

Mank, Gregory William. *It's Alive! The Classic Cinema Saga of Frankenstein.* San Diego/New York: A.S. Barnes, 1981.

_____. *The Hollywood Hissables.* Metuchen, N.J.: Scarecrow, 1989.

_____. *Karloff and Lugosi: The Story of a Haunting Collaboration.* Jefferson, N.C.: McFarland, 1990.

_____. *Hollywood Cauldron: Thirteen Horror Films from the Genre's Golden Age.* Jefferson, N.C.: McFarland, 1994.

Martin, Pete. *Hollywood Without Make-up.* Philadelphia: J.B. Lippincott, 1948.

Marx, Samuel. *Mayer and Thalberg: The Make-Believe Saints.* Hollywood: Samuel French, 1975.

_____, and Joyce Vanderveen. *Deadly Illusions: Jean Harlow and the Murder of Paul Bern.* New York: Random House, 1990.

Massey, Raymond. *A Hundred Different Lives.* Boston: Little, Brown, 1979.

Matzen, Robert D. *Carole Lombard: A Bio-Bibliography.* New York: Greenwood, 1988.

Miller, Don. *B Movies.* New York: Ballantine Books, 1973.

Moore, Dick. *Twinkle, Twinkle, Little Star (But Don't Have Sex or Take the Car).* New York: Harper & Row, 1984.

Morella, Joe, and Edward Z. Epstein. *Paulette: The Adventurous Life of Paulette Goddard.* New York: St. Martin's, 1985.

Morley, Sheridan. *Tales from the Hollywood Raj: The British, the Movies, and Tinseltown.* New York: Viking, 1983.

Moss, Robert F. *Karloff and Company: The Horror Film.* New York: Pyramid, 1974.

Murphy, Michael J. *The Celluloid Vampires: A History and Filmography, 1897–1979.* Ann Arbor, Mich.: Pierian, 1979.

Noble, Peter. *Hollywood Scapegoat: The Biography of Erich von Stroheim.* London: Fortune, 1950 (reprinted by Arno Press, New York, 1972).

_____. *Ivor Novello, Man of the Theatre.* London: Falcon, 1951.

Nollen, Scott Allen. *Boris Karloff: A Critical Account of His Screen, Stage, Radio, Television, and Recording Work.* Jefferson, N.C.: McFarland, 1991.

Ott, Frederick W. *The Great German Films.* Secaucus, N.J.: Citadel, 1986.

Palmer, Scott. *British Film Actors' Credits, 1895–1987.* Jefferson, N.C.: McFarland, 1988.

Parish, James Robert. *Ghosts and Angels in Hollywood Films: Plots, Critiques, Casts and Credits for 264 Theatrical and Made-for-Television Releases.* Jefferson, N.C.: McFarland, 1994.

_____. *The Hollywood Death Book.* Las Vegas: Pioneer, 1992.

_____, and William T. Leonard. *Hollywood Players: The Thirties.* Carlstadt, N.J.: Rainbow, 1976.

_____, and Michael R. Pitts. *The Great Science Fiction Pictures.* Metuchen, N.J.: Scarecrow, 1977.

_____, and _____. *The Great Science Fiction Pictures II.* Metuchen, N.J.: Scarecrow, 1990.

Pascall, Jeremy. *The King Kong Story.* New York: Chartwell, 1977.

Peary, Danny (ed.). *Close-Ups: The Movie Star Book.* New York: Workman, 1978.

Pitts, Michael R. *Horror Film Stars.* Jefferson, N.C.: McFarland, 1981.

Quigley, Martin. *Decency in Motion Pictures.* New York: MacMillan, 1937.

Ragan, David. *Who's Who in Hollywood 1900–1976.* New Rochelle, N.Y.: Arlington House, 1976.

Riley, Philip J. (ed.). *Frankenstein: Universal Filmscript Series Classic Horror Films, Volume 1.* Absecon, N.J.: MagicImage Filmbooks, 1989.

_____. (ed.). *The Bride of Frankenstein: Universal Filmscript Series Classic Horror Films, Volume 2.* Absecon, N.J.: MagicImage Filmbooks, 1989.

_____. (ed.). *The Mummy: Universal Filmscript Series*

Classic Horror Films, Volume 7. Absecon, N.J.: MagicImage Filmbooks, 1989.

_____. (ed.). *Dracula: Universal Filmscript Series Classic Horror Films, Volume 13.* Absecon, N.J.: MagicImage Filmbooks, 1990.

Robertson, Patrick. *Guinness Movie Facts and Feats.* Enfield, Middlesex, England: Guinness, 1988.

Romani, Cinzia. *Tainted Goddesses: Female Film Stars of the Third Reich.* New York: Sarpedon (English translation), 1992.

Seabrook, W. B. *The Magic Island.* New York: Literary Guild of America, 1929.

Senn, Bryan, and John Johnson. *Fantastic Cinema Subject Guide: A Topical Index to 2500 Horror, Science Fiction, and Fantasy Films.* Jefferson, N.C.: McFarland, 1992.

Sennett, Ted. *Masters of Menace: Greenstreet and Lorre.* New York: E.P. Dutton, 1979.

Sherriff, R. C. *No Leading Lady: An Autobiography.* London: Victor Gallancz, 1968.

Shipman, David. *Movie Talk: Who Said What About Whom in the Movies.* New York: St. Martin's, 1988.

Siegel, Scott, and Barbara Siegel. *The Encyclopedia of Hollywood,* New York: Facts on File, 1990.

Singer, Kurt. *The Laughton Story.* Philadelphia: John C. Winston, 1954.

Skal, David J. *Hollywood Gothic: The Tangled Web of Dracula from Novel to Stage to Screen.* New York/London: W. W. Norton, 1990.

_____. *The Monster Show: A Cultural History of Horror.* New York: W.W. Norton, 1993.

Smith, David C. *H.G. Wells: Desperately Mortal.* New Haven: Yale University Press, 1986.

Smith, Ronald L. *Comic Support: Second Bananas in the Movies.* New York: Citadel, 1993.

Steinberg, Cobbett: *Reel Facts.* New York: Vintage, 1982.

Steinbrunner, Chris, and Burt Goldblatt. *Cinema of the Fantastic.* New York: Galahad, 1972.

Taves, Brian. *Robert Florey, the French Expressionist.* Metuchen, N.J.: Scarecrow, 1987.

Taylor, John Russell. *Strangers in Paradise: The Hollywood Emigres 1933–1950.* New York: Rinehart and Winston, 1983.

Truitt, Evelyn Mack. *Who Was Who on Screen.* New York: R.R. Bowker, 1984.

Tudor, Andrew. *Monsters and Mad Scientists: A Cultural History of the Horror Movie.* Cambridge, Mass.: Basil Blackwell, 1989.

Turner, George E. and Michael H. Price. *Forgotten Horrors: Early Talkie Chillers from Poverty Row.* New York: A.S. Barnes, 1979.

Turner, George (ed.). *The Cinema of Adventure, Romance and Terror.* ASC, 1989.

Underwood, Peter. *Karloff.* New York: Drake, 1972.

Von Gunden, Kenneth. *Flights of Fancy: The Great Fantasy Films.* Jefferson, N.C.: McFarland, 1989.

Watters, James. *Return Engagement: Faces to Remember—Then and Now.* New York: Clarkson N. Potter, 1984.

Weaver, Tom. *Science Fiction Stars and Horror Heroes.* Jefferson, N.C.: McFarland, 1991.

_____. *Poverty Row Horrors: Monogram, PRC and Republic Horror Films of the Forties.* Jefferson, N.C.: McFarland, 1993.

_____. *Attack of the Monster Movie Makers: Interviews with 20 Genre Giants,* Jefferson, N.C.: McFarland, 1994.

Weld, John. *Fly Away Home: Memoirs of a Hollywood Stuntman.* Santa Barbara: Mission, 1991.

Wells, H. G. *Experiment in Autobiography: Discoveries and Conclusions of a Very Ordinary Brain (Since 1866).* Philadelphia: J. B. Lippincott, 1934 (reprinted 1967).

Westmore, Frank, and Muriel Davidson. *The Westmores of Hollywood.* Philadelphia: J.B. Lippincott, 1976.

Willis, Donald C. *Horror and Science Fiction Films: A Checklist.* Metuchen, N.J.: Scarecrow, 1972.

Wolf, Leonard. *A Dream of Dracula: In Search of the Living Dead.* Boston: Little, Brown, 1972.

Wray, Fay. *On the Other Hand: A Life Story.* New York: St. Martin's, 1989.

Youngkin, Stephen D., James Bigwood, and Raymond Cabana, Jr. *The Films of Peter Lorre.* Secaucus, N.J.: Citadel, 1982.

Periodicals

The American Cinematographer
Bioscope
The Candlelight Room
Castle of Frankenstein
Cinefantastique
The Cinema
Cult Movies
Famous Monsters of Filmland
Fangoria
Fantastic Monsters of the Films
Film Weekly
Filmfax
Films and Filming
Films in Review
Harrison's Reports
The Hollywood Reporter
Illustrated Daily News
Kinematograph Weekly
London Times
Look
Los Angeles Examiner
Los Angeles Times
Midnight Marquee
Modern Monsters
Monthly Film Bulletin
Motion Picture
Motion Picture Classic
The Motion Picture Guide
Motion Picture Herald
Movie Monsters
New York Daily News
New York Evening Post
New York Times

The New Yorker
Oakland Tribune
Phantasm
Photon
Scarlet Street

Seattle Times
Shriek
Sight and Sound
The Spectator
Starlog

Time
TV Guide
Variety
Video Watchdog

Index

Numbers in **boldface** refer to pages with photographs.

Abbott and Costello Meet Dr. Jekyll and Mr. Hyde 416
Abbott and Costello Meet Frankenstein 153, 307, 389, 421, 456
Abbott and Costello Meet the Invisible Man 416
Abbott and Costello Meet the Killer, Boris Karloff 153
Abbott and Costello Meet the Mummy 416
Ackerman, Forrest J 211, 489
Adams, Stella **155**
Adamson, Ewart 347, 351
Adrian 273–274
The Adventures of Robin Hood 416
The Adventures of Tarzan (1921 serial) 443
Ainsley, Norman **283**
Alberni, Louis 480
Alda, Robert 49
Alexander, J. Grubb 480
Alexander, Sam "The Man with No Face" 63
Alice Sit-by-the-Fire (play) 487
Alien 6
All My Sins Remembered 480
All Quiet on the Western Front (1930) 19, 30, 158
All This and Heaven Too 416
Allan, Elizabeth 104–105, **106**, 108–109, 272, **273**, 274, 276
The Alligator People 151
Always Tell Your Wife 255
Amadeus 128
The Amazing Colossal Man 429
American Cinematographer Manual 246
Ames, Leon **45**, 48, 51, 116
Amy, George 94
And Sudden Death 477
Andersen, M. A. 325
Andress, Ursula 478
Andrews, Robert 347
Angels with Dirty Faces 98
The Angry Red Planet 351
Anna Christie (1923) 101
Antoine, LeRoi 246
Antonia (play) 475
Anything for a Quiet Life 107

The Ape 448
The Ape Man 461
Argento, Dario 241
Arlen, Richard 150, 151, 153, 484
Armstrong, Robert 114, 115, 117, 173, 177, **224**, 225, 232
Arnold, Edward 474–475
Arsenic and Old Lace 232
Arsine Lupine 41
Asher, E. M. 18, 50, 358
Atkinson, Brooke 246, 434
Atom Man vs. Superman (serial) 408
Attack of the Puppet People 367
Atwill, Lionel 7, 41, 95–96, 101, **155**, 156, **157**, 158, 162, 165, **166**, 168–169, 191, 192, **194**, 194–195, 269, 390–391, 393, 394, 408, 428, 446, 474–475, 476
Auer, John 331–332, 333, 334, 336, 337
Auer, Leopold 327
Auer, Mischa 324–325, **324**, 326, **326**, 327, 328, 457
August, Joseph 432
Averill, Anthony **403**
Axcelle, Carl 85
Ayers, Lew 345

Back from the Dead 193
Baclanova, Olga 60, 64–65
Bad Girls of the Silver Screen 42
Bagnold, Enid 211
Balcon, Michael 210–211, 384
Balderston, John L. 19, 26, 142, 144, 218, 280, 287, 359, 361, 380, 382, 384–385
Baldwin, Earl 96, 98
The Bamboo Saucer 352
Bankhead, Tallulah 246
Banks, Leslie 111, 113–114, 115, **116**, 117
Bansak, Edmund G. 490
Bara, Theda 135
Barnell, Jane (aka Olga Roderick) 66
Barnum, P. T. 67

Barrie, Elaine 263
Barrymore, Diana 143–144, 480
Barrymore, Elaine 480
Barrymore, Ethel 91, 471, 472
Barrymore, John 41, 65, 91, 143, 263, 321, 471, 480, 481
Barrymore, Lionel 41, 269–270, **273**, 274, 345, 370–371, **371**, 372, 373–374, **375**, 376, 449, 471, 472
Barton, Charles T. 153, 456
Barty, Billy **283**, 287
The Bat (play) 232
The Bat Whispers 1, 18
Batman and Robin (1949 serial) 408
Bauer, Harry 445
Baxter, Anne 336
Beal, John 434
The Beast with Five Fingers 49, 232, 327
Beaudine, William 475
Beck, John 183
Becky Sharp 99
Beddoe, Don **400**
Bedford, Barbara 327
Bedlam 307, 384
Before I Hang 4, 327, 347, 401, 402
Belden, Charles 167, 169
Bellamy, Madge 87, 90
Belle of the Yukon 264
Belmore, Lionel 394
Ben-Hur (1926) 134, 151
Benighted (novel) 125
Bennett, Charles 250, 253, 254, 255, 436
Bennett, Leila 269, 484
Beresford, Harry 192
Berger, Carl 469
Berger, Ralph 83
Bergerman, Stanley 240
Bergman, Ingrid 42
Bergman, Sandahl 478
Berman, Pandro S. 450
Bernds, Edward 319, 401
Best, Willie (aka Sleep 'n' Eat) 457–459
The Best Man 100
Best Man Wins 468
The Best Years of Our Lives 314
Between Flops 221
Biberman, Herbert 434
Bickel, Fred (aka Fredric March) 41
Biggs, Douglas 364, 366
A Bill of Divorcement (play) 220
Billy the Kid vs. Dracula 18
The Birds 30
Birth of a Nation 256, 335, 376, 401
Bishop, Julie (aka Jacqueline Wells) 409
The Black Cat (1934) 5, 18, 19, 50, 85, 87, 140, 151, 234–241, **236**, **239**, **240**, 258, 286, 287, 298, 305, 316, 320, 335, 345, 359, 376, 409, 472; see also *The Vanishing Body*
The Black Cat (1941) 241, 351
The Black Cat (1966) 241
The Black Cat (1981) 241

The Black Cat (1990) 241
"The Black Cat" (short story) 235, 264, 452
The Black Doll 101, 159, 361, 431
Black Dragons 327, 461
The Black Forest 115
Black Friday 4, 342
Black Moon 90, 244, 319, 431–433, **432**, 470
The Black Room (1935) 314–322, **317**, **230**, 358, 401, 432, 459, 468
The Black Scorpion 180
The Black Stallion (1979) 90
Black Tower (play) 167
Blackbirds of 1933 (play) 246
Bloch, Robert 6, 490
Blondie (series) 328
Blood and Sand 99
Blood Feast 263
Bloodlust 115
Bluebeard's Ten Honeymoons 423
Blystone, Stanley **403**
The Body Disappears 457
Body Parts 314
The Body Snatcher 4, 345
Boehm, David 301–302, 305
Boese, Carl 445
Bogart, Humphrey 424, **426**, 427, 428, **428**, 429
Bohus, Ted A. 490
Boles, John 24, 447, 479
Boleslawski, Richard 135
Bond, Lillian **124**, 126
Bondi, Beulah **344**, 345
Bonomo, Joe 52, 152–153
Bordwell, David 80
Borland, Carroll 268, 269, 270, 271, 272, 273–274, 274–275,
Boris Karloff: A Critical Account of His Screen, Stage, Radio, Television, and Recording Work 136
Boris Karloff and His Films 6, 390
Borst, Ronald V. 490
Bowery at Midnight 461
Bowman, Laura 244, 246
Boy! What a Girl! 439
The Boy and the Pirates 336
Brabin, Charles 133, 134, 135, 136, 472
Bradbury, Ray 175, 180, 490
Brain of Blood 65
Brando, Marlon 352
Brennan, Walter 221
Brewster's Millions (1935) 256
Bride of Frankenstein 3, 6, 19, 22, 23, 30, 122, 123, 125, 127, 207, 215, 217, 241, 272, 276–288, **277**, **280**, **283**, **286**, 294, 307, 319, 326, 339, 345, 372, 377, 385, 386, 389, 392, 394, 431, 454, 470, 485, 490
Bride of the Monster 262
The Bridge on the River Kwai 107, 255
Bring 'Em Back Alive 469
Bristow, Billy 250, 253
British Intelligence 429
Bromley, Sheila (aka Sheila Fulton; Sheila Manners) 409

Brooks, Jean (aka Jeanne Kelly) 336
Brophy, Edward 67
Brown, Karl 399, 401
Brown, Tom 487
Brown, William 152
Browning, Tod 11, 14–15, 16, 17, 19, 55–57, 60–61, 63, **64**, 66, 68, 215, 267, 268, 269, 270, 271, 272, 273, 274, 275, 276, 301, 358, 372, 374, 376, 377, 440
Bruce, Virginia 311
Brunas, John 46, 342–343, 390, 490
Brunas, Michael 46, 342–343, 491
The Brute Man 408
Buck Rogers (serial) 282
Bunco Squad 352
Bunston, Herbert 14, 19
Burgess, Dorothy 431, 432
Buried Alive (1939) 408
Burke, Kathleen **145**, **148**, 150, 151, **152**, 153, 191, 192, **194**, 194
Burn Witch Burn 376
Burn Witch Burn (novel) 376
Burroughs, Edgar Rice 246
Busch, Mae 100
Bushell, Anthony 208, 211
Butterworth, Charles 481
Byron, Arthur S. **283**

The Cabinet of Dr. Caligari (1919) 47
Cabot, Bruce 117–118, 176, 182
Callow, Simon 126, 152
Calthrop, Donald 381, 382, **383**, 386
The Camels Are Coming 384
Captain Blood 98
Captain Kidd 416
Captains Courageous 467
Captive Wild Woman 416
Carewe, Arthur Edmund **162**
Carmilla 11
Carnival Lady 367
Carpenter, Horace **259**, 260, 263–264
Carradine, John 18, 30, 221, 241, 259; *see also* Richmond, John Peter
Carrel, Alexis 350
Casablanca 30, 98, 170, 220, 348
Castle, William 128
Castle of Doom see *Vampyr*
The Cat and the Canary (1927) 18, 19, 89, 433, 443, 447
The Cat and the Canary (1939) 96, 101, 269, 433–434, **433**, 446
The Cat and the Canary (1978) 434
The Cat and the Canary (play) 433
The Cat Creeps (1930) 433, 456
The Cat Creeps (1946) 1, 416
Cat People (1942) 4, 307
Cawthorn, Joseph 87, 88, 91
Cellier, Antoinette 386
Cellier, Frank 381, 382, **383**, 385–386
Chamber of Horrors (1941) 424

Chandler, Helen 13–14, 143, 272
Chandu on the Magic Island 434–435, 470, 472, **473**
Chandu the Magician 376, 435
Chaney, Lon, Jr. 7, 116–117, 292, 293, 449
Chaney, Lon, Sr. 18, 22, 153, 275, 276, 292, 372, 376, 449, 450
Chang 172, 177, 178
Chaplin, Charles 98, 193, 312, 434
Charles Laughton: A Difficult Actor 152
Charles Laughton: A Pictorial Treasury of His Films 151, 152
Charles Laughton, An Intimate Biography 151
Charles Laughton and I 126
Charlie Chan at the Opera 169
Un Chien Andalou 429
Chivra, Alex 293
Churchill, Marguerite **349**, 350, 351–352, 357, 359
The Cinema of Adventure, Romance, and Terror 117, 119
The Cinema of Fritz Lang 6
The Citadel 109
Citizen Kane 229, 314
Clair, Rene 80
The Clairvoyant 107, 176, 255, 386, 435–436, **436**
Clare, Mary 435
Clarence, O. B. 423
Clarens, Carlos 453
Clark, Carroll 113
Clarke, Mae 24, 29, 30, 287
Classic Movie Monsters 178
Classics of the Horror Film 1, 377, 390
Clemento, Steve 117
The Climax 352
Clive, Colin 3, 27, 29–30, 220, **277**, 281, 287, 311, 314, 359, 390, 394
Close-Ups: The Movie Star Book 126, 199, 203
Clymer, Jack B. 125
Cobra Woman 307
Cohn, Harry 313
Coleman, C.C. 319
College Humor 448
College Swing 434
Collyer, June 443
Colman, Ronald 203, 449
Colossus of New York 360
Colton, John 293, 340–341, 342, 367
Column of Fire 478
Comstock, Howard W. 98
Condemned to Live 91, 159, 263, 322–328, **324**, **326**, 331, 355, 445
Confessions of a Nazi Spy 63, 429
Conjure Wife (novel) 376
A Connecticut Yankee (1931) 204
Connell, Richard 111
Considine, John W., Jr. 311
Contner, J. Burgi 246
Cooper, Merian C. 115–117, 118, 168, 172, 173, 177–178, **178**, 179–180, **181**, 181–183, 215, 227, 232, 456, 458, 477, 478
Cooper, Violet Kemble 221, 340, 342, 345

Cooper, Willis 389, 393
Corman, Roger 241, 416
Cornish, Robert E. 350, 400, 451, 452
The Corpse Vanishes 65, 461
Corridors of Blood 19
Cortez, Ricardo 350, 351, 471, 484, 486
Cortez, Stanley 351
Counselor-at-Law 430, 480
Courtenay, William 18
Cox, Jack 381, 385
Cozzi, Luigi 241
Crabbe, Buster 118–119, 443
Crabbe, Byron L. 182
The Crawling Hand 153, 462
Creation (unproduced) 170, 177, 179
Creation of the Humanoids 352
Creelman, James Ashmore 111, 112, 115, 172, 173, 179
The Creeper 327, 416
Cregar, Laird 109
Cremer, Robert 90, 272
Crime and Punishment 312
The Crime of Doctor Crespi 7, 328–337, **330**, **333**
Crime School 430
The Crimes of Stephen Hawke 255, 436–437, 442, 482
Crisler, B.R. 230, 334, 423
Cronjager, Les 458
Cronyn, Hume 143
The Crooked Circle 232, 437–438
Crosby, Bing 101, 195, 394
Cross, Eric 252
Crowley, Aleister 240–241
Cunningham, Jack 240
The Curse of Frankenstein 259
Curse of the Demon 255
Curse of the Fly 107
Curse of the Werewolf 152, 305, 377
Curtis, Dan 211
Curtis, James 220, 221, 284, 285, 287
Curtiz, Michael 4, 94–95, 96, 97, 98–99, 163, 164, 166–167, 168, 215, 348, 350, 352, 429
Cushing, Peter 478
The Cyclops 159

Dade, Francis 438
D'Agostino, Albert 302–303, 307, 339
The Damned 109
Dante, Joe 491
Darby O'Gill and the Little People 384
Darien, William 471
The Dark Eyes of London 6, 416–424, **419**, **422**, 463
The Dark Eyes of London (novel) 423
Dark Victory 193
The Darling of Paris 448
Daughter of the Dragon 144, 438
David O. Selznick's Hollywood 115
Davis, Bette 41, 42, 50
Dawn, Jack 274
The Dawn Patrol 167
Day-Lewis, Daniel 384

Dead Eyes of London (Die Toten Augen von London) 424
Dead Men Walk 159, 408
Dead of Night (1945) 109
Deadly Game 115
Deadly Illusions: Jean Harlow and the Murder of Paul Bern 377
The Deadly Mantis 361
Deane, Hamilton 19
Dear Boris 29, 136
Death Takes a Holiday (1934) 194, 440, 456
Decency in Motion Pictures 55
De Cordoba, Pedro 324, 325, 326, **326**, 327, 372
DeForrest, Kansas 283
De Gunzburg, Nicolas *see* West, Julian
De Laurentiis, Dino 183
Delehanty, Thornton 166, 433
Delgado, Marcel **171**, 231, 254, 457
Delgado, Victor **171**
Del Rio, Delores 467
DeMille, Cecil B. 153, 321, 367
DeMille, Katherine **317**, 321
The Demon Barber of Fleet Street (1936) see *Sweeney Todd, the Demon Barber of Fleet Street*
De Reszke, Jean 479
Destination Moon 117, 361, 409
Destry Rides Again 352
The Devil and the Deep 125–126
The Devil Bat 4, 91, 408, 447
The Devil Commands 401
The Devil-Doll (1936) 14, 68, 215, 270, 284, 327, 336, 368–377, **371**, **375**,
The Devil Girl from Mars 385
The Devil's Daughter 438–439, 470
The Devil's in Love 468–469
De Wolfe, Karen 325, 355
Dieterle, William 480
Dinehart, Alan 201, 202, 204
Dinner at Eight 480
Dione, Rose **55**
Disney, Walt 177
Dr. Cyclops 232, 240
Dr. Gillespie (series) 345
Dr. Jekyll and Mr. Hyde (1931) 1, 6, 30–43, **32**, **33**, **36**, **39**, 151, 152, 187, 199, 204, 295, 421, 456, 476
Dr. Jekyll and Mr. Hyde (1941) 35, 40, 42, 43, 416
Dr. Jekyll and Mr. Hyde (novel) see *The Strange Case of Dr. Jekyll and Mr. Hyde*
Dr. Jekyll and Mr. Hyde (play) 481
Dr. Kildare (series) 345
Dr. Mabuse the Gambler 484
"Doctor Tarr and Professor Fether" (short story) 452
Dr. Terror's House of Horrors (1943) 445
Dr. Terror's House of Horrors (1965) 483
Doctor X 91–102, **97**, **100**, 158, 163, 164, 166, 167, 168, 169, 180, 187, 215, 352, 427, 428–429, 484
The Doctor's Secret (short story) 428
Doktor Mabuse der Spieler 484
Donlevy, Lillian Lugosi *see* Lugosi, Lillian

Dore, Gustav 181–182
Dorian, Ann 400–401
Double Door 439–440, **440**, 456
Double Door (play) 439
Douglas, Melvyn **124**, 127, 156, **157**, 158–159, 478
Dracula (1931) 1, 3, 6, 7, 9–19, **10**, **15**, **17**, 21, 22, 26, 30, 35, 50, 57, 60, 61, 78, 79, 83, 85, 87, 88, 89, 90, 138, 139, 140, 143, 144, 151, 159, 187, 215, 233, 267, 268, 271, 272, 276, 285, 298, 306, 336, 341, 345, 353, 355, 356, 357, 358, 359, 361, 374, 375, 376, 385, 392, 393, 438, 440, 465, 472, 493
Dracula (1931; Spanish language version) 15, 18–19, 51, 440, **441**
Dracula (novel) 11, 19, 46
Dracula (play) 273, 469
The Dracula Scrapbook 19
Dracula vs. Frankenstein 65
Dracula's Daughter 15, 41, 117, 193, 339, 342, 343, 352, 352–361, **356**, **359**, **360**, 376, 408, 416, 431, 456, 472
Dragonwyck 203
Drake, Frances 49, 99, 143, **310**, 311, 313–314, 340, **340**, 341, 344–345, **344**, 456, 477
Dreier, Hans 150
The Dress Doctor 202
Dreyer, Carl-Theodor 73–75, 77, 78, 79, 80, 361
Drums o' Voodoo 7, 241–246, **243**, **245**, 258
Duck Soup 448
Dudgeon, John *see* Dudgeon, Elspeth
Dudgeon, Elspeth 125, 127, 476
Duggan, Andrew 434
Dunagan, Donnie 392
Duncan, Arletta 287
Dunne, Irene 486
Dunne, Peter 359
Durante, Jimmy 462
Duvivier, Julien 445
Dwan, Allan 202
The Dybbuk (1937) 440–441

Earles, Bert 65
Earles, Daisy 60, 65, 66
Earles, Harry 60, 61, 65, 66
East Side of Heaven 394
Eastman, John 450
Ebson, Buddy 488
Eck, Johnny 66, **67**
Edeson, Arthur 22, 24, 122–123
Edgar Wallace: The Biography of a Phenomenon 424
Edison, Thomas 26
Edwards, Roy 122
Edwards, Ted 260
Eisner, Lotte 484
The Electric Man (unproduced) 3
Elsa Lanchester, Herself 126
Elvey, Maurice 105, 106, 107, **108**, 436
Emmott, Basil 105, 107
The Emperor and the Golem 445
End of the World 367

Endore, Guy 274, 305, 372, 376–377
Ensign Pulver 352
Entwistle, Peg 487
Erickson, Carl 164, 165, 167
Esmeralda 448
Esmond, Jill 126
Esper, Dwain 7, 58, 63, 258–259, 260, **261**, 261, 262, 263
The Eternal Jew 453
Everest, Barbara 109
Everson, William K. 1, 6, 73, 90, 211, 377, 390, 491
Every Day's a Holiday 193
The Evil Mind see *The Clairvoyant*
Experiment in Autobiography 219

The Face at the Window (1920) 443
The Face at the Window (1932) 441–442, 443
The Face at the Window (1939) 437, 442–443, **442**, 481
The Face at the Window (play) 443
A Face in the Fog 443, 474
Face of Marble 457
Fahrmann Maria (1936) 79, 443–444
Fairbanks, Douglas, Sr. 264
Fairbanks, Douglas, Jr. 448
Farnum, William 203, 204
Farrell, Glenda 96, 164, 166, 167, 168
Farrow, John 376
Farrow, Mia 376
Farrow, Tisa 376
Fassbinder, Rainer Werner 80
Fast Workers 68, 272
Faust (1926) 480
Ferryboat Pilot Maria see *Fahrmann Maria*
Ferryboat Woman Maria see *Fahrmann Maria*
Fields, Joseph 347, 351
Fields, Mrs. Salisbury 41
Fields, W.C. 193, 394
Fiend Without a Face 109
The Films of Bela Lugosi 50
The Films of Carl-Theodor Dreyer 79, 80
Fingers at the Window 345
Fisherman's Wharf 394
Five Graves to Cairo 336
Flash Gordon (1936 serial) 119, 282
Flash Gordon's Trip to Mars (serial) 443
Fleming, Victor 488
Flesh and Fantasy 90, 351
Fletcher, Bramwell 143–144, 456, 480
Flight to Mars 430
The Florentine Dagger 232, 444
Florey, Robert 26–27, 30, 46, 49, 50–51, 218, 293, 339, 444
Flotsam and Jetsam 437
The Fly (1958) 151
Fly Away Home 219
The Flying Deuces 193
The Flying Saucer 19
The Flying Serpent 408
Foolish Wives 335
For Her Children's Sake (play) 168

Forbidden Love (aka *Freaks*) 63, 263
Ford, Wallace **55**, 60, 461
Forster, Robert 135
Fort, Garrett 16, 218, 355, 356, 357–358, 359, 372, 376
Forties Film Talk 18
Forty-Second Street 165
Foster, Preston 100–101
Foulger, Byron **398**
The Four Feathers 179
Four Sided Triangle 109
Fox, Sidney **45**, 49, 50
Foy, Bryan 430
Foy, Eddie, Sr. 430
FP1 Doesn't Answer 6, 79
Francen, Victor 451
Francis, Arlene 46, 51
Franco, Jess 115
Frankenstein (1910) 26
Frankenstein (1931) 1, 3, 11, 19, 19–30, **25**, **28**, 50, 51, 61, 89, 92, 97, 122, 125, 128, 131, 140, 149, 158, 159, 187, 209, 215, 218, 233, 239, 256, 260, 276, 279, 281, 282, 283, 284, 286, 287, 288, 304, 311, 316, 319, 336, 342, 353, 355, 359, 376, 385, 392, 393, 394, 414, 423, 446, 447, 448, 470, 479
Frankenstein (or, the Modern Prometheus) (novel) 26, 46, 111
Frankenstein and the Monster from Hell 483
Frankenstein Meets the Wolfman 27, 319, 389, 416
Frazer, Robert 91, **155**, 327–328
Freaks 1, 5, 6, 14, 52–68, **55**, **59**, **64**, 149, 187, 192, 215, 263, 271, 272, 312, 377, 476, 478, 490; see also *Forbidden Love; The Monster Show; Nature's Mistakes*
Freaks: Myths and Images of the Secret Self 66
Freud, Sigmund 23, 311
Freund, Carl 4, 7, 11–12, 14, 47, 49, 50, 52, 80, 99, 139, 142–143, 215, 309–310, 311, 313–314, 358, 377
Friedlander, Louis 300, 301, 305, 307; *see also* Landers, Lew
Friedman, David F. 63, 68, 263
Frisco, Joe 445
Fritz Lang 484
From Here to Eternity 402
The Front Page (play) 100
Frye, Dwight **10**, 13, 16, 19, 24, 26, 156, 158, 159, 221, 283, 287, **330**, 333, 334, 335, 336, 353, 394, 446
Frye, Dwight, Jr. 336
Fulci, Lucio 241
Fulton, John P. 217, 220–221, 284, 289, 295, 339, 341, 342, 345, 470
Fulton, Sheila (aka Sheila Bromley) 409

Gable, Clarke 203, 464, 467
Gahagan, Helen 478
Galaxina 65
A Game of Death (1945) 115, 385, 478
Gance, Abel 450, 451
Garbo, Greta 98, 351
Gardner, Shayle 109
Gargan, William 447
Garland, Judy 487, 488
Gawthorne, Peter 109
Gemora, Charles **45**, 51–52
Genius at Work 180
Gérard, Henriette **72**, 79
Gerrard, Charles 14, 16
Gerrard, Henry 114
Getting Married (play) 487
The Ghost Breakers 233, 269, 237, 434, 457
Ghost Catchers 345
The Ghost in the Invisible Bikini 351
The Ghost of Frankenstein 151, 389, 394, 421
The Ghost of John Holling (novel) 463
Ghost Ship (1943) 406
The Ghost Walks 91, 159, 328, 443, 444–445
Ghosts on the Loose 461
The Ghoul (1933) 21, 205–212, **209**, 384
The Giant Behemoth 249
The Giant Claw 402
Gibbons, Cedric 370, 372, 376
Gift of Gab 345
Gilliat, Sidney 380, 382
Give Me a Sailor 434
Gleason, James 327
Gleason, Russell 327
Glen or Glenda? 262
Glut, Donald F. 178, 180
Goddard, Paulette, 433, **433**, 434, 446
Goebbels, Joseph 79
Goldbeck, Willis 61
Golden, Nina 302–303
Goldner, Orville 458
The Golem (1915) 445
The Golem (1916) 445
The Golem (1920) 241, 445, 452
The Golem (1936) 445
The Golem and the Dancing Girl 445
The Golem's Daughter 445
The Golem's Last Adventure 445
Gone with the Wind 99, 183, 193, 313, 416
The Good Earth 313
Goosson, Stephen 316
Gordon, Alex 211
Gordon, Bert I. 336
Gordon, Richard 19, 142, 491
The Gorilla (1927) 446
The Gorilla (1931) 430, 445, 446
The Gorilla (1939) 445–446, 476
The Gorilla (play) 445, 446, 476
Gowland, Gibson 251, 256
Graft 27
Graham, Lewis 333–334
Grand Hotel 480
Grant, Cary 484
The Grapes of Wrath 314, 336
Grass 172, 177
Gray, Charles 107

Gray, Lorna 400, **400**
The Great Dictator 151
Great Expectations (1934) 293, 326
Great Expectations (1946) 255
The Great Impersonation 232, 446
The Great Man Votes 395
The Great Rupert 360
Greed 256, 335, 377
Greene, Graham 319, 478
Greenhalgh, Jack 408
Grey, Nan 361, 431
Griffith, D.W. 210, 335, 376, 401
Grinde, Nick 4, 399, 401
Grip of the Strangler see *The Haunted Strangler*
Grot, Anton 95, 99–100, 163, 164, 168, 480
Grundgens, Gustav 80
Guilfoyle, Chubby 192
Guilfoyle, Paul 336
Gunga Din 395
Gwenn, Edmund **349**, 350
Gynt, Greta **419**, 421, 423

Haggard, H. Rider 478
Hale, Rex 409
Haley, Jack 488
Hall, Charles D. 14, 19, 23, 47–48, 50, 122, 236, 240, 282, 357
Hall, Huntz 429
Hall, Mordaunt 16, 40, 96, 98, 115, 151, 166–167, 201, 218
Hallelujah 439
Hallenbeck, Bruce G. 491
Haller, Ernest 189, 193
Halloween 156
Halperin, Edward 83, 88, 90, 91, 200, 202, 367
Halperin, Victor 7, 83, 84, 85, 88, 90, 91, 198–199, 200, 201, 202, 203, 215, 358, 363–364, 366, 367, 406, 406–407, 408, 409
Hamilton, George 274
Hamilton, Margaret 488
Hamilton, Neil **483**, 484
Hamlet (1949) 211
Hammerstein, Oscar 282
Hands of a Stranger 312
The Hands of Orlac (1925) 211, 312
Hands of Orlac (1935; aka *Mad Love*) **310**
The Hands of Orlac (1965) 312
The Hands of Orlac (novel) see *Les Mains D'Orlac*
Hard Target 115
Harding, Ann 452
Hardwicke, Cedric 211
Hardy, Oliver 100
Harlow, Jean 63, 439
Harrigan, William 217, 220
Harrington, Curtis 128
Harris, Robert 293
Harrison, Kathleen 211
Harrison, P. S. 484
Harron, John 91
Harryhausen, Ray 229, 491

Hart, Ferdinand 445
Hatfield, Hurd 18
Hauer, Rutger 115
The Haunted Strangler 19, 109
A-Haunting We Will Go 457
Hawkins, Jack 107–108
Hawks, Howard 307
Haxan (aka *Witchcraft Through the Ages*) 260
Hayes, Helen 246
Hays, William H. 5
Hayward, Lillie 347
Hayworth, Rita 275
Head, Edith 202
Hearts of Dixie 90
Heath, Percy 40, 41
Heitfeldt, Heinrich 207
Hellavision 446
Hell's Angels (1930) 321
Helm, Brigette 287
Hepburn, Katherine 142
Herbert, Holmes 204
Herbert, Hugh 125, 476
Herman, Al 477
Hersholt, Jean 134
Hickox, Sid 426–427, 430
Hicks, Seymour 251, 255
Hieronimko, Jan **72**, 79
Higgin, Howard 342, 367
Higham, Charles 151
Hill, Bob 443, 473–474
Hillie, Verna 448
Hillyer, Lambert 15, 319, 339, 341, 343, 358, 359, 361
Hilton, Daisy 65–66
Hilton, Edith 66
Hilton, Mary 66
Hilton, Violet 65–66
Himm, Carl 472
Hinds, Samuel 301, 307, 478
History's Great Women 98
Hitchcock, Alfred 255, 364, 384, 467
Hitler, Adolf 312–313, 423, 484
Hobart, Rose 37–38, 40, 41–42
Hobbes, Halliwell 38, 456
Hobson, Valerie 282–283, 292, 293–295, 446
Hodges, Douglas 342
Hoerl, Arthur 244, 245–246
Hoffberg, J. H. 469
Hoffenstein, Samuel 40, 41
Hohl, Arthur 151, **371**
Hold That Ghost 328
Holden, Eddie 406
Holden, Gloria 355, 356, **356**, 358, **359**, 360
Holden, Lansing C. 117, 477
Hollywood Anecdotes 7
Hollywood Cameramen 43, 61
Hollywood Gothic 11
Hollywood Without Makeup 94
Holm, Ralph 79
Holt, Jack 432
Hope, Bob 96, 195, 269, 433–434, 446, 457

Hopkins, Anthony 43
Hopkins, Miriam 32, **33**, 35, 37, 40, 41–42, 246
Hopper, DeWolfe 424, 429
Hopper, Hedda 361, 429
Hopper, William 361, 424, 429
Hopton, Russell 127, 406
Horsley, David 295
The Hound of the Baskervilles (1939) 204
The Hounds of Zaroff see *The Most Dangerous Game*
House of Dracula 18, 151, 159, 389, 416, 452
The House of Fear 446–447
House of Frankenstein 18, 151, 159, 232, 389, 416
House of Horrors 4
House of Mystery 91, 447–448
The House of the Seven Gables (1940) 361, 447
House of Wax 430
The House That Dripped Blood 211
Houseman, John 142
How to Make a Monster 367
How to Undress in Front of Your Husband 63, 263
Howard, Cecil 313
Howard, Leslie 27
Howe, James Wong 60–61, 267–268, 275, 435
Hugo, Victor 448
Hugo the Hunchback 448
Hull, Henry 5, 290, 292, **292**, 293, **294**, 295, 433
Hull, Warren 350
The Human Duplicators 153
The Human Monster 424; see also *The Dark Eyes of London*
The Hunchback 448
The Hunchback of Notre Dame (1923) 19, 90, 159, 345, 448–449
The Hunchback of Notre Dame (1939) 3, 415, 432, 448–450, **450**, 480
A Hundred Different Lives 126, 486
Hunt, J. Roy 478
Hunter, Ian 412, 416
Hunter, T. Hayes 207, 210–211
Hurlbut, William 280, 287
Huston, John 51
Hutchinson, Josephine 394
Hyams, Lelia 60, 63–64
Hyde, Edith 67
Hyer, Bill 474
Hyman, Bernie 472
Hyson, Dorothy 211

I Lived with You 107
I Lived with You (play) 107
I Married a Witch 465
I Walked with a Zombie 4, 478
I Was a Teenage Frankenstein 367
I Was a Teenage Werewolf 367
An Illustrated History of the Horror Film 453
International House 193
Intolerance 401
Invasion of the Saucer Men 65, 474
Invisible Agent 430

The Invisible Ghost 90, 461, 474
Invisible Invaders 367
The Invisible Man (1933) 19, 22, 23, 30, 122, 127, 128, 204, 209, 212–221, **214**, **217**, 283, 284, 286, 295, 307, 342, 343, 359, 376, 431, 454, 470
The Invisible Man (novel) 218, 219–220, 221
The Invisible Man Returns **217**, 361, 447
The Invisible Ray 131, 221, 232, 307, 337–345, **340**, **343**, **344**, 358, 367, 376, 380, 465, 470
The Invisible Woman 193
Irena, Princess 472
Irving, Henry 386
The Island of Dr. Moreau (1977) 153
The Island of Dr. Moreau (novel) 153
Island of Doomed Men 402
Island of Lost Souls 5, 52, 64, 83, 144–153, **145**, **147**, **152**, 187, 192, 194, 195, 203, 219, 448, 492
It 445
It Happened One Night 467
It's Alive! The Classic Cinema Saga of Frankenstein 390
It's Never Too Late to Mend 442, 482
Ivanhoe (1952) 475

J'Accuse! (1918) 451
J'Accuse! (1937) 450–451
Jack the Giant Killer 384
Jack the Ripper (play) 481
Jacobs, W. W. 456, 457
Jagger, Dean 363–364, 364–365, **365**, 366, 367
Jailhouse Rock 475
James, Ida 438
James Whale (biography) 128, 284
Jannings, Emil 41
The Jazz Singer (1927) 430
Jenkins, Allen 476
Jensen, Paul M. 6, 390, 491
Jerome, Stuart 480
Joan of Arc (1948) 467
Johann, Zita 138, 142–143, **143**, 486
John, Graham 456
Johnson, John 492
Johnson, Noble **48**, 51, 117, 232–233, 458, 478
Johnson, Tom 492
Jordan, Dorothy 118
Journey's End 3, 27, 208
Journey's End (play) 219
Joy, Jason S. 479
Judge, Arline 461–462
Jul, Christen 79
Jungle Captive 360
Jungle Woman 307

Karl Struss: Man with a Camera 42
Karloff, Boris 2, 3, 4, 7, 19, 21, 22, **25**, 27–29, **28**, 85, 87, **121**, 125, 126, **127**, 128, 130, 131, **132**, 133, 134, 135, 136, 138, **139**, 141, **141**, 142, 143, **143**, 207, 208, 209, **209**, 211, 218, 219, 220, 221, **236**,

237, **239**, 240, **240**, 241, 274, **277**, 281–282, 285, 286, **286**, 287, 288, 293, 298, 299–300, 300–301, 303, 304, **304**, 305, 306, **306**, 307, 309, 316, **317**, 318–319, 319–320, **320**, 320–321, 335, **340**, 341–342, **343**, 344, 345, 347–348, 349, **349**, 350, 352, 359, 379, **380**, 382–383, **383**, 384, **385**, 387–389, **388**, 390–392, **391**, 393, 394, 395, **396**, 397, 398, **398**, 399, 400, **400**, 401, 402, 407, 409, **410**, 412, 413–414, 415, 421, 427, 429, 438, 445, 448, 457, 459, 468, 470, 479, 481, 486
Karloff, Sara Jane 394
Karloff (biography) 135, 210
Karloff and Company: The Horror People 56
Karloff and Lugosi: The Story of a Haunting Collaboration 142–143, 307, 313
Katz, Lee 426
Katzman, Sam 65
Kauffman, Al 313
Keith, Ian 18
Kelly, Jeanne (aka Jean Brooks) 336
Kelly, Patsy 446
Kennedy, Edgar 431
Kent, Robert 470
Kent, Ted 278–279, 285
Kenton, Erle C. 83, **145**, 150, 151, **152**, 152, 153, 492
Kerr, Frederick 24
Key Largo 313
Kill or Be Killed 115
Kilpatrick, Tom 240
King, George 437, 442, 443, 481
King Kong (1933) 6, 7, 21, 51, 96, 114, 115, 117, 125, 168, 169–184, **171**, **174**, **176**, **178**, **181**, 215, 222, 224, 225, 226, 227–229, 231, 232, 233, 243, 249, 254, 374, 424, 435, 436, 439, 456, 457, 458, 477, 478, 490, 491
King Kong vs. Godzilla 183
The King of Kings 183
King of the Underworld 430
King of the Zombies 4, 63
Kingsford, Walter **343**, **344**, 345
Kinnell, Murray 476
The Kiss Before the Mirror 219
Klemensen, Richard 492
Kline, Benjamin 399, 402
Knaggs, Skelton 406
Knights of the Round Table (1953) 475
Kohner, Paul 440
Korda, Alexander 80
Kosloff, Theodore 302–303
Krampf, Gunther 207, 211
Kronos 151
Kruger, Oom Paul 360
Kruger, Otto 357, 359, 360
Kuhn, Irene 131
Kurten, Peter 453

The Lady and Monster 153, 335
The Lady Vanishes (1938) 385

Laemmle, Carl, Jr. 2, 26, 49, 50, 126, 142, 220, 221, 240, 283, 294, 361, 449
Laemmle, Carl, Sr. 2, 29, 219, 287, 295, 361
Lamarr, Hedy 385
Lanchester, Elsa 126, 280, 284, **286**, 287
Landers, Lew (aka Louis Friedlander) 307, 319
Landis, John 492
Lane, Frankie 361
Lane, Margaret 424
Lane, Rosemary 427, **428**, 429
Lang, Fritz 80, 310, 335, 453, 484
Langan, Glenn 429
Langley, Bryan 420
La Plante, Laura 447
Larrinaga, Mario 182
Lasky, Jesse 475
The Last Joke (play) 211
The Last Man on Earth 204
The Last Warning (1929) 447
The Last Will of Dr. Mabuse see *Das Testament des Dr. Mabuse*
Laughton, Charles **124**, 125–126, **127**, **145**, 147, 149–150, 284, 448, 449–450, **449**
Laurel, Stan 100
Lawrence of Arabia 107, 255
Lawton, Frank 340, **344**, 345, 372, 376
Lean, David 252–253, 254, 255
Lease, Rex 457
Lederman, Ross 319
Lee, Anna 381, 382, 383, 384, **385**
Lee, Bernard 483
Lee, Christopher 478
Lee, Norman 458
Lee, Robert N. 412, 416
Lee, Rowland V. 389, 390, 392, 393, 394, 395, 412–413, 414, 415, 416, 452
Le Fanu, Sheridan 11
Leiber, Fritz 376
Leisen, Mitchell 456
Leni, Paul 18, 447
Leonard, Arthur 438, 439, 470
Leonard, Sheldon 469
The Leopard Man 336
LeRoy, Mervyn 100, 488
Lesser, Sol 435, 472
Levy, Ben 122, 125
Lewis, Emory 434
Lewis, H. G. 68
Lewton, Val 4, 307, 336, 406, 478
Life Returns 350, 451–452
Life Without Soul 26
The Light in the Dark 153
Lights of New York 430
Lilies of the Field (novel) 287
Lincoln, Pamela 448
Lindbergh, Charles A. 350
Lindsay, Cynthia 29
Litel, John 427, **428**, 429–430
Little Caesar 168, 416
The Living Dead (1932) 241, 452
The Living Dead (1933) 452

Loder, John 381, 382, 385
Lodge, John 192, 194, 456
The Lodger (1926) 109
The Lodger (1932) 6, 102–109, **103**, **106**, **108**, 209, 272, 436
The Lodger (1944) 109, 430
The Lodger (novel) 109
Lombard, Carole 199, 201, 202–203, 484
London After Midnight 276, 376, 456
Long, Audrey 115
The Long Dark Hall 211
Long Day's Journey into Night (play) 434
Lord of the Rings 65
Lorre, Peter 307, 310–311, **310**, 311–312, 312–313, **313**, 393, 449, 453, 490
The Lost Continent (1951) 408
Lost Horizon (1937) 204, 476, 477
The Lost World (1925) 30, 135, 177
The Lost World (1960) 254, 255
Louise, Anita 446
Louisiana (play) 245, 246
Louisiana see *Drums o' Voodoo*
Love at First Bite 274
Love from a Stranger (1937) 385, 386, 452, 481
Love from a Stranger (1947) 452
Love from a Stranger (play) 452
The Love Wanga 469; see also *Ouanga*
The Loves of Edgar Allan Poe 430
Lowe, Edmund 435, 446
Lowe, Edward T. 159
Lowndes, Mary Belloc 109
Lowry, Ed 447
Loy, Myrna 64, 131, 133, 136, 438, 486
Lubin, Arthur 4
Lubitsch, Ernst 153
Lucas, Tim 492
Lucky Boy 168
Luff, William 105
Lugosi, Bela 2, 3, 7, **10**, 11, 13, 16, **17**, 18, 19, 26, 27, **45**, 46–47, **48**, 50, 51, 52, 65, 83, 85–87, 88, **89**, 90, 91, **147**, 150, 193, 201, 237, **239**, 240, 241, 259, 260, 268, **268**, 271, 272, 273, 274, 275, 276, 286, 288, 293, 298–301, **299**, 303, **304**, 305, 306, **306**, 307, 339–340, 341, 342, **343**, 344, **344**, 345, 353, 359, **360**, 363, 364, 390, 391, **391**, 392, 393, 394, 395, 407, 408, 420, 421, 422, **422**, 423, 429, 434, 435, 440, 446, 447, 449, 458, 460, 461, 462, **463**, 464–465, **464**, 467–468, 468–469, 470, 471, 472, 473, 476, 482, 490, 493
Lugosi, Bela, Jr. 465
Lugosi, Hope 241
Lugosi, Lillian 274, 342, 394
Lugosi, the Man Behind the Cape 90, 272
Lukas, Paul 474–475
Lyon, William 402
Lys, Lya 429

M (1931) 6, 56, 107, 453, 484, 490
M (1951) 135

McCarty, John 467
McCrea, Joel **113**, 114, 115, **116**, 117, 118–119, 182, 203, 477
MacDonald, Wallace 401
McDowall, Roddy 136, 445
McGill, Barney 480
McHugh, Catherine 168
McHugh, Edward A. 168
McHugh, Frank 166, 167, 168
Mack, Helen **224**, 225–226, 232, **477**, 478
MacKenzie, Jack 459
McKim, Josephine **283**
McKinney, Morris 244–245
McKinney, Nina Mae 438, 439
MacLane, Barton 350
Macready, George 434
The Mad Doctor 327
The Mad Doctor of Market Street 233, 474
The Mad Genius 321, 480–481
The Mad Ghoul 38, 232
Mad Love (1935) 67, 99, 139, 143, 192, 215, 305, 308–314, **310**, **313**, 377, 385, 397, 476; see also *Hands of Orlac*
The Mad Magician 430
Mad Max Beyond Thunderdome 65
The Mad Monster 408
Madison, Julian **403**
The Magic Island 88
The Magic Sword 65
The Magnificent Ambersons 351
Mahon, Patrick 467
The Main Event (1927) 232
Les Mains d'Orlac (novel) 312
Makin, William J. 429
The Making of King Kong 115
Malandrinos, Andreas **106**, 109
Malden, Karl 51
Malika Salomi 478
The Maltese Falcon (1941) 30
Mamoulian, Rouben **32**, 34, 35–37, **36**, 37–38, 40, 41–42, 153
Man in the Attic 109, 126
Man Made Monster 7, 307
Man of Destiny (play) 220
The Man They Could Not Hang 4, 131, 320, 347, 395–402, **396**, **398**, **400**, 468, 469
The Man Who Changed His Mind 377–386, **380**, **383**, **385**, 481
The Man Who Could Work Miracles 453–454
"The Man Who Could Work Miracles" (short story) 454
A Man Who Fights Alone 204
The Man Who Knew Too Much (1934) 255
The Man Who Laughs (1928) 18, 19, 305, 447
The Man Who Lived Again see *The Man Who Changed His Mind*
The Man Who Reclaimed His Head 454
The Man Who Reclaimed His Head (play) 220, 454
The Man Who Turned to Stone 402
The Man with Nine Lives 4, 401, 402

Mandel, Rena 79
Maniac (1934) 7, 63, 241, 256–264, **259**, **261**; see also *Sex Maniac*
Mank, Gregory William 138, 142–143, 307, 313, 314, 390, 492
Manners, David 11, 14, 16, 18, 24, 140, 144, 201, 238, 357
Manners, Sheila (aka Sheila Bromley) 409
Mannix, E. J. 377
March, Fredric 32, 35, **36**, 37, 38, 39, 40, 41–43, 152, 421, 449; *see also* Bickel, Fred
Maria Marten, or, the Murder in the Red Barn (play) 481
Marihuana, Weed with Roots in Hell 63, 263
Mark, Michael 394
Mark of the Vampire 14, 60, 68, 108, 215, 264–276, **268**, **270**, **273**, 305, 358, 361, 376, 377, 484
Marks, Clarence 305
Marlow, Brian 199–201
Marsh, Joan 169
Marsh, Marian 320–321, **320**, 480
Marshall, Herbert 355
Marshek, Archie 115–116, 183
Marston, John 226, 232
Martin, Al 474
Martinelli, Arthur 83, 84–85, 91, 199
Martinelli, Enzo 84, 88, 91
Marx, Samuel 377
Mary Poppins 384
The Mask of Diijon 307, 335
The Mask of Fu Manchu 87, 129–136, **132**, **134**, 142, 195, 316, 435, 438, 439, 461, 471
Mask of the Golem 445
Mason, James 475
Massey, Raymond **124**, 126, **127**, 442, 443, 486, **486**
Masters of Menace 313
Maté, Rudolph 74, 75, 80
Matthews, Lester 292–293, 307
May, Joe 447
Mayer, Louis B. 61, 63, 65, 108–109, 312
Mayer and Thalberg: The Make-Believe Saints 62
The Maze 126
Mead, Margaret 4
Meet Boston Blackie 66
Melford, George 15, 19, 51, 440
Menace 454–456, **455**
Mendoza, Peter 253
Menzies, William Cameron 435
Mercer, Beryl 200, 204
Merritt, Abraham 376
Mesa of Lost Women 65, 151
Mescall, John J. 238, 241, 279, 281, 285–286
Metropolis 139, 287, 484, 485
Metzger, Radley 434
Meyer, Abe 91
Michael Balcon Presents ... A Lifetime of Films 211–212
Micheaux, Oscar 246
Midnight Warning 91

A Midsummer Night's Dream (1935) 248
Mighty Joe Young 168, 229, 232, 336, 478
Milland, Ray 117, 454
Miller, Allen C. 98
Miller, John 406
Miller, Mark A. 493
Miller, Seton I. 189–190
Milne, Peter 347
The Miracle Man (1932) 135
Miracles for Sale 68
The Missing Guest 456, 475
Mr. Peabody and the Mermaid 361
Mr. Skeffington 220
Mr. Smith Goes to Washington 204, 220
Modern Motherhood **261**, 263
Mohr, Hal 348, 352
Monagus, Lionel 246
The Monkey's Paw (1915) 457
The Monkey's Paw (1923) 457
The Monkey's Paw (1933) 144, 175, 193, 232, 456–457, 462
The Monkey's Paw (1948) 254, 457
"The Monkey's Paw" (short story) 456, 458
The Monkey's Paw (play) 456, 481
The Monster Maker 327
The Monster Show 3, 18, 374
The Monster Show (aka *Freaks*) 63
The Monster Walks 159, 328, 445, 458–459
Monsters and Mad Scientists 5
Montgomery, Robert 465, 466
Moore, Eva 122, **124**, 125, 126–127, 128
More Classics of the Horror Film 7
Morgan, Dennis 427, 428, 429–430; *see also* Morner, Stanley; Stanley, Richard
Morgan, Frank 327
Morgan, Ira 156, 159, 324
Morgan, Ralph **324**, 326–327, **326**
Morley, Karen 133, 134, 135, 471
Morley, Robert 210
Morner, Stanley (aka Dennis Morgan) 429
Morris, Chester 18, 66, 220
Morris, Gouverneur 218, 239
Morris, Mary 439, **440**
Morris, Wayne 424, 427, 428, 429
Moss, Robert F. 56
The Most Dangerous Game 5, 51, 109–119, **113**, **116**, **118**, 175, 180, 182, 191, 215, 232, 233, 360, 385, 409, 476, 477, 478
"The Most Dangerous Game" (short story) 111, 115
Il Mostro di Frakestein 26
Movie Psychos and Madmen 467
Mowbray, Alan 466
Mower, Jack 424
Mudundu (unfinished film) 80
Mullaly, Don 164, 165, 167
The Mummy (1932) 7, 18, 50, 51, 137–144, **139**, **141**, **143**, 151, 207, 208, 209, 215, 233, 301, 305, 309, 313, 359, 385, 478, 486
Mummy's Boys 457, 458
The Mummy's Curse 138, 204
The Mummy's Ghost 138, 232

The Mummy's Hand 138
The Mummy's Tomb 138, 232, 416
The Munchkins Remember 65
Muni, Paul 18, 351, 449
Murder at Midnight 328
Murder by Television 87, 443, 459
Murder by the Clock 6, 117, 458–461, **461**
Murder in the Blue Room 430, 456, 475
Murder in the Red Barn (1935) 482
The Murderer Invisible (novel) 218, 219
Murders in the Rue Morgue (1914) 51
Murders in the Rue Morgue (1932) 26, 27, 43–52, 45, **48**, 116, 128, 187, 218, 233, 444, 478
Murders in the Rue Morgue (1971) 52
The Murders in the Rue Morgue (1986) 52
"Murders in the Rue Morgue" (short story) 46, 51–52, 257, 264
Murders in the Zoo 158, 184–195, **186**, **188**, **194**, 203, 359, 456
Murphy, Ralph 167, 456
Muse, Clarence 90, 407
My Man Godfrey 327
Myers, Carmel 480
Myrna Loy: Being and Becoming 136
The Mysterious Dr. Fu Manchu 438
The Mysterious Island (1929) 65, 256
The Mysterious Mr. Wong 448, 461–463, **463**
Mystery Liner 91, 448, 463–464, 482
Mystery of Edwin Drood 293, 326, 345, 454
Mystery of the Mary Celeste 255, 256, 300, 464–465, **464**, 482
Mystery of the Wax Museum 96, 98, 99, 158, 159–169, **162**, **166**, 180, 194, 215, 352, 436
The Mystic 57

The Naked Prey 115
Narcotic 263
Naron, Lynn 493
Nature's Mistakes (aka *Freaks*) 63, 263
Naughty Marietta 287
The Navigator 233
A Negro's Ambition 232
Neill, Roy William 317–318, 318–319, 321, 401, 431
Neumann, Kurt 286, 293
Newman, Joseph 14, 60
Nigh, William 448, 463
Night Life of the Gods 465–466, **466**
Night Life of the Gods (novel) 167
Night Monster 232, 327
Night Must Fall (1937) 204, 467, 475
Night Must Fall (play) 467
Night of Terror 467–469, **468**
Night of the Hunter 351
The Nights of Prague 445
The Ninth Guest 307, 319
No Leading Lady 218
No Place Like Homicide 211
Nocturna, Granddaughter of Dracula 18
Nolan, William F. 211
The Norliss Tapes 211–212

Nosferatu (1922) 11, 211
Notorious 220
Notre-Dame de Paris (novel) 448
Novello, Ivor 104, 105, 106, 107, 109
Nugent, Elliott 433, 434
Nugent, Frank S. 272, 350, 358, 366–367, 374, 414–415

Oakman, Wheeler 406
O'Brien, Darlene 175, 229
O'Brien, Edmond 448
O'Brien, George 351
O'Brien, Willis 135, 170, 173–175, 177, **178**, 179–180, 181–182, 183, 229, 230, 231–232, 249, 253, 478
O'Connor, Una 283–284, 285
O'Donnell, Joseph 458, 459
The Offspring 65
O'Hara, Maureen 448
Okuda, Ted 466, 493
Oland, Warner 290, 291, 293, **294**, 438, 463
The Old Dark House (1932) 2, 5, 19, 22, 30, 119–128, **121**, **124**, **127**, 131, 142, 158, 207, 215, 283, 343, 446, 476
The Old Dark House (1963) 128
Old Man Satan (play) 246
Old Mother Riley (series) 255
Old Yeller 384
Oliver, Henry 267
Oliver Twist (1948) 255
Olivier, Lawrence 126, 211, 443
Olmstead, Edwin 333–334
On the Other Hand 98, 158, 168, 180
On the Threshold of Space 367
One Is Guilty 430
One Million B.C. (1940) 249
One Night in the Tropics 193
O'Neil, Barbara 416
O'Neil, Nancy 251, 255–256
O'Neill, Henry 350
An Open Book 51
Osborne, Vivienne **197**, 200, 202, 203
O'Sullivan, Maureen 370–371, 372, **375**, 376
Otterson, Jack 389, 412, 456
Ottiano, Rafaela 372, **375**
Ouanga 438, 439, 469–470
Outside the Law (1921) 18, 276
Outside the Law (1930) 276
Owen, Arthur E. **422**

The Painted Desert (1931) 367
Pal, George 117, 409
Palance, Jack 109
Paradise Lost 181
Parnum, John E. 6, 493
Parsons, Louella 361, 376
The Passion of Joan of Arc 80
Patrick, Gail 192, 194
The Patriot 135

Paul, Val 117
Peach, L. du Garde 380, 382
Peisley, Frederick 251, 256
People Will Talk 64, 117
Pepper, Barbara 473
A Perfect Crime 202
Perkins, Anthony 475
Perkins, Gil 182
Perkins, Osgood 475
Pertwee, Jon 211
Pertwee, Roland 210, 211
The Perverse Countess 115
The Phantom Creeps (feature) 470
The Phantom Creeps (serial) 470
The Phantom Fiend see *The Lodger* (1932)
The Phantom of Crestwood 204, 232, 470–471
The Phantom of the Opera (1925) 18, 19, 256
The Phantom of the Opera (1943) 3, 4, 109, 352
Phantom of the Rue Morgue 51–52
Phantom Ship 463; see also *Mystery of the Mary Celeste*
Pichel, Irving 41, 111, 113, 117, 355–356, **356**, 360–361, **403**, 406, 408–409, 460, **461**, 477
Pickford, Mary 376
Picnic 402
Picture Mommy Dead 384
The Picture of Dorian Gray (1916) 63
The Picture of Dorian Gray (1945) 3, 18, 126, 327, 376
Pierce, Jack P. 21, 22, 85, 123, 128, 138, **141**, 143, **240**, 290, 292, 293, 295, 305, **388**, 414
Pip **55**
"The Pit and the Pendulum" (short story) 297, 298, 307
Plan Nine from Outer Space 262, 263
Poe, Edgar Allan 46, 51, 235, 255, 256, 257, 264, 296, 298, 300, 302–303, 305, 307, 334, 335, 337, 452
Poelzig, Hans 241
Polglase, Van Nest 477
Pommer, Erich 80
Powell, William 202
"The Premature Burial" (short story) 334, 335
Prest, Thomas Preskett 11
Previn, Charles 415, 431
Price, Vincent 28, 204, **217**, 415, 416
Pride and Prejudice (1940) 313
Priestly, J. B. 125
Prince Randian *see* Randian
The Prisoner of Zenda 475
The Private Life of Henry VIII 284
The Private Lives of Elizabeth and Essex 429
Profumo, John 295
Public Defender 151
Putnam, Nina Wilcox 142

Quigley, Martin 55
Quinn, Anthony 321

Rachmil, Louis 460
Racket Squad 151
Radio Patrol (serial) 282
Rain (play) 293
Rains, Claude 128, 176, **214**, 215, 216–217, 220, 254, 255, 281, 352, 435, 436, **436**, 454
Ralston, Vera 335
Randian 53, 67
Rango 172
Rapf, Harry 61, 65
Rardin, Glen A. **152**
Rasputin and the Empress 135, 327, 328, 471–472
Rathbone, Basil 241, 372, 390–392, 393, 394, 395, **410**, 412, 413, 414, 415–416, 452
The Raven (1912) 51
The Raven (1935) 2, 87, 139, 237, 296–307, **299**, **304**, **306**, 319, 320, 335, 337, 342, 345, 359, 377, 423, 431, 478
"The Raven" (poem) 296, 300, 302, 303–304, 305, 307
Rawlins, Jack 456
Ray, Fred Olen 493
Raye, Martha 433–434
Reckless 439
Red Planet Mars 19
Reed, Oliver 152
Reefer Madness 408
Reeves, George 377, 429
Reeves, Kynaston 109
Reicher, Frank 226, 232
Reinhardt, Max 236
Renard, Maurice 312
Rennahan, Ray 95, 99, 163
Rescher, Jay 439
"Resurrection Morning" (short story) 351
Retakes: Behind the Scenes of 500 Classic Movies 450
The Return of Chandu (1934 feature) 434, 435, 470, 472–473, **473**
The Return of Chandu (serial) 183, 434, 435, 472, 473, **473**
The Return of Dr. Fu Manchu 438
The Return of Dr. X 424–430, **426**, **428**
Return of the Ape Man 461
Return of the Frog 482
The Return of the Phantom (unproduced) 18
Return of the Vampire 307, 421, 468
Revere, Anne 439
Revolt of the Demons (aka *Revolt of the Zombies*) 367
Revolt of the Zombies 83, 88, 91, 199, 215, 263, 331, 361–367, **365**, **366**, 407
Richard III (1955) 211
Richardson, Ralph 211
Richmond, John Peter (aka John Carradine) 241
Rietti, Robert 107
Rio 415
Ripley, Robert L. 66
The Ritz Brothers 446, 476
Roach, Bert **45**, 48, 49
The Road Back 423

The Road to Frisco (aka *They Drive by Night*, 1940) 485
The Road to Hollywood 434
Robbins, Tod 61, 67
Robinson, George 339, 342, 356–357, 358, 412–413, 416
Robinson, Peter 66
Robinson Crusoe (1922) 233
Robot Monster 408
Robson, Flora 210
Robson, Mark 4
Rocketship X-M 151
Roderick, Olga (aka Jane Barnell) 66
Rodion, John **410**, 415
Rogell, Al 319
Rogers, Charles 2, 167
Rogers, Stan 370, 372
Rogge, Rudolf Klein 484
The Rogues Tavern 91, 443, 473–474
Rohmer, Sax 135
Roll On Sweet Chariot (play) 246
Rollerball 211
Romero, Cesar 359
A Room with a View 128
Rope 467
Rose, Ruth 172, 173, 179, 225, 477
Rosemary's Baby 376
Rosener, George **97**, 98
Rosmer, Milton 250, 251, 253–254
Rosse, Herman 23
Rossitto, Angelo 65, 66
Ruggles, Charlie 187, 191, 192, 193, 195, 483
Ruggles, Wesley 193, 456, 458, 462
Run for the Sun 115
Ruric, Peter 235, 240
Russell, Rosalind 109, 466
Ryan, Edmond 423
Ryder, Loren L. 153

Sabu 210
Safe in Hell 439
The Saint (series) 336
Salkow, Sidney 199, 203, 204
Salter, Hans J. 393–394
Sanders, George 423, 454
Satellite in the Sky 255
Saulter, William 332
Saum, Cliff 424
Saunders, John Monk 118
Savalas, Telly 434
The Saxon Charm 465
Sayre, George 405–406, 407
Scared to Death 65
Schayer, Richard 27, 142, 240
Scheer, Phillip 367
Schlitze **55**, 66
Schmitz, Sybille 73, 79–80, 443
Schoedsack, Ernest B. 111, 113, 115–117, 118, 119, 172, 177, **178**, 179, 182–183, 215, 226, 227, 231, 456, 457

Schutz, Maurice 79
The Scotland Yard Mystery (aka *The Living Dead*, 1933) 452
Scott, George C. 52
Scott, Randolph 192, 201, 202, 203–204, 477
Scouts to the Rescue (serial) 395
Scrooge (1913) 255
Scrooge (1935) 255
The Sea Hawk (1924) 401
The Sea Wolf 348
Seabrook, W. B. 88
Secret Agent 255, 312
Secret of the Blue Room 127, 158, 343, 456, 474–475, 474
Secret of the Chateau 232, 475
The Secret of the Loch 7, 247–256, **252**, 258, 436
Secrets of the French Police 175, 187, 193, 232, 475–476
See You at the Movies: The Autobiography of Melvyn Douglas 158
Die Sehnucht der Veronika Voss 80
Seitz, John 479
Selznick, David O. 41, 170, 179, 182, 183, 313, 456
Senn, Bryan 474, 493
Sennett, Mack 151, 448
Sennett, Ted 312–313
Sennwald, Andre 142, 192, 311, 312
Sepia Cinderella 439
Seton, Bruce 385, 481–482
The Seven Faces of Dr. Lao 274
Seven Footprints to Satan 65
The Seventh Cross 143
The Seventh Victim 336
Sex Maniac (aka *Maniac*, 1934) 263
Sh! The Octopus 127, 476
Shadow of a Doubt 467
Shadow of the Cat 109
The Shaggy D.A. 384
The Shape of Things to Come (novel) 485
Shaw, Peter **283**, 288
She (1908) 478
She (1911) 478
She (1916) 63, 478
She (1917) 478
She (1925) 478
She (1935) 117, 183, 232, 233, 307, 360, 409, 463, 476–478, 477
She (1965) 478
She (1985) 478
She (novel) 478
She Devil (aka *Drums o' Voodoo*, 1934) **245**
She Devil (1957) 151
She Freak 68
Shelley, Mary 26, 279–280, 285, 287
Shelley, Percy Bysshe 26
Sherlock Holmes and the Secret Weapon 63
Sherlock Holmes in the Great Murder Mystery 51
Sherman, Lowell 466
Sherman, Vincent 426–427, 429, 430
Sherriff, R. C. 27, 125, 215, 216, 218–220, 286, 287, 359

INDEX 515

Shimada, Teru **365**
Shirk, Adam Hull 448
Siegfried (1923) 260
Siegler, Allen G. 316–317, 318
The Silence of the Lambs 43
Simmons, Michael 305
Simpson, Ivan 269
Six Hours to Live 204, 456, 478–480
Skal, David J. 3, 374
Skinner, Frank 393–394, 415
Skull Island see *The Most Dangerous Game*
Slaughter, Tod 436, 437, 442, 481, 482, **482**
Slave Girls from Beyond Infinity 115
Sleep 'n' Eat (aka Willie Best) 457–459
The Sleeping Car (1932) 107
Sloman, Edward 459, 460
The Smiling Ghost 457
Smith, Bunny 66
Smith, C. Aubrey 443, 444
Smith, Don G. 493
Smith, J. Augustus 244, 245, 246
Smith, Leonard 372
Smith, Thorne 167, 466
So Sad About Gloria 367
Something Wicked This Way Comes 65
Son of Dracula 307, 416
Son of Frankenstein 3, 233, 320, 339, 345, 372, 386–395, **388**, 415, 416, 421, 452, 470
The Son of Kong 3, 180, 221–233, **224**, **230**, 249, 254, 435, 477, 478
Sondergaard, Gail 434, 488
Sonney, Dan 258, 264
Sonney, Louis 264, 446
Soul of a Monster 38
South Pacific 282
Soutten, B. Graham 255, 437
Soutten, Ben see Soutten, B. Graham
Spence, Ralph 445, 446
The Spider Woman 65
The Spider Woman Strikes Back 4
The Spoilers 204
Spooks Run Wild 65, 461
"Spurs" (short story) 61–62, 67
Stadie, Hildegarde 263, 264
Stagecoach to Fury 246
Standing, Guy 440
Stanley, Richard (aka Dennis Morgan) 429
Star of Midnight 478
Star Quality 100
Starrett, Charles 133, 136
Steiner, Max 175, 226–227, 232
Stephenson, James 429
Stevens, Onslow 452
Stevenson, R. L. (nephew of Robert Louis Stevenson) 41
Stevenson, Robert (director) 381, 384
Stevenson, Robert Louis (author) 35, 40, 286, 288, 452, 487
Stewart, Jimmy 352
Stone, Lewis 133, 134, 135–136
Straight to Heaven 439

The Strange Adventure of David Gray see *Vampyr*
The Strange Case of Dr. Jekyll and Mr. Hyde 35, 40, 111
The Strange Case of Dr. RX 307
Strange Holiday 232
Strangler of the Swamp 408, 443
Strangler's Morgue see *The Crimes of Stephen Hawke*
Strayer, Frank 156, 159, 324, 325, 328, 355, 358, 445, 457
Strenge, Walter 246
Strickfaden, Kenneth 24, 288
Strickling, Howard 377
Stromberg, Hunt 133
The Strongman 152
Struss, Karl 35, 41, 42–43, 150, 151, 152, 193, 460
Stuart, Gloria 22, 49, **121**, **124**, 126, 127–128, 220, 221, 284, 343, 474, **474**, 475
The Student of Prague (1926) 211
Stumar, Charles 139, 301, 474–475
Sturges, Preston 218, 221
"The Suicide Club" (short story) 286, 452, 487
Summers, Walter 420, 421, 423
Sunrise (1927) 151
Supernatural 7, 83, 91, 195–204, **197**, 215, 407
Surviving the Game 115
Sutherland, Edward 187–189, 191, 193, 343, 359, 476
Sutton, John 414
Svehla, Gary 493
Svengali (1931) 99, 144, 321, 471, 480–481
Sweeney Todd, the Demon Barber of Fleet Street (1936) 255, 385, 436, 437, 481–482, **482**
Sweeney Todd, the Demon Barber of Fleet Street (1979 musical play) 482
Sweeney Todd, the Demon Barber of Fleet Street (play) 481

Talbot, Lyle **403**, 405, 408
Talbot, Stephen 408
A Tale of Two Cities (1935) 108
Tales from the Crypt 211
Tales of Terror 241
Tales That Witness Madness 107
Tandy, Jessica 107–108
Tanz auf dem Vulkan 80
Tarantula 416
Tarzan the Ape Man (1932) 64, 66
Tarzan the Fearless 443
Tashman, Lilyan 461
Tasker, Robert 96, 98
Taurog, Norman 153
Taves, Robert 50
Taylor, Kent 439, 440
Taylor, Marjorie 442–443
The Tell-Tale Heart 255
"The Tell-Tale Heart" (short story) 264
Temple, Shirley 65, 487
The Ten Commandments (1923) 42
The Ten Commandments (1956) 204
Terror (play) 98

The Terror (1938) 482–483
The Terror (novel) 98
Terror Aboard 193, 195, 483–484, **483**
Terror Is a Man 153
Terror of the Tongs 211
Terwilliger, George 438, 469, 470
Das Testament des Dr. Mabuse (*The Testament of Dr. Mabuse*) 484
Tevya 331
Thalberg, Irving 61, 65, 335, 449, 471
That They May Live see *J'Accuse* (1937)
Theatre of Blood 107
Them! 430
Thesiger, Ernest 122–123, 125, 126, 128, 207, **209**, 210, 211, 280–281, **280**, **283**, 285, 288, 381, 454, 485
Thew, Harvey 199–201
They Drive by Night (1938) 107, 484–485
They Drive by Night (1940) 485
The Thief of Bagdad (1924) 233
The Thing (1951) 6, 307
Things to Come (1936) 6, 454, 485–486, **486**
Thirteen Women 486–487
The Thirteenth Chair (1929) 63
The Thirteenth Chair (1937) 135–136
The Thirteenth Guest 408
The Thirty-Nine Steps 255
This Island Earth 60
Thomas, Augustus 487
Thompson, William 259, 262
Thorpe, Richard 466, 475, 488
Those Crazy Wonderful Years When WE Ran Warner Bros. 480
Ticket of Leave Man 442
The Time Travelers 101
The Tingler 448
Toland, Gregg 314
The Toll of the Sea 99
Too Many Crooks 443
Top Hat 478
Topaze 480
Topper 6, 465
The Torrent 351
Torture Ship 83, 88, 117, 199, 215, 356, 402–409, **403**
Die Toten Augen von London (aka *Dead Eyes of London*) 424
Totter, Audrey 465
Tourneur, Jacques 4
Tovar, Lupita 19, 440, **441**
Tower of London 3, 6, 38, 320, 339, 361, 392, 409–416, **410**, **413**, 431
Towers, Richard 99
Tracy, Lee 96, 98, 100, 163, 427
Tracy, Spencer 43, 467
A Trip to Mars (unproduced) 286–287
Tritschler, Conrad 83
Trooper of Troop K 232
Trouble for Two 288, 452, 487
Trytel, W. L. 106
Tudor, Andrew 5

Tully, Jim 305
The Tunnel 107
Tuttle, William 274, 275
Twelve O'Clock High 367
Twentieth Century 202
20,000 Leagues Under the Sea 475
Twice Told Tales 204
Twilight People 153
Two Evil Eyes 241
2001: A Space Odyssey 6

Ulmann, Emil 3, 233
Ulmer, Edgar G. 235, 236, 238, 240–241
Underwood, Peter 135, 210
The Unearthly 19
The Unholy Three (1925) 57, 61, 65, 375
The Unholy Three (1930) 61, 65
The Uninvited (1944) 109
Universal Horrors 46, 50, 342, 390
The Unknown 57
Unnatural ... The Fruit of Evil 335
Up Pops the Devil 193

"The Vagabond King" (play) 429
Valentine, Joseph A. 467
Valentino, Rudolph 351
The Valiant 351
Valley, Richard 494
The Vampire (1913) 210
The Vampire (1957) 434
The Vampire Bat 91, 153–159, **155**, **157**, 180, 194, 324, 325, 327, 328, 426, 436, 445
The Vampire's Trail 210
Vampyr (*The Dream of Allan Gray*) 68–81, **70**, **72**, **76**, 140, 331, 337, 361, 443
Van Every, Dale 240
The Vanishing Body (aka *The Black Cat*, 1934) 241
Van Sloan, Edward 1, 13, 19, 24, 26, 46, 138, 144, 269, 307, 357, 360, 470
Variety (1925) 52
Varney the Vampire 11
Veidt, Conrad 18, 305
Venable, Evelyn 439, 440
The Vengeance of She 478
Very Special People 66
Vetchinsky, Alex 381
Victor, Henry 60, 63, 144, 478
A Victorian in Orbit 211
Vidal, Gore 100
Vidor, Charles 134, 439
Villarias, Carlos 440, **441**
Vincent, Allen **162**
Visaroff, Michael 16, 275–276
Von Harbou, Thea 453, 484
Von Seyffertitz, Gustav 463
Von Stroheim, Erich 307, **330**, 331, 332–333, **333**, 334, 335–336, 372, 377, 436
Voodoo Man 461

Vosper, Frank 452
Voteur, Ferdinand 351
Voyage to the Bottom of the Sea 255, 430

Walker, Stuart 153, 291, 292, 293, 294, 342–343
The Walking Dead 99, 164, 204, 208, 215, 320, 345–352, **349, 351**, 427, 471, 479
Wallace, Bryan Edgar 436
Wallace, Edgar 98, 115, 178, 423–424, 436, 463–464, 482
Wallace, Emmett 439
Walter, Wilfred **419**, 421, 423
Walthal, Henry B. 376
War Gods of the Deep 255
Ware, Irene 301, 302, 307
Warner, Charles 203
Warner, H.B. **197**, 201, 203
Warner, Jack 429
Warren, E. A. 463
Warren, F. Brooke 443
Warwick, John 442
Waxman, Franz 282, 286, 374
Waxworks (1924) 18, 480
Waycoff, Leon *see* Ames, Leon
Weaver, Tom 46, 342–343, 494
Webb, Kenneth 88
Webling, Peggy 26
The Wedding March 335, 377, 436
Wegener, Paul 445, 452
Weihmayr, Franz 444
Weird Woman 327
Weismuller, Johnny 376
Weiss, Louis 245, 246
Weld, John 219
Welles, Orson 229, 259
Wells, H.G. 149, 153, 218, 219–220, 221, 454, 485, 486
Wells, Jacqueline 238, **403**, 409; *see also* Bishop, Julie
Werewolf of London 7, 139, 288–295, **290, 292, 294**, 301, 307, 340–341, 342, 431, 433
The Werewolf of Paris (novel) 305, 377
West, Julian **70**, 77, 78, 79
West of Shanghai 135, 409
The Westland Case 431
Westmore, Frank 450
Westmore, Perc 165, 166, 168, **426**, 427, 429, 449–450
Westmore, Wally 42–43, 150
The Westmores of Hollywood 450
Weston, Garnett 83, 88
Whale, James 4, 5, 21–23, 26–27, 29, 50, 122–124, 125, 126–127, 128, 200, 215–216, 217–218, 219, 220, 221, 240, 272, 278–280, 281, 283, 284–285, 286, 286–287, 319, 342, 358, **360**, 392, 423
What a Carve Up! 211
What Ever Happened to Baby Jane 193
"Whatever Became Of...?" 63
"Whatever Became Of ...?: 4th Series" 142

"Whatever Became Of...?: 9th Series" 66
"Whatever Became Of...?: 11th Series" 90
Wheeler, Leonard 332, 334
Wheeler and Woolsey 458
When Worlds Collide 80
The Whistler (series) 336
White, Mary 336
White Zombie 81–91, **86, 89**, 187, 198, 201, 215, 244, 327, 363, 364, 367, 407, 420
Whittier, John Greenleaf 358
Whitty, Dame May 466
Wilcox, Colin 434
Wilcox, Robert **400**
The Wild One 352
Wilde, Cornel 115
Wilder, Billy 336
Willard, John 131, 433
Williams, D. J. 482
Williams, Emlyn 466
Williams, G. Mac 436
Williams, Hugh 421, 423
Williams, Larry 331, 334, 337
Willis, Edwin B. 267, 370, 372
Wills, Brember 125, 127, **127**, 128
Wilson, Eleanor 440
Wilson, James 251–252, 255
Wilson, Woodrow 91
Wings 118, 153, 167
Wise, Robert 4
Witchcraft Through the Ages (Haxan) 260
The Witching Hour (1921) 487
The Witching Hour (1934) 487
The Wizard of Oz 65, 327, 475
The Wolf Man 5, 256, 290, 291, 292, 293, 467
Wolfe, Ian 306, 307, 314
Wollstonecraft, Mary *see* Shelley, Mary
A Woman of Paris 193
Woman to Woman 384
The Woman Who Came Back 360, 385
Women of the Prehistoric Planet 180
The Wonderful World of the Brothers Grimm 65, 360
Wong, Anna May 438
Wong, Victor 232
Woo, John 115
Wood, Ed 259, 303, 341
Woodbury, Joan **283**
Woods, Bill 259, **259**, 260
Woods, Donald 444
Wray, Fay 49, 96, 98–99, 100, **113**, 114, 115, 117, 118, 156, **157**, 158, **166**, 168, 176, 177, **178**, 180, **181**, 183–184, 255, 335, 431, 432, 435, 436, **436**
Wray, John 101
Wuthering Heights (1939) 314
Wyatt, Jane 359, 457
Wylie, Philip 150, 189–190, 195, 218
Wyndham, Bray 254
Wysbar, Frank 443, 444

X the Unknown 367

Yarbrough, Jean 4
Yates, George Worthington 183
York, Cal 25
You Can't Cheat an Honest Man 394
You Can't Take It with You 204, 327
You'll Find Out 342
Young, Roland 454
Young, Waldemar 150
Youssoupoff, Prince 472
A Youth in Babylon 63, 68

Zeller, Wolfgang 75–77
Zip **55**
Zombie 376
Zombie (play) 88
Zombies of Mora Tau 402
Zombies on Broadway 307
Zucco, George 159, 408, 454
Zulu 107

www.ingramcontent.com/pod-product-compliance
Lightning Source LLC
Chambersburg PA
CBHW081532300426
44116CB00015B/2596